NEW OXFORD HISTORY OF MUSIC

VOLUME IX

THE VOLUMES OF THE
NEW OXFORD HISTORY OF MUSIC

ROMANTICISM
(1830–1890)

EDITED BY
GERALD ABRAHAM

OXFORD   NEW YORK
OXFORD UNIVERSITY PRESS

1990

Oxford University Press, Walton Street, Oxford OX2 6DP

Oxford New York Toronto
Delhi Bombay Calcutta Madras Karachi
Petaling Jaya Singapore Hong Kong Tokyo
Nairobi Dar es Salaam Cape Town
Melbourne Auckland

and associated companies in
Berlin Ibadan

Oxford is a trade mark of Oxford University Press

Published in the United States
by Oxford University Press, New York

British Library Cataloguing in Publication Data

The New Oxford history of music.
Vol. 9: Romanticism (1830–1890).
I. Abraham, Gerald, 1904–1988
780'.9
ISBN 0-19-316309-8

Library of Congress Cataloguing in Publication Data

New Oxford history of music.
Includes bibliographies.
v. 9. Romanticism, 1830–1890/ edited by Gerald Abraham
1. Music—History and criticism.   I. Oxford
history of music.
ML160.N44   780'9   54–12578
ISBN 0-19-316309-8

Set by Oxford Text System
Printed in Great Britain by
Richard Clay Ltd., Bungay, Suffolk

CONTENTS

PUBLISHER'S NOTE

Gerald Abraham died shortly after sending the typescript of this book to Oxford. We wish to pay tribute to his incalculable contribution to the whole of the *New Oxford History of Music*, for much of which he served as the general editor. We wish also to acknowledge the assistance of Professor Robert Pascall of the University of Nottingham, in assuming the responsibility for seeing this volume through the press.

ILLUSTRATIONS

I. THE PARIS OPÉRA
Interior of the Paris Opéra during the Act 3 finale (designed by Cicéri) of the
first production of Meyerbeer's *Robert le diable* in 1831. Lithograph by J.
Arnout.
Bibliothèque de l'Opéra, Paris

II. INSTRUMENT MANUFACTURE
The Adolphe Sax factory in Paris. Engraving from *L'illustration* (5 Febrary
1848).
Mary Evans Picture Library, London

III. BERLIOZ: *GRANDE MESSE DES MORTS*
Opening of the *Dies irae*, showing the range of instruments required, from
the autograph score (1837).
Bibliothèque Nationale, Paris

IV. CHAMBER MUSIC
Anthony (the artist's husband, facing centre) and friends playing a string
quartet at his Frankfurt home (*c*.1843). Watercolour by Mary Ellen Best.
Private Collection

V. AUBER: *LA MUETTE DE PORTICI*
Riot sparked off by the performance of Auber's *La Muette de Portici* (1828)
at the Théâtre de la Monnaie, Brussels, on 25 August 1830. Engraving by
Hebert after Henri Hendrick.
Bibliothèque Royale Albert Ier, Brussels

VI. WAGNER: *TRISTAN UND ISOLDE*
Closing scene of Act 1 in the first production of Wagner's opera at the
Königliches Hof- und Nationaltheater, Munich (1865). Engraving after a
drawing by J. Noerr from the Leipzig *Illustrirte Zeitung* (15 July 1865).
Mary Evans Picture Library, London

VII. GOUNOD: *SAPHO*
Pauline Viardot (centre) in the première of Gounod's opera at the Paris Opéra
on 16 April 1851; this work's return to Classical subject matter and novel
musical features make it a significant landmark in French opera. Engraving
from *L'illustration* (26 April 1851).
Mary Evans Picture Library, London

VIII. VERDI: *OTELLO*
Costumes designed by Alfredo Edel for Othello and Desdemona in the
première of Verdi's opera at La Scala, Milan, on 5 February 1887.
Boston Public Library (photos Richard Macnutt)

IX. MUSSORGSKY: *BORIS GODUNOV*
Opening scene (designed by Shishkov) for the first performance of Mussorgsky'
s opera at the Mariinsky Theatre, St Petersburg, on 8 February 1874.
From V. N. Tumanina: *M. P. Musorgskiy: zhizn' i tvorchestvo* (1939)

X. HUNNENSCHLACHT
Wilhelm von Kaulbach's painting *Hunnenschlacht* (1835–7) inspired Liszt's

symphonic poem of the same name (1857). Engraving by J. L. Raab after the
original now in the Muzeum Narodowe, Poznań.
Archiv für Kunst und Geschichte, Berlin

XI. JOHANNES BRAHMS
Brahms accompanying a solo singer in the Bösendorfer Hall of the Liechtenstein (Winter) Palace, Vienna; this building was converted into a concert
hall in 1872, but demolished in 1913. Watercolour by an unknown artist.
Archiv für Kunst und Geschichte, Berlin

XII. LISZT: *DIE LEGENDE VON DER HEILIGEN ELISABETH*
Liszt conducting the first performance of his oratorio in the Redoutensaal,
Budapest, on 15 August 1865. Engraving after a drawing by Jean Hubert
Reve from the Leipzig *Illustrirte Zeitung* (16 September 1865).
Mary Evans Picture Library, London

INTRODUCTION

By GERALD ABRAHAM

'ROMANTICISM' is a concept more easily recognized than defined. 'The general idea of romanticism' subsumes 'music as a record of the most subtle and intimate personal emotions and impressions' and 'music as a rhetorical language addressed to large audiences'.[1] Wyzewa and Saint-Foix thought they had detected symptoms of Mozart's 'grande crise romantique' as early as 1773[2] and Abert also found 'ein romantischer Zug' in the quartets K 136-8.[3] 'Romantic symptoms' certainly appear in Haydn's minor-key symphonies of the 1770s and in C. P. E. Bach. They are obvious in much of Beethoven and still more in his younger contemporaries. All the same there is a case for regarding the years 1830-90 as the 'Romantic period' *par excellence*. It was in March 1830 that Goethe complained pettishly to Eckermann that 'everybody talks now about Classicism and Romanticism—which no one thought of fifty years ago'. Berlioz was then composing his *Symphonie fantastique*, Schumann his Op. 1, and Chopin his E minor Concerto (he had already written his earliest nocturnes, mazurkas, and *études*). One full-blooded Romantic, Weber—who as early as 1800 had styled his boyish *Waldmädchen* 'romantisch'—had died at a comparatively early age, but his almost exact contemporary, Spohr, lived until the middle of the century and a whole generation born during the decade 1803–13—not only Berlioz, Chopin, and Schumann but Mendelssohn, Liszt, Wagner, and Verdi—came to maturity in the 1830s. These composers were to develop new concepts of form and harmony, extend and elaborate orchestral and pianistic techniques, and re-volutionize operatic structures, which were further exploited by their juniors.

However, the first phase of the period was more or less over by the mid-century: Bellini had died in 1835, Glinka produced little after 1848, while Mendelssohn died in 1847, Donizetti in 1848, and

[1] Vol. X, p. 1.

[2] Théodore de Wyzewa and Georges Saint-Fox, *Wolfgang Amédée Mozart: Sa vie musicale et son œuvre, de l'enfance à la pleine maturité*, i (Paris, 1912), 497.

[3] Otto Jahn, *W. A. Mozart* (Leipzig, 1856-9); rev. 5th edn. by Hermann Abert, *W. A. Mozart: Neu bearbeitete und erweiterte Ausgabe von Otto Jahns 'Mozart'* (1919–21), i. 348.

Chopin in 1849. Schumann's creative career ended with his attempted suicide in 1854. Wagner produced his last Romantic opera, *Lohengrin*, in 1850 and offered the world nothing further for more than ten years. What we may call the second phase of Romanticism was twice as long and included the mature Wagner and Verdi, such giants as Brahms and Bruckner, the Russians and—particularly after 1871— the French.

As for the *terminus ad quem* of the period, in 1890 Wagner, Liszt, and César Franck had recently died while Bruckner and Brahms had only a few years to live, and in 1893 Verdi and Tchaikovsky produced their final masterpieces. It is true that the spirit of Romanticism lived on and was embodied in fresh techniques for another quarter of a century,[4] but

the symptoms of decay and exhaustion were already apparent years before 1914. Sumptuousness of sonority, hypertrophic harmony, emotional intensity, music-as-a-language could be carried no further. The future of music lay in other directions, which other composers—indeed sometimes the late Romantics themselves—had long been pointing to and exploring.[5]

There had been a return to the ideals of 'absolute music', to the cultivation of techniques and sonorities for their own sakes. Reger's cerebral fugal writing and Debussy's floating, non-functional harmonies were both symptoms of the reaction against Romantic expression.

Goethe touched on the essential problem of musical Romanticism when he wrote to Zelter (letter, 6 March 1810) of the 'symbolism for the ear in which the object ... is neither imitated nor painted but presented to the imagination in a quite peculiar and incomprehensible way in that there seems to be no relationship at all between the symbol and the object symbolized'. The emotions and extra-musical meanings that 'Romantic' composers sought to convey often needed more than such tone symbols or even titles to communicate them more precisely. Music and words were brought into a closer symbiosis than had generally existed before except in opera—and even in opera this was brought still closer by Wagner in particular. In solo song, particularly in German song, the piano part tended to be less merely supportive, and was more expressive, even pictorial. Through the later Schubert and Schumann to Hugo Wolf and Mussorgsky a new conception of solo song was brought into existence. In instrumental music the effort to convey the interplay

[4] See Vol. X, pp. 1–79.
[5] Ibid., p. 79.

or conflict of emotions, the narrative or even the pictorial, tended to disrupt the 'Classical' forms of musical architecture and resulted in compromises: the piano ballade, the hybrid form of 'programme symphony', the dissolution of the 'concert overture' on sonata lines into the freer structures that after the mid-century began to be entitled 'symphonic poem' or 'fantasia' or 'tone picture'. The composer of such larger structures—symphony, sonata, concerto—was faced with a problem unknown to composers of 'absolute' music: the establishment of overall unity in works consisting of markedly differentiated ideas—even conveying extra-musical ones. And the usual solutions—themes metamorphosed from movement to movement, or a single 'motto' introduced in each, as in Berlioz's *Symphonie fantastique* and Schumann's D minor Symphony—were apt to betray their inorganic nature. In many of the most successful large-scale works of the period the composer simply evaded the issue of overall unity.

The 'Romantic period' of course covered many degrees of Romanticism from the carefully modified (Mendelssohn, Brahms) to the strongly emphasized (Berlioz, Liszt, Wagner, Tchaikovsky). It was qualified by national characteristics in France, Italy, Hungary, the Slav and Scandinavian lands. It even paradoxically mated with Realism (Mussorgsky) and invaded religious music (Berlioz, Liszt, Franck). But, although it was not peculiarly German, Romanticism had struck deeper in German literature—Novalis, Wackenroder, Tieck, Jean Paul, Hoffmann—than elsewhere and saturated German music more thoroughly than any other. English literary Romanticism flourished in a period when English music was in a poor way, whereas Hugo and Berlioz were almost exact contemporaries. While Romanticism impregnated opera everywhere and the instrumental music of Berlioz, Liszt, and other non-Germans, it subtly infused that great quantity of German music in which the aural symbolism is, as Goethe put it, 'quite peculiar and incomprehensible'. It is a fundamental paradox of Romantic music that much of it remained 'incomprehensible' while composers were striving more and more to widen its expressive powers.

Romanticism flourished earliest in opera, with Méhul, Spohr, and (above all) Weber, because text and action not only generated music but supplied it with meaning, although the earliest Romantic operas to be so called, notably the youthful Weber's *romantisch-komisch*, *Das Waldmädchen* (1800) and *Romantische Oper*, *Silvana* (1810) were more Romantic in subject than in musical substance. The same may be said of the *Undine* (1816) of E. T. A. Hoffmann[6]—who gave the 'noun' 'Romanticism' wider currency. Actually Méhul's *Mélidore et Phrosine* (1794) and *Ariodant* (1799)[7] and Le Sueur's *Ossian* (1804)[8] had more Romantic substance, but it was Weber's *Der Freischütz* (1821), his *grosse-heroisch-romantische Oper*, *Euryanthe* (1823), and *Oberon* (1826)[9], with Spohr's *Faust* (1816), *Jessonda* (1823), and *Berggeist* (1825),[10] that were to lead through Marschner to Wagner and his evolution of 'music drama'. Moreover, Romantic opera supplied instrumental composers with a 'vocabulary' derived from it, even when it did not, as in the case of Berlioz's *Symphonie fantastique*, frankly borrow stage music. By the middle of the century they were borrowing directly from the words of poets.[11]

The other area in which music could be charged with specific meaning was solo song. Eighteenth-century song was essentially melodious, an affair of vocal melody that would have lost comparatively little by transference to an instrument; nineteenth-century song became more and more a true marriage of music with poetry. There had, of course, been such marriages before—for instance, Mozart's 'Abendempfindung' (1787), and, just a month before this, 'Als Luise die Briefe ihres ungetreuen Liebhabers verbrannte', which anticipates that perfect union of the 'Sphear-born harmonious Sisters' which we find in some of the greatest songs of Schubert, Schumann, and Brahms. Even more 'subtle and intimate personal emotions and impressions' were to be conveyed in the *Lieder* of Hugo Wolf, while in Russia words and music were united realistically rather than Romantically in the songs of Modest Mussorgsky, notably in his cycle *Detskaya* [The Nursery], based on the inflections of a child's speech. Wolf's bold piano harmonies and Mussorgsky's empirical ones did almost as much to enlarge the harmonic vocabulary as the chromaticism of *Tristan* and the Prelude to Act III of *Parsifal*.

---

[6] See Vol. VIII, pp. 474 ff.
[7] Ibid., pp. 53–60 and 55–61.
[8] Ibid., pp. 86–91.
[9] Ibid., pp. 496 ff.
[10] Ibid., pp. 483 ff.
[11] See chap. 7.

I

NEW TENDENCIES IN ORCHESTRAL MUSIC: 1830–1850

By Gerald Abraham

THE CONCERT OVERTURE

THE composers of the 1830s inherited a magnificent instrument from Beethoven and Weber: the Classical orchestra brought to its highest development in the hands of the former and already subtilized, its colour effects extended, its sensuous gloss heightened, by the latter. One cannot add Schubert's name to these two, for his scores were practically unknown in the 1830s, but we should certainly add the names of several other opera composers, such as Spontini, with his muted woodwind—their bells in leather bags[1]—in *Fernand Cortez* (1809), his divided strings, some with mutes, some without, in *Olimpie* (1819), and the rest of his colour devices. The fertilization of instrumental music by expressive and descriptive resources first employed in dramatic music, though a fairly constant process, was never more noticeable than during the second quarter of the nineteenth century. Opera even supplied Romantic orchestral music with what is perhaps its most characteristic form: the independent descriptive overture. For once, history literally repeated itself. Just as a hundred years earlier the three-movement Italian opera overture, the *sinfonia avanti l'opera*, had won independent popularity once it had broken away from its parent opera and become an important genre in itself, so too the one-movement dramatic overture in more or less modified sonata form now also won its independence. Both Beethoven and Weber had set precedents for the independent overture. Beethoven had written redundant overtures for his one opera, superb overtures such as *Coriolan* and *Die Weihe des Hauses* for short-lived plays and unimportant dramatic occasions, and one— the C major, Op. 115—'for any occasion—or for concert use' [*Ouvertüre zu jeder Gelegenheit—oder zum Gebrauch im Konzert*], as

---

[1] See Vol. VIII, p. 81.

the first sketch is headed (the connection with the 'name-day' of the Emperor Franz appears to have been quite fortuitous.[2] Weber had drastically recast the overtures to the stillborn operas *Peter Schmoll* and *Rübezahl* years later as a *Grande Ouverture à plusieurs instruments* and *Ouvertüre zum Beherrscher der Geister*, and had composed an independent *Jubel-Ouvertüre* to commemorate the fiftieth anniversary of the accession of Friedrich August I of Saxony. Between 1812 and 1819 the young Schubert wrote no fewer than eight overtures, unnamed and unconnected with any dramatic work.

The abstract and independent overture seems to have come into existence at about the same time as its miniature counterpart, the independent prelude for piano. The overture itself became so popular that it too was annexed by piano composers, once a precedent had been set by transcription of orchestral overtures, precisely as J. S. Bach had annexed the orchestral forms of his day in the Italian Concerto and in its companion in the second part of the *Clavier-Übung*, the *Ouvertüre nach Französischer Art* in B minor. Even if Schubert's overtures in G minor and F minor for piano duet are transcriptions of lost orchestral works (and there is little to suggest that they are) the piano overture established itself and maintained its existence for several decades. In 1842 we find the 18-year-old Smetana writing overtures in C minor and A major for piano duet;[3] he had already composed an overture for string quartet the year before.

MENDELSSOHN'S OVERTURES

The outstanding composers of the 1830s were men of wider culture than most of their predecessors. Berlioz (1803–69), Mendelssohn (1809–47), Schumann (1810–56)—with whom we may link their elder contemporary, Spohr (1784–1859)—all had marked literary gifts and it was natural that they should seek and even proclaim inspiration in literary masterpieces. The overture form lay ready to their hands and, if Mendelssohn began in 1826 by writing an overture to *Ein Sommernachtstraum* [A Midsummer Night's Dream] without the slightest intention of its being played as an introduction to a stage performance, it was only a very small step to the composition of an overture to a short lyrical poem by Goethe (*Meeresstille und glückliche Fahrt* [Calm Sea and Prosperous Voyage], 1828), to an island (*Ouvertüre zur einsamen Insel*, the title of the original (1830) version

---

[2] See A. W. Thayer, *Ludwig van Beethovens Leben* (rev. 2nd edn., Leipzig, 1911), iii. 477.
[3] *Souborná díla Bedřicha Smetany*, i (Prague, 1924).

of the overture, *Die Hebriden*), and to a legend (*Ouvertüre zum Märchen von der schönen Melusine*, 1834).[4] Indeed, as early as 1824–6 he had written two nameless overtures in C major, one for wind-band, the other the so-called 'Trumpet' Overture in which the most interesting passages are not for trumpet but those in which first and second violins, and violas, are all divided. But it is worth noting that he did not always adopt the title and form of 'overture' entirely without hesitation. While he writes to his friend Klingemann (letter, 5 February 1828) that he has 'a big overture to Goethe's *Meeresstille und glückliche Fahrt* . . . already complete in the head', his sister Fanny tells the same correspondent four months later that 'Felix is writing a big instrumental piece *Meeresstille und glückliche Fahrt* after Goethe . . . He has tried to avoid an *overture* with *introduction* and to keep the whole in two juxtaposed pictures.' Even when the piece was completely rewritten [*ganz umgearbeitet*] and made '30 times better' (letter to Schubring, 6 August 1834), although the 'becalmed' 'adagio' may sound like a slow introductory passage, the 'prosperous voyage' ('molto allegro e vivace') is by no means cast in conventional sonata form; one may trace in it passages equivalent to the normal exposition (after a longish transition) and recapitulation, but they are relatively insignificant, only sixty or seventy bars each, and between them lies an enormous 'development' of more than three hundred bars which centres on the tonic key and is itself framed by passages based on the most familiar theme in the whole piece, the dolce cello melody beginning at bar 185. The result is an archlike structure:

> Transition
> > Two themes in D and A
> > > Cello melody in A
> > > > Middle section with D as its centre of gravity
> > > Cello melody in C
> > Two themes in D
> Coda

a form often to be met with in later nineteenth-century music. Nevertheless *Meersstille* was published with the *Dream* and *Die Hebriden* (now finally retitled *Fingals Höhle*) in 1834 as *Drei Concert-Ouvertüren*.

Its two predecessors are less unconventionally cast in free sonata

---

4 Although it was originally conceived as an overture to an opera by Conradin Kreutzer: see Donald M. Mintz, '*Melusine*: A Mendelssohn Draft', *Musical Quarterly*, 43 (1957), 480.

form, as is the fourth concert overture, *Melusine*. *Die Hebriden* is the most closely knit thematically,[5] *A Midsummer Night's Dream* the most episodic though apparently the original form was much less so. (The critic A. B. Marx claimed[6] that the music of the rude mechanicals and other features were inserted later at his suggestion.) But Mendelssohn had found the right approach as well as the right generic name—if indeed he was the first to use it—for this type of composition. The concert overture provided a convenient framework within which themes or orchestral effects suggested by literature or landscape or other extra-musical sources could be extended and worked out more or less in accordance with conventional methods of musical construction. There was nothing particularly new in the kind of associative symbolisms used by Mendelssohn to suggest fairies, lovers, and clowns, the dreary waste of waters in *Meeresstille* (which employs more or less the same means as Beethoven in the first section of his choral setting of the poem), the flowing river of *Melusine*; nothing new in his direct imitation of a natural sound, the donkey's bray, in the *Dream*. What was new in Mendelssohn was, above all, the orchestral magic—such things as incessant staccato quavers of divided violins supported only here and there by nothing but pizzicato violas. The mosaic of musically diverse ideas is fitted into a sonata-form frame, very much as Weber had fitted together diverse ideas in his opera overtures, but sonata form is here no more than a ready-made convention, very different from the living organism of Beethovenian sonata form. *Die Hebriden* is in several respects a special case: it is not only more organically conceived than any of its companions; the pictorially evocative quality of the opening motif and its orchestral setting was something entirely new in music, seldom paralleled, and never surpassed since. A few points in the orchestration are Weberian—the second subject in the reprise (clarinet over sustained string chords), the soft staccato brass chords, the rushing semiquavers on all the strings in octaves—but much is unique even in Mendelssohn's own work. Such effects as the sustained *pp* F sharps of the trumpets at the end, continued into silence by the oboes, seem to be completely novel.

The evocative power concentrated in the opening motif set Mendelssohn a problem which was to confront later nineteenth-century composers and was first satisfactorily solved only by Debussy. If a motif can by itself conjure up a mood or a landscape, that

---

[5] See R. Larry Todd, 'Of Seagulls and Counterpoint: The Early Versions of Mendelssohn's *Hebrides* Overture', *19th-century Music*, 2 (1979–80), 197.

[6] *Erinnerungen: Aus meinen Leben* (Berlin, 1865), ii. 231 ff.

power may easily be destroyed by treating it as a theme for development and it says much for Mendelssohn's skill and perception that throughout this extended movement he contrives to weave an always fresh and interesting texture from the almost unchanged initial motif, with little pendants, related subsidiary motifs, and one major contrasting theme (the second subject) that do not seriously weaken the initial impression, and with a wealth of picturesque orchestral writing that continues and even heightens it. Passages in the original version where he had lapsed into conventional 'thematic working', which brought with it conventional scoring, were excised from the final version.

MENDELSSOHN'S FOLLOWERS

Most of Mendelssohn's disciples followed him in the cultivation of the concert overture though few of them achieved conspicuous success. Of the *Overture to Lord Byron's Poem of Parisina* (1835), *The Naiads* (1836), *The Wood-nymphs* (1838), and *Paradise and the Peri* (1862) by William Sterndale Bennett (1816–75), only the second is still—very occasionally—heard; it is certainly the best. As its predecessor *Parisina*—a very similar 'moderato' also in 6/4 time—demonstrates beyond doubt, *The Naiads* is not indebted to Mendelssohn's *Melusine*, as Schumann suggested, so much as to Weber's *Beherrscher der Geister*; the 12/8 'allegro' of *The Wood-nymphs* is more Mendelssohnian. Sterndale Bennett's affinity with contemporary German Romanticism is particularly marked in the second subjects of *The Naiads* and *The Wood-nymphs*, of which the former has a note-for-note resemblance to the parallel passage in Wagner's earliest operatic overture *Die Feen*, which Bennett could not have known. (Perhaps both derive from a common model.) Bennett's handling of form and orchestration is very conventional but his harmony sometimes surprises by such asperities as that from the second bar of a passage in *The Naiads* (Ex. 1), which particularly pleased both Mendelssohn and the composer.[7] He had little power as a tone

Ex. 1

---

[7] Henry Davison, *From Mendelssohn to Wagner* (London, 1912), 30.

painter; no one would suspect that the 'adagio' introduction to *The Wood-nymphs* was intended to suggest sunrise if the composer had not let us into the secret. Yet he was not devoid of artistic personality, a personality that appears in the peculiarly limpid sweetness of passages in *The Naiads* which have the charm of paintings by Cotman, Crome, and Samuel Palmer.[8]

From the same year as *The Naiads* dates another British overture, the *Chevy Chace* of George Macfarren (1813–87). Written for a play by J. R. Planché, it introduces the old ballad tune of that name to 'God prosper long Our Noble King'. Mendelssohn conducted it at the Leipzig Gewandhaus in 1843 and Wagner in London in 1855 when he was struck by its 'eigentümlich, wild-leidenschaftlich' character;[9] it was still performed in London in the 1890s.

Ex. 2

---

[8] Bennett's symphonies are markedly inferior to his overtures and concertos. The best, in G minor (1864), has been ed. Nicholas Temperley (New York, 1982).

[9] *Mein Leben* (Munich, 1911), 619, where he calls the composer Mac Farrinc and the work *Steeple-Chase*.

Beside these essays of the British Mendelssohnians we may place the Op. 1 of a Dane of the same school, Niels Gade (1817–90). Gade's later overtures, *I Højlandene* [In the Highlands] (another Scottish subject), No. 3 in C, *Hamlet*, and *Michel Angelo* are of less account but *Efterklang af Ossian* [Echo of Ossian] (1839) (Exx. 2–3) does achieve epic breadth and strength at any rate in the twin passages that frame the sonata form, where a striking motto-like theme for solo horn, clarinet, and bassoon gradually emerges from the Celtic twilight and finally disappears into it again. These 'frame' passages are not differentiated in any way from the main sonata movement, into which the motto-theme, usually with brass colouring and harp accompaniment, is woven at several points Exx. 2 and 3; the violins in Ex. 2 are playing the 'true' first subject. The treatment of the harp in these two passages, indeed throughout the overture, is in striking contrast with Mendelssohn's in *Athalie* (1844), where its part suggests simple piano music. On the other hand, Gade himself writes pianistic passages for strings as accompaniment to the second subject of *Ossian*; the fault is common to most of the German and non-German composers of what we may call 'the Leipzig group'.

BERLIOZ'S OVERTURES

Complete freedom from pianistic idioms is one of the principal marks of the orchestral writing of their French contemporary, Berlioz. But Berlioz shared their predilection for the same Romantic subjects: Shakespeare's plays, Byron's poems, nature impressions (particularly of sea or river), fairies, and Scotland—affection for Scotland being a special manifestation of affection for the exotic in general. Like them he found a convenient and congenial form in the concert overture: his *Le Roi Lear* (1831) expressed his direct reaction to a reading of the play and was no more intended to be played before a stage performance than Mendelssohn's *A Midsummer Night's Dream*; with his *Waverley* ('Grande ouverture caractéristique de Waverley, dédiée au Colonel Marmion', 1827) and *Rob Roy* ('Intrata

Ex. 3

di Rob Roy Macgregor', 1832) he was probably the first to compose overtures 'to' novels. His *Grande ouverture des francs-juges* (1826) was certainly intended for a never-completed opera but *Le Carnaval romain* (1844) was simply a convenient means of using up material from the opera *Benvenuto Cellini*, which appeared to have failed and already possessed an overture of its own. As for *Le Corsaire*, it began its existence in 1844 as *La Tour de Nice*, the building in which he was lodging (though sketches date from 1831, when he had first stayed there), and was reconstructed in 1852, first as *Le Corsaire rouge*—Fenimore Cooper's *The Red Rover*[10]—though he afterwards deleted the adjective, no doubt to suggest Byron whose poem he had read in Rome.

Berlioz's concert overtures differ from those of the Leipzig group, not only in his treatment of the orchestra (on which, see below) but in his conception of form. Only in *Meeresstille und glückliche Fahrt* does Mendelssohn make a really drastic modification of sonata form;

---

[10] See Jacques Barzun, *Berlioz and the Romantic Century* (London, 1951), ii. 49–50.

in *Die Hebriden*, for instance, he merely compresses the recapitulation rather severely; Gade's *Ossian* places an orthodox sonata movement within a frame. But Berlioz sometimes abandons sonata form altogether, as in *Le Carnaval romain* which is laid out on a free yet perfectly satisfactory plan, an archlike form very different from that of *Meeresstille*:

> 'Allegro assai con fuoco'
>> 'Ah, sonnez trompettes' (from Act II of *Benvenuto Cellini*; A)
> 'Andante sostenuto', 'Fête chez Capulet'
>> Love duet from Act I (C, E, and A)
> 'Allegro vivace'
>>> 'Venez, venez, peuple de Rome' (from Act II; A)
>>> 'Ah, sonnez trompettes' (E)
>>> 'Venez, venez' (A)   ⎫ with different
>>> 'Ah, sonnez trompettes' (E)   ⎭ scoring
>> Brief development of love duet, with rhythm of 'Venez'
>> (various keys)
> 'Ah, sonnez trompettes' (A)

Even when Berlioz preserves the sonata layout as a structural convenience, he never shows any appreciation of the Classical meaning of sonata form and makes its apprehension by the unaided ear more difficult by his interpolation of fresh episodes, as in the recapitulatory sections of *Les Francs-juges* and *Le Corsaire*. In *Le Roi Lear* not only is the slow introduction subtly related to the 'allegro disperato',[11] but its principal theme returns in the course of the recapitulation. Indeed Berlioz's slow sections are, like those of one or two Haydn symphonies, always thematically related to, or interwoven with, the 'allegro' sections; and in a number of cases— *Rob Roy*, *Le Carnaval romain*, *Le Corsaire*, *Cellini*, and *Béatrice et Bénédict*—the slow section is not an introduction but an interlude early in the 'allegro'. The combination of these devices in his last concert overture, *Le Corsaire*, results in a plastic but perfectly clear and satisfactory form:

> 'allegro assai': Introduction (C and A flat)
> 'adagio sostenuto' (A flat)
>> Transition of repeat of Introduction (C and A flat)
>> Principal subject (C and D flat)
>> Principal subject (G, etc.)

---

[11] See Tom S. Wotton, *Hector Berlioz* (London, 1935; repr. 1970), 90–1.

Secondary theme (fragments of 'Adagio'; B flat, etc.)
Theme of 'Adagio' in full (C)
Transition and repeat of Introduction (C and A flat)
Principal subject (E flat)
Principal subject (C)
Secondary theme (G, etc.)
Coda, long; based on principal subject in various shapes (C).

It was natural for Berlioz's contemporaries to account for such forms by ascribing them to control by concealed programmes. But, despite its various titles, *Le Corsaire* is simply a sea piece with no relation to Nice or Byron or Fenimore Cooper. Such bold and unorthodox forms sprang solely or mainly from the bold and unorthodox thought of their creator—who at the same time liked to give his works attractive literary titles. That was certainly the case with the early *Waverley* with its half-jesting dedication (for there was a genuine Colonel Marmion, the composer's Uncle Felix). 'Berlioz has now written a music to *Waverley*,' said Schumann, reviewing the published score in 1839. 'One will ask: to which chapter, which scene, wherefore, to what end? For critics always want to know what the composers cannot tell them. . . .' Although Berlioz scribbled on the manuscript, 'a long text made up of sentences from the novel',[12] all he actually tells us is that

> Dreams of love and lady's charms
> Give place to honour and to arms.

So we can identify the 'larghetto' with dreams of love and the 'allegro vivace' with honour and arms, but to no great advantage. And it is useless to seek in the 'larghetto' melody any significance beyond Berlioz's love of canon at the octave (cf. *Le Corsaire*, the Andante of *Le Carnaval romain*). In *Les Francs-juges* there may be references to points in the opera that was to have followed it, and there are certainly similar ones in *Le Roi Lear*;[13] but the greater part of *Le Carnaval romain* consists, as we have seen, simply of a long excerpt from the carnival scene in *Cellini* arranged for orchestra and played through twice. Berlioz's creative imagination was actually less pictorial than the imaginations of the Leipzig composers, who possessed in varying degrees a real power of pictorial evocation in themes that were then treated somewhat statically on fairly orthodox lines. Berlioz commanded little evocative power of this kind; indeed

[12] Hugh J. Macdonald, *Berlioz Orchestral Music* (London, 1969), 12.
[13] Ibid., pp. 17–18.

he once confessed to Wagner[14] that he was not musically stimulated by landscape. *Waverley* conveys no sense of Scotland as *Die Hebriden* does (admittedly he had not *seen* Scotland, as Mendelssohn had); in *Rob Roy* he has to help himself out by quoting 'Scots wha hae' and the melody of the slow section is so little characteristic that he was able to use it as the 'Harold' theme in *Harold en Italie*. (Another theme from *Rob Roy* was transferred to the first movement of *Harold*.) *Le Corsaire* is perhaps Mediterranean in quality but as an evocative seascape is not comparable with *Die Hebriden*. Berlioz's imagination was dramatic rather than pictorial and its products are consequently dynamic rather than static; the tremendous brass outbursts in *Waverley* seem to depict specific incidents in an unfolding drama and we know that the similar, even more powerful, ones in *Les Francs-juges* are associated with the villain Olmérik.

WAGNER'S EARLY OVERTURES

Wagner, like Schubert, began his career as an orchestral composer by writing abstract overtures without titles, of which two—in D minor and C major (the latter with a fugal coda suggested by the corresponding part of the 'Jupiter' Symphony)—have been published.[15] Then came a *Polonia* (1836), inspired by contact with Polish political refugees in 1832, and an essay in another variety of the genre: the overture on some more or less familiar melody, in this case 'Rule Britannia!' (1837) (cf. Macfarren's already mentioned *Chevy Chace*, the *Grosse Festouvertüre* on 'God save the Queen' with which Marschner saluted the birth of the Prince of Wales in 1842, Schumann's *Fest-Ouvertüre mit Gesang über das Rheinweinlied* for orchestra and chorus of 1853). Wagner did not anticipate Schumann by introducing optional voices as he himself did many years later in his *Kaiser-marsch*, but he did give the 'Rule, Britannia!' Overture a foil in the shape of a second subject (Ex. 4) which, from its similarity to the 'veto on love' theme in his opera *Das Liebesverbot*, composed

Ex. 4

[14] *Correspondance inédite*, ed. Daniel Bernard (Paris, 1879), letter, 10 Sept. 1855.
[15] First by Michael Balling in his Wagner *Gesamtausgabe*, xx (Leipzig, 1926); more recently ed. Carl Dahlhaus, *Richard Wagner: Sämtliche Werke*, 18, I (Mainz, 1980).

Ex. 5

coll'8va

just before (Ex. 5) may be taken to represent the forces of tyranny and Britannia's enemies in general. *König Enzio* (1832) and *Christoph Columbus* (1835) were both written for actual plays; the former a weak but orthodox attempt to ape Beethoven and Cherubini, the latter a curious experiment in both structure and orchestration betraying the influence of Mendelssohn's recently published *Meeres-stille und glückliche Fahrt* but also forecasting a characteristic trait of Wagner's mature orchestral style: the multiplication of one particular orchestral group (the brass in the first Walhalla scene of *Das Rheingold*, harps in the final one). In *Christoph Columbus* he employs four horns, six trumpets (at first pairs in E flat, D, and C, finally all six in E flat), three trombones, and tuba.

All these early and immature overtures are completely over-shadowed by the powerful *Faust* Overture of 1840. It is true that in its original form this was cruder in detail, much more heavily scored, and lacked (among other things) the beautiful twenty-bar passage which Wagner added at the very end in place of a sudden brutal D minor chord, tutti, when he revised the work as *Eine Faust-Ouvertüre* in 1855,[16] but all the essentials, practically the entire substance, were already there. They are remarkable. The influences of Beethoven (first movement of the Ninth Symphony) and of Weber had not yet been completely digested but the piece as a whole has not only great power in depicting emotional states but a curious felicity in suggesting that they are the states of one individual: Faust. The opening theme of the 'allegro' from the *Faust* Overture (Ex. 6) is not only a very early, perhaps the earliest, instance of octave displacement of

Ex. 6

Sehr bewegt

p

ausdrucksvoll

[16] See Gerald Abraham, 'Wagner's Second Thoughts', in *Slavonic and Romantic Music* (London, 1968), 294–7.

chromatic intervals, not only wonderfully suggestive of painful brooding, but also the first stroke of a musical portrait more striking than any of those in his earlier operas. As he was painting a portrait, he did not need to strain the useful conventions of sonata form. We have his own authority for taking the second subject as a suggestion of Faust's yearnings or aspirations, not of Gretchen. She was to be painted in the second movement of a symphony of which the overture was intended to be the first movement. That, at any rate, was Wagner's story in later years, but the cover and first page of the original score fail to confirm it. The latter is inscribed simply

> Ouvertüre
> Goethes Faust erster Teil

while the former drops the word 'overture' in favour of a new and, for the future, important addition to musical nomenclature:

> Der einsame Faust (oder Faust in der Einsamkeit)
> ein Tongedicht für das Orchester

With the *Faust* Overture Wagner practically ceased to compose independent orchestral works. In later years he produced only the *Siegfried Idyll* and three marches, all three 'occasional' works of little or no value, though one might add to this short list the overture to *Die Meistersinger* which came into existence before the opera.

SCHUMANN'S OVERTURES

In the year after that in which Wagner turned away from the concert hall, another German musician—hitherto known only as a piano and song composer—decided to enter it. It is true that Schumann had seven or eight years before composed a symphony and begun other orchestral works, but this G minor Symphony, though performed, was suppressed for many years[17] and we may date Schumann's real début as an orchestral composer from the B flat Symphony, the first version of the D minor, and the *Symphonette* (later revised as 'Ouvertüre, Scherzo, und Finale'), all 1841. Schumann turned to the independent overture only towards the end of his life, in the 1850s, and his overtures to Schiller's *Die Braut von Messina*, Shakespeare's *Julius Caesar*, and a projected *Singspiel* on Goethe's *Hermann und Dorothea* (based largely on the 'Marseillaise'),[18] with

---

[17] An edition of the two completed movements has been published by Marc Andreae (Frankfurt, London, and New York, 1972).

[18] Reasons for doubting the connection between the overture and the *Singspiel* are suggested in Abraham, *Slavonic and Romantic Music*, p. 288.

the already mentioned overture on the 'Rheinweinlied', like that to the *Szenen aus Goethes Faust*, show his genius in sad decline. The only interesting point concerning them is that Schumann set out to write *Die Braut von Messina* in absolutely free form, following the dictates of his fancy, and ended by producing a thoroughly conventional sonata movement.[19] None of these bears comparison with his earlier opera overture, *Genoveva*, or the overture written in 1848 to Byron's *Manfred*.

As a character study the Manfred Overture may be put beside Wagner's *Faust*. It does not bear comparison as a piece of orchestral writing; like so much of Schumann's orchestral music, it sounds like piano music scored, and it is marked by other characteristic Schumannian miscalculations, such as the famous opening chords which are syncopated before any beat has been established. But as a musical portrait of a gloomy and passionate poetic hero it yields little to Wagner. There are even musical traits in common: the Berliozian use of identical material for slow introduction and 'allegro', the bold, free handling of sonata form with enormous development (presumably the apparition of Astarte), and a very fine coda (evidently Manfred's death), even the characterization by an angular theme (Ex. 7) which may be compared with the *Faust* 'allegro' (Ex. 6) and the theme in which Liszt was to personify the brooding Faust a few

Ex. 7

years later. The subjective element in both the Wagner and the Schumann is typical of German Romanticism and in both works finds expression not only in melody but in harmony overloaded with appoggiaturas. Wagner could see himself as Faust, Schumann as Manfred. There is no such element in, for example, Berlioz's *Le Roi Lear*.

[19] Wilhelm Joseph von Wasielewski, *Robert Schumann: Eine Biographie* (rev. and enlarged 4th edn., Leipzig, 1906), 461.

INCIDENTAL MUSIC

Schumann composed not only an overture but incidental music for *Manfred*, despite the total unsuitability of Byron's play for stage performance. He certainly wished his music to be used in connection with a stage adaptation and Liszt actually produced it at Weimar in 1852. Several numbers consist of 'melodrama' in the technical sense of the word and two of them may have been not without influence on later music: the cor anglais solo, now slow, now quick, accompanying Manfred's

> Hark! the note,
> The natural music of the mountain reed—

may have influenced the parallel passage in *Tristan*; the waterfall scene with the Witch of the Alps may have influenced Tchaikovsky and other Russian composers. One passage, 'Rufung der Alpenfee' [Call of the Alpine Fairy] from the waterfall scene (Ex. 8) is worth quoting both for its charm and because it demonstrates that Schumann could sometimes write felicitously for the orchestra. Schumann's *Manfred* music occupies a midway position between normal incidental music for a stage play, like that which Mendelssohn produced in 1843 for *A Midsummer Night's Dream* and Meyerbeer in 1846 for his brother's *Struensee*, and such a piece as Berlioz's *Marche funèbre pour la dernière scène d'Hamlet* (1848), which was certainly never intended for the theatre and was essentially a personal reaction to a specific performance. Despite the fact that Mendelssohn was able to draw an effective concert suite from his *Dream* music, as Schumann could never have done from *Manfred*, his approach here was different from Schumann's, from Berlioz's and from his own younger self who had written the *Dream* overture—and the difference is perceptible in the music. Then he was musically reacting to a poetic masterpiece; now he was executing with brilliant technique a piece of work required of him. The latter was the traditional approach, the former the Romantic.

Music intended to record and transmit a mood or an impression of poem or landscape naturally tends to be cast in smaller moulds and for an intimate medium; consequently the most successful early Romantic music consists of comparatively short works for piano. We have seen how Mendelssohn confronted the difficulty of reconciling personal impression with large-scale structure in *Die Hebriden*; in the Romantic symphony this difficulty increased in proportion to the size of the canvas, with the result that some of the Romantic

Ex. 8

symphonists found themselves willy-nilly thinking mainly in terms of construction and design like their Classical predecessors. Except in the compromise of the concert overture, Romantic orchestral music had not yet found suitable forms. But during the 1840s the short orchestral piece, counterpart of the more extended kind of piano miniature, began to appear as 'characteristic piece' or idealized dance or march. Berlioz's 'Marche hongroise', which was inserted in *La Damnation de Faust*, not taken from it, and his funeral march for *Hamlet* are symptomatic. And no doubt the success of Mendelssohn's *Dream* pieces in the concert hall encouraged composers to experiment on these lines.

GLINKA

The earliest really notable achievements in this field came from Russia, a country that had hitherto remained on the fringe of European musical culture. The earliest Russian composer to make any substantial contribution to this culture was Mikhail Glinka (1804–57) and his claim to be considered the founder of Russian orchestral music is stronger than his title as the first Russian opera composer. His earliest complete surviving orchestral piece is a scherzo, *Valse-fantaisie*, a pastiche in the manner of Joseph Lanner (1801–49) or the elder Johann Strauss (1804–49) dating from 1839, though it survives only in the revised and reorchestrated version of 1856. It is quite overshadowed by the overture and incidental music to Nestor Kukol'nik's ephemeral tragedy *Knyaz' Kholmskiy* [Prince Kholmsky] (1840), his *Capriccio brillante* on the Jota aragonesa, afterwards renamed Spanish Overture, No. 1 (1845), his *Recuerdos de Castilla*, later revised and renamed *Souvenir d'une nuit d'été à Madrid*, Spanish Overture, No. 2 (1848), and a *Wedding Song and Dance Song* afterwards named *Kamarinskaya* after the second melody (1848). The *Prince Kholmsky* music reveals the influence of Beethoven (cf. Prelude to Act III of *Kholmsky* with the Andante agitato of Entr'acte IV of *Egmont*, and the Prelude to Act IV with the march in Entr'acte III) and perhaps of Weber's *Beherrscher der Geister*; together with the score of Glinka's second opera, *Ruslan i Lyudmila* (1842), it provides ample testimony of the Russian composer's achievement of an individual orchestral technique derived mainly from Mozart and Cherubini some years before he became acquainted with Berlioz's music. In the *Kholmsky* Overture he had even hit independently on the typically Berliozian transformation of the slow introductory theme in the main 'agitato vivace'. But the influence of Berlioz on the scoring of *Kamarinskaya* and the two Spanish pieces is undeniable; the canon between first violins and cellos in *Souvenir d'une nuit d'été à Madrid* also sounds very Berliozian.

The *Capriccio brillante* combines the principles of variation and sonata,[20] the outline and key scheme being that of a sonata form but with little sonata feeling; the music unfolds in terms of (mainly instrumental) variations. *Recuerdos de Castilla*, an occasional piece composed for the orchestra of the Russian viceroy in Warsaw, appears to be much more in the nature of a pot-pourri but is by no means shapeless.[21] *Kamarinskaya* consists mainly of instrumental

---

[20] See David Brown, *Mikhail Glinka: A Biographical and Critical Study* (London, 1974), 247–8.
[21] See Brown's parallel analyses of both versions, ibid., pp. 267–8.

variations or changing backgrounds to the two folk themes. In these three works, especially *Kamarinskaya*, Glinka provided models adopted by most later Russian composers not only for the variation treatment of folk material but for brilliant orchestration and clean, transparent harmony and part writing. Equally characteristic of the great bulk of later Russian music is Glinka's objective approach. The Spanish overtures are the fruits of travel but they are not— even *Souvenir d'une nuit d'été à Madrid* is not—subjective travel impressions like Mendelssohn's Scottish and Italian pieces; they are simply musical treatments of melodies heard in Spain. Glinka went there with the deliberate intention, suggested by study of Berlioz and of Parisian taste, to write

concert pieces for orchestra, under the designation of *fantaisies pittoresques*. Up to now instrumental music has been divided into two opposite categories: quartets and symphonies, valued by a few, but intimidating the mass of listeners by their depth and complexity; and concertos, variations, etc. which tire the ear by their lack of connection and their difficulties. It seems to me that it should be possible to reconcile the demands of art with those of the age and, taking advantage of improved instruments and performance, to write pieces equally acceptable to connoisseurs and the general public. . . . In Spain the originality of the melodies will be a considerable help, the more so as up to now no one has trodden this path.[22]

Similarly he wrote *Kamarinskaya* after discovering an affinity between the two tunes and 'guided', as he insisted, by his 'inner musical feelings' without thought of any programme.

Glinka never managed to complete a symphony. He began one in B flat in his youth, significantly introducing a folk tune in the first Allegro; in 1834, while studying in Berlin with Siegfried Dehn, he worked at a *Sinfonia per l'orchestra sopra due motivi Russi*[23] 'developed in the German style'; and again in 1852 he began a 'Ukrainian symphony', *Taras Bul'ba*, but soon abandoned it, 'being unable to get out of the German rut in the development'. That was Glinka's way of stating the already mentioned problem that confronted most of his contemporaries, German as well as non-German: the problem of the incompatability of their ideas—evocative motifs or instrumental effects, square-cut lyrical melodies, popular tunes—with the traditional techniques of large-scale musical construction.

---

[22] Letter, 18 Apr. 1845, in *Literaturnoe nasledie Glinki*, ed. Valerian M. Bogdanov-Beryozovsky (Leningrad, 1953), ii. 276.
[23] In *Polnoe sobranie sochineniy*, i (Moscow, 1955), 193. And see Brown, *Mikhail Glinka*, pp. 69–71.

MENDELSSOHN'S SYMPHONIES

As we have seen, Mendelssohn himself was conscious of the need 'to get out of the German rut in the development' in which he had stuck in the original version of *Die Hebriden*. Berlioz cut a passage of precisely the same nature from the beginning of the development of the first movement of the *Symphonie fantastique*. The problem, if difficult in the overture, was aggravated in the symphony. The only symphonists untroubled by it were the epigones and the future masters who had not yet found themselves. It will suffice to quote in skeleton the opening Allegros of Mendelssohn's First Symphony, in C minor (1824) (Ex. 9), Wagner's in C major (1832) (Ex. 10), and Schumann's in G minor (1833) (Ex. 11). Such material could scarcely be harmed by any method of treatment whatever, and could be cast in almost any mould. But if Mendelssohn began his public career as a symphonist conventionally—one writes 'public' advisedly, for the autograph of this first published symphony is marked 'Sinfonia No. XIII'—he continued on lines very characteristic of the period. The 6/4 time of the Minuetto, actually an Allegro molto scherzo which he replaced in 1829 with an orchestral version of the Scherzo from his Octet in E flat, op. 20, is almost the only noteworthy feature of the work, though the sentimental Spohr-like nature of the Andante

Ex. 9

Ex. 10

Ex. 11

is a Romantic symptom. But his next symphony, misleadingly numbered 5 owing to late publication, the *Reformations Symphonie* (the 'Reformation') of 1830 (Exx. 12 and 13), marks a new departure. It was a *pièce d'occasion* intended for performance in connection with the tercentennial commemoration of the Augsburg Confession, and Mendelssohn thought little of it in later years; but it is in many respects characteristic of the composer and the period. For one thing, it is semi-programme music. The quiet string introduction to the first movement, ending with two quotations of the 'Dresden Amen', is cut through with challenging calls of the wind, and the Allegro con fuoco which follows—a movement not so distantly related to Wagner's *Faust* Overture in the same key—irresistibly suggests conflict, spiritual or actual, with the old faith symbolized by the 'Amen'. Its opening theme, despite its virile leap of a fifth, reminding one of Haydn and Beethoven, is essentially elegiac in character as is demonstrated beyond doubt at the beginning of the recapitulation (Ex. 12), after another reference to the 'Dresden Amen'. But the actual course of the music is not controlled in any way by extra-musical considerations. The only unconventional feature of the first-movement structure is the curtailed recapitulation, but that feature is common to *Die Hebriden*, the first movements of the 'Italian' and 'Scottish' Symphonies, and other of Mendelssohn's symphonic movements. Neither of the two middle movements appears to have any connection with the Reformation: the Allegro vivace is a Classical scherzo, the Andante an elegiac 'song without words' that was to have sister-pieces in the Adagio of the 'Scottish' Symphony and *Lobgesang*. The Finale celebrates the triumph of the

Ex. 12

Ex. 13

Reformation in a movement compounded of sonata form and a chorale-prelude on 'Ein' feste Burg', Luther's hymn or variations on it or parts of it being interrupted by an independent sonata exposition and sonata recapitulation. The Weberian first subject (Ex. 13) is only one of the numerous traces of that composer's influence on Mendelssohn's melodies and orchestration (for example, the end of the *Dream* Overture, the Nocturne from the *Dream* incidental music, the Trio of the Con moto moderato of the 'Italian' Symphony, the codetta of the first movement of the 'Scottish').

In the same year as the 'Reformation', Mendelssohn began these two other symphonies, of which the A major (No. 4, the 'Italian') was not completed till 1833, and much revised after that,[24] the A minor (No. 3, the 'Scottish') actually not until 1842. Both are typical of the Romantic love of the exotic, for Mendelssohn approaches Italy as a tourist and writes 'Italian music', the Finale of the A major Symphony with its saltarello and tarantella rhythms, as a record of travel experiences, not in the least in the spirit of northern composers of earlier times, who went to Italy to study and absorb the Italian style as an important part of European musical culture. On the contrary Mendelssohn had little but contempt for contemporary Italian 'art' music; his 'Italian music' is imitated from that of the people. So with the 'Scottish' Symphony: the theme of the Vivace non troppo in 2/4 time which occupies the place of a scherzo is pentatonic except for one note at the cadence and embodies a faint reminiscence of 'Charlie is My Darling', while the opening of the 'Andante con moto' introduction to the first movement records his immediate impression of the Palace of Holyrood on 30 July 1829, precisely as the opening of *Die Hebriden* records his immediate impression of the sea-trip from Fort William to Tobermory eight days later.

The nature of the musical material of both symphonies and

---

[24] See Wulf Konold, 'Die zwei Fassungen der "Italienischen Symphonie" von Felix Mendelssohn Bartholdy', *Bericht über den Internationalen Musikwissenschaftlichen Kongress Bayreuth 1981* (Kassel, 1982–3), 410–15.

Mendelssohn's handling of it are equally typical. Almost all the themes are lyrical in nature—and too many are in 6/8 time—and proceed in symmetrical phrases like those of a song; it is seldom possible to extract from them the pregnant motif—particles from which Haydn and Beethoven built symphonic movements. Nor did Mendelssohn command lyricism equal in quality to Schubert's or a gift for generating one melodic shape naturally from another such as Mozart had; even his second subjects hardly contrast at all, sounding like continuations rather than foils. In trying to imitate the plastic *motivische Arbeit* of the Viennese masters, he can only dismember song melodies and either distort the fragments or repeat them in different keys. These weaknesses are particularly noticeable in the first movement of the 'Scottish' Symphony. The opening of the 'Italian' is saved by its exuberance and brilliant, light-handed scoring, and its momentum carries off a great deal of skilful padding. Both works include movements—the Con moto moderato of the 'Italian', the Adagio of the 'Scottish'—which, like the inner movements of the 'Reformation', seem to have no connection with the rest of the work and help to give it an almost suite-like character. It was perhaps recognition of this that led Mendelssohn to experiment in the 'Scottish', not only connecting the movements as in his concertos but contriving subtle near-relationships, as between the introduction (Ex. 14), the first movement (Ex. 15), and the conclusion of the fourth movement (Ex. 16).

In his last symphony, the *Lobgesang* ('No. 2'), Mendelssohn attempted to follow Beethoven in the composition of a symphony with vocal Finale. The differences are considerable, apart from those in the quality of the invention. Like the 'Reformation' Symphony,

Ex. 14

Ex. 15

Ex. 16

Allegro maestoso assai

the *Lobgesang* was a quasi-occasional work commissioned for the Gutenberg Festival at Leipzig in 1840, sometimes thought—erroneously—to have originated in a purely instrumental symphony in B flat, to which Mendelssohn frequently refers in letters of 1838–39.[25] The vocal part for two sopranos, tenor, and chorus, on words from the Psalms, so far overweighs the three instrumental movements—particularly in the revised form of December 1840, when the three numbers of the 'Watchman' episode were inserted—that Mendelssohn wisely adopted his friend Klingemann's suggestion and restyled the work as a *Symphonie-Cantate*, instead of *eine Symphonie für Chor und Orchester* as he had done originally. Nevertheless the *Lobgesang* is in most respects typical of the symphonic tendencies of the period; there is a basic extra-musical idea—'first the instruments praise in their manner, and then the chorus and single voices';[26] there is a movement, the Allegretto un poco agitato, equivalent to a scherzo and placed second as in the 'Reformation' and 'Scottish' Symphonies, which seems to have no connection with the basic idea; and there is a motto-theme, the first bar of which is based on a plainsong *Magnificat*,[27] which recurs at the end of the first movement in its original form (as in the 'Scottish' Symphony), after playing an important part in that movement, and reappears in the Finale to the words 'Alles was Odem hat, lobe den Herrn'.

BERLIOZ'S SYMPHONIES

Profound though the differences are between Mendelssohn's music and Berlioz's, between their whole conceptions of, and approach to, the art, the Frenchman's four symphonies—*Épisode de la vie d'un artiste* (*Symphonie fantastique*) (1830), *Harold en Italie* (1834), *Roméo et Juliette* (*Symphonie dramatique*) (1839), and *Grande Symphonie funèbre et triomphale* for military band with strings and chorus *ad lib.* (1840)—share the same characteristics: basic extra-musical ideas, loose suite-like structure, employment of motto-themes (*Fantastique*

---

[25] See R. Larry Todd, 'An Unfinished Symphony by Mendelssohn', *Music and Letters*, 61 (1980), 293–309.

[26] *Felix Mendelssohn Bartholdys Briefwechsel mit Karl Klingemann* (Essen, 1909), 245.

[27] Tone 8, *Liber usualis*, p. 218.

and *Harold*), compositions for special occasions (the *Fantastique* for a projected concert at the Théâtre des Nouveautés, the *Funèbre et triomphale* for the inauguration of the July Column in the Place de la Bastille), introduction of voices (*Roméo et Juliette*), travel impressions (*Harold*, like Mendelssohn's 'Italian' even has a 'Marche des pèlerins'), plainsong themes (the 'Dies Irae' in the Finale of the *Fantastique*). The most obvious superficial difference is that, whereas Mendelssohn refrained from giving any but vague general clues to the extra-musical significance of his works, Berlioz sought by titles to the separate movements, even in the case of the *Fantastique* by a detailed programme intended for distribution to the audience, to attach more or less precise meanings to music sometimes originally conceived for quite other purposes. The original programme of the *Fantastique* was given by the composer in a letter to Humbert Ferrand (16 April 1830):

 I 'Rêveries—Passions' (double, consisting of a short Adagio im-
    mediately followed by a developed Allegro; a void of passions; aimless
    reveries; delirious passion, with all its paroxysms of tenderness,
    jealousy, fury, fears, etc., etc.).
 II [later III] 'Scène aux champs' (Adagio, thoughts of love and hope
    troubled by dark presentiments).
III [later II] 'Un bal' (brilliant and seductive music).
 IV 'Marche au supplice' (wild music, pompous).
  V 'Songe d'une nuit du sabbat'.

At present this is how I have contrived my novel, or rather my narrative, the hero of which you will recognize without difficulty.[28]

And he goes on to give the literary fleshing out of this skeleton: an artist falls violently in love with his ideal woman whose mental image is always accompanied by a musical *idée fixe*; his thoughts of her in the country and at a ball: his opium dreams—result of an attempt at suicide—that he has killed her and is being led to execution, that they meet at a witches' sabbath. When the symphony was first performed (5 December 1830) an expanded form of this programme was handed out with a prefatory note:

The composer's aim has been to develop *the musical aspects* of different situations in an artist's life. The plan of the instrumental drama, deprived of the assistance of words, needs preliminary exposition. The following programme should therefore be considered as the spoken dialogue of an opera [i.e. of an *opéra comique*], serving to introduce the musical numbers whose character and expression it motivates.

[28] *Lettres intimes* (Paris, 1882), 65.

He had already transposed the positions of the country and ball scenes. In the revised version of the programme[29] prefixed to the published score, all five movements, not merely the last two, are supposed to be opium dreams but Berlioz now insisted that the printed programme was indispensable only when the symphony was given 'dramatically' with invisible orchestra and followed by the *monodrame lyrique* of *Lélio: Ou le retour à la vie*, which completes the *Épisode de la vie d'un artiste*; otherwise 'one might even if necessary dispense with the distribution of the programme, preserving only the title of the five movements: the symphony (the composer hopes) being able to offer in itself a musical interest independent of all dramatic intention'. No doubt Berlioz borrowed the idea of a printed programme, which must in any case have appealed to his temperament as a device for attracting public notice, from his old master Le Sueur, who had published a descriptive brochure for his *Messe de Noël*,[30] just as he almost certainly got the conception of his motto-theme, his *idée fixe*, a theme associated with a character, from the operas of Le Sueur and Méhul. But his music was certainly not composed in conformity with the programme, as his contemporaries supposed; rather, the programme seems to have been invented as a pretext for the compilation of a large-scale instrumental work from *disjecta membra* of the most heterogeneous early compositions. The 'largo' introduction is based on a song of 1816, a setting of some verses from Jean-Pierre Florian's *Estelle et Némorin*:

> Je vais donc quitter pour jamais
> Mon doux pays, ma douce amie . . .

The *idée fixe* itself was taken from the Prix de Rome cantata of 1828, *Herminie*; the 'March au supplice' originated as a 'Marche des gardes' in *Les Francs-juges* and the 'Scène aux champs' probably from a pastoral scene in Act II of the same opera;[31] even the ball scene and the witches' sabbath may have been conceived for a projected Faust ballet. Similarly the sequel to the Symphony, *Lélio*—in which the rhetorical extravagance of French Romanticism of the post-*Hernani* period is carried to its absurdest extreme—is only another, far less successful, literary pretext for the salvage of yet other early compositions. At the end of the symphony, which in these circumstances must be played behind a curtain, Lelio staggers feebly

---

[29] Both versions are printed in full in *The New Berlioz Edition*, xvi (Kassel, 1972).
[30] See Donald H. Foster, 'The Oratorio in Paris in the 18th Century', *Acta musicologica*, 47 (1975), 116 ff.
[31] Adolphe Boschot, *La Jeunesse d'un romantique* (Paris, 1906), 247–8.

on to the stage, his attempted suicide by opium poisoning having failed, and soliloquizes:

Heavens! I am still alive! ... Then it is true, after all! Life, like a serpent, has crept into my heart again to rend it anew.... But, even though that treacherous poison deceived my despair, how could I survive such a dream? ... Why was I not crushed by the horrible pressure of the iron hand that had seized me? ... That scaffold, those judges and executioners, those soldiers, the clamours of that populace, those grave and cadenced steps falling on my heart like Cyclopean hammers ... And the inexorable melody sounding in my ear even in that heavy sleep to recall to me her image and revive my dormant suffering ... What a night! in my torment I must have cried out, Horatio must have heard me? ... No, there is still the letter I had left for him; if he had come in, he would have taken it ... Poor Horatio! I seem to hear him still, so calm and quiet yesterday at his piano, while I was writing him this last farewell ... He knew nothing of the torments of my heart and my fatal resolve; and with that sweet voice of his, poet untouched by cruel passions, he sang his favourite ballad—

This was Berlioz's setting of a translation of Goethe's 'Der Fischer'. ('It is five years since Horatio [probably Albert Duboys] wrote this ballad in imitation of Goethe, and I set it to music,' explains Lélio after the first strophe. 'We were happy then ...') In the same naïve way he introduces numbers from his other Prix de Rome pieces, *Cléopâtre* and *La Mort d'Orphée*, a 'Chanson de Brigands', and his *Grande Ouverture pour 'La Tempête'* (now styled *Fantaisie sur la 'Tempête'*), till at the end the *idée fixe* is heard for the last time and Lélio leaves the stage, murmuring 'Encore, et pour toujours!'

   The method of the pasticcio was not confined to the *Épisode de la vie d'un artiste*. (Nor to Berlioz among Romantic composers: Schumann compiled his F sharp minor Piano Sonata in a not dissimilar way.) The origin of parts of *Harold en Italie* in the *Rob Roy* Overture has already been mentioned; they only just escaped incorporation in *Les Derniers Instants de Marie Stuart*, a projected *fantaisie dramatique pour orchestre, chœurs et alto principal*, instead. The Larghetto ('Tristesse de Roméo') and ball at the Capulets in *Roméo et Juliette* are based on themes from the fourth and last Prix de Rome cantata, *Sardanapale*, and the end of the 'Grande fête chez Capulet' may well be identical with the lost 'conflagration' in *Sardanapale*. Material so dissimilar in origin was hardly to be welded into a musical entity comparable with the Classical symphony either by introducing a common motto-theme in each movement or by recalling all the earlier movements of the Finale ('Souvenirs de scènes précédentes' in the 'Orgie de brigands' of *Harold*). And Berlioz took even less account of key as a source of unity than Mendelssohn, who in the 'Reformation' (in D) had put his Scherzo in B flat, his slow movement in G minor, and the opening of his Finale in G major, and in the B flat *Lobgesang* had written the second movement in G minor and the third in D major. (Admittedly these are related keys but the usual Classical practice had been to desert the main tonic in only one of the 'inside' movements.) The *Fantastique* is in C but the three 'inside' movements are in A major, F major, and G minor. The key plan of *Harold* is closer to orthodoxy:

I   'Harold aux montagnes' (scenes of melancholy, happiness, and joy; Adagio leading to Allegro, G).
II 'Marche des pèlerins' (singing their evening prayer; Allegretto; E).
III 'Sérénade' (of a mountaineer of the Abruzzi to his mistress; Allegro assai alternating with Allegretto, C).
IV 'Orgie de brigands' (G minor and major).

The *Funèbre et triomphale* neglects key unity, though not key relationship, altogether:

I   'Marche funèbre' (F minor).
II 'Oraison funèbre' (modulating, but ultimately G major).
III 'Apothéose' (B flat).

while *Roméo* pays only lip-service to the key principle by beginning in B minor and ending in B major. With its loose key scheme, its additional movements, and the introduction of voices, it buries the vestiges of the Classical symphony—its second, third, fourth, and sixth movements are almost purely orchestral—and proposes a new conception of 'symphony', which was to be defined many years later by Mahler as 'the building up of a world, using every available technical means':

I   'Introduction. Combats—tumulte—intervention du Prince' (orchestra only; B minor).
    Prologue (contralto, chorus, and orchestra; various keys, ending in E).
    Strophes (contralto, chorus, and orchestra; G).
    Recitative and Scherzetto: 'La Reine Mab' (tenor, chorus, and orchestra; F with coda in A minor).
II 'Roméo seul—tristesse—bruit lointain de concert et de bal; grande fête chez Capulets' (orchestra only; F).
III 'Scène d'amour' (serene nights; Capulet's garden silent and

empty—the young Capulets leaving the ball and singing reminiscences of the dance music; short Allegretto with male chorus, leading to Adagio for orchestra only; A).

IV Scherzo: 'La Reine Mab ou la fée des songes' (orchestra only; F).

V   'Convoi funèbre de Juliette' (chorus and orchestra; E).

VI 'Roméo au tombeau des Capulets' (invocation—Juliet's awakening—delirious joy, despair—final anguish and death of the two lovers; orchestra only; beginning in E minor, ending in A major).

VII Finale (the crowd rushes to the cemetery—quarrel between Capulets and Montagues—recitative and aria of Friar Laurence—oath of reconciliation; bass, chorus, and orchestra; beginning in A minor, ending in B major).

It is a curious plan, the second, third, and fourth parts of the first movement performing the function of the printed programme of the *Fantastique* in explaining what the whole thing is about (so that Queen Mab appears twice in the symphony, unimportant though the passage is in relation to the tragedy). A certain amount of thematic cross-reference helps to connect the movements. Yet, despite the very great beauty of many of the parts, *Roméo* is a very unsatisfactory whole. Sometimes, especially in the sixth movement, Berlioz actually does that of which he has often been wrongfully accused: writing music the whole course of which is dictated by a literary programme and makes sense only in terms of the programme. Berlioz's own subheading tells only half the tale; there can be little doubt that his musical imagination was controlled by a more detailed visualization of the scene—not as in Shakespeare, however, but closely following Garrick's version of 1750.[32]

Otherwise the strictly programmatic element in Berlioz's music (for example, the cutting short of the *idée fixe* in the 'Marche au supplice' of the *Fantastique* by the guillotine stroke of the tutti chord) is not very large. With all the relationship of his music to literary or pictorial conceptions, it is generally no more controlled by them than Beethoven's 'Pastoral'. The formal unorthodoxies of the *Fantastique* and *Harold*, like the similar ones in the overtures, are to be accounted for, not by incidents in some detailed but concealed programme, but as inspirations of a bold mind working from point to point. One might almost describe a great deal of Berlioz's

[32] See Roger Fiske, 'Shakespeare in the Concert Hall', in Phyllis Hartnoll (ed.), *Shakespeare in Music* (London, 1964), 192–5, particularly 194.

symphonic texture as melodic passage-work, sometimes merely orchestrally effective passage-work, heedless of structural conventions inherited from the classical past.

THE FRENCH *ODE-SYMPHONIE*

Roméo et Juliette seems to have appealed to contemporary French taste, for during the next twenty years it produced some rather feeble progeny in the form of so-called *odes-symphonies*, of which *Le Désert* (1844) by Félicien David (1810–76), with words by Auguste Colin, was the earliest and most successful. As late as 1859 we find the 20-year-old Bizet sending home from Rome an *ode-symphonie*, *Vasco de Gama*. They were even less symphonic in the Classical sense than *Roméo et Juliette*. The plan of *Le Désert* is typical:

I Chorus 'Allah! Allah!' (C major); 'Marche de la caravane' (A minor); 'La tempête au désert; la caravane reprend sa marche' (reciting voice, chorus, and orchestra; A minor).

II 'La Nuit' (reciting voice, tenor, and orchestra; E flat); 'La fantaisie arabe', orchestra; C major); 'Danse des almées' (orchestra; A minor); 'La liberté au desert' (chorus and orchestra; E minor); 'La rêverie du soir' (tenor, chorus, and orchestra).

III 'Le lever du soleil' (reciting voice and orchestra; A major); 'Chant du muezzin' (tenor and orchestra; B minor); 'Dépont du caravane' (reciting voice, chorus, and orchestra; A minor and C major—recapitulating the caravan music and hymn to Allah from I).

David had travelled in the Middle East and René Brancour suggested that the Andante of his light, suite-like Symphony in E flat (1841), his third purely orchestral symphony, may have been 'inspired by the memory of one of those lovely nights spent on the terrace of the house at Smyrna' and likens the Scherzo to 'a dance of *djinns*'.[33] He certainly introduced genuine Arab melodies in *Le Désert* ('Chant du muezzin', 'La rêverie du soir', and the two orchestral pieces of II), though his harmonization is pitifully limited and unimaginative (Ex. 17). The orchestration of the once-celebrated 'Lever du soleil'— woodwind soli against a high shimmering background chord played only by divided violins, who remove their mutes desk by desk— shows the influence of Berlioz in the use of orchestral colour for its own sake.

---

[33] René Brancour, *Félicien David* (Paris, 1911), 39.

Ex. 17

The 27-year old Ernest Reyer (1823–1909) similarly brought back from Algeria travel impressions which he embodied in his four-movement *Le Sélam* (1850), with words by Théophile Gautier. It is constructed on similar lines to *Le Désert*:

   I Serenade, *Razzia* (choruses of warriors and shepherds), Pastoral.
   II Conjuration of djinns.
   III Evening song (including the *muezzin*'s call).
   IV The *Dhossa* (ceremony of the return of pilgrims from Mecca).

David himself failed in *Christophe Colomb* (1847) to repeat the success of *Le Désert*. The *odes-symphonies* of Louis Lacombe (1818–84)—*Manfred* (1847) and *Arva* (1850)—are worth mentioning only to show the temporary popularity of the genre.

SPOHR

The only German composer of the period who rivalled Berlioz as a composer of frankly programmatic symphonies was Ludwig Spohr (1784–1859), who followed three normal symphonies with *Die Weihe der Töne* (*Charakteristiches Tongemälde in Form einer Sinfonie*) [The Consecration of Sounds] (1832). This is a four-movement work inspired by a poem by Karl Pfeiffer that Spohr had originally intended to set as a cantata.[34] Its programme, if not the actual music, is considerably more abstract than that of Berlioz's *Fantastique*. The separate movements bear no headings but the following points are easily deducible from the poem prefixed to the score, which Spohr

---

[34] Louis Spohr, *Selbstbiographie* (Kassel and Göttingen, 1860–1), ii. 191.

like Berlioz wished to have read aloud or distributed to the audience before a performance:

I Largo: unbroken silence of Nature before the creation of sound (F minor).
   Allegro: subsequent active life; sounds of Nature, tumult of the elements (D minor).
II Cradle song: dance; serenade (B flat).
III Martial music: departure for battle; feelings of those left behind; return of the victors; prayer of thanksgiving (D).
IV Funeral music (F minor): comfort in tears (F major).

After a non-programmatic Fifth Symphony (1836), with a first movement based on an overture to Raupach's tragedy *Die Tochter der Luft*, Spohr composed in 1839 a curious *Historische Symphonie* (the 'Historical') 'in the style and taste of four different periods. First movement: Bach–Handel period, 1720. Adagio: Haydn–Mozart period, 1780. Scherzo: Beethoven period, 1810. Finale: latest period of all, 1840'. Then in 1841 he composed Symphony No. 7, a 'double symphony' for two orchestras, *Irdisches und Göttliches im Menschenleben* [Earthly and Divine in Human Life]. This is in three movements, each headed by a stanza of verse: 'The World of Childhood', 'The Time of the Passions', 'Final Triumph of the Divine'. His Eighth and Tenth Symphonies have no programme, but the Ninth (1850) is entitled *Die Jahreszeiten* [The Seasons] and is in two main parts:

Winter (Sonata form in B minor)—Transition to Spring—Spring (Minuet in G).
Summer (Largo in B major)—Introduction to Autumn—Autumn (Allegro vivace in D).

Thus Spohr's programmes are either generalized and ideal or of such a nature that music could easily suggest them without enlarging or straining its most familiar associative resources; there is, in fact, nothing in them that would have puzzled an eighteenth-century composer to translate into music. He approaches most nearly to the Romantic style of tone painting in the first movement of Symphony No. 4, *Die Weihe der Töne* (bird-calls take the place of 'second subject', duly recapitulated in the tonic, and a storm that of the development section), in the 'Transition to Spring' (bird-calls) and 'Autumn' (hunting sounds) of *Die Jahreszeiten*, and in the Finale of the 'Historical' Symphony where he brings in piccolo, trombones, and other additional brass, with triangle, side-drum, bass-drum, and cymbals to produce a noise presumably intended as a parody of Berlioz and Meyerbeer.

Novel instrumentation plays an important part in other of Spohr's symphonies. In the early *Irdisches und Göttliches in Menschenleben* the divine is symbolized by a small orchestra of solo woodwind, two horns, and solo strings, the earthly by a larger one of double woodwind, horns, and strings, plus trumpets and trombones in the Finale, and the forces of 'good' and 'evil' are used antiphonally or together—often with striking effect, as at the end of the first movement where the major subdominant of the 'divine' orchestra contradicts the minor subdominant of the 'earthly' one (Ex. 18). Spohr had a marked affection for antiphonal effects—witness his double quartets—and in the second movement of *Die Weihe der Töne* he combines lullaby, dance, and serenade (Ex. 19) in a manner reminiscent of the ball scene in *Don Giovanni* and a passage in the third movement of Berlioz's *Harold*. He divides his violins into three in the pastoral middle section of the first movement of the 'Historical' Symphony, writes quasi-thematically for three timpani in its Scherzo

Ex. 18

(Ex. 20) and introduces a solo violin in the Trio of the non-programmatic Eighth. Points of affinity with Mendelssohn and Berlioz include the use of a motto-motif, three rising notes followed

Ex. 19

by the fall of a perfect fifth in several of the themes of *Die Weihe der Töne*, and the quotation of a plainsong melody, 'the Ambrosian song of praise', in the third movement of the same symphony. The

metrical treatment is typical of the period (Ex. 21). In one instance
Spohr was bolder than his younger contemporaries, ending *Irdisches
und Göttliches* with an Adagio. Like them he was essentially a lyrical
symphonist and his gentle under-vitalized lyricism, sentimentally

Ex. 20

Ex. 21

underlined by his notorious tendency to incessant chromatic movement in inner parts, becomes monotonous when stretched to symphonic proportions. It was perhaps from the initial Allegro and Larghetto of his Third Symphony in C minor (1828) that Mendelssohn caught the habit of writing elegiac movements in 6/8 or 9/8 time.

MINOR SYMPHONIC COMPOSERS

The same warm, sometimes lukewarm, lyricism, unrelieved by effective thematic contrasts, characterizes much of the work of the minor Central Europeans of the period: the two symphonies of Spohr's pupil Norbert Burgmüller (1810–36), the seven by the Czech Jan Václav Kalliwoda (1801–66), the eight by Schubert's friend Franz Lachner (1803–90), eldest and most gifted of three distinguished brothers, who turned in later years to the composition of orchestral suites more interesting than his symphonies. In France, apart from Berlioz, the form was represented only by the few Gallicized counterfeits of Viennese Classicism produced by George Onslow (1784–1852) and Napoléon-Henri Reber (1807–80). Scandinavia could show a more original symphonist, and a more symphonic symphonist, in the Swede Franz Berwald (1769–1868) whose *Symphonie sérieuse* in G minor, No. 2 (1843), and *Symphonie singulière* in C major, No. 5 (1845)—particularly the latter—show more originality and virility than most of the symphonies of the Dane Niels Gade. Of Berwald's six symphonies, the First, A major (1820), is incomplete, the Third, D major, was completed in 1913 from the composer's four-stave composition sketch by Ernst Ellberg who called it *Capricieuse*, while the Fourth, the real *Capricieuse*, is lost.[35] There is perhaps an element of self-conscious originality in the *Symphonie singulière*, as the title suggests, but Berwald's other scores show the same dryness and energy, the same bold handling of instrumental blocks and long ostinato-like passages. In Ex. 22 from the Finale of the *Singulière* the astringency of the violin melody and the marcato accompaniment are equally characteristic; but in the course of the movement it is the latter which becomes decidedly the more important and it is one of the two main elements that triumph in the coda (Ex. 23).

There is nothing comparable in Gade, though it is true he sounds a national, even heroic, note in his First Symphony (1842), echoing the *Ossian* Overture, and again in his Eighth (1871). But for the most part Gade's symphonies are those of a naturalized Leipziger, conventionally post-Classical or lyrical. Even his First Symphony

Ex. 22

[35] On Berwald's symphonies and other orchestral works, see Robert Layton, *Franz Berwald* (London, 1959).

Ex. 23

opens lyrically with an orchestral version of one of his own songs, 'King Waldemar's Hunt'; his Fourth (1850), at one time the best known, is appropriately dedicated to Spohr; the Allegro con fuoco of the Fifth (1852) opens like a Schumann piano piece. (The score includes a part for piano, a noteworthy innovation.)

SCHUMANN AS SYMPHONIST

In Schumann's own symphonies the problem of discrepancy between square-cut lyricism and symphonic architecture may be said to have reached a crisis, if for no other reason than that Schumann faced it instead of evading it like most of his contemporaries. He shows most of the other characteristic traits. His first mature symphony, in B flat (1841), is a typical reconciliation of a programme with traditional form. According to his wife it was originally entitled *Frühlingsymphonie* [Spring Symphony] and inspired by 'a spring poem',[36] and the separate movements originally bore titles, 'Frühlingsbeginn' [Spring's Opening], 'Abend' [Evening], 'Frohe Gespielen' [Merry Playfellows], and 'Voller Frühling' [Spring at the Full], though Wasielewski[37] says the first movement was called 'Spring's Awakening', the Finale 'Spring's Farewell'. Schumann's Third, in E flat (1850), although he did not give it its nickname, the 'Rhenish', admittedly 'reflects here and there' aspects of life in the Rhineland,[38] and it is well known that the fourth movement was inspired by the ceremony of Archbishop von Geissel's elevation to the cardinalate in Cologne Cathedral. (Although Schumann's symphonic works contain no quotation of plainsong, this movement betrays a tendency to that Catholic mysticism of which interest in plainsong was a symptom.) We find again in Schumann the suite-like structure (the Scherzos of both First and Second Symphonies have two Trios; the Third Symphony has five movements), and use of the rather mechanical devices of the motto-theme, quotation from one movement to another, and the elimination of breaks between movements to counteract it. Trombones at the end of the Larghetto of the First Symphony solemnly anticipate the theme of the Scherzo which then follows without a break. The C major Symphony, No. 2 (1846), has a motto-theme stated by the brass at the very beginning and recalled—always on the brass—at or near the ends of the first, second, and fourth movements; the main subject of the Adagio reappears in the Finale, an unconventional movement of which the principal feature is an entirely new theme (Ex. 24) that appears

Ex. 24

---

[36] By Adolf Böttger. It is given complete in Berthold Litzmann, *Clara Schumann: Ein Künstlerleben nach Tagebüchern und Briefen* (6th edn., Leipzig, 1920), ii. 27.

[37] *Robert Schumann*, p. 298.

[38] Ibid., p. 456, and letter to Simrock in Hermann Erler, *Robert Schumanns Leben Aus seinen Briefen geschildat* (Berlin, 1886–7), ii. 139.

Ex. 25

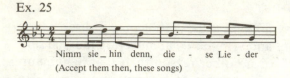

Nimm sie _ hin denn, die - se Lie - der
(Accept them then, these songs)

half-way through and soon dominates everything. It is a near-quotation from the last song of Beethoven's cycle *An die ferne Geliebte* (Ex. 25), which also appears in the piano *Phantaisie*, Op. 17. The violins have already referred to 'wo ich dich, Geliebte, fand' from the first song.

Introduction of a completely new, song-like theme at the end of a movement is a favourite symphonic device of Schumann's: cf. the coda of the first movement of the B flat Symphony and the first and last movements of the D minor. The introduction to the First Symphony states the main theme of the Allegro molto vivace in slow tempo, that to the C major foreshadows practically the whole material of the following Allegro, and even the string counterpoint to the motto-theme turns out to be thematically important. Thematic links are less evident in the E flat Symphony, though there are several references to the fourth movement in the Finale. But Schumann's most determined attempt to knit together all four movements is his D minor, originally composed in 1841 but revised and rescored ten years later, first as a *Symphonistische Phantasie*, later styled 'Fourth Symphony'.[39] Here again the slow introduction to the first movement is of great importance. Its opening theme (Ex. 26), reappears in the slow second movement and throws out tendrils on a solo violin (Ex. 27). Inverted, it generates the theme of the Scherzo while the Trio

Ex. 26

Ziemlich langsam

Ex. 27

Ziemlich langsam

p dolce

---

[39] On the two versions see Abraham, 'The Three Scores of Schumann's D minor Symphony, in *Slavonic and Romantic Music*, p. 281. But the score of the first version published in 1891 is inaccurate.

Ex. 28

Ex. 29

is a rhythmic transformation of Ex. 27. The semiquaver motif that
emerges towards the end of the slow introduction is still more vital;
it at once becomes the chief theme of the Allegro first movement,
to which in the definitive version Schumann gave a German
tempo-indication, 'Lebhaft'. It is more like pianistic passage-work
than germinal 'theme' (Ex. 28). In the relative major it does duty as
second subject and in the development acquires a mate (Ex. 29).
Indeed in the original version it acquired two mates, for it then ran
in counterpoint with the new dolce violin melody which appears at
bar 147. The wind chords of Ex. 29 accompany the inversion of Ex.
26 at the beginning of the Scherzo and, after the solemn passage

connecting Scherzo and Finale—another structural innovation[40]—together they open the Finale itself and provide the binding elements of the entire movement. All in all, this was the most important of all attempts to give the Romantic symphony coherence and unity, as *Roméo et Juliette* is the most important essay in the opposite direction.

Despite their great interest and numerous beauties—among which the 'Cologne Cathedral' movement of the Third and Adagio espressivo of the Second, with its poignant chromatic appoggiaturas, are outstanding—Schumann's symphonies are by no means unqualified masterpieces. They are handicapped not so much by their frequently thick and generally unimaginative scoring and the doubtfully successful structural innovations as by the nature of the material: the typical Romantic difficulty of the song-like theme in the symphonic setting. The types of theme that sprang naturally from Schumann's mind were the symmetrically balanced phrases of song melody and the kind of rhythmic aphorism composers are apt to find at the piano; neither is well adapted for expansion in the grand paragraphs that seem to be demanded by a large-scale orchestral composition. Schumann is most true to himself in the naturally lyrical slow movements and naturally aphoristic scherzos; when, following the lead of Mendelssohn's A minor Symphony, he writes scherzos in 2/4 time (first Trio of the B flat Symphony, entire Scherzo of the C major), the result is a satisfactory substitute for the Classical scherzo: a Schumann miniature for orchestra instead of piano. But his first movements, with the very notable exception of the E flat, and his finales are very seriously weakened by the over-repetition of rhythmic patterns and melodic phrases too complete in themselves to demand, even allow, expansion or indeed any sort of continuation except symmetrical answering phrases. He can do little but repeat them sequentially with varied scoring and in different keys. Only in the first movement of the E flat does he find a long-breathed opening theme with well-defined features which he can expand in the spacious periods of a truly symphonic style.

---

[40] The sketches of the C major Symphony show that here also Schumann originally contemplated a connecting section between Adagio and Finale. See Wolfgang Boetticher, *Robert Schumann: Einführung in Persönlichkeit und Werk* (Berlin, 1941), 542, and also Jon W. Finson, 'The Sketches for the Fourth Movement of Schumann's Second Symphony, Op. 61', *Journal of the American Musicological Society*, 39 (1986), 143.

PROBLEMS OF THE ROMANTIC CONCERTO

Schumann's much greater success in his Piano Concerto (1845) is due above all to his abandonment of any attempt to copy Classical models. He was content in the first place to write a single-movement *Fantaisie* for piano and orchestra (1841), the present first movement, based on frankly lyrical themes—indeed almost entirely on one lyrical theme which, slightly transformed and with different continuations (as in Mendelssohn's *Die Hebriden*), supplies the material for a movement in sonata form though devoid of sonata feeling. The form is simply a framework for the laying out of a series of delightful ideas that would have served equally well for short piano pieces; but here they are set even more delightfully against an unobtrusive orchestral background which strengthens the climaxes; in particular a wind instrument sings a melody, perhaps instead of the piano, or with the piano, or even picking up one that the piano is only implying. Still less is there any question of rivalling the subtleties of Classical concerto structure. This first movement is something *sui generis* or, as Schumann himself put it,[41] 'something between symphony, concerto and grand sonata'. The addition, five years later, of an Intermezzo and Finale did not alter that.

After the sentence quoted, from a letter written in January 1839, he goes on: 'I see that I can't write a concerto for the virtuosi; I must think of something different.' That need either to write for the virtuosi or to think of something different was the major problem for every composer who at that period wished to write for solo instrument and orchestra. Writing for the virtuosi, particularly the piano virtuosi, had for years not only debased the concerto style itself but brought into existence a quantity of loosely constructed showpieces—fantasias, sets of brilliant variations—in which the orchestra was reduced to the role of menial, by no means indispensable accompaniment. For his *Krakowiak* (*Grand Rondeau de concert*) (1828) Chopin provided here and there an alternative left-hand part to use when playing without an accompaniment; the orchestral part, except for an occasional noisily interjected tutti, consists of quiet string harmonies with here and there a solo wind instrument (almost invariably marked dolce) winding its way, sometimes thematically, often rather aimlessly, through the piano figuration (Ex. 30). Such was to be the basis of much of the scoring of Schumann's Concerto. The *Krakowiak*, with Chopin's 'La ci darem' Variations (1827), his *Fantaisie sur des airs nationaux polonais* (1828), and his *Grande*

---

[41] *Jugendbriefe von Robert Schumann* (Leipzig, 1885), 297.

Ex. 30

Polonaise brillante (*précédée d'un Andante spianato*) (1831), with Liszt's *Grande Fantaisie symphonique* on themes from Berlioz's *Lélio* (1834) and *Fantasie über Motive aus Beethovens 'Ruinen von Athen'* (*c*.1852), stands on a higher plane than most pieces of this type. Indeed the *Krakowiak* itself approximates to the better organized, less superficial type of composition most successfully practised by Mendelssohn and Schumann: the former in his *Capriccio brillant* (1832), *Rondo brillant* (1834), and *Serenade und Allegro giojoso* (1838), the latter in his *Introduction und Allegro appassionato* and *Konzert-Allegro* for piano (1849 and 1853) and *Phantasie* for violin (1853).

These hardly differ from their composers' concerto movements; as we have seen, Schumann was able to use such a movement as the basis of a concerto.

Programmatic tendencies had already shown themselves earlier in the century, more noticeably in the concerto than in the symphony: in Weber's *Konzertstück* and in concertos by Steibelt, Field, and others.[42] They quickly disappeared from serious music but were still exploited by showmen of the concert platform, particularly in the Paris that could be excited by the programme of the *Symphonie fantastique*. Mendelssohn reported to Zelter (letter, 15 February 1832) that he had just heard in Paris Friedrich Kalkbrenner (1785–1849) play his *Grande Fantaisie*, '*Le Rêve*':

This is a new piano concerto he has composed, in which he has gone over to romanticism; he explains beforehand that it begins with indefinite dreams, goes on to despair, then to a declaration of love and finally a military march. Henri Herz had no sooner heard it than he also made a romantic piano piece and explains it too beforehand: then a storm, then a prayer with the angelus and finally a military march. You won't believe it; but it really is so.

Although such ephemera are hardly to be seriously connected with contemporary tendencies in the symphony, it was only natural that the symphonists should apply their favourite solutions also to the structural problems of the concerto as Mendelssohn and Schumann did. (Berlioz neglected the concerto, for *Harold en Italie* is emphatically a symphony with solo viola, not a viola concerto.) The Classical—or more precisely Hummelian—piano concerto nearly died with Chopin's two essays in F minor and E minor (1829 and 1830). It can hardly be said to be still alive in the last works of Ferdinand Ries or in the elegant—and really very seldom programmatic—platitudes of Kalkbrenner. However, Hummel's pupil Adolph Henselt (1814–89) was to develop it powerfully in his remarkable Concerto in F minor (1844). Henselt's work is warmly Romantic in idiom, nearly Lisztian in technique; the Chopinesque Larghetto (Ex. 31) has an extraordinary middle section in C sharp minor where four staves are needed for the unprecedentedly full piano writing.

The new type of piano concerto was launched with Mendelssohn's G minor in 1831, its first movement without introductory ritornello, simply a piece for piano and orchestra in curtailed sonata form—

---

[42] See Vol. VIII, pp. 206–54.

Ex. 31

the recapitulation compressed even more drastically than usual with
Mendelssohn. All three movements are played without a break, and
the first and third thematically connected by their common link with
the slow movement and by the reappearance of the second subject
of the Molto allegro near the end of the Finale. The material is as
Romantic as the form in which it is cast: the slow movement a
prototype of the nocturne in the *Midsummer Night's Dream* music,
the second subject of the first movement a typical Romantic
melody alike in its structure, its modulations, and its plastic curves.
Mendelssohn's friend Moscheles (1794–1870) tightened up this general
concerto pattern with more theme-transformation and much less
display of virtuosity in his Concerto No. 7 (the 'Pathétique') (1836)
whereas Mendelssohn himself was content to repeat it in his D minor
Piano Concerto (1837) and his ever popular E minor Violin Concerto
(1844).[43] Both of these dispense with introductory ritornellos and
both have carefully composed links between the slow and the two
outside movements. (The first violinist to perform the E minor,
Ferdinand David (1810–73), had already in 1837 published a concerto
on the same lines and in the same key.) This was the pattern that
Schumann borrowed in most essentials in his Piano Concerto (1841
and 1845) and worked out more faithfully and with finer artistry in
the linking passages in his Cello Concerto (1850). Only in the D
minor Violin Concerto (1853), for many years suppressed by his
heirs on the ground of its inferiority, did Schumann surprisingly

[43] Work on which was delayed by an attempt at a piano concerto in the same key; see R.
Larry Todd, 'An Unfinished Piano Concerto by Mendelssohn', *Musical Quarterly*, 68 (1982),
80–101.

revert to the old ritornello—or, rather, to a somewhat inept 'double exposition' in the tutti of which the second subject already appears in the relative major. In its compression the Cello Concerto—which Schumann originally in the catalogue of his works called not 'concerto' but *Konzertstück für Violoncello mit Begleitung des Orchesters*—is the counterpart of the D minor Symphony. In all these works the solo part remains very difficult but ceases to be a vehicle for mere virtuosic display. The cadenza—as essential a feature of the Classical concerto as the introductory ritornello—is either dropped altogether or drastically shortened to a few bars or even, in Schumann's Piano Concerto, transformed into a slow and dreamy improvisatory passage. Even the more conventional cadenza of Mendelssohn's Violin Concerto provides a completely unconventional and immensely effective return to the recapitulation.

ENLARGEMENT OF THE ORCHESTRAL PALETTE

The unusually rich fertilization of pure orchestral music by resources drawn from opera has already been mentioned. (At the same time symphonic music was already beginning to repay its debt to the theatre.) As we have seen, the latter part of Berlioz's *Roméo et Juliette* is very nearly operatic; the 'marche au supplice' and probably the 'scène aux champs' of the *Fantastique* actually originated in opera. Even the more conservative, least operatically inclined composers introduce dramatic elements in their symphonies and concertos, particularly in the transitional passage linking movements (Mendelssohn's G minor Concerto, Schumann's D minor Symphony and Cello Concerto). And the enrichment of concert music by the results of experimentation in the theatre is even more noticeable in the medium itself than in the forms.

New instruments and additions to the Classical orchestra with its pairs of wind and timpani plus strings appeared in opera orchestras and scores earlier and more frequently than in concert orchestras and scores. By about 1830 the additional wind (piccolo, cor anglais, bass clarinet, ophicleide, trombones), percussion of indefinite pitch, and harp or even two harps, were almost universal in opera scores but still exceptional—though they soon grew less so—in concert music.[44] In the early 1830s the only usual addition to the Classical orchestra was a second pair of horns, generally crooked in a different key from the first pair in order to give a wider choice of notes, though Mendelssohn does without them in the 'Reformation' and

---

[44] Adam Carse, *The History of Orchestration* (London, 1925), 220 and 245.

'Italian' Symphonies and in most of his overtures. The 'Italian' Symphony, the Violin Concerto, *Die Hebriden*, and *Melusine* are all written for the pure Classical orchestra. In other works Mendelssohn augmented it: in the *Dream* Overture with an ophicleide, the new 'keyed serpent' which now tended to displace the old serpent (it seems to have reached England only in 1834) and was itself gradually displaced by the tuba about the middle of the century;[45] in the 'Scottish' Symphony with a second pair of horns, in the 'Reformation' with serpent and double-bassoon (playing the same part) and three trombones; in *Meeresstille* with piccolo, serpent, and double-bassoon, and a third trumpet; and in *Ruy Blas* with a second pair of horns and three trombones. Similar forces, with harp or triangle, bass-drum, and cymbals for special effects, satisfied almost all symphonic composers of the period, but not opera composers—or Berlioz. Berlioz's 'extravagance', except in some quite abnormal works—such as the *Requiem*, the *Te Deum*, the *Symphonie funèbre et triomphale*, and the cantata *L'Impériale*, written for special occasions and perpetuating a French tradition of 'monumental' works dating from the Revolution and First Empire (for example, Gossec's *Requiem* and second *Te Deum*, Le Sueur's Coronation Mass for Napoleon)—consists mainly of writing concert music for the normal orchestra of the Paris Opéra, the orchestra commonly employed by Halévy and Meyerbeer, with piccolo, cor anglais, four bassoons (a peculiarity of French orchestras), four horns, a pair of cornets (another French peculiarity), trombones, one or two ophicleides, additional timpani and other percussion, and a harp or harps. Even his insistence that his string parts must be played by at least fifteen first violins, fifteen seconds, ten violas, ten to twelve cellos, and nine (in *Roméo* only seven) double-basses means only that he would be content with no smaller body of strings than Habeneck had for the Société des Concerts in 1828: fifteen firsts, sixteen seconds, eight violas, twelve cellos, and eight basses.[46] He originally scored *Waverley* for four clarinets, two in C, two in A, but changed his mind although Habeneck had them.

The invention of valve-mechanism which gave trumpets and horns a full chromatic scale made itself felt too late to influence most of

---

[45] Modern editions of scores of this period often indicate a tuba where the composer specified an ophicleide or serpent. Thus in the 'Songe d'une nuit du Sabbat' in the *Fantastique* Berlioz originally wrote a part for a B flat serpent; in the first French edition (Schlesinger, 1846), this was given to a second ophicleide, in B flat, and a note elsewhere in the score authorizes the playing of this second ophicleide part on an E flat tuba. But most modern editions give both ophicleide parts to tubas in C.

[46] Georg Schünemann, *Geschichte des Dirigierens* (Leipzig, 1913), 319.

the orchestration of this period, though Meyerbeer introduced a whole band of saxhorns on the stage in *Le Prophète* (1849). The *trompette à clefs* used by Meyerbeer in *Robert le diable* (1831) and Halévy's *trompette à pistons* in *La Juive* (1835) were short-lived instruments of a different type, the former a keyed bugle, the latter related to the cornet; indeed Pierné and Woollett[47] have suggested that composers of this period often wrote *trompettes à pistons* when they meant *cornets à pistons*. Berlioz began by writing for *trompettes à pistons* in *Waverley* and *Les Francs-juges* but when he transferred the *Francs-juges* march to the *Fantastique* he substituted B flat cornets for the single E flat piston trumpet. In any case, composers had little idea what to do with the piston instruments, often using them melodically with rather vulgar effect (for example, 'Réunion des deux thèmes, du Larghetto et de l'Allegro' in the second movement of *Roméo et Juliette*), though Berlioz does often employ them in conjunction with a pair of natural trumpets. In the little known and never used additional cornet part for 'Un bal' in the *Fantastique* he gives the instrument a pungent rhythmic figure (See Ex. 32, bars 106 ff).[48] The much more important mechanization of the horns, which ultimately revolutionized the nineteenth-century orchestra by giving mobility to the Romantic instrument *par excellence*, was completely ignored by Mendelssohn and almost completely by Berlioz until late works (*Les Troyens, Béatrice et Bénédict*) where he sometimes admits a pair of valve-horns beside a pair of natural instruments. Yet earlier he would take elaborate pains to get horn melody, sometimes employing four natural horns all in different crooks, as in the Prince's recitative in the introduction of *Roméo* where the theme of the fugal 'Combats' appears in augmentation (though they really only support cornets, trombones, and ophicleide). Mendelssohn's ingenuity is fully exercised in the invention of a lovely melody in the Nocturne of the *Dream* based entirely on the open notes and with the few closed sounds very carefully placed. Oddly enough, one of the first important symphonic composers to employ a pair of valve-horns in addition to a pair of natural ones was Schumann; he had made a singularly unlucky use of closed notes for horns and trumpets in the original opening of the B flat Symphony. We know from both Berlioz's *Memoirs*[49] and Wagner's *Rienzi* that the Dresden orchestra, unlike

---

[47] 'Histoire de l'orchestration' in Albert Lavignac (ed.) *Encyclopédie de la musique*, 2/4 (Paris, 1929), 2532.

[48] See *The New Berlioz Edition*, xvi (ed. Nicholas Temperley) (Kassel, 1972), 197.

[49] *The Memoirs of Hector Berlioz*, trans. David Cairns (New York, 1969), 306.

Ex. 32

that of the Leipzig Gewandhaus, possessed valve-horns and trumpets early in the 1840s, so when Schumann moved there at the end of 1844 he was naturally encouraged to write his first and second horn parts, sometimes all four, and his trumpet parts for valve-instruments as a matter of course, although he almost always treats them as Classical horns with extra notes at their disposal, not as flexible new voices in the middle register. Only in conjunction with the trombones, as in the famous fourth movement of the 'Rhenish' Symphony and at the beginning of the *Neujahrslied* for chorus and orchestra (also 1850), does he take advantage of the new resources of the horn quite freely; indeed his quiet use of trombones, sometimes at dangerous heights,[50] as a real, freely moving choir employed neither for noise

---

[50] Like most of his German contemporaries, he scores for alto, tenor, and bass; elsewhere three tenors were more usual.

nor for dramatic effect, was a feature of his scoring after his discovery of Schubert's C major Symphony: see, for instance, his First Symphony, particularly the end of the Larghetto. In the Scherzo, however, he reverts to the early nineteenth-century practice, condemned by Berlioz, of underlining the string bass part with a single bass trombone—a practice that survived also in Sterndale Bennett's *Naiads* and the scores of Chopin, Glinka, and others. But in the *Valse-fantaisie* Glinka allows his trombone to play cantabile phrases unsupported, like those of the unison trombones in the *Capriccio brillante*.

The improvements in woodwind mechanism introduced by Theobald Boehm and others had even less immediate influence on orchestral technique than Adolphe Sax's improvements to the brass, and such experiments as Berlioz's muting of the clarinet in 'La Harpe éolienne' in *Lélio* by wrapping it in a leather bag, as Spontini had done long before in *Fernand Cortez*, never passed into ordinary practice. But composers did make ever heavier demands on wind-players' agility and general resourcefulness; the flute solo in the Scherzo of Mendelssohn's *Midsummer Night's Dream* music is famous, and some of the clarinet passages in the same movement were at first found almost unplayable. In the third movement of *Die Weihe der Töne* Spohr did not hesitate to plunge his A clarinets deep into a flat key. Similarly the strings, with their centuries-old 'mechanism' unchanged, found their upward compass being continually extended. Devices employed exceptionally by the masters of the two previous decades—the picking out of a solo violin, division of violins or cellos into four or even more parts, various kinds of tremolo, playing sul ponticello—now became quite common, particularly in the scores of Berlioz and the opera composers. They too, rather than the more conservative symphonists, began to use percussion more subtly; Berlioz wrote chords for the timpani (end of the 'Scène aux champs' in the *Fantastique*, the overture to *Cellini*); Meyerbeer uses four timpani thematically in one of the entr'actes of *Le Prophète*, and an example from Spohr has already been quoted (Ex. 20). In the 'Grande fête chez Capulet', the Andante of *Carnaval romain*, and Glinka's Spanish pieces even the percussion of indefinite pitch cease to be mere contributors of noise and are scored with subtlety.

It is more difficult to generalize on tendencies in the handling of the orchestra as a whole, thanks to the fact that orchestration was becoming far more obviously than ever before a matter of personal

style and texture, not of semi-routine. The influence of Weber is
apparent in the work of all the outstanding orchestrators of the
period: on Mendelssohn and Berlioz, Meyerbeer, Glinka, and
the young Wagner. Of all these, Mendelssohn advanced least from
the post-Classical style of Weber, though he used it with supreme
skill and added numerous happy refinements of his own: the rapidly
repeated wind chords against which the octave violins outline the
opening theme of the 'Italian' Symphony, the pianissimo passage for
all the strings in octaves against the harmonies of the woodwind and
brass—a contrast used by Weber only in brilliant tuttis—in the first
movement of the 'Scottish', the organ-like layout of bars 11–19 of
the Andante con moto of the 'Italian' where the violins seem to

Ex. 33

represent one manual, the flutes another, and the staccato basses the pedals, to name three instances at random, though all three, as it happens, illustrate that clear differentiation of string and wind colouring which is one of the marked characteristics of the period as a whole.

Schumann's timid tendency after the B flat Symphony and the first version of the D minor to play for safety by constant doubling of strings and wind was exceptional. The valve-mechanism enabled him to use the horns (even more than in the earlier works) as inside padding, but unfortunately this reduced far too much of his orchestration to an opaque mass of strings, woodwind, and horns, sounding all the thicker because of the frequent lack of fluidity in the separate parts. Schumann's pianistic approach to the orchestra often shows not only in the invention of pianistic figures but in a too 'vertical' conception of texture. In rescoring the D minor Symphony he even injects pianistic effects, like the percussive figure on second violins, violas, and cellos at the beginning of the first Allegro, into music originally conceived orchestrally. Or he will double and thicken, and substitute pianistic repeated chords on second violins and violas for true orchestral texture. However he did not always mute his imagination in later years. One very different instance has already been quoted from *Manfred* (Ex. 8); another is the 'Sonnenaufgang' that opens the second section of the *Szenen aus Goethe's Faust* (Ex. 33), an example of what were then the most modern orchestral tendencies: division of the strings, limpid texture, with primary colours alternated or contrasted simultaneously, occur on many pages of Glinka, the best of Wagner's earlier operas, and Meyerbeer—to say nothing of Berlioz the supreme master. Wagner's tromboning of themes against glittering backgrounds in the *Tannhäuser* Overture of 1845 and the Prelude to Act III of *Lohengrin* (written in 1848), for which there were Berliozian precedents in *Le Roi Lear* and *Benvenuto Cellini*, illustrate the same tendency at its coarsest. Ex. 34 from the *Prince Kholmsky* Overture, showing Glinka at much less than his most brilliant, is a typical mixture of strings, woodwind, and brass.

The opening of Meyerbeer's *Struensee* Overture illustrates the love of primary yet novel colours (Ex. 35). The passage is immediately repeated in staccato quavers, *ff* and *pp*, by an entirely unsupported brass choir of two horns, *trompette à pistons*, three trombones, and ophicleide—and the carefully balanced dynamic markings now often thought necessary.

Such subtleties of balance, like the rhythmic complications of Ex. 34, could never have been achieved under the old system of joint 'conducting' by continuo-player and principal violinist which had survived well into the first quarter of the nineteenth century and even beyond it; modern conducting was introduced at Leipzig, for instance, by Mendelssohn, only in 1835—and Schumann at first disliked it. The music of Berlioz and Wagner, above all, needed the independent specialist conductor with his baton and it is significant that both wrote treatises on the new art.[51] By 1848 Wagner had in *Lohengrin* developed an individual orchestral style which nevertheless was only a preliminary stage in the evolution of his mature handling of the orchestra. By the same date Berlioz had closed his career as a symphonic composer with the *Marche funèbre pour la dernière scène d'Hamlet*, though he was still to use the orchestra with consummate

---

[51] Berlioz, 'L'Art du chef d'orchestre' in the 2nd edn. of his *Grande Traité de l'instrumentation et d'orchestration modernes* (Paris, 1855); Wagner, 'Über das Dirigieren' (1870); repr. in *Richard Wagner: Gesammelte Schriften und Dichtungen*, viii (Leipzig, 1873), 325–410.

Ex. 34

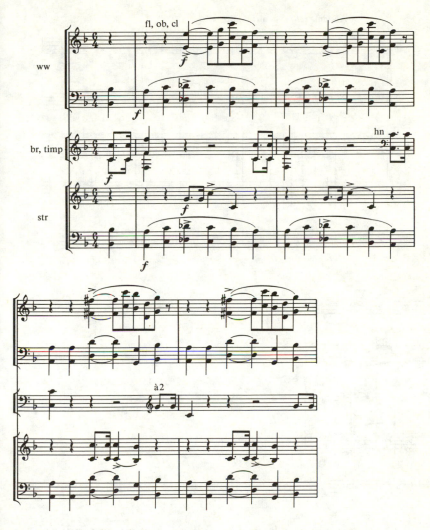

skill in *L'Enfance du Christ* and the *Te Deum*, in *Les Troyens*, and *Béatrice et Bénédict*.

BERLIOZ AND THE ROMANTIC ORCHESTRA

It was Berlioz who summed up and refined upon every new tendency in Romantic orchestration. He often learned from such contemporaries as Halévy and Meyerbeer and such immediate predecessors as Weber, Spontini, and Rossini, but he subtilized their devices and in turn bequeathed a whole encyclopaedia of orchestral conceptions to those who came after. He scattered the seed of ideas

Ex. 35

so lavishly that some was bound to fall upon stony ground; neither the already mentioned muting of the clarinet nor the famous combination in the *Requiem* of high flute chords with the pedal notes of eight tenor trombones playing in unison has probably ever been adopted by anyone else. But his fertilizing influence generally was incalculable, though its action was oddly delayed in his own country. A few favourite, characteristic, or strikingly novel effects may be mentioned: the pizzicato arpeggios with thumb glissando in Mephistopheles' serenade in *La Damnation*, the violin harmonics in the 'Queen Mab' Scherzo of *Roméo*, the suspended cymbal struck softly with a sponge-headed drumstick (probably first used in the

Francs-juges Overture), the drawing of scales in one instrumental group across the solid texture of another group, semiquaver arpeggio accompaniment figuration in one orchestral group, division of melodic interest between first and second violins (as in *Waverley*), suggestion of bells by flute, oboe, horns, and harp (end of the 'Marche des pèlerins' in *Harold*), shimmering rapid passages on woodwind or muted strings as accompaniment to a melody (introduction to the *Fantastique*, 'larghetto' of the *Cellini* Overture). *Roméo et Juliette* and *La Damnation de Faust* are specially rich in new devices. Yet it is, after all, not in these 'effects' that Berlioz's real greatness as an orchestrator lies, and certainly not in his essays in the titanic, such as the four additional brass bands in the 'Tuba mirum' of the *Requiem* which, like the *Symphonie funèbre et triomphale*, revive the tradition of 'monumental music'[52] and astonished even in those days of Meyerbeerian extravagance. It was in his 'normal' orchestration, his intimate knowledge of the resources and capabilities of every instrument and combination, his careful weighing of every detail of execution and of the dynamic balance, spacing, and colour of every chord and figure and instrumental line, above all in the fact that he was seldom an 'orchestrator' at all in the sense of one who scores material conceived abstractly or unconsciously as keyboard music. He thought and wrote directly in terms of the orchestra more consistently than any of his predecessors or contemporaries.

[52] See Vol. VIII, pp. 67 and 650–1.

II

CHAMBER MUSIC: 1830–1850

By John Horton

AMATEUR AND PROFESSIONAL PLAYERS

THE practice and enjoyment of chamber music was widespread during the first half of the nineteenth century. Among its most influential patrons in Germany, Austria, and Russia were aristocratic dilettanti of the kind who helped to make possible the achievements of Beethoven's last decade. Their beneficent tradition was kept alive beyond the mid-century by such enthusiasts as Count Mateusz Wiełhorski, the Polish–Russian amateur cellist to whom Mendelssohn dedicated his D major Sonata, Op. 58, and Schumann his Piano Quartet, Op. 47. But the most rapid growth of interest was now to occur among the middle classes, with their accumulating wealth, their social aspirations, and their increasing artistic sensibility. Domestic music-making was a prominent feature of the Biedermeier scene, where families and friends gathered to read through duos, trios, quartets, and quintets for their own pleasure or for the entertainment of guests. Their activities created an insistent demand for new compositions, especially those that made no unreasonable calls on technique or comprehension, a market that prolific and industrious composers toiled to supply. The quartets of Ignaz Pleyel (1757–1831),[1] the pianoforte trios of Karl Reissiger (1798–1859), and the string quintets of George Onslow (1784–1853) were among the most popular of their time, though the more discerning connoisseurs based their repertoires on what were already accepted as the foundations of Classical chamber music: Haydn, Boccherini, Mozart, and the early Beethoven of the Op. 18 quartets (1800). While much of this amateur participation can hardly have reached a high level of technical or interpretative skill, it steadily nurtured a potential audience for chamber music as performed by serious artists, who were now beginning to turn their attention more and more in that direction, while usually combining it with solo and orchestral playing.

---

[1] See Vol. VIII, pp. 304–5.

In both amateur and professional fields the German-speaking lands claimed superiority. Playing at Strasbourg in 1821 before a particularly responsive audience, Spohr observed that this was a town 'to which the taste for quartet music has more readily penetrated from its contiguity to Germany'.[2] It was Germany also that produced the earliest professional touring quartets, like the Müller brothers from Brunswick who set out on their travels in 1831.

CHAMBER MUSIC IN FRANCE

In other countries interest tended to be concentrated in the capital cities. Thus in France, as Mendelssohn soon discovered, most professional expertise was to be found in Paris,[3] where the violinist Pierre Baillot (1771–1842) flourished as orchestral and quartet leader and professor at the Conservatoire. Baillot was versed in the Viennese classics, which meant to him originally Haydn and Mozart, but he was progressive in outlook, giving public recitals of Beethoven's earlier quartets, studying the later ones in private with his colleagues, and encouraging contemporary composers. Visiting Paris in 1832, Mendelssohn was gratified to find that the Conservatoire students had been made to study his works, and were 'practising their fingers off to play *Ist es wahr?*' (Quartet in A, Op. 13). In 1835 Baillot's enterprise was carried further by the cellist P. A. Chevillard, who in association with the violinist J. P. Maurin formed a society for the study of Beethoven's last-period quartets.[4] Standards of string playing were in fact nowhere higher at this time than in Paris; besides Baillot, there were Kreutzer and Rode, for both of whom Beethoven had written sonatas (Op. 47 and Op. 96 respectively). Nor were the wind instruments neglected: the prolific and versatile Anton Reicha (1770–1836) had been teaching composition at the Conservatoire since 1818, and through his own works for woodwind and horns with or without strings was ministering to the French taste for wind and mixed ensembles. On the other hand, native French composers of chamber music were few; Reicha, Cherubini, Onslow, and Kalkbrenner were all expatriates, but among the exceptions may be mentioned Rodolphe Kreutzer (1766–1831), who was French-born in spite of his name, Félicien David (1810–76) whose twenty-four string quintets entitled *Les Quatre Saisons* have no pretensions beyond salon entertainment, and Louise Farrenc (1804–74), a

---

[2] Louis Spohr, *Selbstbiographie* (Kassel, 1860–1), ii. 143.
[3] Letter to Zelter, 15 Feb. 1832.
[4] Even before this, the late Beethoven quartets had been introduced to Parisian audiences by the Bohrer brothers in 1827.

redoubtable pianist, teacher, anthologist (*Le Trésor des pianistes*), and composer of a considerable amount of serious chamber music— duet sonatas, piano trios, two piano quintets, a sextet, and a nonet— which has always been respectfully noted by historians but no longer has a place even in the national repertoire.

CONDITIONS IN ENGLAND

England characteristically followed a path of compromise in musical life, with social distinctions scrupulously observed.[5] The aims of the Philharmonic Society included under the terms of its foundation in 1813 'the performance . . . of the best and most approved instrumental music, consisting of Full Pieces, Concertantes for not less than three principal instruments, Sestetts, Quintetts and Trios; excluding Concertos, Solos and Duets . . .'.[6] Such intermingling of what would now be considered distinct genres, against which Moscheles protested in vain ('Grand orchestral works and quartet music are played at one and the same concert, third-rate singers are engaged . . .'),[7] persisted for another forty years or so. Chamber music began to drop out of the programmes during the decade 1840– 50, but did not finally disappear until after 1861, in which year the Hummel Septet, Op. 74, was still among the items. The English tradition of heterogeneous programmes was followed by early American concert organizers, the ubiquitous Hummel Quintet being performed at the first concert of the Philharmonic Orchestra of New York City, founded in 1842.[8]

Meanwhile, London was becoming better provided with specializing chamber recitals, such as Henry Blagrove's in the Hanover Square Rooms (1832–42), Joseph Dando's in the same hall and later at Crosby Hall, Bishopsgate (1842–53), and above all the Musical Union (1845–81) founded by John Ella (1802–88), who believed in educating his audiences, taking as a motto Baillot's assertion, 'It is not enough for the artist to be well prepared to face the public: it is also necessary for the public to be well prepared for what it is about to hear', and giving them analytical programme books

[5] 'There were large numbers of English amateurs who counted it a special honour to associate with artists and to play by their side at their private soirées. Thus Sir W. Curtis on the violoncello, Mrs Oom and Mrs Fleming on the piano. Prince Leopold and Princess Sophia, sister to King George IV, were always attentive listeners to the performers.' (Charlotte Moscheles, *The Life of Moscheles*, trans. Arthur D. Coleridge (London, 1873), i. 77–8.)

[6] Myles B. Foster, *History of the Philharmonic Society of London 1813–1912* (London, 1912), 4.

[7] C. Moscheles, *Life*, i. 261.

[8] Paul Henry Láng, *Music in Western Civilisation* (London, 1942), 934–5. A Mendelssohn Quintet Club was founded in Boston, Mass. in 1849.

containing notes on specific works and music-type illustrations. Mention must also be made of the series of chamber concerts arranged by Sterndale Bennett during the years 1843–56, and the founding of the Beethoven Quartet Society in 1845 by T. M. Alsager of *The Times* in order to promote better understanding of Beethoven's later works.[9]

COMBINATIONS OF STRINGS AND WIND

The larger mixed groupings of solo strings and wind popular at this time were in some sense the successors of the serenade, divertimento, and cassation of an earlier epoch, though they now usually conformed to the four-movement pattern of the symphony, string quartet, and piano trio. Their influence on conditions of performance is brought out in Schumann's account of musical life in Leipzig in the winter of 1839–40. Writing about a series of *Abendunterhaltungen* or soirées, given by Ferdinand David's quartet with other artists, he says:

in response to the wishes of the public the scope of these recitals was enlarged to include works for larger ensembles and also solo items. And for the sake of the music, as well as of the audience, the small anteroom [of the Gewandhaus] hitherto used for chamber music was abandoned in favour of the large concert hall . . . quartets by Mozart, Haydn, Beethoven, Cherubini, Franz Schubert and Mendelssohn were played. In addition there were performances of Spohr's Nonet and a double quartet, Mendelssohn's Octet, a Quintet by Onslow, trios by Beethoven, Mendelssohn, and Hiller, and duo sonatas and similar works by Mozart, Beethoven and Spohr.[10]

This season included the first public performance of Mendelssohn's D minor Trio, and Mendelssohn himself played accompaniments he had written to some of Bach's solo violin movements.

The quasi-orchestral character of much of the chamber music of the period is emphasized by the common use of the double-bass to strengthen the foundations of the larger ensembles, as in Viennese music of the divertimento kind, as well as the Beethoven Septet, Op. 20, Schubert's Octet, D 803, and 'Trout' Quintet, D 667, and minor works by Ferdinand Ries, Hummel, Moscheles, and Spohr.[11] Even where a second cello was originally specified in string ensembles the double-bass was often substituted, an expedient that is said to have

---

[9] The Philharmonic, Musical Union, and Alsager institutions are vividly described in Hector Berlioz, *Les Soirées de l'orchestre* (Paris, 1852).
[10] Schumann, *Gesammelte Schriften über Musik und Musiker*, ed. Martin Kreisig (5th edn.; Leipzig, 1914), i. 510–11.
[11] See Vol. VIII, pp. 320–1.

arisen fortuitously in London when Dragonetti deputized at short notice for a missing second cellist in one of Onslow's quintets. The result was judged so successful that Onslow himself came to prefer the cello–bass pairing, and even such carefully balanced works as Spohr's double quartets were subjected to similar treatment. Conversely Félicien David scored his quintets *Les Quatre Saisons*, four sets of six (1845-6), for the combination with bass, but allowed a second cello as alternative.

The growing ascendency of the virtuoso performer, especially the solo violinist and pianist, was not altogether to the advantage of idiomatic chamber-music composition and interpretation. Haydn had been fortunate in his daily association, over many years, with select groups of musicians who were used to working together, and Beethoven came to rely on that most dedicated of teams, the string quartet led by Ignaz Schuppanzigh. But Spohr's autobiography reveals a very different aspect of current performing practice. The virtuosi who toured Europe in the 1820s and 1830s often treated the string quartet as a vehicle for the leader's personal display, or the concerted piano ensemble as a medium for the keyboard executant aided by subordinate instrumentalists. Describing how he tested the abilities of the 13-year-old Joachim in 1844, Ella 'mustered a notable assembly of musical lions to hear him play [*sic*] Beethoven's posthumous Quartet in B flat'.[12] And Mendelssohn, who had introduced Joachim, discharged his obligation to Ella by 'playing' his own D minor Trio, stipulating only that the Moravian violinist Heinrich Ernst should 'accompany' him. Although a few permanently constituted quartet groups were already to be found in the more important centres, and some even toured, it was not until after the middle of the century that it ceased to be taken for granted that a recitalist ought to be willing to take his place as leader of a chamber ensemble with little more concern than he would feel in playing a concerto with an unfamiliar orchestra.

Executants still availed themselves of their traditional licence to add ornamentation, and early nineteenth-century chamber performance was by no means exempt from such liberties. The London quartet leader Joseph Dando is said to have ornamented the repeats of the variation movement of Beethoven's Quartet Op. 18, No. 5, and even Ferdinand David was 'given to "decorating" chamber music with trills and grace notes'.[13] When Liszt played the piano

[12] John Ella, *Musical Sketches Abroad and at Home* (3rd edn.; London, 1878).
[13] *Cobbett's Cyclopedic Survey of Chamber Music* (London, 1929–30), i. 314.

part of the Hummel D minor Septet at a Philharmonic concert in 1841, he 'so embellished Hummel's passages that the author himself would scarcely have recognized them'.[14]

The most potent influence on performing and compositional styles and textures during this period was the dominating position occupied by the pianoforte in musical and social esteem. It was a golden age of Romantic piano literature and a heroic age of keyboard technique, aided and encouraged by the inventions and improvements of instrument makers. With few exceptions, such as the violinists Spohr and Berwald and the woodwind player Reicha, almost every composer approached chamber music primarily through the piano. It is true that one of the most illustrious of the pianist–composers, Hummel, had the intelligence and sensitivity to control his virtuosity and to co-ordinate the piano with other instruments in his ensembles, but on the other hand Friedrich Kalkbrenner (1785–1849) well-nigh submerged his 'accompaniment' under torrents of brilliant but empty passage-work and stated the priorities unequivocally by publishing his Op. 81 (c.1826) as *Grand Quintett pour le piano-forte*, *avec accompagnement de clarinette, cor, violoncelle et contrebasse*.

SCHUMANN'S CHAMBER MUSIC

While Kalkbrenner and his kind hardly survive except as historical figures, Schumann's chamber music lives on to demonstrate how far the technical and expressive qualities of the piano could permeate a Romantic imagination. Up to 1842, when Schumann turned his attention seriously to chamber music, he had written comparatively little that was not keyboard-based, for the outpouring of songs in 1840 must surely be included in that category. Now, at the age of 32, he was stimulated by the example of Mendelssohn and by an intensive study of Classical quartet literature to attempt string-quartet composition on his own account. His three essays in that medium, Op. 41, No. 1 (nominally in A minor), No. 2 in F, and No. 3 in A major, were the outcome of hard self-discipline.[15] Their creative vitality and constructional ingenuity go far to disarm criticism arising from such stylistic blemishes as the constriction of much of the string writing within the grasp of a pianist's hands. He actually arranged

[14] Foster, *History*, p. 164.
[15] For a close study of Schumann's chamber works, the sketches and the many alterations they underwent during composition, see Hans Kohlhase, *Die Kammermusik Robert Schumanns: Stilistische Untersuchungen* (Hamburg, 1979); also A. E. F. Dickinson, 'The Chamber Music', in Gerald Abraham (ed.), *Schumann: A Symposium* (London 1952), 138, and Joan Chissell, *Schumann* (rev. edn.; London, 1977), 155–68.

Nos. 1 and 2 for piano solo in 1853. The Quartet in A, Op. 41, No. 3, is perhaps the most interesting of the set in spite of suffering from a *klaviermässig* Finale; the whole work is unified through the motivic use of the initial falling perfect fifth and its inversion. Yet, although Schumann had entered upon quartet composition with all the enthusiasm and concentration characteristic of his most fertile periods, he returned in this very same year to the piano as the basis of the rest of his chamber music. 'For Schumann the quartet was a stimulating novelty, not an essential thread, and once tried it gleamed no more in his mind.'[16]

It is worthwhile to look a little further into Schumann's reliance on the piano. A clue can be found in the remark he made to Clara Wieck in 1838: 'The pianoforte has become too limited for me. In the compositions I now write I hear many things I can hardly indicate.' In the following year he told his former teacher Heinrich Dorn that he felt the piano was too narrow for his ideas. Although these remarks are usually taken as heralding the symphonic compositions of 1841, they may also apply with equal relevance to the chamber works that quickly followed upon the three string quartets of 1842. From this time onwards he often appears to use other instruments as a way of enriching and extending the eloquence of the piano, enabling chords and arpeggios to be sustained, melodies to be given new colours, and the inner parts of contrapuntal textures to be enriched. The search for novel shades of colour through the addition of middle-range instruments was to continue to the end of Schumann's career. Thus the horn entered into partnership with the keyboard in the *Adagio and Allegro*, Op. 70, the clarinet in the *Fantasiestücke*, Op. 73, the oboe in the *Drei Romanzen*, Op. 94, the cello in *Funf Stücke im Volkston*, Op. 102, the viola in the *Märchenbilder*, Op. 113, both clarinet and viola in the *Märchenerzählungen*, Op. 132. Of earlier date, but showing a similar tendency, is the first version of the *Andante and Variations*, Op. 46 (1843) (Ex. 36), laid out for two pianos, horn, and two cellos. The supplementary instruments are used sparingly, and chiefly to reinforce or colour the inner voices and basses of the piano parts. The alternative two-piano version has obvious practical advantages, but the original scoring represents the composer's real intentions. The antiphonal variation between horn and cellos on the one hand and the pianos on the other (see Ex. 36), which had to be sacrificed in

---

[16] Dickinson, 'Chamber Music', p. 140.

Ex. 36

the revision, must have had special significance, based as it is on the motto-theme of the song cycle *Frauenliebe und -leben*.

The two major works for piano and strings written immediately after the Op. 41 quartets broke fresh ground by combining the now fully developed concert grand piano with bowed strings, treated in a manner that attempts to reconcile Classical quartet or trio textures with quasi-orchestral density. In the Quintet, Op. 44, the piano is *primus inter pares*, throwing out ideas which the strings have no difficulty in adopting for themselves. In the march-like second movement, indeed, violin and cello are allowed to take the initiative, while the piano is held in check, though maintaining a presence with discreet idiomatic figuration. The Scherzo favours the keyboard player, but its bold construction, with two trios, and its pulsating energy carry all before it. In the Finale the piano again takes the lead, but thins out its texture, so that for much of the movement the keyboard part is reduced virtually to a single melodic line, broken from time to time by passages of full chordal harmony, with cumulative power building up to a climax when, in the coda, the principal theme of the Finale is combined with that of the first movement—an idea that Schumann may have borrowed from Mendelssohn's Op. 12 String Quartet or his Octet in E flat. This work was to become a prototype for examples of the genre by Brahms, Dvořák, Franck, and Fauré. Schumann's Piano Quartet, Op. 47, offers the strings fewer opportunities to distinguish themselves. Frequent doublings with the piano result in a certain monotony of sound, though the falling sevenths and harmonic suspensions of the Andante cantabile and the luscious cello melody forming a tribute to the dedicatee, Count Mateusz Wiełhorski, cannot fail to haunt the memory.

DUET SONATAS

Schumann's achievements in two other fields of chamber music with piano are noteworthy. Important sonatas for a single stringed instrument and piano are uncommon between those of Beethoven and Brahms, but Schumann's examples for violin, Op. 105 in A minor and Op. 121 in D minor, both written in 1851,[17] enrich the repertoire of the violin as much as Mendelssohn's Op. 45 (1838) and Op. 58 (1845-6) enrich that of the cello. Mendelssohn's sonatas, grateful as they are to play and listen to, do not altogether lack rivals: Chopin's Op. 65 in G minor (1845-6) has claims that are still sometimes underrated, being splendidly written for both instruments, probably with the help of Franchomme over the cello part;[18] and Sterndale Bennett's Sonata-duo, Op. 32, while technically unambitious, has a melodic charm that is seldom absent from his slender output. Moreover the Mendelssohn cello works contain much that is fluent rather than inspired, even if we except the chorale movement of Op. 58, which may have had its origin in a study of 'Es ist vollbracht' in Bach's *St John Passion*. But Schumann's violin sonatas have a more full-blooded quality that transcends their curious restriction of the violin parts to the lower range of the instrument, yet another example, presumably, of the effects of subconscious feeling through pianist's hands. The passionate outer movements of the A major Sonata are separated by a poetical Allegretto with constantly fluctuating tempo, one of Schumann's most imaginative conceptions, which Brahms must have had in mind when he wrote the Andante tranquillo of his own A major Sonata thirty-five years later, just as César Franck seems to have been indebted to Schumann's Op. 121 for a number of ideas: the close relationship between movements, the whirling, darkly coloured figuration of the *lebhaft* section of Schumann's first movement, and even the canonic episodes of the Finale. The third movement of Op. 121, a delightful set of variations on a theme (foreshadowed near the close of the Scherzo)

---

[17] A third, also in A minor, dating from 1853, was edited by Oliver Neighbour (London, 1956).

[18] Moscheles, when commissioned to make the piano-duet arrangement of Chopin's sonata, found it 'a wild overgrown forest, into which only an occasional sunbeam penetrates' (C. Moscheles, *Life*, ii. 213).

that is itself a free variant of the chorale 'Gelobet seist du, Jesu Christ', makes use of a kaleidoscope of delicate colours—violin pizzicato chords, arco double stopping, and sul ponticello, with the una corda of the piano and great variety of keyboard textures.

THE PIANO TRIO

Of all the standard chamber music ensembles it was the trio for keyboard, violin, and cello that had the longest pedigree, had undergone most fluctuations of intention and style, and was (with the possible exception of the string quartet) the most prolific in examples during the late Classical and early Romantic periods. In Haydn, and in Mozart's greatest trio, K 542 in E major, the cello is still occupied for most of its time in reinforcing the bass of the fortepiano. Beethoven brought about the complete emancipation of both violin and cello, and in his Op. 70 and Op. 97 treated all three instruments as equals, at the same time enlarging every dimension of the ensemble to attain a spaciousness, grandeur, and emotional depth never before realized. These two Beethoven trios, together with Schubert's in B flat and E flat, formed the heart of a legacy bequeathed to the 1840s and 1850s.

Few composers of those decades were equipped to take up the challenge. Amateur players asked for much less formidable material such as Reissiger, with his twenty-seven trios, was quite able to turn out. The virtuoso pianist–composers, the Hummels, the Moscheles, and the Kalkbrenners (and also Chopin in his early Op. 8), wrote their own pieces for keyboard display, usually with perfunctory 'accompaniment' parts that were seldom included or even fully cued into the published piano scores, as Schumann complained when obliged to review these, or unscored sets of parts, for his Neue Zeitschrift. The occupation must have been almost invariably depressing, as his scathing comments revealed: 'A clearer example of the best intentions towards higher regions, while seated firmly on prosaic earth ... would be difficult to find anywhere in the world' (of a Grand Trio by Anton Halm, 1789-1872); 'Take the key of E minor and an easy-going triple time, imagine yourself an ardent pianist, get two gentle understanding friends to accompany you, suffuse the picture with a rosy dawn, and you have what amounts to a trio' (by Jacob Rosenhain, 1813-94);[19] 'salon-trio, during which one can just gaze around [lorgnettiren], without completely losing the thread of the music' (of an early Trio, Op. 2, by Ambroise

[19] *Neue Zeitschrift*, 5 (1836), 4.

Thomas (1811-96).[20] Schumann wrote a long and mainly laudatory review of Spohr's Trio in E minor, Op. 119, welcoming it not so much for its intrinsic merits but because it gave further evidence of Spohr's productivity over a wider field than ever, the sure mark of a fidelity to German tradition and therefore to be warmly encouraged. But it was Mendelssohn's D minor Trio, Op. 49, that received, in 1840, the famous accolade of 'the master-trio of the present age, as Beethoven's in B flat and D, and Schubert's in E flat, were supreme in their own time'.[21] Yet the D minor Trio, for all its suavity, its balanced sonorities, and its masterly craftsmanship,[22] was to be surpassed six years later by the more closely integrated and emotionally more profound Op. 66 in C minor. The opening Allegro energico e con fuoco evolves from a single motif by means of contrapuntal working, variation, and tonal transition while exploiting all three instruments technically to an even greater degree than in the earlier Trio. Only in the Finale is there some falling away from the generally high quality of idiomatic writing, when Mendelssohn allows himself to be lured into a gradiose peroration based, like the first of the Six Preludes for piano, Op. 35, on a chorale.[23] The success of Mendelssohn's trios, and perhaps Clara Schumann's attempt at a Trio in G minor on her own account, encouraged Robert Schumann also to try his hand.[24] In 1847 he completed the first two published trios, Op. 63 in D and Op. 80 in F (Ex. 37). The third, Op. 110 in G minor, followed four years later when his stamina had begun to fail, and, despite the moving eloquence of the second movement, a loss of concentration and of sensitivity to the independence and balance of the instruments is apparent. But Op. 80 is a particularly attractive work with some happy interchanges among the instruments and a verve that launches the first movement on its way with an impetus resembling that of the E flat Symphony written three years later. Captivating also are the subsidiary F major themes and the C major material of the second subject distributed

[20] Leon B. Plantinga, *Schumann as Critic* (New Haven, 1967), 189-190, quotes passages from this work by Thomas.

[21] *Neue Zeitschrift*, 13 (1840), 198.

[22] 'A movement so compact and so convincingly launched as the first in the Trio is not matched by any composer of the romantic era until Brahms' (Láng; *Music in Western Civilisation*, p. 822).

[23] Both Mendelssohn and Schumann sometimes reflect their trio styles in solo piano pieces: Mendelssohn, for example, in the *Lieder ohne Worte*, Op. 19, no. 5, in F sharp and Op. 38, no. 6, in A flat, Schumann rather more imaginatively in the F sharp *Romanze*, Op. 28, no. 2, spreading himself over three staves.

[24] The *Fantasiestücke*, Op. 88, for piano, violin, and cello, consist of the dismembered and retitled movements of a piano trio drafted towards the end of 1842, about the same time as the Piano Quartet in E Flat, Op. 47.

Ex. 37

among the players. The slow movement of this Trio in F recalls Schumann's impassioned *Lieder*, and explores magical realms of harmony (Ex. 37). The *Ländler*-like Intermezzo looks forward to Brahms, but also contains in its last four bars yet another affectionate quotation from the motto-theme of *Frauenliebe und -leben*. In the Finale the piano over-asserts itself, making the string parts almost redundant.

The accessibility of the piano trio as an ensemble for easy diversion, concert display, or serious communication, earned it popularity over a wide geographical area and allowed it to reflect national characteristics. For example, Sterndale Bennett's later Trio in A, Op. 26 (1839), nearly contemporary with Mendelssohn's in D minor, shows an originality in Bennett's handling of the instruments, and a touch of humour as in the 'Serenade' (Ex. 38), that lift it well above the average.[25]

Interesting in other ways is the 18-year-old César Franck's Trio in F sharp (1841), which d'Indy claimed as introducing new concepts of form into mid-century instrumental music.[26] While discounting d'Indy's hyperbole, one can regard this particular work as a distinctive essay in the medium, abounding in thematic metamorphoses and other cyclic devices. Such procedures, however, were very much in the air at this time, and not only in the orchestral compositions of Liszt and Berlioz; Mendelssohn's experiments in his earlier quartets and in the Octet were already well known in Paris in the 1830s; even before then Glinka's *Trio pathétique* (1826) for piano, clarinet, and bassoon employs *idées fixes* with thematic transformations.

SCANDINAVIAN CHAMBER MUSIC

Scandinavian composers associated with the Leipzig group transported its styles and ideals back to their own countries. Niels Gade (1817–90), a viola player, served as Mendelssohn's right-hand man at the Gewandhaus and adopted features of his compositional practice, showing a particular interest in string ensembles including a quintet (1845) and an octet (1848). Returning to Denmark at the height of a national Romantic movement that embraced all the arts, Gade met the needs of the time by combining sincere workmanship and moderate technical demands with a breath of the gentle pastoral atmosphere that frequently characterizes Scandinavian music and probably takes its origin from a native tradition of lyric song. Several Swedish composers also advanced the cause of chamber music in their country. Adolf Fredrik Lindblad (1801–78) produced, among other chamber works, a Trio in G minor for violin, viola, and piano

---

[25] Ed. with the Cello Sonata, by G. Bush, *Musica Britannica*, 35 (London, 1972).
[26] Cobbett, *Survey*, i. 419–20.

Ex. 38

Andante ma un poco scherzando
The pizzicato quite piano throughout, and without the slightest harshness

(1843), a string quintet, and two quartets. But the most original native composer of the period was Franz Berwald (1796-1868).[27]

While Berwald's chamber music cannot compare in importance with the symphonic works he was writing in the 1840s, it shows much of the freshness of outlook that attracted the attention of both Swedish and German critics: melodic fluidity, unpredictable harmonic movement (to some extent indebted to Spohr), and above all an interest in experiment with design. Even so, the trios and the two piano quintets hardly show him at his best, owing to his lack of keyboard expertise. It is only when he writes for strings alone that his constructive imagination takes wing, as in the String Quartet No. 3 in E flat (1849), where not only is a 'scherzo' episode introduced into the slow movement, but this already complex structure is itself embedded in the exposition, development, and recapitulation of a single large-scale sonata form. At the same time, the string writing has much elegance (Ex. 39).

CHAMBER MUSIC FOR STRINGS BY MENDELSSOHN AND SPOHR

Whereas the string quartet was for Schumann a transitory interest, though productive of three works of enduring value, Mendelssohn was fascinated by the medium almost throughout his career. Except for the two piano trios and the later duet sonatas, he abandoned chamber music with piano after his fifteenth year. Between completing his first and second piano quartets he wrote the earliest of his string quartets (in E flat), though it did not reach publication until more than thirty years after his death. The Quartet in A, Op. 13 (1827), remains, despite its early date, one of his most revolutionary compositions. Quotations from a song 'Ist es wahr?', written earlier in the year, frame the beginning and end of the work, and pervade the whole of it through subtle derivatives and variations.[28] Much of the writing is strongly and even harshly linear, though lyrical and dramatic elements appear in the Intermezzo and Finale, with a

[27] Ludwig Norman's 'Franz Berwalds Kammermusik-verk', *Tidning for teater och musik* (1859), nos. 7, 8, 10, is reproduced in German translation in *Franz Berwald: Die Dokumente seines Lebens*, ed. Erling Lomnäs (Kassel, 1979), 490-7.

[28] Mendelssohn wrote to A. F. Lindblad in 1828: 'The song I append to the Quartet is the theme. You will hear it note for note in the first and last movements, but its mood pervades all four of them' (Friedhelm Krummacher, *Mendelssohn—der Komponist: Studien zur Kammermusik für Streicher* (Munich, 1978), 87). Krummacher (ibid., p. 592) reproduces in facsimile the title-page of the holograph manuscript in the Berlin Staatsbibliothek. Here the quartet is explicitly described as 'sopra il tema . . . [followed by two bars of the song 'Frage'— 'Ist es wahr?'] Another manuscript of the quartet exists in the British Library (Add. MS. 32179, fos. 45-64). Although this is not confirmed as the composer's autograph, it shows a number of erasures and alterations, with several attempts at a suitable speed indication for the scherzando section of the Intermezzo.

Ex. 39

'scherzando' episode incorporated in the former. An encounter with Beethoven's great A minor Quartet, Op. 132, written barely two years earlier, must be assumed.[29]

Mendelssohn's String Quartet, Op. 12—again in E flat—which he finished in London in September 1829, is less unconventional than Op. 13, which preceded it in order of composition, but none the less has some unusual features of structure. Its second movement is the Canzonetta, with another 'scherzando' middle section, that was for long the most popular single movement of the composer's chamber works, but the whole quartet is notable for the beauty of its string writing, as in the passage leading to the reprise in the first movement (Ex. 40). The Finale is happily rounded off with a return of the principal theme of the first movement.

With the three Op. 44 quartets (in order of composition, No. 2 in E minor, No. 3 in E flat, and No. 1 in D) Mendelssohn reached

[29] Mendelssohn's indebtedness to Beethoven in this and other early works is discussed by Joscelyn Godwin, 'Early Mendelssohn and Late Beethoven', *Music and Letters*, 55 (1974), 272, and with more detail in Krummacher, *Mendelssohn*, pp. 309 ff.

Ex. 40

what may be regarded as the apex of his powers in this field. Relationships with his orchestral music of the same period are easy to point to: the E minor Quartet looks forward to the Violin Concerto in the same key, and the D major Quartet, for which the composer showed his own preference by having it published before the others, looks backward to the 'Italian' Symphony of five years earlier; both symphony and quartet begin with a springing violin theme over repeated chords, both have one middle movement in the style of Haydn (actually called Menuetto in the quartet), with the other taking the form of a grave song without words, and both end with a saltarello. But perhaps the E flat Quartet, Op. 44, No. 3, is the most completely satisfying of the three, with its unobtrusive but strong cyclic links and a most original Scherzo combining contrapuntal mastery with the lightest touch imaginable.[30]

It can hardly be doubted that the Op. 44 Quartets owe much of their finish and assurance to the presence in Leipzig of Ferdinand David (1810–75), who, after leading a private quartet for six years, joined the Gewandhaus orchestra as leader in 1836. Seven years later he was appointed head of the violin department in the new Conservatory, formed his own quartet there and gave the first performances of Mendelssohn's three Op. 44 and Schumann's three

[30] The apparent spontaneity of this group of works hides a considerable amount of revision and emendation, as shown with the help of a facsimile in Krummacher, *Mendelssohn*, pp. 593–612.

Op. 41 quartets. As a pupil of Spohr and a teacher of Joachim he links the Classical and Romantic schools of German violin playing, and stands at a turning-point in the evolution of nineteenth-century instrumental technique and interpretation, establishing once and for all the concept of the permanent, unified chamber music team as a prerequisite for maintaining the highest standards. His visit to London in 1839 appears to have been a revelation to English musicians: Moscheles noted that 'his quartet playing at Mori's and Blagrove's soirées delighted everyone with a genuine artistic taste; before he came, such a perfect *ensemble* had never been realised'.[31]

In 1847 Mendelssohn produced, under severe emotional stress, his last string quartet, Op. 80, which, taking its departure from Beethoven's Op. 95 in the same key (F minor), sounds depths of introspection and spiritual drama that might have heralded a new phase of creative development, as presaged in the searing dissonances of the opening, the weird *Totentanz* of the Scherzo ('allegro assai'), the tortuous elaboration of the Adagio, and the impressionistic fragmentation of the Finale.

In his two String Quintets, Op. 18 in A and Op. 87 in B flat, Mendelssohn used the instrumentation with two violas preferred by Mozart and Beethoven (both of whom, like Mendelssohn himself, were violists) rather than the two cellos adopted in quintets by Boccherini, Schubert, and Onslow. Both the Mendelssohn quintets have associations with famous violinists of their time: Op. 87 dates from 1845, the year of the C minor Piano Trio, and its dedication to Spohr may account for the prominent first violin writing in the first, third, and fourth movements. The second movement, Andante scherzando, is noteworthy for its refinements of string technique and for some lively rhythmic displacements and syncopations. The Op. 18 Quintet was originally a carefree product of Mendelssohn's early life, but acquired an elegiac character when, before publication in 1832, its original second movement was replaced with an Intermezzo in memory of the two violinists to whom, up to that time, Mendelssohn had been most indebted—Eduard Rietz and Baillot. Their virtuosity seems to be acknowledged in the florid violin and viola passages of the quintet.[32]

The unique Octet for strings[33] may appear to stand on the

---

[31] C. Moscheles, *Life*, ii. 47.

[32] The original second movement was a Minuetto with a Trio in double canon. Krummacher, *Mendelssohn*, pp. 586–90, reproduces it from a set of parts in the Bibliothèque Nationale, Paris (Cons. MS 204), except for the missing second viola part.

[33] A facsimile of the holograph score, formerly the property of Eduard Rietz, and now in the Whittall Foundation Collection, has been published by the Library of Congress (Washington

borderline of orchestral and true chamber music, but it belongs to
the latter even more surely than Schubert's mixed string and wind
Octet composed in the same year, 1825. Mendelssohn at the age of
16 treats his eight instruments on terms of impartial equality, while
ensuring that their most telling registers are interlaced to obtain every
possible shade of colour and density. The Andante is particularly rich
in such effects, and the Scherzo, whether or not it has behind it a
programme such as Goethe's Walpurgis scene, weaves a tapestry of
pure sound extending at a few points into twelve real parts and
surpassing in brilliance the much later *Midsummer Night's Dream*
Scherzo. The Finale comes perilously close to satirizing Beethoven
by juxtaposing ethereal fantasy with the grotesque, besides bringing
off a *coup de théâtre* with its fleeting reminiscence of the Scherzo.
The Octet remains unchallenged in its inventive distinction, even
though it had its would-be imitators such as Gade, whose String Octet
appeared in 1848. Spohr's four double quartets, while employing the
same instruments as those of the Mendelssohn Octet, were not
intended as competitors, as Spohr himself made quite clear:

My four double quartets remain the only ones of their kind. An octet for
stringed instruments by Mendelssohn-Bartholdy belongs to quite another
kind of art, in which the two quartets do not concert and interchange in
double chorus with each other, but all instruments work together.[34]

The distinction, so frankly and fairly stated, should allow Spohr full
credit for his own kind of originality. In his earlier experiments with
the medium he was inclined to make one of the quartets subservient
to the other, but they are treated more equally in the fourth of the
series (Op. 136 in G minor) (1847). The opening Adagio of the
Double Quartet No. 3, Op. 87, written in 1833, testifies to Spohr's
keen ear for instrumental and harmonic colour (Ex. 41). These four
works represent only a small fraction of Spohr's assiduous cultivation
of the string quartet. In all he left more than thirty examples, ranging
from marketable *Gebrauchsmusik* to display pieces specified as
Quatuor brillant. Most, if not all of these must be assumed to have
long outlived their usefulness, but the double quartets and the violin
duets—another genre he exploited most ably—constitute subspecies
of string chamber music that should not be entirely neglected. A

DC, 1973), with a critical introduction by Jon Newsom, who lists the cuts and other alterations
made by the composer between completing the manuscript in Berlin on 15 October 1825 and
publishing the string parts with Breitkopf and Härtel in 1832. The first printed full score was
published in 1848, the year after Mendelssohn's death.

[34] Spohr, *Selbstbiographie*, ii. 162.

Ex. 41

great violinist, Spohr helped to preserve and indeed advance string technique in an age dominated, as we have seen, by the piano.[35]

[35] Yet such a comparatively late work as Spohr's Piano Trio, Op. 133 (1846), shows not only a virtuosic violin part but also a good deal of empty keyboard rhetoric, which he plainly regarded as proper to the genre though he disclaimed any pianistic skill.

THE PERIOD IN PERSPECTIVE

It would be easy to regard the period between the death of Beethoven and the beginning of Brahms's career in the 1850s as a trough of depression in chamber music, relieved only by the complementary talents of Mendelssohn and Schumann. Such a view would be both superficial and unhistorical. Mendelssohn's precocity can give rise to a distortion of perspective. He was writing his first published works—the Piano Quartets, Opp. 1, 2, and 3)—at a date when Beethoven was producing his late quartets and Schubert had not yet written his Octet, his three finest string quartets, the Quintet with two cellos, and the B flat and E flat piano trios. On the other hand, the tragic brevity of the lives of both Schumann and Mendelssohn (and of Schubert) contrasts poignantly with the longevity of many of their contemporaries who were born in the last decades of the previous century. Cherubini died in 1842 at the ripe age of 82, Kalkbrenner at 64, Spohr at 75, and Moscheles at 76, the last two surviving both Mendelssohn and Schumann. Ferdinand Hiller, one of Hummel's most successful pupils, was born in 1811, only two years after Mendelssohn, but lived until 1885, and Gade, born in 1817, had seventy-three years before him. While a cynic might contend that all these were men who avoided the proverbial effects of being beloved by the gods, they were nevertheless able to amass great volumes of work (whatever judgements may be made on its quality), to set fashions, and to control taste over many decades, and their influence must be taken into account in surveying the period, a point well made by Leon Plantinga. Emphasizing the need to 'investigate a full cross-section of the repertory' on the ground that 'the commonplace is often of special value in determining the prevailing norms and procedures of an era', he notes that 'what most interested Schumann was the best achievements of his romantic contemporaries; but he always saw their work against the backdrop of contemporary musical culture as a whole'.[36]

High among the secondary masters of the 1830s, must be placed Hummel, who in 1834 took Schumann to task for 'abrupt changes of harmony'. In fact Hummel was far from being devoid of a spirit of adventure; his E flat Quintet, Op. 87 (1821), for violin, viola, cello, double-bass, and piano, has a thoroughly unconventional key scheme, starting as it does in the tonic minor and soon modulating enharmonically to A major—a gesture that Schumann himself might have envied. In his sense of instrumental colour Hummel had shown

---

[36] Plantinga, *Schumann as Critic*, pp. 137–8.

highly Romantic tendencies even earlier, when in 1816 he produced his already mentioned D minor Septet. He could equal Weber in evoking the magic of the natural horn; he had a partiality for viola tone; he wrote admirably for woodwind; and in the second septet, *Septett militaire*, Op. 114 (1830), he anticipated Saint-Saëns by including the trumpet in a chamber ensemble. Despite the Scandinavians and the modest contributions of Sterndale Bennett, Félicien David, and the young César Franck, chamber music was essentially a Teutonic field. The only prolific non-Germans were two wealthy English amateurs who both studied with Reicha in Paris, George Onslow (1783–1852) and John Lodge Ellerton (1807–73). Onslow settled permanently in France where he composed thirty-six string quartets, thirty-eight string quintets,[37] and other chamber music, including one or two works for wind. The Finale of his *Sextuor*, Op. 77 (b), for flute, clarinet, bassoon, horn, double bass, and piano, offers a good example of his handling of this medium (Ex. 42). As exacting a judge as Mendelssohn could enquire through Moscheles whether Cherubini and Onslow had recently produced anything new,[38] and Schumann coupled Onslow's name with Mendelssohn's as a preserver of the authentic Classical quartet style.[39] Ellerton also cultivated that style in his fifty-four quintets, witness the slow movement (Ex. 43) and the Scherzo (Ex. 44) of his Op. 62.

Yet while all these, with other second- or third-rank figures, must be taken into account, nothing can diminish the overriding significance of the brief and meteoric careers of Mendelssohn and Schumann. It was largely through their efforts that by the end of the half-century there had come about a regeneration of instrumental composition in the forms of duet sonata, piano trio, and string quartet. They had realized, and lost no opportunity of impressing on their contemporaries, that the way to ensure a bright future for German music was dependent on taking a long, respectful, but by no means antiquarian look at the past, now revealed as containing not only the great masters of the age of the sonata, but also the supreme contrapuntist, J. S. Bach. Armed with a ready if sometimes extravagant pen, Schumann had almost completely routed the philistine army of showy keyboard virtuosi whose exhibitionism was

[37] Two of Onslow's quintets are discussed, with quotations, by H. Woollett in Cobbett, *Survey*, ii. 195–9.
[38] Letter, 30 Nov. 1839, Felix Mendelssohn, *Letters*, trans. Gisella Selden-Goth (London, 1946), 286.
[39] Discussing the paucity of good quartet writing after Beethoven, Schumann sums up in these words: 'Onslow allein fand Anklang, und später Mendelssohn, dessen aristokratisch-poetischem Character diese Gattung auch besonders zusagen muss' (*Neue Zeitschrift*, 16 (1842), 160).

Ex. 42

Ex. 43

Ex. 44

Allegretto vivace

in danger of debasing the European inheritance of instrumental forms. Mendelssohn through his executant skills and his rigorous educational ideals—and especially through the founding of the Leipzig Conservatory—had struck powerful blows against amateurism, while providing amateurs with material and standards of performance that might be within their reach, given sincere endeavour. These were policies that had their limitations, one of the most serious being an excess of zeal for the German tradition and a failure to discern the distinct but positive qualities of French art. The flowering, less than a quarter of a century later, of a national French school of instrumental music, including chamber music, was to take the form of a conscious reaction against the German aesthetic hegemony that Mendelssohn and Schumann (and Brahms after them) had made strenuous efforts to preserve.

III

ROMANTIC OPERA: 1830–1850

(a) GRAND OPÉRA

By DAVID CHARLTON

THE phrase *grand opéra* had been applied to French recitative opera since the eighteenth century, but it subsequently came to apply particularly to serious French works in the Romantic period. One significant milestone in the genre's evolution was *Fernand Cortez* by Spontini (1809; rev. 1817), in whose preface the librettist, Etienne de Jouy, wrote: 'French *grand opéra* has at least as much connection with epic as with tragedy.' Napoleon and the Bourbons who succeeded him gave the Paris Opéra the traditional role of presenting operas inherently symbolizing the 'grandeur' of the State. This was done as much through richness of material means as through what was considered proper subject-matter from mythology or history. Those responsible for *grand opéra* after 1830 did not abandon such criteria, but the various developments in public taste, in theatrical technique, and in musical language coalesced with them, resulting in a remarkably potent series of works.

STAGING AND COSTUME

Since *grand opéra* was the product of unusual cultural and political factors, its evolution can be understood only with reference to the conditions of the 1820s. Although the Paris Opéra received much subsidy under Louis XVIII (d. 1824) and Charles X (reigned 1824–30), it had lost artistic credibility in most spheres of its activity. Rossini's presence in Paris[1] brought about the development of modern vocal technique, and the nurture of young voices was to be continued by Meyerbeer, who arrived there in January 1825. The erection of a new building (rue Le Peletier, 1822) could not disguise the basic absence of co-ordination between internal departments, resulting in anachronistic costumes and sets, inexact props, and poor

---

[1] See Vol. VIII, pp. 103 ff.

lighting. The transformation and artistic reconnection of these elements occurred little by little, as did the evolution of the required new type of opera libretto.

Gas stage lighting was available from 1822. The principal set designer, Pierre Luc Charles Cicéri, tried out at the same time atmospheric settings which reorganized stage space on different levels (for example, diagonal staircases) and made the actors seem part of their stage environment, using three-dimensional scenery that could be walked on. These sets were not at first for the Opéra but for the Théâtre de la Porte Saint-Martin—for example, *Le Château de Kenilworth* (1822).[2] The 1820s saw the gradual perfection of huge painted canvases, lit by changing sources of light, and giving the illusion of a transformation before one's eyes.[3] Standards of public expectation in visual matters inevitably rose.

Historical accuracy, in the interests of local colour, was tentatively explored in the Opéra's troubadour costumes and Cicéri's and Daguerre's 'château d'Eidelbert' in *Alfred le Grand* (1822), a ballet-pantomime of no musical importance. But only eight out of thirty-two works from 1822 to 1830 adopted medieval settings, and very often, as in the eighteenth century, sets were reused from work to work; it was traditional for the Opéra to spend more on costumes than sets.[4] These priorities were to be reversed in Meyerbeer's *Robert le diable* (1831), although Rossini's *Guillaume Tell* (1829) had also had completely new painted sets.

The official beginnings of the attempt to unify the constituent elements of opera (a unification such as Weber had dreamed of) lay in the creation in April 1827 of the 'Comité de mises-en-scène' on which sat the architect and stage designer Duponchel, and its appointment of a staging manager in 1828.[5] In fact this manager, Solomé, published the first full account devoted exclusively to an

[2] Marie-Antoinette Allévy, *La Mise en scène en France dans la première moitié du dix-neuvième siècle* (Paris, 1938), Plate 8; Nicole Wild, 'La Recherche de la précision historique chez les décorateurs de l'Opéra de Paris au XIXème siècle', in Daniel Heartz and Bonnie Wade (eds.), *Berkeley 1977: Zwölfter Kongress der Gesellschaft für Musikwissenschaft* (Kassel, 1981), 453–63.

[3] They were first developed by L. J. M. Daguerre in his Diorama (Paris, 1822–39). Daguerre designed for the Théâtre de l'Ambigu-Comique (1816–22) but also worked for the Opéra (1820–2) with Cicéri.

[4] Catherine Join-Diéterle, '*Robert le diable*: Le premier opéra romantique', *Romantisme*, 28/9 (1980), 147–66; ibid., 'La Monarchie, source d'inspiration de l'Opéra à l'époque romantique', *Revue d'histoire du théâtre*, 35 (1983–4), 430–41.

[5] H. Robert Cohen, 'On the Reconstruction of the Visual Elements of French Grand Opera: Unexplored Sources in Parisian Collections', in Heartz and Wade (eds.), *Berkeley 1977*, pp. 463–80.

opera's staging, that of Daniel Auber's *La Muette de Portici*, in the same year, and so inaugurated a long-lasting custom.

AUBER'S *LA MUETTE DE PORTICI*

Auber's *Muette* (1828) takes its place as the prototype of *grand opéra* because it was not just a musical triumph, but a carefully integrated joint enterprise. The libretto was by Eugène Scribe (1791–1861), already a seasoned and eclectic popular dramatist, and Auber's operatic partner since 1823. Its five-act scheme was evolved from a more conventional three-act one, and six different settings were stipulated.[6] The chorus evoked scenes from popular life, supposedly in 1647, local colour being promoted by national dances: guaracha and bolero in Act I, tarantella in Act III. The sensational close of Act V, the eruption of Vesuvius, required 'machinery never before used in Paris'.[7] Evidence of a flexible, modern use of the stage, borrowed, like all the foregoing visual elements, from popular theatre practice, exists in the published production book.[8]

While the choice of a subject from history was not a surprise, its theme of revolution was quite untypical. The political orientation of the Opéra under the Restoration was often overtly monarchic blatantly seen in various allegories by lesser composers.[9] If public interest in the Masaniello subject was strong, Scribe's first (three-act) version of the libretto, probably dating from 1825, shows the Revolution in a more sentimental light than the final one. With the expansion to five acts came the greater integration of the story of Fenella (the dumb girl, wooed and rejected by the viceroy's son) with that of the Revolution (Masaniello's leadership of the revolt of the Neapolitans against the Spaniards). This fictional interweaving— Fenella was a character taken out of Walter Scott's *Peveril of the Peak*—confirmed the way forward for *grand opéra* by playing off the theme of a doomed love against the backdrop of inexorable historical forces.

Scribe and (we must assume) Auber granted a limited role to

---

[6] The settings, all different, alternated between the court environment (Acts I, III, V) and the people's environment. This itself dramatized the theme of separation between rulers and ruled. On the three-act version, see Jean Mongrédien, 'Variations sur un thème: Masaniello', in Michael Arndt and Michael Walter (eds.), *Jahrbuch für Opernforschung 1985* (Frankfurt am Main, 1985), 90–121.

[7] Hellmuth Christian Wolff, *Oper: Szene und Darstellung von 1600 bis 1900* (Musikgeschichte in Bildern, IV/1; Leipzig, 1968), 166.

[8] Karin Pendle, 'The Boulevard Theaters and Continuity in French Opera of the Nineteenth Century', in Peter Bloom (ed.), *Music in Paris in the Eighteen-Thirties* (New York, 1987), 509–35.

[9] See Join-Diéterle, 'La Monarchie'.

conventional solos, duets, or trios, but an expanded part for the chorus both alone and in combination with soloists. All the solos and ensembles except the Princess Elvire's Act I showpiece have a directly dramatic function—whether actively or ironically—and the chorus, after dominating Act I, leads musically and dramatically in the climaxes of the next three acts. This ensures the popular tone of the whole, counterbalancing the facts that Masaniello is murdered as a counter-revolutionary and that the Spaniards are finally victorious.

Events surrounding many performances of *La Muette* in Europe— not just the one that sparked the Belgian Revolution of 1830—prove the correctness of Wagner's recollection that 'seldom was an artistic phenomenon more closely related to events of world importance'.[10] But one must acknowledge, with Wagner, that the opera's power stems from Auber's intense, imaginative score. (The work was seen at the Opéra until 1882 in 488 performances.[11]) Just as Scribe respects the unities (those of place and time would in future often be broken), so Auber confers unusual unity upon his score and the drama by scrupulously responding to each event, (especially in harmony), by using flexible verbal–musical rhythms, by the subtle transfer of motifs from act to act, and by expert pacing of events. The simplest and most effective example of such pacing is the withholding of the theme epitomizing Masaniello's revolutionary triumph in Act IV until a long way into the final sequence (Ex. 45), suddenly raising the whole temperature. Auber, in the tragic fifth act, shrank neither from a five-note dissonance, nor from the use of a gong, nor from extended

Ex. 45

(Honour and glory)

[10] Richard Wagner, 'Erinnerungen an Auber' (1871); repr. in *Richard Wagner: Gesammelte Schriften und Dichtungen*, ix (Leipzig, 1873), 51–73; trans. in *Richard Wagner's Prose Works*, ed. and trans. William Ashton Ellis, v (London, 1896), 35–55. See too Ludwig Finscher, 'Aubers *La Muette de Portici* und die Anfänge der Grand-opéra', in Jürgen Schläder and Reinhold Quandt (eds.), *Festschrift Heinz Becker* (n.p., 1982), 87–105.

[11] Totals for all operas to 1892 are given in Albert Soubies, *Soixante-sept ans à l'Opéra en une page* (Paris, 1893); they are updated in Stéphane Wolff, *L'Opéra au Palais Garnier (1875– 1962)* (Paris, 1962; repr. Geneva, 1983); Wolff gives the total as 489 for *La Muette*.

periods of free, through-composed irregularity. These tendencies, and the habitual transformation of conventional Italianate forms in set pieces, showed that French artists could offer a serious alternative to the Rossinian styles that had predominated for a decade.

EXTERNAL TRAITS

The success of *La Muette* and of *Guillaume Tell* (the latter was shown every year in Paris until 1892) determined essential traits of *grand opéra* before the July Revolution of 1830: however, the regime of Louis-Philippe (the 'bourgeois monarch') until 1848 placed entrepreneurs in charge of the Opéra, though it limited their freedom by means of an appointed committee. Louis Véron[12] budgeted large sums for costumes and scenery (Cicéri's pupils Séchan, Philastre, and Cambon could create extravagantly realistic backdrops) and introduced real waterfalls, better gas lighting, etc. Against a different background for each act, singers, chorus, and dancers in appropriate costumes—metal armour was created for Halévy's *La Juive*—moved in carefully rehearsed grouped masses, whose disposition (always published) was integral to the whole.[13] Véron wrote: 'When one has . . . an orchestra of more than eighty musicians, nearly eighty chorus members, male and female, eighty supernumeraries, not counting children, a company of sixty stage hands [*machinistes*] for moving sets, the public listens and expects great things from you'.[14] Stage sets became very realistic in the 1840s, attracting Delacroix's criticism that they were therefore un-Romantic and puerile.

So *grand opéra* came to refer to a type of large-scale work at the Opéra, typically having a tragic or melodramatic ending. It often consisted of five acts (so renewing Baroque practice), but sometimes four. Its dramatic sources rejected Classicism in favour of history, whether medieval (*Robert le diable*), Renaissance (*La Juive*), or modern (*Gustave III*).[15] In dramatic handling, *grand opéra* utilized

[12] Véron, a doctor and pioneer of patent medicine, was chosen on payment of 250,000 francs to run the Opéra as a private enterprise, with some state subsidy; he was succeeded in 1835 by Edmond Duponchel. Véron's methods included contractual penalty clauses for composers who did not deliver on time. The exact relation between government, its *Commission de Surveillance*, and the entrepreneur-directors, is explored in Jane Fulcher, *The Nation's Image: French Grand Opera as Politics and Politicized Art* (Cambridge, 1987).

[13] Cohen, 'Reconstruction'; Wild, 'La Recherche', p. 454, shows that the designer for *La Juive* undertook research trips in order to achieve a faithful picture of the art and architecture of South Germany between 1400 and 1430.

[14] Louis Véron, *Mémoires d'un bourgeois de Paris* (Paris, 1853–55), iii. 252, translated and discussed in Karin Pendle, *Eugène Scribe and French Opera of the 19th Century* (Ann Arbor, 1979), 50.

[15] Historically informative footnotes appeared in the printed librettos, and are sometimes essential to the understanding of a work.

the chorus to a high degree, giving it different roles within one work, and incorporated at least one ballet sequence, woven into the action with greater or lesser plausibility, in any act, as in earlier *tragédie lyrique*. Certain operas included large ceremonial processions, occasionally using horses, and enabling composers to invent effects on the largest scale; stage bands found a natural place.

Aspects of *grand opéra*, including visual local colour, overlapped with concerns of the Romantics: first, the concern with contrasts, for example, freedom to jump forward in time, to break the unity of place, or to exploit enormous contrasts in musical scale, say between the monumental tutti and the use of only one or two instruments and a voice; second, the use of musical local colour in conceiving certain scenes, for example, the Nightwatchman scene in *Les Huguenots*; third, the choice of themes involving religion, reflecting intense Romantic preoccupations with 'new religious formulations';[16] and last, but certainly not least, the portrayal of individuals in relation to a given society. Without arguing that *grand opéra* attained any philosophical depth, one may claim that an abiding concern (beneath the trappings of history) was morality in relation to society. Its main characters are placed—often as ordinary people caught up in events—so that in some sense they are projected as representatives of groups. This reflected the tendency of French Romantics 'less to the particular and private than to the general and impersonal'.[17] Against fateful human decisions, not excluding political *force majeure* (as in *La Muette de Portici*), themes of doomed love are played out.

At the same time *grand opéra* did not aspire to Victor Hugo's formulation of the Romantic contrast between the 'sublime and grotesque', at least so far as juxtaposing tragedy and comedy, following Shakespeare. And Hugo's desire for a truly all-pervasive use of local colour was one that only the greatest composers could hope to attain on a five-act scale. Some operas concentrated on the tribulations of leaders more than those of society at large (*Gustave III*, *Charles VI*), and it has been aptly observed that every Paris Opéra work from 1840 to 1848 made allusion in some degree to royalty.[18]

Eugène Scribe, who wrote the texts for all four of Meyerbeer's

[16] D. G. Charlton, 'Religious and Political Thought', in D. G. Charlton (ed.), *The French Romantics* (Cambridge, 1984), i. 33 ff.

[17] Charlton, 'The French Romantic Movement', in *The French Romantics*, i. 24. *Robert le diable*, however, stems from a different type of plot.

[18] Join-Diéterle, 'La Monarchie', p. 437: she sees here 'a nostalgia for royal ceremonies'. Berlioz's *Benvenuto Cellini*, which is *sui generis*, comes nearest to all Hugo's formulations.

grands opéras was the dominating librettist during the period. That he worked to a rigid formula is far from the truth; he was ready both to modify his work for his composer and permit others to make small text changes, subject to his approval.[19] His marked artistic limitations in language and characterization were made up for by his eye for piquant situations, and certain techniques from the 'well-made' plays which were his trademark: the high point prepared by events before the story begins; the central misunderstanding (or *quiproquo*) clear to the audience but not to all the characters; the logical progress of each act.[20]

A NEW DESIGN ELEMENT

Scribe did, however, develop one particular type of dramatic coup as he gained *grand opéra* experience. Typically it is melodramatic, and springs a problem on a character, the nature of which we already suspect. But it was found—even by Verdi—most suitable as a central focus in a long five-act structure. In *La Muette de Portici* Scribe created such a focus in Act IV by juxtaposing the 'private' and 'public' strands of the story in one climactic episode, using the massed forces of the Opéra company (see Ex. 45, above). Subsequent librettos by Scribe, and his emulators, refined the management of this type of coup so that it became not merely a juxtaposition, but an absolute, even shocking intersection of the private dilemma and the public ceremony. The vast stage forces thereby earned their validity through the greater or lesser worth of the dramatic irony present in a given case.

The coup is still fairly simple in *La Juive*, Act III. Rachel realizes Léopold's true identity and denounces him in the midst of state celebrations in his honour. The *locus classicus* of the Scribe coup occurs in Meyerbeer's *Le Prophète*. Jean, the Anabaptist leader, has captured Münster. In a spectacular scene in Act IV he is crowned in the cathedral, as the son of God. Unknown to anyone, his mother has sought him out; at a crucial moment she recognizes him and exclaims, 'My son!' The whole edifice of the Anabaptists (and of history: the Münster episode is authentic) is about to be set tumbling, when Jean simply out-dares his mother by denying her, pronouncing her silence as a 'miracle'. The ceremony continues.

Verdi never ceased to be haunted by this coup. In *Les Vêpres*

---

[19] Léon Halévy, *F. Halévy: Sa Vie et ses œuvres* (2nd edn.; Paris, 1863), 23–5. Occasionally the printed libretto will show significant divergencies from the score. Scribe's career in *opéra comique*, before 1828, is described in the following section.

[20] Pendle, *Eugène Scribe*, p. 85. Yet *Gustave III* is episodic in structure and *Guido et Ginevra* has its intrigue curtailed by the disruptive effects of the Florentine plague.

siciliennes, Act IV, a character reveals his paternity to the assembled public, forced to do so by his private dilemma. Act III of *Don Carlos* contains the equivalent scene of the *auto-da-fé*. Only in works without a pronounced public political element is the coup superfluous: *Robert le diable*, *Guido et Ginevra*, *L'Africaine*, and others.

INTERNAL MUSICAL TRAITS

Important vocal features of *grand opéra* were the extensive role of the chorus and the nature of the duet. First acts tended to form an exposition with chorus present throughout; last acts often harnessed ensemble and chorus variously with solos; tableaux, processions, or festivals gave purely musical prominence to the chorus. The duet often replaced the solo form as the essential vehicle for the voice, both in ubiquity and variety. In an operatic genre where dramatic tension was an ideal, duets forwarded the action in myriad ways, ranging from the imparting of information to argument and separation of characters, from the most stark confrontation of good and evil to the most passionate expression of love. Although it seems possible to relate duet forms (and finale forms) in France to the four-section Italian outline of active, static–lyrical, active, static-cabaletta, in practice such formalism is left behind by the dramatic and musical responses to the individual situation.[21] Solos, on the other hand, were more relevant to the action through narrative content (strophic forms could be used, as in *opéra comique*), or by being interrupted in some way, or by being ceremonial. The basic matrices of A (slow) B (fast) and ABA could be adopted, disguised, or developed infinitely, particularly in an age of contrast and experiment in the field of harmony.

Ensemble scenes could be built up from a sequence of linked sections. In fact, as the early nineteenth century developed the sectional solo scena, so one might say that *grand opéra* applied the same principle to ensemble scenes. Different soloists could pursue an action against a background continuum; in the librettos the latter was indicated by blocks of regular verse, alternating with conversation in freer form.

The use of the 'allegro' choral finale in various act endings (whether for perplexity, shock, triumph etc.) was necessary in a genre where the chorus claimed an almost equal part alongside principals. Yet

---

[21] Steven Huebner, 'The Second Empire Operas of Charles Gounod' (Diss., Princeton, 1985), fos. 75–84. The 'static' sections involve parallel strophes for the singers in turn, with more periodic phrasing. The 'active' sections use a variety of textures. Much research remains to be done on formal aspects of French opera in this period.

finales were not over-abundant, if sometimes over-extended. Taken as a whole, probably too little fresh thought went into their composition before Meyerbeer's *Le Prophète*.

Textural imagination was shown in the accompaniment to recitatives, helping to liberate composers from limitations of either the plain, secco style or the dramatic accompanied style. Halévy, in particular, used a new 'lyrical recitative' style, often with solo instruments or lower strings, half-way between recitative and arioso. Such blurring of formal distinctions was typical of the genre.

Immense care was lavished on details of orchestration and choral textures; technical difficulties in all parts could be numerous. The cellos played an independent and figurative melodic role. New instruments became standard participants: *trompettes à pistons*, cornets, valve horns, bass clarinet. The cor anglais, organ, gong, and various bells became regular extras, as did substantial stage bands. Halévy used anvils (*La Juive*), col legno bowing (*Guido et Ginevra*), the *mélophon*, a portable free-reed instrument invented in 1837 (ibid.), the musette (*La Reine de Chypre*), and four saxophones in *Le Juif errant* (1852). Saxhorns appeared in the same opera, as they had in 1849 in *Le Prophète*.

The more popular works could attain around 500 Parisian performances in a half-century (*La Muette, La Juive, La Favorite, Le Prophète*), while the most popular of all could reach 700–800 (*Les Huguenots, Guillaume Tell, Robert le diable*). The next average level of some 150 performances was reached by Halévy's *La Reine de Chypre* and Auber's *Gustave III*. Other works earned some thirty to sixty performances. Verdi's *Les Vêpres siciliennes* attained eighty-one between 1855 and 1864.

MEYERBEER'S *ROBERT LE DIABLE*

The first phases of Meyerbeer's career have been described elsewhere.[22] After the Paris success of *Il crociato in Egitto* (1825), Meyerbeer eventually began work with Scribe on an *opéra comique, Robert le diable*, in 1827. The conception outgrew the genre, but its reworking from three to five acts was ultimately less successful than the parallel process undergone by *La Muette de Portici*; the première was in November 1831. Comparison shows that the scenario and character relationships were little changed, resulting in loss of dramatic tension, especially in Acts II and IV.

The medieval source tells of Robert, duke of Normandy, who

[22] See Vol. VIII, pp. 426–9.

terrorized the region until his conversion and visit to Rome.[23] Scribe added the figure of Bertram, a fallen angel who has until midnight to escape perdition by securing Robert's everlasting loyalty. He is taken for Robert's bosom friend, but thwarts his path to legitimate happiness, revealing himself as his father in Act V.[24]

The dramatic focus of the opera is blurred since Robert evinces no moral position, except chivalric patriotism, but is thrust between the forces of evil and good. The latter is personified by Alice, the peasant who brings a testament from Robert's dead mother which finally causes him to abandon Bertram. Alice is well pitted against Bertram (whose satanic nature she immediately senses), in both Act III and V, where she has important trios with him and Robert. This leaves Princess Isabelle of Sicily (where the action is set) in a poor dramatic position, even though she sings opposite Robert (whom she loves) in Acts II and IV.

Robert le diable was perceived at the time as a revolutionary totality of stage effect, dramatic substance, and music. Its highly-wrought score exploits great contrasts of timbre (from un-accompanied Act III trio to full orchestra plus stage band), form, and harmony; the veteran composer Le Sueur praised not just 'les magiques effets de mélodie et d'harmonie' but also the 'étonnant ensemble simultané' of soloists, chorus, dancers, orchestra, and décor. Meyerbeer's painstaking preparatory work shows that, although he was part of a team, his own aim in *grand opéra* was to be musically original in every way: his word setting, form, timbre, and melody are best understood as original developments, appropriate to the dramatic subject, forged out of a marriage between Italian (Rossini) and German (Weber) opera types. He took it for granted that his subject-matter would be original in opera, that it would allow for local colour, and for sufficient choral scenes. And he habitually demanded alterations to the libretto as he proceeded.[25]

In detail, Meyerbeer's scores confirm that music, not words, took primary responsibility for the effect; that is, Scribe's text was cut,

[23] The legend comes down in various publications, detailed in Join-Diéterle, '*Robert le diable*', p. 154. The opera's composition history is shown in Pendle, *Eugène Scribe*, pp. 438–42.

[24] The likeness with Faust and Mephistopheles is obvious. Other sources were Latouche's novel *Le Petit Pierre* (1820), Matthew Gregory Lewis's *The Monk*, and Charles Robert Maturin's *Bertram*.

[25] The larger ones were by Scribe, the smaller ones by anonymous assistants. See Heinz Becker, 'Giacomo Meyerbeers Mitarbeit an den Libretti seiner Opern', in Carl Dahlhaus *et al.*, *Bericht über den internationalen musikwissenschaftlichen Kongress Bonn 1970*, Gesellschaft für Musikforschung (Kassel, 1972), 155–60.

repeated, and redivided sectionally in the interests of dramatic truth as Meyerbeer saw it. This led, for instance, to the happy combination of chorus with aria in Bertram's Act III solo ('O mon fils'); and in ensemble or duet scenes Meyerbeer would attain impressive forms of continuum, unified often by the developing presence of an orchestral motif. In set pieces, *Robert le diable* employed more straightforward slow–fast forms than did the composer's later French works. A rearward-glancing technique was the use of a strophic ballade in Act I, as often in *opéra comique*, to provide essential exposition (the legend of Robert, Ex. 46), together with its later ironic use in thematic recollections (Ex. 47). Meyerbeer also gives a recurring motif to Robert's rival, the prince of Granada, which is instantly recognizable if morally neutral (Ex. 48). However, in Weber's manner, strong moral qualities were given to various keys; perhaps Meyerbeer's most ambitious desire was to project this conception on to a lengthy five-act work: F major ends Acts I and V, while B minor/major is associated with Bertram and his influence. In a remarkable section of Act III, Alice's B flat major ('Quand je

Ex. 46

(Long ago, in Normandy, ruled a noble, valorous prince)

Ex. 47

Ex. 48

quittai la Normandie') is intercut with diabolic B minor passages, indicating the presence close by of demons.

Delacroix noted his preoccupation with local colour: 'it depends on an indefinable thing, which is not at all the exact observation of usages and costumes,' Meyerbeer said in 1853.[26] In the most carefully designed orchestral timbres, he sought to impart an individual tone to all significant utterances. *Robert le diable* already demanded *trompettes à clef*, poignantly deployed under the stage as the hero's mother's testament is recounted in the last act (Ex. 49).

Were it not for the image of forbearance imparted by the cor anglais in Act IV (Ex. 50) we should not be half-disposed towards Isabelle's professed love for Robert, nor towards his decision to follow the path of virtue which she symbolizes. Perhaps typical of the opera's problems is that its most celebrated episode is dramatically tenuous: the moonlit cloister with its eerie *frisson* of the blasphemous mixed with the erotic, as spirits of dissipated nuns dance and seduce Robert into stealing a sacred twig.[27] There can be no comparison

Ex. 49

The keyed trumpets must be placed outside the orchestra pit: their sound must produce the effect of distance, and as if below ground. In Paris they are placed under the stage, below the prompter.

Ex. 50

[26] *Journal de Eugène Delacroix: Nouvelle édition publiée d'après le manuscrit original*, ed. André Joubin (Paris, 1932); Eng. trans., Walter Pach, *The Journal of Eugène Delacroix* (New York, 1937), 360.

[27] The bill for painting sets (37,474 francs) amounted to more than the budget for *Guillaume Tell* (Join-Diéterle, '*Robert le Diable*', p. 161).

with Berlioz's *Ronde du sabbat* of 1830, for Meyerbeer is obliged to paint rather the inner dialogue between male and female, which he does with great orchestral sensibility, anticipating Berlioz's love scene in *Roméo et Juliette*.

Meyerbeer's conception of a given role was always bound up with the voice of a particular singer. This did not, however, make for self-indulgent display so much as allow him to stretch technique in pursuit of new musico-dramatic ideas.

MEYERBEER'S *LES HUGUENOTS*

Les Huguenots (1836), Meyerbeer's finest French opera, was also a popular one. The source was a Romantic text: Mérimée's *Chronique du règne de Charles IX* (1829). Of all *grands opéras*, it comes closest in every way to the acid truth about politics and persecution; not only are the Protestants Raoul and Marcel killed, but also the Catholic-born Valentine (who dies loving Raoul and abjuring her religion) and Valentine's Catholic husband Nevers (who dies for his humanity towards Marcel). The work ends with the St Bartholomew Day massacre (24 August 1572) portrayed with brutal force in Act V; its theme is religious fanaticism, too strong to be quelled by royalty (in the form of Marguerite de Valois)[28] and destined to be fanned into flame by a tragic misunderstanding between Raoul and Valentine. The couple's recent meeting and incipient love is told in Raoul's Act I romance, 'Plus blanche que la blanche hermine', with viola obbligato. It is abundantly clear that the sympathies of librettist and composer lay with the Protestant minority; unexpectedly, perhaps, their engagement transcended historical limitations by avoiding sentimentality as regards the main characters. They thus created a masterpiece of Romantic tragedy.

Meyerbeer's fertile musical invention is tailored in an unusually focused way. The drama commences, in both a spatial and temporal sense, on a relaxed, idyllic, even lightly humorous plane; but, from the moment of the (unsuccessful) reconciliation of parties ending Act II, the work steadily concentrates time, place, and action into a relentless spiral that ends with cold-blooded murder in a Paris gutter when Valentine is shot as a Protestant by her fanatical father; he recognizes her too late. This process is determined by the music both superficially and internally: the first part of Act II adopts, for example, a showy, effusive style for Marguerite and includes one of

---

[28] Marguerite's wedding to Henri IV of Navarre (actually 18 August 1572) is represented in the interrupted ball scene, Act V, sc. i. Henri is not impersonated.

the obligatory ballet sequences, that of bathing courtesans in the gardens of Chenonceaux. This and Marguerite's sentimental approach towards religious reconciliation—blindfolded Raoul is ushered in to meet his arranged match—merely reinforces the weak impression of the monarchy. True power lies with the Catholic conspirators: their music in Act IV is a depiction of righteous blood-lust, set as a through-composed ensemble scene and unified by recurrences of a melody whose similarity to the 'Marseillaise' is musically and politically self-explanatory and abiding (Ex. 51). Yet more chilling, in the same scene, is the music for the benediction of swords by monks, as stark, alienating, and horribly inevitable as the gesture itself (Ex. 52). Its tonal relationship of flat VI to tonic (E to A flat) exists also simultaneously on a higher structural level (benediction scene in A flat within general tonic E) and it is no accident that we have already heard it in Act II at an earlier Catholic ritual: the wedding procession of Valentine and Nevers (Ex. 53).

In *Les Huguenots* Meyerbeer attained the Romantic ideal of pervasive local colour. This was possible through the unique character

Ex. 51

(For this holy cause obey my God and my king without fear!)

Ex. 52

(Pious, holy swords)

Ex. 53

of Marcel, Raoul's old retainer. Marcel is not only a bluff, implacable, slightly grotesque veteran of the religious battle of La Rochelle (Act I aria, 'Piff, paff'). He personifies religious faith at a depth that makes religion's other manifestations in the opera seem unworthy. This touches both his vocabulary and his music. Indeed, in Raoul's and Valentine's last hour, Marcel catechizes them in the faith that will make them all martyrs. Meyerbeer's extraordinarily futuristic music is accompanied here by a single bass clarinet (Exs. 54–5). For his recitative utterances, Marcel has a personal tone-colour: triple-stopped cello, with double-bass, alternating with very simple unisons or contrapuntal lines, giving an 'ancient' effect.[29] Finally, and most importantly, Marcel is often given the music of Luther's chorale, 'Ein' feste Burg',[30] which provides the musical material of

Ex. 54

(Have you cast off all mortal fetters?)

Ex. 55

(Yes, faith at last governs our hearts in peace)

[29] In a letter to Scribe (2 July 1834) Meyerbeer recalls that Scribe's 'execution of the role of Marcel did not agree with the idea of the musical character of the role' that the composer had desired. 'I have rewritten the whole of Marcel's part for my musical needs.' This proves the composer's unified view of Marcel's function. See *Giacomo Meyerbeer Briefwechsel und Tagebücher*; ii. *1825–1836*, ed. Heinz Becker (Berlin, 1970), 376-7.

[30] Noted in the full score as 'Seigneur, rempart et seul soutien'. Thus, 'sublime' musical material issues from a 'grotesque' character.

Ex. 56

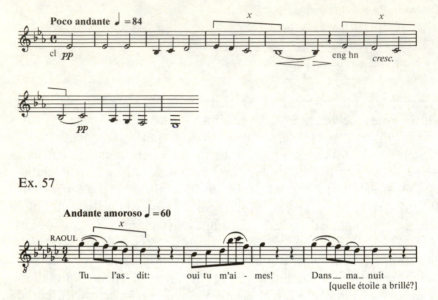

Ex. 57

(You said so: yes, you love me! In my darkness [what star has shone?])

the opera's prelude-like overture (Ex. 56). At first, when sung in Act I, it appears in gross musical distinction from other material. But, as matters proceed, Meyerbeer is able to make its scalic motifs form the basis of important themes, tightening the musical fabric like an enveloping net in order to form a musical analogue of the resilience of Huguenot faith, as in the cavatina in Act IV (Ex. 57).[31]

Many other scattered musical correspondences add to the force of this score, as do the beauty of the duet 'Tu l'as dit', sung by the hapless lovers as the hour of the massacre approaches, and the improved unity of style as compared with *Robert le diable*. Colourful invention ran high, too, in the crowd scenes in Act III (Huguenot soldiers, Bohemian dancers, the calling of the curfew, final festive music).

AUBER'S *GUSTAVE III, OU LE BAL MASQUÉ*

Auber's and Scribe's five-act *opéra historique* appeared in 1833 but the libretto stems from before 1830. Telling of the love of the Swedish

---

[31] One need hardly recall the difficulties still faced socially in many quarters by those of Meyerbeer's own (Jewish) faith.

king for Amélie, wife of his adviser Ankaström, it ends with Gustave's assassination (actually in 1792) at a spectacular masked ball. The libretto was adapted by Rossi for Gabussi, by Cammarano for Mercadante, and by Somma for Verdi, *Un ballo in maschera*. Even on the French stage the employment of a fortune-teller, a ball scene, and a page role sung in *travesti* was probably influential: both the latter reappear in *Les Huguenots*, for example. Seemingly composed in some haste, Auber's score lacks the richness and psychological truth of *La Muette*, particularly in the ensemble scenes that include Gustave's enemies.[32] Auber also seems to have been less than inspired by the character of Amélie herself. However, he covered a wide spectrum of musical expression in the score as a whole, from Gustave's love of the arts, seen in his rehearsal of *Gustave Wasa* in Act I, to the stark E flat minor opening of Act III, set in a horrifying snowbound landscape at night. Auber's fluency was suited to the many dances and dance-influenced ensembles, yet he persistently employed augmented-sixth progressions too, as in Ex. 58, the moment in Act III when Ankaström first realizes that his wife has met the king alone.

Ex. 58

HALÉVY'S *LA JUIVE*

The outstanding aspects of Halévy's style in his *grands opéras* are, first, a vocal melody of completely un-Italian cast (except in certain nostalgic pieces or love duets), produced not by elimination of symmetry but by elimination of ornament, and a propensity for syllabic setting; second, a keen sense of choral and orchestral timbre; and, third, a conscientious approach to dramatic setting, whether in the matter of altering the layout of a libretto in detail, or, for example, in the investing of subtle forms of musical local colour.[33] Halévy's scores now seem wanting in stylistic subtlety and

---

[32] There may have been political reasons for this. Auber had been made aware by the King of the delicate consequences of the popularity of *La Muette*.

[33] This was strongly appreciated by Wagner: 'To solve this problem, it was no question of consulting antiquarian documents . . . [but] to lend the music the perfume of the epoch.' '*La*

melodic originality; but this is potentially less damaging than the way his psychological insight seems to fall prey to a certain formalism in organization. One unexpected correlative of this is Halévy's reluctance (after *La Juive*) to build up effective contrapuntal ensembles which would express essential differences of motivation.

La Juive (1835) has a finely designed libretto, set in Constance in 1414, where the historical Cardinal Brogni presided over a grand council to heal the Church's schisms and thus assert its authority in a Germany menaced by the teachings of John Hus. Although the Hussites were used elsewhere in Romantic art to evoke the desire for freedom,[34] Scribe chose to highlight the persecution of Jews. The five acts alternate smoothly between public and private events. Against the massive public celebration of the Council and eventual entrance of the emperor, Sigismond, Act I depicts the courageous independence of Eléazar, who is set on by the mob for working (he is a goldsmith) and for entering the cathedral portico.[35] His supposed daughter, Rachel, is in love with 'Samuel', actually the popular military leader Léopold, who confesses his Christianity to her in Act II. His true identity and alliance with Princess Eudoxie is realized by Rachel only in Act III. Rachel publicly condemns him, but is herself arraigned. Eléazar refuses to save her life and his own by abjuring his faith, revealing to the Cardinal at the last moment that the girl was Brogni's lost daughter, sole vestige of a tragic earlier life before he entered the Church.

Although it contains the apotheosis of the Scribean *quiproquo*, *La Juive* employs perhaps the least amount of stage action possible in a *grand opéra*, giving it an unusually Classical temper. A series of well-contrived duets exploits the many layers of irony available (Rachel–Léopold, Brogni–Eléazar, Brogni–Rachel) and Scribe allowed the development of the character of Eléazar: religious persecution finally determines his course of vengeance, for he is deeply attached to Rachel. Brogni is a tolerant figure, not a caricature, leaving fanaticism as the common enemy.

The three 'public' acts are framed in different ways: Act I by a grand Te Deum, with full organ (Ex. 59), Act III by G minor, and

---

Reine de Chypre d'Halévy' (1842); repr. in Richard Wagner, *Sämtliche Schriften und Dichtungen*, ed. H. von Wolzogen and R. Sternfeld, xii (Leipzig, 1911); trans. in Ellis, *Prose Works*, viii. 181.

[34] For example, Carl Friedrich Lessing's painting *The Hussite Sermon* (1836), reproduced in Hugh Honour, *Romanticism* (Harmondsworth, 1981), 227.

[35] In the original libretto Eléazar was ducked in the lake by the drunken crowd and reappeared bleeding and with torn clothes.

Ex. 59

Te De-um lau - da - mus te Do-mi-num confi - te - mur

(+organ)   (organ holds
                   chord)

Ex. 60

LE CRIEUR Des Hus-si - tes a - yant châ-ti - é l'in-so-len - ce de par le saint con - ci - le

I   IV   ♭VII

(Having punished the arrogance of the Hussites, in the name of the Holy Council . . .)

Ex. 61

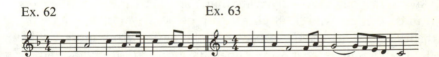

O   Dieu, Dieu de nos pè - res,   par-mi nous des-cends

[principals repeat
the phrase]

(O God of our fathers, come down among us)

Ex. 62   Ex. 63

Act V by B minor. The 'ecclesiastical' flattened leading-note chord in Ex. 59 represents an element of local colour recurring elsewhere, for example the chorus, the Crieur in Act I (Ex. 60), and Brogni. In the intimate setting of Act II (which contains no chorus) Jewish prayers at supper (Ex. 61) echo certain known chants: 'Akedah' (Ex. 62), and 'Shofet Kol hoaretz' (Ex. 63).[36]

Halévy's use of chromaticism became subtler, but he already commanded a forceful rhetoric, using brass techniques both loud and soft. Liberal use of the 'anger' rhythm ♩ ♪♪♪ emphasizes the score's debt to Cherubini and Méhul; less happily traditional

[36] Halévy composed seven now little-known settings in S. Naumbourg's *Chants Religieux des Israelites* (Paris, 1847), a publication intended to revitalize the music of Jewish services.

was the choice of a 'march duet' in Act IV where Brogni and Eléazar argue over the one true God.[37]

HALÉVY'S *GUIDO ET GINEVRA*

Active, picturesque, and episodic, with a happy ending and no *quiproquo*, *Guido et Ginevra* (1838) forms a complete contrast with *La Juive*. Scribe rationed solos to the minimum, organizing the action into duets and ensembles. Its Renaissance Florentine setting, atmosphere of contrasting extremes, and character of a sculptor (Guido) invite comparison with Berlioz's *Benvenuto Cellini*. The latter is an ever-pertinent fable on the subject of art, while *Guido et Ginevra* emulates the Romantic historical novel, laid out in vividly sketched scenes surrounding the plague of 1552–3. Act IV concludes with the burning of Cosimo de' Medici's palace at night, seen from a snow-filled square; Act V affords a spectacular view of the Apennines, a symbol of rebirth. Though exceedingly melodramatic, the plot also took the theme of potential adultery further than had *Gustave III*; Alexandre Dumas *père*'s play *Antony* (1831) had been an influential attack on the institutions of marriage and the family, in favour of individualism. The aristocratic heroine of *Guido et Ginevra*, twice given up for dead, forms a love match with her young sculptor, perhaps—we are not told—ignorant that her husband Manfredi has succumbed to the plague after wounding her in Act IV.

Halévy responded vividly, catching the tone of Forte Braccio's brigands in their wild 12/8 chorus, or of courtly pomp, or of the cathedral crypt in Act III; orchestrally he never wrote more richly. Bells of different pitches, sometimes harmonized subtly, sound in every act save the last. The high piston trombone has an obbligato; recitatives can attain a new fluidity with chamber scoring, such as at the opening of the second act (Ex. 64). Ingenious modulatory passages are worked into set pieces (e.g. Guido's Act I romance) instead of staying within recitative. His Act I duet with Ginevra modulates to the flat mediant (G flat major from E flat) in only two chords, continuing as though nothing had occurred. The B major Act III burial chorus jumps to F minor for Cosimo's affecting prayer. In older *opéra-comique* fashion Guido's Act I romance becomes a musical identity motif, announcing his presence even before we notice

---

[37] 'Ta fille en ce moment.' These male-voice, dotted-rhythm duets had appeared in Spontini, Rossini, *La Muette*, Act II, *Robert le diable*, Act III, and so on. See Leopold M. Kantner, 'Zur Genese der Marschduette in der Grand Opéra', *Österreichische Akademie der Wissenschaften, Mitteilungen der Kommission für Musikforschung*, 25 (Vienna, 1976), 322–34.

Ex. 64

(Since the auspicious day when I rescued her whom I adored, all seems to smile on me and lend prosperity)

him.[38] These details, however, merely complement the way Halévy articulates the score through harmonically organized sequences acting analogously to the drama in their own right. In this sense it is a descendant of *La Muette de Portici*.

HALÉVY'S *LA REINE DE CHYPRE*

The librettists of *La Reine de Chypre* (1841), C. and G. Delavigne, based their work freely on the career of Caterina Cornaro (1454–1510); it describes her separation from her fiancé Gérard de Coucy through the edict of Venice's Council of Ten, and her enforced marriage to Jacques de Lusignan, the Council's chosen king of Cyprus. Gérard follows her to Cyprus, intent on vengeance, as he has been kept in ignorance of the truth about Venetian influence. This he exposes in Act V, after two years have passed and Lusignan is dying, poisoned by Venice for pursuing an independent political policy. Caterina leads the Cypriots successfully against the Venetians; Gérard resumes his solitary life as a Knight of Rhodes.

The fatalism and menace of the work, and its literary quality, were highly regarded in its own time; Wagner particularly admired its contrasted local colour for Italy (Acts I and II) and Cyprus. The lovers' powerful duet of separation—one of several memorable duets—crowns a second act of distinction. This proceeds from the scene-setting (off-stage gondoliers) through Caterina's monologue, balancing traditional forms and use of tonality with modern 'free'

---

[38] This is especially effective in Act IV. Meyerbeer had made Raimbaut's romance in *Robert le diable* (Ex. 46) a recurring symbol of Bertram's satanic influence.

forms and chromaticism, to a surging coda expressing Gérard's uncomprehending fury (Ex. 65). Halévy's almost Verdian eloquence in Caterina's Act V aria—she cannot forget Gérard—sums up the pain of loss (Ex. 66).

Ex. 65

(To Cyprus!)

Ex. 66

(Gérard—and he is the one who calls for him—that name which echoed in my heart immediately)

Ex. 67

An orchestral motif symbolizing the insidious power of the Council was adopted, winding against its agent Mocénigo's threats in Act I (Ex. 67), or informing us in Act V of Venice's connection with the dying king.[39] Yet, though Halévy's fluid harmony and mature willingness to avoid cadential closure were undeniably useful, they could not replace that final necessary degree of discrimination in melody and dramatic irony. And the gigantic ceremonial scenes for the Act III celebrations in Cyprus or the Act IV disembarkation of Caterina at Nicosia seem inadequately balanced by developing musical portraits of the principals.

HALÉVY'S *CHARLES VI*

Charles VI (1843) marked a sharp break in substance and style away from the *grand* tradition, and almost turned that tradition to ironic account. The text, by the Delavignes, expresses a French nationalist response to foreign intervention.[40] Moreover, it portrays Charles VI of France (reigned 1380–1422) in his last year, episodically insane and a helplessly pathetic figure. The historical monarch married his daughter to England's Henry V. The opera makes Charles's wife, Isabella of Bavaria, into a schemer in league with the English, and introduces an *ersatz* Joan of Arc character in the form of Charles's faithful attendant, Odette.[41] A freely Shakespearian method of approach to the subject was used: the verses are relatively informal; royal characters can be bereft of all dignity; the king is visited by ghosts of assassinated acquaintances, including John the Fearless, in Act IV; other historical characters are brought into the last act, ready to be rallied by Odette;[42] but, above all, the figure of Charles VI was conceived in complex terms requiring a singer–actor

[39] Wagner drew attention to this motif and its function in '*La Reine de Chypre d'Halévy*', Ellis, *Prose Works*, viii. 195. Wagner's translator here confused Ex. 67 with a vaguer, semitonal one that recurs in the score but is not proper to one person or one emotion.

[40] It may have been inspired by the threat represented by the attempted coup in 1840 of Louis Napoleon Bonaparte (the future Napoleon III), and there was an obvious parallel between the ageing Louis-Philippe and the fictional Charles VI. By 1850 it had become politically too problematic to be shown in Paris: Léon Halévy, *F. Halévy*, p. 37.

[41] The historical Joan of Arc was to bring about the last major event of the Hundred Years War, the anointing of Charles VII at Rheims in 1429.

[42] Including Tannegui du Chatel and Jean Dunois, count of Orléans (John the Bastard).

capable of portraying a confused old man, yet one still a king and at times conscious of the awful consequences of his own madness. He dies at the end, fulminating against the English.

However, the overall tendency was towards a patriotic spectacle, not a tragic drama. The initial love-story of Odette and the Dauphin is soon abandoned. The typical *grand opéra* processional scene, the entry of English leaders on horseback into 'old Paris lit by brilliant autumn sunlight', ends in chaos as the king unexpectedly rejects Lancaster. The same tendency relieved Halévy from a problematic musico-dramatic task: he could throw certain 'national songs' into relief instead, such as 'Guerre aux tyrans' and 'À toi, France chérie'.

Apart from such public statements, Halévy's most successful music was in Act IV, not, unfortunately, for the ghosts but in Odette's childlike lullabies sung to the declining king. The all-important first solo for the king, the Act I romance, is sentimental (Ex. 68) and not effectively redeemed by its motivic relation to the trio in Act III (where Odette reconciles Charles with the Dauphin, Ex. 69), the ghost scene in Act IV (Ex. 70), and the overture (Ex. 71).

BERLIOZ'S *BENVENUTO CELLINI*

Benvenuto Cellini (1838) fits into no generic category, but is best discussed at this point. A work of supremely high musical invention, victim of its own originality, it still awaits publication in a form

Ex. 68

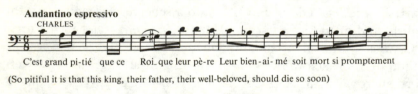

(So pitiful it is that this king, their father, their well-beloved, should die so soon)

Ex. 69

(To rob him of his inheritance)

Ex. 70   Ex. 71

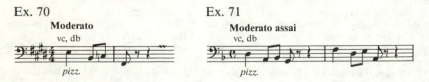

permitting the author's first intentions to be fairly judged or performed. Berlioz was not wanting in operatic experience when— prompted perhaps by Farjasse's translation of Cellini's *Autobiography* (1833)—he fastened on this subject for a two-act *opéra comique* in 1834.[43] *Estelle et Némorin*, his first opera (1823), is lost. Since 1822 he had learnt his craft by frequent attendance at the Opéra, and the year 1826 saw the completion of his second operatic work, *Les Francs-juges*. This was never accepted for performance and parts of it were utilized elsewhere. Refused at the Opéra-Comique, the libretto of *Cellini* was accepted for the Opéra late in 1835 and the score written in 1836 (scoring completed in April 1837).[44] The work had four complete performances (1838–9) between which cuts were made; there were then three performances of the first act only. It was shortened and revised in three acts in 1852, for Weimar.

In a sense the work did well to get so far in 1838, since its score was explosively modern and remains a breathtaking experience to hear. Aesthetically it was a Trojan Horse which carried the full armoury of Berlioz's sardonic genius into the bourgeois stronghold. The dramatic design has nothing in common with *grand opéra*. Admittedly it ends with a stage spectacle; yet the casting of the *Perseus* makes its own ironic comment on the catastrophic machines ending *La Muette* and other operas. Instead, it fuses three complementary impulses: first, the energy and colour of Cellini's own story, first written in 1558–66; second, Berlioz's Romantic self-identification with Cellini as one who will liberate his art, and whose statue of Perseus, which we see physically created at the climax of the opera, symbolized 'the artist's conquest over a grudging intellectual environment';[45] and, third, the evident desire to put into operatic practice some essential tenets of modern Romantic drama, as professed in Victor Hugo's 1827 Preface to his play *Cromwell*. This last impulse explains, for example, the work's constant exploitation of all types of contrast, whether of dramatic event (buffoonery to manslaughter), or of scoring; its use of some unconventional operatic diction, and rejection of periphrasis; its being imbued with a single, governing 'local colour' in Berlioz's extrovert 'Italian' style; and its

[43] Hector Berlioz, *Correspondance générale*, ed. Pierre Citron (Paris, 1972-), ii. 184. The work's early vicissitudes, including one project for a serious opera, are discussed in Thomasin K. La May, 'A New Look at the Weimar Versions of Berlioz's *Benvenuto Cellini*', *Musical Quarterly*, 65 (1979), 559–72.

[44] Hector Berlioz, *Correspondance générale*, ii. 184, 248, 263, 319, 341. The authors were Léon de Wailly and Auguste Barbier, with some contribution from Alfred de Vigny, Berlioz's friend and (apparently) first choice as his poet.

[45] Gary Schmidgall, *Literature as opera* (Oxford, 1977), 157.

sheer uniqueness, following Hugo's dictum, 'Il n'y a ni règles, ni modèles'.

The opera rejects the structure of intrigue in favour of a spontaneously linear sequence, almost reminiscent of a fairy-tale. In Act I (Tableaux I, II) Cellini plans to elope with his love, Teresa, daughter of Balducci, the Pope's treasurer. His commissioned statue (the *Perseus*) awaits casting; in the escape with Teresa from the Mardi Gras carnival, Cellini scuffles with his laughable rivals in art and love (Fieramosca and Pompeo), killing the latter. Act II (Tableaux III, IV), next day, sees escape again thwarted as the Pope orders Cellini to complete his statue forthwith, on pain of death. Fieramosca fails again to spoil the hero's plan, the statue is successfully cast, and Cellini and Teresa are triumphant.

Clearly this is basically a comedy, but one projecting a serious, vivifying philosophy of life: Hugo's 'soul beneath the body, a tragedy beneath a comedy'. The coruscating surface of satire, wit, buffoonery, colour, and rapidity comes from Berlioz's music; almost a riot of impressions is created, yet is genially ordered by the recurring chorus of master metalworkers, a kind of popular hymn to the eternal truth of art first heard in Tableau II (Ex. 72) (cf. *Die Meistersinger*). An opposite pole of energy is the anarchic gaiety of the Mardi Gras carnival music. There are audacious harmonic episodes everywhere, for example, for the whining innkeeper enumerating payments due, also in the second Tableau (Ex. 73). The seemingly endless orchestral *trouvailles* entail great individual virtuosity in the pit, but eschew the

Ex. 72

(If the earth, in summertime, is crowned with corn-sheaves, fruits, flowers)

Ex. 73

The sequence is sung first a tone, then a further semitone, higher.

(White Orvieto wine — Aleatico — and Mareschino — thirty flasks)

current fashion for stage bands, bells, and new-fangled instruments. Berlioz instead adopted a pair of guitars for local colour in Tableaux I and IV. But it is the dimension of rhythm that attracts most attention; probably no score since the Renaissance had played against the barline more determinedly. In this respect, the *locus classicus* of the score is Fieramosca's wish-fulfilling anticipation in Act II of a duel with Cellini that never occurs (Ex. 74). It is entirely typical of *Cellini* that the hardest music to execute requires the lightest touch by the performer.

Ex. 74

Berlioz's love for Gluck's later operas perhaps predisposed him to writing arias as well as dramatically vivid ensembles; in fact a 'Classical' articulation of his opera is perceptible; there are well-developed solos for all main characters, including the Pope (in a variety of ABA, slow–fast, and non-regular forms), and virtually no duets involving action. Recitative, orchestral but often secco in style, moves the action from point to point, and each tableau culminates in its own ensemble finale, containing (except the last) more perplexity than action.

By 1839 Berlioz was communicating with Scribe about a new opera, and prophetically declared, 'I should very much like an *antique* subject but am afraid of our actors' costumes, as well as the determined prosaicness of our public.'[46] Over the years 1841 to 1847 the two worked on *La Nonne sanglante*, in which an unwitting elopement with the ghost of a murdered nun sets the dramatic dilemmas in train. Having composed the music for two acts, Berlioz returned the libretto (eventually set by Gounod, 1854) in the aftermath of a dispute with the directors of the Paris Opéra.

DONIZETTI IN PARIS

Having laid the groundwork for Parisian commissions through third parties as early as 1835, Donizetti found the way clear with the success of *Lucia di Lammermoor* at the Théâtre Italien (1837). He arrived in October 1838 with *Poliuto*, recently prohibited in Naples but written with an eye to Paris.[47] Scribe expanded the work to four acts as *Les Martyrs* and restored the primacy of religious conflict to the action, conforming to Corneille's source-play, *Polyeucte*. In view of Donizetti's professed view (when returning another Scribe libretto by post earlier in 1838) that 'love treated almost as an episode' was displeasing to him as a composer, the limited success of *Les Martyrs* on 10 April 1840 must have reinforced his faith in the values he knew. However, Ashbrook reckons that only about one-fifth of *Poliuto* was actually altered, including all the recitatives. These changes he described in formalistic terms to his old mentor, Mayr: 'For example, banished are the *crescendi*, etc., etc., banished are the usual cadences, *felicità*, *felicità*, *felicità* [i.e. hackneyed V–I

[46] *Correspondance générale*, ii. 575. See also A. E. F.Dickinson, 'Berlioz's "Bleeding Nun"', *Musical Times*, 107 (1966), 584–8. Berlioz also entered into a contract for a three-act opera in French projected for Drury Lane in 1849.

[47] Letter, 8 May 1838, cited in William Ashbrook, *Donizetti and his Operas* (Cambridge, 1982), p. 132. Important prefaces to the three serious French operas of Donizetti, by Philip Gossett, are found in the facsimile scores issued in *Early Romantic Opera* (London and New York, 1980, 1982).

formulas]; then between one verse of the cabaletta and the other you should always have lines that heighten the emotion . . .'[48]

Two new trios were added (end of Acts I and IV). An applied lesson in French formal freedom was the way that Severo's cabaletta in Act II, in becoming 'Je te perds', was divorced from its original cantabile and recomposed into a mixed complex including arioso and ensemble. However, the old *Poliuto* score already contained the 'French' feature of a climactic last-act duet for the doomed lovers, whereas Italian *opera seria* traditionally favoured a final exit aria for the prima donna. Donizetti made good use of the orchestral resources of the Opéra, for which he was praised by Berlioz in the *Journal des débats*.

Donizetti toiled hard in Paris: during the eighteen months it took *Les Martyrs* to come into existence he wrote the four-act *L'Ange de Nisida* for the new Théâtre de la Renaissance, half of *Le Duc d'Albe* for the Opéra, plus *La Fille du Régiment* (1840) for the Opéra-Comique.

This last, the first of Donizetti's works written specially for Paris, may be mentioned here although it properly belongs to the next section. A brilliantly superficial text by Jules-Henri Vernoy de Saint-Georges and J.-F.-A. Bayard offered Donizetti a series of diverse set pieces, not just for Marie (brought up from infancy by the regiment) and her lover Tonio, but also for that collective 'character', the regimental chorus itself; the chorus displaces both older, potentially sadder characters (Sergeant Sulpice and Marie's long-lost mother) in musical terms. Donizetti's score sparkles with memorable tunes, which were quickly pressed into the service of French patriotism. But the score also has the now traditional extended opening sequence, plus many later passages of recitative and mixed conversational textures. These help reduce the amount of spoken dialogue, and give the work its air of effortless fecundity. However, the gaiety and joy would not have half their effect without Donizetti's technical mastery. (Ex. 75).

The Théâtre de la Renaissance went bankrupt and Donizetti recast *L'Ange* in Summer 1840 for the Opéra: it thus become *La Favorite*, whose original libretto by Alphonse Royer and Gustave Vaëz was revised by Scribe. Its perennial success shows that the French were happy to accept a basically Italian product, especially in conjunction with a sentimental fantasy about a free woman. For Donizetti's language remained that of bel canto and his dramatic organization

---

[48] Ashbrook, *Donizetti*, p. 141.

Ex. 75

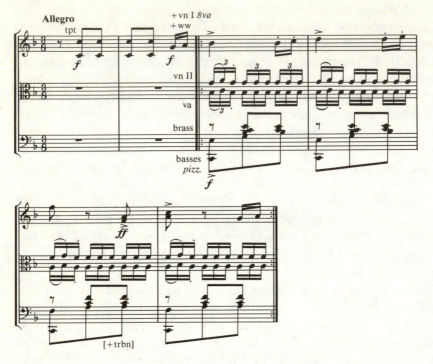

was still articulated through the disjunct technique of recitative-set piece, however this might be modified through the insertion of short arioso sections, or the unexpected omission of a cabaletta, or the addition of an organ part.[49] There is no disguising the contrivances of the plot, set in 1340. Alfonso XI of Spain has taken Léonor de Gusman as his mistress, a fact known to all except the newcomer, Fernand. The latter has rejected his religious calling after a chance encounter with Léonor, and is loved by her. When pressure is applied on Alfonso by the Church, and after Fernand's triumphs in battle, the former willingly allows Fernand to marry Léonor. Immediately afterwards Fernand is informed he has married the 'favourite'; he smashes his sword at the king's feet and returns to his monastery. Finally Léonor comes in disguise requesting her due forgiveness (she had sent a message revealing the truth, which was intercepted) but dies even as Fernand reasserts his love for her. The matrix is thus close to *La traviata*, the Romantic cliché of 'the fallen woman

[49] Winton Dean describes the modifications in 'Donizetti's Serious Operas', *Proceedings of the Royal Musical Association*, 100 (1973–4), 123–41. There is no shortage of cabalettas in *La Favorite*.

rehabilitated by a pure love',[50] a theme set forward in Hugo's early play *Marion de Lorme* (1831). Donizetti writes mixed recitative-arioso continuum textures for the action sequences, for example, surrounding the Act III wedding, using the chorus of courtiers as a character in its own right. Likewise, Act IV attains an excellent continuity between its varied textures, ranging from the penitential religious chorus with organ through to the lovers' duet (Ex. 76).[51] But admirable parts cannot add up to a whole worthy of the pungent ironies inherent in the fable: the work's basic sentimentality is well captured in the aria sung by Fernand in Act IV as an apostrophe

Ex. 76

(Come, I give in, passionately, to the rapture that intoxicates me)

Ex. 77

(Angel so pure, whom in a dream I thought I found; happiest dream)

---

[50] W. D. Howarth, 'Drama', in Charlton (ed.), *The French Romantics*, ii. 215, 240-1.
[51] A theme they do not sing together, however. Donizetti had already given it to the cellos in the Prelude to Act IV as if to suggest that this love had merely been diverted underground.

to his past, but *before* Léonor has even reappeared at the monastery (Ex. 77).[52]

The five-act *Dom Sébastien* (1843), the last opera to be completed by Donizetti, was the only one of his works originally conceived for the Opéra: it is that which most closely approaches *grand opéra*, being a tale of lost love, a lost kingdom, and ultimately the political murder of both main characters. It is based on King Sebastian of Portugal's death in the Moorish crusades (1578), the character of the poet Luís de Camões (d. 1580), and the loss of Portuguese independence to Spain in the same year. In the opera Sébastien survives the battle in Morocco only to fall victim, together with his Arab friend Zaïda, to the usurpers Don Antonio (his uncle) and Juan da Silva (head of the Inquisition). Each act has a separate setting (Act II is in Morocco).

Donizetti, as usual, composed rapidly, and was later obliged to make unwelcome changes at the peremptory behest of his librettist, Scribe; the music is mostly in a full-blown Italian idiom, organized around a more or less dramatic arrangement of set pieces, though with a particularly unconvincing ballet sequence at the beginning of Act II. After the battle, which is not portrayed, Donizetti explores his main figures in extended duets for Sébastien and Zaïda in Acts II and V. Romances for Zaïda (Act I), Sébastien (Act II), and Camões (Act III) eschew cabalettas, but the work remained in many ways a vehicle for the tenor Gilbert Duprez, whose soft high D flat *in alt* came in the second of these, and Rosina Stoltz, who was notable for creating in Zaïda (and Léonor in *La Favorite*) a new type of mezzo-soprano role, both dramatic and vocally wide-ranging. However, Donizetti also made efforts to characterize Camões, who sings a 'prophecy' in Act I, and explore the relationship between Zaïda and her jealous Arab husband Abayaldos, in their Act III duet; this piece also exemplifies the French Romantic tendency to give duets the character of an exploratory scena. The septet in Act IV (the inquisition scene) and its two succeeding ensembles formed an outstanding last example of Donizetti's art as a master of vocal drama.

MEYERBEER'S *LE PROPHÈTE*

Besides the works by Halévy and Donizetti already described, the 1840s saw the quickly forgotten *Richard en Palestine* of Adolphe

---

[52] This famous aria stemmed from *Le Duc d'Albe* (1839) which Donizetti abandoned. Its torso was twice completed by other hands (1882; 1959). See Ashbrook, *Donizetti*, p. 692, for table of musical sources of *La Favorite*.

Adam and Louis Niedermeyer's *Marie Stuart* (both 1844). However, the unquiet spirit of Meyerbeer's *Le Prophète* lurked in many minds: this had been composed by 1840 but held in abeyance largely owing to its exceptional demands on leading singers. Meyerbeer was finally inspired by Pauline Viardot-Garcia's contralto voice and revised the score for performance (16 April 1849).

Le Prophète (text by Scribe) is one of the most ambitious canvases attempted by any composer, and represents the *ne plus ultra* of *grand opéra*.[53] The fable traces the fate of Jean (John of Leyden), his mother Fidès, and his fiancée Berthe, from their obscure beginnings to Jean's coronation as son of God in Münster Cathedral, following the capture of Münster by the radical Anabaptists under Jean's command.[54] In the cathedral he denies knowledge of his mother, but is reconciled with her before finally causing a holocaust that consumes the forces of reaction and revolution alike. The opera fails in its attempted synthesis of tragedy, comedy, maternal love, religious and political history, and the spectacular (the attempt was extraordinary enough); but with the exception of the 'skating' ballet sequence of Act III (at the Anabaptist army camp outside Münster), gratuitous musical or visual display is confined to certain parts of Act V, where the constructive tension lessens and one even finds residual Italianate cabalettas. In general the drama is expressed not through 'machines' but in terms of human characters, of whom Fidès is the most interesting.

Jean himself is an unusually complex operatic figure whose actions, as with most people, are motivated by a mixture of personal and social impulses: Berthe's abduction by Comte d'Oberthal; his own religious disposition; his natural talent for military leadership; his Messianic vision, narrated in Act II. It is symptomatic that the chorus plays a relatively restricted role throughout, sketching in the background as needed.

Meyerbeer's harmonic language became markedly fluid; it roves frequently through more distantly related keys, especially a third apart, and through enharmonic progressions, as with Jean's words to his mother in Act IV (Ex. 78); it employs numerous chromatic progressions over pedal points and chromatic discords in sequence.

---

[53] Unlike *Robert le diable* and *Les Huguenots* it stretches the unity of time considerably. Acts III, IV, and V consist of two main scenes each. The sites of action are, respectively, countryside near Dordrecht (Holland); a suburb of Leyden; a Westphalian forest; and the cathedral and palace of Münster.

[54] The historical John of Leyden (Jan Beuckelszoon) (1509–36) was executed following the German recapture of Münster in 1535.

Ex. 78

(May holy light descend upon you, poor madwoman, and enlighten you!)

The music avoids cadential closure in discursive or active dramatic sections, either by modulating or simply side-stepping chromatically. The first two acts achieve also a flexibility of musical forms that comprises undemonstrative solo styles and is almost continuous in effect; articulating the drama as though unfolding a narrative, they remain Meyerbeer's most forward-looking achievement. The coronation march in Act IV, Scene ii, stands at an opposite pole, yet with a masterly five-bar opening phrase (Ex. 79) that looks forward to Mussorgsky's 'Great Gate of Kiev'.

Local colour is readily perceptible in *Le Prophète*, though it is of subtle application. There are distinct traits of material associated with, first, the Dutch countryside, and Jean's roots in peasant culture (this uses types of drone and is effectively recalled in Act V when the main characters long to return home); second, the Anabaptists, who have their own motif (Ex. 80) and various contrapuntal textures;

Ex. 79

Full orchestra, including 4 trumpets and percussion

Ex. 80

(Come to us again, wretched ones, to the water of salvation)

and, third, the military world of Jean's period as leader: types of horn-call material apply here.

The religious world of the Anabaptists tends to be expressed in flat keys, while the 'true' religion of Fidès adopts the very sharp side; but Meyerbeer is not restricted to a rigorous plan and ultimately ranges as far as the key signature of seven flats (A flat minor) in Act V.

Meyerbeer assists the work's conceptual unity by using three themes of recollection (untransformed)[55] and two that are transformed: the Anabaptists' ubiquitous refrain heard first during their preaching (Ex. 80) and the couplets of Zacharie in Act III ('Aussi nombreux') recalled in Act V. Other shorter ideas, especially using the flat supertonic or flat submediant, act on a subtler unifying level.

The score possesses a wealth of orchestral interest, ranging from sinister divided basses to four harps soli, from tutti with children's choir and organ duet to the '*Petits timbres en La* (*Campanelli*)' struck by several children while singing in the coronation scene. (This scene uses a stage band including eighteen saxhorns.) Yet Meyerbeer's chamber textures are equally memorable, just as his finely chiselled arioso sections are to be savoured as much as the large tableaux. One's appreciation of musical ideas is modified by their constantly changing timbre, to an even greater degree than happens in *Benvenuto Cellini*.

[55] The Act II 'Pastorale' ('Pour Bertha'); the Coronation hymn 'Le voilà, le roi prophète'; and the march quoted in Ex. 79.

(b) OPÉRA COMIQUE

By David Charlton

THERE were no great liberalizing changes in theatre government as a consequence of the July Revolution of 1830. As before, three Parisian theatres continued to be responsible for three main types of opera. The Opéra gave (apart from ballet) serious opera and some comedy, using recitatives; the Théâtre-Italien existed to display the best singers in Italian-language opera; and the Opéra-Comique gave the whole range of opera using spoken dialogue. Such, by and large, had been the situation in 1789; and the remaining theatres, as before the Revolution, put on a wide range of comedy, melodrama, vaudeville, and some concerts.[56] Repeated attempts were made to create a second Opéra-Comique theatre where young composers' work could be presented (1820, 1829, 1842, 1844) but all were rejected by the government of the day. The Opéra National founded in 1847 by Adolphe Adam fell victim to the upheavals of 1848. Taste outside Paris differed somewhat from city to city: but all important musical premières were the prerogative of the capital.

The Opéra-Comique company had been founded in 1801 and so had at its disposal the whole repertoire from that date, as well as earlier *opéras comiques*.[57] New works from 1830 therefore competed with successes such as Boieldieu's *La Dame blanche* (performed virtually every year to 1893), Auber's *Le Maçon* (performed frequently up to 1887), and Isouard's *Les Rendez-vous bourgeois* and *Joconde*.[58] Public taste was inclined to be traditional; the Opéra and the Opéra-Comique catered for a predominantly moneyed audience whose furious enthusiasm for music existed almost in spite of the simultaneous flowering of French Romanticism.

Music, then conceived of as an art of fashion and variety, of fine tone-colour and the exercise of virtuosity, both satisfied performers receiving the highest degree of adulation and reinforced in the bourgeois mind the taste for sensualism and spectacle, changeable attitudes, puerile vanity. In 1856 Scudo [a well-known musical journalist] ... showed French society divided into

---

[56] See François Lesure (ed.), *La Musique à Paris en 1830–1831* (Paris, 1983).

[57] i.e. from the Théâtre Feydeau and the Opéra-Comique National, earlier Comédie-Italienne.

[58] Albert Soubies, *Soixante-neuf Ans à l'Opéra-Comique en deux pages 1825–94* (Paris, 1894); but, because the author's statistics were compiled from newspapers, they are subject to errors of detail.

two antagonistic classes: the minority of music-lovers very keen on classical concerts, and the solid bourgeois class devoted to virtuosos, fashion, facile music exploited by professional entertainers.[59]

So ruthlessly applicable were the laws of supply and demand that even a successful *opéra comique* composer like Adam complained, 'If one says, "The Government encourages the arts", that means that the Government is ordering statues, paintings, is constructing monuments . . . Of poor musicians no mention is to be made,'[60] and so men of genius were becoming lost amid the drudgery of teaching and earning their living. Young and skilful players were available to restock the orchestral desks of the Opéra-Comique only once the problems of the July Revolution had been solved: in the words of Mendelssohn in 1832, 'few German theatres are so bad or in so dilapidated a condition as the Opéra-Comique here, where one bankruptcy succeeds another'.[61]

THE COMPOSERS AND LIBRETTISTS

In terms of success, *opéra comique* was dominated by Daniel Auber (1782–1871), with only two failures out of fourteen works given in this period; Adolphe Adam (1803–56), with only a handful of failures out of twenty works; Fromental Halévy (1799–1862), with two unsuccessful works out of ten; and Ambroise Thomas (1811–96), whose eight *opéras comiques* from 1837 all had greater or lesser success. However, very successful works were also produced by Hippolyte Monpou (1804–41) in *Les Deux reines* (1835) and *Le Luthier de Vienne* (1836), and by Albert Grisar (1808–69) in *Sarah* (1836), *L'Eau merveilleuse* (1839), *Gille ravisseur* (1848), and *Les Porcherons* (1850). François Bazin (1816–78) and Louis Clapisson (1808–66), too, had sporadic successes.

Opéra comique as a dramatic genre signified not comedy as such, but opera with spoken dialogue (occasionally spoken over music to form *mélodrame*), designed to give pleasure rather than instruction. By contrast with the eighteenth century, this produced a concentrated avoidance of contemporary manners as a subject, let alone contemporary politics. Instead, there was a typical exploitation of

[59] Joseph-Marc Bailbé, 'Le Bourgeois et la musique au XIXe siècle', *Romantisme*, 13 (1977), 124.
[60] Adolphe Adam, 'Les Musiciens de Paris' (1834) in *Souvenirs d'un musicien* (Paris, 1868), 52–3. Cf. Fétis in 1831: 'We have started down the English road, where nothing is done for art and artists' (Lesure (ed.), *La Musique à Paris*, p.3).
[61] Letter to his father, 21 Feb. 1832, in *Letters*, trans. Gisella Selden-Goth (London, 1946), 194.

imaginative escape, whether in time or geographical location. Whereas the smaller theatres mounted much satire and reflected, in Mendelssohn's words, the 'extreme bitterness and deep disgust' of the people,[62] the Opéra-Comique dealt in comedy of manners (Halévy's *L'Éclair*, 1835), comedy of situation (Thomas's *La Double échelle*, 1837, or his *Le Panier fleuri*, 1839; Adam's *Le Toréador*, 1849), fantasy (Auber's *Le Cheval de bronze*, 1835), and sentimental comedy, whether set in Switzerland (Adam's *Le Chalet*, 1834), or at the court of Louis XIII (Halévy's *Les Mousquetaires de la reine*, 1846) or of Louis XV (Adam's *Le Postillon de Lonjumeau*, 1836) or of Aboul-y-far of Algeria (Thomas's *Le Caïd*, 1849). A more melodramatic strain of *opéra comique* employing definite historical settings and at least the implication of potential seriousness of theme was represented, *inter alia*, by Auber's *Haydée ou Le Secret* (1847) and Adam's *Giralda ou La Nouvelle Psyché* (1850). These librettos, both productions of Eugène Scribe, portrayed leaders of men such as the Venetian admiral Lorédan who is elected Doge at the end of *Haydée*, and the queen of Spain and her court in *Giralda*; however both are really comedies of intrigue in which a series of adventures revolves round a central character (bearing a guilty secret) and his hoped-for lover, who herself is the object of desire to one or more further characters.

Scribe himself was the best-known librettist of the period, but was far from the only successful one. The most notable of his rivals were Jules-Henri Vernoy de Saint-Georges, Adolphe de Leuven, his collaborator Léon-Lévy Brunswick, and Thomas Sauvage.[63] Scribe's range and output were so considerable that in some ways the period 1830–50 in French opera is inseparable from his name. He had begun by writing vaudevilles and plays, creating about eight new works every year.[64] Although his first librettos (for Luc Guénée and others) date from 1813–16, his long and important partnership with Auber began in 1823 with *Leicester*; by 1828 his and Auber's *La Muette de Portici* was mounted at the Opéra. Scribe's *opéra comique* librettos naturally exploited the principles that had first made his spoken dramas successful: ingenious yet transparent construction; focus on motivation and reverses of fortune instead of the development of character; colourful choice of setting; and a central misunderstanding or *quiproquo* made obvious to the spectator but withheld from certain

[62] Letter to Karl Immermann, 11 Jan. 1832, in *Letters*, pp. 185–6.
[63] Brief biographies are given in Thomas Joseph Walsh, *Second Empire Opera: The Théâtre Lyrique, Paris, 1851–1870* (London, 1981), appendix D. For a complete list of Scribe's librettos see *The New Grove*, 'Scribe, Eugène'.
[64] Pendle, *Eugène Scribe*, p. 6.

participants.[65] His sources were inevitably eclectic, although the final results (whether Scribe's alone or produced in authorial collaboration) had notable consistency. It appears that he remodelled, for example, his own vaudevilles, Goethe's *Singspiel*, *Jery und Bätely* (it became *Le Chalet*), and selected themes from contemporary prose fiction such as Scott's *Guy Mannering*[66] or Dumas's *Count of Monte Cristo*. This helped to give certain librettos the flavour of Romanticism through local colour and strangeness of incident.

Other librettists, who at times could not but follow certain of Scribe's innovations, developed the more elegant character-comedy of eighteenth-century tradition, sometimes infusing it with original strokes of incident (Saint-Georges's *L'Éclair*) or, for example, boldly separating the first two acts by an imagined interval of ten years and a change of place (de Leuven's and Brunswick's *Le Postillon de Lonjumeau*). A few comic characters of enduring quality were occasionally happened upon, such as Angélique and Beausoleil in the same authors' *Le Panier fleuri*. An important shift of orientation occurred in de Leuven's and Rosier's *Le Songe d'une nuit d'été* [A Midsummer Night's Dream], set by Ambroise Thomas (1850). Although it has nothing to do with Shakespeare's play—Shakespeare and Elizabeth I both appear on stage—it blends historicism and fantasy with the assumption that an audience will also be interested by artistic inspiration itself, and in hearing a composer depict this by analogy; in the event the musical means used were quite radical for the genre. The work itself proved popular.

Le Songe d'une nuit d'été also discarded assumptions concerning the disposition of characters in *opéra comique*. Normally, a three-act work portrayed a main couple and either a subsidiary pair or else a single lover who is left.[67] However, the character of Shakespeare is paired not with a lover but with the inspirational figure of the queen, while the subsidiary female role of Olivia unexpectedly gains in emotional depth as the opera reaches its final act.

AUBER

Auber's career at the Opéra-Comique began in 1813 with *Le Séjour militaire* (a virtual failure), which was followed by another twelve works to 1830 including the highly successful *Le Maçon* (1825)

[65] Steven S. Stanton, quoted in ibid., p. 85.

[66] Ibid., pp. 273–84. See Vol. VIII, p. 100, for *La Dame blanche* by Scribe and Boieldieu, partly taken from *Guy Mannering*.

[67] Variations readily occurred among subsidiary figures. In *Le Postillon de Lonjumeau* the same actress plays both leading female characters.

and *Fra Diavolo* (1830), both seen regularly to the end of the century. *Le Cheval de bronze* of 1835 demonstrated the freshness of a fantastic and oriental subject, not far removed from the more innocent gaiety of similar comic works of the Napoleonic and Restoration eras. Typically, however, the actual motifs and relationships might have suited the *ancien régime*: a farmer's daughter (Péki) to be married to an official (the mandarin Tsing-Sing) when she really loves the local boy, Yanko; and a prince searching for his ideal beloved. But whereas earlier *opéra comique* tended to possess a core of three central characters to which two or three peripheral ones were added, the newer convention was to have five central characters in addition to peripheral ones. This consequently gave rise to many more possibilities for developing subplots, whether or not closely integrated with the primary fable. In *Le Cheval de bronze*, for example, Tsing-Sing's jealous fourth wife assists in furthering the plot against his marriage with Péki.

Scribe, the librettist, incorporated certain sharp contrasts that are representative of the period: exotic settings, fanciful events, the divulging of information when a person is supposedly asleep. The bronze horse of the title bears both Yanko and Tsing-Sing away by air to a Venus peopled only by women; on returning, both men unintentionally reveal this secret destination and are turned into statues. In a parody of the Orpheus myth, Péki (dressed as a man) resists Venusian blandishments and so succeeds in bringing her lover back to life.

The musical planning of this and other works at first sight resembles earlier *opéra comique*: sixteen numbers distributed over three acts, comprising nine solos, five ensembles, and several choruses either alone or combined with other numbers. It is true that simpler traditional solo items continued to be composed: stanzaic solos (called couplets) that not infrequently provided essential background information,[68] and arias falling into sectional moulds of two or four parts (ending more rapidly) or three parts (ending how they began). Although the beginning and ending of sections could at times be blurred, the basic ABA form remained discernible in *opéra comique* arias even in works by Massenet fifty years later. However, the ensemble and the choral items frequently attained an elongated sectional construction that existed to provide musical development for its own sake, unified only by the dramatic conundrum and the musical logic of its component parts. As if to counter this, *Le Cheval*

---

[68] In *Le Cheval de bronze* Péki's stanzaic solo No. 6 is entitled 'Ballade'.

de bronze and other works brought back at the close of Act III a memorable theme from much earlier (in this case the opening chorus) to provide a superficial sense of wholeness. This technique is not to be confused with the occasional recollection of musical material as an ironic or other type of dramatic reminiscence.

The *opéra comique* chorus conventionally sang in the first and last numbers of an act; to omit them thus became a means of creating special dramatic tension. First and second acts normally concluded with a finale sequence anchored to a major incident (for example, the arrival of Yanko on the bronze horse) that occurred within the duration of the music. The full resources of voices and orchestra would then be marshalled and united by a theme suitably designed for repetition.

Auber's music seems never far from the inspiration of movement or dance; one might even draw a comparison between it and Baroque music, since it falls into readily perceptible sections, it places a premium on melody, and it fixes a dominant mood in the hearer by developing a certain *Affekt* through rhythm as well as theme. On the other hand, like much *opéra comique*, Auber's music tends to avoid counterpoint, thematic conflict, and the minor mode. Lively melody, Auber's greatest asset, was still in 1835 (*Le Cheval de bronze*) filtered through the experience of Rossini and Weber, as in the Prince's Act I air (Ex. 81); particularly in earlier works he applied a bold intervallic spread. There is an attractive strength in Auber's use of melodic sequence, causing a line to 'fall into place' yet managing to overcome the inherent predictability of the process. His least original melodies were the slowest ones. The atrociously insensitive word setting in Ex. 82 (taken from the Act I quintet) also reflects Auber's allegiance to Italy; his French rivals were not so cavalier, fortunately.

Le Domino noir (1837), the most popular of all Auber's productions, shows his musical strengths reflecting Scribe's escapism most clearly.

Ex. 81

(O night, my greatest fortune, O sleep of enchantment)

Ex. 82

(How beautifully she walks, how elegant and attractive [she is])

Ex. 83

(O terror that overwhelms me, what have I done, poor wretch, guilty in the eyes of all, what shall become of me?)

The plot, set in Madrid, is based on a ridiculous premise: Angèle (the queen's cousin) is a nun who pursues her worldly interests in society disguised in a black domino (a masquerade cloak); she finally becomes free to marry, thanks to a timely royal ordinance. For two acts Angèle is on the run, first from a Christmas Eve ball and then from a private house; Act I, like Verdi's *Rigoletto*, sets the action against a sequence of dance music played by an off-stage orchestra, and closes after an interlinked series of duets with Angèle's fearful escape as midnight strikes (Ex. 83). Forced into adopting a maid's disguise in Act II, she is obliged to perform a 'Ronde aragonaise' complete with castanets (Ex. 84). (Similarly bright 'Spanish' colours also came to the fore in Adam's *Le Toréador*, *Giralda*, and elsewhere.) The opera became a vehicle for leading singers, its drama an updated reworking of *Cinderella*.

One of Auber's most successful and interesting *opéras comiques*

Ex. 84

(Beautiful Inès, belle of the ball, is alluring, virtuous, and—what's more—has plenty of money)

was *Haydée ou Le Secret* of 1847.[69] Scribe's sources—a combination of Dumas and Mérimée—provided material for a work which itself has the episodic excitement of a Romantic novel.[70] Each act is set in a different location, the second being on board the vessel of Lorédan, a *quinquecento* Venetian admiral. Lorédan's 'secret' refers to a youthful act which has caused both death and suffering, and which he expiates in the course of the opera. The music remains largely genial, so that utterances of hatred and irony in particular fall short of any undue realism. The formal confrontation duet between Lorédan and his enemy, Malipieri, suffers thus in Act II. But the broader ground of solo and ensemble is admirably designed, and in closing Act I Auber even stood Scribe's intended conventional finale on its head in favour of a chromatic coda, its thematic distortion symbolizing the hero's plight. The musical scope and continuity in the more private episodes of Act III (nos. 15 to 17) enable the tension to reach its climactic level with the self-destructive urge of Lorédan and the self-sacrifice of Haydée, the slave whom he loves, powerfully opposed. Auber's increased range of expression may be seen in Lorédan's music: a revealing aside during the Act I finale (Ex. 85); the hero's more public remorse, uttered during the Act II confrontation duet (Ex. 86); and his public farewell to a beloved Venice in Act III, when he thinks all is lost (Ex. 87). This dignified solo is heard against the memory of the massed choral welcome sung to Venice by his crew at the end of Act II, 'Salut cité chérie', a melody which exemplifies Auber's considerable suggestive skill in this medium (Ex. 88).

[69] By 1890 it had been performed 483 times at the Opéra-Comique. *Le Domino noir* was given every year except four up to 1890, by when it had had 1,114 performances.

[70] Sources identified as Mérimée's story 'La Partie de trictrac' and Dumas's *The Count of Monte Cristo*, in Pendle, *Eugène Scribe*, pp. 222–6.

Ex. 85

(Leading their bravery, I thought I would find death)

Ex. 86

(Punishment for crime, a just torment, yes, I see the abyss open beneath my feet.)

Ex. 87

(Farewell for ever, noble city which recognised my worth)

Ex. 88

(Hail, beloved city, O Venice our home)

HALÉVY

Halévy's first-performed *opéras comiques*, *L'Artisan* and *Le Roi et le batelier* (1827) were not successes, but over the next two decades Halévy wrote at least five durable works: *Le Dilettante d'Avignon* (1829), *L'Éclair* (1835), *Les Mousquetaires de la reine* (1846), *Le Val d'Andorre* (1848), and *La Fée aux roses* (1849).[71] His most constant librettist was Saint-Georges, though in 1835 he began an intermittent collaboration with Scribe. Had he so desired, Halévy could have given *opéra comique* a new sense of musical purpose for, as Henry Chorley said, 'Among skilled living musicians, there was no one to be found more available than M. Halévy. If he was rarely fanciful, he was never vulgar in his music; if seldom spontaneous, he was always ingenious, and wrote like one to whom all the resources of his art are known.'[72] These resources were manifest most obviously in his orchestration, which is discussed below. Perhaps the surest proof of Halévy's musico-dramatic imagination in *opéra comique* remains *L' Éclair*. The drama, by Saint-Georges, is unusually restricted to four characters without chorus; it is set in Boston, USA. The young English graduate George has been invited to stay with the young widowed Lucy, and her sister Henriette. Lionel, a young American naval officer on shore leave, encounters George and is then recalled on board; but he is thwarted by a sudden storm and blinded by a flash of lightning. In time Henriette falls in love with Lionel as she nurses him, and he with her, though he has never seen her. But when his bandages are removed he embraces the attractive Lucy. Henriette's humiliation and Lionel's error are put to rights by time, a little subterfuge, and marriage.

Halévy's music can be opposed to Auber's in several ways: it respects verbal prosody and responds rapidly to the meaning of single words; it modulates more often and more richly, often using keys a third apart, in order to build transitional or contrasting sections; its melody, taken alone, does not always imply or determine one obvious chord at any point, and it is equally comfortable in slow love-songs and fast ensembles. Although counterpoint as such plays little part in *opéra comique*, Halévy's ensembles and orchestral inventions are often articulated through contrapuntal means. *L'Éclair* thus emerges with the emotional and musical range of a serious comedy: George remains a little ridiculous, Henriette always sensitive

[71] In addition to five partly successful ones he also composed an Italian *opera semiseria*, *Clari*, and a second Italian work, *La tempestà* (after Shakespeare), was written for London, 1850.

[72] *Thirty Years' Musical Recollections* (London, 1862), ii. 115.

and Lionel by turns active, anguished, or sentimental. Halévy's talent for stylistic parody, having lent success to *Le Dilettante d'Avignon* through its mock-Italianisms, could respond more creatively to tradition, for example in Lionel's 'Grand Air' in Act I, for this account of the sailor's life is related to Philidor and Grétry.[73] On the other hand, the Lionel–Henriette duet in Act II is a fine epitome of Romantic sensibility, containing both a supposed Provençal melody and an archetypical declaration of passion (Ex. 89).

Ex. 89

(There is no lord, no prince, no king, who can love better than I.)

Ex. 90

---

[73] Philidor's arias descriptive of various trades, and Pierrot's nautical aria 'Notre vaisseau' in Grétry's *Le Tableau parlant*.

Ex. 91

Ex. 92

(A sweeter day dawns at last, bringing hope to my heart)

L'Éclair even provides the stricken Lionel with an orchestral motif, heard first on brass as he is led on stage by Henriette; it is not sung but is used for his entrances in Acts I and II. It captures the tragic implications of his blinding (Ex. 90), but these are also expressed in the tortuous harmonies that illustrate the first reactions to it (Ex. 91).

Les Mousquetaires de la reine (1846) had words by Saint-Georges, but took its cue from Scribe through being set in the 1620s and the anti-Huguenot reaction. But the context is confined to courtly gallantry and Halévy adapted himself to a relaxed evocation of 'the air of the old French court' as Chorley observed, to set pieces, and to extrovert melody. When the need to express personal feeling arose, the composer well satisfied it; but sentimentality was the order of the day. This provoked the repetition of the hero's third-act romance, No. 11, at the end (Ex. 92). This melody also betrayed a new syllabic style in *opéra comique*, intimate and yet transparent, which could be seen as the direct ancestor of Debussy's in *Pelléas et Mélisande* (see 'Heightened lyrical speech' on p. 362 below). Overall, however, as in *Le Val d'Andorre*, the composer stayed within the usual limits of his medium: vocal forms as summarized above, and the occasional use of local colour.

ADAM

Whereas Halévy made important contributions to *grand opéra*, Adam worked almost wholly in *opéra comique*, and for the smaller theatres. He had twenty-five works staged before 1830, fifteen *opéras comiques* staged in the next decade, eight various operas in the next, and thirteen *opéras comiques* in the six years before his death. Like Balzac, he served art to pay his debts—a kind of martyrdom made inevitable by the failure of his Opéra National (1847–8).[74] Adam worked at some time with most of the leading librettists, who helped him to successes: Scribe in *Le Chalet* (1834) and *Giralda* (1850), de Leuven and Brunswick in *Le Postillon de Lonjumeau* (1836), and Thomas Sauvage in *Le Toréador* (1849).

Adam's music was less demanding than that of his rivals: its texture, harmony, and orchestration are less varied. Comparatively uninterested in developing structures, he preferred to build by starting new sections or using a simple variation principle. His melodic facility was considerable, typically taking either a dance-rhythm or a reminiscence of Weber as its starting-point, as can be seen in Ex. 93, from Act II, No. 8, of *Le Postillon*. His melody almost seems to be generated by the simplicity of its accompaniment and static quality of its bass line. One of Adam's melodic fingerprints was the beginning of a phrase outside the tonic, giving an informal, optimistic effect. Local colour did not play a large part in his work, and would be sufficiently provided by a token song or by suitable themes in the overture.

The Swiss troops and returning soldier Max in *Le Chalet*, however, gave ample opportunity for exploiting the pseudo-military style that was such a weakness of the 1830s and to some extent the 1840s. The uproarious 'Vive le vin' (brought back at the end simply as a good tune) may stand for many comparable examples by Adam and Auber (Ex. 94). Conversely, although her supplies have been ransacked and her very safety is at risk the heroine Betly can sing no more frightened

Ex. 93

(Thanks to good fortune, madam, I can [here reveal to you the intensity of my love])

---

[74] Walsh, *Second Empire Opera*, Introduction and Appendix E.

Ex. 94

(Long live wine, love and tobacco)

Ex. 95

(Despite myself, I tremble. She trembles for fear)

Ex. 96

(Oh! oh! oh! how handsome he was, the postilion of Lonjumeau)

phrases in the ensemble, No. 4, than that of Ex. 95; this echoes the deft humour of the whole.

The musical identification of an *opéra comique* with one memorable theme was happily brought about in *Le Postillon de Lonjumeau,* a sentimental comedy about the coachman whose voice is 'discovered' by Louis XV's administrator of opera, and becomes a leading tenor anxious to conceal his past in order to avoid prosecution for bigamy. Chapelou's theme (first heard in Act I, No. 3) shows, however, the extent to which purely vocal quality and technique were now essential to *opéra comique*: the singer is not celebrating the past through pastiche, but the present through his living artistry and (later) his top B natural (Ex. 96). Indeed, a convention developed of allowing leading characters to make their first-act entrance with the dramatically meretricious aid of lavish vocalises or cadenzas.

The immense popularity of *Le Postillon de Lonjumeau* was earned by the superior variety of Adam's score and the ingeniousness of its libretto. Adam even gave the postillion's neighbours a fugue to sing. In the two-act *Le Toréador*, set in the same period, witty musical reference to eighteenth-century *opéra comique* played an essential part of the plot. Quotation from Grétry in particular both revived the spirit of vaudeville and paid homage to a composer certain of whose works still held the boards, and whose *Richard Cœur-de-lion* and *Zémire et Azor* were newly orchestrated for modern consumption by Adam himself.[75] Moreover *Le Toréador* contains a miniature *divertissement* for all three characters in the form of variations for voice and flute on the nursery tune 'Ah! vous dirai-je maman'. With this may be compared the closing scene of Auber's *Jenny Bell* (1855) which contains vocal variations on 'Rule, Britannia!'[76]

Le Toréador's gay lack of pretension was carried over into *Giralda*, but could not appropriately fill a large three-act canvas. Scribe's tedious reverses of fortune are too well mirrored in repetitive vocal lines and cadences; the massive second finale comes to resemble the monstrous fusion of an *opera buffa* with the resources of *grand opéra*. Only the chromaticism of Manoel's Act I aria (Ex. 97) seems to suggest an emergent change of sensibility.

THOMAS

Ambroise Thomas's career extended to the 1880s and he only set one Scribe libretto (*Le Comte de Carmagnola*, Opéra, 1841), preferring instead the wit and finesse of Sauvage, François Planard, or de Leuven. Several distinctive qualities emerged in his first, and successful, *opéra comique*, *La Double échelle* (1837). They included the capacity to write as attractively carefree melodies as his elders could; respect for accurate prosodic word setting and distaste for gratuitous vocal display; command of contrapuntal lines in ensembles; and a liking for subtle harmony. Thomas's more personal themes had greater rhythmic flexibility and subtlety than those of his elder rivals, particularly in steady 6/8 metre. Moreover, he was willing to employ thematic interconnections of a more contrived nature, though always

[75] *Le Toréador* quotes from Grétry's *L'Amant jaloux*, *Le Tableau parlant*, and *L'Ami de la maison*; the dramatic situation ending Act I appears to be inspired by the second act close of the first of these.

[76] The action takes place in England. Act III also includes variations on 'God Save the King'.

Ex. 97

(Sweetest dream, you who always soothe me, Happy enchantment of discreet amours)

Ex. 98

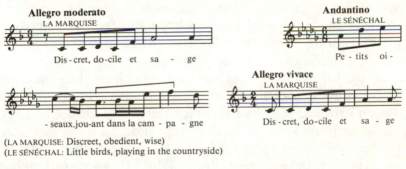

(LA MARQUISE: Discreet, obedient, wise)
(LE SÉNÉCHAL: Little birds, playing in the countryside)

Ex. 99

with a light touch: Ex. 98 draws on three successive sections of the opening trio of *La Double échelle*. Equally lightly worn was the learned harmonic sequence (Ex. 99) used as the basis for a mere *mélodrame* during the serenade, 'Ah! si j'avais'. This sort of intelligence set Thomas apart, but for the moment he remained content to stay within orthodox forms. *Le Panier fleuri* (1839), another one-act piece, almost equally successful, again demonstrated his penchant for character-comedy and traditional dramatic values. He took up current musical styles and applied them zestfully. For

example, the opening double chorus of soldiers and drinkers does
not only take in a plethora of conversational details (the scene is a
Parisian bar in 1760) but also goes on to include further action
matched with musical development. Like Adam, Thomas is ready to
parody older styles such as the minuet; like Auber, he can invent a
brazen melody to carry an ensemble (in this case No. 4) triumphantly
through (Ex. 100).

Thomas's next major success was not until 1849, with *Le Caïd*.
Sauvage's reworking of the *papataci* episode from Rossini's *L'italiana in Algeri* naturally provoked some Italianate parody, especially
near the end. However, it also demonstrated the composer's fertile
use of varied accompaniments and ritornellos, his artful melody
contrasting with Adam's simpler one. But still the traditional forms
obtained: air, duet, ensembles, finales. It was with *Le Songe d'une
nuit d'été* (J. B. Rosier and de Leuwen, 1850) that a new orientation
appeared, pointing to future *opéra comique* librettos that would move
away from novelettish adventure towards something more ambitious
(later undisguised in the form of direct literary adaptation) and more
pretentious treatment of adult relationships. Thomas's work begins
conventionally enough with a celebration in a London tavern given
by Falstaff in honour of Shakespeare's latest success. But a masked
Queen Elizabeth and her maid Olivia are obliged to shelter there
from a storm, having been to the première also. The volatile poet,
unmoved by various entreaties, takes refuge from loneliness in
alcoholic confusion. Act II, set in Richmond Park by moonlight,
contains an extended sequence in which the still-masked Elizabeth
calls on Shakespeare as his muse to reform and return to poetry. In
the half-light Shakespeare seizes Olivia's hand in error, only to
become involved with her noble suitor in a duel. He escapes, thinking
he has killed Latimer. Not until Act III does the queen reveal her
identity and give the poet her friendship in return for his rededication

Ex. 100

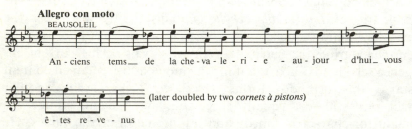

(Good old days of chivalry, today you have returned)

Ex. 101

(With them, one's soul bewitched, ah, then one can hasten to battle)

to art. (There are probably direct connections with Offenbach's *Les Contes d'Hoffmann* of 1881, discussed later.)

Thomas at first seems to search for a stylistic way; there are echoes of Weber and Berlioz (among others), notably a sterling version of the 'Marche de Pélerins' from the latter's symphony, *Harold en Italie* (Ex. 101), which occurs in the introductory ensemble. But there is also a pompous theme for the London revellers that is closer to *grand opéra*, and prominent use of *mélodrame* to lend heightened reality to Elizabeth's pleading in the first two acts. The atmosphere changes in Act II, No. 8, with the 'dream' sequence. In a sense it is childishly sentimental, but in another it anticipates Act II of *Tristan und Isolde*. The music persistently employs enharmonic modulation by thirds (G flat—A—F, etc.), requires the use of a harmonium to create an apparently endless harmonic flux, and adds the disembodied vocalises of Elizabeth to complete its strange beauty (Ex. 102). Enharmonic change continues to forestall cadences, and also applause, as the sequence moves through its duet of principal characters (in E), the challenge, and the duel itself, which ends the act in D (an enharmonic third below G flat, which began the 'dream'). Almost as suggestive of the future are the third-act duet for Olivia and Latimer, set to a sobbing B minor, and the discordant openings of both Nos. 12 and 13.

ORCHESTRATION

The conventional 1830s *opéra comique* orchestra included double woodwind and piccolo, four horns (crooked in separate keys), two

Ex. 102

(I breathe in the sweet perfume of flowers.)

natural trumpets, three trombones, percussion, and strings. A harp was regularly but not always included. Adam used a *cornet à pistons* in the overture to *Le Chalet* but this was exceptional. In the 1840s the chromatic (piston) trumpet was specified, the same players regularly turning to natural trumpet in the course of the same work (for example, Adam's *Le Roi d'Yvetot*), or else doubling trumpet and *cornet à pistons* (Auber's *Haydée*).

We can see Thomas's early use of the harmonium (patented only eight years before in 1842) in Ex. 102. However in 1834 Halévy

Ex. 103

created a not dissimilar effect in *L'Éclair*, the finale of Act II, when Henriette shows her Aeolian harp to her sister (Ex. 103). The music passes through several enharmonic modulations and requires the use of both a harp and a 'piano expressif', evidently a type of free-reed instrument inspired by Anton Haeckl's physharmonika.[77]

Orchestration in *opéra comique* was an essential ingredient of its colourfulness, commonly using the full possibilities of wind (solo, doubling, etc.) and strings (pizzicato, muted, and occasionally solo, including cello). Adam's orchestration was the least imaginative, Halévy's probably the most; Halévy and Thomas evidently thought of material in terms of orchestral colouring, consequently writing more flexibly and incorporating more interesting detail, even in the tutti. *Cornets à pistons* were used to suggest both solemnity and

[77] See Alfred Berner, 'Harmonium', in *The New Grove*. Halévy's full score, title-page, explains: 'Pour faciliter l'exécution ... qui se fait à Paris avec un piano expressif, ou fisharmonika, Mr Marix, Passage des Panoramas No. 47, a fabriqué sous le nom d'*accordéon éolien*, un instrument ayant le forme d'un accordéon.'

menace, and of course to double main themes in the largest tuttis. Stage orchestras were fairly regularly used, drawn from the pit group.[78] Inferior scores, it need hardly be said, succumbed to the crude rhetoric of bass drum and cymbals.

(c) ITALY

By David Kimbell

ITALIAN ROMANTICISM: ART AND POLITICS

In 1830 Italy was little more than what Metternich was to call it: 'a geographical expression'.[79] At any rate the word had no political reality, for the peninsula was still divided into the multiplicity of kingdoms, duchies, and grand-duchies, and provinces of the Austrian Empire that had been restored at the Congress of Vienna in 1815. Nor to outward appearance did 'Italy' mean much more in 1850. For in that year, following the failure of the revolutions and wars of independence of 1848–9, a second Restoration had been effected.

But, if the political map of Italy was little changed, it was otherwise in the minds of men. The 1830s and 1840s were crucial decades of the Risorgimento; and the Risorgimento—the 'rising-up-again' of the Italian people to liberty—was at this period more an achievement of intellect and imagination than of direct political action. Many of its heroes were intellectuals or artists: the political philosopher Giuseppe Mazzini, who in an unending stream of writings proclaimed his belief that nothing could stand in the way of the growth into nationhood of people who shared a common religion, a common way of life, and a common culture; the poet Alessandro Manzoni, who spent more than a decade refashioning his great novel *I promessi sposi* in such a way that it might help provide Italians with an accepted national language; the composers, Bellini, Donizetti, and Verdi, whose operas were acclaimed in theatres all over the peninsula and regarded as part of the patrimony of all Italians. Such men, directly and indirectly, persuaded their compatriots that 'Italy' was more than a geographical expression: it was an intellectual and emotional and spiritual reality as well, and once that was well

---

[78] e.g. *Le Domino noir, Les Mousquetaires de la reine, Haydée.*
[79] Letter to Count Apponyi, 12 Apr. 1847.

understood social and political reorganization must inevitably follow.

The Italian Romantic movement acquired much of its distinctiveness from its social and political dimensions. Of course, Romanticism had complex ramifications in Italy no less than in other parts of Europe. It entailed a rejection of the past, of Classical and mythological subject-matter, and the premium put on harmonious formalism of design. Italians became more enthusiastically cosmopolitan than ever before, keenly interested in artistic developments in those northern countries where Romanticism was most at home: France, Germany, and Britain. But they did not imitate them slavishly: not the clamant individualism of the artist-hero, nor the preoccupation with the supernatural, nor the curious relish for remote periods of history were generally typical of them. Mazzini, in his literary essays, insisted that the age of artistic egotism was a thing of the past, and that the age to come would be one of 'socialized humanity'.[80] The history with which Manzoni dealt in his plays or D'Azeglio in his novels interested those authors not for its strangeness and remoteness, nor because they had an objective curiosity to know what the past was really like, but because of the light which it shed on the contemporary plight of Italy. As D'Azeglio quite specifically put it, 'I conceived the plan of influencing people through a patriotically inspired literature.'[81] In Italy Romanticism was the cultural arm of the Risorgimento.

THE PLACE OF OPERA IN ITALIAN SOCIETY

Most Italian artists were, then, not solitary dreamers but men keenly aware of their social role. To communicate with their fellow men vividly and attractively was a first priority, and throughout the period opera remained a popular art form loved by Italians of all classes and conditions. The number of theatres where opera was performed was prodigious; and outside the theatre operatic music was a mainstay in the repertoire of town and military bands, of church organists and of barrel-organ grinders. That coachman who drove Dickens into Italy in 1846, and who had 'a word and a smile, and a flick of his whip, for all the peasant girls, and odds and ends of the Sonnambula for all the echoes' was a quintessential figure of the period.

In the larger cities, where opera was performed regularly at most

---

[80] See, for example, 'Della fatalità considerata com'elemento drammatico', *Edizione nazionale degli scritti di Giuseppe Mazzini*, viii (Imola, 1910), 169–200.

[81] Massimo d'Azeglio, *I miei ricordi*, with posthumous completion by Giuseppe Torelli (2 vols.; Florence, 1867); Eng. trans., E. R. Vincent, *Things I remember*, (London, 1966), 311.

seasons of the year, the theatre occupied a central place in social life. The still flourishing box system, whereby tickets were purchased not for individual performances but for, usually, the season, encouraged people to regard the opera-house as the normal place of public resort in the evening. Except in those theatres that were attached to a court, such as the Teatro Regio in Turin and the San Carlo in Naples, where etiquette was severely formal, such a state of affairs naturally disposed audiences to treat opera-going as a convivial activity as much as an artistic one.

DRAMATIC AND MUSICAL PRINCIPLES

In the ever-shifting balance of power between words and music, the first half of the nineteenth century was, in Italy, an age in which the primacy of the musicians was overwhelming and largely uncontroversial. Above all else opera meant the theatrical rendering of impassioned song: 'carve in your head in letters of adamant,' wrote Bellini to the librettist of *I puritani*, 'the music drama must draw tears, inspire terror, make people die, through singing.'[82] Moreover, despite the violence of the dramatic themes that Romanticism brought into fashion, this singing was accommodated within an operatic structure that was still highly formalized, and dominated by musical values.

An Italian Romantic opera made no attempt to present its subject in consistent detail or depth. The dramatic action was concentrated on a comparatively small number of cardinal incidents, and each of these was structured in the way that Rossini had standardized. To begin with, a brief instrumental prelude; then a recitative in which the dramatic business is expounded; this first section of the scene, generally static in character, culminates in a lyrical aria or ensemble, the cantabile. After the cantabile there is a marked change of mood, sometimes brought about by the arrival of more characters, sometimes by a shift from reflection to decision in the mind of the protagonist. The transitional passage (tempo di mezzo) that accompanies this transformation issues in the cabaletta (or stretta as it is usually called in the case of large-scale ensembles), a fast and brilliant aria, sung twice to bring the scene to its conclusion. In ensembles the cantabile is often proceeded by another lyrical movement in a more animated and erratic style, the primo tempo. The pattern also affects those numbers of an opera that already in the eighteenth century had been

---

[82] Letter to Count Carlo Pepoli, *Vincenzo Bellini: Epistolario*, ed. Luisa Cambi (Verona, 1943), p. 400.

multipartite—the introduction and the grand finale—for composers now tended to concentrate the dramatic and musical interest on just two movements, one slow and one fast. Only the choruses and the occasional single-movement aria, often distinguished by some such special term as canzona or romanza, were unaffected.

Within the individual sections of the scene more had changed since Rossini. Some composers, like Saverio Mercadante and Giovanni Pacini, still favoured the 'chainlike' aria structures of Rossini, in which one musical idea succeeded another in a loose succession to which only the internal balance of the phrases and, often, the increasingly florid character of each succeeding phrase gave any firmness. Ex. 104, from Act I of Pacini's *Ivanhoe*, illustrates this.

But Bellini popularized a tighter form, in which the aria culminates in a varied reprise of its opening phrase, and this became the favourite of Verdi's early years (see Ex. 105 from *Oberto*, Act II). During the 1840s Verdi tended increasingly to convert this largely formal reprise into a climactic phrase in which the initial lyrical impulse returns intensified and transformed; indeed he often reverted to the evolving form of Rossini and Pacini, but with a closer expressive relationship between each succeeding couplet of verses and each succeeding phrase of song.

At the beginning of this period the freer sections of the operatic design—recitative or scena, primo tempo, tempo di mezzo—were very much subordinate to cantabile and cabaletta. But they contained the seeds of some of the most significant developments in the second part of the century. Dramatic and expressive considerations often prompted composers to pack into their 'recitatives' sections of lyrical arioso or of evocative orchestral music, and the primo tempo and tempo di mezzo—particularly the latter, in which the momentum is often sustained by the orchestra—were the places where quasi-symphonic skills were already being applied to dramatic ends.

Only very slowly did Italian composers begin to avail themselves of the expressive resources of chromatic harmony, or of the Romantic orchestra. The primacy of the singing voice gave a certain one-dimensionality to the musical language, and melodic, rhythmic, and formal considerations therefore weighed heaviest. Harmony was used to clarify form, and to underline the rhythmic and dynamic incidents in an aria or ensemble. It is a singular trait, *vis-à-vis* other musical traditions, that the most complex chord progressions and the most abstruse modulations are rarely used to underline the expressive climaxes of a song; more often they give an almost physical vehemence to the tutti cadences that follow a cabaletta. The orchestral

Ex. 104

(My only comfort amid such bitter sorrows is the sweet thought that his heart loves me;
Ah! to see him for a moment before dying! to hear the voice of tender love; then let the
harshness of my fate be fulfilled, sweet is death in the arms of love.)

Ex. 105

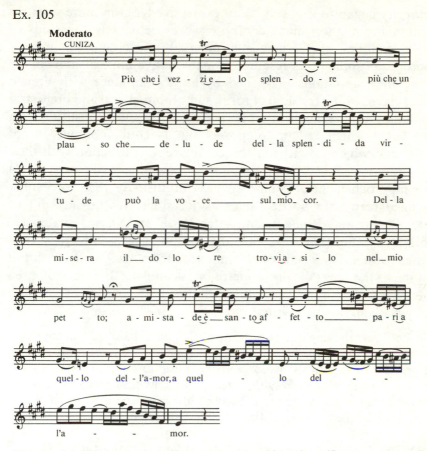

(The voice of glorious virtue has more effect on my heart than riches and magnificence,
more than deluding praise. Let the sorrow of the unhappy woman find refuge in my bosom;
friendship is a holy affection just as surely as love is.)

writing likewise seldom provides the kind of detailed expressive
commentary that had become fashionable in Germany and France.
When composers sought to diversify their conventional style of
scoring it was to employ devices more typical of eighteenth century
orchestral practice: an obbligato instrument, or a reduction of the
full orchestra to some distinctive chamber grouping.

REAPPRAISAL

For good and for ill, the force of musical tradition was stronger
in Italy than anywhere else in Western Europe. But the Romantic
age brought a series of reappraisals of the tradition which, slowly
and unspectacularly, transformed the language of opera. Composers
grew more confident in imposing their wills on singers; Rossinian

virtuosity began to give way to an expressive lyricism more sensitive
to dramatic nuance; many composers became acutely conscious of
the splendours of German instrumental music and anxious to
appropriate some of its resources for the native musical style; many
found their ambitions sharpened by an acquaintance with French
grand opéra, whose freedom of form, sumptuous choral and orchestral
resources, and grandiosity of spectacle together constituted an
allurement which Italian composers simply could not put out of
mind, and which unsettled a too complacent satisfaction with their
own tradition. But perhaps the most important development was a
new rapprochement of composer and librettist. By 1830 so cavalier
an unconcern with poetic values as Rossini's was already out of
date. Bellini and Romani, and later Verdi and Piave, established
working relationships in which the composer was intimately concerned with every detail of the libretto, from its broad structural
outline to the finest details of metre or vocabulary. Before 1850 even
Salvatore Cammarano, the leading librettist in the bastion of tradition
that was Naples could write:

Did I not fear the imputation of being an Utopian, I should be tempted to
say that to achieve the highest degree of perfection in an opera it would
be necessary for both the words and the music to be the product of one
and the same mind; and from this ideal follows my firm opinion that when
it has two authors, they must at least be like brothers, and that if Poetry
should not be the servant of Music, still less should it tyrannize over her.[83]

DONIZETTI'S MATURE OPERAS: GENERAL CHARACTERISTICS

An account of Donizetti's early career and of his first masterpiece,
Anna Bolena (Milan, 1830), has been given elsewhere.[84] The distinction of that opera was apparent both to popular audiences and
to the subtlest minds of the period. Mazzini admired it for the
way in which it cast off Rossinian lyricism and concentrated on
truthfulness of characterization;[85] and old Simone Mayr, Donizetti's
teacher in Bergamo, at last began to address his former pupil as
maestro. The first of his operas to be performed in Paris and London,
Anna Bolena, marked the beginning of Donizetti's international
career. Until 1837 (*Roberto Devereux*) his activities continued to be
centred in Naples, forming the last significant chapter in the glorious

[83] Letter to Verdi, 17 July 1849, *I copialettere di Giuseppe Verdi*, ed. Gaetano Cesari and
Alessandro Luzio (Milan, 1913), 473.
[84] See Vol. VIII, pp. 44-9.
[85] Cf. the passage from his 'Filosofia della musica', quoted in Herbert Weinstock, *Donizetti
and the World of Opera* (London, 1964), 75-6.

operatic history of the city; thereafter he was drawn away increasingly to Paris and Vienna.

Donizetti's maturity was not marked by any decisive rejection of his Rossinian inheritance. To the end of his working life he recognized that he and 'every Italian composer lived and continues to live on the knowledge, the taste and the experience born from the style created by that genius'.[86] He never outgrew the operatic structures established by Rossini's example; and even in matters of style, old-fashioned traits remained well after *Anna Bolena*. Chainlike aria forms still heavily outweighed those in rounded, recapitulatory forms; as late as *L'assedio di Calais* (Naples, 1836) Donizetti still used female singers for heroic male parts; and a delicate and graceful floridity was still often to be heard in the writing for tenor and bass voices. But about 1830 he came under the influence of the slightly younger Bellini, whose style had matured earlier than Donizetti's own. Gradually the aria structures became more compact; coloratura encrusted the melodies less thickly; and instead the lyricism acquired a new expressive intensity, partly attributable to the profusion of slow, dissonant appoggiaturas, partly to the scrupulous matching of word and tone. Soon Donizetti no less than Bellini himself was a master of a style of which one might say, 'we do not know whether it should be called sung declamation or declaimed song'.[87] See, for instance, Ex. 106 from *Sancia di Castiglia*, Act II.

Donizetti was typical of his age in that, in maturity, he concentrated on the composition of serious opera. The range of subjects he handled was wide, extending from neo-Classical tragedy in the French style (*Belisario*, Venice, 1836) to historical romance (*Lucia di Lammermoor*, Naples, 1835); from homely sentimentality (*Linda di Chamounix*, Venice, 1843) to themes of national and religious conflict (*Sancia di Castiglia*, Naples, 1832). But he had a particular partiality for sanguinary intrigue, usually focused upon some kind of love triangle. While some operas—including *Belisario* and *Sancia*—dispense with a conventional love interest altogether, Donizetti's own recorded views on librettos endorse the taste of the period for Romantic melodrama: 'I want love—because without it subjects are cold—violent love.'[88]

---

[86] 'Scritti e pensieri sulla musica', manuscript notes, possibly for a lecture in Austria in 1843, Museo Donizettiano, Bergamo.

[87] From a review of Bellini's *La straniera*, in *L'eco*, Milan, 20 Feb. 1829, quoted in Bellini, *Epistolario*, p. 196.

[88] Letter to Giuseppe Consul, 21 July 1835, Guido Zavadini, *Donizetti: Vita—musiche-epistolario* (Bergamo, 1948), 379.

Ex. 106

(SANCIA: We separated? Ah, no! that horrible thought alone is enough for me. I understand no other feeling if I must lose you . . .
IRCANO: Yes . . . and for ever. He who drives me out must die at last. Let him die!)

As Italian composers turned from the archetypal Classical themes that had dominated the first two hundred years of operatic history to subjects that were more violently passionate and psychologically more lifelike, and as they aimed to match ever more closely the musical expression to the meaning of the words, the tension that had always existed in opera between 'dramatic truth' and musical beauty entered a critical phase. Donizetti often emphasized his desire to 'serve the words';[89] but the dramatic illumination is in fact fleeting and fragmentary, for a deeper desire, namely to create beautifully fashioned artefacts of impassioned song is never repudiated. In the cantabile of the duet in Act II of *Lucrezia Borgia* (Milan, 1833) the disagreement between the friends Orsini and Gennaro is faithfully reflected in the openings of their solo phrases (Exx. 107 and 108). But as well as being a juxtaposition of character, a duet was seen as a musical form which required the harmonization and reconciliation of its constituent elements; and, notwithstanding the

Ex. 107

(So that you may show yourself grateful to her)

Ex. 108

(You know, you are fully aware. . .)

[89] For example, in the letter to Antonio Dolci, 10 Jan. 1839, ibid., p. 493.

Ex. 109

(ORSINI: Negroni is a noble lady . . .
GENNARO: But now in this court . . .)

sense of the words, Orsini and Gennaro are soon simply 'making music' together (Ex. 109). Such constraints on dramatic fidelity have been observed in some degree by most opera composers; but Italian Romantic opera imposed a further one. In another letter Donizetti speaks of his habit of 'serving the situation and giving the artists scope to shine';[90] and it is the sense that some of the music has been written with no other object than that of 'giving the artists scope to shine', to earn the admiring applause of their dazzled audience, that occasions a more destructive tension between music and drama. The cabaletta at the end of *Lucrezia Borgia* provides a striking example. Starting in the grandest tragic style, with plunging arpeggios, and broken gasps of song, the aria culminates—*più mosso*, in the major key—with a mere *tour de force* of virtuosity.

The fact of the matter was that Italian opera composers could not long lose sight of their singers or audiences in pursuit of an ideal dramatic vision. Operas were still bespoke for a particular company of performers, and it was essential for the composer to make the most of their strengths and minimize their shortcomings. When operas were revived by different companies, it was a quite normal procedure for the arias to be adapted to suit them—*puntature* was the technical term for such adaptations. It was not the least of the innovations of *Macbeth* that it marked Verdi's break with that custom. That the consequences of such complaisance were not always deplorable is shown by Donizetti's response to the talents of Giorgio

90 To Antonio Vasselli, 24 Oct., 1841, ibid., p. 558.

Ronconi, in *Torquato Tasso* (Rome, 1833); a great singing actor, Ronconi prompted Donizetti to explore the dramatic potential of the hitherto neglected baritone voice, thus introducing to Italian Romantic opera an invaluable new expressive resource.

DONIZETTI AS MUSICIAN AND CRAFTSMAN

Early in his career Donizetti had entertained reforming ambitions: a fellow-student, Marco Bonesi, tells of his impatience with 'the predictable situations, the sequence of introduction, cavatina, duet, trio, finale, always fashioned in the same way'.[91] What impresses in his mature operas, however, is not so much any clear purpose of reform as the extraordinary resourcefulness he showed while working within the tradition. Some of this resourcefulness is the result of the pleasure of the master craftsman in his material: Donizetti's aria structures are frequently extended and elaborate, far more so than the merely effective presentation of the text demands, and give an altogether more leisurely impression than those of the young Verdi. But more often some dramatically apt point is made by the inventive stroke in question. Most noticeable, because they occur in what is normally the most stereotyped part of the opera, are the transforming touches that Donizetti often introduces into the cabaletta: the rewriting of its second statement; the temporary transference of the theme from voice to orchestra; the replacement of the usual exuberant release of energy by a slow plain kind of song more apt to a scene of tragedy. But in fact, such felicities are to be found in every part of his scores; Donizetti's knack of handling the conventional forms in novel ways that served to illuminate the dramatic task in hand was inexhaustible.

In 1834 Rossini was quoted by Bellini as expressing the view that Donizetti was 'the composer in Italy with the most skill ... in working out his pieces' [*per la tiratura dei pezzi*].[92] Donizetti himself attributed to his knowledge of the quartets of 'Haydn, Beethoven, Mozart, Reicha, Mayseder' the fact that he was able to 'economize on imagination and work out a piece from few ideas',[93] and there are indeed many examples of arias and ensembles in which he pursues a motif with Beethovenian single-mindedness. The stretta from the quartet in Act II of *Parisina* provides an example (Ex. 110). Another aspect of Donizetti's thematic economy is his handling of recurring

---

[91] Quoted by William Ashbrook, *Donizetti* (London, 1965), 42.
[92] Letter to Francesco Florimo, 4 Oct. 1834, Bellini, *Epistolario*, p. 443.
[93] Letter to Antonio Dolci, 15 May 1842, Zavadini, *Donizetti*, p. 602.

Ex. 110

(PARISINA: Go, fly } and let Italy be spared an atrocious spectacle
ERNESTO: Come, fly}
UGO: It is not life, it is protracted death, eternal torment, which you give me
AZZO: Go away: as long as in my heart . . .)

themes. Some such themes are dramatically emblematic, as, for example, the ballata of Pierotto, the orphan-boy organ-grinder in *Linda di Chamounix*; some are largely formal, as when the orchestra takes up in the tempo di mezzo material already heard in the primo tempo or scena preceding the cantabile—a feature hardly more common in Donizetti than in the music of his contemporaries. But there are many examples that are as unusual and as apt expressively as they are deft in terms of musical craftsmanship. For example, in the duet for Giovanna and Enrico in Act I of *Anna Bolena* the haunting climactic phrase of the cantabile 'Di un ripudio avrò la pena' recurs to crown the cabaletta; and the primo tempo of the

Lucrezia–Alfonso duet in Act I of *Lucrezia Borgia* is a parlante set against an orchestral theme developed out of the Prelude to Lucrezia's solo scena in the Prologue—a theme associated, therefore, with her love for Gennaro.

Donizetti was the master-harmonist among Italians of the age, though he paraded his skills less ostentatiously than Mercadante. He made effective play with the wide range of tonal relations that arise from the Italian habit of regarding each key as having two equally valid equivalents—relative and parallel—in the opposite mode. Particularly deft with enharmonic and 'Neapolitan' effects, he often introduced delicious harmonic and tonal shifts to give relish to repetitions of phrase (see Ex. 111, from *Maria Stuarda*, Act II). Typical of much of his mature music was a popular songlike simplicity which, except as a special effect, was new in Italian opera. Sometimes this *popolaresco* note was emphasized for dramatic purposes—as in the music of Gennaro in *Lucrezia Borgia* or Pierotto in *Linda di Chamounix*; but more generally it appears that Donizetti was seeking in the full-blooded sentimentality of popular song— especially Neapolitan popular song—that same antidote to Rossinian floridity that Pacini confessed himself to have been seeking in the same place at about the same time.[94] His instrumentation was firmly within the Germano-Italian tradition established by Mayr, largely dependent upon a 'variegated pattern of wind colour over a neutral string background'.[95] Several operas, notably *Lucia di Lammermoor*, allotted an unusually prominent role to the horns, as if they had for Donizetti the same associations with the Romantic as they did for Weber.

Donizetti's facility was legendary; tradition reports that *L'elisir d'amore* (Milan, 1832) was written and composed in the space of two weeks, to help out an impresario who had been let down by another composer.[96] In the 1830s and 1840s, however, many critics regarded such facility with more suspicion than admiration, and Donizetti—shown in a celebrated caricature in the Paris *Charivari* composing with both hands at once[97]—did not escape their sneers. While he was far from blind to the abuses of the age and deplored the compromises with circumstance which he was continually having to make, Donizetti took pride in his work and resented the insulting

---

[94] Giovanni Pacini, *Le mie memorie artistiche* (Florence, 1865), 93.

[95] Julian Budden, 'Donizetti', in *The New Grove Dictionary of Music* (London, 1980).

[96] F. Alborghetti and M. Galli, *Gaetano Donizetti e G. Simone Mayr: Notizie e documenti* (Bergamo, 1875), 77–8 (quoted in Weinstock, *Donizetti and the World of Opera*, p. 83).

[97] Reproduced in Weinstock, *Donizetti and the World of Opera*, plate 9.

Ex. 111

(Through you I hope that my plight will not be as wretched as this . . .)

and unjust criticism to which he sometimes was subject: he was particularly hurt when Schumann described *Lucrezia Borgia* as 'music for a marionette-theatre'.[98] Apart from his musical talents, he was a writer sufficiently accomplished to complete the libretto of *Fausta* (Naples, 1832) after the death of the librettist Domenico Gilardoni, to write the librettos of several of his comic operas himself, and to translate into French both *Belisario* and *Linda di Chamounix*. One of the most fastidious of the artists who worked with him, Giuseppina Strepponi, later Verdi's second wife, remembered him as a man of 'goodness and vast culture . . . a truly superior artist and gentleman'.[99]

MERCADANTE'S REFORM OPERAS

The works of both Bellini and Donizetti showed unmistakably that a spirit of reform was in the air. But it was not until the late 1830s that a group of operas appeared that were actually claimed by their composer, Saverio Mercadante (1795–1870), to be revolutionary.

Mercadante was perhaps particularly well placed to make an objective reappraisal of the tradition, for twice in mid-career he withdrew from the hurly-burly of Italian operatic life. From 1827 to 1831 he was in Spain, and in 1835–40 he worked at Novara—'a provincial city where no-one talks about anything but rice, wheat, wine and maize'[100]—as director of music at the cathedral. At all events it was in the first operas composed after his return from Spain, particularly in *I Normanni a Parigi* (Turin, 1832), that a new character begins to be perceptible: the music is less brilliant, less stereotyped in form, and suggests a close study of the text. And it was during his service at Novara that Mercadante produced the series of 'reform operas' for which he is still dimly remembered: *Il giuramento* (Milan, 1837), *Le due illustri rivali* (Venice, 1838), *Elena da Feltre* (Naples, 1838), *Il bravo* (Milan, 1839), and *La vestale* (Naples, 1840). Thereafter, with his return to Naples as director of the Conservatory, his vision of a reformed melodrama seemed to fade.

In the late 1830s Mercadante's programme for reform was very much in line with the thinking of (earlier) Bellini and (later) Verdi. Conventional stereotypes were to be eliminated, the music was to be more responsive to the dramatic theme, and singers were to be

---

[98] Letter to an unknown friend, 15 Aug. 1839, Zavadini, *Donizetti*, p. 502.

[99] Writing in *Gaetano Donizetti, numero unico nel primo centenario della sua nascita, 1797–1897*, cited and trans. Weinstock, *Donizetti and the World of Opera*, p. 162.

[100] Letter to Francesco Florimo, 10 July 1835, Naples, Biblioteca del Conservatorio di Musica.

disciplined to perform strictly in accordance with the wishes of the composer. A letter to Florimo, written while Mercadante was working on *Elena da Feltre*, has often been quoted:

I have continued the revolution begun in *Il giuramento*: the forms varied—trivial cabalettas banished, crescendos eliminated—concise working-out—few repetitions—some novelty in the cadences—proper attention paid to the drama: the orchestra rich, without covering the voices—the long solos in the ensembles, which compel the other parts to stand coldly by and damage the action, removed—little bass drum and very little *banda* . . .

But the most important thing is . . . not to allow my score to be altered in the slightest, whether by additions or cuts or transpositions. The singers should study it carefully and neglect nothing in the ensembles, putting their whole heart into declaiming and accentuating it, without any arbitrariness in tempo or in the addition of fioritura.[101]

Almost from the beginning of Mercadante's career critics commented on the resourcefulness of his orchestral writing. In his reform operas this quality is unmistakable: particularly characteristic are the woodwind solos that he uses, sometimes to introduce, sometimes to act as obbligatos to his vocal numbers and, more than any of his contemporaries, to punctuate and support the recitative; he is fond too of entrusting a section of music exclusively to a somewhat recherché combination of instruments. Another aspect of Mercadante's orchestral skill is the fascinating density of some of the instrumental patterns set up in more declamatory parts of the score. Ex. 112 from the primo tempo of the Act II duet in *La vestale* is typical of the driving energy which he achieves by such means.

Apart from this orchestral elaboration, the reform operas can boast a structural freedom that has no parallel among Mercadante's contemporaries. Indeed few of the formal innovations generally associated with Verdian scores of ten years later—*Macbeth*, *Luisa Miller*, or even *Rigoletto*—are not in some way adumbrated here. The conventional patterns are always liable to be overturned: in Foscari's aria in Act I of *Il bravo*, an off-stage romanza is heard between the two statements of the cabaletta; while Ubaldo's aria in Act III of *Elena da Feltre* merges cantabile, declamation, cabaletta and chorus into a flexible whole that pays as little heed to the formal layout of Cammarano's text as do some of Verdi's great scenes to their literary frames. At the same time as loosening the structure of the individual numbers, Mercadante strove for a more natural sense of continuity. In ensembles he liked to engage all the singers virtually

101 Letter, Jan. 1838, Naples, Biblioteca del Conservatorio.

Ex. 112

(No, the sword which spilt my blood was not pitiless . . .)

from the outset, avoiding long solos—as the above-quoted letter to Florimo confirms. And as Verdi was to do, he tended drastically to reduce the number of extended arias: there is none in Act I of *La vestale* and only a one-movement preghiera in the second; in all acts of this opera the music is composed in one virtually unbroken sweep, each number dovetailed smoothly into the next.

The most personal of Mercadante's structural innovations was his transformation of the cabaletta. Even when he retained the fast final movement to round off a scene, it rarely had the gaily dancing rhythms, the florid vocalism, or the repetitive design typical of the form. The vocal lines tended to be declamatory rather than lyrical or brilliant; the accompaniments to avoid stereotyped 'vamping' patterns; in duets and trios the voices are clearly differentiated in style and scrupulously avoid repeating one another. In *Giuramento*, *Elena da Feltre*, and *La vestale* he transforms the convention of the brilliant concluding aria for the prima donna far more radically than Bellini or Donizetti had ever done, composing in each case a tiny cantabile that breaks down into graphic declamation as the hand of death takes firmer hold of the singer (see Ex. 113 from Act III of *Il giuramento*).

But even in the late 1830s, when, briefly, Mercadante was the nearest thing to a great composer permanently based in Italy, there

Ex. 113

(For me there is no hope, and I leave love to you. Ah, do not weep . . . smile at me . . . your hand . . . here . . . on my heart. I die happy)

were features in his music to suggest that he was no born progressive. Despite his concern for musico-dramatic continuity, he elaborated the individual movements with a care more typical of the eighteenth than of the mid-nineteenth century. Introductions to arias are often long and elaborate, with florid cadential material following the thematic *incipit*, and not infrequently he rounds off the design with carefully wrought instrumental postludes. His harmonic and modulatory resources, much admired by Italian contemporaries, are also strangely old-fashioned in effect. There is no trace of a new sensibility, opening up new worlds of feeling by harmonic means; rather traditional harmonic patterns are elaborated to the verge of abstruseness; we are still closer to Corelli than to Weber (see Ex. 114 from *Elena da Feltre*, Act III).

Ex. 114

Mercadante's correspondence with Florimo confirms the suspicion that his impulse to reform neither welled up from any deep internal urge nor was inspired by any keen dramatic vision. 'If I had not followed your advice, I should still be stuck with those confounded cabalettas, repetitions, and tedious procedures [*lungagini*] etc. This new career of mine I owe to you, who shook me out of my lethargy and restored me to new musical life.'[102]

And his reform of the cabaletta proves to be not the sovereign gesture of one who was a past master of the style—as Donizetti's and Verdi's cabaletta reforms were—but rather the refuge of one who had always been ill at ease with it.

If you should have any good new cabalettas to send me you would be doing me a pleasure, because I can compose the first movements—the adagios—but these confounded *cabalettas*, ... ruin everything for me. The more I strive to be original, the more antiquated they seem to turn out.[103]

The object of this remarkable request was presumably to stimulate

---

[102] Letter, 7 Jan. 1839, Naples, Biblioteca del Conservatorio.
[103] Letter, 23 Nov. 1831, Naples, Biblioteca del Conservatorio.

Mercadante's creative juices rather than to embark on wholesale plagiarism: behind a redoubtable exterior hid an artist always painfully aware of the limitations of his talent. 'Others with greater flair and more imagination can complete [the work of reform] and I shall be content to have initiated it, and that in pursuit of your suggestions.'[104]

A very perplexing question is, however, what kind of completion of his work he might conceivably have wished for. He detested such innovations in style as he associated with the 'northerners', Donizetti and Verdi; and such general artistic principles as he proclaimed were nostalgic rather than prophetic. Naples was still 'the fatherland of composers', and on assuming the directorate of the Conservatory there in 1840 he saw his task as being that of 'restoring the ancient fame of Neapolitan composers . . . establishing a school founded on the Old Neapolitan school, but free from prejudice and enriched with the advances which the art has made'.[105] Despite Mercadante's admiration for Rossini and Bellini, it sounds as if his old teacher Zingarelli, together with Cimarosa and Paisiello, had never ceased to be the chief divinities in his artistic pantheon. Long before his death he had become a reactionary notorious even by the standards that are supposed to have prevailed in nineteenth-century conservatories. The nearest thing he left to an artistic testament, an extraordinarily ill-informed paper entitled 'Breve cenno storico sulla musica teatrale da Pergolesi a Cimarosa', delivered to the Royal Academy of Archaeology, Literature and Fine Arts in Naples in 1867, bears witness to a feebly Platonic view of the aesthetics of his art. In music 'the idea of the *Beautiful* and the *True*' must never be lost: the way of the great Neapolitans of the past was that of 'the effective expression of the words rendered sublime by simple melodies'.[106]

His total indifference to literature was another anachronism in the Romantic age. He felt most at home with the Metastasian and post-Metastasian subjects on which he had been brought up, and had a particular sympathy for themes from Roman history. In his best years he set more fashionable librettos, apparently because he was given them: *La gioventù di Enrico V* (Milan, 1834) is based on Shakespeare, *Il giuramento* on Victor Hugo's *Angelo*. But Mercadante showed absolutely no interest in their literary pedigree, and nothing survives to suggest that he ever discussed them with his librettists

[104] Letter, 1 Jan. 1838, Naples, Biblioteca del Conservatorio.
[105] Letter, 4 July 1840, Naples, Biblioteca del Conservatorio.
[106] *Atti della Reale Accademia di Archaeologia, Lettere e Belle Arti*, iii (Naples 1867), 34–5.

with any kind of critical acumen. One cannot imagine Bellini, Donizetti, or Verdi happily harnessing their best music to so clumsy and obscure a libretto as Gaetano Rossi's for *Il giuramento*; nor empowering a third party—Florimo again—to act on his behalf in getting Cammarano to revise the libretto of *Elena da Feltre* (it had too many solo arias). 'I am too far away to go into such details, and you know the game better than anyone—I shall approve everything . . .'[107] In later years he abandoned Romantic librettos altogether, returning to such archaic themes as *Orazi e curiazi*, *Medea*, and *Statira*.

THE INSPIRATION OF EXTRA-MUSICAL IDEAS: POLITICS

In their different ways, Bellini, Donizetti, and Mercadante all helped ensure that in the years after Rossini's exile and retirement the Italian operatic tradition did not stagnate. The choice of dramatic theme, the musical language and formal design, the relationship of words and music, the style of performance, all underwent a gradual change, a slow but perceptible development towards a more Romantic ideal of music-drama. In addition, certain extra-musical factors played a part in increasing the dramatic and emotional range of opera; it was made to function as the vehicle for new ideas, and it was subjected to unprecedented ideological and imaginative influences. In the central decades of the Risorgimento it is not to be wondered at that one of these extra-musical factors was politics.

Censorship rarely allowed composers to write operas that were explicitly political. While the censors' duties were interpreted with varying degrees of severity in the different parts of Italy, it was everywhere agreed that of all their responsibilities—political, religious, moral, and 'philological'—the first was of primary importance. Besides having the power to veto the choice of subject, they could emend or expurgate a finished libretto; and at performances in the theatre, the effect of an opera on its audience was carefully supervised by the police. In 1847 Angelo Mariani, directing a series of performances of Verdi's *Nabucco* in Milan, was reprimanded by the police 'for having given to Verdi's music an expression too evidently rebellious and hostile to the Imperial Government'.[108]

Despite these precautions, the theatre was too central a feature of Italian life to be kept free from political contamination. If the deliberate provocation of patriotic riot can have been only very rare,

---

107 Letter postmarked 27 Apr. 1837, Naples, Biblioteca del Conservatorio.
108 Frank Walker, *The Man Verdi* (London, 1962), 151.

there clearly was some mysterious link between the opera and the nationalist and libertarian emotions of the age. Even in Rossini's heyday, Heine had linked the delirious Italian enthusiasm for opera with the abject political condition of the country, and with the passing of the years the link became more specific. Many of the operas Verdi composed in the 1840s contained not only the idiosyncratic characters and the stirring dramatic confrontations that were to remain typical of the mature Verdi; works like *Nabucco* (Milan, 1842),[109] involving the fate of the Jewish people in their Babylonian exile, or *Giovanna d'Arco* (Milan, 1845), set against a background of the fifteenth-century wars that followed the English invasion of France, had a political and national dimension besides. If censorship largely banished Italian themes from the stage, librettists, composers, and audiences alike were adept at perceiving in apparently remote and exotic subjects analogies to the contemporary Italian condition.

The emphasis placed on the nation in the librettos of such operas is matched in the music by a profusion of choral scenes. Indeed, on the strength of the choruses in *Nabucco* and its sequel *I Lombardi alla prima crociata* (Milan, 1843), Verdi was dubbed *il padre del coro* by his Milanese admirers. The term implies nothing elaborately contrapuntal. On the contrary, the effectiveness of the choruses in *Nabucco* was due in no small part to their technical simplicity. Verdi perceived that if the chorus was to embody the idea of the nation—not only the Jewish or French nation ostensibly represented on the stage, but the potential Italian nation among his audience—the manner of its utterance must be as popularist as possible. This ideal is realized by writing for it predominantly in unison. Whether echoing the religious sentiments of their high-priest Zaccaria, or denouncing the traitor Ismaele, or dreaming nostalgically of their distant homeland, or glimpsing visions of the downfall of tyranny, the Jews of *Nabucco* regularly sing what Rossini was to call 'arias for chorus'. The fervour of Verdi's early lyrical style, especially in moods of militaristic aggression and nostalgic melancholy, combined with the technical resource of the unison chorus, accounts for much of the electrifying impact of this early masterpiece. There were precedents, for example in Donizetti's *Belisario* or Vaccai's *Maria Visconti* (Turin, 1838), but no one before Verdi had employed the choral unison so extensively or with so clear a perception of its demagogic possibilities. *Nabucco* also sets the tone for later Risorgimento-

---

[109] *Nabucco* is in fact an abbreviation of the original full title *Nabucodonosor*.

inspired operas by the prevalent brassiness of its orchestral colouring: 'Pourquoi nous annoncer Nabucodonos-or Quand c'est
Nabucodonos-cuivre?' enquired a satirical Frenchman on the appearance of the opera in Paris. Such a movement as 'È l'Assiria',
where the choral unison is doubled by woodwind, trumpets, and
trombones, and accompanied by softly thudding chords for strings,
horns, bassoons, and serpent, introduces into Italian opera a new
note of quietly menacing aggression (Ex. 115).

While *Nabucco* is the opera most fully representative of the political
aspirations of much Italian Romantic art, it certainly cannot be
regarded as a comprehensive political allegory; still less can the
operas that followed it. The 'political' scenes are generally passing
incidents in the dramatic design, Risorgimento odes, as it were,
embedded in operas which as a whole lack any specifically political
ideology: the conspiracy scene in Act III of *Ernani* (Venice, 1844);
the chorus of Scottish exiles in Act IV of *Macbeth* (Florence,
1847). With the revolutionary upheavals of 1848–9, however, the
opportunity for a full-blooded patriotic opera did arrive. *La battaglia
di Legnano*, performed in Rome in January 1849 in the heady weeks

Ex. 115

(Assyria is a queen as powerful on earth as Bel)

Ex. 116

(Long live Italy! A sacred covenant binds together all her sons.)

that followed the abolition of the temporal power of the papacy, is Verdi's celebration of the Revolution. The censorial restraints had been removed; the patriotic note no longer needed to be episodic and ambiguous: it was strident and all-pervasive. The subject—telling how once, by forgetting their traditional petty rivalries and working in a common cause, the Italian communes had been able to expel the German emperor Barbarossa from the land—was hotly topical, and in virtually every scene the nationalist message was driven home. The music of the opening chorus (Ex. 116) serves as a kind of national anthem to which Verdi returns again and again during the course of the opera. Choral scenes, processions, and tableaux make up a greater part of the score than in any other Verdi opera, early or late.

After 1849 long years of political struggle still lay ahead for the Italian nationalists; but as an artist Verdi was no longer interested. His patriotic duty honourably done, he moved off to new fields: intimacy and psychological nuance were to be his preoccupations in the following years. But scores like *Nabucco*, *I Lombardi*, and *La battaglia di Legnano* had made him, still only in his mid-30s, a national hero such as few of the great figures in the history of opera have been.

THE INSPIRATION OF EXTRA-MUSICAL IDEAS: LITERATURE

Of more enduring significance was the influence on Italian opera of literary fashions. While pre-Romantic tastes survived surprisingly long, the literary heroes of Italian Romanticism began to exert some influence on librettos even as early as Rossini. Rossini's own works include a Shakespeare adaptation, *Otello* (Naples, 1816), a Scott adaptation, *La donna del lago* (Naples, 1819), and, among his French operas, a version of Schiller's *Wilhelm Tell* (*Guillaume Tell*, Paris, 1829). The effect of these admired authors on the character of Italian opera was at first negligible: so free were the librettists' adaptations, so little was Rossini interested in the sources of his operas, and so unsystematic was the relationship between text and music, that it is difficult to attribute any musical features specifically to their influence. But this state of affairs was soon to change. By the 1830s and 1840s the Italian Romantics' enthusiasm for such authors could no longer be dismissed as an irrelevance: the spirit of literature was beginning to have its effect on the actual style of operatic music.

Particularly was this the case with Verdi. After he had established himself as a national figure with *Nabucco* and *I Lombardi*, almost all his operas originated in his own literary enthusiasms. Reading widely in the dramatic literature of most of Western Europe, sometimes stimulated in his searches by such friends as Giulio Carcano, Andrea Maffei, and Francesco Piave, Verdi had an unerring eye for the operatic potential of what he read. Like every great *operista* of the age he was particularly thrilled by powerful and bizarre scenes of confrontation: Pope Leo I partitioning the world with Attila the Hun, in Zacharias Werner's *Attila, König der Hunnen*; the adulterous Lina in the middle of a church service submitting herself to the judgement of her husband, the Lutheran pastor Stiffelius, in Souvestre's and Bourgeois's *Le Pasteur*. More than any of his senior contemporaries. Verdi had the kind of imagination that tended to become obsessed by certain of the characters he discovered: by Lady Macbeth or Triboulet (who became Rigoletto) or Azucena, for example. But what was unique to Verdi was his conviction that a composer could find in his literary sources more than a plot, a series of powerful situations, and a handful of memorable characters. A good play has an atmosphere all its own which the opera might aim to recreate; even the dramatist's language—the full, detailed sequence of ideas, the choice of imagery and metaphor, the sheer poetry of his verse—might, if faithfully imitated in the libretto, inspire flights of fancy unimaginable as long as opera continued to employ the mannered 'libretto-ese' of the age. Exhortations to his librettists to 'do it exactly as in the original' run through Verdi's correspondence like a leitmotif. To discover the point of this we must examine the operas inspired by three of the most potent literary influences of the age: Hugo, Shakespeare, and Schiller.

HUGO AND VERDI

The operas with which Verdi had established his reputation, *Nabucco* and *I Lombardi*, had both been examples of that kind of Italian Romanticism that placed Church and State at the centre of human affairs. *Ernani* (Venice, 1844), his first Hugo-inspired opera, marks a change of direction. Verdi had tired of the monumental and statuesque, and was in search of something 'very fiery, packed with action and concise'.[110] He found it—at any rate he found the fire and the action—in contemporary French Romantic drama, of which Hugo was the most distinguished practitioner, and *Hernani* (Paris, 1830), the most notorious specimen; and the effect on his operatic style was immediate. For it was the perfervid passions of Hugo's characters that gave Verdi the stimulus to explore the scope of musical characterization, and it was the profusion of astonishing incidents and strong situations that prompted him to refine his skills in the writing of dramatic ensembles. The three men who battle for the heart of Elvira—Ernani, a Romantic rebel; Don Ruy Gomez da Silva, an addled and vindictive old aristocrat; and Don Carlo, King of Spain, a prince in whose breast private passions and public responsibilities struggle for mastery—formed a triad which pressurized Verdi, after he had deliberated long and hard about it, into a 'definition ... of his male vocal archetypes',[111] tenor, bass, and baritone, a definition so persuasive that it served Verdi for the rest of his career. Indeed it has proved difficult for any subsequent opera composer to escape from it. And it was in such scenes of confrontation as the Act I finale, where bandit, grandee, and monarch stand face to face in Elvira's chamber, that Verdi proved his mastery of the large-scale ensemble which translated dramatic climax, theatrical tension, and stage spectacle alike into song.

It is certainly no accident that the list of Italian operas inspired by Hugo includes several of the most stylish in the repertoire: Donizetti's *Lucrezia Borgia*, Mercadante's *Il giuramento*, Verdi's *Ernani* and *Rigoletto* (Venice, 1851). The peculiarities of technique in these plays, which, as Hanslick was to remark, make them resemble 'less tragedies against which music would do violence, than librettos which have not yet been composed',[112] highlighted certain qualities that had long been inherent in Italian opera. Hugo's protagonists are vividly and melodramatically overdrawn in a way that opera,

---

[110] Letter to Domenico Bancalari, 11 Dec. 1843, Franco Abbiati, *Giuseppe Verdi* (Milan, 1959), i. 469.

[111] Julian Budden, *The Operas of Verdi*, i. *From Oberto to Rigoletto* (London, 1973), i. 147.

[112] *Die moderne Oper*, i. *Kritiken und Studien* (Berlin, 1875), 222.

where characterization depends upon a tiny number of confessional emotional outbursts, can reinforce with perfect aptness. The relationship in Hugo between dramatic action and outpourings of eloquence is also more akin to operatic techniques than to earlier models of poetic drama. For, as in an opera, where the recitatives link and motivate the arias and ensembles, so too in these plays the dramatic action seems contrived primarily with a view to providing openings for the poetic 'tirades'. It is not the dynamic of action nor the illumination of character that are Hugo's primary concerns, but passion and eloquence; and something of these still resounds in the aria texts that Romani, for Donizetti, and Piave, for Verdi, derived from them. Finally, it is typical of Hugo's dramatic style that his acts should culminate in blood-tingling tableaux of confrontation: the exposure of the disguised Lucrezia at the Venetian carnival in the Prologue of *Lucrèce Borgia*; Don Carlos stepping from the tomb of Charlemagne to confound the conspirators in Act IV of *Hernani*. How much more convincing are such scenes when translated into operatic ensembles than in their original spoken form where most of the participants, for most of the time, have to stand by in silence! No wonder Hugo is reported to have envied Verdi the resources of a medium that made possible the quartet in *Rigoletto*; and no wonder that, on reading *Hernani*, Verdi perceived in a flash the opera latent within it.[113]

SHAKESPEARE AND VERDI

While Hugo helped Italian composers to realize the Romantic and melodramatic potential of their most characteristic art form, Shakespeare offered them more problematic assets. Nineteenth-century Italian critics tended to emphasize two qualities in Shakespeare's art: Manzoni commended him for the freedom and naturalness of his style, remarking how much more spontaneous and truthful it seemed than the regimented drama of the French tradition; Mazzini, on the other hand, was eloquent in his praise of Shakespeare's genius for characterization: 'he brings to the stage life and being in the most real, the most true, and the most perfect way that it has ever been granted a man to achieve. . . .'[114] But structural freedom and lifelike characterization were the most difficult of attributes to transpose into the profoundly stylized medium of Italian opera. Ostensibly Shakespearean operas were composed even before

---

[113] Letter to Count Mocenigo, 5 Sept. 1843, Abbiati, *Verdi*, i. 473-4.
[114] 'Della fatalità considerata com'elemento drammatico,' p. 186.

Rossini's *Otello*, and continued to be composed during the next thirty years; but it is not until we reach Verdi's *Macbeth* (Florence, 1847) that we find an opera which can be described as Shakespearean in any very meaningful sense.

Macbeth is Shakespearean precisely because of Verdi's ideal of fidelity to the literary original, even when—perhaps especially when— that entailed unprecedented technical and imaginative challenges. The composer took an active part in the preparation of the libretto, providing Piave with a full prose synopsis and explaining exactly how he wanted the musical numbers distributed;[115] and he did this, one feels sure, so that the amount of conventionalizing undergone by Shakespeare's tragedy should be reduced to a minimum. Verdi was determined that its awe-inspiring characters should not be watered down into stereotypes of Romantic melodrama; and he was determined that the evocative power of Shakespeare's language should not be abandoned in favour of the standardized vocabulary and circumscribed imagery of the professional librettist. The result of Verdi's participation was a libretto in which all but a handful of phrases are closely modelled on Shakespeare's own.

This reverence of one great artist for another working in an alien tradition remote in time was an unprecedented phenomenon in Italian opera. But it was an issue of real historical moment because of the impact it had on Verdi's musical imagination. This impact is clearest seen in the two movements that the composer described as 'the most important in the opera',[116] the 'gran scena e duetto' in Act I and the 'gran scena del sonnambulismo' in Act IV.

The duet is a recreation of the dialogue between Macbeth and Lady Macbeth following the murder of Duncan in Act II, Scene ii, of Shakespeare's play; but anything less like a conventional conspiratorial duet could hardly be imagined. Verdi has retained virtually all the evocative details in which the original is so rich, and for each of these poetic images he has fashioned a musical analogy: the owl cry (Ex. 117); the perturbed dreams and prayer of Donalbain and his attendants and the 'Amen' that stuck in Macbeth's throat (Ex. 118); the voice that cried 'Sleep no more! Macbeth doth murder sleep' (Ex. 119); and so on throughout the scene. The result is that, with Verdi's mediation, the pressure of Shakespeare's imagination begins to wreak havoc on the established forms of Italian opera. The ensemble no longer has space for fallow interludes and tame

---

[115] Cf. his letter to Tito Ricordi, 11 Apr. 1857, *Copialettere*, p. 444, n. 2.
[116] Letter to Cammarano, 23 Nov. 1848, ibid., p. 62.

Ex. 117

(I heard the owl scream . . . what was it you said just now?)

Ex. 118

dis - se - ro; *A - men* dir vol - li an - ch'i o,

(I heard the courtiers praying in their sleep, and they cried 'God help us always'; I wanted to say 'Amen' too.)

Ex. 119

(O Macbeth, you will have only thorns for your pillow! Glamis, you murder sleep for ever.)

symmetries; it has become as densely packed with significantly expressive music as the Shakespearean dialogue with poetry.

The received conventions of nineteenth-century opera were treated more freely in *Macbeth* than in any of Verdi's operas before *Rigoletto*, and, fired by a dramatic vision more haunting than anything Italian Romanticism had yet afforded, the composer made unprecedented demands on the performers. The score has some extraordinary directions for interpretation: '*staccate e marcate assai*: and don't forget that they are witches who are singing'; 'the whole of this duet must be performed *sotto voce e cupa* by the singers, with the exception of a few phrases, which have been marked *a voce spiegata*'. The original Lady Macbeth, Mariana Barbieri-Nini, described in her memoirs how 'for three months, morning and evening, I attempted to impersonate those people who speak in their sleep, uttering words (as Verdi used to tell me) almost without moving their lips, the rest of the face motionless, including the eyes', and how the Act I duet 'was rehearsed, you may think I am exaggerating, one hundred and fifty times: to get the effect, as the maestro said, of being more *spoken* than *sung*'.[117]

SCHILLER AND VERDI

Shakespeare was one of the great discoveries resulting from the cosmopolitan enthusiasms of Italian Romanticism. So too was Schiller. In the early years of the Risorgimento his plays and essays were a favourite topic of discussion in the pages of the *Conciliatore*, the leading literary journal of the age; and translations of the plays began to appear from 1813. Although too young to be involved in the early stages, Verdi had direct links with later developments of this kind. Both the first translator of the complete Shakespeare, Giulio Carcano, and the first translator of the complete Schiller, Andrea Maffei, were personal friends of his, a fact that was probably more important in the latter case. In 1845, in collaboration with Temistocle Solera, Verdi had composed *Giovanna d'Arco*, apparently quite oblivious of its associations—admittedly vague—with Schiller's *Jungfrau von Orleans*. But from the time Maffei interested Verdi in making a setting of *Die Räuber* (*I masnadieri*, London, 1847) Schiller became one of the most enriching influences on his art.

Compared with Hugo-inspired and Shakespeare-inspired operas, the number inspired by Schiller is small. The greatest of them, *Guillaume Tell* and *Don Carlos*, are not Italian operas at all, but *grands opéras* written in French for Paris. The currency of another of the most distinguished, Donizetti's *Maria Stuarda*, was restricted by censorship. Mercadante, Pacini, and Vaccai all wrote operas more or less closely modelled on Schiller, and the closing scene of Bellini's *Beatrice di Tenda* (Venice, 1833) was inspired, to some extent, by the

---

[117] Translated from Eugenio Checchi *Giuseppe Verdi: le genio e le opere* (Florence, 1887), quoted in David Rosen and Andrew Porter (eds.), *Verdi's Macbeth: A Sourcebook* (New York and Cambridge, 1984), 51.

matching scenes of *Maria Stuart*, the most popular of Schiller's plays in Italy. But really the only Italian operas closely modelled on Schiller and widely performed in Italy were *I masnadieri*, *Luisa Miller* (Naples, 1850) and, much later, the Italian revision of *Don Carlos*. This is a modest harvest, considering the prestige Schiller enjoyed. It must have disappointed Mazzini; for he regarded Schiller as the ideal model for young dramatists, who were to help build the new Italy with 'a profoundly religious, profoundly educative social drama . . . greater than Shakespeare by as much as the idea of Humanity is greater than the idea of the individual'.[118]

In 1846, after the production in Venice of *Attila*, Verdi suffered what seems to have been a nervous breakdown. From the period of enforced repose that followed, he emerged mentally and imaginatively renewed. He put aside the styles of opera in which his earliest successes had been gained—whether Romantic melodramas like *Ernani*, or Risorgimento-inspired pageants of national life like *Nabucco*—and addressed himself to more ambitious tasks. In particular he was preoccupied with two issues. The first was how to escape from the restrictions of conventional characterization, how to create characters who were as unique and as 'real'—to use Verdi's own favourite term of commendation—as those in the poetic drama he most admired. A second, complementary ambition was to set these 'real' characters in a 'real' world—to make society part of the subject of the drama. If Shakespeare was the principal source of inspiration in the first case, Schiller surely was in the second.

In Verdi's first Schiller opera, *I masnadieri*, the relationship between the hero Carlo and society is still sketchy. But it is there, and is important, since Carlo is a classic early example of an outsider, tragically alienated from the world in which he finds himself. With *Luisa Miller* and *Don Carlos* the aim of setting 'real' characters in a 'real' world is more fully achieved: Verdi does recreate something of a lifelike complexity in the relationship between the realm of personal feelings and that of social organization. To paraphrase one of his own remarks—and he was echoing Mazzini—he has moved on from the type of opera that is made of arias and duets to a new type made of ideas: ideas like the conflict of class structure and humane feeling (*Mode* and *Menschheit*) in *Luisa Miller*, or of dogmatism and libertarianism in *Don Carlos*. Real characters in a real world, with the emphasis on the characters, was Verdi's diagnosis of what verismo involved—or ought to involve. After *Luisa Miller* he was to

---

[118] 'Della fatalità considerata com'elemento drammatico', p. 196.

carry this preoccupation into other kinds of real world where Schiller might have been ill at ease, notably in *La traviata*. But the three Schiller operas, *I masnadieri*, *Luisa Miller*, and *Don Carlos*, are conspicuous landmarks on the road towards Verdi's very individual brand of realism.

LESSER MASTERS

The demand for new operas remained insatiable. In most theatres Rossini, Bellini, Donizetti, and Verdi shared the repertoire not with such classics of an earlier era as Cimarosa or Mozart, but with a host of minor contemporaries. In 1846 an Italian correspondent of the *Allgemeine Musikalische Zeitung* provided statistics to show that during the previous eight years (1838–45) 342 new operas had been produced in Italian theatres, and no fewer than 130 new maestri had made their débuts (Verdi and 129 others).[119] Most of these men enjoyed only ephemeral or local success; but some—like Pacini or the Ricci brothers—were immensely popular for many years, and all of them played a part in helping sustain opera as a living art in virtually every corner of the land.

Because the music of even the greatest composers of the period amply partook of the naïvety and vulgarity that was undeniably part of the Italian tradition, it is not easy to approach their lesser contemporaries without condescension. But some of them were formidable musical craftsmen and men of wide culture. In the former category Pietro Raimondi (1786–1853) is remembered. His prodigious contrapuntal exertions produced not merely vast quantities of fugue, but a cycle of three oratorios, *Putifar*, *Giuseppe*, and *Giacobbe* (completed 1848, performed Rome 1852), designed to be performed first separately and then simultaneously. Among his operas, some fifty in number, is to be found a comparable *tour de force*: the *opera seria*, *Adelasia*, and the *opera buffa*, *I quattro rustici*, may also be performed both separately and in combination. In fact, as Raimondi died before orchestrating them, they seem not to have been performed at all.

Perhaps more generally fruitful were the talents of Nicola Vaccai (1790–1848). An outstanding literary gift—in his adolescence he produced four Alfieri-inspired tragedies in verse—led him to take an interest in the translation of foreign musical works, including Méhul's *Joseph* and Bach's *St. Matthew Passion*. As a musical educationalist he was particularly influential during his period as *censore* at the

---

[119] *Allgemeine Musikalische Zeitung*, xlviii (1846), cols. 141–2.

Milan Conservatory (1838–1844), where he introduced student opera performances on the Naples model, founded a new choir school, and spread enthusiasm for the German classics. His textbook on singing— *Metodo pratico di canto italiano* (1832)—remains a classic work. Rossini described Vaccai as a composer 'in whom sentiment was allied to philosophy'; and something of his superiority of mind is perhaps suggested by his tendency to overstrain the medium. The scoring of his mature operas has a Mercadantean ponderousness, and from time to time one alights upon little touches of musical erudition that are scarcely typical of the genre. The quasi-fugal duet cabaletta quoted in Ex. 120 is from *Marco Visconti* (Turin, 1838).

The career of Giovanni Pacini (1796–1867) might be cited as an epitome of the activities of the best and most successful of the minor masters of the age. By 1830 he had already produced some forty operas in little more than fifteen years, and was a popular figure throughout Italy. But in the early 1830s, as the superior talents of Bellini and Donizetti came into full flower, Pacini suffered something of an eclipse; and in 1834 he retired from the theatre for some years

Ex. 120

(OTTORINO: I know you well, faithless man, because of your other treacheries, but I shall be able to render vain your insane envy.
LODRISIO: O faithless man, there is more than one offence that you must atone for with me.)
(NB Ottorino and Lodrisio are denouncing not one another but a rebellious third party, who is not on stage.)

Ex. 121

(My heart cannot control the fulness of its delight! At every beat I feel a new joy in my breast.)

to devote himself to musical education. Having surmounted this creative crisis he resumed his operatic career in 1839. He now adopted a new manner and was 'baptized by public opinion as no longer the composer of facile cabalettas, but rather of elaborate works, the product of much meditation'.[120] Thanks to his early works Pacini was known as *il maestro della cabaletta*. Many of his cabalettas are indeed outstanding for their verve and rhythmic originality. This, the composer emphasized, was not due to instinctive genius, but to his careful study of the rhythms and metres of the verse (see Ex. 121, which is from *Saffo*).[121]

Saffo (Naples, 1840) is Pacini's masterpiece. This noble work is in many ways a representative reform opera of the period. The structures are notably flexible and in many scenes conventional recitative is abandoned in favour of a dense profusion of ariosos and parlantes that reflect the flux of emotion with scrupulous care. The orchestration is full and resourceful; the chorus has a conspicuous dramatic role; and there is no lack of harmonic felicities. But perhaps the most remarkable thing about *Saffo* is that, at the height of the Romantic movement, Pacini, like Mercadante, should discover the best in himself in exploring the Classical world. What he has to say about *Saffo* in his Memoirs reads more like the reflections of a Renaissance humanist than of an opera composer of the 1840s:

Reading and re-reading the history of that race which was the torch of all human learning, and trying to discover what sort of music was employed by that heroic nation ... I was able to establish that the Greeks attributed to the word *music* a wider sense, embracing not only that art which excites emotion by means of sound, but also poetry, the art of beauty, rhetoric,

---

[120] Pacini, *Le mie memorie artistiche*, pp. 98–9.
[121] Ibid., p. 84.

philosophy, and that science which the Romans called *politior humanitas*. Taking note of the modes which the Greeks used, Dorian, Ionian, Phrygian, Aeolian and Lydian, and of their intermediaries, Hypodorian etc., I formed for myself an idea of their system. And always bearing in mind what *Aristides* says about the qualities of the three genera, diatonic, chromatic and enharmonic, that is that the first is noble and austere, the second very sweet and plaintive, the third mild and exciting (*mansueto ed eccitante*), I tried . . . to approximate to their Melopea.[122]

THE DECLINE OF *OPERA BUFFA*

Rossini had produced his last *opera buffa*, *La Cenerentola*, as early as 1817, concentrating in his last composing years in Italy on the *seria* and *semiseria* genres. Most of his younger contemporaries followed suit. Though there was a brief revival of the form in the 1850s, the pure *opera buffa* was all but extinct by 1830. For the greater part of Bellini's career, during Donizetti's maturity and Verdi's early years, the Italian repertoire was virtually monopolized by heroic and tragic themes. Only the *opera semiseria* such as Bellini's *La sonnambula* and Donizetti's *Linda di Chamounix* provided a widely enjoyed alternative, and that too was often heavily pathetic in tone. In the smaller Neapolitan theatres dialect operas with spoken dialogue were popular. Stylistically they were often of the most naïve artlessness, even in the hands of so experienced a master as Luigi Ricci, and apparently they drew on the rich store of Neapolitan popular song, which enjoyed one of its vintage periods in the middle decades of the century (see Ex. 122, from Act I of Luigi Ricci's *Piedigrotta* (Naples, 1852)). But while the decline of *opera buffa* was unmistakable and in the long run irreversible, Donizetti ran counter

Ex. 122

[122] Ibid., p. 95.

Vie-ne, ca chiam-ma am-mo - re   Ed a- spet -tà non pò.

(Look from your window, dove of my heart. Come, for love calls and cannot wait.)

to the tendency of the age in composing two masterly specimens
that must be regarded as his most nearly perfect works: *L'elisir
d'amore* (Milan, 1832) and *Don Pasquale* (Paris, 1843).

So completely had the serious opera of Rossini's day absorbed
the musical language of the *opera buffa* that there was little in terms
of form and style to distinguish the genres. Generally *opera-buffa*
lyricism was a little simpler, the forms a little more concise and the
orchestration a little lighter; and in many scenes composers continued
to employ recitativo semplice, accompanied by a keyboard player
reading from a figured bass. *Don Pasquale* is exceptional in scoring
all the recitatives for strings. Just a few resources remained unique
to *opera buffa* and were dependent upon the peculiar skills of the
buffo bass. Dulcamara in *L'elisir d'amore*, for example, makes his
entrance not with the kind of lyrical sortita that was typical of the
serious genre, but with a comic aria, 'Udite, udite, o rustici', in
which mock-rhetorical declamation and rapid patter are the principal
elements. Often in cantabiles and slow cabalettas patter from the
comic bass is combined in duet with lyrical singing from soprano or
tenor, creating a mocking or pathetic ambiguity of mood.

Echoes of the great age of Rossinian *opera buffa* are frequent, and
sometimes reminiscence reaches back even into the eighteenth century.
Only rarely was Mozart to be heard in the public theatres at
this time, but all Italian composers knew and studied at least a
representative number of his major works, including the operas. In
1832 Pacini treated the theatre-goers of Viareggio to a new version
of the Don Giovanni legend, *Il convitato di pietro*, in which allusions
to Mozart's score are frequent and unmistakable (see Ex. 123 from
Act II).

The comedy of the *opera buffa*, even in this final phase, remained
rooted in the *commedia dell'arte*. The four principal characters of
Don Pasquale might have been borrowed straight from a seventeenth-

Ex. 123

(COMMENDATORE: You invited me to dinner; I came here without difficulty. Now I shall invite you: will you come to dine with me?
FICCANASO: O dear! O dear! His lordship cannot.
DON GIOVANNI: I have no fear in my heart; yes I accept the invitation.)

century *commedia scenario*. True, there is no *zanni*, but Don Pasquale —'an old bachelor, set in old-fashioned ways, parsimonious, credulous, obstinate, but a good fellow at heart', as the libretto describes him—is clearly next of kin to Pantalone; and his friend and confidant, Malatesta, is a doctor. Numerous are the movements modelled on the *tirate* or even the *lazzi* of the *commedia*. The primo tempo of Pasquale and Malatesta's duet 'Cheti, cheti, immantinente' is a delicious example of such a musical *lazzo*. In the comfort of Pasquale's home, the two men enact in imagination the furtive course of action which they are planning: as the imagined events take place in the dark, they provide the same pretext for virtuoso miming as had the night-scenes beloved of the *commedia*. The duet 'Mio signore venerato' from *Il campanello* (Naples, 1836) is an excellent example of a piece modelled on the *commedia tirata*, for in it Enrico simply reels off an interminable list of ailments, followed by the prescription for a spoof remedy.[123]

To the last, *opera buffa* was composed according to properly dramatic principles. When Romani reworked Scribe's *Le Philtre* into *L'elisir d'amore* the kinds of change he felt moved to make bring this out very well. Not satisfied, as Scribe in his operetta-like original had been, to treat the characters as a group of entertainers periodically breaking into musical 'turns', he could not refrain from the exercise of the dramatist's prerogative of empathy, entering into their dilemmas and thereby much enlarging the emotional scope of the opera: both 'Adina credimi', the cantabile of the Act I finale and 'Una furtiva lagrima', Nemorino's romanza in Act II, are Romani additions of this kind. At the same time he dispensed with those numbers in the French original which were simply repeated after an intervening stretch of dialogue. It was alien to Italian operatic manners to have characters twitching into and out of song without the developing action having the least impact on the style of that song. In *L'elisir d'amore* such numbers are replaced by Italianate multisectional forms, in which the dramatic action is embodied in the succession of musical styles. But while *opera buffa* remained unquestionably a species of music drama, it surpassed other genres in its accommodation of what some critics have described as *ludus*— the sense that its characters, as well as being involved in a dramatic action, are also engaged in a diversionary game. The primo tempo of the duet 'Signorina, in tanta fretta' from Act III of *Don Pasquale* provides a good example. The movement begins with close and nicely

---

[123] This movement is not included in the autograph score of *Il campanello*.

observed analogies between music and drama: Norina's retorts to Pasquale's questions acquire their verve from the occasional repeated words which make a more rapid and zestful enunciation possible: and the supreme insult, 'quando parla non s'ascolta', is thrown into harsh emphasis by stripping away the softening harmonies, and by Pasquale's incredulous echo. But as the scene continues, such analogies are gradually abandoned; Norina is swept along in the exhilaration of the game, and music drama yields to lyrical and virtuoso 'sporting' (Ex. 124).

Ex. 124

(Go to bed, sleep well, then we can talk about it tomorrow.)

THE PERFORMANCE OF ITALIAN ROMANTIC OPERA

In an age that knew neither conductors nor, in the modern sense, producers, the singers were the principal figures in the performance of an opera. The 1830s and 1840s saw the fulfilment of changes in the art of singing that had been preparing since the turn of the century. The disappearance from the stage of the castrato, Rossini's attempts to limit the singer's freedom to embellish, the taste for more violently emotional dramas and therefore for heavier orchestral scoring and louder singing—all contributed to this transformation. Singing became more directly expressive, but coarser, and left less to spontaneous inspiration. The expansion of the chest-range of the tenor voice to top C'' (before about 1830 notes above G' had been taken falsetto), and the undiscriminating use of vibrato, were two conspicuous symptoms of the new style. In the absence of a producer, and given an operatic structure in which substantial musical numbers alternate with short and sometimes madly eventful recitatives, the style of acting, in serious opera at least, can hardly have been naturalistic. It must have been stylized and statuesque, a matter primarily of grouping, of pose and gesture.

There was as yet no need for a conductor, because of the long survival of orchestral practices associated with the continuo. A contract for a new work usually committed a composer to directing the first three performances of his opera from the keyboard. Normally he would have had nothing to play except the figured bass sections of the recitative in opera buffa; but, particularly in smaller theatres where orchestras were tiny and amateurish, it may have been useful for the keyboard player to flesh out the music occasionally and to be able to intervene in cases of emergency. The layout of Italian orchestras varied a good deal from city to city and was often changed during the course of the century.[124] One effective arrangement was introduced by Donizetti at La Scala in 1834: around the keyboard sat the principals of the four string sections, and, strategically placed in this way, the composer could 'whenever he wishes, give the leader, both by word and gesture, the indication of the tempos he desires'.[125] Once the composer's three performances were up, the direction of the opera fell to the leader—*primo violino, capo e direttore d'orchestra*, as contemporary librettos described him. He directed with his bow, sometimes using it as a baton, sometimes,—according to the reports

[124] Cf. Gregory W. Harwood, 'Verdi's Reform of the Italian Opera Orchestra', *19th-Century Music*, 10 (1986), 108–34.
[125] Letter from Donizetti to Duke Visconti, 17 Jan. 1834, Zavadini, *Donizetti*, p. 343.

of both Berlioz and Mendelssohn—tapping out the beats of the bar on his music stand: 'it sounds something like obbligato castanets, but louder.'[126] Not until the 1860s did the leader's bow give way to the conductor's baton.

The large professional orchestras attached to the chief theatres in Milan and Naples represented Italian instrumental skills at their best, and were good enough to be admired by such connoisseurs as Spohr and Berlioz. But in most smaller cities the professional ranks were diluted with dilettantes. In these circumstances, not only were standards of performance lower; relics of earlier usages—notably impromptu ornamentation—survived at least into the 1830s and the whole atmosphere of the performance was more casual and easily sociable. Like the orchestras, the choruses too were generally dependent on amateur and—where a local school of music made it appropriate—student performers. Yet another body of people was brought into the theatre for those operas that required a stage band. This, a military-band formation of upward of twenty players, was normally supplied by musicians from a local garrison.

The staging of an opera was the responsibility of the librettists attached to most of the leading theatres. They supervised the work of costume and set designers and directed the rehearsals. In these particulars, as in so much else, Italy was no longer in the van of European developments. Traditional types of stage set—the townscape, the sumptuous interior, the natural (often woodland) setting—long continued to satisfy most requirements, and traditional styles of design—notably the elaborate perspective compositions, of which Sanquirico at La Scala was the last great exponent—survived into the 1830s. The Romantic movement did, however, lead to a keener awareness of the picturesque and atmospheric, to an interest in historical realism, and a new sensitivity to the relationship between a drama and the landscapes and buildings in which it was set. In these respects the historical novels of Scott and the new developments in lighting introduced by Daguerre in Paris were deeply influential.[127]

THE APPRECIATION OF OPERA

There were financial advantages to all concerned and artistic advantages too in the survival of the box system: 'a certain degree of private self-communion is essential to savour the sublimest charms

---

[126] Mendelssohn, *Briefe aus den Jahren 1830 bis 1847* (7th edn., Leipzig, 1899), 116.
[127] Cf. Mary Ambrose, 'Walter Scott, Italian Opera and Romantic Stage-setting' *Italian Studies*, 36 (1981), 58–78.

of music.'[128] But to modern eyes its most remarkable consequence was the effect upon theatrical tone. To own a box in the opera-house was tantamount to having a private salon in a public place. One behaved accordingly, listening to the opera with as much attention as one wished to give it, but free every moment to draw the curtain and withdraw into one's own private world, or to tour the theatre calling upon friends and acquaintances in their boxes. Under these circumstances many people were so preoccupied with the social aspects of opera-going that they lost sight of its artistic purpose altogether; the capacity to listen to music with sustained concentration was rare. Even in northern Europe the phenomenon of the silent audience was a late nineteenth-century one. But only in Italy do we read of such scenes as Berlioz witnessed in Milan at a performance of *L'elisir d'amore*; he found

the theatre full of people talking in normal voices, with their backs to the stage. The singers, undeterred, gesticulated and yelled their lungs out in the strictest spirit of rivalry. At least I presumed they did, from their wide-open mouths; but the noise of the audience was such that no sound penetrated except the bass drum. People were gambling, eating supper in their boxes, etcetera, etcetera.[129]

Nevertheless all composers of the period accepted the fact that it was the acclaim of these easily distracted audiences, not the considered assessment of critic or connoisseur, that set the seal on an opera's reputation. What they dreamed of was the sort of reception accorded the first performances of *Lucia di Lammermoor*, when 'every piece was listened to in religious silence, and celebrated with spontaneous shouts of applause'.[130] It was to accommodate such applause that the composer closed each phase of the musical action with those loudly reiterated cadences which have no bearing on the dramatic purpose of the scene, and which are such an embarrassing encumbrance in modern performances of Italian Romantic opera. Audiences were sometimes cruel and sometimes irrational when they exercised their prerogative to whistle new operas from the stage; as yet they approached even the music they loved with no trace of hushed reverence. But, at its best, opera provided them with an intoxicating delight which for its spontaneity and conviviality has no parallel in the modern appreciation of music:

---

[128] Stendhal, *Life of Rossini*, trans. Richard N. Coe (London, 1956), 428.
[129] *The Memoirs of Hector Berlioz*, trans. David Cairns (New York and London, 1969), 208.
[130] Donizetti to Giovanni Ricordi, 29 Sept. 1835, Zavadini, *Donizetti*, p. 385.

In the few performances of *La sonnambula* given before the theatres closed, Pasta and Rubini sang with the most evident enthusiasm to support their favourite maestro; in the second act the singers themselves wept and carried their audiences along with them so that in the happy days of carnival, tears were continually being wiped away in boxes and parquet alike. Embracing Shterich in the Ambassador's box I, too, shed tears of emotion and ecstasy.[131]

(d) GERMANY

By Siegfried Goslich

STAGE AND COMPOSER

The German-speaking lands were not lacking in theatres. the ruling princes maintained them in the large and medium-sized capitals; in 1857 there were said to be nineteen.[132] They were financially secure and commanded resources for casting and production which attracted composers. But the intendants of the court theatres were as a rule conservative and seldom willing to take artistic risks. In many Imperial and Hanseatic towns and other prosperous large towns, there were numerous other theatres catering for mixed repertoires and therefore staffed with dramatic, operatic, and ballet ensembles, chorus, and orchestra. These municipal and commercially run theatres also tried to get outstanding artists under contract and were to some extent able to compete seriously with the court theatres. Indeed their managements often displayed a pioneering spirit which those lacked. But they often had to cope with economic problems and, in order to compete with the state theatres, were obliged to adjust their repertoire in accordance with public taste.

The heyday of Italian opera in Germany was over. The Italian ensembles were dissolved in Munich in 1826, in Vienna in 1828, and in Dresden in 1832; the Spontini era at the Berlin Royal Opera came to an end in 1841. All the same the stylistic influence of the Italians and French on repertoires and taste was still considerable—and remained so until the middle of the century. From 1830 to 1849 twenty-five Italian and forty-five French operas were given, the most

---

[131] Mikhail Ivanovich Glinka, *Memoirs*, trans. Richard B. Mudge (Norman, Oklahoma, 1963), 61. (I have substituted 'maestro' for Mudge's 'conductor'.)
[132] F. G. Paldamus, *Das deutsche Theater der Gegenwart* (Mainz, 1857), 87.

popular being the works of Rossini, Bellini, Donizetti, and Auber. A few British operas also were produced in the German-speaking countries; Henry Hugo Pierson's *Der Elfensieg* was given at Brünn (Brno) in 1845 and his *Leila* at Hamburg in 1848; the Irishman Michael Balfe's *Bohemian Girl* was produced as *Das Zigeunermädchen* at Vienna and Hamburg in 1846, and Brünn, Prague, Frankfurt, Munich, and Berlin during the next three or four years, while his *Les Quatre Fils Aymon* (*Die vier Haymonskinder*), which had preceded it in Vienna (1844), was even more successful with the German public. As for the operas of living German composers, the most popular around 1850 were Spohr's *Faust* and *Jessonda*, Marschner's *Der Vampyr*, *Templer und Jüdin*, and *Hans Heiling*, Conradin Kreutzer's *Das Nachtlager von Granada*, Lortzing's *Zar und Zimmermann* and *Der Wildschütz*, Flotow's *Alessandro Stradella* and *Martha*, Wagner's *Rienzi* and (already) *Der fliegende Holländer*.

The number of German composers who concerned themselves with opera was astonishing. Many of them spent their lives mainly as court opera conductors, municipal music directors or theatre intendants, but soloists, music-pedagogues, and writers also tried their hands occasionally at opera composition. Many of their works never reached the stage at all; others achieved one or two performances—usually in the town where the composer was living—and were then forgotten. Turning the pages of such operas that have fallen by the wayside, one comes across already outworn melodic clichés, conventional cavatinas, romances, and arias, mechanically constructed ensembles, and well-worn modulations, side by side with a striving for individual expression in the harmony, motivic detail, and attempts at scenic composition on the lines of Weber and Spohr. One often gets an impression of a struggle towards a musical-dramatic ideal carried out with unsuitable material, where the composer's creative inspiration was insufficient to breathe genuine life into his characters and rouse interest in their fates.

THE THEATRE CONDUCTORS

Some of the court conductors in the major capitals also earned distinction as composers. Schubert's friend Franz Lachner (1803–90), conductor at the Kärntnerthor Theatre, moved in 1836 to Munich as *Hofkapellmeister*, becoming, in 1852, *Generalmusikdirektor*; his chief work, *Catarina Cornaro*, was produced there in 1841. The Berliner Wilhelm Taubert (1811–91), assistant conductor of the court concerts at the age of 20, made his operatic debut there in 1832 with his one-act *Die Kermes* to a libretto by Eduard Devrient, who also supplied him with the text of its successor *Der Zigeuner* (1834); he showed the same assured, light-handed technique in music to plays based on Ludwig Tieck's *Der gestiefelte Kater* (1844) and *Blaubart* (1845). The Darmstadt *Hofmusikdirektor* Carl Amand Mangold (1813–89), best known for his male voice choruses, followed Wagner with a *Tannhäuser* (1846) on a libretto by the journalist Ernst Duller, while his colleague at Stuttgart, Peter Josef von Lindpaintner (1791–1856), continued his long career as an opera composer with *Die Amazone* (1831). Weber's successor at Dresden, Karl Gottlieb Reissiger (1798–1859), first made his mark with *Die Felsenmühle zu Etalières* (1831), the effective overture to which became very popular. *Turandot* (1835), *Adèle de Foix* (1841), and *Der Schiffbruch der Medusa* (1846) never achieved much success.

As *Hofkapellmeister* at Weimar from 1848 onwards, Liszt was an outstanding champion of contemporary opera; during his ten years in that post he performed forty-three operas, twenty-four of them by living composers but none by himself. He thought of composing a *Jeanne d'Arc*,[133] and a Hungarian opera, *Janos*;[134] the Liszt Museum at Weimar possesses the prose sketch in French of an opera *Sardanapal*, after Byron, dated '9 Decembre 1846'; but nothing came of any of these projects. He served German opera by performing it, giving the *premières* of *Lohengrin*, Raff's *König Alfred*, Schubert's *Alfonso und Estrella*, and Cornelius's *Der Barbier von Bagdad*, and also by his writings on its problems and its masters, and by piano transcriptions (particularly of excerpts from Wagner).

Conradin Kreutzer's *Nachtlager in Granada*—still occasionally performed—has already been mentioned. In his youth Kreutzer (1780–1849) had been *Hofkapellmeister* in Stuttgart and Donaueschingen, later conductor at the Kärntnerthor and Josephstadt Theatres in Vienna, at Cologne, and then again, as Nicolai's successor, in Vienna. The long list of his operas includes *Der Lastträger an der Themse* (1832), *Melusine* (after Grillparzer, 1833), *Fridolin, oder Der Gang nach dem Eisenhammer* (after Schiller, 1837), *Die beiden Figaro* (by G. F. Treitschke, 1840),[135] *Des Sängers Fluch* (after Uhland, 1846), and *Aurelia, Prinzessin von Bulgarien* (1849). Very successful was *Des Adlers Horst* (1832) by the German-Bohemian Franz Gläser (1798–1861), which Wagner conducted at Magdeburg in 1835; Gläser was conductor at the Königstadt Theatre, Berlin, where his opera was performed five times by 1837. The

---

[133] See *Franz Liszt: Briefe an die Fürstin Sayn-Wittgenstein* (Leipzig, 1900), 414–88 passim.
[134] Ibid., pp. 420–41 passim.
[135] The reviser of the third version of *Fidelio*.

libretto was by Karl von Holtei, later theatre director at Riga where he crossed swords with the young Wagner. Glaser moved to Copenhagen in 1842, soon became court conductor there, and composed three Danish operas (two with librettos by Hans Christian Andersen).

It was not only conductors who tried their luck on the stage. One such was Carl Loewe (1796-1869), the master of the ballade. His comic opera *Die drei Wünsche* (after Raupach) was given in Berlin in 1834, but his four other operas were never performed. And two gifted 'outsiders' deserve mention in this survey. Ernst II, duke of Saxe-Coburg-Gotha (1818-93), elder brother of the Prince Consort of England, had studied theory and harmony with Heinrich Breidenstein, music director at Bonn University, and embarked on opera composition with *Zayre* (after Voltaire) (1846) and *Tony* (1848). His most successful work, *Santa Chiara*, was one of those brought out by Liszt (1854); it was produced in many German cities as late as the 1890s, in French translation at the Paris Opéra in 1855, and at Covent Garden in Italian in 1877. Johann Vesque von Püttlingen (1803-83), an Austrian civil servant who playfully adopted the pseudonym Hoven (suggesting that he was less than Beethoven), studied composition with Simon Sechter in Vienna. His operas, *Die Belagerung Wiens durch die Türken* (1833), *Turandot* (after Gozzi, 1838), *Johanna d'Arc* (after Schiller, 1840), *Liebeszauber* (after Kleist, 1845), *Burg Thaya* (1847), and *Ein Abenteuer Carls II* (1850), are above the average. The last named work, and *Der lustige Rat* (1852), were given by Liszt at Weimar.

THE LEADING MASTERS

Of Spohr's *Faust*,[136] Weber, who conducted the first performance (Prague, 1816), wrote that 'a few melodies ... weave like delicate threads through the whole work and hold it together artistically'.[137] In this key work Spohr opened the way to systematic employment of constituent motif, a direction in which he was to go further. In *Jessonda* (1823)[138] he enriched the recitative by the quasi-gestural nature of the accompaniment and the insertion of metrically articulated sections, while in *Der Berggeist* (1825)[139] he reached the zenith of his dramatic method. That was as far as he was prepared

[136] See Vol. VIII, pp. 485-6.
[137] *Carl Maria von Weber: Writings on Music*, ed. John Warrack and trans. Martin Cooper (Cambridge, 1981), 193.
[138] See Vol. VIII, pp. 486-7.
[139] Ibid., p. 487.

to go for the present; in *Pietro von Abano* (1827) he turned back to number opera. And in its successor, *Der Alchymist* (1830), based on a story in Washington Irving's *Conquest of Granada* by his brother-in-law Karl Pfeiffer (the librettist of *Pietro*), he made no stylistic progress. Spohr then abandoned his operatic career for fifteen years except for three numbers—overture, song, and finale— contributed in 1839 to a collective work, *Der Matrose*, by Moritz Hauptmann and two others. Then in June 1843 he conducted *Der fliegende Holländer* at Kassel—a few weeks before Wagner had described himself as Spohr's 'admiring pupil'—and, impressed by its innovations, returned to through-composed opera in *Die Kreuzfahrer* (1845). This had a libretto based on Kotzebue by his wife and himself, but it lacks both the striking general idea and the gripping details needed to inspire music.

'Giacomo' (properly Jakob) Meyerbeer (1791–1864), a Berliner by birth, composed unsuccessful German operas until 1814 and Italian operas during 1817–24 before turning to French *grand opéra*. But his first great success, *Robert le diable*, was quickly translated and given in Berlin in 1832, and Friedrich Wilhelm III made him *Hofkapellmeister*. *Les Huguenots* was produced in translation in several German cities before it reached Berlin in 1842, where for six years Meyerbeer held the post of *Generalmusikdirektor*, producing the works of Mozart, Gluck, Spohr, and others for the Prussian court as well as a masque, *Das Hoffest in Ferrara* (1843), based on accounts of the life of Friedrich II, and a *Singspiel*, *Ein Feldlager in Schlesien* (1844), for the reopening of the Berlin opera-house after a fire. He pleaded with the king for the performance of three new German operas a year and directed a gala performance of *Euryanthe* in aid of a Weber memorial.

Heinrich Marschner (1795–1861) was in 1830 appointed *Hofkapellmeister* at Hanover where his *Vampyr* had been given in 1828. After the comic opera *Des Falkners Braut* (1832), he wrote his masterpiece *Hans Heiling*, of which he conducted the Berlin première (1833). (After the Leipzig performance the university gave him an honorary doctorate.) *Das Schloss am Aetna* (Leipzig, 1836), *Der Bäbu* (Hanover, 1838), and *Kaiser Adolph von Nassau* (Dresden, 1845) followed. Marschner was one of the founders of German national opera; Wagner was indebted to him on several accounts. The relationship between voice and orchestra was frequently reversed, the accompanying orchestra now conveying moods and thoughts, the formerly predominant voice becoming the reciting member in the 'total orchestra'. Marschner further developed Weber's style of declamation, was a master of motivic work, and decisively advanced the method of scenic composition after Spohr. *Kaiser Adolph* has some magnificently conceived scenes.

LORTZING

Gustav Albert Lortzing (1801–51) was highly thought of in the German-speaking lands for his remarkable many-sidedness, his dramatic talent, and his humour. As a child he had had his earliest theory lessons from Friedrich Rungenhagen but was largely self taught. His father was a strolling player and he himself appeared on the stage at an early age, acting and singing. At Detmold he played the cello in the orchestra; in Leipzig he was both actor and *buffo* tenor, as well as occasional producer, and in 1844 was appointed conductor. Despite his swiftly growing reputation as a stage composer, he settled nowhere. In 1846 he became conductor of the Theater an der Wien but was unpopular with the Viennese, and, after the 1848 rising, he returned to Germany where he was obliged to take up acting again to support his family. In 1850 he was engaged as conductor at a third-rate Berlin theatre but died in poverty in less than a year. Lortzing was his own librettist, and his repertoire as an actor included the Fool in *King Lear*, Kosinsky in Schiller's *Räuber*, the Prince in Lessing's *Emilia Galotti*, and Valentin in Raimund's *Verschwender*. At the first performance of Grabbe's *Don Juan und Faust*, for which he provided instrumental music, he played Don Juan. As librettist Lortzing distinguished himself by his sensitivity to the material and its treatment; his characters are full of life and the dramatic events skilfully carried to climax. He was a master not only of grace and wit but of musical structure and instrumentation. Independently and in unmistakable fashion he realized the ideas of the *Gesamtkunstwerk*. His great successes are *Zar und Zimmermann* (Leipzig, 1837), *Hans Sachs* (Leipzig, 1840), *Der Wildschütz* (Leipzig, 1842), *Undine* (Magedeburg, 1845), and *Der Waffenschmied von Worms* (Vienna, 1846). But also in the now forgotten works such as *Zum Grossadmiral* (1847) and *Rolands Knappen* (1849) he made significant contributions to the romantic musical theatre. In *Regina oder die Marodeure* (1848) he handled a theme with contemporary political overtones.

MENDELSSOHN AND NICOLAI

Outstanding among the composers who, despite repeated efforts, never managed to find a suitable libretto, was Felix Mendelssohn-Bartholdy (1809–47). After the six comic operas of 1820–9, he sought

one in vain. His negotiations with Charles Duveyrier over Schiller's
Jungfrau von Orleans and with Scribe over Shakespeare's *Tempest*
were no more successful than his discussions with the actress–poetess
Charlotte Birch-Pfeiffer on a *Genovefa* (*sic*). He was unable to make
up his mind over his friend Devrient's *Hans Heiling* libretto and it
went to Marschner instead. But he participated in the efforts of the
Prussian court to revive the dramas of classical antiquity and
composed and conducted music to Sophocles' *Antigone* and *Oedipus
at Colonus* and also that to Racine's *Athalie*. When at last he decided
on Emanuel Geibel's *Loreley* he had composed only the finale of
Act I, a chorus of vintners, and an 'Ave Maria' when he died.

Otto Nicolai (1810–49), a student at the Royal Institute for Church
Music in Berlin and a member of the Singakademie, lived in Rome
during 1833–6 as organist of the Prussian Embassy chapel and
studied Palestrina very thoroughly. But he became interested in opera
and in 1837 secured a post as conductor at the Hoftheater in Vienna,
where he was appointed principal conductor in 1841. In the interval
he had returned to Italy and begun a career as an opera composer,
scoring his first important success with *Il templario* (after *Ivanhoe*:
Turin, 1840). In 1845 this was adapted in German for Vienna as
Der Tempelritter, and *Il proscritto* (Milan, 1841) was similarly given
as *Die Heimkehr des Verbannten* (Vienna, 1844). The translator of
both works, Siegfried Kapper, drew his attention to the figure of
Falstaff in Shakespeare, who had already appeared in operas by
Peter Ritter, Dittersdorf, Mercadante, and Balfe; a libretto was
begun by Jacob Hoffmeister, though the lion's share of *Die lustigen
Weiber von Windsor* was the work of the Viennese dramatist Salomon
von Mosenthal. In 1849 Nicolai conducted the first performance at
Berlin, where he had been appointed *Hofoperndirigent*, and two
months later suffered a fatal stroke. Despite the later competition of
Verdi's *Falstaff*, *Die lustigen Weiber* has kept its place on the German
stage by the originality of Nicolai's invention, the ease of the diction,
and its polished humour.

SCHUMANN

Robert Schumann (1810–50) wrestled all his life with the subject
of opera. In 1842 he wrote to the theatre conductor Carl Kossmaly:
'Do you know my morning and evening prayer as an artist? It is
German opera. There's something to be done there.' He had already
in 1840 failed to get a libretto out of E. T. A. Hoffmann's story
Doge und Dogaressa. In 1842 he busied himself with *Die Braut des
Kadi* but turned to another oriental subject, *Das Paradies und die*

Peri, a translation of Thomas Moore's poem; then, having failed to make an opera from it, he composed it as a 'secular oratorio'. In 1844 he contemplated Byron's *Corsair* and Goethe's *Wilhelm Meister*. In vain he asked Annette von Droste-Hülshoff to write him a libretto. He himself rejected Julius Słowacki's *Mazeppa*. Then at last in 1847 his choice fell on Hebbel's play *Genoveva*, from which Robert Reinick extracted a libretto; this dissatisfied him and in the end he himself compiled a text from Reinick's attempt, Hebbel's play, and a play on the same subject by Tieck. (Its weaknesses were pointed out to him by Wagner.) The score was finished in 1848 and he conducted the first performance himself at Leipzig in 1850. In that year he was attracted by a libretto by Richard Pohl based on Schiller's *Braut von Messina* but composed only the overture. Among his other opera projects were *Faust*, *Maria Stuart*, *Die Nibelungen*, *Der falsche Prophet* (from Moore's *Lalla Rookh*), and *Sardanapal* (Byron).

FLOTOW

Friedrich (Freiherr von) Flotow (1812–83) studied composition with Reicha in Paris. He made himself a master of French charm and owed a great deal to that nation, but even during his longer stays he never lost touch with his German roots. His first comic opera, *Pierre et Catherine* (1831), was produced in German at Ludwigslust as *Peter und Kathinka* (1835). In 1833 he composed two librettos by Theodor Körner, *Die Bergknappen* and *Alfred der Grosse*. Several French operas were given in translation in German theatres and followed by three original works: *Alessandro Stradella* (Hamburg, 1844), *Martha, oder Der Markt zu Richmond* (Vienna, 1847), both with librettos by Friedrich Wilhelm Riese, and *Sophie Katharina* (Berlin, 1850) to a text by Charlotte Birch-Pfeiffer. When the material for the three-act *Le Naufrage de la Méduse*, composed with Auguste Pilati (Paris, 1839), was destroyed by fire at the Hamburg theatre, Flotow rewrote it as *Die Matrosen* in four acts to a libretto by Riese (1845). *L'Esclave de Camoëns* (Paris, 1843) was similarly enlarged as *Indra* (1852). His numerous later works were less successful. Flotow not only conquered Paris; he appealed to the *Biedermeier* taste of his fellow-countrymen. Nothing is problematic; everything is solid and effective. Flotow's melodies catch the ear and some have become opera-house hits. *Martha* was internationally successful and even critical audiences were captivated by the composer's wealth of ideas and technical ability.

WAGNER

In 1832 Wagner (1813–83) based the text and music of the first scenes of an opera, *Die Hochzeit*, to some extent on Johann Gustav Büsching's *Ritterzeit und Ritterwesen*.[140] The next year he founded on Carlo Gozzi's *La donna serpente* the libretto of *Die Feen*, which he composed while chorus director of the Stadttheater at Würzburg. Beethoven and Weber were, according to his *Autobiographische Skizze*, his models. 'A great deal was successful in the ensembles; in particular the finale of the Second Act bid fair to be very effective.' The 'forbidden question' we know from *Lohengrin* was already anticipated here; the fairy Ada commands Arinfal, the mortal she wishes to marry, never to enquire about her origin. When the work was not accepted at Leipzig, Wagner reflected resignedly that 'the performance of an opera by a German composer was evidently something one had to beg for'. It was not until five years after his death that *Die Feen* had its first performance, at the Munich Nationaltheater. In 1834 he based the libretto of *Das Liebesverbot* on Shakespeare's *Measure for Measure*. (Already in the overture lively carnival music is confronted with the gloomy theme of the 'ban on love'.) As music director at Magdeburg Wagner was able to produce his opera there in 1836, though not without a concession to the censorship which insisted on the title being changed to *Die Novize von Palermo*. From this period dates a prose scenario on Heinrich König's opera, *Die hohe Braut*.

Two articles dating from 1837[141] show Wagner as a close observer of contemporary opera. Impressed by the art of Wilhelmine Schröder-Devrient (who was later to 'create' the roles of Adriano in *Rienzi*, Senta, and Venus), Wagner wrote in 'Der dramatische Gesang' that the basis of vocal performance lay in purity of tone and enunciation, precision and labialization as well as the smoothness of passage-work—a very necessary admonition in view of the dull routine that reigned in German theatres of that period. In the article 'Bellini' he attacked 'the boundless confusion of forms, style and modulation of so many German opera composers'.

The dissolution of the Magdeburg company obliged him to move to Königsberg where he was music director for a short time; in 1837 he became conductor of the Stadttheater at Riga. His experience as a conductor was widened but his personal situation was wretched and his relations with the theatre director Karl von Holtei were

---

[140] See Max Koch, 'Die Quellen der "Hochzeit"', *Richard Wagner-Jahrbuch*, iv (1912), 105.
[141] 'Bellini', and 'Über Meyerbeers *Hugenotten*' (both 1837), both in Richard Wagner, *Sämtliche Schriften und Dichtungen*, ed. H. von Wolzogen and R. Sternfeld, xii (Leipzig, 1911).

strained. In 1839 he saw no way out but flight—with Paris as his goal. At Königsberg he had written the libretto of a comic opera, *Männerlist grösser als Frauenlist* (from the *Arabian Nights*), after which Bulwer Lytton's novel, *Rienzi*, suggested the libretto of *Rienzi, der letzte der Tribunen*. The bay of Sandwike in Norway, where Wagner's ship sheltered from storm on the voyage from Pillau to London, became the scene of *Der fliegende Holländer*. Nature impressions and his own experiences accelerated Wagner's creative imagination; in representing the wanderings of the Flying Dutchman, descendant of Odysseus and the Wandering Jew, he realized the idea of a new poetic-musical form of opera. He was about to make a complete reformation. But bitter necessity forced him to make concessions. He wrote both poem and music of the *Holländer* but, being unable to get it performed, sold the scenario to the director of the Opera who commissioned a French libretto, *Le Vaisseau-Fantôme*, long thought to have been set by Pierre Dietsch.[142] In the intervals of hack work he wrote prose scenarios for *Die Sarazenin* (on Manfred and his father Friedrich II) and *Die Bergwerke von Falun* (on E. T. A. Hoffmann's story). But in 1842 the bad days in Paris ended. Wagner moved to Dresden where *Rienzi* had been accepted for performance. As the *Kapellmeister*, Reissiger, complained of the lack of good librettos Wagner offered him *Die hohe Braut*; when Reissiger turned it down, it was offered to Johann Kittl (1806–68) who composed it as *Bianca und Giuseppe oder Die Franzosen vor Nizza* (Prague, 1848). But the success of *Rienzi* led to production of the *Holländer* (1843), which Wagner conducted himself—as he did the Berlin production in 1844. The success of *Rienzi* also earned him appointment as second conductor at Dresden.

The sight of the Wartburg and the Hörselberg near Eisenach on the journey from Paris to Dresden reawakened his interest in an opera subject that had been in his mind for some years. Two characters were fused into one. The first was Tannhäuser, a thirteenth-century poet who in the medieval legend became a knight, followed the love-goddess Venus into her magic mountain, and, as a penitent pilgrim to Rome, sought forgiveness for his sins. Tieck had introduced him in his story *Der getreue Eckart und der Tannhäuser* (1800). The other character was Heinrich von Ofterdingen who is mentioned in the thirteenth-century poem *Singerkriec uf Wartburc* and since the fifteenth century connected with St Elisabeth of Thuringia. He is also mentioned by the Romantic writers, in a

---

[142] According to *The New Grove*, v. 470, the libretto of Dietsch's opera was based on a novel by Marryat, presumably *The Phantom Ship*.

fragment by Novalis (1802) and by La Motte-Fouqué in his play *Der Sängerkrieg auf der Wartburg* (1828). In his *Sagenschatz des Thüringer Waldes* (1835) Ludwig Bechstein had connected the Tannhäuser and song-tournament stories and three years later a Königsberg professor, C. T. L. Lucas, in a study *Über den Wartburgkrieg*, suggested that Tannhäuser and Ofterdingen were identical.

Wagner began to work on his poem, originally called *Der Venusberg*, in May 1842 and completed the full score of *Tannhäuser und der Sängerkrieg auf Wartburg* in April 1845. He conducted the first performance on 19 October. Later the work underwent various changes. In the original version neither Venus nor Elisabeth's funeral procession were shown on the stage; the drama ended with a glow from the Hörselberg while torches on the Wartburg and a passing-bell suggested Elisabeth's death. The new ending was first performed on 1 August 1847 and the work underwent far more drastic changes when it was given in Paris in 1861.

With *Tannhäuser* Wagner turned his back on fashionable taste. The public was either puzzled by it or rejected it. It was condemned for lack of melody, formlessness, and excessive modulation. Professional judgements were hesitant or contradictory; the Berlin *Generalintendant* von Küstner considered it too epic, a Dresden critic too dramatic, one at Leipzig too lyric. The fundamental idea of the sinner's redemption was not understood. It was the performances under Liszt at Weimar (1849) and Spohr at Kassel (1853) which substantially furthered understanding of the work's unprecedented structure. Berlin did not decide on *Tannhäuser* until 1856 when it had already been given on fifty other stages.

As early as July 1845 Wagner had written the rough draft of a comic counterpart to the Wartburg tournament of song—*Die Meistersinger von Nürnberg*—but less than three weeks later he set down another prose sketch, for *Lohengrin*. The text was finished in November. Wagner composed the third act first and the Prelude last; he completed the full score in April 1848. Here again he conflated two sources: the legend of the Swan Knight, armed with supernatural powers who fights wrong-doing; and the myth of the Grail. In essentials Wagner followed the thirteenth-century Lohengrin epic published by Joseph Görres, in which the legend is placed in the time of Henry the Fowler.

Discontent with conditions in Dresden led Wagner, with his colleague the conductor August Röckel, to become involved in subversive politics and after the May rising of 1849 he fled to Switzerland to avoid arrest. Yet the artistic fruits of this turbulent period were considerable. Besides *Lohengrin* they included plans for an opera *Wieland der Schmied*, traces of which appeared in the *Ring*, and a prose sketch for a work on the Nibelung myth itself. By the end of 1848 he had completed the libretto of a 'grand, heroic opera', *Siegfrieds Tod*—the original form of *Götterdämmerung*—and during 1850–1 composed some music for it.[143] As for *Lohengrin*, the projected production in Dresden was of course impossible, and when Liszt gave it in a model performance at Weimar on 28 August 1850 Wagner was unable to be present. He heard it for the first time in 1861, in Vienna.

LIBRETTISTS

German librettists were in an unfortunate position; it was long before they had copyright protection. But in 1842 the Hamburg Stadttheater took the bold step of trying to introduce a system of royalties and the following year Meyerbeer arranged at the Berlin Opera that authors should receive 10 per cent of the box-office takings at each performance. Léon Pillet, director of the Paris Grand Opéra, paid 500 francs for the prose sketch of the *Holländer*, while Lachner paid Henri de Saint-Georges 2,000 for the libretto of *Catarina Cornaro*. Other—artistic—problems faced German authors of opera librettos. Whatever their literary powers, they were lacking in dramatic instinct. They offered series of pictures and scenes but were incapable of conjuring up an exciting stage happening. Their texts lacked tense representation of action, concentration, logical build-up, the hot breath of passion, Dionysian fire. The constant complaints of composers from Mozart to Mendelssohn that they could find no suitable libretto in their native country were not unfounded.

The suitability of a libretto cannot be judged merely by its literary value; it is more important that it should offer music every possibility for the development of expression. The librettist of Romantic opera should have commanded the ability to think in musical relationships, to write music-inspiring verses, to offer the composer stimuli to new kinds of theme and harmonic progression, to lend rhythmical and metrical wings to his fancy. But he had also to be willing and able to agree with the wishes of his partner in matters of text and dramaturgy. The ability of a Calzabigi or Hofmannsthal to do this is not an inborn gift. It can hardly be acquired, at most perfected

---

[143] Published by Robert Bailey in Harold S. Powers (ed.), *Studies in Music History: Essays for Oliver Strunk* (Princeton, 1968), 485–94.

and refined by collaboration with the composer. Ideally text and music should be the work of one person. In his preface to Hoffmann's tale *Der goldene Topf* Jean Paul wrote that one hoped for a man who would 'write both the poem and the music of an opera' [*der eine Oper zugleich dichtet und setzt*]. Yet even such personalities as Spohr and Schumann were unsuccessful in this field. But two other musicians, thanks to their literary skill, poetic imagination, comprehensive knowledge of the stage repertoire and dramatic ability were able to do just that: Lortzing and Wagner. Their works were in totally different genres—they met only in homage to Hans Sachs—but both achieved works of strong vitality on the stage thanks to the successful co-ordination of word and sound. In both the text produces suitable music.

In many librettos words and dramatic content were equally weak and colourless. The four-stress line became the rule. The average composer was content with humdrum verses, feeble rhymes, and schematic stresses. However, Weber had shown how the words could be associated with characteristic, rhythmically distinct melodies, themes, and harmonies. Rhyme, which Mozart had already eschewed in opera, was avoided by Spohr in his *Berggeist* as cramping. Wagner rejected it after *Die Feen* almost completely but gave his librettos varying metres and compressed power of expression; he explained his method in *Oper und Drama* (Leipzig, 1851), and soon after came the poem of the *Ring des Nibelungen* written in a new style marked by assonance and alliteration. A considerable number of other authors—respectable poets and men connected in some way or another with the stage, even music critics—sought subjects in the fields of Romanticism or national history.

While various stylistic elements were common to French and Italian opera as well, much was specifically German. The German Romantic had a quick ear for wind and storm; he peopled rustling forests, sea, springs, and waterfalls with sprites, woods and meadows with elves and gnomes and spirits, heaven and earth with angels and fairies. He saw phantoms, trafficked with the other world and hell, felt himself at the mercy of dark powers, despaired, fell prey to illusions. Or life became a dream. Myths and folk-tales spoke to him and he found inspiration in his country's past. Extremes met; deep devoutness and pious simplicity came up against the demoniac in men and spirits. Fantasy was unlimited. Every kind of magic was taken seriously. Hysterical and clairvoyant characters were represented and also those endowed with supernatural powers. Purely literary skill was hardly sufficient to present them convincingly on the stage. E. T. A. Hoffmann in 'Der Dichter und der Komponist'[144] wrote that 'a truly romantic opera can be written only by the inspired poet of genius, for only he can bring to life the marvellous apparitions of the spirit world'. And according to the young Wagner 'the essence of dramatic art . . . lies in the successful grasping and representation of the inner nature of all human life and affairs, the idea'.[145] The Romantic view of art is admittedly élitist and demanding, not easily taken by those who—for instance, at the opera—merely wish to be entertained. Such people preferred the homely style later known as Biedermeier, marked by pathetic sentimentality and the simply idyllic; they were breathed on by the spirit of the age but soon abandoned its higher flight. They were satisfied with the triviality of mere pseudo-Romanticism—the pseudo-Romanticism of many opera plots. Anton Reicha considered that in the German view music was suitable only for the depiction of bizarre, preposterous situations in which the main part was played by witchcraft, ghostly goings on, and similar stupidities.[146] But there were librettos of undeniable quality: Grillparzer's *Melusine* was written for Beethoven who forwent it,[147] and it was finally composed by Conradin Kreutzer in 1833. Friedrich de la Motte-Fouqué arranged his tale *Undine* for E. T. A. Hoffmann and made a fresh version for Christian Girschner (1794–1860) whose work was given a partial performance in Berlin (1830) and complete at Danzig (1837). Lortzing also set it in 1845 and three years later a *Rolands Knappen* based on a tale by another well-known author, the Weimar poet Johann Karl Musäus. And, as we have seen, Tieck's *Phantasus* contributed to *Tannhäuser* while his *Leben und Tod der Genoveva* together with Hebbel's drama was the basis of Schumann's opera.

Heinrich von Kleist was another source of inspiration. His *Die Hermannsschlacht* provided the basis for an opera (1835) by the Bavarian *Hofkapellmeister* Hippolyte Chélard (1789–1861) and *Das Käthchen von Heilbronn* inspired both 'Hoven' (Vesque von Püttlingen) (1803–83) and the Dessau *Hofmusikdirektor* Friedrich Lux (1820–95),[148] and the scenes of the trial-by-ordeal and the wedding procession gave Wagner material for *Lohengrin*. Heine also con-

---

[144] Originally published in the *Allgemeine musikalische Zeitung* (1813).

[145] 'Pasticcio', *Neue Zeitschrift für Musik*, 6 and 10 Nov. 1834; repr. in Richard Wagner, *Sämtliche Schriften und Dichtungen*, xii (Leipzig, 1911).

[146] *L'Art du compositeur dramatique* (Paris, 1833); trans. Carl Czerny, *Die Kunst der dramatischen Komposition* (Vienna, 1835).

[147] See, for instance, Alexander Thayer, *Ludwig van Beethovens Leben*, iv (rev. 4th edn., Leipzig, 1923), 413–14.

[148] Hoven's work (1845) was entitled *Liebeszauber*, whereas Lux's (1846) was named after the play.

tributed; Wagner knew Heine's version of the *Holländer* story in the *Memoiren des Herrn von Schnabelewopski* and it must have been a passage in 'Götter im Exil' that drew his attention to the *Singerkriec uf Wartburc*. Wilhelm Hauff's 'Geschichte von dem Gespensterschiff' (in *Die Karawane*) was yet another source for the *Holländer*.

Eduard Devrient's libretto *Hans Heiling*, intended for Mendelssohn who rejected it and admirably composed by Marschner, was inspired by Theodor Körner's tale 'Hans Heilings Felsen'. But *Heiling* was Devrient's only successful libretto; in this field he was completely overshadowed by August von Kotzebue (1761-1819), whom Beethoven considered to possess a 'unique genius' and whose librettos were set by Spohr (*Die Kreuzfahrer*), Marschner (*Der Kyffhäuser Berg*), and Lortzing (*Der Wildschütz*).

The Berliner Ernst Raupach—whose name is familiar because of the young Wagner's overture and finale music for Act V of his tragedy *König Enzio*—provided the libretto for Loewe's *Singspiel*, *Die drei Wünsche* (1834) and the text of Ferdinand Hiller's *Ein Traum in der Christnacht* (1845) is based on one of his plays. The poet and critic Ludwig Rellstab provided the libretto of Meyerbeer's *Ein Feldlager in Schlesien* (1844) and translated Scribe's for *Le Prophète*. Some of the most original librettists had no professional connection with the theatre, for instance Eduard Gehe supplied the books not only of Spohr's *Jessonda* but of three operas by the now forgotten Joseph Maria Wolfram (1789-1839) and Johann Christian Lobe's *Die Flibustier* (1829); his planned *Rübezahl* for Spohr remained unfinished. J. F. Kind never repeated his success as the librettist of *Freischütz*, but the book of Konradin Kreutzer's very popular *Nachtlager in Granada* (1834) was based on a play by him. One of the most successful practitioners of the day was Otto Prechtler who supplied the librettos of Franz Lachner's *Alidia* (after Bulwer Lytton) (1839), Hoven's *Johanna d'Arc* (after Schiller) (1840), *Liebeszauber* (after Kleist) (1845), and Joseph Netzer's *Mara* (1841). He must be counted among the above-average librettists, together with Friedrich Wilhelm Riese ('W. Friedrich'), Flotow's partner in *Alessandro Stradella* and *Martha*.

THE FATE OF THE 'NUMBER OPERA'

The long threatened decay of the old opera convention was now completing itself. The hitherto admissible categories proved more and more unsuitable for the expressive aims of the new age. If the Baroque opera and its architectonic forms might be regarded as statuesque, the Romantic may be described as dynamic. Instead of the representation of types, situations, and narrowly circumscribed emotions, we find the interrelation of individuals and psychological developments. The man acting on the stage is, like Tannhäuser, 'dem Wechsel untertan'. What he has to sing and say embraces a wide scale from tender feeling to the expression of unbridled passion. Changes of mood demand compositional flexibility beyond the capability of the conventional 'number'.

THE OVERTURE

The practice of anticipating in the overture attractive themes from the opera led as in Italy and France to the worthless pot-pourri form, although the leading masters knew how to give a theme announced in the orchestral introduction the character of an important motto. Alternatively the overture would be replaced by a short introduction leading directly into the first scene. The short overture to Spohr's *Die Kreuzfahrer* is given a warlike stamp by ophicleide and military drum, a character which dominates Act I in the camp of the Christian army before Nicæa. Even the position of the overture in the general structure was questioned. In Marschner's *Heiling* it is placed not at the beginning but after a scenic *Vorspiel* performed on the open stage and before the first act actually so called. It thus has the character of an entr'acte in which the composer symbolizes the unbridgeable conflict of the two spheres—of mountain spirit and man—which characterizes the action. The familiar overture of Nicolai's *Die lustigen Weiber* is an outstanding essay in Romantic representation in sound. The depiction of moonrise, Falstaff's appearance as Herne the hunter, and themes from the 'fairy' ballet (all from Act III) transport the listener into Shakespeare's fantastic world. The general tendency is to foreshadow the main lines of the action in the orchestral introduction. In the overture to *Undine* (Ex. 125) Lortzing anticipates some of the thematic material of the last finale (Exx. 126 and 127).

In January 1841 Wagner had contributed an extensive article 'De l'Ouverture' to the *Gazette musicale*,[149] outlining the development of

Ex. 125

bn, trbn, vc, db

---

[149] Repr. in Richard Wagner, *Sämtliche Schriften und Dichtungen* (Leipzig, 1911), 241–56.

Ex. 126

Ex. 127

the form from the abstract music of earlier times to the 'poetic' overtures of Cherubini (particularly *Les Deux Journées*) and Beethoven, and the 'dramatic fantasia' of Weber's *Oberon*. 'The history of the pot-pourri begins to a certain extent with Spontini's overture to *La vestale*.' As a composer Wagner had at first followed the custom of the day. In *Die Feen* and *Das Liebesverbot* he extracted important themes in order to give the audience concise symbolic indications of the action. In the *Rienzi* Overture, introduced by the 'freedom' fanfare, he presents as essential themes Rienzi's prayer, the motif of his heroic will, the call to battle against the nobles ('Santo Spirito Cavaliere'), and the theme of the people's homage to the Tribune. But the overture to the *Holländer*, begun a few months after the *Gazette* article, foreshadows the substance of the action as a whole; Senta's ballad lies at the heart of the tempestuous drama. A similar idea of 'redemption' determined the *Tannhäuser* Overture. With it, Wagner felt he had exhausted the genre; he called the introduction to Act I of Lohengrin *Vorspiel*.

THE LIED

The simple Lied was significant as a species of counterbalance to the more sophisticated operatic forms. J. A. Hiller and Reichardt had made their marks as composers of *Liederspiele* and *Singspiele*,[150] and Mozart had indicated the role of the Lied in opera with Papageno's 'Vogelfänger' song in *Die Zauberflöte*. Given to simple folk—peasants, hunters, soldiers—it served to characterize the singer, as with Friar Tuck and the fool Wamba who have two each in Marschner's *Der Templer und die Jüdin*. Tuck's second song is typical (Ex. 128). When sung by operatic heroes the Lied became a symbol of momentary reflection or characterized a situation. The naïve obviousness of the text distinguished it from the other numbers of an opera. Drinking songs were always particularly popular (for example, Plunkett's in Flotow's *Martha*, Falstaff's 'Als Büblein klein' in *Die lustigen Weiber*). Key, metre, and accompaniment were always kept simple. The Tsar's song 'Einst spielt' ich mit Szepter' in Lortzing's *Zar und Zimmermann* and Stadinger's 'Auch ich war ein Jüngling' in his *Waffenschmied* are among the most popular operatic pieces in Germany. Schumann burst open the form in *Genoveva* when he dissolved the Lied-duet 'Wenn ich ein Vöglein war' into passionate declamation.

The young Wagner introduced the Lied as a cheerful, delaying contrast in the course of serious actions. For instance the libretto of *Die hohe Braut* (1837) includes a specimen of grim humour, the song of the two hermits, 'Ein armer Sünder liess mich rufen'. And the sketch for the projected *Bergwerke zu Falun* (1842) shows that Joens, just before the catastrophe, was to sing a merry Lied about how things would go when he married. The helmsman's Lied, 'Mit Gewitter und Sturm', in Act I of the *Holländer* characterizes the

Ex. 128

(Brothers, wake! Look out! Horns are sounding, dark night's out. Off to the greenwood!)

---

[150] See Vol. VII, pp. 76 and 81–5. In 1830 Lortzing made a new version of Hiller's *Die Jagd* and in 1832 composed two *Liederspiele* of his own, *Der Pole und sein Kind* and *Szenen aus Mozarts Leben*.

simple young sailor in contrast with the curse-laden world wanderer whose aria follows. Two years later in *Tannhäuser* we no longer find the term Lied; in his list of numbers the composer calls the shepherd's little song *Gesang*; it is indeed unlike the typical opera Lied.

THE ROMANZE

The Romanze was still at the height of its popularity—in opera, in the concert hall, and in the drawing-room. As an operatic number it was indispensable; in Germany hardly any opera was without one or more. Kreutzer's *Nachtlager* has three and Lindpaintner's *Macht des Liedes* five. It often expressed love—including love of the homeland—and chivalry, as well as the legendary, fabulous, or awesome. In contrast with the Lied it is more 'characteristically' accompanied, often with solo instruments or instrumental groups (for example, woodwind and horns or pizzicato strings), and modulates further (often alternating major and minor) as in Hugo's 'Ich ritt zum grossen Waffenspiele' (Lortzing's *Undine*, Act I). Emmy's *Romanze* 'Sieh, Mutter, dort den bleichen Mann', in Marschner's *Vampyr*, is exceptional; its five recitando stanzas, with changes of tempo, have a choral refrain:

> Denn still und heimlich sag ich's dir,
> der bleiche Mann ist ein Vampyr.

Wagner employed a similar ironic refrain in Gernot's Romanze 'War einst 'ne böse Hexe wohl' in *Die Feen*, a witch hideous yet wearing a ring which makes her appear young and fair. His last Romanze, very different, was Wolfram's song to the evening star in *Tannhäuser* where the harp, with *pp* trombone and bass tuba chords, portend death.

BALLADE, CAVATINA, AND PREGHIERA

The ballade appears rarely but always in an explanatory role, often with reference to the mysterious: for example, the heroine's 'Fur solche Schmach zu wacker' in Ferdinand Ries's *Liska* (1831),[151] John's 'Wenn alles schläft um Mitternacht' in Hiller's *Traum in der Christnacht* (1843), Frau Reich's 'Vom Jäger Herne die Mär ist alt' in Nicolai's *Die lustigen Weiber* (1849). It might be said that Wagner developed the whole of the *Holländer* from Senta's 'Traft ihr das Schiff im Meere an?'

The lyrical, predominantly elegiac cavatina in German romantic opera, something between Lied and aria, had ideal prototypes in

---

[151] There is a lengthy excerpt in Siegfried Goslich, *Beiträge zur Geschichte der deutschen romantischen Oper* (Leipzig, 1937), 118.

'Porgi amor' in *Figaro* and 'Und ob die Wolke' in *Freischütz*. It differs from the aria in being cast in a single movement and in avoidance of word repetition. Its special fields are amorous longing, pious simplicity, and gentle melancholy. It tends to be in flat keys and compound triple time, and associated with solo instruments of elegiac timbre. (But Lindpaintner's *Vampyr* has two cavatinas, the second of which parodies the first.) Wagner gave Ada in *Die Feen* an Italianate cavatina, 'Wie muss ich doch beklagen', and Erik's cavatina in the *Holländer* is not without traces of the older style.

The preghiera borrows the form of the cavatina, as in Marschner's *Kaiser Adolf von Nassau* (Ex. 129). As solo, ensemble, or chorus

Ex. 129

(When the anxious heart despairs, it has always found with thee consolation for its wounds.)

Ex. 130

(Go with God! May he protect you! My prayer ascends urgently!)

number, it was an indispensable requisite of opera. The declamatory prayer of the imprisoned Rebekka in Marschner's *Templer* is untypical in its modulations and rising passion, which were to be echoed in the middle section, 'O Gott, vernichte nicht das Werk', of Rienzi's prayer. Closely related to this again—even melodically at one point ('Lass mich im Staub vor dir vergehen')—is Elisabeth's prayer in *Tannhäuser*. The key of the latter, G flat, was a favourite for German operatic prayers, for example, in Lindpaintner's *Genueserin* (1839) and the *Mara* (1841) of Joseph Netzer (1808-64) (Ex. 130). The ensemble or choral prayer was another popular feature, which the young Wagner employed from *Die Feen* (Act III) onwards.

THE ARIA

The principal form of earlier opera, the aria, often degenerated after 1830 into commonplace melody without particular textual relevance, with poverty-stricken rhythms, weak suspensions, and expressionless accompaniment. This is true even of such skilful composers as Kreutzer, Lindpaintner and Reissiger. But with the leading Romantics the fate of the aria signified a crisis in thinking. Lortzing in particular was distinguished by his originality. Van Bett's aria 'O sancta justitia' in *Zar und Zimmermann* and the Schoolmaster's '5000 Thaler' in *Der Wildschütz* are gems. Marie's aria in the Act I finale of *Der Waffenschmied* (Ex. 131) is enlarged into a scena with such characteristic details as the door-knocking motif and the pianissimo orchestral reminiscence of the previous quartet, 'Ich weiss vor Zagen kein Wort zu sagen'.

With Spohr and Marschner the introductory recitative is often more important than the aria itself, for example, *Jessonda*, Act I, No. 7, where the recitative is one of the finest passages in Spohr while the aria is relatively weak. The clearest example of the change

Ex. 131

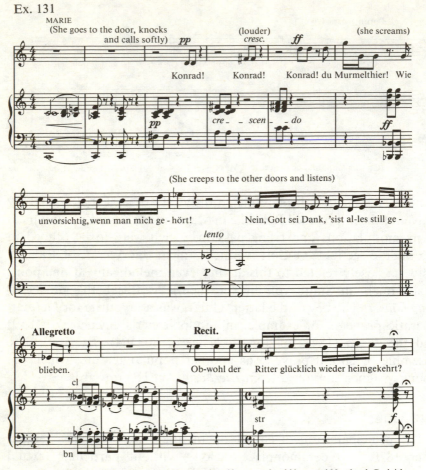

(Konrad! Konrad! You dormouse! How careless, if anyone should hear me! No, thank God, it's
all quiet. I wonder whether the knight got home again safely?)

of style is Guilbert's 'scene and aria' in Act II of *Templer und Jüdin*,
concerning which Marschner wrote to his librettist Devrient 'the
public are not to expect anything aria-like'. The destiny of the form
could hardly have been expressed more brutally. But he brought off
a fine stroke in Heiling's aria 'An jenem Tag' where the goblin–king
expresses his passion through the repetition of short chromatic motif
fragments at intervals of tone or semitone. Three years later, in the
terzet, No. 14, of *Das Schloss am Aetna*, he was to use repetition of
a rising chromatic motif in the orchestra with even more telling effect
(Ex. 132).

In Act III of *Die Feen* the young Wagner gave the delirious Arindal
an aria which in one section approaches the expressive level of Weber
(Ex. 133). And in the *Holländer* the orchestral exposition of themes

Ex. 132

(Knowest thou the Sicilian's blood? Thou dost not — or that boy would long ago have fallen on thy own dagger!)

Ex. 133

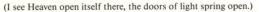

(I see Heaven open itself there, the doors of light spring open.)

in 'Die Frist ist um' is similarly more important than the voice part. In the climactic waves of a short motif, taken over from Marschner, lie the germ of a technique that was to be more fully developed later. From *Lohengrin* on, the concept of *Arie* was to disappear. And Schumann applied the term in *Genoveva* to what is really a prayer-cavatina ('O du, der über Alle wacht').

ENSEMBLE AND CHORUS

In their ensembles many composers were content with melody rendered insipid by chromaticism and sentimental coloratura, and with indefinite accompanying rhythms. The choruses of the average opera lacked dramatic punch; the singers are scarcely ever participants in the action but merely spectators. Exceptionally, Meyerbeer knew how to handle large groups of soloists and choral masses. And not only in his *grands opéras*; in the *Feldlager in Schlesien* he brought four groups of soldiers into a quadruple chorus. Lortzing excelled in lively character sketches and strong effects; in the introduction to Act III of *Caramo* (1839) an entire family council of aristocrats swoons at the mention of the word 'Mésalliance!' and in the Act I finale of *Casanova* (1841) the *fugato* of the timorous policemen is irresistibly comic. The billiard-playing scene in the second act of *Der Wildschütz*, and the introduction to Act III of *Zar und Zimmermann*, in which the conceited burgomaster attempts with remarkable lack of success to conduct a choir, are masterly essays in a kind of musical humour rare in Germany.

As for Wagner, he had already planned the introduction to Act I of *Das Liebesverbot* as a grand ensemble and then built up great climactic complexes in both acts. In *Rienzi* he produced a majestic effect with the double chorus in the Lateran, and Act II of *Tannhäuser* after Elisabeth's 'Dich, teure Halle' consists, with the exception of Wolfram's and Tannhäuser's songs, almost entirely of ensemble writing. Only a few remnants of the old kind remain beside new forms determined by connecting motifs and changes arising from the situation. Harmonic energy-fields give the extended ensembles in *Lohengrin* contrast, profile, and dynamism. Male and female choirs provide a complete scale of scorings and groupings; they participate in the action so that everything becomes a scenic happening.

SCENE COMPOSITION

Spoken dialogue was still preserved in comic opera but was in retreat. The day of secco recitative was also over. After Weber and Spohr the dominance of measured, orchestrally accompanied recitative was established and thus became an essential factor in the through-composition of larger complexes. The declamatory principle became highly significant. Melodrama, which Schumann was to make an independent form in his music to Byron's *Manfred*, was given a special task in opera. Following the precedent of the dungeon scene in *Fidelio*, it was employed for the representation of the marvellous and sinister: by Conradin Kreutzer when Raimund stands before his own grave in *Melusine*; by Ferdinand Hiller for the churchyard scene in *Der Traum in der Christnacht*; by Lortzing in the scene of the Mountain Queen in *Rolands Knappen*. Marschner was an outstanding master of the melodrama. The moonlight scene in *Der Vampyr* was an exemplar. In *Hans Heiling* Gertrude is waiting for her daughter on a stormy night: from the whistling and whispering of clarinets, bassoons and horns, of muted violas and cellos, a melody emerges which the old woman begins to hum—an effect which is still gripping to this day. In 1832 Wagner, in his settings from Goethe's *Faust*, composed Gretchen's prayer as melodrama but he found no use for the device in opera.

Voice parts tended to follow Weber's model in giving more attention to the emphasis of sense by verbal accentuation. Composers broke away from the flourishes of secco and melodic melismas. Wagner said that a singer, to be worthy of the name, must combine

careful declamation with other basic accomplishments.[152] This prosodic manner of performance was to be given significance in the
future by the ever closer connection with the melos of the orchestra
which would take over the sound symbolism and the establishment
of logical connections.

The network of cross-connections between the different sections
of the opera, including the overture, leads to overall coherence. In
Melusine Grillparzer points out that Raimund must call to mind the
heroine's words by imitating her earlier song. Spontini in *Nurmahal
oder Das Rosenfest von Kaschmir* (1822) anticipates themes from the
aria No. 27 in the arioso 'Ha, welch ein Traum' (No. 21). Examples
of recurring 'situation themes' are to be found in Kreutzer's *Der
Taucher* (1813, rev. 1823) (the 'roaring of Charybdis') and in Lachner's
Catarina Cornaro (1841) (the entry of the Venetian ambassadors). A
whole scene, the hiring of the maids in the finale of Act I of Flotow's
Martha, is recapitulated after the words 'Gerade, wie es damals war'
[Just as it was before] at the end of the opera. Thematic reminiscences
may be attached to objects, happenings, persons, or supernatural
apparitions, and may prepare, urge on, or delay the course of the
action. Wagner of course was vastly to develop this technique,
though he speaks only of 'thematic germs' and the 'repetition of a
theme with the character of an absolute reminiscence'.[153]

While the aria became less important, the 'scene' expanded as a
connected, through-constructed section of an action. The first five
scenes of Act II of Spohr's *Berggeist*, a through-composed, unified
complex, represent a high point in this development, and Marschner—
particularly in the second act of *Der Templer*—shows his command
of an idiom with expressive tone-symbols, as in the Templar's great
scena (the chromatic harmony at his 'Grausam, lieblos nennst du
mich?' and the *pp* wind triplets at 'War ein Ritter', specially admired
by Wagner) and the chorus in the act finale. He further heightened
this style in the finale of Act III of *Heiling* (Ex. 134). Recitative,
arioso melody, instrumental stimulus, and motif-work are combined
in a new organic whole. Schumann treated the personal motifs of
Genoveva and her adversary Golo with the same logical consistency
and thereby earned Spohr's approval.[154] We are here at a turning-
point in the history of opera.

[152] In 'Pasticcio'.

[153] The term leitmotiv appeared for the first time in Friedrich Wilhelm Jähns, *Carl
Maria von Weber in seinen Werken: Chronologisch-thematisches Verzeichniss seiner sämmtlichen
Compositionen* (Berlin, 1871).

[154] Louis Spohr, *Selbstbiographie* (Kassel and Göttingen, 1860–1), ii. 334.

Ex. 134

In 1834 the young Wagner had objected that German operas consisted only of a mass of musical numbers with no psychological connection. While he still composed in these categories himself, he mixed them with motifs and declamatory elements. He employed personal themes and 'fate' themes throughout and these carry the new architecture of musical drama. In *Tannhäuser* the threads of the

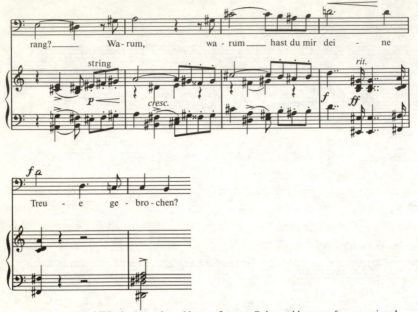

(HEILING: Anna! Why have you done this to me? ANNA: O do not blame me for your misery!
HEILING: Do you not remember the day you promised me loyalty, when I struggled in joy and
pain to your feet? Why, why have you broken faith with me?)

action are all gathered in the last finale: the Rome narrative signifies
a definitive supersession of the 'number' by the scene. The orchestra
in a hitherto almost unknown manner becomes the partner of the
singer; it fills out the content of his story, carries his declamation,
and elucidates the spiritual connections. Yet many composers still
clung to the traditional keys for separate numbers. The 'revenge'
aria was usually in D minor; F sharp minor was the demonic key.
The Lied was commonly in simpler keys than the Romanze and, as
we have seen, G flat major was often chosen for the preghiera. The
recitative had to intervene between such tonal areas. In contrast
to this practice the harmony of progressive composers directly
characterizes the person, the power of nature or destiny. It determines
the overall formal structure. In *Die lustigen Weiber* Nicolai constructed broadly conceived finales. That to Act I is in C major, the
dominant of the opening and concluding key of the opera, F major.
The separate sections logically modulate to other keys, the tonal
organization giving the work the impress of compelling consistency.
Looking far ahead, Weber had based the Wolf's Glen finale of
Freischütz on four degrees of the scale a minor third apart and
compressed them into the Samiel motif which dominates the whole
opera as a *Leitharmonie*. Wagner achieved another functional

construction of an entire action in *Lohengrin*. A major is not only the key of the Grail, the Prelude, and the final Grail Narrative, it is the 'starting-point' of the whole work. The dark counterpart of this bright world (Telramund's and Ortrud's vow of vengeance) is in the relative minor. A neighbour tonic, A flat (Lohengrin's personal theme and Elsa's dream in A flat major, the 'forbidden question' in A flat minor), is pertinently contrasted with the main key. The basic key of *Die Meistersinger* is C major, that of the *Ring* D flat.

In the three works before the mid-century Wagner's expressive style became ever bolder and more original. The main element was now accompanied recitative. He generally abandoned melodic melismata. His motifs not only underwent rhythmic and harmonic metamorphoses; they were shortened or lengthened, closely following the course of the drama, and thus ensured an enrichment and deepening of the psychic content, and tightening of the action. The orchestra provided a running commentary on the inner and external happenings; in his treatise *Oper und Drama* (1851) he called it the equivalent of the chorus in Greek tragedy.

He used the designation 'Romantic opera' for the last time for *Lohengrin* and soon afterwards announced 'I write no more operas'.[155] The 'number' structure was replaced by the unbroken succession of big scenes. Liszt praised the work above all for its unity of conception. No melodic phrase, no ensemble number can be understood apart from the whole. Wagner was creating a new music out of speech-rhythm and word-melody, freed from the periodization of Classicism. Its aim is 'unendliche Melodie', the infinite spinning on of the line.[156]

(e) RUSSIA AND EASTERN EUROPE

By GERALD ABRAHAM

RUSSIA

The history of Russian Romantic opera—more precisely, of Russian opera written under the influence of Weber—begins with the *Pan Twardowski*, produced in Moscow on 24 May–5 June 1828, of Aleksey Nikolaevich Verstovsky (1799–1862).[157]

---

[155] 'Eine Mittheilung an meine Freunde' (1851); repr. in *Richard Wagner: Gesammelte Schriften und Dichtungen*, iv (Leipzig, 1872), 285–418.

[156] The expression appeared in the 'open letter to a friend', *Zukunftsmusik*, written in 1860.

[157] See Vol. VIII, pp. 533–4, and Gerald Abraham, 'The Operas of Alexei Verstovsky', *19th-Century Music*, 7 (1984), 326–35.

VERSTOVSKY

Freischütz had been performed in St Petersburg and Moscow in 1824 and 1825, *Preciosa* in the northern capital in 1825, and Verstovsky, a typical aristocratic dilettante who had studied the piano with Steibelt and Field, was duly impressed by them. In 1826 he published an essay entitled 'Excerpts from a history of dramatic music', in which he says one might have had to agree with the admirers of Mozart, Cherubini, and Méhul who are convinced that the age of music is over 'if Weber had not written his *Freischütz*'. As Inspector of the Imperial Theatres in Moscow, he was able to express his admiration in practice. A colleague in theatrical officialdom, the historical novelist Mikhail Zagoskin, supplied him with a libretto on the legend of the so-called 'Pol'skiy Faust'—here rather a Polish Caspar—who sold his soul to the devil. The heroine is rescued from his power by her former lover, Krasicki, when he returns from the Turkish war, and Krasicki's Act I aria[158] shows Verstovsky's lyrical invention at its best. Twardowski's aria in the same act[159] is powerful, Julia's polonaise romance[160] much inferior. The introduction of a gypsy element may well have been suggested by *Preciosa*, though the music is not particularly Weberian. Verstovsky's harmony is commonplace, his scoring heavy-handed—though he followed Cherubini and Méhul by writing for an ensemble of solo cellos (which alternates with the full orchestra in the opening of the overture). But scenically the Wolf's Glen was paralleled by flood and an earthquake that destroys Twardowski's castle.

Like *Twardowski*, Verstovsky's later operas belong to the *Freischütz* genre of Romantic *Singspiel*. In his second, *Vadim ili Dvenadtsat' spyashchikh dev* [Vadim or The Twelve Sleeping Maidens] (1832), even the eponymous hero has only a speaking part. The libretto was cobbled up by a Moscow university professor from the second part of a poem by Zhukovsky, the first part of which was to provide the basis of Verstovsky's last opera, *Gromoboy* (1858). The subject of *Vadim* is Russian but even the quasi-epic song of the old Slavonic bard Boyan[161] is devoid of genuine Russian flavour despite Verlody's claim to have introduced 'Russian characteristics'. These came only with *Askol'dova mogila* [Askold's Tomb] (16–28 September 1835),[162]

---

[158] Excerpt in Vol. VIII, Ex. 195; complete in Semyon L'vovich Ginzburg, *Istoriya russkoy muziki v notnïkh obraztsakh* (Moscow and Leningrad, 1952), iii. 39.

[159] Ginzburg, *Istoriya*, p. 47.

[160] Ibid., p. 62. Krasicki also has a polonaise romance.

[161] In Ginzburg, *Istoriya*, p. 69.

[162] Overture and eight other numbers in Ginzburg, *Istoriya*, pp. 82–165. There are several editions of the vocal score.

for which Zagoskin fashioned a libretto from one of his own novels, with the substitution of a happy ending for a tragic one and the demotion of the heroine's father from former courtier to simple fisherman. The plot[163] is a farrago of tenth-century Russian history and pagan witchcraft, with a typical Romantic mystery figure, a bass 'Unknown' who seems to be an incarnation of the conservative Slavophilism of the librettist, the composer, and their friends. The influence of *Freischütz* is still perceptible not only in the music but in the first scene of Act IV where the witch Vakhrameevna, another speaking part, brews a magic potion. The night scene of the 'Unknown' on Askold's tomb, with an invisible chorus of Christians in the ruins of a church, also belongs to the world of German Romantic opera—as do the occasional polonaise rhythms. Verstovsky rests under the suspicion of having borrowed operatic numbers from his early vaudevilles, and the heroine's first song in Act I and the 'allegro agitato' section of her Act III aria certainly originated in earlier romances with piano. But it was the imitations of Russian popular song, albeit of the urban rather than the peasant variety, in the choruses of fishermen and peasants (Ex. 135) and the songs of *gudok*-player Toropka in Act I (Ex. 136) and Act III (Exx. 137 and

Ex. 135

(Come, brothers, quickly haul up the nets.)

Ex. 136

(Bright is the moon at midnight, bright the sun on a spring day, fa-la-la!)

[163] Mikhail Samoylovich Pekelis's summary of the plot is translated in Gerald R. Seaman, *History of Russian Music*, i (1967), 279.

Ex. 137

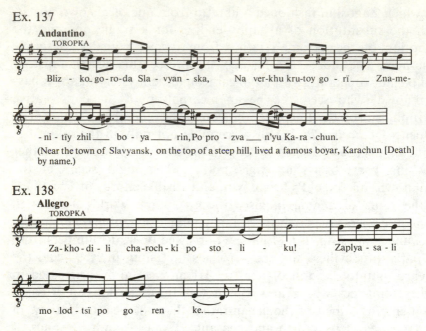

(Near the town of Slavyansk, on the top of a steep hill, lived a famous boyar, Karachun [Death] by name.)

Ex. 138

(Cups were passed along the table! The lads danced about the room.)

138) that won for *Askol'dova mogila* its quick and lasting popularity. (It had four hundred performances in Moscow alone during the last century.) The work which followed it the following year and has totally eclipsed it in the pages of history enjoyed nothing like the same immediate success with the general public.

GLINKA

Zhizn' za Tsarya [A Life for the Tsar] as it was called originally, and, since the Revolution, *Ivan Susanin*, by Mikhail Ivanovich Glinka (1804–57) was the first durable Russian opera, though it remained unperformed in the West, except Prague, until the 1870s and 1880s. (*Askol'dova mogila* was given in New York in 1868.) Although essentially a dilettante like Verstovsky, Glinka was not only very much more gifted but commanded a much wider and deeper musical culture. Before he embarked on his first opera he had had practical experience with an orchestra, spent a considerable time in Italy and Germany mixing with composers and singers of the first rank, and lived in Berlin for some months studying composition with the distinguished theorist Siegfried Dehn. Above all, he was by then obsessed with 'the idea of writing music in Russian'. He had already, about 1824, employed three folk melodies in a jejune attempt to write a symphony in B flat, and in Berlin in 1834 based other instrumental compositions on folk material; but his music had hitherto been essentially Italianate though not without French influence. The catalyst, suggested by the poet Zhukovsky, was the story of the heroic peasant Ivan Susanin who in 1613 sacrificed his life to save the founder of the Romanov dynasty from the Poles.[164]

Glinka set to work in the most extraordinary way, sometimes composing passages of music to which the librettist—or, rather, librettists for more than one lent a hand—had to fit the text.[165] Vanya's song at the beginning of Act III, 'When they killed my mother', is one instance. An unmistakably Russian idiom is established at once in Act I in the opening choruses of male and female peasants, first separately, then combined. The coloratura element in Antonida's cavatina which follows, though Italian in origin, is subsumed in the general Russianness of her cantilena (Ex. 139) and nothing could be more racily Russian than the chorus of the approaching boatmen with its pizzicato accompaniment suggesting balalaikas. Susanin has made his first entry between the cavatina and the boatmen's chorus to music that begins with, and grows out of, a snatch of actual folk-song which will be echoed by him in the finale of Act IV when he is awakened by the Poles before they murder him (Ex. 140).[166]

Ex. 139

(I gaze into the open country, fix my eyes far off, on my native river.)

---

[164] On the earlier opera on the same subject by Cavos, see Vol. VIII, pp. 530–3. Devoid of jealousy, Cavos championed Glinka's work and conducted the first performance.

[165] The post-Revolution *Susanin* (1939) has an entirely new libretto by S. M. Gorodetsky.

[166] The many, and more subtle, melodic relationships throughout the score—to say nothing of the extensive use of reminiscence-themes—are discussed by David Brown, *Mikhail Glinka: A Biographical and Critical Study* (London, 1974), 115–18. Brown's book, with its copious musical examples, is the best non-Russian study of Glinka.

Ex. 140

(Wedding! There'll be no wedding! One wave comes after another and calamity succeeds calamity.)

Ex. 141

(A lovely bride awaits you, darling. We'll find your father for you and bring him home.)

A *Life for the Tsar* is the earliest Russian opera with no spoken dialogue; Glinka replaced it by brief fragments of recitative quickly flowering into arioso or what he called 'not recitative but characteristic song *non motivé*', the national quality of which is perceptible but hardly definable. The same may be said of Sobinin's love-song in Act IV, a perfect fusion of Italian and Russian elements (Ex. 141; note the motif *x* common to this passage and Ex. 140). In later years Glinka himself became painfully conscious of such vestiges of Italian influence. Most purely Russian is the 5/4 bridal chorus in Act III, most anti-Russian, of course, the polonaise and mazurka rhythms which characterize the Poles. But the drama of *A Life for the Tsar* goes deeper than this crude antithesis. Glinka conceived real characters in real situations. He wishes Vanya's song in Act III to be sung without expression; the boy is singing thoughtlessly to himself as he works. Susanin's great monologue as he waits for the dawn that will bring his death recalls no fewer than six themes heard earlier in association with those he loves and thus cumulatively sums up the hero's whole character.

Verstovsky was not impressed by his rival's work. 'Each kind of music has its own forms, its own limits,' he sourly remarked. 'People don't go to the theatre to pray.'[167] And in his own later operas— *Toska po rodine* [Longing for the Homeland] (1839), on another Zagoskin novel, *Churova dolina* [The Valley of Chur] (1841), and *Gromoboy*, all very inferior to *Askol'dova mogila*—he made no attempt to follow the example set by *A Life for the Tsar*. Nor, for that matter, did Glinka himself in *Ruslan i Lyudmila* (1842). Turning from Russian history to Russian mythology (as seen through Pushkin's playfully ironic spectacles), he set a hopelessly undramatic subject to music more excitingly novel than that of his first opera. The opening scene of the wedding feast with the song of the bard Bayan (Verstovsky's Boyan in *Vadim*), its warm cantilena accompanied by piano and harp imitating the *gusli*, the transparent, slightly chromaticized part-writing, the bright pure orchestral colours highlighted by triangle and cymbals, presents all the essentials other than folk melody of Russian lyrical expression during the next half-century. Folk melody itself is reflected in Finn's ballad in Act II, which Glinka had heard in Finland, and in the choral lullaby when the sleeping Lyudmila is fanned by feathers plucked from the Firebird. And it is hardly too much to say that the later Russian 'oriental' convention is entirely based on such things as the Persian chorus in Act III (Ex. 142) and the *romans* of the Khazar prince Ratmir in Act V (Exx. 143 and 144). The tinting of Ex. 144 with chromatic passing-notes in the harmony illustrates a favourite device of Glinka's. A much more startling element in *Ruslan*, quite as influential as the pseudo-oriental idiom, is the harmonic vocabulary associated with the magical and fantastic. The descending whole-tone

---

[167] 'Avtobiografiya kompozitora A. N. Verstovskogo', *Biryuch petrogradskikh gosudarstvennïkh teatrov* (Petrograd, 1921), 231.

Ex. 142

(You will find with us a swarm of beauties.)

Ex. 143

(She is life to me, she is joy to me! She has returned to me anew my lost youth.)

Ex. 144

(Beauties have loved me, but in vain the lips of the young captives promised me delights.)

Ex. 145

scale of the evil magician Chernomor is familiar from its appearance near the end of the overture, where its nakedness is veiled by the harmony; it is used more daringly in the music of Lyudmila's abduction, entirely in the whole-tone mode (Ex. 145). Glinka makes great play with augmented and diminished triads, simultaneous seconds or sevenths, unrelated chords with a single note in common. In Act IV the processional march of Chernomor and his train and the final vivace of the *lezginka* are *loci classici* of mid-nineteenth-century harmonic daring.

Not everything in *Ruslan* is so original. The Italian *buffo* nature of the cowardly Farlaf's rondo is, of course, intentional. But the chorus of flowers in Act IV and the latter part of the finale of V suggest the influence of *Euryanthe* and *Oberon*. Glinka was always apt to be critical of Weber, but Liszt, who had just heard *Ruslan* at Petersburg, told him, 'You and Weber are like two rivals courting the same woman.'[168]

---

[168] Glinka, *Literaturnoe nasledie Glinki*, Valerian Mikhaylovich Bogdanov-Beryozovsky (ed.) (Leningrad and Moscow, 1952–3), i. 230.

DARGOMÏZHSKY

During the years between *Life for the Tsar* and *Ruslan* a young
friend of Glinka's, Aleksandr Sergeevich Dargomïzhsky (1813–69)
had also been working on an opera which he completed in 1841 or
1842.[169] This was an *Esmeralda* based on Hugo's *Notre-Dame de
Paris* and composed in the first instance to a libretto which Hugo
had prepared for a French woman-composer, Louise Bertin. Instead
of Esmeralda being hanged, Hugo substituted a proclamation of her
innocence by Phébus, who has been mortally wounded by Frollo
and dies in her arms. When Dargomïzhsky's work, for which he
now made his own Russian version, was produced in Moscow in
1847, the censorship imposed further changes: Notre-Dame became
a city hall and Frollo a lay official. The interest of *Esmeralda* is
twofold. Unlike the work of Verstovsky and Glinka it is a true *grand
opéra*, considerably influenced by Halévy's *La Juive* which had been
heard in St Petersburg in 1837, and of course completely un-Russian.
But it is the first opera of a composer who was the inferior of Glinka
as a musician, but was nevertheless to exercise an influence on the
evolution of Russian opera hardly less than Glinka's own. Already
in *Esmeralda* he shows dramatic sense, as in the duet for Phébus and
Frollo in Act III, Scene i, each rival wrapped in his own thoughts
and fears (Ex. 146). He had, of course, models for this in *opera*

Ex. 146

(PHÉBUS: I'm in confusion, suspicious.
FROLLO: Fearful, undecided whether to ruin oneself for love!)

---

[169] The dates in Dargomïzhsky's autobiography, written in 1866, are inaccurate (see Mikhail
Samoylovich Pekelis, *Aleksandr Sergeevich Dargomïzhskiy i ego okruzhenie* (Moscow, 1966–
71), i).

buffa, but before long he was to develop much more subtle powers of characterization and treatment of the Russian language.

POLAND

Between Kurpiński's *Zamek na Czorsztynie* [Czorsztyn Castle] in 1819[170] and the first version of Moniuszko's *Halka* in 1854, the history of Polish opera is a chronicle of very small beer. Kurpiński's protégé Józef Brzowski (1805–88) produced no more than a single one-act work, *Hrabia Weseliński* [Count Merrymaker] (1833). Józef Damse (1789–1852) was much more prolific. Encouraged by Kurpiński, he brought out from 1820 onward a stream of operettas, comedy operas, and melodramas (including two on *The Bride of Lammermoor* and *Kenilworth*), mostly on librettos translated from the French and aiming no higher than pleasing the Warsaw public. To aim higher was to court failure. In 1838 Ignacy Feliks Dobrzyński (1807–67), like Chopin a pupil of Elsner, completed a three-act work *Monbar*, based on K. Van der Velde's novel *Der Flibustier*, which reflects Italian and *grand-opéra* styles, but it had to wait until 1863 for its first performance. Example 147, an excerpt from Donna Maria's aria, greeting the dawn of a spring morning, exemplifies Dobrzyński's not strikingly original talent. The rather older Franciszek Mirecki (1794–1862) had gone to Italy where he spent most of his time from 1816 to 1838 conducting and composing Italian operas, one of which, *Evandro in Pergamo* (Genoa, 1824), had some success. When he returned to his native land he wrote only one opera, the comic two-act *Nocleg w Apeninach* [Night Quarters in the Apennines] (Cracow, 1845), the vocal score was published by Ricordi (Milan, 1850),[171] but this failed to keep it alive.

Ex. 147

(Oh the dawn has broken, the dawn of the sun has broken, the spring morning has begun.)

[170] See Vol. VIII, p. 528.
[171] Mirecki justly claimed in the Preface that it was conceived 'nello stile e nel gusto italiano'.

NON-GERMAN OPERA IN THE HABSBURG EMPIRE

Vernacular opera in Bohemia and Moravia was handicapped by the fact that the official language and language of the upper classes was German and the paramount operatic language Italian. Public performances in Czech were actually forbidden for a time after 1815. However Weigl's *Schweizerfamilie* was performed in a Czech translation at Prague in 1823, *Les Deux Journées* and *Freischütz* in 1824, and *Don Giovanni* in 1825. These seem to have emboldened František Škroup (1801–62), who had taken part in these productions, to try his hand at an original Czech *Singspiel*. This was *Dráteník* [The Tinker], produced in 1826.[172] It is a modest work, without choruses or ballet, but its humour and local colour, the tinker himself singing in Slovak, long kept it alive. Vojtěch's song in Act I bemoaning the happiness he has lost so early (Ex. 148), is typical of the opera's naïve tunefulness, well suited to an anecdote of a young lover, Vojtěch, who changes clothes with a travelling tinker—a part played by the composer himself at the first performance—in order to get access to his sweetheart's house. Škroup's second opera, *Oldřich a Božena* (1828), with the same librettist, J. K. Chmelenský, was a failure, but the composer had a German version prepared and set it to new music as *Udalrich und Božena* (1834). Then came a number of German operas, one of which, *Der Prinz und die Schlange* (1829), was later translated into Czech by Chmelenský. Škroup's third and last Czech work, *Libušin sňatek* [The Marriage of Libuše] (1835, fresh version 1850), also to Chmelenský's text, was more

Ex. 148

(Is my star burning out so soon, that led me into the grove of love? Where I learnt to know the saving joys, where the May of my days began, where the May of my days began!)

172 Vocal score (Prague, 1913; 2nd edn., 1926).

ambitious but a total failure. His most enduring composition was a song, 'Kde domov můj?' [Where is my home?], sung by a blind fiddler in J. K. Tyl's farce, *Fidlovačka* [The Carousel] (1834), popular from the first, introduced in a later version of *Dráteník*, and finally adopted as the Czech national hymn in 1918.

The Hussite theme in Czech history was first turned to operatic account by František Kott (1808–84) in the two-act *Žižkův dub* [Žižka's Oak], produced at Brno as *Žižkas Eiche* in 1841 but in Czech in 1842. The libretto by Václav Klicpera was set again by Jiří Macourek (1815–after 1863) and produced at Prague in 1847, but neither his work nor Kott's was successful enough to get into print.[173]

The history of vernacular opera in the other non-German Habsburg dominions is similar. Nationalist feelings were strongly developing in all of them and national themes were treated in the national languages—at first with little success. German was not the only obstacle; in Slavonic Croatia Hungarian was even more dangerous to national culture and when Croatian opera emerged with the *Ljubav i zloba* [Love and Malice] (Zagreb, 1846) of Vatroslav Lisinski (1819–54), it had a weak champion, an amateur unable to orchestrate his work. In Hungary itself vernacular opera had started earlier. One of the first was József Ruzitska's *Béla futása* [Béla's Flight] (Kolozsvár/Cluj, 1822; Pest, 1826), adapted from a play by Kotzebue dealing with the escape of Béla IV from the Tatars in 1241. The aria of the warrior Kálmán[174] has a national flavour (Ex. 149), and the

Ex. 149

Lassan (slow)

---

[173] One aria from Macourek's setting was published in *Zlatý zpěvník* in 1857.
[174] Complete vocal score in Bence Szabolcsi, *A Concise History of Hungarian Music* (Budapest, 1964), musical appendix, no. XIII (i). This English edition is a somewhat abridged version of the original Hungarian (2nd edn., Budapest, 1955).

(My forefathers [gave many warriors] to this house of sorrow.)

soprano aria 'Hunnia nyög letiporva' [Hungary groans under the yoke] became almost a folk-song. Although the music as a whole alternated between Italian, German, and Hungarian styles, even the foreign ones are sometimes decorated with the ornamental characteristics of *verbunkos*,[175] and it was accepted as genuinely Hungarian, performed all over the country for many years, and revived at Buda as late as 1862.

In the 1840s a whole group of opera composers emerged: Ferenc Erkel (1810-93), György Czászár (1813-50), Károly Thern (1817-86), Ferenc Doppler (1821-83). Thern's *Gizul* (1841) and *Tihany ostroma* [Siege of Tilhan] (1845), Czászár's *A kunok* [The Cumanians] (1848), and Doppler's *Benyovszky*, yet another Kotzebue opera (1847), and *Ilka* (1849) had only temporary success. Erkel's first opera, *Báthori Mária* (1840), marked him as an outstanding talent,

---

175 From the German *Werbung* [recruitment], the gypsy-style dance music used by the Imperial officers to attract recruits.

Ex. 150

Ex. 151

Ah mily va-dul szá-guld-ja át lel-ke-met_ a_ fé-le-lem!

Vá-rat-la-nul el-ra-ga-dák keb-lem-ről_ két_ gyer-me-kem.__

(Ah, how fiercely fear runs through my heart! My two children suddenly torn from my arms.)

Ex. 152

and his second, *Hunyadi László* (1844), is the first real masterpiece of Hungarian opera. Ladislas Hunyadi, brother of Matthias Corvinus, executed as the result of a palace intrigue in 1457, was a memorable historical figure popularly transfigured into a national hero and the national note is sounded at the very beginning of the overture when a trumpet plays (Ex. 150), a theme associated throughout the work with the patriotic Hunyadi family in general. Much of the music is undeniably Italianate: Erzsébet's second big coloratura aria in Act II, inserted in 1850, breaks into the *verbunkos* idiom (Exx. 151 and 152). The national strain is particularly strong in the third act, for instance in the wedding chorus in the second scene; and the final chorus of Act I, 'Meghalt a cselszövő' [The Plotter is Dead], was popularly adopted as a revolutionary song in 1848. Of the less national passages the finest is the scene of László V's soon-to-be-broken oath at the end of Act II. Erkel's third opera, *Bánk Bán* [The Palatine Bánk], composed in 1852, was suppressed owing to the political climate and performed only in 1861 when the absolutist monarchy was beginning to make concessions.

(f) BRITAIN AND THE UNITED STATES

By NICHOLAS TEMPERLEY

THE 1830s witnessed a determined and not unsuccessful effort to launch a serious school of English Romantic opera. In 1830 English opera was perhaps at the lowest point in its uneven history. Between 1826 and 1834, as the critic George Hogarth wrote in 1838, 'no English composer produced a single musical piece of the smallest importance ... and the stage was supplied with importations from abroad'.[176] Thus the principal 'English' theatres, Drury Lane and Covent Garden, devoted their energies to garbled versions of foreign operas, while the King's Theatre, which alone attracted the wealth and prestige of aristocratic audiences,[177] was strictly confined to opera in Italian.

The event which sparked the revival was the opening of the rebuilt Lyceum Theatre, London, in 1834 as the English Opera House. The lessee, S. J. Arnold, was the son of the eighteenth-century composer[178] and was himself a dramatist, who had since 1809 used the old Lyceum theatre for the production of burlettas, melodramas, 'musical dramas' (plays with songs and incidental music), and the like. Now, in the summer of 1834, he opened the new theatre for 'the representation of English operas and the encouragement of indigenous musical talent', and it was soon apparent that there was indeed a fund of indigenous musical talent waiting for just such an opportunity. The composers who played the chief part in establishing English Romantic opera were John Barnett (1802–90), Edward James Loder (1813–65), Michael William Balfe (1808–70), and William Vincent Wallace (1812–65). Benedict and Macfarren, though of similar age, did their most important work after the mid-century, and so will be considered in Chapter VI.

BISHOP

The operatic tradition inherited from the previous generation, represented chiefly by the works of Henry Bishop (1786–1855), was one in which the music was still to a great extent episodic. Most,

---

[176] *Memoirs of the Musical Drama* (London, 1838), ii. 456.
[177] See Nicholas Temperley, 'The English Romantic Opera', *Victorian Studies*, 9 (1966), 294 n.
[178] See Vol. VII, pp. 263–5.

but not all, of the action took place in spoken dialogue. Each of the three acts would include several musical numbers, such as strophic ballads, duets, glees, choruses, or instrumental pieces; there would be one or two full-scale arias, or grand scenas incorporating recitative, or *mélodrames*;[179] and there was always a full-length overture, and a short musical finale to each act. Occasionally the musical numbers might be quite ambitious—for instance, the Act II finale of Bishop's *Cortez* (1823), depicting, in several movements, a wild scene of human sacrifice interrupted before its consummation. In *Clari* (1823) Bishop attempted to unify his work by using the ballad 'Home, sweet home' as a sort of leitmotif, but the experiment did not catch on. What was lacking was any cumulative musico-dramatic effect; and the style of Bishop's music was deferential and undemanding, hardly attempting to sweep the audience along by its emotional force. Bishop's operas generally had some principal characters who did not sing at all: the only exception was *Aladdin* (1826).[180]

The one precursor of the new style was Weber's *Oberon* (1826), which was performed at Covent Garden during the closing months of the composer's life, and made a profound impression on the English public, already greatly excited by English adaptations of *Der Freischütz* that had appeared in 1824. The *Oberon* libretto by James Planché was entirely typical of its time and place, but Weber's richly Romantic score had shown how much emotional depth music could add even to a spoken drama.

BARNETT AND LODER

Barnett's *The Mountain Sylph* (1834), which was the most successful of the new works commissioned by Arnold for his first season, is strongly influenced by both *Freischütz* and *Oberon*. Based on the ballet *La Sylphide*, it concerns interactions between mortals and supernatural beings, and has several Weberian motifs which appear in the overture and reappear at telling moments later on: most notable is the opening theme, heard over diminished sevenths tremolando. The music of the two acts is still broken by spoken dialogue,[181] but it includes several connected scenes in which action,

---

[179] A *mélodrame* was an instrumental number accompanying action or dialogue, whereas a *melodrama* was a spoken play with some musical numbers.

[180] See Bruce Carr, 'Theatre Music: 1800–1834' in Nicholas Temperley (ed.), *Music in Britain: The Romantic Age 1800–1914* (London, 1981), 292–3.

[181] Until recently it was thought that *The Mountain Sylph* was sung throughout, but this notion was dispelled by Bruce Carr in 'The First All-sung English 19th-century Opera', *Musical Times*, 115 (1974), 125–6. According to an 'Advertisement' prefacing the published vocal score, Barnett first wrote the work as a 'musical drama' for the Victoria Theatre, which he then 'heightened' into a 'romantic grand opera'.

conflict, and character development are carried on with the full
collaboration of music. Most of these scenes belong to types well
established in continental opera—there is a fortune-telling scene, a
marriage contract, an invocation scene (the Act I finale), and so on.
A certain British colouring is given by occasional pentatonicism, for
instance in the unison melody of the Act II finale: this suits the
setting of the drama, which is in the Western Isles of Scotland. It
can hardly be said that any of the characters has much depth. But
there is a passionate warmth and vehemence about some of Barnett's
music, for instance the song 'Oh! no, 'twas no deceptive spell' (Ex.
153), that goes well beyond anything achieved by Bishop, and does
indeed herald a new era for English opera.

Ex. 153

A month before *The Mountain Sylph*, Loder's *Nourjahad* was
produced at the English Opera House, so becoming, in Macfarren's
words, 'the inaugural work of the institution of modern English
Opera'. Barnett never again approached the heights he had reached
in *The Mountain Sylph*, but Loder went on to write two more full-scale
operas, *The Night Dancers* (Princess's, London, 1846) and *Raymond
and Agnes* (Theatre Royal, Manchester, 1855). *The Night Dancers* is
another fairy opera—it is a version by George Soane of the story
better known from the ballet *Giselle*—and indeed it is the 'fairy'

parts of the work, those most influenced by *Oberon*, that are the most delightful. Many of the ballads and waltz songs are of the trite, conventional sort in which Loder was all too fluent, but an exception must be made for the beautiful serenade, 'Wake, my love, all life is stirring';[182] here Loder has captured some of the same passionate musical language that stirred Barnett at his best.

The fairy conventions of the early Victorian period have unfortunately succumbed to the satire of *Iolanthe*, and are hardly acceptable now unless allied to the music of a Weber or a Mendelssohn. In *Raymond and Agnes* Loder found a plot of more enduring value, however dated the style of Edward Fitzball's verse. Beneath the Gothic and supernatural overtones, it is a classic conflict between a middle-aged guardian (the Baron) and a young lover (Raymond) for control of the heroine; and the centrepiece is a long scene for the two male characters, which builds dramatic tension to a degree unique in English opera of the nineteenth century. In a full twenty minutes of compelling music, the men move steadily from chilly politeness, through mutual suspicion and dismay, to a quarrel of mounting intensity. At last Raymond recognizes the Baron as his father's murderer, the two men fight, and a chorus rushes on stage to a unison tune of positively Verdian energy (Ex. 154). The opera also boasts a beautiful terzetto in the Act I finale, a fine bass aria, and a superb sleep-walking scene with a quintet that has been compared with the quartet 'Mir ist so wunderbar' from *Fidelio*.[183] There are also—in addition to the normal quota of spoken dialogue, insipid ballads, and predictable choruses—several songs that successfully invoke the appropriate Gothic mood of fear and horror.

Ex. 154

BALFE

The English opera movement was soon taken up by other theatres,

[182] Reprinted in *Musica Britannica*, xliii. 92.
[183] See Michael Hurd, 'Opera: 1834–1865', in Temperley (ed.), *Music in Britain*, p. 323 (an excerpt from the quintet appears on pp. 324–7).

and in 1835 Balfe's first opera, *The Siege of Rochelle*, originally intended for the English Opera House, came out at Drury Lane. Balfe was the most successful of this group of composers, producing some two dozen English operas for London, several of which became popular all over the Western world, and also winning commissions from Trieste, from Vienna, from the Paris Opéra and Opéra-Comique, and even from Her Majesty's (formerly the King's) Theatre, London, which produced his Italian opera *Falstaff* in 1838.

Balfe was Irish by birth and upbringing, and was a successful baritone singer; in his youth he spent several years in Italy. For all these reasons, perhaps, he was blessed with a greater flow of spontaneous melody than any of his rivals, and this, as almost all commentators agree, is the strongest quality of his operas. He knew how to make the most of his singers—and the success of his second opera, *The Maid of Artois* (Drury Lane, 1836), was in very large measure due to the singing of Maria Malibran. After a series of more moderate successes, an abortive attempt to establish his own English opera company, and a foray to Paris, Balfe brought out his masterpiece, *The Bohemian Girl*, at Drury Lane in 1843. This work was so well and so universally known to the English-speaking public for the next two generations that at last it seemed that opera in English had won a place in popular esteem beside the Italian variety. It was still in the repertoire during the first three decades of the present century.

The Bohemian Girl, which shares a plot with Weber's *Preciosa*, is about noblemen and gipsies; the love between hero (Thaddeus) and heroine (Arline) can only be brought to a happy resolution when Arline's father, Count Arnheim, learns that Thaddeus is not a gipsy but a Polish gentleman (albeit a rebel) in disguise. An interval of twelve years separates the first two acts. The basic plan of Alfred Bunn's libretto is quite orthodox: there is still spoken dialogue,[184] and most of the musical numbers are self-contained and episodic, but there are substantial connected introductions as well as finales to each of the three acts. Without a doubt, the great pillars of the opera's unprecedented fame are the two principal tunes, the chorus 'In the gipsy's life you read', and Arline's ballad, 'I dreamt that I dwelt in marble halls'.[185] Both are used in the overture; 'In the gipsy's life' recurs many times as a leitmotif in the Bishop manner.

---

[184] Of Balfe's operas only *Catherine Grey* (1837) and *The Daughter of St Mark* (1844) are all-sung. See Carr, 'The First All-sung English 19th-century Opera'.

[185] For a detailed discussion of this song, see Nicholas Temperley, 'Ballroom and Drawing-room Music', in Temperley (ed.), *Music in Britain*, p. 126.

There is a third song of almost equal popularity, Thaddeus's 'When other lips and other hearts'.[186] Balfe's tunes, simply constructed and accompanied, show his understanding of the human voice, for they allow the singer to exercise sway over the audience's feelings without competition. He is also very much at home in the love duets. In other parts of the opera—in the scenas, concerted numbers, instrumental movements—Balfe is a competent craftsman, no more. But he does quite as well as Donizetti does in many recently revived works, and provides just as much tuneful music. He went on to write another half-dozen successful operas for the Pyne-Harrison Company (1857-64); they show little or no development of style or technique.

WALLACE

Wallace was also an Irishman, but his career was very different from Balfe's. He was first a pianist, second a violinist. He spent much of his youth in adventures that took him as far afield as Australia and Chile; he made his name in New York and Holland before he at last reached London, and his first opera, *Maritana* (Drury Lane, 1845), was by far the most successful of the six he produced—indeed for a time it was a rival to *The Bohemian Girl*. *Maritana* is a *macho* story about male honour and heroism set in Spain. The most popular song from it is not an amorous or nostalgic ballad, but Don Cesar's blustering 'Yes! let me like a soldier fall'. In plan it follows the usual pattern. Apart from the ballads the general style is more Italianate than Balfe's, but Wallace added a more unusual element of Spanish colouring, possibly derived from his experiences in Latin America. This is most evident in the romance 'It was a knight' (Ex. 155), anticipated in the overture, and the gipsy chorus 'Pretty Gitana'. Such use of harmonic colouring of the flamenco type goes far beyond anything to be found in contemporary operas set in Spain, such as *La favorita*, *Ernani*, or *Don Pasquale*, and it faintly heralds the spirit of *Carmen*. Wallace is far more

---

[186] Sims Reeves wrote, in *My Jubilee, or, Fifty Years of Artistic Life* (London 1889), of one of Thaddeus's songs in *The Bohemian Girl*: 'The words of Mr. Bunn's extraordinary poetical effusion run literally as follows:

> When the fair land of Poland was ploughed by the hoof
>   Of the ruthless invader; when Might
> With steel to her bosom and flame to her roof,
>   Completed the triumph o'er Right, etc.

. . . It was bad enough to have a pause after the word "hoof", which thus became separated from the words "ruthless invader"; but it was intolerable that the nominative "Might" should be separated from its verb by drums and trumpets.' (As a matter of fact the score shows no pause after 'hoof', but the trumpets and drums after 'Might' are actual.)

Ex. 155

ambitious than Balfe in his finales. The Act I finale is based on a tune which is first heard as a quiet prayer ('Angels that around us hover') and then rises to a climax à la Meyerbeer—an innovation as far as English opera was concerned.

Two of Wallace's later operas, *Lurline* (composed 1848, produced Covent Garden, 1860) and *The Amber Witch* (Her Majesty's 1861), continue the trend of building large-scale scenes in the French manner; one also detects a new Mendelssohnian flavour, especially in some of the instrumental music (the F sharp minor tune from the overture to *Lurline*, for example). One of the best songs of Victorian opera also occurs in *Lurline*, the richly accompanied 'Sweet form that in my dreamy gaze'.

These four composers—Barnett, Loder, Balfe, and Wallace— championed the cause of serious opera in English, but they did little to make their operas English in character, apart from continuing to incorporate the traditional ballads, glees, and dialogue. Their plots were usually taken from continental sources and were set in foreign lands or in fairyland; they were content to set execrable verse, and, often enough, paid little attention to verbal accent. They were not worried by the falsity and irrelevance of the situations and emotions portrayed in the stories they set. The feeling in their music, however, is strong and convincing, especially in songs of love. As Bernard Shaw wrote after hearing a revival of *Lurline*, 'there are several moments in the opera in which the string of hackneyed and trivial shop ballad stuff rises into melody that surges with genuine emotion'.[187] Perhaps it should be seen as a release of the pent-up feelings in many a Victorian breast, at a time when direct expression of love was so painfully circumscribed. All four of these composers relied primarily on the intuitive, emotional values of their music, unlike their contemporary George Macfarren.

THE UNITED STATES

The operatic stage in the United States in this period continued to be almost wholly dependent on imports from London, both of indigenous English operas and of continental works that had already appeared on the London stage. After the visit of the Garcia troupe to New York in 1825, there was a growing taste for Italian opera in fashionable circles. With such slender foundations the difficulties of producing an 'American' serious opera were vastly greater even than those faced by composers in Britain.

The first fully-fledged opera ('grand opera' as it was usually termed in America) actually composed in the United States is believed to have been *Ahmed al Ramel* by Charles Edward Horn (1786-1849), an English composer who had produced a score of operas for the London stage between 1810 and 1830. It was produced at the New York National Theatre on 12 October 1840, with a libretto by H. J. Finn after Washington Irving's *Tales of the Alhambra*, but unhappily the music has not survived.

Only one 'grand opera' by an American-born composer is known to have been produced before 1850: *Leonora*, by William Henry Fry (1813-1864), first performed at the Chestnut Street Theatre, Philadelphia, on 4 June 1845. It ran for twelve nights. This was certainly a historical landmark. But, despite the composer's later expressed views of musical nationalism, there is nothing very American about *Leonora*. It is based on an English novel set in France, Bulwer-Lytton's *The Lady of Lyons*, and the music is

---

[187] *London Music in 1888-89 as heard by Corno di Bassetto* (London, 1937), 351.

thoroughly Italian in style: a contemporary critic called it 'a study in the school of Bellini'.[188] There is little sign even of the English ballad, which had been adopted by many American composers. What is remarkable, however, is the degree of technical skill that Fry displays in this ambitious score.[189] His second opera, *Esmeralda* (after Hugo's *Notre Dame de Paris*), was produced at Philadelphia in 1864.

On the whole, opera was still an alien growth in the Anglo-Saxon cultures; they had their own flourishing forms of theatre in which music was only a perfunctory element. Strong and distinctive English-language opera came only with the rise of musical nationalism, which was a latecomer in both Britain and the United States.

[188] Gilbert Chase, *America's Music* (New York, 1955), 331.
[189] For a study of this opera, see K. E. Gombert, ' "Leonora" by William Henry Fry and "Rip Van Winkle" by George Frederick Bristow' (Ph.D. Diss., Ball State University, 1977).

IV

ROMANTIC PIANO MUSIC: 1830–1850

By WILLI KAHL

THE PIANO OF THE 1830s

WHEN in February 1837 Ignaz Moscheles gave three piano recitals in London, his programmes included not only recent piano music but works by Domenico Scarlatti and his contemporaries, which he performed on a 1771 harpsichord from the Schudi workshops placed at his disposal especially for these concerts by the firm of Broadwood. This was probably the first time in the nineteenth century that the harpsichord was introduced into the concert hall in the role of 'historical' instrument. In the course of the preceding decades the *Hammerflügel* had undergone structural improvements which naturally influenced performing technique and composition. One of these was the repetition mechanism invented by Sebastien Erard and patented in London in 1808, followed in 1821 by his double escapement which permitted the same note to be struck several times in rapid succession. A most important step towards strengthening the structure of the *Hammerflügel,* and one which opened up many new possibilities in the field of dynamics, was the introduction, from America where it was patented in 1825, of the iron frame cast in a single piece which gradually superseded the older wooden frame, and the overstringing of the bass strings. Of far-reaching effect on the styles of piano music in these decades were the opposing influences on the one hand of the so-called Viennese school and on the other of English technical progress which played an increasingly incisive role in piano manufacture after 1800. All other types of mechanism developed during this time are variants of these two: the English mechanism, whose deeper key action gave correspondingly fuller tone, enabling the pianist to combine a singing melodic line with a sonorous mobile accompaniment; and the Viennese action, which, though it produced a thinner tone, was better suited to performing passages of a sparkling, rippling nature by virtue of its shallower key movement, which necessitated a lighter touch. The effects of these contrasting actions on piano style during the first half of the century are revealed by comparison of Field's nocturnes, and later those of Chopin, with Hummel's style of playing and writing, which was entirely based on the Mozartian tradition.

Among the attempts made towards establishing the *Hammerklavier* as a serious competitor to the harpsichord and clavichord, one of the most interesting was the introduction of such devices as register stops.[1]

These modifications, which reached a climax in the first two decades after 1800, were still in evidence after 1830, though only the usual three pedals have survived, owing undoubtedly to a reaction against a superabundance of devices which soon set in. The great piano teachers of those years, in particular Czerny, Hummel, and Moscheles disliked them on the grounds that the forte, piano, and una corda pedals were all that was necessary. Nevertheless the demand for pianos with built-in modifications persisted; a list of the patents taken out for such instruments between 1801 and 1851 in Europe, the United States, and Canada shows that no fewer than twenty-three were applied for after 1830.[2] All the same, they made little or no impact on composition.

THE CRISIS OF THE SONATA

Even a brief survey of the keyboard music written between 1830 and 1850 shows that the relationships between the various genres had altered fundamentally since Classical times. With Mendelssohn single-movement forms predominate. But the development of the one-movement piano piece into a musical genre did not begin in 1830. The ground had already been prepared, particularly in the second decade of the new century: one-movement piano pieces started to take shape as forms in their own right and appeared in ever increasing numbers, a process which accelerated after 1830. In these circumstances the fate of the post-Beethoven piano sonata as the epitome of the cyclic form in solo piano music of the Classical era was soon decided. Schubert still patterned his sonatas on those of Beethoven and produced twenty-one, some completed, others not. With Weber's sonatas, however, which were written between 1812 and 1822, the whole aspect of the genre changed.[3] The same change

---

[1] On the mechanical development of the piano see, for instance, Rosamund Harding, *The Pianoforte* (Cambridge, 1933), and Ernest Closson, *Histoire du piano* (Brussels, 1944; trans. Delano Ames, London, 1947).

[2] Harding, *Pianoforte*, pp. 147–50.

[3] Walter Georgii, *Karl Maria von Weber als Klavierkomponist* (Leipzig, 1914), 16–27; William S. Newman, *The Sonata since Beethoven* (Chapel Hill, 1969), 249 ff. On Weber and his longer-lived contemporaries, Cramer (1771–1858), Kalkbrenner (1785–1849), Czerny (1791–1857), and Moscheles (1794–1870), see Vol. VIII, pp. 354–5.

is visible in Mendelssohn if the three early sonatas are set against the fifty *Lieder ohne Worte*, while Schumann and Chopin produced no more than three piano sonatas each. In this context it is interesting to note what Schumann said in 1839 with reference to the piano sonatas of his contemporaries:

Most sonatas of this type should be regarded as kinds of academic exercise, as studies in form; they are scarcely products of strong inner impulse. But if the older composers no longer write them, then they must likewise have good reasons for not doing so.

Hummel zealously trod in Mozart's footsteps but left only one sonata, the F sharp minor, that will survive, while Beethoven's chief disciple was Franz Schubert, who strove to break new ground, and succeeded. Ries[4] worked too hastily, Berger,[5] like Onslow,[6] was incapable of working out the full implications of his occasional flashes of inspiration. Most fluent and fiery of all was Karl Maria von Weber, who evolved his own style and is in turn influencing several younger composers. This is how the sonata stood about ten years ago, and the situation has not changed. A few fine but isolated examples of the genre will certainly emerge from time to time— some have already done so. On the whole it seems as though, as a form, the sonata has run its course, and this is in the nature of things; instead of a century of repetitions we should turn our thoughts to something new. By all means write sonatas or fantasies—what's in a name!—but don't forget the music, and your own genius will do the rest.[7]

Already, eight years before, the 18-year-old Wagner had in two long unknown works explored the divergent paths large-scale piano composition might follow. In 1831 he composed a quite respectable Sonata in A,[8] following dutifully in the steps of Beethoven and even demonstrating his knowledge of Op. 110 and Op. 111. Then in November of the same year he wrote a *Fantasie* in F sharp minor,[9] in which, beside more echoes of Beethoven, appear passages foreshadowing the idiom of the mature Wagner (Ex. 156). In 1833 Mendelssohn composed a *Sonate écossaise*, also in F sharp minor, Op. 28, which (with the uncertainty typical of the period) he restyled *Phantasie* before publishing it. But with Wagner there was no uncertainty. His *Fantasie* pointed decidedly in another direction, his own true way, the way of largely instrumental drama.

---

[4] Newman, *Sonata*, pp. 170 ff.
[5] Ibid., pp. 454–5.
[6] Ibid., pp. 475–7.
[7] *Neue Zeitschrift für Musik* 11/1 (1839), 134; Robert Schumann, *Gesammelte Schriften über Musik und Musiker*, ed. Martin Kreisig (5th edn.; Leipzig, 1914), i. 395.
[8] First published by Otto Daube, '*Ich schreibe keine Symphonien mehr*' (Cologne, 1960), 230–57. Also in *Richard Wagner: Sämtliche Werke*, ed. Carl Dahlhaus, xix (Mainz, 1970).
[9] Leipzig, 1905; also in *Wagner: Sämtliche Werke*, ed. Dahlhaus.

Ex. 156

Any further evolution of the sonata after Beethoven could only proceed from the quite different conception of form held by the succeeding generation, one quite opposed to the Classical ideal.[10] 'In contrast to Beethoven, the Romantic composer proceeds in a way that is associative rather than functional.'[11] This associative attitude, closely allied to a basic lyricism, permeates the whole range of instrumental music of that time; themes typical of the *Lied ohne Worte* are frequently introduced even in 'allegro' movements[12] and are not easily accommodated in the formal structure of a sonata in the Classical tradition. Thus traits emerged which had the effect of radically modifying the traditional concept of sonata form. Similar characteristics occur in Romantic chamber music: 'reversal of the tensional relationship between theme and counter-theme', 'division of thematic energy between theme and counter-theme',[13] resulting in an episodic type of sonata, breakup of the traditional norm of four movements by introduction of new formal elements such as the canzonetta or intermezzo, which often disrupt the sonata sense.

These diverse alterations eventually affected the formal cycle as a whole, by reversing the usual order of movements or by adding to them. Beethoven's pupil Carl Czerny had produced a five-movement sonata, Op. 7, in 1820. His Op. 124 (1827) expands to seven

[10] Gustav Becking, 'Zur musikalischen Romantik', *Deutsche Vierteljahrschrift für Literaturwissenschaft und Geistesgeschichte*, ii (1924), 581–615.

[11] Arnold Schmitz, *Das romantische Beethovenbild* (Berlin and Bonn, 1927), 114.

[12] Ibid., pp. 124–7.

[13] See Hans Mersmann, 'Sonaten Form in der romantischen Kammermusik', in Walter Lott, Helmuth Osthoff, and Werner Wolffheim (eds.), *Musikwissenschaftliche Beiträge: Festschrift für Johannes Wolf* (Berlin, 1929), 112–17.

movements, but his Op. 788 for four hands (1847) is a one-movement work 'in the style of Domenico Scarlatti'. To this haphazard process of evolution Carl Loewe (1796–1869) made a unique contribution with his E major Sonata, Op. 16 (1829), the second movement of which introduces *ad libitum* tenor and soprano voices singing a French romance, 'Toujours je te serai fidèle'.[14] Loewe styled his Op. 47 (comp. 1824; pub. 1835) 'Tondichtung in Sonatenform, Le Printemps',[15] and his *Zigeunersonate*, Op. 107 (1847), has five movements, each with a title.[16]

SCHUMANN'S SONATAS

The extent to which the piano sonata had declined as a commercial proposition is perhaps best illustrated by the position in which Robert Schumann (1810–56) found himself, when, in 1836, he offered his F minor, Op. 14, to the Viennese publisher Haslinger in its original five-movement form with two scherzos. Haslinger insisted that it should be described as a 'Concert sans orchestre' (a good selling title in that golden age of the virtuoso concerto) and that the two scherzos should be omitted. When the second edition was brought out in 1853, the second Scherzo was restored, now as the second instead of the fourth movement,[17] and the four-movement piece appears, as it did in the third edition (1862), as 'Troisième grande sonate'.[18] It is a personal confession dating from the time of the composer's unhappy courtship of Clara Wieck and the variation movement is based on an Andantino composed by her.

Despite disruptive tendencies which threaten the Classical form, Schumann's sonatas do convey a sense of unity. In the F minor Clara's variation theme provides the material and Walter Georgii has demonstrated[19] the subtle interrelationship of motifs in the definitive form (1839) of the G minor Sonata, Op. 22, begun in 1830.[20] See Ex. 157 from the first movement, Ex. 158 from the second, and Ex. 159 from the fourth.

---

[14] See Paul Egert, *Die Klaviersonate im Zeitalter der Romantik* (Berlin, 1934), 134–6. On Loewe's sonatas in general, see also Newman, *Sonata*, pp. 282–6.

[15] See Egert, *Die Klaviersonate*, pp. 132–4.

[16] Ibid., p. 138.

[17] The original first Scherzo was published separately in 1866 and later included in the Supplementary Volume of the *Gesamtausgabe* in 1893.

[18] For the whole complicated history of the work, see Linda Correll Roesner, 'The Autograph of Schumann's Piano Sonata in F minor, Opus 14', *Musical Quarterly*, 61 (1975), 98.

[19] *Klaviermusik* (3rd edn.; Zurich and Freiburg im Breisgau, 1956), 308–9.

[20] On the various operations in which Schumann refashioned the movement, see Linda Correll Roesner, 'Schumann's Revisions in the First Movement of the Piano Sonata in G minor, Op. 22', *19th-century Music*, 1 (1977–8), 97.

Ex. 157

Ex. 158   Ex. 159

Schumann's method of constructing even a first movement suggests the assembling of a mosaic, and his sonatas as wholes are assembled partly from independent pieces. The F sharp minor, Op. 11 (1832–5) introduces new types of movement. The first began its existence as a fandango, *Rhapsodie pour le piano*,[21] which he thought of publishing in 1832 as Op. 4; the second Trio of the Scherzo is a gently ironic polonaise, marked 'Alla burla, ma pomposo', though he also labels it 'Intermezzo' as if to emphasize still further the presence of an intruder among the sonata movements. The Trio ends with an unbarred recitative-like passage marked 'quasi oboe'. It is not so much a traditional scherzo trio as a kind of 'characteristic piece' disrupting the conventional structure.

As might be expected, Schumann's sonatas also offer examples of the *Lied ohne Worte* style which so strongly influenced the instrumental works of the Romantic composers. The slow movements of Op. 11 and Op. 22 have very decided affinities with the Lied, being indeed based on actual songs: the Aria of the F sharp minor Sonata goes back to Schumann's song 'An Anna' (1828), while the Andantino of the G minor is a transcription of another song, 'Im Herbste', written in the same year.

[21] Facsimile of the autograph of the first page is in Hermann Abert, *Robert Schumann* (Berlin, 1903), 57.

SCHUMANN'S C MAJOR *PHANTASIE*

Schumann might well have published his F sharp minor Sonata as a *fantasie*, as Mendelssohn had done; he took this step with his Op. 17, written in 1836. Its earlier titles, *Grosse Sonate für Beethoven* and *Obolen auf Beethovens Monument*, are explained by the fact that it was intended as a contribution to an appeal for funds to erect a Beethoven monument at Bonn. The link with Beethoven must have made the description of the three movements as a 'sonata' seem appropriate, but the original titles of the movements—'Ruins', 'Trophies' (later 'Triumphal Arch'), and 'Palms' (later 'Constellation')—are characteristic of the poetic language so dear to the romantic composer. However, when the work was published in 1839, Schumann entitled it simply *Phantasie* and replaced the separate movement headings with a 'Motto' by Friedrich Schlegel for the whole work:

> Durch alle Töne tönet
> Im bunten Erdentraum
> Ein leiser Ton gezogen
> Für den, der heimlich lauschet.

The *Phantasie* also demonstrates the originality of Schumann's piano style: for instance, the increased sonority obtained by full chords anticipating the bass beat as in the middle movement, the bold use of the pedal, and the intricate interplay of rhythms.

Until the advent of this work by Schumann the connection of the keyboard fantasia with the sonata is more or less clear. When Beethoven described each of the two sonatas of Op. 27 as 'quasi una Fantasia' this only referred to irregularity in the disposition of the movements (which recurs in other of his sonatas). And when Schubert varies the conventional sonata cycle, as in the *Fantaisie* Op. 15 (the 'Wanderer' Fantasia), and the four-hand *Phantasie*, Op. 103, he still preserves its basic shape. As we have seen, Mendelssohn's Op. 28 was originally entitled *Sonate écossaise*; apart from one or two improvisatorial features in the Andante first movement, the free reversal of the movements approximates to what Beethoven intended to express by the phrase 'quasi una Fantasia'. With Schumann it was different.

SCHUMANN AND THE VARIATION PRINCIPLE

While the production of piano sonatas declined steadily after 1830 and the small-scale single piano piece proliferated beyond measure, new cyclic genres were coming into being. Single piano pieces could be linked together superficially, like mosaics, to form collective wholes with no inner connection, but they could also form planned structures, often under the influence of poetic concepts. As well as this, of course, there were the traditional sets of variations based on purely musical ideas,[22] to say nothing of arrangements of songs and fantasias on operatic melodies, which were at the height of their popularity at this time.

Schumann's piano music is rich in examples of the variation principle.[23] His first set, Op. 1 (1830), dedicated to a semi-fictitious 'Pauline, Comtesse d'Abegg', appears at a superficial glance to follow absolutely the traditions of the genre. The models for the variation technique—even in many details—are obvious (Weber, Hummel, Moscheles, as well as Beethoven),[24] but there are already signs of a new element, based on a complete change in the whole concept of thematicism. For Schumann the theme was no longer to be varied as a whole; instead, motifs were extracted from it and plastically remoulded. Thus emerged what has been called the *Gefühls-* or *Fantasievariation*,[25] whose inner connection, according to Schumann himself, required 'poetic completeness'.[26] Thus the theme of the ABEGG variations is not first and foremost a musical structure but a name symbol with implications reaching beyond the series of notes A, B, E, G, G, the nucleus of a 'poetic completeness'.

Several other sets of piano variations from this early period were considered unworthy of publication: on an original theme in G (1831–2); on the Allegretto of Beethoven's Seventh Symphony (1832),[27] from which one variation was published in 1854 as Op. 124, No. 2; on Schubert's so-called *Sehnsuchtswalzer* (1833), and on Chopin's Nocturne, Op. 15, No. 3, (1834).[28] The theme of the next set to be published, *Impromptus sur une romance de Clara Wieck*, Op. 5 (1833),[29] was borrowed from the *Romance variée*, Op. 3, of

[22] On Romantic variations in general, see Martin Friedland, *Zeitstil und Persönlichkeitsstil in den Variationenwerken der musikalischen Romantik* (Leipzig, 1930); Robert U. Nelson, *The Technique of Variation* (Berkeley and Los Angeles, 1948), Joseph Müller-Blattau, *Gestaltung-Umgestaltung: Studien zur Geschichte der musikalischen Variation* (Stuttgart, 1950).

[23] See Werner Schwarz, *Robert Schumann und die Variation* (Kassel, 1932).

[24] See Wolfgang Gertler, *Robert Schumann in seinen frühen Klavierwerken* (Wolfenbüttel and Berlin, 1931), 66–7.

[25] Müller-Blattau, *Gestaltung-Umgestaltung*, p. 57.

[26] Schwarz, *Robert Schumann*, p. 21.

[27] Ed. Robert Münster, with Schumann's additional variations (Munich, 1976). Kathleen Dale quotes the theme of the G major set, 'The Piano Music', in Gerald Abraham (ed.), Schumann: A Symposium (London, 1952), 19.

[28] The second Chopin variation was published in Wolfgang Boetticher, *Robert Schumann: Einführung in Persönlichkeit und Werk* (Berlin, 1941), 588.

[29] A revised edition, omitting two variations but including a new one, appeared in 1850.

Schumann's future wife. The bass—announced first as in Beethoven's *Eroica* set, Op. 35, then presented with the theme—figures in subsequent variations, which are thus a new version of the older type of ostinato variation, hardly impromptus. The work ends like Beethoven's Op. 35 with a fugue, though it is not isolated but framed within a prelude and postlude which again refer to the theme. But all these earlier works are completely overshadowed by one based on a theme by an amateur flautist, Baron von Fricken, and successively thought of as *Zwölf Davidsbündler Etuden*, *Etuden im Orchester Character*, *von Florestan und Eusebius* (differing projections of his own character), and *Études symphoniques* which in the second edition (1852) became *Études en formes de variations*. As with Op. 5, this second edition was marked by alterations and additions, and in 1893 Brahms published five more variations in *Robert Schumanns Werke: Supplementband*. As the titles show, Schumann was still deliberately employing the variation principle to combine two kinds of 'study' in compositional technique and in pianistic technique.

More numerous than these variations on purely musical themes—to which should be added the *Andante und Variationen* for two pianos, Op. 46 (1843)—are the poetic cycles in which the musical ideas are much more freely varied.[30] Even one group of sketches for *Papillons*, Op. 2, written between 1829 and 1832, was headed 'Variationen', though the finished work shows little or no trace of musical-variation technique. Its unity derives from its poetic background, the ball scene, 'Larventanz', which is the penultimate chapter of the *Flegeljahre* of Jean-Paul Richter, whom Schumann greatly admired.[31] In his copy of the novel Schumann marked in the margin the passages that have musical counterparts in *Papillons*.[32] The cycle is a series of miniatures, teeming with imagery; incidentally, some of the material was adapted from the four-hand *Polonaises* of 1828.[33]

The letter symbolism of the ABEGG variations, translated into notes, was a pretext rather than a theme for variations. But in *Carnaval: Scènes mignonnes sur quatre notes*, Op. 9 (1833–5), a free cycle of twenty musical vignettes with a 'Préambule', it became 'an intellectual game, romantic and ironic, built on a small group of

---

[30] Cf. Richard Hohenemser, 'Formale Eigentümlichkeiten in Robert Schumanns Klaviermusik', *Festschrift zum 50. Geburtstag Adolf Sandberger überreicht von seinen Schülern* (Munich, 1918), 21, and Dale, 'The Piano Music', pp. 33–41, 51–3, 56–7, 59 ff.

[31] Hans Kötz, *Der Einfluss Jean Pauls auf Robert Schumann* (Munich, 1918), 21.

[32] Dale, 'The Piano Music', pp. 37–8.

[33] Ed. Karl Geiringer (Vienna, 1933), and see Dale, 'The Piano Music', pp. 25–7.

notes'.[34] The notes are the letters AE♭CB♮ = ASCH, home of a young woman, Ernestine von Fricken, the Baron's illegitimate daughter, to whom Schumann was briefly engaged; at the same time they are the only letters in his own name which have musical equivalents. *Carnaval* has been described as an 'improvement and expansion' of *Papillons*,[35] 'expansion' particularly as regards the richer imagery of the separate movements, which are now given titles and so become character pieces. Beside such types as 'Coquette', 'Arlequin', and 'Pierrot', Schumann portrays people close to him and composers who had influenced him—'Chiarina' (Clara), 'Estrella' (Ernestine), 'Chopin', and 'Paganini'—as well as himself in 'Florestan' and 'Eusebius'. The more introspective *Davidsbündlertänze*, Op. 6 (1837)—in the second edition of 1851 they appear simply as *Die Davidsbündler*[36]—never became as popular as *Carnaval*. As with the first draft of the *Études symphoniques*, Schumann toyed with the idea of putting the names of Florestan and Eusebius on the title-page as the actual composers, but in the end compromised by inserting the initials 'F' or 'E', sometimes both together, at the end of each piece. Instead of titles, the pieces are given mood descriptions: for example, 'Hitzig' [ardent], 'Etwas hahnebüchen' [rather heavy-handed], 'Wie aus der Ferne' [as if from a distance]; No. 9 is headed 'Here Florestan remained silent, though his lips trembled with emotion', No. 18, 'Eusebius thought as follows and his eyes expressed much happiness'.

This list should properly include some of Schumann's other piano works which are held together by musical threads as well as by a 'poetic unity'. To a greater extent even than the *Davidsbündlertänze*, with their shades of Florestan and Eusebius, the *Kreisleriana*, Op. 16, of 1838 offer 'the most successful self-portrait of Schumann, and of the Romantic artist in general as symbolized by the *Kapellmeister*'.[37] The musical unit of this cycle is assured by the key plan; and here, after the motley contrasting images of the earlier cyclic works, Schumann introduces a new element, interspersing the basic passion with dark, tortuous, and enigmatic ingredients suggested by the character of E. T. A. Hoffmann's fictitious musician. The *Kinderszenen*, Op. 15 (1839),[38] are not really 'pieces for children' as were the subsequent *Album für die Jugend*, Op. 68, and the three

[34] Friedland, *Zeitstil*, p. 68.

[35] Gertler, *Robert Schumann*, p. 70.

[36] Originally the title of a novel begun in 1831, in which Florestan and Eusebius were the principal characters. The aim of the 'David league' was, of course, to fight philistinism in music.

[37] Werner Korte, *Robert Schumann* (Potsdam, 1937), 64.

[38] Rudolf Steglich, *Robert Schumanns Kinderszenen* (Kassel and Basle, 1949).

Sonaten für die Jugend, Op. 118. Schumann himself later described them as 'retrospective reflections of an adult and for adults',[39] and they are a most beautiful document of Romantic love of children; the 'adult' himself speaks in the recitative-like 'Epilog'.

The *Faschingsschwank aus Wien*, Op. 26 (1840), might perhaps be considered as a five-movement sonata with an unorthodox first movement compounded of Rondo and Variation; it is one of Schumann's most important free cyclic works.[40] And finally there are the *Waldszenen*, Op. 82 (1848–9), where the collective title itself implies a 'poetic unity' between the separate parts, and Schumann's last composition for the piano, the *Gesänge der Frühe*, Op. 133 (1853), a late example of a cycle with fairly strict motivic unity.[41]

On the borderline between cycle and single piece are two works not expressly conceived as cycles with independent parts: the *Blumenstück*, Op. 19 (1839), like the first movement of Op. 26, which is a synthesis of variation-and-rondo form with snatches of each overlapping and alternating with one another, and the *Humoreske*, Op. 20, dating from the same year, whose 'tiresome hotchpotch of forms',[42] is revealed by closer analysis as an artistic unity.[43]

LISZT

In his large-scale piano cycles Franz Liszt (1811–86) deviates from Schumann's models. He could never have emulated Schumann's introduction of 'Romantic–ironic' elements in his cycles. Schumann loved to infuse poetry with psychological refinements, while Liszt inclined more to the material. The sets of *Années de pèlerinage* (1835–6; 1839–49; 1877) are basically different from, say, Schumann's self-portrait in his *Davidsbündlertänze*. Instead he assimilates the world around him and reflects the impressions conjured up on his travels by nature, art, and poetry. Thus the last piece in the second part of the *Années de pèlerinage*, 'Après une lecture de Dante: Fantaisie quasi sonata', sketched in 1837 and rewritten in 1849, follows the three 'Sonetti del Petrarca' as homage to a poet. It is a

[39] *Robert Schumanns Briefe: Neue Folge*, ed. Friedrich Gustav Jansen (2nd edn., Leipzig, 1904), 290.

[40] Hohenemser, 'Formale Eigentümlichkeiten', pp. 31–3.

[41] Ibid., pp. 27–8, and Wolfgang Boetticher, '*Gesänge der Frühe*. Schumanns letztes Klavierwerk', *Neue Zeitschrift für Musik*, 107 (1956), 418.

[42] Georgii, *Klaviermusik*, p. 314, And see Kahl, in *Die Musik in Geschichte und Gegenwart*, vi, col. 938.

[43] Hohenemser, 'Formale Eigentümlichkeiten' pp. 37–40. Kathleen Dale adjudicated nicely: '*Humoreske* is not a sonata, neither is it a set of variations, even in the Schumannesque meaning. It is, however, invested with attributes of rondo-form in that one or two of the sections recur in part or in whole' ('The Piano Music', p. 60).

kind of symphonic poem for the piano, written as a result of the impressions which later inspired his *Symphonie zu Dantes Divina commedia*. Thus the *Années* is not a musical cycle but an enormous collection of separate pieces. The *Harmonies poétiques et religieuses*, composed at various dates between 1834 and 1852, with a title borrowed from a collection of Lamartine's poems, are something else again. They are a set of ten characteristic pieces, predominantly religious in content, each with its own title. The *Consolations* (*c.*1849), a more closely knit cycle, probably taking its name from a book of poems by Sainte-Beuve, is perhaps Liszt's nearest approach to Schumann's ideal of a 'poetic unity'; the individual pieces were not given titles.

Liszt was to turn again to the characteristic piano piece in his last years, and in such pieces as *Csárdás macabre*, *Nuages gris*, *La lugubre gondola I and II*, *Richard Wagner—Venezia*, and *Unstern*, all from the 1880s, he embodied some of his most far-reaching tonal, structural, and textural experiments.

The essence of Liszt's keyboard style can be understood only against the intellectual backgrounds of his music and his urge to make it 'speak'. Anxiety to express the underlying poetic idea often results, understandably, in a superfluity of performance marks. It may be said that in his piano writing he was emulating what Paganini had done for violin technique. But that was only part of his intentions; what concerned him most was to exploit the potential versatility of the piano at that stage of its structural development, for instance by suggesting orchestral sound through use of the extreme registers, while filling the intervening space with sonorous repeated chords or diatonic and chromatic scales. Among the hallmarks of his technique and keyboard writing are a highly developed leaping technique; frequent transposition of the melody from treble to tenor register (here also in octaves); stretches of a tenth; and, above all, absolute perfection in the interlacing and alternation of the hands. The increasing subtlety of his textures appears in the transformation of the *Études* of 1827 (see Ex. 160),

Ex. 160

Ex. 161

Ex. 162

first into the *Grandes Études* published in 1839 (see Ex. 161), and then into the *Études d'exécution transcendante* (1852) (see Ex. 162).

The same techniques were employed in a great number of keyboard fantasias—for the most part, operatic in origin—and also produced transcriptions of, for instance, Beethoven's symphonies, many Schubert songs, Berlioz's *Symphonie fantastique,* which have been happily described as 'translations into the sphere of the piano'.[44]

The importance of this type of piano music in the years between 1830 and 1850 is shown at its highest level by what Liszt contributed to it. Of his sixty-seven fantasias,[45] composed at intervals from 1824 until his last years, half date from the period before 1850 and include such masterpieces as *Réminiscences des puritains* (1836, after Bellini), *Grande Fantaisie sur la cavatine de l'opéra Niobe de Pacini* (1835-6), the *Réminiscences de Lucia di Lammermoor* (written during the same two years), and, above all, the *Réminiscences de Don Juan* (Mozart's *Don Giovanni*) (1841). During 1824-47 Liszt's operatic fantasias

---

[44] Diether Presser, *Studien zu den Opern- und Liedbearbeitungen Franz Liszts* (Diss. Cologne, 1953); id., 'Die Opernbearbeitung des 19. Jahrhunderts', *Archiv für Musikwissenschaft*, 12 (1955), 228.
[45] Six in the Liszt Museum at Weimar are still unpublished.

ranged from the traditional to the increasingly virtuosic, but thereafter this element tended to fade out more and more until in its final stage (1871–82) virtuosity is often subordinated to spiritual content. Towards the end, most of Liszt's themes are taken from Verdi (*Don Carlos* and *Boccanegra*) and Wagner (Isolde's 'Liebestod', 'Walhall' from the *Ring*, the Grail procession from *Parsifal*).

CHOPIN

The triad of near contemporary masters of piano composition was completed by Frédéric (originally Fryderyk) Chopin (1810–49). His reputation as one of the greatest melodists of Romantic piano music is based particularly on his nocturnes. Influenced by Italianate melody, they also provide numerous examples of the variety of his ornamentation,[46] which he develops to the point where ornament becomes a constructive part of the compositional technique. Beside the nocturnes, only Chopin's four impromptus are connected with types in the early history of the lyrical piano piece—and they have little in common with those of Schubert and Jan Voříšek.[47] One innovation, however, was the establishment of the large-scale scherzo as a separate entity outside the framework of the sonata. In Chopin's four scherzos (1832–9) the passages of gloomy, passionate feeling once prompted Schumann to wonder in his review of the first, in B minor, 'how seriousness should be dressed if "Scherz" (jesting) goes darkly veiled'.[48] At all events, this was the first appearance of the piano scherzo as a large-scale single piece, written in a free form in many respects related to sonata form and devoid of humour. Another of Chopin's new creations were his four Ballades (1835–42), the earliest instrumental compositions to be so called. Instrumental counterparts of the poetic ballad but extended in free rondo or sonata form, they often adopt a quasi-narrative tone, as in the introduction to the G minor Ballade, Op. 23. (Chopin confided to Schumann that his ballades had been inspired by the ballads of Adam Mickiewicz.)[49] Side by side with these are the *Berceuse*, Op. 57 (1843–4), with its highly developed ostinato technique, and the *Barcarolle*, Op. 60 (1846). All of these characteristic pieces by Chopin, with the exception of the nocturnes, were published separately, since their scope made it impossible to group them together.

Like Schumann, he composed 'concert studies': two collections,

[46] See particularly Maria Ottich, *Die Bedeutung des Ornaments im Schaffen Friedrich Chopins* (Berlin, 1937).
[47] See Vol. VIII, pp. 370–1.
[48] *Neue Zeitschrift für Musik*, 2 (1835), col. 156; Schumann, *Gesammelte Schriften*, i. 111.
[49] *Neue Zeitschrift für Musik*, 15 (1841), col. 41; Schumann, *Gesammelte Schriften*, i.

Op. 10 (comp. 1829–32; pub. 1833), and Op. 25 (comp. 1832–6; pub. 1837). With all their poetic qualities, they might be described as an advanced course in the innovations he had made in the technique of piano playing, for instance the role of the tenth, obliging the hand to stretch wide intervals, particularly in arpeggios. In Op. 10, No. 2, chromatic scales have to be played with only three fingers of the right hand. Op. 10, No. 5, sets the performer an entirely new task: every bar but one must be played by the right hand on the black keys. Several studies exercise passages in thirds, sixths, or octaves. Chopin's approximation of the *étude* to the 'characteristic piece' is paralleled in the Preludes, Op. 28 (1839), which are on a smaller scale and, like the Studies, mostly monothematic, often presenting special technical difficulties; despite their title, they have no connection with the *praeludium* as a musical prologue.

It was more difficult for Chopin than for Schumann to group his single pieces in collections, since his scale was larger. As for cycles based on the concept of poetic unity of all the parts, Chopin hardly touches the areas of programme music or poetic association; his pieces are characterized sufficiently by the genre—as, for instance, are his waltzes, mazurkas, and polonaises. His dance music was, almost from the first, idealized. The waltzes and polonaises of Schumann's *Papillons* are still very close to actual dance music although they were placed in a poetic, or rather novelistic, frame before they were published. Chopin's are stylized dances, dance poems in which florid ornamentation, bravura passages, and changes of tempo often disguise the actual dance melody. It was not for nothing that Chopin called his Op. 61 (1846) *Polonaise-fantaisie*;[50] the F sharp minor Polonaise, Op. 44 (1841), actually incorporates— with masterly workmanship—a full-length mazurka.

Chopin's reputation as one of the greatest melodists of Romantic piano music and master of the bel canto of the piano is based particularly on his nocturnes. Influenced by Bellini's melody,[51] they also provide numerous examples of the variety of his ornamentation. But, despite the importance of ornamental variations in his style, his variations *per se* are limited to insignificant early works and *Variations brillantes* on a rondo from Herold's *Ludovico*, Op. 12 (1833).

Chopin's relationship to the Classical sonata is different from Schumann's. Leaving aside the early C minor, Op. 4 (1828), first published posthumously in 1851 and frequently dismissed as an

---

[50] On this remarkable work, see Jeffrey Kallberg, 'Chopin's Last Style', *Journal of the American Musicological Society*, 38 (1985), 264.
[51] See Vol. VIII, pp. 359–60.

immature early work, there remain the sonatas in B flat minor, Op. 35 (1839), and B minor, Op. 58 (1845), which, unlike Schumann's, show few breaks with tradition. The four-movement form, with the central movements reversed, is in itself unremarkable, while the Marche funèbre of Op. 35, though composed earlier as an independent piece, can scarcely be regarded as a new departure since Beethoven had set the example with his Op. 26. All the more striking, therefore, is the Finale of the B flat minor, an uninterrupted flow of quaver triplets to be played by both hands in a passionless *sotto voce*. Whereas Schumann was given to describing the content of his movements by eloquent titles and directions for the player, Chopin is content to mark this movement 'Finale. Presto non tanto'. Nor does he show a conscious preoccupation with unity. Deviating only slightly from the Classical tradition, Chopin's sonatas always remain sonatas, and their balance of form and content makes them outstanding in the context of the time although they are surpassed by the great single-movement Fantaisie in F minor, Op. 49 (1841).

OTHER SONATA COMPOSERS

Chopin's and Schumann's sonatas occupy nothing like the central position in their piano music that, for instance, Beethoven's occupy in his. The picture is everywhere the same in this period. Of the 150 or more works published by Stephen Heller (1813–88)—who wrote exclusively for the piano—between 1829 and 1877, only four are sonatas, though he described a fifth (c.1847) as a *Fantasie in Form einer Sonate*.[52]

The first, in D minor, Op. 9 (1838) excited enthusiastic recognition from Schumann.[53] Both in this and in the second sonata, Heller undermines the traditional cycle by making the third movement an Intermezzo. The second, in B minor, Op. 65 (c.1846), includes new material in the shape of a Ballade and an 'Epilogue' Finale[54] marked 'äusserst lebendig und mit charakteristischem Ausdruck' [very lively and with characteristic expression], a direction typical of Heller whose nature was akin to Schumann's. In sonata movements of this kind, and still more in his later characteristic pieces, Heller emphasizes the 'speaking' element in the music as clearly as possible; it gave variety to the lyrical principle underlying instrumental music all through the Romantic period.[55]

[52] See R. Schütz, *Stephen Heller. Ein Künstlerleben* (Leipzig, 1911), and Newman, *Sonata*, pp. 498–502.
[53] *Neue Zeitschrift für Musik*, 11/2 (1839), 186; *Schumann: Gesammelte Schriften*, i. 453.
[54] See Newman, *Sonata*, p. 501.
[55] The eccentric but prolific Alkan, whose birth and death dates were the same as Heller's, wrote a sonata, *Les Quatre Âges*, Op. 33 (c.1847).

Ex. 163

Spohr's A flat major Sonata, Op. 125 (1843), shows the *Lied-ohne-Worte* type of melody characteristic of Romantic thematicism, actually used as the main idea in the first movement. As Egert puts it, 'organic work' is replaced by 'harmonic successions' [harmonische Reihung],[56] and the violinist–composer was unable to think in terms of pianistic ideas. But the supple chromaticism of the Trio of the Scherzo is very typical of Spohr (Ex. 163).

Spohr's gifted but short-lived pupil Norbert Burgmüller (1810–36)[57] showed a greater understanding of the piano. His F minor Sonata, Op. 8 (comp. 1834 or 1835, pub. posthumously 1840), came at the point where his style was maturing in the Classical mould, when he was preoccupied with the problem of form. The Spohr-like sensuousness of his early works recedes and the sonata occasionally sounds quite harsh. But the middle movement, a Romanze in D flat major, is on the pattern of Spohr's 9/8 larghettos. With Burgmüller's death, which Schumann thought 'the most grievous since Schubert's',[58] the piano music of the 1830s lost one of its greatest hopes.

The much larger contributions of Cramer and Hummel to the sonata repertoire belong to an earlier period,[59] although they were still writing until 1858 and 1837 respectively. The piano sonatas of Mendelssohn, who died in 1847, were composed in his youth.[60]

MENDELSSOHN'S *LIEDER OHNE WORTE*

Mendelssohn never returned to the piano sonata in his maturity. Instead he produced capriccios (Op. 33, 1833–5), preludes and fugues (Op. 35, 1832–7), and sets of variations—of which the *Variations sérieuses* (Op. 54, 1841) are by far the finest. But these have been eclipsed in popularity by the eight books of *Lieder ohne Worte*,

[56] *Die Klaviersonate*, p. 102.
[57] Heinrich Eckert, *Norbert Burgmüller. Ein Beitrag zur Stil- und Geistesgeschichte der deutschen Romantik* (Augsburg, 1932), 89.
[58] Schumann, *Gesammelte Schriften*, i. 430.
[59] See Vol. VIII, pp. 356–8.
[60] See Vol. VIII, pp. 374–5.

Opp. 19, 30, 38, 53, 62, 67, 85, and 102, produced during the last fifteen years of his life.[61] Most have no titles or other clues; the three Venetian barcaroles, Op. 19, No. 6 (dated Venice, 1830), Op. 30, No. 6, and Op. 62, No. 5, are exceptions. The popular title of the 'Spring Song' is completely justified by the inscription on the autograph, 'Ein Frühlings-Lied ohne Worte'; another album inscription testifies that Op. 53, No. 4, is an 'Abendlied'. On 17 January 1835 Mendelssohn wrote to Klingemann that, a few weeks before, he had written 'by far his best' *Lied ohne Worte* and asked whether he should call it 'der Sommerabend oder gar nicht',[62] to which his correspondent evidently advised against a title. The dedication of Op. 62, No. 1, to Clara Schumann speaks for itself. To what extent the *Lieder* were inspired by verbal texts, if at all, it is impossible to say, but part of their musical ancestry can be traced from the *Études* of his teacher, Ludwig Berger[63]—compare, for instance, Op. 38, No. 2 (Ex. 164), with Berger's Op. 12, No. 11 (Ex. 165)—and from the *Acht Minnelieder für das Pianoforte*, Op. 16, of another Berger pupil, Wilhelm Taubert (1811–91), which are headed by quotations from Goethe, Heine, and others. Fresher than these are the Three Musical Sketches (1836) of Sterndale Bennett (1816–75) and the *Mélodies orientales* of Félicien David (1810–76).

Ex. 164

Ex. 165

---

[61] In addition to the general literature on Mendelssohn, see Willi Kahl, 'Zu Mendelssohn's *Liedern ohne Worte*', *Zeitschrift für Musikwissenschaft*, 3 (1920–1), 460.

[62] *Felix Mendelssohn-Bartholdys Briefwechsel mit Legationsrat Karl Klingemann in London* (Essen, 1909), 167.

[63] See Vol. VIII, p. 357.

THE SLAV LANDS

During the first half of the nineteenth century the dominant influence on piano music in Russia had been that of Field, which was superseded after the late 1830s by that of the Bavarian Adolf von Henselt (1814–89). A pupil of Hummel, Henselt composed *Douze Études caractéristiques de concert*, Op. 2 (1837), and *Douze Études de salon*, Op. 5 (1838), all with poetic titles or quotations (for example, 'Wenn ich ein Vöglein wär') and a very fine Ballade, Op. 31 (1846). The leading native composer, Mikhail Glinka (1804–57), showed little interest in the piano and wrote mainly lightweight pieces, though his *Capriccio on Russian Themes* (1834) for piano duet is noteworthy, and his 'Thème écossais varié', No. 4 of *Privet otchizne* [A Greeting to my Native Land] (1847)—really the Irish song we know as 'The Last Rose of Summer'—has a period charm. But his friend Ivan Laskovsky (1799–1855), an official in the War Ministry, left a number of compositions published posthumously in 1858. They include an impressive Ballade (Ex. 166), some bold variations on 'Kamarinskaya' (Ex. 167), and a passionate *Pensée fugitive*.

Polish piano music of this period is of course completely dominated by Chopin. The piano compositions of his teacher Józef Elsner (1769–1854) practically all date from an earlier period of his life, and his own contemporary, Stanisław Moniuszko (1819–72), distinguished composer of songs and operas, produced for piano only polonaises, mazurkas, a few bagatelles, and other pieces of no great significance.

Ex. 166

Ex. 167

In the Czech lands Jan Bedřich Kittl (1806–68) published a quantity of idylls, scherzos, impromptus, three sets of *Aquarelles*, a Notturno, Op. 8, a Romanze, Op. 10, and a *Grande Sonate* for four hands, in F minor (1847). But he was completely overshadowed by his younger contemporary, Bedřich Smetana (1824–84) who precociously wrote a piano galop at the age of 8 and went on to compose a vast quantity of piano music: *Bagatelles et impromptus* (1844), a set of *Characteristic Pieces* (1848), fugues, marches, a great number of polkas from 1840 onwards, and a set of *Svatebni sceny* [Wedding Scenes] (1849), of which the second piece, 'Bridegroom and Bride', is—typically—a polka,[64] long before any of the operas by which he is generally known.

---

[64] For an edition of the complete piano works, see *Klavírni dilo Bedřicha Smetany*, ed. Mirko Očadlík *et al.* (Prague 1944–73).

V

WAGNER'S LATER STAGE WORKS

By ARNOLD WHITTALL

LIFE AND WORKS

WAGNER'S life can scarcely be considered in other than Romantic terms, as a highly eventful affair of opportunism, intrigue, intransigence, and the dogged pursuit of the ideals and ambitions which ultimately found fruition in the Bayreuth Festival. And dangerous though it is to search for simple parallels, there can be little doubt that the composer's life and works match each other in their eager embrace of restlessness and rhetoric, and their reliance on that 'instinctive impulse' which, Wagner believed, characterized the nature of the creative artist's gift.[1] Nevertheless, the more one examines his life, from the time he completed *Lohengrin* in 1848 until his death thirty-five years later, the more amazing it seems that Wagner found either the time or the inclination to undertake any creative work at all. The works are more a triumph over the life than a mere illustration of it.

When Wagner fled to Switzerland from Dresden in May 1849, after the political upheavals in that city, he took with him the text of *Siegfrieds Tod*, written in 1848, and his first four years of exile were devoted almost entirely to the writing of words. In 1850 came *Das Kunstwerk der Zukunft*; in 1851 he completed *Oper und Drama* and *Eine Mitteilung an meine Freunde*. In 1850 there was an abortive attempt to begin the composition of *Siegfrieds Tod*, and the following year, completing the text of *Der junge Siegfried*, he also made a few musical sketches for that work. By now, however, he had decided that the material he had first discussed in *Der Nibelungen-Mythus als Entwurf zu einem Drama* (1848) needed to be presented as a four-part stage work and performed in special, festival circumstances, to achieve the necessary break with the evils of the Italian-dominated

---

[1] See 'Zukunftsmusik' (1860), repr. in Richard Wagner: *Gesammelte Schriften und Dichtungen*, vii (Leipzig, 1873), 121–80; trans. as 'Music of the Future', in *Three Wagner Essays*, trans. Robert L. Jacobs (London, 1979), 13–44.

operatic tradition in Germany. Between 1851 and 1857, while still living primarily in Zurich, he completed the full text of the *Ring*[2] and composed the music through to the end of Act II of *Siegfried*; this act apart, the music was also fully orchestrated. But in 1857 *Siegfried* was set aside in favour of *Tristan*, a work which Wagner had conceived three years previously. *Tristan und Isolde* was begun at the Asyl near Zurich, continued in Venice, and completed in the Hotel Schweizerhof, Lucerne, in August 1859.

From September 1859 to April 1861 Wagner was based in Paris, preparing the revised version of *Tannhäuser* for its notorious trio of performances at the Opéra. Also in 1861 he began to work on *Die Meistersinger*, a prose sketch for which he had drafted in Dresden sixteen years earlier, in 1845. Wagner settled for a time in Vienna, but in 1864 he was obliged to leave in haste in order to escape his creditors. That same year King Ludwig II of Bavaria summoned him to Munich, offering him enthusiastic and generous patronage. Wagner lived there until the end of 1865, by which time his relationship with Cosima von Bülow and his general unpopularity with those who saw him as a malign influence on the impressionable and unstable young king drove him back to Switzerland, and the relative peace of the Villa Tribschen near Lucerne. Here he finished *Die Meistersinger* in 1867, and *Siegfried* in 1869. Wagner's first wife Minna died in 1866, and he finally married Cosima in 1870, a year after the birth of their son Siegfried. Also in 1870 Wagner began to consider Bayreuth as a suitable location for his *Ring* Festival.

The Wagners moved to Bayreuth in 1872, and *Götterdämmerung* was completed in their new house, Wahnfried, in 1874. The first Festival took place in 1876, with three complete cycles of *Der Ring des Nibelungen*. In 1877 Wagner returned to the subject of *Parsifal*, for which he had made prose sketches in 1857 and 1865. The work was completed on 13 January 1882 in Palermo, and first performed at the second Bayreuth Festival on 26 July 1882. A little over six months later, on 13 February 1883, Wagner died in Venice.

THEORIES

Even from such a sketchy summary, it is clear that Wagner's life was one of success as well as struggle, fulfilment as well as frustration.

---

[2] The poems of the four works were completed in reverse order, but two points should be noted: first, *Das Rheingold* and *Die Walküre* were conceived at the same time, and Wagner wrote his prose drafts for *Das Rheingold* first; second, the poems of *Der junge Siegfried* and *Siegfrieds Tod* were revised after the poems of *Das Rheingold* and *Die Walküre* were completed. See Robert Bailey, 'The Structure of the *Ring* and its Evolution', *19th-century Music*, 1 (1977-8), 48-61.

It is probable that the personal and financial problems he continued to experience after 1864 were not entirely compensated for either by the satisfaction of seeing his works performed in something like suitable conditions, or by the joys of family life with Cosima, the children, and his close circle of devotees and acolytes. As far as his creative work was concerned, however, this later phase of Wagner's life saw frustration swept aside with notable rapidity, for once he had begun to compose the music for *Das Rheingold* in 1853 he was able to sustain a remarkable level of originality and inventiveness. Wagner's own memory of the frustrations of the years between 1848 and 1853 is evident in his reference to the 'abnormal state of mind' in which his principal prose works were produced: 'I was straining to formulate theoretically what I could not communicate in the infallible form of a convincing work of art, owing to the disparity between my outlook and the one generally held concerning the present state of opera.'[3] There is no space to discuss here the full ramifications of Wagner's theories; but it is clear that he came to see himself as a very practical and specific kind of reformer. Looking back in 1860, he claimed that it was through the artistry of the celebrated soprano Wilhelmine Schröder-Devrient that he had first sensed 'the poetic and musical shape of a work of art which I could hardly call by the name of opera'.[4] And during the period of 'sustained reflection', in which, as an exile, he attempted through theoretical writings to eliminate the 'great obstacle' to instinctive creation which his misgivings about the state of opera in Germany had erected, he came to realize that the 'perfect opera' could be achieved only by a 'complete transformation of the poet's role',[5] and by channelling 'into the bed of music drama the great stream which Beethoven sent pouring into German music'.[6] But this theorizing was not completely detached from work of creative significance: in 1860 Wagner argued that

the most daring of my theoretical speculations concerning the form of music drama were brewing within me precisely because at that very time I was carrying in my head the plan of my great Nibelung drama ... Thus my theories were virtually little more than an abstract expression of the artistic process then at work within me.[7]

But there was bound to be a vital distinction between abstract and

[3] 'Music of the Future', p. 29.
[4] Ibid., p. 19.
[5] Ibid., p. 23.
[6] Ibid., p. 19.
[7] Ibid., p. 32.

actual expression. Wagner was also convinced that 'the unthinking sense of absolute certainty, which I experienced when I was creating *Tristan*' was a consequence of the fact that 'here at last I was able to proceed with such freedom and disregard of all theoretical considerations that while writing it I was myself aware that I was going far beyond my own system'.[8] A composer whose ultimate ideal was the 'sublime naïveté' of Beethoven's Ninth Symphony[9] could only be happy instinctively transcending theories rather than consciously illustrating them. As Wagner put it in a letter to Berlioz in 1860:

My aim thus became to demonstrate the possibility of a work of art in which the highest and deepest sentiments that the human spirit is capable of conceiving could be communicated in a readily comprehensible manner to minds receptive only to the simplest of purely human sympathies, and to communicate them moreover so definitely and convincingly that no critical reflection would be needed for their absorption.[10]

The transformation of the poet's role in the new drama would be achieved by the use of verse-forms less narrowly poetic than those requiring regular stress-patterns and neatly matching end-rhymes, and of subject-matter drawn from myths and sagas. Wagner regarded this as the 'ideal subject-matter' because 'here all that smacks of convention and all that pertains to abstract reason is completely missing: all we have is the eternally comprehensible, the purely human, albeit presented in that inimitably individual concrete form which is immediately recognizable in every genuine myth'.[11] Moreover,

from the poet's point of view a legendary subject has another essential dramatic advantage. Not only does the simple, easily grasped action spare him the necessity of retarding explanations; it provides the greatest possible scope for revealing those inner psychic motives which alone can bring home the inevitability of the action since we ourselves feel them in our own hearts.[12]

In his own later texts, Wagner was in general to remain faithful to text lines of variable length, though he did not invariably exclude end-rhyme, or show such devotion to alliteration (*Stabreim*) as he did in the *Ring*.

As both theorist and poet, Wagner had a shrewd understanding

---

[8] Ibid., p. 33.

[9] See *The Diaries of Cosima Wagner*, trans. Geoffrey Skelton, ii (London, 1980), 994.

[10] Herbert Barth, Dietrich Mack, and Egon Voss (eds.), *Wagner: A Documentary Study*, trans. P. R. J. Ford and Mary Whittall (London, 1975), 192.

[11] 'Music of the Future', p. 24.

[12] Ibid., p. 34.

of what was wrong, for him, with the subject and style of the typical libretto. But as a composer of genius he was well placed to misunderstand the achievements and intentions of other composers, especially those he most admired. It seems clear that only someone with very strong convictions about what the musical stage work should become would talk, with respect to *Don Giovanni*, of 'looseness, lack of cohesion', and complain that it was 'all so lacking in integration'.[13] Wagner discoursed at length about his desire to achieve a new kind of unity and coherence, and the eventual results, as demonstrated for example in *Die Meistersinger*, struck Hanslick as 'the conscious dissolution of all fixed forms in a formless, intoxicating sea of sound. . . . Anxiously avoiding every concluding cadence, ever renewing itself from itself, this form without bone or muscle flows on indefinitely.'[14] Although Stravinsky for one has repeated this charge in more recent times,[15] it is rarely thought necessary today to defend Wagner against accusations of form-lessness: indeed, Pierre Boulez's praise of *Parsifal* is couched in what might well be deliberately Hanslickian terms.[16] But it is still possible to question whether Wagner really understood the one composer who seemed to mean the most to him: Beethoven. Or, to put it more melodramatically, whether Wagner could possibly have achieved what he did achieve had he really understood the essence of Beethoven's own concerns and achievements.

Not only did Wagner believe that 'art, in order to be art, must conceal itself and appear in the guise of nature'.[17] He also believed that 'absolute music', which was not motivated by dramatic, poetic imperatives, and which could manifest itself at times even in as important a precedent for his own work as Weber's *Euryanthe*, could not communicate in the way that music in the middle of the nineteenth century was destined to communicate.[18] If lack of unity

[13] *The Diaries of Cosima Wagner*, ii. 493.

[14] *Wagner: A Documentary Study*, p. 215.

[15] In *Poetics of Music*, trans. Arthur Knodel and Ingolf Dahl (Cambridge, Mass., 1947), 64–5 and 80–1.

[16] 'This music which is in perpetual *evolution* is probably the most highly personal musical invention of Wagner—it places the emphasis for the first time on uncertainty, on indetermination. It represents a rejection of immutability, an aversion to definitiveness in musical phrases as long as they have not exhausted their potential for evolution and renewal' (Pierre Boulez, notes to recording, DG 2713 004).

[17] See Carl Dahlhaus, *Die Musikdramen Richard Wagners* (Velber, 1971); trans. as *Richard Wagner's Music Dramas*, trans. Mary Whittall (Cambridge, 1979), 69.

[18] See Wagner's comments on *Euryanthe* in 'Oper und Drama' (1851; rev. 1868); repr. in Richard Wagner: *Gesammelte Schriften und Dichtungen*, iii and iv (Leipzig, 1872), 269–394 and 3–284; trans. in *Richard Wagner's Prose Works*, ed. and trans. William Ashton Ellis, ii (London, 1893), 83–7.

was one evil, lack of meaning, and failure to communicate, were others. And Wagner's zeal for communication was ferocious. As he belligerently put it near the end of *Zukunftsmusik*: 'My primary aim is to compel the public to focus its attention upon the dramatic action so closely that it is never for a moment lost sight of: all this musical elaboration must be experienced simply as the presentation of this action.'[19]

From his early perception, as recollected in *Mein Leben*, that Beethoven's Ninth Symphony 'surely held the secret to all secrets',[20] Wagner's sense of almost mystic communion with the composition which was 'the redemption of Music from out of her own peculiar elements into the realm of Universal Art'[21] remained consistent. And Beethoven's preference for purely instrumental music made him the more tantalizing as an ideal who might become a model.

The characteristic of the great compositions of Beethoven is that they are veritable poems, in which it is sought to bring a real subject to representation. The obstacle to their comprehension lies in the difficulty of finding with certainty the subject that is represented.[22]

Wagner, the scourge of 'absolute music', proposed to remove the obstacle and provide the certainty, with the profoundly simple thematic material and powerfully progressing variation form of the Ninth Symphony's Finale as a particular stimulus. But Wagner was well aware of the distinction between the inspiring example of Beethoven and the actual musical elements from which he could build his reforms: 'I could not have composed in the way I have done if Beethoven had never existed, but what I have used and developed ... are isolated strokes of genius in my dramatic pre-decessors, including even Auber.'[23] Predecessors were important enough: but there was also the immediate stimulus of at least one sympathetic contemporary. Having written the text for *Der junge Siegfried* in 1851, Wagner told a friend that 'I am now tired of theorizing: Liszt has inspired me to new creative work.'[24] And

[19] 'Music of the Future', p. 44.

[20] *Mein Leben*, ed. Martin Gregor-Dellin (Munich, 1976); Eng. trans., Andrew Gray, *My Life* (Cambridge, 1983), 36.

[21] 'Das Kunstwerk der Zukunft' (1849); repr. in Richard Wagner: *Gesammelte Schriften und Dichtungen*, iii (Leipzig, 1872), 51–210; trans. in Ellis, *Prose Works*, i (London, 1892), 126.

[22] Letter to Theodor Uhlig, 13–15 Feb. 1852; *Richard Wagner: Sämtliche Briefe*, ed. Gertrud Strobel and Werner Wolf, iv (Leipzig, 1979), 285; trans. in *Wagner on Music and Drama*, ed. Albert Goldman and Evert Sprinchorn (New York, 1964), 160.

[23] *The Diaries of Cosima Wagner*, ii. 572. For an illuminating discussion of Wagner's musical sources and debts, see John Warrack, 'The Musical Background', in Peter Burbidge and Richard Sutton (eds.), *The Wagner Companion* (London, 1979), 85.

[24] *Wagner: A Documentary Study*, p. 182.

Wagner recalled in *Mein Leben* that, at the time when he was completing the *Ring* poem, 'my joy in everything I heard by Liszt was as profound as it was genuine, but above all it was productively stimulating; for after such a long interval, I was myself about to begin composing again'.[25]

A full exploration of the whole subject of Wagner's possible debts to predecessors and contemporaries remains to be undertaken, and anyone doing so will be faced with formidable difficulties. Certainly the first hundred years after Wagner's death saw more determined efforts to analyse his harmony and form than to anatomize his possible influences. The first major analytical study of the later works, by Alfred Lorenz, attempted to demonstrate the 'secret' of their formal coherence through Wagner's apparently consistent use, on both large and small scales, of tripartite models (AAB, ABA) involving repetition and contrast.[26] More recently, scholars have sought more diverse means of identifying those elements of thematic process, phrase structure, and harmonic organization with which, in the later works, the composer's theories were transformed through new technical considerations, in order thereby to clarify the sense in which Wagner builds on fundamental formal precedents to create his radically new flexibility. The central issues raised by attempts to interpret such large structures analytically will be discussed below. But Wagner scholarship has also become increasingly concerned with the 'background' to the finished works—with the interpretation of the voluminous surviving sketches and other documentary material.

COMPOSITIONAL PROCEDURES

It might seem reasonably safe to assume that Wagner wrote his texts first, then set them to music, sometimes many years later, always moving logically from beginning to end, with occasional omissions and alterations, but without major modifications. Robert Bailey, noting that 'with his later operas, at least, there is precious little documentary evidence showing how he planned them in musical terms', goes on to argue that 'an important feature of Wagner's later works is the preparation of their musical structure in the structure of the poem itself; musical decisions were made in the act of turning into verse the dramatic conception which he had written out in detail

25 *My Life*, p. 495.
26 Alfred Lorenz, *Das Geheimnis der Form bei Richard Wagner* (Berlin, 1924–33). See David R. Murray, 'Major Analytical Approaches to Wagner's Musical Style: A Critique', *Music Review*, 39 (1978), 211.

in a complete Prose Scenario'.[27] And elsewhere Bailey asserts that 'a great deal of the musical setting' suggested itself to Wagner as the poems were taking shape.[28] Wagner did occasionally jot down musical ideas on the manuscripts of his poems, but not all scholars accept Bailey's interpretation of their importance. In John Deathridge's view, for example, Wagner's musical ideas were only 'rudimentary when he was writing his librettos'.[29]

There has also been disagreement among scholars as to what the various stages of Wagner's creative process should be called. But the first comprehensive catalogue of Wagner's compositions includes an authoritative discussion of the issue, and a set of terms likely to be accepted as definitive.[30] This involves a basic distinction between 'sketch' (*Skizze*), which normally refers to material relating to parts of a work or an entire work in outline, and 'draft' (*Entwurf*), which refers to fuller, more complete material. For the four stages in the writing of the poem, the catalogue proposes the following: prose sketch (*Prosaskizze*), prose draft (*Prosaentwurf*), first copy of the complete poem (*Erstschrift des Textbuches*), and fair copy of the poem (*Reinschrift des Textbuches*). As for the music, what emerges in broad outline is a process with three principal stages. First, after various separate, short sketches (*Einzelskizzen*), a complete draft (*Gesamtentwurf*), the vocal line supported by one or two instrumental staves. For all the music dramas after *Die Walküre*, Wagner produced two such drafts, the second with fuller indications of instrumentation and amounting, often, to a short score. The final stage in all cases was a fair copy of the full score (*Reinschrift der Partitur*), but for the first two acts of *Siegfried* and the *Tristan* Prelude Wagner made a draft of the full score (*Partiturerstschrift*) before the fair copy.

It must be stressed that this is only the barest outline of a complex and varied process, the full and fascinating details of which are provided in the *Wagner Werk-Verzeichnis*. As John Deathridge has pointed out,

when Wagner began sketching the music of his later works he had broken completely with the number convention of traditional opera. He therefore had little difficulty in first making a rough, through-composed draft of an

[27] Robert Bailey, 'The Method of Composition', in Burbidge and Sutton (eds.), *The Wagner Companion*, p. 271.
[28] 'The Structure of the *Ring* and its Evolution', p. 48.
[29] *19th-century Music*, 5 (1981), 83.
[30] John Deathridge, Martin Geck, and Egon Voss, *Wagner Werk-Verzeichnis* (Mainz, 1986).

entire work (or single acts at a time) which was continuous from beginning to end.[31]

In particular, the surviving sketches of the *Ring* show a remarkable fluency, reflecting that 'unthinking sense of absolute certainty' which Wagner himself described;[32] and differences between complete draft and final score are rarely of major significance. Wagner's own comments on his following of unconscious impulse are confirmed by the apparent spontaneity of the compositional process, inasmuch as this is accurately represented by what is actually written down: 'one even has the feeling that, with fundamental motifs already in mind, Wagner literally improvised from one moment to the next, often too engrossed in smaller forms and immediate effects to pay much attention to larger formal relationships.'[33] It is certainly not easy to proceed from a discussion of Wagner's technique of through-composition to an argument that unity on the largest scale in either conception or perception is essential to the fabric of his work as executed in the score and performed in the theatre. Yet the technique of composition is the direct result of rejecting what he described as the 'mish-mash of petty undeveloped forms cramped by meaningless conventions' found in earlier opera.[34]

In *Oper und Drama* Wagner did not merely place a theory of music alongside a theory of poetry. In the new drama, he argued, it was necessary for the two to come together, to fuse into musico-poetic periods, sections not self-contained like traditional operatic 'numbers', but integrated around specific textual and tonal elements. Text and melody together would break out of the old constraints, producing something akin to Classical drama, as Wagner understood it. His theoretical ideal was for music and poetry to coexist, contributing equally to the drama. But, despite occasional glimpses of this ideal in *Das Rheingold* and *Die Walküre*, music—and especially orchestral music, providing a rich harmonic and tonal context for the new, flexible melody—came to dominate the completed compositions, even if it did not literally generate them. The extent of this distinction between theory and practice is another matter of dispute among Wagnerians, and discussions of the works will naturally reflect the convictions of the writer. The account that

[31] 'The Nomenclature of Wagner's Sketches', *Proceedings of the Royal Musical Association*, 101 (1974–5), 75–7.
[32] 'Music of the Future', p. 33.
[33] John Deathridge, 'Wagner's Sketches for the *Ring*: Some Recent Studies', *Musical Times*, 118 (1977), 386.
[34] 'Music of the Future', p. 16.

follows is an attempt to combine some consideration of the poetic—
those psychological, metaphysical issues so exhaustively discussed by
Deryck Cooke with reference to the *Ring*—with technical, musical
issues, in an analytical commentary concerned most essentially with
what has been described as 'perhaps the thorniest of all subjects to
lay hands on, . . . the form-defining function of tonality in Wagnerian
music drama'.[35] The aim is mediation between the poetic and the
structural, but it may be difficult to avoid contradiction. Cooke, for
one, put the weight of his considerable authority behind the
implication that, in dealing with the *Ring*, a work whose creator's
original intention 'was to set forth the evils of modern civilization
and adumbrate a possible ameliorization of them',[36] it is belittling,
if not entirely irrelevant, to concentrate on abstract, absolute
structural features which, for Wagner, were very much the technical
means to expressive, communicative ends. Certainly it cannot be
argued that tonalities as such—however explicitly associated with
particular characters, objects, or moods—can bear the unambiguous
symbolic and psychological import of the principal thematic ideas
(the *Grundthemen* or leitmotifs) *when* these are correctly understood.
Carl Dahlhaus has argued powerfully that one of the fundamental
reasons for distinguishing earlier from later Wagner is that it was
only after *Lohengrin* that leitmotifs become 'essential structural
factors'.[37] But even if the motifs determine the harmony, rather than
the other way round, the finished product is tonal music whose
evolutionary unfolding is the result of thematic and harmonic
interaction. As Wagner put it, referring to the chorus-like role of
the orchestra in his later works, 'it will embody the harmony which
alone makes possible the melody's specific expression; it will maintain
the melody in a state of uninterrupted flow so that the motifs will
be able to work with the maximum effect upon the audience's
feelings'.[38]

TONALITY

Any analysis which seeks to advance beyond description into
interpretation must explore the whole question of whether and how
successive tonalities relate to each other, and the ways in which the
various harmonies which establish and express those tonalities

[35] Anthony Newcomb, 'The Birth of Music out of the Spirit of Drama. An Essay in
Wagnerian Formal Analysis', *19th-century Music*, 5 (1981), 48.
[36] Deryck Cooke, *I Saw the World end: A Study of Wagner's Ring* (London, 1979), 12.
[37] *Richard Wagner's Music Dramas*, p. 108.
[38] 'Music of the Future', p. 40.

actually function in the context of music whose dramatic subject must always be absolutely explicit. Many writers have observed that tonality was as important to Wagner as to any symphonist. But there is little point in comparing Wagner's use of tonal relations with that of a symphonist whose purpose was to demonstrate how a single key could retain its primacy throughout the complete structural span of a movement, so that all other keys occurring within that span have the kind of subordinate status to the tonic which leads them to be described as dominant, relative minor, and so on. Indeed, it is often argued that, in the most truly symphonic symphonies, a single hierarchy of related keys will function throughout. But even when Wagner does begin and end a work in the same key, as with *Die Meistersinger* and *Parsifal*, it is difficult to feel that C major and A flat major actually function as tonics throughout the enormous spans of these works, so that, for example, Act I of *Die Meistersinger* could be said to end in 'the subdominant', and Acts II and III to begin in 'the dominant'.

Wagner's use of tonal relations and oppositions are always more dramatic than symphonic, and governed as much by ideas of remoteness as of relatedness. This was shown at an early stage of his career by the use of E major and E flat major in *Tannhäuser*. Neither is the tonic of the entire work, but both contribute as distinct tonics, at particular stages, to a dramatic, symbolic harmonic process involving many other tonalities as well. E and E flat are perhaps the most important keys in *Tannhäuser*, but that does not justify describing every other key in terms of its subordinate relation to either E or E flat.

Bailey discusses the tonalities of *Tannhäuser* as a preliminary to his claim that the whole of the *Ring* has an underlying plan 'based on the principle of associative tonality'.[39] It is not surprising that in so large and complex a work themes should often recur in the keys in which they were first presented; and from time to time tonalities which are close relatives in the symphonic sense may be given prominence to make a dramatic point—for example, the use of D flat major for Valhalla and B flat minor for Nibelheim. The extent to which tonality functions associatively—thematically—may be debated: analysts will also argue over such details as whether it is any longer possible to separate major from minor keys, or whether the frequently found large-scale associations between keys a third apart justifies talk of a 'tonic complex', such as might embrace, for

[39] 'The Structure of the *Ring* and its Evolution', p. 61.

example, the A minor/major and C major/minor of Act I of *Tristan*. But such debates are incidental to the essential matter of acknowledging the existence of tonal structures which, however 'opportunistic' or 'unsymphonic', underpin and promote the gradually evolving coherence and continuity of the whole. These structures may prolong an established tonality diatonically or, more commonly, extend it chromatically, with emphasis on more remote regions;[40] and such structures are more fundamental than those which progress from, or float between, one established tonality and another without clear commitment to alternatives, however many possible keys may be hinted at in the process. Wagner's later works are magnificent examples of such structures, and matters of form, thematic process, and even orchestral and textural presentation can best be understood in relation to this most fundamental of compositional entities: the prolongation and extension of tonal progressions and their placement as the essential building-blocks of the total structure.

DER RING DES NIBELUNGEN

Wagner begins the *Ring* with a celebration of fundamentals. His initial, scene-setting stage direction contains a mass of diverse details, but these come together to stress matters relating to space and light. The Rhine is depicted as something more than amorphous, uniform: just as the area nearer the surface is lighter than that nearer the river bed, so it is nearer the surface that one is most conscious of the actual flow of the water: 'towards the bottom the waters resolve themselves into a fine, humid mist.' And yet the music which accompanies and portrays this stage picture is radically confined with respect to the element which tonal composition most commonly possesses—harmonic progression. Up to the entry of the voices, the music prolongs a single chord, and only with Flosshilde's words 'Des Goldes Schlaf' does the bass-note change. But the prolongation lacks nothing in purposefulness; there is a gradual, inexorable increase of power and intensity. The form of the Prelude might be described as variations on a chord, or studies in the transformation of an arpeggio into a scale. Without either harmonic progression or thematic contrast, it could scarcely be held to set a structural precedent for the music of the entire cycle, still less for the later Wagner as a whole; it might seem rather to provide that sense of perspective against which all the later progressions and contrasts function. But

---

[40] See Schoenberg's discussion of extended tonality in *Structural Functions of Harmony*, ed. Leonard Stein (rev. 2nd edn., London, 1969), 76–113.

the Prelude is so far from an abstract statement of purely harmonic, pitch factors that its function as a precedent is by no means to be entirely excluded. It shows that evolutionary, cumulative variation of a thematic element is possible even when harmony is prolonged without progression, and the resultant emphasis on matters of register, tone colour, and rhythm should act as a caution against any tendency to ignore such features when harmonic progressions *are* present.

Wagner's account in *Mein Leben* of the inspiration, the 'vision', of this opening music, which came to him at La Spezia on 5 September 1853 and sent him rapidly back to Zurich to resume serious composition after the frustrations of the previous four years, is too dramatic and too Romantic to have been accepted without question. Deathridge has suggested that the account is 'a later interpretation most likely influenced by his reading of Schopenhauer's *Parerga und Paralipomena* which discusses similar phenomena'; and he quotes a sketch sheet containing the opening of the Rhinemaidens' song and two arpeggio figures which dates from 'at least 14 months before the composition sketch was begun, as the form of its text predates the verse draft of *Rhinegold* (begun on 15 September 1852)'.[41] It could be that what drove Wagner so precipitately back to Zurich was the realization of how such a basic, previously sketched musical formula could actually be made to work, generatively, at the outset of his revolutionary tetralogy. But the most common subject for debate is not how the work was begun, but what it is actually about.

Cooke places *Der Ring des Nibelungen* alongside *Hamlet* and *Faust* in the category of the 'problematic': 'works in which their creators have attempted to delve so deep into the springs of human action that they have been unable to make their findings absolutely clear'.[42] He attaches particular importance to the idea that in the *Ring* 'Wagner's social and political vision is concerned with the struggle of love against power'. Dahlhaus gives greater emphasis to the antithetical elements which 'link Wotan's drama with Siegfried's, the divine myth with the heroic tragedy'[43]—that is, fear and fearlessness, and the means whereby love is equated with the latter and lovelessness with the former. Dahlhaus is certainly the most persuasive recent exponent of the argument that, despite all his later tinkerings with the text and his various written remarks, the *Ring* as Wagner

[41] 'Wagner's Sketches for the *Ring*', p. 387.
[42] *I saw the World end*, p. 13.
[43] *Richard Wagner's Music Dramas*, p. 99.

completed it remained faithful to his original conception, in which we witness 'the downfall of a world of law and force, and the dawn of a utopian age; though Siegfried and Brünnhilde fall victims to the old order, they are the first representatives of the new'.[44] And Dahlhaus concludes:

In the prose sketch of 1848 Wagner had written that the gods' purpose 'will have been achieved when they have destroyed themselves in this human creation, namely when they have had to surrender their direct influence, faced with the freedom of the human consciousness'. The music Wagner wrote in 1874 to bring *Götterdämmerung* to its conclusion expresses just that. His first conception was also his last.[45]

The more detailed the accounts of the meaning of successive events in the plot of the *Ring* become, the more likely they are to diverge in their interpretations. Fortunately, there is less cause for dispute when it comes to the identification of Wagner's literary sources and the uses to which he put them. I will not attempt to summarize the painstaking and fascinating work of Cooke in this field. But it is clear that, however numerous and diverse these sources, Wagner was very much in command of materials and methods, as in his adaptation of the 'ancient alliterative verse' to his own purposes, and the way in which aspects of distinct myths or sagas—primarily the Volsunga Saga—were fused, transformed, and complemented by material of Wagner's own. For example, the very first scene of *Das Rheingold*, 'despite its profoundly mythic character, is Wagner's own invention'.[46] So is the character of Fasolt, and what Cooke describes as 'the law-enforcing, civilizing aspect of Wotan'.[47]

DAS RHEINGOLD

The first scene of *Das Rheingold* is dominated by the flowing contours of the music depicting the Rhine and the three Rhine-daughters—or Rhinemaidens, as they are invariably known in English. As the disturber of the peace, Alberich is characterized by more angular, more purposefully animated material: and the dramatic crux of the scene occurs when Alberich 'steals' the Rhinemaidens' own least characteristic music. They know that the gold *can* be stolen by anyone who will 'renounce the power of love' and they dismiss the possibility as too improbable, at least as far as the lovesick Nibelung is concerned. But it is the brief solemnity of Woglinde's

[44] Ibid., p. 81.
[45] Ibid., p. 141.
[46] Cooke, *I saw the World end*, p. 134.
[47] Ibid., p. 147.

music when that possibility is first acknowledged which is recaptured with terrible economy at Alberich's moment of decision and action. It is also a moment of purely musical clarification, as Wagner reinforces the shift between the scene's two principal tonal centres of E flat and C in favour of the latter, but delays the resolution from the dominant on to the tonic of C minor until the uproar has subsided and the process of transition—tonal as well as scenic—to Scene ii has begun (Ex. 168). The focusing of tension on a prolonged

Ex. 168

dominant (thirty-nine bars in this case) and the use of resolution on to the tonic to initiate a new stage of the musical structure is one of the most fundamental features of Wagner's mature musical language.

If the crucial event of Scene i is Alberich's theft of the gold, that of Scene ii is Wotan's realization of his own need to possess it, and therefore to rob the robber. In its confrontation between gods and giants, Scene ii parallels the confrontation between Rhinemaidens and Nibelung in Scene i; and one may even argue that, because Scene ii also progresses through a 'minor third' (D flat major to E minor), its detailed musical processes subtly parallel those of Scene i. But the second scene is much longer and more diverse than its preludial predecessor, its length and complexity stemming not only from the greater number of events and characters, but from their more varied characteristics. In Scene i the Rhinemaidens are of one mind: they act and react in concert. But in Scene ii both gods and giants argue among themselves; and not only the giants, but also Fricka and Loge, who refuse to do Wotan the courtesy of accepting his every word as law. It is a scene of many subtleties, since the gods possess much of the giants' aggressiveness, and the giants—Fasolt, at least—the capacity for finer feelings. But it has a less explicit musical continuity than Scene i, and Bailey has argued that, as a result of Wagner writing his first draft on two staves only, 'many vocal portions of the *Rheingold*, particularly in Scenes ii and iv, sound like little more than accompanied recitative'.[48]

Bailey suggests that Wagner's tendency, from *Die Walküre* onwards, to use two instrumental staves as well as the vocal stave for his first draft was the result of a desire to avoid such 'sketchy' passages. But the textural diversity which this occasional sketchiness promotes can contribute positively to the formal flexibility of Scene ii of *Das Rheingold*, and there is no appreciable loss of momentum. Even at such a point of extreme contrast as that between the rich yet concentrated lyricism of Wotan's greeting to Valhalla and Fricka's ensuing recitative, the nature of the plain harmony which occurs in the non-motivic passages has a purposefulness which rarely produces any feeling of meagreness, or loss of direction. The circling round the D minor triad at Fricka's words 'Herrschaft und Macht | soll er dir mehren' may seem harmonically relatively perfunctory, but it is not dramatically inappropriate for Fricka's somewhat unimaginative sentiments (Ex. 169).

---

[48] 'The Method of Composition', p. 295.

Ex. 169

(It is to increase your power and authority; the towering fortress was built
only to provoke greater outbursts of discontent.)

On the larger scale, this exchange establishes a contrast between
the D flat major of Wotan's untroubled delight in the fortress and
the D minor of Fricka's doubts and questions, a tendency to favour
rapid transitions to remote harmonic regions which is reinforced
when the first reminiscence of the Valhalla theme, at Wotan's words
'dass, in der Burg gebunden', occurs in C major, not D flat. As the
scene develops, it is D major which becomes the principal centre for
the lyrical music associated with Freia, the goddess of love hymned
by both Fasolt and Loge. Clearly, therefore, it was not one of
Wagner's concerns to employ only a small group of closely related
tonalities in any particular scene. Just as the drama thrives on
argument and conflict, so the music depends on a wide range of tonal
perspectives, some centres firmly established with the appropriate
cadences and diatonic harmonies, others only hinted at—a diversity
complementing that of the motifs themselves. Such deeper structural
elements may be less immediately apparent to the listener than the
balance the scene strikes between more active and more reflective
episodes; but they are vital in creating that sense of inevitability
which ensures that, for all its fluctuations, the drama never sags or
stagnates.

The third and fourth scenes of *Das Rheingold* present the confrontation between the work's central pair of characters, Wotan and Alberich. Scene iii is dominated by Alberich, whose over-confidence in his own repressive rather than benevolent power leads directly to his capture. The transition from the second scene (spanning a tritone from E minor to B flat minor) is achieved through a powerful compilation of motifs referring to the gold, the ring, and Freia, but not to Wotan himself: he will remain in the background, and leave the tackling of Mime and Alberich to Loge. Since Wotan himself says so little, the Valhalla theme is most evident in Alberich's mockery and Loge's sarcasm: in particular, the improbable idea of the slavery of the mightiest to the Nibelung is underlined by a skittish fusion of this theme with Loge's own much less melodic motif. This material returns to express the triumph of the gods as Alberich is captured, in a way which confirms Wagner's already impressive skill at the flexible treatment of his basic, always recognizable themes: and the exchanges between Loge and Alberich in this scene show that the emphasis on a web of motifs in the orchestra need not result in characterless vocal writing, or short-breathed, regularly cadencing phrases.

At the end of Scene iii B flat minor reappears only briefly and ambiguously through the agency of a semitone sideslip after a protracted dominant preparation in A major: the F natural is of course needed by the monotonal anvils. And the transition to Scene iv is achieved without cadential progression on to tonics; instead the dominant of C is hugely prolonged and only resolved, almost incidentally, when the scene has begun, after Loge's words '. . . bestimmst du drin mir zum Stall?' Wagner's postponement of the decisive exchange between Wotan and Alberich until the beginning of the final scene shows his sure dramatic instinct. Wotan still has relatively little to say, but he radiates great power, as in the moment immediately after he wrenches the ring from Alberich, where triumphant, chromatically ascending triads are framed by the still potent menace of the ring's own theme. The essential dissonance of that theme achieves full expression in Alberich's curse, which gradually clarifies its B minor tonality only to postpone the tonic at the final climax —'meinem Fluch fliehest du nicht!'—and resolve on to it (not a fully emphasized root position, in this case) only as a process of transition begins to take place.

As the final scene proceeds, the contrasts between triumph and tragedy, optimism and foreboding are brilliantly focused and integrated, and nowhere with greater refinement than at the point

Ex. 170

(LOGE: Did you listen to his loving salute?
WOTAN: Let him vent his rage!)

shown in Ex. 170, where the sustained B and D from the end of Alberich's curse prepare the modulation to C major as, in the brightening light, Freia is brought back by the giants. Once again, particular significance attaches to a semitone relation in this scene— C and C sharp/D flat. And its most striking small-scale use comes, appropriately, in the final stages of the scene. The rainbow-bridge theme cunningly reflects the Valhalla theme's rhythms: but the use of the chord of G flat major for its first appearance—Froh's 'Zur Burg führt die Brücke'—ensures that the prompt return of the Valhalla theme in D flat has a quality of understatement hinting at instability: the effect of its final return in *Götterdämmerung* will not be dissimilar. And that instability, belying the confident words, is what Wotan's great final statement reveals. The flourishing of the

Ex. 171

(Thus I salute the fortress, secure from fear and dread. Follow me, wife: live in Valhalla with me!)

sword could seem like an act of crowning confidence, so clearly and carefully is the modulation to C major prepared. But the suddenness with which D flat is restored (Ex. 171) has so disorienting an effect that this final tonic seems less than ideally stable and secure. The chromatic colouring of the Rhinemaidens' lament, which follows, and what some see as the essentially hollow triumph of the entry into Valhalla itself, could support this view. But there is an undeniable and deeply stirring grandeur in the final bars, not just because of their pure diatonicism and opulent orchestration, but because it is clear that the gods have achieved their goal, at a price. It is a poignant rather than hollow triumph.

DIE WALKÜRE

Das Rheingold begins with a theft and ends with the gods taking possession of their fortress; its emphasis is on power and property. In *Die Walküre* human feelings and relationships are given far greater importance: the power of love now looms larger than the love of power. The power of love is by no means absent from *Das Rheingold*: Loge's reminder to the gods of its existence, and Fasolt's acknowledgement of it, are two of the work's most haunting moments. But in *Die Walküre* the dangers and delights of passion are placed at the centre of the action, and the phrase 'the power of love' —'der Minne Macht' or 'der Liebe Macht'—recurs in Wotan's lines, as in the later stages of Act III:

Du folgtest selig	[You were happy to follow
der Liebe Macht:	The power of love:
folge nun dem,	Now follow him
den du lieben musst!	Whom you must love!]

Dahlhaus has argued that, as a drama, *Die Walküre* 'is disjointed, whether considered as a work on its own or as a part of the tetralogy';[49] and Cooke has shown that Wagner 'had greater difficulty in fashioning a convincing dramatic framework for Act I than for any other act of the tetralogy'.[50] Yet the ultimate power of the drama derives from the single element at its heart, the process whereby Wotan isolates himself—from Fricka, Siegmund, Brünnhilde. Indeed, *Die Walküre* is as much about isolation as relationships, from its initial image of the solitary fugitive Siegmund to the presentation, in Act III, of three characters about to experience separation: Sieglinde, Brünnhilde, Wotan.

It is Act I which expresses 'der Liebe Macht' with the most obvious inevitability and force, and many commentators have rhapsodized over the effortlessness of its lyrical flow and steadily mounting excitement; perhaps only in the extended passage of dumb show near

---

[49] *Richard Wagner's Music Dramas*, p. 110.
[50] *I saw the World end*, p. 290.

the end of the second scene, as Hunding retires to bed, do music and action temporarily hang fire. The text contains a high proportion of narration, but Wagner never falters in the musical imagination with which past events—Siegmund's earlier life, in particular—are made to contribute positively to the actual situation as it develops on stage. The composer's mastery of form is especially striking on the large scale, where widely separated climaxes are connected by music whose moments of extreme simplicity are no less arresting than the climaxes themselves. For example: in the third and final scene, the first climax comes early, as Siegmund calls on his father for a sword with which to defend himself against Hunding. Very gradually, after this, the music subsides to the point at which Sieglinde returns. 'Der Männer Sippe' is the moment of maximum simplicity, and dangerously close to 'sketchy' recitative; but in context it comes as a suppression of the outburst of more passionate music in Sieglinde's preceding lines, an outburst which anticipates the mood and material which will erupt extensively and conclusively to end the scene. It is this checking of momentum, both in order to allow for further reflection and narration, and to enhance the power of momentum when resumed, which is at the heart of Wagner's musico-dramatic technique, his 'endless melody' shaped and controlled by the ebb and flow of his harmonic processes. As Bryan Magee sees it, it is a kind of drama whose 'chief requirement was for situations which remain unchanged long enough for the characters' full inner experience of them, and response to them, to be expressed'.[51] Act I of *Die Walküre* reveals complete mastery of the expression of these crucial inner experiences, even in a character as unsympathetic as Hunding; and it balances action and reflection, anticipation and reminiscence, in ways which powerfully increase the evolutionary power of the whole, and render the eventual, postponed resolutions as inevitable as they are exciting.

As might be expected, such a process is underpinned not only by striking motivic development, but by a progressive tonal scheme which itself embodies a principle of transformation and enrichment. The overall motion from D minor to G major is notable for the resource with which its successive stages are elaborated, and the first scene is especially remarkable for its harmonic restraint; the exploration of closely related regions of its D minor/major tonic ensures that the function of that tonic is sustained throughout. The process of extension reaches its climax when the dominant key,

[51] Bryan Magee, *Aspects of Wagner* (rev. 2nd edn., Oxford, 1988), 8.

A major, leads on to its own relative minor at Siegmund's words 'Schmecktest du mir ihn zu?' This key of F sharp minor—the diatonic mediant of D major—is defined briefly but distinctly through a dominant-tonic-dominant progression. But Wagner brings the music back to the more basic tonic of D minor in one of the most intensely expressive phrases of the entire work, showing his reliance on two particularly fruitful techniques: sequence, and stress on a dominant (of B flat in this case), which generates further linear, modulatory motion rather than resolving cadentially on to its 'proper' tonic. The actual resolution on to D minor's root-position tonic is also delayed until Siegmund is four lines into the next stage of his narration (Ex. 172). And from the end of this scene onwards, it ceases to be possible to speak of D minor as 'the tonic' at all.

Wagner's use of different cadence forms has been the subject of much comment. Certainly it would be convenient if it could be argued that straightforward perfect cadences are always relatively

Ex. 172

with growing warmth. Still gazing, he removes the horn from his lips and lets it sink slowly,

whilst his features express strong emotion.)

(He sighs deeply and gloomily lets his eyes sink to the ground.)

(SIEGLINDE: You will not refuse this sweet drink of rich mead.
SIEGMUND: Will you taste it first? You have been caring for an ill-fated man. May you be spared
such misfortune! My rest has done me good: now I must be on my way.)

inhibiting to momentum, and therefore invariably increase the sense of a sectionalized form, while such 'evasions' as occur at the 'Langsam' (Ex. 172) ensure a more positive musical continuity. But rhythmic and general textural contexts often make such interpretations seem seriously over-simplified. Perfect cadences like those which frame Wotan's monologue in Act II, Scene ii (the first in A flat minor, the second in A minor) are both in their very different ways points of emphasis and definition, while such obvious evasions of prepared cadences as those at the end of Act I, Scene iii, or during Wotan's despairing monologue in Act II, Scene ii, after the words 'den Freien, erlang' ich mir nicht', ensure the continuation of tension and momentum, though in this case the 'true' cadence is not long delayed (Ex. 173). But emphasis and definition do not in themselves inhibit forward movement, any more than the postponement of a root-position tonic in favour of a submediant or some more complex and remote harmony need create genuine tonal ambiguity. The evolving tonal process is served by both procedures, and, since there is no serious doubt that the fundamental tonal goal will eventually be established by consonant cadential harmony whose finality is utterly explicit, it is the use of a variety of means to dramatize progress towards that goal which matters most—not arguments about whether or not such a goal actually exists.

Act I of *Die Walküre* is skilfully shaped to reach its point of highest excitement and greatest musical concentration at the very end. Wagner himself had doubts about the very different structure of Act II, in which two distinct 'catastrophes' occur: catastrophes 'which are so important and severe that they would really serve for an act each'.[52] Not all commentators agree that Wagner rose

[52] Letter to Liszt of 3 Oct. 1855, quoted in Dahlhaus, *Richard Wagner's Music Dramas*, p. 121.

Ex. 173

doch der in Lieb' ich frei - te, den Frei-en er-lang' ich mir nicht.

(Rising up in bitter wrath.)

So nimm mei-nen Se - gen, Nib - lungen Sohn! Was tief mich

e-kelt, dir geb' ich's zum Er - be, der Gott - heit

nich - ti-gen Glanz: zer - na-ge ihn gie - rig dein

più p

str

timp

Etwas lebhafter

Neid!

p   *cresc.*

(Although I wooed with love, I could not beget a free man. So take my blessing,
son of the Nibelungs. What revolts me deeply, I bequeath to you: eat your envious
fill of the empty glory of the gods!)

adequately to the occasion in the music which prepares the first of
these climaxes—the long second scene for Wotan and Brünnhilde
which the composer regarded as the most important 'for the evolution
of the whole, great four-part drama'. But it would be difficult to
argue that the second climax, and the way it is prepared in Scenes
iii and iv, suffers in conviction or impact from following on directly
from the earlier part of the act. The first climax, Wotan's great
outburst of bitterness and despair, grows out of reflection; the
second, linking Brünnhilde's conversion to Siegmund's cause with his
subsequent death, is embedded in action; and this action is not only
the culmination of the steady growth of tension throughout Scene
iv, but the vital counterpart to Brünnhilde's passive role during
Wotan's earlier scene of self-examination and self-accusation. Both
Brünnhilde and Wotan are driven to action in Scene v, and Wagner
guides the final stages of that action to their close with no sense of
anti-climax. To slow up and thin out the texture to the extent that
he does just before Wotan's final outburst is to concentrate and
intensify rather than dissipate the tension of the scene (Ex. 174).
And the act is only structurally complete as Wotan's wrathful exit
balances, with well-nigh ironic force, the warlike confidence with

Ex. 174

(*At this moment the clouds divide, so that Hunding, who has just drawn his spear from the fallen Siegmund's breast, is clearly seen.*)

WOTAN (*surrounded by clouds, stands on a rock behind leaning on his spear and sadly gazing on Siegmund's body.*)
(*to Hunding*)

Geh' hin, Knecht! Kni - e vor Fricka:

(Go, slave! Kneel before Fricka.)

which the act began. At the start of the act, Wotan has urged
Brünnhilde to ensure Siegmund's victory. At the end he himself
declares war on Brünnhilde for forcing him to cause Siegmund's
death directly, through his own intervention in the fight with
Hunding. The full extent of Wotan's shame and disgrace becomes
apparent only at this point.

Act I of *Die Walküre* begins with a storm, Act II with an
anticipation of the fight to come, and Act III develops this fight

music in its first scene, the most extendedly turbulent set piece in the whole cycle. In the case of Act III, however, the ending does not concentrate or outdo the initial turbulence, but dissolves it. The climax of the act's animated music comes with Brünnhilde's last words, 'dem freislichen Felsen zu nah'n!', the apex of an extended process of gradual intensification from the point of repose at 'War es so schmählich?' at the start of Scene iii, which also establishes the E tonality fundamental to the entire final scene. Wagner's technique in Scene iii shows the most powerful, large-scale control of tension and resolution, through motivic development and tonal extension. He is able to let the almost unbearable excitement generated up to Brünnhilde's final phrases flow out into the broader, more reflective final section of the work, from Wotan's 'Leb' wohl, du kühnes herrliches Kind!', achieving a dramatic fulfilment founded on finely proportioned musical architecture. E major is established at an early stage of this final section, at the line 'der freier als ich der Gott!' (Ex. 175), and its subsequent enrichment is a superb example of the purposeful interaction of diatonic and chromatic, consonant and dissonant elements. The extended major mode of the ending clearly represents not only Loge's warm, protective glow, but Wotan's own

Ex. 175

sinks in ecstasy on Wotan's breast: he holds her in a long embrace.)

p *molto cresc.*   ff

(One freer than I, the god!)

transfiguring compassion. Yet the ending, like that of *Das Rheingold*, is also poignant. Wotan and Brünnhilde may be reconciled, but he is still unable to let her go free. His sorrow is as much for himself as for her. The essential image is therefore of isolation, and profound, helpless regret.

SIEGFRIED (1)

The preferred modern reading of the *Ring* is likely to be one which finds Wotan more sympathetic than Siegfried. And, whereas we may welcome Wagner's remark, with reference to the Wanderer, that 'he resembles us to a tee; he is the sum of the intelligence of the present', the thought of Siegfried as 'the man of the future willed and sought by us, but who cannot be made by us and who must create himself through *our destruction*' is remote in tone and temper from the later twentieth century. For Wagner, Siegfried was 'the most complete man I could conceive of, whose highest awareness is that all awareness can be expressed only in the utmost immediacy of life and action'. In the scene with the Rhinemaidens in Act III of *Götterdämmerung*, 'Siegfried is immeasurably knowing, for he knows the most important thing, that death is better than living in fear'. And Wagner exclaims that 'the gods in all their glory must pale before this man!'[53] A hundred years after Wagner's death, we would probably prefer to stress what Dahlhaus calls 'the tragic contradictions of Siegfried's situation', and to note that the cause of his downfall

lies in the tragic contradiction that his instinct and independence, which single him out to save himself and others from the entanglements of contracts and laws and the consequences of reflection, also invite disaster. The route that avoids catastrophe leads directly to it.[54]

[53] Letter to August Röckel, 25–6 Jan. 1854. See *Wagner: A Documentary Study*, p. 184.
[54] Dahlhaus, *Richard Wagner's Music Dramas*, p. 91.

Dahlhaus goes so far as to describe *Siegfried* as 'a fairy-tale opera rather than a heroic myth',[55] and yet it contains the encounter which is the crux of the cycle, a scene more decisive, as action, than Act II, Scene ii, of *Die Walküre*—the meeting of the Wanderer and Siegfried in Act III, Scene ii. Siegfried and the Wanderer are the only two characters to appear in all three acts of *Siegfried*, and Wagner delays their meeting until the later stages; yet differences and similarities between them are essential to the structure of the whole drama. In Act I, for example, the vital contrast is not between Siegfried's strength and Mime's weakness, or between the Wanderer's wisdom and Mime's stupidity: it is between the fearless energy of Siegfried and the potent resignation of the Wanderer. Act II confirms that the Wanderer is capable of Siegfried-like humour and harshness, while Siegfried himself can be tender and thoughtful. But it is only when they meet in Act III that it is clear that any potential they might have for thinking and behaving alike—like Wälse and Siegmund—will have no chance to prosper. Although the Wanderer has belied his claim to watch, rather than to act, in the way he has tricked Mime, mocked Alberich and Fafner, and harangued Erda, there is a ritualistic quality to the actions with which he actually attempts to prevent Siegfried from passing him which demonstrates the consequences of his recent admission to Erda that he will gladly yield his place to the young hero.

The richness of *Siegfried* lies in the opportunities for contrasts and elaborations which these dramatic elements provide. The music of action, with its less developmental song and rondo forms, is most dominant in Act I. Yet 'development' can take various forms: for example, the obvious reiterations of the forging song (Ex. 176) transcend their own potential banality, not only by the sheer power with which they generate a hectic, very un-song-like atmosphere,

Ex. 176

(Nothung, Nothung! Glorious sword! . . .
I have reduced your sharp splendour to chaff)

[55] Ibid., p. 128.

Ex. 177

(As whimpering child, I brought thee up, . . .
the impatient boy torments and hates me!)

but in the way they slyly offer themselves as derivatives of the
corresponding, limp repetitions of Mime's earlier lament (Ex. 177).
Nor is all the music fast and furious: the very first scene links Mime's
own forging music with Fafner's motif, and contrasts both with
reminders of Sieglinde, using more lyrical material which will receive
fuller treatment in Act II. In Act I, Scene ii, the use of question
and answer provides Wagner with a golden opportunity for large-scale
musical reminiscence, motivic and tonal, but the effect of this is the
reverse of mechanical or predictable. The scene becomes an extended
process of development and integration in which mere repetitions
are consistently overridden, and its subtle variations of pace as well
as its inexorably cumulative tension are carried over into Scene iii.
Today we may have some difficulty in seeing such naked delight in
weapons and violence as comic, in true scherzo fashion, but the
delight of the hero in his own skill and strength is the more forcibly
apparent in the way the final D major music offers the closest parallel
in the *Ring* to Beethoven's 'Ode to Joy'.

Like Act I, Act II begins with sinister foreboding, but its course
is very different. Although it embraces the violent deaths of Fafner
and Mime, and reveals that Alberich has not deviated in the slightest
from his demonic determination to regain the ring, it is the less
portentous elements which predominate: Wotan's wit, Fafner's
humour and humility, Mime's comic self-betrayal, and the
Woodbird's decoded messages. As for Siegfried, it may be felt that
Wagner tried too hard to give the hero humanity, as well as certain
skills as an instrumentalist, in this act. But the sublime idyll of his
reflection on maternity is composed with sovereign economy: the
music flows ecstatically out of its references to Mime and Sieglinde,
and leads effortlessly into the business with bird and dragon.
Moreover, it is at once clear, when Siegfried emerges from the dead
dragon's cave, with the ring and the Tarnhelm, that the mood of

lyrical exaltation to which he has gained access has not been lost. Rather it has intensified, as the economy with which the music extends two dominants (a whole tone apart) demonstrates (Ex. 178). A more strenuous, heroically Romantic quality emerges later as

Ex. 178

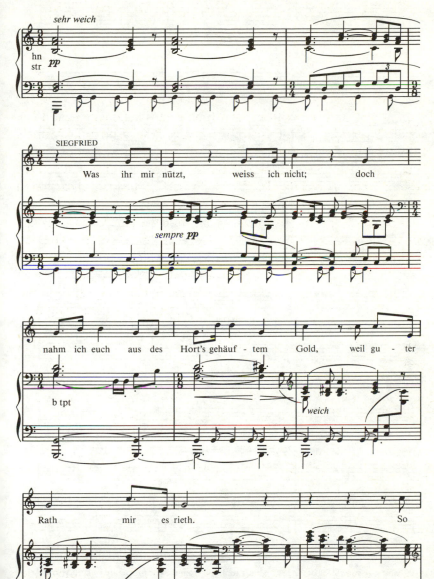

(I don't know how you will be of use to me; but I took you from the piled-up hoard of gold because of good advice; your decoration can witness to this day's deeds, your glitter recall that I fought and killed Fafner without yet learning what fear is.)

Siegfried begins to act out his destiny as the rescuer, lover, and betrayer of Brünnhilde. But the whole act ends playfully, the sudden, loud chord of E major offering a foretaste of the still more playful music (the end of Act II of *Die Meistersinger*) which Wagner would compose before completing *Siegfried* itself.

TRISTAN UND ISOLDE

The Wagner literature staggers under the weight of discussions about the similarities and contrasts between the essential dramatic theme of *Der Ring des Nibelungen* and *Tristan und Isolde*, a topic made the more tantalizing by the knowledge that in his sketches Wagner was at one stage unsure whether to use certain material in *Tristan* or in *Siegfried*; after all, both were concerned with expressions of passionate love and the crossing of an 'old man' who tries to stand in the way of that love. It is in the literature which stresses purely musical considerations that arguments favouring the view that *Tristan* represents a fairly radical break with the past are likely to be found. It will be claimed not only that the dramatic theme is much less concerned with political, social issues than that of the *Ring*, but also that the music seems to be driven by the sheer force of its symbolic potential to question its own most fundamental stabilizing functions: if night is the time of true illumination, if death is the only true fulfilment of love, then the triad and tonality itself must be challenged by the greater expressiveness and necessary ambiguities of a chord which encapsulates tension so potently that all resolutions of it seem illusory.

It cannot be denied that the structural significance of the *Tristan* chord extends beyond its frequent surface occurrence as a vertical entity and its various resolutions. The individual pitch-classes—F, B, E flat, and A flat—are all of importance in acting as tonics for substantial areas of the work, notably the A flat major at the centre of the Act II love scene, and the spanning of Act III by F minor and B major. But for all its evident dependence on those intervals which divide the octave symmetrically—tritone and minor third— the chord does not in practice promote a harmonic language which has no points of contact with traditional distinctions between consonance and dissonance, still less a musical language which is positively motivic and only negatively harmonic: in *Tristan* the functional distinctions between chromaticism and diatonicism, as well as between consonance and dissonance, are ultimately reinforced. The effortless and persistent superiority of tonics as controlling consonances can no longer be taken for granted, but traditional relationships are reshaped rather than eliminated. In Act II, Scene i, for example, the necessary excitement of expectation is created by prolonging the dominant of the principal tonality (B flat major) and giving little or no attention to the root-position tonic triad of that key.

To argue for the unprecedented radicalism of *Tristan* by detaching the famous chord from its various contexts of preparation, transposition, and resolution is to over-simplify, and prejudge the issue. The prominence which Wagner gives to the chord is clear evidence of the special intensity and concentration of the work's atmosphere. But the nature of its treatment is evidence of a heightened linearity in which assertions of 'unity' by means of strategically placed repetitions are less vital than the continuous process of transformation. The scale on which Wagner was operating made it psychologically more satisfying if his perorations, in particular, could be recognized as recollections—or developments—of material heard earlier. Repetition is absorbed into transformation—as, most obviously, in Isolde's final 'transfiguration'—but the listener is as likely to be aware of balanced contrasts as of an integrated unity in which contrasts are somehow of inferior status to substantial passages of repetition.

There are certainly many contrasts and conflicts in *Tristan* which cannot be explained away as serving some higher unity. In several places Wagner exploits the effect of a sudden intrusion to increase tension or destroy a mood. At the start of Act I the sailor's song provokes Isolde, and Isolde's own interruptions of Brangäne illustrate the vital role of harmony in turning potentially mollifying cadences into new provocations (Ex. 179). The most celebrated example in *Tristan* of the combination of a sudden intrusion with a thwarted cadence is the appearance of King Marke and his followers at the

Ex. 179

(BRANGÄNE: on this calm sea we're sure to reach land by evening.
ISOLDE: What land?
BRANGÄNE: Cornwall's verdant strand.
ISOLDE: Never! Not today nor tomorrow!)

start of Act II, Scene iii. But Wagner's technique was as well adapted to the exploitation of expectation as of intrusion; to portraying reproachful, resentful, or guilty silence as well as angry, feverish, or passionate volubility; and the musical means vary according to the dramatic effect required. Thus, for Tristan's reluctant approach in Act I, Scene v the initial plain cadence on to the tonic of F minor generates not a process of expansion within that tonality but a powerful progression across the tritone, outlined with relative rapidity (Ex. 180), though B major is only cadentially confirmed thirty-seven bars later at Tristan's 'Gehorsam einzig hielt mich in Bann'. But the very different use of F minor at the beginning of Act III, with chromaticism strongly controlled by recurrences of diatonic triads, is no less expressive of silent suffering; the difference is that here Tristan himself is physically motionless—indeed the curtain has not yet risen (Ex. 181).

Ex. 180

(Sir Tristan may approach.)

Ex. 181

In a description of Act III of *Tristan* Wagner referred to 'the ceaseless play of musical motifs, emerging, unfolding, uniting, severing, blending anew, waxing, waning, battling each with each, at last embracing and well-nigh engulfing one another'. These motifs 'have to express an emotional life which ranges from the fiercest longing for bliss to the most resolute desire for death, and therefore required a harmonic development and an independent motion such as could never be planned with like variety in any pure-symphonic piece'.[56] This should be sufficient to demolish the stale old argument

[56] 'Meine Erinnerungen an Ludwig Schnorr von Carolsfeld' (1868); repr. in *Richard Wagner: Gesammelte Schriften und Dichtungen*, iii (Leipzig, 1872), 221–41; trans. Ellis, 'My Recollections of Ludwig Schnorr von Carolsfeld', *Prose Works*, iv (London, 1895), 235.

about whether or in what way *Tristan und Isolde* is 'symphonic', at least in its tonal structures. As with all Wagner's later works, what is most essential with respect to its musical organization and dramatic expression is the existence of a process of tonal enrichment; and this leads away from the essentially symphonic idea of one governing key or single hierarchy of related keys to an overriding concern on both small and large scales with an evolutionary process, with progressive changes which in fact unify the work more effectively and decisively than regular, if diverse, references to a single centre. It is the process which matters more than the idea of a fixed point of reference. *Tristan und Isolde* may indeed be so radical in its fundamental pitch structures that, to quote a present-day analyst, it is 'not only "12-tone" in a special sense, but also "serial" in a special sense'.[57] But it is also tonal in a relatively normal, if far from precisely 'symphonic' sense. The novelty and richness of the music are not the result of a sudden rejection of tradition, but of the remarkable way in which new possibilities are opened up within the framework of the old relationships.

DIE MEISTERSINGER VON NÜRNBERG

Nowhere in later Wagner do 'new' and 'old' confront each other more directly and disconcertingly than in Act I of the Paris *Tannhäuser*, where the distance between the Venusberg and Thuringia is so much greater than in the original version. The Paris *Tannhäuser* is very much an appendix to *Tristan*. But the manifold and obvious contrasts between *Tristan* and *Die Meistersinger* can be manipulated to make the latter seem a necessary antidote to the former—an antidote the more explicit for its use of a passing reference to *Tristan*'s plot and music in order to reduce rather than heighten tension. The way in which Hans Sachs addresses the assembled company at the end, and receives their acclaim, is indeed the representation of a very different dramatic denouement from that of Isolde's solitary 'transfiguration', just as the triadic amplitude of *Die Meistersinger*'s opening contrasts pointedly with the tonally allusive linearity of the *Tristan* Prelude's first bars. It would scarcely be surprising if both chromaticism and dissonance were more prominent in the surface detail of *Tristan* than of *Die Meistersinger*. But a study of the ways in which both works prepare and establish their principal points of tonal emphasis and resolution might discover aspects of

---

[57] Benjamin Boretz, 'Meta-Variations, Part IV: Analytic Fallout (I)', *Perspectives of New Music*, 11 (1972), 216.

process and technique which are both more fundamental and more similar than obvious differences of subject-matter and surface detail might lead one to expect.

Tristan is unambiguously concerned with the power of love, but *Die Meistersinger* is arguably more ambitious in theme. The love of Walther and Eva is real enough, but—because that love inspires Walther to invent some remarkably powerful, passionate music, and Walther's radicalism in turn inspires Sachs to meditate on the life of art in society—the work seems more fundamentally concerned with the power of music, and its capacity to advance when a new naturalness and spontaneity are allowed to sweep away arid and excessively literary conventions. It may even be held to demonstrate that such changes can best be achieved by aristocrats arriving from outside to live purposeful lives within a hierarchically ordered society; no wonder T. W. Adorno described it disapprovingly as 'the blueprint of a pristine bourgeois world'.[58]

Such a world seems to depend on the recognition that some intellects are superior to others, and that a superior intellect may mislead and humiliate an inferior for the greater social good. It will probably never be possible to attempt to disentangle Wagner's works from his own beliefs, and their apparent connections with early twentieth-century German ideology, without accusations of special pleading, and the unease about Sachs's treatment of Beckmesser— Sachs standing for Wagner and Aryan Germany, Beckmesser for the Jews and all persecuted minorities?—is understandable. Post-war producers have tended to make the final reconciliation more com-prehensive than Wagner intended, by bringing back a crestfallen Beckmesser to witness the final jubilation, showing that he has learned his lesson and bears no lasting grudge. But Wagner was probably not very interested in treating Beckmesser as naturalistically as many of the work's other characters. As a senior mastersinger, his incompetence when trying to improvise appropriate music for the new poetry of Walther is more comprehensible than his inability to turn out a satisfactorily simple serenade in Act II; but then, as Dahlhaus shrewdly points out, 'Beckmesser does not represent any sector of art, not even mastersong. . . . The Marker is nothing but a caricature of a critic.'[59] One may, in the interests of dramatic credibility, attribute Beckmesser's elementary errors in his serenade and prize song to emotional disturbance, and something is certainly

[58] Theodor Adorno, *In Search of Wagner*, trans. Rodney Livingstone (London, 1981), 96.
[59] *Richard Wagner's Music Dramas*, p. 68.

Ex. 182

(Mild and gentle, how he smiles; how sweetly he opens his eyes.)

Ex. 183

(St John stood by the Jordan to baptize the people of every nation.)

lost if we feel no sympathy whatever for him at this point. But it is not necessary to accept without qualification Dahlhaus's view that 'his role in the action is allegorical' to sense that dream-like wish-fulfilment matters as much as soberly naturalistic reality in the unfolding of the dramatic scheme. Wagner's desire to make Beckmesser 'a caricature of a critic' conquers Sachs's desire for him to be a genuine mastersinger whose gifts have been atrophied by unthinking adherence to 'the rules'.

To juxtapose the first four bars of Isolde's 'transfiguration' (Ex. 182) with the first four bars of David's 'Sprüchlein' from Act III of *Die Meistersinger* (Ex. 183) is to highlight two very different examples of Wagner's characteristic simplicity of shape and rhythm. Although the first two intervals happen to be the same in both melodies, the first is harmonically open-ended, the second purely diatonic. Both are instances of the composer's aspiration to that 'sublime naïveté' which he valued so highly in Beethoven, and which perhaps achieved its finest expression at the end of the Good Friday music in Parsifal's phrase 'du weinest—sieh, es lacht die Aue!' *Die Meistersinger* marks a particularly important step along the road to that ideal of communicating directly to the feelings with the greatest naturalness and simplicity, since its plot involves the argument that there is a fundamental difference between old and new musical styles, centring on the contrasts between simplicity and complexity, orthodoxy and unorthodoxy. But *Die Meistersinger* is not a documentary, in which two stylistically incompatible kinds of musical authenticity are demonstrated. Rather it is a composition in which Wagner displays his versatility, his ability to represent both sterility and vitality within the bounds of his own style. *Die Meistersinger* contrasts the stolidity and pomposity of those who support lack of change with the impetuosity, open-mindedness and more elevated expressiveness of those—Sachs and Walther—who see no virtue in blind adherence to old-established procedures which have outlived their usefulness, at least for a younger generation. But the essential difference between the two modes of expression is not, as a documentary might be obliged to demonstrate, in the nature of their basic materials as represented by generative thematic ideas, but in the way the materials are treated; in a sense, after all, the basic motif of Walther's prize song is scarcely more promising or memorable than that of Beckmesser's.

Wagner's composition of the entire work in his own style results in many moments of delightful and pointed dramatic irony, and as soon as the curtain rises Wagner hints at the possibility that the music might involve disorienting shifts between moods which even his supremely flexible and diverse idiom might not be able to accommodate comfortably. There is something wilfully un-sophisticated about the Romantic instrumental interpolations in the hymn, and it is perhaps just as well that the issue of the relation between sacred and secular in sixteenth-century Nuremberg is not further pursued. As for the earthy yet conservative masters, how, we might ask, can they take such exception to Walther's Act I spring song in F major when they have sat without flinching through the extraordinary modulation across a tritone with which Pogner recovers that key in his earlier address (Ex. 184)? Are they making the point that Pogner is not offering a 'song' as such and that only Art must cherish tradition, leaving Life to be as contemporary as may be?

It can be claimed with some confidence that Act II of *Die Meistersinger* is Wagner's greatest single achievement in the art of drawing large-scale continuity out of a brilliantly balanced diversity

Ex. 184

(So hear, Masters, what prize I have decided to bestow!
The singer, who [is the victor] in the song contest, . . .)

of character and event. The continuity is not one in which incidental discontinuities need to be explained away. Just as the 'small' is integrated into the 'large' without losing its identity, so the evolutionary progress of the whole may be enhanced by occasional interruptions and disruptions, such as that which Sachs provides with the first stanza of his cobbling song. Wagner's particular enthusiasm for transition was rooted in the obvious point that such a feature provides the opportunity for heightened expression, not a merely mechanical 'continuity'. In Act III of *Die Meistersinger* some of the most expressive music of all is concentrated into passages which cross maximum tonal space between C major and G flat major (or vice versa). Every commentary on the work remarks on the way the quintet seems to have been placed on a remote tonal plateau, and the progression which precedes it—from the dominant of C to the dominant of G flat—is achieved through the most direct stepwise descent (Ex. 185). As the quintet ends, there is a much more extended progression away from G flat to prepare the C major of Scene v.

Ex. 185

(*He moves from the middle of the half-circle which the others have formed round him, so that Eva stands now in the middle.*)

Spruch.

poco rall.

Langsam, doch leicht fliessend

EVA

Se - lig, wie die_ Son - ne mei-nes_ Glü - ckes lacht,___

(SACHS: Now may it grow large, without hurt or injury.
Let the youngest Godmother speak the fitting words.
EVA: Brightly, as the sun breaks upon my fortune, . . .)

And just before Sachs's final address there is a last, concentrated reminder of the material of the quintet as an even more basic stepwise motion drags Walther and Eva back from their dream world to the solid reality of Nuremberg and its well-ordered society (Ex. 186).

Adorno singles out the quintet as what he terms a moving, but

Ex. 186

Langsam

WALTHER (*refusing the chain impetuously.*)   (*He looks tenderly at Eva.*)

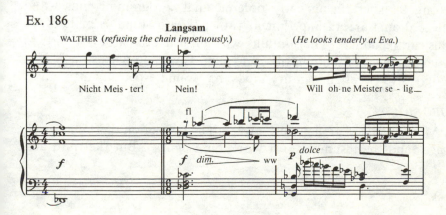

Nicht Meis - ter!   Nein!   Will oh - ne Meister se - lig_

(All look at Sachs in great perplexity.)

Mässig bewegt
(Sachs comes to Walther and takes him impressively by the hand.)

(Not Master, no! I will be happy without Masterdom!)

impotent gesture, which 'after a few bars of a tender luminous beauty
. . . falls back on the stock of motives of the Prize song' and 'fails
to develop from the new idea'.[60] Apart from its insensitivity to
tonal and textural transformations within the quintet itself, this
interpretation fails to detect the pervasive relationship between
'modulation', which for Adorno 'never quite escapes from the sense
of side-stepping', and 'seems peculiarly arbitrary', and the large-scale
generators and goals which shape and control the actual language
of the music. The analytical custodian of the purely symphonic tonal
tradition, Heinrich Schenker, was quite right to see Wagner as an
opponent rather than a continuer of that tradition, but he was quite
wrong to assert in an early polemic that 'programme music and
music drama are an impediment rather than a stimulus or boon to
musical freedom'.[61] The stimulus which music drama did provide to
a development of more flexible and expressive materials is one which
progressive twentieth-century music has found especially attractive.

SIEGFRIED (2)

More than a year elapsed between the completion of *Die Meistersinger* and the resumption of work on *Siegfried*. But the third acts

[60] *In Search of Wagner*, p. 125.
[61] Heinrich Schenker, 'Essay on Ornamentation', trans. Hedi Siegel, *Music Forum*, 4 (New
York, 1976), 36.

of both works have at least one fundamental common factor: in both, the overall tonal motion is from G to C. Nevertheless, the contrast between Sachs's contemplative G major and the Wanderer's turbulent G minor could hardly be greater. Once again, as in Act I, the Wanderer comes seeking information, asking questions to which he does not, this time, appear to know the answers already. But the 'all-knowing' Erda is as ineffective a respondent as the foolish Mime, and the Wanderer is again forced to provide the crucial answer for himself. Siegfried has already claimed two victims—Fafner and Mime; Wotan will be his third, but only because the god himself wills it to be so. In Scene ii the 'Alter Frager' assumes the role of questioner for the last time, and the effect is only to delay, rather than divert, the inevitable course of events. The Wanderer's anger is no more effective than his affability; since the moment in *Das Rheingold* when he confessed that 'care and fear fetter my mind', he has ultimately been powerless in the face of fearlessness.

Siegfried himself knows that the will of the enemy who contrived his father's death is powerless to prevent his own progress. The two enact a ritual to represent the momentous transfer of power which has already been accepted by Wotan, and is acknowledged by him with the brief benediction, 'Go on, I cannot restrain you.' It is as if, at the end of *Die Meistersinger*, Walther were to supplant Sachs as the prime object of the crowd's acclaim. There the 'young', having made his point, stands back in respect for the 'old'. But Wotan is allowed no aria of farewell, no further prophetic peroration, before Siegfried advances through the fire (Ex. 187). Wagner's abrupt dismissal of such a significant character may seem disturbingly casual, but it has an unsparing dramatic truth. As the scene has unfolded we have come increasingly to see the god through Siegfried's eyes,

Ex. 187

(*He suddenly disappears in complete darkness.*)

Ich___ kann dich nicht hal - ten! —

più **p**

SIEGFRIED

Mit zer - focht' - ner Waf - fe floh mir der

pp

bn
d bn

Fei - ge?

poco cresc.

(WANDERER: Go on! I cannot restrain you!
SIEGFRIED: With his spear shattered, has the coward run away?)

and Wotan's last decision is not to impose his presence a second longer. The sooner he returns to Valhalla, the sooner preparations can begin for 'the end'. After all, as Wagner wrote to King Ludwig in 1864, 'he knows . . . that he lives on in Siegfried, as the artist lives on in his work'.[62]

Wotan now sees nothing but 'the end': yet Siegfried himself has barely begun. In one of Wagner's most extended and extreme transitions, a huge slowing up of tempo and thinning out of texture takes place, in total contrast to the rapid replacement of Erda by Siegfried at the start of the previous scene. The transition begins with one of Wagner's most emphatic perfect cadences, in F major,

[62] *Wagner: A Documentary Study*, p. 206.

then extends that key—with particular reference to the dominant of
G flat major—before reaching E major, the correct chord for the
repetition of the reposeful 'fire music' which ended *Die Walküre*.
Now, however, the E major triad and its dominant together form
just one salient feature in a flux involving the dominants and tonics
of C and D majors as well. The transition reaches its moment of
maximum withdrawal from the fierce energy of its beginning with
the broad unfolding of D major's dominant seventh, which begins
Scene iii. But instead of resolving directly on to its tonic, this
dominant moves up a tone to the dominant of E major as the violin
line reaches its apex. The resolution to the D major tonic is then
achieved, an effect which is not merely texturally understated, but
structurally unstable; far from being the starting-point for a section
of music in that key, it initiates a still more elaborate quest for a
genuine point of stability (Ex. 188).

Ex. 188

(Blessed solitude on the sun-lit summit!)

The immensely sustained moment of Brünnhilde's awakening is notable for the way in which Wagner extends the fundamental C major with special reference to the dominant of its mediant, E minor, thereby establishing a third relation which is treated in greater depth as the scene proceeds: the E major/minor music of the Siegfried 'Idyll' episode provides the most stable alternative to C in this long third scene. The first main diatonic cadence in C occurs when the couple formally acknowledge each other by singing together (Ex. 189). Only here is the process of progression from the transition's initial F major to a new stability complete, and this type of cadence, complete with trills and pauses, returns to create the exalted finality of the very end. The cadence seems joyous rather than banal because its diatonic purity is a genuine resolution of the chromatic enrichments with which the music is principally concerned. Wagner may have shown a ruthless capacity for cutting harmonic corners when a sudden shift of perspective was dramatically appropriate, but the juggler was always guided by the architect, and effects of the moment never undermine the strength of the edifice as a whole.

Ex. 189

(SIEGFRIED: . . . that I behold these eyes which laugh on me now in my joy!
BRÜNNHILDE: Your eyes alone were permitted to see me, you alone could waken me!)

GÖTTERDÄMMERUNG

In Act I of *Götterdämmerung* contrasts between action and reflection
are delineated with the clarity and sense of impending doom necessary
to this late stage of the drama. The first significant event in the
Prologue—the breaking of the Norns' rope—sets up a terrible irony
which sustains the drama of the act across the long spans which

separate this from the two other principal events, Siegfried's drinking
of the potion and his theft of the ring from Brünnhilde. The irony
is clearest in the plain text, where Brünnhilde's cheerful talk of the
hero's longing for new exploits immediately follows the Norns'
despairing conclusion about the loss of their eternal wisdom. The
Norns seem to know little of Siegfried, beyond the fact that it was
'a bold hero' who shattered Wotan's spear. Their attention is fixed
on the more fundamental issue of what Wotan will eventually do
with those spear fragments, and the evolution of the scene through
its refrains and tonal recurrences is as inexorable as the workings of
Alberich's curse.

The second part of the Prologue, the scene for Brünnhilde
and Siegfried, anticipates the action exuberantly portrayed in the
transitional music of Siegfried's Rhine journey. By bringing in the
most direct reference since *Das Rheingold* to the tonality and theme
of the Rhinemaidens' music (the tonality of E flat has dominated
the whole Prologue), and dissolving it into the third-related anticipation of the Gibichungs' B minor music, Wagner not only
contrasts primal lyricism with human villainy, but focuses with great
and timely precision on the images which will only reach their
fulfilment when the Rhinemaidens drag Hagen down to a watery
grave. There is indeed a powerful harmony between all the elements
present in *Götterdämmerung*:

the scenes in which the divine myth dominates the action ... do not so
much directly influence the course of the action as imbue the events taking
place in a temporal setting with a mythic significance—providing them, as
it were, with a reverberation spreading far beyond their immediate sphere.[63]

The first two scenes of Act I demonstrate what Siegfried's principal
exploit is to be—the winning of Brünnhilde for Gunther. Of the
large-scale musical factors through which this action is charted,
special emphasis is given to the opposition between semitones. Scene
i begins in B minor, but, after its ending in an extrovert B flat major
with Siegfried's arrival, the tonality is twisted back to B minor
through an emphatic harmonization of the 'curse' motif (Ex. 190).
Scene ii therefore begins in the same key as Scene i, but with a
transformation of Siegfried's own motif, not that of the Gibichungs;
the change of identity has already begun. The end of Scene ii is a
kind of reversal of that of Scene i, as Siegfried departs with Gunther,
and the tonality moves away from B flat minor into the long
transition from action to reflection in Hagen's hopeful brooding. As

---

[63] Dahlhaus, *Richard Wagner's Music Dramas*, p. 135.

Ex. 190

(Hail! Siegfried, dearest hero!)

the music rediscovers elements from the early stages of the first scene it is clear that Brünnhilde remains optimistic, and content to wait for Siegfried's return. At the very end of the transition, indeed, the music recalls her original awakening in Act III of *Siegfried*. But then a rapid conflict ensues between these recollections and the stormy approach of Waltraute, the B minor of the original Valkyrie music serving to reassert the act's principal point of tonal reference.

One important dramatic function of Scene iii is to make the horror of Brünnhilde's eventual betrayal by Siegfried seem the greater by provoking her to an extravagant affirmation of faith in the power of his love—something she values to a degree which leaves her impervious to, though not unmoved by, Waltraute's pleas. Waltraute's description of the broken Wotan in Valhalla is indeed one of the most moving episodes in all Wagner's work, and seems the more powerful when one realizes that the musical as well as the dramatic foundations are being laid for the final stages of the cycle. It is a structure which, for all the intensity of its chromatic detail, is founded on the significant relation between a tonic (F sharp minor/G flat major) and its dominant of D flat; and it is one of the finest examples in Wagner of a structure placed at the service of a situation 'which remains unchanged long enough for the characters' experience of it, and response to it, to be expressed'.[64] But the brutal events which end the act are portrayed in music of such gripping concentration that there is no sense of anti-climax.

Act II begins like a continuation of Act I, with music in an extended B flat minor, which is the apotheosis of brooding malevolence: the entire first scene expands on the material of Hagen's 'watch'. Alberich constantly alludes to the fact that Hagen is his son, but his appearance serves principally to clarify Hagen's determination to win the ring for himself. Although at the end of Act II Hagen does refer to Alberich as the Lord of the Ring, 'des Ringes Herrn'—the Nibelung will play no more direct a role in the drama's climax than will Wotan.

After Scene i, Act II is notably eventful, dominated by arrivals and accusations. Siegfried's return is magically abrupt, so much so that the music, which has begun to move decisively away from F major, has to be brusquely returned there for the appropriate horn-call. By contrast, the arrival of Brünnhilde and Gunther is prepared by an extrovert and extended choral ensemble, skilfully structured so that clarification of the long-promised C major is itself

---

[64] Magee, *Aspects of Wagner*, p. 8.

finally swept aside by the approach of B flat major, a basic confrontation between the act's first and last tonal centres. After the diatonic emphasis of the welcome for Gunther and Brünnhilde, the central part of the act employs an intense chromaticism for Brünnhilde's denunciation of Siegfried, and the oaths; nevertheless, this chromaticism does not override such strongly cadential points of tonal reference as that to the E flat and B centres (which dominated Act I) at the end of Brünnhilde's oath (Ex. 191). After this, the blithe restoration of a diatonic C major at the end of Siegfried's conciliatory peroration seems appropriately ingenuous.

Accusation, self-accusation, and the most concentrated chromaticism permeate the final scene of Act II as the plot for Siegfried's death is hatched. At the very end of the ensemble passage, C major re-emerges as the act's final arrival, that of the wedding procession, takes place. The sense of a fusion of extremes—the kind of jubilation achieved at the very end of *Siegfried* blended with the threatening jocularity of Hagen's rousing of the vassals—makes this a complex

Ex. 191

(BRÜNNHILDE: . . . this man has sworn falsehood.
VASSALS: Help, Donner!)

but powerful representation of the evident failure of 'true love' to survive the determined assault of human barbarity. There is a pervading hollowness, disturbing simply because it is dramatically so convincing.

Like the first scene of *Das Rheingold*, the first scene of Act III shows an encounter between the three Rhinemaidens and a solitary male. Siegfried is initially as reluctant to return the ring to them as Alberich was eager to steal the gold. The Rhinemaidens had themselves provided Alberich with the motive for effecting the theft, telling him about the powers conferred by the renunciation of love; and Siegfried comes to claim that, although the ring may have given him great power, he could in fact be prepared to renounce all that power for the pleasures of love—'der Minne Gunst'. The Rhinemaidens provide a Norn-like prophecy of Siegfried's imminent death, and they describe with powerful economy the all-too-human weakness of the hero. In one basic respect, however, they seem to be under his spell, and their dependence on his fate is represented in the music by this scene's use of F major as its basic tonic—the F of Siegfried's horn-call. There is no decisive return here to the primal E flat of the Rhine itself. That particular innocence is irrecoverable.

In Scene i Siegfried is still under the spell of Gutrune's potion—though able to remember Fafner's dying warning—and in Scene ii the gradual lifting of the spell does not result in a sudden access of cautious common sense, but a suicidal embrace of the ecstasy of memory. The hero rediscovers the truth in a narration whose stages summarize the events of *Siegfried*. First he recounts his relationship with Mime, the reforging of Nothung, the death of Fafner, and the first words of the Woodbird (remembered exactly) about the treasure. Then, prompted by Hagen and the vassals, he recalls the bird's warning about Mime and its subsequent description of Brünnhilde. The confirmation of C major towards which the music moves during Siegfried's own description of the woken Brünnhilde (he omits any mention of the Wanderer, or of his long struggle with fear) is now postponed, so that Hagen's attack takes place in a structural parenthesis. C major is asserted first as Siegfried begins his final lines (the music from *Siegfried*, Act III) and then, finally, at the overwhelming climax of the funeral march. But the struggle from minor to major tonality is then reversed, not to provide a simple symmetrical design, but with an intensified chromaticism in the final phase, and the return of C minor is touched on only in passing (Ex. 192).

In the theatre it is occasionally possible to feel that the rest of the

Ex. 192

(Was that his horn?)

work after the funeral march is an anticlimax. The mechanics of the action, from the re-entry of Hagen to the burning of Valhalla and the flooding of the Rhine, are all too obtrusive. But even if the staging of these final events presents producers with well-nigh insuperable problems, the need for a musical resolution is explicit from the point at which the march itself fails to resolve conclusively, and the progress to suitably incontrovertible resolution is superbly sustained to the very end. On the level of recall, transformation, and combination of motifs, Wagner reveals his full mastery, but this in itself would count for little without the harmonic framework which enables the material to unfold with all the necessary expansiveness and inevitability.

Only two particularly significant aspects of this process can be mentioned here. First, the fact that the very opening of Brünnhilde's final scene—the first paragraph to the line '. . . des hehrsten Helden verzehrt'—moves from one unstable chord to another by way of more conventional triadic harmony; at this stage things are in a sense 'inside out', and only on the largest scale will this tendency be conclusively reversed. The second point concerns the establishment and elaboration of the final tonic, D flat major; something so powerful can only be accomplished in stages, and the first stage uses the moment of most profound repose—Brünnhilde's 'Ruhe, ruhe, du Gott!'—to launch (with a perfect cadence) the entire final phase of the scene; here the principle of the generating harmony being stable is established. The second phase of the scene moves away from D flat again, and this returns at the end in what might seem a dangerously plain, conventional cadential preparation. But Wagner diverts the tonic note into an augmented triad, and the full D flat major triad finally appears at a moment of relative understatement, six bars into a section in which its function might at first seem subordinate—that is, subdominant—to that of the A flat major Rhine music (Ex. 193). Here Wagner brilliantly casts a slight, highly effective shadow of doubt over the tonal direction, through a

Ex. 193

(Strings and harps omitted.)

significant modification of the passage as first sketched.[65] Never-theless, the remaining music prolongs and confirms that D flat tonic without any further extensive reference to its dominant. There is no more decisive perfect cadence, and the final confirmation of D flat is achieved through coloration of more passive plagal and Neapolitan harmony.

For Dahlhaus, the inescapable optimism of this ending is enshrined most essentially in Brünnhilde:

It is only in Brünnhilde that freedom grows to self-awareness: she was divine and has become human, that is, the gods' self-destruction and their superseding by the 'freedom of the human consciousness' have actually taken place in her; and it is through her that 'the new world dawns'.[66]

It follows that there is also a sense in which she acts as a model for—or relative of—Parsifal, who grows in a rather different way to self-awareness and who makes possible, not the birth of a new world but the survival, healed and reinvigorated, of the old. Even so, trying at all costs to link all Wagner's later stage works in an unbroken chain in which each link explores a different aspect of the same theme is not entirely satisfactory. There are also similarities between the ending of *Parsifal* and that of *Die Meistersinger*. But the differences may prove to matter, and mean, rather more.

PARSIFAL

As a *Bühnenweihfestspiel* [a Festival Drama of Consecration or Dedication], *Parsifal* has a concern with religious belief and ob-servance whose precise significance and extent have consistently diverted commentators into such matters as the possible relation between Buddhist and Christian elements in Wagner's thought. Dahlhaus declares that 'Wagner's faith was philosophical, not religious', and cites the composer's comment in *Religion und Kunst* (1880) that 'where religion is becoming artificial it is for art to salvage the nucleus of religion by appropriating the mythic symbols, which the former wished to propagate as true'.[67] The debate around these issues is not likely to be easily or quickly resolved. Yet religious belief and religious ritual are scarcely in the foreground of the events which motivate and propel the drama. The theme of *Parsifal* is not the nature and function of religion in a particular society, but the nature and qualities of leadership, and the need of a rather special

---

[65] See Curt von Westernhagen, *Die Entstehung des 'Ring'* (Zurich, 1973); trans. as *The Forging of the Ring*, trans. Arnold and Mary Whittall (Cambridge, 1976), 263 ff.

[66] *Richard Wagner's Music Dramas*, p. 98.

[67] Ibid., pp. 143–4.

kind of religious community to find a new Priest–King worthy of the office. The drama depicts the process whereby one holder of that office, Amfortas—whose unworthiness is demonstrated and explained—is replaced by someone who becomes worthy. Amfortas has been corrupted by the temptations of the flesh, and the knights have lost their most prized possession (after the Grail itself) to an evil magician. Parsifal, first encountered as a 'pure fool', who acts without premeditation even when his actions are destructive, begins to achieve enlightenment through observing the sufferings of Amfortas as he reluctantly fulfils the functions of his office; and this enables Parsifal to withstand the temptations to which Amfortas succumbed, take back the spear, and return to Monsalvat to assume Amfortas's office. It is not necessary to argue that Parsifal is renouncing all contact with the 'real' world, or even with the legitimate delights of the flesh—as Wagnerians well know, he becomes Lohengrin's father—but the drama turns on the fact that what traps Amfortas frees Parsifal. It is a plot which provides adequate opportunity for stage action, and Wagner is sometimes felt to have been unnecessarily austere in the emphasis given to narration by Gurnemanz, a character whose sole function seems to be to recall events at which he was only an observer. But the narrations in *Parsifal* perform a musico-dramatic function complementary to that of the more active episodes which they prepare and frame. In making such a clear distinction between those events which are enacted, and those which are described, Wagner achieves an effect of concentration in which the contemplativeness appropriate to the theme is balanced and irrigated by a variety of actions, ranging from the brief, hectic events surrounding Parsifal's killing of the swan, to the more extended enactments of the sacramental celebrations, in which action itself becomes meditative.

For all its contemplative emphasis, however, *Parsifal* is not a static triptych in which the outer acts perform parallel, subordinate framing functions. It is a structure whose internal evolution overrides simple symmetric correspondences; one need only examine the textual and musical differences between the two Grail scenes to appreciate this point. No doubt *Parsifal* is more symmetrical than Wagner's other later stage works in the way the actual settings of Act III parallel those of Act I. But such special features do not invalidate the argument that the *Bühnenweihfestspiel* confirms and refines the essential techniques of composition employed in the earlier works.

Most fundamentally, *Parsifal* coheres around tonal and thematic recurrences, and most of the principal tonal centres are in a major or minor third relation to the A flat major in which the work begins and ends. The way in which A flat major is used, as the basis for music depicting the flower-maidens as well as the knights of the Grail, suggests that its significance is more than merely associative; in any case, Wagner's ability to advance beyond the idea that particular tonalities should be reserved for single characters, objects, or moods had been demonstrated before, as in Act I of *Die Meistersinger*, where Walther uses D major ('Am stillen Herd') and F major ('Fanget an!') in rather different ways from David and Pogner respectively. In *Parsifal* the large-scale third relations around A flat focus the extended tonality of the work—a tonality in which the symmetry of dividing the octave into equal intervals (tritones and minor thirds) coexists with the traditional diatonic hierarchies. These large-scale third relations are paralleled on the small scale by the prominence of powerfully expressive non-triadic chords constructed from thirds—the diminished seventh, the *Tristan* chord (a 'secondary' seventh), and various 'dominant quality' chords. In *Parsifal* an increase of tension can be sensed between forces making for hierarchy and forces making for symmetry, but Wagner's flexible, evolving harmonic processes continue to favour the subordination of the latter to the former, just as dissonance ultimately gives way to consonance.

Act II of *Parsifal* is exceptional in Wagner's later works for beginning and ending in the same key, B minor. We might therefore expect any sense of a constant relation to a single, central key to be most evident here. But even this relatively concentrated musical span takes a little over an hour to perform, and confirms the contention that there is a very great difference between the statement that the act begins and ends in the same key, and any claim that B minor functions as an 'extended' tonic throughout. Anthony Newcomb has argued that 'contrast between stable and unstable tonality is a stronger tonal shaping force in some units than any sense of pull against and return to a single central key';[68] and when the unit is a complete act, the fundamental importance of that contrast is the greater. It is almost as if Wagner decided to return to B minor at the end of the act not merely for reasons of motif but because he wanted to compensate for the exceptional amount of tonal instability which occurs during its course. The analyst must work on a very small scale to justify any talk of 'atonality'. But the first stage of Parsifal's sudden, sustained outburst of self-understanding shows the

[68] 'The Birth of Music', pp. 54–5.

Ex. 194

(Amfortas! The wound! It burns here in my side. Oh! grief, terrible grief!
It cries from the depths of my heart.)

harmony at its least diatonic (Ex. 194). Allusions to keys—F major
or minor, in particular—can certainly be detected, but the harmonic
emphasis is on chords whose piled-up thirds prevent pure major and
minor triads, and any progressions based on them, from emerging
as stabilizing forces. This music most certainly does not extend and
prolong the fundamental diatonic triads of a particular tonality in
the way that Kundry's previous lulling paragraphs do, over a span
of some ninety-two bars. The primary role of tonal relations in all
Wagner's later works is to ensure an evolving musical continuity,
employing both remoteness and relatedness, within which the motifs
can function symbolically and structurally. The quality of the motifs
themselves, as memorable representations of a person, a mood, or
an object, is obviously vital to the aesthetic quality and effect of the
drama. But such ideas can only function structurally, and therefore
expressively, through Wagner's supremely flexible and coherent
techniques of evolutionary harmonic continuity.

WAGNER'S HERITAGE

Martin Cooper has argued that 'opera during the years between
1890 and 1918 was dominated by Wagner's shadow',[69] and Gerald
Abraham has claimed that 'in *Salome* (1905) Strauss created perhaps
the greatest of all Wagnerian music-dramas not actually written by
Wagner himself'.[70] The full impact of Wagner's influence was
certainly not felt until some time after his death; his later works
were not frequently staged during his lifetime, and an achievement

[69] See Vol. X, p. 145.
[70] *A Hundred Years of Music* (4th edn.; London, 1974), 214.

of such magnitude naturally took time to make its full effect. Moreover, what immediate influence there was, in the years up to 1890, was almost wholly unfortunate; the fact that 'Wagner's most ambitious and unabashed imitator'[71] was a virtual nonentity—August Bungert (1845–1915)—confirms that coming to terms with Wagner's genius would be a difficult, even traumatic affair. Before 1890 perhaps only Chabrier, in his *Gwendoline* (1886), produced something strongly under Wagner's influence which does contain some worthwhile music, while far from its composer's best and most personal idiom. As Hugo Wolf showed in his songs, the best way to profit from Wagner's example at that early stage of assimilation was to divert some of his technical and expressive innovations into channels which Wagner himself had ignored. As early as 1893, with Humperdinck's *Hänsel und Gretel*,[72] it was possible to claim that even a very different kind of opera could profit from Wagner's example, and with Richard Strauss and Schoenberg the possibility of fuelling expressionism with Wagnerian kindling was shown to be real and valuable. But the whole history of twentieth-century music, from Debussy and Stravinsky to Boulez, Stockhausen, and beyond, has been deeply involved with—if not always dominated by—reactions and responses to the challenge of Wagner himself, and those who claim to have learned most directly from him.

Wagner's greatness seems far from diminished either by the passing of time or by the persistence of controversy, and that greatness must depend on something more than the apparent failure of those who have followed to make a comparable impact. In this chapter his achievement has been described and explained through an interpretation of a highly personal compositional technique in the service of a particular poetic and dramatic ideal. But many would prefer to talk of the uniqueness of what the works express, and no one has done this with more conviction than Magee with his observation that

Wagner gives expression to things that, in the rest of us, and the rest of art, are unconscious because they are repressed. . . . Wagner's music expresses, as does no other art, repressed and highly charged contents of the psyche, and that is the reason for its uniquely disturbing effect.[73]

One does not need to translate Wagner's subject-matter into the language of Feuerbach, Schopenhauer, Marx, Jung, or anyone else

---

[71] John Warrack, 'Opera', *The New Grove*, xiii, 596.
[72] See Vol. X, p. 146.
[73] *Aspects of Wagner*, pp. 34 and 39.

to appreciate and experience the force of this effect which, even if it is less immediately 'disturbing' than that of much twentieth-century music, seems to strike deeper and sustain its impact for so much longer. This effect is achieved by means of one of the most elaborate, consistent, and coherent fusions of words and music ever devised. And while scholars and performers alike continue to remain aware of the special challenges and rewards which Wagner's works present to them, it seems possible that his relative stature will actually increase, as true understanding deepens.

VI

OPERA: 1850–1890

(a) GERMANY

By GERALD ABRAHAM

Two operas produced in 1850 mark a turning-point in the development of German opera: Schumann's *Genoveva* (Leipzig, 25 June) and Wagner's *Lohengrin* (Weimar, 28 August). *Lohengrin*, Wagner's last 'Romantic opera', soon proved to be a success; *Genoveva*—with all its fine passages, such as Golog's 'Frieden, zieh' in meine Brust' near the beginning, and its recurrent 'reminiscence themes'—never was.[1] Schumann died and Wagner's next stage work, *Tristan und Isolde*, was not published until ten years later and performed five years later still. It was not styled 'opera' but—curiously—*Handlung*, an 'action'.

CORNELIUS

Throughout Wagner's lifetime he was, of course, unrivalled; but outstanding among his younger contemporaries was a Liszt pupil at Weimar, Peter Cornelius (1824–74), who admired him and whose individual talent saved him from being a mere camp-follower. His first, and best, work was a comic opera, *Der Barbier von Bagdad*, on a subject from the *Arabian Nights*, for which he provided his own libretto; the only performance in his lifetime was given under Liszt at Weimar in 1858—and ruined by a theatre riot. In 1882 the 26-year-old conductor Felix Mottl found the score, produced a drastically cut one-act version, and also substituted the alternative overture in D major—the original is in B minor and major—which Cornelius composed in 1874 and Liszt orchestrated. In this form the opera quickly made its way on the German stages.[2]

Cornelius left two other operatic works: the *lyrisches Drama*, *Der*

---

[1] For a discussion of *Genoveva* see Abraham, *Schumann: A Symposium* (London, 1952), 272–82.

[2] A vocal score was published by Kahnt of Leipzig in 1877. The original version was published by Breitkopf in 1904 and produced at Weimar the same year.

Cid (1864; produced at Weimar the following year), and the unfinished *Gunlöd* (completed by Max Hasse and Waldemar von Bausznern; an earlier attempt at completion, by Karl Hoffbauer, was performed at Weimar in 1891). But despite some beautiful passages in *Der Cid*—for instance, in Chimene's lament, Act II, Scene ii (Ex. 195), not influenced by Wagner—the work lacks dramatic vitality. The composer's statement that 'the music is always the foundation and provides the inner definition of the text'[3] is hardly necessary. *Der Cid* was revived from time to time from 1891 but never enjoyed anything like the belated success of *Der Barbier*.

Cornelius's first opera is a real masterpiece, arguably the best German comedy—as distinct from operetta—of the second half of the century. Nureddin's first song (Ex. 196) sounds the note of

Ex. 195

(O what salvation! God where thy breath is! Our father which art in heaven!)

Ex. 196

(Come to water your flowers, O Margiana!)

[3] *Peter Cornelius: Literarische Werke*, ed. C. M. Cornelius, E. Istel, and A. Stern, i. *Ausgewählte Briefe* (Leipzig, 1904), 463.

Ex. 197

spontaneous lyricism that permeates many pages of the score. The harmony is generally Lisztian, but here and there, as for example in Ex. 197, the Barber's words and music anticipate both Gilbert and Sullivan, as does Nureddin's

> Das Fieber ihn schuttelt
> Und ziehet, und ruttelt,

in Act II, Scene x. The pseudo-oriental element is more or less confined to the music of the three *muezzins*.

Cornelius admired the work of an almost exact contemporary, Johann Strauss (1825–99), who was later to win much greater popularity with a lighter genre, operetta. But it was Strauss the waltz composer—his first operetta came in 1871—whom Cornelius 'loved': 'Ich liebe diese Dinge sehr', he wrote in 1861.[4] He never knew the operettas, for he died three months after the production of Strauss's first great success, *Die Fledermaus* (1874). Here, and particularly in *Der Zigeunerbaron* (1885), Strauss raised operetta to the level of true opera—though their popularity was based largely on their dance rhythms.

GOETZ

Just six months after the appearance of *Die Fledermaus* a more ambitious but much less successful comedy was produced at Mannheim: *Der Widerspänstigen Zähmung* [The Taming of the Shrew] by Hermann Goetz (1840–76). Goetz himself prepared the libretto in collaboration with Joseph Viktor Widmann, later a friend of Brahms. They unfortunately tamed Shakespeare as well as his Katharina; the buffoonery was toned down, Katharina's shrewishness was reduced

---

[4] *Ausgewählte Briefe*, p. 579.

to a 'Brünnhilde-like' unwillingness to submit to a man, and Petruccio was to be no more than a mere 'cursing *Landsknecht*'. Even Shakespeare's purely comic characters are made more sympathetic. An audience can laugh at Shakespeare's play but only smile at Goetz's opera. He was a highly talented craftsman but not the genius as which he was hailed ninety years ago.[5]

Der Widerspänstigen Zähmung is a beautifully crafted score: light-handed—the end of Act II, Scene iv, is the only passage (except in the overture) where trombones are employed—and sometimes charming—as, for example, in the Bianka-Lucentio scene in Act I, Scene ii (Ex. 198)—and reaching its emotional climax with Kathar-ine's E major reply to Petruchio's 'Let me entreat you!' (Ex. 199) which has the ring of *Meistersinger*. (Indeed his 'Komm! Liebes Käthchen!' at the beginning of Act IV, Scene v, is nearly a quotation from *Meistersinger*.) The scene in which Lucentio makes love to Bianka while pretending to give her a Latin lesson is amusing; it was actually this which induced the Mannheim conductor, Ernst Frank, to perform the work. But there are many uninspired passages:

Ex. 198

(LUCENTIO: I want to embark on a new life, and a new life will open for you.
BIANKA: A new life! Ah how gladly!)

[5] See, for instance, Bernard Shaw, *Music in London 1890–94* (London, 1932), iii. 94.

Ex. 199

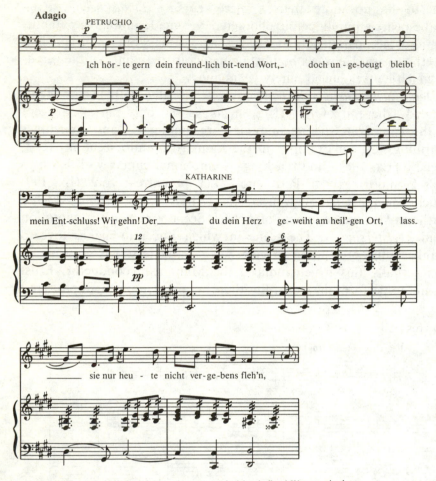

(PETRUCHIO: I gladly heard your plea, yet my decision is firm! We are going!
KATHARINE: Let her to whom you vowed your heart at the holy place, let her not
plead in vain today.)

for instance, the Lucentio–Hortensio duet in Act I, Scene iv,
Katharine's Lied in Act II, Scene i, the ensemble in Act II, Scene
iii. And Goetz was unable to make up his mind about the end of
the opera; after the first performance he added a septet and just
before his death he worked out another ending which remained
unpublished. Conversely, performances have sometimes been ended
with the duet in Act IV, Scene v.

The success of the *Der Widerspänstigen Zähmung* encouraged
Goetz to embark on a second opera, *Francesca da Rimini*. This was
cut short by his death and, although it was completed and performed
in 1877 by Ernst Frank, it never established itself.

GOLDMARK, BRUCH, AND RUBINSTEIN

The composition of serious German opera in the latter part of the century was paralysed by the shadow of Wagner. Mild Wagnerian influence is apparent in the *Königin von Saba* (1875), the best of the half-dozen operas of Cornelius's Hungarian friend Karl Goldmark (1830–1915). Max Bruch (1838–1920), whose work lay mostly outside the field of opera, based his *Die Loreley* (1863) on a libretto intended for Mendelssohn, who died with it only just begun. Brahms's friend Ignaz Brüll (1846–1907) composed a pleasant lightweight work, *Das goldene Kreuz*, in 1875, French in subject and even in style. Another gallicized work was *Der Trompeter von Säkkingen* (1884), enormously popular in its day, by the Alsatian Viktor Nessler (1841–90). Two second-rate masters were not even German: Franz von Suppé (1819–95), a composer of successful operettas, born in Dalmatia of a family Belgian in origin, and Anton Rubinstein (1829–94), son of a Russian Jew and Silesian mother, a much more substantial figure. Most of his operas were settings of Russian librettos, but two were German: *Feramors* (1863), based on Thomas Moore's *Lalla Rookh*, and *Die Makkabäer* (1875), produced at Dresden and Berlin respectively. The 'dances of the Cashmerian brides' in *Feramors* (Ex. 200) sound more

Ex. 200

authentic than Cornelius's *muezzins* in *Der Barbier*. But neither of Rubinstein's German works won any lasting success.

(*b*) FRANCE

By DAVID CHARLTON

THE 1850S AND 1860S

The 1850s bear the hallmarks of a transitional period. Major composers produced penultimate operatic works (Meyerbeer's two *opéras comiques*; Berlioz's *Les Troyens*); Adam (d. 1856), and Halévy

(d. 1862) produced their last operas. Verdi wrote *Les Vêpres siciliennes*, his first for the Opéra (1855). Meanwhile, Gounod was producing the works culminating in *Faust* (1859); a new, fourth, opera house was opened in Paris; and Jacques Offenbach became established as a composer of operettas with his own company: *Orphée aux enfers* (1858) was his thirtieth stage work. As the Opéra-Comique company was improving its scenic and vocal resources, the conditions were set generally for the emergence of a new and intermediate operatic genre: *opéra lyrique*.

In 1851 the Opéra National was restarted in Dumas's Théâtre Historique (which had possessed a partial music licence). Being without state subsidy it could not afford to alienate audiences, yet managed to build up a viable new repertoire of *opéra comique* (by Adam, Ferdinand Poise, Victor Massé, Halévy) amid the revivals. It took the name Théâtre Lyrique in 1852.[6] Under the directorship of Léon Carvalho (1856–60, 1862–68) a number of significant works by Gounod and Bizet were staged, together with a cut version of *Les Troyens* (last three acts) in 1863.

The 1860s, the decade in which Bizet's art grew to maturity, produced many notable works, though not in general at the Opéra. Through-composed operas of importance were produced at the Théâtre Lyrique (Bizet's *Les Pêcheurs de perles*, Gounod's *Roméo et Juliette*) in addition to works with spoken dialogue, while the Opéra-Comique's first production set to music all through was seen in 1873. Verdi, whose Italian operas were popular in Paris, wrote *Don Carlos* (set in French) for the Opéra, first seen in 1867.

OPÉRA COMIQUE TO 1862

A number of light works created in the 1850s attained immense success: Massé's *Galathée* (1852) and *Les Noces de Jeannette* (1853) were performed until 1911 and 1942 respectively; François Bazin's *Maître Pathelin* (1856) was perennial. Middlebrow comedy, tending towards farce, was Adam's favoured medium in *Si j'étais roi* (1852) and *Le Bijou perdu* (1853). The music is 'tuneful' yet diverse in scope: *Si j'étais roi*, for example, contains a full-scale aria and duet in Act II, both in several linked sections; the same act ends with a furious ensemble and chorus in D minor. There is a tendency to group different numbers together to produce continuous, varied sections incorporating action. The 'Duetto, scène et trio', No. 14, for

---

[6] Thomas Joseph Walsh, *Second Empire Opera: The Théâtre Lyrique, Paris, 1851–70* (London, 1981), 5–12, 260. He describes it as 'the opera house of the working man and woman and the hard-up artist'.

example, comprises a sentimental strophic duet; a linking 'allegro'; a conversational 'plus lent' for the arrival of a third character; a linking recitative; and a final ABA' trio. Such techniques prepared the way for the achievements of *Faust* and *Carmen*, as well as for the elimination of spoken dialogue in *opéra lyrique*.

Opéra comique in the grand, melodramatic manner of Scribe was continued in Auber's main success, *Marco Spada* (1852). Although Auber sometimes used Italianate vocal style (for example, in cadenzas), his music had now attained a colourful yet indigenous character, with predominantly syllabic melodies. Its technical assurance is admirable, and Auber occasionally used harmonies more surprising than Donizetti's. An unaccompanied vocal trio (finale of Act II) contains simultaneous arpeggios of the diminished seventh. The dramatic climax resides in the dying confession of Spada (a 'noble villain' character), where the directions state there is to be a tableau modelled on Horace Vernet's painting *La Confession d'un bandit*.

Auber was less successful with *Jenny Bell* (1855), incorporating the English national anthem and 'Rule, Britannia!', but his *Manon Lescaut* of the following year was appreciated; Scribe rewrote Prévost's tale in order to appeal to mid-nineteenth-century taste, adding new characters.[7] Nevertheless, Manon still dies in Des Grieux's arms in Louisiana. This ending, and that of *Marco Spada*, exemplifies the shifts in public taste which helped make Gounod's *Faust* possible in its original *opéra comique* form, and also a 'literary', demi-character type of work, which included *opéras lyriques* such as Gounod's *Roméo et Juliette* and Massenet's *Manon*.

Two notable attempts at 'exotic' operas were made: Félicien David's *La Perle du Brésil* (1851)[8] and Halévy's *Jaguarita l'indienne* (1855), both at the Théâtre Lyrique. The first suffers from an inexpert libretto, rather too close to Scribe's *Haydée*, but is distinguished by the sea storm ending Act II and the setting of Act III in virgin Brazilian forest. A Brazilian woman, Zora, who has been brought to Lisbon and educated, saves the lives of a Portuguese expeditionary force. David's score, often routine or salon-like in character, rises to the occasion in Act III in Zora's 'Couplets du Mysoli' (Ex. 201). In the case of *Jaguarita*, the whole work takes place on 'foreign' soil, Dutch Guyana, and the eponymous native heroine plays

---

[7] Albert Gier, '"Manon Lescaut" als Fabel von der Grille und der Ameise', in Michael Arndt and Michael Walter (eds.), *Jahrbuch für Opernforschung 1985* (Frankfurt am Main, 1985), 73–89.

[8] With parts for organ, bells, harp, ophicleide and cannon, David's score shows the extent of resources at the Opéra National, later Théâtre Lyrique. Berlioz praised the 'melodious dreamer' but castigated 'lazy' aspects of the score: Walsh, *Second Empire Opera*, p. 17.

Ex. 201

(Mingled with azure and ruby!)

Ex. 202

(Silently in the bosom of night, the tribe presses forward, Like the creeping snake it advances in the darkness, Under the black vault of evening let us walk joyfully, At last we shall catch and hold our victim)

Ex. 203

(Kind humming-bird, O sweet friend who calls me from afar, I come, here I am, sweet friend, if only I had your wings)

a leading role: she outwits the Dutch—who are led by comic incompetents—and exerts emotional fascination over the European, Maurice. Portions of the music are as tedious as the outworn humour, but other parts allow us to glimpse a forerunner of *Carmen*, and hear anticipations of Fauré. Halévy uses some novel metrical constructions, particularly in 'Au sein de la nuit' in Act II where Jaguarita leads a dance (Ex. 202). Maurice administers a love potion to her later in Act II, which leads to an evocative phrase using the chord II[9], second inversion. In Jaguarita's song of the Colibri in Act I, No. 5, the music captures her insouciant, dance-like physique (Ex. 203).

The transitional nature of the 1850s was also reflected in a return to Classical sources, in markedly different dramatic genres. Examples by Gounod and Berlioz are discussed below (*Philémon et Baucis*; *Sapho*; *Les Troyens*); Ambroise Thomas's *Psyché* (1857) was a light comedy that became the most performed of his five *opéras comiques* of this decade.

Félicien David's greatest success was the two-act *Lalla-Roukh* (1862), after Thomas Moore's 'oriental romance' of 1817. Its charm lay chiefly in its dramatic setting; there are pleasant enough songs, but David's musical language was very conventional and did not take up the piquant techniques of Halévy, or indeed Meyerbeer.

MEYERBEER'S *OPÉRAS COMIQUES*

Meyerbeer's *opéras comiques* stand in a class by themselves. *L'Étoile du nord* (1854) originated in an occasional work, *Ein Feldlager in Schlesien* (1844), for the Berlin court theatre.[9] This was based by the librettist Rellstab on one of Frederick the Great's campaigns, and was subsequently seen in Vienna as *Vielka* (1847), the action now in Bohemia instead of Silesia. For Paris, Scribe wove a story around Peter the Great and his courtship in Finland of Catherine; she is represented as the more mature character and he as the impulsive, slightly dissipated partner. Dressed as a soldier, she learns of an incipient mutiny in the army, but, having saved Peter's position, she is shot at for a misdemeanour and barely escapes with her life. Peter, who has been drunk when this occurs, restores her to sanity some time later, as Tsar, by the display of tableaux evoking Finland. Although disposed in fifteen numbers separated by dialogue (made later into recitative), Meyerbeer's music has a unique density of texture. It is particularly inventive in harmony, and can be seen as a genuine growth of his language; the uses of enharmonic modulation are Schubertian in their ease. The composer's constant changes of rhythmic pattern (involving limited use of 4/16, 6/16 and 8/16 time signatures) add to the density and extend often to the choral writing, whose interest is well above the routine style of most *opéra comique*. In the second finale two stage bands help in the grandiose counterpointing of four militaristic themes. The 'star' of the work's

---

[9] Max Loppert, 'An Introduction to "L'Étoile du nord"', *Musical Times*, 116 (1975), 130–3. Only the overture and four vocal numbers (including the Act II and part of the Act III finales) were taken over from *Ein Feldlager* (Loppert, 'Introduction', p. 132 n. 7).

title refers to an astrological prediction of Catherine's great destiny
by her mother; the long-breathed cantabile associated with it occurs
(apart from the overture) twice in Act I and once each in Acts II
and III. There are also thematic repetitions of a growling idea sung
by Peter in anger, and of many Act I ideas during the final tableaux.

In *Dinorah* or *Le Pardon de Ploërmel* (1859) the pendulum of
subject-matter swung to the naïve and folkloric, akin to the *pay-
sanneries* of a hundred years before—eighteenth-century *opéras
comiques* were still revived in the 1850s—but with a regional (Breton)
accent. The librettist Michel Carré, who collaborated with Jules
Barbier for *Dinorah*, was soon to prepare the Provençal subject
Mireille for Gounod. Incident, of which there is too little spread
over the three acts, has given way to beautifully polished musical
pictures of characters in whom we are not asked to believe. Dinorah
herself, for the most part harmlessly mad, is accompanied by a pet
goat. The musical density of *L'Étoile du nord* was now concentrated
more on the sensuous sophistication of the orchestral writing,
especially high violins. Rhythmic irregularity was also pursued, as
in the 5/4 bars and other ambiguities of Corentin's Act I couplets,
'Dieu nous donne'. The 'bitonal' cadences to end Act I (Ex. 204)
are as arresting here as similar ones in Verdi's *Otello*, while Act II
ends with real orchestral violence. All Meyerbeer's harmonic magic
is concentrated on Dinorah's healing and recollection of the 'Ave

Ex. 204

Ex. 205

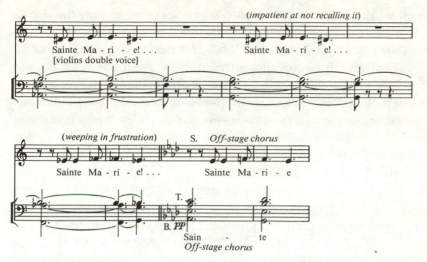

(They said . . . Holy Mary!)

Maria', with which the tale comes full circle in Act III, No. 21 (Ex. 205).

OFFENBACH AND OPERETTA

Jacques Offenbach (1819–80) made initiatives in operetta that affected *opéra comique* in several ways. In 1855 he was granted a licence to start his own company, the Bouffes-Parisiens, and rapidly produced a string of successful one-act works. They blew a welcome gust of fresh air into musical Paris; even Meyerbeer was a regular attender. Offenbach published in 1856 a lengthy preamble to a competition of his own for new works (the joint winners were Bizet and Lecocq with *Le Docteur Miracle*), expressing the need to return to the simplicity, wit, and grace of *opéras comiques* before 1790. The genre, he wrote with obvious justice, 'has taken on proportions that often make it unrecognizable'.[10] *Orphée aux enfers* (1858), originally in two acts, was Offenbach's largest-scale piece to date, involving six principal singers and extensive chorus work. It rudely burlesqued not only the Orpheus story but the whole pantheon of Greek gods, and commandeered Gluck's aria 'Che farò senza Euridice' to boot. The brilliant 'Galop infernal' (not originally 'Cancan') accompanied a wild bacchanal in Hades. A new, four-act version of *Orphée aux enfers* was mounted in 1874; it had already earned some 1,800,000 francs.

Although Offenbach lived until 1880 and compulsively produced

---

[10] See Alexander Faris, *Jacques Offenbach* (London and Boston, 1980), p. 50 etc.

several works every year, his main successes came within the decade of *Orphée*: *La Belle Hélène* (1864), *La Vie parisienne* (1866), *La Grande-Duchesse de Gérolstein* (1867), *La Périchole* (1868). After the basically straightforward and satirical musical language of *Orphée*, the subtlety of Offenbach's use of discords increased, as did the economy of his best melodies. In *Robinson Crusoé* (1867) Offenbach signalled his desire to write *opéra comique* of wider, more traditional scope.

GOUNOD'S MINOR WORKS

Although Offenbach's operettas were frequently execrated, as was the treatment of Classicism in *Orphée aux enfers*, they seem to have encouraged more decorous lightweight *opéras comiques*; among these are Gounod's *Le Médecin malgré lui* (1858), *Philémon et Baucis*, and *La Colombe* (both 1860). The first is a close adaptation of Molière; the second is a comedy woven around the Classical tale; the third adapts La Fontaine and Boccaccio.[11] All are unpretentious. *Le Médecin malgré lui* avoids imposing sentiment on Molière and, though it has quite prolonged ensembles containing action, never musically overwhelms the text. Yet Gounod's fresh melodic genius was still apparent.

The plot, but not the dramaturgy, of *Philémon et Baucis* evokes the eighteenth century (cf. Philidor's *Le Bûcheron*). The chorus proved more of a problem than in *Le Médecin* (where it closed off Acts I and II), and in the original three-act version was chiefly confined to Act II for the orgy and then destruction of Philémon's sacrilegious neighbours. In 1876 it was reduced to two acts by simple elimination.[12] The music is pleasurable and varied, rather than memorable, probably because the old couple of the title are hardly given a chance to be individuals.

La Colombe, for all its wonderfully contrived harmonic side-steps, seems over-artificial, and so to lack dramatic conviction. Its successful première in Germany was followed by a less enthusiastic reception for the somewhat revised Paris version of 1866.

BERLIOZ'S *BÉATRICE ET BÉNÉDICT*

Composed almost as a relaxation after *Les Troyens*, *Béatrice et Bénédict* (1862) as an *opéra comique* related closely to current trends:

[11] *Le Faucon*; *The Decameron*, Day 5, Story 9. The librettos of all three were by Barbier and Carré.

[12] Fuller details in Steven Huebner, 'The Second Empire Operas of Charles Gounod (Diss., Princeton, 1985), fos. 236 ff. Most of Gounod's stage works entail complex questions of revision and publication that have still not been resolved by scholarship.

literary distinction of its source; modest use of chorus; small number (three) of main soloists; emphasis on lightness and wit. The text was, however, fashioned by the composer, from *Much Ado about Nothing*.[13] True to form, Berlioz produced something unique: it was not staged in Paris until 1890, though it was successful in Baden-Baden (1862) and Weimar (1863). The almost-tragic plot to stain Hero's character was omitted, as was the villainous Don John; Hero's betrothed, Claudio, sings only in the trio, No. 5, and 'Marche nuptiale', No. 13. To substitute for the immortal wit of Dogberry and the singer Balthasar, Berlioz created Somarone, prototype of the opinionated bad musician. The chorus performs Somarone's 'Épithalame grotesque', No. 6, in academic fugue style, then repeats it with equally grotesque ornamentation for oboe, sketched on the spot. However, Somarone's second contribution beginning Act II rather overplays the musical style of joke, and its position in the drama creates a gap between the gulling of Béatrice (off-stage, before the 'Duo-Nocturne', No. 8), and her great aria of reaction, 'Il m'en souvient', No. 10.

Such things, however, can be overcome in production. Berlioz's spoken dialogue is concise and his purpose sure: to portray and develop the characters of his eponymous principals. In particular, 'Berlioz has to reconcile Béatrice to the very conception of true love, tenderness and constancy',[14] of which her cousin Hero becomes the example. The early sparring-match (the Duo, No. 4, 'Comment le dédain'), Shakespeare's 'What, my dear Lady Disdain! Are you yet living?', excellently captures the badinage of Béatrice and Bénédict, but also its emotional sub-text, entrusted to the orchestra. There are many haunting pages that paint a valediction to Berlioz's 'great, strong Italy'.[15] The ending (Scherzo–Duettino, No. 15) is conceived in the moral vein of vaudeville *opéra comique*, after the spirit in *Much Ado* of Benedick's 'For man is a giddy thing, and this is my conclusion'; but its cyclic return to the evanescent music of the overture lends it the Shakespearian ambiguity of 'Life's but a walking shadow' (also the postscript of the *Memoirs*) (Ex. 206).

[13] Apparently the first attempt to make this play into an opera. Berlioz's plans for such a work went back to an Italian setting (1833) and a much adapted version (*c*.1852), the scenario of which is printed in the *New Edition of the Complete Works*, ed. Hugh Macdonald, iii. 299–300.

[14] Julian Rushton, 'Berlioz's Swan-song: Towards a Criticism of *Béatrice et Bénédict*', *Proceedings of the Royal Musical Association*, 109 (1982–3), 113–14: 'Thus Berlioz's Béatrice is his own character, not Shakespeare's, just as his Friar Laurence, Faust, or Dido are his own.'

[15] David Cairns (trans.), *The Memoirs of Hector Berlioz* (New York and London, 1969), 175.

Ex. 206

(Love is a flaming torch)

BERLIOZ'S *LES TROYENS*

Les Troyens (partial staging, 1863) is obviously a Romantic epic, its resources matched to those of Parisian *grand opéra*. Literary epics, though avoiding antiquity, were perfectly characteristic of French Romanticism. But they, like Wagner's music dramas, strove for an encompassing expression of unity. Berlioz had no philosophical predisposition towards mysticism or renewal. David Cairns has written:

> Remorse and redemption, the *leitmotiv* of so much Romantic drama, have no place in Berlioz's scheme of things. Unlike Goethe, he does not redeem his Faust. . . . The heroic figures of *The Trojans* live their lives without repining, accept their fate and go down to eternal night, driven by forces beyond the reach of man. Such a vision is Classical, not Romantic.

The work is, on probably every level, the finest French opera composed during this period. Its Classical setting was not a novelty; moreover its five-act format, divided into two 'dark' (Trojan) acts, two 'bright' (Carthaginian) acts, and a tragic fifth act, compares closely with that of *La Reine de Chypre*. In length—some four hours of music—it does not exceed larger works by its contemporaries. Yet it has stood virtually outside musical history since its conception. The score was composed mainly in 1856–8 but for a century after its partial staging in 1863 at the Théâtre Lyrique was frequently known as a bipartite work.[16] Publication of the full score had to wait until 1969.

Les Troyens is based on Books I, II, and IV of Virgil's *Aeneid*. Berlioz, who had been profoundly inspired by this epic since

---

[16] The Théâtre Lyrique staged Acts III–V (cut) as *Les Troyens à Carthage*. Vocal scores are still common of this, and of Acts I–II as *La Prise de Troie*, first heard in 1879. Not until 1908, in Munich, was *Les Troyens* given in the theatre in reasonably complete form on one evening. See Ian Kemp (ed.), *Hector Berlioz, 'Les Troyens'* (Cambridge, 1988), Appendix D.

childhood, wrote the opera (words as well as music) purely from inner compulsion. The dramaturgy is not only expert, but reflects all aspects of Virgil's source—not least the concept of a ruling fate. It was articulated in a succession of strongly contrasted types of scene; this aspect, together with the appearance of the shades of Hector and others, plus the large cast and gently comic duet scene, 'Par Bacchus' (No. 40) before the final tragedy, was Berlioz's own, mature borrowing from Shakespeare. Contrast, however, was balanced by objectivity, the more necessary since the opera does not want for action and excitement. Acts I and II, in which the wooden horse is brought inside the walls of Troy, and the city sacked, are given their ironic distancing by Berlioz through the repeated, unheeded warnings of Cassandra. Aeneas plays his heroic part, but not so as to predominate. The destruction of a city, its rituals and its history, are the real themes. Trojan character is established through the people's initial jubilation, their religious ceremony mourning Hector, 'Pantomime' (No. 6), their determined 'Marche Troyenne' (No. 11), and the heroic mass suicide of Trojan women in the 'Final' to Act II. The sheer force and grandeur of all this music establishes for us that ideal background which Aeneas must keep alive by pursuing his destiny and winning a kingdom in Italy. In Act III he is fated to meet Dido; during the 'Chasse royale et orage—Pantomime', No. 29 (Act IV) they are fated to become lovers; in Act V they part and Dido kills herself, prophesying future vengeance on the race of Aeneas.

Berlioz did not need Scribe. The dramatic motivation of Aeneas is welcome, following the feeble escapism of so many previous tenor heroes. None the less, *Les Troyens* takes what it wants from him: the acts each build well from first to last, reaching a dramatic climax expressed in choral and ensemble terms (Acts II, III); however, in Act I the *grand opéra* set piece—the 'Final', No. 11, with three off-stage ensembles at differing distances—is capped by the cries of Cassandre. Act IV is concluded by the main love duet, 'Nuit d'ivresse', No. 37, and an imminent sense of departure (cf. *Les Huguenots*). There are exotic, interpolated dances in Acts I, III, and IV. Yet *Les Troyens*, with never-flagging musical quality, creates constant surprises. This is because Berlioz thought out the requisite musical form, as well as content, anew at each stage: 'The hardest task is to find the musical *form*, this form without which music does not exist, or is only the craven servant of speech. . . . I am in favour of the kind of music you call *free*.'[17]

---

[17] Letter of 12 Aug. 1856, cited in Hugh Macdonald, *Berlioz* (London, 1982), 185.

Sometimes tripartite structure is chosen (Cassandre's Air, No. 2); sometimes non-repeating dramatic monologue (Didon's 'Je vais mourir', No. 47); sometimes rondo (the love duet, No. 37); sometimes strophic ('Chanson d'Hylas', No. 38). The most brilliant stroke was the dance pantomime inspired directly by Virgil (the 'Chasse royale et orage').

Dido and Troy's chieftain found their way to the same cavern. Primaeval Earth and Juno, Mistress of the Marriage, gave their sign. The sky connived at the union; the lightning flared; on their mountain-peak nymphs raised their cry. On that day were sown the seeds of suffering and death.[18]

However, there is also the large-scale application of recurring motivic features: an upward-rushing scale and a lower mordent figure, sometimes combined with it (see Ex. 207 from Act I and Ex. 208 from Act II), and a certain rhythmic pattern (see Ex. 209, drawn

Ex. 207

Ex. 208

Ex. 209

from Acts I and V). These devices do not denote an exact person or thing, but 'cluster in certain scenes, turning-points in the fate of the Trojans and their victim, Dido'.[19] Their fateful associations permit Berlioz to intensify given situations, or underscore ironic references, as in the otherwise serene duet, No. 37, in Act IV (Ex. 210), or the quintet, No. 35. Another aid to musical consistency is

[18] *The Aeneid*, Book IV, trans. W. F. Jackson Knight (Harmondsworth, 1956), 102.
[19] Julian Rushton, 'The Overture to *Les Troyens*', *Music Analysis*, 4 (1985), 128. Rushton gives comprehensive tabular enumerations of motifs, and pursues his analysis in chapter 10 of Kemp (ed.), '*Les Troyens*'.

Ex. 210

the free foreshadowing of set-piece material (Cassandre–Chorèbe duet, No. 3, bars 308 f.) in the preceding dramatic dialogue (ibid., bars 165 ff., 210). The score also reflects Berlioz's late interest in novel musical scales or modes, notably in his music for the doomed Trojan women in the 'Chœur-Prière', No. 14, in Act II (Ex. 211).

Ex. 211

CHORUS OF TROJAN WOMEN

It is safe to predict that *Les Troyens*, for its unique moral integrity no less than its ineffable beauty, will gradually assume a leading place in all assessments of the nineteenth century's artistic legacy.

GOUNOD'S GENIUS REVEALED

Gounod's *Sapho*, libretto by Émile Augier, was first acted at the Opéra in 1851.[20] That it had the first libretto there since 1823 using a Greek subject is but one of its points of significance. Augier decided on a three-act structure and a virtually domestic approach to the

---

[20] Revised in 1858, much cut; revised 1884 with extensively rewritten text and music. See Huebner, 'The Second Empire Operas', fos. 87 ff.

subject. Phaon, whose affections have switched from the woman of beauty, Glycère, to the woman of music and poetry, Sapho, is involved in a plot to murder the tyrant Pittacus. (The *coup* never happens and the tyrant never sings.) Glycère discovers the plot, blackmails her rival into silence, and escapes with a deceived Phaon into exile. Sapho drowns herself.[21]

Although there are various choruses, representing people, priests, and so on, they are not given much sense of realism. Musically, they are routine. The aesthetic focus of the work repudiated *grand opéra* in order to concentrate on a musical world of ritual and sensuous beauty. Both required to be captured in the style of pure song (as befitted Sapho's Lesbos). Gounod's melodic and harmonic genius was manifest in a series of individual and subtle lyric utterances. The entire opera, in fact, ends not histrionically but with neo-Classical control: Sapho's art expressed as song. In a sense this is the first *opéra lyrique* of its period. Avoiding linear extremes, Gounod's melody found its *cachet* in the small scale, in balancing repetition, in the use of one or two pitches as a centre of gravity (see Ex. 212 from Act III, No. 17).

Ex. 212

(Be blessed by a dying woman)

---

[21] Glycère extracts the plot from a weak conspirator, Pythéas. His open request for favours from Glycère as the price of his secret, and the generally revolutionary undertones, caused problems with the censor.

Gounod's harmony revealed several future paths for French music
and its consistency in this respect may well have caused its lack of
success in 1851 (only nine performances). Several melodies tend
towards the subdominant area, so robbing them of expected forward
motion, as in the 'Ode', Act I, No. 6 (Ex. 213). More strikingly,
several vital passages are built up by a piquant or hypnotic circling
round a tonic chord: one simple recitative example from Act I, No.
4, is shown in Ex. 214, while Ex. 215 (reduced from Phaon's 'Quand
ce qu'on voit' from Act II, No. 10) has its tonic rooted inside the
harmony. Ex. 216, Sapho's 'Cantilène' in Act II, No. 13, illustrates
the end of an eight-bar period consisting of a single oscillation
between I and V, and how, lulling the hearer into security, the
composer steps elliptically on to G major. Above the oscillation
Sapho's melody, 'Ma vie en ce séjour', was articulated in a quite
un-classical manner. It was revolution from within.

The composer was willing to apply sequential treatment to
secondary dominants, and write sequential and chromatic pro-

Ex. 213

(O Liberty, severe goddess, your noble altar has been broken)

Ex. 214

Ex. 215

Ex. 216

(Is a limpid stream which runs over moss and reflects the light)

Ex. 217

gressions of sevenths. In Ex. 217, where the Act II trio, No. 15, sees Glycère's trap close around Sapho and Phaon, the seven consecutive sevenths in the context of passionate dialogue (shown in reduced form) show positively Wagnerian sensibility. Authentically Wagnerian diction, nevertheless, appears only briefly, in the heightened recitative prior to the final ensemble of Act II. But contained, disciplined, linearly clear dissonances in Sapho's solo of forbearance (see Ex. 212) point to Fauré and Debussy.

Gounod's second recitative opera, *La Nonne sanglante* (1854), was set to Scribe's five-act melodrama stemming from Lewis's *The Monk*. A passage occurring in Act II before the Bleeding Nun first speaks broke new ground by exploring a sequence of unrelated triads a whole tone apart (Ex. 218). But much of the score is conventionally operatic, with solo parts written for the effect of a high note, several 12/8 movements of traditional cut, and an Italianate finale to Act IV in the normal four sections. However, a waltz for the peasants beginning Act III anticipated *Faust*. Following the publication of a government enquiry into the Opéra, which attacked (*inter alia*) the

Ex. 218

way the public had been seduced into accepting 'the trickery of insincere expression', its new director, Crosnier, had *La Nonne sanglante* withdrawn after eleven performances.[22] The two above works had nevertheless revealed Gounod to be dramatically radical as well as flexible, and the most outstanding French creative talent since the advent of Berlioz a generation earlier.

FAUST

In 1859 this long-awaited masterpiece brilliantly deployed Gounod's dramatic and musical intelligence. Its diversity of emotion, which faithfully followed Goethe's spirit, enabled Gounod's superior range to be concentrated within a single work: learnedness, *naïveté*, dances, love music, demonic energy, and an apotheosis. He created a totally original sequence of musical forms. Taken in conjunction with the flowering of his musical idiom into a degree of chromaticism as yet unheard on the French stage, these features explain the feeling behind Gounod's words to Charles Réty in 1859: 'I am most anxious that M. R. Wagner hears my score of *Faust*. His approval as well as his criticism are of the kind one seeks.'[23]

The opera was first heard, with a modest quantity of spoken dialogue, at the Théâtre Lyrique. The substitution of recitative (1860) was only one of many early adjustments, but these could not overbalance the work's coherence. The dramatic source had been Michel Carré's play *Faust et Marguerite* (1850); the opera, with libretto by Carré himself and Barbier, added other scenes from Goethe's *Faust*.[24] If Carré's play emphasized the popular and everyday, Gounod's music gave it convincing poetry. These in combination (particularly in the spoken dialogue version) produce

[22] 'Rapport de la Commission chargée d'examiner la situation de l'Opéra', *Le Moniteur universel*, 2 July 1854. Private enterprise, as initiated by Véron, had not respected 'the authority of good taste'. See Huebner, 'The Second Empire Operas', fo. 157.

[23] Walsh, *Second Empire Opera*, p. 105 n. Wagner arrived in Paris in September 1859. Full and vocal scores of his *Der fliegende Holländer*, *Tannhäuser*, and *Lohengrin* had been published in 1844, 1845/6, and 1851/2 respectively.

[24] i.e. *Faust*, Part I; see Huebner, 'The Second Empire Operas', fos. 169 ff.

changes of dramatic speed and texture wholly faithful to Goethe.
Indeed, given the limitations inherent in the operatic genre, it is
difficult to imagine a more expert adaptation of the latter half of
Faust, der Tragödie erster Teil.[25] Gounod's protagonist is admittedly
the sensualist rather than the Doctor. This, however, allowed the
authors to impose a larger theatrical (and indeed thematic) symmetry
on material which in itself might have been too diffuse:

Act I	Act V
Faust's pact;	Madness and death;
vision of Marguerite	redemption of
	Marguerite

(Musically characterized by free, lyrical *parlante* texture; formal
solos are truncated.)

Act II	Act IV
Valentine's departure;	Valentine's murder;
public scenes;	church scene
first contact with Marguerite	

(Musically characterized by mixture of shorter set-piece solos
(often ABA and strophic forms), ensembles, and some chorus
work.)

Act III

Faust's courtship of Marguerite;
garden scene with Mephistopheles and Martha;
love duet

(Musically dominated by the freely continuous, increasingly
chromatic quartet and duet; no chorus.)

All-important, however, was the internal musical design, its
subtlety and unity. Gounod's language accepted the expressive
discord (often in the form of melodic appoggiatura or neighbour note)
and, unlike Meyerbeer's, applied advanced chromatic progressions to
all parts of the score as needed, i.e. from climactic moments down
to merest recitative. With this went the virtual dissolving of the ancient
antithesis between set-piece (e.g. aria) texture and conversation
(recitative) texture. The fluidly alternating pattern of Lully's operas
could have been the model for a heightened, accompanied recitative

---

[25] The opera differs most by having Mephistopheles bribe Faust with a vision of his ideal
woman in Act I. Obviously scenes like the Walpurgisnacht were impractical, though Gounod
at one point wrote an orchestral piece to represent it. Valentine is shown before his departure
for the wars. Siébel is made into Marguerite's adolescent admirer, but this role also personifies
the close-knit environment, both poor and pious, from which Goethe's Margarete comes.

that gave way freely to brief, memorable solos or ensembles. Fortunately, Gounod's themes (more diatonic than Wagner's) had the strength of his harmonic repertoire, certain melodies attaining that brazen power which for decades had seemed the prerogative of Italian music.

Building on the spirit of the times, Gounod made thematic recollection an essential part of the score. Faust's urgent demand for the return of youth and its pleasures (Act I, 'À moi les plaisirs') returns in Act II (arioso connecting Nos. 5 and 6) and Act III (after Siébel's 'flower' song, 'Faites-lui mes aveux', No. 7). The basic returning image, however, is the music for the Act I vision of Marguerite (Faust's 'O merveille' in No. 2), which is woven with immense skill into the Act III love duet, No. 11, at 'O nuit d'amour', and will also be recalled, with other painful musical memories, by the unbalanced Marguerite in prison in Act V (duet No. 19, at 'Non! Reste!', Ex. 219). But this theme itself has a three-note conjunct motif (marked *y*) that is found in several other diverse themes throughout the opera: the final ritornello of the love duet, No. 11 (Ex. 220); 'Le Veau d'or', Act II, No. 4 (Ex. 221); the off-stage

Ex. 219

(Stay awhile, and let your arm clasp mine, as in times past!)

Ex. 220

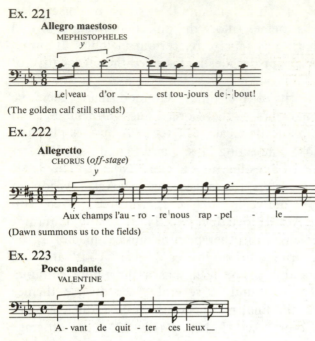

Ex. 221

Allegro maestoso

MEPHISTOPHELES

Le|veau   d'or _____ est tou-jours de-|bout!

(The golden calf still stands!)

Ex. 222

Allegretto

CHORUS (*off-stage*)

Aux champs l'au - ro - re|nous rap - pel - le_____

(Dawn summons us to the fields)

Ex. 223

Poco andante

VALENTINE

A - vant de quit - ter ces lieux___

(Before I leave this place)

chorus near the opening of Act I (Ex. 222); and Valentine's celebrated cavatina in Act II (Ex. 223).

Gounod's orchestration attained a high level of refinement, and embodied a hitherto unheard-of importance relative to the material given to the voices. These aspects may be seen in Ex. 224 from the close of Act III, with its Debussy-like ecstasy. As Martin Cooper has written, 'this scene . . . set a standard that influenced composers for the rest of the century'.[26] Another novel ingredient was the 'learned' contrapuntal music introducing Faust, which probably reflects the Bach revival but is aptly reinterpreted with Romantic harmonies.

GOUNOD'S LATER WORKS

Faust was followed by two problematic operas. At the Opéra *La Reine de Saba* (1862) suffered from Gounod's habitual over-writing and indiscriminate cutting in rehearsal. Its concentration on recitative and solo was found confusing, even a 'vast physiognomy of vaporous and fleeting contours'.[27] More promising was *Mireille* (1864), first

[26] 'Charles Gounod', in *The New Grove*, vii. 582.
[27] Cited in Huebner, 'The Second Empire Operas', fo. 260. The work was successful only in Brussels. It derived from Gérard de Nerval's *Le Voyage en Orient*. Several revised versions exist.

Ex. 224

(Does the petal tremble and quiver with love? Tomorrow!)

produced at the Théâtre Lyrique. Its originality lay in the subject of a love tragedy provoked by social differences but set in a timeless, perhaps modern, rural community. Designed as a five-act *opéra comique* with its limited amount of dialogue—in verse—it was derived from Frédéric Mistral's provençal poem, *Mirèio* (1859). Unfortunately, Gounod's conscientious visit to the area was not enough to transmute the artlessness of the subject into music, and the characters fall into operatic clichés. There are, naturally, patches of local colour; but even the ghosts of the Rhône in Act III could be mistaken for angels. Act II has a *grand opéra* sectional finale which inflates the tale as much as the sanctimonious style of the last act.[28] The 'Chanson de Magali', set entirely in alternate 9/8 and 6/8, looks more original than it sounds. The fragility and inner depth of the subject could easily, however, be related to the later world of *Pelléas et Mélisande*; the mystic forces which destroy the bullying Ourrias exist as much outside conventional reality as do Maeterlinck's subtly ambiguous underground scenes.

[28] *Mireille* was long known in a three-act version with happy ending (from 1864). The Henri Busser recitative edition (1939) does not represent Gounod's original intentions.

Planned, like *Mireille*, to contain dialogue, *Roméo et Juliette* (1867) was given recitatives in time for the first performance at the Théâtre Lyrique.[29] (For the first time since the Revolution of 1789, a law had in 1864 decreed the liberty of the theatres, inasmuch as a director could now mount a stage work in any genre at will.) Barbier and Carré followed Shakespeare quite closely, to the extent of including an 'Ouverture-Prologue, avec chœur', a token part for Paris, and a Queen Mab solo ('Ballade') for Mercutio.[30] But by concentrating attention on the lovers in Acts II, IV, and V, telescoping events towards the end (Roméo arrives at the Capulets' vault without our knowing how or why), and omitting the reconciliation of families, the authors reduced the whole conception; the play's more abrasive elements find no place. Indeed the music before Juliette swallows her sleeping-draught has little of Shakespeare's expression of panic at this point, and Roméo's music before taking poison is lyrically passive. The opera is articulated with formal orthodoxy, for example, closed ABA solo forms and ensemble finales to Acts I and III, the first of which is wooden in effect. Fortunately, Gounod's music regained much of its harmonic originality, which was lavished on the love idylls. Their extent and intensity (almost filling Acts II and V) entitle us to speak of a French response to *Tristan und Isolde* (scores published 1860). Gounod's phrase structures are persistently symmetrical, but not his modulation. He now admits seventh chords functionally on degrees of the scale such as III and VII (see the asterisks in Ex. 225 from Roméo's Act II cavatina), which can lead to a series of exotically related tonal resting places. This music leads directly to the balcony scene, itself built up as a series of exalted dialogues and small solos which culminate in two repeated strophes for the lovers together, making their bitter-sweet farewells: this vestigial cabaletta (Ex. 226) has been absorbed formally and expressively into a free-sounding sequence, concluded by Romeo's solitary valediction.

Ex. 225

Bb: I   I♭7   VI   Vb   V7   I
  Gb: III♭7 V7c   I   I♭7
                          G: VII♮7 I

[29] Joël-Marie Fauquet, 'Quatre versions de *Roméo et Juliette*', *L'Avant-scène*, 41 (1982), 66–9.

[30] It was the first operatic setting with such a piece or with a Prologue. See Winton Dean, 'Shakespeare and Opera', in Phyllis Hartnoll (ed.), *Shakespeare in Music* (London, 1964), 151.

Ex. 226

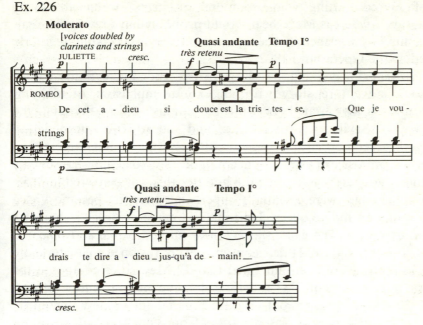

(So sweet is the sadness of this farewell, that I would bid you farewell until tomorrow!)

In Act V much is sung by the lovers either as musical recollection or accompanied by such recollection (cf. *Tristan*): 'Sois béni' (Act III); 'Non, ce n'est pas le jour' (Act IV); the 'embrace' theme which follows the preceding; the 'Anges du ciel' theme opening and closing Act IV, Scene i; and a transformation of 'Le Sommeil de Juliette' (beginning Act V) as she awakens. And, for once, Gounod concluded an operatic love-death without either bombast or more than four bars of sanctimoniousness.

MEYERBEER'S *L'AFRICAINE*

The original contract for a five-act opera entitled *L'Africaine* was signed by Scribe and Meyerbeer in May 1837. Neither man lived to see its première in 1865 so the preparation was placed in the hands of Germain Delavigne and others (for the text) and the octogenarian François Fétis (for the score).[31] As Meyerbeer had habitually modified his music in rehearsal, and since *L'Africaine* as he left it lasted four and a half hours exclusive of intervals, the Fétis version represents only one attempt at an unobtainable authenticity;

---

[31] Fétis left a record of his procedures both in the published full score and a vocal score entitled *Deuxième Partie de l'opéra en cinq actes L'Africaine*, containing twenty-two deleted fragments.

he favoured cutting whole sections or items—when absolutely necessary—whereas Meyerbeer would probably have rewritten smaller units.[32] Nevertheless, the opera was very successful, regularly acted at the Opéra until 1902.

L'Africaine began and, to a large extent, ended its evolution as an episodic adventure story with an exotic emphasis. Originally it concerned a love triangle between the Spanish officer Fernand, the viceroy of Seville's daughter Inès, and the African queen Sélica. Meyerbeer composed a certain quantity of music but then, under the fresh influence of Camões's account of Vasco da Gama's discovery of India, got Scribe to rewrite the libretto; this was delivered in 1853. But his changes were essentially superficial: Fernand became Vasco and Sélika an Indian queen. Nothing was made of Vasco's character as an explorer. (The work was by now entitled *Vasco de Gama* but Fétis insisted on the old title, geographical confusion notwithstanding. His Sélika rules over an unnamed island.) Meyerbeer composed the music during parts of 1857 and 1860-4; some music from the version of 1837-43 was re-used, but was itself often substantially revised.[33]

The action begins as Vasco returns from Diaz's failed expedition with Sélika and her chieftain, Nélusko. Vasco's rival Don Pédro is given charge of a new expedition and also obtains the hand of Vasco's beloved, Inès. In Act III, set at sea, Pédro's vessel is wrecked, in spite of Vasco's warnings. Sélika has always loved Vasco; she now saves his life from the revenge of her people (who execute Pédro) but, when Vasco goes back to Inès, dies by inhaling the noxious perfume of the flowers of a great manchineel tree. The opera may have been attractive precisely because it retained a totally sentimental attitude to its material.[34] As the character-motivation becomes steadily less satisfactory, so the picturesque elements become progressively more important: the storm and shipwreck; the obeisance to and celebrations for Sélika in Act IV; Vasco's duet with her, sung under the influence of a love potion; and the unique final tableau. 'Oriental' local colour was, naturally, featured all through, but not all-pervasively: it can resemble Halévy's music for *Jaguarita l'indienne* (cf. Ex. 203), as in Act II, when Sélika in an 'Air du sommeil' fans

[32] Extensive details of *L'Africaine*'s history are found in John H. Roberts, 'The Genesis of Meyerbeer's "L'Africaine"' (Diss., Berkeley, 1977). Meyerbeer died on 2 May 1864, shortly after finishing his work.

[33] Ibid., fos. 28-30, 161; Roberts notes that Meyerbeer's *visual* imagination enriched the 1853 conception in many details (fo. 134).

[34] Nélusko remains implacably opposed to the Westerners, even delivering a defiantly ironic salvo in Act I to the Portuguese assembly, aimed at their practices in slavery. But, though he causes the shipwreck, he is not allowed a solid identity.

Ex. 227

(On my knees, son of the sun, victor on the field of battle)

Vasco while singing (Ex. 227). Orchestral effects exploit both the rich low wind timbres (two cors anglais and two bass clarinets are required) and the percussion world of tam-tam and glockenspiel (see Ex. 229). The four-part off-stage choir vocalises as part of the accompaniment to Sélika's 'Un cygne au doux ramage' in Act V. The concentration on such things in the final two acts helps lift the work out of the realms of history or verisimilitude on to its perfumed plateau and fantastic love-death (Ex. 228).

The opera's whole fabric supports the same central ethos of fragmentation and loss of personal will; that is, Meyerbeer uses a mosaic-like sequence of abbreviated set pieces, minimising assertion and personal conflict. His actual language becomes maturely lyrical, relaxing the intensity of rhythmic and chromatic drive seen in the composer's 1849–59 works. Old-fashioned act endings have almost gone. The finale of Act I is the most traditional, yet it arises unobtrusively out of dramatic exchanges. Act II concludes in resigned

Ex. 228

(What heavenly chords)

Ex. 229

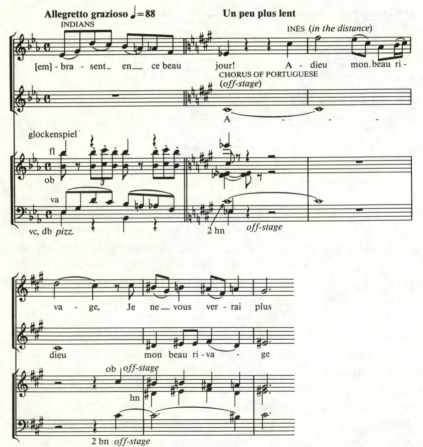

(INDIANS: Set ablaze on this fine day! INÈS: Farewell, fair shores, that I shall never see again)

mood with an 'andante' septet, Act III with a terse chorus of conquering Indians, and Act IV with a striking juxtaposition of East and West, for, while dancers prepare the nuptials of Sélika and Vasco, the off-stage voice of a supposedly-dead Inès breaks in almost bitonally (Ex. 229), singing a motif which we recognize from Act I as Vasco's faithful farewell to her before his departure two years before the opera's action starts (Ex. 230). Meyerbeer's harmony could also follow Vasco into intoxicated regions (Ex. 231, from the Act IV Duo, No. 17), or, briefly, express narcotic ecstasy in the same duet using a chromatic seventh chord on the flat leading-note (Ex. 232). The work fails in so far as its construction requires us to believe in decisions people make; thus Act III and its weakly characterized Don Pédro fare the least well.

Ex. 230

(Farewell, gentle shores, farewell my only love!)

Ex. 231

(Like a flaming beam has entered my heart)

Ex. 232

(I feel as though in heaven)

Each of Meyerbeer's *grands opéras*, therefore, presented a different dramatic and even technical milieu. The guiding theme of *Robert le diable* is redemption; *Les Huguenots* is an important Romantic tragedy; *Le Prophète* amounts to an epic concerning a failed revolution; and *L'Africaine* celebrates the unworldly aspects of love and death. They influenced the public because they contained a wealth of good music; the profession because they translated ideas into new musico-dramatic terms; and both because in Paris they set the highest standards of contemporary operatic stagecraft.

VERDI IN PARIS

Verdi wrote or rewrote four operas for Paris: *Jérusalem* (4 acts, Opéra, 1847); *Les Vêpres siciliennes* (5 acts, Opéra, 1855); *Macbeth* (4 acts, Théâtre Lyrique, 1865); *Don Carlos* (5 acts, Opéra, 1867). The first and third of these were revisions and are discussed elsewhere. Paris attracted Verdi both financially and artistically. He was to reside there or nearby at Passy from July 1847 for two years, for the winter of 1851–2, from October 1853 for over two years, for parts of 1856 and 1863, and for much of the fifteen months leading up to *Don Carlos*.

A contract for an opera with Scribe was ready early in 1848; in 1852 Verdi signed such a contract for a work, yet to be agreed, in four or five acts.[35] The third subject offered by Scribe, *Les Vêpres siciliennes*, was accepted late in 1853 as a recasting of the old text prepared for Halévy and begun by Donizetti as *Le Duc d'Albe*. Verdi's ambitions as to scale were as decided as was his preference

---

[35] Frank Walker, *The Man Verdi* (London, 1962), 184; Andrew Porter, '*Les Vêpres siciliennes*: New Letters from Verdi to Scribe', *19th-century Music*, 2 (1978), 96. This article contains Verdi's draft plan for the end of Act IV.

for Scribe: the latter recorded, 'Verdi wanted a great big opera in five acts, a work as big as *Les Huguenots* or *Le Prophète*. I agreed to everything.'[36] A sixteenth-century Flemish revolt against the Spaniards became a thirteenth-century revolt against the French. Though this revolution is successfully accomplished at the end of the opera, the work concentrates in its last three acts on the loyalties of the duchess Hélène (whose brother has been executed as a rebel by the French) and her lover Henri (a Sicilian patriot who turns out to be the son of the hated French governor, Guy de Montfort). In variety and dramatic situation the libretto is good: Verdi's active part in its arrangement is beyond doubt. The French are quickly seen as irresponsible rulers while Henri, Montfort, and Hélène are established strongly. Procida, the Sicilians' political leader, returns from a mission to Spain. A first Sicilian revolt (Act II) is avoided only by Henri's arrest, while the latter's paternity is revealed in Act III. Torn between filial duty and patriotism, he foils Montfort's assassination. Hélène and Procida are saved from execution when, in Act IV, Henri publicly acknowledges his father, who turns matters to French advantage by arranging the surprise marriage of Hélène and Henri. But, as the bells ring out for this ceremony at Vespers, Procida leads a massacre of the unarmed enemy: the principals are slain.

Acts I and II are full of brilliant musical *trouvailles*, concisely expounding both individual and national characters. Musical forms are variously employed (including ternary, strophic, and free form); where slow–fast aria form (Procida, Act II) or duet form with strophic main sections (Montfort–Henri, Act I) are perceptibly Italianate, they are fleshed out with various irregularities and designed to sit as justly proportioned parts of a larger whole. A 'new manner' of Verdian melody appears in the 'three-limbed' cut of AA′B; it has been shown to be typical of the composer from the 1850s onwards.[37] The second act, a fine musical and dramatic entity, grows steadily in power and complexity towards a double-choir finale juxtaposing enraged Sicilians with insouciant French officers and women going to a ball. Additionally, the Sicilians' music is shot through by a dactylic rhythm that Verdi had long identified internally with the

[36] Letter of 3 Dec. 1853: Porter, 'Les Vêpres siciliennes', p. 100. The original authors' preface, by Scribe and Charles Duveyrier, is reprinted in the French–Italian edition of the libretto edited by Massimo Mila (Turin, 1973).

[37] Julian Budden, *The Operas of Verdi*, ii. *From Il trovatore to La forza del destino* (London, 1978), 40, 198; Luigi Dallapiccola, 'Words and Music in Italian 19th-century Opera', in William Weaver and Martin Chusid (eds.), *The Verdi Companion* (London, 1980), 200–1.

Ex. 233

Ex. 234

Dans l'ombre et le si - len-ce, pré-pa-rons   la ven-gean-ce!

(In darkness and silence, let us prepare for vengeance!)

Ex. 235

(Ah, let us celebrate, our spirits elated)

concept of vengeance (see Ex. 233 from the overture and Act II finale; Ex. 234 from Procida's Act II 'Palerme, ô mon pays', and Ex. 235 from the Act II finale).[38] On the other hand, the fatalistic quality of the lovers' emotions is economically conveyed through a kind of tragic lullaby within their duet, 'Comment, dans ma reconnaissance' (Ex. 236).

Act III is hindered by the long obligatory ballet ('Les Quatre Saisons'), splitting the action into two. From here on certain problems also emerge: their basis lies in the text, which, having aligned the characters well, fails to make them utter or interact in an adult manner. For example, Montfort becomes almost totally absorbed with the idea of filial affection. The music thus begins to sound

[38] More generally the motif signifies death, the adopted meaning for Budden, *The Operas of Verdi*, ii. 51–2, drawing on Frits Noske, 'The Musical Figure of Death' in *The Signifier and the Signified: Studies in the Operas of Mozart and Verdi* (The Hague, 1977), 171–214.

Ex. 236

(Near, perhaps, the tomb into which we shall descend, I could not respond to such self-sacrifice!)

Ex. 237

(To die loving you, ah, I die happy)

unjustifiably rich in the set pieces. The work's intended Meyerbeerian Act IV climax (cf. *Le Prophète*), where public ceremonial and private agony so intimately intersect, is also adversely affected. This is not to deny the great beauty of music like Henri's romance, 'O jour de peine' (though not its modified cabaletta section), or of the lambent farewells of Hélène in her romance, 'Ami! le cœur d'Hélène', also in Act IV (Ex. 237).

Les Vêpres siciliennes is characterized by (1) avoidance of simple repetition, (2) thematic development, (3) flexible rhythmic structure, and (4) a psychologically detailed approach to texture and scoring. All these, together with the frequent use of a conceptual motif (the 'vengeance' rhythm), were traits more subtly and ambitiously employed in *Don Carlos*.

Although *Don Carlos* (1867) obviously exists in one sense as one of the last and greatest of five-act *grands opéras*, it also exists in an oblique relation to the *grand* tradition, as does *Les Troyens*. On the one hand, Verdi definitely achieved that freedom from musical formalism already noted in Opéra works from 1830: *Don Carlos* shares many of the external traits seen earlier as characteristic of the genre. On the other, the political background of the opera, though consistently felt, is not normally dramatized through the chorus, or by changing sites of action (cf. *La Muette*, *Le Prophète*). The focus instead is on a group of principals who tend to use such political forces as exist to attempt to exorcise personal demons or repressions. While the central thread is certainly the 'doomed love' of Carlos and Elizabeth de Valois, pitted against 'fateful human decisions', the essence of the work is in the emotional interaction of a complex group of characters. This allowed the composer to make a successful four-act revision of the work (Milan, 1884). Moreover, it made for a Paris original that was consistently intense in feeling and rich in action, while also being rather lengthy. Its demands on audiences made for a run of only forty-three performances, all in 1867.

The libretto by Joseph Méry and Camille du Locle, after Schiller's eponymous verse drama, was accepted as a theme by Verdi in summer 1865.[39] Its wealth of suggestiveness has prompted mention of Oedipus, Hamlet, and the 'Saul–David–Jonathan syndrome',[40] and presented the musician with the challenge, successfully met, of translating a rambling structure by Schiller into a musical experience with a high degree of unity. As in the case of *Les Troyens*, we can speak of a late-twentieth-century flowering of knowledge and appreciation.[41] In terms of Verdi's art, the composer believed that in *La forza del destino*, *Don Carlos*, and, later, *Aida*, 'he had composed

---

[39] It had been mentioned by the Opéra as an idea already in 1850 as part of the preliminaries leading to *Les Vêpres siciliennes*.

[40] See the masterly account in Budden, *The Operas of Verdi*, iii. *From Don Carlos to Falstaff* (London, 1981), pp.4–157.

[41] Many publications have documented the actual discovery of forgotten music and related letters: Budden, *The Operas of Verdi*, iii; Andrew Porter, 'The Making of *Don Carlos*', *Proceedings of the Royal Musical Association*, 98 (1971–2), 73–88. The two-volume vocal score ed. U. Günther and L. Petazzoni (Milan, 1980), contains the music of all the versions, but the extensive preface is only in Italian and German.

operas of a new kind, "modern operas" made with ideas, not made up of numbers. Their production . . . should be undertaken only by an ensemble company. . . . He had read Wagner's theoretical works and approved of many of the ideas expressed in them.'[42]

Set around 1560, the action of Act I is located in France, the remainder in the Spain of Philip II. The privations of winter and war with Spain are at once exposed. Carlos (free and happy for the only time) encounters his fiancée, Elizabeth. Their idyll is destroyed when she is given in marriage by her father (the king of France) to Carlos's own father, Philip II. The drama plays itself out in two directions: the attempt by Carlos to cope with lost love, his rejection of the infatuated Princess Eboli, and the consequences of her vengeance; and the rise and fall of Carlos's bosom friend, the Marquis of Posa. Posa harbours libertarian beliefs concerning the Spanish subject people of Flanders, though he also becomes the king's confidant. 'Flanders', as a place of destiny whither Posa and Carlos are drawn, may be compared to 'Rome' in *Les Troyens*, but the later work ends darkly as the mystical apparition of Charles V (Philip's father, whose death was memorialized in Act II) enfolds Carlos, saving him from murder at the hands of monarch and Inquisition.[43]

The identity of Flanders is not evident in Verdi's music as Rome becomes a reality in Berlioz's opera. However, in an essential episode of Act III, all worldly and spiritual powers merge in a spectacular scene that allowed Verdi, finally, to match *Le Prophète*, Act IV. Before the cathedral of Valladolid, public rejoicing in the presence of the monarch will include the burning of three men by the Inquisition. (Stage music with brass and saxhorns was incorporated, the results foreshadowing *Aida*.) Suddenly six unknown deputies from Flanders enter with Carlos to beg for relief from the ravages of occupation. When Philip dismisses his son's plea to be sent hither, Carlos draws his sword; only Posa can save the situation. Carlos is led off to detention and the *auto-da-fé* resumes. The half-madness to which he is provoked was captured in a five-note discord of the ninth (Ex. 238), while the almost ferocious gaiety of the people seems musically lit by the flames of the stake. Likewise, music of pathological suggestiveness occurs in Carlos's tortured Act II duet with Elizabeth

[42] Porter, 'Verdi', *The New Grove*, xix. 654.
[43] Porter notes (*The New Grove*, xix. 654) that Carlos himself is the 'common point of three emotional triangles': Elizabeth–Carlos–Eboli; Philip–Posa–Carlos; Philip–Elizabeth–Carlos. These relationships are essentially chaste; since Eboli is seduced by the king, we can posit the carnal triad of Elizabeth–Philip–Eboli.

Ex. 238

Ex. 238

(By the God who hears me, I shall be your deliverer, noble Flemish people!)

Ex. 239

Ex. 240

[timpani, bass drum omitted]

(one which Budden calls 'one of the most impressive fusions of music and drama to be found in all opera').[44] The orchestral imagery illustrates the chasm in his mind between reality and fantasy.[45] Other of the opera's most memorable phrases also turn out to be orchestral: the Act IV opening (Ex. 239) summing up the icy depths of loneliness in Philip, and the mixture of dogmatism and age in the person of the nonagenarian Grand Inquisitor, slightly later in the act (Ex. 240).

[44] Budden, *The Operas of Verdi*, iii. 75–8. Verdi 'took infinite trouble with both the scoring and the distribution between voice and orchestra'.
[45] It is in D flat major, 'always for Carlos the key of illusory happiness' (ibid., p. 107).

Verdi's technique was founded on a fertile supply of ideas that developed or changed in response to word or act. The frequency of AA′B vocal themes is less evident to the listener than are the consequences of an aesthetic formulation by Verdi in a letter to Cammarano dating from 1851: 'If only in opera there could be no cavatinas, no duets, no trios, no choruses, no finales, etc., and if only the whole opera could be, so to speak, all one number, I should find that sensible and right.'[46] None the less, he did not reject traditionally static ensembles, such as that in Act III in reaction to the Flemish deputies, the Act IV quartet, or the Act V finale ensemble with its chorus of Dominicans.

We are more deeply conditioned by subtleties contributing to a pervasive emotional local colour—that unyielding, depressed atmosphere of the Church-dominated Spanish court: low clarinet tones; low orchestral mixtures; a ubiquitous acciaccatura figure (seen in Exx. 239–42, the last two from passages opening and closing Act I) that attains the status of a governing *topos* of lament; and the tendency of melodic phrases to fall, even in ostensibly happy passages. (Antithetically, Carlos's Act I Romance 'Je l'ai vue' and Act I duet are characterized by climbing phrases, joy still unalloyed. In the *auto-da-fé* the hysterical upward scales of the orchestra become psychologically as well as materially suggestive.) Additionally, Frits Noske has identified 'two distinctive elements dominating the score: (a) a motive ascending from the tonic to the sixth . . . and then descending to the fifth . . . (b) non-ornamental, chromatic rotation around the fifth'. Rare in contiguous Verdi works, these elements are present in proportion as a given character suffers psychological frustration.[47]

Obvious concessions to outward Spanish local colour occur in Act II, Scene ii (Eboli's song), and Act III, Scene i (off-stage ball scene with castanets). And an extensive ballet, called 'La Peregrina', bisects the first half of Act III without adding much to its value.

Ex. 241   Ex. 242

[46] Porter, 'Verdi', *The New Grove*, xix. 642.

[47] Frits Noske, ' "Don Carlos": The Signifier and the Signified' in *The Signifier and the Signified* (The Hague, 1977), 294–308.

'HEIGHTENED LYRICAL SPEECH'

This important melodic style of later nineteenth-century French opera was not characteristic of the period's greatest melodist, Bizet; but it was typical of demi-character works, especially those sung throughout (*opéra lyrique*), by Thomas, Massenet, and, to a lesser extent, Delibes. Perhaps, in part, it was a response to Wagnerian 'continuous melody'; certainly, especially in later Massenet, it helped to blur divisions between formal set piece and non-formal declamation to the point of extinction. But it had national roots. These are seen by reference to its properties of (1) syllabic setting of words, and (2) commencing with small, stepwise intervals which gradually open out. The syllabic setting derived from Classical *opéra comique*, where Grétry found a way of giving shared importance to the meaning of sung verse by moulding the line around the most significant words it contained. Commencing a melody with small intervals was typical of the eighteenth-century French song, particularly the romance as it stemmed from Rousseau (see Ex. 243, from his *intermède*, *Le Devin du village*), and was also used in opera. These twin elements were only partially submerged later by the taste for periodically structured cantabile.

The revival of syllabic values (see Ex. 92, above) was, therefore, a kind of neo-Classicism, opposed to the rhetorical German–Italian

Ex. 243

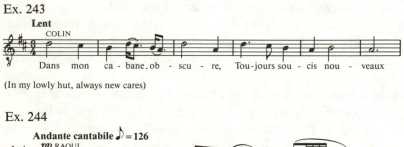

(In my lowly hut, always new cares)

Ex. 244

(Whiter than white ermine)

Ex. 245

(He is gentle, he is good, his speech is calm)

melody style here represented by a romance by Meyerbeer from Act I of *Les Huguenots* (Ex. 244), conspicuously different in its use of wide intervals, non-syllabic setting, and stress on musical symmetry. Meyerbeer's approach to word setting was in fact dominated by musical values. He wanted Scribe 'to construct his verses in such a way that they [could] be consistently broken down into smaller units for musical purposes',[48] and often composed vocal music before the precise words were available from the librettist.

The loosening of melodic syntax in Gounod's *Sapho* (see Ex. 216) had marked a revolutionary stage; in fact his habitual avoidance of symmetrical or angular rhythms was criticized for incoherence. Gounod's willingness to fragment a vocal line, while giving more complete syntactical material to the orchestra, also pointed the way forward (cf. Ex. 285). But *opéra lyrique* did not greatly develop the domestic scale of its lyricism: thus the line of resemblance between late-eighteenth- and late-nineteenth-century style is perceptible in, for example, a celebrated melody from Act I of Massenet's *Hérodiade* (1881) (Ex. 245). In his later works, such as *Werther* (1892), the line was broken up into 'heightened lyrical speech, strongly reinforced by the orchestra';[49] such a language was typical of Puccini and other early twentieth-century composers.

THOMAS'S LATER WORKS

We have already seen Ambroise Thomas's predilection as early as 1837 for subtle harmony, rhythmic flexibility, and thematic interconnections in *opéra comique*. *Mignon* (1866) was his fifteenth such work, over thirty years of composition, and it became successful to a degree enjoyed by only a handful of others: *Carmen*, *Lakmé*, *Manon*, *Le Pré aux clercs*.[50] Barbier and Carré took their central character, the 'mysterious child', from Goethe's *Wilhelm Meisters Lehrjahre*, and 'ingeniously conflated other characters and incidents to provide an *opéra comique* setting'.[51] Although it is possible that *Mignon* would have succeeded merely thanks to several melodies, sentimental and dance-like, that are hard to forget, the very slightness of its dramatic intrigue is at one with a fascinating amorality. No

[48] See John H. Roberts, 'The Genesis of Meyerbeer's "L'Africaine"' (Diss., Berkeley, 1977), fo. 116.

[49] Martin Cooper, 'Jules Massenet', *The New Grove*, xi. 805.

[50] *Mignon* had 1,833 performances at the Paris Opéra-Comique to 1950; *Carmen*, 2,607; *Lakmé*, 1,265 to 1945; *Manon*, 2,000 to 1952; *Le Pré aux clercs*, 1,608 to 1949. See Stéphane Wolff, *Un Demi-siècle d'opéra-comique (1900–1950)* (Paris, 1953).

[51] Andrew Porter, 'Travels with Mignon' in *Music of Three Seasons: 1974–1977* (New York, 1978), 52, an essay which provides information concerning an anterior manuscript version in the Bibliothèque Nationale.

character has responsibility for anything except their own transitory emotions; Mignon herself is an explicitly asexual figure. She grows emotionally richer as events proceed; Wilhelm comes to understand his emotions; Lothario (the Harper) regains his memory and finds his daughter.[52] The music, which is quite often melancholy, combines affective melodies with the glimpses of profundity which modern harmony could suggest, as in Mignon's Act II duet with Lothario (Ex. 246). Thomas's cadential pauses became a stylistic mannerism in Massenet; and the polished balance between the final security of

Ex. 246

(Have you suffered? Have you wept? Have you languished without hope? Your soul grieving, your heart broken? Then you know my suffering!)

[52] Such growth makes the happy ending almost inevitable. Thomas did, however, compose a tragic ending for Germany. The breeches role of Frédéric was also a later adaptation, from the original tenor part.

F major and the excursions to A flat and A minor may be taken as typical of the language of *opéra lyrique*. Commencing with smaller intervals and moving to larger ones, this melody also provides a point of reference regarding 'heightened lyrical speech', discussed above, as does Ex. 247.

Recitatives composed in lieu of dialogue (1869) were an unconvincing distortion of *Mignon*'s genre, and its fragile essence. The atmosphere of complete debility opening Act III (Mignon lies ill, sleeping in a deserted palace) was, after all, a precedent for *Pelléas et Mélisande* (first seen at the Opéra-Comique), as indeed were Thomas's discreet orchestration and dreamily suggestive use of thematic recollection. Chief among such material was 'Connais-tu le pays' ('Kennst du das Land'), first heard in Act I (Ex. 247), and given a Berliozian wistfulness in its modulation from D flat to F minor.

Barbier and Carré cast *Hamlet* (1868) as a five-act recitative work. An accomplished score, it had steady success at the Paris Opéra. If the cues for its literary pedigree and general design were those of *Faust*, its predecessors in adapting Shakespeare's play were Italian: Mercadante (1822), Antonio Buzzolla (1848) and Franco Faccio (1865), the last of whom had the distinction of setting Boito's first libretto.[53] For Thomas the plot was telescoped and the ending changed: the Ghost appears to Hamlet for the third time at Ophelia's funeral, finally inducing him to kill Claudius and serve his people by becoming king. Although the tone of the libretto is predictably operatic, several main scenes are authentically rendered: for example the Ghost upon the battlements, the Players, the gravediggers, 'To be or not to be', and—most successfully—Hamlet's great interlocution scene with Gertrude. Since the leading male roles were for baritone voice or lower, the work gains an interesting sombreness of colour.

Thomas derived ideas shrewdly. His basic construction kept solos and duets simple and brief, while heightening the connecting tissue sometimes to a sustained arioso level. However, clichés of recitative

Ex. 247

(Do you know the land where the orange-tree blossoms?)

---

[53] These works, and Aristide Hignard's *Hamlet* (1888, but composed before Thomas's), are discussed in Winton Dean, 'Shakespeare and Opera', pp. 163–8.

Ex. 248

Ex. 249

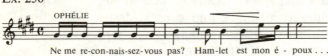

Dou - te de la lu - miè - re   Doute du so-leil et du jour

(Doubt thou the living day, doubt thou the sun and light)

Ex. 250

OPHÉLIE

Ne me re-con-nais-sez- vous pas? Ham-let est mon é - poux . . .

(Do you not recognize me? Hamlet is my husband . . .)

could not be avoided, especially given the traditional nature of the
text. Easily recognized recurring themes play a significant part: that
for Hamlet (Ex. 248) is used in Acts I, II, and V, while the motif of
his Act I avowal 'Doute de la lumière' to Ophelia (Ex. 249)[54] is
recalled four times in different forms (see Ex. 250 from Act IV). This
was the legacy of *Faust* and of Meyerbeer. But Thomas went
further, recalling (to moving effect) the orchestral theme of Hamlet's
self-dedication in avenging his father; recalling a motif from the
Players' scene in Hamlet's Act III monologue; juxtaposing earlier
fragments (sung by Hamlet) with deliberately alienating effect in the
ensemble finale to Act II; and making the Ghost's Act I 'Invocation'
music return with that spectre in Act III.

Elsewhere, Thomas's style is excessively formalistic. Ophelia's
character is limited by her symmetrical, short phrases laid over a
static bass; ingenious harmonic progressions are sometimes wasted
in linking material instead of infusing major scenes with greater
interest. The opera succeeds because the main role is so convincingly
created in music, particularly Hamlet's emotions towards his father:

[54] Cf. 'Doubt thou the stars are fire; | Doubt that the Sun doth move' (*Hamlet*, II. ii. 115–
16).

Ex. 251

(Sweet ecstasy! Adieu!)

Ex. 251, for example (Shakespeare's 'Adieu, adieu, remember me'
speech), finely encapsulates the quality of his 'noble heart' near the
end of Act I. In the scene with Gertrude, Thomas created an
altercation of rare psychological conviction, building up at length
from a discontinuous start. Its force was surely not lost on Bizet, a
known admirer of *Hamlet*.

The use of a solo alto saxophone in the Players' scene could have
been suggested by Fétis's addition of a baritone saxophone part to
L'Africaine (which was heard at the time but not published). However,
Jean Georges Kastner's opera *Le Dernier Roi de Juda* (concert
performance, 1844) and Halévy's *Le Juif errant* (1852) preceded both
in using the instrument, though not soloistically.

BIZET'S YOUTHFUL WORKS

Georges Bizet (1838–75) was, almost from the first, a precociously
original composer, whose colours, rhythmic interest, and forcefulness
marked him out from the prevailing qualities of French opera. Thus
he inherited the mantle of Berlioz, who, in fact, lived long enough
to review and praise *Les Pêcheurs de perles* (1863) in many particulars
as a score that did Bizet 'the greatest honour'. Others, to a degree
that is at first hard to comprehend today, found Bizet's music
incomprehensible, or heretically Wagnerian.

Bizet was a child prodigy who entered the Paris Conservatoire
before his tenth birthday. He had close connections with Gounod,
his teacher and mentor, and Halévy, whose daughter Bizet married
and whose brother (Léon) and son (Ludovic) both acted as his
librettists. An early *opéra comique* remains unpublished (*La Maison*

du docteur, *c.*1855).[55] The one-act *Le Docteur Miracle* attained eleven
performances as joint winner, in 1857, of Offenbach's competition
intended to lead *opéra comique* back into the fold of traditional
gaiety. Ironically it was Bizet who was destined to revolutionize the
genre with a new type of tragedy: *Carmen*. The music of *Le Docteur
Miracle* indicates both very competent handling of vocal forces and
also embryonic examples of later creative traits: driving rhythm;
piquant harmonies—asterisked—as upbeats to the dominant chord
(see Ex. 252, *Le Docteur Miracle*, Overture, Ex. 253 from *Les
Pêcheurs de perles*, Ex. 254, the opening of *Djamileh*, Ex. 271, and
Ex. 272 from *Carmen*); and, most significantly, the ability to write
extended, shapely melody. This gift, denied to Meyerbeer and
Gounod, is discussed separately below. There was no room for
harmonic innovation—later so important in Bizet's art—though
Pasquin enters in G minor in his couplets, No. 3, whereas the
ritornello is in B flat. But hints of future dissonances appeared in
the 'Omelette Quartet', where chords of G, C minor, A, and D
minor succeed one another over an F pedal.[56]

The Roman years (1858–60) as Prix de Rome winner saw the
completion of *Don Procopio*, a two-act comedy which Bizet set in

Ex. 252   Ex. 253

Ex. 254

[55] The libretto, by Henri Boisseaux, has recently been identified by Lesley Wright: see 'Bizet before "Carmen"' (Diss., Princeton, 1981), fo. 9, n. 19.

[56] Compare Ex. 264, one of many characteristic pedal passages in Bizet. One might observe that another fingerprint, the held note as part of a melody, can be regarded as an upper or middle pedal point.

Ex. 255

(What a precious scheme, charming idea!)

the original Italian. Although apparently modelled on Donizetti's *Don Pasquale*, whose plot it echoes closely, *Don Procopio* had sufficient originality to provide material for several self-borrowings in *Les Pêcheurs de perles*, *La Jolie Fille de Perth*, and the Symphony in C. Of these the most significant was Odoardo's serenade 'Sulle piume', No. 7, which became (not without changes) Smith's serenade, no. 13, in *La Jolie Fille de Perth*. This is because it possesses a characteristic form of melodic construction which may be termed 'additive'. But more standard Italianisms became important too, typified in the trio, No. 4 (Ex. 255). A second operatic *envoi*, *La Guzla de l'émir*, was completed and even rehearsed, but seems to have been destroyed. At the same juncture (1862) Bizet apparently commenced his five-act *grand opéra*, *Ivan IV*. It survives only in a putative early version (rather than an assumed 1864–5 version which was refused by the Opéra;[57] Bizet was in fact the first great French composer to have none of his operas originally staged there).

No greater contrast can be imagined than between the dramatic falsities of *Ivan IV*, and the triumphs of characterization and timing achieved in *Djamileh* (composed 1871). The former has an inept libretto by F. H. Leroy and H. Trianon that Gounod had tried out in 1855–6. The abduction in Act I by the Russians of Marie, and the chance meeting in Moscow of Marie's father and brother in Act III, recall *Le Prophète* (Acts I, IV). Marie marries Ivan; her family's naïve rescue plan fails; Ivan survives an attempted usurpation. There is no coherence of political or personal motivation; even a duet for Ivan and Marie is lacking.

Bizet, at least in the surviving score, developed an appropriate language mainly in the impersonal set pieces: the Act I ensemble of

---

[57] See Winton Dean, 'Bizet's "Ivan IV" ', in Herbert Van Thal (ed.), *Fanfare for Ernest Newman* (London, 1955), 58–85. The published vocal score (1951), among many other liberties, silently conflates the original Acts I and II.

Ex. 256

Caucasian mourning (not printed in the 1951 vocal score); the Act
II serenade; the ensemble finales to Acts II and IV; and ceremonies
and a Russian hymn in Act III. Here Bizet gave some individual
flavour to the manipulation of stock outlines, and his facility is
illustrated in the bold if misjudged string of seventh chords used in
the finale of Act II (Ex. 256). But the principals' music merely bears
witness to Bizet's impulses towards extended melody. This song
impulse—a Mozart-like trait—embarrasses the flow of action; the
melodic influence of Verdi seems incontrovertible,[58] though is kept
within bounds.

Wagner's example surfaced in different ways: a *Lohengrin*-inspired
ending to Act I; several large closing cadences interrupted by a
diminished seventh; some declamatory recitative using the gestures
of the *Ring*.[59] There was a loose response to recurring motifs, with
ideas associated with Marie and Yorloff. Displaying his genius for
music suggesting action, Bizet gave a passage to Marie fetching
spring water for the traveller Ivan that parallels *Die Walküre*, Act
I, Scene i.[60]

BIZET'S STYLE

We can perceive Bizet trying and testing new aspects of musical
language with each completed opera, evidently aiming to forge a
unity between the type of drama and its appropriate score. But his
strong compositional personality, which matured early, permits us
to examine three aspects of his style—melody, harmony, rhythm—
with examples all predating *Carmen*.

Bizet exploited many melodic schemes. From Classical practice he
used both 'periodic' construction (ABA′B′) and 'sentence' construction (AA′B): the terminology is Schoenberg's. The former, in
its simplest layout of 2+2+2+2 or 4+4+4+4 bars, is most

---

[58] See the arching form and grace notes of 'Ah! par ces larmes' (vocal score, p. 97), Ivan's
'Je t'aimais' (ibid., p. 264), or the cadential formula used in 'J'aimais l'aspect' (ibid., pp. 212–
13). Bizet is known to have admired *Rigoletto*.

[59] E.g. vocal score, p. 92.

[60] Vocal score, p. 22, where Marie's motif is first heard in the orchestra.

extensively found in *Djamileh*. The latter, which is inherently inclined towards growth, occurs in unusual proportions even in *Ivan IV*: this work was in fact one of melodic discovery for Bizet. In Ex. 257 ('Fatigué d'incertitude' from *Ivan IV*), the 'sentence', as normal with the composer, cadences outside the tonic to begin with, maintaining harmonic tension and interest over its span.

However, Bizet created at least two other types of structure. One was the extension of periodic form so that its final segment grew outwards. It is seen as early as *Le Docteur Miracle*, No. 5 (Ex. 258), where it evinces secure grasp of harmonic tension at the same time as employing unusual phrase lengths. This was a resource regularly used as needed. All Bizet's operas used the extended periodic form.

The second extended structure was an additive one. It too was ubiquitous, but was chiefly evident in *Les Pêcheurs de perles*. Bizet might write any number of segments, and each segment could be short or long: whichever pattern was selected for a given melody, its internal pattern was repeated in each segment. *Les Pêcheurs de perles*,

Ex. 257

Ex. 258

Ex. 259

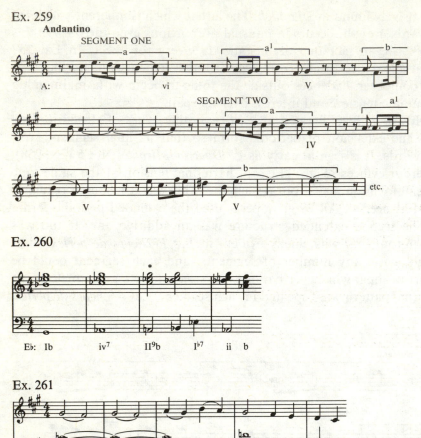

Ex. 260

Ex. 261

No. 5, contains seven two-bar segments. No. 3B of the same work, however, contains five eight-bar segments, each segment itself comprising three phrases deployed as a miniature 'sentence' (Ex. 259). The final held note is a Bizet fingerprint. Later, in *Djamileh*, the additive principle was refined to create non-parallel segments: Haroun's 'Dans la blonde fumée' in No. 1, and Splendiano's 'À la fleur près de naître', No. 2.

It was in its harmony that Bizet's modernism was most abruptly felt. He had a most refined sense of key relationships and the most vivid harmonic responsiveness to a dramatic situation. In a reduction from *Ivan IV*, Act III (vocal score, p. 178) (Ex. 260) we see his use of the established linear approach to dissonance and the appoggiatura. Ten years later the more dissonant, Tristanesque appoggiatura style played a part in *Djamileh* (Ex. 261 from No. 2). Bizet always fastened on the ii⁷ configuration (asterisked in Ex. 260) in pursuit of tonal ambiguity. The jump in language from *Ivan IV* to *Les Pêcheurs de perles* is seen in the advanced way Bizet used three such chords (asterisked in Ex. 262) in the later work as strange, haunting substitute dominants in the 'oath' sequence, No. 3C. In fact they provide the only 'cadences' in the whole thirty-nine-bar scene, interpretable as one large V–I in B major, and a fine example of Bizet's precocity.

He often built up dissonant progressions over (or under, or surrounding) a pedal note. The principle exists in Exx. 260 and 261, but many more individual examples occur. The reduction in Ex. 263 is from a conversational passage in *Les Pêcheurs*, Act I: Zurga's words to Léila in No. 3C: 'C'est bien; à tous les yeux tu resteras voilée.' The languid luxury of *Djamileh*'s opening (Ex. 264) led to

Ex. 262

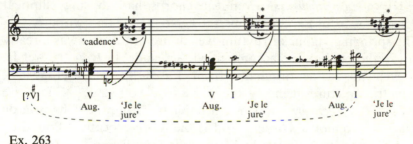

Ex. 263

Ex. 264

Ex. 265

(It's Nadir, wanderer of the forests)

multiple layers of dissonance passing like opium puffs over a held chord; here, as always in Bizet, the timbre of orchestra and voices finely complemented the total effect. But ambiguity could even dispense with a pedal. Gounod's daring opening to Act V of *Faust* (a brassy, shocking augmented chord) found more than one echo in Act III of *Les Pêcheurs*. Even the chorus had to sing elliptical progressions, as in Ex. 265 from Act I, No. 1B of that work.

The springing vigour of rhythm we admire in *Carmen* was already heard in the tambourine-accompanied 'Sérénade' in *Ivan IV*, Act II, but even this came originally from *Vasco de Gama* (1859–60). Polymetric picturesqueness—the 12/8 / 9/8 off-stage 'Chanson', No. 8, in *Les Pêcheurs*—was heard publicly before the 'Chanson de Magali' in Gounod's *Mireille*, and is the more evocative. Pounding duple rhythms characterize the St Valentine revellers of *La Jolie Fille de Perth* and such rhythmic ostinatos produce many 'local' or 'characteristic' Bizet effects. Rhythmic counterpoint, however, was also essential; the best Bizet choruses all contain vividly juxtaposed rhythms (although those in *Ivan IV* contain almost none). The technique may have stemmed from Berlioz, whose Mardi Gras music in *Benvenuto Cellini* seems to lie behind the brilliant tarantella rhythm in Bizet's own 'Chœur dansé', No. 13 of *Les Pêcheurs de perles*. In *Carmen* new paths opened out thanks to the aptness of dance and movement to the drama: the 'Habanera' (Act I, No. 5), the 'Séguedille' [*sic*] (Act I, No. 10), the 'Chanson bohème' (Act II, No. 12), and creative reminiscences of flamenco.[61] Bizet's genius for mimetic suggestion, noted above, became fused with his natural rhythmic vigour; and both elements were harnessed to his incomparable melodic invention. The step cannot have been easy, because the melodic style of *Carmen* actually represents a new technical stage of development in Bizet.

[61] Edgar Istel, *Bizet und 'Carmen'* (Stuttgart, 1927), pp. 112 ff., considers the un-Spanish rhythm of Bizet's 'Habanera', and his Spanish sources elsewhere in the score.

LES PÊCHEURS DE PERLES

From Bizet's letters to his pupil Edmond Galabert concerning compositional methods in opera, we know that he possessed acute theoretical awareness of psychology and dramatic timing. From his manuscripts we know that theory became practice in the extensive revisions made during the experience of rehearsals.[62] In fact he turned *Les Pêcheurs de perles* (1863) from an *opéra comique* to a through-composed work in its final rehearsal month.[63] The richness of the score has concealed any suspicion of this until recently. Scoring and rhythmic energy in the linking dialogue sections do not belie the personality of the whole, which combines vigour with a brilliant sense of coloration, harmonic and orchestral. In its fine melodies, Bizet absorbed and extended the language of Verdi. Because the drama contains so little intrigue, and so few important ensembles, Bizet was free to spread himself in picturesque solos and choruses; they contrast sharply with the violently active choral dances of the Ceylonese pearl fishers.

The libretto is poorly designed in its accommodation of character. Chance brings the virgin priestess Léila, Zurga (the chief pearl fisher), and his friend Nadir together. Both men had seen and desired Léila some time before, in Candy, but agreed to forswear this love. In Act II Nadir seeks Léila out; they are discovered and condemned to death, but finally allowed to escape by Zurga, whose life Léila had once saved as a girl. Bizet endows this cheap romance with a beautiful sense of fantasy. Where action is required, Bizet's suggestion of movement and response is sure; he brings a Germanic kind of power to the simple passions enunciated. Tying together the threads of past and present, suggesting dimensions of time and personality so otherwise lacking, Bizet invented a languid melody symbolizing the kernel of the tale: the numinous moment in Candy when friendship, love and circumstance were set on their inevitable course (Ex. 266, from the Nadir–Zurga duet in Act I). This concept, and its musical realization, turned Gounod's parallel example in *Faust* (see Ex. 219) to much-needed advantage. Unfortunately, the composer somewhat

---

[62] Wright, 'Bizet before "Carmen"', fos. 102, 226 ff.; Winton Dean, *Georges Bizet: His Life and Work* (London, 1948; enlarged 3rd edn., 1975), p. 60. The work Galabert was attempting, in 1868, was *La Coupe du Roi de Thulé*. Bizet's own interest in the libretto became such that he set it himself and submitted it anonymously in the 1869 competition set by the Opéra. The manuscript now comprises only fifteen fragments. Dean estimates that it would have ranked 'second only to *Carmen*': ibid., pp. 79, 185 ff.

[63] Wright, 'Bizet before "Carmen"', fos. 260–1, citing evidence of censor's manuscript libretto. Falsifications were perpetrated silently in virtually all vocal score editions of Bizet's operas other than *Le Docteur Miracle*. See Dean, *Georges Bizet*, Appendix F and p. 162 n. 1.

Ex. 266

overplays its recollection, for example, in No. 12C, where dramatic attention is focused on a quite different aspect of the plot; but he does sometimes transform its metre.[64]

LA JOLIE FILLE DE PERTH

Problems of finding a good libretto persisted, despite Bizet's fastidious approach to literary subjects—or because of it. (He habitually took a hand in modifying a text, and rhymed his own libretto for the early *L'Amour peintre*, after Molière, which does not survive. Later, he was to invent words as well as music for the 'Habanera' in *Carmen*.) The veteran librettist Vernoy de Saint-Georges worked with Jules Adenis to formulate a conventional plot from Scott's *The Fair Maid of Perth*; the result—produced in 1867—bears only a passing resemblance to episodes and characters in this long novel.[65] Though the Scottish setting is maintained, it seems reflected only in the dour A minor tune beginning Act II. As a comedy of intrigue it was the most conventional of Bizet's opera plots, a fact reflected in some public approbation. It earned, even in eighteen performances, more exposure than other novelties at the Théâtre Lyrique, only excepting *Roméo et Juliette* and Flotow's *Martha*.[66] The dramatic ancestry was the good humour of early nineteenth-century *opéra comique*; harmony, recitative, and rhythm were more conventionally handled than in *Les Pêcheurs de perles*.

Although the libretto is best described as unconvincing (if not downright silly), it afforded a certain amount of characterization for Bizet to exploit. After a two-year courtship, the union of Henry

---

[64] The Zurga-Nadir duet in Act I should not in fact end with this famous melody; Bizet's subsequent music throws the emphasis away from it and therefore makes its recollection less obvious.

[65] Jerome Mitchell, *The Walter Scott Operas* (University of Alabama, 1977), pp. 341-9. Mab's character was adapted from Louise the glee-maiden; see Scott's chapters 2, 11, 12, 16, 19, 23.

[66] Walsh, *Second Empire Opera*, pp. 232-5 and 319-21. Verdi's *Rigoletto* and *Violetta* (*La traviata*) were still very popular at the same theatre at the time. They left their mark in Bizet's gaming scene, Act III.

Smith and Catherine Glover is further delayed by unlikely interventions from the gypsy Mab and the profligate Duke of Rothsay. In the last act Catherine has a brief mad scene (cf. *L'Étoile du nord*). But for the first time Bizet tested his character depiction in terms of ensemble writing. There was little occasion for the expansive solo. In rehearsal, he both changed smaller set pieces (often making symmetrical structures irregular) and improved larger ensemble sequences.[67] Little development is given to Catherine's character, but Smith, his rival Ralph, and Mab are memorable enough. There was a subtle use of recurring themes, particularly the waltzing melody we associate with Rothsay's flirting with Catherine—the mainspring of the action. In shape, key, and function it relates to the waltz in Act II of *Faust*.[68]

Bizet's score, which awaits accurate editing, eventually satisfied its composer; Ex. 267, a passage in her Act I aria 'Vive l'hiver', gives Catherine a Carmen-like quality that explains her response to the

Ex. 267

(Make the most of every moment, for all passes, all will die!)

---

[67] Lesley Wright considers that perhaps seven numbers, including three of the finales, were thus rewritten ('Bizet before "Carmen"' fo. 328). Bizet altered the celebrated Act II Serenade in design to integrate it dramatically. Most scores present a corrupt (regular strophic) version.

[68] The rhythms and patterns of Weber are also audible, especially in Act I and II. *Oberon* had been revived at the Théâtre Lyrique in 1863; *Der Freischütz* was seen there throughout the same decade.

duke and, perhaps, her temporary instability later in the opera. It is absent from current editions.[69] Bizet's ability to give a work a unique overall sense of flavour and dramatic propriety gives *La Jolie Fille de Perth* its chief distinction.

DJAMILEH

Djamileh (1872), like *Le Docteur Miracle*, was a one-act *opéra comique*. It had been preceded by various projects during which Bizet's operatic art matured further.[70] The text, by Louis Gallet, is a simple variation on the Scheherezade idea, in which the slave discovering that, like her predecessors, she is about to be rejected after one month by Haroun, convinces him of their genuine love. But the story is almost the least important element. Immense musical sophistication, skilled pacing and the lightest handling of material and orchestration created a miniature masterpiece. The species of opening music is illustrated in Ex. 264, depicting the palace at sunset as Haroun reclines, smoking, and is the most authentic counterpart to Hugo's *Les Orientales* or Ingres's *Odalisques*.[71] If the source, de Musset's poem *Namouna* (1832), actually concerned 'vulnerability, the effort to describe the deepest promptings of the quest for happiness, the inconclusive pursuit of art',[72] much the same cultivated ambiguity infuses the opera. Particularly interesting were the through-composition techniques used for scenes of interaction, Nos. 2, 3, and 9. None of these begins or ends in the same key. Bizet certainly retained traditional forms such as the verse song (couplets), the duet, and the trio, but blended one into the other with free declamatory passages infused by capricious emotional oscillation; we are close to the world of Debussy's *Jeux*. The idea of a waltz theme, ironically recalled near the end and symbolizing love's gaiety, reappeared from *La Jolie Fille de Perth*.[73] Djamileh has her own orchestral theme, whose yearning was derived from the ii^7 chord itself. It alone accompanies the heroine on her silent first appearance in Scene iii, attaining high eloquence through its scoring, which is absurdly simple on paper (Ex. 268): such economy is typical of the

[69] The corruptions in various scores of the work are discussed in Jack Westrup, 'Bizet's *La Jolie Fille de Perth*', in J. Westrup (ed.), *Essays presented to Egon Wellesz* (Oxford, 1966), 157–70.

[70] *La Coupe du Roi de Thulé; Clarissa Harlowe; Grisélidis*. Some music from the first was introduced in *Djamileh* and *Carmen*.

[71] The visual setting had been anticipated in the opium-smoking scene that opens Reyer's *opéra comique*, *La Statue* (1861) discussed later in this chapter.

[72] J. C. Ireson, 'Poetry', in D. G. Charlton (ed.), *The French Romantics* (Cambridge, 1984), i. 143.

[73] Vocal score p. 65, 'Enfant, laissons dans les buissons', recalled on p. 114.

Ex. 268

Ex. 269

(Your perfumed lip)

score. The Wagnerian potentiality it embodies comes to the fore in the last scene, where Haroun's solo of self-realization transforms the intervals diatonically as the scales fall from his eyes (Ex. 269).

Two refinements of melodic style must be mentioned: Haroun's twenty-six bars of non-repeating melody 'Dans la blonde fumée' in No. 1, a perfect analogue of narcotic indecision, and Djamileh's 'Ghazel', No. 3. (This acts as a tale within a tale, just as, say, 'Une fièvre brûlante' from Grétry's *Richard Cœur de lion* in 1784 or the ballade in Act I of Meyerbeer's *Robert le diable*. In all three cases

Ex. 270

(Nour-Eddin, king of Lahore, is proud like a god, is handsome)

Ex. 271

the music in question is used in a varied and recalled form later in
the work.) The 'Ghazel', of the subtlest beauty, opens with a
fourteen-bar melodic span that is but the first segment of a 'sentence'
form. It is, further, dispossessed both of a firm down-beat and an
anchoring bass line (Ex. 270). Hardly surprisingly, *Djamileh* left
audiences at the Opéra-Comique uncomprehending, and was seen
only eleven times. The critics were naturally scandalized by the music
of Ex. 271, which opens the heroine's 'Lamento', No. 6.

CARMEN

The commission by the Opéra-Comique for a new piece, text by
Meilhac and Ludovic Halévy, was received by Bizet at the time of
Djamileh: the composer himself proposed *Carmen*, a short novel by
Mérimée (1845). The incidental music for Daudet's *L'Arlésienne*
came later in 1872; work on *Carmen* stretched from 1873 to 1874,

being itself interrupted by composition of a five-act opera, *Don Rodrigue* (1873), intended for the Opéra but not accepted.[74]

Although *Carmen*, produced in 1875, scandalized many in France, it experienced no delay at the Censor's office.[75] But Bizet was obliged to insist that his collaborators (both literary and theatrical) maintain the integrity of their subject. He intended to regenerate *opéra comique*. In this one catalyst was Gounod, whose heroines in *Faust* and *Mireille* (originally *opéras comiques*) die tragically. Another was the Verdi of *La traviata*. Carmen was scandalous because she was an unrepentantly free spirit, quite beyond the pale of bourgeois experience, and because Don José is both rejected and destroyed after his affair with her. There was no rescuing bosom in sentiment, the Church, or the family. '*Carmen* was a landmark because it asserted that the deeper passions *were* a matter of every-day life and therefore a fit subject for *opéra comique*. The substitution of recitative with its unnatural grand-opera associations falsifies the entire work.'[76]

The drama is articulated with the relentless force of a Classical tragedy. Action and character are built up rather gradually: Don José deserts the army only at the end of Act II; no time is wasted (dramatically or musically) on any idyll between Carmen and him. By Act III they are quarrelling and Carmen foretells her death in the cards. Her murder, on stage, posed no legal problem since the liberalization of 1864, but it assaulted convention just as did the unified design. As one dissatisfied old witness put it, 'there ought to be surprises, happenings, incidents, things that make you say, "What is going to occur in the next act?" '[77]

The Spanish setting took Bizet beyond the fitful liveliness of Perthshire and Cairo, and beyond simple rhythmic ostinatos. He actually adopted Spanish folk material and a song by Yradier (for the Act I 'Habanera'), thinking it was traditional. In all cases, however, he does not quote verbatim, but alters notes and rhythms. It is the rhythmic vitality of the whole score that projects a certain image of Spain on to almost every page.

But the new conjunction of rhythm, kinetic suggestion, and melody

[74] Bizet again suggested the subject: 'It's not Corneille's *Cid*, it's the original Cid with real Spanish colouring.' The autograph is preserved but lacks most of the accompaniment details. See Dean, *Georges Bizet*, pp. 106–7.

[75] Lesley A. Wright, 'A New Source for *Carmen*', *19th-century Music*, 2 (1978–9), 68.

[76] Winton Dean, 'The Libretto' in *Carmen: A Romance by Prosper Mérimée* (London, 1949), 90–1. In Mérimée the whole story is narrated from his condemned cell by Don José. The original characters were more rough-hewn: José, for example, kills both the lieutenant and Carmen's husband, a character excluded from the opera.

[77] Douglas Charles Parker, *Bizet* (London, 1951), 47. The imperial decree of 6 Jan. 1864 enabled any genre of work to be acted on any French stage.

had of course a directly dramatic purpose. Carmen and Escamillo are creatures of movement; Micaela and José creatures of sentiment. Thus, Carmen is pictured in her 'Habanera', her mocking 'Coupe-moi, brûle-moi', her ' Séguedille', her castanet dance, and the 'Chanson bohème'. This pattern is then broken; she sings the slowest music in the opera in the F minor 'En vain pour éviter' in Act III, and in the final Act IV confrontation she rises to a vocal eloquence that confirms her moral strength in the face of fate. Escamillo 'exists' in the Toreador's song and, by extension, in the rowdy glory of the march, 'Les voici', in Act IV and the overture.

Bizet was censured by some for continuing to be too cerebral in harmony and melody but, by contrast with *Djamileh*, he chose not to dwell on 'learned' chords, rather to use them sparingly to highlight the diatonic colour of the main 'Southern' idiom: see Ex. 272 from Escamillo's Act II couplets, 'Votre toast'.

The stress on continuity in *Djamileh*, however, was developed in *Carmen*. As in any Romantic recitative opera, the emotional crises unfold in extended duet sequences (Acts I, II, IV), not self-contained numbers. In Act III the 'public' and private dilemmas are focused in the finale into opposition within an ensemble context. This, too, reflects the Scribe tradition of *grand opéra* on a small scale. How

Ex. 272

(It's the festival of noble hearts! Toreador, on guard!)

conscious it was remains matter for speculation, though Micaela's revelation that José's mother is dying was a *coup de théâtre* owing nothing to Mérimée. Certainly the continuities of design were found disturbing: 'There are three pieces in it which contain music, and make some effect because *they come to an end*', was one representative view,[78] and presumably these were the three set pieces to be applauded at the première: Act I, Micaela-José duet; Act II, Toreador's song; Act III, Micaela's aria.

Two significant threads of stylistic development are evinced in *Carmen*: thematic unity and melodic concision. There is an abundance of melodic interest but Bizet controls it motivically, using a basic cell with the intervals of a perfect fourth, a second, and a third; often, but not invariably, the second and the third are grouped or 'contained' within the perfect fourth. Exx. 273 and 274 illustrate this cell as it relates to the twin main recurring motifs of the opera: the first represents Carmen, the second her fateful effect on Don José. The cell is also bracketed in Ex. 272. Other themes built on the same intervals are the 'Marche et chœur des gamins' in Act I (Ex. 275), Don José's 'Ma mère je la vois' from his Act I duet with Micaela (Ex. 276), and the Act II duet 'Je vais danser en votre honneur' (Ex. 277).

Bizet's new melodic conciseness in *Carmen*, whether in 'sentence', 'period', or additive form, made for memorability and a proper balance between personal utterance and the development of material by another or by an ensemble. Periodic form is most common, but

Ex. 273   Ex. 274

Ex. 275   Ex. 276

Ex. 277

[78] Ibid.

Bizet also used a new form, the ABCA or ABB′A melody.[79] Even when sentence form was used (for example, the refrain of the Toreador's song) the length was only twelve bars. By contrast, Micaela's music is in the older, lengthier style, especially 'Je dis que rien' in Act III.

Bizet recast much of *Carmen*'s music during intensive rehearsals.[80] The chorus found its part impossibly difficult; its music had to be reduced. In general Bizet honed the score so that it became the infallible cutting edge of the drama at all points, never surer than in the closing scene. Here, as everywhere, use of thematic recollection was made with great economy and irony; the culminating entries of Ex. 274 possess almost physical impact; so do the choral shouts from the bullfight in its simultaneous climax.

Bizet died (from complicated causes) during the first run of *Carmen*, which attained merely forty-five performances, not to be revived in Paris until 1883. But the opera quickly gained fame. It particularly influenced Tchaikovsky, Chabrier, the Italian realists, and, presumably, Alban Berg, while Bizet as a whole affected Fauré, Debussy, Saint-Saëns, and others. *Carmen* was to become the modernist stick with which Nietzsche beat Wagner in *Der Fall Wagner*:

Bizet's work also saves; Wagner is not the only 'Saviour'. With it one bids farewell to the *damp* north and to all the fog of the Wagnerian ideal. Even the action in itself delivers us from these things. From Mérimée it has this logic even in passion, from him it has the direct line, *inexorable* necessity; but what it has above all else is that which belongs to subtropical zones. . . . Here another kind of sensuality, another kind of sensitiveness, and another kind of cheerfulness make their appeal. . . . I envy Bizet for having had the courage of this sensitiveness, which hitherto in the cultured music of Europe has found no means of expression.[81]

Recitatives were added to *Carmen* by E. Guiraud in 1875. They remove much of the motivation, plot, and character of the work, and ruin the point of Carmen's insolent chanson in Act I (which must contrast with speech).

---

[79] Heard in Micaela's 'Et tu lui diras' from her Act I duet with José, and in the 'chanson bohème' commencing Act II.

[80] The finales, except the second, 'were revised several times' and 'more than half the pieces in Act I were cut or revised' (Wright, 'A New Source for *Carmen*', p. 68). The Oeser full score edition confuses the status of these and other cuts; see Winton Dean, 'The True "Carmen"?', *Musical Times*, 106 (1965), 846–55.

[81] See *The Philosophy of Nietzche*, ed. Geoffrey Clive (New York, 1965), 259–60.

THE 1870S AND 1880S

The 1870s was a decade of limited achievement, and that took place at the Opéra-Comique. The Théâtre Lyrique had closed in May 1870; it had been in decline before Carvalho's bankruptcy in 1868, though its spirit of enterprise flashed intermittently: *Rienzi* was staged in 1869. The Paris Opéra was in a period of sclerosis; Massenet's *Le Roi de Lahore* (1877) and *Le Cid* (1885) were the principal world premières. It delayed productions of significant works such as Saint-Saëns's *Samson et Dalila* (Weimar, 1877), Massenet's *Hérodiade* (Brussels, 1881), Reyer's *Sigurd* (Brussels, 1884) and Chabrier's *Gwendoline* (Brussels, 1886). The new spirit was, however, manifest at the Opéra-Comique, where the most important premières were: *Djamileh* (1872); *Le Roi l'a dit* (Delibes) (1873); *Carmen* (1875, not revived until 1883); *L'Étoile* (Chabrier) (1877); *Les Contes d'Hoffmann* (Offenbach) (1881); *Lakmé* (Delibes) (1883); *Manon* (Massenet) (1884); *Le Roi malgré lui* (Chabrier) (1887); *Le Roi d'Ys* (Lalo) (1888); *Esclarmonde* (Massenet) (1889).

While Bizet assimilated or cast off aspects of Wagner's music, others could not but succumb, as Wagner's influence widened in Paris both behind the scenes and on the stage. His actual works did not appear at the Opéra between the *Tannhäuser* fiasco of 1861 and the year 1891 (*Lohengrin*). But French musicians visited Bayreuth from 1876 (d'Indy, Saint-Saëns, Widor) and 1882 (Delibes)[82] while César Franck's hearing of the *Tristan* Prelude in 1874 had a permanent effect on his work, including the opera *Hulda*. This was written in 1881–5 but not performed until after Franck's death (Monte Carlo, 1894, shortened version).[83] Chabrier, the most committed French Wagnerian of genius, became a full-time composer after seeing *Tristan und Isolde* in Munich in 1880. *La Revue Wagnérienne* (1885–8) acted as a cultural focus, its contributors including the musicians Saint-Saëns, d'Indy, Fauré, Hahn, and Schmitt.

Opera on the threshold of the modern period therefore became primarily eclectic in subject-matter, form, and musical language, with equally interesting contributions from both Opéra and Opéra-Comique traditions. Only Massenet was to bridge all operatic genres successfully, but Chabrier and Saint-Saëns both made significant advances in actually extending the art-form.

[82] See Albert Lavignac, *Le Voyage artistique à Bayreuth* (Paris, 1897), which both typifies and documents the French interest in all aspects of the 'pilgrimage'. Nevertheless Wagner's scores were available for study at the keyboard much earlier.

[83] By G. Franck and S. Rousseau. Restored version by D. Lloyd-Jones (Reading University performance, 1978). See *19th-century Music*, 2 (1978), 162–4.

SAINT-SAËNS

A prodigiously gifted pianist (like his friend Bizet), Camille
Saint-Saëns (1835–1921) was a polymath of a composer. His two
early operas, which both employ spoken dialogue, experienced
production delays and were unsuccessful. *La Princesse jaune*, in one
act, stems chiefly from 1866 (performed 1872); *Le Timbre d'argent*,
in four acts, was begun in 1864 but not staged until 1877. Both are
comic moralities involving elements of the surreal. The former—it
involves a Japanese figurine—uses several pentatonic melodies for
local colour, as in the duet, No. 5 (Ex. 278). However, it also pointed
in the direction of *Samson et Dalila* in its 'modern', extended
love duet, complete with enharmonic progressions and passionate
crescendos. The work is long-winded and unsubtle beside *Djamileh*,
which also had only two main characters. *Le Timbre d'argent* is out
of the world of E. T. A. Hoffmann, its text by the authors of the
1851 play that was to become *Les Contes d'Hoffmann*: Barbier and
Carré. (The Hoffmann-inspired ballet, *Coppélia*, was Delibes's first
great success in 1870.) Saint-Saëns's figure of Dr Spiridion plays the
same 'evil genius' role as Lindorf in Offenbach's work, which was
begun in the year during which *Le Timbre d'argent* was first seen.

Ex. 278

Sur l'eau claire et sans ri - de Glis-se mon ba-teau

(My boat slips over the clear, calm water)

Ex. 279

(God of Israel!)

The main character, Conrad, pursues the love of the dancer Fiametta with the supernatural aid of a silver bell that also brings death. The music is energetic, though without a markedly personal stamp, and sometimes repetitive. Structurally it tends towards continuous chaining-together of numbers; there is some use of spoken *mélodrame*.

Samson et Dalila occupied Saint-Saëns for a decade before its performance in 1877: the authorities made difficulties, disconcerted by the biblical material. The dramatic design of the piece is extremely original, its musical structures unpredictable, and its music, of unflagging quality, is an unlikely though successful amalgam unified by certain Wagnerian methods. Baroque neo-Classicism expresses the sorrows of the Children of Israel, opening Acts I (Ex. 279) and III. The chorus is given fugue and fugato. The opening, indeed, could only have made sense to a generation basically familiar with Bach's church music. Later, the Israelite elders have chant-like music (Act I, Scene v), involving only four notes over thirty-two bars (Ex. 280). In Act III the Philistines' dances are given a pungent Middle

Ex. 280

(Hymn of joy, hymn of deliverance, ascend to the Eternal One)

Ex. 281

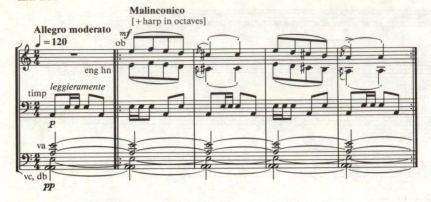

Eastern flavour (Ex. 281). Elsewhere in the act the glockenspiel, wood and metal castanets, and crotales add gaudy colour to the merrymaking.[84] Because these and other devices remain in command, proceeding within a dramaturgy that is only to a limited degree realistic, the opera creates something fresh out of its debt to Wagner. The structure is chiefly neo-Classical, in that solos, choruses, or dances are built up in separate blocks, while the more psychologically realistic—and typically Romantic—duet texture is reserved for the Dalila–Grand Prêtre scene and the Dalila–Samson seduction, which form the bulk of Act II. Of course, even here, Dalila's utterances to Samson are a 'device', not genuinely passionate.

More than any before him in France, Saint-Saëns in this work adopted Wagner's style of motif identity and transformation for dramatic purposes. He also used a species of 'unending melody'

Ex. 282

---

[84] The glockenspiel, in some form, appeared briefly in the Coronation scene (Act IV, No. 24B) of *Le Prophète*, in which Delibes had been one of the boy sopranos in 1849. In 1852 Adam used the instrument in the Act II finale of *Si j'étais roi* for a Bayadères' dance; and in *Lakmé*, Act II, Delibes used a glockenspiel in his own Bayadère scene (1883).

(With a last farewell, without regret, bravely, we must break the sweet bond of our love!)

texture in the seduction scene, borrowing many Wagnerian formulae of declamation, orchestral continuity, and interrupted cadences. Their effect was the more natural since Saint-Saëns shared Wagner's proclivity for stolid rhythmic patterns (Ex. 282). In sum, though, the opera remained *sui generis*, with the oratorio-like use of chorus and even a canonic duet in Act III.

Henry VIII, composed in 1881–2 and produced in 1883, was Saint-Saëns's second most popular opera in France.[85] The librettists, Léonce Détroyat and Armand Silvestre, tried to breathe life into the four-act *grand opéra* mould, but could not give the king sufficient personality or make the intrigue other than conventional. Saint-Saëns used flexible recurring motifs but these seem predictable in themselves and the composer's language too slack in spite of the efficient chromaticism and up-to-date use of unrelated triads. Local colour appeared in the Act II 'Fête populaire' with Scots tunes and 'The Miller of Dee'. Recurring throughout was a melody the composer

---

[85] Originally in four acts and six tableaux, it was rapidly reduced to five tableaux, and afterwards to three acts in 1889. Two vocal score editions exist.

Ex. 283

Ex. 284

(It is all over then! He has severed your bonds)

found in an English manuscript.[86] It is identifiable as 'The New Medley' on p. 143 of 'Will Forster's Virginal Book' now in the British Library (Ex. 283). This symbolizes the schism with Rome, and acts as a climax in the Act III Synod scene, the ceremony which also sees the annulment of Henry's marriage to Anne Boleyn (Ex. 284).

Ascanio (five acts; text by L. Gallet), produced in 1890, was based on Paul Meurice's 1852 play about Benvenuto Cellini and his favourite pupil Ascanio. The action, unlike Berlioz's *Benvenuto Cellini*, takes place in Paris in 1539. Though including a traditional *divertissement* using, as we might expect, an original melody,[87] the opera is lively and conversational in tone. Saint-Saens found a comfortable mixture of neo-Classical diatonic music, which neatly avoids pastiche, and post-Wagnerian warmth for the romantic sections. The stress on realistic dramatic continuity, in this context, points to the later style of Richard Strauss.

MASSENET

Like Saint-Saëns, Jules Massenet (1842–1912)[88] met the challenge of writing viable through-composed opera in the wake of Wagner.

[86] Saint-Saëns reported 'I went and rummaged in the library at Buckingham Palace.... There I found a big sixteenth-century manuscript volume containing a harpsichord arrangement of an extremely beautiful melody buried under thickets of pointless ornamentation. This melody supplied, as it were, the framework of the opera.' See James Harding, *Saint-Saëns and his Circle* (London, 1965), 162.

[87] From Arbeau, *Orchésographie*, supplying dance no. 5. The original edition of *Ascanio* consists of seven tableaux, the second of six.

[88] Jules Massenet's later career is discussed in Vol. X, particularly p. 164.

Like Saint-Saëns, he was eclectic in choice of subjects and varied his musical language to some degree in the appropriate way, though not all-pervasively. The quality of Massenet's ballet music deserves particular mention: bold of colour, memorable of motif, it took on the mantle of Meyerbeer's 'skating' ballet in *Le Prophète*. (Of course, he had before him Delibes's masterpieces of *Coppélia* and *Sylvia* too, dating from 1870 and 1876.) At its sporadic best, Massenet's opera is a major synthesis of the continuous texture of modern chromatic harmony and a vocal line developing by short phrases with a passionate freedom of expression.

Partly owing to his compulsive industry, the quality of Massenet's operas is distinctly variable. Another cause was the low technical and artistic level of certain librettos, for Massenet was content to set supernatural, sentimental, and stupid ones by turns. Hand in hand with this went his limited ability to suggest character in music. Massenet also found no reason to reject ABA′ arias, traditional recitative, the aesthetic of the *divertissement*, the full close inviting applause, or the choral and ensemble clichés of his *grand opéra* predecessors. Such choral episodes can become locked into fixed tonalities.

Much of Massenet's style was secure by 1877 when he produced *Le Roi de Lahore*. Several early works had been composed and rejected, while the *opéra comique* of *Don César de Bazan* (1872) already displayed vivid Spanish rhythms and melodies even before *Carmen*. Dramatically speaking, *Le Roi de Lahore* is a farrago resembling, in basis, *Les Pêcheurs de perles*: an Indian leader in rivalry for the love of a temple girl. The *truc* is that the king dies at the end of Act II but is given a new life by the Hindu divinity in the heavenly fields of Act III. However, he is united in death with his beloved at the end. A certain essential musical polarity was evident: attractive melodic episodes (here indebted to Gounod) on one side, and various 'effects without causes' on the other. Striking ideas tended not to be developed; there were bombastic and warlike choral ensembles in a manner to be reused in *Le Cid*.

Hérodiade (1881), derived from Flaubert's 'Hérodias' (*Trois Contes*, 1877), was the most accomplished libretto Massenet set in this period,[89] and it produced his best score. Unlike Strauss's libretto for *Salomé* (a translation of Oscar Wilde), *Hérodiade* contains substantial motivation drawn from a state political theme—the domination of Jerusalem by the Romans—forming a *grand opéra* antithesis with

---

[89] The librettists were Paul Milliet, Georges Hartmann, and Angelo Zanardini.

Hérode's passion for Salomé.[90] The opera is built up in briefer scenes
than normal, which suited Massenet's gifts; the tendency to bombast
in choruses was mitigated by the presence of the 'religious' element
associated with Jean (John the Baptist); and the inevitable *divertissement* was most unusually banished to the last act, so that it
avoids a hiatus during the development of the intrigue. The power
of the passions displayed, and their variety, seem to have prompted
a greater musical sense of continuity and development. There was a
suppleness of language, which is easily seen in the flexible motif
signifying Salomé's love for Jean, quoted here from the end of Act
I (Ex. 285). If the underlying harmonic language and diction were
in debt to Gounod, Massenet imposed his own unity on the score.
One fingerprint was the dominant 13th chord (Ex. 285 relies on it).
Another was the 'false dominant' expressive excursion prior to a
tonic cadence; this has already been illustrated in Ex. 246 from
Mignon. A third was Massenet's unexpected way of beginning a

Ex. 285

(In that mystic fervour, immersed in the ideal)

---

[90] There is even a *grand opéra* ensemble scene (Act III, sc. xii) juxtaposing private and
public concerns: Hérode, having first decided to save Jean for political reasons, condemns
him on discovering that he is loved by Salomé.

Ex. 286

(Salomé, let me gaze upon your lovely, proud beauty!)

melody with basically straightforward harmony, as seen in the Act III duet for Hérode and Salomé (Ex. 286).

The libretto of *Manon* (1884), by Henri Meilhac and Philippe Gille, was cast as a five-act, through-composed *opéra lyrique*, but with brief spoken episodes over music. Based on Prévost's novel (already the source of a version by Auber), the opera tones down Des Grieux's original nature as a duplicitous moral coward; we see him on the verge of taking Holy Orders. The character of Manon is also less shockingly fickle in the stage work than the novel; she dies, from no clear malady, before leaving France. *Manon* begins slowly; here and in Act III the music associated with de Brétigny is unengaging, as are the many pastiche rococo elements. Massenet was proud of using some fifteen motifs, which he said 'kept the characters distinct until the end', but the effect is often of patchwork and a naive succession of textures. Often the music is either at high pressure or no pressure at all.

Ex. 287

(Is it no longer my hand that presses this hand, is it no longer my voice? Is there [no longer a caress] for you?)

The individuality of the score lies in the tragic heroine and her mixture of innocence, gaiety, remorse and passion. She conveys a kind of fluttering physicality, especially in her melody of Act III, Scene ii, in which the composer takes rhythmic freedom perhaps further than he had hitherto (Ex. 287).

Le Cid (1885) demanded character depiction of an order denied to Massenet, for the drama hinges on a profound dilemma: whether Chimène may accept Rodrigue even after the latter has slain her father over disputed family honour. Much of the score is given over to inflated ceremonial scenes with effects such as tuned bells and organ, or even an enacted vision of a benediction sung by St James himself. The Spanish dance sequence in Act II provides the best music.

Fantastic manipulation of time, place, and history reached new extremes in Esclarmonde (1889), a five-act recitative opera about a Byzantine princess who uses magic to ensnare the French knight Roland. Since she knows of him at the outset, and he does not object to the obvious fact that she is an enchantress, who for certain reasons will not reveal her identity to his face, the opera has a very

Ex. 288

episodic structure. The styles of Wagnerian love music, of triumphal choruses, and of strife had all been used by the composer before. New ideas included extensive fantastic music in Acts I and IV; while Massenet disliked composing full-length overtures, he always set a scene with the orchestra to good effect. Both the phantasmagoric and the love music gave rise to certain new chords in Massenet's palette, though any piquant passage would always resolve diatonically before long, frequently via the hackneyed diminished seventh. *Esclarmonde* also rejected the tedium of dry recitative passages for a permanently active 'endless melody', which helps avoid the patchwork effect of its two predecessors. The heroine is given a coloratura treatment aptly suggesting her nature. The unaccompanied passage in Ex. 288 announces her approach in Act III, tableau 6: the complete solo is three times as long.

OFFENBACH'S *LES CONTES D'HOFFMANN*

Three masters whose best works were produced at the Opéra-Comique in the 1880s, either at or near the end of their respective careers, were Offenbach, Lalo, and Delibes. Offenbach, as mentioned earlier, had ambitions beyond operetta. Writing *Les Contes d'Hoffmann* with deliberation from 1877, he left part of Acts IV and V unfinished at his death in 1880. The work was orchestrated by Ernest Guiraud, who also wrote some recitatives plus whatever he felt necessary for the première in 1881. Since the work has never been published in a scholarly edition, there remain many critical questions.[91] No surer evidence of the opera's stature exists, however,

---

[91] See Hugh Macdonald, 'Hoffmann's Melancholy Tale', *Musical Times*, 121 (1980), 622–4. The vocal score edited by Fritz Oeser as *Hoffmanns Erzählungen* (Kassel, 1977) does not distinguish between the work of Offenbach, Guiraud, or Oeser himself; it is in other respects the most reliable version, and the one to which reference is made in this account. The problem is compounded by the fact that Offenbach habitually revised works following the experience of production: Alexander Faris, *Jacques Offenbach* (London, 1980), 203.

than the fact that each generation has felt impelled to stage or publish the piece in some way.

The work presents a highly original scheme and an anti-realistic dramatic subject. It stemmed from a play of the same name, in whose first production Offenbach had been involved in 1851, by Jules Barbier and Michel Carré. This in turn bore strong similarities to Thomas's unusual *opéra comique*, *Le Songe d'une nuit d'été* (1850). Whereas the latter presented a quasi-realistic framework for Shakespeare and his muse, the former ingeniously created a symbolically imaginative one, and this was taken over in Offenbach's setting.

Acts I and V provide an outer frame with Hoffmann, his Muse, his mistress Stella, and his rival in love, Lindorf. The Muse, a chorus of spirits of beer and wine, even Lindorf, are allegorical characters posing metaphysical questions: the distinction between appearance and reality, and the relation of these twin forces in the life of a creative artist, the writer E. T. A. Hoffmann. The Muse transforms herself into Hoffmann's young companion, Niklausse. Stella is the opera singer who, in the course of Acts II to IV, is understood to be performing *Don Giovanni* in the adjoining theatre. At the conclusion Stella leaves with Lindorf; Hoffmann, somewhat drunk, abjures the outer world in favour of his Muse and art.

Acts II to IV are three independent acts, based freely on three Hoffmann tales,[92] representing the poet's telling of these stories to his drinking friends. But a system of parallels and duplications also transforms these acts into cumulative variations on the central theme, Hoffmann's internal nature. This is made clear by having Hoffmann and Niklausse appear as characters in the tales, and by having the singers representing Lindorf and Stella also impersonate Coppelius and Olympia in Act II, Dr Miracle and Antonia in Act III, and Dapertutto and Giulietta in Act IV.[93] Offenbach's music follows the rising curve of tension simply and effectively, and is admirably free from any system of recurring motifs. There are set-piece solos, sometimes with chorus, generally ABA' in form. However, many of them are filled with stage action, as are the two duets and two trios of Act III. As Offenbach's melody is euphonious yet apt, the whole opera possesses an unusual mixture of lyricism and movement.

[92] *Der Sandmann*; *Rat Krespel*; *Die Abenteuer der Silvester-Nacht*. The framing acts draw on *Don Juan*, and the tavern setting reflects Hoffmann's actual life, particularly the final Berlin period, 1814–22.

[93] Many other subtleties of design, with an interpretation including notions of the beautiful and grotesque, outer and inner perception, and the death of the ideal figure, are discussed in Richard S. Huffman, '*Les Contes d'Hoffmann*: Unity of Dramatic Form in the Libretto', *Studies in Romanticism*, 15 (1976), 97–117.

I.   THE PARIS OPÉRA

Interior of the Paris Opéra during the Act 3 finale (designed by Cicéri) of the first production of Meyerbeer's *Robert le diable* in 1831. Lithograph by J. Arnout.

II. INSTRUMENT MANUFACTURE

The Adolphe Sax factory in Paris; note the completed baritone saxophone hanging up (right), supporting the theory that Sax made the baritone of the family first, and the 'Berliner-pumpen' valves being assembled (centre foreground). Engraving from *L'illustration* (5 February 1848)

III.   BERLIOZ: *GRANDE MESSE DES MORTS*

Opening of the *Dies irae*, showing the range of instruments required, from the autograph score (1837).

IV. CHAMBER MUSIC

Anthony (the artist's husband) and friends playing a string quartet at his Frankfurt home (c.1843). Watercolour by Mary Ellen Best.

V.   AUBER: *LA MUETTE DE PORTICI*

Riot sparked off by the performance of Auber's *La Muette de Portici* (1828) at the
Théâtre de la Monnaie, Brussels, on 25 August 1830. Engraving by Hebert after Henri
Hendrick.

VI.   WAGNER: *TRISTAN UND ISOLDE*

Closing scene of Act 1 in the first production of Wagner's opera at the Königliches Hof- und Nationaltheater, Munich (1865). Engraving after a drawing by J. Noerr from the Leipzig *Illustrirte Zeitung* (15 July 1865).

VII. GOUNOD: *SAPHO*

Pauline Viardot in the première of Gounod's opera at the Paris Opéra on 16 April 1851; this work's return to Classical subject matter and novel musical features make it a significant landmark in French opera. Engraving from *L'illustration* (26 April 1851).

VIII.   VERDI: *OTELLO*
Costumes designed by Alfredo Edel for Othello and Desdemona in the première of
Verdi's opera at La Scala, Milan, on 5 February 1887.

IX. MUSSORGSKY: *BORIS GODUNOV*

Opening scene (designed by Shishkov) for the first performance of Mussorgsky's opera at the Mariinsky Theatre, St Petersburg, on 8 February 1874.

X. HUNNENSCHLACHT

Wilhelm von Kaulbach's painting *Hunnenschlacht* (1835–7) inspired Liszt's symphonic poem of the same name (1857). Engraving by J. L. Raab after the original now in the Muzeum Narodowe, Poznań.

XI.   JOHANNES BRAHMS

Brahms accompanying a solo singer in the Bösendorfer Hall of the Liechtenstein (Winter) Palace, Vienna; this building was converted into a concert hall in 1872, but demolished in 1913. Watercolour by an unknown artist.

XII. LISZT: *DIE LEGENDE VON DER HEILIGEN ELISABETH*
Liszt conducting the first performance of his oratorio in the Redoutensaal, Budapest, on
15 August 1865. Engraving after a drawing by Jean Hubert Reve from the Leipzig
Illustrirte Zeitung (16 September 1865).

Ex. 289

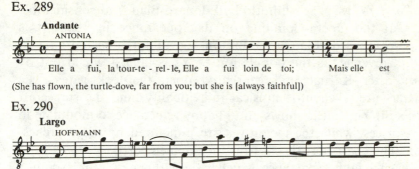

(She has flown, the turtle-dove, far from you; but she is [always faithful])

Ex. 290

(Oh God! With what exultation you inflame me! Like a heavenly concert)

(There are dances in Act II and Offenbach's style is suffused with dance rhythms anyway.)[94] This movement is also a consequence of the greater amount of action present than was normal in a musical work.

The individuality of Offenbach's melody sometimes took the form of unusual intervals over straightforward harmony (see Ex. 289, the romance, No. 11, from Act III, and Ex. 290, the duet, No. 21, from Act IV). But this may reflect a traditional trait at the Opéra-Bouffe, since we find similar things in Chabrier's comedies and operettas by Hervé, Lecocq, and others.[95] At least in Acts I to III (where Offenbach's score is most reliably free from accretions) the composer found a rapid, heightened recitative style that surely reflects the experience of decades in capturing the ironic Hoffmannesque cut and thrust of conversation and the rapid musico-dramatic timing demanded by the slightly surreal speed of events.

LALO

The three-act opera *Fiesque* by Édouard Lalo (1823–92), derived from Schiller, was never produced after its completion in 1868. It provided most of the material for the composer's Symphony in G minor (1886).[96] Lalo is described by Hugh Macdonald as representing 'the more red-blooded streak in French music. His harmony [uses] ... frequent chromatic alterations that never approach the more fluid chromaticism of Wagner, largely because the rhythmic pulse is strong.'

[94] Offenbach, like many others, pressed parts of earlier works into service: *Die Rheinnixen* (Vienna, 1864; his first through-composed work) furnished the famous barcarolle and other sections; *Le Papillon* (ballet, 1860); *Fantasio* (1872). See Faris, *Offenbach*, pp. 216–17.

[95] See Gervase Hughes, *Composers of Operetta* (London, 1962).

[96] Description in Hugh Macdonald, 'A Fiasco Remembered: *Fiesque* Dismembered', in Malcolm H. Brown and Roland J. Wiley (eds.), *Slavonic and Western Music: Essays for Gerald Abraham* (Ann Arbor and Oxford, 1985), 163–85.

Le Roi d' Ys (1875–88), libretto by Edouard Blau, had considerable success at the Opéra-Comique on its appearance in 1888. It is through-composed. Blau used Breton legend for a melodrama of love and revenge, as the population of Ys is almost wiped out by the sea after Karnac and Margared open the lock gates. The characters are given little musical individuality, and the stagecraft can be stiff. The music shows an unhappy reluctance to modulate in the set pieces, while the recitatives are punctured by noisy orchestration. The characteristic chord is the augmented triad, which Lalo places even in fanfare passages. Much in the earlier acts is underpinned by fanfares apt to the warlike situation but essentially beside the point of the drama: Margared's obsessive character. Lalo introduced a Breton theme in the Act III wedding scene, labelled accordingly (Ex. 291). Doubtless in this, as in 'Spanish' operas of the time, we see transitional evidence of the folk-song revival which would stretch so potently into the twentieth century.

DELIBES

The career of Léo Delibes (1836–91) as theatre composer divides into his sixteen early operettas and light *opéras comiques*, often in one act (1856–69); his contribution to the ballet *La Source* (1866) and his important ballet scores of *Coppélia* (1870, after E. T. A. Hoffmann) and *Sylvia* (1876); and the following three *opéras comiques*.

Le Roi l'a dit (1873) is basically an operetta in style, with the dramatic development residing in its farcical plot, set in the period of Louis XIV, rather than in complicated musical units. Traditional forms such as couplets are still present, and the choral writing is chiefly homophonic. The idiom often falls into the 'patter' style of repeated-note motifs. In 1885 the work was revised for the Opéra-Comique, several numbers being moved to a different act,

Ex. 291

(Why resist like that, do you think I would want to leave a lover at the door when love has entered in! Since an unruly spirit can break so noble a heart . . .)

and a fresh score was issued.[97] The music added in 1885 includes the interesting opening to No. 11 (Ex. 292) and the 'Musique de scène', No. 17 *bis* (Ex. 293), prefiguring Poulenc. Delibes's invention was obviously stimulated by the factor of rhythm in itself and he added to the irregularities noted earlier in Meyerbeer, Gounod, and others with a comic solo in 5/4, 'C'est un fait acquis'.

The second opera, *Jean de Nivelle* (1880), a semi-comic burlesque set in Louis XI's reign, was initially very successful. Musically Delibes's piece was cast as an updated but limited evocation of Adam (his teacher), extrovert to the point of boisterousness. Older forms recur in abundance: couplets, romance, march, ensemble. There was a new essay in irregular metre, but one which dared to combine 2/4 and 3/4 in asymmetrical patterns of accretion (see Ex. 294, the Act I finale).

Lakmé, the third work (1883), brought together modern tendencies in a palatably sentimental way. Designed with dialogue scenes and a secure sense of the individual number which 'comes to an end' (cf.

Ex. 292

Ex. 293

Ex. 294

---

[97] Descriptions of the two versions, together with those of an early unpublished version and a posthumous version arranged by P. Gille, are in Henri de Curzon, *Léo Delibes, sa vie et ses œuvres* (Paris, 1926), 117–42.

(We are queens for the day, our king leaves us on a whim, before the festivity ends he must rule in our court!)

Carmen), it also contained strong 'Indian' local colour, enharmonic progressions (kept under cadential control), a recurring motif, and love duets in the impassioned style. The latter betray the dull rhythmic structures of an unpretentious work of art; yet they suit the English officer-class stiffness of Gérald. He is mostly interested in his own 'ironic dilettantism, [his] sceptical curiosity',[98] and the one true dramatic stroke is that Lakmé, the Brahmin's daughter, sees through him. Like Sélika in *L'Africaine*, Lakmé kills herself (by eating a poisonous leaf).

Delibes's orgiastic dances in Act II almost anticipate Stravinsky's ballets: the fourth of these ('Coda') uses two extra tuned drums (Ex. 295); elsewhere there are crotales. Although the style may owe a debt to *Samson et Delila* (see Ex. 281)—not however staged in France until 1890—it is worth recalling that Berlioz had created an extraordinary 'Nubian' dance in *Les Troyens*, Act IV, No. 33c, whose throbbing bass, non-cadential harmony, quasi-modal melody, and use of percussion (petites cymbales antiques, tambourin, tarbuka) were a generation ahead of their time (Ex. 296).

Later in Act II, when the Hindu festival provides the cover for Gérald's would-be murderer, Delibes combined energy with harmonic ambiguity: five of the six notes in the violin figure in Ex. 297 move by whole-tone intervals. To the modern ear these 'orientalisms' are the most innovative parts of the score; the path to Debussy, via Chabrier's *Gwendoline*, was swift and direct. Many other places in

Ex. 295

[horns omitted]

[98] Ibid., p. 178.

Ex. 296

Ex. 297

Lakmé use the flat seventh and the supertonic to create ambiguity; for this reason the heroine's own cantillation prior to her 'Bell' song (the 'Scène et Légende', Act II, No. 10) cannot be assigned to any definite single key. By contrast, the cheap fife-and-drum tune, signifying the British army's hold over Gérald's loyalties, has a boldness of character and application worthy of its probable inspiration: *Carmen*, Act II.

REYER

Ernest Reyer (1823–1909) was an unrepentant, intelligent individualist. He was a later friend of Berlioz and a music critic, inheriting Berlioz's column on the *Journal des débats* in 1866 when d'Ortigue died. From his first performed *opéra comique*, *Maître Wolfram* (1854), Reyer's musical qualities were manifest: a gift for extended melody; conscious development of new rhythmic ideas; rejection of Italianate melody; readiness to create freshness through modulation; and an affinity with the German tradition, particularly

in echoes of Weber. Even in this one-act, essentially domestic piece
about a young man, organist of Bonn cathedral, who seeks solace
in composition and the gift of music, Reyer showed that he favoured
the construction of ensemble numbers containing dramatic action
and musical continuity. The score includes an organ part at the
beginning and end, when Wolfram is playing.

Both *Maître Wolfram* and *La Statue* (1861) enjoyed revivals. The
latter began as a substantial *opéra comique* in three acts and was
later given recitatives.[99] It is an oriental and magic comedy, somewhat
in the vein of Auber's *Le Cheval de bronze* or Adam's *Si j'étais roi*;
but it is more dependent than these upon spectacle.[100] Reyer's music
is fluent and enjoyable; if ultimately lacking in melodic originality,
the score is certainly never dull. (One example of its wit is a *buffo*
canon at the unison for two characters claiming to be the same
person: the duo No. 9.) Within the conventional system of separate
numbers, the emphasis was on continuity and musical development.

The tenor part of Sélim, the main character, was conceived rather
grandiosely, somewhat like the role of Catherine in Meyerbeer's
L'Étoile du nord. Recurring motifs were used for Sélim's and
Margyane's love, and for a prophetic chorus of spirits. More unusual
was the use of a flexible anapaestic motif whose musical intervals
and character constantly varied according to their context. Although
not unlike the Mephistopheles motif in Berlioz's *Damnation de Faust*,
Reyer's could be woven in and transformed as a symbol of the genie
Amgiad's controlling influence on the plot at all levels (Ex. 298,
showing No. 5, No. 6, No. 12, and the Act III finale). Such an
organic concept, quite exceptional for its date in French opera,
reflected Reyer's knowledge of modern German music.

Ex. 298

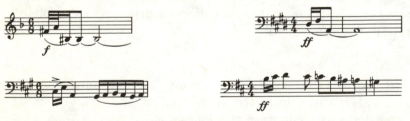

[99] Two vocal score editions were published. The recitatives were composed for a German
production in 1864, and subsequently translated into French.

[100] The opium-smoking chorus and its similarity to Bizet's in *Djamileh* has already been
noted. The first production at the Théâtre Lyrique was lavish, and newspapers reported that
the décors would be 'based on photographs brought back from Baalbek itself [the site of part
of the opera] by the French writer Maxime Du Camp'. See Walsh, *Second Empire Opera*,
pp. 133–6.

Erostrate (1862; première at Baden-Baden) was Reyer's first through-composed opera; such recitatives as there are differ greatly from orthodox French formulas and approach a Germanic cut. The two-act libretto is a bizarre mixture of legend and history, hinging unfortunately on the loss of the Venus de Milo's arms and ending with self-sacrifice through pride. Its musical substance did not encourage its revival.

Sigurd (1884), on the contrary, was a major French work which was to hold the stage by the side of Wagner for half a century. Reyer's friend Edouard Blau submitted a scenario to him in the early 1860s, based on the Edda and the Nibelungen sagas. It was versified and polished by Camille du Locle, and a significant portion of the music written by about 1866. But Act IV was not completed until shortly before the première, and the chronology of the work's progress is obscure. Reyer was committed in his approval of Wagner, from 1857 if not before, and *Sigurd* comes by far the closest of any French opera of its period to reproducing the musico-dramatic experience of mature Wagner. That said, however, and Reyer's individuality begins to become apparent.

Sigurd draws mainly on the Eddas and its plot is close to that of *Götterdämmerung*, but it stresses qualities of the chivalric and of clarity rather than of myth and fatalism.[101] It marked a daring break with prevailing French subject-matter. Blau and du Locle succeeded well in their venture: the epic material is logically shaped and motivated, the characters varied and consistent. The score, which is on an epic scale, creates its own musical and dramatic terms of reference. In *Sigurd* the existence of Brunehild in her magically defended palace is recounted by a bard (in the separate librettos his speeches are given to Hagen). Gunther's sister, Hilda, ensnares Sigurd's affections by means of a potion concocted by her nurse, Uta. Sigurd wins Brunehild for Gunther, concealing his identity by his visor. She marries Gunther, but is instinctively drawn to Sigurd (for love of whom she was punished by Odin). After her only duet with Sigurd, and at Hilda's jealous urging, he is murdered. He ascends with Brunehild to Valhalla in an apotheosis.

Reyer's main achievements can be summarized as harmonic command to create interest and pacing over very long spans; virtual elimination of the aesthetic of the set piece; use of a set of some twelve recurring motifs with fluency and in some cases

---

[101] Henri de Curzon, *La Légende de Sigurd dans l'Edda: L'Opéra d'E. Reyer* (Paris, 1890), 85. Sigurd himself is presented as 'son of Sigemon'.

in transformation;[102] avoidance of rhythmic stagnation; and the
maintenance of overall tension and increase in dramatic feeling in
Act IV as fate closes in on the hero and heroine.

It is easy to criticize aspects of Reyer's art by almost inescapable
reference to Wagner: Reyer is occasionally prolix; his range of chords
has limits; he is less successful depicting evil and anger than heroism
and love. The music for Norns, Kobolds, and spirits defending
Brunehild in Act II looks back to *Robert le diable*. But this approach
does not reveal the nature of *Sigurd*, which is elevated and tragic in
the unsentimental way of *Les Troyens*. Certain passages, indeed,
recall Berlioz's rhythmic surge and shape in that work. The close of
Sigurd borrows from *Les Troyens* the idea of a vision of future
retribution: Hannibal is prophesied by Dido, and Attila (whose
image is supposed to be seen) by Hilda.

Something of the flavour of *Sigurd* may be seen through its motifs.
Certain ones are not much transformed on rehearing, being associated
with fixed things like the potion or Attila's envoys. However, a
typical exception is the motif of Sigurd's deliverance of Brunehild,
seen both in an early appearance (Ex. 299, from Act I) and then in
ironic recollection as Gunther, kneeling before Brunehild, claims the
right to marry her (Ex. 300, from Act III). Reyer's orchestra
comments on the action.

The pithiness and expressive style of his motifs was as Wagnerian
as the irony of their application. But the overall balance between

Ex. 299

Ex. 300

Ex. 301

Reyer's lyrical invention and motivic working reflects middle-period, not late Wagner. At the same time the Frenchman's long compositional concern with the work seems to have enabled him to attain more maturely concentrated effects in Act IV. In Ex. 301, when Sigurd realizes his true emotions, the motif of Hilda's love (x) is dramatically subordinated to a development of that of Brunehild (y).

Reyer's *Salammbô* (1890), a work Flaubert had wished him to compose, following Verdi's refusal, was also planned in the 1860s. It too was successful, and confirmed Reyer's exceptional place in French opera.

CHABRIER

While the musical languages of Reyer, Massenet, and Saint-Saëns presented syntheses of current practice, that of Emmanuel Chabrier (1841–94) was a catalyst: his work became the cradle of French modernism. Debussy's middle-period orchestral style is audible in parts of *Gwendoline*, while for his part Ravel asserted, 'It is from [Chabrier] that all modern French music stems. His role was as important as that of Manet in painting'.[103]

Chabrier's music possesses irrepressible qualities of joy and satire, which were heard in several light operettas. The two early incomplete

[103] Roger Delage, 'Ravel and Chabrier', *Musical Quarterly*, 61 (1975), 546–52.

collaborations with Paul Verlaine (*Fisch-Ton-Kan* and *Vaucochard et Fils 1ᵉʳ*) probably date from 1865–9 (not *c*.1864, as often stated); they mock the politics and personality of Napoleon III. Thus, when the operetta librettists E. Leterrier and A. Vanloo, who had been working with Lecocq, offered Chabrier *L'Étoile* (1877), the notion must have been particularly attractive. Written with dialogue, it is set in the fantasy dictatorship of the fatuous king, Ouf 1ᵉʳ, and prompted a richly humorous score. There are subtle passing harmonies, entrancing pieces of word-play, and musical parodies of Offenbach and Donizetti. The one-act operetta *Une éducation manquée* (1879) suffered from a weak libretto; an attempt to rescue the work by the addition of recitatives was made by Milhaud (1934).[104]

The experience of seeing *Tristan und Isolde* in Munich in 1880 did not cause Chabrier to imitate Wagner, but it did produce a problem piece, *Gwendoline*, produced in 1886. The composer admitted he thought it would be such, even during its composition; yet this is merely to confirm that the problem lay with the drama, by Catulle Mendès, which is indeed naïve: 'As to *Gwendoline* being a flop, it will be one in a big way, but I'm certainly going to risk it. Opera librettos are always terrible: look at the "book" for [Massenet's] *Le Roi de Lahore* . . .'[105]

In Act I a Saxon community in Britain, led by Armel, is invaded by the Danes, led by Harald. Armel's daughter Gwendoline quells Harald with her beauty and personality, and he asks for her hand in marriage. Armel hatches a plot. Act II sees the wedding, but during the feasting the unarmed Danes are slaughtered by the Saxons. Harald is mortally wounded and Gwendoline stabs herself. (She has been given a dagger by Armel to kill Harald, but she does not realize this until too late.)

Perhaps Chabrier actually thought of the action as a peg on which to hang his astonishing music: the dramatic proportions are awkward, the wedding scene is over-long, and the work falls into sections with sometimes disparate musical material. It is certainly not dominated or unified by the presence of recurring motifs, though Gerald Abraham has pointed out that 'it has a dozen or so genuine *Leitmotive* which are modified, transformed, combined and woven into a more or less continuous orchestral texture'.[106] The score is,

[104] Francis Poulenc, *Emmanuel Chabrier*, trans. Cynthia Jolly (London, 1981), 32; Rollo Myers, *Emmanuel Chabrier and his Circle* (London, 1969), 21.

[105] Myers, *Chabrier*, p. 57.

[106] Gerald Abraham, *The Concise Oxford History of Music* (London, 1979), 741. He adds that 'some of the modifications of the "Gwendoline" motive . . . are almost too subtle to be noticed'.

finally, a treasure-trove of infinite promise. It expresses Chabrier's great range and sophistication, from the fine *Tristan*-like love duet to an almost bitonal yell (Ex: 302, vocal score, p. 81); from folk-tune to floating tonality (Ex. 303, vocal score, p. 152); and from a superb evocation of dawn to impressions of hand-to-hand combat in Act II, with trumpets purely Debussyan yet over ten years before the *Nocturnes* (Ex. 304, vocal score, p. 264).

The *opéra comique Le Roi malgré lui* (1887) was Chabrier's last

Ex. 302

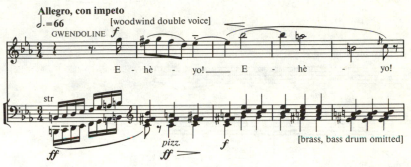

Ex. 303

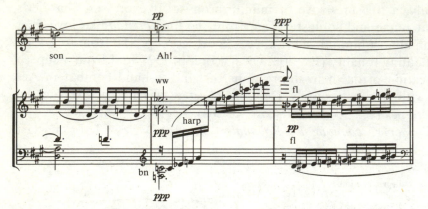

(And repeat word and sound with me: 'Spin, spin, blonde beauty . . .')

Ex. 304

completed stage work, and he once again stumbled on the literary side.[107] Although it returns to the theme of an irresponsible king (the historical Henri III of France when king of Poland), the work was a full-length attempt to infuse many emotional nuances into a light framework.[108] Gaiety dominates, and the score parodies Offenbach

[107] The libretto by Émile de Najac and Paul Burani, derived from an 1836 vaudeville, was revised by Jean Richepin; Chabrier himself had to help with it. The plot is both weak and confusing. See Myers, *Chabrier*, p. 70 and also Poulenc, *Chabrier*, pp. 53–4, for summaries.

[108] Changes were made at revivals in 1888 and 1929; the vocal score edited by A. Carré follows the latter version, altering the order of some items and also changing the words.

Ex. 305
Moderato
ww, brass

Ex. 306
Maestoso
ww, brass

(the *Barcarolle*), Berlioz (the Hungarian March), and Meyerbeer's bold chords in *Les Huguenots* (cf. Ex. 52), in Chabrier's own conspirators' ensemble, No. 13 (Ex. 305). These chords were brazenly developed in the overture (Ex. 306) and apparently influenced Satie as well as Ravel, who would often say to Poulenc, 'The première of *Le Roi malgré lui* changed the direction of harmony in France.'[109] For Chabrier freed seventh and ninth chords and second inversions from their orthodox functions; threw in unexpected passing notes; explored modal relationships; and refused to remove the supertonic from the final chord of No. 2. Yet the result maintains its fine poise and taste; Chabrier's goal was the listener's pleasure, his method conceived of perhaps like an impressionist painting (he owned a discriminating collection of such works and was very close to Manet) in which the realistic outline would be broken up by momentary inflexions and sensations.[110] It is our great loss that he never found the appropriate dramatic medium to contain the expression of his extraordinary sensibility.

(c) ITALY

By JULIAN BUDDEN

THE period which followed the fall of Venice in August 1849 was one of profound demoralization; in no other part of Europe had the insurgents of 1848 gained so little. The extent to which patriots such as Verdi had been harassed by the Austrian rulers has understandably been exaggerated; outside the Kingdom of the Two Sicilies and the Papal States the most 'Risorgimental' of his operas encountered only

---

[109] Poulenc, *Chabrier*, pp. 54–5.
[110] This general idea is discussed by Myers, who also reproduces the list of works of art owned by Chabrier: *Chabrier*, pp. 146–54.

minimal interference from the censorship. When the publisher of *Attila* charged the management of La Scala, Milan, an exorbitant hire fee for its performance, it was the Austrian police who compelled him to lower it. During the 1850s Verdi's difficulties with the censors were continual, and only his personal eminence sufficed to overcome them; for the lesser composer there was no such remedy. The 'enlightenment' dramas of Vittorio Alfieri were frowned upon no less than the works of that arch-liberal Victor Hugo, which is why Mercadante had to wait fifteen years for his *Virginia* of 1851 to be performed. New ideas, new dramatic stimuli from contemporary European literature were barred to the average composer of the time.

All of this would matter less if, Verdi apart, the stagnation of Italian Romantic opera had not already begun. The tradition inaugurated by Rossini and his immediate successors had reached its apogee around 1840. By 1845 Donizetti was confined to an asylum, Mercadante and Pacini were turning out ever more elaborate versions of the same product. Federico Ricci was never to regain the heights scaled in 1841 with *Corrado d'Altamura* and *Luigi Rolla*. Only Verdi continued his steady ascent. Indeed during the next two decades Italian opera, conservative in the 1830s, was to become well-nigh anachronistic. Throughout the nineteenth century opera shows a continuous progress in the direction of dramatic continuity. The convention of frozen time, essential to eighteenth-century *opera seria*, operates less and less in the age of Romanticism. In Italian opera with its highly formal basis this process was, if not entirely halted, effectively slowed down. In a type of opera whose twin principles are balance and contrast, the 'art of transition' in Wagner's phrase, can make little headway. Here the drama is still conceived as a succession of situations rather than a continuously evolving action; it moves through a sequence of finite numbers, each designed to be followed by applause and curtain calls. Linking material normally takes the form of a so-called scena—a mixture of recitative, arioso, orchestral gesture, and the type of instrumental melody known as the 'parlante',[111] in which the voices engage sometimes on the top line (though not for long), at others on the harmony notes. Duets and trios are set out in contrasted movements, each marked by a change of mood. Plots are constructed centripetally, working

---

[111] The term 'parlante' is defined at length in Abrame Basevi, *Studio sulle opere de Giuseppe Verdi* (Florence, 1859), 30-2. Originally used with reference to the voice part only, it came to embrace the vocal–orchestral design as a whole, of which the orchestral part is the most important. A parlante melody should not be confused with those short orchestral themes, often of no more than two or three bars in length and of a cadential character, with which composers before 1860 liked to punctuate and round off long passages of recitative.

towards a grand confrontation of principals in one of the middle acts, the resulting pezzo concertato and associated stretta forming the architectural pinnacle of the score and allowing the composer to demonstrate his skill in massive part writing. From then on everything leads to the death of the hero or heroine, usually amid a crowd of sympathetic bystanders.

With the proclamation of the Italian state in 1861, censorship was lifted from most of the peninsula. However, conditions could hardly change over night; and the tyranny of the prima donna was less easy to shake off than that of the Austrian rulers. But she already had a rival in the nascent star conductor,[112] a species long familiar north of the Alps but unknown in Italy where the musical direction was normally divided between the *maestro concertatore* (at premières usually the composer himself), who rehearsed the singers, and the *primo violino* who guided the performance from a cued violin part with occasional gestures of his bowing arm.

If the new breed of conductors could not directly bring about the renewal of Italian opera, it at least facilitated that invasion of Italian theatres by foreign operas that began during the 1860s. The latest works of Gounod, Thomas, and Meyerbeer, now assured of adequate performance, began in their turn to influence contemporary Italian opera. One of them, *L'Africaine*, would become seminal, inaugurating a taste for exotic idioms from which native music had up till then been free. Italy was no longer immune from the contemporary trend towards dramatic continuity in opera. The solo cabaletta with its obligatory repeat fell slowly into desuetude. Prima donnas with a penchant for brilliance were usually accommodated with a genre-piece in the manner of French opera. Duet cabalettas continued to flourish but the threefold statement became increasingly rare. Aria and romanza were now identical, both cast in French ternary form with a long middle section which modulates widely. The pezzo concertato was still *de rigueur* for a central finale; but the stretta might occur in another act.

In sum the architectural nature of post-Rossinian Italian opera was being at last undermined; but no alternative system of construction had been found to replace it. Most Italian operas of the 1860s were amorphous and unsure. It was a state of affairs against

---

[112] After reading an unfavourable report of Toscanini's *Falstaff*, Verdi wrote, 'When I began shocking the musical world with my sins there was the disaster of the prima donna's rondos; now we have the tyranny of the conductors. The first was the lesser evil.' (Letter to Giulio Ricordi, 18 Mar. 1899, quoted in Franco Abbiati, *Giuseppe Verdi* (Milan, 1959), iv. 638.)

which the idealistic Boito railed to little effect. But behind the general confusion of the time one trend can be discerned, namely towards *grand opéra* on the French model; and Verdi would be part of it.

THE LATER TRAGIC OPERAS OF MERCADANTE AND PACINI

By 1850 both Saverio Mercadante (1795-1870) and Giovanni Pacini (1796-1867) had passed their meridian. Apart from a single excursion into the *semiseria* genus, Mercadante continued to turn out the same massive product, suitably tailored to the singers at his disposal. His plots are now invariably neo-Classical, with their suspended weddings (*Virginia*, 1866), oracular pronouncements (*Statira*, 1853), and heroines torn between allegiance to father and husband (*Pelagio*, 1857). Arias in two contrasted movements are still the rule, though the tenor may be granted a romanza (normally in 3/8) and the soprano a preghiera in a later act. The cantabile will be in 9/8 or 12/8 with woodwind filigree between the phrases and a few interesting if unmotivated modulations; the cabaletta will be in common (occasionally triple) time with an accompaniment of alternating pulsations and a few 'darting' interventions from solo wind including trumpet and piccolo. Here the tonal orbit is wider than the material warrants and the rhythm often too contrived. Duets are in the usual two or three movements, the material divided between the two singers in an eminently traditional manner. Yet, even when each is allotted a different melody, the contrast is rarely sufficient to convey the dramatic situation. Too much is sacrificed to mellifluence. Choruses are heavily scored with abundant use of full brass. Preludes for one or two concertante instruments treated in sub-Paganinian style are often to be found.

In two fields, however, Mercadante retains a certain distinction. The transitional passages (scene, tempi di mezzo) are always finely wrought, arioso, recitative, and parlante being combined in a manner which serves to carry the action purposefully forward. Then again, Mercadante remained a master of the slow pezzo concertato—the short-breathed declamatory opening that planes out into a broad period, from which in turn a succession of lyrical ideas unfurl, all moving with effortless momentum to the final cadence. The finale to Act II of *Statira* is a particularly fine example.

Amid much that is predictable—including the maddening tic (♪♪ ♪) which runs through all the later operas as a call to attention— Bianca's prayer from *Pelagio* ('D'un infelice accogliere') with its interweaving of voice and obbligato cello stands out as a magnificent late flowering of Mercadantean melody (Ex. 307). To the end of his

Ex. 307

(Oh Heaven, thou shouldst receive [the prayers] of an unhappy one)

career Mercadante remained one of the few composers to write florid music for baritone.

A mere practitioner by comparison, Pacini likewise continued to produce operas in much the same mould as Mercadante. If his melodies flow more freely, they are more banal and loosely constructed, the 'andante' in particular showing a tendency to wander aimlessly through two or three related keys. The 'allegros' however, display an unusual rhythmic variety; and in certain cases the cabaletta repeats are shortened. As in Mercadante the style is unremittingly bland and subservient to the demands of star singers. The duet between the prima donnas in *Malvina di Scozia* (1851) reverts to the *canto fiorito* of Rossini's *Semiramide*; while the choral narration of

Wortimer's (*sic*) crime proceeds in a sunny B flat major undisturbed by discord or the minor mode. The instrumental experiments of such late works as *Margherita Pusterla* (1856) and *Don Diego de Mendoza* (1867) show no advance save in elaboration. Of Pacini's output of over ninety operas, only *Saffo* continued to hold the stage throughout the century; and much of his later activity was devoted to providing new arias for exponents of the title role.

OPERA BUFFA AND SEMISERIA

One consequence of the escapist mood of the 1850s was a resurgence of the lighter forms of opera. Yet in form, style, and expression *opera buffa* and *semiseria* were no less stereotyped than their sister genre. *Buffo* basses and baritones still chatter either by themselves or beneath lyrical sopranos and tenors, cavatinas tend to be in two short movements without tempi di mezzo, and, unbelievably, recitative secco is still the main connecting tissue. The *Piedigrotta* (1852) of Luigi Ricci (1805-59), remembered today for its lively tarantella, reverts to a no less antiquated convention of spoken dialogue in Neapolitan *patois*. The *Amori e trappole* (1850) of Antonio Cagnoni (1828-96) is consciously archaic, borrowing its plot from Rossini's early *farsa, L'occasione fa il ladro*, and even including in the heroine's cavatina an instance of the Rossinian 'open melody' with showy, declamatory flourishes which give way to a smooth, periodic motion. Elderly cuckolds, amorous Turks, heavy fathers, and bubbling coloratura sopranos still form the staple ingredients of *buffo* plots. The only difference between the comedies of the 1850s and those of twenty years earlier lies in a certain thickening of the instrumental texture and a somewhat exaggerated use of parlanti— the besetting sin of the otherwise lively *Il carnevale di Venezia* (1851) by Errico Petrella (1813-77).

The wonder is that composers still occasionally found something new to say in the manner of Donizetti and Rossini and that the young Bizet was sufficiently attracted by the genre to write an opera such as *Don Procopio* (1859) for his *envoi* for the Prix de Rome. The *Tutti in maschera* (1856) of Carlo Pedrotti (1817-93) shows refined harmonic workmanship and has one genuinely original number in which the mezzo-soprano Dorotea in two alternating movements devises various ways of vamping the susceptible Abdala. A minor classic of the period is *Crispino e la comare* (1850) by the brothers Luigi and Federico Ricci. Piave's morality, about a poor cobbler who with the aid of a fairy godmother becomes a rich doctor until pride and avarice return him to his former state, combines a touch of Molière with those elements of the fantastic hitherto banned from Italian operatic comedy and thus provides a relief from the regular *buffo* stock-in-trade. The music, if not especially original, has a certain high spirited spontaneity, in which Luigi's superior vigour is offset by Federico's more refined craftsmanship. Waltz rhythms abound and many of the numbers end with an attractive teasing out of the final cadence.

All the operas cited above represent the rump of an Italian tradition that reaches back into the eighteenth century and which failed to survive the 1850s. The comedies of the next decade, such as Cagnoni's *Michele Perrin* (1864) and *Papa Martin* (1871) and Federico Ricci's *Una follia a Roma* (1869), are very different in character: more individual, freer in structure and richer in individual personalities. A distinctly Parisian influence is apparent—indeed *Una follia a Roma* suggests a French *opéra comique* with Italian recitative added. Recitativo secco is now finally obsolete; only the chattering *buffo* bass, a remarkably resistant growth, remains as a link with the past.

The *semiseria* genre has always been more difficult to define; but by the 1850s its models would appear to be Bellini's *La sonnambula* and Donizetti's *Linda di Chamounix*. Constant features were a rural ambience, a happy ending, and a heroine variously accused of theft (Mercadante's *Violetta*, 1853), infanticide (Petrella's *Elena di Tolosa*, 1852), or mere inconstancy (Pedrotti's *Fiorina*, 1851). Pacini's *Il saltimbanco* (1856) anticipates *Pagliacci* with an Act I finale for an actor whose genuine distraction at being deserted by his wife is mistaken for brilliant acting by an admiring crowd. The forms are nearer those of tragic opera; but there is usually an abundance of choruses in 6/8, still the traditional rhythm for peasants, huntsmen, and the lower orders generally. In *Violetta* and *Fiorina*, both set in Switzerland, there are excursions into a *montanaro* style. (The latter even includes a *ranz des vaches*.) Orchestrally accompanied recitative prevails, the one exception being *Violetta*, presumably since it was intended as a show-piece for the two veteran *bassi buffi*, Giuseppe Fioravanti and Leopoldo Cammarano, whose comic bravura would emerge more clearly from the older convention.

THE MIDDLE GENERATION: PETRELLA, PEDROTTI, AND CAGNONI

All three of these composers first made their name in comedy and all came into national prominence in the 1850s. Errico Petrella was born in Palermo the same year as Verdi. He made his operatic début as early as 1829, before Verdi had even begun his studies in Milan, but for many years his works had only limited and local success. With *Il carnevale di Venezia* (1851) all this changed. Entirely traditional in design, it shows a spontaneous gift for melody, and a genuine resource in adapting stock procedures to a particular situation. (A hilarious 'hydrophobic' aria for the *primo buffo* remains in the mind, as does a quartet in which three women make up to a bewildered Neapolitan.) With the chain of serious operas that begins with *Marco Visconti* (1854) the defects in his musical technique become apparent. Inept progressions, pleonastic fillings out of bars, lapses into banality are all too frequent. Certain of his works rely on spectacular stage effects: a storm at sea (*Marco Visconti*), the flooding of the Netherlands (*Elnava*, 1856), an eruption of Vesuvius (*Jone*, 1858); which is not to deny them occasional moments of power, as in the duet finale to the second act of *Jone* where the hero's growing delirium is reflected in an increasingly busy accompaniment and chromatically inflected line, only, alas, to culminate in the reprise of a trivial *brindisi*. In the first act finale of *Morosina* (1859) both concertato and stretta are dominated by an unusually forceful tenor solo.

During the 1860s Petrella's activity was confined chiefly to Naples where he produced a string of works often described rather unfairly as 'cabaletta' operas. True, they never failed to satisfy the requirements of a virtuoso prima donna. *Celinda* (1865) contains two scenes of laughing madness for the heroine, one feigned, the other genuine. In *Giovanna di Napoli* (1869) Ghislanzoni's queen abandons her regal manner for a showy bolero. In *La Contessa d'Amalfi* (1864) the baritone's cavatina ('Non sai tu che il genio chiede') is in one movement only but with the gait of a cabaletta (a solution adopted by Verdi twice in *Un ballo in maschera*). Leonora's cavatina in the same opera is an andante in the traditional binary form but with an extended coda decorated with coloratura. But of the old-style cabaletta with ritornello and repeat there is not a trace. Duets consist mainly of alternating solos from each singer with brief interventions from the other; only in the final movement do they both join. Throughout old-fashioned binary cantabili jostle with French-style *couplets*, strophic romanze and ternary arias with no sense of overall design. Concertati are still constructed on the 1830s model with a Bellinian groundswell towards the final cadence. *Manfredo* (1872) shows a half-successful attempt to come to terms with the plainer, more massive style of the 1870s.

If Petrella's operas founder on the lack of musicianship, the same cannot be said of those of Carlo Pedrotti. His comedies show a refined craftsmanship, an elaboration of detail which in no way detracts from their freshness. Even in the early *Il parucchiere della reggenza* (1851)—another of those operas involving Peter the Great— there are memorable ideas, including a parody of Verdi's early manner in an aria for the Tsar. His masterpiece, *Tutti in maschera*, could well bear revival today. But his serious operas from *Isabella d'Aragona* (1859) to *Olema* (1872) lack even the vigour that helped to sustain those of Petrella; and he ended by forbidding their performance ('old men's stuff').

Working entirely in the north where French influence was at its strongest, Antonio Cagnoni (1828–96) brought a certain welcome crispness to the prevailing Italian idiom. Throughout the 1850s and 1860s he rarely strayed far from comedy. Most of his operas have substantial overtures showing a skill in development rare for an Italian composer of the time. *Giralda* (1852), *Michele Perrin* (1864), as well as the more serious *Claudia* (1866), *Un capriccio di donna* (1870), and *Francesca da Rimini* (1878) make use of 'labelling' themes. Yet like many of his generation Cagnoni found it hard to maintain consistency of style; his comedies oscillate between Rossinian facility and an attempt at harmonic piquancy that often results in mere ugliness. None the less his *Papa Martin* (1871), known in England as *The Porter of Havre*, enjoyed a certain success in Italy and abroad; and in the later tragedies there are moments of heavily charged lyricism which anticipate the language of verismo.

Among the more lasting success of the period was the *Ruy Blas* (1869) of Filippo Marchetti (1831–1902). Though clearly influenced by Meyerbeer, the style is Marchetti's own—somewhat over-sweet and with a penchant for long pedal points, but musically well nourished and often haunting. He anticipates Puccini in preparing well beforehand the obvious gem of the score, the duet 'O dolce voluttà', and using it as a reminiscence theme thereafter. Casilda's ballata in the Andalusian style breaks new ground for an Italian opera.

But to certain bold spirits in the north all such innovations were far too timid. The time had come, they insisted, for a far more drastic reform.

REFORM FROM THE NORTH: FACCIO AND BOITO

In Milan, with the proclamation of the Italian state, the dawn of intellectual freedom came up like thunder. The prevailing cultural movement was that of the so-called *Scapigliatura*—a loose association of writers, artists, and musicians dedicated to the overthrow of established canons whether of art or religion. Much of what they produced is merely bizarre, a kind of avant-gardisme for its own sake; but among their more positive beliefs was that in a regeneration of the arts through mutual intermingling. The chief musical representatives of the *Scapigliatura* were Arrigo Boito (1842–1918) and Franco Faccio (1840–91), both determined to make a bonfire of traditional Italian opera. Of the two, Faccio had the greater musical facility. 'He is a good musician,' Mariani wrote to Verdi, 'but unfortunately what is good in his work is not new, and what is new is rather boring.'[113] Certainly there is nothing very new about *I profughi fiamminghi* (1863), written to a text by the *scapigliato* poet Emilio Praga. Yet this was the opera which prompted Boito to hail the composer as 'perhaps the man who is destined to clean the altar of Italian opera, now befouled like the walls of a brothel'. For Faccio's *Amleto* (1865) Boito himself supplied the libretto. It scored no more than a *succès d'estime*, and the vocal score was never published in full; but from certain excerpts—the funeral march and the monologue 'Essere o non essere'—one can discern a rich, carefully wrought harmonic and orchestral style and a consciously elevated tone, as of one whose range extended into symphony and chamber music as well as opera.

Meantime Boito had been active as propagandist in the musical journals of Milan. He preached the revival of Italian instrumental tradition, the cultivation of Beethoven, Mozart, and Mendelssohn; he declaimed against the formulae of Italian operas, likewise the outworn system of metres which, it seemed, no composer had been able to shake off. Opera remained his goal and Meyerbeer his chief model. It remained to be seen how far Boito's ideals would measure up to his own practice. The original *Mefistofele* of 1868—so long that it was decided to give its second performance in two halves played on successive nights—is now lost beyond recovery. The *Mefistofele* that we know today is the revision of 1875 with improvements added the following year; the autograph does however allow us to see which passages passed over intact from the first version to the second. From the reviews alone it is clear that the first *Mefistofele* was altogether more radical, avoiding where possible everything that recalled the formal arias of the past. Several of the well-known lyrical plums are missing from it—not however, Mefistofele's Meyerbeerian couplet 'Son lo spirito che nega' each

---

[113] Letter from Mariani to Verdi, 20 May 1865 (Abbiati, *Verdi*, iii. 17–18). He was referring to *Amleto*, of which he conducted the première.

verse ending with prolonged whistling, the traditional sign of
disapproval. Faust was a baritone, not a tenor; and the fourth act
contained a scene from Goethe's Part II, where Mefistofele appears
at the Emperor's court as a jester, followed by a symphonic
intermezzo descriptive of a battle, which Boito subsequently published
in an arrangement for piano duet. Even from an unaltered passage
such as Ex. 308, taken from the Prologue in Heaven, with discords
resolving on discords, an unceasing circle of modulation and the
final cadence continually withheld, one can imagine the effect on
contemporary Italian ears.

Boito's ideas are usually distinguished; they never contain a
superfluous note; but they are curiously infertile. They lead either

Ex. 308

(accompaniment only)

nowhere or back upon themselves. The result is that every act lacks
a sense of scale proportionate to its length. We seem to be hearing
a succession of miniatures. As a musical influence on Italian opera
Boito is negligible. He would have remained a mere footnote of
history but for his collaboration with a genius of a wholly different
calibre.

THE VERDIAN SYNTHESIS

The qualities which raise Verdi's operas so far above those of his
Italian contemporaries are various and interdependent; fundamental
to them all, however, is his determination to treat each work as a
separate problem requiring its own unique solution, using traditional
means where they could serve his purpose, striking out in a new
direction where they did not. Having chosen his subject, he devoted
his energies to realizing the drama in music with as few concessions
as possible to the kind of sonorous hedonism in which so many of his
fellow countrymen indulged. In a word Verdi's music is dramatically
functional. Of this *Rigoletto* (1851), that masterpiece of his middle
years, furnishes a good example. At the point where Rigoletto mocks
Monterone the music indulges in a series of grotesque cabrioles of
no melodic interest (Ex. 309). Yet not only do they express to
perfection Rigoletto's malign ribaldry; they detonate the hugely
powerful marching periods of Monterone's anger. This is not a case
of music humbly serving drama, but rather of drama taking musical
shape.

Ex. 309

- ste, voi con-giu-ra-ste con-tro noi, Si-gno-re;

(My lord, you did conspire against us.)

Not that *Rigoletto* is entirely free from concessions to singers and public. The Duke's aria 'Parmi veder le lagrime' is hardly appropriate to a rake; it does however offer the first instance of a typically Verdian melodic economy whereby the third and fourth phrases are run together in a single flight. Three-limbed melodies with the lyrical emphasis thrown on the final limb were to become a regular feature of Verdi's mature operas.

Every number of *Rigoletto* shows the same ability to say as much as possible in the fewest notes. The first duet between Rigoletto and Gilda shows traces of the old tripartite scheme; but everything is inflected towards the unique dramatic situation, so that each fresh idea occurs as a natural result of what has gone before. Certain of the recitatives achieve musical parity with the arias. Nowhere except briefly at the end of the first scene is there a static ensemble. The famous quartet in Act III, though bearing a family likeness to Bellini's 'A te, o cara' from *I puritani*, is in fact an action piece in which every character receives sharp musical definition. Indeed the third act is the most obviously original of the three. Operatic storms were common enough; but they occurred mostly by way of prelude or interlude. The storm in *Rigoletto* is the first to proceed *pari passu* with the action in a free association of characteristic motifs reaching its climax with the murder of Gilda. The use of the stage song 'La donna è mobile' to bring about the anagnorisis is justly celebrated but there is nothing very new about it. How many operatic heroes and heroines have been brought back to sanity through hearing 'our tune'!

Il trovatore (1853) operates on a quite different principle. Here is no steadily developing action but a sequence of contrasted situations with no immediate connection between them. In the person of Azucena Verdi first exploits the mezzo-soprano voice as the female equivalent of the baritone. Indeed the whole opera is based on the polarity between her and the soprano heroine Leonora. Each inhabits her own tonal area and speaks her own musical language, lyrical, aristocratic in Leonora's case, popular and dramatic in Azucena's; and each dominates alternate scenes of the opera, holding it in a dynamic equilibrium. The Count belongs naturally to the aristocratic world of Leonora; Manrico is divided between her and Azucena; and the turning-point of the drama is where he crosses from Leonora's sphere into Azucena's with the rousing cabaletta 'Di quella pira'. In contrast to those of *Rigoletto* the arias and duets are divided in the traditional manner and there is a minimum of recitative, all of which gives *Il trovatore* a somewhat old-fashioned air. But abundance of melody, insistent rhythmic vitality, moments of grandeur such as the 'Miserere' scene with its distant echoes of the Parisian stage all combine to make of *Il trovatore* the fiery essence of Italian Romantic opera and its *ne plus ultra*.

In *La traviata* (1853) it was said that Verdi brought chamber music into the opera house.[114] The reference is of course not to instrumental texture but rather to its style of vocal melody, which approached that of the *aria da camera*. This is the most intimate of Verdi's operas, a drama of three characters in which the chorus always appears as an intrusion. The melodies move by small intervals; the prevailing rhythm is that of the waltz. At a time when Mercadante and Pacini were still writing long-limbed melismatic lines in 9/8 and 12/8, Alfredo's declaration of love (Ex. 310), later to become the

Ex. 310

(Of that love which is the heartbeat of the whole universe — lofty, mysterious, the heart's cross and its delight.)

[114] Basevi, *Studio*, p. 231.

main reminiscence theme of the opera, must have sounded disconcertingly bare—the Italian lyric style pared down to its simplest.

For *Simon Boccanegra* (1857) Verdi found a very different *tinta* (his own term, denoting a certain combination of harmonic, melodic, and rhythmic attributes which stamps each opera with an unmistakable character of its own).[115] For him fourteenth century Genoa was an age of blood and iron. Accordingly the tone of *Simon Boccanegra* is unusually dark and austere. The Prologue is confined to basses, baritones, and male chorus. The leading character dominates the opera without a single aria, while in his opponent, Jacopo Fiesco, Verdi creates his most remarkable bass role so far—a character as rugged and unyielding as the basalt rocks of his native Liguria. His cavatina ('Il lacerato spirito') demonstrates how in Verdi formal concision and harmonic ellipsis go hand in hand. The succession of 6-4 and 6-4-3 chords may be unorthodox, but it is the only possible harmonic solution to Verdi's brief but highly charged melody (Ex. 311). The central pezzo concertato is conceived naturalistically with no concessions to melodic charm, while the stretta abounds in harsh counterpoint. The chief moment of lyricism is reserved for the ensemble that marks the Doge's death, where it lights up the end of the opera like a radiant sunset after a stormy day.

Verdi made use of French ternary form with modulating central episode for Amelia's cavatina in *Simon Boccanegra*. French forms are still more in evidence in his many-faceted *Un ballo in maschera*

Ex. 311

[115] Alarmed by rumours that an opera based on *Le Roi s'amuse* would not be allowed, Verdi wrote to the management of the Teatro la Fenice, Venice: 'the whole idea and the musical colour (*tinta*) of it have been settled in my mind and I may say that the principal part of the work has already been done.' (Letter to Marzari 20 Aug. 1850, quoted in Gaetano Cesari and Alessandro Luzio (eds.), *I copialettere di Giuseppe Verdi* (Milan, 1913), 106–7.) For a further definition of *tinta*, see Basevi, *Studio*, pp. 121–2.

Re - sa al ful-gor de - gli an-ge - li,   pre - ga, Ma-ria, per me

(Heaven in its mercy granted her the crown of martyrdom. Gathered to the splendour of the angels, pray, Maria, for me)

(1859). The light soprano page Oscar (a novelty for the Italian stage where *travesti* roles were traditionally given to mezzo-sopranos) has two solos in *couplet* form, the tenor Riccardo one with choral refrain (the central concertato 'È scherzo od è follia' is wonderfully buoyant). Much of the score sparkles with Gallic charm and gaiety, beset however by menacing shadows. The part of the heroine Amelia is conceived wholly in tragic terms. The centrepiece of the opera is the love duet, Verdi's finest next to that of *Otello* and certainly his most incandescent. Here the old threefold division is maintained but with more than one difference. The end of the first movement, instead of forming a contrast with the cantabile, anticipates its rhythm in the final bars; the cantabile itself proceeds through the development of a single thematic cell, which becomes transformed into the following essentially instrumental culmination. Verdi was clearly learning the 'art of transition' (Ex. 312). The same idea recurs, fortissimo, in the cabaletta—so completely altering the conventional balance. Here for

Ex. 312

Più lento ♪ = 100

the first but not the last time Verdi uses the duet cabaletta form to create theatrical tension—as in Act I of *La forza del destino* and Act III of *Aida*, not to mention Act V of *Don Carlos*; it is his favourite form for the portrayal of lovers who outstay their own safety.

Verdi's only Italian opera of the 1860s—excluding the revision of *Macbeth* (1865)—is *La forza del destino*, first given at St Petersburg in 1862 and revised for La Scala, Milan, in 1869. This is an essay in epic music drama, in which characters as fantastic as those of *Il trovatore* are set against a background of ordinary, diverse humanity. Here Verdi is sometimes accused of musical self-indulgence at the expense of drama, especially in such peripheral numbers as the 'Rataplan' chorus; and the charge would certainly hold good if the subject required the concentration of *Otello*. But dispersal is fundamental to the premiss of Rivas's play in which the hand of fate must pursue its victims through scenes of the utmost variety. *La forza del destino* is Verdi's nearest approach to a Shakespearean chronicle play, embracing the highest and the lowest in the land. The richness and diversity of language that enabled him to encompass such a scheme is due partly to lessons learned from Paris and partly to a renewed study of the musical classics. Among the novelties of *La forza del destino* may be noted an aria which begins outside the home key and only moves into it on the second phrase ('O tu che in sen agli angeli') and a style of declaimed melody with its origins in the recitatives of *Rigoletto* and *Macbeth* for the punning sermon of Fra Melitone, a comic character entirely *sui generis*. With its choruses, dances, and range of characters *La forza del destino* is more than half-way towards *grand opéra* on the French model. By 1870 the age of Italian 'grand opera' had arrived.

ITALIAN 'GRAND OPERA'

'Grand opera' may be defined as opera in four or five acts involving lavish spectacle, an abundance of chorus, at least four principals, and a central ballet. Originating in Paris around 1830, it had come to dominate the European scene in the latter part of the century, though surprisingly few of its products have survived today. In Italy the vogue received a stimulus from the popularity of Meyerbeer's *L'Africaine*, which was played in almost every major season in the late 1860s; indeed in Lauro Rossi's theatrical satire, *Il maestro e la cantante* (1867), it is the only modern opera that rates a quotation by the plagiarizing composer. In 1871 *Lohengrin* was performed in Bologna, the first of Wagner's operas to reach Italy; and by 1876 the entire early Wagner canon had been heard. If *Der fliegende*

Holländer was the least liked, *Lohengrin* was to acquire honorary Italian status. Though it lacks a ballet, its slow majestic pace, its total lack of *fioritura*, its spectacular pageantry would leave its mark on many Italian operas of the 1870s and 1880s, with the ironical result that though Wagner himself was a foe to grand opera his own music was doing more than anyone else's to keep the genre alive. Not until Giuseppe Martucci conducted the first Italian performance of *Tristan und Isolde* in Bologna in 1888 did native composers have the chance of coming to grips with Wagner's mature idiom.

During the 1870s and after, the promotion of operas, both native and foreign, was in the hands of the publishers. Where earlier a composer would have been contracted by the management of a theatre, he now wrote for a publisher, who would assume responsibility for mounting the opera in a worthy manner and at the same time allow him a percentage of the hire fees. At the time Italy was divided between the rival firms of Ricordi and Lucca. Each had its own house magazine and each its chief theatrical showcase: Ricordi, La Scala Milan; Lucca, the Teatro Comunale, Bologna. Ricordi held a stronger suit in native composers with Verdi as his ace of trumps; Lucca could muster no one of greater consequence than Petrella (the firm's attempt to boost Gobatti's old-fashioned and incompetent *I Goti* (1873) as the 'music of the future' failed lamentably), but he had an impressive tally of foreigners—Gounod, Meyerbeer, Goldmark and Wagner. The sensation of the late 1870s was Massenet's *Roi de Lahore*, first given in Milan in 1870; its success convinced Ricordi that he had found in Massenet the answer to Wagner; and he commissioned his next opera, *Hérodiade*, for Italy. Both operas, grand and exotic, exercised an influence on composers of the day, as did Goldmark's *Die Königin von Saba*.

Many factors contributed to the new interest in all things foreign. The reform of the conservatories in 1870 laid a new emphasis on the study of German instrumental music, past and present. For part of every year Liszt held court at the Villa d'Este near Rome. Florence had become Bülow's home since the break-up of his marriage: he was even considered as a candidate for the Directorship of the Milan Conservatory. Thus, during the 1870s and 1880s Italian opera became less recognizably Italian than before. Critics drew attention to influences from Schubert, Liszt, and Gounod. Lauro Rossi (1810-85) in *La contessa de Mons* (1874) quotes the melody of the jota aragonesa, something unheard of in the 1860s.

By this time all traces of the post-Rossinian tradition have been obliterated. The forms are those of French *grand opéra*. Arias are in ternary form; *fioritura* and *melisma* have vanished and with them all trace of the broad compound rhythms typical of the mid-century cantabile. If the formal numbers are still basically finite, they show an increasing tendency to merge into the surrounding tissue. Cadenzas are obsolete. By the beginning of the 1880s the act or tableau has become the formal unit, as can be seen by comparing Verdi's revised *Simon Boccanegra* (1881) with its original of 1857. All the conventional applause points have gone; cabalettas are either removed or so altered as regards form that the term itself becomes a misnomer. Only the central concertato remains *de rigueur* as the musical coping-stone.

THE LATER VERDI

It was unfortunate that by far the greatest of the Italian grand operas appeared near the beginning of the vogue, making most of its successors look like poor imitations. Verdi's *Aida* (1871) has been justly described as the only grand opera from which not a note can be cut. The problems of proportion which had sometimes eluded him in *La forza del Destino* and *Don Carlos* are here triumphantly resolved. The two prime ingredients of grand opera—grandeur and exoticism—are held in perfect equilibrium. In the finale to Act II three themes are piled on top of one another with an ease and naturalness that Meyerbeer might have envied. The central ballet springs directly from the trumpet march like an arrow from a bow. In the trial of Radames monumental use is made of the threefold statement. The third act, which Verdi wished to be printed without division into arias and duets (he was over-ruled however), shows a rare delicacy of harmony and scoring; but Verdi never allows description to get the upper hand of drama. As usual, old and new blend in a personal synthesis. In accordance with contemporary practice Verdi uses labelling themes for Aida, Amneris, and the priests but always with discretion. The aria 'Celeste Aida' is a perfect instance of Verdian three-limbed melody evolved into a ternary design. But where the composer most conspicuously draws ahead of his countrymen is in his subtle handling of poetic metre as a means to melodic self-renewal. The so-called eleven-syllable metre was traditionally considered more suitable for recitative than aria. Verdi however treats it lyrically in three numbers in *Aida*, of which the most striking is the final duet. Here it is set as a widely arched melody of such simplicity and beauty that Verdi repeats it three times in the form of an old-style cabaletta; what is more, three of

Ex. 313

its five phrases are identical (see Ex. 313). Not since Bellini had any composer ventured so much repetition of a single strain.

For ten years Verdi did not write another opera. Then came the revision of *Simon Boccanegra* including an entirely new scene set in the Council Chamber of Genoa, in the course of which orchestral motifs are developed in a strictly personal manner. The concertato is a lyrical pendant to Simone's noble plea for peace between the Italian cities, a superbly controlled melodic paragraph with the majestic, march-like gait characteristic of the Italian grand opera style. The act ends with a bout of powerful recitative reinforced by brutal unison gestures from the orchestra as the villain is made to curse himself. The revised *Simon Boccanegra* softens without lifting the darkness of the original score. It is also one of the finest expressions of political idealism in all opera.

The *Don Carlo* of 1884 was written for performance at La Scala, Milan; but to call it on that account 'the Italian *Don Carlos*' is like calling the *Macbeth* of 1865 French because it was designed for the Théâtre Lyrique, Paris, and first sung in French. Both operas were revised to a text in the original language and in neither case was the fundamental character altered. The principal innovation of the four-act score is the duet between Philip and Posa, in which an intellectual argument about freedom, originally a chain of essentially lyrical periods, is rewritten as a dramatic dialogue in which all traces of closed form have gone and each singer reacts to the other at a length appropriate to his thought—a technique which figures prominently in Verdi's last tragic opera.

OTELLO AND *FALSTAFF*

Otello (1887) is the Everest among Italian operas but without the surrounding Himalayas. No other work of the 1880's compares with it, either in form or in stature. The opening bars present an unheard of harmonic audacity—a dominant eleventh which never resolves but merely loses definition (Ex. 314). For all that, *Otello* cannot be said to anticipate the more freely dissonant style of the *veristi*. What Verdi called the 'vent-hole' of a perfect concord quickly arrives; and even here he does not fail to wind up the profusion of heterogeneous storm motifs with a simple, regular melodic period ('Dio fulgor della bufera') just as he had done in *Rigoletto*. Written at a time when Italian composers were laying ever greater emphasis on the orchestra, *Otello* remains a drama for the voice. Thematic recall is restricted to two ideas: the first phrase of 'È un'idra fosca, livida', and the 'kiss' motif, an epigram of lyrical magic which ends the love duet and recurs twice in the last act, bringing down the final curtain (Ex. 315).

Again the musical organization is entirely personal. Motivic transformation, bar form ('Inaffia l'ugola' and 'Piangea cantando'), the projection of three-limbed cantilena into a larger design ('Dio mi potevi scagliar'), declaimed melody ('Credo in un Dio crudel'), dramatic dialogue, whether tense, as between Iago and Otello in Act

Ex. 314

Ex. 315

II, or calm and radiant as in the love duet—all play their part. The ghost of a cabaletta stalks the oath duet and the last movement of the handkerchief trio. The concertato of Act III is of a symphonic grandeur and complexity. External influences can be felt as a distillation of past experience. The gait and phrase-formation of the soprano–tenor duet of *Lohengrin* is reflected in that of *Otello*, though at 74 Verdi was more successful than the young Wagner in avoiding monotonous regularity. Domenico Scarlatti is present in the handkerchief trio; and there is even a recollection of Meyerbeer's 'Adieu, mon doux rivage' (*L'Africaine*) in the 'willow' song, that strangest and most haunting of melodies, half modal, half diatonic, here harmonized, there totally resistant to harmony. That the sympathetic Dannreuther should have preferred Rossini's setting[116] shows how far Verdi had outstripped conventional notions of Italian lyricism.

If *Otello* stands apart from the contemporary Italian scene this is still more the case with *Falstaff* (1893). Produced in the first flush of the verismo age—Maurel, the first Falstaff, had created Tonio the year before in Leoncavallo's *Pagliacci*—Verdi's comic masterpiece has a wit and elegance entirely Classical. The musical continuity is at last seamless, the texture as alive as that of a Beethoven quartet. Each idea merges into its neighbour, such motifs as recur being always derived from a line of text ('Può l'onore riempirvi la pancia', 'Dalle due alle tre', 'Te lo cornifico'). Boito's *recherché* vocabulary, often irritating in *Otello*, is here a source of constant delight; and

[116] *Oxford History of Music*, vi (2nd edn., London, 1932), 64.

Ex. 316.

(And your countenance shall shine upon me, like a star upon the vast universe)

the opera abounds in verbal and musical play. To demonstrate his slightness as page to the Duke of Norfolk, Falstaff sings an aria all of thirty seconds long.

All the conventions of Italian opera are turned on their head. Instead of being given each an 'entrance', all the women are thrown on to the stage together. Ford and Falstaff dispute as to which shall leave the stage first and finally exeunt arm in arm. The idiom is clear and simple throughout, excesses of Romantic harmony being reserved for moments of irony, as when Alice comes to the end of Falstaff's letter (Ex. 316). Yet not even Mendelssohn evoked nocturnal magic more delicately than Verdi in the Windsor Forest scene.

All this may seem out of tune with the times. But once the tumult and the shouting of verismo had died Verdi's last opera could be seen as a work linked more to the future than the past. For Casella, *Falstaff* was the starting-point for modern Italian music.[117]

THE CONSERVATIVES: PONCHIELLI AND GOMES

Inevitably the older composers found the most difficulty in keeping up with the new trend. In *Cleopatra* (1876) and *La contessa di Mons*

[117] *I segreti della giara* (Florence, 1939), 300.

(1874) Lauro Rossi merely burdens his essentially old-fashioned schemes with stodgy rhythms and clogged harmonies. Marchetti followed up his *Ruy Blas* with *Gustavo Wasa* (1875) and *Don Giovanni d'Austria* (1880), in which the orchestra takes an ever increasing part in the organization but to no better purpose than before.

His contemporary Amilcare Ponchielli (1834–86) achieved much greater distinction, even if he took longer to arrive. Born in Cremona, his operatic career began modestly in the lesser theatres of the north and included a setting of *I promessi sposi* (1856). A typical product of the 1850s it none the less made the composer's name when revived in 1872 at the Teatro Dal Verme, Milan, in a more or less updated version. The public was enthusiastic, the critics were cautious; and it was not until after the success of his ballet *Le due gemelle* (1873) that Ricordi decided to publish the score. He then commissioned from Ponchielli the ambitious drama *I lituani* (1874) based on Mickiewicz's *Konrad Wallenrod*. Ponchielli rose to the challenge with a remarkably grand, dark-hued work, in which thematic recall is used flexibly and to good effect. Outstanding are an overture in full sonata form, a duet of farewell for Walter and Aldona, and a scene for the heroine with a subterranean chorus of the *Vehmgericht* (added for a later revival). But it was with his next opera, *La Gioconda* (1876), to a libretto by Boito based on Hugo's *Angelo*, that Ponchielli enjoyed his one lasting triumph. Less musically adventurous than *I lituani*, it allows greater scope to the lyrical vein in which Ponchielli excelled. The aria 'Cielo e mar' remains one of the plums of the tenor repertoire—a strophic song whose second verse begins as an abbreviation of the first and ends as an expansion of it by way of codetta. Ponchielli has a recognizable melodic line, sinuous and tending to move by wide intervals, and a gift for pictorial atmosphere which his pupil Puccini would inherit. Much of the score is unashamedly old-fashioned. The opening chorus is almost Donizettian in its 6/8 swagger. La Cieca is clearly based on Meyerbeer's Fidès and sings the same language. Barnaba's 'O monumento' is sometimes described as an anticipation of Iago's 'Credo', but its bland harmonies rather recall the recitatives of *Rigoletto*. Two other features are worth noting: the incorporation of the 'rosary' theme, first heard in the Prelude, into the lyrical framework of La Cieca's aria; and the grand orchestral resumption, fortissimo, of the most memorable idea in the concertato to bring down the curtain on Act III. Both devices would be exploited by Puccini. *La Gioconda* stands in much the same relation to late Verdi as Webster does to Shakespeare. It is vital, rich in ideas, and in a sonorous poetry, yet in the last resort too sensational to reach the depths. But it has sufficient merit to keep it in the repertoire of the opera-houses that can afford its lavish resources. The ballet 'La danza delle ore' has remained a classic of light music since the time it was written.

Of Ponchielli's later works *Lina* (1877), revised from an earlier *Savoiarda*, is, like the *Dolores* (1875) of Salvatore Auteri-Manzocchi (1845–1924), a late reversion to the *semiseria* genre with all the laughs removed and a tragic denouement. *Il figluolo prodigo* (1880) is once again in the grand tradition, touched this time by the influences of Massenet and Goldmark. Here Ponchielli sets out to define two contrasted worlds—that of the frugal Judean patriarch and the wild debauchery of Nineveh—an effect that the French composer would achieve with far greater economy in *Thaïs*. *Marion Delorme* (1885) aims at a lighter style, akin to that of *opéra comique*. Although these works are musically accomplished, they lack the pace and vitality and the sureness of touch of *La Gioconda*. A leading critic of the 1880s described Ponchielli as 'the Mercadante of our time'.

The career of the Brazilian Carlos Gomes (1836–96) traced a somewhat similar graph. He burst upon La Scala, Milan, with *Il Guarany* (1870), a spiritual offspring of *L'Africaine*, mingling elements of his native folk-dance with the current Italian idiom. The ideas are often naïve and the scoring brash but the drama moves and grips. *Fosca* (1873) is a powerful grand opera comparable to *I lituani*, the second act containing what must be the most elaborately designed finale concertato before that of *Otello*, Act III. The thematic organization is tight, reaching far beyond the limits of the individual number. A broad motif of crotchets and crotchet triplets, representing the corsairs' honour (Ex. 317) remains a constant point of reference throughout the score; and the cast includes a particularly subtle villain in the person of Cambro (first sung by Victor Maurel). Yet the opera was coolly received; and, like Ponchielli, Gomes lowered his sights for its successor *Salvator Rosa* (1874), a drama of love and politics in the picturesque Neapolitan setting of Masaniello's revolt. With its wealth of barcaroles, tarantellas, and marches, not to

Ex. 317

mention a ballata for the pert apprentice Gennariello (a *travesti* role) which became a popular hit, *Salvator Rosa* proved the greatest success of Gomes's career; but it was soon offset by the disastrous failure of *Maria Tudor* (1879). Unlike Ponchielli, Gomes enjoyed no salaried post; his wealth melted away and he was forced to return to Brazil where his next opera, *Lo schiavo*, was produced in 1889. Its most distinguished feature is a dawn prelude, a brilliant essay in orchestral colouring; but the opera moves ponderously. Certain melodic traits seem to anticipate the style of the *veristi*, especially Leoncavallo, the most formally minded of the school. But the harmonic style remains old-fashioned, never going beyond that of Verdi in the 1860s. Lively and fluent in his earlier works, Gomes, like Marchetti, allowed his vital spark to be extinguished beneath the apparatus of grand opera.

THE RADICAL ELEMENT: CATALANI AND FRANCHETTI

Born in Lucca in 1854, Alfredo Catalani belonged from the start to the ranks of the *esterofili*. Before studying at the Milan Conservatory he had spent some months in Paris, where he absorbed the influence of Massenet long before that composer had been heard of in Italy. He was a devoted Wagner enthusiast; and at first despised Verdi and all he stood for. Characteristically the one-act eclogue *La falce* (1875), his passing-out piece for the Milan Conservatory, starts not with an overture but with a symphonic poem, in which the influence of Liszt is patent. Throughout, *La falce* shows a far wider harmonic vocabulary than anything of Ponchielli or Gomes; the lines are more supple and flexible; and in the final duet there is a foretaste of the most famous aria from his masterpiece *La Wally* (1893). But, like his contemporaries, Catalani was forced to grapple with the demands of grand opera; and both in *Elda* (1880) and *Dejanice* (1883) the individual voice is heard only by fits and starts, though the musical resource is considerable. In *Edmea* (1886) Catalani won through to a more intimate type of drama and a consequent refinement of musical thought. The opening scene is dominated by a spinning chorus of Mendelssohnian delicacy. In the heroine's mad scene he achieves a kind of bizarre disjointedness that owes nothing to Donizetti and his successors. Yet the style remains too eclectic for the opera to make a strong impression. Moreover Catalani's grip of the formal aria is not as strong as that of Ponchielli or Gomes. In his hands the standard ternary structure tends to fall apart in the middle. Not until his last two operas did Catalani as last find the organization that suited him. *Loreley* (1890) is a revised version of

Ex. 318

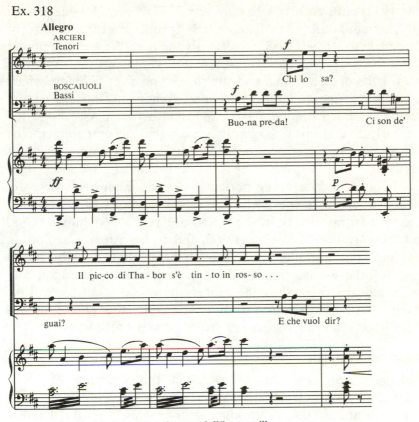

(FORESTERS: Good hunting! HUNTSMEN [BOWMEN]: Who can tell!
FORESTERS: Is anything amiss? HUNTSMEN: The summit of Mount Thabor is tinged with red . . .
FORESTERS: What should that mean?)

Elda with all the dead weight of conventional grandeur removed and a quasi-symphonic working of orchestral motif taking the place of the scena as the main connecting tissue. The opening chorus scene (Ex. 318) is a case in point. If this is a parlante, it is of the Wagnerian variety.

By the time of *La Wally* (1892) operatic verismo had already affirmed itself; but, despite the language of Illica's libretto and its setting amongst the dour peasants of the Tyrol, the opera does not really belong to that category; Catalani's brand of lyric poetry was too sensitive. *Loreley* and *La Wally* alone among Italian operas reflect, if somewhat palely, the world of German *Naturromantik*. With *La Wally* it was said that Catalani had brought the 'high mountain' into Italian opera.[118]

If Catalani died before his talent matured, Alberto Franchetti

[118] The phrase is Carlo Gatti's, taken from *Lettere di Alfredo Catalani a Giuseppe Depanis*, ed. Carlo Gatti (Milan, 1946), 40.

(1860–1942) outlived his. A baron, possessed of considerable private means, he could afford to take endless trouble over his operas, of which the first, *Asrael* (1888), is certainly the best. Wagner is a potent influence. Leading themes are sharp and characteristic, especially those for the demon Asrael and the redeeming Suor Clotilde, which Franchetti manages to insert at unexpected moments into the texture in true Wagnerian fashion. The grand duet between Asrael and the gipsy girl Loreta, with its gently syncopated accompaniment, its chromaticism, its huge tonal orbit, and its sensuous interweaving of vocal lines is clearly inspired by 'O sink' hernieder'. Wagner's, too, is his habit of side-stepping perfect cadences. Elsewhere there are spectacular choral scenes, which owe much more to Meyerbeer. Indeed a natural facility in the grandiose vein stood him in good stead for *Cristoforo Colombo* (1892). But in his attempt to find an individual style he failed; and, though he continued to be hailed as one of the *giovane scuola* along with Puccini, Mascagni, and Leoncavallo, by the end of the century he was a spent force. Like Catalani and Faccio's pupil, Antonio Smareglia (1854–1929), he was too fastidious to draw sustenance from the verismo tradition.

TOWARDS *VERISMO*

Verismo began as a literary movement, the equivalent of Zola's 'naturalism'. Its foremost literary representatives, Giovanni Verga and Luigi Capuana did not produce their best work until the 1880s; but well before that the term was in general circulation.[119] A number of chance events, occurring about 1880, sowed the seeds of musical verismo. The first was the arrival on the scene of Edoardo Sonzogno, an enterprising publisher determined to rival the reigning dynasties of Lucca and Ricordi. His first move was to invest in such ultramontane composers as had escaped the Lucca net. His most important catch was Bizet's *Carmen*. A failure at its première in 1875, it proved the success of the season at the Teatro Bellini, Naples, in 1880 and within the next two years had gone the rounds of the Italian *teatri di cartello*, totally eclipsing the operas of Massenet. Its impact was twofold. A colourful *opéra comique* for most of its length, it convinced audiences and managements that grandeur was no longer essential to the success of an opera; while the last act, with its naked passion and violence, had a theatrical immediacy that Italian opera had not known for many years. Shrewdly drawing the

---

[119] Verdi described Massenet's *Le Roi de Lahore* as 'an opera eminently suited to this age of *verismo* in which there is not a scrap of verity' (letter to Faccio, *c*. January 1879, quoted in R. De Rensis, *Franco Faccio e Verdi: Carteggio e documenti inediti* (Milan, 1934), 182–5).

correct conclusion, Sonzogno then announced a competition for a one-act opera. The prize was allotted jointly to Guglielmo Zuelli (1859–1941) for his *La fata del Nord*, and Luigi Mapelli (1885–1913) for his *Anna e Gualberto*, an entry by the young Puccini—*Le Villi*—having been turned down because of its illegibility. Friends of the composer, however, among them Boito, helped him to mount a performance at the Teatro dal Verme in 1884. It was at once taken up, together with its author, by Giulio Ricordi. From now on, if Verdi was his king, Puccini would be his crown prince.

Le Villi, like *La fata del Nord*, was based on one of those subjects taken from northern mythology that were in vogue at the time. But the germs of a new, Massenet-inspired manner are clearly present: instead of the march of grand opera, a softer more sinuous style of melody propelled by gentle syncopated pulsations with phrases that often end in flurries of semiquavers (see Ex. 319 from Act I). This was to be in essence the lyrical language of verismo.

In *Edgar* (1889) Puccini develops this style still further increasing his harmonic range to include unresolved dominant sevenths, extending his ideas in an ever larger continuity and making imaginative use of 'labelling' themes. Indeed *Edgar* might well have proclaimed the new style throughout Italy had not an impossible libretto hindered its circulation. The honour went instead to Puccini's fellow pupil, Pietro Mascagni (1863–1945).

Mascagni's *Cavalleria rusticana* (1890) won the same competition to which *Le Villi* had been submitted six years before. Apart from its swift, naturalistic pace, its main novelties were two. First, the direct language of the libretto; it may not be that of the Sicilian peasants among whom the action is set but it is recognizably that of everyday life in contrast to the traditional fustian of a Ghislanzoni

Ex. 319

(Be not so sad, Anna mine; a few days will pass and I shall return.)

Ex. 320

or the preciosity of a Boito. 'Il cavallo scalpita,' cries Alfio on his first entrance; previously the 'cavallo' would have been a 'destriere'. More important is a reckless lyricism that takes no account of good manners: see, as an illustration, Ex. 320, an extract from the introduction to Santuzza's aria 'Voi lo sapete'. Here after two decades of uncertainty was Italian opera once more striking out boldly.[120]

(d) RUSSIA AND EASTERN EUROPE

By GERALD ABRAHAM

RUSSIA

During the 1850s Russian opera stagnated. Glinka composed no more operas after *Ruslan i Lyudmila*; Dargomïzhsky produced only *Rusalka* (1854), and Verstovsky his last work, *Gromoboy* (1857). The early attempts of the rising star of Russian music, Anton Rubinstein (1829-94), were mostly insignificant or total failures. The exception was the first, *Dmitriy Donskoy* (1852), based on Ozerov's tragedy. (On the insistence of the censors, the names of all the characters had to be changed and the title altered to *The Battle of Kulikovo*.) Verstovsky's *Gromoboy*, like his *Vadim*, was based on Zhukovsky's

---

[120] On Mascagni's later works see Vol. X, pp. 154–5, 162, and 193.

Twelve Sleeping Maidens and is said to show a more advanced treatment of the orchestra particularly in the 'bright and cheerful overture and the spirited "Wallachian dance" ';[121] it was still being performed at the end of the century. But none of his operas had anything like the lasting success of Dargomïzhsky's *Rusalka* which reached Paris in 1911, New York in 1922, and London in 1931.

In *Rusalka*, a variation on the *Donauweibchen/Undine* theme, Dargomïzhsky turned his back on the *grand-opéra* style of his *Esmeralda* and, making his own adaptation of Pushkin's unfinished dramatic poem, tried to follow in Glinka's footsteps—with a difference:

The more I study our folk elements, the more diversity I find in them. Glinka, ... in my view has touched only one aspect—the lyrical. Drama with him is too melancholy, the comic side loses national character. I speak of the character of his music for his technique is always superb. To the best of my ability I am trying in *Rusalka* to develop our dramatic elements. I shall be happy if I succeed half as well as Glinka.[122]

In his lyrical music—for example in the Princess's aria and Olga's couplets in Act III—he succeeded no more than half as well; it was in the dramatic element that he scored, above all in the characterization of the Miller,[123] driven out of his mind by his daughter's suicide. When the seducer Prince addresses him as 'miller', he says he is no miller; he has sold the mill to the devils behind the stove and given the money to the *rusalka*, his daughter, for safe-keeping (Ex. 321).

Ex. 321

Ikh rïb-ka od-nu-glaz - ka sto-ro - zhit   Kha,kha,kha,kha,kha, kha!   O-ne v pes -

---

[121] Ol'ga Evgen'evna Levashova, in *Istoriya russkoy muzïki*, i (Moscow, 1972), 348.

[122] Letter to V. F. Odoevsky, 3 June 1853; see *A. S. Dargomïzhskiy: Izbrannïe pis'ma*, ed. Mikhail Samoylovich Pekelis (Moscow, 1952), 41.

[123] First sung by the famous bass Petrov, the original Susanin in *Life for the Tsar* and Ruslan in Glinka's second opera.

ke Dnep-ra za - rï - tï ikh rïb-ka sto-ro - zhit.

(The one-eyed fish guards them, ha, ha, ha, ha, ha, ha! Buried in the sands
of the Dnieper, the fish guards, them.)

And Dargomïzhsky can also catch subtler nuances, as when in
Act I the false Prince makes smooth excuses to the girl for jilting
her.[124]

After *Rusalka* and *Gromoboy* Russian opera showed no signs of
life until 1863, and even then Rubinstein's *Feramors* did not contribute
to a revival. Its quasi-oriental libretto was based by a German poet
on an English poem by an Irishman, Moore's *Lalla Rookh*; it was
first produced in Germany and reached the Mariinsky stage only in
1884.

SEROV

Yudif [Judith] (1863) of Aleksandr Serov (1820–71), given three
months after the Dresden première of *Feramors*, had a better fate,
although it was equally non-Russian.[125] The heroine is Jewish. Serov
was attracted to the subject by an Italian play, Paolo Giacometti's
Guiditta, and he began by commissioning an Italian libretto which
became the basis of the Russian one. Serov was then in his forties
and had failed even to complete several earlier operas, but *Judith*
was an immediate success and for nearly a decade he was the leading
composer of Russian opera.

Although Serov had been profoundly impressed by *Tannhäuser*,
which he heard in 1858, his real model was his earlier hero,
Meyerbeer; *Judith* and its successor *Rogneda* (1865) were *grands
opéras*.[126] So also would have been the *Salammbô* begun by the 24-
year-old Modest Mussorgsky (1839–81) in 1863 after he had written

---

[124] Quoted in *The Concise Oxford History of Music*, p. 729.
[125] Serov's operas and their cultural ambience are studied in detail in Richard Taruskin,
Opera and Drama in Russia as Preached and Practised in the 1860s (Ann Arbor, 1981).
[126] See Gerald Abraham, 'The Operas of Serov', in *Essays on Russian and East European
Music* (Oxford, 1985), 40.

a long, detailed and sarcastic account of *Judith*.[127] Flaubert's Salammbô is another heroine who penetrates an enemy camp to seize a precious trophy and the one passage in *Judith* that Mussorgsky admired, the swift transition from *ff* to *pp* in the chorus at the end of Act I, was echoed at the end of Act I of *Salammbô*.[128] And there are other musical parallels: between Judith's prayer in Act II and Salammbô's in the temple of Tanit, and between the opening of the odalisques' scene in Act III and the scene of Salammbô prostrating herself before the image in the temple. From Serov's next opera, *Rogneda* (1865), Mussorgsky derived ideas for naturalistic handling of the chorus in a later and much greater work, *Boris Godunov*. Even in *Judith*, where it is generally treated as a mass, Serov indicates in the first chorus of Act I that 'not all' are to participate in certain passages, or '2 voices', 'another 2', '4 voices', mainly for musical variety; but in the last finale of *Rogneda*, when the people of Kiev flock into the streets at the sound of an alarm bell, the point is dramatic rather than musical: '3 basses ("Hark! Listen, they're coming here!")', '1 tenor ("People are coming in crowds!")', '1 bass ("Look!")', '1 tenor ("Look!")'.

Meyerbeerian opera was nothing if not spectacular and Serov confessed that

the music of this opera (*Rogneda*), like that of *Judith*, was composed *not according to the words of the text*, which did not yet exist, but according to 'situations' which were clearly defined in the author's imagination. Thus the words had often to be invented for already prepared or half-prepared music.[129]

The figure of Rogneda herself was borrowed from a poem by Rïleev; she also appears in Verstovsky's *Gromoboy*. The opera has plenty of spectacle, including the ballet in the audience-chamber of Vladimir of Kiev, a hunting scene for which dogs were borrowed from the Imperial Kennels, the sacrifice to the idol Perun. (The time is that of *Askol'dova mogila* [Askold's Grave]; indeed, Serov extracted the subject from the same Zagoskin novel Verstovsky had drawn on in *Askold*.) And the Russian subject demanded Russian-flavoured music which Serov achieved most successfully in the duet for Vladimir and Dobrïnya Nikitich in the hunt scene, in Rogneda's Act IV monologue

---

[127] Translated in Jay Leyda and Sergei Bertensson (eds.), *The Musorgsky Reader: A Life of M. P. Musorgsky in Letters and Documents* (New York, 1947), 48–57.

[128] *M. P. Musorgskiy: Polnoe sobranie sochineniy*, iv (Moscow and Leningrad, 1939), 36–7. This volume contains all the *Salammbô* fragments.

[129] 'Avtobiograficheskaya zapiska', in *A. N. Serov: Izbrannïe stat'i*, ed. Georgy N. Khubov (Moscow and Leningrad, 1950), i. 75.

Ex. 322

(Mother dear princess, my own! Why are you weeping bitterly?
You're tiring your eyes! Enough, leave off, my own one.)

(although the sketch was marked 'imitation of Gounod'), and most beautifully in the music of her little son, a contralto role, just before it (Ex. 322).

But Serov had been mostly interested in Ukrainian folk song; it was only when in 1867 he had begun work on his last opera, *Vrazh'ya sila* [Hostile Power] that he set about serious study of Great Russian folk-music—and even then its urban rather than its peasant forms.

Vrazh'ya sila is based on a play, *Ne tak zhivi kak khochetsya, a tak zhivi kak Bog velit* [Don't live as you'd like to, but live as God commands], by Ostrovsky, whose masterpiece the tragedy *Groza* [The Storm] had already inspired an absurdly Italianate opera (1867) by Vladimir Kashperov (1827–94) and an overture by the young Tchaikovsky (1840–93). (Tchaikovsky was now also working on an Ostrovsky opera, *Voevoda*.) The dramatist himself took a hand in all three opera librettos but his collaborations with Serov and Tchaikovsky both broke down. *Ne tak zhivi kak khochetsya* is a realistic play, but in the opera Ostrovsky wanted to treat the *maslyanitsa* [carnival] scene in Act IV as a fantasy with diabolical characters, while Serov insisted on realism and also turned the resigned ending into melodrama: instead of renouncing suicide, Peter murders his wife.

THE NEW GENERATION

New tendencies were invading Russian opera during the 1860s; not the influence of Wagner, as might have been expected in Serov, a professed Wagnerian, but interest in 'the people' as a result of the recent emancipation of the serfs and insistence on dramatic—even prosaic—truth. Dargomïzhsky worked from 1866 until his death in 1869 on a setting of Pushkin's 'little tragedy' in verse, *Kamennïy Gost'* [The Stone Guest],[130] 'just as it stood, without altering a single word', and his young friend Mussorgsky emulated him with a setting of Gogol's prose comedy *Zhenit'ba* [The Marriage] (1868),[131] which he fortunately abandoned after one act in favour of a far more important work: the initial version of *Boris Godunov* (1869). Serov himself in the preface to *Rogneda* had stated as his aim '*dramatic truth* in sounds', if necessary at the expense of ' "conventional" beauty'. In fact there is a great deal of ' "conventional" beauty', mostly folk-song flavoured, in *Vrazh'ya sila* (as there is in *Boris*) and also a certain amount of bold empirical harmony (see Ex. 323, from

Ex. 323

130 See Taruskin, *Opera and Drama*, pp. 249 ff. and Jennifer Baker, 'Dargomïzhsky, Realism and *The Stone Guest*', *Music Review*, 37 (1976), 193.
131 See Taruskin, *Opera and Drama*, pp. 307 ff.

Vrazh'ya sila).[132]   Tchaikovsky's *Voevoda* (1869) on Ostrovsky's comedy, *Son na Volge* [Dream on the Volga], was, despite initial success, destroyed by the composer after he had transferred some of the material to later works—it itself includes borrowings from earlier ones[133]—but has been restored from the performing material.[134] The plot might be described as a Russian version of *Die Entführung* but Tchaikovsky shows little sense of musical characterization; the dramatic element is conventional and the score rises above the commonplace only when the composer borrows or skilfully imitates folk melody. In this respect *Voevoda* is naturally more Russian than the *Vil'yam Ratklif* [Wiliam Ratcliff] of the avowed 'nationalist' César Cui (1835–1918), which was produced a fortnight later. But Cui was half-French, half-Lithuanian; *Ratcliff* is a Heine play on a Scottish subject and most of his other operas are non-Russian except in text. The exceptions are *Kavkazskiy plennik* [The Caucasian Prisoner] (Acts I and III, 1857; Act II, 1881), based on Pushkin's poem and most successful in its oriental element, and the act Cui contributed to the 'collective *Mlada*' of 1872.[135] He admitted to Felipe Pedrell in 1897: 'Je n'ai pas le sens de la musique russe dans mes veines. . . . C'est pourquoi, à l'exception de mon premier opéra *Le Prisonnier du Caucase*, tous les sujets de mes opéras sont et seront étrangers.'[136]

It was very different with Cui's friends, Mussorgsky, Aleksandr Borodin (1833–87), and Nikolay Rimsky-Korsakov (1844–1908)—all, like him, non-professional musicians. In 1868 Rimsky-Korsakov began an opera based on Lev Mey's *Pskovityanka* [The Maid of Pskov] and Mussorgsky one on Pushkin's *Boris Godunov*; the next year Borodin was attracted by the old Russian epic, *Slovo o polku Igoreve* [The Tale of Igor's Campaign]. And Tchaikovsky began his *Oprichnik*, on a tragedy by Ivan Lazhechnikov, in 1870. All are historical or quasi-historical. *Pskovityanka* was the first to reach the stage (1873); *Boris* had a curious history: it was rejected by the Mariinsky opera committee in 1871, drastically recast, and performed in 1874. Rubinstein also reappeared on the scene with his *Demon*, after Lermontov, which he played over to the Cui–Mussorgsky–

---

[132] The brief last act of this 'national-Russian musical drama' was written by his widow, Valentina Serova, a not totally negligible composer, on the basis of what he had often played to her.

[133] On both points see Gerald Abraham, 'Tchaikovsky's Operas', in *Slavonic and Romantic Music* (London, 1968), 123–6.

[134] *P. Chaykovskiy: Polnoe sobranie sochineniy*, i (*dopolnitel'nïy*) (Moscow, 1953).

[135] The other composers of this never performed opera-ballet were Mussorgsky, Rimsky-Korsakov and Borodin. See Abraham, *On Russian Music* (London, 1939), 91–112.

[136] Higinio Anglès, 'Relations épistolaires entre César Cui et Philippe Pedrell', *Fontes Artis Musicae*, 13/1 (1966), 15.

Ex. 324

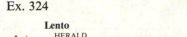

(Hey, where are you, good lads? Make sport for the tsar, our father!)

Rimsky-Korsakov group in 1871; it was produced in 1875. Its pseudo-orientalism (Caucasian) is more successful than that of *Feramors* (Indian), and in *Kupets Kalashnikov* [The Merchant Kalashnikov] (1880), another Lermontov subject, he often draws near to the deeply Russian idiom of the young nationalists, as in the chorus of Kalashnikov's neighbours trying to console him after the rape of his wife by an *oprichnik*, or the herald's proclamation before the fatal fight in the last act (Ex. 324).

The misdeeds of Ivan the Terrible and his dreaded bodyguard had already provided the plot of Tchaikovsky's *Oprichnik*: rape of the heroine and execution of the hero, as in *Kalashnikov*. In *Pskovityanka* the heroine is duly abducted but saved by Ivan's discovery that she is his daughter. In contrast with these melodramatic plots, *Knyaz' Igor'* [Prince Igor] and *Boris Godunov* are as nearly plotless as possible.

BORODIN'S *PRINCE IGOR*

Prince Igor was based on a scenario by V. V. Stasov,[137] long and detailed enough for a *grand opéra*. But Borodin, a distinguished chemist, was constantly distracted by professional and other nonmusical affairs and sometimes cooled towards the project and transferred large blocks of music to other compositions. After his death a performable torso had to be completed by Rimsky-Korsakov and his young disciple Glazunov.[138]

Thus *Igor* is not so much a drama as a series of strikingly original, gorgeously orchestrated tableaux among which the barbaric festival in the Polovtsian camp in Act II is outstanding. Borodin was not incapable of suggesting characters in music: the magnanimous Khan Konchak, Igor's lovesick son, and above all Igor's devoted wife, who has some of the most touching music in the opera and participates in its few passages of genuine drama—but she appears only in Acts I and IV, and briefly in the Prologue.

---

[137] Printed in full in Serge A. Dianin, *Borodin*, trans. Robert Lord (London, 1963), 58.

[138] Glazunov published an account of his stewardship in *Russkaya muzïkal'naya gazeta*, iii (1869), col. 155; translation in Abraham, *On Russian Music*, p. 165.

MUSSORGSKY

Boris Godunov is also essentially a tableau opera but with the difference that Mussorgsky possessed that gift for penetrating and expressing character in which Borodin was weak. And, whereas Igor remains a simple, rather negative figure, Pushkin's play offered a subtle, complicated principal character whose various facets are fully shown even in the original seven-scene version, as well as a far from simple anti-hero, the False-Dmitry. The very first scene shatters the conventions of *grand opéra*; the crowd in the courtyard of the Novodevichy Monastery are not only fragmented like Serov's in *Rogneda*; they are individualized, and bullied by a police officer to make them show enthusiasm they are far from feeling. And in the second, the acclamation of Boris is not brilliantly coloured as in Rimsky-Korsakov's well-intentioned but misguided versions of 1896 and 1908. After two scenes presenting the anti-hero—in the Chudov Monastery where he hears the story of the true Dmitry's murder and gets the idea of his imposture, and in the frontier inn where he escapes from the police officers—Boris is brought forward again, as loving but guilt-ridden father, denounced by a holy simpleton in St Basil's Square in the Kremlin, and dying beside his son to music which, like other passages in *Boris*, he adapted from *Salammbô*.[139] Unfortunately this initial 1872 version of *Boris* underwent a number of changes before performance in 1874, the major ones being a wholesale rewriting of the scene with the Tsar's children, the insertion of two new and musically weak scenes showing the False-Dmitry in Poland wooing an aristocrat who despises him (a lapse into *grand opéra*), and the deletion of the St Basil's scene except for the 'holy simpleton' episode, which was now placed at the end of the opera after a scene in a wood showing peasant anarchy and the passing of the Pretender with his troops. Even when the musical substance is the same in both versions, the carrying out is very different. *Boris* is not a drama in the normal sense in either version but a sequence of dramatic scenes with characters portrayed, except in the Polish act, in music of exceptional power and beauty.[140]

In 1872 Mussorgsky began another opera on a historical subject, *Khovanshchina*, the plot of the Princes Khovansky against the Romanov dynasty, and in 1874 *Sorochinskaya yarmarka* [Sorochintsy Fair], a comic opera based on one of Gogol's stories of peasant life

---

[139] See Abraham, 'The Mediterranean Element in *Boris Godunov*', in *Slavonic and Romantic Music*, p. 188.

[140] The best edition is that edited by David Lloyd-Jones (vocal score, London, 1968; full score, London 1975.)

in the Ukraine, but he died in 1881 with both unfinished.[141] *Khovanshchina* was drastically rewritten and completed by Rimsky-Korsakov,[142] while several composers have tried their hands with *Sorochinskaya yarmarka*. Some of the *Khovanshchina* fragments—the instrumental introduction suggesting dawn in the Red Square, the music associated with Marfa, Shaklovity's aria in Act III, the scene of Golitsïn going into exile—are very fine and there are some powerful melodramatic strokes (for example, the murder of Ivan Khovansky), but the work is non-existent as genuine drama. So, too, is *Sorochinskaya yarmarka* despite some effective comic scenes. As an opera composer Mussorgsky stands, but stands very high, on *Boris Godunov*.

RIMSKY-KORSAKOV

Rimsky-Korsakov's first opera, *Pskovityanka* [The Maid of Pskov] was produced before *Boris* in 1873. Later he became very dissatisfied with it, made a second version in 1878 which was never produced, and a third mainly in 1892. This is the one generally known but it is the original form[143] that must be considered here.[144] Based on a play by Mey, it may be described—like Serov's *Rogneda* and Rubinstein's *Kalashnikov*—as 'Russian *grand opéra*'. (In the later versions Rimsky-Korsakov even borrowed from the grandest of Parisian operas, Berlioz's *Les Troyens*, a 'Chasse royale et orage'.)

Ex. 325

---

[141] *Khovanshchina* is published in *M. Musorgskiy: Polnoe sobranie sochineniy*, ed. Pavel Lamm (Moscow, 1931); *Sorochinskaya yarmarka*, ibid., iii, vi, p. 1 (Moscow, 1933).

[142] This version was published at St Petersburg in 1883 and performed in 1886.

[143] Full score in *N. Rimskiy-Korsakov: Polnoe sobranie sochineniy*, 1a and b, ed. A. N. Dmitriev (Moscow, 1966). Vocal score (St Petersburg, 1872).

[144] For a detailed discussion of all three versions, see Abraham, '*Pskovityanka*: The Original Version of Rimsky-Korsakov's First Opera', *Musical Quarterly*, 54 (1968), 58; reprinted in *Essays on Russian and East European Music*, p. 68.

go   o-din vla-dï- ka,   kak vo e-di-nom sta-de   e- di-nïy pa-stïr'

(Only that realm is vigorous, strong and great where the nation knows it has
one ruler—as in a single flock a single shepherd)

Ex. 326

Unlike Mussorgsky and Tchaikovsky, Rimsky-Korsakov was not a
musical dramatist by nature but in *Pskovityanka* he achieved at least
one passage not too far from *Boris*, that in which Ivan, after looking
back to his love for Olga's mother, reflects on his conception of
regal duty (Ex. 325). And just before, after Olga's abduction, at the
end of Act IV, Scene iv, the curtain has fallen on a long quite
Mussorgskian passage ending (Ex. 326). There are effective reminiscence themes—a harsh one, often heard on trombones in
octaves, characterizing the Tsar, a naïvely beautiful suggestion of
Olga (employed as second subject of the overture), and defiant ones
for her lover and the other young rebels of Pskov. More anticipatory
of Rimsky-Korsakov's later works are the girls' folk-songish
raspberry-gathering chorus in the first scene and Vlasevna's fantastic
'tale of the Tsarevna Lada'. The big choral scene, almost the whole
of Act II, as the people of Pskov await the Tsar, is true *grand opéra*,
but Acts I and II both end with total instrumental etiolation and
the five *pp* bars for strings on which the final curtain falls, however
justified dramatically, are not remotely comparable with the quiet
end of *Boris*. (A *grand-opéra* end was substituted in the version
completed in 1894.)

   If Rimsky-Korsakov sought to rival Mussorgsky in *Pskovityanka*,
the rivalry is even more obvious in his next opera, *Mayskaya noch'*

[May Night], composed in 1879 while his friend was working
on *Sorochinskaya yarmarka*, and based on another Gogol story.
(Tchaikovsky's *Kuznets Vakula* [Vakula the Smith], on 'Christmas
Eve' in the same Gogol collection, had already been produced in
1876.) In *Mayskaya noch'* there is no question of 'drama', only of a
young peasant's love-affair and the tricks played by him and his
friends on the rascally village-elders. The score is light-handed, full
of charming melodies—including at least half-a-dozen borrowings
from authentic Ukrainian folk-music[145]—and the hero's encounter
with *rusalka*s bathing in the moonlight at the beginning of Act III
gave an opportunity for Romantic orchestration (Ex. 327). *Mayskaya
noch'* is a fulfilment of Dargomïzhsky's wish for 'Glinka with national
comedy'.

Ex. 327

[145] Taken from A. I. Rubets, *216 narodnïkh ukrainskikh napevov* (Moscow, 1872; 2nd edn.,
1882).

There is little comedy and no conventional drama in *Snegurochka* [Snowmaiden], composed in 1880. 'Dramatic truth' had gradually ceased to be the watchword. Rimsky-Korsakov based his third opera on a poetic play by Ostrovsky which had been produced in 1873 with incidental music by Tchaikovsky. It is situated in the never-never land of the Berendeys, ruled by a kindly autocrat whose court music is provided by blind *gusli*-players. The characters include both mortals and symbolic figures such as the shepherd Lel who personifies music. The heroine is only apparently mortal; daughter of the Spring Queen and Grandfather Frost, she dies when touched by the rays of the sun god Yarila. The whole work is permeated by ancient Slavonic pantheism and its rites (preserved in Christianized forms down to the nineteenth century); the score is woven from folk-music, lyrical melody, and what it is tempting to call micro themes,[146] and saturated with translucent orchestral colour. *Snegurochka* is a work *sui generis*. Rimsky-Korsakov never attempted to recapture its unique qualities. He composed no more operas for nine years and by then he was a changed man; the performances of the complete *Ring* at St Petersburg by Angelo Neumann's touring 'Richard-Wagner-Theater' in 1889 had opened his mind to new concepts both of orchestration and of opera in general. The great series of works begun with *Mlada* (produced in 1892) belong to another chapter in the history of Russian opera.[147]

TCHAIKOVSKY

The outstanding opera composer, from 1876, when he produced *Kuznets Vakula* [Vakula the Smith], until his death, was Pyotr Il'ich Tchaikovsky (1840–93). As we have seen, his first opera, *Voevoda*, was condemned by himself; his second, *Undine* (comp. 1869), was rejected by the Mariinsky opera committee and never performed; his third, *Oprichnik* (1874), to which he transferred a great deal of the *Voevoda* music, had more success, although in later years he became dissatisfied with this too and tried in vain to forbid its performance. It conforms in every respect to the conventions of *grand opéra*, but the music itself is as Russian as that of *Pskovityanka*, not only borrowing actual folk melodies but employing intensely Russian cantilena as in the melody to which the hero's mother pleads with him (Act II, Scene ii), one of the reminiscence themes of the

---

[146] See the detailed analysis in Nikolaus van Gilse van der Pals, *N. A. Rimsky-Korssakow: Opernschaffen nebst Skizze über Leben und Werken* (Paris and Leipzig, 1929; repr. 1977), 111–62.

[147] See Vol. X, pp. 174–7.

Ex. 328

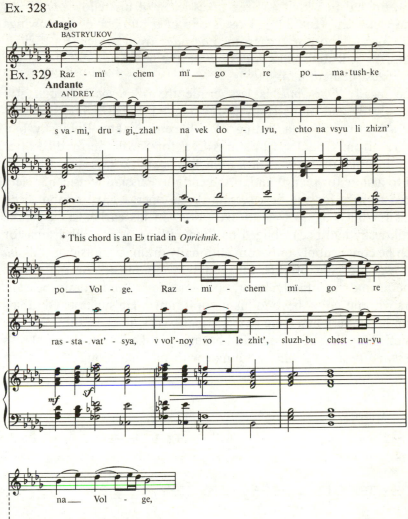

Ex. 329

* This chord is an E♭ triad in *Oprichnik*.

(We banish sorrow on Mother Volga.)
(I'm sorry to leave you, friends, sorry I may not freely live in honorable service celebrating the Tsar.)

opera, or that in which Andrey takes leave of his fellow *oprichniks* in the last scene (Ex. 328). This is one of a number of borrowings Tchaikovsky incorporated from *Voevoda*, from which Ex. 329 is taken. (As in Rubinstein's *Kalashnikov*, the hero is executed and the Tsar seizes the heroine.)

Technically *Oprichnik* is less crude than *Voevoda* though still harmonically and orchestrally heavy-handed, but it is far surpassed by *Vakula*. This was a setting of a libretto Yakov Polonsky had prepared from Gogol's 'Christmas Eve' for Serov. Serov died after making a quantity of sketches (which his widow was able to work up into a suite for piano) and in the end the Russian Musical Society offered a prize for the best setting. Prize operas have seldom been successful but *Vakula* was an exception. In his earlier stage works Tchaikovsky had been obliged to cope with conventional drama for which he could supply only conventionally dramatic music; in *Vakula* there was nothing of this. He could invent music for the village coquette and her manly lover, a comic devil, and comic peasant elders without going beyond his natural range. He suggests Oksana's charm in her very first song (Ex. 330). and very much of the score has the same limpidity of melody and harmony. Like Rimsky-Korsakov's *Mayskaya noch'*, *Vakula* is 'Glinka with national comedy' and the

Ex. 330

(An apple-tree bloomed in the little garden, bloomed but faded; the mother spoiled her daughter, dressed her up and disappeared!)

scene at court where Vakula flies on the devil's back to secure the Empress's 'little boots' (the Ukrainian word is *cherevichki*) gave Tchaikovsky a pretext for a curiously haunting minuet, an early essay in the pseudo-rococo in which he delighted.

Yet, partly because of a poor Oksana, the early performances disappointed the public and Tchaikovsky himself felt his work was 'too clogged with details, too densely orchestrated, too poor in vocal effects'.[148] Accordingly, for a revival in 1878 he made cuts and other changes[149] and in 1885 he undertook a drastic revision in four acts, the fourth being the last scene of the original Act III,[150] which he entitled *Cherevichki*. The action was speeded up by the substitution of recitative for arioso: for example, compare Ex. 331 from *Vakula*

Ex. 331

[148] *P. I. Chaykovskiy—S. I. Taneev: Pis'ma*, ed. Vladimir Aleksandrovich Zhdanov (Moscow, 1951), 11. Two days before, Cui had reported in the *Sanktpeterburgskiya vedomosti* that the music was 'completely beautiful' but 'almost completely melancholy, elegiac, sentimental', ibid., n. 4.

[149] See K. Yu. Davïdova *et al.*, *Muzïkal'noe nasledie Chaykovskogo* (Moscow, 1958), 34–6.

[150] For particulars of the changes, see Abraham, *Slavonic and Romantic Music*, p. 137.

(Odarka! Oh, what marvellous little ornamented boots you have! And new ones!)

Ex. 332

(Odarka! Oh, what marvellous little ornamented boots you have! And new ones!)

with Ex. 332 from *Cherevichki*, a dramatic gain entailing a musical loss. To the end of his life Tchaikovsky considered *Vakula/Cherevichki*, as 'so far as music is concerned, almost my best opera'.[151]

The qualification 'almost' is accounted for by the work that followed the original *Vakula*. A few months after its production Tchaikovsky was discussing possible opera-subjects with the contralto

[151] Letter to his publisher, 2 July 1890. *P. I. Chaykovskiy: Perepiska s P. I. Yurgensonom*, ed. Vladimir Aleksandrovich Zhdanov and Nikolay Timofeevich Zhegin, ii (Moscow, 1952).

Elizaveta Lavrovskaya when she said, 'What about "Evgeny Onegin"?' The idea of an opera on near contemporary, mostly everyday life first struck him as 'wild', but little by little he felt drawn to it, re-read Pushkin's 'novel in verse' and after a sleepless night began to rough out a scenario.[152] Without waiting to prepare a libretto—which he did later with a little help from friends—he set Tatyana's letter to Onegin just as it stands except for lines 11–21 where he substituted two or three sentences in which Tatyana breaks off to consider what she is doing. He was 'in love with the image of Tatyana' and dreaded her impersonation by some veteran of the Mariinsky stage. Actually the part was first taken by Mariya Klimentova, a 23-year-old student at the Moscow Conservatory in 1879, who pleased him by her 'warmth and sincerity'; the first public performance of *Onegin* was also given in Moscow (1881); it reached the Bolshoy at Petersburg only in 1884. Tatyana's letter might almost be described as the *clou* of the whole opera. The instrumental 'writing' figures may be compared with Pimen's in *Boris* and the clerk's in the first scene of *Khovanshchina*; indeed the instrumental share in the scene is as important as Tatyana's and the segments of the recurring horn phrase (an echo of John Field's eleventh Nocturne) which is to rise to the climax of the whole scene, stamps its image on a number of other passages: the end of the quartet (Ex. 333), the end of the Olga–Lensky duet (Ex. 334), most important of all, the letter scene (Ex. 335), Gremin's aria in Act III (Ex. 336), and

Ex. 333   Ex. 334

Ex. 335

Ex. 336

i   mo-lo-dost', da   mo-lo-dost'

(and youth, yes youth)

[152] Translated in Abraham, *Slavonic and Romantic Music*, p. 143.

Ex. 337

(Onegin, in your heart there are both pride and candid honour!)

Tatyana's 'Onegin, in your heart are pride and candid honour' at the end of the opera (Ex. 337).

After *Onegin* Tchaikovsky reacted violently against 'Russianism' with a spectacular work, *Orleanskaya deva*, on a non-Russian subject, Schiller's melodramatic *Jungfrau von Orleans* which existed in a superb translation by Zhukovsky—though, probably influenced by the anglophobia of the period, he replaced Schiller's 'rose-coloured death scene' with her burning by the English. From a musical 'novel in verse' he turned to *grand opéra* in the true Meyerbeerian tradition, but also with hints of contemporary French lyric opera—he greatly admired Gounod's *Faust*; for example, in Act II Agnes Sorel's 'If strength is not given thee' (Ex. 338) and Ioanna's recitative on her presentation to the King (Ex. 339).

Tchaikovsky's next two operas, *Mazepa* (comp. 1881-3; perf.

Ex. 338

(If thou art not given strength to wash away from the fatherland the stain of abasements)

Ex. 339

(I saw you — but only where you were visible to none but God)

1884), based on Pushkin's poem 'Poltava' and introducing some passages from it in Viktor Burenin's libretto, and *Charodeyka* [The Sorceress] (comp. 1885–7; perf. 1887), on a tragedy by Ippolit Shpazhinsky, seem to have been composed because, as he wrote to his publisher, opera was 'now the only form of composition capable of arousing my enthusiasm'.[153] In *Mazepa*, as in *Onegin*, he began in the middle with a scene between the heroine and Mazepa (Act II, Scene ii). But he confessed that he 'felt no particular attraction to the characters',[154] and he lacked the dramatic power to portray the divided character of Mazepa as Mussorgsky portrayed Boris, so that he emerges simply as a villain who occasionally breaks into beautiful music (his arioso in Act I, Scene i; the beginning of Act II, Scene ii). *Mazepa* ends with the heroine going mad over her lover's dead body; its successor, *Charodeyka*, ends with the hero's father going mad after killing his son. It is an absurd melodrama centred on an innkeeper whose beauty bewitches every man who comes her way, a Russian Carmen. But, as Tchaikovsky saw her, 'in the depths of this loose woman's soul there is *moral strength and beauty*',[155] and in his music he equates 'moral strength and beauty' with Russianness. Her music, for instance the song in which she expresses her love for the young prince Yury (Ex. 340), is intensely Russian; indeed the earlier part of the opera, beginning with the folk-song instrumental introduction, is saturated in folk idioms. But the ghost of Gounod appears in the old prince's arioso, 'Net sladu s soboyu' [I cannot master myself] in Act III, and the last three acts as a whole seldom lifted Tchaikovsky's invention above competent commonplace.

[153] *Perepiska s P. I. Yurgensonom*, i (Moscow, 1938), 193.
[154] *P. I. Chaykovskiy: Perepiska s N. F. fon-Mekk*, ed. Vladimir Aleksandrovich Zhdanov and Nikola Timofeevich Zhegin, iii (Moscow and Leningrad, 1936), 62.
[155] Modest Tchaikovsky, *Zhizn' P. I. Chaykovskogo*, iii (Moscow, 1900–2), 38.

Ex. 340

(Everywhere, my darling, hiding from all, I furtively watched thee!)

Pikovaya dama [The Queen of Spades] (comp. and perf. 1890) is another matter. By a curious transference Tchaikovsky identified the weak-willed hero with the tenor Nikolay Figner, for whom he felt intense sympathy, and the libretto—largely by his brother Modest— transformed Hermann from the merely ridiculous figure he cuts in Pushkin's story into a tragic if contemptible one. A number of additional characters are introduced and the transference of the period from the contemporary, as in the story, to the eighteenth century gave Tchaikovsky a pretext for the insertion of any amount of rococo padding: Tomsky's ballade in Act I, and his song, a setting of verses by the eighteenth-century poet Derzhavin, in Act III; the duet for Liza and Polina (on a poem by Zhukovsky) in Act I; the old countess's 'Je crains de lui parler la nuit' (borrowed in its entirety from Grétry's *Richard Cœur de Lion*); and the four-movement interlude 'The Faithful Shepherdess' in Act IV.[156] The opening scene, with the boys playing at soldiers, was probably suggested by the opening scene of *Carmen* with its soldiers and *gamins*. But there are also things in *The Queen of Spades*, notably Plina's romance in Act I, Scene ii, and Liza's 'Akh, istomilas' ya gorem' [I am worn out with grief] before her last meeting with Hermann, that only Tchaikovsky could have written.

There is little of Tchaikovsky's unique invention in his last opera, *Iolanta* (comp. 1891; perf. 1892), which is based on a translation of Henrik Hertz's *Kong Renés Datter*, a dramatic elaboration of a story by Hans Andersen. It is a one-act work commissioned by the Director of the Imperial Theatres to be performed together with a two-act ballet, *Shchelkunchik* [The Nutcracker], on E. T. A. Hoffmann's

[156] On the adaptations from Mozart, Bortnyansky, and others in the interlude, see Abraham, 'Tchaïkovsky's Operas', p. 172.

'Nussknacker und Mausekönig'. Tchaikovsky had already entered the field of full-length ballet with *Lebedinoe ozero* [Swan Lake] (comp. 1875-6; perf. 1877) and *Spyashchaya krasavitsa* [Sleeping Beauty] (comp. 1888-9; perf. 1890). (In *Swan Lake* he borrowed an entr'acte and the opening of the final scene from the condemned *Voevoda* of 1869, and a love duet from the destroyed *Undine*.)[157]

Nutcracker has long been a popular work, but *Iolanta*, which has numerous musical affinities with it, has never—despite various productions in Germany and Scandinavia—won general acceptance. The setting is fifteenth-century Provence, so that French attributes in the music are appropriate, but the influence of French opera first apparent in *Orleanskaya deva* and very much more in *The Queen of Spades* is overwhelming in *Iolanta* despite traces of Tchaikovsky's personal idiom. Rimsky-Korsakov rightly judged it to be 'one of the weakest of Tchaikovsky's works' with 'shameless borrowings' and 'topsyturvy orchestration'.[158]

Ironically, the ghost of Tchaikovsky's very Russian first opera had appeared in 1890. Some years before he had given the libretto to his young friend Anton Arensky (1861-1906) who restored Ostrovsky's original title, *Son na Volge* [Dream on the Volga], and also characters and episodes that Tchaikovsky had excised. Arensky's score is enriched by skilful borrowings from folk-song but his own pleasant invention was not strong enough to establish the work in the repertoire.

POLAND AND MONIUSZKO

The history of Polish opera during the 1830s and 1840s has been described in Chapter III as 'a chronicle of very small beer' and the work which drew a line under that chronicle, Stanisław Moniuszko's *Halka*, emerged only tentatively and gradually in two acts in a concert performance by amateurs at Wilno in 1848, with a stage performance also at Wilno in 1854, and did not reach the Warsaw Opera—drastically rewritten and in three acts—until 1858. Moniuszko (1819-72) had composed more than half a dozen operettas before his masterpiece, but *Halka* aimed higher and immediately established itself as a milestone in Polish operatic history. Włodzimierz Wolski's libretto is melodramatic and the subject is the not unfamiliar one of peasant girl abandoned by aristocratic lover when he wishes to marry into his own class. Halka goes mad and

---

[157] See Vladimir Vasil'evich Protopopov and Nadezhda Vasil'evna Tumanina, *Opernoe tvorchestvo Chaykovskogo* (Moscow, 1957), 48-9 and 52-3.

[158] *Letopis' moey muzïkal'noy zhizni* (5th edn., Moscow, 1935).

drowns herself and her baby after singing to it a lullaby which is one of the most beautiful pages of the score. She is a real character, simple and passionate (as is her faithful peasant lover Jontek), and Moniuszko skilfully embodied her in generally appropriate music. It is sometimes Italianate—he had to remember that his Halka at Warsaw was an Italian, Paulina Rivoli—but on the whole unmistakably Polish (Ex. 341). And the Polish ambience is emphasized in the polonaises, mazurkas, *dumki*, and the *tańce góralskie* [mountaineers' dances] in Act III (Ex. 342).

Ex. 341

(One cannot see how, one cannot see whence, the Sun will rise.)

Ex. 342

MONIUSZKO'S LATER OPERAS

Between the two versions of *Halka* Moniuszko produced two or more operettas for Wilno—*Cyganie* (afterwards renamed *Jawnuta*) and *Bettly* (on a translation of the Scribe-Melesville *Le Châlet*, first composed by Adolphe Adam and later in an Italian version by Donizetti)—and after *Halka* the Warsaw Opera also wanted a one-act work. He quickly composed *Flis* [The Raftsman], a pleasant peasant comedy in which the heroine is in danger of being forced to marry a fop from Warsaw instead of her raftsman lover. (Like Halka, Zosia was sung by Rivoli who was again provided with unsuitable coloratura.) She is saved by the discovery that the fop is the raftsman's long-lost brother, who gladly resigns her.

Moniuszko's second major work was a Romantic comedy, *Hrabina* [The Countess] (1860), set in the period of the Napoleonic Grand Duchy of Warsaw. The hero is a young lancer officer, just returned from the Peninsular War, who nearly falls into the embrace of the beautiful eponymous young Countess. The third act is set in the country house where Kazimierz has gone to the girl he really loves, the Countess's protégée Bronia, and where the Countess follows him. Two melodies from this act give an idea of Moniuszko's characterization: the song in which Bronia tells how the chance mention of Kazimierz's name when he was in Spain would bring tears to her eyes (Ex. 343), and the Countess's pretended surprise at finding him at Bronia's home (Ex. 344).

Yet another soldier returned from the wars is the hero of the one-act *Verbum nobile* [A Nobleman's Word] (1861). Two old

Ex. 343

Gdy mi kto z bo-ku wspom-ni Ka-żmie-rza, łez na-gle w o - ku po-tok u - de - rza

(When someone mentions Kazimierz to me in passing, then all at once a stream
breaks forth in my eye)

Ex. 344

Ah! *quelle sur-pri-se!*   co za spo-tka-nie!   i cóż wy - ró - wna ra - do - ści mej

(Ah! what a surprise! What an encounter! and what is equal to my joy)

gentlemen have long ago pledged their words that one's son shall
marry the other's daughter; now the young couple, unknown to each
other, have met by chance and fallen in love. But the hero, Michał,
has stupidly and incomprehensibly told Zuzia that his name is
Stanisław. Her father has given his *verbum nobile*, his word as
nobleman, that she shall marry no one but Michał and even the
revelation that Michał and Stanisław are the same is no immediate
solution, for her father has now given his *verbum nobile* that she
shall never marry 'Stanisław'. However Zuzia's ingenuity solves the
problem and all, of course, ends happily. For this piece of nonsense—
Moniuszko was unlucky in his librettists—the composer supplied
delightful sparkling music with serious, but not too serious, treatment
of the lovers' plight. (He replaced his original setting of Zuzia's sad
dumka with a less passionate and elaborate one.)

Moniuszko's real masterpiece of comedy was the four-act *Straszny
dwór* [The Haunted Chateau] (1865) which has two heroes, brothers
who, like Kazimierz in *Hrabina* and Michał in *Verbum nobile*, are
yet again soldiers just back from a war. They also are bound by a
pledge: they have sworn never to marry lest they should fall under
feminine domination. But they visit the chateau of their dead father's
friend, who has two daughters—with the inevitable consequence.
The chateau has the reputation of being haunted and the two lively
girls contrive some haunting, with pictures that come to life and a
mysterious chiming clock. The heroes are for a time slightly less
than heroic but they happily surrender their independence in the
end. *Straszny dwór* offers plenty of opportunities of national colour,
comedy, and vocal display—the part of Hanna, one of the sisters,
is a terrific coloratura role—but Moniuszko could also strike a more

serious note, as in Stefan's midnight vigil when the carillon of the clock plays an old polonaise tune reminding him how in childhood his blood used to be fired when in their family circle their father sang to him or Zbigniew 'that Sarmatian song' (Ex. 345).

Ex. 345

(O God! That melody reminds me of such a time as fires the blood in my breast!
So often did my father in our family circle, teaching me or Zbigniew, his elder son,
how to wield the wooden broad sword, hum that Sarmatian tune!)

After *Straszny dwór* Moniuszko accomplished little of note. He worked on the three-act *Parja*, based on Casimir Delavigne's tragedy *Le Paria*, from time to time for ten years until it was produced in 1869, but the subject, the Portuguese in fifteenth-century India, was foreign to him in every sense. It was a complete failure, as was the one-act operetta *Beata*, performed in 1872 just before his death.[159]

MONIUSZKO'S SUCCESSORS

Polish operas of the post-Moniuszko period were not particularly distinguished. The best comic ones were the *Paziowie królowej Marysienki* [Queen Mary's Pages] (1864) of Stanisław Duniecki (1839–70) and *Duch Wojewody* [The Spirit of the Voivode] (1873) by Ludwik Grossman (1833–1915). (Duniecki also embarked (*c.*1866–70) on a 'great Slavonic opera', taking its subject from the medieval Russian epic of *Igor* [Igor's Campaign], but completed only one act.) More important are the *Mazepa* (1876), *Mindowe* (1880), and *Jadwiga, królowa polska* [Jadwiga, Queen of Poland] (1886) of Moniuszko's pupil, Henryk Jarecki (1846–1918), who directed opera at Lwów from 1872 onwards, and the first opera of Władysław Żeleński (1837–1921), *Konrad Wallenrod* (1885), after the poem by Mickiewicz from which he borrowed a number of passages in the libretto. Żeleński was musically the most gifted composer of that generation— but not dramatically. And in the case of *Konrad Wallenrod* he was not helped by the lack of dramatic action. The result was a belated historical *grand opéra*, eclectic in musical style. Yet he has been hailed as 'the standard-bearer of the Moniuszko tradition'

equally in the national subject of the opera and in the similar approach to the problem of text/music (melody as the point of reference to which the text is moulded) and also in the connection with Polish folklore. From this point of view the libretto of *Konrad Wallenrod* did not offer major possibilities . . . nevertheless in some passages we already find stylisation of folk-melodies (the ballet in Act III) and even quotations ('Święty Boże' in the second scene of Act IV).[160]

CZECHOSLOVAKIA

The history of Czech opera was markedly different. Bohemia lost her independence two centuries earlier than Poland, at a time when opera existed only as princely entertainment in half a dozen Italian cities; the numerous Czech musicians of European repute were

---

[159] On Moniuszko's later operas, see Abraham, 'The Operas of Stanisław Moniuszko', in *Essays on Russian and East European Music*, pp. 160 ff.

[160] Włodzimierz Poźniak, in *Z dziejów polskiej kultury muzycznej*, ii (Kraków, 1966), 284.

instrumental performers and composers, while the Bohemian aristocracy gravitated to Vienna and became German-speaking. The vernacular operas of František Škroup and others were all, except Škroup's naïve *Drátenik* [The Tinker], complete failures.

Škroup himself turned to German opera and scored a modest success with *Der Meergeuse* on the Dutch 'sea beggars' of the 1570s (1851). The four-act *Vladimír, bohů zvolenec* [Vladimir, God's Chosen One] of František Skuherský (1830–92)[161] was, like his later operas, originally composed to a German libretto but was translated in time to appear in 1863 as the first new Czech work to be given in the Prague Provisional Theatre. Then Karel Šebor (1843–1903) produced a series of operas: *Templáři na Moravě* [The Templars in Moravia] (1865), *Drahomír* (1867), *Husitská nevěsta* [The Hussite Bride] (1868, but later rewritten), which introduced the Hussite hymn familiar from Smetana's use of it, and *Zmařená svatba* [The Ruined Wedding] (1879), which the conservative Old Czech Party vainly hoped would overshadow Smetana's *Prodaná nevěsta*. But Šebor's bent was for *grand opéra*, not scenes from popular life. Bedřich Smetana (1824–84) essayed both in two operas produced in 1866: *Braniboři v Čechách* [The Brandenburgers in Bohemia] (5 January) and *Prodaná nevěsta* [The Bartered Bride] (30 May).[162]

SMETANA

The action of *Braniboři* passes in late thirteenth-century Prague when Bohemia had a temporary Prussian ruler; the Prussians and Bohemian Germans are the villains. Yet it is, ironically, in some respects a late 'German Romantic opera' employing not very striking reminiscence themes and a Lisztian musical idiom. And, final irony, Smetana (like all well-to-do Czechs of the time) had been brought up to speak and write German; he was never sure of Czech grammar or pronunciation, so that the original libretto of *Braniboři* had sometimes to be altered to fit the music. But, whereas *Braniboři* enjoyed only short-lived success, *The Bartered Bride*, after a doubtful start, quickly became popular in its native land and, after translation into German by Brahms's biographer Max Kalbeck in 1892, all over the world. The original *The Bartered Bride* was in two acts with spoken dialogue; in 1869 new numbers, including the polka, were inserted and later in the same year the first act was divided into two

---

[161] The subject is an episode in ninth-century Bulgarian history. Smetana wrote a severely critical notice on the first performance in *Národní listy* (3 Jan. 1865), reprinted in V. H. Jarka (ed.), *Kritické dílo Bedřicha Smetany, 1858–65* (Prague, 1948), 147.

[162] On Smetana's operas generally, see Brian Large, *Smetana* (London, 1970), and John Clapham, *Smetana* (London, 1972).

and more dances were added; finally in 1870 Smetana replaced the
spoken dialogue with recitative.[163] Very little of the music employs
actual folk material—the furiant near the beginning of Act II, partly
based on the tune 'Sedlák, sedlák, sedlák' is an exception—for
Smetana considered quotation, even imitation, of folk-song as skin-
deep nationalism; but the whole score has, as he justly claimed in a
notebook entry (23 April 1864), 'a completely *národní* [national or
popular] character', though he might have admitted some influence
from Gounod's *Faust* which he, like Tchaikovsky, greatly admired.[164]
But even when he borrows a folk melody, as in the Furiant (Ex.
346), he soon introduces a touch of his personal magic. The
'vivacissimo' overture is a perfect comedy overture and, while the
comedy is nearly reduced to farce by the stuttering character Vašek,
it is raised well above it by the charm of Mařenka's music. Their
juxtaposition in their Act I duet is piquant.

   In his next two operas, *Dalibor* and *Libuše*, Smetana abandoned
the librettist of *Braniboři* and *The Bartered Bride*, Karel Sabina, and
found a new collaborator in the German Josef Wenzig, whose texts
had to be translated. *Dalibor* (1868) is a tragic counterpart to

Ex. 346

[163] For a full account of the various versions, see Abraham, 'The Genesis of *The Bartered
Bride*', *Slavonic and Romantic Music*, p. 28.

[164] After one performance he is reported to have said, 'That's fabulous. I've only one wish:
sometime to write something like it.' See František Bartoš, *Smetana ve vzpomínkách a dopisech*
(Prague, 1939), p. 69.

Braniboři. The fifteenth-century hero is condemned to life-imprisonment—and, later, death—for trying to avenge the execution of his friend, the musician Janko (changed after the composer's death to Zdeněk). In an attempt to rescue him the heroine Milada disguises herself as a boy and penetrates his prison, but unlike Leonora/Fidelio she fails and the opera ends tragically. Smetana here develops the musico-dramatic technique of *Braniboři* but with more use of reminiscence themes so that these nearly become true leitmotifs; the one first heard when the curtain rises—as in *Braniboři*, there is no overture—reappears again and again in numerous Lisztian metamorphoses.[165] And Milada and the jailer Beneš converse in Act II over a play of motifs (Ex. 347), like characters in *Meistersinger* (which was performed a month after *Dalibor*).

Libuše is similar in style but different in nature. It was completed in 1872 but set aside first for the celebration of the expected coronation of the Emperor Franz Josef as king of Bohemia, then for the also cancelled wedding of the Archduke Rudolf, and at last performed in 1881 for the official opening of the National Theatre, by which time the composer was stone deaf. As Smetana himself wrote some years later, '*Libuše* is not an *opera* in the old manner but a *festive tableau*.'[166] The legendary Czech princess had already been the heroine of a number of plays and operas, including

---

[165] Some of which are shown in Clapham, *Smetana*, p. 97.
[166] Bartoš, *Smetana*, p. 221.

Ex. 347

(MILADA: Eat and drink; help yourself, do!
BENEŠ: I get great pleasure from you when
I look at you like this, my lad.)

můj,   když tě tak zřím,

Grillparzer's *Libussa*. She took as her husband a peasant farmer,
Přemysl, and pointed out to the Czech chieftains the site on which
they were to build a fortress city, Prague. Dramatic action is slow
and limited mainly to the quarrels of rivals. The work is crowned
by 'Libuše's prophecy', a series of six tableaux representing episodes
of Czech history: the fourth, the Hussites, naturally introduces their
hymn, 'Kdož jste Boží bojovníci' [You who are God's Warriors],
which continues through the fifth and sixth, in the last of which,
showing the royal castle of Prague, the Hradčany, the entire company
echoes Libuše's affirmation, 'The Czech nation is imperishable; it
will survive the horrors of hell!' The score tends to be static and
monumental; even the plentiful combinations of leitmotifs have no
polyphonic vitality. But Přemysl has some fine lyrical monologues
and his address to his loved lime-trees in the second scene of Act II
is accompanied by unmistakably Wagnerian 'forest murmurs'.

Dvě vdovy [The Two Widows] (1874), based by a new librettist,
Emanuel Züngel, on Félicien Mallefille's one-act farce *Les Deux
Veuves*, is a total contrast: a charming light-handed 'number opera',
originally with only four characters and spoken dialogue. But in
1876 Smetana had the libretto revised, replaced the spoken dialogue
with recitative, and added two new characters, a peasant couple who
join in a newly composed finale to Act I and a new trio in Act II.
This second version was produced in 1878. In it, he wrote in 1882,
he had 'combined salon elegance with tenderness and refinement'.[167]
Smetana's melodic invention is here at its best, though characteristically it is often shown in the orchestral writing as much
as in the vocal part it is supposed to 'accompany'. The music in

Ex. 348

[167] Ibid., p. 197.

(Love — powerful, noble, ardent, even crazy — led me here; now I'm a prisoner here,
I want to flee but cannot.)

which Ladislav confesses to one widow his love for the other is typical (Ex. 348).

The original form of *Dvě vdovy* was the last opera composed by Smetana before, in October 1874, his deafness became total. Yet he produced three more: *Hubička* [The Kiss] (1882), *Tajemství* [The Secret] (1878), and *Čertova stěna* [The Devil's Wall] (1882), all with librettos by Eliška Krásnohorská. There is nothing in *Hubička* to suggest any aural handicap; this peasant comedy is one of his finest scores. Indeed he himself considered the heroine's meditation in Act I (Ex. 349) 'decidedly the most beautiful passage in my dramatic works, whether as regards most perfect fusion of words and melody or, in the orchestral accompaniment, most complete truthfulness of the melancholy mood that dominates the deserted Vendulka's soul'.[168] Another favourite of his was Vok's aria near the end of

[168] Ibid., p. 140.

Ex. 349

(How should I forget the lovely time when the moon saw us together, then under the alder in the dusky valley!)

Act I of *Čertova stěna*, 'which always *carries me away* when I sing it inwardly ... it always moves me to tears'.[169]

These last two works show no decline in technical accomplishment; indeed the leitmotif technique is developed even further and the theme of the 'secret' in *Tajemství* in various transformations permeates much of the score. But there is a decided falling off in inspiration.

SMETANA'S CONTEMPORARIES

Operas by Smetana's younger contemporaries include the one-act *V studni* [In the Well] by the somewhat Mendelssohnian Vilém Blodek

[169] Ibid., p. 175.

(1834–74), with a libretto in which Sabina vainly tried to repeat the success of *The Bartered Bride*. And he tried again in the *Starý ženich* [The Old Bridegroom] (1882), composed by Dvořák's friend Karel Bendl (1838–97). Bendl's gifts lay in the direction of big French opera, as he showed in his first work, the five-act *Lejla* (1868) on a libretto by Krásnohorská, though he made at least one essay in nationalism, the tragic Hussite opera *Dítě Tábora* [A Child of Tábor] (comp. 1888; prod. 1892), also on a Krásnohorská text. Rather younger was Vojtěch Hřimalý (1842–1908) whose comic opera *Zakletý princ* [The Bewitched Prince] appeared in 1872 and kept a place in the repertoire for several years.

DVOŘÁK

Though far more gifted than any of these, Antonín Dvořák (1841–1904) began his operatic career with a number of false starts: a Wagnerian 'heroic opera', *Alfred*, on a German libretto by Körner (comp. 1870 but never produced in his lifetime), and *Král a uhlíř* [King and Charcoal-burner] (comp. 1871), which he suppressed after rehearsal making an entirely new setting of Bernard Lobeský's feeble libretto three years later; even this was not very successful and Dvořák composed Act III afresh in 1887. For the comic one-act *Tvrdé palice* [The Pig-headed Ones] (comp. 1874) he had a better text (by Josef Štolba), but before it was performed in 1881 he had tried his hand with a five-act tragic opera, *Vanda*, to an appallingly bad libretto on a subject from Polish myth-history. It was not until the comic two-act *Šelma sedlák* [The Rascally Peasant], with a libretto by J. O. Veselý (1878) that Dvořák scored some success. Essentially an instrumental composer, his voice parts had tended to be moulded to the orchestral underlay; now he composed for the voice first and foremost. But he was still fatally drawn to *grand opéra* and in *Dimitrij* (1882) he returned to it. Based on the historical events that followed the death of Boris Godunov, *Dimitrij* had a good libretto by Marie Červinková-Riegrová, largely on Schiller's unfinished *Demetrius*. Dimitrij and Xenie both have leitmotifs which are heard immediately at the beginning of the overture: his, powerful and doom-laden, on the strings; hers, gentle and submissive, on the oboe echoed by the bassoon. But the opera is most memorable for its massive choral scenes, for example the opening double chorus in the Kremlin square, one body hailing Boris's son as tsar, the other supporting the pretender Dimitrij (Ex. 350).

It was only in *Jakobín* (1889) that Červinková gave Dvořák a totally congenial subject: a simple tale set in a late eighteenth-century

Ex. 350

(I: Glory to Tsar Fyodor, mighty monarch.
II: What do we want with Godunovs? What do we want with tyrants?
Dmitry is the true son of Ivan.)

village where the typically Czech musician–schoolmaster is a secondary hero. The eponymous hero is a one-time Jacobin who returns with wife and child to the Count his father, who has disowned him. A most effective dramatic stroke is the pianissimo singing of a lullaby by the ex-Jacobin's wife (Ex. 351), overheard by her father-in-law. It is the lullaby that had been sung to his own baby son and it melts his heart. The whole score is rich in pure Dvořákian melody and colourful orchestration, handled with that unobtrusive technical mastery which so impressed Brahms.

FIBICH AND KOVAŘOVIC

Dvořák wrote no more operas for ten years,[170] but two notable talents came to the fore during the last quarter of the century: Zdeněk Fibich (1850–1900) and his pupil Karel Kovařovic (1862–1920). Kovařovic's first opera was *Ženichové* [The Bridegrooms] (1884) and he made a strong impression with the one-act *Cesta oknem* [The Way through the Window] (1885), for which Züngel, as in *Dvě vdovy*, went back to a French original, this time by Scribe and Lemoine. But Kovařovic's masterpiece came later, the tragic *Psohlavci* [The Dog-heads] (1898), on a historical novel by Alois Jirásek.[171]

[170] See Vol. X, p. 177.
[171] On *Psohlavci*, see Rosa Newmarch, *The Music of Czechoslovakia* (London, 1942), 178.

Ex. 351

(Little son, my flower, my happiness, my world, my heaven!)

Fibich was a more important figure; indeed Czech critics have hailed him as the third figure among the creators of their native opera. Unlike his compatriots, he had studied in Leipzig, Paris, and Mannheim, come under the influence of Weber and Wagner, and composed three unpreserved operas. His first Czech opera, *Bukovín* (1874), on a weak Sabina libretto, was heavily influenced by *Freischütz* though the second act duet for Dobka and Bukovín has a slightly Wagnerian flavour (Ex. 352).

For his next work, *Blaník*, Krásnohorská gave him a better poem. He was now familiar with mature Wagner and *Blaník* shows the consequences: leitmotifs, a very large orchestra, Wagnerian harmony, and polyphony with triple theme combinations, as in the finale of Act II and introduction to Act III. *Nevěsta Messinská* [The Bride of Messina] (1884), the libretto by Otakar Hostinský on Schiller's *Braut von Messina*, is still more Wagnerian, arguably more Wagnerian than any earlier opera not by Wagner himself. The funeral march for Manuel at the end of Act III, Scene iv (Ex. 353) is very impressive. Yet after this fine work Fibich abandoned opera for eleven years and turned to the composition of *melodramy*, spoken plays with

Ex. 352

(Moment of joy, moment of love)

Ex. 353

orchestral accompaniment,[172] before returning to opera with *Bouře* (1895), a version of Shakespeare's *Tempest*, and other works which may not unfairly be described as a reaction from Wagner to Smetana and Dvořák.

[172] See Vol. X, pp. 177–9.

HUNGARY

The Hungarian opera composers who had come to the fore during the 1840s, Erkel, Thern, and Ferenc Doppler, were still active during the next half-century and were soon joined by another master, Mihály Mosonyi (1814–70). The leader was still Erkel, who collaborated with the Doppler brothers, Ferenc and Károly, Poles by birth, in *Erzsébet* (1857), and equalled the success of *Hunyadi László* with another historical work, *Bánk Bán* [The Palatine Bánk] (comp. 1852; perf. 1861), which Béni Egressy, the librettist of *Hunyadi*, based on a tragedy by József Katona set in 1213. In the absence of Andrew II, his evil queen Gertrud and her relatives have offended the nobility and oppressed the serfs; the final crime is the violation of Melinda, wife of Bánk, the ousted palatine of the southern marches, by the queen's brother; Bánk rebels and kills the queen. One of the finest passages of the opera is the opening of Act III, where Melinda, delirious and fleeing with her child and the old attendant Tiborc, is held up on the bank of the flooded river Tisza (with two pipe-playing boatmen) while a storm approaches. She sings to the child (Ex. 354).

Erkel never achieved equal success with his later works. After *Bánk Bán* he attempted comic opera in *Sarolta* (1862) but returned to historical tragedy in the five-act *Dózsa György* (libretto by Ede Szigligeti after Mór Jókai) (1867), in which he may have had the collaboration of his youngest son, Sándor (1846–1900).[173] Here he

Ex. 354

---

[173] Sándor Erkel produced an opera of his own, *Csobáncz*, in 1865, but he was primarily a conductor.

an - gya-lom te, an - gya-lom te! Ál - modj sze-li-den, é - des - de-den.... an - gya-lom ah, an - gya-lom ah!

(Dream calmly, sweetly, my angel!)

turned away from the set numbers of his earlier works in favour of continuous music and recitative in a style compounded of Hungarian folk declamation, Italianate recitative, and Wagnerian speech melody. The hero was the leader of a sixteenth-century peasant revolt crushed by the nobles who tortured him to death by crowning him with a red-hot crown while seated on a red-hot throne. *Brankovics György* (1874) was another historical work, based on the treachery of the eponymous Despot of Serbia, Djordje Branković—whence the introduction of Serbian melodies—which led to the defeat and capture of János Hunyadi (the father of László) at Kossovo in 1448. Here the Hungarian element in his declamation is more marked, as it is also in the lighter and more popular *Névtelen hősök* [Nameless Heroes] (1880), which celebrates the soldiers of the 1848 war for independence. His last work, *István király* [King Stephen] (1885), celebrating the triumph of Hungary's first king, was his most nearly Wagnerian; intended for the inauguration of the Pest Opera House in 1884, it was completed too late.

After Károly Doppler's *A gránátos tábor* [The Grenadiers' Camp], with spoken dialogue, and Ferenc's *A két huszár* [The Two Hussars] (both 1853), the brothers left Hungary and contributed no more to opera there. The only notable works other than Erkel's were two by Mosonyi and the *Zrínyi* (after Körner) (1868) of Ágost Adelburg

(1830–73). Mosonyi was the most uncompromisingly nationalistic composer of the period, basing his style on *verbunkos*. His *Szép Ilonka* [Pretty Ilonka] after Vörösmarty (1861) is a charming fantasy but his Romantic, heroic *Álmos*, composed in 1862, was never performed in his lifetime.

(e) BRITAIN AND THE UNITED STATES

By NICHOLAS TEMPERLEY

BRITISH OPERA

Changing conditions in London were not particularly favourable to the continuing development of English opera. The 1843 Act for Regulating Theatres had taken away the monopoly on Italian opera hitherto enjoyed by Her Majesty's Theatre, allowing Covent Garden to open in 1847 as a rival 'Royal Italian Opera' and soon surpass the older house in prestige and success. At the same time, the two 'patent theatres', Drury Lane and Covent Garden, lost their monopoly for 'legitimate drama' (spoken plays), which allowed the 'minor' theatres to give up their practice of disguising plays as burlettas by the addition of a few songs. Thus both Italian opera and spoken drama were assisted by the new law; English opera, inevitably, suffered.

Special efforts were needed, therefore, to consolidate the success of the English romantic opera school, and various schemes were brought forward during the rest of the nineteenth century. The most successful was the company formed in 1857 by Louisa Pyne and William Harrison. It kept the flag flying with annual commissions of new operas by Balfe, Wallace, and others. After the first two seasons it found a home at Covent Garden as the Royal English Opera. Its winter season of English operas alternated with the Royal Italian Opera in the summer, until its demise in 1864.

One of the triumphs of the Pyne–Harrison company was *The Lily of Killarney* (Covent Garden, 1862) by Julius Benedict (1804–85), the German-born pupil of Weber who had been resident in Britain for more than thirty years and had produced several Italian and English operas earlier in his career. It was an adaptation of Dion Boucicault's already very successful play *The Colleen Bawn*, set in Ireland, and in a tragic mode. It can be called the first Irish nationalist opera. The story has no political overtones, but Benedict's music, especially for the humbler characters, deliberately evokes that nostalgia for old Ireland whose musical conventions had been established by Moore's *Irish Melodies*. Several themes are pentatonic, including the sinister 'murder' motif (anticipated in the overture) as well as such purely decorative melodies as the boatsmen's chorus, 'Across the Broad Waters 'tis Pleasant to Row'.[174] Benedict could write as good a ballad as anyone, and he could also produce extended scenes of dramatic tension, such as the Act II finale. The scene for the hunchback servant Danny Mann, wrestling with conflicting feelings of devotion to his master and love for his master's wife, is especially powerful.

MACFARREN

Another opera commissioned by Pyne–Harrison was *She Stoops to Conquer* (Covent Garden, 1864) by George Alexander Macfarren (1813–87). Macfarren also had a long career in English opera behind him, including an early success at the English Opera House, *The Devil's Opera* (1838), with a libretto by his father, an established dramatist. But Macfarren was a composer of a different stamp from the Balfe–Wallace school. His gifts were intellectual rather than lyrical. Endowed with a deep reverence for the Viennese classics by his teacher, Cipriani Potter, he generally avoided the pervasive Italian and French influences, modelling himself on Mozart.[175] He also possessed a strong feeling for English literature and history, and in his later years particularly he set out to forge a style of opera that was really English in character, tending to choose subjects drawn from English history or literature, to draw on folk idioms as one element in his musical style, and to pay careful attention to word setting. This last point is illustrated in Ex. 355, from *Don Quixote* (Drury Lane, 1846), where Don Quixote replies to an aggressive challenge ('Who art thou?') by Camacho and the chorus that forms the end of the preceding section of spoken dialogue.

In short Macfarren was the unrecognized founder of the English school of nationalist opera, as Benedict was of the Irish. Tendencies in this direction are already to be seen in *King Charles II* (Princess's, 1849) and *Robin Hood* (Her Majesty's, 1860). In the latter work, the

[174] A good example of a folklike, though not consistently pentatonic, song from *The Lily of Killarney* is quoted by Michael Hurd, 'Opera: 1834–1865', in Nicholas Temperley (ed.), *Music in Britain: The Romantic Age 1800–1914* (London, 1981), 328.

[175] Henry Charles Banister, *George Alexander Macfarren: His Life, Works and Influence* (London, 1891), 221–3. See also Nicholas Temperley, 'Musical Nationalism in English Romantic Opera,' in Temperley (ed.), *The Lost Chord: Essays on Victorian Music* (Bloomington, 1989).

Ex. 355

Act II finale illustrates Macfarren's experienced sense of the theatre, as well as his penchant both for learned musical devices evoking the past (the 'round dance' is on a ground bass; the Sompnour's plainsong-like chanting is combined with lively dialogue over a dance rhythm) and for modal references to English folk-music.

LATER ROMANTIC OPERAS

The Romantic school continued in the next generation with such works as *Pauline* (Lyceum, 1876) by Frederic Cowen (1852–1935); *Esmeralda* (Drury Lane, 1883), by Arthur Goring Thomas (1850–92); *Colomba* (Drury Lane, 1883), by Alexander Mackenzie (1847–1935); *Ivanhoe* (Royal English Opera House, 1891), by Arthur Sullivan (1842–1900); and *Shamus O'Brien* (Opéra-Comique, 1896), by Charles Villiers Stanford (1852–1924). The basic traditions of the school were maintained, with the simple strophic ballad never entirely superseded, but with more ambitious connected scenes added, and with new influences coming from the Continent—first of Gounod and Verdi, then of early Wagner, whose *Der fliegende Holländer* [The Flying Dutchman], *Tannhäuser*, and *Lohengrin* had been introduced to London audiences (in Italian) in the 1870s.[176] *Ivanhoe*, though ultimately a failure, excited great interest during its one season; it is Sullivan's most ambitious score and a rare example of a through-composed Victorian opera. *Shamus O'Brien* takes up Benedict's vein of Irish nationalism, in which Stanford was becoming something of a specialist, and this time with political connotations: the story is set in the context of the Irish rebellion of 1798.

---

[176] The *Dutchman* was given in English in 1846, *Lohengrin* in 1880, *Tannhäuser* in 1882. *The Ring* cycle in German had to await the visit of Angelo Neumann's Richard-Wagner-Theater in 1882, in which year the earlier operas were also performed in German.

COMIC OPERA

Comic opera in the 1850s and 1860s was largely dominated by Parisian *opéra bouffe* and operetta. The only native English type of any consequence was burlesque, and here the leading figure was the librettist F. C. Burnand, who produced a series of 'hearty, rumbustious entertainments' at the Royalty and Royal Strand theatres.[177] In some cases the music was merely cobbled together by an anonymous hack, but *Windsor Castle* (Royal Strand, 1865) had a respectable score by Frank Musgrave, who also collaborated with Burnand in *L'Africaine; or the Queen of the Cannibal Islands* (1865) and *Der Freischütz; or A Good Cast for a Piece* (1866). The success of these shows depended on satire of *grand opéra*, topical jokes, puns, sexual humour and extravaganza; the music, though indispensable, had to be quite undemanding.

The beginnings of a more significant form of light opera were planted by Thomas German Reed (1817–88) and his wife Priscilla Horton (1818–95), who in 1855 started a new type of entertainment; from 1856 they used the Gallery of Illustration, Marylebone. The 'German Reed Entertainments' appealed to a large new public by providing respectable and innocuous pleasure in a building that was not a theatre, and was thus free of the disreputable associations that kept a large section of the Victorian public away from theatres and opera-houses. The Reeds commissioned chamber operas on a small scale, designated *opera di camera*, for singers of modest accomplishments, generally accompanied on a piano and a harmonium. Two such were *Jessy Lea* (1863) and *The Soldier's Legacy* (1864) by Macfarren. The situation suited Macfarren's particular gifts and tastes; he was relieved of the normal need to appeal to a 'gallery' of unsophisticates who only wanted amorous ballads, heroic crowd scenes, or low humour. He could deal here with a limited number of characters, in a good English story made up of credible situations, and could use his not inconsiderable powers to develop them musically: for instance in the catty duet 'You wicked gipsy girl' (*Jessy Lea*). In one scene from *The Soldier's Legacy* the character keeps trying to recall a tune he knows; when at last it appears, it is indeed a reminiscence (no doubt unconscious) of the slow movement of Mozart's Piano Trio in E major, K 542, which happens to have a pentatonic first phase. Macfarren's 'folk-song' idiom was erected on a foundation of Classical style, whereas Vaughan Williams was to base his on the style of the sixteenth century. (Neither conjunction

[177] A good account of burlesque in this period is Andrew Lamb, 'Music of the Popular Theatre', in Temperley (ed.) *Music in Britain: The Romantic Age*, pp. 92–108.

has any special historical authenticity, but each is valid if artistically successful.)

SULLIVAN

By far the most successful English operas in this period, of course, were Sullivan's comic operas, and here the German Reeds had played an early part, for they commissioned *The Contrabandista* (1867) and revived *Cox and Box* (1869), Sullivan's first comic stage pieces (with librettos by Burnand), as well as some of W. S. Gilbert's early efforts. From the start, Gilbert and Sullivan both set themselves against the *risqué* humour of burlesque and French operetta and hence could win and hold the affections of the middle-class Victorian public. The famous pair came together in *Thespis* (Gaiety, 1871), but it was a failure and the music is lost.

The great series of Gilbert and Sullivan operas or operettas began with the one-act, all-sung *Trial by Jury*, commissioned by Richard D'Oyly Carte for the Royalty Theatre and performed there in 1875 (as a curtain-raiser to Offenbach's *La Périchole*). Its success induced D'Oyly Carte to form a syndicate to produce Gilbert and Sullivan operas, first at the Opéra-Comique, then, after 1881, at his own theatre, the Savoy. From this the name 'Savoy Operas' has become attached to the series of eleven collaborations, of which the most famous are *HMS Pinafore* (Opéra-Comique, 1878), *The Pirates of Penzance* (Royal Bijou, Paignton, 1879), *Patience* (Opéra-Comique, 1881), *Iolanthe* (Savoy, 1882), *The Mikado* (Savoy, 1885), *The Yeomen of the Guard* (Savoy, 1888), and *The Gondoliers* (Savoy, 1889).[178]

There is much to link these works to the past history of English opera—the spoken dialogue interspersed with musical numbers; the custom of including two or three strophic ballads and one glee or 'madrigal' in each work; the *mélodrame*; other standard numbers, such as the chorus of maidens beginning the second act; and so on. Sullivan, however, had had the benefit of a more thorough and more German training than most of his operatic predecessors. He could command technical resources that they lacked, and the detectable influence of Mendelssohn may have reinforced, for many Victorians, the reassuring propriety of Gilbert's librettos. Sullivan had also imbibed something of Schubert's techniques, most notably the felicitous use of remote modulations.

The wide appeal and unique staying power of these masterpieces is in no way lessened by their very clear association with a particular

---

[178] Miniature full score, ed. David Lloyd-Jones (London, Paris, and New York, 1984).

time and place. It has often been pointed out that Gilbert and Sullivan were temperamental opposites. Each modified the other's psychology towards compatibility with his own; the result was not a bland compromise, but a meeting ground in which dynamic tension continued to flourish. Gilbert's biting wit, shown in unadulterated form in the spoken dialogue, treats emotion as something to be observed, analysed, and subjected to logic and satire, but never shared. Music is scarcely capable of partaking in this process, though it may accompany it in a neutral way, as Sullivan's does well enough in the patter songs. But when the music is given its head, its direct emotional appeal tends to overwhelm Gilbert's verbal wit—as he found to his annoyance—and to give the audience a necessary outlet for feelings that Gilbert checked in the spoken passages. Sullivan was capable of musical parody—many of his recitatives are obvious examples. It is debatable whether Sullivan, like Gilbert, was making fun of fashionable orientalism in *The Mikado*; perhaps he was revelling in the romance of it all. His most valuable contributions are often in an entirely serious vein, whether sentimental, as in the gorgeously orchestrated girls' chorus from *The Yeomen of the Guard* (Ex. 356); quasi-religious, as in the unexpected choral outburst 'Hail, Poetry!' in *The Pirates*; or merely pictorial, as in 'The Moon and I' from *The Mikado*.

Ex. 356

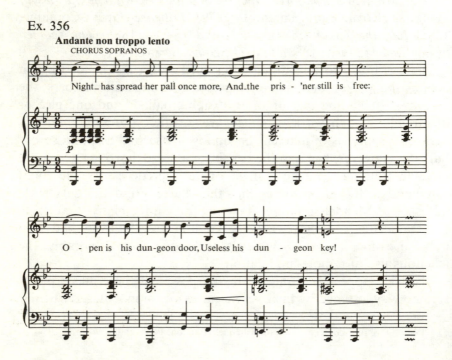

A great attraction of the Savoy operas was that they broadened the possible range of subject matter of light opera, appealing to sophisticated tastes. *Princess Ida* dealt with feminism, *Patience* with the aesthetic movement, *Ruddigore* with *nouveau-riche* snobbery; all the operas are full of pungent commentary on British institutions, prejudices, and social customs. These matters often excite more interest than the inevitable love story, though the latter may have the best music.

THE SAVOY OPERAS IN THE UNITED STATES

The unprecedented popularity of the Savoy operas, both in Britain and, after the introduction of *HMS Pinafore* in New York (1879), in the United States, overwhelmed the craze for French *opéra bouffe* which had dominated the London and New York musical stages in the previous decades. They had many imitators, but no serious rivals for a long time. In England, Frederic Clay (1838–89) and Alfred Cellier (1844–91) had some success, as did John Philip Sousa (1854–1932) and Reginald De Koven (1859–1920) in America; but it was not until Victor Herbert's career in light opera began with *Prince Ananias* (New York, 1894) that a serious challenge to Sullivan's hegemony was brought forward. And even Herbert's pieces have succumbed like the rest while Sullivan's live on.

Deane Root has asked 'why *HMS Pinafore*, alone of all the popular musical stage works performed in the United States between 1860 and 1880, continues to be performed regularly and widely a century later'. He suggests an answer: 'it is still popular partly because the musical and textual styles and the methods of performance which it represented have been perpetuated in American musical theater.'[179] The reason may be simpler: that Gilbert and Sullivan's individual and complementary abilities were far superior to those of any of their rivals, and were peculiarly suited to the Anglo-Saxon temperament. Gilbert was one of the wittiest dramatists of all time. The British were quite ready to laugh at themselves; the Americans took themselves more seriously, but had no objection to laughing at the British, as Root points out.[180] But if, in the long run, opera must depend primarily on its music, let us admit that Sullivan was one of the most richly endowed composers of the century.[181]

[179] Deane Root, *American Popular Stage Music 1860–1880* (Ann Arbor, 1981), 169.
[180] Ibid., p. 167.
[181] A German critic, Robert Papperitz, thought that Sullivan's natural musical talent was greater than Brahms's, but—less perceptively—regretted that he had 'prostituted his talents for money-making works'. Samuel Midgley, *My 70 Years' Musical Memories* (London, 1934), 21–2.

AMERICAN OPERETTA AND OPERA

American operetta had, however, established an independent existence before the '*Pinafore* fever' began. Entertainments at the Boston Museum in the 1860s seem to have fulfilled a function similar to the German Reed entertainments, in reaction to the pervasive French operettas and burlesques. *The Doctor of Alcantara*, an operetta by the German immigrant Julius Eichberg (1824–93), was first performed there in 1862, and was soon widely popular both in theatres and in church associations.[182] Its music was simple-minded but effective, and it was followed by other American works of similar type. *Evangeline* (Niblo's Garden, New York, 1874) by Edward Everett Rice (1848–1924) also maintained accepted standards of propriety, but was more directly in the burlesque tradition in its reliance on satire and extravaganza.

The foothold of 'grand opera' in American life was more precarious. Many cities boasted opera houses in the later nineteenth century, but their repertoire was almost exclusively imported; few indeed were the operas by American composers that managed to reach the stage, and not one had an unequivocal success. *Rip Van Winkle*, by George F. Bristow (1825–98), was produced at Niblo's Theatre, in New York, in 1855, and ran for four weeks: it had one revival, at Chicago in 1870, and has been staged again in more recent times.[183] Considering that this was only the third American 'grand opera' on record, and the first on an American subject, it shows a rather astonishing degree of technique and invention. Bristow uses set-piece arias, choruses, ballads, recitatives and melodrama as well as spoken dialogue. Genuine feeling infuses Rip's third-act song, after he has

Ex. 357

---

[182] Root, *American Popular Stage Music*, p. 139.
[183] At the University of Illinois, Urbana, under the direction of Neely Bruce (1974).

awoken from his long sleep (Ex. 357), and the misunderstandings that follow are cleverly depicted in the finale.[184]

Other American 'grand operas' of the period, now almost wholly forgotten, include *Antonio* (Chicago, 1874), revived in 1887 as *Lucille*), and *Zenobia* (Chicago, 1883), by Silas G. Pratt (1846–1916), and *Otho Visconti* (com. *c.*1877, prod. Chicago, 1907), by William W. Gilchrist (also 1846–1916).[185]

INCIDENTAL MUSIC

One other type of stage music that aspired to high art should be briefly mentioned. The long tradition of incidental music, especially to the plays of Shakespeare, continued to flourish throughout the Victorian period. John Liptrot Hatton (1809–86) supplied several fine examples in the 1850s, while Sullivan wrote some of his most distinguished music for *The Tempest* (1861) and four other Shakespeare plays. A newer development was the provision of incidental music for Greek plays acted at universities: this attracted the interest of composers such as William Sterndale Bennett (1816–75) and Hubert Parry (1848–1918) who were not men of the theatre. Bennett's *Ajax* (1872) never progressed beyond the Prelude, but

---

[184] For a study of this opera, see K. E. Gombert, ' "Leonora" by William Henry Fry and "Rip Van Winkle" by George Frederick Bristow' (Ph.D. Diss., Ball State University, 1977).

[185] For further details see Edward Ellsworth Hipsher, *American Opera and its Composers* (Philadelphia, 1927).

Macfarren's music for the same play (Cambridge, 1882) is vigorous and convincing. Parry contributed fine scores to Aristophanes' *Birds* (1883) and *Frogs* (1892) for Oxford, while Stanford continued the Cambridge line with *Eumenides* (1885) and *Oedipus Tyrannus* (1887). Typically these consist chiefly of instrumental numbers and choruses, and do not demand the kind of 'operatic' writing for which experience in the theatre is indispensable. An effective American work of the same genre was *Oedipus Tyrannus*, by John Knowles Paine (1839–1906), produced at Harvard in 1881.

VII

THE SYMPHONIC POEM AND KINDRED FORMS

By GERALD ABRAHAM

IT has been remarked in an earlier chapter that perhaps the most characteristic form of Romantic orchestral music was the concert overture, and at the middle of the century, as music aspired still more ardently towards the qualities of the other arts, the programmatic concert overture began to develop new characteristics and acquired a new generic title: 'symphonic poem'. (It was first employed by Liszt, on the occasion of a performance of his *Tasso* Overture at the Weimar Court on 19 April 1854.) Under its cover composers felt freer to indulge in structural licences like those taken by Mendelssohn in *Meeresstille und glückliche Fahrt* and Berlioz in *Le Carnaval romain*, and in the devices of tone symbolism and tone painting that were still regarded with suspicion, if not hostility, by many musicians at the middle of the century. It is impossible to draw a defining line between the early symphonic poems and contemporary concert overtures; the terms were for some time almost interchangeable. It is true the scores of symphonic poems were generally prefaced by literary programmes like those to Berlioz's *Symphonie fantastique* and Spohr's *Die Weihe der Töne*, but so too, occasionally, were the scores of overtures. The Anglo-Alsatian Henry Litolff (1818–91) issued his overture to Griepenkerl's *Maximilian Robespierre* (1850) with a lengthy explanation that 'the tone poem [*Tondichtung*] not merely forms the musical introduction to Griepenkerl's tragedy, but also—quite independently of the content of the play—gives its own picture of the life and character of the hero', every detail of which is then made clear.

A number of the earliest symphonic poems actually began their existence as concert or theatre overtures. The Lisztian symphonic poem was indebted to Berlioz's programme symphonies only for the idea of the printed literary programme and the wealth of new orchestral resources which facilitated and encouraged tone painting. Even Liszt's favourite device of transforming a basic theme into surprisingly different shapes each serving as material for a different section of a work is derived not only from the motto-themes of the *Symphonie fantastique* and *Harold en Italie* but from such works as Schubert's *Fantaisie*, Op. 15 (the 'Wanderer' Fantasia), and the first movement of Schumann's Piano Concerto, with their ancestry in the pavane–galliard relationship of the sixteenth century and the variation suite of the seventeenth. Berlioz's programme symphonies had important progeny during the second half of the century, but the one-movement symphonic poem was not among them.

Liszt too wrote programme symphonies, *Eine Faust-Symphonie in drei Charakterbildern* (the 'Faust' Symphony) (first version 1854; choral Finale added in 1857) and *Eine Symphonie zu Dantes Divina commedia* (the 'Dante' Symphony), which stand in much the same relationship to his symphonic poems as Berlioz's to his concert overtures. The 'Faust' Symphony is indeed less programmatic than the Berlioz symphonies. Instead of attempting to illustrate specific episodes from Goethe as Berlioz had done with Shakespeare in *Roméo et Juliette*, he made three character studies on the lines of Schumann's *Manfred* Overture and Wagner's *Faust* Overture; indeed he may have owed the conception to Wagner's project. As musical portraits, the movements are more effective than psychologically penetrating; yet they compose into an impressive, thematically unified triptych. The expansion of the ending into an 'andante mistico' setting of the closing words of Goethe's Second Part, for tenor solo and male chorus, was a not altogether happy afterthought. The greatly inferior 'Dante' Symphony also ends chorally and was also conceived as a triptych,[1] but on Wagner's advice Liszt substituted a setting of the *Magnificat*, for women's or boys's voices, as a coda to 'Purgatory', and scrapped 'Paradise'.

LISZT'S OVERTURE POEMS

Liszt's earlier symphonic poems, up to the spring of 1854, were with two exceptions originally concert or theatre overtures—several of them for official celebrations at Weimar—scored in the first place by the operetta composer August Conradi or by Liszt's young factotum Joachim Raff. *Ce qu'on entend sur la montagne* was roughed out in 1848 and at first described as a 'concert overture' with that title, or alternatively as *Bergsymphonie* or *Méditation symphonie*.[2]

---

[1] In a letter to Rubinstein (3 June 1855) Liszt announces that he has sketched the plan: 'Symphony in three parts: the two first, "Hell" and "Purgatory", exclusively instrumental, the third, "Paradise", with chorus', *Briefe*, ed. La Mara (Leipzig, 1893–1905), i. 201.

[2] See Helene Raff, 'Franz Liszt und Joachim Raff im Spiegl ihrer Briefe, *Die Musik*, 1 (1901–2), particularly pp. 389 and 1163.

Tasso was composed the following year as an overture to a festival performance of Goethe's play at Weimar; in 1851 Liszt speaks of it as '*Lamento e Trionfo* (Tasso Ouvertüre)' and '*L'Ouverture du Tasse*'. A concert overture of 1848, *Die vier Elemente*, was based on earlier settings of poems by Joseph Autran, 'La Terre', 'Les Aquilons', 'Les Flots', and 'Les Astres', for male voices and piano (collectively entitled *Les Quatre Éléments*), and still bearing that title in 1851 though it was performed at a Weimar concert in 1854 as a *symphonische Dichtung*. *Prometheus* was composed in 1850 as the overture to a set of eight choruses from Herder's *Der entfesselte Prometheus*, with which it is to some extent thematically connected: *Festklänge* in 1853 as a simple *Festouvertüre*, though it was first performed as an introduction to Schiller's *Huldigung der Kunste*; *Orpheus* in 1854 as a prologue (with an epilogue on the same themes)[3] to a gala performance of Gluck's *Orfeo*.

LISZT'S EARLIER DISCIPLES

A number of the earlier symphonic poems of Liszt's disciples also originated in theatre overtures and acquired programmes, sometimes incongruous ones, *ex post facto*. Thus the youthful Hans von Bülow (1830–94), one of the closest of his immediate followers, wrote an overture to an unsuccessful tragedy, *Ein Leben im Tode*, by Karl Ritter. Having become detached from the play, it then existed for several years as a *Fantaisie* without title; for a performance at Berlin in February 1859 it was described on the advice of Liszt, who was worried by this lack of a name, as 'a Symphonic Prologue to Byron's *Cain*'. A couple of years later we find Liszt proposing yet another title: 'What do you think of "Symphonischer Prolog zu *den Raübern*" (or "zu Byrons *Cain*")??? It seems to me well suited to the work.'[4] In the end it became *Nirwana*, an 'orchestral fantasia in overture form'.

Similarly, though with more fidelity to his original subjects, Liszt's Czech admirer Bedřich Smetana (1824–84), then a conductor at Göteborg in Sweden, wrote his first three symphonic poems under the direct influence of three plays and in at least one case was prepared for his music to be used as a theatre overture. He tells Liszt: 'I have finished the music for Shakespeare's *Richard III* and am now working on music to Schiller's *Wallensteins Lager* as first

---

[3] Peter Raabe, *Franz Liszt: Leben und Schaffen* (Stuttgart, 1931), ii. 299.
[4] *Briefwechsel zwischen Franz Liszt und Hans von Bülow*, ed. La Mara (Leipzig, 1898), 307. See also C. F. Barry, 'Hans von Bülow's *Nirwana*', *Zeitschrift der Internationalen Musikgesellschaft*, 2/9 (June, 1901).

part and *Wallensteins Tod* as second part.'[5] *Wallensteins Tod* was never finished, perhaps never even begun, but when its companion, *Valdštýnův Tábor* [Wallenstein's Camp], was completed three months later Smetana provided it with an alternative ending for use in the theatre. Whether or not he thought of *Hakon Jarl* (1861) as an actual overture to Oehlenschläger's tragedy it is impossible to say, but it was certainly inspired by the play which had made a 'powerful impression' on him. None of the three works is described on the autograph score as a symphonic poem, but as 'To Shakespeare's Richard III', 'Wallensteins' Camp/by Fr. Schiller/orchestral composition' and '*Hakon Jarl* for full orchestra'. A letter to Smetana's former teacher Josef Proksch, makes it clear that he had not yet heard the new term: *Richard III* 'is a sort of musical illustration, composed in one movement yet neither overture nor symphony, in short something that awaits a name'.[6] The term 'symphonic poem' was first used when *Richard III* was performed—in a sixteen-hand piano arrangement—at Göteborg in 1860, yet two years later when it and *Valdštýnův Tábor* were first performed in Prague both were described as 'fantasias'. In his diary during his Swedish period (1856-61) Smetana refers to all three works as 'symphonies'; it is only later that he begins to speak of them in his correspondence as 'symphonic poems'.[7]

LISZT'S *SYMPHONISCHE DICHTUNGEN*

Having hit upon the term *symphonische Dichtung* for the 1854 performance of *Les Préludes*, Liszt applied it in the same year to *Hungaria* (which has no programme) and proposed it to Breitkopf and Härtel for the collection of his orchestral works—which included *Mazeppa* (based on a piano *étude*) and *Héroïde funèbre* (1850) (based on sketches for the first movement of a 'revolution symphony' projected twenty years before). The term itself may have been suggested by Wagner's *Faust* Overture, described as *ein Tongedicht für das Orchester* on the cover of the original score, but it should be remembered that such descriptions had earlier Romantic roots: Carl Loewe in 1835 had styled his *Der Frühling* for piano *eine Tondichtung in Sonatenform*.

After *Hungaria*, the earliest symphonic poems to be actually

---

[5] Letter, 24 Oct. 1858, František Bartoš, *Smetana ve vzpomínkách a dopisech* (9th edn.; Prague, 1953), no. 24.

[6] 9 Sept. 1958, quoted by Josef Plavec in his introduction to the miniature score (Prague, n.d.).

[7] I am indebted for this information to the late Alfons Waissar, formerly Director of the Smetana Museum at Prague.

created as such were the *Hunnenschlacht* inspired by Kaulbach's painting in the Altes Museum, Berlin, and *Die Ideale* after Schiller's poem (both 1857). (The main theme of *Ideale* was borrowed from an earlier choral setting of Schiller's *An die Künstler*.) *Hamlet* (1858) was originally intended as a prelude to the play. The last of the important orchestral works Liszt wrote at Weimar were the *Zwei Episoden aus Lenau's 'Faust'* (1860)—'Der nächtliche Zug' and 'Der Tanz in der Dorfschenke' (sometimes known as 'the first *Mephisto Waltz*')—miniature symphonic poems in all but name. After leaving Weimar Liszt wrote only one more symphonic poem actually so called, *Von der Wiege bis zum Grabe* (1882), inspired by a design by the Hungarian painter Mihály Zichy, although several of his later orchestral works belong to the same genre of poetically inspired music which the composer wished to be listened to in the light of the actual poem; thus, for *Le Triomphe funèbre du Tasse* (1866), an epilogue to the *Lamento e Trionfo*, he wanted the description of Tasso's funeral in Pierantonio Serassi's biography to be printed in concert programmes. But these compositions are neither more nor less unorthodox in form than those which began their existence as overtures.[8]

Liszt's symphonic poems are as heedless of sonata form as *Meeresstille* and *Carnaval romain* but their changes of tempo and other formal unconventionalities were not dictated by the prefatory programmes as was supposed by Liszt's adversaries and even by his disciples. Neither *Orpheus*, *Héroïde funèbre*, *Festklänge*, *Hungaria*, nor *Hamlet* has anything one could call a programme; the last three lack even prefaces and, as we have seen, several of the others came into existence before the programmes were invented. Nor are the programmes or prefaces, whether written by Liszt himself or the Princess Sayn-Wittgenstein, necessarily reliable accounts of the origin of the works. That to *Tasso*, for instance, tells us that

Tasso loved and suffered in Ferrara, was avenged in Rome, and still lives today in the folk-songs of Venice. These three moments are inseparable from his imperishable fame. To remember them musically, we called up first his great shade as it still haunts the lagoons of Venice; then we saw his proud, sad face pass through the festivities of Ferrara, where he created his masterpieces; finally we followed him to Rome, the Eternal City, which by giving him the crown of fame glorified in him the martyr and poet.

But the first conception was certainly not threefold; the Ferrara

---

[8] For detailed formal analyses, see Joachim Bergfeld, *Die formale Struktur der Symphonischen Dichtungen Franz Liszts* (Eisenach, 1931).

section, 'quasi menuetto', was inserted some five years after the composition of the original overture—and the logical position of a Venetian section would hardly be at the beginning of the work. The truth is that Liszt began with the idea of a twofold overture reflecting Tasso's sufferings and triumph, and musically founded on the melody to which he had heard the Venetian gondoliers sing the opening of *Gierusalemme liberata*.[9] The printed programme was devised later to fit existing musical facts.

Liszt's printed programmes serve as extensions of the titles, giving the listener a general clue to the extra-musical sense of the scores; he never used them as blueprints for the layout of compositions. They are also symptoms of his general culture (typical of musicians of the period) and of his wish to advertise it (a more personal characteristic). There is no reason to doubt the sincerity of his statement to Agnes Street-Klindworth in 1860 that during his dozen years at Weimar he had been upheld by 'a great idea: that of the renewal of Music by its more intimate alliance with Poetry; I have always been spurred on by the idea of a freer development, more *adequate*—so to speak—to the spirit of this age'.[10]

But this 'renewal of music' was not to be effected by subordination of music to literary details. Such passages of tonepainting as the rising storm in *Les Préludes*, the galloping of Mazeppa's horse and the walking of Faust's in the first of the Lenau *Episodes*, are relatively few. Still fewer are such as that at the end of Mazeppa's ride and before his release by the Cossacks or that near the end of the second Lenau *Episode*, 'Der Tanz in der Dorfschenke'—Faust slipping out into the night with the innkeeper's daughter while a nightingale sings (Ex. 358).

Ex. 358

[9] Already used in a piano piece, No. 1 of a set of four entitled *Venezia e Napoli* (*Gesamtausgabe*, ii. 5). The form of the melody employed by Liszt is given in Werner Danckert, *Das europäiische Volkslied* (Berlin, 1939), 306.
[10] *Liszt's Briefe*, iii. 135.

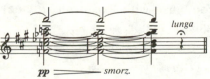

Here Liszt writes programme music in the strictest sense, an attempt to depict a succession of events, each section headed with the relevant lines of the poem. The score of *Die Ideale* is similarly sprinkled with quotations taken at random from Schiller's poem, but the extra-musical ideas are less specific and concrete; *Die Ideale* was first conceived as a *Symphonie en trois parties*[11]—'Soaring' (Allegro spiritoso), 'Disillusion' (slow movement), 'Occupation' (Scherzo)—with final 'Apotheosis', all on transformations of the same themes, and it remains a condensed symphony closely parallel in form to the earlier E flat Piano Concerto (1849; rev. 1853 and 1856).

While the different sections of *Die Ideale* thus correspond to those of the Classical symphony, those of the majority of Liszt's symphonic poems are grouped in monistic patterns, enlargements and elaborations of the square-cut, sectional forms typical of Romantic piano music. The only real exception is *Mazeppa* in which the concluding section (Allegro marziale) is unrelated to the main part of the work, the ride. On the other hand in *Hunnenschlacht*, built on a similar plan, the final section (beginning at Letter I, Maestoso assai) is related thematically. Even the apparent three-movement form of *Tasso* is really a monistic pattern and the three clearly defined movements of *Von der Wiege bis zum Grabe* are arranged in the clearest ternary form, ABA′. These ground-plans for the layout of thematically related sections in different keys and tempos, while they lack the organic cohesion of sonata and cognate forms, generally— as Bergfeld was the first to demonstrate—have their own, perhaps rather mechanical, symmetry. One need not agree with the details of Bergfeld's analyses to endorse his general conclusion. The broad plan of *Les Préludes* is typical:

Introduction (on theme A: C major)
  Andante maestoso (on theme A: C major)
    Theme A ('cantando': C major, E, etc.)
    Theme B ('amoroso': E major)
      Transition (Allegro ma non troppo, on theme A)
        Allegro tempestuoso (on theme A: A minor, etc.)
      Transition (Un poco più moderato, on theme A)
        Allegretto pastorale (E major)
      Transition (theme B combined with 'pastorale' theme)
    Theme A (Allegro marziale: C major, etc.)

---

[11] Ibid., p. 83. See also *Briefwechsel zwischen Liszt und Bülow*, p. 248.

Theme B (similarly transformed: C major, etc.)
Andante maestoso (on theme A: C major)[12]

The predominance of 'theme A' almost justifies Liszt's claim[13] that *Tasso* is *construirt* with Ex. 359 and the *Préludes* with Ex. 360. Liszt went too far; these scores are not literally monothematic. But the ingenuity of his theme-transformations does enable him to squeeze the maximum value from such unpromising scraps as these[14] and partially to counteract the effect of scrappiness that would otherwise be produced by his sectional structure in contrasting tempos.

Ex. 359   Ex. 360

While this technique of motif transformation goes beyond anything of the kind attempted by the symphonic composers of the 1830s and 1840s and reminds one rather of Wagner's exactly contemporary development of the leitmotif, much of Liszt's actual material belongs to some of the same categories as those of the symphonists: melodies of lyrical origin—*Die Ideale, Tasso, Les Préludes, Prometheus*;[15] and plainsong: 'Crux fidelis' in *Hunnenschlacht*, 'Der nächtliche Zug', the 'Dante' Symphony. And his treatment of it is generally very like Schumann's: by harmonic sequence and wholesale repetition in fresh keys (most characteristically in keys a third apart). Like Schumann, he attaches enormous importance to the theme for its own sake rather than as a part of a larger whole, but he savours actual sound effects far more intensely than Schumann ever did. Liszt's own

Ex. 361

Allegro

---

[12] Bergfeld's analysis, *Die formale Struktur*, pp. 76 ff. is much more detailed.

[13] *Liszt's Briefe*, viii. 127.

[14] Cf. Alfred Heuss, 'Eine motivisch-thematische Studie über Liszts sinfonische Dichtung *Ce qu'on entend sur la montagne*', *Zeitschrift der internationalen Musikgesellschaft*, 13 (1911-12), 10.

[15] In *Prometheus* the cello theme (Ex. 361) is modified from a setting of the words 'und du allein bist, ja du allein bist, die sie ordet, göttliche, menschliche, weise Themis!', in the original *Chöre zu Herders 'Der entfesselte Prometheus'*.

defence of repetition as exemplified in Schumann was that 'from the point of view of the public it is indispensable for the understanding of the thought, while from the point of view of art it is almost identical with the demand of clarity, structure and effectiveness'.[16] A certain sinuous and angular type of theme of which Liszt was rather fond also seems to derive from Schumann and other German Romantics (Weber, early Wagner); others of his melodies, such as the second theme, for horns and divided violas, of *Les Préludes* and the middle section of *Orpheus*, derive from Italian opera either directly or through Chopin. Most typical of all are the numerous chromatic recitative-like or ejaculatory themes, slivers of Liszt's frequently Chopinesque and boldly dissonant harmony. Sometimes the verbal inspiration of these instrumental recitatives and ejaculations is frankly avowed, as in the opening of the 'Dante' Symphony where the words of Dante's inscription on the portal of Hell are printed under the notes in the score. Sometimes it can be demonstrated: the 'recitativo', actually so marked, for cor anglais, bassoon and muted violas, in *Prometheus*, originated in an alto solo of the *Prometheus* choruses (Exx. 362 and 363).

Ex. 362

Ex. 363

(The altars of the gods stand deserted in the grove. Foreboding dreams. . .)

[16] *Gesammelte Schriften von Franz Liszt*, ed. Lina Ramann (Leipzig, 1880–3), ii. 103.

Liszt's unsureness as an orchestrator has already been mentioned. When he gained enough confidence to do his own scoring, his orchestration,[17] brilliant as it is, is always that of a pianist.[18] He very frequently felt the need of the harp, more even than Berlioz. In *Ce qu'on entend sur la montagne* he gives it glissandos. Even when he dispenses with it, he likes to write arpeggio figuration for the strings and sometimes (the Minuet in *Tasso*, both *Episoden aus Lenau's 'Faust'*, and the first and second movements of the 'Faust' Symphony), with curiously silvery effect for woodwind.

His scoring in general owes much to Berlioz and to *Lohengrin*, though his employment of completely triple woodwind in *Mazeppa* is exceptional. In his melodic use of brass and his sharp differentiation and contrast of pure instrumental colours, he is very close indeed to Berlioz and fairly early, even mature, Wagner; but he is distinguished from them by his essentially homophonic texture. Berlioz thinks directly in terms of his orchestral medium. In the most characteristic pages of *Lohengrin* horizontal tendencies are everywhere perceptible; the parts 'sing'. Liszt often has to use in his scoring all the ingenuity acquired in his years of piano writing to elaborate blocklike chordal textures, as in Ex. 364 from *Mazeppa*.

Like Berlioz, he attached the highest importance to fine balance and flexible rhythm in the performance of his orchestral music.[19] His scores are very carefully marked. Sometimes he asks for a gradual acceleration spread over nearly fifty bars, as in *Les Préludes*; he occasionally uses fresh signs 'R . . .' and 'A . . .' to indicate 'slight crescendi and diminuendi of the rhythm'. In all these respects his example was enormously effective, for his disciples were numerous and often influential in turn.

LISZT'S INFLUENCE IN RUSSIA

Perhaps the most important instance of the transmission of Liszt's orchestral influence and its crossing with other strains is to be found in the semi-amateur young Russian school which emerged during the 1860s under the somewhat despotic leadership of Mily Alekseevich Balakirev (1837–1910), Glinka's closest disciple. Balakirev and his group were very consciously 'progressive' as well as nationalist, and Balakirev himself as a conductor was the principal champion of

---

[17] See H. Woollett and Gabriel Pierné, in Albert Lavignac (ed.), *Encyclopédie de la musique et Dictionnaire du Conservatoire* (Paris, 1920–31), II. iv. 2602–5.

[18] See the facsimiles at the end of Raabe, *Franz Liszt*: Leben und Schaffen, ii: (a) Liszt's pencil sketch for *Tasso*; (b) Conradi's orchestration; (c) Raff's more genuinely orchestral conception.

[19] See his general preface to the symphonic poems, particularly the original, French version.

Berlioz, and later of Liszt, in Russia. Russian orchestral music of this period shows all the hesitations, compromises, and varieties characteristic of contemporary programme music in Western Europe, and Balakirev's early works again illustrate the interchangeability of the terms 'overture' and 'symphonic poem', together with the fact that the existence or lack of a programme is no touchstone for distinguishing them. Following Glinka's example, the young Balakirev composed a number of overtures on folk themes: *Overture on the Theme of a Spanish March* (1857), *Overture on Three Russian Themes* (1858), a *Second Overture on Russian Themes* (1864), and an *Overture on Czech Themes* (1867). Their several histories are enlightening. The autograph score of the *Spanish* Overture was inscribed in pencil 'To the drama, *The Expulsion of the Moors from*

Ex. 364

Spain.[20] No such play is known; this title was never published; but when in 1887 Balakirev revised and reorchestrated the piece for publication he gave it a programme which does not mention a play but indicates content:

The composer had in mind the history of the tragic fate of the Moors, persecuted and finally driven from Spain by the Inquisition. The first theme is therefore given an Oriental character; the orchestra at certain places depicts the organ, the singing of the monks, the burning pyres of the *auto-da-fé* with the ringing of bells and the rejoicings of the people.

The first *Russian* Overture remained without programme or descriptive title, but the second underwent two changes. It appears[21] to have been inspired to some extent by a passage in an article of Herzen's on the Russian student agitation of 1861:

Give ear, for darkness does not prevent hearing: from every part of our

[20] Cf. Grigory Timofeev, 'M. A. Balakirev: Na osnovanii novïkh materialov', *Russkaya Mïsl'* (1912), no. 6, p. 50.

[21] V. Karenin (ed.), *Perepiska M. A. Balakireva s V. V. Stasovïm* (Moscow, 1935), i. 270.

vast fatherland, from the Don and the Urals, from the Volga and the Dnepr, swells a groan, rises a murmur; it is the first roar of the sea-waves that are beginning to rise, pregnant with storms after the dreadfully weary calm. To the people! To the people!—there is your place. . . .

But when the overture was published in 1869 it became a 'musical picture', *1000 let* [1000 Years], in allusion to the founding of the Russian state by Rurik in 862; and in 1887, when it was issued by a different publisher in a slightly revised and completely reorchestrated form as the 'symphonic poem' *Rus'*—the old name for Russia— Balakirev went even further, asserting in a prefatory note that the composition had been 'occasioned by the inauguration in 1862, in Novgorod, of the millenary monument of Russia' and that by the three folk themes he had

wished to characterize three elements of our history: paganism, the Muscovite way of life, and the semi-feudal, semi-republican elements later revived among the Cossacks. Their conflict—terminated by the fatal blow dealt by the reforms of Peter I to religio-national aspirations—provided the content of the instrumental drama.

It is true that by 1868 Balakirev had some such characterization in his mind, but no conflict and no suggestion that the Petrine reforms were 'fatal'. There is certainly not much 'conflict' of themes in Rus and nothing that can be called an 'instrumental drama'. Nor does the 1887 programme account for the two appearances of a lyrical theme of Balakirev's own; according to Stasov, this 'delightful, truly inspired melody depicts the new life beginning'.[23] The composer's political views had changed by 1887 but the music remained unchanged in every essential. The *Overture on Czech Themes* underwent a more effortless change into the symphonic poem *V Chekhii* [In Bohemia] when it was belatedly published in 1906. It was revised and rescored but, as the composer put it, he wanted 'to call it a *symphonic poem* because of its scope and treatment' (letter, 5 June 1902) and the programme he devised could hardly have been more naïve: 'A Russian musician visits Bohemia; he hears about him the sound of Czech songs, arousing in his soul a mighty whirlpool of memories and reflections on his distant land and the songs of the Russian people.'

Balakirev's only 'true' symphonic poem, the only work initially conceived as such and attempting picturesque description, is the later *Tamara* (begun 1867, completed 1882, and published with a dedication

---

[22] 'The Giant Awakens', *Kolokol* 110 (1 Nov. 1862).
[23] 'Nasha muzïka za posledniya 25 let', *Vestnik Evropï* (Oct. 1883), 597.

to Liszt) after Lermontov's poem. On the other hand, the theatre overture to *King Lear* (1859) is almost equally episodic in structure and the episodes are unmistakably associated with characters and scenes in the play. To Balakirev the terms 'overture' and 'symphonic poem' were equivalent. The essential ground-plan of each of these works is the same: an Allegro framed, except in the case of the Czech piece, by a slow opening and close based on identical material. The Allegros themselves, in their combination of variation and sonata principles, acknowledge as their parent Glinka's *Capriccio brillante* on the Jota aragonesa. (Liszt's example began to influence the Russians only after 1865 when Balakirev conducted *Les Préludes*.) They are not so much 'in sonata form' as referable to sonata form. The themes or groups tend to be self-contained episodes rather than parts of a whole and the key systems bear little relation to those of a sonata movement. *Rus'* has an 'allegro' first subject in D major; the equivalent of a second-subject group is in B flat minor and major in the exposition but mainly in B flat, D, and D flat major in the recapitulation, while a 'larghetto' frame opens and closes the work in B flat minor. The frame of *Tamara*, a tone picture of the Daryal Gorge and the rushing river Terek, is heard in B minor at the beginning and D flat major at the end, while the main 'allegro moderato', the orgy in Tamara's castle, has two recapitulations, one beginning in the orthodox key (D flat), the other in B major.

The theme of Tamara herself stands outside the sonata plan, like a Berliozian motto-theme, and is sometimes heard in independent episodes which break into the plan, sometimes interwoven with the other themes. But the impression of almost complete dissolution of sonata form is due mainly to the nature of the material generally and its treatment: a number of tiny quasi-oriental motifs forming themes initially rather alike and made even more confusingly alike by subtle variation or remoulding (Exx. 365–7, bars 78–80, 137–9, 329–32). Balakirev's mosaic glows with the colours of Chopinesque

Ex. 365

Ex. 366

Ex. 367

harmony and the subtle, brilliant scoring of a natural orchestrator who learned everything that Glinka, Berlioz, and Liszt could teach him. The melting kaleidoscopic motif-technique made Tamara an important archetype of orchestral impressionism.[24]

TCHAIKOVSKY

Similar lack of distinction between overture and symphonic poem, and similar treatment of both in terms of very free and episodic sonata outline with all sorts of excrescences, mark the programme music of Balakirev's young compatriot Pyotr Il'ich Tchaikovsky (1840-93), the earliest Russian composer of note to receive orthodox academic training. But his teachers at the newly founded Petersburg Conservatory failed to plant in him the conception of organic form— or at any rate the ability to realize it. His earliest essay in programme music, an overture to Ostrovsky's drama *Groza* [The Storm] (1864),[25] is almost exceptional in that its programme was conceived before the music. It exemplifies the kind of rough guiding plan a composer is likely to extract from a literary work:

Introduction; 'adagio': Katerina's childhood and all her life before marriage; 'Allegro': hints of the storm; her longing for true happiness and love (all 'appassionato'); her spiritual conflict;—sudden change to evening on the banks of the Volga; again conflict, but with a trace of a kind of feverish happiness; foreboding of the storm (repetition of the motif after the 'adagio' and its further development); the storm; climax of desperate conflict and death.[26]

On the other hand the symphonic poem *Fatum* [Fate] of four years later has no programme; the verses by Konstantin Batyushkov prefaced to the score were added later by a friend who, according to one version of the story,[27] had not even heard the music. But, although the *Storm* Overture is still referable to sonata form, it includes a number of passages comprehensible only in the light of the programme and is quite as patchily episodic as *Fatum* which is

---

[24] See Vol. X, pp. 92 and 94-5.
[25] Better known outside Russia in Janáček's operatic version, *Kát'a Kabanová*.
[26] K. Yu. Davïdova *et al.*, *Muzïkal'noe nasledie Chaykovskogo* (Moscow, 1958), 272.
[27] *Ibid.*, p. 278.

in a freely symmetrical form on Lisztian lines. As regards musical substance, however, the young Tchaikovsky leaned not on Liszt but on Schumann, the cosmopolitan Litolff (who was enjoying a certain vogue in Russia at that time) in *Groza*, and Balakirev in *Fatum* and most of his other programme pieces.

Fatum is Tchaikovsky's only symphonic poem actually so called. *The Tempest* after Shakespeare (1873) and *Francesca da Rimini* after Dante (1876) are both styled 'fantasia'. The symmetrical arrangement of the sharply differentiated episodes of *The Tempest* is evident from the programme:

> The sea (F minor)
> > Prospero orders Ariel to raise the storm (F minor to E major)
> > (The storm)
> > > Miranda and Ferdinand fall in love (G flat and B flat)
> > > > Ariel—Caliban (G minor, etc.)
> > > > > The full passion of Ferdinand and Miranda (A flat and C)
> > Prospero renounces his magic powers (C major and A flat)
> The sea (F minor)

One cannot say that the form is conditioned by the programme; rather, as in Liszt, the programme is laid out in a quasi-musical pattern. Also as in Liszt, the most crudely realistic episode, the storm, is a formal excrescence. It is the same in *Francesca* where the returning husband's hunting horns, the discovery, and the killing are naïvely suggested in a twenty-bar parenthesis:

> Introduction (Andante lugubre)
> Whirlwind of Hell (Allegro vivo, E minor)
> > Paolo and Francesca (Andante cantabile, A minor)
> > > Second love theme (perhaps the story of Lancelot)
> > Paolo and Francesca
> > (The surprise)
> Whirlwind of Hell

In two other programme compositions, *Romeo and Juliet* (1869, rev. 1870 and 1880) and *Hamlet* (1888), the episodes are arranged on a plan derived from sonata form for which Tchaikovsky adopted the term 'overture-fantasia'. In *Manfred* (1885) he produced a frankly Berliozian programme symphony—on a programme originally devised by Stasov for Balakirev[28]—in four movements with a motto-theme for the hero appearing in each. Only in a later work, the

---

[28] See Gerald Abraham, foreword to miniature score of *Manfred* (London, 1958).

'symphonic ballad' *Voevoda* (1891), after Mickiewicz's *Wojewoda*, did Tchaikovsky adopt a somewhat looser framework. But by that time the whole nature of the symphonic poem had begun to change and there were German and French precedents for the narrative orchestral 'ballad'.

'MUSICAL PICTURES'

Exceptionally brilliant orchestration in the Berlioz–Balakirev tradition is the most striking characteristic of Tchaikovsky's contemporary Nikolay Rimsky-Korsakov (1844–1908). His earliest essay in programme music was an *Epizod iz bïlinï o Sadko* [Episode from the Legend of Sadko] (1867), a title obviously suggested by Liszt's *Episoden aus Lenau's 'Faust'*, one of which, the 'Tanz in der Dorfschenke', confessedly served as a model. But the second and third versions (1869 and 1892) are styled *Muzïkal'naya kartina—Sadko* [Musical picture—*Sadko*] and that title, too, is of some interest. The 'musical picture' was a favourite genre in Russia from the late 1860s for a decade or so. The *Ivanova noch' na Lïsoy gore* [St John's Night on the Bare Mountain] (1867)[29] of Modest Mussorgsky (1839–81) was a 'musical picture', like Balakirev's *1000 let (Rus')*. The nomenclature suggested something static, the absence of any of those attempts at musical narrative which were then believed to have fatally affected the musical form of the symphonic poem, and even the anti-Lisztian Anton Rubinstein (1829–94), who had composed a Mendelssohnian *Océan symphonie* without programmatic indications (1851; three additional movements, including a storm, later), painted 'musical characteristic pictures' of *Ivan Groznïy* [Ivan the Terrible] (1868) and *Faust* (1871). In his *Don Quixote* ('Humoresque for orchestra') (1871) he went further and depicted the hero's adventures with the sheep, the three village-women and the galley-slaves, and his death in a series of variations (not actually so called). The piece is skilful and not without humour but Rubinstein's characterization of the hero (Ex. 368) first announced in bare octaves, and the ideal Dulcinea (Ex. 369) are not particularly apt. Even the final scene with Quixote's dying thought of Dulcinea lacks pathos (Ex. 370).

Aleksandr Borodin's *V sredney Azii* [In Central Asia] (1880) is one of the most successful of these Russian 'musical pictures'; it is a landscape with a simple action proceeding, an easier musical subject than a portrait. And the term 'musical picture' was still used by

---

[29] First published in 1968. The work which long passed as 'Mussorgsky's *Night on the Bare Mountain*' is a composition by Rimsky-Korsakov on Mussorgsky's somewhat altered themes.

Ex. 368

Ex. 369

Ex. 370

Aleksandr Glazunov to describe his *Kreml'* [The Kremlin] (1890) and *Vesna* [Spring] (1891).

Tchaikovsky had written his *Manfred* Symphony under strong pressure from Balakirev and the same formidable mentor had been responsible for the composition of Rimsky-Korsakov's *Antar* Symphony (1868; revised 1875 and 1897),[30] also on Berliozian lines with a motto-theme for the hero. But the composer was in later years troubled by the thought that, unlike Berlioz, he had neglected to cast his first movement in something like sonata form, and in 1903 he restyled *Antar* a 'symphonic suite', like its later companion-piece, that still more resplendent display of orchestral virtuosity, *Sheherazade* (1888), which is just as much, or as little, a 'programme symphony' with a personal theme for the story-teller herself. Both *Sheherazade* and the one-movement *Skazka* [Legend] (1880) typify an attitude towards programme music by no means peculiar to Rimsky-Korsakov: unwillingness to acknowledge—even inability to decide—to what extent certain borderline works really are programmatic. The four movements of *Sheherazade* were first thought of as Prelude, Ballade, Adagio, and Finale; they were then given titles—'The Sea and Sinbad's Ship' and so on—'in order to give the hearer a hint as to the direction taken by my own imagination'; finally the titles were removed because people made too much of the hints. Just as *Sheherazade* was intended to give a general impression of fantastic oriental tales, the earlier *Skazka*—prefaced by a famous passage of Pushkin on the character of Russian folklore—was meant to give a similar impression of Russian fantasy. But in both cases the composer, while insisting on his aim of 'general impressions', admitted to his Boswell, V. V. Yastrebtsev,[31] a good many more details of programmatic illustration than he confessed to in his autobiography:[32] for instance in the *Skazka* the voice of a *rusalka* [water-nymph], the witch Baba Yaga and her hut 'on fowl's legs', the whistle of some legendary bird, forest voices, and so on, are 'not a complete, organically developed programme but a series of musical images from Russian legendary lore'. These fantastic images are reflected in music that is thematically and harmonically dry and brittle but orchestrated with the utmost virtuosity. Even the

---

[30] See Gerald Abraham, *Slavonic and Romantic Music* (London, 1968), 199–201.

[31] *Rimskiy-Korsakov: Vospominaniya V. V. Yastrebtseva* (2 vols.; Moscow, 1959–60), i. 81–2, 99–100. The first of these passages is given in Florence Jonas's abbreviated translation, *Reminiscences of Rimsky-Korsakov* (New York, 1985), 31.

[32] *Letopis' moey muzïkal'noy zhizni* (St Petersburg, 1909); the third edition (Leningrad, 1928) is the earliest to give the full, nearly unexpurgated text; Eng. trans., by Judah A. Joffe, *My Musical Life* (New York, 1942).

scoring, though motivated by 'fantastic images', exists for its own sake rather than for its evocative power.

The programme symphony, though seldom as closely modelled on *Harold en Italie* and the *Symphonie fantastique* as Tchaikovsky's *Manfred* and Rimsky-Korsakov's *Antar*, made a special appeal also in Western Europe to those moderately progressive composers such as Joachim Raff (1822-82) who disliked the 'excesses' of *Zukunftsmusik* and the 'formlessness' of the symphonic poem. Their ideal was music that made no pretence at absoluteness yet which could be cast in fairly traditional forms with continuous, as opposed to episodic, structure: programme music in the sense that Beethoven's 'Pastoral' is programme music. Raff had been befriended by Liszt and served as his factotum, but he expressed his 'need to gain the terra firma of a neutral terrain' in a letter to the *Neue Zeitschrift für Musik* (11 February 1853) even before Liszt had hit on the term *symphonische Dichtung*. Nine of his eleven symphonies are counterparts of Spohr's programme symphonies of a generation earlier.

The same path of compromise was trodden by a score of German composers during the 1860s and 1880s in such once-popular but now forgotten works as J. J. Abert's *Kolumbus* (1864), Rheinberger's *Wallenstein* (1866), Goldmark's *Ländliche Hochzeit* (1876) and Hans Huber's *Eine Tell-Symphonie* (1881). It was a dull path and it was not that of the symphonic poem.

THE SYMPHONIC POEM IN GERMANY

The true symphonic poem found little favour in Germany at first, even in Liszt's immediate circle. (It is noteworthy that both Hans von Bülow (1830-94) and Felix Draeseke (1835-1913) eventually followed Raff in his apostasy from the so-called New German school.) The most talented member, Peter Cornelius (1824-74), wrote no independent orchestral music. Draeseke contributed once-celebrated analyses of Liszt's symphonic poems to the 'New German' organ *Anregungen für Kunst, Leben und Wissenschaft* (1858-9) but did not venture beyond the concert overture himself. Carl Tausig (1841-71) and Bülow were both more notable as pianists than as composers, and Tausig's *symphonische Ballade, Das Geisterschiff* (which survives only in his piano transcription), with Bülow's *Nirwana* (1854, rev. later) and his 'Ballade für Orchester', *Des Sängers Fluch* (after Uhland) (1863) are typical specimens of epigonism. The material of *Nirwana* is completely Lisztian, consisting largely of ejaculatory fragments from which only the second subject (Ex. 371)

Ex. 371

stands out. The form, too, is that of the Lisztian arch: a sonata Allegro with the second subject recapitulated before the first, framed by two 'grave' passages. *Des Sängers Fluch* shows the impact of Wagner and is constructed in free strophes as becomes a ballad.

Historic importance as the direct link between Liszt and Richard Strauss has been claimed for one always loyal Lisztian, Alexander Ritter (1833-96), Bülow's friend and brother of that Karl Ritter whose *Leben im Tode* had been the original inspiration of *Nirwana*. But the claim hardly bears investigation. Ritter's close friendship with the younger man from 1886 onwards may have helped to wean him from his conservative upbringing but his own earliest essays in programme music are even later than Strauss's. It is true that his *Olafs Hochzeitsreigen* (1891), a 'symphonic waltz' on a grim programme, ending with the striking of midnight (five years before it struck in Strauss's *Zarathustra*), derives from an opera—on a play by his brother Karl—projected and partly sketched as early as 1868,[33] but the *Erotische Legende* of 1890 is essentially a concert-overture and *Sursum corda!* (1894), despite its portentous subtitle, *Eine Sturm-und Drangphantasie*, has no programme and is really the third incarnation of a work which had begun its existence as a violin concerto in 1860 and then been transformed into a *Phantasie und Fuge* for orchestra alone in 1863. The thematic material of these early conceived works, the sinuous principal theme of *Sursum corda!*, with its rhythmic vitality and wide range (Ex. 372) and the waltz theme of *Olafs Hochzeitsreigen* (Ex. 373) may possibly have influenced

[33] Siegmund von Hausegger, 'Alexander Ritter: Ein Bild seines Charakters und Schaffens', *Die Musik* (Berlin, 1907).

Ex. 372

Ex. 373

the young Strauss, but Ritter shows no structural enterprise. Only his last work, the unpublished *Kaiser Rudolfs Ritt zum Grabe* (1895), is, according to Hausegger,[34] 'a symphonic poem in the strictest sense of the word', that is to say 'a work deriving its organic structure entirely from the poetic impulse'. But by that time a symphonic poem of this type was far less uncommon than thirty years earlier, when it was represented only by a few quite exceptional pieces: Liszt's 'Der nächtliche Zug' and such experimental freaks as the English Henry Hugo Pierson's 'Symphonic poem to the tragedy *Macbeth*' (*c*.1865).

ENGLISH PROGRESSIVES

Long resident in Germany, Pierson (1815–73), though not a member of the Liszt circle, was a camp-follower of the New German school. He was certainly the only English member of the avant-garde, although in 1862 the more conservative Sterndale Bennett (1816–75) produced a 'fantasy-overture', *Paradise and the Peri*, which went

---

[34] Ibid.

beyond his usual Mendelssohnian mean of picturesque music in orthodox moulds, abandoned the sonata-form scheme, and laid out the work as an introduction, depicting the 'Peri at the gate of Eden', and three 'scenes' corresponding to the three episodes of Moore's poem: the Indian patriot, the Egyptian lovers, the repentant Syrian. The music of the three scenes corresponds to three great strophes in D minor, F minor, and G minor, the last returning to the material and key (D major) of the opening. Each section is headed by a short quotation from the poem and the music sometimes hints at programmatic details, for example, the oboe's plaint, 'quasi recitativo, con passione', in the introduction.

Pierson was progressive in everything but harmony. His orchestration is Berliozian, the course of his music almost entirely dictated by a succession of extra-musical ideas. His *Macbeth* is far more heavily peppered with poetic quotations than Liszt's *Ideale* or 'Der nächtliche Zug'; nothing is developed at any length; one brief episode is succeeded by another so quickly that, despite recurrence of themes, the music is incoherent; and Lady Macbeth is characterized by a feeble theme played on the clarinet (Ex. 374), followed by the rubric, 'This have I thought good to deliver thee, my dearest partner of greatness . . .'. The later and shorter *Concert-Ouverture zu 'Romeo und Julie'* (pub. 1874) shows the same qualities in a better light. Though styled 'overture' it is not in sonata form but an agglomeration of episodes (this time unlabelled). They are not quite so short but there are ten different tempos on thirty-seven pages of full score, and, though thematically connected, the episodes are neither well balanced nor integrated. The ejaculatory nature of much of Pierson's material, his over-detailed markings, and his disastrous over-reliance on the explicit expressiveness of his music expose it to every objection raised by the hostile critics of programme music. Nevertheless, in orchestral imagination he stands easily first among the British composers of his day.

THE SYMPHONIC POEM IN FRANCE

Nothing could be in stronger contrast with Pierson's daring, untidy, semi-amateurism than the cautious, polished, professional

Ex. 374

assurance of Camille Saint-Saëns (1835–1921). Although well acquainted with Berlioz, Wagner, and Liszt, both musically and personally, Saint-Saëns showed no inclination to outdo them. Quite the contrary. He himself placed it on record that Liszt's 'first symphonic poems ... pointed out to me the road on which I was later to meet the *Danse macabre*, *Le Rouet d'Omphale* and other works of the same nature',[35] yet in these works he seems the heir not so much of Liszt or Berlioz as of the older French tradition of graceful pictorialism.

The subject of his earliest symphonic poem, *Le Rouet d'Omphale* (1872), based on an earlier rondo for piano, he tells us, is

feminine seductiveness, the triumphant struggle of weakness against strength. The spinning-wheel is only a pretext chosen solely from the point of view of the rhythm and the general style of the piece. Those interested in the search for details will detect at letter J Hercules groaning in the bonds he is unable to break and at letter L Omphale mocking the hero's useless efforts.

(Yet the oboe's 'mocking' transformation of the hero's groans is marked 'tranquillo'.) The whole piece is in a slightly modified ternary form, with these pictorial details forming the middle section. The ternary form of *Phaéton* (1875), the best of Saint-Saëns's four symphonic poems, is equally clear, with the launching of Jove's thunderbolt as the climax; the ride itself is suggested by traditional tone symbolism. *Danse macabre* (comp. 1874; pub. 1875) consists of two themes from one of Saint-Saëns's songs, framed by two short realistic passages—midnight and the tuning of Death's fiddle; cockcrow and the dispersal of the skeletons—and once interrupted by the 'Dies Irae' in waltz rhythm. But this is no companion-piece to Liszt's *Totentanz*; the words of the original song, by Henri Cazalis—of which only a few lines are printed in the score—'have nothing of the romantic ballad about them; they are familiar and ironic'.[36] The ironic smile is fatal to the Romantic *frisson*; the true Romantics never smiled at themselves.

Only in *La Jeunesse d'Hercule* (1877) did Saint-Saëns essay a more truly Lisztian type. The programme lends itself less easily to refined tone-painting; the subject is the young Hercules' choice between the paths of pleasure and of virtue 'disregarding the seductions of the

---

[35] *Portraits et Souvenirs* (Paris, 1899), 34. The novelty of the symphonic form in France in the early 1870s may be judged from the fact that Saint-Saëns found it necessary to tell the readers of the periodical *La Renaissance littéraire et artistique* (28 Dec. 1872) that the symphonic poem, created by Liszt, is 'un nouveau moule qui fera époque dans l'histoire de l'art'.

[36] Georges Servières, *Saint-Saëns* (Paris, 1923), 124–5.

nymphs and bacchantes, the hero takes the road of struggle and combat at the end of which he sees, through the flames of the pyre, the reward of immortality'.

The free symmetrical arrangement of the episodes of 'voluptuousness' and 'striving', suggested by themes that are not so much transformed as presented in different tempos; the recitatives in which Hercules rejects pleasure and decides for virtue; many details of the transparent scoring: all suggest Liszt. But it is Liszt with the Romantic element left out. Even Saint-Saëns's orchestration really rests on the older Classical tradition, for instance in the handling of the brass. One has only to compare the climax of the bacchanale in *La Jeunesse d'Hercule* (Ex. 375) with (Ex. 376) a parallel passage in another French symphonic poem, *Lénore*, written three years earlier, in 1874, by Duparc, the composer to whom (as it happens) *Hercule* is dedicated, to see how far Saint-Saëns was

Ex. 375

Ex. 376

from being the leader of the French avant-garde.[37] Henri Duparc (1848–1933), had learned not only from Liszt but from Wagner, as other pages of *Lénore* show still more clearly, and the real flowering of the French symphonic poem in the 1870s and 1880s was due to

[37] It is difficult to believe that Saint-Saëns advised Duparc on the orchestration of *Lénore* (cf. Léon Vallas, *Vincent d'Indy* (Paris, 1946–50), i. 227). But we must remember that *Lénore* underwent considerable revision before its published form. Owing to illness, Duparc composed hardly anything after 1885.

the band of Wagnerians who acknowledged César Franck (1822–90) as their leader.

Outside the Franck circle there was plenty of pictorial and dramatic French orchestral music at this period when French instrumental music in general was enjoying a remarkable efflorescence in the early days of the Third Republic. There were the *Patrie* Overture of Bizet and Massenet's *Phèdre* (both 1873). Bizet's *Roma* Symphony (1868; rev. 1871), a decidedly suite-like symphony—originally performed as

a *fantaisie symphonique* and originally published as a *suite de concert*—
was one of the earliest of the 'topographical' orchestral pieces—
Spanish symphonies, Norwegian rhapsodies, Algerian suites, impressions of Italy, Alsatian scenes—which poured from Lalo, Saint-
Saëns, Massenet, Chabrier, Charpentier, and others during the next
quarter of a century and continued in a new idiom even in the
impressionistic pieces of the next generation.[38] But these compositions

[38] See Vol. X, pp. 1–79.

remain on the very fringe of programme music; they are never quite programme symphonies or symphonic poems; *Roma* differs from *Harold en Italie* in that it is a landscape without a figure. Chabrier's dazzling orchestral *tour de force*, *España* (1883), is no mere pot-pourri; after some hesitation, he rightly called it a rhapsody—'*C'est un morceau en* fa, *et rien de plus.*' But Duparc's *Lénore* is unquestionably a symphonic poem.

FRANCK AND HIS CIRCLE

Lénore was the earliest symphonic poem of the Franckist group, for Franck's own *Rédemption*, sometimes described as a symphonic poem, is really part of the middle portion of a *poème-symphonie* (original version 1872; rev. 1874) in the line of Félicien David's *odes-symphonies*. Even Duparc's choice of a German subject, Bürger's famous ballad,[39] is characteristic of a period when France seemed to have been conquered musically almost as thoroughly as she had been militarily, and for a longer period. Franck himself illustrated Bürger ('Der wilde Jäger') in *Le Chasseur maudit* (1882); his most prominent disciple Vincent d'Indy (1851-1931) was inspired by Uhland ('Harald') in *La Forêt enchantée* (1878), and by Schiller in the three pieces that constitute the *Wallenstein* trilogy (1879, 1873, and 1874). But it was, above all, the employment of a modern German musical technique that makes *Lénore* remarkable. It is not only the orchestration that is Wagnerian; the plastic types of theme and texture, the sensitively changing harmonies, which Duparc had observed in 1869-70 when he heard *Tristan*, *Das Rheingold*, and *Die Walküre* in Munich, gave him the means to fuse his episodes into a genuine dramatic narrative without obliterating the purely musical form. Lenore and Wilhelm are not represented by Lisztian motto-themes ingeniously but mechanically transformed, but by Wagnerian leitmotifs emotionally moulded and shaded from point to point. Thus the mourning Lenore of the opening (Ex. 377) becomes the

Ex. 377   Ex. 378

[39] Its special popularity as a programmatic subject in the early 1870s was due to the centenary of the poem, written in 1773. Besides Duparc's piece and Raff's symphony, there was a *Lénore* Symphony by a younger Liszt disciple, August Klughardt (1847-1902) (see Otto Klauwell, *Geschichte der Programmusik* (Leipzig, 1910), 204-7).

Ex. 379

terrified Lenore of the climax of the ride (Ex. 378), and the broken, dying Lenore of the end (Ex. 379).

The course of the narrative is clear: the mourning Lenore, the appearance of Wilhelm, the ride, the mounting terror, the stroke of midnight (which Duparc does *not* render literally with twelve strokes), the disappearance of the ghosts, and Lenore's death. Yet there is a clear and satisfactory musical plan: framed within the two slow passages of the mourning Lenore and the dying Lenore, the ride music is played twice—but with many changes. (It grows more terrifying, see Ex. 376.) And the recurrences of the 'Lenore' theme in its original form but in changing settings, at letters H, F, and X, suggest an articulation of the whole piece in ballad-like stanzas.

César Franck's earliest symphonic poem so called,[40] *Les Éolides* (1876), though inspired by a poem by Leconte de Lisle, is not so much programme music as an orchestral scherzo. The orchestration is Berliozian—Berlioz's influence on Franck, notably in the *Ruth* of thirty years earlier, has never been sufficiently recognized—and as becomes music addressed to

> brises flottantes des cieux,
> Du beau printemps douces haleines

more transparent and fanciful than Franck's scoring often is. The Wagnerian element is limited to the harmony and to the chromatic sighs of the 'baisers capricieux' (Ex. 380); Franck had heard the Prelude to *Tristan* not long before.

Le Chasseur maudit (1882), on the other hand, is frankly narrative and descriptive. Its subject inevitably provokes comparison with Duparc's *Lénore*: an unfortunate comparison, for the master was far more naïve than his disciple. The situations of *Le Chasseur maudit* are colourfully depicted—the orchestral procedure this time is

---

[40] The Bibliothèque du Conservatoire possesses the autograph full score of an orchestral piece by Franck entitled *Ce qu'on entend sur la montagne* (MS 8561). The score, which has been dated '1846' by another hand, seems to bear no relation to Victor Hugo's poem nor any indication of genre. See Julien Tiersot, 'Les Œuvres inédites de César Franck', *La Revue musicale*, 4/2 (1922), 117–24.

Ex. 380

Lisztian—in easily comprehensible musical terms: church-bells and hunting horns, the chase, the curse, the Hell-hunt. But the whole piece remains an aggregation of picturesque episodes. *Les Djinns* (1884) is more generalized, like *Les Éolides* to which it is a kind of demonic companion-piece. According to d'Indy,[41] it is 'only rather remotely connected' with Victor Hugo's poem, though Cortot, in his penetrating study of the work,[42] sees analogies between the musical structure and the 'lozenge' shape of the poem. The chief interest of the music lies in the introduction, for no extra-musical reason, of a piano in the orchestra—a lady-pianist had asked Franck for a short work for piano and orchestra[43]—but, although the piano and the orchestral writing are both somewhat Lisztian, there is no noticeable relation to Liszt's *Totentanz*, his nearest approach to a symphonic poem with piano.

Franck's last essay in this field, *Psyche* (1888), is nominally a still more curious experiment, a *poème symphonique pour chœur et orchestre*, though like *Rédemption* it really owes its origin to the *ode-symphonie*. It is in three 'parts', each of which is subdivided into sharply differentiated sections:

> I Psyche's sleep (orchestra only: Lento, B major)
> Psyche carried off by the Zephyrs (orchestra: Allegro vivo, modulating from G major to D flat; based on themes from *Les Éolides*)

[41] *César Franck* (8th edn.; Paris, 1919), 143.
[42] *La Musique française de piano* (Paris, 1930–48), i. 80–91.
[43] Léon Vallas, *La Véritable Histoire de César Franck* (Paris, 1950); Eng. trans., Hubert Foss (London, 1951), 176–7.

II The gardens of Eros (orchestra and chorus: Poco animato
and Lento, beginning and ending in D flat)
Psyche and Eros (orchestra only: Andante ma non troppo
lento, A major)

III The Punishment—Psyche's sufferings and lamentations—
Apotheosis (orchestra and chorus: Lento, beginning in F
sharp minor and ending in E major)

The conception is essentially orchestral, the chorus—which Franck
wished to be invisible—entering to comment or to address Psyche
only at certain points to clarify the action:

'Mais, Psyche, souviens-toi que tu ne dois jamais de ton mystique amant
connaître le visage . . .'
'Amour, elle a connu ton nom. Malheur sur elle! . . .'
'Eros a pardonné . . .'

But the general effect is very patchy and, despite the sensitively
sensuous beauty of certain passages—if *Psyche* is Wagnerian it is
influenced by the Wagner who wrote the love-music for Eva and
Walther, not the composer of *Tristan und Isolde*—it is an incident
rather than a milestone in the history of the symphonic poem.

The symphonic poems of the other members of Franck's circle—
Chausson's *Viviane*, Lekeu's *Hamlet*, and the *Irlande* of Augusta
Holmes—are overshadowed by those of their more vigorous comrade
d'Indy, whose *Forêt enchantée* and *Wallenstein* have already been
mentioned. The central piece in the *Wallenstein* trilogy, the first to
be composed, was *Piccolomini*, in which, anticipating his friend
Duparc in *Lénore*, he employed Wagnerian means (personal leitmotifs, plastic texture, quasi-polyphony) to suggest the course of a
dramatic action,[44] but the form is not completely free—it begins
with an Andante-and-allegro-risoluto in orthodox sonata form—and
d'Indy employed a similar grafting of free to traditional form in *La
Forêt enchantée*, which was styled successively *symphonie-legende*,
ballade symphonique, and *symphonie-ballade*. A comparison with
Tchaikovsky's exactly contemporary *Tempest* illustrates the difference
between what may be called the Wagnerian and the older, Lisztian
type of symphonic poem. The love scenes in *The Tempest*, though
more convincingly erotic than d'Indy's, are two passages of impersonal 'love music' connected by purely musical methods to the
episodes which precede and follow them, with which they have no

---

[44] The first edition of the *Ouverture des Piccolomini* was headed by a definite programme,
printed by Vallas, *César Franck*, i. 185. But the music is so explicit that such guidance is
hardly necessary.

dramatic connection. D'Indy has already established his hero and heroine as two musical characters so that when, in the course of Thekla's music, Max's theme enters in counterpoint, the narrative is as comprehensible as if it were accompanied by action on the stage. And their idyll is shattered in Wagnerian style by the entry of cornets and trombones with a new theme on an interrupted cadence: the leitmotif of Wallenstein.

In 1874 d'Indy produced a second *ouverture symphonique* inspired by Schiller, *La Mort de Wallenstein*, and in 1879 a third, *Le Camp de Wallenstein*. *Les Piccolomini* was now revised and renamed *Max et Thecla* and took its place as the central *partie* of *Wallenstein: Trilogie d'après le poème dramatique de Schiller*. This is sometimes spoken of as a symphony; but, although d'Indy had in earlier days dreamed of a *Wallenstein* Symphony,[45] his descriptions of the existing work are the only accurate ones; it is a trilogy or *suite d'ouvertures* connected by common themes.

D'Indy essayed other forms of programme music: the programme symphony in the never published *Jean Hunyade* (1875), the older, Lisztian type of poem in the *légende*, *Saugefleurie*, on a poem by Robert de Bonnières (1884)—despite his description of it as an *allégorie musicale avec personnages thématiques*[46]—and the curious experiment of programmatic variations in *Istar* (1896), where the theme, the musical equivalent of the heroine of the Assyrian epic of *Izdubar*, is revealed in ever clearer simplicity and finally appears in naked unison.

SMETANA AND DVOŘÁK

Problems of nomenclature in mid-century bothered others besides Smetana in the Czech lands. In 1858 Alois Hnilička (1826–1909) composed an overture, *Táborita* [The Taborite], later described as a symphonic poem. And in the same year Smetana's friend and pupil Ludevít Procházka (1837–88) conceived an *Alfred* symphony inspired by Vítězslav Hálek's poem, the first movement of which survived as a 'symphonic poem'. Smetana himself, after ten years almost exclusively devoted to opera, returned to the symphonic poem in the 1870s. The idea of a whole cycle of pieces inspired by Czech landscape and Czech history under the general title *Má Vlast* [My Country] was suggested by the conclusion of the opera *Libuše*,[47] where the

---

[45] Vallas, *Vincent d'Indy*, p. 105.

[46] *Cours de composition musicale*, II. ii. 327.

[47] Otakar Zich, *Symfonické Básně Smetanovy: Hudebně estetický rozbor* (Prague, 1924), 61; Otakar Šourek, *Smetanova 'Má Vlast': Její vznik a osudy* (Prague, 1939), 9–10; Brian Large, *Smetana* (London, 1970), 260–88; John Clapham, *Smetana* (London, 1972), 75–84.

heroine has a prophetic vision of a series of episodes in her country's history; indeed opera and cycle are related thematically as well as in general mood; one of the themes of the first poem, *Vyšehrad* (bars 21 ff.), comes from a passage in the opera (Act II, Scene v) where a character mentions 'the tower of Vyšehrad', and both opera and cycle close in D major with the Hussite hymn 'Kdož jste Boží bojovníci' [Ye who are Warriors of God]. The six poems differ considerably in type of subject and treatment, but are generally Lisztian in structure as in orchestration, though individual in other respects. *Vyšehrad* (1874) is a general evocation of Czech history, symbolized by the ancient citadel, a vision of chivalry, war, and ruin, while *Vltava* (also 1874) traces the course of the river in a series of tone pictures defined by headings in the score and held together only by the refrain-like appearances of the main 'river' music. *Šárka* (1875) narrates a historical legend and is frankly programmatic, though Smetana objected to attempts at over-detailed exegesis. *Z českých luhů a hájů* [From Bohemian Fields and Forests] (1875) is, according to Smetana himself, an attempt to 'sketch life in songs and dances, what the Germans call *Volksweisen* or *Tanzweisen*'[48] against a pastoral background; there is no definite programme, though the composer no doubt followed some such train of thought as that outlined by V. V. Zelený in his authorized programme for the first performance.[49]

Tábor (1878) and *Blaník* (1879) may be regarded almost as two halves of a single piece, being united by key and based on the same material, including the Hussite hymn of *Vyšehrad*; the first looks back to the heroic days of the Hussite wars, the second forward to the time when the Hussite warriors shall emerge from the mountain where they sleep their centuries-long sleep and bring back freedom and glory to the Czech land. In addition to this close connection between the last two poems of *Má Vlast*, a looser association is established by the introduction of themes from *Vyšehrad* at the culminating points of *Vltava* and *Blaník*. More important: *Má Vlast* as a whole amounts to something more than the sum of its parts. The cycle opens and closes in a lofty, heroic vein, while the picturesque legend of *Šárka* is flanked by the two mainly pastoral pieces.

The only other notable Czech exponent of the symphonic poem at this period, Zdeněk Fibich (1850-1900), shows much less in-

---

[48] *Bedřich Smetana a Dr. Lud. Procházka: Vzájemná korespondence*, ed. Jan Löwenbach (Prague, 1914), 13. Zich, *Symfonické Básně Smetanovy*, p. 85, misquotes 'in *work* and dance'.
[49] See Zich, *Symfonické Básně Smetanovy*, p. 86.

dividuality in his *Othello* (1873), *Záboj, Slavoj a Luděk* (1873)—from which Smetana inadvertently borrowed his 'Vyšehrad' theme—and *Toman a lesní panna* [Toman and the wood-nymph] (1874), as well as two 'symphonic pictures', *Bouře* (Shakespeare's *Tempest*) (1880) and *Vesna* [Spring] (1881). The far more gifted Dvořák (1841–1904) was late and at first tentative in turning to programme music. The three overtures now known as *V přírodě* [Mid-nature] (1891), *Karneval* (1891), and *Othello* (1892) really constitute a trilogy originally entitled *Příroda, Život a Láska* [Nature, Life, and Love]. They are connected by a common musical motto and the idea of 'nature as the source of life': the bliss of solitude on a summer night, the joy of mingling with a happy crowd, and the bitterness of love poisoned by jealousy.[50] But it was only at the very end of his career as an orchestral composer that Dvořák arrived at the symphonic poem proper, producing a group of five. Even so, the last of these, *Píseň bohatýrská* [Heroic Song] (1897), is not programmatic except in the most general sense. But its four predecessors, all dating from 1896 and all based on ballads from K. J. Erben's *Kytice*, are curious attempts by an essentially 'abstract' musician to write detailed narrative music. They are *Vodník* [The Water-sprite], *Polednice* [The Noon Witch], *Zlatý kolovrat* [The Golden Spinning-wheel], and *Holoubek* [The Little Dove]; all are peasant tales of the type we associate, in Germany, with the brothers Grimm. The music is correspondingly naïve, orchestrated in primary colours of extreme brilliance, sharply episodic and following closely the details of the story, many of which Dvořák indicated in his composition-sketches,[51] though none appear in the published scores. Yet, paradoxically, it lacks true narrative power; the descriptive element is conventional and superficial. The material is for the most part frankly lyrical and often charming, but the peculiarly interesting feature of these four works is that the themes and melodies are in a number of cases moulded on Erben's actual words.[52]

Dvořák knew his Wagner very well and sometimes succumbed to his influence but here he turned his back on Wagner completely; the themes of his symphonic poems are more or less arbitrary symbols, not leitmotifs. Yet, as in the cases of Duparc and d'Indy a Wagnerian technique offered far the best means available for writing music that could really suggest narrative without loss of musical coherence.

[50] Otakar Šourek, *Dvořákovy skladby orchestrální* (Prague, 1944–6), ii. 86.

[51] See Antonín Sychra, *Estetika Dvořákovy symfonické tvorby* (Prague, 1959), 43–54, 114–30, and the facsimiles following p. 520.

[52] Gerald Abraham, *The Tradition of Western Music* (London and Berkeley, 1974), 83.

THE WAGNERIAN LEGACY

The German Wagnerians were strangely slow in turning to the symphonic poem, being perhaps inhibited by reverence for Wagner's own rejection of programme music as an independent, self-sufficient form of art. But it was impossible not to observe that orchestral excerpts from Wagner heard in the concert hall often made highly effective and unusually comprehensible pieces of programme music; it was increasingly tempting to compose original programme music on similar lines. Yet the earliest important Teutonic symphonic poem deriving from Wagner rather than Liszt, the *Penthesilea* (1883)[53] of Hugo Wolf (1860-1903) is a triptych comparable with d'Indy's *Wallenstein* rather than a narrative. It consists of three distinct, though connected and thematically related, movements: the departure of the Amazons for Troy, Penthesilea's dream of the Rose Festival (Ex. 381), and 'Combats, Passions, Madness, Annihilation'. (Wolf's programme is derived from Kleist's tragedy in which Penthesilea kills Achilles, whom she loves, instead of being killed by him.) Except in the first movement with its trumpet-calls and its 'ride' theme—so like the 'ride' themes of *Le Chasseur maudit* and *Saugefleurie*—Wolf seeks not to suggest a series of events but to express the savage and hysterical emotions of his heroine.

Wolf's solitary essay, after a notorious rehearsal by the Vienna Philharmonic Orchestra (15 October 1886), was never performed in his lifetime. In any case it would have been eclipsed by the series of works by Richard Strauss (1864-1949) begun in 1886 with the 'symphonic fantasia' *Aus Italien*. It was Strauss, a far more assured master of the Wagnerian orchestra than Wolf, who in *Macbeth* (1887; rev. 1890), *Don Juan* (1888), *Tod und Verklärung* (1889), *Till Eulenspiegels lustige Streiche* (1895), *Also sprach Zarathustra* (1896), *Don Quixote* (1897), *Ein Heldenleben* (1898) and the *Symphonie Domestica* (1904) gradually carried orchestral programme music to what still appear to be its extreme limits so far as narrative is concerned. In psychological character drawing on Wagnerian lines, also, Strauss was most skilful; in evocation of mood and setting and landscape much less so. Yet it was as a landscape-painter that the 22-year-old Strauss, under the intellectual influence of Alexander Ritter, first broke away from the Classical leading reins that had held his earlier compositions. *Aus Italien* is a symphonic suite of four

---

[53] Authentic text published only in 1937, in the series of *Nachgelassene Werke*, ed. Robert Haas and Helmut Schultz (Leipzig and Vienna). The score published by the Hugo-Wolf Verein (Leipzig, 1903) was a much shortened version with a great deal of rescoring, made by the younger Josef Hellmesberger and Ferdinand Löwe.

Ex. 381

Ex. 382

travel impressions,[54] like Berlioz's *Harold* and Bizet's *Roma*. (Italian travel had been a source of orchestral inspiration during much of the century; d'Indy wrote an Italian symphony with tarantella Finale, never published, in 1872.) With all its debts to Liszt and, to a lesser extent, Wagner, *Aus Italien* sounds some completely original notes. Such passages as Ex. 382 from the third movement, 'On the Beach at Sorrento', show that the orchestral technique of impressionism

[54] Strauss's own description, written three years later, is given in Michael Kennedy, *Strauss Tone Poems* (London, 1984), 11.

was already to hand although the real impressionists did not lavish such colour on simple triads.

Strauss's earliest *Tondichtung* actually so called—he never used the term *symphonische Dichtung*—was *Macbeth*, although the revised version ultimately published was made after the composition of *Tod und Verklärung*. It is in many respects a near relative of Wolf's *Penthesilea*, a character study powerfully executed in rather grey colouring. Macbeth's personal theme is actually marked as such in the score; Lady Macbeth, whose appearance is indicated by the quotation

> Hie thee hither,
> That I may pour my spirits in thine ear;
> And chastise with the valour of my tongue
> All that impedes thee from the golden round
> Which fate and metaphysical aid doth seem
> To have thee crown'd withal,

is a function (in the mathematical sense) of Macbeth rather than an independent character. There is little or no attempt to suggest the outward events of the play and Strauss clearly did right to suppress his original ending: the D major triumph of Macduff. Strauss's natural gifts as a musical dramatist and his command of a far more flexible means of expression lifted *Macbeth* above earlier character studies; technically, the portrait of Macbeth is more subtly, less theatrically drawn than Liszt's Faust, and the musical material, if much less striking, is better organized. *Macbeth* is organic music, apart from the circumstance that its organism is distantly sonata-like.

In *Don Juan*, inspired by Lenau's dramatic fragment, Strauss attempted to combine a character study with some suggestion of a narrative sequence. The hero is depicted with all his boundless energy, his boundless erotic desires, his moods of satiety, but he is also shown in action, flirting with a country-girl, making love to a countess, nearly conquered by Donna Anna, at a masked ball, mortally wounded by Don Pedro. Strauss made none of this explicit in a literary programme; he was content to reveal the source of his inspiration and, after the first performance, to print in the score excerpts from Lenau's poem,[55] expressing his hero's erotic philosophy and his sense of its failure; the music itself is explicit enough. Dramatically the episodes are subsumed into the portrait of the hero; musically they are fused into an organic form so original and unconventional that attempts have been made to refer it now to

[55] See ibid., p. 18.

sonata form,[56] now to rondo;[57] yet practically all critics have agreed in finding it totally satisfactory. Orchestrally the score is notable for a rich and warm brilliance that Strauss in later years often outbid but never really surpassed. *Don Juan* was written at a time when brilliant orchestration was becoming more and more common—Rimsky-Korsakov's *Sheherazade* and Tchaikovsky's Fifth Symphony both date from the same year—but its opening (a tremendous C major 'up-beat' to E major, typical of Strauss's masterful treatment of key) is as outstanding amid the music of its period as the opening of Berlioz's *Carnaval romain* in the music of the 1840s. Throughout the score the Wagnerian thematic polyphony is lightened by a Berliozian–Lisztian vivacity; the broad diatonic melodies at the heart of the typically post-Wagnerian texture, with its chromatic harmony and abrupt key changes, are sweet and sensuous.

Similar qualities, but with dry, grotesque humour in place of lush Romanticism, inform *Till Eulenspiegel*, a rather more restrained display of orchestral virtuosity, though the forces employed are even larger, including triple woodwind, eight horns, and six trumpets. Here the hero's character is displayed almost entirely in action and a series of definite events is narrated with the aid of two leitmotifs for the hero, wonderfully transformed, and a number of subsidiary themes in a species of freely varied sonata rondo. And two years later he frankly adopted the variation form for his much greater *Don Quixote*, 'fantastic variations on a theme of chivalrous character' or, rather, on two themes—one for the Don and one for Sancho: yet another series of specific events, with far more subtle psychological treatment of the hero than in *Till*. And just as Berlioz's Harold had been impersonated by a solo viola, Quixote and his squire appear not only as leitmotifs but as solo cello and viola. In *Till* and *Don Quixote* suggestive symbolism and realistic suggestion are carried as far as it is possible to carry them in music; the bleating of sheep in the second variation of *Quixote* is a *ne plus ultra*—as, in a different way, is the pathos of the hero's death. Yet even in these essays in extreme explicitness Strauss was as unwilling as Rimsky-Korsakov to avow the details of his programme. Neither *Till* nor *Quixote* has a printed programme, not even section headings. When the conductor Franz Wüllner asked Strauss to supply a programme note for the first performance of *Till*, he replied that it was 'impossible' for him

---

[56] Cf. Max Steinitzer, *Richard Strauss* (13th edn.; Berlin, 1922), 82; Reinhold Konrad Muschler, *Richard Strauss* (Hildesheim, 1925), 263, 266; Fritz Gysi, *Richard Strauss* (Potsdam, 1934), 45; Klauwell, *Geschichte der Programmusik*, p. 230.

[57] Cf. Richard Specht, *Richard Strauss und sein Werk* (Vienna and Leipzig, 1921), i. 181.

Ex. 383

to give a programme, that what he had thought in composing the various parts would appear 'often rather odd' if clothed in words and would 'perhaps even give offence'.[58] Yet he afterwards allowed every detail to be made known and placed the autograph score with his marginal annotations at the disposal of Wilhelm Mauke for his guide to the work.[59] Without such a guide it would be impossible to guess that Ex. 383 is intended to suggest Till creeping into a mousehole; with it, one can be amused by Strauss's ingenuity. Considered from a purely musical point of view, *Till* is a brilliant orchestral scherzo or humoresque while many pages of *Don Quixote* contain passages unsurpassed in the whole range of post-Wagnerian orchestral polyphony.

Between these realistic narratives Strauss produced two tone-poems of a less definite character. *Tod und Verklärung*, a deathbed scene, is still a narrative—of the thoughts and pictures that throng the brain of a dying man. But the two explanatory poems by Alexander Ritter[60] were written after the music; he obviously versified a rough scenario given him by the composer. Yet several critics[61] have seen in it a partial retrogression to Lisztian thought, types of material,

[58] The letter is given in full in Muschler, *Richard Strauss*, p. 315, Gysi, *Richard Strauss*, p. 50, Steinitzer, *Richard Strauss*, p. 133, and elsewhere. And see *Richard Strauss und Franz Wüllner im Briefwechsel*, ed. Dietrich Kämper (Cologne, 1963).

[59] In the series of Meisterführer, *Richard Strauss: Symphonien und Tondichtungen* (Berlin, n.d.)

[60] The first ('Stille, einsam öde Nacht!'), copied on the title-page of the autograph full score (cf. the facsimile reproduction, Vienna, n.d.), printed in the programme books of the first two performances, and reproduced in Muschler, *Richard Strauss*, p. 275; the second ('In der ärmlich kleinen Kammer') printed in the published score and also given by Muschler, pp. 276–7.

[61] Cf. Muschler, *Richard Strauss*, p. 274; Gysi, *Richard Strauss*, p. 48. Rey M. Longyear has detected the influence of the last section of Moszkowski's *Johanna d'Arc* (1879), 'Schiller, Moszkowski and Strauss', *Music Review*, 28 (1967), 209.

and even scoring. *Also sprach Zarathustra* ('freely after Friedrich Nietzsche') is in some respects even more Lisztian in style (e.g. the opening passage) and in its episodic structure, each section being headed by a chapter-title from Nietzsche's book despite the general irrelevance of the music to the content of the chapter. The episodes are neither symmetrically balanced as in Liszt's own works nor fused into a satisfactory organic whole; there is no narrative, only a sequence of general ideas or, musically, a torrent of rhetoric. The most striking features of *Zarathustra* are its inflated orchestra— Strauss here writes for quadruple woodwind, and adds the organ— and its tonal antithesis of totally unrelated keys. B major or minor asserts itself throughout against C major or minor as the principal key, not only in the subject of the fugue 'Concerning Science'. And this dualism persists to the very end, where a trombone chord (C, E, F sharp) is resolved in different senses simultaneously: by the lower strings, pizzicato, whose F sharp moves to G, and by the harp and upper wind which resolve the C and E to B and D sharp.

The culmination of Strauss's work in this field was reached in two quasi-autobiographical compositions, *Ein Heldenleben* and *Symphonia domestica*. (The title of the latter implies that its four sections correspond to the movements of a Classical symphony.) Each narrates with the aid of a complex of leitmotifs a series of generally idealized events, those of the hero's career and those of a few hours of his domestic life. The orchestra in both is larger even than that of *Zarathustra*: the quadruple woodwind are augmented by fifth members of the clarinet and bassoon groups and a quartet of saxophones in the *Domestica*, and both works call for eight horns— which are treated with all the flexibility of violins. These vast forces are employed in the weaving of a thematic polyphony so sumptuous, so loaded with colour, that the ear is liable to be satiated even in relatively quiet passages.[62] Such scores threaten to break down under the weight not only of their orchestra[63] but of their structure. Recognition that there could be no further progress in this direction is implicit in Strauss's abandonment of the symphonic poem (except for the *Alpensymphonie* of 1915) after the *Domestica*. He who had carried the precise expressiveness of purely orchestral music as far, probably, as it can be carried, now had to call in the aid of words and action. The Wagnerian aesthetic had avenged itself.

[62] See, for instance, Vol. X, p. 5, Ex. 2.
[63] On Strauss's orchestra, see H. Woollett and Gabriel Pierné, 'Histoire de l'orchestration: Max Reger et Richard Strauss', in Lavignac (ed.), *Encyclopédie*, II. iv. 2620–35; Egon Wellesz, *Die neue Instrumentation* (Berlin, 1928), ii. 36–47, and Norman Del Mar, *Richard Strauss: A Critical Commentary on his Life and Works* (London, 1962–72).

VIII

MAJOR INSTRUMENTAL FORMS: 1850–1890

By ROBERT PASCALL

HISTORICAL PERSPECTIVES

BEETHOVEN continued to dominate musical creativity for many years after his death—in choice of genres and instrumental forms, in the preservation of stylistic essentials based on thematic drama in a tonal context, and in increased emphasis on originality and significance (rather than technique and entertainment). Wagner, in one of the greatest public tributes by any composer to another, wrote in 1870 that Beethoven had lifted music 'far above the aesthetically beautiful into the sphere of the totally sublime' by the emancipation of melody 'from the influence of fashion and changing taste' and its elevation into an 'eternally valid type for all humanity'.[1]

Brahms learnt the core of his creative equipment from Beethoven, rather than his own immediate predecessors, Mendelssohn, Schumann, and Spohr; Lalo took part from 1856 in professional performances of Beethoven's chamber music; Berlioz wrote on Beethoven and published a selection of his writings in 1862, including studies of all the Beethoven symphonies;[2] Liszt finished his transcriptions of the symphonies for piano solo in 1865, in spite of the near-impossibility he felt of doing justice to the Finale of the Ninth; and Wagner chose his essay on the hundredth anniversary of the composer's birth, cited above, to present his own deepest philosophy of music. Meanwhile, the scholars von Lenz, A. B. Marx, Nottebohm, and Thayer were at work on Beethoven, and Breitkopf & Härtel published a Complete Edition in 1862–5.

Wagner's accolade may be seen in the context of the generally enhanced awareness in the second half of the nineteenth century of the present value of past achievements, an awareness which encompassed not only Classical music but also that of the Baroque

---

[1] Richard Wagner, *Gesammelte Schriften und Dichtungen*, ix (2nd edn.; Leipzig, 1888), 102.
[2] Hector Berlioz, *À travers chants* (Paris, 1862).

and late-Renaissance. While the latter mainly influenced choral genres, the continuing rediscovery of Baroque music had a powerful effect on some of the instrumental genres selected by composers, especially in the revivification of the suite, prelude and fugue, and chorale-prelude. It also affected styles in other genres, by the assimilation of Baroque sequences, imitations, canon, fugue, developmental processes, and figurations into sonata and other forms. Such assimilation is especially significant in the styles of Bruckner and Brahms. Just how far it could extend is well shown by the Adagio of Brahms's Clarinet Quintet (1891), where a fully contemporary movement in ternary form has its opening lyrical theme based on the Baroque harmonic progression of the chromatically descending fourth, tonic to dominant, and the theme beginning in canon; the point is reinforced by the genetic history of this theme, which is a reworking of an early neo-Baroque Sarabande (1854) by Brahms.

Bach's music had been in part known to small circles of cognoscenti ever since his death; but Mendelssohn gave important impetus to increased public awareness of this great repertoire with his justly famous performance of the *St Matthew Passion* in 1829, and in the first half of the nineteenth century, particularly Bach's keyboard music became quite widely known. In 1851 the Bach Gesellschaft began work on its publication of the Complete Edition; similarly a Handel Complete Edition was founded in 1858, both editions running throughout this period. Chrysander included works by Carissimi, Corelli, and Couperin in his *Denkmäler der Tonkunst* (1869–71)— Brahms editing one of the volumes of Couperin's keyboard music (he also contributed significantly to the Handel Complete Edition). Spitta's great biography of Bach appeared in 1873–80 and Chrysander's unfinished Handel biography in 1858–67.

There were other important strands of historical perspective in this period. Schubert's achievements as an instrumental composer had, even during his life, been largely eclipsed by his *Lieder*. Mendelssohn's performance of the great C major Symphony in 1839 and Schumann's critique of the work in the subsequent year were landmarks in the discovery of Schubert as an instrumental composer of the first rank. In 1846 Liszt played the *Fantasie*, Op. 15 (the 'Wanderer' Fantasia), which he later arranged for piano and orchestra; Hellmesberger gave first performances of some of the chamber-music masterpieces during the early 1850s in Vienna; the Symphony in B minor (the 'Unfinished') was first performed in 1865 by Herbeck, and Kreissle von Hellborn's biography appeared the same year. Much of Schubert's instrumental music had to wait until the 1880s for public rediscovery, and the Complete Edition ran from 1884 to 1897; but those works known earlier became important sources of influence on Liszt, Bruckner, Brahms, and Dvořák among others. Mozart also exerted real power over the musical consciousness of the period; Jahn's biography appeared in 1856, Köchel's Catalogue in 1862, and the Complete Edition ran from 1877 to 1883. Brahms and Tchaikovsky both viewed Mozart as an example of perfection and purity in composition.

Historicism in this period must be understood primarily not as antiquarianism, but as a trend towards the recognition of universal, a-temporal significance in works of previous times. The musical horizons of the age thus became very broad and the possibilities for stylistic influence correspondingly diverse. Naturally this historicism did not exclude modern composers from exerting influence over compositional concepts and techniques: the importance of Berlioz and Liszt, particularly for Russian and French composers, and the continuing Mendelssohnian styles of Raff, Lachner, and Rheinberger are cases in point.

PROGRAMMATICISM

An important part of the background to programmaticism as a way of composing is programmaticism as a way of hearing and receiving. Specifically musical gestural flux was regarded as analogous to, and even as incorporating, the flux of felt life. The main thrust of Hanslick's famous study *Vom Musikalisch-Schönen*[3] is sometimes oversimplified into a purely formalist one (by concentration on his aphoristic paragraph 'The essence of music is sound and motion'), but his broad argument, largely concerned with consideration of music as a referential code, establishes an analogue between expressive change within a musical work and the general dynamics of emotion. Liszt went further and defined music in his essay on Berlioz's *Harold en Italie* as 'the embodied, palpable manifestation of feeling'.[4] The flux of felt life could naturally be attached to words and concrete ideas, and the play of ideational fancy around music was a recognized and valued mode of appreciation. E. T. A. Hoffmann had been one of the early masters of 'poetizing criticism', and the exegesis of music

[3] Leipzig, 1854.

[4] 'Verkörperte, fassbare Wesenheit des Gefühls' (Franz Liszt, 'Berlioz und seine Haroldsymphonie', *Neue Zeitschrift für Musik*, 43 (1855), 41a). Discussed in Detlef Altenburg, 'Eine Theorie der Musik der Zukunft: Zur Funktion des Programms im symphonischen Werk von Franz Liszt', in Wolfgang Suppan (ed.), *Liszt Studien 1: Kongress-Bericht Eisenstadt 1975* (Graz, 1977), 9–25.

not overtly programmatic by a speculative interpretative programme was an established form of private and public critical writing. Clara Schumann wrote in her diary, of the last movement of Brahms's First Symphony, 'the Introduction so shadowy, in a truly staggering way it then clarifies so gradually up to the sunny theme of the last movement, at which one's heart literally swells, as if refreshed by spring air after long and dismal days ...'.[5] Joachim saw in the last movement of Brahms's Third Symphony the story of Hero and Leander, as he told Brahms in his letter of 27 January 1884; and Clara Schumann wrote of this whole symphony to its composer: 'How one is from beginning to end surrounded by the secret magic of the life of the forest!'[6] Wagner, who maintained in his open letter *Über Franz Liszt's symphonische Dichtungen* 'Nothing is (*nota bene*: for its appearance in life) less absolute than music',[7] wrote *Programmatische Erläuterungen* [Programmatic Elucidations] of instrumental works by Beethoven and himself; he also included an interpretation of Beethoven's C sharp minor Quartet, Op. 131, in his essay on the composer (quoted above) in which he treated the work as paralleling a day in Beethoven's life.

Interpretations of this kind must be viewed as conditioned by, and in some sense appropriate to, the musical work; but they are also free and inconclusive. Such hermeneutic reception does not necessarily show *naïveté*; the interpreter felt the need to discuss music in a manner that was thought to go further than purely structural analysis by integrating it into the totality of his experience.

Within the context of this marked tendency to hermeneutic reception, a given programme attached by its composer to an instrumental work could act partly as a limitation on receptive fantasy; indeed Liszt's own definition of programme music draws on this idea. In the essay on *Harold en Italie* he wrote that a programme was a 'preface by means of which the composer intends to guard listeners against wilfulness in poetic interpretation, and to direct his attention to the poetic idea of the whole or to a particular point in it'.[8] We should remember that *Poesie* was a nineteenth-century term indicating imaginative value in general, though programme music often called upon works of literature, and Liszt himself wrote of his

[5] Berthold Litzmann, *Clara Schumann: Ein Künstlerleben nach Tagebüchern und Briefen*, iii (4th edn.; Leipzig, 1920), 347.

[6] *Johannes Brahms Briefwechsel*, vi. *Johannes Brahms im Briefwechsel mit Joseph Joachim*, ed. Andreas Moser (2nd edn.; Berlin, 1912), 211–12; *Clara Schumann–Johannes Brahms: Briefe aus den Jahren 1853–1896*, ed. Berthold Litzmann (Leipzig, 1927), ii. 273.

[7] Richard Wagner, *Gesammelte Schriften und Dichtungen*, v (2nd edn.; Leipzig, 1888).

[8] Cited and discussed in Roger Scruton, *The Aesthetic Understanding* (London and New York, 1983), 41.

innovative thrust at Weimar during the 1850s that his aims had been 'the renewal of music by its deeper connection with the poetic art'.[9]

However one defines programme music, the programmatic function consists of a verbal ideational premiss acting as at once subject and metaphor for a composition; this is so even in those somewhat rare cases where a programme has been written after the completion of the composition, when a specific interpretation is elevated into a formal premiss. Mostly, however, the generation of music by a programme is actual; composers of programme music composed to a programme. Yet music, even vocal, can never be fully generated by words alone; it always has its own purely musical generating factors.

We may recognize a distinction between narrative and meditative modes of the programmatic function. The narrative mode often shows a high degree of conditioning by a programme, for a narrative programme helps generate both the substance and the sequence of the differentiations in a musical structure. This narrative mode finds a natural home in the symphonic poem (Liszt's *Mazeppa* and Smetana's *Šárka* are examples), though it did penetrate the symphony, as in Raff's *Lénore*. The meditative mode is rather in the nature of either a facet exploration or a mood parallel; the differentiations of musical substance are not ordered according to a prestated or pre-existent narrative, and are not necessarily concretely descriptive. The first movement of Liszt's *Eine Faust-Symphonie* (the 'Faust' Symphony) is an extensive but clear sonata form, while at the same time being a character study of Faust himself, as the titles of the work and movement make plain: *Eine Faust-Symphonie in drei Charakterbildern. I. Faust*. The title of Rubinstein's *Océan symphonie* (in which the separate movements do not carry further titles) invites the listener to play with ideas of immensity and elemental motion. In the meditative mode the programme is usually condensed into a title or titles only. But a title can of course incorporate a work of literature by referring to it, as is the case with Liszt's 'Faust' Symphony and Rheinberger's symphonic tone picture *Wallenstein*.

Another form of verbal ideational premiss is the poetic motto; this appears, for instance, in the second movements of Brahms's Piano Sonatas, Opp. 2 and 5, and in the first pieces of his collections Opp. 10 and 117, in Sterndale Bennett's Piano Sonata (where there

---

[9] Letter to Agnes Street-Klindworth, 16 Nov. 1860; cited and discussed in Carl Dahlhaus, 'Zur Problematik der musikalischen Gattungen im 19. Jahrhundert', in Wulf Arlt, Ernst Lichtenhahn, Hans Oesch (eds.), *Gattungen der Musik in Einzeldarstellungen: Gedenkschrift Leo Schrade* (Berne and Munich, 1973), 861.

are also titles for the movements), and in two of the movements from MacDowell's *Erste moderne Suite*. Poetic mottoes should usually be taken as in the meditative mode. But some scholars have controversially unpacked Brahms's mottoes as narrative programmes, and the sequence of movement titles and mottoes in Sterndale Bennett's Sonata creates a narrative programme for the work as a whole.

While poetry, literature, and legend provided important sources of programmatic material, so too did the physical environment. Following Mendelssohn's example in his 'Italian' and 'Scottish' Symphonies, composers made countries the titles and subjects of their symphonies and suites: Sullivan's Symphony in E, the Irish, Lalo's *Symphonie espagnole*, and Massenet's *Scènes hongroises*. Regions or types of environment (sea, forest, mountains) could also be specified: for example, Charles Bordes's *Suite basque*, and Raff's Symphony No. 7, *In den Alpen*. The seasons of the year also appeared: Tchaikovsky's Symphony No. 1, *Winter Daydreams*, Lange-Müller's *Symphonie Efteraar* [Autumn], and Raff's Symphonies 8–11 (which form a cycle based on all four seasons). In programmes drawn from the physical environment the subject could be an environment alone, or include delineations of events in that environment. Such inclusions could be highly picturesque, and also employ elements of make-believe: Raff's Symphony No. 8, *Frühlingsklänge* [Sounds of Spring] has 'In der Walpurgisnacht' as its second movement. Where countries or regions are specified, national or exotic colour is often present in the music, sometimes borrowing folk-song, as in Bordes's *Suite basque*.

In programme music, words and ideas are unequivocally incorporated into a musical work, but there are a significant number of examples of private, secret, or suppressed programmes. Schumann told his wife through their communal diary that his Fourth Symphony was to be about her, and the principal theme of this essentially monothematic work is derived cryptographically from her name.[10] Tchaikovsky wrote of his Sixth Symphony that it was to be a 'programme symphony; but with a programme that should remain an enigma for everyone but myself'.[11] And Mahler's First Symphony,

[10] Litzmann, *Clara Schumann*, ii (5th edn.; Leipzig, 1918), 30: 'My next symphony shall be called "Clara", and I will depict her therein with flutes, oboes, and harps.' For work on the 'Clara' theme, see Eric Sams, 'Did Schumann use Ciphers', *Musical Times*, 106 (1965), 584; 'The Schumann Ciphers', *Musical Times*, 107 (1966), 392; 'The Tonal Analogue in Schumann's Music', *Proceedings of the Royal Musical Association*, 96 (1969–70), 103.

[11] Letter to 'Bob' Davidov, Feb. 1893; cited in John Warrack, *Tchaikovsky Symphonies and Concertos* (London, 1969), 34. See also Gerald Abraham, *On Russian Music* (repr. New York, 1980), 143–6, where a fascinating private sketch of a more detailed programme is given.

while it was still entitled 'Symphonic Poem', had a published programme for its second and third performances only; this extensive specification differed slightly in detail between the two performances, but in any case was completely withdrawn on the subsequent publication of the work. In these kinds of programme specific ideational surrounding for the hearing of the work is not part of the work as given to the world in its finally valid form. However, together with the tendency to hermeneutic reception previously discussed, such programmes underline that music takes place in an essentially human arena, and show something of the proximity of programme music to non-programme music. In the light of historical knowledge we should be wary of over-emphasizing the distinctions between the two.

NATIONALISM

National boundaries offer a rationale for the writing of national history in music. Nations possess distinctive creative styles, even though a national style is at root a generalized conceptual construct based on groupings of individual composers and their personal styles. Yet, while nationalism could be a strongly felt force (particularly by prominent non-German musicians), the genres which concerned composers in this period remained supra-national, and nationalism manifested itself in music as inflexions of them. Literary and legendary national heritages would be natural resources for all kinds of texted music, including programme music. And differing language characteristics have a powerful effect on national musical styles, even indirectly on instrumental music—for instance, the tendency in Czech to stress initial syllables militates against up-beat openings to instrumental themes.

Political oppression often led to extra pressure on composers to create a distinctive national music, as was particularly the case for Smetana. It might further lead to political uses for music. Nations could be politically independent yet culturally oppressed, and such oppression was clearly felt by many Russian composers.

The national schools of France, Italy, and Spain had distinctive bases in opera and church music, though in all these countries some pressure was felt to create an instrumental musical culture. In Italy and Spain responses to this pressure were mostly made by minor composers, and neither the formal nor the informal socio-musical institutions were sufficiently developed to sustain and nourish such a culture at all strongly. In France, however, there were powerful moves towards national instrumental music, and the works of contemporary French composers were particularly favoured by the Société de Jeunes Artistes du Conservatoire (founded by Pasdeloup in 1853) for orchestral music, and by the Société de Quatuor Français (1862) for chamber music. Further impetus came from the founding of the Société Nationale de Musique in 1871, which encouraged the composition of both orchestral and chamber music. Instrumental genres in France were primarily Teutonic but this did not prevent César Franck, Saint-Saëns, Fauré, d'Indy, and others from creating important and highly original works in them.

The thrust towards a national music could characteristically take strong impetus from the use of folk-song. This was particularly so in Russia, where, following Glinka's example, composers used such songs as themes in large-scale instrumental works of elevated import; Borodin's String Trio in G minor is based on the folk-song 'Chem tebya ya ogorchila' [With what did I vex you]; Tchaikovsky's Second Symphony is one of his most nationalistic works and introduces three Ukrainian folk-songs, which led to the establishment of its nickname ('Little Russian', a term very offensive to Ukrainians);[12] the Finale of his Fourth Symphony uses the tune 'Vo pole beryozon'ka stoyala' [In the field stood a birch tree]; and Rimsky-Korsakov's *Sinfonietta* (from an unpublished string quartet) is based entirely on eight folk-tunes, which have been identified by Abraham in his essay on the folk-song element in Russian music.[13] In that essay he also outlined the incongruity between folk-song and symphonic forms and described some of the solutions offered by Russian composers to this compositional problem. The problem is how the self-enclosed completeness of a folk-tune may be opened into large-scale symphonic argument. The development section of Tchaikovsky's Second Symphony shows the coming together of Russian folk-song and German symphonism, for the opening folk-song of the symphony is fragmented and modified in a fully Germanic manner.

In the instrumental field Czech nationalism through use of folk material was principally based on peasant dances: Smetana used the polka (actually an urban dance in the nineteenth century) and *furiant*; Dvořák the *furiant*, *skočná*, and *dumka*. The *dumka* was originally a Ukrainian folk-lament which penetrated Poland during the first part of the century, and Dvořák's use of it is a product of the consciously Panslavonic element in his own nationalist position.[14] When actual

---

[12] David Brown, *Tchaikovsky: A Biographical and Critical Study*, i. *The Early Years* (*1840–1874*) (London, 1978), 256.

[13] Gerald Abraham, *Studies in Russian Music* (London, 1935), 55–6.

[14] I am greatly indebted to John Tyrrell for this view, as also for his wide-ranging and invaluable comments on the chapter as a whole.

folk material was not present, inflexions derived from such material could nevertheless form part of a composer's personal style; these inflexions often manifested themselves as specific melodic figures, as incidental uses of modality, and as dance-derived rhythms.

Folk melodies were usually regionally localized within a country, and almost always belonged to rural peasant cultures. In taking such material into nationalist art-music, composers were therefore lifting folk-music out of its immediate social context—its locality and its class confines—in order to renew aristocratic-bourgeois city culture. Thus there is an element of cross-cultural quotation involved in the basing of nationalist aspiration in art-music on folk material, as likewise an element of Romantic glorification of the populace and countryside. In this sense nationalism flourished as a form of programmaticism. Further, audiences could well read specific nationalist programmes into such stylistic features as peasant drones, lydian fourths, dance rhythms, or irregular metres, while such features were in reality common to the peasant cultures of more than one nation.

Nationalism is close to exoticism (the use of regional colour from a nation other than that of the composer), and exoticism formed a significant resource for nineteenth-century composers, as it had for eighteenth-century masters (Mozart's interest in Turkish music, Haydn's in Hungarian Gypsy music). Liszt and Brahms were particularly interested in this so-called Hungarian Gypsy music—the music of the *Verbunkos*, which had already become part of city culture around the close of the eighteenth century. Lalo, Bizet, and Rimsky-Korsakov all borrowed Spanish styles. But exoticism tends towards the picturesque, and cannot support a similar weight of signification as nationalism.

BRAHMS AND THE PIANO SONATA

In 1839 Schumann had written of the piano sonata: 'it seems the form has run its course . . .'[15] Yet, when Brahms and Liszt met for the first time in the summer of 1853, each had recently finished a piano sonata. In Brahms's case his Opp. 1 and 2 are among his earliest surviving works; in Liszt's, his only work in the genre marked the interim end, as he put it at the time, of his concern with the piano.[16] Brahms had learnt how to compose sonata movements as

---

[15] Robert Schumann, *Gesammelte Schriften über Musik und Musiker*, ed. Martin Kreisig (5th edn.; Leipzig, 1914), i. 395.
[16] As stated in Liszt's letter of Spring 1854 to Louis Köhler (*Letters of Franz Liszt*, ed. La Mara, trans. Constance Bache (London, 1894), i. 187).

part of his early training, by modelling them after specific Classical examples,[17] and detailed similarities of theme, harmonic structure, and development between his Op. 1 first movement and Beethoven's Op. 31, No. 1, 'Waldstein', and 'Hammerklavier' Sonatas are outward signs of a fundamental inclination to Beethovenian style in both these works. This includes general considerations of form, of texture (extremes of register, especially the low bass, are important in their sound world, as is the virtuoso element), and of the varied and energetic rhythmic surface, which is more violent than in subsequent Brahms works; indeed Brahms wrote in 1856 that these sonatas were 'sometimes raging'.[18] These characteristics are also to be found in the Third Sonata, Op. 5 (1853); more massive yet, it has a five-movement form and wide-ranging exploitation of the keyboard.

Brahms's piano sonatas are based on sonata and variation forms, which interact; thus at the very beginning of his creative life he staked out for himself principles of thematic integration and modification which were to be central to his musical thought, and to have profound consequences for the development of musical style in the early part of the present century. The Finale of Op. 2 shows variation ideas applied in a sonata form, since one theme appears in the six distinct guises: introduction (Ex. 384, bars 1–4); first subject (Ex. 385, bars 25–8); bridge (diminished; Ex. 386, bars 61–5); second

Ex. 384

Ex. 385

[17] Gustav Jenner, *Johannes Brahms als Mensch, Lehrer und Künstler* (Marburg, 1905), 39.

[18] *Johannes Brahms Briefwechsel*, v. *Johannes Brahms im Briefwechsel mit Joseph Joachim*, ed. Andreas Moser (3rd edn.; Berlin, 1921), 158.

Ex. 386

Ex. 387

Ex. 388

Ex. 389

subject (further diminished in the left hand, reorganized in the right hand; Ex. 387, bars 71–3); codetta (Ex. 388, bars 95–7); and coda (Ex. 389, bars 258–61).

All these sonatas also contain similar transformations across movements; in Op. 2 all the material of the third movement is evolved from the second (thus also extending the variation structure of that second movement), while in Op. 1 the opening becomes, in compound triple time with syncopations, the first theme of its Finale. Op. 5 has the second and fourth sections and coda of its slow movement built on a thematic shape from the development section of the first movement, and the progressive tonality of this slow movement (A flat to D flat majors) is a further 'composing out' of the same tonal plan for the second subject group of the first movement. The opening of the second movement is then transformed into the additional slow fourth movement, entitled 'Rückblick' [Retrospect]. Brahms was probably unaware of the contemporary Lisztian uses of these techniques (before their meeting), as also of Schubert's 'Wanderer' Fantasia; in which case he was following earlier models, including Classical variation writing, especially when the last variation is in rondo style. The variation-form Andante of Op. 1 uses the folk-song 'Verstohlen geht der Mond auf' as theme and, unusually, modifies its harmony, texture, and structure in the variations, leaving the melody as cantus firmus. The slow movement of Op. 2 duplicates this design, using an original theme based on the words of a *Minnelied*. The design of these two movements has a sonata-form resonance, with variation 2 as development—it is significantly longer than the themes in both cases—and variation 3 as a transfigured recapitulation.

Brahms wrote no further piano sonatas; in the field of solo piano writing he turned to variation sets and the poetic miniatures of the *Balladen*, Op. 10 (which are nevertheless grouped in a pseudo-sonata format). In the field of multi-movement instrumental composition, his ideas became too colossal for two hands on one piano and, via an incomplete duet sonata, he encountered other, orchestral genres. (Schumann had indeed called Op. 1 and 2 'veiled symphonies' in his laudatory article *Neue Bahnen*.)

LISZT AND THE SONATA

An important work for Liszt was Schubert's 'Wanderer' Fantasia; as we have seen, he performed it, then arranged it for piano and orchestra (he called this arrangement *symphonisch bearbeitet*); and its combination of multi-movement with single-movement design had much influence on Liszt's structural concerns around this time, as evidenced in the *Grosses Konzertsolo* (1849) and the two piano concertos. In his B minor Piano Sonata (1852–3) he created a highly subtle compressed structure which is both multi-movement and single-movement, with thematic unification of diversity by motivic and transformational relations. The structure is thus a combination of: (1) introduction, Allegro first movement, slow movement, Finale, and coda, with: (2) introduction, exposition and development, slow episode, altered recapitulation, and coda. The opening of the work draws unambiguously on traditional sonata structure: a tonally adventurous slow introduction (Ex. 390, bars 1–4) leads to a sonata-form exposition with two subject groups, each with two separate constituent themes (Exx. 391–4: Ex. 391 shows the first theme of the first subject, bars 8–13; Ex. 392 the second theme of the first subject, bars 13–17; Ex. 393 the first theme of the second subject, bars 105–12; Ex. 394 the second theme of the second subject, bars 153–60). Neither does the ensuing development section yet explicitly open into the overall structural ambiguity outlined above; this ambiguity begins with the appearance of the Andante theme in bar 331 (Ex. 395, bars 331–40).

Ex. 390

Ex. 391

Ex. 392

Ex. 393

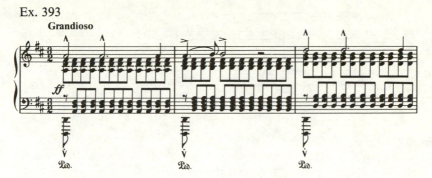

Ex. 394

Ex. 395

The six examples show the six primary themes of the whole work. While these have separate identities and structural functions, the second themes of the first and second subject groups (Exx. 392 and 394) are closely related by simple transformation, and all the themes are related by their sharing of the motivic elements: repeated-note initiation, scalic descent, and ascending leap. The introduction theme and Andante theme are particularly close motivically. Although the slow movement/slow episode is separated from its surroundings by tempo, metre, and theme, much of its substance is created from lyrical–decorative versions of the second subject material of the preceding Allegro; by this means the slow movement/slow episode is given distinct developmental aspects which serve further to integrate it into the overall structure of the work. The Finale/altered recapitulation is heralded by the introduction theme, now more regularly placed (tonally considered) on F sharp; the Finale/altered recapitulation then follows the thematic course of the first movement/exposition and development, with modifications, expansions, some omissions, and some literal repetitions. The most powerful of modifications is that the Finale/altered recapitulation continues after the introduction theme with the first-subject themes of the opening of the Sonata as a fugue in B flat minor, thus following in thematic and structural matters Liszt's Schubertian model. The Andante theme reappears in the tonic major near the close of the work. By these means Liszt created a cogent and positive ambiguity between multi-movement and single-movement designs.[19] The pianistic virtuosity involved is extreme, but is always for clear structural purposes of development and elaboration; here virtuosity finds a truly dramatic role, and the spectacular is tamed and enhanced by its integration into the heroic–lyrical.

Wagner wrote his less differentiated *Sonate für das Album von Frau M. W.* in 1853, and Liszt's example was followed in structure and virtuosity by Rudolf Viole in his Op. 1 (1855) and Reubke in his B flat minor Sonata (1857). But in the following decades the trend towards the re-establishment of the structure of the symphony in four separate movements was also reflected in the piano sonata: Grieg's Op. 7 (1865); Tchaikovsky's early Sonata in C sharp minor (1865), and his mature but problematic Op. 37 in G (1878); Rheinberger's Sonatas Nos. 1 (*Sinfonische Sonate*), 3 (1883), and 4 (*Romantische Sonate*); Robert Fuchs's Sonata in G flat, Op. 19; Parry's Opp. 71 and 79 (1877–8), and Richard Strauss's Op. 5 all have this structure. The title *Fantasie-Sonate*, deriving from Beethoven and Schubert, found some further use: Raff's Op. 168 (1872) is so titled, and Draeseke's Op. 6 (1862–7) is headed *Sonata quasi fantasia*.

The piano sonata, in spite of the precedents of Beethoven's *Lebewohl* and Alkan's *Grande sonate: Les quatre âges* (1848), was not generally a vehicle for programmaticism, and highly significant here is the fact that Liszt, the most progressive and committed of the programmatic composers of the 1850s, wrote his great sonata without a programme. The genre was closely surrounded by more established programmatic genres: the cycle of piano miniatures, the symphonic poem, and the symphony (later the suite also became programmatic). Yet there are some rare programmatic piano sonatas in our period. Sterndale Bennett's Sonata Op. 46 (1873) is entitled *The Maid of Orleans*, and each of its four movements has a title, together with a superscription from Schiller's play: (1) In the Fields;

---

[19] For detailed studies of the form of the Sonata and its precedents, see Rey M. Longyear, 'Liszt's B minor Sonata: Precedents for a Structural Analysis', *Music Review* 34 (1973), 198; Sharon Winklhofer, *Liszt's Sonata in B minor: A Study of Autograph Sources and Documents* (Ann Arbor, 1980). (Winklhofer does not concur with my view of the importance of Schubert's 'Wanderer' Fantasia for Liszt.)

'In innocence I led my sheep | Adown the mountains silent steep';
(2) In the Field: 'The clanging trumpets sound, the chargers rear, |
And the loud war cry thunders in mine ear'; (3) In Prison: 'Hear me
O God in mine extremity | In fervent supplication up to thee | Up
to thy heaven above I send my Soul'; (4) The End: 'Brief is the
sorrow, endless is the joy'. The indication 'alla tromba' occurs during
the second movement and a further quotation during the course of
the third.

BRAHMS'S PIANO VARIATIONS

Piano variations had been Brahms's chosen genre for his earliest
publicly performed composition (now lost), and, after the piano
sonatas, he returned to the genre in the years 1854–65 with his
most Schumannesque work, Op. 9, his earliest essay incorporating
Hungarian influence, Op. 21, No. 2, his only free-standing set on a
theme of his own, Op. 21, No. 1, and the masterpieces of the early
1860s (Variations on a Theme of Handel, Op. 24, Variations on a
Theme of Schumann, Op. 23, and the two books on a Theme of
Paganini, Op. 35). In a letter of 1856 he wrote to his friend Joseph
Joachim of his underlying attitude to variation writing:

I sometimes ponder on variation form and find variations must be made
stronger, more pure. The ancients held to the bass of the theme, their actual
theme, strongly. With Beethoven melody, harmony and rhythm are all so
beautifully varied. But I sometimes find that moderns (both of us!) more
(I don't quite know how to put it) rummage about over a theme. We
anxiously retain the melody but do not treat it freely, do not create anything
new from it, just punish it. But the melody is nevertheless not recognizable
. . .'[20]

This letter also has significance for his maturing style in general.
However these private thoughts were not in any sense developing a
theory of variation writing, and Brahms offers no view on the overall
structuring of a variation set—an aspect of his composition in the
genre which is always highly organized and significant.

Such organization was well established in Classical times for
variation sets as movements in multi-movement works. And after
the somewhat experimental movements in his first two piano sonatas,
Brahms reclaimed the general shape of Classical models in the slow
movement of his Op. 18 String Sextet—which he immediately
arranged for piano solo as a free-standing set. This general plan
runs: theme + variations 1–3: increase in animation; variation 4:

[20] *Brahms Briefwechsel*, v. 150.

change of mode and slowing of animation; variation 5: increase in animation, perhaps with reversion to the old mode; coda (in which the form of the theme, having been retained for the variations, is broken). This plan remained a generalized basis for Brahms's movements in variation form right through to his latest works. The overall structure for free-standing variation sets is naturally more varied, but the organization in particular works is nevertheless strong. In this respect Brahms seems to have placed his Op. 23 set close to Beethoven's Op. 34 (the tonal schemes of both show much variety of key), and in Op. 24 he may have had Bach's Goldberg Variations as a background, not only in the placing of related variations at regular intervals during the course of the set, but also in the diversifying of the series by character variations.

The work consists of twenty-five variations and a massive fugue as finale. Hans Gál has described it as 'one of the most important piano works he ever created'. And Wagner said, after hearing the piece played by its composer at their only known meeting (at Penzing in February 1864): 'One sees what may still be achieved in the old forms when someone comes who understands how to handle them.'[21] This was the temperate but nevertheless post-*Tristan* Wagner who spoke, recognizing the two types of originality represented by the two composers, both types cogent and deeply expressive—the one radical in structure and foreground detail, the other firmly rooted in Classical tradition yet winning significant artistic newness within that tradition. (Wagner of course became less temperate in his comments on Brahms as Brahms grew in fame.) The variations in Op. 24 maintain the form of the theme, though developmental intricacies of phrase structure and harmony are pervasive. The placement of the minor variations and thematically linked variation pairs are primary sources of overall structure, and suggest Brahms thought in three large groups of eight variations each, with variation 25 as a peroration. Perhaps nowhere else is Brahms's desired creative newness in individual variations more apparent, and his set includes a number of character variations: a quiet siciliano, a cheeky musette, and the following rich and strong response to Hungarian gypsy music. The examples show how the first half of the theme (Ex. 396, bars 1–4) was moulded into the first half of variation 13 (Ex. 397, bars 1–4), exemplifying how Brahms was able to win newness by following closely the form of the theme. They offer an instructive

[21] Hans Gál, *Johannes Brahms: His Work and Personality* trans. Joseph Stein (London, 1963), 124; Max Kalbeck, *Johannes Brahms*, ii (3rd edn.; Berlin, 1921), 118.

Ex. 396

Ex. 397

comparison with Ex. 398 from Dvořák. Brahms's fugue follows a scheme based on episodes, inversions, and augmentations, and its climax is a remarkable and deep synthesis of Baroque counterpoint with modern idiomatic piano writing.

This idiomatic pianism as a basic premiss of composition became even more refined and poetic in the thirty shorter characteristic pieces Brahms wrote between 1871 and 1893. They were grouped in the collections *Clavierstücke*, Op. 76 (publ. 1879), *Zwei Rhapsodien*, Op. 79 (1880), *Fantasien*, Op. 116 (1892), *Drei Intermezzi*, Op. 117 (1892), and *Clavierstücke*, Opp. 118 and 119 (1893). The pieces are individually titled Rhapsodie, Capriccio, Ballade, Romanze, or Intermezzo. Brahms used the title Rhapsodie for extended, vigorous fast movements; Op. 79, No. 2, is a fully articulated sonata-form movement with a tonally allusive opening, and Op. 119, No. 4, an expanded ternary form with a particularly intensifying coda ending in the tonic minor. The Capriccii and Ballade are smaller in scale but also characteristically fast; the Intermezzi are mostly slow and

Ex. 398

THEME

VARIATION 3

meditative, as is the Romanze (the original title of which was indeed Intermezzo). The three Intermezzi, Op. 117, were referred to by Brahms as *Wiegenlieder meiner Schmerzen* [cradle-songs for my sorrows], and the first is prefaced by a verse of a Scottish ballade.

Brahms used sonata or ternary forms in the main for these pieces, but, as is so characteristic of his larger-scale works, variation techniques pervade the continuity; for instance, the contrasted theme in D flat in the Intermezzo, Op. 117, No. 2, is a legato major simplification of the opening arpeggiated theme in B flat minor, and the waltz-like middle section of the Intermezzo, Op. 119, No. 2, is a rhythmically and harmonically altered major variation of the opening theme. All these pieces grow out of and develop what may be achieved with two hands on a keyboard, with rich instrumental melody, imaginative and varied textures; the resonance of the harmonies is also intimately connected with the charateristics of the piano. The Intermezzo, Op. 119, No. 1, for instance, one of the most inwardly reflective of all these pieces, combines elaborately constructed diatonic discords with the sonic values of the decay-envelope of piano sound.

PIANO VARIATIONS BY BRAHMS'S CONTEMPORARIES

Dvořák's most substantial work for solo piano is the Variations, Op. 36 (1876) and, unlike his earlier Piano Concerto, it shows a full command of idiomatic keyboard writing. Commentators have drawn attention to the resonances of Beethoven, Schubert, and Brahms in this work; those of Beethoven are particularly strong from the variation movements in the Piano Sonatas, Opp. 26, 109 and 111 (involving the type of theme, use of trills and registral contrasts, and the return to the unadorned theme for a quiet ending, as well as particular features of certain of the variations; for example, Beethoven's Op. 26, variation 1, gives Dvořák his own rhythmic division in variation 1). Dvořák's original theme has complex imitation and chromaticism, and the forms of his variations show a radical contrast with Brahms's variation writing, for Dvořák nowhere adheres to the formal confines of the theme but stretches areas of tonality and figuration, and thus forces the form of the theme into background structure. In Ex. 398 the opening statement-and-response structure of the theme (bars 1–12) is shown mapped on to the equivalent structure (bars 1–23) in his variation 3. Dvořák may have been encouraged in this radicalism by his recent encounter with the music of Liszt and Wagner.

Other contributors to the genre of piano variations in this period were Stephen Heller, Alkan (*Le Festin d'Aesop*), Bizet (the *Variations chromatiques* of 1869, one of his most powerful instrumental works), Rimsky-Korsakov, whose six variations on BACH are an original combination of variation, prelude and fugue, and suite, Robert Volkmann, Busoni, and Sergey Taneev.

GERMAN ORGAN MUSIC

Little significant organ music had been written during the Classical and early Romantic periods in Germany and Austria, save for Mendelssohn's great set of six Organ Sonatas, his three Preludes and Fugues, and Schumann's Fugues on BACH. But during the 1850s both Liszt and Brahms turned to the organ. Liszt's Fantasia and Fugue on the chorale 'Ad nos, ad salutarem undam' (1850) (from Meyerbeer's *Les Huguenots*), and Prelude and Fugue on BACH (1855) successfully adapt virtuosic piano writing to the organ, with full awareness of the sustaining power of the instrument; sectionalized transformative structures are fused with inputs from Baroque style. Julius Reubke's Organ Sonata, from the same year as his Piano Sonata, is close to the model of Liszt's Piano Sonata, and follows a movement scheme of introduction, slow, fast, slow, fast (fugue) which is compressed into the ambiguity of a one-movement structure depending on an almost exclusive monothematicism (diversified by thematic transformation). This Sonata on the 94th Psalm quotes verses of the Psalm 'O Lord God to whom vengeance belongeth . . .' as preface, and is thus programmatic; attempts to show a narrative programme on the text, however, have not met with success; the work belongs to the type of 'meditative programme music'. Though Reubke's sonatas are Lisztian in structure and rhetoric, they have a creative power of their own, and one can only lament their composer's tragically early death at the age of 24.

Brahms's early organ music comprises two Preludes and Fugues (A minor and G minor), a fugue in A flat minor (all composed in 1856-7), and the Chorale-prelude and Fugue on 'O Traurigkeit, o Herzeleid'. These works stem from Brahms's dissatisfaction with his compositional abilities, following his early public recognition by Schumann, and the concomitant period of self-imposed re-education. Indeed some of these works were included in the correspondence course in counterpoint that he conducted with his friend Joachim in 1856; but they are all much more than exercises, and it is rare, even among great composers, to find such original and expressive works written for study purposes. Their style is of great contrapuntal intricacy, at its most intense in the A flat minor Fugue, with its many inversions, strettos, multiple countersubjects, augmentations, and diminutions. There is Baroque influence not only in contrapuntal technique but also in themes and structures: material based on decorated scales and sequences proliferates, and Bach's organ-fugue designs, involving a central thinning of texture combined with an increase in animation and new countersubject material, are taken over by Brahms. A fundamental effect on Brahms's later style surely stems from his early organ works, which confirmed and accentuated the forceful influence of Bach; from them grew such music as the great sequences at the openings of the A major Serenade, Fourth Symphony, and Clarinet Quintet.

The title and genre 'organ sonata' had really been established by Mendelssohn for subsequent nineteenth-century composers; he drew on the Baroque forms of the chorale, chorale-prelude, chorale variations, and fugue, as well as on the English voluntary tradition, mediated principally through Samuel Wesley, and created multi-movement works quite different in structure and scope from the contemporary piano sonata. In the second half of the century, his lead was followed particularly by Rheinberger, and Gustav Merkel (1827–85).

Rheinberger's sequence of twenty organ sonatas span the years 1868–1901, and was unfinished at his death, for each is in a different key and he was clearly working towards a set of twenty-four. He did not use chorales or chorale-related structures, though in Sonata No. 3 the 8th psalm tone appears as a theme in the outer movements. But fugue is very common: twelve of the sonatas conclude with fugues, No. 15 with a ricercar; two more begin with fugues (No. 8, which ends with the justly famous passacaglia, and No. 10, which actually begins with a prelude and fugue); No. 14 begins with a ternary Präludium in which the middle section is a fugue. Sonata form is also used: No. 7 begins with a clear and powerful example (again called Preludio), and the first movement of No. 11 (entitled Agitato) uses sonata form with combined and reordered response. Suite-like middle movements of lyrical import abound: Marcia religiosa (Sonata No. 6, movement ii), Romanze (9, ii), Cantilena (11, ii), Pastorale (12, ii; 20, iii), Idylle (14, ii; 18, iii), Skandinavisch (16, ii), Provençalisch (19, ii). Rheinberger was a pupil of F. Lachner, one of the important composers of orchestral suites during our period. Preludes and fugues also formed a significant part of Lachner's conception of the orchestral suite, and there is a proximity in movement types and styles between Rheinberger's organ sonatas and Lachner's suites. Fourteen of these sonatas are in three move-ments, the remainder in four.

In 1896 Brahms turned again to the organ, with death and religion much on his mind, and following the *Vier ernste Gesänge* [Four Serious Songs] came the posthumously published eleven Chorale-preludes, Op. 122. They do not really form a set; manuscript evidence suggests Brahms originally thought in groups of three, but he then sent the first seven as a group to his copyist, in a revised order. This grouping in seven itself suggests Brahms had more than another four pieces in mind, and there survives a sketch for a canonic prelude on 'Es ist ein Ros' entsprungen'. Brahms himself described these works as rare, and they come at the end of a barren century for the chorale-prelude (such pieces were mostly by insignificant musicians). But these are no mere freak appendage to Brahms's life's work; they are fine, widely underrated music, and a significant development from the *Vier ernste Gesänge*. They push towards the objectivity of liturgical forms, but in spite of this retain a deep expressiveness, all the more powerful for being regulated and generated within long-established precepts.

All preludes treat the chorale as cantus firmus, mostly in the top part. The chorale itself could be spaced, including in the gaps: fugue (No. 1), imitation (No. 3), pre-echo (Nos. 4, 7, 10), and double after-echo (No. 11); or the chorale could be continuous. There are two important kinds of expressive opposition to the structure of the chorale as formal determinant: (1) Brahms could introduce change in the third quarter of the prelude, followed by the restoration of the old texture/figuration in the last quarter; and (2) he could create an end climax. The elaborative parts surrounding the chorale are derived from the chorale by either diminution, or decorative variation, or by a combination of these.

FRENCH INNOVATIONS

Alkan's *Symphonie* for solo piano is a unique work in many ways. It is part of his most substantial opus: twelve *Études* in all the minor keys, Op. 39 (1857). Perhaps following Clementi's grouping of movements into suites in his *Gradus ad Parnassum*, Alkan grouped Nos. 4–7 of his *Études* into a four-movement symphony (with progressive tonality—the keys of the movements are C, F, B flat, and E flat minors). Alkan's symphony cannot be regarded as mistitled: it shows orchestral effects by variation of register, and the second movement begins with a quasi-cello melody. There are motivic relationships across movements, and the movements themselves show a clear command of structures associated with the genre of the symphony: sonata form in first and last movements, and ternary for the middle movements. Nevertheless the title is an innovation, which possibly inspired subsequent French composers to overcome accepted genre boundaries, for Alkan must not be underestimated as a composer; Liszt and Busoni valued his music highly, and (according to d'Indy) César Franck called him a 'poet of the pianoforte'.[22]

Franck's own *Grand pièce symphonique* (1860-2) for organ was dedicated to Alkan, and formed the first of a line of French organ symphonies continued by Widor and, after 1890, by Vierne and Dupré; these organ works were related to the new large-scale, so-called 'symphonic' organs being built in France by Cavaillé-Coll. Franck's *Grand pièce* has a multi-sectional differentiated structure in a modified palindromic design, with a motivic principal theme, a chorale element, fugal textures, andante episodes, and a climactic conclusion. It had a number of sequels: the organ symphonies already alluded to, Franck's own orchestral Symphony (for which it provided the opening motif), and his later original keyboard works (particularly the three *Chorals* for organ). It was, however, another piece in the same collection as the *Grand pièce symphonique* which formed the first of Franck's three famous tryptichs: the *Prélude, fugue et variation*, a simple but none the less original combination of prelude and fugue, variation, and ternary forms. Franck arranged this work in 1873 as a duet for piano and harmonium, in which form he seems to have preferred it. In 1884 he wrote the *Prélude, choral et fugue* for piano; d'Indy narrates how this was originally planned as just a prelude and fugue.[23] The *Prélude, aria et final*, which followed in 1887, moves away from the prelude and fugue as basis, towards the piano sonata. Both these works depend on cyclic thematic principles which include recall of themes at the close, including one theme in augmentation. This tryptich form was taken up by Pierre Bréville in his *Fantaisie* (1888) consisting of introduction, fugue, and finale. Franck's last works were his three *Chorals* for organ (1890); these are types of extended one-movement sonatas and have nothing directly to do with the Lutheran chorale, though each includes stately hymnic writing. The overall forms are substantial, distinctive, and discursive, but unified and closed: No. 1 fuses variation, ternary, and sonata-form inputs, No. 2 is a highly diversified binary form, including chaconne, lyrical themes, recitative, and fugue, and No. 3 is ternary overall,

[22] Vincent d'Indy, *César Franck*, trans. Rosa Newmarch (London and New York, 1910), 95.

[23] Ibid., p. 164.

again with strong input from sonata form. All three have a climactic version of a principal theme near the end. Experimental is surely a misleading term for Franck's structural innovations (and we shall have occasion to note further such innovations in the fields of symphony and chamber music); 'experimental' makes a judgement on the enterprise and implies the results of that enterprise are lucky or unlucky. Franck's use of tradition as a background to his creation was more controlled than this; he made significant major structural originalities which were nevertheless formally cogent and comprehensible. Because they were at the highest levels of structure, they occasionally altered the genre system itself (as in the great tryptichs), and always altered traditions within genres.

Charles-Marie Widor's organ symphonies are a further example of French genre alteration, related even more closely to the suite than are Rheinberger's sonatas. Widor noted the justification of their title in his preface to his Op. 13 collection of such symphonies, by reference to the new Cavaillé-Coll organs: the dynamic volume and tonal variety of these instruments (with many pseudo-orchestral instrument stops) allowed works written for them to adopt a similar grandeur to orchestral music. Widor's symphonies in his Op. 13 (1876) and 42 (1880), eight symphonies in all (he wrote a further two organ symphonies after 1890), have resonances from the suite in their overall movement structures and in their movement types. Three symphonies from this series are in five movements, four in six movements, and one (No. 1) in seven; the movement types are a mixture of symphonic analogues together with preludes, toccatas, fugues, marches, and poetic movements (just how characteristic such a mixture is for the Teutonic suite will become apparent in the following section of this chapter). Examples of the poetic movements are 'Meditation', 'Pastorale', and 'Salve Regina'. While these works are not profound, they have a distinct originality and nobility, based on an expert understanding of the idiomatic possibilities of the organ.

THE SUITE

In the second half of the century, the suite was a genre much cultivated by composers, indeed the level of production is comparable with that of the symphony. But the genre has heretofore hardly provided a central topic for historians. It has an important, distinctive, and distinguished role in the genre system of this period, and draws on many cultural concerns of composers; investigation of the genre casts fresh light on historicism, programmaticism, and nationalism at a general stylistic level which is neither as elevated as that of the symphony nor as trivial as that of the salon piece. It is particularly related to the symphony, sonata, serenade, and set of character pieces. The late Romantic suite is a multi-movement work with internal differentiation of movement types which could be extracted from Baroque, Classical, or modern models. Within certain limitations, which themselves changed through these years, the genre offered relative freedom to composers and manifested a large degree of diversity. We may, however, postulate four basic tendencies: the neo-Baroque, the modern dance, the symphony/sonata substitute, and the programmatic tendencies. This typology has a chronological validity, as we shall see. While these four tendencies may exist each in relative isolation as the chief constitutive rationale of a work, they are also often mixed with each other in various ways within a single work. It is the possibility and practice of this mixture which allows the genre to cohere, for, separately used, these four tendencies could give rise to highly disparate types of suite. The extract suite has not been regarded as one of these tendencies, since it is properly a form of arrangement rather than composition, and in any case is itself subject to these tendencies (especially the latter three); it will be considered later in this chapter.

As in the Baroque period the primary performing resources for the late Romantic suite were orchestra (Lachner, Raff, Saint-Saëns, Massenet, Tchaikovsky, Debussy) or keyboard—now, of course, piano (Rubinstein, Raff, d'Albert, Debussy). But suites were also written for concerto forces or chamber combinations from about the mid-1860s on, after the re-establishment of the suite for piano or orchestra. Raff's Op. 180 is for violin and orchestra, Op. 200, for piano and orchestra; Gounod's *Suite concertante* is for pedal piano and orchestra, and Rheinberger's Op. 149 is for organ, violin, cello, and string orchestra; Raff's String Quartets Nos. 6 and 8 (1874) are both suites (and so titled); Goldmark's Suites, Op. 11 (1869) and Op. 43 (1893) are for violin and piano, as is Ignaz Brüll's Suite, Op. 42 (1882); Rheinberger's Op. 166 (1891) is for violin and organ (or piano).

The idea that the term 'suite' is synonymous with 'collection' has to be considered and modified. It is based in part on the separate publication of suite items which was common for piano suites; further, Tchaikovsky performed the variations from his Third Suite as a separate concert item. But such separation does not deny a unity operating across movements: several suites from this period have related movements with thematic recall (Raff's Op. 72, which was issued in separate offprints, Massenet's *Scènes alsaciennes*, Strauss's Suite, Op. 4, for wind (1884), Rimsky-Korsakov's *Sheherazade* (1888), Bordes's *Suite basque*, Dvořák's orchestral Suite in A (originally for piano, 1894)), and movement schemes for suites were clearly of creative significance and subject to compositional choice of a decided kind. Further, the Andante and Scherzo of Brahms's Piano Sonata, Op. 5, were performed separately, by both Brahms and Clara Schumann, and the Andante published as an offprint; but no commentator could wish to suggest that any of this compromises the unity of the sonata. Similarly the 'Deuxième Morceau de la Symphonie Océan' of Rubinstein was issued separately in score, parts, and two arrangements. It is, however, clear that some suites were more loosely connected than others. Raff's Op. 75 is a collection of character pieces for small hands; it shows a rare use of the term 'Suite' in this period (most character-piece sets of this kind were not so titled), and an earlier title for this particular work was 'Bibliothèque';[24] it was clearly designed at least in the main for domestic use, where it would naturally be excerpted; whereas to extract a movement from *Sheherazade* would be to do violence to a unified cyclic work.

THE RE-EMERGENCE OF THE SUITE IN MID-CENTURY

The term 'Suite' was used very rarely in the nineteenth century before 1855. Clementi had grouped pieces in his *Gradus ad Parnassum* into suites; Sterndale Bennett's *Suite de pièces*, Op. 24 (1842), is a free-standing composition in the genre, consisting of six pieces, with titles for Nos. 2 and 4 ('Capricciosa' and 'Alla fantasia' respectively); the special form of the title of the work indicates the independence of the constituent movements (now described as pieces) and the work displays a progressive tonality overall. Schumann knew it, wrote about it, and considered titling as Suite his Overture, Scherzo, and Finale. But the flowering of the late Romantic suite was a post-Schumann phenomenon, and one to which Sterndale Bennett contributed no further.[25]

In 1851 the Bach Gesellschaft began its monumental publication of the complete works of Bach, and in 1853 issued volume i of the

---

[24] I am much indebted to O. W. Neighbour for this information from annotations on a Raff autograph in his possession; the autograph is of a piece once intended for inclusion in Op. 75.

[25] The form of title of the Sterndale Bennett work derives from an English tradition of publication titling of keyboard music by Handel and Domenico Scarlatti. The latter composer was particularly important to Sterndale Bennett, as Schumann noted in his review of Bennett's Op. 24 (Robert Schumann, *Gesammelte Schriften*, ii. 108-9).

clavier works, including the six Partitas. The earliest neo-Baroque suites soon followed; Rubinstein's Op. 38 for piano (comp. 1855; pub. 1856) has ten movements: Prelude, Minuet, Gigue, Sarabande, Gavotte, Passacaille, Allemande, Courante, Passepied, and Bourrée. In September 1855 Brahms finished a Suite in A minor, as we know from private papers of his friends; it had at least Prelude, Aria, Sarabande, Gavotte, and probably a Gigue. Brahms destroyed it as a work, though some of its constituent dances survive, including the Sarabande and Gavotte, which were played as a concert item by Brahms and by Clara Schumann in 1855 and 1856, and constituted the first music of Brahms to be publicly performed in Danzig, Vienna, and London. In the programme for the London performance the pieces were described as 'in the style of Bach'; Ex. 399 shows the first eight bars of the Sarabande, in its earliest form (written in 1854 in A major). Brahms did not publish any of this music, but recognized its power and potential by using it as a thematic quarry for later chamber works (Second String Sextet, First String Quintet, and Clarinet Quintet); in so doing he provided a compelling example of the living generative power of historicism. Clara Schumann's half-brother, Woldemar Bargiel, wrote a Suite, Op. 7, for piano duet in the late 1850s; it consists of Allemande, Courante, Sarabande, Air, and Gigue, and thus follows the German Baroque movement plan for the suite, which had been so conspicuously denied by Rubinstein. Both Rubinstein and Bargiel use key contrasts between movements, though their last movements return to the keys of their first; Rubinstein particularly uses a heavily Romantic pianism, which contrasts markedly with the delicacy of Brahms's response to Baroque style; and Bargiel begins with a ternary-form Allemande. One cannot

Ex. 399

help but be reminded of Heidegger's telling phrase, that it is the 'exclusive privilege of the greatest thinkers to let themselves be influenced. The small thinkers, by contrast, merely suffer from constipated originality.'[26] Brahms's little pieces are both closer to Baroque forms and styles than the works of Rubinstein and Bargiel and at the same time much greater and more original music.

The pure neo-Baroque suite had a continuing history during this period, sometimes attracting the title-modifier '. . . in olden form'; thus Raff's suite for string quartet, Op. 192, No. 1, is entitled *Suite älterer Form* (it has the movements Präludium, Menuett, Gavotte mit Musette, Arie, and Gigue-Finale). Eugen d'Albert's Op. 1 (1883) is a suite in the old style; its movements are Allemande, Courante, Sarabande, Gavotte and Musette, and Gigue—all in the one tonic, D minor. They are in Baroque-style binary forms, and show real expressive power. Grieg, in his suite *Fra Holbergs Tid* [From Holberg's Time] for piano (1884; arr. for strings 1885), and d'Indy in a *Suite en Ré dans le style ancien* for trumpet, two flutes, and strings (1886) made subsequent use of the 'suite in olden style'. And this particular input from the Baroque directly into the late-Romantic was surely the basis for the various neo-Classical tendencies of the twentieth century; it brought with it, even in late Romantic times, a certain impetus for rhythmic renewal, to some extent countering the arhythmical implications of Wagnerian chromaticism. Debussy's Sarabande (1894) in *Pour le piano* is a magnificent creative use of the old form, with its composer's distinctive harmonic blend of discord, parallelism, and modality.

The modern dance—*Ländler*, waltz, mazurka, and polka were favoured types—entered the suite first as a mixture with the neo-Baroque tendency.

Between 1857 and 1879 Raff wrote his seventeen surviving suites: eight for piano, four for orchestra, two for concerto forces, and three for chamber groups. In his first contributions to the genre, the three suites for piano, Opp. 69, 71, and 72 (1857–8) he established a five-movement form mixing Baroque and modern elements. All three begin with a Preludio and end with a Fuge; they have a mazurka or polka or minuetto as second movement, toccatina or toccata as third, and aria or romanza as fourth. Apart from his Op. 75 (the twelve-piece collection referred to above), Raff's subsequent suites range from four to seven movements with a clear preference for five. And, though there are examples of pure neo-Baroque suites,

---

[26] Martin Heidegger, *What is called thinking?*, trans. J. Glenn Gray (New York, 1968), 95.

programme suites, and one sonata-substitute suite, his preference for the mixed neo-Baroque and modern type with which he had begun, is noteworthy. The Rigaudon from his last piano suite, Op. 204 in B flat (1876), may be taken as an example of his reinterpretation of Baroque models, involving heavily Romantic colouring; this movement follows the old couplet form of rigaudons for its initial stages, then appends a modern development section, a varied recapitulation, and coda—the whole in distinctly unbaroque keyboard textures. Ex. 400 shows the end of the recapitulation and beginning of the coda (bars 106–32).

The great waltz sequences of Johann Strauss the younger were not called suites. These, such as *An der schönen blauen Donau* [The Blue Danube] Op. 314 (1867), or *Seid umschlungen Millionen* [Be

Ex. 400

[Allegro]

Embraced Ye Millions] Op. 443 (1892), dedicated to Brahms, characteristically open with an introduction, beginning in non-waltz rhythm, followed by a linked series of separately numbered waltz-movements (five was a favoured number), and a concluding coda drawing on previous themes. The individual waltzes would be in binary or ternary form, related by key but not obviously by theme, and each waltz would characteristically include thematic contrast within itself. Many of Strauss's works enjoyed immediate, widespread, and enduring popularity; Brahms was a particular admirer of Strauss's music, and Schoenberg arranged his *Kaiser-Walzer*, Op. 437 (1889), for chamber ensemble in 1925.

Suites (so titled) including modern dances had differentiated movement types. Franz Lachner's *Ball-Suite* (1874) has Introduktion und Polonaise, Mazurka, Waltz, Intermezzo, Dreher, and Lance.

Arensky's Op. 15 consists of Romance, Waltz, and Polonaise. Both these examples of course show a slight mixture with other modern elements, since each contains one character piece which is not a dance.

A quantity of artistic and biographical data shows the proximity of the suite to, though at the same time separation from, the genres of symphony and sonata. A suite need not include any dance movements: Lachner's Seventh Suite has Ouverture, Scherzo, Intermezzo, Chaconne, and Fuga. Julius Otto Grimm's Op. 10, *Suite in Canonform*, has four unnamed movements—Allegro con brio, Andante lento, Tempo di minuetto, and Allegro risoluto—and although this work includes a dance, the particular placing of a minuet as third movement in a four-movement work enhances rather than contradicts its approximation to a symphony. Raff's first Suite for Orchestra, Op. 101, includes as its last two movements two movements of his (now otherwise lost) first symphony.[27] Lachner turned from writing symphonies to writing orchestral suites, and allowed the latter genre to substitute for the former, as did Tchaikovsky between his Symphonies 4 and 5. Rimsky-Korsakov's Second Symphony *Antar* was renamed 'symphonic suite' many years after its composition; 'symphonic suite' is also the subtitle of *Sheherazade*.

After composing eight symphonies between 1828 and 1851, Franz Lachner turned to the orchestral suite and produced eight works in this genre between 1861 and 1881. His seven numbered suites have an extension and grandeur which confirm their status as symphony-substitutes (or analogues) in four to six movements. They are characteristically based on the mixture of neo-Baroque and modern movement types already noted in Raff's suites. Nos. 2-5 include Baroque dances, of which No. 3 is the most strongly based on this tendency (its movements are Praeludium, Intermezzo, Ciaconne, Sarabande, Gavotte, and Courante). Fugues were used as first movements (Suites 2 and 6) or finales (Suites 1, 4, and 7); No. 1 begins with a Praeludium in fully worked-out sonata form with repeated exposition. Marches occur in Nos. 1 and 6; No. 6 concludes with the programmatic Finale ('Trauermusik und Festmarsch'), which was Lachner's response to the outcome of the Franco-Prussian war of 1870-1. This finale has many Mendelssohnian resonances; it begins in C minor with an oboe recitative, leading to an 'andante

---

[27] In E minor of 1854, which predates his published Symphony No. 1; see Theodor Müller-Reuter, *Lexikon der deutschen Konzertliteratur* (Leipzig, 1909), i. 393-4.

maestoso', during which the chorale 'Ein' feste Burg' enters as cantus firmus; the 'Festmarsch' is a C major 'allegro'. Kretzschmar was a Lachner enthusiast:

Lachner speaks in the authentic tone of the suite; even when sophisticated, he remains clear and approachable; and when he has to choose he prefers the trivial to the esoterically complex ... his preferred speech-form [in minuets and andantes] seems to grow from the idioms of the old Viennese school, especially that of Schubert, then those of Spohr and Mendelssohn, to make a new fourth in the constellation.[28]

Generally, the symphony/sonata substitute suite would be more likely to include a prelude and fugue (or the more modern equivalent, introduction and fugue) than a symphony or sonata. From the symphony and sonata themselves the suite took over the scherzo, march, variations, romanza, and, most importantly, the variation of the tonic through the work. All Lachner's suites vary the tonic, though some more adventurously than others. The generally lighter musical discourse of a suite would tend towards separated and thematically distinct movements. In a discussion which arose after the appearance of Goldmark's *Ländliche Hochzeit* Symphony in 1876 as to whether the work should more properly be called a suite, Brahms was of the view that the two genres differed primarily in 'character' and 'treatment'.[29] Rimsky-Korsakov's reasons for his change of title for *Antar* lay emphasis on the first movement which 'has no thematic development whatever; only variations and paraphrases'.[30] A work of lighter musical discourse needed either a significant dance component, or other Baroque contrapuntal component, or a programme, to avoid overlap with the genre serenade; indeed Goldmark's two violin suites, which do not have such a component, are indistinguishable from serenades.

As with the programme symphony and the symphonic poem, the programme suite could base itself on literature or legend, or on subjects from the physical environment (which is indeed a common type of material for the programme suite). Among the first of the programmatic suites are: Raff's Op. 75 (1858–9); his *Italienische Suite* [Italian Suite] (1871), with the movements Ouverture, Barcarole, Intermezzo ('Pulcinella'), Notturno, and Tarantelle; his Suite No. 2, 'in ungarischer Weise' [In the Hungarian manner] (1874), with

[28] Hermann Kretzschmar, *Führer durch den Konzert-Saal*, i. *Sinfonie und Suite* (5th edn.; Leipzig, 1919), 661.

[29] Karl Goldmark, *Erinnerungen aus meinem Leben* (Vienna and Munich, 1922), 89–90.

[30] Nikolay Andreevich Rimsky-Korsakov, *My Musical Life*, trans. Judah A. Joffe (3rd edn.; London, 1974), 93.

the movements 'An der Grenze' (Ouverture), 'Auf der Puszta'
(Träumerei), 'Bei einem Aufzug der Honved' (Marsch), 'Volkslied
mit Variationen', and 'Vor der Csarda' (Finale); and his Suite *Aus
Thüringen* [From Thuringia] (1875), with the movements 'Salus
intrantibus', 'Elisabethenhymne', 'Reigen der Gnomen und Sylphen',
'Variationen über das Volkslied', and 'Ländliches Fest'.

Massenet wrote his seven numbered orchestral suites between 1865
and 1881. Only No. 1 has no programmatic title; the others are No.
2, *Scènes hongroises* (1871); No. 3, *Scènes dramatiques* (1873); No. 4,
Scènes pittoresques (1871); No. 5, *Scènes napolitaines* (1876); No. 6,
Scènes de féerie (1879); and No. 7, *Scènes alsaciennes* (1881). No. 3
is based on Shakespeare; its three movements are headed: i. Prélude
et divertissement (la tempête—Ariel et les Esprits); ii. Mélodrame (le
sommeil de Desdémone); iii. Scène finale: Macbeth (les sorcières—
le festin—l'apparation—les fanfares du couronnement). This last
movement is highly successful in treating the picturesque elements
of *Macbeth* while not in any sense being either a résumé of the play
or a disquisition on its serious import. No. 4 has the four movements:
i. Marche, ii. Air de ballet, iii. Angelus, and iv. Fête bohème; the
Angelus depends on an opening alternation of chant-like material
with bell imitations, and shows well Massenet's gift for succinct,
picturesque vignettes (Ex. 401).

Ex. 401

Massenet's Suite No. 7 seems initially to be a physical-environment suite, but took its inspiration from a story by Daudet, and lengthy quotations appear for each of its four movements, creating a narrative programme. This work also has a nationalist aspect as does Daudet's story, for Alsace had been lost to France in the Franco-Prussian war.

Some of these programme suites, especially those with three or four movements, partake strongly of the symphony/sonata-substitute tendency, for that tendency and programmaticism are of course by no means mutually exclusive. The chief distinction between a three- or four-movement programme suite and a programme symphony would be in the size of movements, probably in the form of the movements (for instance, the first movement of Massenet's *Scènes pittoresques* is a brief ternary March), and weight of musical discourse. Other composers of the programme suite were Saint-Saëns, *Suite algérienne* (1880), Charpentier, *Impressions d'Italie* (1890) and Debussy.

THE SUITE IN THE 1880s

Tchaikovsky's suites are in many ways highpoints in suite composition; they not only contain great music, but show their composer moving freely within the field of tendencies already discussed, elevating and modifying traditions. His four orchestral suites come from the eleven-year gap between Symphonies Nos. 4 and 5. Early in the preparation of his First Suite, Op. 43, he wrote to Nadezhda von Meck (25 August 1878) that, after sketching the scherzo, 'it came into my head to write a whole row of pieces for orchestra, from which I could form a *suite* in Lachner's manner'—an interesting acknowledgement of the importance and priority of Lachner as example. Modifications to the order and substance of the movements during the compositional process show that something more than a haphazard agglomeration of movements was involved. His letter to Nadezhda von Meck of 16 April 1884 concerning his Third Suite describes how he was

collecting some materials for a future symphonic composition, the form of which is not yet defined. Maybe it will be a symphony, on the other hand it may be a suite. The latter form has for some time been particularly sympathetic to me because of the freedom it allows a composer not to be hampered by traditions, conventional examples and established rules.[31]

---

[31] These two letters to Madame von Meck are cited and discussed in Gerald Abraham's Foreword to the Eulenburg Edition of Tchaikovsky's Suite No. 3 (London, 1978).

These remarks from one of the period's foremost composers are of course extremely important to the definition of the suite in relation to the symphony (for Tchaikovsky the proximity was close, but the alternative real): but at the same time they also warn against too rigorous a delineation of types of suite.

Tchaikovsky began his first suite 'in Lachner's manner' (1878–9) with an 'Introduzione e fuga', followed it with the Classical or Romantic movements—Divertimento, Intermezzo, Marche miniature, and Scherzo—and concluded with a further neo-Baroque movement, a Gavotte—originally called 'Giants' Dance'. A programmatic tendency emerged quite strongly in his Second Suite, Op. 53 (1883): 'Jeu de sons', Valse, Scherzo burlesque (including parts for four accordions), 'Rêves d'enfant', 'Danse baroque (style Dargomizhsky)'. The first movement contains a massive central fugue. The Third Suite, Op. 55 (1884), opens with an 'Élégie' in which the tone of lament has become mere wistfulness; it begins with a three-bar phrased tune which shows all the subtlety, originality, and generative power one expects of an elevated-style piece; the ambiguity between tune and accompaniment, as the tune is reiterated over changing underparts, is a particularly telling sophistication (Ex. 402). This theme opens an original sonata-form structure with a many-themed exposition, all themes being related by motif, and with a partial and reordered recapitulation. The subsequent movements in this suite are Valse mélancolique, Scherzo, and Tema con varazioni (with twelve variations).

Ex. 402

The suite, particularly the programmatic variety, played a highly important role in Debussy's early period—perhaps partly as a result of his teacher Guiraud's interest in the genre. A surviving Intermezzo (1882) (published in 1944) is part of a projected suite for cello and orchestra. His four-movement orchestral suite *Triomphe de Bacchus* (*c*.1882) is mostly lost, and his *Première suite d'orchestre* (*c*.1883), with the movements 'Fête', 'Ballet', 'Rêve', and 'Bacchanale', remains unpublished. The original score of *Printemps*, symphonic suite for female chorus, orchestra, and piano (1887), is also lost; the work appeared arranged for piano duet in 1904 and was reorchestrated from this version by Büsser under Debussy's supervision in 1912. The *Petite Suite* (1886–9) for piano duet has 'En bateau', 'Cortège', 'Menuet', and 'Ballet'; and the *Suite bergamasque* (1890; rev. 1905) for piano solo consists of Prélude, Menuet, Clair de lune, and Passepied. In the later suite *Pour le piano* Debussy turned to Baroque models for the three movements Prélude, Sarabande, and Toccata.

THE EXTRACT SUITE

Although primarily an original and self-sufficient genre during this period, the suite lent itself to the presentation of concert excerpts from larger works for the theatre—incidental music, ballet, opera. Bizet's *L'Arlésienne* suite, No. 1 (1872), and Grieg's two *Peer Gynt* suites (1874–5) are early examples of the type. All three show a strong symphonic–analogue tendency: Bizet's includes some recomposition, with a conflation of two originally separate numbers, and all three suites are four-movement works. Thus, Grieg included in his two suites only eight of the original twenty-three numbers of the incidental music. Tchaikovsky's ballet-suite *Shchelkunchik* [The Nutcracker], Op. 71a, is a further example of the extract suite made by the composer. Others could also create such arrangements, as is the case, for instance, with Bizet's *L'Arlésienne* suite, No. 2, arranged by Ernest Guiraud.

In his suite *Mozartiana*, Op. 61 (1887), Tchaikovsky created something new in this field, for it consists of arrangements of four unrelated pieces by Mozart. Perhaps prompted by the 6/8 beginnings of his own Second and Third Suites, Tchaikovsky here took the bold step of beginning *Mozartiana* with a gigue (*Eine kleine Gigue für das Klavier*, K 574), which he orchestrated and lightly arranged with fuller harmonies. The second movement is a similar treatment of the *Menuett für Klavier*, K 355. The third movement is entitled Preghiera and is Mozart's late Motet 'Ave Verum Corpus', K 618, in an overtly Romantic arrangement 'd'après une transcription de F. Liszt'. And the fourth, 'Thème et variations', is an arrangement of Mozart's *Zehn Variationen für Klavier*, K 455 (on 'Unser dummer Pöbel meint', from Gluck's *Singspiel, La Rencontre imprévue*); here the arranging is again done with a light hand, but includes alterations of cadenzas, and of variation 9 to make it more virtuosic for a solo violin.

The late-Romantic suite was, then, a distinct and significant genre, arising as a multi-faceted response to a historicized musical environment, a response free but controlled, liberating but enriching.

THE SERENADE

The serenade is a more recent genre than the suite, and had flourished, along with its close relatives the divertimento and the cassation, during the Classical period as a lighter version of the symphony/chamber music/sonata genres. Heinrich Christoph Koch had indeed defined the divertimento by comparison with sonata types; it was 'not polyphonic or so extensively worked-out as sonata-types',[32] nor was it, in his view, so organically unified. And the serenade had a strong life in our period again as a lighter version of these more weighty genres. Its orientation was towards charming, entertainment music apt for an evening greeting; the name has resonances of outdoor performance, and Kretzschmar called the genre *Garten-musik*.

Unlike a suite, a serenade might consist of one movement: Rubinstein's Op. 22 (1855) for piano has three such as a collection, of which No. 2, in G minor, is in 5/4 time, with a suggestion of folk-instruments, *gusli* and *balalayka*; Tchaikovsky's *Sérénade mélancolique*, Op. 26 (1876), is a single-movement work for violin and orchestra; Wolf's Italian Serenade is in one movement, and so is Strauss's Serenade for thirteen wind instruments. But the serenade was more usually multi-movement, with four or more movements thematically and temporally distinct—not so organically unified. However, Robert Volkmann's serenades use multi-

---

[32] Cited and discussed in Dahlhaus, 'Zur Problematik', p. 855.

movement/single-movement structure, involving substantial thematic unification. Dvořák's D minor Serenade, Op. 44 for wind, cello, and bass (1878) in four movements, includes a recall of the opening movement at the end of the Finale.

The serenade was not a genre which included Baroque dances or other Baroque contrapuntal forms (there is, however, a canonic serenade by Salomon Jadassohn), though it characteristically included the Classical minuet or modern dances, particularly march and waltz. Nor was the serenade so often a vehicle for programmaticism or national flavour as was the suite; though Wolf's Serenade for string quartet (1887), orchestrated as *Italienische Serenade* in 1892, is an example. The serenade and suite touch as sonata or symphony substitutes; Goldmark's two violin suites are cases in point, and Tchaikovsky's Serenade for strings, Op. 48 (1880) consists of 'Pezzo in forma di Sonatina' (which he confessed was deliberately Mozartian), Valse, Elegia, and Finale (introducing two folk-tunes). The serenade was usually for orchestra (Brahms, Jadassohn), string orchestra (Volkmann, Fuchs, Tchaikovsky, Dvořák), woodwind ensemble (Dvořák, Strauss), solo with orchestra (Volkmann, Bruch), or chamber grouping (Théodore Gouvy, two for flute and strings, one for piano quartet; Carl Reinecke, two for piano trio).

Brahms's early contributions to the revivification of the genre mark an important aspect of the relationship of symphony and serenade. By September 1858 he had written a four-movement serenade for flute, two clarinets, horn, bassoon, and strings; but by 8 December, persuaded by friends, he had resolved 'finally to turn the first Serenade into a symphony'. However, eight days later he had added two scherzos and was again calling the work a serenade. It was thus prevented from becoming a symphony by its alteration into a six-movement work; Brahms clearly recognized that, in their reliance on Haydnesque and middle-period Beethovenian models, the four original movements could not form a work of sufficient import to be a 'beautiful, grand' post-Beethovenian symphony.[33] His Second Serenade also shows Classical leanings, firstly in its five-movement structure, with a Scherzo and Quasi menuetto organized around a central Adagio, secondly in the purity of its harmonic resource in the four fast movements, and thirdly in the setting, for, although the scoring is often commented upon as being a Romantic innovation (based on a precedent in Méhul), the effect of omitting violins from the orchestra is suggestive of an accompanied woodwind serenade.

---

[33] *Brahms Briefwechsel*, v. 226–8; *Clara Schumann–Johannes Brahms Briefe*, i. 254.

The first three Serenades of Robert Fuchs (1847–1927) are four-movement works for string orchestra; No. 4 adds two horns and is in five movements, and No. 5 is for small orchestra, again in four movements. All are significantly smaller in extent than Brahms's serenades and than Fuchs's own symphonies. A particular differentiation from the symphony is also Fuchs's tendency to begin with a slowish movement (Andante or Allegretto); his Third Serenade begins with the graceful melody shown in Ex. 403. The Fifth Serenade was written as a tribute to Johann Strauss the younger, and includes themes from his *Fledermaus* in its last movement. These were among Fuchs's most successful and popular works, so that in Viennese circles he acquired the nickname 'Serenaden-Fuchs'.

VARIED CONCEPTIONS OF THE SYMPHONY

The term 'symphony' was now mostly reserved for orchestral works of serious and substantial musical import in from one to seven movements. As already noted, the title was used in France also for

Ex. 403

solo keyboard works which took over something of the textural weight and stylistic substance of the orchestral symphony. The genre had a strong relationship and some overlap (again particularly in France) with the concerto; and there is one case, also in that country, of the title being used for a chamber work: Gounod's *Petite Symphonie* (1885) for nine woodwind instruments.

The unitary movement for orchestra is primarily found with the designations 'overture', 'symphonic poem', or 'fantasia'. Wagner titled his *Siegfried Idyll* (1870) 'Symphonie' in his manuscript fair copy, and towards the end of his life conceived the unrealized project of writing some (further) one-movement symphonies.[34] Puccini's *Capriccio sinfonico* (1883) may be regarded as a one-movement symphony, with 'capriccio' added to the title to excuse any irregularities in this first major orchestral essay by the student composer. But where the designated movements of a symphony are fewer than three, there is usually some marked differentiation of musical material to suggest an underlying larger number. Schumann's Fourth Symphony (1851) was published as a 'Symphony . . . in one movement' with five specified parts. Arensky's Second Symphony (1889) is in one movement with slow and scherzo episodes. Liszt's *Eine Symphonie zu Dantes Divina Commedia* (the 'Dante' Symphony, 1855–6) is in two movements, the second comprising two distinct sections. Saint-Saëns's Third Symphony (1886) groups an underlying four-movement design of 2 + 2 into a designated two-movement structure. True three-movement symphonies are Liszt's 'Faust' Symphony (1854–7) (though the Finale has a differentiated choral epilogue), Bruch's F minor Symphony (1870) (its central Adagio leading directly into the final Allegro), Dvořák's Third Symphony (1873), d'Indy's *Symphonie cévenole* (1886), César Franck's Symphony (1888) (where the composer included slow and scherzo elements in the middle movement), and Chausson's Symphony (1890). Raff could allow his programme for a symphony to group essentially four-movement works into three 'divisions'. But the norm of four movements inherited from Classical and early Romantic times was maintained during this period, and re-emphasized by the great symphonists of the 1860s to 1880s: Bruckner, Brahms, Borodin, Tchaikovsky, and Dvořák. This norm derives from, and is a mark of, the reverence in which the genre was held, and it embodied the highest aspirations of instrumental composition. Following

---

[34] Curt von Westernhagen, *Wagner: A Biography*, trans. Mary Whittall (Cambridge, 1978), ii. 468, 589–90.

Beethoven's precedent in his 'Pastoral', the symphony could be expanded to five movements: Schumann's Third (1851), Raff's First, *An das Vaterland* (1861), Lalo's *Symphonie espagnole* (1874), Tchaikovsky's Third Symphony (1875), and Goldmark's *Ländliche Hochzeit* (1876), but only very exceptionally any further. Rubinstein's popular *Océan Symphonie* exists in three versions, in four movements (1851), six movements (1863), and seven movements (1880).

While the symphony remained normally purely orchestral, it could, since Berlioz's *Harold en Italie*, readily incorporate a solo instrument: Gade's Symphony No. 5 (1852), Giovanni Pacini's 'Dante' Symphony (1865), and d'Indy's *Symphonie sur un chant montagnard français* (*Symphonie cévenole*) are for orchestra with solo piano; Lalo's *Symphonie espagnole* is for orchestra with solo violin; and Saint-Saëns's Third Symphony is for orchestra with piano duet and organ. In this type of symphony there is already a mixture of the primary genres of symphony and concerto. Lalo's work is indeed more like a five-movement concerto than a symphony because of its substantial and dominating virtuoso writing for the violin; the virtuoso writing for piano in d'Indy's *Symphonie* is perhaps less dominant, but none the less real. As always, the title becomes an important part of the composer's artistic statement. This mixture of genres also occurs in works which are primarily concertos but entitled *concerto symphonique*.

Since Beethoven, composers had also been interested in including voices, but, perhaps because of proximity to choral genres such as the ode and cantata, the choral symphony remained a rarity during this period, though a highly characteristic one. Following Beethoven and Mendelssohn, Liszt used voices in the final movements of both his symphonies. But between then and Mahler's Second Symphony (1894) very few major works of this type were written. Paul Lacombe's *Sapho* (1878), Augusta Holmes's *Les Argonautes* (1880), and Cecile Chaminade's *Les Amazones* (*c.*1888) are all entitled *symphonie dramatique* and draw on models by Félicien David and Berlioz. Elgar's Op. 25 is entitled 'Symphony for Chorus and Orchestra *The Black Knight*' (1889–92), and is in four scenes (perhaps as movement parallels). It belongs in the English choral cantata tradition, and Elgar later called his Symphony in A flat Op. 55 'Number 1'. And when it became clear to Bruckner that he would not finish his Ninth Symphony, he suggested performance of the three completed movements with his Te Deum added; this was however substitutive, and extensive sketches remain for an instrumental Finale.

The diminutive sinfonietta seems to have been first used by Raff

for his Op. 188 (1876) for ten woodwind instruments.[35] Cowen and
Théodore Gouvy wrote orchestral sinfoniettas in 1881 and *c*.1886.
Rimsky-Korsakov's String Quartet of 1879, entirely based on Russian
folk-tunes, was subsequently scrapped, and its first three movements
revised and orchestrated as Sinfonietta on Russian Themes, Op. 31
(1884).

STYLISTIC CHARACTERISTICS

The nature of the work of composition and performance, the
imposing and varied sound world involved, together with the very
strong traditions of the genre, made the symphony the 'apex-work'
for late-Romantic composers. Elevated style was axiomatic, and such
style characteristically involved some kind of integration of movement
structures, which could be effected by various techniques in isolation
or combination: movements or movement types flowing into one
another, thematic quotation or transformation across movements,
motivic unification of themes of different movements. This thrust to
continuity and fusion had its roots in Beethoven (especially in his
Symphonies Nos. 5, 6, and 9); and it nourished a tendency to the
climactic finale (as in Beethoven's Fifth and Ninth). Where one
theme, by prominent quotation or transformation between movements, comes to dominate a complete work, it can be called a
motto-theme (even if other themes also cross movement boundaries
in a less obvious manner); Berlioz had established the use of
motto-themes in symphonies, and his example was followed particularly by Tchaikovsky.

Thematic materials for symphonies would ideally have epic quality,
often with motivic prominence, elemental ethos, complex phrase
structures, internal developmental processes, integrated contrapuntal
elements, and dependence on instrumental idioms. Sonata form
remained the generating thought process of the symphonic drama;
it was almost always used for first movements, often for finales and
for the sections of scherzo and trio movements, and it also appeared
in slow movements. Where contrast-based forms (ternary and rondo)
or variation form or fugue were used, these were often inflected by
sonata-form influences in types of development and types of relations
between themes. The sense of symphonic pacing thus involved
pregnance, dramatic unfolding, evolution, and *rapprochement* at all

---

[35] After abandoning his initial title 'Suite' for the *Overture, Scherzo and Finale*, Schumann
referred to the work in 1841 as 'Symphonette', though by the end of that year it had acquired
its present title; see Gerald Abraham, 'Robert Schumann', *The New Grove* (London, 1980),
xvi. 839.

levels of structure. This could take place in an extended time-span, related again to the Beethovenian precedents of the *Eroica* and Ninth Symphonies; and Bruckner in particular explored such monumentality. Typical expansions of Classical tonality would involve the use of remote tonal regions (Tchaikovsky's B major second subject in the first movement of his F minor Symphony is an extreme example), the multiplication of tonal areas (the three-keyed sonata-form exposition was a commonly used resource by Brahms and Bruckner), and the veiling of tonal areas (as in the second subject of Brahms's Second Symphony first movement, the opening of Bruckner's Eighth Symphony, or the Finale of Dvořák's Fifth—where the first subject has its opening fifty bars in the mediant minor, which key also opens the recapitulation). Developmental techniques drew on Classical precedent (fragmentation, extension, intervallic modification, variation), and Baroque devices (inversion, diminution, augmentation, fugato, contrapuntal combination). Characteristically, late-Romantic developmental procedures would use such techniques in the service of expressive alteration; a powerful example is the manner in which the strongly pastoral second subject of the first movement of Brahms's Third Symphony becomes an epic–heroic gesture in the subsequent development section.

The breadth of true symphonic pacing was enabled and enhanced by the great timbral variety inherent in the orchestral sound world, as also by the grandeur of the orchestral tutti. Orchestration depends on the play of timbral colour, but orchestration in these years was much more than a varied presentation of abstract ideas. The disposition of themes and their derivations across the available sound resources becomes part of the thematic substance itself, and orchestration must be regarded as an element of structure. This could involve particular emphasis on the idiomatic nature of themes; Bruckner's trumpet first subject for his Third Symphony, Dvořák's flute theme within the first subject of his Eighth, grow out of the instruments concerned, and embody musical aspects of the very being of these instruments. Tchaikovsky offered a different perspective on this matter when he wrote 'the musical idea carries with it the proper instrumentation for its expression'.[36] Use of the possibilities of chamber-music-related dialogue appear especially in Dvořák and Brahms; indeed in Dvořák's mature symphonic style, antiphony of an integrated instrumental–thematic nature was a mode of pregnance early in a symphony. Structural orchestration could involve certain

---

[36] Cited and discussed in Warrack, *Tchaikovsky Symphonies and Concertos*, p. 8.

differentiated orchestrations for specific formal areas: Dvořák favoured an orchestral tutti after the opening of a fast movement as
an early climactic restatement (often marked grandioso); Bruckner
favoured a string contrast for the initiation of his second subjects,
and a quiet string or woodwind initiation of his development sections;
Brahms employed a solo effect for his second-subject initiations. The
block-like orchestration of the third movement of Tchaikovsky's
Fourth Symphony clearly and simply articulates the structure, as
well as the private programme of the movement.

Within the concept of structural orchestration, composers developed their individual sound preferences. Commentators have noted
Tchaikovsky's fondness for primary colours; Brahms's doublings of
melody line across instruments from different sections are highly
characteristic, especially of his later orchestral style; Bruckner's
treatment of woodwind, brass, and strings as separate departments
to be used *en bloc* is often related by commentators to his abilities
as an organ virtuoso. Although the writing-out of the full score was
usually the last part of the main compositional effort for a symphony,
this does not of course in any way deny a structural value to
orchestration. And a continuity sketch for the opening of Dvořák's
Sixth Symphony shows already that flute and oboe were to provide
the initial antiphony to the bass in this theme; indeed Dvořák's note
of the instrumentation was entered before the tempo-marking of the
movement, which therefore had to be squeezed in.[37]

PROGRAMME SYMPHONIES OF THE 1850s: SCHUMANN, LISZT

Beethoven's concerns with programme and structural matters
involving fusion of movements, expansion of confines, and climactic
finales had been developed by composers up to 1850; Berlioz, Spohr,
Mendelssohn, and Schumann had used some or all of these concepts.
Schumann continued this line into the 1850s with his Third and
Fourth Symphonies (respectively 1850 and 1841; completely rev.
1851). The Third, the 'Rhenish', has an additional movement inspired
by a 'solemn ceremony' in Cologne Cathedral, a stately slow
movement before the Finale, which uses measured imitative counterpoint on trombones to parallel the solemnity of the programme.[38]
The Fourth Symphony has great thematic cohesion tending towards
monothematicism. Although it remains possible to identify separate

[37] Antonín Hořejš, *Antonín Dvořák: The Composer's Life and Work in Pictures* (Prague, 1955), unpaginated.
[38] For the sources of the nickname and programmatic associations of this Symphony, see Linda Correll Roesner's Preface to the Eulenburg Edition of the work (London, 1986).

themes, the five-note Clara motif stated at the outset of the introduction dominates the work, and from it all subsequent themes may be seen to be derived (even the seemingly new theme of the development of the first 'movement' includes this motif). The work is also fused by being continuous. Though it was published in this, its second version, as *Symphonie No. IV D moll, Introduction, Allegro, Romanze, Scherzo und Finale in einem Satze*, it is customarily regarded as having the four traditional movements with introductions to the first and last.

Liszt's two symphonies come from his Weimar period, and are part of his programmatic and idealistic concerns of this decade. In them, as in his other great 'multi-movement' work of these years, the Piano Sonata, Liszt dispensed with any kind of dance movement. His 'Faust' Symphony was completed in three instrumental movements in 1854; they have been described as 'a triptych of three of his finest symphonic poems',[39] and each movement depicts a principal character from Goethe's drama in a meditative, non-narrative programmatic manner: the first movement is Faust himself, the second Gretchen, the third Mephistopheles. But the work also coheres as a symphony. The first movement is a large-scale sonata form, clearly articulated on Classical precepts (thus less radical than the Piano Sonata); the second movement uses some first-movement themes as subsidiary material; and the third movement is a demonic parody of the first, involving transformation of its themes with the expressive purpose of representing Mephistopheles as a non-originating, negative, distorting force. (In this, the processes of the movement have some kinship with those of the Finale of Berlioz's *Symphonie fantastique*.) Liszt's third movement follows the formal and thematic course of the first; it is also, therefore, in sonata form, but it acts on a higher formal level as a variation of the first movement, which is only departed from by a quotation of the principal slow-movement theme just prior to the Finale's recapitulation. In 1857, after completing his next symphony chorally, Liszt added to the 'Faust' the 'Chorus mysticus', a short choral epilogue which sets Goethe's hymn to the 'eternal feminine'; this epilogue is based on the principal theme of the second movement, and the general large-scale thematic plan of the Symphony thus becomes ABA_1B_1.

Liszt's *Symphonie zu Dante's Divina commedia* (the 'Dante' Sym-

---

[39] For this stimulating view, see Gerald Abraham, *The Concise Oxford History of Music* (Oxford, 1979), 684.

phony) is also based on a great literary work, and in some ways may be viewed as more dependent on its programme for coherence than his 'Faust' Symphony. It is in two designated movements ('Inferno' and 'Purgatorio'), but the second falls into two distinct parts. The first movement opens with a trombone setting of the inscription over the gates of Hell. Although the 'allegro' sections of this movement are strongly based on sonata-form procedures, the overall form is ternary, with a central slow section depicting the lovers Francesca and Paolo. The almost unrelenting use of discord in the allegro sections often forces the tonal basis into the background; this basis is D minor, written without a key signature. The Symphony as a whole has a progressive tonal scheme, for B minor emerges as the tonic of the instrumental part of the second movement (also ternary), and B major as the tonic of the subsequent vocal part of this movement. The work increases in foreground tonal clarity during its course, which is clearly a feature of the programmatic depiction. The last part of the work is a choral *Magnificat* for women's or boys' voices—actually a meditative setting of the first verse of the *Magnificat* only, with quiet 'hosannas' and 'hallelujas' appended. Although it is neither designated a separate movement, nor separated from the preceding music by a rest, it stands in place of a movement on Dante's *Paradiso* and draws its highly distinctive themes in part from three plainsong psalm-tones. Wagner, who had suggested this kind of ending to Liszt, called the Symphony 'one of the most astounding deeds of music'.[40]

RAFF'S PROGRAMME SYMPHONIES

Joachim Raff carried the programme symphony into the next two decades. Of his eleven surviving symphonies (an early one of 1854 is partly lost) only two are non-programmatic. His First Symphony is entitled *An das Vaterland*, his Third *Im Walde*, his Fifth *Lénore*, while his Sixth has a poetic motto, the programmatic implications of which Raff detailed in a letter to von Bülow.[41] His Seventh Symphony is *In den Alpen* and his last four form a cycle on the seasons of the year: No. 8, *Frühlingsklänge*; No. 9, *Im Sommer*; No. 10, *Zur Herbstzeit*; No. 11, *Der Winter*. These surviving symphonies were composed in the period 1859–79 and published soon after completion, for Raff was celebrated during these years as one of the leading composers of Germany.[42] He was a fluent stylist in the

[40] Richard Wagner, *Gesammelte Schriften und Dichtungen* x (2nd edn.; Leipzig, 1888), 100.
[41] Müller-Reuter, *Lexikon*, pp. 388–9.
[42] Markus Römer, *Joseph Joachim Raff (1822–1882)* (Wiesbaden, 1982), 36–7, 55.

Mendelssohn–Spohr tradition, and Liszt had thought highly enough of his early abilities at instrumentation to enlist his help in the orchestration of some of his own symphonic poems.

Raff's symphony of 1854 was in five 'divisions' [*Abtheilungen*], two of which (Scherzo and March) became the last two movements of his First Orchestral Suite. *An das Vaterland* is also in five 'divisions'—his term *Abtheilung* seems to have been equivalent to 'movement' at this time; but thereafter Raff favoured the four-movement symphony, though he could allow his programme to dominate this structure in a grouping of movements by larger 'divisions'—the term now used in a different sense. This feature may be seen in his two most popular symphonies, *Im Walde* (1869) and *Lénore* (1872). The former, properly entitled *Im Walde Sinfonie Nr. 3* (the order is significant), has:

1st Division: Daytime. Impressions and Feelings. Allegro; 2nd Division: At twilight. A. Dreaming. Largo. B. Dance of the Dryads. Allegro assai; 3rd Division: Night. Still murmuring of the night in the forest. Entry and Exit of the wild hunt with Frau Holle (Hulda) and Wotan. Daybreak. Allegro.

The second division is thus linked by its programmatic siting 'at twilight', for the Largo and Allegro assai are separated, self-enclosed, ternary-form movements in different keys, corresponding to the traditional middle movements of the symphonic genre.

The first movement is in a clear sonata form, beginning with a highly poetic anticipatory 'curtain'—twenty-six bars in the main allegro tempo, which adumbrate in lightly sketched form the principal thematic material of the movement. (The idea of an introduction in the main tempo, which Raff used again in the last movement, had a precedent in Mendelssohn—for instance in the piano concertos.) Raff's first subject shows aspects of his compositional fluency and ingenuity (see Ex. 404, bars 23–36). It grows imperceptibly out of the 'curtain', and has a structure of statement + semi-palindromic

Ex. 404

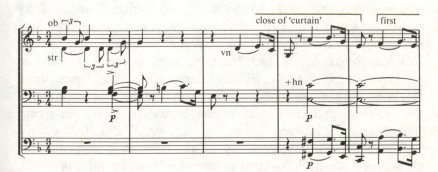

response, in which the eight-bar basis is blurred by motivic means; its bass is a typically smooth motion paralleling the melody. The second subject group has two themes, the second a 'hunting' theme; the group is stated in the subdominant, and recapitulated in the dominant (a lengthy coda re-establishing the tonic). This tonal plan has a strategic purpose, for the true recapitulation of the second subject comes at the very end of the Symphony, where it appears, as apotheosis, in the tonic for the first time. The Finale has another original introduction in the main tempo: an eleven-bar theme is stated five times in a mixture of fugue and variation. The main body of the movement has little to do with this theme, being a fully worked-out sonata form of vigorous, even raucous tone, owing much in its portrayal of the supernatural to Weber and Berlioz.

In *Lénore* movements 1 and 2 are grouped in the first division, 'Joy of Love', the next two divisions ('Separation' and 'Reuniting in Death') consisting of one movement each. Again the four movements follow Classical precedent, the opening Allegro and subsequent Andante portraying different aspects of the Joy of Love. In the third movement an army arrives to carry off the beloved in its ranks; the march makes a steady long-term crescendo depicting the approach, and, after a central section on the passionate farewell of the lovers, a corresponding decrescendo to the close of the movement depicts the departure. This is a simple poetic idea, but is nevertheless very powerful, almost theatrical in effect. The central part of the fourth movement portrays Lenore's horse-ride with her dead lover in a macabre *perpetuum mobile* incorporating recall of themes from previous movements; a discordant climax leads to a slow quasi-religious ending.

REVITALIZATION OF CLASSICAL FORMS: BRUCKNER

Although Bruckner began composing multi-movement in-strumental works during the 1860s (the C minor String Quartet (1862), *Studiensymphonie* (1863), Symphony No. 0 (1864 and 1869), and Symphony No. 1 (1866)), his instrumental music did not have a significant public impact until well into the 1880s, and by 1885 only two of his multi-movement instrumental works were in print. This slowness of recognition was partly due to performance diffi-culties, partly due to Bruckner's adherence to Wagner, which antagonized the powerful critic Hanslick from 1873 on, and partly due to the very substance of his music itself. His symphonic style became so individual that the greatness, expressive coherence and intensity of his music, now beyond question, were subjects of controversy; and even Brahms at the very end of his life still could not comprehend them.[43] Bruckner's dedicated cultivation of the symphony was thus a triumph of faith over experience. Some encouragement came in the form of a government grant to assist in 'the composition of major symphonic works'[44] when he moved to Vienna in 1868, but undoubtedly Bruckner regarded his creativity as very separate from worldly concerns and within the context of his deep religious faith. Symphonies Nos. 2–5 belong to the years 1871–8, and Symphonies Nos. 6–8 to the years 1879–87; No. 9 remained unfinished at his death in 1896.

His symphonic style may be seen as an integrated synthesis of experience in three different sound worlds. His education, his appointments prior to the move to Vienna, and many aspects of his life in Vienna were dominated by the world of the church musician, and sacred musical styles of the late-Renaissance, Baroque, and Classical Mass remained a fundamental background to his own musical thought processes. Bach formed an important part of his musical education; he copied the *Art of Fugue*, studied the

[43] Richard Specht, *Johannes Brahms*, trans. Eric Blom (London, 1930), 262.
[44] Ernst Decsey, *Bruckner: Versuch eines Lebens* (Berlin, 1921), 57.

chorale-harmonizations and the '48'. During a period of study under the theorist Sechter he was compelled to forego free composition and concentrate on contrapuntal expertise. He remained a practising virtuoso on the organ until near the end of his life, becoming internationally famous as such during the 1870s, well before his fame as composer spread beyond local confines. He was particularly celebrated for his grand improvisations, which were characteristically, though not exclusively, fugues. Aged 37, he sought to acquire command of symphonic form and orchestration, turning to Otto Kitzler as teacher, with whom he studied particularly sonata form. Beethovenian precedent, especially in the Ninth Symphony, and Schubertian instrumental style were to become very important ingredients of his creativity, and these early nineteenth-century examples formed the second sound world of the Brucknerian synthesis. It was also through Kitzler that Bruckner became acquainted with the third—that of Wagner's music. Kitzler mounted a performance of *Tannhäuser* in 1862; Bruckner attended the first performance of *Tristan und Isolde* at Munich in 1865, meeting Wagner. From these beginnings Bruckner became an ardent Wagnerian, dedicating his Third Symphony to Wagner, using some Wagner themes in improvisations and symphonies, and visiting Bayreuth in later years.

The proximity of Bruckner's symphonies to liturgical choral music is suggested by the self-quotations from his Masses and other church music in his symphonies (these are particularly prominent in Symphonies Nos. 2, 7, and 9), by his thematic recourse to pseudo-chorales with measured sostenuto block harmony—especially in Finales (e.g. in the last movement of Symphony No. 5, where Bruckner refers to the theme concerned as *Choral* in the score itself), by modality (e.g. in Symphony No. 6, which opens with phrygian-mode inflexion), and by certain similarities between his method of orchestration and the way organists register. But by far the most important and fundamental influence from the *Kapellmeister* sound world is manifest in Bruckner's chosen ways of treating and extending material. Inversions, diminutions, augmentations, sequences, ostinati, scalic basses, pedals, fugatos, contrapuntal combinations (often involving rhythmic complexity) were all Baroque modes of extension, and Bruckner applied them within the context of late-nineteenth-century harmonic and formal structures in a manner which is one of the chief marks of his individuality in symphonic thought.

The unchanging basis of Bruckner's symphonies is the Classical model of four separated movements, with slow movements placed second, except in Nos. 8 and 9 where they are third. Bruckner did, however, follow contemporary trends by using thematic links between movements, which could be motivic (e.g. in Symphonies 2 and 8), transformational (e.g. in Symphony No. 5 between movements 2 and 3), or by quotation. A characteristic linkage of this last kind is the climactic quotation of the opening theme of a symphony at the close of its Finale, as it were in triumphant resolution. Bruckner does this in Symphonies Nos. 3–7, while at the close of the Finale of the Eighth Symphony the principal themes of all previous movements are brought back in contrapuntal combination. Sonata form remained the central basis for movements 1 and 4, as for the sections of the scherzo and trio movements; the slow movements are ternary in the *Studiensymphonie* and Symphonies Nos. 1 and 3, sonata form in Symphony 0, and follow Bruckner's favoured $ABA_1B_1A_2$ form in Symphonies Nos. 2 and 4–9.

Sonata form in Bruckner's first and last movements was given massive internal expansion, often involving three separated thematic groups with differing keys. His first movements characteristically open with an elemental theme against a tremolo background. The second subject group is more lyrical (called by Bruckner *Gesangsperiode*), often involving extended tonality, in which a seemingly roving modulatory scheme is nevertheless anchored at structurally important moments, the main key becoming a reference point which prevents large-scale instability. The *Gesangsperiode* of the first movement of the Seventh Symphony is an example of this, where the B major of its opening in bar 51 is neither prepared nor established, but provides a reference point consolidated by thematic return (in bars 69, 89, and 103) within the otherwise widely modulating structure. As Bruckner said: 'during the audacities I allow myself here and there in my works, I always return to, and never lose complete sight of, the basic key.'[45] The third subject group (referred to by Bruckner as *Schlussperiode*) often involves impressive orchestral unison or heterophonic writing. First-movement expositions are not repeated, except in the *Studiensymphonie*. The development sections characteristically begin quietly; points of recapitulation are usually clear, but not so in Symphonies Nos. 3 and 4 because of tonic statements in the development sections, in Symphony No. 8 because of powerful subsequent development within

---

[45] August Göllerich, *Anton Bruckner: Ein Lebens- und Schaffens-Bild*, ed. Max Auer (Regensburg, 1922–37, repr. 1974), iv/2, p. 644.

the recapitulation, and in Symphony No. 9 because of a conflation of development and recapitulation into a unified responsive second half of the total structure. Such conflation is effected by having a single pass through the thematicism of the exposition, combining restatement and development. Redlich has called this type of structure 'telescoped',[46] but the term is somewhat misleading, because the movements concerned are not necessarily shorter than more normally structured movements; here this type of structure is called 'sonata form with combined response'.

While the forms of Bruckner's slow movements differ, they have in common the return of sections or themes much varied both by sonata-style developments and by elaborative figural decoration. In his later style Bruckner effected stupendous climactic moments by these means, particularly in the slow movements of Symphonies Nos. 7-9. The sonata form of the scherzo and trio sections is characteristically 'neo-primitive', in which the exposition ends in a related key but with only slight thematic differentiation, which has been evolved gradually during the course of the exposition. The thematic substance of the scherzos relies on insistent ostinato-like repetition of short figures, and scalic and sequential materials proliferate. By such means Bruckner generated immense energy in his scherzos, and created a new aesthetic value for foreground repetition itself. The Scherzo of the Ninth Symphony makes a new chord into a thematic idea (E, G sharp, B flat, C sharp).[47] The trios are characteristically more relaxed and resonant of *Ländler* style.

Finales have similar structures to first movements. The *Choral* element can be introduced as part of the *Gesangsperiode* (as in the Finales of the Third Symphony, where it is counterpointed with a polka, and of the Seventh), or as part of the *Schlussperiode* (as in the Finales of the Second and Fifth Symphonies). The Finale of the Fifth is unique for Bruckner in two structural respects: it begins with a review and dismissal of the openings of movements 1 and 2, and the first subject group of the subsequent sonata form is a fugue, which comes to dominate later stages of the form in combination with the *Choral* of the *Schlussperiode*. Bruckner used 'sonata form with combined response' in the Finales of Symphonies Nos. 6 and 7 (in the latter this form is further complicated by a final restatement of the first subject), and in the 1889 revision of the Finale of the Third Symphony.

---

[46] Hans Ferdinand Redlich, Foreword to the Eulenburg Edition of Bruckner's Symphony No. 9 (London, 1963; Foreword dated 1963), p. vii.

[47] Dika Newlin draws attention to Schenker's analysis of this chord in *Bruckner, Mahler, Schoenberg* (rev. edn., London, 1979), 95.

Fundamental to his symphonic thought is the Classically derived concept of the four-bar phrase, and his manuscripts show numberings of bars in accordance. His phrases naturally differ in function through a movement (statement, response, liquidation, contrast, restatement, etc.), and form thus macro phrase complexes. Such processes may clearly be seen at work in the exposition of the first movement of the Fifth Symphony, which relies heavily on four-bar structures. But in the first movement of the Seventh Symphony, his first real public triumph, Bruckner seems positively to avoid this four-bar basis to his discourse. His modulations to third-related keys are derived from Schubertian style.

From Wagner, as well as from the last symphonies of Beethoven and Schubert, Bruckner received the impulse towards monumentality based on length and scale, resulting in a renewal of the late-nineteenth-century symphony as a noble, even sublime, expressive genre combining lyricism with music of elemental grandeur and power. His often slow harmonic rhythm, chromatic harmony, and epic themes also had strong precedents in Wagner; indeed, Bruckner signalled his discipleship with quotations from Wagner's music. Yet in a significant respect—the aesthetic—Bruckner can by no means be called a Wagnerian. Bruckner's programmaticism was usually of a private, somewhat trivial kind; and, though he spoke of his symphonic music freely among friends in representational terms (the first movement of the Fourth Symphony is 'dawn in a medieval town', its Scherzo 'portrays the hunt', the second movement of the Eighth Symphony is 'der deutsche Michel'), these programmes were never seriously or formally presented to the world, nor can it be held that they match up to or generate the music in any significant way. One of Bruckner's descriptions of the first movement of the Fourth Symphony (the only one to carry a subtitle—'Romantic') concludes: 'and so the romantic picture develops.'[48] Bruckner had no need for the Wagnerian dependence on the fusion of words and music, being, like Brahms, concerned with the self-signification of discourse based on sonata form.

Although the Eighth Symphony is a profoundly mature master-piece, it has not escaped the textual problems which affect all Bruckner's symphonies except the *Studiensymphonie*, and Nos. 0 and 9—in part resulting from well-meaning but inadequate advice from friends and well-wishers, and the action of this advice on Bruckner's deep-seated humility and propensity for self-doubt. The Eighth exists

[48] Max Auer, *Anton Bruckner* (Vienna, 1923), 146.

in two versions. Robert Haas viewed the second as containing both
deterioration and improvement, and therefore conflated Bruckner's
two versions in his own edition; his pupil, Leopold Nowak, separated
the versions again; the following remarks on the opening movement
refer to Bruckner's second version of 1889–90.

For this Symphony Bruckner chose the order of movements of
Beethoven's Ninth, and indeed began the work with the characteristic
rhythm of Beethoven's opening. But Bruckner's first subject (Ex.
405) is otherwise very different; it has an immediate, prominent,
and grinding dissonance in an allusive preparatory tonal setting.
(Attempts to analyse the opening as defining the key of B flat minor
are over-determined and inappropriate.) The subject, involving
auxiliary formations and successive seventh-chords, is organized by
and under a rising scalic top part which moves from the subdominant
to the leading-note; C minor is well established by the end of the
subject, but not until its very last note is there a cadence on to the
tonic, and even then this is on a weak beat with reduced texture.
The subject shows a basis in four-bar phrase structure. It is given a
fortissimo varied repeat which avoids cadence and leads forward
into the *Gesangsperiode* second subject (Ex. 406) at bar 51. This is

Ex. 405

Ex. 406

one of the most hymnic, least dance-influenced of Bruckner's second subjects; however, it does use a characteristic Brucknerian rhythm, which has already appeared prominently in the first subject. The G major tonality of the *Gesangsperiode* is defined clearly at its beginning and end, though this key is quickly left at the opening by means of scalic bass-motion leading to a widely modulating middle. Again the subject is repeated with variants and without closure, moving to the heterophonic third subject (Ex. 407) in E flat minor at bar 97. This includes a huge rising scalic and chromatic bass (ascending through an augmented eleventh), which culminates in a codetta on the first subject, now in E flat major. The development section has Bruckner's characteristic quiet opening, and involves augmentations, inversions, imitations, and combinations of first and second subjects. At bar 225 the recapitulation begins with the first subject at original pitch, but reharmonized to cadence on to a chord of C major in its fifth bar. The subject is then further developed by sequence and fragmentation, so that the original twenty-two bars of the opening of the exposition are recapitulated with development as a seventy-eight-bar period. The *Gesangsperiode* returns in E flat major, the third subject in C minor; the codetta is expanded into a climax, followed by a quiet 'winding-down' ending, which Bruckner privately called the *Totenuhr*. Hugo Wolf wrote that the Eighth Symphony 'towers over all the other symphonies of the master in spiritual dimensions, in fecundity and greatness'.[49]

---

[49] Letter to Emil Kauffmann, 23 Dec. 1892; cited in Leopold Nowak's Foreword to *Anton Bruckner Sämtliche Werke: VIII. Symphonie C-moll, Fassung von 1890* (2nd edn.; Vienna, 1955).

Ex. 407

BRAHMS'S SYMPHONIES

At the beginning of the 1870s Brahms remarked to his friend, the conductor Hermann Levi: 'I shall never write a symphony, you have no idea what it feels to the likes of us constantly to hear such a giant [Beethoven] marching behind one.'[50] This was the time of Brahms's struggle with two genres of supreme importance to Beethoven, string quartet and symphony. Some of his early difficulties with the symphonic genre have already been noted; but in 1862 the first version of the first movement of his eventual First Symphony, Op. 68, without its slow introduction, was shown to friends (attempts by Kalbeck to affix an earlier date to this movement are speculative and unconvincing).[51] Much interest attached to this movement in Brahms's circle, and he was constantly being pressed by friends to finish the work. During the struggle to do so Brahms was nevertheless able to found a new genre by writing the first free-standing variation set for orchestra. His Variations on a Theme of Haydn (1873) consist of eight figurative and character variations followed by a passacaglia finale. The genre became important for subsequent composers—

[50] Kalbeck, *Johannes Brahms,* i (3rd edn.; Berlin, 1912), 165.
[51] Ibid., pp. 233–6; iii (2nd edn.; Berlin, 1912), 92–3.

Johann Herbeck, Iwan Knorr, Dvořák, Jean Louis Nicodé and Ernst Rudorff within this period, and d'Indy, Parry, Elgar, and Reger shortly after.

It may well have been the opening of Bayreuth in 1876 which provided Brahms with the final impetus to finish his First Symphony; Wagner was much in his thoughts that summer, and it is as if the First Symphony should form a politico-musical counter-statement to Wagnerian ideals. Brahms worked at the Symphony with a will that summer, and, most unusually for him, even fixed a performance before finishing the work. Brahms's triumph over the shadow of Beethoven in his First Symphony liberated him in the genre, and he was able to complete his Second within a year of the First. The Third, composed in 1883, and Fourth, 1884-5, also form a pair. Brahms did struggle with further projected symphonies in the late 1880s, and some surviving sketch material relates to this struggle; but he ultimately excused himself by claiming 'more than four symphonies are not really possible any longer for the musician wishing to give them a particular content; after that one is forced to repeat oneself'.[52]

The overall structure of the symphony for Brahms remained that of four separated and formally closed movements, albeit with integration of movements by thematic quotation, transformation, and motivic unification. The thematic–motivic intricacy and cogency so characteristic of Brahms's instrumental music from the very beginning remains fundamental to his symphonic style. But a special characteristic of his treatment of this genre is the importance of what may even be described as pre-thematic material, which appears at the opening of each symphony and has long-term ramifications over the whole succeeding work.[53] The First Symphony begins with two contrapuntally diverging lines over a rhythmically articulated pedal (Ex. 408). These not only surround the arpeggiaic first subject of the subsequent 'allegro' section, but form one of the main thematic links between all movements, appearing in the slow second movement at bar 5 (Ex. 409, which shows bars 4-7), the third movement at bars 23 and 30 (Ex. 410, which shows bars 22-33), and at the beginning of the slow introduction to the Finale, where they are integrated with a prefiguring of the main theme of the 'allegro' (Ex. 411).

[52] Ibid. iv (2nd edn.; Berlin, 1915), 216. For a brief discussion of the sketch material, see Robert Pascall, 'Brahms und die Gattung der Symphonie', in Christiane Jacobsen (ed.), *Johannes Brahms: Leben und Werk* (Wiesbaden, 1983), 114.

[53] The concept of pre-thematic necessity in Brahms's symphonies is introduced and discussed in Siegfried Kross, 'Brahms the Symphonist', in Robert Pascall (ed.), *Brahms: Biographical, Documentary and Analytical Studies* (Cambridge, 1983), 125-45.

Ex. 408

Ex. 409

Ex. 410

Ex. 411

In the Second Symphony the pre-thematic material is the auxiliary-note figure in bar 1, which is itself derived from the Finale of the First Symphony, and which comes to dominate the thematic material throughout the Second. This domination is obvious in the first and last movements (and has indeed been studied by Réti);[54] in the second movement the figure is more hidden, being decorated and elaborated, while the third movement has the figure in inversion. The pre-thematic material of the Third Symphony is the F–A flat–F motif at the opening, and in the Fourth it is the concept of the falling third behind the first subject.[55] This pre-thematic element in the symphonies is not found to nearly such a marked extent in Brahms's sonatas, concertos, or chamber music. Its use in symphonies did not eliminate other links between movements: one of the thematic units of the First Symphony is a 'Clara' theme, as Michael Musgrave has pointed out, and this appears prominently in the first and last movements;[56] the Third Symphony, after using transformations of material from the slow movement in its Finale, ends with a quiet valedictory quotation of the opening of the first movement; in the Fourth Symphony the first theme of the first movement is quoted towards the end of the Finale in canonic entries over the passacaglia bass.

Brahms used sonata form for all his symphony first movements, with three thematic groups having motivic elements in common, the second and third characteristically being in major and minor versions of the same contrasting key (the First Symphony has C minor,

[54] Rudolph Réti, *The Thematic Process in Music* (2nd edn.; London, 1961), 78–81, 163–5.

[55] The opening of the Fourth Symphony formed the material of one of Schoenberg's analyses in his famous article 'Brahms the Progressive', in Dika Newlin (ed.), *Style and Idea* (London, 1951), 62.

[56] Michael Musgrave, 'Brahms's First Symphony: Thematic Coherence and its Secret Origin', *Music Analysis*, 2/2 (July 1983), 117–33.

E flat major, and E flat minor; the Third F major, A major, and A minor; the Fourth E minor, B minor, and B major). The Second Symphony uses more distinct tonal areas: D major, F sharp minor, and A major. Expositions are repeated in the first movements of the first three symphonies, but never in last movements. The character of the thematic profile of his first-movement expositions varies from symphony to symphony; in the Second, for instance, the themes become increasingly more vigorous, pointing towards a climactic and contrapuntal development section. Development sections characteristically include some change of ethos: in the First Symphony the development includes a new chorale-like tune which clarifies the extreme chromaticism of the exposition; the Third Symphony's development turns the pastoral second subject into an epic–heroic gesture, and the vigorous first subject into a restrained, veiled, somewhat brooding passage just prior to the recapitulation. Recapitulations are clear and usually straightforward, though in the first movement of the Fourth Symphony the recapitulation begins with a greatly stretched version of the first subject in a moment of powerfully dramatic calm.

Codas are important and can include the drawing out of new poetic aspects of thematic material within a strong thrust to closure. The horn solo in the coda of the first movement of the Second Symphony is the *locus classicus* of this feature, and it is followed by material related to a contemporaneous song, which Brahms recognized by writing in his personal copy of the printed score 'Love is so lovely in Spring'.

The slow movements are always placed second. That of the First Symphony was initially a rondo form, but between first performance and publication it underwent a major structural revision, and was converted in a highly sophisticated way into a ternary form.[57] Subsequent slow movements are ternary in Symphonies Nos. 2 and 3 (both movements including developmental material), and sonata form with combined response in Symphony No. 4. They are lyrical and melodic, but not to the exclusion of compositional complexity in themes, relations between themes, and treatments of them. Even the simplest thematic opening of a slow movement, that in the Third Symphony, has the phrase structure 4 + 4 + 6 + 9. The Fourth Symphony's slow movement opens modally. Brahms was working on the Complete Edition of Schubert's works at the time of composing this Symphony, and its second movement shows some specifically

---

[57] Robert Pascall, 'Brahms's First Symphony Slow Movement: The Initial Performing Version', *Musical Times*, 122 (1981), 664–7.

Schubertian traits: the horn introduction, the pizzicato accompaniment to the subsequent sustained theme, the very great
melodic beauty of the second subject, and the explosive developmental
outburst late in the movement.

Brahms's third movements were often innovatory, not only in his
symphonies. The restrained Intermezzo of the First Symphony,
beginning with five-bar phrases and melodic inversion, has a conflation of rondo and ternary formal types. The non-recurring and
brief first episode of the rondo plan is integrated more with previous
material than the longer second episode, which therefore establishes
itself as the main contrasting section, and the overall form of the
movement may also be viewed as ternary with shortened return. In
his Second String Quartet Brahms had combined minuet and scherzo
elements in a way which led directly to the third movement of the
Second Symphony. This movement has the plan $ABA_1B_1A_2$, where
the scherzo-like B section is motivically extracted from the minuet-like
A section, and B_1 is a rhythmic transformation of B. A_2 opens in a
colouristically variant tonality, F sharp major, which is related to
the tonic of the movement as its under auxiliary-note key; this is an
example of a motif (the pre-thematic opening of the Symphony)
generating large-scale tonal ramifications. The Scherzo of the Fourth
Symphony is in sonata form with combined response, and no trio-like
contrasts are established.

Save for the special case of the last Symphony, Brahms's symphonic
Finales are in sonata form, with combined response in Symphonies
Nos. 1 and 3. The Finale of the First Symphony has a wide range
of expressive content. The dark, chromatically inflected introduction
clarifies at the announcement of an 'Alphorn' melody (so characterized by Brahms in a postcard to Clara Schumann before
the Symphony was completed), which is followed by a stately
pseudo-chorale. The 'Alphorn' melody is integrated into the subsequent Allegro, while the pseudo-chorale recurs climactically and
frame-like near the end of the movement. The Allegro has a
three-themed and three-keyed exposition (C major, G major, E
minor); the first subject carries undoubted resonance of the principal
theme of the Finale of Beethoven's Ninth, and this movement has
been a primary focus for critics wishing to emphasize Brahms'
continuity with Beethoven. Von Bülow called this Symphony 'the
Tenth', since when many commentators have taken him to have
meant Beethoven's Tenth, though von Bülow himself was at pains
to point out he had not intended any such implication.[58] Perhaps

[58] Hans von Bülow, *Briefe und Schriften*, ed. Marie von Bülow, iii (Leipzig, 1896), 369.

following what they thought was his lead, Hanslick called Brahms's Second Symphony his 'Pastoral', and Richter the Third his 'Eroica'. Brahms seemed to lay especial weight on the finale in symphonies. Thematic links, while existing between most movements of each symphony, are at their most obvious in finales, and all finales include intricate contrapuntal work. In his First Symphony Brahms completed the first and last movements before completing the middle movements; in the Second he turned to the composition of the Finale immediately on finishing the first movement.

The passacaglia Finale to the Fourth Symphony is a special creative moment in Brahms's instrumental output. It is based on a theme from Bach's Cantata 150, 'Nach dir, Herr, verlanget mich', to which Brahms added a chromatic passing-note, A sharp, that seems to entail the F natural in the bass two bars later. See Ex. 412, where the last section of the Bach Cantata is shown mapped on to the opening of the Brahms Finale. There follow another thirty statements of this theme, which is often disguised by being embedded deep within the harmony, followed by a terse, developmental, and climactic coda. Brahms had earlier arranged for piano left hand Bach's D minor Chaconne from the second solo violin partita. It was a movement he very greatly admired, and it gave him the impulse towards his own highly organized overall structure for the Finale of the Fourth Symphony. Brahms followed Bach in using a basic overall ternary design, with a middle section involving the major tonic key. (In Brahms's movement this middle section is really defined by an augmentation of the harmonic rhythm, and begins with a poignant flute solo, still in the minor.) Also following Bach, Brahms used recapitulatory variations, and the grouping of variations in fours and pairs. This Symphony was to prove Brahms's valediction to the genre, and it is in certain ways retrospective and summatory; Bach, Beethoven, and Schubert had formed the greatest sources of influence

Ex. 412

on his instrumental music, yet here, as elsewhere, these influences are totally assimilated and transformed into mature, compelling and intensely expressive originality.

THE SYMPHONIES OF STRAUSS AND MAHLER

It was within the context of the revitalization of Classical symphonic structure that Richard Strauss and Mahler produced their early symphonies. Strauss's F minor Symphony (1883–4) belongs to his young traditionalist phase. Its four-movement design has thematic integration across movements; Del Mar draws attention to influences from Schumann and Mendelssohn, and detects 'more than a hint' of Bruckner in the Finale (though the possibility of establishing any biographical basis for this as direct influence seems unlikely).[59] Strauss moved away from the ideals expressed in this Symphony in his programmatic symphonic fantasia *Aus Italien* (1886), which nevertheless takes the four-movement symphony and sonata form as points of departure; he himself described it as a transitional work, 'the connecting link between the old and the new methods'.[60]

Mahler's First Symphony seems to have been preceded by four other youthful symphonic attempts, now lost. It evolved from 'Symphonic Poem in two parts' without programme (1888), to '*Titan* a tone-poem in symphony-form in two parts' with programme after Jean Paul Richter (1893–4), to 'Symphony (*Titan*) in five movements (two parts)' with individually titled movements (1894), to 'Symphony' in four movements (1896).[61] This evolution demonstrates clearly the gravitational pull of the four-movement symphony of Classical structure, especially as the discarded second movement, 'Blumine', is very fine. Mahler said in 1895 'to me "symphony" means constructing a world with all the technical means at one's disposal', but it is clear from letters of 1896 to Max Marschalk that he had come to regard explicit programmes as inadequate for the genre and misleading.[62] The first movement of his First Symphony makes already a personal and distinctive approach to sonata form, for the basic thematic duality is between introduction and exposition, the exposition itself showing no marked thematic differentiation; further,

[59] Norman Del Mar, *Richard Strauss: A Critical Commentary on his Life and Works*, i (2nd edn.; London, 1969), 26; cf. Willi Schuh, *Richard Strauss: A Chronicle of the Early Years, 1864–1898*, trans. Mary Whittall (Cambridge, 1982), 158.

[60] Del Mar, *Richard Strauss*, i. 41.

[61] See Donald Mitchell, *Gustav Mahler: The Wunderhorn Years* (London, 1975), 158–9, for a useful summary chart of this complex history.

[62] Natalie Bauer-Lechner, *Recollections of Gustav Mahler*, trans. Dika Newlin (London, 1980), 40; *Gustav Mahler: Briefe (1879–1911)*, ed. Alma Maria Mahler (Berlin, 1924), 185, 187.

although the exposition begins in D major, A major is very quickly adopted within that first subject itself. The evocative introductory material, 'Wie ein Naturlaut' [like a Sound of Nature], returns in the development to establish a hold over the Symphony, which reaches into and generates much of the structural originality of the Finale; there is also in the development an F minor treatment of the first subject, which provides the tonal and thematic starting-point of the Finale. The Scherzo-and-trio movement shows well Mahler's sublimation of popular culture and even perhaps vulgarity, with its fast *Ländler*-type Scherzo and gentler café-music styled Trio, followed by a curtailed da capo. The third movement was (and in a sense remains) 'a funeral march in Callot's manner', with an ostinato-like treatment of 'Brüder Martin' as its opening, and a parody of Bohemian village music in some of its subsidiary material. The Finale opens with a sectionalized sonata-form exposition; an extensive, intense F minor 'storm', based on material from the development of the first movement, serves as first subject, followed by a slow lyrical D flat major second-subject area. Both sections are self-enclosed, which is part of Mahler's highly personal solution to the finale problem here. The development recalls the introduction to the first movement before treating finale material, but it is in the 'recapitulation' that expressive originality based on formal innovation reaches its highest mark. An unexpected D major eruption offers a chorale-like transformation of part of the first subject and of part of the introduction to the first movement; after a restatement of this introduction in its original guise, the Finale's own material is recapitulated—second subject in F major and first subject in F minor. A second parallel D major eruption then forms a gigantic culminative gesture. The Finale is thus really in F minor as far as traditional elements of its structure are concerned; but intrusions of D major material subvert its own closure into a closure for the Symphony as a whole. Mahler said of the first of the D major eruptions: 'My D major chord, however, had to sound as though it had fallen from heaven, as though it had come from another world.'[63]

This work thus lays a basis which has many implications for Mahler's future symphonic style—a cosmic inclusion of strongly differentiated and evocative material, including the elevation of the everyday into higher art (bird sounds, trumpet calls, military and

[63] Bauer-Lechner, *Recollections*, p. 31. For a recent extensive discussion of this movement, see Bernd Sponheuer, 'Der Durchbruch als primäre Formkategorie Gustav Mahlers: Eine Untersuchung zum Finalproblem der Ersten Symphonie', in Klaus Hinrich Stahmer (ed.), *Form und Idee in Gustav Mahlers Instrumentalmusik* (Wilhelmshaven, 1980), 117–64.

other marches, chorales, café and folk-music resonances), effected by abrupt and expressive contrasts, sinuous contrapuntal line-weaving, flexible tempos, and a highly personal approach to traditional forms (including sonata form). This Symphony also demonstrates Mahler's characteristic drawing together of instrumental and vocal music, for it is in many ways a counterpart to the four-movement song cycle *Lieder eines fahrenden Gesellen* [Songs of a Wayfarer] (1883–5), from which it draws much thematic material, together with an interest in progressive tonality. The work's beguiling but brittle and psychologically significant glamour forms a strong prelude to the expressionist tendency in early twentieth-century Austrian music.

THE SYMPHONY IN RUSSIA

The basic polarity in Russian musical circles during this period is marked by the opposing figureheads of Anton Rubinstein and Balakirev. Rubinstein, the established piano virtuoso and composer, influential founder of the Russian Musical Society and director of the St Petersburg Conservatory, was ambitious for Russian music, but saw its development as best served by professional Teutonic training. For him, music was 'a German art', and he antagonized particularly Glinka, Balakirev, and the critic Stasov by an article of 1855 announcing his programme. It was as a direct counter to this that Balakirev gathered about him the group known as the *kuchka*, 'the handful', and founded the Free Music School. The symphony was important to both parties. Balakirev began his own First Symphony in 1864, abandoned it for thirty years and completed it only in 1897, but encouraged Borodin to begin a symphony in 1862 while Rimsky-Korsakov laboured on his First at intervals from 1861 to 1884. The later circle around Rimsky-Korsakov included the symphonists Arensky and Glazunov, whose First Symphony was produced at Weimar in 1884 under the auspices of Liszt. Rubinstein wrote six symphonies, of which his second was also an ongoing project, its number of movements being incremented at intervals.

Tchaikovsky was a pupil of Rubinstein and sought to distance himself from the *kuchka* (though he was influenced by Balakirev in two periods of his life, culminating in the orchestral fantasy *Romeo and Juliet* and the *Manfred* Symphony). Yet Tchaikovsky was steeped in Russian folk-song (saturating himself 'from earliest childhood with the inexplicable beauty of the characteristic traits of Russian folk-song'), used folk-songs in some of his symphonies, and related, as did the *kuchka*, particularly strongly to Glinka. (The Russian symphonic school is 'all in *Kamarinskaya*, just as the whole oak is in the acorn'.[64])

Both Borodin and Tchaikovsky, the greatest Russian symphonists of the period, realized that the Teutonic tradition of the symphony had to be harnessed rather than rejected; and it is a mark of their greatness that they took aspects of this tradition and blended them with specifically Russian characteristics. Borodin's two completed symphonies (composed in 1862–7 and 1869–76), are in four distinct movements with the Scherzo as second; the slow movement and Finale of the Second Symphony are joined. His unfinished Third Symphony was also to use the four-distinct-movement plan. Both its first movement (Moderato, opening with a simple folk-song-derived plaint) and its substantial 5/8 Scherzo were originally written for string quartet, and Glazunov, following Borodin's intentions, completed and orchestrated these two movements, adding the beautiful coda to the first movement and the Trio to the Scherzo (using material rejected from *Prince Igor*). Borodin's primary Germanic influences came from Beethoven, Mendelssohn, and Schumann, and his symphonies show a strong Beethovenian vitality based on terse, rhythmically distinctive motifs, often using syncopation, intricate motivic developments, and an overall exuberance with concision.

He retained Teutonic forms; each of his symphonies for instance opens with a sonata-form movement. But his themes are specifically Russian, including folk-song-like material, sometimes together with irregular metres, quasi-oriental figures, and modality. Whether of lyric beauty, energetic allegro or scherzo types, these themes characteristically rely on short-breathed phrases rotating round and elaborating a single pitch. Though his developmental techniques derive from Beethoven in their reliance on motivic fragmentation, these were employed in original ways. With regard to the first movement of the First Symphony, Abraham has pointed out that the 'allegro' opens with a fragmentation of the modal introduction, accompanied by an insistently reiterated modern chord, B flat, E flat, A flat, C, F (which resolves ultimately on the dominant), and that the concluding 'andantino' of this movement synthesizes the thematic duality of the movement also by motivic means.[65] Borodin's harmonic context also is Teutonic in basis, but with a Russian

---

[64] Letter to Madame von Meck, 5 (17) Mar. 1878, cited and discussed in Warrack, *Tchaikovsky Symphonies and Concertos*, p. 9; diary entry, 27 June (9 July) 1888, cited and discussed in Richard Taruskin, 'How the Acorn Took Root: A Tale of Russia' *19th-century Music*, 6/3 (Spring 1983), 190.

[65] Gerald Abraham, *Borodin: The Composer and his Music* (London, 1927), 24–9, and *Studies in Russian Music*, pp. 109–15.

surface inflected by both modality and contrapuntal elaboration around referential pitches. The enormously powerful opening of the Second Symphony (Ex. 413) shows this well. Like all profoundly original music, it challenges normal analytical categories. The first subject depends on three widely spaced statements on the original pitch of the opening imposing unitary gesture, bars 1, 25, and 52,

Ex. 413

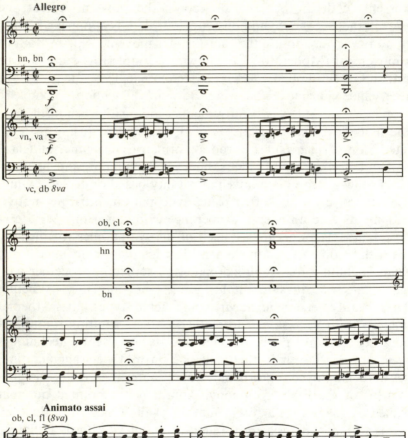

each quitted by sequence. Bars 1–3, incorporating the gesture, show the elaboration of the pitch B by a phrygian auxiliary C natural, mixed with an 'upper part' descent E–D sharp–D; there is motivic concentration on semitone and third (major and minor). Bars 5–7 shift the 'upper part' descent to the lower part, and the gesture is repeated on A. Bars 11–16 are harmonically centred on an ambiguity between A sharp/B flat in the bass, resolved finally on to a dominant chord, over which ambiguity a new motivic theme centred on F sharp re-explores the intervals of the third and auxiliary semitone. The dominant chord is decorated with the opening gesture, prepared in bars 15–16 by semitone auxiliary G naturals, before an extension of the same material leads to the restatement at bar 25. The primary bass-motion of bars 1–23 is thus B, A, G, F sharp. While firmly based, therefore, on an underlying Teutonicism in thematic and harmonic techniques, the original thematic and harmonic immediacy is of a very distinctive order.

TCHAIKOVSKY'S SYMPHONIES

There is some case for regarding Tchaikovsky's symphonies as his most characteristic utterances. Though he was a committed opera composer, he wrote in 1878 'What you say about words harming music, often dragging it down from unscalable heights is absolutely true and I have always felt it deeply—perhaps that is why I have succeeded better with instrumental compositions than with vocal.'[66] He was nevertheless always worried about his formal abilities, and there are many oft-quoted remarks of his, relating to self-doubt in this respect; perhaps as a result of this self-doubt his symphonies show a wide variety of forms both overall and within movements, a high degree of formal and stylistic originality. He was also, of course, a fine composer of ballets (as well as operas), but the symphony remains a profounder form, and already he had included sublimated ballet influences in symphonies before the two great ballets he wrote between Symphonies Nos. 5 and 6. Tchaikovsky's mature view of the symphony was that it was 'the most lyrical of forms'.[67] This view helps explain the absence of explicit programmes for his symphonies after the First (except for *Manfred*), and the prominence he gave in them to what he called 'the lyric idea'. His genius particularly shone in the lyric idea, though there are many other elements in the Tchaikovsky symphony. He was the most highly trained of all the nationalistically inclined Russian composers of the period, and he brought to the symphony a deep understanding of German music, with an especially pronounced love for Mozart, sensitivity to and enthusiasm for French music, particularly of Berlioz, Bizet, and the ballets of Delibes, which he combined with the Russian folk element and emotionalism. From the Germanic tradition he drew an interest in sonata form, scalic basses, pedals, and contrapuntal developments; from the French a lightness of touch, especially but not exclusively in middle movements, and scintillating orchestration.

His First Symphony (1866) shows nationalist aspiration in its inclusion of a folk-song in the Finale and a folk-style melody as the principal theme of its slow movement, and the way in which these make the programme of the title refer to Russia: the Symphony is called 'Winter Daydreams', with subtitles for its first two movements—'Daydreams on a Winter Road' and 'Dreamy Land, Land of Mists'. In the substantial sonata-form first movement Tchaikovsky

[66] Letter to Madame von Meck, 9 (21) Feb. 1878; cited and discussed in Warrack, *Tchaikovsky Symphonies and Concertos*, pp. 7–8.

[67] N. S. Nikolaeva, *Simfonii P. I. Chaykovskogo* (Moscow, 1958), 285.

begins with a large tonic first-subject area including development within itself; such enclosed subjects remained a distinctive feature of his sonata forms, and perhaps helped give rise to his worry about formal technique. For the third movement Tchaikovsky used the Scherzo from his C sharp minor Piano Sonata, and added as Trio the first of a long line of symphonic waltzes. The Finale uses the folk-song 'Tsveli tsvetiki' [Little Flowers Blossomed] in its introduction and also as second subject of the ensuing sonata form.

The nationalist inclination of this work reached its culmination in the Second Symphony (1872: rev. 1880), though folk-song is also used in the Fourth. The Second found much favour with both Rubinstein and the *kuchka*. In it Tchaikovsky used three folk-songs. The introduction to the sonata-form first movement begins with one, which is extended by variation and development. It acts like the first subject, for the succeeding 'allegro' first subject proper is short and non-lyric—these remarks concern the second version of the movement, for which Tchaikovsky composed a new first subject, transferring his previous first subject to act as the new second subject—and the development section is much concerned with the folk-song of the introduction extended by counterpoint and sequence. The slow movement uses the wedding march from Act III of the abandoned opera *Undine* (1869), as the outer sections of a ternary form; the central section is another folk-song, extended by 'changing background' technique. After a characteristically vital Scherzo as third movement, the fourth uses the folk-song 'Ta vnadyvsya zhuravel'' [The Crane] as the first subject of its sonata form; this four-bar melody appears twenty-two times within the first subject, and provides the *locus classicus* of Tchaikovsky's 'changing background' technique. These twenty-two appearances are interspersed with contrasts and developments; Ex. 414 shows the first group of six appearances.

Ex. 414

Thus Tchaikovsky's use of folk-song in this Symphony is very far from being simply a matter of quotation; folk-songs are used as themes, subjected to localized variation treatment, and developed with all the techniques of sonata style. The localized variation treatment has sometimes been seen as 'anti-symphonic', acting against the proper integration of folk-elements into symphonism. But we must hear with Russian ears: the tune-ostinato, or 'changing background' technique itself comes from Russian folk-music and had already been taken into the world of nationalist art-music. As a primary activity of Russian folk musicians, short instrumental dance tunes would be repeated *ad libitum* as the basis for extemporized variations. Glinka had taken such structure into that most influential work, ultimately itself called *Kamarinskaya* (after the name of just such a folk-tune which it uses). In Glinka's work this tune appears seventy-five times with 'changing background'; he also connects two folk melodies and uses motivic extraction and development.[68]

This aspect of Tchaikovsky's deployment of folk-song within the symphony influenced his structures when he did not use folk-song, and the Third Symphony (1875), which in other respects betokens a retreat from nationalism towards Schumannesque models and styles, begins with a funeral march subjected to 'changing background' elaboration. The sonata-form Allegro has a three-theme, three-key exposition. The work is in five movements, the addition being the second, Alla tedesca, which is a waltz in all but name. In the Finale Tchaikovsky moves away from sonata form; the movement is ternary, yet it begins with a sonata-form exposition as its first section.

The Fourth, *Manfred*, and Fifth Symphonies (1878, 1885, and

---

[68] See Taruskin, 'How the Acorn Took Root'.

1888 respectively), are based on motto-theme structures. The 'fate' motif of the Fourth Symphony is an emergence into thematicism of previously appearing 'arrests' and bridges (for instance at the end of the development of the first movement of the First Symphony). This 'main idea' of the Fourth recurs between exposition and development, between recapitulation and coda in the sonata-form first movement, and before the coda in the rondo-form last movement. The first subject of the first movement is perhaps the most serious and significant waltz ever written, while the secondary material is related to the delicacy of the ballet. The key scheme of this movement is highly original, with F and A flat minors and B major forming the basic tonalities of the exposition, and the recapitulation beginning in D minor and moving to F major; the overall tonal progression is thus by ascending minor thirds. The motto-themes of *Manfred* and the Fifth Symphony recur in all the movements of their respective works. Balakirev, the instigator of the *Manfred* project, pointed Tchaikovsky towards specific models in Berlioz's and Tchaikovsky's own previous works, but the great chromatic complication of this work is reminiscent also of Liszt.

The Sixth Symphony, the *Pathétique* (1893), is Tchaikovsky's culminating masterpiece. The first movement is again in sonata form, and raises chromatic scalic writing and large self-enclosed subject structure to the highest expressive power. The two subjects are here contrasted by tempo, the furious pithy first subject yielding to a lyrical and richly suave 'andante' second subject. The 'allegro' development allows Tchaikovsky to embed the recapitulation of his first subject seamlessly within it. The use of andante tempo within the first movement has strategic structural implications in its preparation for the closing slow movement. The second movement is a further apotheosis of the waltz, a further exploration of the remote expressive possibilities of this dance within the symphonic context, for it is a 5/4 'allegro' waltz, with a melancholic trio bearing the same time signature. The third movement builds on Tchaikovsky's use of the march in symphonies, and shows a highly original blend of scherzo and march within one structure: the march as a fragmentary accompaniment to the scherzo gives way gradually to the scherzo as accompaniment to the fully emerged march, this process being repeated. The chromatic scalic accompaniment to the opening of the Symphony, which had been transformed into the trio of the second movement, gives rise to the scalic theme at the beginning of the 'adagio' Finale. The theme here is spread between first and second violins, and requires their spatial separation in the orchestra. (This expressive and telling movement order had already been used by Spohr and was later followed by Mahler.) Tchaikovsky wrote a pensive 'lamentoso' Finale in ternary form, with a broad cantabile 'lyric idea' as central section, which recurs briefly as coda, now in the tonic minor and with its scalic initiation extended downwards to a very low *pppp* ending, echoing the opening of the work. Though it does not incorporate folk material, this Symphony is in other respects a summation, blending structural originality at work and movement levels, lyric ideas, and ballet influence, in a vivid and profound emotional profile.

THE SYMPHONY IN FRANCE

The symphony in France during this period took a generally opposite course of development from that in Germany and Austria. Partly because the French symphonists of the 1850s were largely composers towards the beginning of their careers still learning traditional form, and partly because Berlioz remained a peripheral figure in French culture, much more honoured and influential in Germany and Russia, the characteristic design for French symphonies at the beginning of the period was of four separated movements— as in Gounod's Symphonies Nos. 1 and 2, Saint-Saëns's Symphonies Nos. 1 and 2, and Bizet's Symphony in C. (Saint-Saëns's Second Symphony shows signs of his later originality; it begins with a fugue, and themes from the second and third movements cross into the Finale.) Thereafter the genre was expanded particularly by proximity to the concerto, and by a significant influence from Liszt. This influence impinged not at all on Bruckner, and only negatively on Brahms, but in France it channelled itself strongly through Saint-Saëns, who wrote his symphonic poems in the 1870s, and César Franck. Both of these composers were important, dominating leaders in the evolution of French instrumental styles. French symphonies from the latter part of the period characteristically show movement conflations (Saint-Saëns's Third Symphony, Franck's Symphony), and thematic quotation and metamorphosis between movements (Saint-Saëns' Third, d'Indy's *Symphonie cévenole*, Lalo's G minor Symphony (1886), Chausson's Symphony, Franck's Symphony). As Saint-Saëns said of his Third (actually his fifth completed symphony)—with its 2 + 2 movement construction, poetic and grandiose use of the organ, and thematic transformation between movements and sections—his object was 'to avoid the endless resumptions and repetitions which more and more tend to disappear from instrumental

music under the influence of increasingly developed musical culture'.[69]
This Symphony was dedicated to the memory of Liszt, though
finished just before Liszt died.

Franck's Symphony is part of the corpus of structurally original
works particularly associated with his last period. Its first movement
follows sonata-form outlines, but begins with a massively scaled
sequence: introduction + 'allegro' first subject, D minor; introduction
+ 'allegro' first subject, F minor. This sectionalization is successfully
incorporated into higher symphonic purposes, and the recapitulation
provides a synthesis, with the introduction appearing in D minor in
canon, and the 'allegro' first subject in E flat minor, moving to a
regular recapitulation of the second subject in the tonic major. The
slow movement, Allegretto, introduces harp and cor anglais, and
conflates slow and scherzo elements in a broad and complex rondo
design. The middle return of the opening tune is a kind of scherzo
variation, and the final return combines the original legato version
with the scherzo variation as accompaniment. The Finale has a
sonata-form basis, but after the exposition, the second movement's
main theme returns in B minor; development of the Finale's subjects
leads to recapitulation of the first subject, another return of the
second movement's tune in D minor, and both subjects of the first
movement, before a triumphal ending with the first subject of the
Finale.

DVOŘÁK'S SYMPHONIES

Dvořák hardly ever used actual folk melodies in his works, and,
so far as is known, never in his symphonies. There is nevertheless
real folk influence in his symphonies, which must be sought in
assimilated stylistic features. As he said: 'I myself have gone to the
simple, half-forgotten tunes of the Bohemian peasants for hints in
my most serious work,' and

I study certain melodies until I become thoroughly imbued with their
characteristics and am enabled to make a musical picture in keeping with
and partaking of those characteristics. The symphony is the least desirable
of vehicles for the display of this work, in that the form will allow only of
a suggestion of the colour of that nationalism to be given.[70]

This 'partaking' may be seen in melodic turns of phrase, often with
harmonic implications (pentatonic tunes—involving the 'knight's

---

[69] Arthur Hervey, *Saint-Saëns* (London and New York, 1921), 99.
[70] From interviews given to the *New York Herald*, 21 May 1893, and *Chicago Tribune*, 13
Aug. 1893; see John Clapham, *Dvořák* (Newton Abbot, 1979), 197, 201.

move'[71]—use of the flat seventh, sharp fourth, major-minor mixture, initial upward leaps, absence of anacrusis, 3-2-1 cadences, doublings of melody at the third, 'scotch-snap' rhythms, and elaborate fast ornamentation of slow tunes); also in detailed phrase structure (short phrases, small-scale repetition sometimes involving transposition), and most of all in dance-derived rhythms (from the *dumka*, *furiant*, polka, *skočná*, and *sousedská*).[72] Dvořák's music often has melodic *naïveté* and freshness as primary aesthetic features, and this too may well be a general influence from his interest in folk melodies. A large number of his most beautiful themes show pronounced dependence on arpeggios, repeated notes, auxiliary notes, and scales.

But this inclination to folk-like simplicity is integrated into a profound understanding of the subtleties and intricacies of Classical symphonic thought. Dvořák had a deep admiration for the Classical masters of the symphony, Haydn, Mozart, Beethoven, and latterly particularly Schubert, about whom he wrote a substantial article. In this he said: '[Schubert] is never at fault in his means of expression, while mastery of form came to him spontaneously. In originality of harmony and modulation, and in his gift of orchestral colouring, Schubert has had no superior. . . . I cordially acknowledge my great obligations to him.'[73] From Schubert too came reinforcement of Dvořák's primacy for melody, and his love of major-minor mixture. His early Symphonies, Nos. 1 and 2, both 1865, may be seen as especially influenced by Beethoven's Fifth and Sixth Symphonies respectively. The First, which he supposed lost, was referred to by him as *The Bells of Zlonice*; it shows a grand symphonic sweep, with some motivic connections between movements, and the same key scheme for the movements as the Beethovenian model. But its rather ordinary themes are over-extended in treatment, and these treatments rely on transposition to the virtual exclusion of expressive alteration. Such 'young-man's' features can also be seen in his Second; and he recognized the over-extension in his revisions of this Symphony, which was progressively cut at three different times. (In his article quoted above he commented adversely on the length of Bruckner's Eighth and advocated a 'return to the symphonic dimensions approved by Haydn and Mozart. . . . Modern taste calls for music

---

[71] Gerald Abraham, 'Dvořák's Musical Personality', in Viktor Fischl (ed.), *Antonín Dvořák: His Achievement* (London, preface dated 1942), 205, 222.

[72] The *dumka* is not strictly of dance origin; see John Tyrrell, 'Dumka', *The New Grove*, v. 711.

[73] Antonín Dvořák (in co-operation with Henry T. Finck), 'Franz Schubert', *The Century Illustrated Monthly Magazine* (New York, 1894); repr. in John Clapham, *Antonín Dvořák: Musician and Craftsman* (London, 1966), 300.

that is concise, condensed and pithy.') In the late 1860s and early 1870s Dvořák became susceptible to Wagnerian and Lisztian influences, traces of which can be seen in the cast of the themes, chromatic harmony, and appoggiaturas of his Third Symphony (1873), which has no Scherzo. He retreated from these influences, but an enrichment of his control of chromatic harmony remained with him. His Fourth Symphony (1874) shows increasing concision, and by the Fifth his mastery of symphonic form was mature. Symphonies Nos. 5–9 were published during his lifetime, beginning with No. 6 which appeared as No. 1 in 1882; he did attempt to publish earlier symphonies, but without success.

The Fifth (1875) comes from a strongly nationalist phase, and, after a simple arpeggio opening theme, made subtle by its rhythmic articulation and delicate cadential harmony, the second theme of the first subject group shows clear folk resonance. The second movement is *dumka*-like, but not so titled; though it has a distinct cadence followed by a short pause, the Scherzo begins with a bridge based on it. The Scherzo theme shows folk influence in its repetition of figures. The Finale has that characteristically Dvořákian opening out of the main key, already noted, and the movement has a recall of the opening theme of the Symphony at its end. The Sixth Symphony (1880) shows a particularly strong influence from his friend and supporter Brahms, and commentators have rightly pointed to resonances from Brahms's own Second Symphony. The metre of Dvořák's first movement, its initial modulation, syncopations and developments, the relationships between movements 1 and 4, and the contrapuntal writing (particularly by contrary motion) all have their sources in the Brahms work. Dvořák's now mature powers of development are clearly seen in his slow movement, where the exquisite opening theme is fluently and effortlessly evolved into new expressive shapes, in a sonata form with major–minor mixture in its second subject. The scherzo is the first named *Furiant* in Dvořák's symphonies, with vigorous reliance on mixed 2/4 and 3/4 accentuations, following the well-known folk *furiant* 'Sedlák, sedlák' [Farmer, farmer].

The Seventh Symphony (1885) has been seen by many commentators as Dvořák's greatest symphonic achievement; all diverse influences are sublimated and integrated in his most dramatic, fierce, and forceful symphony. The sonata-form first movement has a narrow-ranged modally inflected opening theme, with prominence for an auxiliary-note figure. The continuation is dark and passionate, setting a tone in which *naïveté* is at its most distant; the chromaticism shows how Dvořák has assimilated the influences of Liszt and Wagner, adapting these to his own purposes. Brahmsian influence is there too, again in the counterpoint, as also in the second subject, which is an echo of the slow movement of Brahms's Second Piano Concerto. Brahms's Third Symphony slow movement influences the course of Dvořák's; a simple theme gives way to subsidiary material using discord and appoggiaturas. The third movement, not titled *furiant*, has nevertheless the characteristic *furiant* mixture of accentuations, here with a 6/4 time signature. The structure of the movement is original; the Scherzo is made up of statement + response + statement + response, each unit with cadence development. This allows the strange Trio, with its brief, reticent themes, to be more discursive; a sonata-form exposition and development lead directly into a return of the Scherzo, now shortened to one statement + response, but with a luxuriant expansion of its final cadence development. The fourth movement is in regular sonata form, the first subject using a sharp fourth and much chromatic development, the second being the only unequivocally joyful tune in the Symphony, with folklike profile in overlapped five-bar phrases.

In the Eighth (1889) Dvořák set out to write 'a work different from the other symphonies, with individual ideas worked out in a new way'[74] and he produced an unobtrusively original work of great beauty. The Symphony represents a return to *naïveté*, but of a very subtle kind! The sonata-form first movement combines diverse materials in its first-subject group: a seventeen-bar irregularly phrased lyrical cello melody in the tonic minor, a five-bar arpeggiaic flute theme in the tonic major, a preparatory development mediating between these two themes, and the initiation of a further cello melody in the tonic major at bar 39, with 3-2-1 opening. The E flat-D background structure of the opening melody is modified to E-D in the flute theme; the 3-2-1 melody recalls the sostenuto and repeated notes of the opening, but is not permitted to progress to full lyricism by developmental accretions of previous material. When the flute theme emerges into a climactic statement at bar 57, it incorporates bridge elements by cadencing on to a mediant 6-4, and the folk-influenced second subject group is in the mediant minor–major. The opening melody returns in its original key for the beginning and the end of the development section; its latter appearance is on trumpet and reharmonized over a timpani dominant, in a new way of obscuring the point of recapitulation. The use of the trumpet here

---

[74] Otakar Šourek, *Dvořákovy Symfonie* (2nd edn.; Prague, 1943), 156.

is a progression towards the opening of the Finale. In the Adagio—
sombre, delicate, charming, and dramatic by turns—material based
on auxiliary-note figures, scales, and arpeggios again features prominently; the movement begins in E flat, but C major becomes the
tonic of most of the remainder of the structure. The third movement
is an Allegretto and Trio, with a continuous stream of simple,
beguiling melody. The Finale is founded on the repeated note and
arpeggio, in a combination of variation and ternary form. A trumpet
introduction, not in the sketches for the movement, leads to a simple
theme, which is a much altered and more solid variant of the flute
theme of the first movement. There are four variations, of which the
second is repeated faster as the fourth. A contrasted episode is
followed by development of the theme, towards the end of which
the introduction returns. The theme is recapitulated and followed by
a further three variations, of which the last is a return of variation
4 and is extended into the final cadence. The theme is present in
many of the variations, which are mainly contrasted by texture and
pacing.

The Ninth Symphony (1893), with the title *Z nového světa* [From
the New World], must be heard in the context of Dvořák's wish to
promote a national American music; though certain melodies in this
symphony are close to specific Indian tunes or Negro spirituals,
many of the modal, pentatonic melodic features and scotch-snap
rhythms Dvořák found in these were already part of his Czech-based
style, as Abraham has pointed out.[75] Dvořák's full symphonic
technique is brought to bear, of which a particular feature here is
thematic integration across movements. The first subject of the first
movement returns in all subsequent movements, and the Finale also
uses the main themes of the other two movements integrated into
its main tempo. The closing combination of the main themes of the
first movement and Finale in a cadential context uses powerfully
discordant auxiliary harmony.

THE CONCERTO

The title 'concerto' was mostly reserved in this period for works
with one soloist and orchestra, making significant use of idiomatic
virtuoso writing for the soloist, in from one to four movements.
Concertos for other forces appeared very rarely indeed. Delphin
Alard published some *symphonies concertantes* for two violins and
orchestra (or piano) in the early 1850s, using a title which had been

[75] Abraham, 'Dvořák's Musical Personality', pp. 205-6.

very popular up to about 1830, and Brahms wrote his Double Concerto in 1887. These works follow a tradition of concertos for more than one soloist established in the Baroque era and carried into Classical and early Romantic times, for instance by Mozart and Beethoven. (In the early twentieth century Bruch and Delius also contributed to this tradition, Bruch with his masterpiece for viola and clarinet, Op. 88, which, though in richly Romantic style, was written in 1911, and his Concerto for Two Pianos, op. 88a (1915); Delius with his Double Concerto in 1915–16.) Alkan, in his solo piano *Études*, Op. 39, grouped numbers 8–10 as a concerto, again (as with his Symphony in the same opus) with progressive tonality. And Chausson's *Concert* for piano, violin, and string quartet (1891) is a chamber work, for the strings are one player to a part.

The one-movement concerto was a popular type, with its influential precedents in Spohr's *Gesangsszene* violin concerto, and Weber's *Konzertstück* for piano and orchestra. Joachim's *Konzert in einem Satze* (for violin), Liszt's Second Piano Concerto, Saint-Saëns's First Violin Concerto, and First Cello Concerto, Vieuxtemps's Fifth Violin Concerto, Hermann Goetz's Violin Concerto, Johan Svendsen's Cello Concerto, and Rimsky-Korsakov's Piano Concerto all contributed to this type. But, as with the symphony, there was a tendency in works where the designated number of movements was less than three for marked differentiation of material to suggest an underlying larger number. Liszt's Second Piano Concerto in its final form (1857) is a complex rhapsodic single-movement structure with much thematic metamorphosis, suggesting a background movement sequence of 'adagio', 'allegro', 'march', and 'finale'. Saint-Saëns's First Violin Concerto, Op. 20 (1859), is an expanded ternary form: 'allegro'-'andante'-'allegro'. His First Cello Concerto (1872) follows this with 'allegro'-'allegretto'-'allegro', where the final 'allegro' is introduced and concluded by the main theme of the opening 'allegro', but otherwise has a separate structure with a transformation of a theme from the 'allegretto' as its own main theme. Svendsen's Cello Concerto (1870) has a slow section between its development and recapitulation. Rimsky-Korsakov's Piano Concerto (1883) is practically monothematic, but varies its Russian theme through different tempos, primarily 'moderato'-'allegretto quasi polacca'-'andante'-'allegro'.

Liszt's First Piano Concerto, conceived and sketched in 1830 but completed in 1849–56, has as background a four-movement design, with the movement elements grouped 1, 2–4. There are strong thematic links across the structure, including the use of a motto-theme, and the last movement element has very little underived material. Saint-Saëns's Fourth Piano Concerto (1875) groups the movement elements 2 + 2. The three-movement structure inherited from Classical and early Romantic times remained the norm during this period, and was used in such important works as Brahms's First Piano Concerto, Violin Concerto, and Double Concerto, and Tchaikovsky's two complete Piano Concertos and Violin Concerto. The movements could be linked: Grieg's Classically shaped three-movement Piano Concerto (original version, 1868, but drastically revised 1907) and Tchaikovsky's Violin Concerto (1878) both link their slow movements to their Finales. Schumann's Cello Concerto (1850) has bridge material joining the three otherwise distinct movements. Strauss's First Horn Concerto (1883) has three short movements played without a break, and thematic metamorphosis from its opening into the principal theme of the rondo Finale. These and suchlike works need strong resonances of traditional movement forms and types in order to be distinguished from the more integrated one-movement concertos discussed above.

However, the concerto was much influenced by the symphony during this period, and the inherited three-movement norm was strongly challenged by a four-movement trend. The extra movement would characteristically be a scherzo type, which would of course be most apt for showing an additional aspect of a soloist's virtuosity. Litolff's four surviving piano concertos (1844–67) are entitled *Concerto symphonique*, and use four-movement form. Liszt admired these works, dedicated his own First Piano Concerto to Litolff, and, like Litolff, included in that work a scherzo movement element. Vieuxtemps's Fourth Violin Concerto (*c*.1850) and Brahms's Second Piano Concerto are both four-movement structures, and were received as examples of the symphonic concerto. Berlioz wrote of the Vieuxtemps work that it was 'a magnificent symphony for orchestra with principal violin'.[76] Brahms's two previous concertos had touched four-movement design during their genesis, the First Piano Concerto as a sonata for two pianos, then a symphony, and the Violin Concerto as a four-movement work (though the assumption that a discarded scherzo from this Concerto then became the Scherzo of the Second Piano Concerto is purely speculative). Lalo's Cello Concerto (1876) is a three-movement work combining slow and scherzo elements in the second, entitled Intermezzo, with the internal structure 'andantino'–'allegro'–'andantino'–'allegro'. In this

---

[76] Boris Schwarz, 'Henry Vieuxtemps', *The New Grove*, xix. 753.

work, as in his four-movement *Concerto russe* (1883) for violin and orchestra, employing Russian themes in both Lento and Finale, the movement structure is further elaborated by slow introductions to first and last movements. Tchaikovsky included a 'prestissimo' in the middle movement of his First Piano Concerto.

However much the soloists were integrated into a symphonic argument—and in many of the greatest concertos of the period this integration was very thorough—the defining nature of concerto texture and continuity was dualist. The principle of opposition and antiphony is ever present, even when one or other side is silent. The soloist's role is virtuosic and positively projected; balance of volume between soloist and a large Romantic orchestra (however lightly used) remains a crux of the genre. The orchestra acts as accompaniment, foil, and carrier of symphonic aspirations. The silences of one or other side vary in length from large-scale orchestral expositions and other ritornelli-residues, and soloist's presentations and cadenzas, to quick alternations between them—within the space of a bar, or even sometimes a beat. The double-exposition structure for first movements was no longer common, but survived in a number of important works, and Brahms used it, subtly modified, in all four of his concertos. Following examples in Mendelssohn and Schumann, the cadenza could be brought more into the prerogative of the composer by being written out; Grieg's Piano Concerto has a written-out cadenza, which remains part of the coda in the orthodox sonata-form first movement, albeit with single exposition. The cadenza could alter this, its traditional position, to appear between development and recapitulation; Tchaikovsky's Violin Concerto follows Mendelssohn's in this respect. It could also appear very near the opening of a work, as in Brahms's Double Concerto; Tchaikovsky's First Piano Concerto has a cadenza in this position, but also one towards the close of the first movement. Short cadenza-like passage-work during the course of movements could substitute for a full cadenza, as in Liszt's Second Piano Concerto, or the cadenza could disappear altogether, as in Brahms's Second Piano Concerto. The disappearances of both the double exposition and the cadenza move the genre closer to the symphony.

The orchestra as accompaniment or foil for the soloist may be treated relatively simply (and detached chords for orchestra were obviously useful in reaching a just balance of forces), or complexly. A particular and characteristic mark of such complexity derives from soloistic virtuosity. An essential of the soloist's part is its difficulty, hence, compared with the same instrument's role in chamber music, there is generally an increase in rhythmic speed and textural density, and a soloist often figuratively divides and decorates simpler but nevertheless structural material in the orchestra. (In such textures a soloist might even be said to 'accompany' the orchestra.)

The increased rhythmic speed usually involves arpeggios, scales, and trills, and the increased textural density octaves and multiple stoppings (strings), double, triple, quadruple octaves and full-hand chords (piano). An important feature of the late-Romantic concerto solo part is increased speed of registral variation, which applies to all instruments, and which may happen in very small durations (in performance, this feature is one of the most visual aspects of virtuosity). The opening of Liszt's First Piano Concerto provides a case in point. Figural music thus has an indispensable role to play in concertos, and a real test of compositional skill was to make this figural music interesting and expressive. Liszt, Brahms, Bruch, Tchaikovsky, Saint-Saëns, and Dvořák had pronounced gifts in this respect, and the genre brought out some of the best music of Bruch and Saint-Saëns. Figural work could be decorative, elaborative, developmental, and thematic: Tchaikovsky's figurations in the first solo entry of his Violin Concerto exemplify well this latter type. Registral difficulty is a marked feature of string concertos, mostly effected by very high writing, but in very low writing tonal strength and penetration also become difficult.

Fewer concertos than symphonies were written, and composers generally felt able to be more structurally innovative in concertos than in the 'apex-genre'; Liszt, Bruch, Dvořák, and the young Saint-Saëns are examples of this tendency. Bruch in his Second Violin Concerto, Liszt, Saint-Saëns, and MacDowell in their Second Piano Concertos found no need to begin with a fast movement. Nevertheless sonata form remained the basis of fast first movements, whether or not with double exposition. Even Bruch's *Vorspiel*, the first movement of his First Violin Concerto, uses it. Tchaikovsky inflected it in his First Piano Concerto and Violin Concerto by opening in each case with a strong lyrical idea which then plays no further direct part in the work. Fused movement structure could give rise to foreshortening of the sonata form, as in Vieuxtemps's Fifth Violin Concerto, Svendsen's Cello Concerto, and Strauss's First Horn Concerto. Liszt avoided sonata form altogether in his First Piano Concerto. The structure of its first movement is original and radical, while owing something to Baroque ritornello form; it depends on the opening theme recurring on E flat (bar 27), E (bar 34), F (bar 73), F sharp (bar 94), G (bar 101), and E flat (bar 108).

Ternary form was favoured for slow movements and rondo for finales.

The concerto in this period was not generally a programmatic genre, though it had had a distinctly programmatic aspect earlier, as in the works of Weber, Field, Steibelt, and Moscheles. Liszt's concertos are non-programmatic. And of Raff's four only one is programmatic: his Second Violin Concerto is a three-movement work with one verse of a poem by Börner attached to each movement. But the concerto could readily be used for nationalist or exotic inflexions. Joachim's Violin Concerto, 'in ungarischer Weise', Op. 11, was one of his most popular and enduring works. Tchaikovsky, Rimsky-Korsakov, and Lalo incorporated Russian themes. Bruch's *Schottische Fantasie* is really an extended concerto with differentiated movements and using Scottish melodies. Brahms assimilated Hungarian resonances in his concerto finales, and this indeed was one of the ways he distanced his 'symphonic concertos' from the symphony. Dvořák's Violin Concerto has Czech folk resonances in all its movements. Saint-Saëns' Fifth Piano Concerto is nicknamed 'the Egyptian', and contains oriental melodic inflections.

VARIATIONS FOR SOLOIST AND ORCHESTRA

Variations for soloist and orchestra, a genre closely related to the concerto proper, were established in the nineteenth century by Chopin's Variations on 'La ci darem' (1827), which Schumann greeted with acclaim.[77] Half a century later Tchaikovsky followed Chopin's example with his Variations on a Rococo Theme for cello and orchestra (1876). This charming work shows the purest expression of its composer's neo-Classicism in an original composition. The work only recently emerged in Tchaikovsky's own version, unmutilated by its dedicatee, Wilhelm Fitzenhagen, whose changes involved the reordering of variations and the deletion of variation 8 altogether.[78] Tchaikovsky wrote a simple binary theme with codetta (treated similarly to Chopin's link between variations), and eight variations upon it, most of which expand its structure; there is a strongly virtuosic element in many of the variations, and several cadenza-like insertions.

César Franck's *Variations symphoniques* for piano and orchestra (1885) is a further structurally innovative work from his late period,

---

[77] 'Hats off gentlemen! A genius', Robert Schumann, *Gesammelte Schriften*, i. 5.
[78] For an account of Fitzenhagen's alterations, together with a useful tabular analysis of the work, see David Brown, *Tchaikovsky: A Biographical and Critical Study*, ii. *The Crisis Years (1874–1878)* (London, 1982), 120–3.

being a continuous structure of introduction, theme and variations, episode, and finale. The introduction has two themes, initially in alternation, the first of which penetrates the latter stages of the central theme-and-variations section, and the second of which forms the basis of the quiet episode and of the extended and spirited sonata-form finale. The theme of the variations, incidentally prefigured in the introduction, emerges as an eighteen-bar binary theme, which is given six unnumbered variations, the earlier ones of which retain the form of the theme. This theme plays only a subordinate role in the finale, as bass to the second subject. The Alsatian Leon Boëllmann followed Franck in writing *Variations symphoniques* (1893) for cello and orchestra.

CHAMBER MUSIC

Chamber music is best regarded as a collection of genres and subgenres, with the common characteristic of having one player per part. The constituent genres may be identified according to title and mode of musical discourse; the central chamber music genre is the multi-movement symphony or sonata analogue normally titled by the specific performing forces, which range from two performers upwards, though more than nine are rare. Strings can form a 'whole' ensemble up to eight, or be joined by the piano up to six players (though the earlier fashion for the piano sextet had now been largely superseded). Woodwind and horn may take part though brass instruments are very rare. (The trumpet had some vogue in French chamber music.) As the forces increase so does the reliance on pseudo-orchestral colour; but chamber music is always prevented from becoming orchestral by the integrity, identity, and continuity of its individual parts. Within the great variety of groupings, the duo sonata with piano, piano trio, string quartet, and string quintet had important Classical precedents and later emphasis; and during the later nineteenth century the piano quintet and particularly the piano quartet became important groupings.

The characteristic of one player to a part had a strong influence on the nature of chamber style itself; its nature was dialogue, founded on Beethovenian precedent. The times of the *quatuors brillants*, consisting of virtuoso solo plus accompaniment, were past. That aspect of late-Romantic instrumental style which might be called 'thematic density', and which formed one of the most significant stylistic continuities between Beethoven and Schoenberg, found its characteristic home in chamber music; and the textural dialogue gave possibilities of great flexibility in thematic manipulation, particularly used by Brahms. Though chamber music was in many ways a conservative genre, this aspect of its style was importantly progressive. The eschewing of the wider timbral range and larger dynamic volume of the orchestra intensified the thematic–structural dialogue, and the small number of parts emerged each in reinforced continuity and individuality. The modes of textural articulation are grouping and distancing. Octave doubling, though a colouristic device imported from orchestration, becomes a form of grouping. Chamber music had its origins, to a large extent its rational base, and a significant part of its use as players' music. But this performers' music was always projectible in private circles or on the public platform as listeners' music, and an immense growth in importance of the public chamber music concert is a distinctive feature of this period; the intimacy of the small group became a public aesthetic object.

Such was the satisfaction of chamber music composers with the traditional format of three or four separated movements that, in spite of the experimental precedent of some of Beethoven's late string quartets, they showed little inclination to explore such possibilities further. Thus the unitary single movement for chamber group (not including variation sets) is a great rarity; there was no real equivalent of the orchestral fantasy or symphonic poem, though Puccini's *Crisantemi* [Chrysanthemums] for string quartet (1890) is an example. Raff's Fourth Violin Sonata (1866) is a single-movement work incorporating fast and slow material, and Dvořák's String Quartet in E minor of 1870 is one of his formally experimental works composed under the influence of Liszt and Wagner, with differentiated movement types in a one-movement structure. Volkmann's B flat minor Trio (1854), which aroused much critical acclaim and was greatly admired by Liszt, combines slow and final movements. Tchaikovsky's Piano Trio in A minor (1882) has two designated movements, the second in two parts, a set of variations, and a finale. Saint-Saëns's First Violin Sonata (1885) shows one of his characteristic groupings of movement types as 2 + 2; and Boëllmann took this up in his Piano Trio, Op. 19 (i. 'introduction', 'allegro', 'andante'; ii. 'scherzo', 'finale'). But three or four separated and formally closed movements remained the norm for the great chamber-music composers of this period: Brahms, Borodin, Tchaikovsky, Franck, Fauré, Smetana, and Dvořák; as also for the minor masters who cultivated the genre (such as Friedrich Kiel, Raff, Heinrich von Herzogenberg, Rubinstein). Of Brahms's twenty-four chamber works, five are in three movements. The First Cello Sonata and Second Clarinet Sonata omit a slow movement (Brahms actually composed one for this Cello Sonata, but deleted it before publication), and the First Violin Sonata omits a scherzo. In his First String Quintet and Second Violin Sonata he compressed slow and scherzo movement types into a single movement with formal integration, in both cases based on an $ABA_1B_1A_2$ design, where A is slow and B fast. More than four movements for a chamber work in the sonata analogue are rare, though Friedrich Kiel's First Piano Quintet has five, as had Dvořák's G major String Quintet in its first version. His *Bagatelles* is a five-movement work; Raff's String Quartet No. 7, '*Die schöne Müllerin*': *cyklische Tondichtung*, and Dvořák's *Dumky* Trio are both six-movement works, and Dvořák's *Cypřiše* [Cypresses], for string quartet, but originally conceived as songs with piano has twelve. The Raff example is close to the suite, and the Dvořák examples are close to 'collections'.

In so far as it was analogous to sonata and symphony, chamber music was elevated in style, though the intimacy of the setting modified some aspects of this style. Integration of movement structures remained, characteristically based not on movements flowing into one another, but rather on thematic quotation, transformation, and motivic unification across movements. Thematic materials would tend to be less epic and elemental than in the symphony, more melodic; a comparison of Borodin's string quartets with his completed symphonies is particularly instructive in this respect. Thematic materials retained other aspects of the elevated style. As in the symphony, sonata form was the generating thought process, again almost always used for first movements (Brahms providing a rare exception in his Horn Trio of 1865), though it could more readily than in the symphony give way to ternary or variation form in slow movements, and rondo or variation form in last movements.

The chamber work was not greatly used for programmatic expression. Carl Reinecke wrote an *Undine* Sonata for piano and flute; Wilhelm Kienzl used a poetic motto for his First String Quartet, Op. 57, as did Wolf for his D minor Quartet (1879); and Lux's String Quartet, Op. 58 (1877), has the title 'Idyll' for its slow movement, with three sub titles. Smetana's Piano Trio in G minor (1855, rev. 1857) was written in memory of his favourite daughter and includes a funeral march in its third (final) movement; his First String Quartet, *Z mého života* [From my Life], has a powerful programme in which nationalist and biographically programmatic elements are combined. Raff's quartet *Die schöne Müllerin* (1874) has six movements: i. 'The Youth', ii. 'The Mill', iii. 'The Maid of the Mill', iv. 'Unrest', v. 'Declaration', vi. 'On the Eve of the Wedding'. Puccini's *Crisantemi* (1890), a lament,[79] and Tchaikovsky's String Sextet *Souvenir de Florence*, simply a recollection of a happy time, have just their titles as programme.

Nationalist and exotic styles were certainly appropriate to chamber music, as they had been for Haydn and Beethoven. Brahms included strongly Hungarian music in the Finales of his First Piano Quartet and Second String Quintet; Dvořák included Czech folk inflexions in his chamber music, and the three chamber masterpieces of his American sojourn (String Quartet, Op. 96, String Quintet, Op. 97, and Sonatina for violin and piano, Op. 100) are part of his attempt to found a national American music. Rheinberger introduced a Hungarian element in his String Quintet (1875) and his C minor Quartet (1876). Karl Schuberth's Third Quartet (1862) is entitled *Meine Reise in den Kirgisen Steppen* [My Journey in the Kirghiz Steppes], and Nikolay Afanas'ev's Quartet in A, *The Volga* (1866), includes songs of the Volga boatmen. Tchaikovsky's First String Quartet, Op. 11, won much of its popularity by its use of a folk-song as the main theme of its slow movement. Glazunov's Third String Quartet (1888), titled *Slav Quartet*, has a mazurka as third movement and a Finale headed 'Slavonic Festival', a vigorous dance-inflected rondo which he afterwards orchestrated.

Self-standing variation sets were also written for chamber groups, but this genre was distinctly overshadowed by the multi-movement chamber work, and did not establish itself at all forcefully. Such sets were written by Fibich (1885), Vincenz Lachner (1875), Massenet (1872), Rheinberger (1876), and Żeleński (1883). Rheinberger's Theme with Variations for String Quartet, Op. 93, has a short eight-bar chaconne-like theme followed by no fewer than fifty variations, all but the last of which (entitled 'Capriccio') keep the eight-bar form. Some variations, especially early in the work, retain the theme as cantus firmus; others are based on decorative and figurative elaborations, harmonic alterations, and contrapuntal devices.

CHAMBER MUSIC IN GERMANY AND AUSTRIA

Chamber works were, of course, still being written in the two decades before 1850, especially by Mendelssohn, Schumann and

---

[79] It was written on the death of Duke Amadeo of Savoy and is dedicated to his memory. Mosco Carner describes it as 'an inspired threnody' (*Puccini: A Critical Biography* (2nd edn.; London, 1974), 305).

Spohr, Lachner and Reissiger, but the genre was not so characteristic of the times as, in the instrumental realm, solo piano music and orchestral music. Some of Schumann's, Spohr's, and Lachner's chamber music is post-1850, including Schumann's three Violin Sonatas and Third Piano Trio, Lachner's Nonet of 1875, and Spohr's last four String Quartets, last String Quintet, some duos for two violins, and his Septet in A minor. For the second half of the nineteenth century in these two countries, reckoned by sheer volume of works produced, chamber music titled by specific performing forces must be regarded as the most characteristic instrumental genre of the times. It was of course in many ways easier to write than symphonies or concertos; but the medium found new vigour, helped by the increase of professional artists and ensembles playing chamber music in public, as also by the increased cultivation of *Haus-Musik*. The following selective list gives some idea of the numbers of composers and works involved; the summations after each composer are of mature completed works in the genre titled by specific performing forces. Significant composers of chamber music in these two countries from the 1850s on included: Woldemar Bargiel (9), Brahms (24), Bruch (6), Eduard Franck (18), Goldmark (11), Friedrich Kiel (20), Raff (25), Reinecke (24) and Volkmann (12). In the 1860s the following composers began their production in the genre: Friedrich Gernsheim (19), Goetz (4), Rheinberger (14); in the 1870s: Brüll (6), Robert Fuchs (40), Heinrich von Herzogenberg (21), August Klughardt (10); and in the 1880s: Wilhelm Berger (12), Felix Draeseke (10), Richard von Perger (6), and Richard Strauss (4). Some of these later composers wrote chamber music in late-nineteenth-century style well into the twentieth century, and Fuchs's serenely beautiful Clarinet Quintet (1917) must serve as an example of this significant part of early twentieth-century musical activity.

Friedrich Kiel (1821–85) was a highly respected master of the genre, whose works in it were all published shortly after composition. Wilhelm Altmann, a Kiel enthusiast, drew attention to his stylistic lightheartedness and its integration with contrapuntal expertise;[80] there is an active Kiel Society in Germany today. His first multi-movement chamber work is the Piano Trio in D (1850), and his last the piano quartets of 1874. He wrote two string quartets, two piano quintets, three piano quartets, seven piano trios, four violin sonatas, a viola sonata, and a cello sonata, thus preferring groupings involving

---

[80] Wilhelm Altmann, 'Kiel', in Walter Willson Cobbett (ed.), *Cobbett's Cyclopedic Survey of Chamber Music* ii. (London, 1930), 49–52.

the piano. He used three- and four-movement forms, though the First Piano Quintet has five movements. In his three-movement works he prefers to omit the slow movement. His Viola Sonata, Op. 67 (1871), is a masterly four-movement work. The opening of his sonata-form first movement (Ex. 415) demonstrates his full understanding of the dialogue basis of chamber music, and his expressive and inventive treatment of this opening at the beginning of the development (Ex. 416), where it is integrated with second-subject material, gives some indication of his compositional expertise. The tonic for each movement descends by a major third (G minor, E flat, B, G); there are motivic connections across all movements, and

Ex. 415

Ex. 416

the Finale, in a 'hunting' rondo style though using sonata form, has a coda which recalls the opening of the work.

Raff wrote a string octet, a sextet, nine string quartets (one of which is lost), a piano quintet, two piano quartets, five piano trios (one lost), five violin sonatas, and a cello sonata. He mostly used four-movement form, though he departed from this in four works: the Fourth Violin Sonata (1866), subtitled *Chromatische Sonate in einem Satz*, begins with recitative, and includes a slow section before the main Allegro; and his group of three String Quartets, Op. 192 (1874), consists of two works subtitled suites (in five and seven movements) and *Die schöne Müllerin*, whose movements have already been detailed. Raff had a particular gift in chamber music of combining lyricism with virtuosity in the context of a convincing grasp of chamber textures.

BRAHMS'S CHAMBER WORKS

Brahms had been involved with chamber music from his earliest years. He played it in a private concert arranged by his father in 1843, the programme including Beethoven's Op. 16 and one of Mozart's piano quartets. He also wrote it early in his composing career; in 1851 two of his (lost) chamber works were played at another private concert: a Duo for cello and piano, and a Piano Trio.[81] His early interest remained with him, and performance and composition in the genre formed central features of his life. It was partly as a chamber music player and composer that he introduced himself to Vienna in 1862 with the Piano Quartets Opp. 25 and 26, and he played in the first performances of his last chamber works, the two Clarinet Sonatas. His surviving chamber works stretch throughout his composing career.

His first surviving multi-movement chamber work is the Piano Trio, Op. 8, of 1854, massively scaled and opening with a lengthy lyrical melody. He soon became dissatisfied with it, and took occasion in 1889 to rewrite it, broadly retaining the second movement (the Scherzo and Trio) and the openings of the other movements. Major points of his reworking were the creation of new second themes in movements 1, 3, and 4, in each case more dynamic in ethos than their predecessors, and the regularization of the recapitulation in the first movement. This reworking offers absorbing insight into Brahms's development over almost his entire creative life.[82] In 1856 he completed a Piano Quartet in C sharp minor in three movements, which in 1875 became his Third Piano Quartet in C minor, Op. 60. James Webster has studied the relationship between the lost early version and its later rewriting.[83] Brahms had composed a deeply personal work reflecting his involvement with Clara Schumann: in

---

[81] An A major Piano Trio published by Ernst Bücken and Karl Hasse (Leipzig, 1938) as an early work of Brahms is not now generally accepted as such; see Margit L. McCorkle, *Johannes Brahms: Thematisch-bibliographisches Werkverzeichnis* (Munich, 1984), 687-8. Other lost chamber works from Brahms's early years are detailed in McCorkle's Anhang IIa Nr. 5, 6, 8, and 10.

[82] For studies of this reworking, see Donald F. Tovey, 'Brahms', in *Cobbett's Cyclopedic Survey of Chamber Music*, i (London, 1929), 159-63, and Ernst Herttrich, 'Johannes Brahms—Klaviertrio H-dur op. 8, Frühfassung und Spätfassung—ein analytischer Vergleich', in Martin Bente (ed.), *Musik, Edition, Interpretation: Gedenkschrift Günter Henle* (Munich, 1980), 218-36.

[83] James Webster, 'The C sharp minor Version of Brahms's Op. 60', *Musical Times*, 121 (1980), 89-93.

both versions it opens with a 'Clara' theme, and Brahms described the later version in terms of Goethe's *Werther*.

The works of the early 1860s, a period named by historians as Brahms's 'First Maturity', show consolidation of influences and an establishment of his stylistic location, particularly *vis-à-vis* Liszt and the New German School. Chamber music was a particular compositional concern at this time, and he produced the First String Sextet (1859-60), First and Second Piano Quartets (1861), Piano Quintet (finished in its first version as a string quintet in 1862, reworked as two-piano sonata and piano quintet in 1864), First Cello Sonata (1862 and 1865), Second String Sextet (1864-5), and Horn Trio (1865). His earlier primarily Beethoven-derived style was now supplemented and modified by a particularly strong Schubertian influence. There are direct thematic resonances from Schubert, especially in the Finales of the Second Piano Quartet (from that of Schubert's String Quintet) and Piano Quintet (again from Schubert's String Quintet and also his Grand Duo); there are structural influences (three-keyed expositions, lengthy chromatic inflexions of second-subject initiations, and sonata form with combined response);[84] and Beethovenian dramatic rhetoric is synthesized with Schubertian lyricism. But these works are far from being epigonal, and show many elements of Brahms's modernity. For instance, the openings of the Second String Sextet and the Horn Trio have clearly new directions in melodic writing, the one immediately registrally expansive, the other restricted, though evocatively so, in an ostinato rhythm; both examples use a motivically based lyricism which is typical of many themes in this group of chamber works. His harmony could draw on fully contemporary chromatic progressions: for instance, the close of the recapitulation of the first movement of the Second Piano Quartet is based on major chords a major third part. Chromatic inflexion plays a large part in the poetry of the slow movement of the Horn Trio, and special moments of structural chromaticism are the developmental continuation of the central fugue and the coda. In the second movement of the First Piano Quartet Brahms initiated a series of innovatory non-slow middle movements, in a veiled scherzo, called Intermezzo, which was continued in the equally original approach to scherzo writing in the second movement of the Second String Sextet, based on his early Gavotte in A minor.[85]

[84] For further discussion of Schubertian influence on Brahms during these years, see James Webster, 'Schubert's Sonata Form and Brahms's First Maturity', *19th-century Music*, 2/1 (July 1978), 18-35; 3/1 (July 1979), 52-71.

[85] Robert Pascall, 'Unknown Gavottes by Brahms', *Music and Letters*, 57/4 (Oct. 1976), 404-11.

This series extends into works of the 1870s and beyond, as has already been noted with regard to the symphonies.

Brahms's use of biographically derived elements in his chamber music continues with the 'Clara' theme of the Intermezzo of the First Piano Quartet, and a similarly evolved 'Agathe' theme in the first movement of the Second String Sextet. He also continued his massive approach to the genre. The broad sense of scale in all these works comes from an internal expansion of movements, a particular mark of which is enlargement of second subject groups in sonata form to include up to five identifiably distinct themes. The first movement of the First String Sextet has four such separate themes, albeit motivically related, but made particularly distinct by each being accorded an immediate variational repeat; the first movement of the First Piano Quartet has five such themes (at bars 50, 79, 92, 101, and 113) followed by a lengthy codetta. Other movements receive similar expansive treatment; for instance the second (slow) movement of the Second Piano Quartet has the diversified structural plan $ABA_1CDA_2BC_1A_3$ (demonstrating a modification of an extended ternary design, by 'relocation' of the C_1 section), and the Scherzo and Trio of its third movement are each a fully articulated sonata form. Brahms's sensitivity towards sound compelled him to vary his instrumental groupings; throughout his life he had no really central chamber-music groupings such as Classical composers had found in the piano trio, string quartet and quintet. Brahms's search for the appropriate instrumentation of his Piano Quintet, with its ultimate integration of string sostenuto and piano percussive nuances, does not deny this sensitivity, rather manifests it—as does the great textural variety he used within his sextets and piano quartets. A particularly scintillating texture from this period is the heterophonic presentation of the first theme of the slow movement in his Second Piano Quartet. His luxuriant, spacious, and imaginative textures at this time act as support and enhancement of the structural breadth of scale.

The decade of the 1870s in Brahms's chamber music may be viewed as that of 'unfinished business'. His productivity in the genre of the 1860s had been interrupted partly by the completion of *Ein deutsches Requiem* (and, in the aftermath of that work's stupendous success, a concentration on large-scale choral genres), and partly by a continuing struggle with the string quartet. He had decided not to publish his early B minor String Quartet, but 'finished' two others by the mid-1860s (one in C minor) which he showed to friends. These did not satisfy him, and he did not properly finish his First and Second String Quartets until 1873, describing them in his own manuscript catalogue of his works as 'written for the second time, Summer 1873'. His struggle with the string quartet parallels his longer and more spectacular struggle with the symphony. Although the core of his creative equipment had been learnt primarily from Beethoven, he clearly felt overawed in both these supremely Beethovenian genres. He casually (and possibly exaggeratedly) mentioned to a friend that he had completed more than twenty string quartets before publishing his Op. 51, No. 1. This, together with the First Symphony, is the most Beethovenian in style of all his mature masterpieces. Particularly the first and last movements of the Quartet show a rigorous concision, a motivic and rhythmic urgency and drive, and a retreat from lyricism. His Second String Quartet, beginning with Joachim's motto FAE, reinstates Brahms's by now natural lyricism, and its third movement continues his innovatory approach to non-slow middle movements with a combination of minuet and scherzo, incorporating intricate canonic links. By the Third String Quartet (1875), written after the reworking of the Third Piano Quartet (1869–75), Brahms had become positively playful in the medium, though the easy charm of the work incorporates great structural polish, originality, and subtlety. Its third movement has what amounts to a viola solo, since the other instruments, though participating in dialogue, are muted throughout.

Brahms had intended to include an early A minor Violin Sonata in his first group of publications, but was prevented by having mislaid the manuscript (the work remains lost); his First Violin Sonata (1878–9) he described as the fourth actually composed. It was written during and after the composition of the Violin Concerto. Brahms's marked tendency to compose pairs of works in close temporal proximity is a commonplace for commentators (piano quartets, variation sets, symphonies, overtures, sonatas), and has important bearing on the artistic significance of the works involved. But the 'disparate pairs' such as the Third Piano Quartet and Third String Quartet, Violin Concerto and First Violin Sonata, Clarinet Trio and Clarinet Quintet (which Brahms himself described as 'twins') have not received so much attention, and show in addition an interplay of genres or sub-genres. The differing types of virtuosic and intimate violin lyricism in Concerto and Sonata, and the forms of the movements (especially since the Sonata is also in three movements without scherzo) are instructive to compare. Brahms distinguished his violin sonatas by relating them closely to songs, and his First Violin Sonata uses the song 'Regenlied' for the main theme of its Finale; this theme is motivically connected to themes of the first and second movements.

Brahms was now entering the period of his ripest maturity, with influences fully assimilated into his lyric–dramatic approach to chamber writing. Themes have a new suavity, economy, and distinction, developmental techniques are at their most meaningful and less separated from thematic presentation, and the rich musical continuum is of overwhelming beauty. In 1882 he completed his C major Piano Trio and First String Quintet. The latter uses two violas, as opposed to the two cellos of his earlier superseded string quintet. The first movement, with its sostenuto opening, was one of very few Brahms works to appeal to Hugo Wolf.[86] The middle movement with its compression of slow and scherzo elements is a recomposition of his early piano Sarabande and Gavotte in A into a self-enclosed formal scheme which nevertheless shows a very rare Brahmsian use of progressive tonality.[87] The Finale combines sonata form and fugue, as had that of the First Cello Sonata. In 1886 he wrote the Second Violin Sonata, C minor Piano Trio, Second Cello Sonata, and Third Violin Sonata (which did not, however, receive its final polishing until 1888). Brahms intended his Second String Quintet (1890), that most poetically Viennese of all his chamber works, to mark his retirement, but his meeting with the clarinettist Richard Mühlfeld in March 1891 provided the inspiration for the rich final flowering of the four clarinet works: Clarinet Trio and Quintet (1891) and the two Clarinet Sonatas (1894).

The Clarinet Quintet is one of the supreme chamber music masterpieces of the nineteenth century. It combines thematic economy and density with a profound range and intensity of expression, relying on the evolution of significant new shapes from simple primary materials. It incorporates the very highest aspirations of late Romantic instrumental music within established forms, and in many ways may be regarded as the summation of Brahms's chamber music style. In it he further explored the remote possibilities of the group of dances that had so obsessed him over many years, and the opening of the Quintet derives distantly from the Gavotte in A minor. The lyrical–motivic four-bar initiation, thematically differentiated but bound together by the descending octave it fills, receives an expansionary developmental response of twenty bars, in which new shapes are evolved so naturally and simply yet so convincingly and

---

[86] See W. A. Thomas-San-Galli, *Johannes Brahms* (Munich, 1912), 214–15.
[87] Pascall, 'Unknown Gavottes by Brahms'; Michael Musgrave, *The Music of Brahms* (London, 1985), 201–2, 204–5.

decisively from the opening, in a paradigm of what Schoenberg
termed 'developing variation'. This response elongates the opening
two bars of the movement by internal expansion over an harmonic
sequence based on the Baroque cycle of fifths; bars 3–4 of the
movement then become evolved into a new shape by internal octave
displacement and a new extension (bars 14 ff). Ex. 417 shows the

Ex. 417

opening twenty-four bars of the Quintet. A bridge theme, based like the opening on a descending octave, then presents the Baroque sequence in a new expressive format, and leads to a second subject group in which Brahms dissects his opening semiquaver shapes, yet simultaneously nourishes them into a new sustained lyricism across the texture. The development section reconciles figurative play on the first subject with a meditative expressive alteration to the bridge theme. The recapitulation is basically regular, as was Brahms's mature custom, and the coda provides further expressive modifications, primarily now to the first subject.

The Adagio has a simple ternary form as its background, which Brahms complicates in three characteristic and far-reaching ways: (1) the middle section is built on a variation of the opening section, (2) developmental bridge passages link the formally closed sections, but are themselves highly expressive, the second containing a climactic development based on further extension of the octave-displacement techniques of the first movement, and (3) a lyrical coda recalls the middle section in tranquillity, thus extending and modifying the central contrast of the structure, which leads to final closure on the first two notes of the movement. The opening section is a recomposition of the piano Sarabande in A, in a new rhythm; the middle section combines Hungarian and concerto elements in its variational technique.

The Adagio provides primary thematic shapes for the subsequent movements. In the Andantino Brahms continues his series of formal innovations for non-slow middle movements by using an intermezzo-like frame in D major with progressive thematicism (that is, without a self-enclosed form) around a central B minor scherzo in fully articulated sonata form. The opening of the movement is a simple decoration of the Adagio theme, which leads into a theme evolved from the second subject of the first movement; the scherzo begins with a nervous, incomplete transformation of the opening of the Andantino, counterpointed against the theme evolved from the first movement.

In the Finale Brahms wrote a theme again extracted from the Adagio, as basis for a set of five variations with coda. The structure across the variations follows Brahms's characteristic grouping by increase of animation over variations 1–3 and 4–5, with a change of animation and mode for variation 4. Here, however, variations 4 and 5 begin a closer definition of earlier movements; variation 4 is a legato lyrical mediation between the second and third movements, and variation 5 reintroduces the semiquavers of the first movement, together with their augmentation. The coda is a culmination of this sophisticated cyclic thrust and recalls directly the opening of the Quintet in a valedictory setting, achieving final closure on the cadence of the first movement itself.

FURTHER CONTEMPORARIES OF BRAHMS

Neither Bruckner, Wolf, nor Richard Strauss can be considered as primarily composers of chamber music, though all three produced significant chamber works during this period. Bruckner's C minor String Quartet of 1862 was published only in 1955 and has not become widely known; although it dates from his student years, it is a compelling and delightful early work. His String Quintet (1879) is, on the other hand, a major mature masterpiece; though closely related to his symphonic style, monumentality here becomes breadth, and the elemental is given a more lyrical aspect. Wolf's D minor String Quartet (1879) carries Faust's insight 'Entbehren sollst du, sollst entbehren' [Renounce, you must renounce] as motto. Eric Sams has drawn attention to its incorporation of Beethovenian and Wagnerian influences, and discussed the proper movement order (the two middle movements were reversed in early editions).[88] Strauss's

---

[88] Eric Sams, 'Hugo Wolf', *The New Grove*, xx. 483.

chamber music in traditional forms consists of a String Quartet (1880), Cello Sonata (1882), Piano Quartet (1884), and Violin Sonata (1888); he did not subsequently cultivate the genre, except in the wonderful sextet included in his last opera, *Capriccio*, and the Sonatines for 16 woodwind instruments of the same period.

RUSSIAN CHAMBER MUSIC

The most prolific composer of multi-movement chamber works in Russia was Anton Rubinstein, with twenty-seven such works, and there are clear indications that some Russian composers regarded the multi-movement chamber music genre as a particularly Teutonic one. Borodin acknowledged his Germanic bases for chamber music more openly than for the symphony. Of his String Sextet (1861) in Mendelssohnian style he said, it was written 'to please the Germans'; his First String Quartet (1879) has on its title-page 'inspired by a theme of Beethoven', and Borodin related how the initial news that he was composing a string quartet had horrified Mussorgsky and Stasov.[89] Rimsky-Korsakov said of his own Quintet for piano and woodwind (1876) that the first movement was 'in the classic style of Beethoven'.[90]

Borodin was a keen chamber-music player, as cellist, from his early years, and his first recorded chamber compositions (both lost) date from 1847. A further nine works date from the period 1850–62; some of these were never completed, some others may have been but survive in a fragmentary state. His String Quintet in F minor (1854) lacks the coda of the Finale; his Cello Sonata in B minor (1860) lacks most of the Finale; of his String Sextet (1860–1) only the first movement and the first half of the second survive. As the complete and incomplete works of this period are in our time becoming better known, so a fuller picture of Borodin as an instrumental composer emerges. They show a predominantly Mendelssohnian stylistic approach to themes and textures, overlaid with other diverse influences in particular works. His Quartet for flute, oboe, viola, and cello (1852–6) is based on works by Haydn, his Trio in G for two violins and cello (1860) on a Russian folk-song, and his Cello Sonata (*c.*1860) on a theme from the second movement of Bach's first unaccompanied Violin Sonata (BWV 1001), which he

[89] For Borodin's comment on the Sextet, see Gerald Abraham, 'Alexander Borodin', *The New Grove*, iii. 55; for details concerning the Quartet, see David Brown's Foreword to the Eulenburg Edition of the work (London, 1976).

[90] Rimsky-Korsakov, *My Musical Life*, p. 169.

used for the openings of his first and last movements and in the middle of his second movement, titled 'Pastorale'.

Borodin's two String Quartets, No. 1 in A (1874–9) and No. 2 in D (1881), are his crowning chamber music achievements, of great beauty and originality. Both are Classical four-movement structures, and both use sonata form for their first and last movements. This form is also used for the Scherzo of the Second Quartet which has no Trio, the second subject being a contrasted waltz. The other middle movements are ternary. Specifically Russian elements are insistent motivic reiteration in themes even when lyrical, slow movement tunes either derived from folk-song and modally inflected (as in the First Quartet) or using more quasi-oriental figures (Second Quartet), changing background technique (as in the first subject of the Finale of Quartet No. 1), and Borodin's centripetal harmonic foreground. (The opening of Quartet No. 1 makes significant use of the ambiguity F natural–E sharp, which takes on a referential value.) The quartet writing in both works shows great maturity, with a very flexible approach to textures (the viola, for instance, can act as bass or high melody instrument in addition to its more normal roles), even thematic distribution over the instruments, pronounced reliance on counterpoint in themes and developments, and some radiantly luminous high writing (such as the harmonics in the trio of the First Quartet, and the luxuriant cello melody at the opening of the slow movement of the Second). The first movements of both quartets are more sustainedly lyrical than the corresponding movements of Borodin's symphonies. The tonal structure of the exposition of the first movement of No. 2, D major–A major–F sharp minor–A major, is altered on recapitulation to D major–E flat major–C minor–D major.

Tchaikovsky wrote several movements for chamber groups during his student years (1863–5); these include five for string quartet, one of which, an Allegro in B flat (1865), has been published. A slow introduction, adumbrating the folk-song first subject of the Allegro, and including counterpoint and recitative-cadenzas for each instrument in turn, precedes a full sonata-form Allegro. Motivic reiteration is characteristic for both subjects, there are orchestral effects with tremolo bowing, and the second subject is recapitulated a semitone higher than its exposition key. Parts of the introduction return at the end of the Allegro, and the movement closes with an unharmonized version of the folk-song first subject. Some of these features find place in Tchaikovsky's five mature multi-movement chamber works—the three String Quartets, Op. 11 in D (1871),

Op. 22 in F (1874), Op. 30 in E flat minor (1876), Piano Trio, Op. 50 in A minor (1882), and String Sextet (*Souvenir de Florence*), Op. 70 (1890–2).

His First String Quartet was written for a specific fund-raising concert. It has first and last movements in sonata form: the slow second movement has a ternary structure, with a folk-song as the first section, and the third movement is a Scherzo and Trio. In the first movement counterpoint is the chief means of extension and development, to the virtual exclusion of expressive alteration. The 'andante cantabile' folk-song of the slow movement made this work immediately and lastingly popular. The Second String Quartet opens with a highly chromatic slow introduction, which includes instrumental recitative. Both subjects of the ensuing sonata-form Moderato are strongly motivic, and there is a notable absence of lyricism in this movement; counterpoint is more integrated into the subjects themselves than in the corresponding movement of the First Quartet, and there are some grand textures with tremolo bowing. The delicate and haunting Scherzo uses a mixture of 6/8 and 9/8 bars to create seven-beat phrases for its theme, and the Trio has resonances of changing background technique in the three presentations of its theme. Even in the slow movement lyricism does not fully emerge; its outer sections are plangently expressive but rely on strongly motivic melody, and the central section has much figurative decoration and a massive climax using orchestrally derived texture. In the Finale an opening motivic melody with ostinato tendencies alternates with a simple lyrical idea (accompanied with the ostinato rhythm) in the overall design $ABA_1B_1A_2B_2$ Coda. B is in D flat, B_1 in A, and B_2 in the tonic of the movement, F. A_1 and A_2 are much expanded, A_2 being a complete fugue; all the A sections are in F. This movement is thus an original and entirely successful derivative of the rondo principle. Tchaikovsky was pleased with this work, and it is an important one in understanding his view of the relationship between chamber music and symphony.

His next two chamber works were written in memory of close associates and include specifically elegiac elements. The Third String Quartet is dedicated to the memory of Ferdinand Laub, the Piano Trio to 'the memory of a great artist'—Nicholas Rubinstein. His last multi-movement chamber work, the String Sextet *Souvenir de Florence*, was written shortly after a visit to that city. All three works are large scale: the sonata-form first movement of the Sextet, for instance, is of 769 bars. The slow introduction of the Third Quartet presages the first subject of the ensuing Allegro sonata form; it has also a theme of its own which recurs in the slow tempo at the end of the movement. The development of the Allegro combines the motivic first subject with the more lyrical second and shows what may be achieved when counterpoint is fused with expressive alteration. A light ternary Allegretto as second movement precedes the emotional core of the work, the Andante funebre e doloroso third movement. Here plangent harmonies, powerfully expressive textures and rhythms in the outer sections of the ternary form are contrasted with a sustained 'lyric idea' in the middle section, which is given much elaborately figural accompaniment. A light sonata-rondo Finale creates an unusual and significant movement balance for the work as a whole.

The two-movement Piano Trio is perhaps Tchaikovsky's greatest chamber work. Its first movement, titled 'Pezzo elegiaco', is in sonata form, but with differentiations of tempos similar to those Tchaikovsky was to use later in the first movement of the Sixth Symphony. The breadth of scale in the first movement of the Trio is enhanced by very slow harmonic rhythms for the first subject and a massive virtuoso piano part. The first subject is 'moderato assai' leading to 'allegro' for the second subject. The development maintains this latter tempo in spite of being concerned initially with the first subject; a new poetic theme is generated towards the close of the development, which returns in the coda of the movement. The recapitulation of the first subject is initially an 'adagio con duolo'. Tchaikovsky divided the second movement into two parts: A. 'Tema con variazioni'; B. 'variazione finale e coda'. He thus followed Classical precedent in the expansion of a variation set into a finale-styled close; here, however, part one of the movement is in E major, part two in A major, a fully articulated sonata form. The theme at the beginning of the movement is often described by commentators as simple, which is an apt description of the diatonic harmony and chordal accompanying texture, but its string of ten two-bar phrases, each with a similar rhythmic shape, has an original internal structure. The first three phrases group as a statement, the next three as response cadencing on to the tonic; a further group of two phrases acts as a new statement in the dominant (the starting-point of the ternary form of some variations), and a two-phrase group concludes. The set of eleven variations begins in a figural decorative mode, maintaining the form of the theme, but already in variation 3 Tchaikovsky veers away into character variations based on elements of the theme only. Variation 5 is a high-pitched musette, 6 an extended waltz, 8 a fully worked-out three-part fugue with the piano in octaves acting as the lowest voice and with imposing use of augmentation, 10 a mazurka, and 11 a modified recapitulation of the theme. For the B section of the movement a transformation of the first phrase of the theme with new extensions acts as the first subject, and phrase 7 of the theme, again with new extensions, as second subject. The movement ends with the opening theme of the entire work set first as a massive culminative gesture, then as a simple funeral march. Both movements of this work are thus of structural originality on traditional bases, and Tchaikovsky's characteristic gifts for blending lyric ideas with counterpoint, intimacy with grandeur, and emotional expression with formalism, create a powerful and deeply felt masterpiece.

Chamber music played an important part in the Friday meetings at the Maecenas publisher Belyaev's in the late 1880s, and a number of light works were produced. The String Quartet for Belyaev's name-day in 1887 was *Jour de Fête*: Glazunov provided the first movement, called 'Christmas Singers'; Lyadov the second, 'Glorification', and Rimsky-Korsakov the third, 'Khorovod'.

FRENCH CHAMBER MUSIC

As in Germany and Austria during this period, so in France more chamber works than symphonies were written. Minor masters such as Henri Bertini, Charles Dancla, Louise Farrenc, Théodore Gouvy, and Paul Lacombe cultivated the multi-movement chamber work, as did Lalo, Saint-Saëns, Castillon, Fauré, Franck, d'Indy, Chausson, and Lekeu. The artistic environment in Paris was one in which chamber music played a large part. In 1856 the *Gazette musicale* announced 'a new era, the era of the quartet', and Jeffrey Cooper's monumental survey of Parisian concert life from 1828 to 1871 shows that in 1856 there were nine established concert series either primarily of chamber music (as Dancla's Concerts and 'Séances', those of the 'Société des Derniers Quatuors de Beethoven', and 'Société des Quatuors de Mendelssohn') or including chamber music in more mixed programmes. In 1870 there were nineteen such series.[91] The 'Société des Quatuors Français' (1862-5) was founded to perform French chamber music composed within the previous thirty years, and the famous 'Société Nationale de Musique' (founded 1871) promoted contemporary French music, concentrating on chamber and orchestral works.

Of Lalo's seven multi-movement chamber works, five belong to

[91] Jeffrey Cooper, *The Rise of Instrumental Music and Concert Series in Paris, 1828-1871* (Ann Arbor, Mich., 1983), *passim*.

the 1850s (two piano trios, the Violin Sonata, Cello Sonata, and String Quartet); thereafter he turned away from the genre until 1880, when he revised his String Quartet, giving it a new opus number, and wrote his Third Piano Trio, which Florent Schmitt extolled as 'held with good reason to be Lalo's finest and most finished chamber composition . . . a splendid and original work'.[92] Saint-Saëns composed a piano quartet in 1853 which remains unpublished; his subsequent multi-movement chamber works in our period are the Piano Quintet (1855), First Piano Trio (1863), First Cello Sonata (1872), Piano Quartet in B flat (1875), Septet (1881), and First Violin Sonata (1885). His Piano Quintet is one of his earliest cyclic compositions, and serves as a reminder that cyclic structures, though arguably more popular in France towards the close of this period, were in fact used throughout. Saint-Saëns's Septet, for trumpet, piano, two violins, viola, cello, and double bass, was written for the chamber music society *La Trompette*; though not so titled, it shows a suite-like tendency, with the movements: Préambule, Minuet, Andante, Gavotte, and Finale. The First Violin Sonata shows the 2 + 2 movement conflation ('allegro'–'adagio', 'allegretto'–'finale'), which Saint-Saëns also used in his Fourth Piano Concerto and Third Symphony; as with his First Cello Sonata, it contains a pronounced virtuosic element. Alexis de Castillon met César Franck in 1868, after a period of despondency about composition, and in the few years from then until his early death in 1873 produced most of his seven multi-movement chamber works: the Piano Quintet, Op. 1; String Quartet, Op. 3; Piano Trio, Op. 4; Violin Sonata, Op. 6; Piano Quartet, Op. 7; Second Piano Trio, Op. 17b; and part of a Second String Quartet (unfinished). Opp. 1 and 7, both in four movements, use cyclism in the inclusion of themes from their slow third movements in their respective Finales. D'Indy wrote of him, 'No man was ever more thoroughly a chamber composer.'[93]

Three of Fauré's ten great multi-movement chamber works were written before 1890: the First Violin Sonata (1875–6), First Piano Quartet (1876–9; Finale rev. 1883), and Second Piano Quartet (?1885–6). He was distinctly less innovative in large-scale structural considerations than some of his contemporaries, but his combination of melody and motif into a passionate lyricism is highly expressive; he also demonstrated a deep understanding of the textural essence of chamber music. His First Piano Quartet opens with a char-acteristically modally inflected theme, the melodic continuity of

[92] Florent Schmitt, 'Lalo', in *Cobbett*, ii. 89.
[93] Vincent d'Indy, 'Castillon', in *Cobbett*, i. 232.

Ex. 418

which depends upon a motivic prominence for the interval of a fifth
(C–G) and two important rhythmic cells (dotted quaver-semiquaver,
and quaver-semiquaver-semiquaver) (Ex. 418). This sonata-form
movement initially opposes piano and strings, but the textural
dialogue becomes more involved at the restatement of the first theme
in bar 18 (Ex. 419, which shows bars 17–21), and the second subject
is based upon imitative sequence across the instruments (Ex. 420,
bars 38–48). The unity of this Quartet does not draw on techniques
of thematic quotation or metamorphosis between movements, rather

Ex. 419

on a subtle exploration of motivic ramifications. The opening two chords of the work become the key relationship between the first two movements, and the main 'scherzo' theme of the second movement depends heavily on them in retrograde for its harmonic and melodic contours. In the Adagio third movement Fauré fills the interval of the fifth with scale figures which become the basis also for the great central melody of the movement. The Finale expands this scale to an octave for its first subject, which also reactivates the dotted rhythm of the opening of the work; indeed all the themes of

Ex. 420

this sonata-form Finale are differing manifestations of the scale as melody, and the high degree of thematic differentiation Fauré achieves is a mark of his greatness as a sonata-form thinker.

Some of Franck's earliest compositions were in the field of chamber music; his First Piano Trio in F sharp minor, Op. 1, No. 1 (1841), has a cyclic approach to thematic structure for which Franck was later to become famous. His Fourth Piano Trio, Op. 2 (1842), was highly regarded by Liszt and dedicated to him.[94] But it was not until

[94] This Trio, in one movement, originally formed the Finale of the Third Piano Trio, Op. 1, No. 3, and it was at Liszt's suggestion that Franck made it into a separate work; see Vincent d'Indy, *César Franck*, pp. 110–12.

his last period that Franck returned to chamber music, and produced
three highly original major works: the Piano Quintet (1879), Violin
Sonata (1886), and String Quartet (1889). The Violin Sonata
modifies a traditional four-movement plan by opening with a short
sonata-form Allegretto, based initially on chord pairs, and following
this with a more extended sonata-form Allegro which, because of its
closely argued motivic style, is much closer to first-movement ethos
than that of a scherzo. In both these movements the second subject
area, so often in late-nineteenth-century music an area of tonal stasis,
is highly modulatory and developmental; these second subjects are
identifiable because of their qualities of thematic initiation in a
suitably prepared and related key, but they quickly progress into
thematic and tonal instability. Ex. 421 shows the opening of the

Ex. 421

second subject of the first movement. The third movement is headed Recitativo–Fantasia, and opens with a transformational précis of the main theme of the second movement, progressing to a transformation of the first subject of the first movement. The Recitativo is tonally fluid; in the succeeding binary Fantasia, parts of the Recitativo become the piano accompaniment to sustained lyrical and dramatic violin melodies. The second part of the Fantasia includes an extension of the main theme of the first movement. The tonally stable Finale begins as if it were a canonic rondo, but becomes an original fusion of rondo with sonata form: A, B (from movement 3), A, B, A (dominant), C (from movement 2), development (movements 4 and 3), A. Themes are here used between movements without transformation, yet they hardly become motto-themes in the Berliozian or Tchaikovskian sense either, for they do not occur as quotations in prominent relief, rather as subsidiary material embedded within the movement structure; this extends 'theme-quotation' into 'theme re-use'.

D'Indy gave a detailed analysis of the String Quartet in Cobbett,[95] demonstrating Franck's innovatory use of a lyrical, self-enclosed, non-preparatory 'lento' introduction to its first movement, which recurs for development after an 'allegro' sonata-form exposition, and as conclusion after the 'allegro' development and recapitulation; d'Indy treated this movement as an interleaving of two separate structures. The 'lento' theme reappears in the second movement, and the Finale begins with a review of movements.

D'Indy's own Piano Quartet, Op. 7 (1878–88), caused him much difficulty, and probably contains residues of a student work severely criticized by Franck. Two of his further eleven chamber works in the symphony-sonata genre belong to this period: the Trio for clarinet or violin, cello, and piano, Op. 29 (1887), and First String Quartet, Op. 35 (1890). Following Franck, d'Indy valued cyclic structure, and these three works all make use of it, the Trio and String Quartet strongly. The Trio has four movements: Ouverture, Divertissement, Chant élégiaque, and Finale.

---

[95] Vincent d'Indy, 'César Franck', in *Cobbett*, i. 426–8.

Chausson is not known today as a chamber-music composer, but Franck liked his four-movement Piano Trio (1881), and it was performed at the Société Nationale de Musique in 1882. His *Concert* for piano, violin, and string quartet (1889–91) is a powerful work, with an original textural basis: the string quartet is treated chiefly *en bloc* as accompaniment, with concerto elements in the writing for solo violin and piano. Both these works have cyclic thematic procedures, though this is not a strong feature of the *Concert*. A significant interest in Wagner developed in France from the mid-1870s; many French composers travelled to Bayreuth or Munich to hear performances, and *La Revue Wagnérienne* (1885–7) provided a focus of this interest not only for musicians but also for poets and painters. Wagner's influence on French music towards the close of the nineteenth century was naturally chiefly manifest in opera, but some of the chromaticism and sequential structuring of Chausson's and Lekeu's instrumental music owes more to Wagnerian than to Franckist harmonic practices—this in spite of distinct elements of love/hate in Chausson's response to Wagner. Lekeu wrote four complete chamber works, of which his poetic Violin Sonata (1891), with cyclic structure, remains the crowning achievement. At his early death a cello sonata and piano quartet were left unfinished, and were completed by d'Indy.

SMETANA'S CHAMBER WORKS

As with Brahms and Tchaikovsky, multi-movement chamber music attracted Smetana to utterances of personal significance in a way that other major instrumental genres did not. Although he wrote only four mature chamber works, Smetana was much involved with the genre from his earliest years. He knew and played many chamber works, especially those by Beethoven, Mendelssohn, and Schumann (whose Piano Quartet was a particular favourite), and the genre formed a vehicle for student writing—music now either lost or suppressed. His three-movement Piano Trio (1855) contains much energetic, even grandiose chromatic and contrapuntal writing in its sonata-form first movement. The Allegro second movement has the opening section of its rondo form based on materials from the first movement; of the two distinct slower episodes, the second is a march. The final Presto is a rondo with one recurring episode, altered on its second appearance to include a funeral march element. His First String Quartet, *Z mého života* [From my Life] (1876), is a classically shaped four-movement work with a programme both nationalist and biographical. Smetana gave several versions of this; in a letter to Srb-Debrnov he wrote:

The first movement depicts my youthful leanings towards art, the Romantic atmosphere, the inexpressible yearning for something I could neither express nor define, and also a kind of warning of my future misfortune. . . . The long insistent note in the finale owes its origin to this. It is the fateful ringing in my ears of the high-pitched tones which, in 1874, announced the beginning of my deafness. The second movement, a quasi-polka, brings to my mind the joyful days of youth when I composed dance tunes and was known everywhere as a passionate dancer. The third movement . . . reminds me of the happiness of my first love, the girl who later became my faithful wife. The fourth movement describes the discovery that I could treat national elements in music, and my joy in following this path until it was checked by the catastrophe of the onset of my deafness, the outlook into the sad future, the tiny ray of hope of recovery; but remembering all the promise of my early career, a feeling of painful regret.[96]

Although the work is clearly programmatic—because of its title, its unmistakable and poignant representation of the onset of deafness in the coda to the last movement and the retrospection this engenders in the subsequent recall of fragments of the first movement—the details of the programme remained private. The two duos for violin and piano, Z domoviny [From my Homeland] (1880), include small-scale multi-movement/single movement fusion, using folk material. The Second String Quartet (1883), a product of his sorely disabled and distracted last years, was described by Smetana in his own catalogue of works as 'String Quartet in D minor (the continuation of From my Life). Composed in the nervous illness which arose out of deafness'.[97] It may thus be heard as a programmatic sequel to the First Quartet, though it has no public or explicit programmatic indications. Like the First Quartet, it is a four-movement work, but now characterized by violent contrasts with much disruption of tempos, and original formal structures in which discontinuity is a notable feature; Schoenberg was greatly drawn to it.[98]

DVOŘÁK'S CHAMBER WORKS

From Dvořák's own listings we know he composed at least thirty-seven multi-movement chamber works, of which five were

[96] Letter of 12 Apr. 1878; see Karel Janeček, Smetanova komorní hudba: Kompoziční výklad (Prague, 1978), 222–3.
[97] Karel Teige, Příspěvky k životopisu a umělecké činnosti mistra Bedřicha Smetany, i. Skladby Smetanovy (Prague, 1893), 109.
[98] František Bartoš's Preface to Bedřich Smetana, Komorní skladby (Prague, 1977), p. xliv.

destroyed, three survived Dvořák's attempt at destruction complete, one survived incomplete, and one remains unfinished. This total includes thirty-three works that are clearly symphony/sonata analogues, a destroyed Octet (Serenade), and the three works which border on the genre 'collection': the *Bagatelles*, Op. 47, *Cypřiše* (without opus-number), and *Dumky* Trio, Op. 90. Dvořák's inclination towards chamber music is a general confirmation of his ready embrace of aspects of Teutonic tradition; nevertheless there was a particularly rich flowering of chamber music production during his most strongly nationalist phase, in the latter half of the 1870s, and the limitations he recognized on nationalist expression in symphonies clearly did not extend fully to chamber music. Dvořák was a viola player, and understood string writing in a double sense from 'inside'. He wrote chamber music throughout his productive life, except for his final years when, in spite of publishers' pressure to produce more chamber works, he turned to symphonic poems and opera. The backbone of his production is the fourteen string quartets, though some of his greatest chamber works are for smaller or larger groupings. He found his most natural form of expression in the three or four separated movement structure, but during the early 1870s he experimented with movement compression, to his evident dissatisfaction, and the three works bordering on the genre 'collection' listed above have five, twelve, and six movements respectively.

His first chamber works, the three-movement String Quintet in A minor, Op. 1 (1861) and four-movement String Quartet in A, Op. 2 (1862), are Classical in form and proportion, with clear sonata-form first and last movements. Dvořák was immediately able to write convincing chamber texture, and the first subject of the first movement of the Quintet is a typically Dvořákian blending of arpeggios, scales, and repeated notes into a memorable lyric theme. The slow movements are richly lyrical, showing early a Schubertian gift for inventive figurative accompaniments.

From the time of Dvořák's greatest susceptibility to influences from Liszt and Wagner came four works which he attempted unsuccessfully to destroy: three String Quartets of *c*.1869–70 (in B flat, D, and E minor) which survived in part-sets, and a Cello Sonata (*c*.1870–1) of which the cello part only survives. The B flat major Quartet is in four separated movements, but shows significant experiment with movement forms, and melodic and harmonic styles. The first three movements are each essentially monothematic, the Finale combining its own material with substantial sections from the first movement. The striving for a Wagnerian emotional temperature made Dvořák evolve radically new forms, and in the first movement ritornello-like recurrences of the theme in the tonic are followed by fertile but prolix sonata-style developments involving much chromaticism and concentration on short thematic fragments; lyricism has no space to shine through, and phrase structures are not articulated. Though locally always vital and convincing, by Dvořák's later standards the movement is severely underdifferentiated for its length, and the resultant somewhat amorphous formal profile suggests improvisation. The work, however, remains a highly original and interesting attempt to write Wagnerian chamber music. The D major Quartet, also in four separated movements, is another extended work; it uses a folk-song for its Scherzo, though the melody is modified by elaboration and variation of its phrase lengths. The E minor Quartet compresses five sections into a one-movement design $ABA_1B_1A_2$, with 'allegro' sonata-style A sections and 'andante' B sections; it concludes in B major. The Cello Sonata is in three linked sections.

Dvořák's lack of assurance in chamber music continued as he retreated from these Wagnerian–Lisztian influences, and of two destroyed piano trios from 1871–2 no details are known. The three-movement Piano Quintet of 1872 was extensively revised in 1887, when Dvořák cut two-fifths of the first movement and modified the others. Motivic and contrapuntal work is already less intense than in the works of 1870, allowing articulate lyricism more place. The Finale begins out of the tonic key, a feature of a significant number of later chamber works. In 1873 a destroyed Violin Sonata in A minor, a prolix F minor String Quartet, and the A minor String Quartet, Op. 12, were composed. Op. 12 is particularly interesting in charting Dvořák's recapture of Classical precepts, since he first wrote the work in one movement and five sections, but soon began to split it into four separate movements, entirely removing one section and rounding the others into closure; he abandoned this revision before completing it, and Jarmil Burghauser has carried the project through in our time. By the A minor String Quartet, Op. 16 of 1874, Dvořák's first chamber work to be published, his retrenchment was achieved, with a concise, restrained work reaffirming delicacy, melodic grace, and articulative clarity of expression.

The next five years were particularly rich in chamber music masterpieces. From 1875 (the year of the Fifth Symphony) come the String Quintet in G, Op. 77, for string quartet and double bass, Piano Trio in B flat, Op. 21, Piano Quartet in D, Op. 23; from 1876 the Piano Trio in G minor, Op. 26, String Quartet in E, Op. 80; from 1877 the String Quartet in D minor (Op. 34, dedicated to Brahms); from 1878 the *Bagatelles*, Op. 47, for two violins, cello, and harmonium, and String Sextet in A, Op. 48; and from 1879 the String Quartet in E flat, Op 51. These years show Dvořák growing into and establishing a distinctly national style in chamber music. The dance-like shaping of fast themes with small-scale rhythmic repetitions and strong accentuation, already noted in the Fifth Symphony, continued in the String Quintet (first and last movements), Piano Quartet (first movement), and the Finales of the String Quartets in E and D minor. The Piano Trio in B flat second movement shows Dvořák inclining towards the ruminative, elegiac *dumka* style; it has a simple slow tune in duple time and minor key, with figurative ornamentation of phrase-endings. The E major String Quartet has a similarly *dumka*-styled slow movement but in triple time. The String Sextet shows the first use of such a movement with title: '*Dumka* (Elegie)'; and the String Quartet in E flat has a titled *Dumka* as second movement, in which a contrasted vivace transforms the main theme into a *furiant*. *Furiant* rhythms appear in the Finale of the Piano Quartet, and third movement of the E major String Quartet; the first named *Furiant* is the third movement of the String Sextet. The polka appears in the third movement of the B flat Piano Trio; though the movement is not so named, it has even quavers in allegretto duple time with upbeat and simple short phrases. The D minor String Quartet has a named 'Alla polka' as second movement, and the E flat Quartet has a polka second subject in its first movement; its *Dumka* second movement and Finale related to the *skočná* make it one of the most nationalistically inflected of these chamber works; indeed it was written in response to a request from the Florentine Quartet for a quartet 'in the Slavonic style'. The *Bagatelles* introduce part of the folk-song 'Hrály dudy u Pobudy' [Bagpipes Played at Pobuda] in the first, third, and fifth.

Though some of these dance-influenced movements are highly sophisticated in their continuations, the general effect is a reinforcement of stylistic simplicity in clarity of phrase structure and a primacy of melody. Large-scale forms continue clear and concise; movements are self-enclosed, though there are examples of thematic transformations across movements in the String Quintet and B flat Piano Trio. The basing of the first and third *Bagatelles* on the same theme, and the transformation of this theme in the fifth, are a compelling reason for regarding the *Bagatelles* as a multi-movement work, in spite of the plural title. It is a slighter, more domestically oriented work than Dvořák's other multi-movement chamber music so far, and in this sense points forward to the *Terzetto*. Sonata form is used for the first movements of all the chamber works of this nationalistic phase, including the *Bagatelles*, where it is foreshortened. Following Schubert's lead, Dvořák included development of the second subject within the exposition, particularly in the B flat Piano Trio and D minor String Quartet, and favoured a three-key exposition. In the String Quintet the second subject is in the key of the flat leading-note, the exposition ending on the dominant; the Piano Quartet has a tonally wide-ranging first subject, a second subject in the dominant, and the exposition closes in the mediant.

Ternary form is the basis of many slow movements and all scherzo-and-trio movements; the form may be expanded by a coda referring to the middle section, as in the *dumka* movements of the String Sextet and E flat String Quartet. The slow movement of the Piano Quartet is a theme with five variations and coda, where Dvořák reconstitutes rather than decorates the theme in the variations. The slow movement of the G minor Piano Trio is a most telling and original monothematic form combining elements of variation and ritornello; the theme is presented in the tonic five times, each presentation leading into new developmental extensions. The resultant sections are of 10 + 16 + 23 + 16 + 27 bars. Finales also show much formal originality. That of the Piano Quartet combines 'scherzo' (A) and 'finale' (B) elements in a sonata-form design: A (tonic first subject + bridge), B (dominant second subject + development), A_1 (extended recapitulation + bridge), B_1 (shortened recapitulation + coda). Finales begin out of the tonic in the B flat Piano Trio, G minor Piano Trio, E major String Quartet, and String Sextet, this last having a theme-and-variation Finale where the theme is mostly in the supertonic minor (a tonal profile replicated in the variations). In such cases the opening of a finale becomes an harmonically auxiliary area to the tonic of the work, the movement requiring and using its context. Most finales of this period blend rondo and sonata principles, that of the G minor Piano Trio being highly innovative: AB (first subject), A_1B_1 (bridge), A_2B_2 (a transformation in second-subject style, tonic major!), development, AB (first subject recapitulation), B_2A_2 (second subject recapitulation).

Dvořák's next three chamber works, the Violin Sonata, Op. 57 (1880), C major String Quartet, Op. 61 (1881), and F minor Piano Trio, Op. 65 (1883), show a partial retreat from nationalism, a new susceptibility to Brahmsian influence (also found in his con-temporaneous Sixth Symphony), and an intensification of expressive power. The Violin Sonata has many Brahmsian resonances: flexible treatment of metre, including different metrical alterations in violin and piano simultaneously, contrapuntal intensifications of themes and developments, sequences involving diatonic discords, and contrary motion arpeggios; the second subject of the Finale is a broad Brahmsian 'chorale' in even crotchets.

The opening of the C major Quartet fuses Schubertian harmony (deriving directly from the opening of the great C major Quintet) with a Brahmsian approach to thematic shape, involving development within presentation. The chief means of this development is an elaborative figure in bar 2, which is also the main feature of the Scherzo; from this figure comes much of the impetus of the sonata-form first movement. It has a three-keyed, three-themed exposition which also derives from Schubert's Quintet. Ex. 422 shows the first subject, Ex. 423 (bars 47-56) its varied return in the exposition, and Ex. 424 (bars 112-25) its treatment at the beginning

Ex. 422

Ex. 423

of the development, demonstrating something of the intensity, complexity, and imaginative idiomatic quartet textures characteristic of this fine movement. The ternary Adagio opens with a sustained melody over a rich rhythmically complex Brahmsian accompaniment; as with several of Dvořák's slow movements there is duetting within the theme. This Quartet was written for Vienna, specifically for the Hellmesberger Quartet, a commission which may have reinforced Dvořák's turning away from nationalist inflections towards overtly Austrian models. But Dvořák could not avoid writing a finale with Czech resonance even here, and *skočná*-styled figures appear in the first subject, initially simple in phrase structure.

The epic, passionate F minor Piano Trio also opens with a sonata-form first subject of particularly Brahmsian cast, conflating presentation and development in a motivically based lyricism. National elements are again combined into Viennese style: the second movement uses an ostinato folk-styled allegretto melody in a monothematic form, and the Finale begins in *furiant* rhythm, with a waltz as second subject.

Ex. 424

Dvořák's remaining chamber music—the *Terzetto*, Op. 74,
Cypřiše, and A major Piano Quintet, Op. 81, of 1887; the E flat
Piano Quartet, Op. 87 (1889); *Dumky* Trio, Op. 90 (1891); the F
major String Quartet, Op. 96, E flat String Quintet, Op. 97, and
Violin Sonatina, Op. 100 of 1893 (his three American chamber
works), and the String Quartets in G and A flat majors (Opp. 106
and 105) of 1895—shows a continuation and enhancement of stylistic
trends already well established.[99] Emphasis on the domestic aspect
of the genre is found in the *Terzetto*, *Cypřiše*, and Violin Sonatina.
The inclusion of nationalist inflexion continued in the *Terzetto*, Piano
Quintet and Quartet, finding its most concentrated expression in the
Dumky Trio, a serious, complex multi-movement work in which each
of the six movements is a *dumka*. The expansion of genre-horizons
is particularly important in *Cypřiše*—an arrangement of twelve songs

[99] The nickname 'American', which is sometimes applied to both the F major String Quartet
and the E flat String Quintet, is not part of Dvořák's own published titles for these
compositions; see Jarmil Burghauser, *Antonín Dvořák: Thematický Katalog* (Prague, 1960),
pp. 307–9.

selected from an early song cycle, in revised order—and in the *Dumky* Trio. And, after the effortless grace of the American works, the G major Quartet must be regarded as the culmination of Dvořák's formal innovation within the separate four-movement structure. Its formal originality is of the very highest order, based on extensive experience and personalization of traditional structures, which are now explored to some of their remotest possibilities, and Dvořák here radicalizes form in a way that can be compared with late-Beethoven. Particularly his fantasia variations on a double theme (the two halves of which are motivically related) as second movement, his obsessive opposition of B and G sharp minors in the Scherzo, and the confrontation of light dance-inflected opening with an integrated retrospective of the first movement as Finale, all demonstrate him to be one of the most expressively innovative formal thinkers of the closing years of the nineteenth century.

IX

SOLO SONG

(a) GERMANY

By LESLIE ORREY

SCHUMANN

SCHUBERT's death in 1828 closed the first important chapter in the history of the Lied. The next is dominated by Robert Schumann (1810–56). Between the two, song as a genre continued to flourish, and we meet some of the composers in the pages of Schumann's periodical, *Die neue Zeitschrift für Musik*, which absorbed much of his time between 1834 and 1844. They include the gifted Norbert Burgmüller (1810–36), Josef Dessauer (1798–1876), Bernardt Klein (1793–1832), Carl Zöllner (1800–60), Josef Klein (1802–62), Wenzel Veit (1806–64), and Heinrich Esser (1818–72).[1] Schumann himself was hesitant to approach the form. As a young man, brought up in the shadow of Beethoven, he valued instrumental art higher than vocal,[2] and he made a reputation with his piano music before any of the songs by which he is universally known had been written. The conversion to song came only a few months after the letter to Hirschbach; another, equally famous, letter to Clara Wieck testifies to his sudden joy in the new medium.[3]

THE 1840 SONGS

During this one year Schumann wrote some 140 songs—that is,

---

[1] See Hans Hermann Rosenwald, *Geschichte des deutschen Liedes zwischen Schubert und Schumann* (Berlin, 1930); W. K. von Jolizza, *Das Lied und seine Geschichte* (Leipzig, 1910); Hans Joachim Moser, *Das deutsche Lied seit Mozart* (2nd rev. edn.; Tutzing, 1968), and Hugo Reimann, *Musik-Lexikon* (12th edn.; Mainz, 1967).

[2] See his letter to Hermann Hirschbach, in *Robert Schumanns Briefe: Neue Folge*, ed. F. Gustav Jensen (Leipzig, 1886), 143.

[3] See *Jugendbriefe von Robert Schumann* (Leipzig, 1885), 309. About a dozen songs had in fact been written before this, *c.*1827–8, and sent to Gottlob Wiedebein for comment. Three were published by Brahms, in a Supplement to the *Gesamtausgabe*; six more were issued by Karl Geiringer in 1933, and one as a Supplement to the *Zeitschrift für Musik*, 1933.

about half his total output.[4] For a comparable burst of song we have to go back to Schubert at his most prolific. Hardly one is unimportant. Some of the poets drawn upon, such as Goethe, Rückert, and Heine, had already been used by Schubert, though none of the poems had been chosen by him; but there were many fresh names—Eichendorff, Chamisso, Reinick, Kerner, Hans Christian Andersen, Burns, Thomas Moore, and Byron. After 1840 Schumann returned only very occasionally to a few of these (Goethe for the *Wilhelm Meister* songs of 1849, Byron for the *Drei Gesänge*, Op. 95, of the same year).[5] Moore and Byron furnished librettos for important works later in his life (*Das Paradies und die Peri* and *Manfred*), but for the solo songs he moved on to other writers such as Lenau, Mörike, Geibel, Heyse, Platen, and some poetical nonentities such as Elisabeth Kulmann and 'Wielfried von der Neun'.

More than any composer before him, and than most after him, Schumann conceived his songs in connected groups or cycles. The 'scenario' was sometimes due to the poet, as in the Heine *Liederkreis*, Op. 24 (nine poems taken bodily from the first part of the *Buch der Lieder* entitled *Junge Leiden*), or in Chamisso's *Frauenliebe und -leben*.[6] In other instances Schumann himself strove to give his selection a thread of meaning. The Eichendorff *Liederkreis*, Op. 39, for example, is drawn from various sources (chiefly the short story *Viel Lärm um Nichts* and his 'Wanderleben' romance *Ahnung und Gegenwart*) to form a series of nocturnes. All are concerned with moods and fears associated with night, whether the supernatural ('Waldesgespräch'—a variant of the Loreley legend), enchantment ('Mondnacht'), eeriness ('Zwielicht'), or distance ('In der Fremde'). His most important song cycle, *Dichterliebe*, Op. 48, is selected from the sixty-five poems of Heine's *Lyrisches Intermezzo* to make a more or less coherent story of love's awakening, rapture, disillusionment, betrayal, and final renunciation. The scheme shows some indebtedness to Schumann's *Die schöne Müllerin*.[7]

[4] The release of Schumann's pent-up emotions in song is inevitably linked with Clara Wieck, but the matter is far from simple. They had become engaged in 1837; 1840 was the blackest year in the struggle with her father, and the marriage was not consummated until September 1840, by which time the bulk of the songs had been written and, indeed, published. See Berthold Litzmann, *Clara Schumann: Ein Künstlerleben nach Tagebüchern und Briefen* (Leipzig, 1902–8), i; also Fritz Feldmann, 'Zur Frage des "Liederjahres" bei Robert Schumann', *Archiv für Musikwissenschaft*, 9 (1952), 246.

[5] All his Heine songs were written in 1840, though some were published later.

[6] Nine poems again, but Schumann set only eight. The gist of the last, not set by Schumann, is 'nought is now left but memories, dreams of days long past', hence Schumann's epilogue, repeating in the piano part the first song of the cycle.

[7] See Raymond Duval, 'L'Amour du poète de Schumann-Heine', *Rivista musicale italiana*, 8 (1901). Schumann originally intended twenty songs, as in *Die schöne Müllerin*, but four

Dichterliebe is a unity, a convincing whole, with a wide-ranging and carefully thought-out key scheme. The first eight songs are linked in obvious sequence: F sharp minor, A major, D major, G major, B minor, E minor, C major, A minor. The move to the flat side continues: D minor ('Das ist ein Flöten und Geigen'), G minor, E flat major. 'Am leuchtenden Sommermorgen' is in B major, related enharmonically to E flat, followed at once by the darkest key, E flat minor, and the nadir from the opening F sharp minor/A major. Another enharmonic change brings us to B major again ('Allnächtlich im Traume'); then follows E major and, for the last song, C sharp minor/major. This is the dominant of the original and in fact the first song had ended *on* its dominant, C sharp major. Thematic connections are present, though subtle. Several songs (Nos. 2, 4, 7, 8, and 10) begin on a mediant in the vocal line; others feature a falling scale passage, d', t, l, s, f (No. 2, opening bass line; Nos. 5, 8, 10, and possibly elsewhere).[8] The rippling waltz tune of No. 9 is hinted at in the postlude to the previous song;[9] the final epilogue is clearly related to the piano postlude of No. 12 (bars 23–6).

Most of the 1840 songs were short, two or three stanzas. Longer poems were often treated in some variant of rondo form, as, for example, 'Er, der Herrlichste von Allen' from Op. 42. Among the longer poems are some ballads, by Heine and Chamisso. Some of these, such as Heine's 'Belsazar', Op. 57—one of the earliest of the 1840 songs—are only half successful; others, such as Chamisso's 'Die röte Hanne' or 'Die Löwenbraut', are among his weaker compositions. But the striking 'Die beiden Grenadiere' Op. 49, No. 1, shows him handling a varied strophic design with much skill and imagination.[10]

In many of the 1840 songs the piano part had already moved away from 'accompaniment', to be fused with the vocal line in a new way. In Op. 48, No. 1 ('Im wunderschönen Monat Mai'), for instance, the evanescent sonorities of the piano are exploited in a

('Dein Angesicht', 'Lehn' deine Wang'', 'Mein Wagen rollet langsam', and 'Es kuchtet meine Liebe') were eventually published separately.

[8] For a discussion of the extra-musical significance of these and many other motifs see Eric Sams, *The Songs of Robert Schumann* (London, 1969; rev. 2nd edn., 1975); also the article by Sams, 'Did Schumann use Ciphers?', *Musical Times*, 106 (1965), 584.

[9] Cf. *Frauenliebe und -leben* where the main vocal line of No. 5 is transformed, in its postlude, into a wedding march.

[10] The poem comes from Heine's *Buch der Lieder* under the heading, *Romanzen*. Its title there is simply 'Die Grenadiere'. Schumann's title may stem from Chamisso who in 1838 translated a poem by Béranger, 'Les Deux Grenadiers'. Béranger's poem is a dialogue supposed to take place in the château de Fontainebleau where Napoleon took leave of his Guards on 20 April before going to Elba.

typically Schumannesque manner, with tender, shy wisps of melody emerging indistinctly from the quasi-extemporary arpeggios. In 'Zwielicht' or 'Muttertraum', Op. 40, No. 2, there are sinuous threads of melody which can be related with some difficulty to the Classically 'correct' harmony of the time.[11] In 'Mein Herz ist schwer', Op. 25, No. 15, this technique, now more chromatic, is combined with a vocal line that embeds such expressive melodic dissonances as the diminished fourth in spacious arches of melody with a total compass of a thirteenth. This was a style fundamentally different from that of most of his contemporaries[12]—a style that was to reach its culmination in Wolf.

SCHUMANN'S LATER SONGS

The standard of the 1840 songs had been extraordinarily high and generally consistent, but Schumann's later work is much more uneven. The songs, more than one hundred, date from 1849 to 1852[13]—years which Gerald Abraham has characterized as the period of 'some of Schumann's finest music'.[14] Yet most critics have been reluctant to recognize masterpieces among these late songs, and it must be confessed that few have the immediate attractiveness of the earlier Schumann. One or two of the 1849 *Liederalbum für die Jugend*, Op. 79 (a parallel to the piano album of the previous year) such as 'Der Sandmann' and 'Marienwürmchen', are vignettes sketched in the best 1840 manner. In other songs new methods are grafted on to old techniques. In the Lenau 'Meine Rose', Op. 90, No. 2, the 1840 style of emotionally charged repeated chords (as in 'Er, der Herrlichste' from Op. 42 or 'Ich grolle nicht' from Op. 48) is combined with hesitant fragments, to form an accompaniment almost completely independent of the vocal line—a development that once again leads to Wolf.

The most important of the 1849 songs are the Goethe set—nine out of the ten lyrics that were interspersed in the novel *Wilhelm Meister*. Although they have tempted dozens of composers, including Schubert, Beethoven, Liszt, and Wolf,[15] they have proved deceptively

---

[11] This linear writing has been linked with his Bach studies.

[12] These include, besides those already mentioned, Heinrich Dorn (1804–92), whose songs were praised by Schumann: Heinrich Marschner (1795-1861); Karl Gottfried Wilhelm Taubert (1811–91), whose long list of compositions includes some 300 songs; Theodor Kirchner (1823–1903); Johann Vesque von Püttlingen (1803–93).

[13] Two excellent settings of Mörike in 1847 must also be mentioned—'Die Soldatenbraut' and 'Das verlassene Mägdlein'.

[14] In Gerald Abraham (ed.), *Schumann: A Symposium* (London, 1952), 260.

[15] The first edition of the novel (1795) contained melodies to eight of them by Friedrich Reichardt (repr. in *Das Erbe deutsche Musik*, lviii). For a list of other settings, see Willi Schuh, *Goethe-Vertonungen: ein Verzeichnis* (Zurich, 1952).

difficult to set. Schumann's settings have come in for some harsh criticism, and have even been written off as 'among Schumann's most conspicuous failures as a song-writer'.[16] This is too severe. Philine's 'Singet nicht in Trauertönen', for example, recaptures the piquant spirit of the earlier 'Die Kartenlegerin'; 'An die Türen will ich schleichen' is a graphic picture of the Harper's shambling gait and pitiful begging (for food, love, and forgiveness), while 'Nur wer die Sehnsucht kennt', though Schumann deals in arbitrary fashion with Goethe's verse and, like every other composer, writes music that is too sophisticated for the child Mignon, catches much of the febrile mood of the poem.

It is clear that here, and in some of the songs in the cycles by Wielfried von der Neun, Op. 89, and Nikolaus Lenau, Op. 90, written in 1850, Schumann, in common with Liszt, Wagner, and others, is striving towards a new relationship between voice and instrumental support.[17] His vocal line had always tended to be declamatory rather than lyrical (the fusion of the two in his best songs is one of his chief glories); it now becomes freer tonally, more chromatic, often enigmatic and fragmentary. The piano part may suggest the orchestra and in 'Es stürmet am Abendhimmel', Op. 81, No. 1, is gloomy, nebulous, with tremolandi and sweeping crescendos and diminuendos. (The song is unusually fully marked.). In the Lenau song 'Kommen und Scheiden' the accompaniment is derived almost entirely from the opening bar, while in 'O Freund, mein Schirm, mein Schutz!' (Rückert, Op. 101, No. 6) the piano pursues its way with the single-mindedness of a Bach prelude.

MENDELSSOHN

The eighty songs of Felix Mendelssohn (1809–47) are of minor importance.[18] His ideal seemed to be a well-turned phrase, supported by an elegantly decorated accompaniment with smoothly managed modulations and no harmonic surprises. His attitude towards the words is suggested by his own *Lieder ohne Worte*; it was no hardship for him to omit them altogether. Examples of such artless songs are 'Frühlingslied', Op. 19, No. 1 (1830–4) (Ulrich von Lichtenstein), 'Der Blumenstrauss', Op. 47, No. 5 (Klingemann), and 'Der Blumenkranz'

[16] By Martin Cooper in Abraham (ed.), *Schumann: A Symposium*, p. 110. For a more sympathetic assessment see Jack M. Stein, *Poem and Music in the German Lied from Gluck to Hugo Wolf* (Cambridge, Mass., 1971). See also Karl Wörner, *Robert Schumann* (Zürich, 1949).
[17] See Wörner, *Schumann*, especially pp. 222 ff.
[18] No critical edition has been published. They were originally issued in sets, six or twelve at a time, by Schlesinger of Berlin or Breitkopf and Härtel. A convenient edition is Peters (plate number 6022).

(1829?) (Thomas Moore). The best of this type is certainly 'Auf Flügeln des Gesanges', Op. 34, No. 2 (1833/4) (Heine).

Occasionally, as in Heine's 'Reiselied', Op. 19, No. 6, the piano's role becomes more significant. A subtler song is the Eichendorff 'Nachtlied', Op. 71, No. 1 (1845),[19] which captures something of Eichendorff's melancholy. One of the tenderest and most delicate of all his songs is 'Das erste Veilchen' Op. 19, No. 2 (1837). Both poem, by Egon Ebert, and setting pay tribute to the Goethe-Mozart 'Das Veilchen', K 476. The song is through-composed, and Mendelssohn seems to have taken unusual care over detail. See, for instance, the long, arched phrase in bars 10-15 at the repetition of the words 'die Botin des Lenzes drückt' ich voll Lust an meine schwellende, hoffende Brust' (Ex. 425). A notable point is the treatment of the motif in bar 6, which goes far to bind the work together. Repeated as an interlude in bars 15 and 16, it is used again, in the tonic minor, for the opening of the second stanza ('der Lenz ist vorüber'); it reappears, with an extension, in bar 33 and, most imaginatively, in the piano postlude.

Ex. 425

[19] About half of Mendelssohn's songs were written before Schumann's 'song year'. The mutual influence of these two composers remains to be fully studied, but see Rudolph Felber, 'Schumann's Place in German Song', *Musical Quarterly*, 26 (1940), 340.

(I joyfully pressed the herald of Spring to my swelling, hoping breast.)

The Goethe settings are all interesting. The two Suleika songs (the first not by Goethe but by Marianne von Willemar, the youthful protégée of his old age) are typical Mendelssohn; the E major section of 'Ach, um deine feuchten Schwingen' Op. 34, No. 4 (1833/4), could be by no other composer. The second, 'Was bedeutet die Bewegung?' Op. 57, No. 3 (c.1840), is more fully developed, and in 'Erster Verlust', Op. 99, No. 1 (1841), there is a wider emotional and musical range than usual. But the most enterprising of all, and the high-water mark of Mendelssohn as a song-writer, is his setting of Goethe's sonnet 'Die Liebende schreibt', Op. 86, No. 3—and incidentally one of the earliest, composed in 1833.[20] It has a wide modulatory range, moving from E flat to the tonic minor (bar 10, 'entfernt von dir . . .'), thence to G flat major, where it stays for a dozen or more bars of entrancing music. The long passage beginning at bar 16, 'die einzige, da fang' ich an zu weinen', has a bloom and a sensuous quality anticipating the idyllic love music of *Tristan* or the hushed, suspended adagios of Mahler (Ex. 426).

Ex. 426

[20] Op. 86 was published posthumously.

an zu wei - - - - nen

(the only one, then I begin to weep)

LISZT

The contribution of Ferenc Liszt (1811–86) to German song has a significance which is only gradually becoming fully recognized.[21] His mixed Hungarian, French, and German background brought a fresh, and refreshing, outlook on song. If it is true that 'Upon the pure soil of German song, which so often touches the deepest recesses of the heart, Liszt did not feel altogether at home'[22] (which could be disputed), on the other hand he rarely lapsed into the sentimentality or the *Gemütlichkeit* that threatened the lesser German composers of the nineteenth century. Even when his choice of poem led him towards the sentimental there was usually some felicity in the piano part as compensation. Of the seventy or so songs[23] there are few without some claim on our attention.

They can conveniently be divided into three periods: (1) songs from the early 1840s; (2) the Weimar period, 1849–58, and (3) a final period from about 1870 until his death in 1886.[24] The early songs, as might be expected, have elaborate piano parts, which in later revisions were often simplified.[25] The writing is always pianistic without being too exacting. One or two call for a certain amount of dexterity ('Es war ein König in Thule' (Goethe, 1843); 'Die Loreley' (Heine, 1841, rev. 1856); 'Die drei Zigeuner' (Lenau, 1860)), but none is so difficult as 'Erlkönig' or some of Jensen's or Wolf's

[21] The literature is fairly extensive. See E. Reuss, *Liszts Lieder* (Leipzig, 1906); Bernhard Vogel, *Franz Liszt als Lyriker* (Leipzig, 1887); Carl Kittel, 'Über das "Gesangliche" in Franz Liszts Vokal-Kompositionen', *Die Musik* (Oct. 1936); Martin Cooper, 'Liszt as a Song Writer', *Music and Letters*, 19 (1938), 171; Christopher Headington, 'The Songs', in Alan Walker (ed.), *Franz Liszt: The Man and his Music* (London, 1970; 2nd edn., 1976), 221–47.

[22] Quoted from the Preface, by Carl Armbruster, to Ditson's Boston edition of thirty songs (1911).

[23] Complete lists in Walker (ed.), *Franz Liszt*, and in Peter Raabe, *Franz Liszt: Leben und Schaffen* (rev. 2nd edn., Tutzing, 1968).

[24] The chronology is based on Raabe, *Franz Liszt*, ii. 341 ff. Many songs were extensively revised.

[25] See Headington, 'The Songs', for a discussion of some of these revisions.

accompaniments. But no composer before Liszt had asked for such detail, control, or nuance in the handling of the piano.[26] Schumann, his contemporary, had certainly demanded great subtlety and intimacy, but both he and Schubert had been modest in their demands on the range of the piano part. Liszt for the first time utilized the whole keyboard, exploiting the tone colours of the upper registers as freely as the sonorities of the bass. Later the piano became terse and laconic; it ceased to be an 'accompaniment' and instead acted as a commentary on the words, often interlocked in dialogue with the vocal line, itself a simple type of recitative.

About two dozen songs come from the first period. They include a setting, c.1840, of Heine's 'Im Rhein . . .', strikingly dissimilar from Schumann's setting, full of deft, pictorial touches such as the fluttering angels' wings at 'Es schweben Blumen und Englein'; and what is probably his most famous song, 'Die Loreley'.[27] This Siren legend, the beautiful Loreley singing her seductive song on the rock high above the Rhine, is due to Clemens Brentano who invented it in 1802; Heine's poem immortalizing the legend was published in his *Buch der Lieder* (1827). Liszt's treatment is highly descriptive, the Rhine flowing majestically in compound time, as in Wagner. The cello-like recitative in the opening bars is a Liszt fingerprint that recurs time and again. Another Heine song, 'Du bist wie eine Blume' (1840), is a little masterpiece. It also opens with a 'cello' melody which is the kernel of the song; it blossoms like a flower in the voice part, the piano muses over it in the middle section, and it forms the most delicate of postludes. Another successful Heine song is 'Vergiftet sind meine Lieder' (1842). The grinding dissonances in the prelude (Ex. 427) anticipate Wolf. The three songs from Schiller's *Wilhelm Tell* (1845) are also attractive examples of his early style.

The songs of the Weimar period, about twenty, show a notable change in subject matter and style. The descriptive, ballad-like poems now had less attraction for him than the more compact form of the

Ex. 427

[26] See Raabe, *Franz Liszt*, ii. 112 ff.
[27] Both were revised c.1856.

lyric, though his treatment did not always correspond. In Goethe's 'Über allen Gipfeln ist Ruh' (pub. 1848, and, somewhat revised, 1859) the scene is set by the tranquil opening chords (the progression includes the out-of-key common chord that is a Liszt fingerprint for 'repose'); but the mood of the poem is shattered by the working up to a forte climax, in a song the essence of which is peace and silence, and by an inexcusable extension: the last two lines of the poem are spun out, by word and phrase repetition, to twenty-nine bars out of a total of forty-five. The same elongation is seen in Heine's 'Anfangs wollt' ich fast versagen' (1856; rev. 1880). Structurally this song is interesting as showing Liszt anticipating Wolf's habit of building a song on an ostinato one-bar motif; the rhythm of the first bar ♩ ♩ ♪ is present with little modification in twenty-nine bars out of a total of forty. But in Heine's 'Ein Fichtenbaum' (1855), one of his best songs, he shows a more artistic restraint. The poem, simple and short, draws two contrasting pictures of loneliness, the pine in the far, frozen North dreaming in its long winter sleep of the palm, equally lonely, in the blistering sand. Once again an opening 'cello' motif plays an important part. The leaning towards the terse and epigrammatic is also observable in the second setting of the Harper's song from *Wilhelm Meister*, 'Wer nie sein Brot mit Tränen ass' (*c*.1860), which is a foretaste of the increasingly experimental work of his last years. 'Die drei Zigeuner' (Lenau, 1860), on the other hand, brilliantly recaptures the zest and exuberance of his earlier, more pictorial manner.

About a dozen songs belong to his last period. They tend to be spare, almost austere, like some of the later piano works. They are increasingly experimental, especially in their cadences; they often end on inversions, or on chords other than the tonic. The coda to 'Die Fischerstochter' (Coronini, 1871) is a typical ending (Ex. 428). Not surprisingly, his choice of poems during these latter years led him

Ex. 428

(the heart is broken.)

to some quasi-religious poetry; gratifyingly, the settings emerged on the whole purged of the religiosity that sometimes marred his earlier work. 'Und sprich' (Beigeleben, 1874) is touchingly simple, but the more involved 'Gebet' (Bodenstedt, c.1878) puts us in mind of the tortuous, self-immolatory penitential songs of Wolf's *Spanisches Liederbuch* [Spanish Songbook].[28]

FRANZ

Though Robert Franz (1815–92) was much admired in his day,[29] few of his three hundred songs have survived the test of time. 'Franz war der erste Liederjournalist,' wrote Oskar Bie;[30] the journalism is occasionally elevated to literature, but on the whole this judgement is just.

His first songs were written c.1842, inspired by and dedicated to one of his pupils. He was persuaded to send them to Schumann, who found a publisher for them and reviewed them in his journal.[31] The gem of this collection is 'Die Lotosblume' (Geibel). The texture is transparently simple, a gently undulating arpeggio figure; but the harmonies are curiously shifting, prophetic of Fauré. In none of the twelve does Franz attempt much realism in the piano part, though in No. 7, 'Sonntag' (Eichendorff), in a song that otherwise moves in solemn four-part harmony, there is just a suggestion of church bells. Franz subsequently declared himself opposed to such pictorialism,[32] preferring to express the meaning and mood of the poem mainly through the melodic line. This, however, presupposes a finer melodic gift than his.

28 Wolf's relationship with Liszt remains unexplored.
29 He was extravagantly over-praised during his lifetime. Thus Franz Brendel wrote, in the *Neue Zeitschrift für Music* (1857): 'Song in Robert Franz has fulfilled what Schubert only anticipated.' Even as late as 1900 the Bostonian William Apthorp could write, 'In the domain of the purely lyrical Lied no greater songs than his can be written' (Preface to *Fifty Songs of Robert Franz* (Boston, 1900)).
30 *Das deutsche Lied* (Berlin, 1926).
31 *12 Gesänge für Sopran oder Tenor mit Pianoforte*, Werk 11. See Schumann, *Gesammelte Schriften* (Berlin, 1888), iii. 135–55.
32 See his opinions quoted in Wilhelm Waldmann (ed.) *Robert Franz: Gespräche aus zehn Jahren* (Leipzig, 1895).

Some of his best songs are found among his Heine settings. 'Allnächtlich im Traume', Op. 9, No. 4, is imaginative and free from sentimentality, and the last one of the same set, 'Auf dem Meere', is a song of some distinction. 'Meerfahrt', Op. 18, No. 4, uses the mannerism of sequence less mechanically than some and by exploiting judiciously spaced harmonies combined with the use of the sustaining pedal also anticipates the sensuous sounds of French impressionistic writing. Another Heine song which stands out is 'Der Fichtenbaum', an attractive miniature which compares favourably with Liszt's setting. Other songs that might be singled out are 'Wonne der Wehmuth', Op. 33, No. 1 (Goethe); 'Die Lotosblume', Op. 25, No. 1 (Heine); and, for its experimental nature, 'Ja, du bist elend', Op. 7, No. 6. This is the poem which, not set by Schumann, follows 'Ich grolle nicht' in Heine's *Lyrisches Intermezzo*. It is the most restless tonally of all Franz's songs; the C major chord at the beginning lasts for only half a bar before the music is swung violently into C sharp minor, thence through D minor, E flat minor, E minor, finally cadencing on E major.[33]

WAGNER, CORNELIUS AND JENSEN

The two or three composers in Wagner's circle made only a small contribution to the history of German song. Richard Wagner (1813–83) himself, though he professed an admiration for the songs of Franz,[34] was very little in sympathy with such a miniature art-form.[35] The five Wesendonck songs, written in 1857–8, are closely bound up with *Tristan*, having much the same musical technique; indeed the third, 'Im Treibhaus', and the fifth, 'Träume', provided some of the raw material for that work. When the simple throbbing quavers of 'Träume' were incorporated into the love duet in Act II of *Tristan* (at 'O sink' hernieder ...') they became the more complex pattern ♪♩ ♩♪♫ —perhaps the prototype of a similar nervous rhythm in a number of Wolf's songs. Wolf is also anticipated in the pulsating secondary sevenths of the first song, 'Der Engel', and by the persistent dissonances of the fourth, 'Schmerzen'.

One of Wagner's faithful disciples was Peter Cornelius (1824–74).

---

[33] Franz's songs, now out of print, have never been published in a critical edition. A selection, in maddening disarray, is published by Peters in five volumes.

[34] In 1857 Franz visited Wagner in Switzerland, and found some of his own compositions in the master's study. Wagner sang his 'Widmung', Op. 14, No. 1, which he 'declaimed with extravagant pathos, dramatically'—and added that Franz ought to write opera.

[35] In 1839–40 in Paris Wagner wrote four songs to French words—'Dors, mon enfant'; 'Mignonne'; 'Attente', and 'Les Deux Grenadiers'. They are discussed, together with the only other German song to be published in his lifetime, 'Der Tannenbaum', in Ernest Newman, *Wagner as Man and Artist* (rev. 2nd edn.; London and New York, 1924).

He had also been close to Liszt in the Weimar days. The song cycles *Vater Unser*, Op. 2 (1854–5)—nine poems meditating on the Lord's Prayer, each with a plainsong *incipit*; *Trauer und Trost*, Op. 3; the *Brautlieder* (1856–9),[36] and the *Weihnachtslieder*, Op. 8 (1856–70) were much admired in their day, but there is little to single them out from the average Lied of the time. Perhaps he found little inspiration in his own verse; at any rate two songs from his Op. 5, 'Zum Ossa sprach der Pelion' (words by Annette von Droste-Hülsdorf) and 'Auftrag' (Hölty), are much more worthy of investigation.

A more interesting figure is Adolf Jensen (1837–79).[37] He was an East Prussian, born in Königsberg; his career as pianist, conductor, and composer was interrupted more and more as time went on by illness, and his last years were spent in a vain struggle against the tuberculosis to which he finally succumbed. For his more than 170 songs he drew on a wide variety of poets including Heine, Eichendorff, Geibel, Heyse (the *Spanisches Liederbuch* was used extensively), Daumer, Chamisso, and Rückert. There was also an array of English, Scottish, and Irish poetry, by Tennyson, Thomas Moore, Walter Scott, Alan Cunningham, and Mrs Hemans, in translations by Ferdinand Freiligrath. Like most composers he is as good as his poets, and some of the lesser writers lure him into a chromatic, saccharine style. A simple melodic line, as in 'Und schläfst du, mein Mädchen', for example, from the *Spanisches Liederbuch* (it is headed 'Im Volkston'), is given a lush accompaniment quite out of keeping. Other songs from the same source, however, hold a comfortable balance between voice and piano, and reveal him as a by no means unworthy forerunner of Wolf. The declamation in 'In dem Schatten meiner Locken' (written in 1853, thirty-six years before Wolf's setting) may not be quite so meticulous as Wolf's, and Jensen is too preoccupied with Spanish local colour to bring out the touching, caressing sweetness of the poem to the extent that Wolf does; but for all that it is a fine song, with the guitar idiom well controlled, and the chromaticisms in this instance not at all obtrusive. More of these Spanish songs were set in 1860 as Op. 4, and again some of them can stand comparison with Wolf. 'Sie blasen zum Abmarsch' and 'Dereinst, dereinst Gedanke mein' are both fine songs; another

---

[36] The *Brautlieder* seem indebted to Chamisso's *Frauenliebe und -leben*—the musings of a bride on her wedding day. By far the best is No. 4, 'Am Morgen'.

[37] See F. Baser, 'Der Nachlass des Liedmeister A. Jensen', *Musica*, 7 (1953). The standard biography is still Arnold Niggli, *Adolf Jensen* (Zurich, 1895), but see also the article by Reinhold Sietz, 'Jensen', *Die Musik in Geschichte und Gegenwart*, vii.

excellent one, with a far more manageable piano part than Wolf's, is 'Klinge, klinge, mein Pandero', Op. 21, No. 1.

Being a pianist, he made considerable demands on the accompanist. Songs such as 'Die Schwestern', Op. 53, No. 1, 'Der letzte Wunsch', Op. 53, No. 6, or 'Eduard', Op. 58, No. 3, require an almost Lisztian technique; nevertheless the writing is always pianistic. But the emphasis is by no means concentrated on the piano, and often, as in 'Murmelndes Lüftchen, Blüthenwind', 'Holde, schattenreiche Bäume', 'Ach, ihr lieben Aeuglein' (Ex. 429), and others from the *Spanisches Liederbuch*, he calls for something of the effortless floating of the soprano voice over the accompaniment that we associate with Richard Strauss.

Jensen indeed had a high talent bordering on genius. He was a composer fastidious within the limits imposed by the climate and conventions of his time. He used the techniques of the period with skill and artistry, perhaps not with boldness but with some originality. His best work does not justify the neglect into which it has fallen.

BRAHMS

Johannes Brahms (1833–99) is most familiar to us in the concert hall as an instrumental composer, but more than half his 122 opus numbers incorporate the voice in one form or another. His interest in the solo song was lifelong: the earliest songs, published as Opp. 6 and 7, date from 1851–3, the last, Op. 121 (the *Vier ernste Gesänge*), appeared in 1896. Publication was largely concentrated in three periods, 1868, 1877, and 1884–8, but these dates give little clue to dates of composition. We have it from Brahms himself that he kept songs by him often for a considerable time before the final polishing preparatory to their appearance. Altogether he wrote about 250 songs.

Apart from folk poetry he drew on the work of some forty-five writers, including Goethe, Heine, Tieck, Mörike, Platen, and Liliencron. His favourite seemed to be the orientalist Georg Friedrich Daumer, who provided texts for nineteen of the solo songs, as well as the words for the two sets of *Liebeslieder* waltzes for four voices and piano duet, Opp. 52 and 65. Another favourite was the North German Klaus Groth, with twelve.[38] His approach was quite the antithesis to that of his junior, Wolf. His concept of the vocal line

---

[38] For further details of the sources of Brahms's texts, see Max Friedlaender, *Brahms' Lieder* (Berlin, 1922; Eng. trans. C. Leonard Leese, London, 1928), and Gustav Ophüls, *Brahms-Texte* (Bonn, 1898; 2nd edn., 1908). There are fifteen songs by Ludwig Tieck, but all are concentrated in one group, the *Romanzen aus L. Tiecks Magelone*, Op. 33.

Ex. 429

(Ah, dear eyes, blue eyes, Heaven grant that you think of me!)

was lyrical, with recitative almost non-existent. There are few attempts at the dramatic, and those not among his best. Nor did he favour the ballad, and indeed his attempt at setting the old Scottish Ballad 'Edward' ended as a piano piece, Op. 10. On the instrumental side he shied away from the overtly graphic and pictorial, preferring to let the accompaniment reflect the general mood of the poem, responding where necessary, as in the masterly 'An ein Veilchen', Op. 49, No. 2 (Hölty), to its varied emotional needs. Sometimes he seems too concerned with purely musical considerations, so that a song such as 'Abschied', Op. 69, No. 3 (Wenzig), gives the appearance of being too pedantically derived from the opening four-note motif in the bass: E flat, F, A flat, G. The unification of a work by means of 'academic' techniques such as inversion, diminution or augmentation, and canonic and other contrapuntal devices was such a feature of his style that it would be strange not to find them in his songs.

Formally he leaned towards the strophic rather than the through-composed—a reflection of his lifelong enthusiasm for the *Volkslied*. Once again the contrast with Liszt, Jensen, and, above all, Wolf is very marked. But he used the basic strophic form with much variety and subtlety,[39] as, for example, in 'Wie Melodien zieht es', Op. 105, No. 1 (on a poem by Hermann Lingg). Moreover the contours and span of the vocal line and the harmonic and rhythmic richness of the piano part often belied or disguised the essential simplicity. The same, incidentally, is true of Wolf.

A Brahms 'fingerprint', not confined to the songs, is the cross-rhythm two against three, which he used more frequently than most composers.[40] There are enough instances in the songs to suggest that this device was used to depict mental conflict, doubt, indecision. These were characteristics of Brahms the man;[41] they guided instinctively his choice of poems. By far the majority are love songs, usually telling of unhappy or unrequited love.[42] 'Liebestreu', Op. 3, No. 1 (Reinick), the finest of his early songs (1853), is of this nature.

---

[39] See the discussion in Paul Mies, *Stilmomente und Ausdrucksstilformen im Brahmsschen Lied* (Leipzig, 1923)—one of the few books in the large Brahms literature to attempt a serious examination of his songs.

[40] In Book I of the *Lieder* in the Peters edition this device occurs more or less prominently in fourteen out of fifty-one songs. By comparison, the first volume of Schumann's songs in the same edition, comprising a large selection of the 1840 songs, has six out of a total of seventy-eight.

[41] 'Many passages in the letters afford touching illustration of his constitutional lack of self-confidence and his desire for sympathy' (quoted in Florence May, *The Life of Johannes Brahms* (London, 1905), ii. 489).

[42] 'Brahms is the greatest master of resignation, pessimism and *Weltschmerz* in nineteenth-century song' (quoted in Walter Niemann, *Johannes Brahms* (Berlin, 1920), 295).

It is a dialogue between mother and daughter: 'O my child, sink your sorrow in the deep, deep sea'—'a stone will stay in the water's depths, my sorrow surges ever upwards.' The melody, in canon with the bass (this in itself is a symbol of stress), evolves from the first three-note motif, and the conflict expressed by the cross-rhythm is emphasized, especially in the third stanza, by chromaticism and harsh dissonances.

Brahms showed comparatively little interest in the song cycle. His principal contributions were the somewhat unsatisfactory *Magelone Lieder*, Op. 33—fifteen songs, written in 1861-9, drawn from Tieck's romance, *Wundersame Liebesgeschichte der schönen Magelone und des Grafen Peter aus der Provence* (1797)[43]—and his farewell to song and last important work, the *Vier ernste Gesänge* for bass of 1896. During the previous few years death had taken a severe toll among his friends—Gottfried Keller (1890), Elisabet von Herzogenberg (1892), Hermine Spies (1893), Billroth and Hans von Bülow (1894). Clara Schumann died in the very month that Op. 121 was completed, May 1896. With words drawn from Ecclesiastes, the Apocryphal Ecclesiasticus, and the first Epistle to the Corinthians, these songs represent a conscious summing up of his thoughts concerning life and death.

A major contribution by Brahms to the art of song lies in the impressionism of his late style, following on from the Schumann of, for example, 'Zwielicht' or 'Mondnacht' (also set by Brahms). Such a song is 'Feldeinsamkeit', Op. 86, No. 2 (Hermann Allmers) (1879)—a summer landscape, the serenity of which is unsurpassed in nineteenth-century song literature. The great 'Sapphische Ode', Op. 94, No. 4 (Hans Schmidt) (1884), is suffused by the same serene but melancholy radiance. All Brahms's late works are characterized by an astonishing sensitivity towards instrumental, vocal, and harmonic colour, which in the songs reached its culmination in two of the Op. 105 set, 'Wie Melodien zieht es' and 'Immer leiser wird mein Schlummer' (1886). The unresolved 6/4 chords at bars 44-6 of the latter illustrate beautifully the colouristic, non-functional harmony which Brahms had been increasingly exploring (Ex. 430).[44]

---

[43] The cycle is discussed in A. H. Fox Strangways, 'Brahms and Tieck's "Magelone"', *Music and Letters*, 21 (1940), 211.

[44] There is a revealing commentary on this song by Elisabet von Herzogenberg, who says of these bars: 'I know of no other passages to equal it for harshness in the whole of your music' *Johannes Brahms im Briefwechsael mit Heinrich und Elisabet von Herzogenberg*, ed. Max Kalbeck (Berlin, 1907), 132.

Ex. 430

(Come, come soon.)

BRAHMS AND THE *VOLKSLIED*

In a letter to Clara Schumann (27 January 1860) Brahms wrote:
'Song is at present following such a wrong course that one cannot
hold up an ideal before one too consistently. And, in my opinion,
this ideal is the *Volkslied*.'[45] He had just been busy on his *Lieder
und Romanzen*, Op. 14, in which he deliberately set out to catch the
flavour of German folk song as it was understood at the time.
He had also (1858) completed the *Volkskinderlieder*, intended for
Schumann's children.[46] Settings of *Volkslieder*, often in translation
from Serbian or Czech, occur from time to time among his songs,
but the culmination was the forty-nine *Volkslieder* published in
1894.[47]

Yet here again there is a contradiction; for the *volkstümlich* style
hardly figures at all among his best songs. The popular 'Vergebliches

[45] Quoted in Niemann, *Brahms*, p. 359.
[46] No doubt conceived as a pendant to Schumann's own Op. 79. A further set, also dating
from 1858, remained unpublished until 1926.
[47] For a discussion of Brahms and the *Volkslied*, see Friedlaender, *Brahms' Lieder*, pp. 192 ff;
also 'Brahms' Volkslieder', *Jahrbuch des Musikbibliothek Peters*, 9 (1902), and *Neue Volkslieder
von Johannes Brahms* (Berlin, 1926).

Ständchen', Op. 84, No. 4, for instance, is not, as Brahms thought, a Rhenish folk-poem;[48] and, if it were, the treatment is far from *volkstümlich*. All the songs so far mentioned—to which might be added 'An eine Aeolsharfe', Op. 19, No. 5; 'Wie bist du meine Königin', Op. 32, No. 9; 'Ruhe, Süssliebchen', Op. 33, No. 9; 'Die Mainacht', Op. 43, No. 2, and many others—display a sophistication far removed from the *Volkslied*.

Writing to Elisabet von Herzogenberg in 1879 he comments, *à propos* some compositions by Herzogenberg: 'I am rather embarrassed on this point, as I am forced to remember the innumerable *Volkslieder* I myself have dabbled with [*verwuzelt*].'[49] This perhaps refers to the posthumous collection (1926), fourteen of which are reworkings of some that appeared in his 1858 collection ('Sandmännchen' and 'Schlaf, Kindlein, schlaf!' are two popular songs from this). The reworkings often transform an appropriately simple piano accompaniment into a more or less elaborate 'art-song'. Brahms, like other nineteenth-century masters, while paying lip service to the notion of folk art, had not yet reached the stage when he could let it stand by itself. The urge to improve was irresistible.

MAHLER

It is impossible even to list more than a few of the German Lied composers of the second half of the century. They include Hugo Brückler (1845–71), Alexander Ritter (1833–96) Albert Fuchs (1858–1910) (about 100 songs), Hans Pfitzner (1869–1949), Martin Plüddemann (1845–97), important in the history of the ballad, as well as non-German composers such as Dvořák and Rubinstein.[50]

Gustav Mahler (1860–1911) almost from the first took the natural and, from his point of view, inevitable step of transferring the accompaniment from the monochrome piano to the multi-coloured, infinitely variable orchestra. His only songs conceived originally for voice and piano were two of the *Lieder und Gesänge aus der Jugendzeit* (1885)—'Frühlingsmorgen' and 'Erinnerung'. All his other songs (*Lieder eines fahrenden Gesellen*; *Lieder aus des Knaben Wunderhorn*; the *Kindertotenlieder*; the *Fünf Lieder nach Rückert*; and one or two isolated songs) were designed with orchestral accompaniment; they

---

[48] It had appeared in *Deutsche Volkslieder* (Berlin, 1840). But this collection, edited by Franz Kretschmar and Anton Wilhelm von Zuccalmaglio, was most unreliable, for it included not only a quantity of verse by Zuccalmaglio himself (including this particular poem) but at least thirty compositions by J. F. Reichhardt and Otto Nicolai. Brahms drew extensively on this volume.

[49] *Briefwechsel*, p. 106.

[50] See Hermann Kretzschmar, 'Das deutsche Lied seit dem Tode Richard Wagners', *Jahrbuch der Musikbibliothek Peters*, 4 (Leipzig, 1897), 45–60.

have moved outside the frame of the 'Lied mit Klavierbegleitung'. They have also, like much of the late nineteenth-century song production, moved out of the domestic sphere into the concert hall. German song in both composition and performance had become highly professional.

STRAUSS

If Mahler and Wolf could be said to have an excess of introspection and an almost morbid sensitivity, the defects of Richard Strauss (1864–1949) lay in the opposite direction. Gifted with the self-confidence that Brahms lacked, he composed rapidly and con-tinually—and, it seems on looking through his copious output of two hundred songs, indiscriminately.[51] Though up to date and 'modern' in his composition, and with an unrivalled command of the technique of his craft, he seems on the whole to have thought of song in the old-fashioned sense of 'voice' and 'accompaniment',[52] as in the early 'Zueignung', Op. 10, No. 1 (1882), and 'Winternacht', Op. 15, No. 2, are examples. The vocal line may become more opulent and exacting, as in 'Cäcilie', Op. 27, No. 2 (1893). While the accompaniment may become highly ornate as in 'Hochzeitlied', Op. 37, No. 6 (1896), or the Lilienkron setting, 'Bruder Liederlich', Op. 41, No. 4 (1899), the genre remains essentially that of Men-delssohn or Jensen, whose songs Strauss almost certainly knew.[53] The best known song of this type is of course the von Schack 'Ständchen', Op. 17, No. 2 (1885), with an accompaniment which is exactly right for the teasing intimacy of the song. Others, such as the Carl Busse 'Wenn', Op. 31, No. 2, or Rückert's 'Anbetung', Op. 36, No. 4, have accompaniments that are obvious, fulsome, or over-blown, suggesting that Strauss has too readily yielded to his own pianistic agility or a desire for an effective climax.

The quieter songs often reveal a more endearing side. The Bierbaum 'Traum durch die Dämmerung', Op. 29, No. 1 (1894), or the Falke 'Meinem Kinde', Op. 37, No. 3 (1897), are remarkably successful in their evocation of atmosphere. Another striking song is Dehmel's '*Leises Lied*', Op. 39, No. 1, which flirts with the whole-tone scale

---

[51] For a discussion of all the songs see 'A Lifetime of Lieder Writing', chap. 22, in Norman Del Mar, *Richard Strauss: A Critical Commentary on his Life and Works* (London, 1962–72), iii. Alan Jefferson deals with a selection in *The Lieder of Richard Strauss* (London, 1971).

[52] In accompanying his wife, Pauline de Ahna, to whom he dedicated the four songs of Op. 27, he often permitted himself to vary his own accompaniments—a procedure one can hardly imagine the fastidious Wolf adopting.

[53] Jensen's songs, written mainly in the decade 1860–70, were highly regarded. Some of the poets he used were also drawn upon by Strauss in his early songs: see *Jugendlieder*, in the Complete Edition (London, 1964), iii.

in language of, for Strauss, unusual simplicity; and when, as in the popular 'Morgen', Op. 27, No. 4, words by John Henry Mackay (1893), both instrumental and vocal parts seem conceived as one indivisible whole, we get a masterpiece. A song such as the Rückert 'Die sieben Siegel', Op. 46, No. 3 (1899), has a compactness of design that puts us in mind of his Austrian contemporary, Wolf, but on the whole the two composers were poles apart, and would seem to have had little sympathy for each others' music.

WOLF

The first songs by Hugo Wolf (1860–1903) to be published were *Sechs Lieder für eine Frauenstimme* and *Sechs Gedichte von Scheffel, Mörike, Goethe und Kerner*, selected by himself and printed in 1887. Other early songs were published in 1903[54] as *Lieder aus der Jugendzeit*; then in 1936 four books containing thirty-seven songs were brought out as *Nachgelassene Werke*. The poets set were Heine, Hebbel, Matthisson (the 'Andenken' set by Beethoven and Schubert), Körner, Lenau, Julius Sturm, and others.

In these early songs one catches only now and then a glimpse of the quality of the mature Wolf. Thus in the Lenau 'Nächtliche Wanderung' (1878; pub. 1903) there is a foretaste of the Goethe 'Prometheus', and the Heine 'Wie des Mondes Abbild ziltert' (1880; pub. 1936) not only looks forward to the Keller 'Wie glänzt der helle Mond', but also introduces the syncopated chord figure, mixed duplets and triplets, that occurs frequently as a nocturne motif, often associated with sleeplessness.[55] In the last few bars of the Hebbel 'Knabenton' (1878; pub. 1936) we find his characteristic acid harmonies (bars 29 and 30), and the first few bars of the Körner 'Ständchen' (1877; pub. 1936) show another Wolf mannerism, the persistent use of a one-bar ostinato figure in the accompaniment.[56] But on the whole it is easier to see influences of earlier composers than premonitions of the later Wolf. Schumann stands behind two

[54] Not supervised by Wolf, as by this time he was in an asylum. Frank Walker in *Hugo Wolf: A Bibliography* (London, 1951; 2nd edn., 1968), lists more than 100 early songs (i.e. before 1880), many of which are incomplete and even fragmentary. Eric Sams, in *The Songs of Hugo Wolf* (London, 1961), does not discuss any of these but limits himself to those published by Wolf himself. Mosco Carner, *Hugo Wolf Songs* (London, 1982), is an excellent general survey.

[55] In addition to songs such as 'Alle gingen, Herz, zur ruh' and 'Sonne der Schlummerlosen', see also the Night Watchman's song in *Der Corregidor* (Act IV, Scene i). Sams, *Songs of Hugo Wolf*, p. 7, cites a similar rhythm as associated with 'worship, submission, self-surrender' and (p. 15) connects 'night and sleep' with a 'rocking, lulling motif, usually a shifting semitone in cross rhythm'.

[56] Familiar instances are 'Die du Gott gebarst', from the *Spanisches Liederbuch*; the Goethe 'Frühling übers Jahr' and the Mörike 'Das verlassene Mägdlein'.

Heine songs of 1876 (pub. 1936), 'Mädchen mit dem roten Mündchen' and 'Du bist wie eine Blume'; two other Heine songs 'Spätherbstnebel' and 'Mit schwarzen Segeln' (both 1878; pub. 1936), suggest Schubert. Goethe's 'Gretchen vor dem Andachtsbild der Mater Dolorosa' (1878; pub. 1936), a free recitative with an elaborate accompaniment, bears Wagner's hallmark, as does one of the largest of these early songs, the Lenau 'Herbstenschluss' (1879; pub. 1936), the dark colouring and foreboding tremolandi of which seem clearly influenced by the gloomy Wagnerian orchestration then in vogue (*Götterdämmerung* had its first Viennese performance on 14 February 1879).

Some of the texts Wolf chose suggest that his literary taste at that time lacked discrimination. 'Ein Grab' (1876; pub. 1903), by his friend Paul Peitl, is a sentimental essay in the watered-down macabre German Romanticism such as attracted the boy Schubert; other songs ('Traurige Wege', 'Nächtliche Wanderung') show a similar leaning. The worst lapse of taste is the Hebbel 'Das Kind am Brunnen' (1878; pub. 1903)—a childish story of a nursemaid who sleeps while her charge totters to the brink of a well.

The only contemporary writer drawn upon was the Swiss Gottfried Keller; the 240 songs on which Wolf's fame rests almost entirely were drawn largely from five earlier poets, Mörike, Eichendorff, Goethe, Geibel, and Heyse. They occupied him during two periods of intense activity, the first and most prolific beginning in 1888 with the fifty-three *Gedichte von Eduard Mörike* and ending in 1890–1 with the first part of Paul Heyse's *Italienisches Liederbuch* [Italian Songbook]; this was completed in 1896 after a gap of five years. His last songs, three poems by Michelangelo (translated by Walter Robert-Tornow), were composed in March 1897, just before his mental collapse and removal to an asylum.[57]

In Wolf's hands, as never before, the Lied became a tone poem for piano with vocal commentary. In comparatively few instances can the singer's part be classed as a 'melody' in the Classical sense of a vocal line obviously related to or derived from predictable harmonic movements of diatonic simplicity. (The vocal lines of Brahms, Strauss, and Mahler are extensions of this.) Examples in

---

[57] On the songs in general see Georg Bieri, *Die Lieder von Hugo Wolf* (Berne, 1935); Sams, *Songs of Hugo Wolf*; Frank Walker, *Hugo Wolf*; Carner, *Hugo Wolf Songs*. On the Mörike songs, see Anton Tausche, *Hugo Wolfs Mörike-Lieder in Dichtung, Musik, Vortrag* (Vienna, 1947); Jack M. Stein, 'Poem and Music in Hugo Wolf's Mörike Songs'; *Musical Quarterly*, 53 (1967), 22; Walter Legge, 'Hugo Wolf's Afterthoughts on his Mörike Lieder', *Music Review*, 2 (1941), 211. See also Rita Egger, *Die Deklamationsrhythmik Hugo Wolfs in historischer Sicht* (Vienna, 1963).

Wolf are 'Der Gärtner' and 'Fussreise' (both by Mörike); and each
has what may be described as a traditional piano accompaniment.
Other songs where the piano part, though little more than a support
to the vocal line, contributes essentially to the mood of the song are
'Das verlassene Mägdlein' and 'Auf ein altes Bild' (both Mörike);
the accompaniments of 'Nun wandre, Maria' (from the *Spanisches
Liederbuch*), 'Epiphanias' (Goethe), and 'Der Tambour' (Mörike)
are more pictorial, but still in line with the Classical style of Schubert
or Schumann. By contrast, 'Der Glücksritter' (Eichendorff) or
'Schweig' einmal still' (*Italienisches Liederbuch*)—and many others
could be cited—have accompaniments that are virtually self-sufficient
compositions.

Wolf's method of composition, broadly speaking, was that of
Wagner—a free declamation in the voice part, the piano complementing and amplifying this in a rich and complex texture, often
monothematic and chromatic. Every inflexion of the poet's thought
is underlined in a careful, indeed sometimes pedantic, manner.
Occasionally, as in Schubert, this had led to a certain aimlessness of
form, but far more often Wolf keeps a tight hold on the structure
of the song. This is most clearly to be seen in the piano part, which
often shows a fairly obvious ABA or rondo form. Even the strophic
form is not entirely abandoned; 'Kennst du das Land' for example
is strophic, appropriately so, while in others the strophic skeleton
can be clearly recognized. The harmonic usage is often unorthodox;
there is much in his harmony that is cryptic. In a song such as 'Die
du Gott gebarst', where a motif involving a high degree of dissonance
is relentlessly pursued, he does not, as earlier composers would have
done, graft this on to a familiar chord progression, but uses harmonies
that are as individual and peculiar to him as the vocal line. On the
other hand the exquisite 'Anakreons Grab' (Goethe) is a model of
orthodoxy.

Wolf set a greater variety of poems than any other of the great
Lieder writers. He was especially at home in the realm of whimsy
and humour—an area that Schubert had avoided, where Strauss was
heavy-handed, but which Schumann occasionally attempted with
success, as, for example, in 'Die Kartenlegerin'. The Mörike volume
is particularly rich in examples, with 'Der Tambour', 'Zitronenfalter
im April', 'Storchenbotschaft', 'Elfenlied', 'Nixe Binsefuss'; but the
charming 'Epiphanias' and some from the *Italienisches Liederbuch*,
such as 'Mein Liebster ist so klein' or 'Du denkst mit einem Fädchen
mich zu fangen', must also be mentioned. His love-songs are
unrivalled; his choice of poem is often unconventional. Mörike's

'Erstes Liebeslied eines Mädchens' is not at all what its title might suggest; nor, one imagines, would the same poet's 'Nimmersatte Liebe' have been acceptable in Victorian drawing-rooms.[58] There is a wide variety in the *Spanisches Liederbuch*, from the conventional 'Auf dem grünen Balkon' (a serenade) through the tender 'In dem Schattem meiner Locken', the mocking 'Treibe nur mit Lieben Spott', and the pert 'Mögen alle bösen Zungen', to the passionate 'Da nur Leid und Leidenschaft'. The religious songs range from the quietly devotional ('Auf ein altes Bild') to the almost hysterical outbursts of the *Spanisches Liederbuch*. The first ten songs in this volume constitute almost a Passion cycle, from the opening prayers to the Virgin—the first, 'Nun bin ich dein', full of passionate adoration, the second, 'Die du Gott gebarst', a rapt contemplation of the mystery of the Virgin birth, flecked with anticipation of the agony of the Cross—through the weary trudge to Bethlehem ('Nun wandre, Maria') to the final agony at Golgotha ('Herr, was trägst der Boden hier' and 'Wunden trägst du, mein Geliebter').

The fifty-one Goethe poems look like a conscious challenge to himself. They open with all ten of the poems in *Wilhelm Meister*—songs that have attracted, and defeated, dozens of composers; even Wolf is not wholly successful. The set ends with three monumental poems, 'Prometheus',[59] 'Ganymed', and 'Grenzen der Menschheit', all set magnificently. There are ballads, a form notoriously difficult to handle; in at least one, 'Der Rattenfänger', Wolf succeeds brilliantly. There is the delightful pictorialism of 'Sankt Nepomuks Vorabend' (lights twinkling on the water, bells tinkling) and the hushed adoration of 'Morgengruss'. There are settings of rococo verse, such as 'Der Schäfer' or 'Die Spröde', and numerous songs from the *Westöstlicher Divan* that seem chosen expressly for their problems. Altogether these songs, written in the space of five months, October 1888 to February 1889, at a time when Wolf was at the height of his powers, offer a remarkably comprehensive survey of his range, power, and inventiveness.

CONCLUSION

The development of the Lied during the nineteenth century can be traced along two lines: the ever-increasing weight thrown on the instrumental side, and the constant drive towards more exact and

---

[58] Mörike's strange personality is discussed in Margaret Mare, *Eduard Mörike: The Man and the Poet* (London, 1957).

[59] For an interesting comparison between Schubert's and Wolf's settings see G. Mackworth-Young, 'Goethe's "Prometheus" and its settings by Schubert and Wolf', *Proceedings of the Royal Musical Association*, 78 (1951–2), 54.

expressive declamation by the singer. Even in the eighteenth century the keyboard part was beginning to emerge from its role as a mere support for the voice.[60] In Schumann's hands it became, characteristically, not so much accompaniment as an instrumental commentary, often a complete entity in itself. The increasing technical demands on the performers have already been mentioned, as has the pressure to replace the piano by the variegated colours of the nineteenth-century orchestra.

The pattern for the song with orchestral accompaniment was Berlioz's *Nuits d'été*, most of which were scored by him in 1856.[61] Wagner followed only a little later with one of the Wesendonck songs in 1857-8.[62] At about the same time Liszt was busy scoring some of his own songs,[63] for example the three songs from *Wilhelm Tell*, 'Mignons Lied', and 'Die Loreley'. The pattern continued in the next generation, especially with Wolf, who orchestrated no fewer than twenty-seven, and Strauss, who scored even more.[64]

With the instrumental side assuming more and more responsibility for musical illustration of the words, a logical further development was for the voice to renounce music altogether. The step from recitative to recitation, in other words to melodrama, was taken in 1849 by Schumann in his setting of Hebbel's 'Schön Hedwig', Op. 106, for voice and piano, and, three years later, Hebbel's 'Ballade vom Haideknaben' and 'Die Flüchtlinge', a translation of Shelley's 'The Fugitives', Op. 122, No. 2. There was precedent for this in *Fidelio* and *Der Freischütz*, as well as in Schumann's own *Manfred* (1848-9). It was later taken up by Liszt, Grieg, Strauss, and Humperdinck, and ultimately developed by Schoenberg in his *Sprechstimme*, first used in the *Gurrelieder*, written in 1900-1 on the very threshold of the twentieth century.

---

[60] See the discussion *re* Naumann, Reichardt, and others in Vol. VIII, pp. 537-43.

[61] At least two songs by Berlioz were orchestrated earlier, in 1834—'La Belle Voyageuse' and 'Le Jeune Pâtre breton'. Concert arias such as Beethoven's 'Ah! Perfido!' come in a quite different category.

[62] The other four were scored later by Felix Mottl.

[63] He also orchestrated several Schubert songs including 'Die junge Nonne', 'Gretchen am Spinnrade', 'Erlkönig', and 'Der Doppelgänger'.

[64] Complete lists in Walker, *Hugo Wolf*, and Del Mar, *Richard Strauss*. The Strauss songs are in the *Gesamtausgabe*, iv. Brahms remained true to the concept of song with piano accompaniment, but his *Vier ernste Gesänge* have been orchestrated by other hands.

(*b*) FRANCE

By DAVID TUNLEY

The history of French song in this period is concerned almost exclusively with the transformation of the simple drawing-room romance, inherited from the later years of the previous century, into the sophisticated mélodie. Like most derived forms, the mélodie retained some traits of the earlier one—in particular, an easy flow of lyricism—so that even in the later songs of Fauré and others where a remarkable closeness lies between text and music, the words (with few exceptions) are not set at the expense of the melodic line. If in the romance the weakest composers could only express their feelings through sentimental music of a most obvious kind, the earliest composers of significance who concern us in this chapter, while still retaining the essential simplicity and lyricism of the form, imbued it with real tenderness and passion. As the century wore on these feelings were increasingly heightened through the sensuous beauty of new-found harmonies, creating that atmosphere of mystery tinged with sadness so characteristic of the later mélodie. The extraordinary beauty of this last manifestation of nineteenth century French song should not blind us, however, to its links with the unpretentious romance, nor to the rich repertoire that preceded the melodies of Fauré, Duparc, and Debussy.

THE ROMANCE

The simple romance must be the point of departure for any study of nineteenth-century French song. Hippolyte Monpou (1804–41) established his reputation as a fashionable song-writer in 1830 with his setting of Alfred de Musset's *L'Andalouse*. He also set six poems by Victor Hugo, his setting of 'La Captive', (Ex. 431) making an interesting comparison with that by Berlioz (Ex. 432). Monpou's setting clearly illustrates the typical features of the popular romance at the beginning of the period.

Simplicity was one of the most highly prized attributes of the romance, but, as can be easily gauged from Ex. 431, it was rarely gained without banality in the hands of the many mediocre and justly forgotten composers who cultivated it. Their names need not concern us here, but by the middle of the century they had produced some thousands of such songs. Another feature of the typical romance was its strophic form. To enable the singer to cope with

Ex. 431

(If I were not prisoner, I would love this land, and this plaintive sea, and these fields of maize, and these countless stars; if the spahee's sabre were not glinting in the shadows along the dark wall.)

Ex. 432

Si je n'é-tais cap-ti-

-ve, J'ai-me-rais ce pa-ys,_____ Et cet-te

mer plain-ti - ve._____ Et ces champs de ma-ïs,_____ Et

ces as-tres sans nom-bre, Si, le long du mur som-bre, N'é-

(If I were not prisoner, I would love this land, and this plaintive sea, and these fields of maize, and these countless stars; if the spahee's sabre were not glinting in the shadows along the dark wall.)

the different verses (called *strophes*), published songs usually included an extra copy of the melody line, rewritten (with modifications where necessary) for each verse, and often offering a modest cadenza at the end. Influenced by late eighteenth century Classical style and by the direct tunefulness of *opéra comique*, the vocal line was invariably symmetrical and repetitive in its phrases, which were generally moulded in two- and four-bar lengths. This effectively inhibited a flow of just that kind of melody which might have caught the Romantic fervour of the texts. One of the changes wrought to the romance by gifted song-writers, who brought the form up to the level of real art, lay in eliminating this disparity.

Monpou's position in the history of French song is obviously a very modest one, despite his popularity in his own day. Perhaps his most significant achievement lay in his being one of the first composers to set the poetry of Victor Hugo and Alfred de Musset, and in so doing ally the genre with the new school of French lyric poetry. The emergence of this school of poetry was symptomatic of a new era in French artistic life after the upheavals of the Revolution and the First Empire. During the 1830s Paris regained her position as Europe's cultural capital and, as in the days of the young Mozart, acted as a magnet drawing artists, musicians, and writers to it from all over the world. For example Heine made Paris his home, exerting an influence over French literature. Inspired by the intensely personal and Romantic poetry of Alphonse de Lamartine (1790–1869) and the innovations of Victor Hugo (1802–85) many poets sought a seemingly more spontaneous and intimate expression. 'I am the first', said Lamartine, 'to bring poetry down from Parnassus, and in place of a seven-stringed lyre have given to the so-called muse the very cords of man's heart touched and set in motion by the countless tremblings of the soul and of nature.'[65] The example of Lamartine

[65] Preface to *Méditations poétiques* (1820).

and Hugo was followed by de Musset, Gautier, Delavigne, Béranger, and others, and the existence of a rich corpus of lyric poetry was to be one of the catalysts of French art song, as it had been in the evolution of German Lied. In fact, the Lied itself was to be a catalyst in the evolution of mélodie, for it was during the 1830s that Paris discovered the songs of Schubert. Through collections in translation (largely by Béranger) and through performances by Adolphe Nourrit, a celebrated tenor at the Paris Opéra, Schubert's songs became well known in France, probably the first country outside Germany to appreciate them.

It was inevitable that the romance would be affected by all these developments. Thus alongside the sentimental drawing-room pieces pouring from Parisian publishing houses there appeared a trickle of more serious songs, usually still called romances but in later years more frequently known as mélodies.

ROMANCE AND MÉLODIE

The term 'mélodie' was used as early as 1829 by Berlioz in his *Neuf Mélodies*, Op. 2, a setting of poetry in imitation of texts found in Thomas Moore's *Irish Melodies*. (The third edition of Berlioz's work changed the title to *Irlande*.) Even when 'mélodie' had gained wide currency by the middle of the century, it was still regarded as just one of the many categories of the romance (like chansonette, pastorale, tyrolienne, valse, nocturne, etc.). In describing 'mélodies rêveuses et graves' in his romance-types, Romagnési wrote 'they recall the German *Lied* in their employment of a richer and more complex harmonic accompaniment than other kinds of romance'.[66] That such songs were still regarded in 1846 as something of a curiosity is suggested by his comments:

Pieces of this kind, especially when the seriousness of the subject rises above sentiment, are especially suited to deep voices like the bass, baritone or contralto. They demand fullness of voice, but should not be sung with too much power, as so often happens with singers. The art is not to sing loudly, but to catch the nuances according to the meaning of the words. This kind of romance, because of the monotony of deep voices and serious subjects, may be embellished with ornaments, but of a very subdued kind appropriate to this special kind of music.

In the light of the tenor Nourrit's celebrated performances of Schubert's songs (which were called mélodies from the first French

---

[66] A. Romagnési, *L'Art de chanter les romances, les chansonettes et les nocturnes et géné-ralement toute la musique de salon* (Paris, 1846), 18.

edition in 1831 onwards), it is puzzling to read of Romagnési's suggestion that the mélodie was better suited to lower voices, something not borne out by the repertoire. What is clear, however, is that in the middle of the century mélodie was still regarded as part of the romance tradition. Even in the later repertoire the relationship was still often so close as to defy terminology. Indeed, to understand that special quality which sets French art-song apart from German Lied we must recognize how the romance fertilized the mélodie. Perhaps no clearer contrast between the two national schools of song writing could be found than by comparing, say, Schubert's 'Heidenröslein' with Berlioz's 'La Captive' (see Ex. 432). Typical of the German school, when Schubert sought simplicity the effect was something of a folk-song; the simplicity of Berlioz's song has its roots, not in folk-music but in the romance of the salon. When Lied composers moved to a more serious style, the folk-song element disappeared; in the French school the romance was absorbed. It therefore matters little whether or not composers called their songs romances or mélodies, for the two came naturally together in a characteristically French expression.

THE 1830s

Nineteenth-century French art-song begins with Hector Berlioz (1803–69). After composing a few youthful romances, neither better nor worse than those by Monpou and others (and which he apparently later withdrew from circulation) Berlioz composed his first songs of quality in 1829: *Neuf Mélodies* (*Irlande*). Only five of the nine pieces belong to the category of solo song, the others being composed for duet or choral forces, and of these five solo songs four belong to the romance tradition by virtue of their strophic form and unpretentiousness. Yet in some of them a rather uneasy balance was struck between melodic simplicity and Berlioz's penchant for unusual harmonic progressions. At the vocal entry in 'Adieu Bessy', for example, there is a striking dissonance over a chromatic chord which seems at odds with the obvious and very conventional treatment of the words which give the song its title. (Berlioz must have recognized this, for he toned down the abrasiveness of this bar when he revised the song a few years later.) It was, however, in the final song 'Elégie' (No. 9) that Berlioz took the romance to a new level of passionate intensity, the wide-ranging vocal line being supported by an expansive piano accompaniment and rich harmony. 'Elégie', in anticipating Berlioz's greatest songs, those of *Les Nuits d'été*, broke new ground in the history of French song. Yet one of the most satisfying songs he composed during the 1830s was a setting of Victor Hugo's 'La Captive' in which the elements of the traditional romance were brought together in perfect balance (Ex. 432). Berlioz's song achieves a degree of rhythmic suppleness through its six-bar phrasing at the beginning, while of course its strong, yet straightforward harmonies and fine melodic span combine to give the work a character quite beyond anything found in the typical romance of that time. Berlioz was to return to this poem ten years later and replace his strophic setting with one in which each verse was treated differently and in which the piano gave way to an orchestra. His first setting, however, remains a splendid example of the early romance in the hands of youthful genius.

Only one other composer contributed significantly to the romance during the 1830s: Giacomo Meyerbeer (1791–1864), many of whose forty songs took on the style of a cavatina. Nevertheless some, like 'Rachel à Nephtali' (1834), shed the simple strophic form and assumed an intensely dramatic character, which, like Berlioz's 'Elégie', demanded considerable vocal power and range. Indeed, most of Meyerbeer's songs, despite their tunefulness, require some agility in execution, not least in the delightful 'Chant de mai' (1837) in which the gentle humour of the text is underlined in music of exquisite irony.

THE MID-CENTURY

If Berlioz and Meyerbeer were the only significant composers of the romance and emerging mélodie during the 1830s, the next decade saw the first songs of a group of composers who were to cultivate the genres over a number of years: Saint-Saëns, Reber, Lalo, Louis Niedermeyer, Félicien David, Victor Massé. Some of them were later to contribute songs that are amongst the finest in the repertoire. It was during the 1840s also that Liszt composed his handful of French songs. But above all, it was the decade in which appeared one of the greatest collections of the nineteenth century: Berlioz's *Les Nuits d'été* (1841). This is a setting of six poems by Théophile Gautier. A collection of songs rather than a true song cycle, it expresses love's eagerness ('Villanelle'), its fantasy and rapture ('Le Spectre de la rose', 'L'Île inconnue'), its despair and grief through separation and death ('Sur les lagunes', 'Absence', 'Au cimitière'), in music which had no precedents in French song and which remained unmatched for many years in the fluidity of its vocal line and in its harmonic originality. Although none of the songs is through-composed, there is a sense of organic growth in each (even those with refrain), for in

Les Nuits d'été Berlioz gave full rein to his gift for melodic variation and transformation. This, together with the motivic interplay of the accompaniment, imparts to the music a remarkable sense of architecture, particularly in the version for voice and orchestra which he made in later years.

The innovations in *Les Nuits d'été* were followed neither in Berlioz's later songs nor in any others composed during the 1840s. The simple romance still held favour, and the early songs of Saint-Saëns, Massé, and others were in this unpretentious style. Félicien David's romances are good examples of the genre at this stage, featuring as they do well-shaped melodies and a degree of suppleness in the phrasing without, however, asserting much personality. The cultivation of French song as a serious pursuit of gifted composers had to wait largely for the second half of the century.

The development of those resources that transformed the romance into mélodie was, of course, no guarantee of quality. In his famous 'Le Lac', as well as 'L'Automme' and 'L'Isolement', the Swiss-born Louis Niedermeyer (1802–1861) extended the structure of the romance by setting the opening verses in declamatory style, while his 'Le Poète mourant' is almost a through-composed piece. But neither the extended structure, nor the greater demands of the accompaniment, nor the enriched harmonies of these works can hide their period mannerisms. Indeed, the greater the resources, the greater the risk there always was of bringing to the surface that cloying sentimentality latent in the nineteenth-century Romantic style. Even Gounod and Massenet were not entirely to avoid these pitfalls, although their later songs included some masterpieces. The best songs of the middle years of the century are those in which the composers recognized the 'miniature' nature of the romance and burgeoning mélodie and worked within its limits. A particularly fine example of this is 'L'Aube naît' by Lalo (1823–92), one of six settings of poems by Victor Hugo which the composer published in 1856. Although the three verses are set differently, the refrain-like ending of each provides a strophic element, and with its mellifluous vocal line, and its simple yet finely wrought accompaniment, 'L'Aube naît' and the other songs of this collection take the romance to one of its highest levels of artistry.

Lalo's later songs, especially those of 1879 which he entitled *5 Lieder*—despite the title they are composed to French texts—are in the more expansive style of the true mélodie.

Other composers who brought artistry to the romance were Henri Reber (1807–80), Victor Massé (1822–84), and Ernest Reyer (1823–1909), who despite his long life wrote most of his music before the age of 40. While these composers also wrote quite ambitious songs, their talents seemed best suited to the simpler style. One indication of the seriousness with which they approached song writing can be seen in the care taken over the accompaniment. Even in the simplest songs the piano writing is finely polished, particularly in those by Reber and Massé who were clearly influenced by the example of German Lied as far as the accompaniment was concerned. The piano part of Reber's 'Au bord d'un ruisseau', with its figuration suggestive of rippling water, is just as indebted to Schubert's example as is his 'A un passant', which, through its relentless rhythmic motif, evokes the popular Romantic image of the 'wanderer'.

NEW DIRECTIONS

Of the composers whose early songs became widely known in the middle years of the century the most important was Camille Saint-Saëns (1835–1921) who wrote more than a hundred, half before 1890. Songs were among the earliest works of this precocious composer, his first group having been written at the age of 6. These were merely in the style of the fashionable drawing-room romance. At the age of 20 he produced a group of separately published mélodies that marked a new direction in French song. One of these was 'La Cloche' (1855). Hugo's poem, likening the poet's soul to a bell hanging solitary in its vault, inspired from Saint-Saëns a song of great grandeur and passion, notable for its complex harmonies and colourful sonorities. Sheer beauty of sound was to fascinate French song writers more and more, and this predilection can be traced to some of Saint-Saëns's songs written in his twenties. For example, later French fondness for the effect created by doubling treble with bass (as in Fauré's 'La Fée aux chansons') is seen as early as 1857 in Saint-Saëns's 'La Mort d'Ophélie'. The opening of another song of the same period, 'L'Attente' (Ex. 433), foreshadows by some twenty years the opening of Duparc's 'L'Invitation au voyage' (Ex. 434).

From the same period comes his 'Extase'. In this remarkable song,

Ex. 433

Ex. 434

perhaps to match Hugo's constant repetition of the word 'puisque' in the first half of the poem, Saint-Saëns sounds the same low note at the beginning of every bar, forcing him to explore chordal relationships that look ahead to later practice in the mélodie. Such harmonic experiments, together with rhythmic ones like the 7/4 metre frequently used in 'La Solitaire' (*Mélodies persanes*, 1870), suggest that Saint-Saëns regarded song writing as a challenging medium, and his works in this genre deserve to be far better known than they are.

With the songs of Georges Bizet (1838–75) there also enters into the emerging mélodie considerable exploitation of colourful harmony. Most of his songs were written during the 1860s, even though their publication was often considerably later. The element of the exotic is found frequently in his songs, such as 'Le Matin', which, with its bolero rhythm and piquant dissonances is like an early sketch for *Carmen*. Composers from Monpou onwards had been drawn to the exotic—'L'Andalouse' and 'La Captive' have already been mentioned—but, except for Berlioz, Bizet seems to have been the first to have gone beyond conventional harmonic practice to evoke it successfully. It is not evident in all his songs, of course—his *Feuilles d'album* (1860), for example, is a collection of six conventional (but charming) romances—but works like 'N'oublions pas' with its unusual chord progressions, and 'Chant d'avril' with its impressionistic accompaniment, are amongst those which reveal Bizet's originality and place in the history of French song.

If Bizet wrote most of his songs during a relatively short period of his life, those of Charles Gounod (1818–93) and Jules Massenet (1842–1912) span both their long careers. In a survey as brief as this the songs of Gounod and Massenet are best treated together, for in many ways they share similar characteristics. The products of composers whose main medium was opera, the songs of Gounod and Massenet reveal, not surprisingly, a true understanding of the voice, and hence are invariably effective as vocal pieces. On the other

hand both possessed a facile technique that was too often turned in
the direction of drawing-room sentimentality and archness.

The songs of Massenet and Gounod can be seen as a culminating
point in the development of nineteenth-century French song before
it moved into its final—and very individual—stage in the hands of
Fauré, Duparc, and Debussy, and few song-writers in France escaped
the influence of their style. Massenet's 'À Mignonne' (Ex. 435), a
song in the romance tradition, shows this style at its most charming.

A move towards that evocative world which Fauré, Duparc, and
Debussy were to make peculiarly their own is found in the songs of
Alexis de Castillon (1838–73), whose untimely death cut short one
of France's most promising musical talents. He wrote six songs—
settings of words by one of Fauré's favourite poets, Armande

Ex. 435

(For whom will it be, Mignonne, the wavy crown of your chestnut-brown hair? For whom will be your smile,
your eyes where I love to gaze, your little roguish feet?)

Ex. 436

(Who knows where flows the blood from our veins? What futile things does our love pursue! Lips of full-blown flowers, who knows where, in the night, the wind carries your sweet breath?)

Sylvestre—composed during the last five years of his life. In 'Sonnet mélancolique' (Ex. 436) one senses those qualities that Baudelaire believed to be the attributes of the Beautiful: 'something passionate and sad, something a little vague . . . mystery and regret.'

Of his six songs 'Renouveau' is perhaps the one that best reveals the composer's gift for evoking the mood of passionate grief so poignantly through melodic and harmonic suggestion. It is certainly not unworthy of the songs which it so remarkably foreshadowed.

THE PERFECTION OF MÉLODIE

The closing decades of the nineteenth century saw songs by Fauré, Duparc, and Debussy. With them French mélodie entered its final stage of development and, in popular estimation, achieved its most characteristic voice. The lyrical element in their mature songs, while ever present, was gradually transformed, the once clear lines of melody more sensitively moulded to the nuances of the text, more subtly blended into the richly suggestive harmonies of the piano part, together creating in each song a tiny world of mystery, enchantment, sadness, and passionate longing, particularly in those of Fauré and Debussy. So palpable the atmosphere, and so strong the impression of shifting scenes bathed in Romantic half-light, that one might be tempted to think of each song as part of a *mise-en-scène*, were it not that the intensely personal and intimate nature of most of the songs seems to remove all associations with opera or stage.

Each of these composers began his song-writing career with romances strongly influenced by Gounod and Massenet. The songs of Gabriel Fauré (1845-1924) in particular illustrate the transformation of the conventional romance into mélodie of a highly individual kind. His first song was 'Le Papillon et la fleur' (1861) to a poem by Victor Hugo which had also been set some twenty years earlier by Reber. Both settings were in the simple romance style, as were the many charming songs that Fauré was to compose during the next fifteen years. During this period there was only the occasional hint of the originality to come. In 1878 appeared 'Après un rêve', in which Fauré's gift for melody began to be matched by his genius for harmony. Yet it was only a beginning, for the richness of 'Après un rêve' was largely the result of chromatic embellishment of traditional devices (such as the cycle of fifths at the opening) rather than innovation. The song also reveals its Italianate inspiration (it can be sung either in the original, anonymous Italian text or—as is invariably the case—in Bussine's French translation) through its clear distinction of vocal line and throbbing chordal accompaniment. More characteristic of Fauré's maturer style is 'L'Automne', written

Ex. 437

ché - e,   Pé - rit l'a - mour

La   main   qui t'a   tou-

ché - e   Fuit   ma   main   sans re - tour.

(The hand which has touched you flees my hand forever. Like the mown flower, love withers.)

in the same year but published in 1880. Here the vocal line and the wonderfully evocative piano accompaniment merge in a song that conveys the grief of the young poet who sees in autumn the symbol of his fading youth. His most original song of this period, however, is 'Fleur jetée' (Ex. 437), in which the voice soars above harmonies of extraordinary power: typical of Fauré's mature harmonic style, the originality lies not in the creation of new chords but in new relationships.

During the 1880s Fauré composed those songs which are amongst his most frequently performed: 'Notre amour', 'Claire de lune', 'Toujours', 'Les Roses d'Ispahan'. Yet perhaps his finest songs are the more austere examples of his art composed after 1890.[67]

Fauré's output of 105 songs stands in marked contrast to the small number composed by Henri Duparc (1848-1933), whose reputation rests upon thirteen songs composed between 1868 and 1884. Although invariably linked with Fauré and Debussy in the history of French song, Duparc's style has its own individuality. Only one song might be mistaken for a Fauré setting—'L'Invitation au voyage'. Duparc's harmony, for all its colour and sometimes unusual progressions, lies far closer to the central European tradition than does Fauré's, being influenced by Wagner (among others), whom Duparc knew personally. What links Duparc's songs closely to the French tradition is the suaveness of the vocal line, evident as much in his extrovert and pictorially explicit ballad songs ('Le Manoir de Rosemonde', 'La Vague et la cloche') as in his early romance-inspired pieces ('Chanson triste', 'Soupir'). This, together with heightened sensitivity towards poetry and the gift for evoking atmosphere and mood, links him to both Fauré and Debussy.

Songs were among the earliest significant compositions by Claude Debussy (1862-1918). Even though his so-called 'impressionist period' came after 1890, in the fifty songs (not all of them published) which he composed up to that date can be traced the evolution of his highly personal style. Working through the conventional romance form in such songs as 'Beau soir', 'Fleur des blés', and 'Paysage sentimentale', he struck a more individual note in 'Mandoline' by Verlaine,[68] whose poetry he began setting in 1882 and who was to inspire some of his finest songs. The best Verlaine settings before 1890 were those which, having been published separately, were put together in a collection of six songs first called *Ariettes, paysage*

---

[67] See Vol. X, pp. 25-9 and 232.
[68] See the quotation in Vol. X, p. 89.

belges et aquarelles and then (in their 1903 edition) *Ariettes oubliées*. Right from the opening bars of the first song of the collection, 'C'est l'extase' (Ex. 438) (originally published in 1887), we recognize those characteristics which were to form the basis of his art: chains of

Ex. 438

(It is languid ecstasy. It is love's weariness. It is the shiver of the woods at the breezes' embrace. It is, in the grey foliage, the choir of tiny voices. O the thin, cold murmur, it warbles and whispers like a gentle cry until the restless grass withers.)

chords recalling the old medieval techniques of *organum* and dissonant rich clusters of sevenths and ninths which, like other chords, were used by Debussy to establish relationships which defied traditional harmonic practice and conjured up a new world of sound and sensation.

Yet what are we to make of the vocal line? Was it, too, so revolutionary in concept that all links with mélodie were severed? The answer is that, while Debussy's melodic line may indeed spring from the harmonies, it is shaped in a way that reveals a true lyrical impulse, and in its gentle undulations is characteristically French. In fact, Debussy was far freer to give shape to his melodies unhampered as they were by the restrictions of harmonic rhythm and sequence which are so closely associated with traditional tonal procedures. Indeed *shape* is the essence of lyricism: phrases follow one another in such a way that one gives meaning to another, the whole melody unfolding in a series of spans that reach out to notes as though seeking a goal before falling back in repose. This Debussy's songs do to perfection, even if on the surface they sometimes, through repeated notes, appear to be almost recitative-like. 'C'est l'extase' is a good example. The third phrase at the words 'C'est tous les frissons des bois' at first glance might give the impression that melody has given way to recitative. As Ex. 439 illustrates, the repeated notes hide in notation what in performance comes through as a superbly

Ex. 439

(It is the shiver of the woods at the breezes' embrace. It is, in the grey foliage, the choir of tiny voices.
O the thin, cold murmur, which warbles and whispers like a gentle cry until the restless grass withers.)

shaped flight of lyricism. In the context of the whole song this
particular span is reaching out for the later climax on top A.

This element of lyricism alone links the *Ariettes oubliées* to the
tradition of mélodie, and if, in the *Cinq poèmes de Baudelaire* (1890),
Debussy produced (as a result of the Wagnerian influence in Paris
at the time) a rather over-rich and convoluted set of songs, it was
the more limpid and clearer style of the *Ariettes oubliées* which the
composer took up in his songs after 1890.[69]

THE LAST DECADE

In a brief survey it is impossible to discuss all the composers who,
while contributing to the repertoire of romance and mélodie, did not
alter the course of its development. Delibes, Chausson, and Franck
were such composers. One composer, however, must be singled out—
Emmanuel Chabrier (1841–94) some of whose songs are unique in
the nineteenth century for their wit and satirical humour. Perhaps
only Meyerbeer's 'Chant de mai' mentioned earlier shares these
qualities, although Chabrier went very much further in this direction.
Songs such as 'Villanelle des petits canards', 'Ballade des gros
dindons', and 'Pastorale des cochons roses' (from the *6 Mélodies* of
1890) anticipated by some years the twentieth-century reaction
against Romantic song.

For much of the nineteenth century, serious song composition in
France held a position vastly inferior to that of opera, yet the best
songs of the repertoire now have a far better chance of survival
than the many *grand opéras* and *opéras comiques* that once reigned
supreme.

[69] On these, see Vol. X, particularly p. 94.

(c) RUSSIA

By EDWARD GARDEN

In the 1830s the majority of solo songs composed in Russia were still of the lyrical Italo-French 'abstract' romance type, with the melody and accompaniment not particularly underlining the meaning of the text, rather than of the 'expressive' German type where the opposite is the case. The so-called 'Russian songs' were of this type too, often settings of folk or pseudo-folk texts by the likes of Kol'tsov, in which the melody, usually in the minor mode, might or might not be reminiscent of folk-song. Many such songs were written by Gurilyov and Varlamov, whose best-known song, a setting of Tsïganov's 'Krasnïy sarafan' [The Red Sarafan], is still sung in Russia today.[70] Glinka and Dargomïzhsky also wrote a number of 'Russian songs' such as the latter's 'Bez uma, bez razuma' [At One's Wits End] to words by Kol'tsov, set in G minor with a very simple stereotyped accompaniment and conventional cadences. More typical of later examples is the same composer's 'Okh, tikh, tikh, tikh, tikh, ti!' (1852) with its pseudo-folklike piano introduction. Other examples are: Balakirev's 'Pesnya razboynika' [Brigand's Song] and 'Mne li, molodtsu razudalomu' [I'm a Fine Fellow], both settings of Kol'tsov written in 1858; Rimsky-Korsakov's setting of Pleshcheev's 'Noch'' [Night] (1868), which has a piano refrain of the 'Russian song' type but then branches out into a more Romantic lyricism; Tchaikovsky's setting of Mey's 'Kak naladili: Durak' [As they kept on saying: Fool] (1875); Borodin's 'U lyudey-to v domu' [Those Folk] (Nekrasov, 1882); and, as late as 1903, Balakirev still showed himself to be addicted to the genre in the song 'Zapevka' [Prologue] (Mey). In all these cases the folk-song imitations, such as they are, are for the drawing-room in the time-honoured salon tradition. They are totally unlike Balakirev's actual folk-song harmonizations *Sbornik russkikh narodnïkh pesen* [Collection of Russian Folk-songs] (1886),[71] which probe the songs to their very depths and give a feeling of authenticity. The art-song of the pseudo-Russian type was in a quite different tradition, not undistinguished in its own way.

---

[70] For instance, it is the first song in a miscellaneous collection, *Romansï russkikh kompozitorov*, ed. V. Zharov (Moscow, 1979).
[71] Published, together with his later collection, in *M. Balakirev: Russkie narodnïe pesni*, ed. E. V. Gippius (Moscow, 1957).

By far the best song-writer amongst Glinka's older contemporaries was Aleksandr Alyab'ev (1797–1851). In 'Lyubovnik rozï, solovey' [Lover of the Rose, the Nightingale] he initiated in song the orientalism later to be exploited so successfully by Balakirev and Rimsky-Korsakov in some of their best songs. But the orientalism in this song is much tamer than the more rugged Circassian element to be found both in his setting of Lermontov's 'Mnogo dev u nas v gorakh' [We have Many Girls in the Mountains] with its augmented seconds and also in other similar songs. Moreover, he anticipated Dargomïzhsky in certain realistic peasant songs, though Alyab'ev's songs in this vein cannot match the best of Dargomïzhsky's, far less Mussorgsky's.

One other important type of song to be exploited by later composers was the dramatic ballad. Aleksey Verstovsky (1799–1862), better known for his operas, wrote a number of ballads extended enough to allow space for development of characterization, changes of key and tempo, and variation of piano accompaniment figures. Besides his setting of Pushkin's 'Chornaya shal'' [The Black Shawl], no less than 219 bars in length, mention must be made of the highly dramatic 'Tri pesni skal'da' (Zhukovsky, after Uhland's 'Die drei Lieder'), the march-like opening of which anticipates many later and more distinguished Russian ballads. His version of the same poet's 'Nochnoy smotr' [Midnight Review] was soon to be eclipsed by Glinka's setting of the text.

GLINKA AND DARGOMÏZHSKY

Though Mikhail Glinka (1804–59) wrote a handful of fine songs, he contributed little to the development of the genre. Most of his songs are at best delicately refined, at worst vapidly superficial if seldom mawkishly sentimental. The one song which is none of these things, 'Nochnoy smotr', stands on its own as a dramatic ballad, composed in one day and immediately sung to Zhukovsky and Pushkin; the subject is the ghost of a general, rising from his grave and surveying his spectral army, and the song shows real power, providing a prototype for such songs as Mussorgsky's 'Polkovodets' [The Field Marshal] from *Pesni i plyaski smerti* [Songs and Dances of Death]. It was written in 1836 shortly before the completion of the opera *Zhizn' za Tsarya* [A Life for the Tsar], and Glinka's other best songs were composed between then and 1840. Two excellent examples of charming lyricism are 'Severnaya zvezda' [North Star], based on the slow 'wedding song' later to be used in *Kamarinskaya*, and 'V krovi gorit' [Fire of Longing in my Blood], the latter originally (in 1838) set to words by Aleksandr Rimsky-Korsakov but with Pushkin verses substituted in 1839. It is a delightful valse, foreshadowing the *Valse-Fantasie* for piano written in the same year, but obviously there is no close correlation between words and music.

Glinka's most sustained effort in the composition of songs resulted in a collection of twelve (not a cycle) published in 1840 with the title *Proshchanie s Peterburgom* [Farewell to Petersburg]. The poems, by his friend Kukol'nik, are not of any great merit, and the music made more impression on Glinka's successors than it can do on us in the twentieth century. The free decorative arrangement for piano solo of 'Zhavoronok' [The lark] written by Balakirev in the early 1860s greatly improves upon the refinedly nostalgic but rather pallid original, in the 'Russian song' tradition. A cradle song, a barcarolle and a 'Hebrew song' were all to have some influence on Balakirev, if only in his choice of the same titles. But none of the songs in the group can compare with 'Gde nasha roza?' [Where is our Rose?], his finest setting of a poem by Pushkin, written three years earlier in 1837. This perfect gem of only seventeen bars, ten in 5/4 followed by seven in 3/4, beautifully matches the tender regret of the poem.[72] Such exquisite laconism was not to reappear until Borodin's song 'Fal'shivaya nota' [The False Note] (1868), which also happens to be exactly seventeen bars long. (As it is a setting of Borodin's own words, this may well have been deliberately contrived.) In Glinka's song the singer's even-flowing crotchets in 5/4 may have provided the starting-point for Mussorgsky's 'Svetik Savishna' [Darling Savishna], in which a similar technique is used for very different ends. But, unlike so many of Glinka's songs, it is a masterpiece in its own right, regardless of its influence on the next generation of song-writers.

Some of the songs of Aleksandr Dargomïzhsky (1813–69) were altogether more innovatory than Glinka's, but, like his, many of the younger man's were equally weak lyrical romances. Although there were some earlier hints of dramatic characterization in, amongst other songs, 'Mel'nik' [The Miller] (1851), a song about a drunken miller scolded by his wife when he comes home very late, it was not in the main until after Serov had written, in a review of Dargomïzhsky's opera *Rusalka* [The Water-nymph] (1856), of the composer's '*truth* of musical expression . . .' (Serov's italics)[73] that Dargomïzhsky consistently aimed for the musical truth which was so to impress Mussorgsky and his friends. Serov wrote that it was

---

[72] The whole of 'Gde nasha roza?' is given in David Brown, *Mikhail Glinka: A Biographical and Critical Study* (London, 1974), 149.
[73] Serov, *Izbrannïe stat'i*, i (Moscow, 1950), 323.

where the requirements of effectiveness coincide with 'musical truth' that Dargomïzhsky's triumph was complete, and in the following year Dargomïzhsky himself wrote his often-quoted letter[74] to the singer Lyubov' Karmalina, in which he emphasized that he wanted the sound to express the word directly. It thus seems to have been Serov who was the first publicly to pinpoint the importance of this aspect of Dargomïzhsky's work, which up till then even the composer himself had not appreciated, valuing just as highly more derivative lyrical characteristics of his style.

It is not surprising, therefore, that it was only after this that Dargomïzhsky's best songs were to appear. In the dramatic song or ballad tradition he produced two masterpieces: 'Starïy kapral' [The Old Corporal] (1857–8), set to Kurochkin's translation of a poem by Béranger, and 'Paladin' (1859), a setting of a poem by Zhukovsky (Ex. 440). The old corporal is condemned to death for insulting a young officer. At the end of each verse the unwilling squad of soldiers, as they march the old campaigner to his execution, are ordered (and the pace quickens): 'In step, lads, one! two! ... don't

Ex. 440

(the corpse was engulfed by the deep river!)

[74] *Aleksandr Sergeevich Dargomïzhskiy (1813–1869): Avtobiografiya, pis'ma, vospominaniya sovremennikov*, ed. Nikolay Fyodorovich Findeisen (Peterburg, 1921), 55, letter of 9 Dec. 1857. See Richard Taruskin, *Opera and Drama in Russia as Preached and Practiced in the 1860s* (Ann Arbor, 1981), 253 and 258.

complain, get in line, one! two!' This simple but striking song is less adventurous than 'Paladin' as far as the harmonies are concerned. Subtitled 'ballad', the poem tells of a knight (paladin) killed by his faithless servant, who throws the corpse down into a deep river, dons the knight's armour, and mounts his horse; but, as they ride off, it refuses to go over the bridge, rears up, and throws itself and its rider down the bank into the river, in which, weighed down by the heavy armour, the murderer sinks and drowns. Near the opening of the song Dargomïzhsky's word-painting as the knight's corpse is engulfed by the river is exceptionally telling (Ex. 440). The reiterated A in the right hand of the accompaniment and the empirical harmonies in the left which sinks with the body, as it were, are just the kind of treatment which might have been given by Mussorgsky at the height of his powers.

It was Dargomïzhsky, more than any other composer before Mussorgsky, who developed the satirical song. 'Chervyak' [The Worm] (1858), another translation of Béranger by Kurochkin, is subtitled 'comic song'. The arioso vocal line carries the words with consummate art, and the plain accompaniment has the effect of aiding the singer to present the grovelling of the flatterer, who is a mere worm in comparison with the Count whose attention he wishes to attract. 'Titulyarnïy sovetnik' [The Titular Councillor] (1859),[75] telling of a councillor who endeavours to court a general's daughter far above him in the social scale, is similarly simple and effective. In neither of these songs does Dargomïzhsky reveal the exceptional character Mussorgsky was to show, but they provide an excellent vehicle for a good singer to make of them what he will.

BALAKIREV AND CUI

The twenty early songs of Mily Balakirev (1837–1910) were written between 1858 and 1864, and Stellovsky had published them all by 1865. His next collection was not composed until the mid-1890s and a further collection appeared a decade or so after that. While there are some distinguished examples in these later collections, they lack the creative intensity evident in the early songs, which, however, do not break new ground in the manner of his overtures. Nevertheless, in the early set his contribution to existing types of song is very important. He was particularly fond of a number of Glinka's romances and examples of this kind of song include 'Pridi ko mne' [Come to me], No. 10 (1858), the most popular of the group during

---

[75] Printed complete in Gerald R. Seaman, *History of Russian Music*, i (Oxford, 1967), 234–5.

Balakirev's lifetime, and 'Vzoshol na nebo mesyats yasnïy' [The Bright Moon], No. 5 (1858), an engaging song in D flat in which the vocal line and accompaniment are perfectly wedded, as is the case also in the beautiful 'Kolïbel'naya pesnya' [Cradle Song], No. 4 (1858), similar in type to Glinka's cradle song in *Proshchanie s Peterburgom*.

Balakirev's three songs with oriental overtones are all masterpieces, far greater than their prototypes in Alyab'ev, Glinka, and Dargomïzhsky,[76] not to mention Anton Rubinstein and his quite appropriate settings of twelve poems by the Persian poet Mirza-Shafi (1854).[77] The earliest of this type is 'Pesnya Selima' [Song of Selim], No. 11 (1858), Balakirev's first setting of his favourite poet, the vividly Romantic Lermontov. It is not so much the augmented second between the third and fourth degrees of the scale in the piano refrain as the economical beauty of the vocal line which gives the song its feeling of restrained power. The other Lermontov setting, 'Pesnya zolotoy rïbki' [Song of the Golden Fish], No. 16 (1860), is a delicate and gentle siren's song in which the fresh, passionately frigid enchantment of Lermontov's words, of the mermaid enticing her victim to the soft sea-bed where the years and centuries will glide past in marvellous dreams, is perfectly caught in the music; the clean, cool chromaticism of the harmony is an enchantment in itself. The frail, brittle beauty of this song was much admired by the other members of Balakirev's circle, and by Tchaikovsky. 'Gruzinskaya pesnya' [Song of Georgia], No. 19 (1863), to words by Pushkin, was written as a result of Balakirev's visits to the Caucasus in 1862 and 1863. It is the first attempt of any of his circle at Caucasian orientalism, and Balakirev's first-hand association with it results in a song of exceptional merit with a gorgeously eastern accompaniment in which the piano introduction and postlude consist of delicate quasi-oriental roulades over a double pedal of tonic and dominant.

Although the sinuous right-hand piano parts which occur there are matched in the vocal line, 'Gruzinskaya pesnya' is a good example of the increasing importance of Balakirev's piano parts, a feature of the songs of Balakirev's circle, the so-called *kuchka*, including those of César Cui (1835-1918), Franco-Lithuanian by parentage. But

---

[76] Dargomïzhsky's 'Vostochnïy romans' [Eastern Romance], which includes a curious whole-tone figure in the left hand of the short piano introduction and postlude, was much admired by Balakirev. The introduction is quoted in Gerald Abraham's chapter on Russian song in Denis Stevens (ed.), *A History of Song* (London, 1960), 355; repr. in his *Essays on Russian and East European Music* (Oxford, 1985), 17.

[77] Originally published in a German translation by F. Bodenstedt, but subsequently translated from this into Russian by Tchaikovsky, and published in this version in 1870.

Cui's songs cannot equal Balakirev's in the quality of their inspiration. He was considerably influenced by Dargomïzhsky. His 'Lyubov' mertvetsa' [A Dead Man's Love], Op. 5, No. 2 (1859), is indebted to 'Paladin', for example. Like Dargomïzhsky, too, he often makes use of arioso and considered correct declamation to be very important, though, in spite of this, his declamation is sometimes faulty. He set a number of poems by Heine in the Russian translation of Mikhaylov, as did all Balakirev's circle, perhaps as a result of their admiration for Schumann's *Lieder*, which influenced them all. One of Cui's earliest songs, dating from 1858, is a setting of a translation of Heine's 'Aus meinen Tränen' (translated as 'Iz slyoz moikh'). Indeed, Balakirev himself was the only one of the *kuchka not* to set this poem; their versions are all inferior to Schumann's delicate morsel in the *Dichterliebe* cycle where its place (as No. 2) is vital. (With the exception of Mussorgsky, none of the *kuchka* wrote songs in cycles.)

In spite of some beautifully written piano parts, Cui's overriding fault is that his powers of invention are cliché-ridden in the extreme, embodying much of what was worst in the romance tradition and of what was most pallid in the Dargomïzhsky style. But an occasional song, such as the 'epic fragment' 'Menisk', Op. 7, No. 4 (1868), does rise above the commonplace, and one very late song is an epigrammatic masterpiece, on a par with Glinka's 'Gde nasha roza?'. This is Cui's masterly setting of Pushkin's 'Tsarskosel'skaya statuya' [The Statue at Tsarskoe Selo] (1899).

RIMSKY-KORSAKOV

With the exception of a 'Barcarolle' composed before he met Balakirev, all the early songs of Nikolay Rimsky-Korsakov (1844–1908) were composed while he was under the influence of Balakirev's songs. That is not to say that they contain nothing original—on the contrary, Rimsky-Korsakov reveals how extensive was the seam of gold discovered by Balakirev in the Glinka–Dargomïzhsky mine; having mined the ore, he himself decorated it prodigiously, showing it in ever-changing colours. But he did not endeavour to dig deeper to discover new seams of his own, as Borodin and Mussorgsky did.

Rimsky-Korsakov's best songs are to be found among the thirty-three composed between 1865 and 1870. The greater sophistication and more obviously 'vocal' approach of the later songs, such as the Op. 39, Op. 43, and Op. 46 settings of the Parnassian poet A. K. Tolstoy, whose works typified the 'art for art's sake' antithesis of the realist writers and poets with a social message, cannot compensate for their lack of youthful freshness and, more importantly, the lack in many of them of the crucial spark of creative energy so apparent in the earlier period.

Balakirev's quasi-oriental vein is explored in a number of songs. 'Plenivshis' rozoy, solovey' [Enslaved by the Rose, the Nightingale], Op. 2, No. 2 (1866), provides an example in which almost all the interest is in the exotic piano accompaniment and the voice has only—often unaccompanied—arioso. While oriental arabesques in 'V tyomnoy roshche zamolk solovey' [In the Dark Grove the Nightingale is Silent], Op. 4, No. 3 (1866), are still allotted to the piano, the vocal line is integrated much more satisfactorily into the overall texture. A setting of Lermontov's 'Kak nebesa, tvoy vzor blistayet' [Thy Glance is Radiant as the Heavens], Op. 7, No. 4 (1867), is very heavily indebted to Balakirev's 'Gruzinskaya pesnya'. There are no less than six settings of Mikhaylov's translations of poems by Heine. One of these, 'El' i pal'ma' [The Fir and the Palm], Op. 3, No. 1 (1866), also introduces oriental roulades at the point where the fir, in the northern wasteland under ice and snow, dreams of a palm tree 'in a far eastern land'; Rimsky-Korsakov revised this song in 1888 introducing, among other things, more elaborate arabesques.

The finest songs are not of the oriental type. The most beautiful of the songs from Op. 2 is No. 3, a Cradle Song in D flat major even more gently lyrical and beguiling than Balakirev's. It contains a quirk of harmony of which Balakirev was very fond at the time, a minor chord of the (flat) leading note used in a tonic context. Another excellent song is the first to be dedicated to Balakirev, 'Yuzhnaya noch'' [Southern Night], Op. 3, No. 2, which Mussorgsky considered to be Rimsky-Korsakov's best song. But the very next one, a magnificent setting of Lermontov's 'Nochevala tuchka zolotaya' [The Golden Cloud has Slept], Op. 3, No. 3, has an even stronger claim to this accolade. Its sombre opening (Ex. 441) owes

Ex. 441

(The golden cloud has slept)

something to the last of Balakirev's folk-song harmonizations of 1866, his arrangement of 'Ey, ukhnem!' [Song of the Volga Hauliers], No. 40, employing as it does gruff low thirds. The piano figure at the end of the song, Ex. 442, includes a folklike final fall from the unsharpened leading-note to the dominant and may well have influenced the close of Varlaam's drunken song in Act I, Scene ii, of *Boris Godunov*. Also written at this time was a fine declamatory setting of Pushkin's 'Na kholmakh Gruzii' [On the Hills of Georgia], Op. 3, No. 4.

Two of the songs written in 1870 are of a very high standard. One was dedicated to his future wife's sister, Alexandra Purgold, a good singer. 'Tayna' [The Secret], Op. 8, No. 3, imaginatively starts with four beautifully tender, halting, tonally equivocal bars before unexpectedly settling on a chord of C major, which turns out to be the tonic (Ex. 443). The other, 'V tsarstvo rozï i vina' [Into the Kingdom of Roses and Wine], Op. 8, No. 5, was dedicated to Borodin's wife. Fet's poem inspired the composer to waft his singer and audience into a fantastic land, a 'kingdom of dreams', with a delicately fragrant accompaniment and sensitive vocal writing far removed from the often harsh world of Mussorgskian reality.

TCHAIKOVSKY

In the vast majority of his songs, from the six in Op. 6, written at the end of 1869, to the six of Op. 73, written in the last year of his life, 1893, Pyotr Tchaikovsky (1840–93) reveals grave limitations as a song-writer. His setting of words was not only often inappropriate from the declamatory point of view, words or sometimes even phrases of the poems being altered to suit the musical needs, but his depiction of mood tended to be static, with only one mood for the whole song, regardless of any change required by the words. These are definite

Ex. 443

(when [you kissed] me on the lips and eyes)

failings in songs, many of which are of the 'expressive romance' type, and one might almost say that Tchaikovsky was all too prone to write a kind of stereotyped romance with the emotional content drawn from the appropriate pigeon-hole. The form is often ternary (as in 'Ni slova, o moy drug' [Not a Word, O my Friend], Op. 6, No. 2, where the opening verse is even repeated at the end to allow a ternary structure), with a piano prelude which recurs at the end, frequently repeated note-for-note (as in the same song). These conventional salon romances are a far cry from the best early romances of Balakirev and Rimsky-Korsakov, to leave out of account altogether the magnificent realistic songs of Mussorgsky. As was not the case with much of his orchestral and other music, including some excellent folk-song arrangements which owe much to Balakirev's 1866 collection, the bulk of these romances were quite out of tune with the Russian art of the period, mere escapist trifles composed, admittedly, by a man whose professional competence was beyond dispute. Nevertheless, they were the kind of songs which sold well, as for example the last from Op. 6, a setting of Mey's translation of Goethe's 'Nur wer die Sehnsucht kennt', 'Net, tol'ko tot, kto znal' [None but the Lonely Heart], which became a popular favourite and has remained so ever since. This is certainly one of the best of Tchaikovsky's songs of the romance type. It reveals, from the delicately drooping downward leap of a seventh onwards, the kind of tenderness which was an essential ingredient of the opera *Eugene Onegin*. The piano prelude is not repeated at the end and the sad mood of the poem is poignantly encapsulated in the music. The same kind of delicate poignancy occurs at the first entry of the voice in 'Zachem?' [Why did I dream of you?], Op. 28, No. 3, with its wayward chromatic descent, like a falling leaf in autumn. Tchaikovsky may have been influenced by the 'fate' motif in *Carmen*, the score of which he had just received before composing this song. But it does not live up to the expectations aroused by its opening. It is very much in the typical mould: the first stanza is repeated at the end, and the piano prelude and postlude are identical, to make a ternary form. He attempted only once to employ a quasi-oriental vein, in 'Kanareyka' [The Canary], Op. 25, No. 4. But formula-type augmented seconds and triplet twiddles are not enough to weave a magic spell in the manner of the Petersburg composers. The sentiments are only skin deep.

Besides 'Net, tol'ko tot, kto znal', good songs of the romance type include the first four of Op. 38 (1878), all expressive settings, composed in the wake of *Eugene Onegin*, of poems by A. K. Tolstoy, and some of the songs in Op. 73, such as No. 6, 'Snova, kak prezhde, odin' [Again, as before, Alone]. And one of the *16 Pesen dlya detey* [Songs for Children], 'Legenda' [The Christ-child had a Garden], Op. 54, No. 5 (1883), is a gem. There are also one or two powerful dramatic songs. The best known is another setting of A. K. Tolstoy, the operatic 'Blagoslavlyayu vas, lesa' [I bless you, Forests], Op. 47, No. 5 (1880), with a piano part which seems to have been conceived in orchestral terms. But Tchaikovsky's finest song of this type is the ballad 'Korol'ki' [The Corals], Op. 28, No. 2 (1875). When endeavouring to write music of an epic nature, it is perhaps not surprising that, whether consciously or subconsciously, he may have turned to Borodin for inspiration. The opening phrase, Ex. 444, the motif of the corals which a young Cossack setting forth to war must bring back to his beloved—who unfortunately dies before his return— is similar to a motif used by Borodin in three of the four movements of his First Symphony, most prominently in the Trio, where it is employed sequentially (Ex. 445). At the end of the song, after the singer has sung climactically of his beloved's death, the 'corals' motif is used in a deeply moving fashion, as they are hung upon an ikon in her memory and the song gradually dies away. 'Korol'ki' proves that Tchaikovsky was not completely incapable of putting his best music into song, but the songs mentioned above and a handful of others hardly compensate for the poverty of real emotion and the commonplace level of invention in the remainder.

BORODIN

In the songs of Borodin and Mussorgsky the Russian solo song reached its zenith. But while Mussorgsky wrote a fair number of

Ex. 444

Ex. 445

songs of different kinds, Aleksandr Borodin (1833–87) produced only sixteen altogether, if one childhood effort is excluded. Of these, four were written before he met Balakirev and are of no importance, while five date from the 1880s by which time there was a distinct fall in Borodin's already meagre output and any really inspired vocal music was destined for *Prince Igor*. His version of 'Iz slyoz moikh' (1870–1) is no more than a charming essay, if more substantial than the settings of this poem by other Petersburg composers. The six songs written between 1867 and 1870 are all lyrical; none has any pretension to realism. Thus Borodin's claim to fame as the song-writer rests on a much narrower base than Mussorgsky's. That he does have such a claim, however, is made clear by the supreme mastery displayed in 'Spyashchaya knyazhna' [The Sleeping Princess] (1867), 'Pesnya tyomnogo lesa' [Song of the Dark Forest], 'Morskaya tsarevna' [The Sea Princess], 'Fal'shivaya nota' [The False Note], 'Otravoy polnï moi pesni' [My Songs are Poisoned] (all 1868); and 'More' [The Sea] (1870). The perfectly balanced 'Otravoy polnï moi pesni', with its unconventional arioso, is a setting of a Russian translation of Heine's 'Vergiftet sind meine Lieder'; the other five are all settings of Borodin's own texts, in which, as was so often the case with Mussorgsky, words and music are a single act of creation.

The most powerful of Borodin's songs is 'Pesnya tyomnogo lesa', subtitled 'staraya pesnya' [Ancient Song]. It seems to rise from the mists of prehistory in exactly the same way as some of Balakirev's folk-song harmonizations, to which it is deeply indebted. Balakirev's imaginatively evocative 'Ne bïlo vetru' [There was no Wind] is combined with the elemental power of the 'Ey, ukhnem!' to create an individual masterpiece. The time signature constantly changes to suit the subtle metre of the words: after four bars of piano introduction in 7/4 there is a bar each of 5/4, 3/4, 7/4, 5/4, 3/4, and so on. Balakirev had used such unconventional metres in No. 17 (2/4, 7/4, 4/4) No. 20 (5/4, 3/4, 4/4), and No. 32 (3/4, 5/4) of his collection. Low bare octaves with some held notes in the accompaniment persist until the middle of the song, 'più animato', where successive empirical unresolved seconds are used. The song ends with a bare chord of F sharp, without the third. Open chords had abounded in Balakirev's folk-song collection, for instance in No. 18 (the one later to be used by Rimsky-Korsakov as the basis of his Piano Concerto). The sensation of epic antiquity evinced by Borodin in this original song, however, is even more remarkable than that demonstrated by Balakirev in his collection.

In all the other settings of his own words, Borodin introduces the whole-tone scale. In 'Spyashchaya knyazhna' it is used in a two-octave descent over a very low reiterated pedal note when the singer tells of a future time when a hero ('bogatïr'') will come, break the magic spell and free the princess. The magic 'lullaby' material of the opening, with its imaginative alternating seconds, periodically returns, giving a satisfactory rounded structure. Whole-tone material occurs in a more chordal manner at the beginning of 'Morskaya tsarevna', in which the second chord on the piano involves alternating seconds a tone apart in the right hand (Ex. 446) over a D flat and A flat

Ex. 446

bass. Later the quavers become more agitated and turn into triplets at a modulation from F major to D flat and finally, as we might expect in this siren's song, the descending whole-tone scale appears in the accompaniment as the luckless male is swallowed by the sea. Debussy, on his summer vacation visits to Russia in the early 1880s as the musician-in-residence of Tchaikovsky's benefactress, Nadezhda von Meck, must surely have come across these songs (published between 1870 and 1873) as well as Mussorgsky's, and such use of whole-tone material as this provided a starting-point from which he could develop. Borodin's vocal material in 'Spyashchaya knyazhna' tends to be rather stiff, matching the princess's inanimation which persists throughout the song—for the hero never actually does come to wake her. It is quite otherwise with 'Morskaya tsarevna', where the seductive melody is as enchanting as the mellifluous accompaniment.

   In 'Fal'shivaya nota', Borodin's finest epigrammatic song, after the singer has protested her undying love, a gently rising whole-tone scale appears in the left hand of the accompaniment at the mention of the 'false note' in her protestations. 'More' is a dramatic ballad, as extended as the previous song is concise. It is a superb piano toccata with vocal obbligato, clearly composed in the immediate aftermath of Balakirev's virtuosic Lisztian *Islamey*, written a few months before. It originally told of a young exile banished from his country, who on his return home is caught in a storm and in sight of his native shore is overwhelmed by the waves. According to Vladimir Stasov, to whom the song is dedicated, the censor rejected

Ex. 447

(but he could not contend with the unrelenting sea)

this,[78] and a much tamer text was substituted. The bold originality of the principal toccata sections, based in G sharp minor, contrast with the slightly more relaxed lyricism of a D flat major passage where the young man's thoughts turn to home and his beloved. Before the final storm section, at a point where the singer relates that in spite of redoubled efforts, 'he cannot contend with the unrelenting sea' and it is realized that there is no hope—a climactically despairing point—whole-tone material is insinuated into the accompaniment (Ex. 447).

MUSSORGSKY

Modest Mussorgsky (1839–81) found it difficult to find inspiration in a purely lyrical vein. In 1866 he gathered together all the manuscripts of his earliest songs in a bound volume. The feeble lyricism of a number of them, such as 'Otchego, skazhi' [Tell me why] (1858), one of only four of the songs to be published in his lifetime, testifies to the difficulty he had in writing such romances. But another of the songs to be published, the second version of

[78] Serge A. Dianin, *Borodin*, trans. Robert Lord (London, 1963), 68.

'Noch'' [Night] (1864), demonstrates his pure lyricism at its best, while the first of two versions of the dramatic 'Tsar' Saul' [King Saul] (words by Kozlov after Byron, 1863), red-blooded though it is, reveals that his technique still lagged behind his ideas.

Mussorgsky's first song to be completely successful in every respect was the bass song 'Kalistratushka' (1864), revised for tenor as 'Kalistrat'. This peasant character study, subtitled 'study in the folk style', was considerably influenced by Balakirev's ideas and methods in dealing with folk-song, for, although Balakirev's collection had not yet been published, many of his versions of the songs (mostly collected in 1860) had been extemporized to his circle. 'Kalistratushka' is a realistic portrayal of a Russian peasant recalling a lullaby his mother sang to him, in which she had foretold that he would 'live in clover' and how true, ironically, her prophecy proved to be. The singer's opening phrase (Ex. 448) is apparently based on No. 30 of Balakirev's folk-song collection (Ex. 449). Melodic shape, modality, and cadence on the (flat) leading note are strikingly similar. *Peremennost'* (tonal variability) between two tonics a tone apart was characteristic of a number of Balakirev's folk-song harmonizations, including No. 18, which, though in the Dorian mode (D minor without a B flat), has its final cadence a tone lower on C. In addition, as with Borodin in 'Pesnya tyomnogo lesa', Mussorgsky was indebted to Balakirev in the use of changing time signatures and the bare chord without the third. Some of these characteristics are also to be

Ex. 448

(Over me my mother used to sing [a lullaby])

Ex. 449

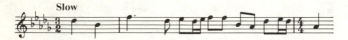

found in the final version of 'Gde tï, zvyozdochka?' [Where art thou, Little Star?].[79]

While it was Balakirev's folk-song arrangements which helped Mussorgsky to achieve maturity, from 1866 onwards he quickly developed his own musical personality which differed widely from any of the other composers in Balakirev's circle. Mussorgsky's writings mirrored his preoccupation with 'truth before beauty', 'the artistic reproduction of human speech',[80] and the importance of original Russian productions 'springing from our native fields and nourished with Russian bread'. This was to be achieved not only by the use of folk intonations, as with Balakirev, but by getting under the skin of the ordinary Russian peasant, representing his true feelings, not idealized travesties of them, and also sometimes by making a social protest about his position in society. The first song in which Mussorgsky achieved these ends was 'Svetik Savishna' [Darling Savishna] (1866), a masterpiece of the front rank. Like the vast majority of Mussorgsky's greatest songs written between 1866 and 1872, it is a setting of his own words. An idiot declares his love to a young woman, knowing that because of his unhappy condition his suit is hopeless. The singer sings uninterrupted crotchets throughout the song, in 5/4 time, and the right hand of the piano part suggests both the physical and mental agitation of the idiot with its incessant ♪♩♩♩ rhythm.

Two other brilliant realistic songs written to his own texts were 'Ozornik' [The Ragamuffin] (1867) and 'Sirotka' [The Orphan] (1868). In 'Ozornik', in which a ragamuffin shouts insults at an old woman, we are treated to a display of comic realism with much use of empirical harmonies (Ex. 450). 'Sirotka' is a song with a 'social' message of the kind to be found in paintings and writings of the period, especially as the Russian word of the title was used in Mussorgsky's day not only with the meaning 'orphan' but also as a collective noun to denote the Russian peasantry.[81] The song ends with an impassioned plea to 'take pity' and dies away in recitative style at the words 'on a miserable little orphan', over a dominant chord (which does not resolve on the tonic).

[79] The version previously thought to have been written in 1857 has now been proved beyond reasonable doubt to date from the mid-1860s. See Richard Taruskin, '"Little Star": An Etude in the Folk Style', in Malcolm Hamrick Brown (ed.), *Musorgsky in Memoriam, 1881–1981* (Ann Arbor, 1982), 57–84.

[80] Mussorgsky's letters of the period are peppered with such references, e.g. a letter of 30 July 1868 to Glinka's sister Lyudmila Shestakova (*M. P. Musorgskiy: Pis'ma* (Moscow, 1981), 68).

[81] See Richard Hoops, 'Musorgsky in the Populist Age', in Brown (ed.), *Musorgsky in Memoriam*, p. 282.

Ex. 450

(Hoy, hoy, granny! hoy, hoy, darling, hoy.)

The apogee of achievement in the setting of his own words is Mussorgsky's song cycle *Detskaya* [The Nursery] (1868–72). He had set Mey's 'Detskaya pesenka' [Child's Song] in April 1868, and in the same month he completed the first and most radical song in the cycle, 'S nyaney' (With Nurse), dedicated to 'the great teacher of musical truth, Aleksandr Sergeevich Dargomïzhsky'. Changing time signatures are at last totally dissociated from any folk-song connections and are used solely in order that the music shall exactly follow the rhythm of the child's speech as he asks his nurse to tell him the story of the bogyman who ate up naughty children, then changing his mind and asking instead to be told about the limping tsar and sneezing tsaritsa who lived in a house overlooking the sea. Mussorgsky makes the most of the opportunities for word painting with a liberal use of empirical harmonies.

The six other songs in the cycle are slightly less radical than 'S nyaney'—there are very few changing time signatures, for example— but they are hardly less unconventional even if their unconventionality sometimes admits of more lyricism. Particularly delightful is 'Po-ekhal na palochke' [On the Hobby-horse], No. 6; the child rides in his imagination to invite his next-door friend to come to play, whoaing and hallooing to a clip-clopping accompaniment. On his way home, he falls off—not in his imagination but in reality—and the singer changes voice to the rounded mature tones of his comforting mother. The music in this central section is a charming skit on a sentimental drawing-room romance, contrasting with the outer sections.

Mussorgsky wrote no more songs until after the first performance of *Boris Godunov* in 1874. Perhaps because he became depressed as a result of the reviews of *Boris*, which were at best equivocal and at worst violently hostile, the songs in his next cycle *Bez solntsa*

[Sunless], settings of poems by Arseny Golenishchev-Kutuzov, show a pessimism not previously to be found in his music. He was never again to write important realist songs unless, as in *Pesni i plyaski smerti* [Songs and Dances of Death] (by the same poet), the realism was imbued with horror.

It has often been pointed out that *Bez solntsa* contains a number of impressionistic features which were to influence Debussy. A passage in 'Okonchen prazdnïy, shumnïy den'' [The Idle, Noisy Day is Ended], No. 3 (starting at bar 17), has been cited as influencing the opening of the first of Debussy's orchestral *Nocturnes*, 'Nuages'.[82] In the most lyrical song, 'Nad rekoy' [On the River], No. 6, there are consecutive 'dominant' sevenths, and it ends where it began, on a tonic seventh. The most radical song is the shortest, 'Menya tï v tolpe ne uznala' [Thou didst not know me in the crowd], No. 2. Only eleven and a half bars in length, this song is on a par with Borodin's 'Fal'shivaya nota'. The typically supple recitative is accompanied by sensitive chords and the song, in D major, ends 'in the air', as it were, on a first inversion of B flat major. This final chord follows one which had appeared near the outset, resolving then on a chord of D major; but Mussorgsky did not make this obvious resolution at the end since this would have destroyed its whole ambience.

In the first song of the cycle *Pesni i plyaski smerti*, 'Kolïbel'naya' [Lullaby], a dying child's mother, with agitated and despairing pleas, and Death, crooning 'hush-a-bye' in soothing tones, vie for the soul of the sick child. Death's serenade itself, in 'Serenada', No. 2, has modal inflections which had by this time become totally integrated with Mussorgsky's style. In the third song, 'Trepak' (a Russian folk-dance), Death dances with a drunken peasant who is lost in a forest at night in a snowstorm. The song is based on a single motif which undergoes a number of metamorphoses including echoes of Liszt's *Totentanz*, for the motif has its origins in the Dies Irae (although the quality of all the intervals is not exact). Compare the opening of the Dies Irae (Ex. 451) with the opening of the song (Ex. 452). Figures *a* and *b* show how two four-note figures are derived

Ex. 451

82 M. D. Calvocoressi, *Modest Mussorgsky: His Life and Works* (London, 1956), 269.

Ex. 452

(Forest and glades are deserted. The snowstorm wails and moans;)

from the Dies Irae. The song is in D minor, with the main motif
starting at the fourth bar of Ex. 452. The three-bar introduction not
only begins completely out of key but proceeds through a chord of
the dominant to one of F sharp minor, as unexpected as it is alien,[83]
depicting starkly the desolation of the scene. (Rimsky-Korsakov's
'correction' of these three bars is one of the curiosities of Russian
music.)[84] After the dance itself, when Death is certain that the
peasant will be his, in a final poignant 'andante tranquillo' section
he croons an ironic lullaby over the recumbent form; the lullaby
periodically ceases for a bar while the piano momentarily increases
the pace as Death seems to give a little gleeful skip, a typical
Mussorgskian pantomimic gesture.

The first three songs in the cycle were all written in 1875. The
last, 'Polkovodets' [The Field Marshal], was added in 1877. The first
section in this tripartite song is a very effective battle painting; in

[83] In choosing this unexpected F sharp minor chord, in the key of D minor, Mussorgsky
may possibly have been subconsciously recollecting Dargomïzhsky's use of the very same
chord in 'Paladin', also in D minor (see Ex. 440, bar 5), though Mussorgsky's approach to
the chord is more startling than Dargomïzhsky's.

[84] See Calvocoressi, *Mussorgsky*, p. 247, for this 'correction'.

the second, the pace moderates to depict the battle field deserted by all but the wounded and dying, and, in the last, Field Marshal Death, in a baleful march, exults over the dead of both sides; only he is the victor. This final section affords another fine opportunity for Mussorgsky to employ empirical harmonies as Death promises never to forget the dead, but to visit them and dance upon their graves to ensure that they never rise again.

Mussorgsky was unique in his ability to produce works which were rooted in the realistic ethos of his period but which, at the same time, transcend their period, remaining timeless masterpieces.

RUBINSTEIN

As well as setting German texts, Anton Rubinstein (1829–94), like Cui a composer of non-Russian origin, wrote songs to Russian words. When 16 or 17 he set Lermontov's famous 'Molitva' [Prayer], Op. 4, and in 1850 composed his 'Zhelanie' [Wish], Op. 8, No. 5. In 1849 he published nine songs by Kol'tsov, Op. 27; in 1850 ten, most of them by Pushkin or Lermontov, Op. 36; in 1864 *Shest' basen I. Krïlova* [Six Fables by Krïlov], composed in 1849 but numbered Op. 64.[85] His Op. 78 (1868) includes five Pushkin settings and one each by Lermontov, Kol'tsov and Maykov; Op. 101 (1877) consists of twelve songs by A. K. Tolstoy; in 1891 he set verses by Semyon Nadson and Dmitry Merezhkovsky.

Of all Rubinstein's Russian songs the most interesting are the early settings of Krïlov's fables, far indeed from the polished textures of his *Lieder* and related to Dargomïzhsky by their humour and characterization. Good examples are 'Kvartet' (in which a monkey, donkey, goat, and bear get hold of instruments and try to play a string quartet) and 'Osyol i Solovey' [The Ass and the Nightingale], in which the amusing characterization is particularly well done (Exx. 453–4).

Ex. 453

O-syol u-vi-del So-lo-v'ya i go-vo-rit e-mu: 'Po-

[85] Rubinstein's opus numbers, often given by German publishers, are wildly misleading. Senff of Leipzig published Op. 64 some years before Op. 3.

(The ass saw the nightingale and said to him, Listen, old friend! They say your singing is very fine.')

Ex. 454

Meno mosso

Tut So - lo - vey yav - lyat' svo-yo is - kus-stvo stal: za-

shchol-kal, za-svi-stal na tï - sya-chu la-dov, tya - nul pe-re - li - val - sya, to

nezh-no on os - la - be-val i tom-noy vda-le - ke svi - rel'-yu ot-da-val - sya.

(Upon which the nightingale began to show off his art; he trilled, he whistled a thousand times, he sang, made roulades, then tenderly relaxed and languidly, as if from far off, echoed his piping.)

The members of the *kuchka* despised Rubinstein and he was a minor composer in comparison with all of them, with the exception of Cui; even his former pupil Tchaikovsky came to regard much of his music with disfavour. Nevertheless his songs to Russian texts contain some of his best music and no account of Russian song would be complete without mention of them.

(d) POLAND

By ROSEMARY HUNT

In the nineteenth century Poland was ruled by the three partitioning powers who had divided her among themselves in 1795: Russia, Prussia, and Austria. Polish education and culture was at best neglected by the authorities, at worst subjected to wide-ranging repression—censorship, the banning of books, travel restrictions— and after the November Rising of 1830, which had repercussions all over the Russian sector, large numbers of intellectuals were forced to emigrate. The Universities of Vilna and Warsaw, both under Russian rule, were closed; Russian was imposed as the official language wherever possible, and numerous other efforts were made to obliterate all traces of Polish culture and national identity.

Polish Romantic poetry, from the 1820s onwards, became the voice of the Polish nation, and at times its only means of self-expression. The new interest in folklore was, in Poland, an important element in the movement to preserve national consciousness. In the first half of the nineteenth century organized cultural life, especially musical activities, faced enormous problems. Public gatherings, such as concerts, were discouraged; there were virtually no facilities for training musicians and it was almost impossible to travel abroad to study. Musical performance was confined principally to the home and to private social gatherings, and was therefore restricted to solo piano and vocal music, and other compositions suitable for small groups of amateurs. Songs held an important position in musical life; they demanded few resources and through the text they could speak to the Polish nation as directly as the poetry itself.

The Warsaw Conservatory which Chopin attended was closed in 1830 and not until 1861 was the violinist, teacher, and composer Apolinary Kątski (1826–79) permitted to open the Instytut Muzyczny

(Institute of Music). After the Warszawskie Towarzystwo Muzyczne (Warsaw Music Society) was founded in 1871 to popularize music and hold public concerts, other societies began to spring up. Music classes were held under their auspices and, in the 1880s, these formed the basis for conservatories in Lvov and Cracow. Musical tastes were unformed compared with those of Western Europe. Songs were written principally for amateur performance and so tended to be technically uncomplicated. Poets and translators of librettos began to study the works of the Polish prosodists, and, in their turn, composers paid closer attention to the specific problems of successfully setting to music an inflected language with a fixed stress.

Polish Romantic songs tend to fall into three groups.[86] The first includes the romance, ballad, and *dumka*; in the second are songs containing strong folk elements, especially dance rhythms; and in the third group are the lyrical songs in which poetry and music are in equal partnership.

The pianist Maria Szymanowska (1789–1831) composed approximately nineteen songs, only three unpublished. Of the earliest group, *Pięć śpiewów historycznych* [Five Historical Songs] to texts by Julian Ursyn Niemcewicz (1757–1841), three were published in Moscow in 1816 and are of little artistic value. In 1820 *Le Départ* and *Six Romances* (one with an Italian text, the others with French texts or translations into French) were published in Leipzig. They are still part of an earlier song tradition. The vocal line in these, over generally similar broken-chord accompaniments, is not always very comfortable and the strophic patterns make no attempt to reflect changes of mood in the texts. The same is true of one of Szymanowska's settings of the work of Adam Mickiewicz (1795–1855), the ballad 'Świtezianka' [The Maid of the Świteź], published in Moscow in 1828. The strict strophic pattern, incorporating two stanzas of the poem, cannot follow the dramatic course of the text.[87] Szymanowska's three other settings of Mickiewicz poems were published in Kiev and Odessa in 1828. Of these, one is more successful: 'Wilija' (Ex. 455) describes the Lithuanian river of that name, and the vocal line is superimposed upon the flowing A flat nocturne, 'Le Murmure'. The song is on the whole prosodically satisfactory.[88]

---

[86] See Alicja Matracka-Kościelna, 'Twórczość pieśniarska warszawskiego środowiska kompozytorskiego w drugiej połowie XIX wieku', in Andrzej Spóz (ed.), *Kultura muzyczna Warszawy drugiej połowy XIX wieku* (Warsaw, 1980), 206, 211.

[87] See Vol. VIII, pp. 577–8.

[88] Of the other two, 'Alpuhara' is unobtainable; 'Pieśń z wieży' appears in Jerzy Gabryś

Ex. 455

(Wilija, the mother of our streams, her depths are golden and azure her face.)

CHOPIN

Fryderyk Chopin (1810–49) probably composed more than the nineteen songs that are known and have been published. The majority appeared in *Siedemnaście pieśni polskich na głos* [Seventeen Polish Songs for Voice], Op. 74, in Berlin 1859, and two, 'Czary' [Spells] and 'Dumka', were published later. Chopin did not attach much importance to his songs, some of which were improvised, and he probably made little attempt to preserve them. Several are mazurkas: 'Życzenie' [The Wish] (1829) with a text by Stefan Witwicki (1802–

and Janina Cybulska, *Z dziejów polskiej pieśni solowej w latach 1800–1830* (Cracow, 1960), 191–3. Szymanowska's daughter, Celina, was married to Mickiewicz.

Ex. 456

(O little barmaid, take care, stop!
There you are smiling, here you are pouring mead over my jacket!)

Ex. 457

(When in a joyous moment my little pet
begins to chirrup, to chirp, and to warble)

47); 'Hulanka' [Drinking Party] (1830) (Witwicki) (Ex. 456); 'Śliczny chłopiec' [Handsome Lad] (1841) (Józef Bohdan Zaleski, 1802–86) and 'Moja pieszczotka' [My pet] (1837) (Mickiewicz) (Ex. 457). Among the more lyrical songs are 'Nie ma czego trzeba' [There is no Need] (1845) (Zaleski); 'Precz z moich oczu' [Away from my Sight!] (1830) (Mickiewicz), and 'Wiosna' [Spring] (1838) (Witwicki), though this last has an uncomfortable vocal line.

Chopin's published songs date from the period 1829-45, yet their style does not develop correspondingly. Most of them are strophic, one or two are prosodically uncomfortable and the accompaniments are uncomplicated. The songs, which were not published until at least ten years after Chopin's death, had little influence on later composers.

MONIUSZKO

The first songs by Stanisław Moniuszko (1819-1872), however, were published in Berlin as early as 1838: *Trzy śpiewy do słów Adama Mickiewicza* [Three Songs to Words by Adam Mickiewicz]. These were 'Sen' [Sleep], 'Niepewność' [Uncertainty], and 'Do D.D.' [To D.D.], later called 'Pieszczotka'.[89] They were the first of an impressive group of Mickiewicz settings, among the best of Moniuszko's several hundred solo songs, and among the best in the Polish nineteenth-century repertoire.

In 1840 Moniuszko settled in Vilna, having completed just two years of study at the Singakademie in Berlin, and began the struggle to make a living as a musician. Two years later his *Śpiewnik domowy* [Home Song book]—the first of six—was published, to be sold on subscription. By way of introduction to the volume he wrote an explanation of his aims in composing the songs, stressing his wish to create music of a Polish character. In order to do this, he had chosen texts by the best Polish poets and considered that vocal music provided the best means of establishing contact with the public.[90] This declaration outlined principles to which he adhered throughout his life.

Another early Mickiewicz setting, one of Moniuszko's most simple lyrical songs, is the second version of 'Rozmowa' [Conversation] (1839). The flowing melody lies over a frequently used accompaniment of repeated chords in one hand, with a second melody in the other at times, echoing the vocal part (Ex. 458). The same pattern is used in 'Znasz-li ten kraj?', the second of two settings of Mickiewicz's paraphrase of Goethe's 'Kennst du das Land?', and composed in or before 1846. Mickiewicz reshaped the love for Italy in the poem into romantic love for a woman, and Moniuszko captures the sensuous quality of the Polish poem in the long, unbroken phrases that soar

---

[89] A poem that attracted not only many Polish composers, but some Russians: Glinka, Rimsky-Korsakov, and Cui (a pupil of Moniuszko).

[90] See Witold Rudziński, *Stanisław Moniuszko: Studia i materiały* (Cracow, 1955, 1961), i. 94-7; the first songbook was artistically quite ambitious but unfortunately Moniuszko heeded the criticism of J. I. Kraszewski and wrote consciously simpler songs after that.

Ex. 458

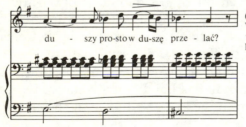

(My darling! What need have we to talk?
Why, when I want to share my feelings
with you, can I not pour them from my
heart into yours?)

over the unelaborate accompaniment to this, possibly his finest song
(Ex. 459).

Moniuszko was always guided by the style or mood of the text
he was setting. A flowing, unbroken melodic line over a continuous
piano part creates a similar effect to that of Schubert's 'Gretchen

Ex. 459

(Do you know that land where the lemon grows,
Where the bright orange gilds the green trees,
Where a garland of ivy decorates the ancient ruins,
Where the laurel flourishes and the cypress tranquil stands?)

Ex. 460

Po no-cnej ro - sie płyń,dźwie-czny gło-sie, niech się twe e-cho roz - sze - rzy,

(Flow over the night dew, melodious voice,
Let your echo spread)

am Spinnrade'—the perpetual motion of a spinning-wheel—in 'Prząś-
niczka' [The Spinner], composed before 1846 to a text by the poet
Jan Czeczot (1796–1847). His most effective setting of a poem by
Władysław Syrokomla,[91] the lyrical 'Pieśń wieczorna' [Evening Song],
captures the tranquility of idealized country life (Ex. 460).

Moniuszko wrote a number of songs in an overt folk style,
including a version of Witwicki's 'Hulanka' (composed between 1846
and 1850), also set by Chopin (Ex. 456). Moniuszko more than once
employed a declamatory style, and in various ways; it is evident
throughout 'Tren III' [Lament III], written between 1843 and 1852
to a text by the sixteenth-century poet Jan Kochanowski, but in
'Świtezianka' it is used in combination with other dramatic effects—
to illustrate the original ballad in a manner very different from that
of Szymanowska's setting.

In two other Mickiewicz ballads, 'Trzech Budrysów' [The Three
Budrys Brothers] (1839 or 1840) and 'Czaty' [The Ambush] (before
1846) (Ex. 461) Moniuszko wisely followed the specific metre of the
original poems,[92] to great effect. Moniuszko, more than any other
composer of the period, spoke directly to his public through his
music, and set a standard that shaped the further development of
Polish song.

Ex. 461

Molto agitato
[p]

Z o-gro - do - wej a - lta-ny wo-je - wo-da zdy-sza-ny bie-ży w za-mek z wście-kło-ścią

trwo - ga.

(From the garden bower the breathless voivode runs into the castle in fury and alarm.)

[91] Pseudonym of Ludwik Kondratowicz (1823–62).
[92] The metre is the anapaest, possibly influenced by Sir Walter Scott's 'The Eve of St John'.

ŻELEŃSKI

The most important composer after Moniuszko was Władysław Żeleński (1837–1921), who represented Polish neo-Romanticism. He studied in Cracow, Prague, and Paris, and in 1872 took over Moniuszko's harmony class in the Instytut Muzyczny in Warsaw. His earliest songs (including 'Moja pieszczotka', which pre-dates the Chopin and Moniuszko settings) are marked by faulty prosody, which Żeleński corrected in his later compositions. These display a lyricism reminiscent of Moniuszko and are often very descriptive of the text. The vocal line is usually closely integrated with a rich, almost independent piano part. Żeleński wrote more than seventy songs, practically all of them to Polish texts. Some are settings of folk-type texts, with the rhythms and melodic patterns of dances such as the mazurka, and some are more lyrical. 'Zawód' [Disappointment], for example, echoes the sensuality of the poem by Kazimierz Przerwa-Tetmajer (1865–1940) (Ex. 462).

LATER NINETEENTH-CENTURY COMPOSERS

Zygmunt Noskowski (1846–1909) was the first really talented

Ex. 462

(I rocked you on the waves of my dreams
Like some stone-pine by the water's edge.)

composer to have studied music in Poland, though he also spent some time abroad, in Germany. He attended Moniuszko's harmony class and himself joined the staff of the Instytut Muzyczny in 1886. He wrote with ease, sometimes carelessly, but although the first ten songs of his *Śpiewnik dla dzieci* [Children's Songbook] (1889) were written in a few hours, they remain popular to this day. He worked on some of these with the author, Maria Konopnicka (1842–1910), and achieved a remarkable blend of words and music. His style of composition was traditional, but melodically displayed greater invention than Żeleński's.[93] He wrote approximately eleven song cycles, none of which is really outstanding, however; see, for example, 'Skowroneczek śpiewa' [The Little Skylark] (1894) (Ex. 463), written in a few minutes on demand!

Ex. 463

(The little lark is singing, the sun is warming,
And the girl in the window is waiting for Jaś.)

[93] See Henryk Swolkień, 'Od Chopina do Szymanowskiego', in Tadeusz Ochlewski (ed.), *Dzieje muzyki polskiej* (Warsaw, 1977).

Both Piotr Maszyński (1855–1934) and Jan Gall (1856–1912) wrote a large number of songs that were very popular in their composers' day. Maszyński studied at the Instytut Muzyczny, under Noskowski for composition, but Gall went to Vienna, Munich, and Italy to study. Both were active in developing choral music and raising singing standards. Maszyński wrote approximately a hundred solo songs. Gall composed about ninety, generally uncomplicated but prosodically very carefully worked, partly as a result perhaps of some vocal training undergone in Italy. One of his most popular songs was 'Barkarola', Op. 13, No. 3 (1890) (Ex. 464).

The music of Eugeniusz Pankiewicz (1857–98), unlike that of his predecessors, was not fully appreciated in his short lifetime, and was criticized as being too intellectual.[94] He studied composition with Żeleński and Noskowski, but was also alert to the way in which music was developing outside Poland. He wrote about fifty songs, which are now considered to bridge the gap between those of Chopin and Szymanowski, through their folk-music elements and advanced, almost impressionistic harmonies. Pankiewicz developed the role of the accompaniment in his songs, some of which on the other hand are treated in a declamatory manner, reminiscent of Schumann and Wolf.[95] Unfortunately, many are marred by slightly faulty prosody.

Ex. 464

(Ah! Come into the gondola, my dearest one.)

[94] See Włodzimierz Poźniak, *Eugeniusz Pankiewicz* (Cracow, 1958).
[95] Ibid.

Ex. 465

(When the last rose had withered, I said to the boy! 'Go!'
The golden thread spun by love had broken.)

His setting of 'Gdy ostatnia róża zwiędła' [When the Last Rose had Faded], to a text by Adam Asnyk (Ex. 465), is in a more stylized folk idiom.

Stanisław Niewiadomski (1859–1936), by contrast, was perhaps the most popular song-writer of his day; he studied in Lvov, Vienna, and Leipzig. His compositions were true to the Romantic tradition, combining folk elements (although never using an actual folk melody) and a pleasing lyricism. His harmonies are uncomplicated and the rich vocal lines reveal faultless prosody. He wrote approximately fifty songs, many of which form cycles of six or twelve, for example: *Kurhanek Maryli* [Maryla's Grave] by Mickiewicz, *Jaśkowa dola* [Jasiek's Fate] by Konopnicka; *Astry* [Asters] by Asnyk; *Piękne tulipany* [Beautiful Tulips]—one of three groups to old Polish texts. Two of the titles from the Mickiewicz cycle are 'Znaszli ten kraj?' and 'Moja pieszczotka', popular among so many composers of the second half of the nineteenth century. One of Niewiadomski's most popular songs, however, was 'Kołysanka' [Cradle Song] (Ex. 466).

Two composers whose music already belongs in part to the 'New Poland' period are Ignacy Jan Paderewski (1860–1941) and Mieczysław Karłowicz (1876–1909). Their songs, however (with the

Ex. 466

(Rock for me, rock, cradle of linden!
May the Lord Jesus watch over you, Jasienko!)

exception of Paderewski's Catulle Mendès cycle), still belong chiefly
to the neo-Romantic tradition. Paderewski employed Chopin-like
harmonies, especially in his Mickiewicz settings (*Sechs Lieder*, Op.
18) (1894) and his writings about Chopin reveal his strong feelings
concerning the national character of Polish music.[96] 'Moja pieszczotka', Op. 18, No. 3 (Ex. 467) is an unexpectedly dramatic version
of the Mickiewicz poem.

Karłowicz studied extensively abroad, principally in Germany, and
also in Warsaw where he attended Noskowski's and Maszyński's

Ex. 467

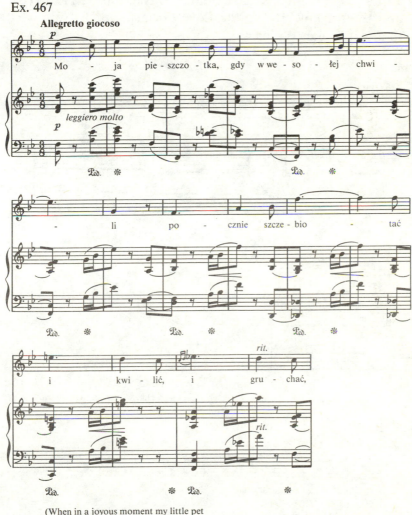

(When in a joyous moment my little pet
begins to chirrup, to chirp, and to warble)

---

[96] See Swolkień, 'Od Chopina'.

classes in composition. His songs are among his early works, when his style had yet to develop from the neo-Romantic towards a style influenced by Grieg and Tchaikovsky, and finally Wagner and Richard Strauss.[97] His songs are lyrical and melancholy, features influenced by his choice of texts, especially those of Kazimierz Tetmajer. Yet he apparently attached little value to them and called them his 'souvenirs' or 'sins of youth'.[98] He was very self-critical, and only some of the songs were published in his lifetime.[99] Amongst these were a Tetmajer setting 'Pamiętam ciche, jasne, złote dnie' [I remember those Tranquil, Clear, Golden Days), Op. 1, No. 5 (Ex. 468), and 'Z erotyków' [From the Love Poems], Op. 3, No. 6 (Ex. 469), to a text by Jan Waśniewski.

Ex. 468

(I remember those tranquil, clear golden days, which now seem to me like some marvellous dream.)

Ex. 469

---

[97] See Feliks Kęcki, *Mieczysław Karłowicz: Szkic monograficzny* (Warsaw, 1934).

[98] See letter from Felicjan Szopski to Adolf Chybiński, 31 Jan. 1934, in Henryk Anders (ed.), *Karłowicz w listach i wspomnieniach* (Cracow, 1960).

[99] See Swolkień, 'Od Chopina'.

łzy i łzy dziś skła-dam ci pod no - gi; prze - bacz, że du - szy mej u -

bo-gie są tak zdro - je, lecz przyj-mij cho-ciaż łzy, bo łzy te, to łzy mo - je.

(And in place of suns and stars, my dear angel,
I lay at your feet only tears now, only tears;
Forgive me, that the springs of my heart are so poor,
But at least accept these tears, for they are my tears.)

When Moniuszko was struggling in Vilna, another composer was active there, writing his own *Śpiewnik* (1855): Wiktor Każyński (1812–67). His thirty songs were popular at the time but have not been reprinted since. A later composer who was also popular in the nineteenth century and who modelled himself largely on Moniuszko was Ignacy Komorowski (1824–57), an excellent performer of his own songs. Another imitator of Moniuszko was Aleksander Zarzycki (1834–95), one of the founder members of the Warszawskie Towarzystwo Muzyczne; unfortunately some of his many songs are spoilt by faulty prosody. The songs of Kazimierz Kratzer (1844–90) were very popular in his day and for many years were in all singers' repertoires.

(e) CZECHOSLOVAKIA

By JOHN CLAPHAM

There were unquestionable artistic advantages for the Czechs, the most westerly of the Slav races, in being encompassed by such rich areas of European culture. To the north and west stood the German states, so strong in music and literature, while to the south and east lay the Austrian empire, to which they themselves belonged. Vienna, acknowledged by many to be the musical hub of Europe, was close at hand, and firm cultural links had been established with Paris and Italy. Nevertheless, when the desire arose to create a repertoire of indigenous art song, the Czechs encountered serious difficulties.

The decisive defeat of the Czechs in 1620 in the battle of the White

Mountain, which sparked off the flight abroad of Komenský (Comenius) and other leading Protestants, brought with it the suppression of the Czech language, and its relegation to a wholly subordinate and insignificant position. German became the official language, and for well over two centuries it remained the dominant language of the Czech towns and cities. Towards the end of the eighteenth century, influenced by the writings of Rousseau and Herder, and affected by the ferment at the time of the French Revolution, the first clear signs of an awareness of national consciousness emerged, with the greatest emphasis being placed on the history of the Bohemian lands and the revival of the Czech language. Progress in building up a repertoire of Czech poetry, suitable for composers of song, took time; and consequently in the early years of the nineteenth century the leading song composer, Václav Jan Tomášek (1774–1850),[100] showed a marked preference for setting the work of Goethe, Schiller, Heine, Bürger, Hölty, Voss, and other German poets.

THE CZECH RENAISSANCE

Owing to the combined efforts of the poet and critic Josef Krasoslav Chmelenský (1800–39) and the composer František Jan Škroup (1801–62), who had already co-operated in the opera *Dráteník* [The Tinker] (1826), the first opera with a Czech libretto to receive public acclaim, a new venture was launched which was warmly welcomed by all those who were eager to reinstate the Czech language. Over a five-year period, 1835–9, these two men issued a collection of 123 Czech songs in monthly parts, under the title *Věnec ze zpěvů vlasteneckých* [A Garland of Patriotic Songs]. It contains settings of verses by thirty-two poets, headed by Chmelenský himself, whose poems appear in one-third of the songs.[101] Twenty-three composers contributed to the collection, and the little-known teacher and organist Václav Josef Rosenkranz (1797–1861) wrote eighteen. Eleven songs are credited to Škroup, and in addition he included fourteen extracts from his works for the stage, which are arias rather than songs with piano accompaniment. Four composers, namely F. Drechsler, J. B. Kittl, A. Růžička, and J. Vorel, each contributed

---

[100] On his songs, with one Czech example, see Vol. VIII, pp. 572–3.

[101] There are 41 settings of verses by Chmelenský, 14 by V. J. Picek, 10 of J. J. Marek, 8 of F. J. Kamenický, 7 of F. L. Čelakovský and 6 of F. B. Trojan. There are in addition two settings each of Karel Sabina (the librettist of *Prodaná Nevěsta* [The Bartered Bride]), Václav Hanka (the author of the forged Dvůr králové manuscript), and K. J. Erben (author of 'Svatební košile' [The Spectre's Bride] and other ballads), and one of K. H. Macha, who wrote the celebrated poem 'Máj' [May].

eight songs, and there are seven by J. Karas. Three of Tomášek's
songs are included in the collection.[102] In 1844, following the death
of Chmelenský, Škroup brought out one further collection, planned
on similar lines and containing twenty-eight songs and two vocal
quartets. The title this time was *Věnec: Sbírka českých zpěvů*
[Garland: A Collection of Czech Songs]. The characteristically Czech
'Jablíčka' [The Little Apples] by Josef Ondřej Novotný (1778–1856)
appeared in the first volume of *Věnec* (Ex. 470).

Ex. 470

[102] Complete contents in Zdeněk Nejedlý, *Bedřich Smetana*, ii (Prague 1925), Appendix B.
A number of Czech social songs of the 1830s and 1840s appear in this book, between pp. 224
and 225; several of these come from *Věnec*, but they lack accompaniments. Josef Vorel's
'Společná' [Sharing] and Jan Nepomuk Škroup's 'Kytka vlastenkám' [A Posy for Patriots]
both from *Věnec*, appear in Jaroslav Pohanka, *Dějiny české hudby v příkladech* (Prague, 1958).
A modern edition of *Věnec*, ed. Josef Plavec, appeared in 1960.

(An apple-tree stands in the broad field on the green grass,
the very green grass; ah, why does my heart ache so under my
red bodice?)

POETIC SOURCES

The emergence of the nature poet Vítězslav Hálek (1853–74), as also of Jan Neruda (1834–91), Svatopluk Čech (1846–1908), and the epic poet Jaroslav Vrchlický (1835–1912), greatly strengthened the standing of Czech poetry, but it was often such lesser figures as Gustav Pfleger-Moravský (1833–75), Adolf Heyduk (1835–1923), Josef Václav Sládek (1845–1912), Karel Jaromír Erben (1811–70), and Eliška Krásnohorská whose work had a special appeal for Czech composers and whose poetry was better suited to their needs. Dvořák set eighteen and Bendl four of Gustav Pfleger-Moravský's *Cypřiše* [Cypresses]. Bendl set thirty of Sládek's *Skřivánčí písně* [Lark's Songs], while Fibich set four of his poems in *Poupata* [Buds]. Krásnohorská, the librettist of Bendl's *Lejla* and of Smetana's last three operas, and also of Fibich's *Blaník*, was the authoress of *Z máje žití* [From the Spring of Life], a collection of poems, at least four of which Dvořák set. Six of her poems were set by Hynek Palla (1837–96). A few of her poems were set by the Slovak composer Ján Levoslav Bella (1843–1936).

Two more composers deserve mention: František Z. Skuherský (1830–92), who published *Tři písně* [Three Songs] from the Dvůr králové [Queen's Court] manuscript, *Drei Gedichte* of H. Heine, Op.

6, *Šest písní* [Six Songs], Op. 8, and *Drei Lieder*, Op. 10; and Leopold E. Měchura (1804–70), who set German texts by G. T. Drobisch, Heine, Mörike, Uhland, and others, and composed *Šest písní* [Six Songs], Op. 103, on poems by Čelakovský.

Especial interest was being shown in the *Zigeunermelodien* [Gypsy Melodies][103] by Adolf Heyduk, seven of which were set by Dvořák. Bella set ten of them, and Bendl twenty-six. For the Czechs the free and easy life of the gypsies was symbolic. As they saw it, the gypsies possessed something which they dearly wanted for themselves, something which they longed for but which eluded them: genuine freedom. Lastly there was the Dvůr králové manuscript, which for many years has been regarded as a forgery, and the work of Václav Hanka (1791–1861). This has proved to be particularly fruitful. It provided the basis for Fibich's symphonic poem *Záboj, Slavoj a Luděk*, served as an important source for Smetana's festival opera *Libuše*, and contained the six poems that were set by Fibich, Dvořák, and Bendl.

BENDL

Karel Bendl (1838–97) was best known for his operas and also as a conductor. He was a fluent composer with a gift for melody, who came under the influence of Mendelssohn,[104] and wrote 150 or more songs to German and Czech texts.

Bendl's *Zigeunermelodien* appear in two sets, the first of fourteen songs in German, the second of twelve songs in Czech. In his setting of the first song, 'Der wilden Steppe Sohn bin ich' [A Son of the Wild Steppe am I], the description of the gypsy's way of life is presented with a defiant ring (Ex. 471). Another song from the German set, 'Wenn einst der Tod mich ereilt' [When Once Death Overtakes me] (Set I, No. 13), expresses a yearning for death by leaning on a dominant minor ninth. Having firmly established the key of F minor from the beginning (Ex. 472), the composer modulates to G minor and, as if to suggest uncertainty as to when he may be granted release, the song ends suspended on the dominant chord in D major. In one of the Czech songs, 'Už dávno tomu dávno je' [That's Already Long Past] (Set II, No. 10), the so-called gypsy scale emphasizes the sorrowful mood.

[103] The title of Heyduk's collection was *Cikanské melodie* (old spelling). Gustav Walter, tenor soloist at the Vienna Court Opera, gave the first performance of two of the songs of Dvořák on 4 Feb. 1881, singing, naturally, in German. Heyduk had written his verses in Czech and then translated them into German. Dvořák set his German version, and consequently the original Czech version does not fit Dvořák's music and cannot be sung.

[104] 'Es will mir oft das Herz verbluten' shows this exceptionally clearly.

Ex. 471

(A son of the wild Steppe am I! My cheeks are brown,
a coarse garment always wraps my free breast!)

Another set of German songs, *Stimmungsbilder* [Mood Pictures],
Op. 101, is dated 1889–90. No. 6 in this set of twelve songs is a
setting of Heine's 'Wir wollen jetzt Frieden machen' [We want now
to Make Peace], in which Bendl responds ecstatically to mention of
the rose, the carnation, and the forget-me-not, while modulating
from E flat to F sharp minor, A major, D flat, and back to E flat.
The setting of Ada Christen's 'Am schwarzen Teich' [At the Black
Pond] (No. 5), which calls to mind 'Der Doppelganger' of Schubert,
depicts the poet contemplating the body of his sweetheart, thrown
down on the shore by rough hands.

Ex. 472

(When one day death overtakes me, let a song ring out.)

Although here and there interesting points arise from Bendl's settings of the verses, it must be admitted that the great majority lack distinction, sequences and repeats are common, the phrases tend to be square, and the introductory bars are perfunctory and unimaginative.

SMETANA

As a young man Bedřich Smetana (1824–84) was first and foremost interested in instrumental music, and in particular in music for his own instrument, the pianoforte. In 1846, however, while studying with Josef Proksch (1794–1864), he composed four songs with German words as an exercise, and seven years later, evidently stirred by the impression Rückert's 'Liebesfrühling' made upon him, he made a setting of Rückert's lines. Having been brought up to speak German with his family, he was seriously ignorant of the Czech language; but this did not prevent him from composing a 'Píseň svobody' [Song of Freedom] to words by Josef Jiří Kolár (1812–96), and two marches, to raise the spirits of those taking part in the revolutionary uprising in Prague in 1848. Only gradually did it become clear to Smetana that, if he were to play a leading part in the music of Bohemia in the years ahead, it would be essential for him to know the Czech language.

After nearly twenty years almost wholly concerned with opera in Czech he was better equipped technically for song composition. So in 1879 he turned to five of Hálek's *Večerní písně* [Evening Songs]; by this time he was completely deaf. The choice of poems was very carefully made, as a reminder of the kind of treatment that had been meted out to the composer by his enemies and by fate. The cycle starts with 'Kdo v zlaté struny zahrát zná' [Honour Him who Knows how to Sound the Golden Strings], and continues with 'Nekamenujte proroky!' [Do not Stone the Prophets!]. It continues with 'Mně zdálo se: "bol sestár' už . . ."' [It Seemed to me: that Pain had Already Grown Old] (Ex. 473) and 'Hej, jaká radost v kole' [Hey, what Fun in a Round Dance!], and concludes with 'Z svých písní trůn Ti udělám za velkých pěvců' [Out of my Songs I shall Build a Throne for you].

Ex. 473

I thought, 'pain has grown old and it will soon be all up with him, and the tears have run out, for their source has dried up.'

Gerald Abraham suggests that, since the words of the first two songs are not reflected in the music, it is quite possible that the music may have been sketched first and the words added later. The first song, with its highly characteristic feminine endings, is extremely typical of the composer, and is a particularly attractive example of a simple and unpretentious song. It would not be difficult to imagine it coming from Smetana's opera *Hubička* [The Kiss], and being sung by Vendulka when puzzled by the strange conduct of Lukáš and left on her own to ponder on the situation. The third song is written in quasi-recitative style, as shown in Ex. 473, making a welcome stylistic change. In the fourth song the composer was obliged to emphasize his love of dancing and show how fate had intervened once again: a lively polka is promptly snuffed out almost as soon as it has begun. The fifth song is twice as long as the others and seems unable to break away from a long succession of two-bar phrases; but eventually Smetana succeeds in ridding himself of the habitual mould.

It will be seen that Smetana lacked a natural aptitude for song writing and needed an inducement of some kind to tempt him to chance his arm in this direction.

FIBICH

Among the leading Czech composers of song during the second half of the nineteenth century, Zdeněk Fibich (1850–1900) appears to have been different in one respect from all the rest: he alone seems to have been almost wholly unaffected by the Czech nationalist movement. In his works for the stage he was indifferent as to whether he should take subjects from Shakespeare, Schiller, Byron, or Greek legend, or from Czech sources; in his songs this stance is even more pronounced. Among his two hundred or so songs with piano accompaniment he made fifty-two settings of Heine, nineteen of Goethe, and fourteen of Eichendorff, and the others include settings of the work of Rückert, Saphir, Lenau, Chamisso, Scheffel, Brentano, Herder, Lingg, Geibel, Sturm, Groth, and Fischer.[105] Compared to these, his thirty settings of Czech verses pale into insignificance. (These include seven settings of Hálek, six of Čelakovský, four of Sládek, and six based on verses drawn from the Dvůr králové manuscript.) His musical studies in Leipzig had equipped him well for what he set out to do, and his admiration for German *Lieder* resulted in his work reflecting the influence of Schumann and Robert Franz. It was customary for him to adopt a semi-strophic structure as a means of achieving unity, allowing for modifications when he deemed these were necessary.

A collection of fourteen songs, bearing the title *Jarní paprsky* [Rays of Spring], may be taken to be fully representative of the composer's song writing in general. The title in Czech, however, is very misleading, for the album contains only one Czech song. The Czech translations were provided by L. Dolanský, and appear immediately above the original German text. In 'Der träumende See' [The Dreaming Lake] (Julius Mosen), the gentle ripple of water is attractively conveyed; and in 'Das Kriegerweib' [The Soldier's Wife] (Ex. 474) from the same collection, to words by the Plattdeutsch poet Klaus Groth, the intensity of feeling is finely controlled.

Like so many other composers Fibich set Goethe's immortal lines 'Kennst du das Land?' Fibich rejected Schumann's strictly strophic solution, because the last stanzas, describing the perilous route across the mountains, demanded a significant change of mood, which could be suggested by changing from the major key to the tonic minor.

Ex. 474

---

[105] Judging by the frequent faulty declamation in the Czech translations of the original German text, it must be assumed that Fibich made settings of the German text, and that the Czech version was then added to the completed composition. A possible exception to this may be seen in 'Wie der Mond sich leuchtend dränget' [As the Moon Pushes her Light] (Heine), in which trochaic rhythms are conspicuous.

Wol - ken ziehn, so denk ich dei - ner Treu, es
zog vor-bei das gan - ze Heer und du warst auch da -
bei,

(When in the evening the clouds are red, I think of your fidelity;
the entire army marched past, and you too were there.)

The four ballads, Op. 7, of 1872–3 mark the composer's vintage
period. 'Der Spielmann' [The Fiddler] (Andersen/Chamisso), No. 1,
and 'Tragödie' [Tragedy] (Heine), No. 4, are settings previously
selected by Schumann; between these come 'Waldnacht' [Night in
the Forest], (Hermann Lingg), No. 2, and Heine's 'Loreley', No. 3.
It is apparent that Fibich is concerned mainly with the poet's moods,
and the balance of the song as a whole, in preference to a sensitive
response to emotive words such as 'Tod' and 'sterben'. The three
separate sections of 'Tragödie' stem directly from the song's striking
opening phrase (Ex. 475). In 'Der Spielmann' the tragic reality of
the wedding festivities is conveyed by means of a lively waltz theme
alternating between C major and C minor, which prevails until the
climax. At this point the totally crushed fiddler intones a despairing
appeal to the Almighty.

Ex. 475

(Flee with me and be my wife)

DVOŘÁK

Antonín Dvořák (1841–1904) wrote rather less than a hundred solo songs. Among these are three settings of liturgical texts, seven of Heyduk's *Zigeunermelodien* using the German text, two folk poems in German, and *Vier Lieder*, Op. 82, using poems by Otilie Malybrok-Stieler. All the rest of his songs are in the Czech language.

Dvořák composed his first solo songs, eighteen in all, as a spontaneous expression of his bitter disappointment and profound sorrow, when in 1865 his charming pupil, Josefina Čermáková, rejected his proposal of marriage. He had taken the verses from Gustav Pfleger-Moravský's *Cypřiše* [Cypresses]. Dvořák's friend Karel Bendl was quick to point out that Dvořák had no notion how to set Czech words to music in accordance with the accepted principles of Czech prosody in favour at that time. If the songs were performed just as Dvořák wrote them, the resulting distortion of the Czech language would be intolerable.

The dilemma has been overcome by providing an alternative text designed to be sung to the composer's vocal line. This has been attempted with some success in the English language, and a similar

attempt with the Czech language is awaiting publication. An
unexpected outcome of these experiments is that it becomes possible
to reassess the state of Dvořák's development from a new angle
during 1865 which was indeed one of the most remarkable years of
his life. Despite his immaturity, here was a keen young musician,
well endowed with a plentiful supply of musical ideas.[106]

Four of the *Cypřiše* were revised and published as *Čtyři písně*
[Four Songs], Op. 2. Two of these, namely 'V té sladké moci očí
tvých' [Overcome by your Powerful Eyes], No. 2, and 'Já vím, že v
sladké naději' [I'm Sure, and Hope Sustains me], No. 6, were revised
a second time, and, together with six other revised *Cypřiše* songs,
were issued as *Písně milostné* [Love Songs], Op. 83. Eager to provide
himself with further memories of the girl he had loved so dearly
(and who was now his sister-in-law), he adapted twelve of these
songs for string quartet, at first with the title *Ohlas písní* [Echo of
Songs], sharing the vocal melody between the first violin and viola,
and in some cases adhering fairly closely to the original song.[107]
Dvořák improved the second of the *Cypřiše* songs, 'V té sladké moci
očí tvých', by changing the key from G major to G minor. If
allowance is made for the faulty declamation, then it will be seen
that, among the early versions of *Cypřiše* 'Ó, duše drahá, jedinká'
[O One and Only Soul so Sweet], No. 4, and 'Zde hledím na tvůj
drahý list' [Here Concealed in a Book's Pages], No. 12, show promise;
in both cases the treatment of the melodies was envisaged by the
composer in 1865.

In the early version of No. 14, 'Zde v lese u potoka' [I Stand here
in Forest Glade], Dvořák was remarkably sure of the powerful
climax he required, but he was uncertain as to how it should be
timed. However, in a later revision of the song (Op. 83, No. 6) he
gave it a better overall balance by ensuring that the climax coincided
with the real climax of the poem, and by shortening the final section
of the song. The early version is shown in Ex. 476. It may seem
strange that 'Nad krajem vévodí lehký spánek' [E'en now the
Countryside Lightly Slumbers], No. 17, overlooks completely the
ultimate pessimism of the poem, and becomes a dance. This is an

---

[106] Radio Prague has a recording of the complete cycle sung by Eva Serning in English,
accompanied by Radoslav Kvapil. These two artists performed all of the songs at the Dům
umělců, Prague, on 1 May 1983.

[107] He used No. 6 and 10 in *Král a uhlíř* and No. 10 in *Vanda*. In 1881–2 he revised Nos.
1, 5, 9, 8, 13, and 11. Starý published the first four of these as *Vier Lieder* (1882), with the
misleading opus No. 2. The composer revised Nos. 8, 3, 9, 6, 17, 14, 2, and 4 (Nos. 9 and 8
for the second time), and Simrock issued these as *Písně milostné* (*Liebeslieder*), Op. 83, in
1889. Dvořák arranged Nos. 6, 3, 2, 8, 12, 7, 9, 14, 4, 16, 17, and 18 for string quartet. The
only song he did not use a second time was No. 15.

Ex. 476

(I see here an old rock on which the waters surge;
that rock without respite begins to sink beneath the torrent.)

exact parallel with Dvořák's overture *V přírodě* [In Nature's Realm],
and so provides an important clue to the composer's attitude to
nature.

The remainder of Dvořák's early songs are as follows: two songs
for baritone (Heyduk; 1865); *Písně na slova Elišky Krásnohorské*
[Songs on words of E. Krásnohorská] (1871); 'Sirotek' [The Orphan]
(Erben; 1871); 'Rozmarýna' [Rosmarine] (Erben; 1871); *Čtyři písně
na slova Srbské lidové poesie* [Four Songs on Serbian Folk Poetry],
Op. 6 (1872?); *Písně z rukopisu Královédvorského* [Songs from the
Dvůr králové Manuscript], Op. 7 (1872); *Večerní písně* [Evening
Songs] (Hálek), Opp. 3, 9, and 31 (1876).

For the most part these are simple and semi-folklike in style, with
comparatively straightforward accompaniments. The *Cypřiše* have
much more character and intensity of feeling because they were
written from the heart. Although ill equipped for the task he had
undertaken, Dvořák composed as well as he was able, and occasionally with modest success.

Early in 1879 the Moravian duets appeared in concert programmes,
followed a little later by performances of 'Das Sträusschen' from

Op. 7 and 'Blumendeutung' from Op. 6 by Amalie Joachim. Other singers followed suit, showing a marked preference for these two songs.[108]

Dvořák had composed his first ballad in 1871, when he set 'Sirotek' by J. K. Erben. His next attempt may perhaps be described as a valiant attempt to master a form for which he was not very well equipped. This time he chose the *Tři novořecké básně* [Three New Greek Poems] (1878). The first two are somewhat repetitive, but the third, a warning that the city of Parga has been betrayed, and calling on the inhabitants to throw away their weapons and dig up the bones of their fathers to prevent the Turks from treading on those they never conquered, is more satisfying. The three ballads were originally written with an orchestral accompaniment, and were first performed in that form by Josef Lev on 17 November 1878.

Early in 1880 Dvořák wrote the *Zigeunermelodien* [Gypsy Melodies]. This cycle of seven songs represents the peak of his song writing. Dvořák favoured minor keys and gave each of the songs a specific and distinctive character. Particularly memorable are the irrepressible spirit of the dance that runs through the second song; the expressive beauty of the melodic line and especially the haunting octave leap and then a further rise of a semitone in 'Rings ist der Wald so stumm und still' [All round about the Woods are Still], No. 3 (Ex. 477), and the subtlety of rhythm in 'Als die alte Mutter' [Songs my Mother Taught me], No. 4. Dvořák has taken a big stride forward in his accompaniments, and the varied accompaniment for each verse in 'Horstet hoch der Habicht' [Give a Hawk a fine Cage], No. 7, shows skill and imagination.

Dvořák set the two German folk poems on 1 and 2 May 1885

Ex. 477

Wer nur den Schmerz be - sin - gen kann, wird nicht dem — To - de

---

[108] Amalie Joachim introduced 'Das Sträusschen' at Leipzig on 8 Jan. 1880 and 'Blumendeutung' in Berlin on 7 Mar. that same year.

(He who can only sing of his sorrow will not curse death.)

while staying at Sydenham during his third visit to England. The first of these, 'Schlaf, mein Kind, in Ruh' [Sleep, my Child, Peacefully], includes an early version of the musical idea that sustains Julie's lullaby in Act III of *Jakobín*, his opera of 1887–8.[109] The lullaby's companion piece, 'Seh' ich dich, mein liebes Mädchen', is a love song. Both songs reflect the simple folk style of their verses. His next songs were again settings of folk poetry, as their title *V národním tonu* [In Folk Style], Op. 73 (1886) suggests; but this time three are Slovak and one, 'Ach, není tu' [Nothing can Change], No. 3, is Czech (Ex. 478). This song is remarkable both for its continuity of line and also for its poignancy and mood of deep despair.

Next came Dvořák's settings of four German poems by Otilie Malybrok-Stieler, the *Vier Lieder*, Op. 82 of 1887–88. Curiously, the second song, 'Die Stickerin' [Over her Embroidery], having opened in C major, shifts halfway through to B major, and concludes with a touch of B minor—for which it is difficult to offer a reason. The first song, 'Lasst mich allein' [Leave me Alone], is perhaps the finest of the set. It was highly regarded by the composer and greatly admired by his sister-in-law, Josefina Kaunizová. When she wrote to America on 26 November 1894, telling Dvořák how seriously her health was declining, and how she was being neglected by those she loved, the composer, conscience-stricken because he had not written to her, immediately introduced two phrases from this song into the Adagio of his B minor Cello Concerto.

During March 1894, following the death of Gounod and of his friends Tchaikovsky and Hans von Bülow, and while his own father lay desperately ill, Dvořák felt a strong urge to reaffirm his religious faith. He selected suitable verses for his cycle of ten *Biblické písně*

---

[109] An extract from his song 'Žežhulice' [The Cuckoo] in *Písně z rukopisu Královédvorského* [Songs from the Dvůr králové Manuscript] reappears in an important transition in the first movement of the F minor Trio, Op. 65, brought to life in a remarkable way.

Ex. 478

(Oh! what would bring me joy is not here; Oh! what brings me joy is not here.)

[Biblical Songs], Op. 99, from the Book of Psalms in the earliest Czech translation, the Kralice Bible of 1613. Although a Catholic himself, he recognized this Protestant translation as a national asset. It is preferable for the accompaniment to be played on an organ, rather than on a piano. However, since Dvořák before long scored the accompaniment of the first five songs for orchestra, this makes a welcome alternative. After setting the Czech text, Dvořák unwisely modified the vocal rhythm to accommodate the German translation, and an English translation was then fitted to the modified rhythm. In the Critical Edition the original rhythm has been restored, and alternative German and English translations are provided. The songs are simple and direct, at times displaying a little American pentatonicism. After the declamatory song 'Oblak a mrákota jest vůkol Něho' [Clouds and Darkness are Round him] (No. 1), comes a charmingly melodious setting of verses from Psalm 23 'Hospodin jest můj pastýř' (No. 4), a forthright 'Bože! Bože! Píseň novou' [I will Sing a new Song unto thee] (No. 5), a moving setting of 'Při řekách babylonských' [By the Rivers of Babylon] (No. 7), with a memorable climax on recalling Jerusalem, and finally a paean of praise, 'Zpívejte Hospodinu píseň novou' [Oh Sing unto the Lord a new song] (No. 10).

(f) SCANDINAVIA

By JOHN HORTON

The main Nordic lands—Denmark, Norway, Sweden, and Finland—experienced during the nineteenth century an abundant flowering of lyric poetry and solo song, with close though shifting relationships between the two arts and many cross-cultural exchanges, both within the region and with foreign countries, the German-speaking ones in particular. Over the period it is possible to trace lines of development from rudimentary models of romance and ballad, revitalized by the recovery and imitation of indigenous traditions, through processes of technical evolution that were eventually to bring Scandinavian art-song very near to the continental Lied, though without complete sacrifice of national identity.

DENMARK

Danish national Romanticism in music might be said to date from 1780, when Johann Hartmann (1726–93) introduced into Johannes Ewald's *syngespil* of *Fiskerne* [The Fishers] a narrative romance, 'Liden Gunver' [Little Gunver], which, with its touching story, melancholy minor tune in 6/8 measure, and *omkvæd* or refrain,[110] appeared to be an ideal pastiche of the medieval Danish ballad. It had a twofold appeal to Copenhagen theatre-goers, since the term romance, already familiar from imported French *opéra comique* and

---

[110] 'O vog dig, mit barn, for de falske mandfolk' [O beware, my child, of deceitful men].

vaudeville, was rapidly becoming naturalized, and was to remain a favourite genre in all the Scandinavian countries during the first half of the nineteenth century.[111]

Christoph Ernst Weyse (1774–1842), the chief exponent of the romance in the first four decades of the century, extended the scope of the simple strophic song-form in two ways: first, by encouraging the current practice of detaching it from its theatre setting and bringing it into the bourgeois parlour, and secondly by giving more attention to the keyboard accompaniment, to which he added preludes, interludes, and postludes. His conservative outlook can be appreciated, however, if one contrasts his unpretentious setting of a German text—Goethe's 'Nähe des Geliebten'[112]—with Schubert's impassioned strophic Lied of 1815.

More functional than the *klaverromance* was the *vise* or social song, much promoted at this time with religious, patriotic, or educational intention. The popular, easily memorized *vise*, together with anthologized 'folk-song' (in the English sense) gathered from literary or oral sources and cherished for its native associations, became assimilated to the general romance convention, thereby providing fertile soil for the growth of free composition in a 'national' idiom.[113] The narrative romance or ballad was cultivated as an art-form by leading composers, who elaborated their primitive models both vocally—as, for example, by introducing passages of recitative— and instrumentally. Specimens of the genre are A. P. Berggreen's setting of Oehlenschläger's 'Skjøterløberen' [The Skater], J. P. E. Hartmann's 'Nøkken' [The Watersprite] to text by B. S. Ingemann, Henrik Rung's 'Valdemars Sang' [Valdemar's Song] to text by Carsten Hauch, and the large-scale, through-composed setting of 'Knut Lavard' by Niels W. Gade (1817–90), also to a text by Hauch.

Gade's years in Leipzig and his association with Schumann and Mendelssohn had their effect on the course of Danish art-music after his return to his native country in 1850. He brought to the lyrical romance and the ballad a practised skill in keyboard and orchestral techniques; in fact, his song writing is distinguished more than anything by its accompaniments, either with orchestra, like the rich

[111] Niels Martin Jensen points out that in the syngespil tradition the romance, unlike the aria, is not 'an arena [tumleplads] for strong emotions or inner conflicts' (*Den danske romance 1800–1850* (Copenhagen, 1964), 19).

[112] Included in Weyse's collected *Romancer og Sange* (1852 and 1860). About a third of the hundred songs are from stage works; the rest are 'keyboard songs', excerpts from occasional cantatas, patriotic songs, children's songs, and narrative ballads.

[113] The most successful early example of ballad opera, Friedrich Kuhlau's *Elverhøj*, contains traditional songs from Danish, Jutlandish, Norwegian, and Swedish sources, all styled *romancer*.

colours of Oluf's ballad 'Saa tidt jeg rider mig under Ö' [Whenever I ride about the isle] in the cantata *Elverskud* [The Elf-King's Daughter] (1853), or with piano in chamber music texture, as in the strophic romance 'Sol deroppe' [Sundown] (to verses by H. C. Andersen), where an innocent eight-bar vocal melody is encapsulated in a total of twenty-five bars of prelude, interlude, and postlude.

The greater demands made on singers and accompanists by Gade and others after the middle of the century reflect the growth of professional recitals and increased awareness of the development of the art-song in German-speaking lands and of Italian bel canto, with which Henrik Rung (1807–71) had become familiar through his travels. The songs of J. P. E. Hartmann (1805–1900), as exemplified in the Ingemann cycle *Sulamith og Salomon* (1847–50), owe much to the contemporary Lied.[114]

A flair for long, flexible vocal lines, rich harmonic colouring, and idiomatic picturesque keyboard figuration characterizes the many romances of Peter Lange-Müller [1850–1926]. Like Hartmann, he set the cycle of Ingemann poems *Sulamith og Salomon*, giving in the third song a charming representation of the message dove and its flight to Sulamith with a palm-leaf letter from her lover. Some of Lange-Müller's later songs show a determination to respond to the painter–poet Holger Drachmann's passion for the sea, as in 'Jeg sejled en Nat over Havet' [I Sailed One Night across the Sea], Op. 54, No. 3 (Ex. 479, with its heaving piano arpegggios and sweeping vocal phrases articulated to accommodate poetic as well as musical rhythm.

Ex. 479

(It was in the radiant summer, when the sun only pretends to go down;
I dozed with open eyes, while the ship glided over the sea.)

---

[114] Nils Schiørring admits that Hartmann's reputation is somewhat faded, but maintains that 'it was through him and him alone that inspiration from the romantic German Lied first entered Danish music' (*Musikkens Historie i Danmark* (Copenhagen, 1977–8), ii. 201).

Ex. 480

(There is an enchantment on thy lip, there is a depth in thy glance,
there is the ethereal music of a dream in the sound of thy voice.)

Danish late-Romantic song reaches its zenith with Peter Heise (1830–79), who like Grieg studied with Moritz Hauptmann in Leipzig, and again like Grieg returned with the technical equipment to put fresh blood into the native lyric tradition. Heise's setting of 'Til en Veninde' [To a Woman-friend] (Ex. 480), a compact four-stanza poem by Emil Aarestrup (1800–56), reveals a command of harmonic tensions that enables him to achieve a perfect match for the poet's erotic verses.[115]

SWEDEN

Whereas the earlier phases of Danish Romantic music were in the hands of professional composers, a number of whom, like Schulz, Kunzen, Kuhlau, and Weyse, were German by birth or training but happy to work in harmony with a golden age of Danish poetry, in Sweden the influence of the dilettante was paramount. The *diktarmusiker* or man of letters with musical interests (a peculiarly Swedish phenomenon going back to C. M. Bellman or even further) was at this time usually a member of the Uppsala coterie led by

[115] Features of this setting, such as its economy and its progressive enharmonic modulations, suggest that Heise knew Schumann's 'Dein Angesicht', Op. 127, No. 2.

Erik Gustaf Geijer (1783–1847), Professor of History and a prominent figure in the so-called Gothic League, which was dedicated to the study and revival of ancient Scandinavian culture and moral virtues. Geijer was a lifelong music lover with a modest though undeveloped talent for composition; he produced a quantity of naïve, amateurish songs, mostly to his own verses, was concerned to maintain the primacy of melody (no doubt as part of aesthetic theories derived from Rousseau), and lent his influential name to a collection of folk-music (*Svenska folkvisor från forntiden* [Swedish Popular Songs from Olden Times]) published between 1814 and 1817 in collaboration with the antiquary A. A. Afzelius. This, and some other pioneer anthologies, though succeeded later in the century by more scientific studies, became the basis of a Swedish national-Romantic style that was by no means extinct by the beginning of the twentieth century.[116]

Other literary members of the Uppsala circle were Gunnar Wennerberg (1817–1901), who wrote both words and music of dialogue songs depicting student life (*Gluntarne*), and Karl Jonas Love Almqvist (1793–1866), a fastidious prose writer whose interpolated dreamlike melodies (called *Songes*) with their affinity to folk-song were innocent of accompaniment of any kind. Professional musicians who associated with the Uppsala dilettanti seem to have fallen under the spell of their aesthetic philosophies. Jacob Axel Josephson (1818–80) and Adolf Fredrik Lindblad (1801–78) may be said to have reversed the roles of the *diktarkomponist*, since both wrote the lyrics for a considerable proportion of their songs. Josephson held the post of *Director Musices* at Uppsala from 1849; Lindblad had a wider range as a composer, and his studies with Zelter in Berlin, his friendship and correspondence with Mendelssohn, and his devotion to the interpretative art of Jenny Lind, who took his songs into her repertoire, earned him a central position in Swedish song during the first half of the century.[117]

Bernhard Crusell (1775–1838), now remembered chiefly for his contributions to instrumental music, was another member of the Uppsala group. He attempted solo settings of lyric poems from *Frithjofs Saga*, the *magnum opus* of Esaias Tegnér (1782–1846), Professor of Greek at Lund University. While Tegnér's writings

---

[116] Carl-Allan Moberg showed that the Geijer–Afzelius collection had acquired the status of a classic by mid-nineteenth century, with the result that 'national-Romantic folk-song had begun to permeate the whole of Swedish musical life, from the infant school to the State Conservatory', 'Från kämpevisa till locklåt', *Svensk tidskrift för musikforskning*, 33 (1951), 5.

[117] Lindblad's collected songs were published by Hirsch of Stockholm between 1878 and 1890, and the composer was the subject of an important critique by C. R. Nyblom, *Adolf Fredrik Lindblad* (Minnesteckning) (Stockholm, 1881).

stand high in Swedish Romantic literature, the vigour of his poetry is but feebly conveyed in Crusell's dozen settings made in 1842. Franz Berwald (1796–1868), whose own lyric songs were comparatively few, considered that association with the Uppsala coterie had inhibited Crusell's talents, and in more general terms Berwald deprecated Swedish composers' preoccupation with *romancer* and *Lieder*, when they should have been grappling with the major instrumental forms.[118]

Events in the 1840s and 1850s, however, marked a turning-point in Swedish song. Geijer died in 1847, Lindblad settled in Stockholm, a strong reaction[119] against amateurism and the *diktarmusiker* set in, and the founding of the Leipzig Conservatory gave Swedish musicians, along with other Scandinavians, opportunities for a thorough musical education, and not least for experience of the more progressive European tendencies. A transitional personality, bridging what might be called the 'Uppsala' and the 'Leipzig' schools, was Ivar Christian Hallström (1826–1901), whose absorption of German Romantic influences, especially from Mendelssohn and Schumann, appears in his freedom of piano writing in such songs as the setting of a 'Serenad' by Stagnelius in 1854. Hallström's eclectic interests led him to experiment with the contemporary French chanson, thereby in a sense reintroducing to Sweden the French-born strophic romance in up-to-date guise, with piquant harmonies. He also made striking advances in the declamation of Swedish verse, as in 'Syarta svanor' [Black Swans] (1879), where every detail of Snoilsky's poem is vividly pointed.

In the works of August Söderman (1832–1876) Swedish song achieved a full measure of national identity through the fusion of contemporary German styles with distinctively Swedish idioms drawn from folk-music, and also with Norwegian national traits, as in his setting of Bjørnson's 'Ingerid Sletten' (Ex. 481).[120] On a much grander scale, though still paying allegiance to traditional models, are Söderman's extended ballads, most with German texts and orchestral accompaniments; a fine example (with Swedish text by Frans Hedberg) is 'Kung Heimer och Aslög' [King Heimer and Aslög] . This was a vein to be exploited by later Swedish composers,

---

[118] Erling Lomnäs (ed.), *Franz Berwald—Die Dokumente seines Leben* (Kassel, 1979), 186 ff.

[119] Led by Albert Rubenson (1826–1901), himself a composer whose songs show originality in harmony and structure.

[120] The importance of Bjørnson's verse to Swedish as well as Norwegian song, especially after 1870, can hardly be overstated.

Ex. 481

(Ingerid Sletten of Sillegjord had neither silver nor gold.)

like Wilhelm Stenhammar in 'Florez och Blanzeflor' (text by Levertin) (1891).

As much of the song production of Emil Sjögren (1853–1918) extends well beyond the limit of 1890, and is further enriched by discoveries among late Romantic poets such as Gustaf Fröding and Erik Axel Karlfeldt, a complete review of his career cannot be attempted here. Sjögren's style, like Söderman's, was grounded in the nationalist folk-music tradition, but was also indebted to a wide variety of European contemporaries—Brahms, Wagner, Liszt, and César Franck among them. He drew upon both Scandinavian and German poets, the latter including the Geibel and Heyse *Spanische Lieder*, settings of which precede Hugo Wolf's by almost a decade and are not altogether put in the shade by them.[121] The two *Tannhäuser* cycles must also be mentioned: the earlier one (Op. 3, 1880) to the Danish verses of Holger Drachmann, and the second (Op. 12, 1883–4) to the German of Julius Wolf. Through an analysis of 'Lad Vaaren komme' [Let Spring Come], a two-page song to words by the Danish poet Jens Peter Jacobsen, Axel Helmer[122] sums up the salient features of Sjögren's style round about 1890, mentioning in particular the way in which the course of the poem is faithfully mirrored in the mounting tension of sequential chromatic harmonies, the elliptic chord progressions of the penultimate section, the singer's final despairing monotone, and the use of a leitmotiv unifying the whole conception.

[121] Sjögren's 'Dereinst, Gedanke mein' can be compared both with the tensely *durch-komponiert* setting by Wolf and with Grieg's Op. 48, No. 2 (1889); the latter is impressive in its way, with a modal, chorale-like setting repeated identically for the second half of the poem, but Sjögren's gains by being through-composed and moving inexorably towards its climax.
[122] *Svensk solosång 1850–1890* (Uppsala, 1972), i. 290–1.

FINLAND

Separated from Sweden since 1809 and made a grand duchy of the Russian Empire, Finland was still in the process of emerging as a cultural entity.[123] The high quality of the Swedish verse of Johan Ludvig Runeberg (1804–77) was, however, recognized throughout Scandinavia and was frequently used by song-writers. Passages from his major work, *Fänrik Ståls sägner* [Ensign Stål's Stories], a cycle of poems dealing with the Russian–Swedish wars of 1808–9, had been set by A. F. Lindblad, but it was the opening invocation 'Vårt Land' [Our Country] that became universally known when it was enshrined as a national anthem with music by Fredrik Pacius (1809–91). Pacius was a pupil of Spohr and one of several German-born musicians who devoted their energies to fostering musical life in their adopted country. No small part of Pacius's service to the nation was his publication of folk-music in the Finnish language.[124]

A fair idea of the state of Finnish song during the first nine decades of the century can be obtained from the anthology *Det sjungande Finland* [Finland in Song], edited in the 1880s by Martin Wegelius (1846–1906), founder of the Helsingfors Institute of Music that was to become the Sibelius Academy. The contents include folk-song arrangements from the two cultures, romance-style compositions like the Tegnér settings by Crusell (who was of Finnish origins), and attempts to naturalize the German Lied and parody the Scandinavian ballad. In 'Paimenessa' [Herding Song] Ilman Krohn (1867–1960) paints a rural idyll with passages in 5/4 time imitative of the shepherd's pipe, Robert Kajanus (1856–1933) sets Runeberg's 'Fly ei undan' [Fly not away] as a strophic Lied, and the 23-year-old Jan Sibelius contributes his first known solo song, a setting of a Runeberg 'Serenad'. Filip von Schantz (1835–65), composer of the *Kullervo* Overture, one of the first orchestral pieces to be inspired by the *Kalevala*, is represented by several songs that testify to the loss Finnish music sustained through his early death. His setting of the Runeberg 'Blomman' [The Flower] (Ex. 482), with its intriguing chiastic structure, seeks to transplant Schumannesque idioms into Finnish earth.

---

[123] Swedish remained the language of administration and higher learning, but since the attainment of political independence in 1979 the country has been officially bilingual. Only about 7 per cent of the population is now Swedish-speaking.

[124] Texts of traditional Finnish songs had been collected by Elias Lönnrot, who also wove into a continuous narrative legendary material he had collected from oral sources, thus creating the national epic *Kalevala* that was to provide composers with so valuable a body of mythology.

Ex. 482

När sig vå - ren

å - ter fö - der klar och ljuf,

Da - gen ler och so - len glö - der, Vak - nar du;

Fä - ster vid din ve - ka stän - gel Blad och

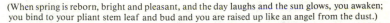

(When spring is reborn, bright and pleasant, and the day laughs and the sun glows, you awaken; you bind to your pliant stem leaf and bud and you are raised up like an angel from the dust.)

NORWAY

For several decades before L. M. Lindeman's great collection of folk tunes (*Ældre og nyere Fjeldmelodier*) [Older and More Recent Mountain Melodies], published between 1853 and 1867, came to the enthralled attention of Edvard Grieg, Norwegian folk-music had already entered the bloodstream of his predecessors and contemporaries. Stylized folk idioms occur frequently in the romances of Halfdan Kjerulf (1815–68) and Rikard Nordraak (1842–66). The latter, a kinsman of Bjørnstjerne Bjørnson, ardently shared that writer's enthusiasm for a regenerated, independent Norway, but his slender output, impatience of technical disciplines, and early death combined to make it difficult even now to assess his creative potential, though it is certain that he awakened Grieg to the possibilities of blending a nationalist style with German Romantic song.

Grieg may have been more realistically indebted to Halfdan Kjerulf, whose romances are miniatures in delicate pastel colours, their voice and keyboard parts integrated with unostentatious skill. Among Norwegian poets, Johan Welhaven (1807–73) inspired some of Kjerulf's most picturesque songs, such as 'Lockender toner' [Luring sounds] and 'Paa fjeldet' [On the Mountain] (Ex. 483), in which crystalline diatonic harmonies float upon sustained pedal notes, and the sounds of traditional instruments are suggested. But

Ex. 483

(Now sits the woodsprite on the hillock and blows on the horn and is so happy.)

it was even more often that Bjørnson brought out the best in Kjerulf, as he did with many another Scandinavian composer—hardly surprisingly, since more than any other major poet of his time he meant his sonorous verse to be sung.[125] Among Bjørnson–Kjerulf settings may be mentioned 'Synnøves sang' with its hummed prelude and postlude, 'Ingrids sang' in the rhythm of a *springdans*, and the magical 'Prinsessen'.

GRIEG

The career of Edvard Grieg (1843–1907) as a song-writer[126] can almost be charted according to the poets from whom he took his texts: German Romantics set in Lied-forms during student days at Leipzig; Danish poets such as Christian Winther and Hans Christian Andersen set chiefly as strophic romances during the stay in Denmark (1863–6) and after the meeting with Nina Hagerup; and Norwegian poets almost exclusively for about a decade and a half after the Griegs' removal to Christiania, the period when the easygoing Danish romance-style gives place to a terse, deeply expressive mode yielding masterpieces like the Bjørnson 'Det første Møde' [The First Meeting] and Ibsen's 'Svanen' [The Swan] and 'Borte' [Departed].

New paths were again opened by the poems of Aasmund Olavsson Vinje (1818–70), written in the broad-vowelled synthesis of regional dialects called *landsmål* (now the basis of Nynorsk or New Norwegian). In setting the Vinje poems (and ten years later in the Garborg *Haugtussa* [The Hillock-Maid] cycle), Grieg reverts to strophic patterns, combining them with a harmonically advanced tonal language to form a medium of poignant nostalgia. Between 1880 and 1890, however, the choice of verse is more diversified, with a miscellaneous collection of *Romancer* (*ældre og nyere*) [Romances Old and New], among them the large-scale episodic setting of 'Fra Monte Pincio', and two sets of songs to texts by the irrepressible Dane, Holger Drachmann. Norwegian verse is represented at this time by settings of poems by John Paulsen, a personal friend who supplied Grieg with more texts than any other writer.

The songs of the 1890s must be mentioned here, however briefly, since they include some of Grieg's finest work: the settings of the late-Romantic Norwegian poet, Vilhelm Krag (among them the

---

[125] Bjørnson wanted to publish his 1870 verse collection under the simple title *Sange*, and only after some argument with the publisher settled for *Digte og Sange* [Poems and Songs].

[126] Grieg's songs are discussed by Astra Desmond in Gerald Abraham (ed.), *Grieg: A Symposium* (London, 1948), 71–99, and by John Horton in *Grieg* (London, 1974), chap. 10. The early German and Danish songs are dealt with by Dag Schjelderup-Ebbe in *Edvard Grieg 1858–1867* (Oslo and London, 1964).

wonderfully impressionistic 'Der skreg en fugl' [A Bird Cried]), some
delightful children's songs, and the *Haugtussa* cycle based on Arne
Garborg's classic of *landsmål* poetry. Finally, Grieg turned to an
amateur Danish poet, Otto Benzon, and in two books of settings
attempted a fusion of Scandinavian traditions with the contemporary
world of Wagnerian declamation and quasi-orchestral keyboard
writing—and by no means without success in such examples as 'Der
gynger en Båd på Bølge' [A Boat is rocking on the Wave] and 'Lys
Nat' [Lucent Night] (Ex. 484), a magical impressionist painting.

A survey of Grieg's entire song production reveals that he made
use of a considerable variety of forms, ranging from the simplest
strophic romance to quite complex through-composed or episodic
structures. Even strophic repetitions may be redeemed from monotony by the introduction of fresh points of interest in the piano part,
by changes of tempo, key, and mode, or by adept transitions, as in
the early Andersen 'Rosenknoppen', Op. 18, No. 8.

Grieg maintained that, with the isolated exception of Solvejg's
repeated song in the *Peer Gynt* theatre music (1876), no quotation
from folk music occurs in the whole of his original song writing.
There are, however, many passages strongly reminiscent of traditional

Ex. 484

(Scarcely come, you depart! Lucent night, why are you so short?)

songs or dances: melodically in head-motifs and cadential formulae, harmonically in the employment of pedal-points and bare fifths (as already noted in the songs of Nordraak and Kjerulf), and rhythmically in the introduction of dance-measures and the frequent mingling of duplet and triplet pulse-divisions.

While Grieg inevitably overshadows other Norwegian song-writers of the nineteenth century, alike in response to a wide variety of poems, in formal diversity, and in harmonic resource, he was generous enough to appreciate merit in a number of his compatriots. The programme book of the first Bergen Festival which he helped to organize in the summer of 1898 provides a roll-call of Norwegians whose songs were included in the recitals: Nordraak, Kjerulf, Eyvind Alnæs (then in the early years of a career in which song writing was to play a prominent part), Johan Backer-Lunde, Per Winge, Otto Winter-Hjelm, the short-lived Sigurd Lie, the rather mannered Johan Selmer, and two composers who stood high in Grieg's esteem: Agathe Backer-Grøndahl (1847–1907) and Christian Sinding (1856–1941). The former, a fine concert pianist, was also a prolific song composer who ranks with the most commanding exponents of Scandinavian Romantic song. Sinding had by the date of the Festival published nearly twenty books of settings of Norwegian, Danish, and German texts, but much of his best work in the field was yet to come. His entire output of about 250 solo songs is overdue for reassessment.[127]

(g) BRITAIN AND THE UNITED STATES

By NICHOLAS TEMPERLEY

Both Great Britain and the United States experienced difficulty, during the nineteenth century, in establishing a native tradition of art-song. Part of the problem was shared with continental Europe: that the song with piano accompaniment had long been regarded as a purely domestic, amateur form of music and, as such, not worthy of the higher creative efforts of the composer. Even Beethoven only occasionally exerted himself when composing *Lieder*. Such views were still held by Schumann in the 1830s, and they also tended to prevail in the English-speaking countries. Thus we find a writer in

---

[127] A beginning has been made with a selection of fifty songs, edited by Øystein Gaukstad and David Monrad Johansen (Oslo, 1978).

1823 illustrating the low state of English song writing with a list of
the 'few English songs' that had 'risen to a high estimation, taken
as compositions for the orchestra or the stage, within the last
twenty-five years';[128] he did not think it worthwhile to mention the
serious domestic songs with piano that had been published by such
composers as Thomas Attwood, John Clarke-Whitfeld, George
Frederick Pinto, and Samuel Wesley.[129] Leading professional singers
performed only with orchestral accompaniment, and in this domain
English or American composers had to compete with the overwhelming prestige of Italian operas and concert arias.

There was, indeed, a large and flourishing market for domestic
songs, but the publishers who controlled it found that only a
comparatively simple-minded product was likely to be profitable.
The drawing-room ballad, or 'concert-household song' as Wiley
Hitchcock has called it,[130] was often launched on the stage or concert
platform by a prima donna with an orchestra; but it was emphatically
aimed at the amateur, who would buy it in sheet-music form with
piano accompaniment, in large numbers if its appeal was sufficiently
broad—hence the term '[music] shop ballad'.

Two important sub-categories of ballad, both destined to influence
art-song, were the national and the exotic. Various collections of
'national songs', mostly of a Celtic flavour, had appeared in the
earlier decades of the century; Thomas Moore's *Irish Melodies* (1807-
34) were the most famous. Again, Isaac Nathan and John Braham's
Hebrew Melodies (1816) are an early musical example of the growing
taste for oriental art.

Of the many successful composers of drawing-room ballads on
both sides of the Atlantic, perhaps the greatest was an American,
Stephen Foster (1826-64).[131] Some devoted their energies entirely to
ballads; some, particularly in Britain, consciously divided their time
between ballads written for profit and 'serious' songs written for
their own satisfaction or the esteem of like-minded musicians. Others
again idealistically confined themselves to serious art-song.

GERMAN INFLUENCE

In attempting to establish the art-song, composers had to contend

---

[128] *Quarterly Musical Magazine and Review*, v (1823), 257 n.

[129] See Vol. VIII, pp. 591-2.

[130] *Music in the United States: A Historical Introduction* (rev. 3rd edn.; Englewood Cliffs,
1988), 69.

[131] See Gilbert Chase, *America's Music From the Pilgrims to the Present* (New York, 1955),
chap. 15. For an account of the ballad in England, see Harold Simpson, *A Century of Ballads
1810-1910* (London, 1910).

not only with the indifference or pessimism of publishers, but also with the attitudes of some critics and fellow-musicians who were inclined to despise the whole genre of keyboard songs because of its association with the ballad. And here the Anglo-Saxon composer faced an additional dilemma: the best models of art-song tended increasingly to come from Germany. Some serious-minded composers responded by whole-heartedly modelling their songs on the German Lied. Others—to be considered later—reacted by asserting the value of the English song tradition, and emphasizing recognizably British or American characteristics.

STERNDALE BENNETT

The tradition of sending young composers to Germany (particularly Leipzig) for their training was established rather sooner in Britain than in the United States. Among early examples were Charles Neate (1784–1877) and Cipriani Potter (1792–1871), both for a time in Beethoven's circle at Vienna. One of the first whose careers were strongly shaped by this process was William Sterndale Bennett (1816–75), a pupil of Potter's. His early friendship with Mendelssohn led to four long visits to Germany in the years 1836–42, where he attracted the admiration not only of Mendelssohn and Schumann, but of the German musical world in general; German publishers pressed him to produce songs. He composed twelve (published in two sets as Op. 23 (1842) and Op. 35 (1856)), which were clearly and consciously modelled on the German Lied. We know from surviving letters that Bennett was determined to have them published simultaneously in England and Germany, and that he held them up for years because of the problem of finding suitable translations (most of the texts were originally English, but some were German). When he had the translations, he took great pains in adapting the melodic lines to suit the varying rhythms of the two languages.[132]

In 'Gentle Zephyr', Op. 23, No. 6[133] (comp. *c*.1837), Bennett adopted the simple strophic form, but constructed the melodic line with a subtlety unknown to the ordinary ballad (Ex. 485). The piano introduction, instead of presenting a plain statement of the first phrase of the song, gives its own transformation of the phrase, shifting the stress and harmonic rhythm; and it is in this form—with still other harmonies—that the phrase returns near the end of each

---

[132] Nicholas Temperley, 'Sterndale Bennett and the Lied', *Musical Times*, 106 (1975), 958–61 and 1060–3.

[133] Geoffrey Bush and Nicholas Temperley (eds.), *English Songs (1800–1860)* (Musica Britannica, 43; London, 1979).

Ex. 485

verse. The accompaniment figuration sweeps through the whole song, carrying over the full closes and breaks between phrases, sections and stanzas, and making the song a single, cumulative experience; and of course at the same time it depicts the wind and the stream.

It is obvious that this song is permeated by German influence. It was the Germans, from Mozart's 'Abendempfindung' [Evening Mood] onwards, who had developed the song unified by its accompaniment. Schubert's *Schöne Müllerin* songs might seem the obvious models. But Mendelssohn loomed larger than Schubert to Bennett in the 1830s, and we can find a similar mood and procedure in Mendelssohn's 'Andres Maienlied' [Another May Song], Op. 8, No. 8, and 'Im Frühling' [In Spring], Op. 9, No. 4, and 'Frühlingslied' [Spring Song], Op. 19, No. 1. None of them, however, is quite like Bennett's: his style had its own character; the harmony of the second bar, for instance, has a piquancy that is quite individual. Within its modest scope 'Gentle Zephyr' was a masterpiece equal to any song Mendelssohn had yet written. Bennett extended the principles established here in the other songs of Opp. 23 and 35, within a fairly wide range of mood and form. All but three of the twelve are strophic; all are amorous or lyrical. From first to last Bennett was greatly concerned with refinement and sensibility, and was extremely sensitive to the problems of bilingual and multi-verse word setting.[134] The Mendelssohnian tradition was carried on in the songs of Bennett's short-lived pupil, Francis Bache (1833–58).

PIERSON

Henry Hugo Pierson (1816–73) was a contemporary of Bennett's, and was briefly associated with him at Dresden (he provided a translation for one of Bennett's songs). Afterwards their paths diverged, and Pierson was, in any case, a very different type by background and temperament. The son of an Anglican clergyman and Oxford don, Pierson's social and educational background was higher than that of most English musicians of the day. He was educated at Trinity College, Cambridge, and was well imbued with the Romantic movement in literature. Without acquiring a degree he left for Germany in 1839, and took private lessons from several German musicians. Though elected to the Reid Professorship of Music at Edinburgh in 1844, he never took up the post, but settled permanently in Germany, where he was briefly a member of

---

134 Temperley, 'Sterndale Bennett', pp. 1062–3.

Mendelssohn's circle but soon repudiated his influence and began to
work out his own methods and ideals in composition. His music was
decisively rejected in England—the leading critics made a determined
attack on his oratorio *Jerusalem* (1852)—but won a good deal of
respect in Germany: his music to the second part of *Faust* (1854),
for instance, was for many years regularly played at performances
of Goethe's drama. Pierson adopted a kind of German nationalism,
but nevertheless constantly returned to Shakespeare and the modern
English poets for inspiration.[135]

About a hundred songs by Pierson were published. There were
some early English settings of Byron, Shelley and Burns. The Burns
songs, Op. 7, published with bilingual texts, were praised by
Schumann, who found their 'strong, manly expression' [*kräftigeren
männlichen Ausdruck*] a pleasant change from fashionable effem-
inacy,[136] though he regarded the music as often too elaborate for
the simple verses. In one of these, 'John Anderson, my jo' (Ex.
486),[137] Pierson respected the simple repeating rhythm of the poem,
but by surprising turns of melody and harmony turned the strophic
'ballad' into an art-song of some sophistication. The second verse
diverges from the first after its opening phrase.

Ex. 486

From 1845 all Pierson's songs were published in Germany, with
German and English texts underlaid, or German only. Unlike
Bennett, he rarely used the simple strophic form, preferring to vary
his verses or to write entirely continuous settings closely following
the changing imagery and emotion of the text. A powerful example
of his later style is the Dirge: 'Fear no more the Heat of the Sun'
(Shakespeare).[138] It has two verses with almost identical music; in
each case the first half is in A minor common time (Ex. 487), the

---

[135] Temperley, 'Henry Hugo Pierson, 1815–73', *Musical Times*, 104 (1973), 1217–20 and
105 (1974), 31–4.
[136] *Neue Zeitschrift für Musik*, viii (1842), 32; repr. Schumann, *Schriften über Musik und
Musiker*, iii (4th edn.; Leipzig, 1891), 113.
[137] *English Songs (1800–1860)*, p. 98.
[138] Ibid., p. 110.

Ex. 487

second, unexpectedly, in D major 6/8, reflecting the refrain-like text 'Golden lads and girls all must | Follow thee, and come to dust', and a similar sentiment in the second verse. For the last verse Pierson suggests the melody of Ex. 487 in the accompaniment, but then, following a metrical change ('No exorciser harm thee'), writes entirely new music, with an extraordinary harmonic progression for the closing lines.

These brief excerpts give only a glimpse of the freedom and boldness of Pierson's writing, particularly in his harmonic unpredictability. It could be said that in many songs his disrespect for convention brings him close to the unintelligible, but this fault is in the opposite direction from those of every other contemporary British composer. Among his most rewarding songs are 'Under the Greenwood Tree' (Shakespeare) (1839); 'Beware the Black Friar' (Byron) (1839); 'All my Heart's thine own' (1844?);[139] 'Heimweh' (Beck) (c.1850); 'Take, oh take those Lips away' (Fletcher) (c.1852);[140] 'Those Evening Bells' (Moore) (c.1854);[141] 'Der gute Kamerad' (1859); 'Thekla's Klage' (Schiller) (c.1861); 'Claribel' (Tennyson) (c.1861); and 'The White Owl' (Tennyson) (c.1868).[142] The last exploits a rare comic vein in Pierson's make-up which was all too little developed. It is entirely individual in style and bears comparison with any song of the period. Another type was classified as a Ballade in Pierson's collected songs;[143] it has no connection with the drawing-room ballad, but is an evocation of medieval chivalry, akin to the *Lohengrin* brand of Romanticism. His best effort in this direction is possibly 'Sturmritt'

[139] Ibid., p. 106.
[140] Ibid., p. 103.
[141] Ibid., p. 106.
[142] Ibid., p. 114.
[143] *15 Liebeslieder; 15 Balladen und Romanzen* (Leipzig, c.1875).

[The Cavalier's Nightsong], to a text by Feodor Loewe beginning 'Zu Ross! zu Ross!'

SULLIVAN

Of the next generation Arthur Sullivan (1842–1900) is perhaps to be classified among the 'Germans': certainly he completed his musical education at Leipzig as the first holder of the Mendelssohn Scholarship, awarded by the Royal Academy of Music. His serious songs are all early in date; among them are five Shakespeare settings of 1863–4, the finest of which is also the best known, 'Orpheus with his Lute' (Ex. 488). Its richly textured accompaniment can be called Mendelssohnian in a general way, but there is much about the song

Ex. 488

that is fresh and original, and it has a youthful forthrightness and confidence perhaps well calculated to appeal to Anglo-Saxon ears. Sullivan was responsible for the first English 'song cycle' in the German sense, *The Window, or The Songs of the Wrens* (1869), in which he collaborated with Tennyson. (The original plan was for Sir John Millais to provide illustrations, but this English *Gesamtkunstwerk* was never fully realized.) Despite the poor quality of the verses, Sullivan produced some very attractive songs, exploiting to the full his natural melodic gift as well as the technical resources he had acquired in Leipzig. No. 8, 'No Answer', shows what he could do with a simple sixteen-bar tune (Ex. 489).

Ex. 489

Winds are loud and you— are dumb: Take my love, for love— will come, Love will come but once— a life, Love will come but once— a life.

WOMEN COMPOSERS

The first woman to hold the Mendelssohn Scholarship, Maude Valérie White (1855–1937), published an *Album of German Songs* which included several successful *Lieder* in the Mendelssohn–Brahms tradition; in Geoffrey Bush's opinion her masterpiece in this genre is 'Die Himmelsaugen' (1885),[144] while her English songs never reached the same level of inspiration. Liza Lehmann (1862–1918), herself a soprano singer of some note, also succeeded in this line, publishing two sets of German *Lieder*, but then went on to produce some excellent songs in her own language. Lacking a great spontaneous gift for melody, she gains her best effects by unexpected harmonic and rhythmic twists, by unusually full and rich piano accompaniments and interludes, and by intelligent text setting. Her highest achievement is the song cycle based on Tennyson's *In memoriam* (1898). It is so continuous as to be almost a cantata, with few decisive breaks between songs, many thematic links and recapitulations, and a predominantly narrative–dramatic tone broken by occasional spells of more regularly phrased lyrical material. The cycle ends with an optional epilogue for spoken voice with piano. A work of this kind may be said to have transcended the direct German influence, and this is still more clearly true of the late-nineteenth-century songs of Parry, Stanford, and Somervell.

ART-SONG IN AMERICA

The American art-song had come even more strongly under German hegemony, as a whole procession of composers, beginning with Richard Willis (1819–1900) in 1841, travelled to Leipzig to

---

[144] Bush, 'Songs', in Nicholas Temperley (ed.), *Music in Britain: The Romantic Age 1800–1914* (London, 1981), 281.

complete their studies; their number was augmented by several
German born and trained composers who settled in the States.[145]
John Knowles Paine (1839–1906) published only eight songs, but
they show a refined skill and a surprising affinity with Sterndale
Bennett: for example, 'I wore your Roses yesterday' (1879), quoted
by Upton. The same may be said of Dudley Buck (1839–1909),
whose 'Sunset' (1877), to a poem by the American poet–musician
Sidney Lanier, attains some melodic distinction. The chief resource
of these German-trained Americans, by then somewhat outdated,
was the continuous accompaniment of broken or repeated chords
sustaining a melody of regular phrase structure. But Buck in his
later songs, such as 'Spring's Awakening' (1893), moved on to freer
and more varied styles. In the songs of Homer Bartlett (1846–1920)
a certain lushness of harmony infuses the texture, and this is further
developed in the work of George Chadwick (1854–1931) and, above
all, Edward Macdowell (1861–1908).

Chadwick, belonging to the school of 'Boston Classicists', perhaps
awaits upward re-evaluation; and two sets of his songs to lyrics by
Arlo Bates (1850–1918) have been reprinted.[146] Boston intellectual
society was in the 1890s experiencing a delayed wave of orientalism,
represented in Bate's poems *Told in the Gate* (1892), some settings
of which Chadwick published in 1897. The other Bates set is a *Flower
Cycle* (1902), each poem a miniature describing a particular flower.
Chadwick writes effective melodies, using the high notes of the voice
to good effect; his harmonies and accompaniment textures are quite
varied, though in all cases German-derived. 'The Cardinal Flower'
has three verses, each divided into a quiet 3/4 section in which the

Ex. 490

---

[145] Details in William T. Upton, *Art-song in America* (Boston and New York, 1930), chaps.
4 and 5.
[146] In *Earlier American Music*, xvi (1980), with an introduction by Steven Ledbetter.

blaze with splen - did fire, their fan - cy stays.___
throws___ while proud as beau-ti-ful she glows.___

voice doubles the lowest note of repeated chords in the piano, and a passionate outburst in 4/4 (Ex. 490). In the first two verses the first section is in D minor and the second in F major; in the last, the keys are respectively D major and F sharp major. Unfortunately the character of this passage is justified only by the words of the first verse. But this is a resourceful song.

MACDOWELL

Macdowell came into early contact with Latin American and French musicians, but the decisive period in his training was spent in Germany (1879–88), where the predominant influence was that of Raff. For some years he contemplated settling in Germany, but he returned to the United States in 1887, and there spent the rest of his short career. Several of his earliest sets of songs were written to German texts. Their accompaniments are almost complete piano pieces in themselves: in 'Oben, wo die Sterne glühen' [In the Skies, where Stars are Glowing], Op. 11, No. 3 (1883) (Ex. 491), for instance, the voice often sings little more than an inner harmonic part, though the rich texture is undeniably attractive.

Ex. 491

Andante, ma non troppo

O - ben, wo die Ster - ne glüh - en, müs - sen
In the skies, where stars are glow - ing, Must___ sweet

zart (teneroso)

The set *From an Old Garden*, Op. 26 (1887), suffers from impossibly arch texts by Margaret Deland; again, each is about a flower. With *Six Love Songs*, Op. 40 (1890),[147] Macdowell comes into his own as a setter of English verse. He begins to write more convincingly vocal melodies (Op. 40, No. 2) and to explore other moods besides the sweetly sentimental (e.g. in 'Folksong', Op. 47, No. 3). In the later sets there is a welcome simplification of the piano texture which forces greater concentration on melody. From Op. 56 onwards Macdowell largely supplied his own verse, and his final mastery of the art-song is well demonstrated in 'Long Ago', Op. 56, No. 1, a sophisticated 'folk' song in simple ternary form; or in 'Fair Spring-tide', Op. 60, No. 2, where a like simplicity is enhanced by the contrasting plunge from D minor to A flat major at the words 'Ah Springtide, thou dost touch the quick of ev'ry creature here below'. Macdowell's edge over other Americans lay chiefly in his mastery of late-Romantic European harmonic style. His songs have been greatly underestimated, chiefly because they are not 'American' enough for such intensely patriotic critics as Gilbert Chase.[148] But he never came to grips with the challenge of setting great poetry to music.

---

[147] Macdowell's songs, Opp. 40, 47, 56, 58, and 60, have been reprinted in *Earlier American Music*, vii (1972).
[148] Chase, *America's Music*, pp. 363–4.

ART-SONG IN THE ENGLISH TRADITION

All through this period there were British and American composers who resisted or ignored the German dominance and achieved some success in the development of art-song in the English tradition. Of course, the line cannot be strictly drawn, either between these composers and the 'German' school, or between the art-song and the drawing-room ballad. But in Britain, at least, there arose a group of composers not without talent who were determined to keep alive a type of song represented in the early nineteenth century by the serious work of composers like Clarke-Whitfeld, Wesley, and Bishop. They tended to find models in stage music, where the predominant foreign influence was Italian rather than German, but where English opera was also experiencing a rebirth; or in the indigenous traditions of church music. The bolder spirits were inspired by the English Romantic poets.

John Barnett (1802–90), Michael William Balfe (1808–70), Edward James Loder (1813–65), and George Alexander Macfarren (1813–87) were all leading figures in the development of English Romantic opera. All composed a fair number of ballads (often the most profitable parts of their operas); Barnett and Loder produced them on a massive scale. In this respect they differed from the 'German' school—Bennett and Pierson regarded ballads as betrayals of their artistic integrity—but all four, given the opportunity, aimed at higher artistic goals.

Barnett in 1834 published an ambitious collection entitled *Lyric Illustrations of the Modern Poets*, which contains some of the earliest settings of Shelley and Wordsworth, in an uncompromising style quite distinct from his facile ballad idiom. He claimed to have written them purely 'for his own gratification' and to have had them 'bitterly abused by the ... Musical Profession and Press',[149] and indeed Henry Chorley in the *Athenaeum* did maintain that 'the dreamy reveries of Shelley are not things to be sung ... Mr. Barnett seems to have been overborne by the fullness and spirituality of the poetry he had selected.'[150] Several of the songs, however, achieve considerable stature without close imitation of existing models: best of all is 'I arise from Dreams of thee' (Shelley).[151]

Balfe and Loder enjoyed a facility in writing memorable melodies that was denied to Barnett. Balfe's famous 'Come into the Garden,

---

[149] Bush, 'Songs', pp. 269–70. Two songs from this collection are in *English Songs (1800–1860)*, pp. 44 and 49.

[150] *Athenaeum* (1834), 753.

[151] *English Songs (1800–1860)*, p. 44.

Maud'[152] is a serious song rather than a ballad, and he also wrote serious settings of Kingsley (e.g. 'The Sands of Dee')[153] and Longfellow ('Goodnight, beloved'). Loder, though trained in Germany, indicated his loyalty to the tradition of Bishop's Shakespeare songs in the preface to his collection *Songs of the Poets* (1844), some of which suggest nationalism by their emphasis on the pentatonic scale. But his outstanding work is elsewhere, particularly in 'Invocation to the Deep' (*c*.1845) (Ex. 492),[154] and 'I heard a Brooklet Gushing' (1850),[155] the latter a setting of Longfellow's translation

Ex. 492

---

[152] Ibid., p. 52.
[153] Ibid., p. 57.
[154] Complete ibid., p. 88.
[155] Ibid., p. 94.

of Wilhelm Müller's 'Wohin?' from the *Schöne Müllerin* cycle. In these songs Loder combines a richness of fundamentally diatonic melody and harmony with well-developed pianism.

Macfarren demonstrated his nationalism by his choice of subjects for operas and texts for songs, and by his undaunted championship of British music. Of his few serious songs, a pair published in 1867 with clarinet obbligato are the most remarkable: 'Pack, Clouds, away' (Heywood) and 'The Widow Bird' (Shelley).[156] Geoffrey Bush has also drawn attention to an unusual set of four songs with prose texts taken from *The Arabian Nights*.[157]

John Liptrot Hatton (1809–86) was also a man of the theatre; he composed operas and incidental music, and developed a one-man show in which he delivered recitations and comic songs at the piano. He also published an important collection of English songs. His *Songs, and other Poems by Herrick, Ben Jonson, and Sedley* (1850) has much in common with Barnett's and Loder's 'serious' collections, including the claims in the preface, in which Hatton said he had written the songs 'for his own amusement'. These are miniatures, and as such can withstand the unvarying four- or eight-bar phrase structure which was Hatton's weakness. They are unpretentious, highly apt for their texts, and benefit from excellent writing for the piano, as in No. 12, 'To Daisies' (Ex. 493), which can claim authentic English roots in the line of Clementi, Field, and Bennett. In the best known song of this set, 'To Anthea',[158] Hatton rises to considerable passion.

Ex. 493

[156] Ibid., p. 80.
[157] One of these ibid., p. 76.
[158] Ibid., p. 59.

let the whole world then dis-pose It selfe to live or dye.

INDIGENOUS SONG IN THE UNITED STATES

This type of song had its parallel in a later generation of American composers. Nationalism ran high in the United States in those times. William H. Fry (1813–64), who wrote the first American 'grand opera', made a strong plea for an indigenous style in American art-music.[159] But he left no independent songs. George F. Bristow (1825–98), also an opera composer, studied with Macfarren in London, and his songs, on the borderline between ballad and art-song, have much affinity with both Macfarren's and Loder's. Francis Boott (1813–1904) was a prolific song-writer who took his main models from Italian opera. His setting of Kingsley's 'The Sands of Dee'[160] makes an interesting contrast with Balfe's.

The most talented American of the 'indigenous' school, however, was Alfred H. Pease (1838–82), whose songs have been woefully neglected despite strong advocacy by William Upton. After his training in Germany, which gave him ample technical mastery, Pease reverted to a style that owed much to the ballad or 'national song', and worked on the problems of setting Romantic English poetry. 'Sea Song' by Kingsley (1872), is modal; 'It's we two for aye' by Jean Ingelow (1874), is pentatonic; many others contain moments of quite individual colouring, for instance 'My Little Love' by Mary H. Higham (1878). The beginning of this last song is shown in Ex. 494. It is ternary in form, the first (and third) parts beginning

[159] *Musical World and Times*, 21 January 1854.
[160] Quoted in Upton, *Art-song in America*, p. 32.

Ex. 494

Moderato

God keep you safe, my lit - tle

love, All thro' the night; Rest close in his en - cir - cling

arms Un - til the light; My heart is with you, as I

kneel to pray, Good-night! God keep you in His care al - way. Good-night! Good-

night! God keep you in His care al - way.

in A minor and ending in C major; the middle section is in B major and E major. Ternary form was often chosen by Pease, but the middle section is often in an unexpected key. Of fifty-four known songs, nine (including Ex. 494) are lullabies, but he explored a number of different veins including a 'Hungarian Air', a 'Bedouin Song', and an Italianate 'Brindisi', and he set poems of Tennyson, Longfellow, and Elizabeth Barrett Browning as well as some of little worth. Unhappily Pease failed to gain recognition from his compatriots, and any further development of a distinctively American art-song had to await the coming of Charles Ives.[161]

THE 'SACRED SONG'

A sub-genre cultivated in Victorian homes on both sides of the Atlantic was the 'sacred song'. Large quantities of simple-minded ones were published, often of still less worth than the average secular ballad. But on occasion serious composers tried their hand. Sterndale Bennett wrote a few sacred songs of some merit ('The Better Land' is the most notable); Loder published a collection of fine and deeply felt *Sacred Songs and Ballads*, dedicated to Bennett, in 1840, the texts being metrical paraphrases of biblical passages by M. D. Ryan. Samuel Sebastian Wesley (1810–76), by profession a church musician, contributed some fine songs that partake of his very individual anthem style, especially 'By the Rivers of Babylon' (1836) and a set of three metrical collects published as *Sacred Songs* in 1851.[162] In the United States, Dudley Buck, also a leading organist and church musician, was the best representative of this tradition; his *Three Offertories*, Op. 91 (1882), bring an unabashed Romanticism, not unlike that of Sullivan's 'The Lost Chord', to the setting of strictly liturgical texts in a way that offends some tastes but shows undeniable skill and resource.

[161] See Vol. X, pp. 575, 582.
[162] 'By the Rivers of Babylon' and one of the collects are in *English Songs* (*1800–1860*) pp. 65 and 70.

PARRY AND STANFORD

In the last three decades of the century foundations for a new flowering of English song were laid by Charles Hubert Hastings Parry (1848–1918) and Charles Villiers Stanford (1852–1924), though the idea that they led an English musical renaissance is perhaps exaggerated since, at least in this branch of the art, a worthy tradition already existed. German influence, by this time chiefly in the person of Brahms, was clearly evident in both men's work, but their powers were of an order to assert strong independent personality. Parry in his youth spent only one long summer in Germany, where, interestingly enough, he studied with Pierson; it was perhaps due to his teacher's example that he composed *Four Sonnets of Shakespeare* with German and English words between 1873 and 1882 (pub. 1887).[163] The Anglo-Irish Stanford studied at Leipzig with Reinecke, and at Berlin under Kiel, and published two sets of Heine *Lieder* (Opp. 4 and 7).

Of the two, it was Parry who made the art-song one of the most important branches of his activity as a composer. He organized seventy-four major songs into a series of books published as *English Lyrics*, Sets 1–10, between 1885 and 1918; two more sets were published after his death, made up of songs from various periods of his life; and there were many more, some published, some left in manuscript.

Parry's superior education and knowledge of literature and aesthetics made him exquisitely sensitive to the rhythms and finer connotations of English poetry. As a result, he wrote few strophic songs; even those that come close to repeating the music of the first verse make slight variations to fit the text. A good example occurs in 'Blow, blow, thou Winter Wind' (1886),[164] one of the most deservedly well known of his Shakespeare settings. Ex. 495 shows

Ex. 495

---

[163] All four pub. in *Hubert Parry: Songs*, ed. Geoffrey Bush (Musica Britannica, 49; 1982).
[164] Ibid., p. 28.

how Parry avoids the first beat of the bar in the second, third, and fourth lines of verse 1, and uses an imperfect cadence before returning to the opening melody at 'Thy tooth . . .'. In verse 2, however, the line 'As benefits forgot' has a different natural accentuation from its correlate in verse 1. Parry shifts the musical phrase accordingly, so that it ends on a G; and he now takes advantage of this change to omit the dominant harmony of the imperfect cadence (Ex. 496).

Ex. 496

Both verses reach a splendid climax on a high G sharp near the end; Parry was acutely conscious of the need to reserve highest notes for a climax near the end of a song, and, indeed, he discussed this matter in one of his essays. There are several other first-rate Shakespeare settings: finest of all, perhaps, is 'Take, O take those Lips away',[165] with voice and piano well integrated, phrase structure perfectly matched to the poem, shapely vocal phrases of slightly uneven length, and a wonderful control of harmony to induce, in a mere twenty-three bars, a mood of mellow reminiscence. In its economy of means this song resembles the best of Hugo Wolf.

Parry responded well to other English classics such as Lovelace and Suckling, and to the Romantic poets, though he could also

[165] Ibid., p. 24.

make something out of second-rate contemporary verse. Although his predominant mood is grave, he could adapt his style to a lighter humour, as in his second, published setting of Suckling's 'Why so Pale and Wan?' (1895). Among the more obviously Brahmsian songs are 'Willow, Willow' (1895), 'There be none of Beauty's Daughters' (1897), and 'O never say that I was False of Heart' (1907).[166] He was also capable, however, of a robust 'English' style, as in 'Under the Greenwood Tree' (1902).[167]

One of his most original, and perhaps greatest, songs is 'Lay a Garland on my Hearse' (1902),[168] to a short text from Beaumont and Fletcher. Again the song is only twenty bars in length; it is in G minor, in a free ternary form, with an unusual piano coda turning to G major. A point of particular acumen is the setting of the line 'My love was false, but I was firm' (Ex. 497): the word 'false' is set on an E to the totally surprising chord of A major, soon followed by 'firm' on an F with a 6/4 harmony of B flat, a more predictable chord in the middle section of such a song.

Ex. 497

For Stanford, songs were a proportionately less significant part of a very large output which included major contributions to opera,

---

[166] All three are ibid., pp. 22, 43, and 77.
[167] Ibid., p. 67.
[168] Ibid., p. 54.

symphony, cathedral music, part-songs, and chamber music. He composed more fluently than Parry and was less critical of the results, so that there are many mediocre songs, though the days when an aspiring serious composer might also publish ballads were now past. Nothing in his work ever surpassed the early 'La Belle Dame sans merci' (1877), a ballad in another sense—a narrative romance. This was extraordinary in several respects. It was virtually the first setting of any poem by Keats, the most difficult of all the Romantics (and indeed, not widely known until the publication of his *Complete Poems* in 1876). The young composer embarked with confidence on the setting of this long, mysterious and difficult poem; and he attempted a feat scarcely known before in English music, the unification of an extended work by deriving the whole from a short opening motif. In the telling of the dream the music mounts to a most powerful and passionate climax (Ex. 498), before returning to the sparse, understated texture of the first verse. It is the obvious way to shape the song, but supremely effective in this instance. There are several other examples of Stanford using his greater fluency to carry off narrative songs on the grand scale, such as Parry rarely attempted: 'Prospice' by Browning (1884) and 'Tears' from Whitman's *Songs of Faith*, Op. 97 (1908), are among the best.

Ex. 498

Stanford could also succeed on a smaller, homelier scale, as in
A Child's Garland of Songs, by Stevenson (1892) and Three Songs,
Op. 43, by Bridges (1897). He also developed a humorous 'dialect'
vein more successfully than Parry, as in Burns's 'Dainty Davie' and
'The Bold Unbiddable Child' (by W. M. Letts) Op. 140, No. 5
(1914).

Stanford devoted much energy to the folk-songs of his native
Ireland. He brought out *Songs of Old Ireland* (1883), then prepared
his own edition of Moore's *Irish Melodies*, Op. 60 (1895), in which
he reharmonized all the songs in a way he considered more
appropriate to the style of the tunes. The harmonic idiom that he
evolved in this process is only lightly coloured by modality and
pentatonicism; it differs from his normal style chiefly in the avoidance
of chromatic dissonance. But it is a significant step towards the more
thorough-going folk idiom of the next generation. It seems to have
had a good deal of influence, for example, on J. A. Fuller Maitland's
settings of folk-songs collected by Cecil Sharp.[169]

Beginning with *An Irish Idyll in Six Miniatures*, by Moira O'Neill
(1901), Stanford brought out several sets of songs with texts in Irish
dialect verse, in which the style he had developed in his folk-song
settings was applied to original compositions with little apparent
difficulty. Often his most effective device was the haunting juxtaposition of two remote chords, as in the best-known example, 'The
Fairy Lough' from the *Irish Idyll*. Greater harmonic originality is
displayed in another from the same set, 'A Broken Song'. The verse
depicts a man wistfully talking to himself about his departed love.
The questions he asks himself ('Where am I from?' 'What o' my
love?' etc.) are all at the same pitch, in A minor,[170] in the first verse;
the second contains a short happy interlude as the speaker remembers
her 'laughin' . . . blushin' . . .'. In the third the questions descend

---

[169] *One Hundred English Folk Songs* (London, 1916; repr. 1975).
[170] The keys mentioned refer to the high-voice edition.

through increasingly dark harmonies on the flat side of the tonic, at one point reaching E flat minor. The masterly closing bars (Ex. 499) return to the tonic in a way that is mysterious, melancholy, and yet expressive of resignation: a perfect representation of the feeling of the verse.

Ex. 499

'Where is she gone?' Och why would I be tel-lin' Where she is gone___
___ there I can nev-er go.___

One other late-nineteenth-century British composer, Arthur Somervell (1862–1937), deserves mention for his contributions to the song cycle, a genre in which neither Parry nor Stanford took much interest. He wrote five cycles for voice and piano, of which by far the most distinguished is *Maud* (1898). Instead of merely extracting the obviously lyrical passages from Tennyson's poem, Somervell chose portions that would allow the songs to represent fully the tragic story, explaining his purpose in the preface. He then produced a series of settings that quite equals the poetry in passion, range of feeling, invention, and psychological depth, taking care to unify the cycle tonally and thematically.

X

CHORAL MUSIC

By GERALD ABRAHAM

THE vast output of choral music, religious and secular, during this period was not only heterogeneous but often hybridized by crossing with symphony and opera. Even the Mass was sometimes affected, but religious music at its best was often extra-ecclesiastical. The most characteristic form was oratorio, exemplified by Carl Loewe's *Die Zerstörung Jerusalems* (1832), *Die sieben Schläfer* (1835), and *Palestrina* (1841)—in which the master himself and part of his *Missa Papae Marcelli* are introduced—and *Johann Hus* (1843). Loewe's *Gutenberg* (1835) is only peripherally religious, but the chorus of printer apprentices as they carry their master's Psalter to the cathedral at Mainz (Ex. 500) is a charming chorale pastiche.

An early champion of Bach was Ludwig Spohr (1784–1859), one of the first to revive the *Matthew Passion*, although his own music shows little Bachian influence. In *Die letzten Dinge* (1826), *Des Heilands letze Stunden* (1835), and *Der Fall Babylons* (1840) he escapes from his notorious chromaticism only into square-cut diatonicism, as in the fugal entry in *Die letzten Dinge* in Ex. 501.

MENDELSSOHN

On a higher plane are the oratorios of Felix Mendelssohn-Bartholdy (1809–47), *Paulus* (1836) and *Elias* (1846). In the former he adopted

Ex. 500

(Thou baptizest the child in the dream; thou baptizest the metal.)

Ex. 501

(Great and wonderful are Thy works, God Almighty!)

from Bach, whose *Matthew Passion* he had resuscitated in 1829, the interpolation of chorales. The overture opens with 'Wachet auf', which recurs later in the work, punctuated by brass fanfares, and one of the finest chorales (sung by a solo quartet instead of chorus) is 'O Jesu Christe, wahres Licht', a simple jewel in a beautifully wrought setting (Ex. 502). Fine in totally different ways are the chorus 'Aber unser Gott ist im Himmel' (sung first by Paul alone) with the chorale melody 'Wir glauben All' an einem Gott' as cantus firmus, and the idyllic chorus 'Siehe, wir preisen selig'. On the other hand the ease with which Mendelssohn could lapse into amiable platitudes is demonstrated in 'Wie lieblich sind die Boten'. Amiable platitudes are depressingly predominant in *Elias*, which has definite characters—not only Elijah himself but Obadiah, Ahab, the widow, and the priests of Baal; musical characterization was not Mendelssohn's forte. Following Handel's precedent in opening *Israel in Egypt* with a recitative, he opened *Elias* with the prophet's

Ex. 502

(O Jesus Christ, true light)

announcement of the coming drought, which is duly suggested by the fugal overture. His genius is displayed only in commentary, above all in the idyllic chorus 'Siehe der Hüter Israels schläft noch schlummert nicht'.

The most ambitious of Mendelssohn's other works for chorus and orchestra was the *Lobgesang* (1840), which he styled *Sinfonie-Kantate*, a disastrous attempt to follow in the wake of Beethoven's Ninth: three instrumental movements followed by ten vocal ones—by far the finest of which is, significantly, the chorale, one verse for six-part choir a cappella and one for unison chorus with orchestral accompaniment. Mendelssohn had been particularly struck by the power of the Lutheran chorales when he was given them in Weimar[1] and he made a setting of 'Aus tiefer Not', Op. 23, No. 1; even earlier he had composed 'Christe, du Lamm Gottes' (1827) and 'Jesu, meine Freude' (1828);[2] 'Ach Gott, vom Himmel sieh' darein'[3] dates from 1832. The finest of his psalms for chorus and orchestra, 'Da Israel aus Egypten zog', was composed in 1839. Much more unusual was a secular work, a setting of Goethe's *Die erste Walpurgisnacht* ,which

---

[1] Letter to Zelter, 16 Oct. 1830.

[2] Ed. Brian W. Pritchard (Hilversum, 1972); facsimile of the autograph, with introduction by Oswald Jonas (Chicago, 1966).

[3] Ed. Pritchard, and see Pritchard, 'Mendelssohn's Chorale Cantatas: An Appraisal', *Musical Quarterly*, 62 (1976), 1.

Ex. 503

(Owl and screech-owl hoot in our hooting round! Come! Come!)

in its original form was 'half-composed' in Rome early in 1831 and completed in July of that year but 'resurrected' in somewhat altered form in December 1842.[4] Its most remarkable number is the chorus 'Kommt mit Zacken' (Ex. 503), which has been described as 'one of the most powerful things that Mendelssohn ever wrote'.[5] A cantata *Lauda Sion* (1846), a quantity of church music, some of it Anglican,[6] and a score or more unaccompanied part-songs are of little account.

SCHUMANN

Robert Schumann (1810–56) was late in attempting choral music and he was never really happy in it. His pianist hands betrayed him into block-chordal writing and he sensibly converted his first choral essay, a setting of Heine's *Tragödie* (1841), into songs with piano. Two years later came the far more ambitious *Das Paradies und die Peri*, possibly suggested by Heinrich Marschner's 'overture, songs and choruses', *Klänge aus Osten*, which he had admired the year before and compared with Berlioz's *Roméo et Juliette*. He described his own work, based on a sometimes very free adaptation of part of Thomas Moore's *Lalla Rookh* by his friend Emil Flechsig, as 'an oratorio but not for the oratory—rather for cheerful people'. The best choral numbers are the chorus of Nile spirits, 'Hervor aus den Wassern' in Part II, and the chorus of houris which opens Part III (Ex. 504). But the solo parts are unlit by the genius which informs so many of Schumann's *Lieder*; Moore-Flechsig was much less inspiring than Heine and Goethe, Ruckert and Eichendorff.

Ex. 504

[4] See his letters, 22 Feb. and 15 July 1831 and 11 Dec. 1842.
[5] Philip Radcliffe, *Mendelssohn* (London, 1954), 139.
[6] See Rudolf Werner, *Felix Mendelssohn-Bartholdy als Kirchenmusiker* (Frankfurt, 1930).

(Deck the steps to Allah's throne; deck them with flowers)

Ex. 505

Lebhaft

(Just look at the mighty wings!)

Schumann seldom breaks away from note-against-note choral writing, even in 'Seht die machtigen Flügel doch an!' in the beautiful *Requiem für Mignon* (1840) from Goethe's *Wilhelm Meister* (Ex. 505), nor in much of the fine second setting of 'Alles Vergängliche' in the *Szenen aus Goethes Faust* (1847). *Der Rose Pilgerfahrt* is notable only for the curiously Wagnerian tenor solo 'Und wie ein Jahr verronnen ist'. From these last years of his sanity, 1851–3, also dated four ballad-cantatas for soloists' chorus, and orchestra, and a Mass and *Requiem* composed in the atmosphere of Catholic Düsseldorf. During his later years, particularly 1849, he also composed choral music for the amateur choirs he conducted in Leipzig and Dresden.

Catholic Bavaria and Austria themselves had nothing more memorable to show. The Masses and oratorios of Sigismund Neukomm (1778–1858)—*Christi Grablegung* (1827), *Auferstehung* (1841), and *Himmelfahrt* (1842)—and the thirty-five Masses of Simon Sechter (1788–1867) only gather the dust of history.

BERLIOZ

Five months before the first performance of *Das Paradies und die Peri*, Wagner had conducted his *Liebesmahl der Apostel* at Dresden with a male choir of 1200 and an orchestra of a hundred, a force no doubt suggested by the *Grande Messe des morts* (1837) and the *Symphonie funèbre et triomphale* (1840) of Hector Berlioz (1803–69). His Te deum ('à trois chœurs avec orchestre et orgue concertants') was composed later (1849) and not performed until 1855 to preface the opening of the Exposition Universelle in Paris. (At the end of the Exposition he conducted a cantata for two choirs and orchestra, *L'Impériale*, dedicated to Napoleon III; it was his last choral composition.) These monster conceptions hark back to open-air festival works of the First Republic which culminated in Méhul's *Chant national* for three choirs and three orchestras and Le Sueur's *Chant du 1er Vendémiaire*[7] for four choirs and four orchestras (both 1800). In strong contrast are the *légende dramatique* of *La damnation de Faust* (1846), and, still more, the touching little oratorio, *L'Enfance du Christ* (1854).

Even the *Grande Messe des morts* conceived for performance at the Invalides, with its four brass orchestras, four cornets, four trombones and two tubas to the north, four trumpets and four trombones to the east, four trumpets and four trombones to the west, four trumpets, four trombones and four tubas to the south in

---

[7] See Vol. VIII, p. 656.

the Tuba mirum, has touching passages: the 'Quid sum miser', the exquisite Sanctus, the Agnus Dei. And nowhere in all music are strokes on bass-drum and cymbals, pianissimo possibile, employed with more thrilling effect. In the 'Tibi omnes' of the Te deum there is similar restraint: the third choir (of sopranos and altos) enters only four times for a few bars to add brightness and strength to the acclamation 'pleni sunt coeli'. None of these effects is as theatrical as the upward sweep of the hitherto silent orchestra in Wagner's *Liebesmahl*, intended to suggest the 'sound from heaven as of a rushing mighty wind' on the day of Pentecost.[8]

In *L'Enfance* the theatrical is limited to the first part of the *trilogie sacrée*, 'Herod's dream', and to the first eight numbers of that. When the Virgin sings 'O mon cher fils' and Joseph adds his blessing, Berlioz prepares to pass into a Pre-Raphaelite vision of the shepherds' farewell (Ex. 506), followed by the Narrator's 'Repos de la Sainte Famille'. The summit of *naïveté* is touched when the Holy Family are entertained by three young Ishmaelites with a very long trio for harp and two flutes, but Berlioz turns from the pleasantly ridiculous to the near sublime at the end of his final, unaccompanied, chorus:

> O mon cœur, emplis-toi du grave et pur amour
> Qui seul eut nous ouvrir le celeste sejour.

La Damnation de Faust is a revised and vastly expanded version of the *Huit scènes de Faust* of seventeen years earlier, the expansion

Ex. 506

(He goes far from the land where in the stable he saw the light.)

[8] Acts 2: 2.

consisting most importantly of the introduction of Faust himself whose 'Nature immense, impénétrable et fière' in Scene xvi is one of Berlioz's finest inventions. But the chorus was rarely a dispensable ingredient in his compositions; the *symphonie dramatique Roméo et Juliette* (1839) has choruses, solos, and a 'prologue en récitatif choral'; the *Symphonie funèbre et triomphale* was given a final chorus; the three *Tristia* are all for chorus and orchestra, although in No. 3 (1848), the *March funèbre pour la dernière scène de Hamlet*, the choir have only one word to sing. Of the six pieces constituting the preposterous *monodrame lyrique* of *Lélio*, which Berlioz appended to the *Symphonie fantastique*, three involve a chorus.

BERLIOZ'S CONTEMPORARIES

In his Conservatoire days Berlioz had incurred the enmity of Luigi Cherubini (1760–1842); nevertheless he admired a great deal in the older man's work, and when his own *Requiem* was preferred to Cherubini's for the Invalides ceremony in 1837 he wrote the old man a touching letter.[9] The veteran died a few years later but younger men were coming along: Félicien David (1810–76), Charles Gounod (1818–93), César Franck (1822–90). Before turning to opera, David composed four choral works: an *ode-symphonie*, *Le Désert* (1844); an oratorio, *Moïse au Sinai* (1846), a second *ode-symphonie*, *Christophe Colomb, ou la découverte du nouveau monde* (1847), and a *mystère*, *L'Éden* (1848). *Le Désert*, for speaker, solo tenor, male choir and orchestra, is notable less for its musical value than for its claim to be one of the earliest European compositions to borrow authentic oriental material. David was in the Middle East during 1833–5 and the 'Chant du Muezzin' which opens the *troisième partie* (Ex. 507) is certainly authentic, as are probably the 'Rêverie du soir' and some of the themes in the 'Fantaisie arabe' and 'Danse des Almées'.

Ex. 507

9 24 Mar. 1837. On Cherubini's D minor Requiem see Vol. VIII, pp. 623–5. The Dies irae, a shattering stroke worthy of the younger man, is quoted in Basil Deane, *Cherubini* (Oxford, 1965), 31.

(Peace be with you)

Gounod was much more gifted by nature, more thoroughly trained, and vastly more prolific. His *envois* from Rome—he had been awarded the Grand Prix in 1839—included two Masses and a Te deum. Plainsong and old Italian church music became lasting influences. On his return from Rome he spent five years as *maître de chapelle* of a Paris church and even contemplated taking orders. He dreamed of restoring religious art in France,[10] and during his long life he composed nine Masses, three *Requiems*, and an enormous quantity of other church music—to say nothing of a dozen operas—and two 'sacred trilogies'. The fine *Messe solennelle à Sainte-Cécile* (1855), with the solo soprano soaring above the chorus *à bouche fermée* (Ex. 508), and the confidently affirmative Credo, are in marked contrast to the saccharine chromaticism and diatonic platitudes of the late trilogies.

As for Franck, his short *églogue biblique en 3 parties*, *Ruth* (1846),

Ex. 508

[10] Letter, 25 Mar. 1843, in J.-G. Prod'homme and Arthur Dandelot, *Gounod (1818-1893)* (Paris, 1911), i. 89.

in ex - cel - sis De - o

shows little promise of the master who was to emerge nearly thirty years later. His *petit oratorio*, *La Tour de Babel* (1865), was not even published, and the only tolerably interesting number of *Ruth* is the chorus of reapers which opens the second part, 'Le Champ de Booz', with its scoring for flutes, clarinets and bassoons, and joyous choral crescendo (Ex. 509).

LISZT

The dominant figure in the world of Catholic music during the latter part of the century was Ferenc Liszt (1811–86). His view was liberal. In 1834 he wrote for the *Gazette musicale de Paris* an article

Ex. 509

(Let's charm away fatigue with joyous songs.)

propounding the idea of 'a new music . . . which shall be devotional, strong and effective, uniting on a colossal scale theatre and church, at the same time dramatic and sacred, splendid and simple, ceremonial and sincere . . . clear and profound'.[11] His own earliest essay in this field was a four-part Mass (1848), which he later revised, with the addition of an organ part, in 1869. Next came a *Missa solemnis* with orchestra for the consecration of the Basilica at Gran (Esztergom) (1856), notable for the composer's favourite device of cross-reference: thus the Christe is quoted at the Benedictus; the orchestral motif which opens the Credo (and is transformed at 'qui propter') reappears at the final 'Amen'; the triumphant 'resurrexit' of the Credo rings out for the 'Hosannas' and for the 'Dona nobis pacem' of the Agnus Dei. This was followed by another *Missa choralis* with organ (1865), a Mass for the coronation of Franz Josef as King of Hungary (1867), using some Hungarian themes and also, for some reason, a Credo borrowed from Henry Du Mont's *Cinq Messes en plain-chant* of 1669,[12] and a *Requiem* for male voices, organ, and brass (*ad libitum*). Another work from the same period is a dramatic, not to say theatrical, setting of Psalm 13 for tenor, chorus and large orchestra (1855; rev. 1859).

Liszt turned rather belatedly to the favourite nineteenth-century form: oratorio. He began *Die Legende von der heiligen Elisabeth*, with a libretto by Otto Roquette, in 1857 and finished it in 1862; it had

---

[11] German translation in 'Über zukünftige Kirchenmusik', *Gesammelte Schriften*, ii (Leipzig, 1881).
[12] See Vol. V, p. 444.

Ex. 510

Ex. 511

to wait three more years for performance. St Elisabeth was a Hungarian princess and the motto-theme pervading the whole work is an antiphon, 'In festo s. Elisabeth' (actually for another Elisabeth, a queen of Portugal) (Ex. 510). Another theme, associated with the mourning of the poor for their benefactress and with her burial, is taken from the *Lyra coelestis* of György Naray (Nagyszombat, 1695).[13] A third quasi-Leitmotif is that of Hungary itself (Ex. 511). *Die Legende von der heiligen Elisabeth* is organized in two parts, each consisting of three scenes: Elisabeth's arrival at the Warburg, her meeting with the Landgraf Ludwig who marries her, parting from her as he sets off on a crusade; and the rage of Ludwig's jealous mother who turns her out of the castle, Elisabeth's death, her burial and canonization. Ex. 510 is treated with exquisite sweetness when the bread and wine she is taking to a dying man miraculously turn to roses. But the music of *Die Legende von der heiligen Elisabeth* is somewhat operatic, with the result that it was later given stage-performances for which it was unsuited. There is very little element of opera in Liszt's second oratorio, *Christus* (1867), where more of the material is based on plainsong but plainsong treated rhythmically. He had quoted the Good Friday hymn 'Crux fidelis' in the *Hunnenschlacht*, and alluded to it, as a symbol of the Cross, in connection with the crusaders in *Die Legende von der heiligen Elisabeth*.

Christus is a triptych: 'Christmas Oratorio', 'After Epiphany', and 'Passion and Resurrection'. The 'Oratorio' opens with the Advent introit 'Rorate caeli' (Ex. 512), a transformation of which, tutti

Ex. 512

[13] Quoted in Bence Szabolcsi, *A magyar zenetörténet kézikönyve* (2nd edn.; Budapest, 1955), musical examples, p. 52.

fortissimo, appears at the end of the work. The Angel's message is delivered by a soprano soloist, unaccompanied; the chorus answers and goes on to sing the 'Stabat mater speciosa' also unaccompanied. The 'Song of the Shepherds at the Crib' and the 'March of the Three Kings', orchestral and mood-shattering, are redeemed by the 'adagio sostenuto' for the Kings' presentation. The Beatitudes—purely vocal except for unobtrusive organ support—are introduced by Ex. 512. The tempest and Christ's stilling of the waves are dealt with in pages of conventional noisy tone-painting, and 'The Entry into Jerusalem' is hardly more impressive until the mezzo-soprano soloist enters with 'Benedictus' (Ex. 513). The third part of the triptych, 'Passion and Resurrection', begins with an impossible task, a setting of Christ's agony, 'Tristis est anima mea usque ad mortem', and then takes up a text that has attracted so many musicians, 'Stabat mater dolorosa'. Next follows the Easter hymn, 'O filii et filiae', to be sung to the traditional tune by a small invisible female chorus, accompanied by flutes, oboes, and clarinets. The work ends with a tremendous 'Resurrexit' with an electrifying entry for solo soprano at 'Christus vincit' (Ex. 514).

Christus is a very uneven work but it has a very high place among the oratorios of the mid-century. It is Liszt's masterpiece among his innumerable religious works, beside which such late ones as the

Ex. 513

Ex. 514

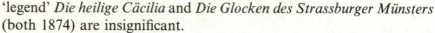

'legend' *Die heilige Cäcilia* and *Die Glocken des Strassburger Münsters* (both 1874) are insignificant.

BRUCKNER

One outstanding church composer who came under Liszt's influence from the 1860s—though as deeply Austrian as Liszt was Hungarian— was Anton Bruckner (1824-96). He was a composition pupil of the great contrapuntist Simon Sechter (1788-1867), himself the composer of a great number of Masses, though only twelve were published. Before his study with Sechter (1855-61), Bruckner had produced a *Requiem*, a *Missa solemnis* and some psalm-settings. Then came a Mass in D minor (1864, three times revised), one in E minor for chorus and wind only (1866; rev. 1885), a *Grosse Messe* in F minor (1868; four times revised), a *Te deum* (1881; rev. 1884), and a setting of Psalm 150 (1892), the power of which—especially near to the end where the fugue theme is combined with its inversion (Ex. 515)—

Ex. 515

Al - les was O - dem hat, Al - les was O - dem hat, Al - les, Al - les,

Al - les was O - dem hat, Al - les was O - dem hat Al - les, Al-[les]
Al - les was O - dem hat, Al - les, Al - les

Al - les was O - dem hat, Al - les was O - dem hat, Al - les, Al-[les]

(All, that has life and breath)

Ex. 516

S. A. Ky - ri - e___ e - le - i - son

T. B. Ky - ri-e, Ky - ri-e, Ky - ri - e

Ex. 517

Allegro moderato

dolce cresc. etc.

makes Mendelssohn's setting of the same words in the *Lobgesang* sound conventionally pompous. The octave leaps and double-dotting are typical of Bruckner: cf. the Kyrie of the D minor Mass (Ex. 516). The fugal 'In gloria Dei patris' in the F minor belongs to the same family of ideas. But Bruckner could also aspire to emotional warmth as in the Benedictus of the same Mass, where the long-drawn cello melody marked 'von Vielen zu spielen' at the beginning (Ex. 517), later taken up by the soloists in close imitation, records a spiritual crisis.

Bruckner's secular choral works are mostly for male choir: unaccompanied, accompanied by organ or wind band, trombones, or choral humming or yodelling, sometimes with soloists and piano. This excerpt from his setting of Heinrich von der Mattig's 'Abendzauber' (1878) is a good example (Ex. 518).

A younger contemporary, Joseph Rheinberger (1836–91), who spent most of his life in Bavaria, was a more conservative talent.

Ex. 518

(The lake dreams among the cliffs)

Immensely prolific, he produced an oratorio, *Christophorus* (1885), twelve Masses, three *Requiems*, two settings of Stabat mater, motets, and numerous small choral pieces both sacred and secular—technically accomplished but low in inspiration.

BRAHMS

The Protestant inverse of Liszt was Johannes Brahms (1833–97), by no means an orthodox Lutheran but ethically Lutheran and an admirer of Luther's translation of the Bible on which he drew for the text of his greatest choral work, *Ein deutsches Requiem*. A certain amount of mystery surrounds the inception of this masterpiece; it has been associated with the death of Schumann; the original two-piano form of the saraband-like second movement, 'Denn alles Fleisches ist wie Gras', came from the same period; but the *Requiem* was not completed until 1868—a year after Liszt's *Christus*. It begins with a beatitude, 'Selig sind, die da Leid tragen', and ends with another, 'Selig sind die Toten, die in dem Herren sterben'; in the middle, No. 4, is the gracious, consoling 'Wie lieblich sind deine Wohnungen'. These are the three pillars of the work. Between Nos. 1 and 4 stand the slow, *marschmässig* 'Denn alles Fleisch' and 'Herr, lehre doch mich' (with baritone solo); between Nos. 4 and 7, two further passages of consolation, 'Ihr habt nun Traurigkeit' (with soprano solo) and 'Denn wir haben hie keine bleibende Statt' (with baritone), with the triumphant fugal

> Herr, du bist würdig zu nehmen
> Preis und Ehre und Kraft.

The final beatitude comes from Revelation (14: 13), a book which

Ex. 519

[Dass er die gro - sse   Hu - re ver - ur-theilt hat]

(That he hath damned the great whore)

Ex. 520

(Bring back once more the golden days of Paradise)

was probably a favourite with Brahms, since he returned to it for the text of his *Triumphlied* (1871), celebrating the recent victory of German arms. His adaptation was not without coarse humour; in setting Revelation, 19: 2, he omitted part of the words but substituted a forte orchestral unison (Ex. 519), which left his listeners in no doubt.

Brahms's earliest choral work was an Ave Maria for female voices and small orchestra (1858), and more part-songs followed. Then, after the *Requiem*, in 1869 came two Goethe settings: *Rinaldo* for tenor, male voice choir and orchestra, and a *Rhapsodie* (from the *Harzreise im Winter*) for alto, male chorus, and orchestra. In *Rinaldo* the hero's almost Italianate lyricism, as in Ex. 520, is more attractive than the choral writing. Conversely, in the *Alto Rhapsody* the soloist has to cope, at 'aus der Fülle der Liebetrank', with the most unvocal writing Brahms was ever guilty of—though he immediately atones when the chorus enters (Ex. 521).

At the time of the *Rhapsody* Brahms was also working on a setting of Hölderlin's *Schicksalslied* for chorus and orchestra, inspired by reading the poem very early one morning and making the first sketch at once on the beach at Wilhelmshaven.[14] It is one of his finest choral compositions, with a masterly final orchestral dissolution

[14] Max Kalbeck, *Johannes Brahms*, ii (2nd edn.; Berlin, 1910), 361.

Ex. 521

(If thy psaltery, loving Father, has a note his ear can catch)

of the poem's pessimism. But the clouds descend again in his last two choral works, short as they are: the gentle *Nänie*, 'Auch das Schöne muss sterben', for the painter Anselm Feuerbach (1881), and the pessimistic *Gesang der Parzen* (1882), from Goethe's *Iphigenie auf Tauris*.

Besides these choral works with orchestra, Brahms composed more than fifty part-songs and motets, and numerous folk-song arrangements, for unaccompanied choir. They culminate in the three *Fest- und Gedenksprüche* of 1889 to Bible texts, and three motets, Op. 110—one of them likewise to a biblical text—from the same period.

DVOŘÁK

Antonín Dvořák (1841–1904), Brahms's friend for nearly twenty years, produced half-a-dozen substantial choral works whereas his compatriot, Smetana (1824–84) composed only one noteworthy choral composition, *Píseň na moři* [Song of the Sea] for un-accompanied male voices. In the same year, 1877, Dvořák made a number of settings of Czech and Moravian folk-poems for the same combination, but was at the same time orchestrating a more substantial composition, a Stabat mater which reached England in 1883 and made a considerable impression on audiences accustomed to such works as Sullivan's *Martyr of Antioch*. Much of the Stabat mater is poor Dvořák, but his personality shows in such passages as that in Ex. 522.

Ex. 522

(Cause me to carry Christ's death, make me a partner in his Passion.)

The Stabat mater so impressed the committee of the 1885 Birmingham Festival that they commissioned a secular work. Dvořák responded with a setting of K. J. Erben's ballad *Svatební košile* [The Bridal Garment], known in England as *The Spectre's Bride*, a brave attempt at *Schauerromantik*, foreign to his genius. At Birmingham it figured beside Gounod's *Mors et vita*, which it eclipsed, and was quickly performed again and again in Britain and the United States. The success of the Bride led to the commission of *St Ludmila* (*Svatá Ludmila* to a text by Jaroslav Vrchlický) for Leeds in 1886, and that in turn to a *Requiem* for Birmingham in 1891. At Leeds *St Ludmila* had to compete with Sullivan's *Golden Legend* and a new work by an Irishman, Stanford's *Revenge*; it added nothing to Dvořák's reputation. The Saint herself is musically colourless and the heathen deities—particularly the three-headed Triglav—are much more lively.

Dvořák's score or more of short choruses are mostly for male voices with or without accompaniment. His last important choral works were a Mass (with organ, 1887; orchestrated 1892), a *Requiem* (1890), and a Te deum (1892). The *Requiem* is by far the finest. Its twelve movements are related by a motto-theme, played at the beginning of the Requiem aeternam by muted violins and cellos (Ex. 523), sung by a solo soprano, unaccompanied, to open the next

Ex. 523

movement, extended in the prelude of Tuba mirum, woven into the bass of 'Quid sum miser', predominant in the Lacrimosa, returning in its original form but now lightly harmonized in the Agnus Dei where presently various soloists take it up, indeed making various other appearances. But the *Requiem* is notable for much more than ingenuity. In sheer beauty of sound the choral Agnus Dei is outstanding—as is the power of the choral response at 'Rex tremendae majestatis' in the 'Quid sum miser'. The fugue subject of 'Quam olim Abrahae' seems to have been suggested by a melody in a *kancionál* of 1541,[15] fitted to a text of forty years earlier and also to later texts.

---

[15] See Jan Kouba, 'Nejstarší cčský tištěný kancionál z roku 1501 jako hudební pramen', in *Studie a materiály k dějinám starší české hudby* (Prague, 1965), 98.

VERDI

More than one writer[16] has drawn attention to Dvořák's indebtedness to the *Requiem* of Giuseppe Verdi (1813–1901). Verdi's
was his earliest choral composition of any note, preceded only by
an *Inno delle nazioni* written for the London Exhibition of 1861 but
not performed there. In 1868 he had suggested that a number of
composers should collaborate in a *Requiem* for Rossini and actually
composed for it the Libera me which he used in his *Requiem* of
1874 'in memory of Alessandro Manzoni'. It is square-cut and
heavy-handed in contrast with the greater part of the work, which
is dramatic (as might be expected) especially in such passages as
'Rex tremendae majestatis' where a 'tremendous' descent of the
basses from *ff* to *pp* in three bars evokes a pianissimo repetition of
the words by the tenors on a repeated three-part chord. And nothing
in all Verdi is more exquisite than the passage in the Offertorio
shown in Ex. 524.

After the *Requiem* Verdi's most impressive choral works were a
dramatic Stabat mater for chorus and orchestra and a Te Deum for
double chorus and orchestra (1898), his last composition, a work of

Ex. 524

---

[16] e.g. Alec Robertson, *Dvořák* (London, 1945), 119–20, and John Clapham, *Antonín
Dvořák: Musician and Craftsman* (London, 1966), 258.

(The standard-bearer St Michael)

great power, as in the 'Salvum fac populum tuum, Domine', and lyrical beauty as at 'Sanctum quoque Paraclitum Spiritum'. On a smaller scale are two *a cappella* Dante settings from 1880, a five-part Pater noster and very beautiful four-part *Laudi alla Vergine Maria*, St Bernard's prayer which Chaucer translated in 'The Second Nonnes Tale':

> Thou mayde and moder, doughter of thi sone,
>
> .   .   .   .   .   .
>
> Humblest and best of every creatúre.

Another *a cappella* piece is a curiosity, the Ave Maria (*c*.1890) headed 'Scala enigmatica armonizzata a 4 voci' on an 'awkward bass' he had come across in the *Gazetta musicale*. As he said himself, 'It isn't real music but a *tour de force*, a charade.'

A curiosity of a different kind was the *Petite Messe solenelle* of Gioachino Rossini (1792–1868), composed in 1863, when he was 71 years old. The original accompaniment was for two pianos and harmonium but it was later orchestrated, in which form it was performed posthumously in 1869. Rossini's only other work of any consequence was the once celebrated Stabat mater (1842), with its strikingly harmonized *a cappella* quartet setting of 'Quando corpus' (Ex. 525).

Ex. 525

(When the body dies)

FRANCE AFTER 1870

The first notable French oratorio after the collapse of the second Empire was Franck's *Rédemption* of 1872—not to be confused with its later versions or compared with Gounod's of 1881. But it was eclipsed by the sensational success of the *drame sacré, Marie Magdeleine*, of Jules Massenet (1842–1912), the following year, a work in which the love duet for Jesus and the heroine impressed Tchaikovsky as 'a *chef d'œuvre*' and made him shed 'whole torrents of tears'.[17] *Ève, un mystère*, for Adam, Eve, and a narrator, with chorus, followed in 1875; its 'note tendre, voluptueuse', so characteristic of Massenet, delighted Gounod. But *La Vierge* (1880), a *légende sacrée*, was a failure. The unison chorus of angels which the Virgin hears at night (Ex. 526) and the later 'Danse galiléenne' are typical of Massenet's saccharine charm. He was well advised to turn to opera in *Hérodiade*.

Towards the end of his long life Camille Saint-Saëns (1835–1921) wrote that Bizet and Delibes had been friends and comrades: 'Massenet était un rival'.[18] But he had come near to Massenet in the solo violin theme symbolizing the anti-Diluvial happiness of

Ex. 526

Le mes - sa-ger du Roi des Rois pa - raît dans la plai - ne é - toi - lé - e, Vo -

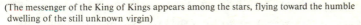

- lant vers le cha - ste ré - duit   de   la   vierge in-con-nue en - co - re

(The messenger of the King of Kings appears among the stars, flying toward the humble dwelling of the still unknown virgin)

Ex. 527

Andante sostenuto

[17] Letter to Nadezhda von Meck, 19 July 1880.
[18] *École buissonnière* (Paris, 1913), 275.

mankind in his *poème biblique*, *Le Déluge* (1876). Before *Le Déluge* he had composed a Mass for chorus, orchestra, and organ (1856), an *Oratorio de Noël* (1863), which reveals the influence of Gounod in the pastoral prelude and elsewhere, and a setting of Psalm 18 (19 in the Authorized Version) for soloists, chorus and orchestra (1875) where again the shadow of Gounod appears in passing. But Bach is more apparent than Gounod in the Psalm and when Saint-Saëns embarked on *Le Déluge*, he suggested Jehovah's displeasure in a fugue (Ex. 527).

After *Le Déluge* Saint-Saëns's interest in choral music declined, although he composed a considerable number of motets, with or without accompaniment, and a noteworthy Hugo setting, *La Lyre et la harpe*, for soloists, chorus, and orchestra (1879).

Gounod himself continued to pour out quantities of religious music, culminating in two 'sacred trilogies', *La Rédemption* (1881) and *Mors et vita* (1884), for both of which he compiled his own texts. Like Liszt's *Christus*, they are triptychs: *Rédemption*—'Passion', 'Resurrection', 'Outpouring of the Holy Spirit'; *Mors et vita*— 'Requiem Mass', 'The Last Judgement', 'Life (The Vision of St John)'. *Rédemption* was first performed at the Birmingham Festival of 1882 and *Mors et vita* was specially written for Birmingham. Gounod is too often weak and cloying but when he breaks into clean diatonic writing he can be very effective; it is said that when *Mors et vita* was first performed in Paris in 1888 the quartet entry with 'Oro supplex et acclinis' in the 'Confutatis' was applauded.

Franck's *poème-symphonie*, *Rédemption* (1872), has already been mentioned. Coming after various motets and Masses for solo voices, it marked his return to oratorio for the first time since *Ruth*. Employing a libretto by Eduard Blau, it is in three parts, the second of which is styled *symphonie* and represents the passing of the centuries and the gradual transformation of the world under the influence of Christ's teaching. A solo mezzo-soprano represents an Archangel. But in its original form the work was a complete failure. Franck withdrew it, but in 1874 published a new edition with a different *morceau symphonique*[19] and a great deal of fresh music in the remaining part. But *La Rédemption* was an interruption to the composition of a much finer, though very unequal, work or series of works, *Les Béatitudes* (libretto by a certain Mme J. Colomb), begun in 1869 and finished only in 1879. Each *Béatitude* is sung by antithetic choirs and soloists: one celestial, with the Voix du Christ

---

[19] The two main themes of the original version are printed in Vincent d'Indy, *César Franck* (Paris, 1906), 127.

Ex. 528

(Blessed are the meek, for they shall inherit the earth)

(baritone) and his motto-theme coming in near the end, as in the second movement (Ex. 528); the other representing money-grubbers, Pharisees, oppressors, warmongers, and persecutors. Franck intended these to be sung separately; indeed the prologue and first *Béatitude* were given in 1878 and the first complete performance in 1891, the year after the composer's death. The *Béatitudes* finished, Franck produced one more oratorio, the *scène biblique*, *Rebecca*, on a poem by Paul Collin, an idyllic counterpart to the *Ruth* of nearly forty years earlier. But he was now much more interested in instrumental composition and even opera. His disciple Vincent d'Indy (1851–1931) composed, mostly during 1879–83, a *légende dramatique—Le Chant de la cloche*—an adaptation of Schiller's 'Lied von der Glocke', which is musically descended from Berlioz's *Damnation*, and he expressed warm admiration of the 26-year-old Debussy's setting of the Rossetti-Sarrazin *La Damoiselle élue* (1888). But the most beautiful French choral work during this period was the *Requiem* (1888) of Gabriel Fauré (1845–1924), intimate and simple throughout. Nothing could be more exquisitely peaceful than the final antiphon, In Paradisum (Ex. 529).

Ex. 529

(Let the angels lead him into paradise)

POLAND

The renaissance of choral music in Poland was due above all to the example and teaching of Józef Elsner (1769–1854), who composed a vast quantity of secular cantatas and Masses with or without orchestra from 1785 onward, and a *Passio Domini Nostri Jesu Christi* (1837), which he misguidedly dedicated to Tsar Nicholas I as King of Poland. The first choral entry is shown in Ex. 530.[20]

---

[20] Taken from Alina Nowak-Romanowicz, *Józef Elsner* (Cracow, 1957), musical supplement, pp. 130 ff. She also gives extended excerpts in full score from the 'Qui passus est' and 'Deus meus es tu'.

Ex. 530

(Compose, my tongue, the laurel of the glorious contest)

But it was Stanisław Moniuszko (1819–72) who was mainly responsible for the revival of Polish church music, infusing national elements and, as Elsner also had done, composing Polish paraphrases of the Mass, including two for female voices in two or three parts, for convent use. His Latin church music includes a *Requiem* in D minor (*c*.1850), four Litanies to the Virgin at Ostra Brama (during the 1850s), and some half a dozen Masses, perhaps the finest of which is the E flat (1865), notable among other things for the intensity of the second Kyrie (Ex. 531). The best of Moniuszko's secular compositions are his settings of Mickiewicz, above all the *Sonety krymskie* [Crimean Sonnets] for chorus, tenor solo, and orchestra (1867); see Ex. 532 from 'Bakczysaraj w nocy' [Bakhchisaray at Night].

In the 1880s Moniuszko was bitterly attacked for his vernacular paraphrases of the Mass by Józef Surzyński (1851–1919), himself a prolific composer of Masses and other church music, who denounced Moniuszko's ecclesiastical music as fit for 'a drawing-room or theatre but not for a Catholic church'. Yet another composer of Masses was

Ex. 531

Ex. 532

(Silver king of the night, hastening to rest with his love!)

Wojciech Sowiński (1805–80), of whose *Oratorio Święty Wojciech* [St Albert] (1845) Chopin wrote that he had now become so easy to please that he could cheerfully listen to it without dropping down dead.[21] But, torn between Orthodox Russia, Lutheran Prussia, and Catholic Austria, Poland was not a fertile soil for vernacular choral music.

RUSSIA

Russian ecclesiastical music was a totally different matter, different above all in the rejection of instrumental participation. The first composer of any note after Bortnyansky,[22] was Aleksandr Alyab'ev (1787–1851), best known for his songs, who composed a Liturgy, two *Kheruvimskie* [Cherubic Hymns], and a psalm-concerto when exiled to Siberia in 1828, while an older contemporary, Pyotr Ivanovich Turchaninov (1779–1856), harmonized ecclesiastical melodies with simple triads, sometimes placing them in the alto or even the bass and sprinkling them freely with flats and sharps. He published four volumes of them towards the end of his life and some survived much later. Glinka (1804–57) wrote little choral music although his brief appointment to the directorship of the Imperial Chapel led to the composition of a short *Kheruvimskaya*, and towards the end of his life he produced a four-part Liturgy, a couple of extremely simple hymns,[23] and a few secular pieces including a setting of Lermontov's 'Molitva' [Prayer], based on an earlier piano piece.

In 1833 Aleksey Fyodorovich L'vov (1799–1870), whose father had succeeded Bortnyansky at the Imperial Chapel, composed a new national anthem, 'Bozhe, Tsarya khrani' [God preserve the Tsar], which led in turn to his own appointment to the Chapel and its sponsorship of a seven volume edition of four-part settings of the *Obikhod* (music for the daily service), introducing more rhythmic freedom (Ex. 533). In this he was probably content to supervise the

Ex. 533

Dos - toy - no est'   ya - ko vo - is - ti - nu bla - zhi - ti

[21] Letter, 18 Aug. 1848.
[22] See Vol. VIII, p. 648.
[23] *Polnoe sobranie sochineniy*, xvii (Moscow, 1968).

(It is truly meet to bless Thee, O Virgin, eternally blessed and immaculate mother of God)

work of Gavriil Yakimovich Lomakin, but L'vov himself composed four *a cappella Kheruvimskie*, a quantity of other church music and a Stabat mater for soloists, chorus and orchestra. Lomakin (1812–85) produced ten *Kheruvimskie* and other church music, and also collaborated with Balakirev (1837–1910) in a Free School of Music which cultivated amateur choral singing.

Balakirev composed no choral music, but his first disciple, César Cui (1835–1918), launched out with secular choruses in 1860 and a 'mystic chorus' for female voices on a text translated from Dante's *Purgatorio* in 1871. Other sets followed in the 1880s and 1890s. His colleagues of the 'Mighty Handful',[24] Mussorgsky and Borodin, produced little or no significant choral music. Mussorgsky's *Porazhenie Sennakheriba* [The Destruction of Sennacherib] (first version 1867, second 1874), on a free prose translation of Byron, and *Iisus Navin* [Jesus Navin] (1874–7),[25] rescued from a projected opera on Flaubert's *Salammbô*, are essentially orchestral conceptions with vocal obbligatos; for more imaginative choral writing one must turn to his operas.

The choral music of the remaining member of the 'Handful', Rimsky-Korsakov (1844–1908), falls into three groups: sets of mostly *a cappella* pieces, some of them folk-song arrangements (1876–9);

[24] *Moguchaya kuchka*, a term coined by Vladimir Stasov in 1867, sometimes referred to in English as 'The Five', originally Balakirev, Borodin, Cui, Mussorgsky, and Rimsky-Korsakov, though the phrase is also used to refer to Dargomïzhsky and Glinka.

[25] *Polnoe sobranie sochineniy*, vi (Moscow and Leningrad, 1939), 56, 97, 113. Mussorgsky is said to have heard the themes of *Iisus Navin* sung by Jewish neighbours celebrating the Feast of Tabernacles.

liturgical music, including eight settings from the *Liturgy of St John Chrysostom* (1883), and three late cantatas, *Svitezyanka* (1897), *Pesn' o veshchem Olege* [Song of Oleg the Wise] (1899), and *Iz Gomera* [From Homer] (1901). The liturgical music was the result of his appointment as assistant director of the Imperial Chapel under L'vov's successor in 1861, Nikolay Ivanovich Bakhmetev (1807–91). Bakhmetev himself was a tentative modernist, who ventured to introduce mildly dissonant chromatic harmony (Ex. 534).

Ex. 534

(We who mystically represent the Cherubim [and sing the thrice-holy hymn to the life-giving Trinity])

Ex. 535

(We who mystically represent the Cherubim [and sing the
thrice-holy hymn to the life-giving Trinity])

Anton Rubinstein (1829–94) is doubly problematic, for he composed what he called 'sacred operas (oratorios)' intended for stage
performance and wrote them to German librettos. But his most
famous pupil, Tchaikovsky (1840–93), was a prolific composer of
choral pieces, many of them short but including the inevitable *Liturgy
of St John* (1878)—written in a more polished idiom than Bakhmetev's
(Ex. 535).

SPAIN

At the other end of Europe the outstanding composer of church
music was Rodríguez de Ledesma (1779–1847) who spent two periods
of his life in England: 1811–14, when he was made a member of the
Philharmonic Society, and 1823–31. His best works date from 1836
onwards, when he was Master of the Capilla Real; they included
three *Misas solemnes*, Responses for the Matins of Epiphany, a
Stabat mater, and striking *Lamentaciones de Semana Santa* (1838)
(Ex. 536).

Prominent in the next generation were Hilarión Eslava (1804–81)
and Benigno Cariñena (d. 1886). Eslava was a scholar as well as
composer. He edited a ten-volume collection of Spanish church
music, *Lira sacro-hispana* (Madrid, 1869), in which he included his
own *Requiem* and Te deum, though not his *Lamentaciones*. Cariñena
also left a *Requiem* and *Lamentaciones* as well as *Misas de Gloria*, a
Miserere, and many smaller works.

Ex. 536

(All they that pass by clap their hands at thee; they hiss . . .)

BRITAIN

At the mid-century the three most notable composers of choral music were Samuel Sebastian Wesley (1810–76), Henry Hugh Pierson (1815–73), and William Sterndale Bennett (1816–75)—a conservative, who composed little but anthems and Anglican services; a radical, whose choral music consisted only of one completed oratorio (*Jerusalem*, 1852), one incomplete (*Hezekiah*, 1869), and the choruses in his considerable music to the second part of *Faust* (1854); and a moderate, who produced anthems, a cantata, *The May Queen* (1858), and an oratorio, *The Woman of Samaria* (1867), both festival commissions. It was the conservative whose work has survived; Wesley's anthems—for example, 'O Lord, thou art my God', 'Cast me not away' and 'Thou wilt keep him in perfect peace'—are masterpieces of their kind. Younger than these was Arthur Sullivan (1842-1900), master of comic opera but a mediocrity in such works as *The Prodigal Son* (1869), *The Light of the World* (1873), *The Martyr of Antioch* (1880), and *The Golden Legend* (1886)—all festival commissions. Only in the last scene of the *Legend*, when Elsie and the Prince listen to the distant bells of Geisenheim does Sullivan come near to real poetry.

Sterndale Bennett and Pierson did, however, contribute to the accomplishment of Hubert Parry (1848-1918) for he studied with both. Parry's virile diatonic idiom informs everything he wrote and breathes life into late Victorian oratorio—the best passages of *Judith* (1888), *Job* (1892), *King Saul* (1894)—but nothing in these surpasses his setting of Milton's *Ode at a Solemn Music* (*Blest Pair of Sirens*) (1887) with its great opening demonstration of the power that still resided in pure diatonicism (Ex. 537), a power that drives the fugal 'O may We soon again renew that Song', which remained with him to the end of his life, and which shows even in unison songs such as 'Jerusalem' and 'England'.

Ex. 537

Second only to Parry was Charles Villiers Stanford (1852–1924), at first, like him, a 'festival composer': for instance, the Whitman *Elegiac Ode* (Norwich, 1884), Tennyson's *The Revenge* (Leeds, 1886), the oratorio *Eden* on a poem by Robert Bridges (Birmingham, 1891). But a greater than any of these was waiting in the wings: the 35-year-old Elgar set about his 'symphony for chorus and orchestra', *The Black Knight*, in 1892. But eight years were to pass before *The Dream of Gerontius* was heard at the Birmingham Festival of 1900 and opened the last phase in the history of a dying form.

UNITED STATES

Two notable American composers of choral music were John Knowles Paine (1839–1906) and Dudley Buck (1839–1909). Paine's Mass in D was given by the Berlin Singakademie in 1867, his oratorio *St Peter* at Portland (Maine) in 1873, a cantata setting of Milton's *Hymn on the Morning of Christ's Nativity* at Boston in 1883, and another cantata, *A Song of Praise*, at the Cincinnati Festival of 1888. Buck, also German-trained, had already appeared at Cincinnati in 1880 with a *Golden Legend* seven years before Sullivan's, and in 1893 a much stronger composer than either—Horatio Parker (1863–1919)—attracted general respect with an oratorio, *Hora novissima* (1893), which six years later was performed at the Worcester Festival, the first American work to be heard there. The rather younger George Chadwick (1854–1931), after the then obligatory German training, produced a number of choral works showing considerable talent, from *The Viking's Last Voyage* (1881) onwards.

A greater than any of these was to visit the United States during 1892–5. Dvořák was invited to accept the directorship of a newly founded National Conservatory of Music in New York and, while he was there, composed some of his most popular and most delightful works. Unfortunately the one he wrote on the eve of his departure for America, *The American Flag* for soloists, chorus, and orchestra, with words by Joseph Drake, is not in that category—and he left the United States before it was performed.

BIBLIOGRAPHY

Compiled by ROSEMARY DOOLEY

GENERAL

(i) Modern Anthologies

GINZBURG, SEMYON L'VOVICH: *Istoriya russkoy muzïki v notnïkh obraztsakh* (Leningrad and Moscow, 1949 and 1952).

KIRBY, FRANK E.: *Music in the Romantic Period: An Anthology with Commentary* (New York, 1986).

PLANTINGA, LEON B.: *Romantic Music: A History of Musical Style in Nineteenth-century Europe*, ii (New York, 1985).

POHANKA, JAROSLAV: *Dějiny české hudby v příkladech* (Prague, 1958).

STEPHENSON, KURT: *Romantik in der Tonkunst* (Das Musikwerk, 21; Cologne, 1961); Eng. trans., Robert Kolben, *Romanticism in Music* (Anthology of Music, 21; Cologne, 1961).

STRUMIŁŁO, TADEUSZ: *Źródła i początki romantyzmu w muzyce polskiej* (Kraków, 1956) [supplementary volume].

WOLFF, HELLMUTH CHRISTIAN: *Die Oper III—19. Jahrhundert* (Das Musikwerk, 40; Cologne, 1972); Eng. trans., A. Crawford Howie, *The Opera III—19th Century* (Anthology of Music, 40; Cologne, 1975).

(ii) Books and Articles

ABRAHAM, GERALD: *A Hundred Years of Music* (London, 1938; 4th edn., 1974).

ARTZ, FREDERICK B.: *From Renaissance to Romanticism: Trends in Style in Art Literature and Music* (Chicago, Ill., 1962).

BARZUN, JACQUES: *Berlioz and the Romantic Century* (Boston, Mass., 1950; rev. 2nd edn., 1956 as *Berlioz and his Century*; rev. 3rd edn., 1969).

—— *Classic, Romantic and Modern* (2nd edn., New York, 1961).

BECKER, HEINZ (ed.): *Beiträge zur Geschichte der Oper* (Regensburg, 1969).

—— *Die 'Couleur locale' in der Oper des 19. Jahrhunderts* (Regensburg, 1976).

BELZA, IGOR': *Ocherki razvitiya cheshskoy muzïkal'noy klassiki* (Moscow, 1951); Czech trans., *Česká klasická hudba* (Prague, 1961).

BLUME, FRIEDRICH: *Classic and Romantic Music: A Comprehensive Survey* (London, 1972).

BÜCKEN, ERNST: *Die Musik des 19. Jahrhunderts bis zur Moderne* (Wildpark-Potsdam, 1929; repr. 1949).

BUJIĆ, BOJAN (ed.): *Music in European Thought 1851-1881* (Cambridge, 1988).

CHASE, GILBERT: *America's Music: From the Pilgrims to the Present* (New York, 1955; rev. 3rd edn., 1977).

CHECHLIŃSKA, ZOFIA (ed.): *Szkice o kulturze muzycznej XIX w.* (Warsaw, 1973-80).

CONRAD, PETER: *Romantic Opera and Literary Form* (Berkeley and Los Angeles, Calif., 1977)

COOKE, DERYCK: *Vindications: Essays on Romantic Music* (London, 1982).

COOPER, MARTIN: *French Music from the Death of Berlioz to the Death of Fauré* (London, 1951).

DAHLHAUS, CARL: *Ästhetik* (Cologne, 1967); Eng. trans., William Austin, *Esthetics of Music* (Cambridge, 1982).

—— *Die Musik des 19. Jahrhunderts* (Wiesbaden, 1980); Eng. trans., J. Bradford Robinson, *Nineteenth-century Music* (Berkeley and Los Angeles, Calif., 1988).

—— *Musikalischer Realismus: Zur Musikgeschichte des 19. Jahrhunderts* (Munich, 1982); Eng. trans., Mary Whittall, *Realism in Music* (Cambridge, 1985).

—— *Studien zur Trivialmusik des 19. Jahrhunderts* (Regensburg, 1967).

—— *Zwischen Romantik und Moderne: Vier Studien zur Musikgeschichte des späteren 19. Jahrhunderts* (Munich, 1974); Eng. trans., Mary Whittall, *Between Romanticism and Modernism: Four Studies in the Music of the Later Nineteenth Century* (Berkeley and Los Angeles, Calif., 1980).

DENT, EDWARD J.: *The Rise of Romantic Opera*, ed. Winton Dean (Cambridge, 1976).

DUCKLES, VINCENT: 'Patterns in the Historiography of Nineteenth-century Music', *Acta musicologica*, 42 (1970), 75–82.

DUMESNIL, RENÉ: La Musique romantique française (Paris, 1944).

EINSTEIN, ALFRED: *Music in the Romantic Era* (New York, 1947; 2nd edn., 1949).

Encyklopedia muzyczna: Część biograficzna (Kraków, 1980–).

FULLER MAITLAND, J. A.: *English Music in the Nineteenth Century* (London, 1902).

GROUT, DONALD J.: *A Short History of Opera* (New York, 1947; 2nd edn., 1965).

HANSLICK, EDUARD: *Die moderne Oper* (Berlin, 1900; repr. 1971); selection ed. and trans. Henry Pleasants, *Eduard Hanslick: Music Criticisms 1846–99* (New York, 1950; rev. 2nd edn., 1963).

HONOUR, HUGH: *Romanticism* (London, 1979).

HUGHES, GERVASE: *Sidelights on a Century of Music 1825–1924* (London, 1969).

ISTEL, EDGAR: *Die Blütezeit der musikalischen Romantik in Deutschland* (Leipzig, 1921; 3rd edn., 1968).

JACHIMECKI, ZDZISŁAW: *Muzyka polska w rozwoju historycznym od czasów najdawniejszych do doby obecnej* (Kraków, 1948–51).

KELDÏSH, YURY: *Istoriya russkoy muïki* (Moscow and Leningrad, 1947–54).

KERMAN, JOSEPH: *Opera as Drama* (New York, 1956).

KNEPLER, GEORG: *Musikegeschichte des XIX. Jahrhunderts* (Berlin, 1961).

KOURY, DANIEL J.: *Orchestral Performance Practices in the Nineteenth Century: Size, Proportions, and Seating* (Ann Arbor, Mich., 1986).

KRAMER, LAWRENCE: *Music and Poetry: The Nineteenth Century and After* (Berkeley and Los Angeles, Calif., 1984).

LANG, PAUL HENRY (ed.): *One Hundred Years of Music in America* (New York, 1961).

LAUDON, ROBERT T.: *Sources of Wagnerian Synthesis: A Study of the Franco-German Tradition in Nineteenth-century German Opera* (Munich, 1979).

LE HURAY, PETER and DAY, JAMES (eds.): *Music and Aesthetics in the Eighteenth and Early-nineteenth Centuries* (Cambridge, 1981; abridged 1988).

LEVASHOVA, OL'GA EVGEN'EVNA, KELDÏSH, YURY, and KANDINSKY, A. (eds.): *Istoriya russkoy muziki* (Moscow, 1970–).

LISSA, ZOFIA: 'Polish Romanticism and Neo-Romanticism', in Stefan Jarociński (ed.), *Polish Music* (Warsaw, 1965), 104–27.

LOEWENBERG, ALFRED: *Annals of Opera 1597–1940* (Cambridge, 1943; 3rd edn., 1978).

LONGYEAR, REY M.: *Nineteenth-century Romanticism in Music* (Englewood Cliffs, NJ, 1969; 2nd edn., 1973).

McGANN, JEROME J.: *The Romantic Ideology: A Critical Investigation* (Chicago, Ill., 1983).

Mała encyklopedia muzyki (Warsaw, 1981).

NEWMAN, WILLIAM S.: *The Sonata since Beethoven* (Chapel Hill, NC, 1969).

NEWMARCH, ROSA: *The Music of Czechoslovakia* (London, 1942; repr. 1969).

Nineteenth-century Music (Berkeley and Los Angeles, Calif., 1977–) [journal].

NOCHLIN, LINDA: *Realism* (Harmondsworth, 1971).

NOWAK-ROMANOWICZ, ALINA *et al.*: *Z dziejów polskiej kultury muzycznej* (Kraków, 1965–).

OČADLIK, MIRKO (ed.): *Československá vlastivěda*, díl IX: *Umění*, svazek 3: *Hudba* (Prague, 1971).

OCHLEWSKI, TADEUSZ (ed.): *Dzieje muzyki polskiej* (Warsaw, 1977); Eng. trans., Magdalena Mierowska-Parzkiewicz, *An Outline History of Polish Music* (Warsaw, 1979).

PLANTINGA, LEON B.: *Romantic Music: A History of Musical Style in Nineteenth-century Europe*, i (New York, 1985).

PRAZ, MARIO: *The Romantic Agony* (London, 1950).

RACEK, JAN: *Česká hudba* (Prague, 1958).

REISS, JÓZEF: *Historia muzyki w zarysie* (Warsaw, 1931).

RICH, NORMAN: *The Age of Nationalism and Reform, 1850-1890* (New York, 1970).

RIDENOUR, ROBERT C.: *Nationalism, Modernism and Personal Rivalry in Nineteenth-century Russian Music* (Ann Arbor, Mich., 1981).

RIEMANN, HUGO: *Handbuch der Musikgeschichte*, ii, ed. Alfred Einstein (Leipzig, 1913; 2nd edn., 1922, repr. 1972).

ROSEN, CHARLES, and ZERNER, HENRI: *Romanticism and Realism: The Mythology of Nineteenth-century Art* (London, 1984).

SADIE, STANLEY (ed.): *Opera* (London, 1988) [part III 'Nineteenth Century'].

SCHMIDGALL, GARY: *Literature as Opera* (Oxford, 1977).

SCHOLES, PERCY: *The Mirror of Music, 1844-1944* (London, 1947).

SIMPSON, ROBERT (ed.): *The Symphony*, i (Harmondsworth, 1966) [chapters on Berlioz, Berwald, Borodin, Brahms, Bruckner, Dvořák, Franck, Liszt, Mendelssohn, Schumann, Tchaikovsky].

Słownik muzyków polskich (Kraków, 1964-7).

SMITH, PATRICK J.: *The Tenth Muse: A Historical Study of the Opera Libretto* (New York, 1970), chaps. 13-19.

SOWIŃSKI, WOJCIECH: *Les Musiciens polonais et slaves anciens et modernes: Dictionnaire biographique* (Paris, 1857; repr. 1971); Polish trans., *Słownik muzyków polskich dawnych i nowoczesnych* (Warsaw, 1874; repr. 1982).

SPÓZ, ANDRZEJ: *Warszawskie towarzystwo muzyczne* (Warsaw, 1971).

STOWELL, ROBIN: *Violin Technique and Performance in the Late Eighteenth and Early Nineteenth Centuries* (Cambridge, 1985).

STRUMIŁŁO, TADEUSZ: *Szkice z polskiego życia muzycznego XIX w.* (Kraków, 1954).

—— *Źródła i początki romantyzmu w muzyce polskiej* (Kraków, 1956).

STRUNK, OLIVER: *Source Readings in Music History* (New York, 1950; repr. in separate vols., including v. *The Romantic Era*, 1965).

Studien zur Musikgeschichte des 19. Jahrhunderts (Regensburg, 1965-).

Szkice o kulturze muzycznej XIX w. (Warsaw, 1971-84).

TEMPERLEY, NICHOLAS (ed.): *Music in Britain: The Romantic Age 1800-1914* (London, 1981).

TIERSOT, JULIEN: *La Musique aux temps romantiques* (Paris, 1930).

TOVEY, DONALD F.: *Essays in Musical Analysis* (London, 1935-9; repr. 1972).

WHITTALL, ARNOLD: *Romantic Music: A Concise History from Schubert to Sibelius* (London, 1987).

WOLF, HUGO: *Musikalische Kritiken*, ed. Richard Batka and Heinrich Werner (Leipzig, 1911; repr. 1976); Eng. trans., ed. Henry Pleasants, *The Music Criticism of Hugo Wolf* (New York, 1978).

ZDUNIAK, MARIA: *Muzyka i muzycy polscy w dziewiętnastowiecznym Wrocławiu* (Wrocław, 1984).

CHAPTER I

NEW TENDENCIES IN ORCHESTRAL MUSIC: 1830–1850

(i) Modern Editions

(a) Anthologies

BROOK, BARRY S. (gen. ed.): *The Symphony 1720–1840* (60 vols.; New York, 1979–86).

ENGEL, HANS: *Das Solokonzert* (Das Musikwerk, 25; Cologne, 1964); Eng. trans., Robert Kolben, *The Solo Concerto* (Anthology of Music, 25; Cologne, 1964).

HOFFMANN-ERBRECHT, LOTHAR: 'The Symphony in the 19th Century after Beethoven', *Die Sinfonie* (Das Musikwerk, 29; Cologne, 1967); Eng. trans., Robert Kolben, *The Symphony* (Anthology of Music, 29; Cologne, 1967).

LANG, PAUL HENRY: *The Concerto 1800–1900* (New York, 1969) [includes works by Chopin, Mendelssohn, and Schumann].

—— *The Symphony 1800–1900* (New York, 1969) [includes works by Berlioz, Mendelssohn, and Schumann].

(b) Works by Individual Composers

BENNETT, W. S.: *Three Symphonies*, ed. Nicholas Temperley (The Symphony 1720–1840, series E, 7; New York, 1982) [symphonies nos. 3–5].

—— *Overture 'Parisiana', Overture 'The Naiads'*, ed. Nicholas Temperley (The Symphony 1720–1840, series E, 6; New York, 1984).

BERLIOZ, H.: *Hector Berlioz: Werke*, ed. Charles Malherbe and Felix Weingartner (Leipzig, 1900–10; repr. 1971): series I *Symphonien*; series II *Ouvertüren*.

—— *New Berlioz Edition of the Complete Works*, ed. Hugh Macdonald *et al.* (Kassel, 1967–): 16 *Symphonie fantastique*, ed. Nicholas Temperley (1972); 19 *Grande symphonie funèbre et triomphale*, ed. Hugh Macdonald (1967); 18 *Roméo et Juliette*, ed. D. Kern Holoman (1988); 17 *Harold en Italie*, ed. Paul Banks; 20 *Overtures*, 21 *Other Orchestral and Instrumental Works* (forthcoming).

—— *Fantastic Symphony*, ed. Edward T. Cone (Norton Critical Score; New York, 1971).

—— *Les Feuilletons de critique musicale par Hector Berlioz*, ed. H. Robert Cohen and Yves Gérard (Vancouver, 1988–).

BERWALD, F.: *Sämtliche Werke*, ed. Berwald Kommittén (Monumenta musicae svecicae, 2nd series; Kassel, 1966–82): *Orchesterwerke* 9 vols.

CHOPIN, F. F.: *Friedrich Chopin's Werke*, ed. Woldemar Bargiel *et al.* (Leipzig, 1878–1902): 12 *Concerte und Concertstücke*.

—— *Fryderyk Chopin: Dziela wszystkie/Complete Works*, ed. Ignacy Jan Paderewski, with Józef Turczyński and Ludwik Bronarski (Warsaw, 1949–61): 21 *Works for Piano and Orchestra* (1962); 19 *Concerto in E Minor* (1961); 20 *Concerto in F Minor* (1961).

GADE, N.: *Sinfonie für das grosses Orchester* (Samfundet til udgivelse af dansk musik, series 3, no. 197; Copenhagen, 1967).

GLINKA, M. I.: *Polnoe sobranie sochineniy*, ed. Vissarion Yakovlevich Shebalin *et al.* (Moscow, 1955–69): 1 *Sinfonia per l'orchestra sopra due motivi Russi, Ouverture* (1955).

KALLIWODA, J. W.: *Symphony No. 2 in E♭ Symphony, No. 4 in C*, ed. David E. Fenske (The Symphony, series C 13, New York 1984).

MACFARREN, G. A.: *Overture 'Romeo and Juliet'*, ed. Nicholas Temperley (The Symphony, series E, 6; New York, 1984).

MENDELSSOHN, F.: *Felix Mendelssohn Bartholdy's Werke: Kritisch durchgesehene Ausgabe*, ed. Julius Rietz (Leipzig, 1874–7; repr. 1967–9): series 1 *Symphonien*;

series 2 *Ouvertüren;* series 4 *Für Violone und Orchester*; series 8 *Für Pianoforte und Orchester*; selection repr. 1975 [Symphonies 3 & 4, and overtures].

—— *Leipziger Ausgabe der Werke Felix Mendelssohn Bartholdys*, ed. Internationale Felix-Mendelssohn-Gesellschaft (Leipzig, 1960-): series 1 *Orchesterwerke*, ed. Hellmuth Christian Wolff (1965-72); series 2 *Konzerte*, ed. Karl-Heinz Köhler *et al.* (1960-1).

ONSLOW, G.: *Symphony in A Major, Symphony in D Major*, ed. Boris Schwartz (The Symphony, series D, 9; New York, 1981).

SCHUMANN, R.: *Robert Schumann's Werke*, ed. Clara Schumann (Leipzig, 1881-93; repr. 1967-8): series 1 *Symphonien für Orchester*; series 2 *Ouverturen für Orchester*; series 3 *Concerte und Concertstücke für Orchester*.

—— *Symphony in G Minor*, ed. Marc Andrae (Frankfurt, 1972).

SMETANA, B.: *Souborná díla Bedřicha Smetany*, ed. Zdeněk Nejedlý (Prague, 1924-36): 1 *Skladby z mládí* (1924).

—— *Studijní vydání děl Bedřicha Smetany*, ed. František Bartoš, Josef Plavec, *et al.* (Prague, 1940-): 13 *Orchestrální skladby sv. 1* (1962).

SPOHR, L.: *Neue Auswahl der Werke*, ed. Folker Göthel and Herfried Homburg (Kassel, 1963-): 5 *Klarinettenkonzert IV*, ed. Heinrich Geuser (1976).

—— *Three Symphonies*, ed. Joshua Berrett (The Symphony, series C, 9; New York, 1980) [in F Major Op. 86, G Major Op. 116, C Major Op. 121].

—— *Selected Works of Louis Spohr (1784-1859)*, ed. Clive Brown (New York, 1987-): 6 *Symphonies* [includes No. 5 in C Minor].

WAGNER, R.: *Richard Wagners Werke: Musikdramen—Jugendopern—musikalische Werke*, ed. Michael Balling (Leipzig, 1912-29; repr. 1971): 18 & 20 *Orchesterwerke*.

—— *Richard Wagner: Sämtliche Werke*, ed. Carl Dahlhaus, Egon Voss, *et al.* (Mainz, 1970-): 18 *Orchesterwerke*, ed. Egon Voss (1973).

(ii) Books and Articles

(a) General

CARSE, ADAM: *The History of Orchestration* (London 1925; repr. 1964).

—— *The Orchestra from Beethoven to Berlioz* (Cambridge, 1948).

DAVISON, HENRY: *From Mendelssohn to Wagner* (London, 1912) [memoirs of James William Davison].

ENGEL, HANS: *Die Entwicklung des deutschen Klavierkonzerts von Mozart bis Liszt* (Leipzig, 1927; repr. 1970).

FINSON, JOHN W., and TODD, R. LARRY (eds.): *Mendelssohn and Schumann: Essays on their Music and its Context* (Durham NC, 1984).

FISKE, ROGER: 'Shakespeare in the Concert Hall', in Phyllis Hartnoll (ed.), *Shakespeare in Music* (London, 1964), 177-241.

HILL, RALPH (ed.): *The Concerto* (Harmondsworth, 1952; repr. 1978).

KLOIBER, RUDOLF: *Handbuch der klassischen und romantischen Symphonie* (Wiesbaden, 1964; 2nd edn., 1976).

—— *Handbuch des Instrumentalkonzerts* (Wiesbaden, 1972-3).

LAVIGNAC, (A. J.) ALBERT, and LA LAURENCIE, LIONEL DE: *Encyclopédie de la musique et dictionnaire du conservatoire* (Paris, 1920-31), part 2, iv. 'Histoire de l'orchestration'.

McCREDIE, ANDREW W.: 'Symphonie concertante and Multiple Concerto in Germany (1780-1850): Some Problems and Perspectives for a Source-Repertory Study', *Miscellanea musicologica*, 8 (1975), 115-47.

MARX, ADOLF BERNHARD: *Erinnerungen: Aus meinem Leben* (Berlin, 1865).

MIES, PAUL: *Das Konzert im 19. Jahrhunderts: Studien zu Formen und Kadenzen* (Bonn, 1972).

NEWMAN, WILLIAM S.: *History of the Sonata Idea*, iii. *The Sonata since Beethoven* (Chapel Hill, NC, 1969; rev. 3rd edn., 1983).

ROSEN, CHARLES: 'Sonata Form after Beethoven', in *Sonata Forms* (New York, 1980), 292-335.

SCHÜNEMANN, GEORG: *Geschichte des Dirigierens* (Leipzig, 1913; repr. 1965).

SIMPSON, ROBERT (ed.): *The Symphony*, i. *Haydn to Dvořák* (Harmondsworth, 1966).

STEINBECK, S.: *Die Ouvertüre in der Zeit von Beethoven bis Wagner: Probleme und Lösungen* (Munich, 1973).

SWALIN, BENJAMIN FRANKLIN: *The Violin Concerto: A Study in German Romanticism* (New York, 1941; repr. 1973).

TOVEY, DONALD (FRANCIS): *Essays in Musical Analysis* (London, 1935-6; repr. 1972 and 1981).

VEINUS, ABRAHAM: 'The Romantic Concerto', in *The Concerto* (New York, 1948; rev. 2nd edn., 1964), 155-235.

WEINGARTNER, (PAUL) FELIX: *Die Symphonie nach Beethoven* (Leipzig, 1897; 4th edn., 1926; repr. 1975); Eng. trans., Arthur Bles, *The Symphony Writers since Beethoven* (London, 1907).

(b) Individual Composers

Beethoven

THAYER, ALEXANDER WHEELOCK: *Ludwig van Beethovens Leben*, ed. and trans. Hermann Dieters, i (Berlin, 1866; rev. 2nd edn., 1901; rev. 3rd edn., Hugo Riemann, 1917); ii–iii (Berlin, 1872-9; rev. 2nd edn., Hugo Riemann, Leipzig, 1910–11); iv–v, ed. Hugo Riemann (Leipzig, 1907-8). Eng. original, ed. Henry Edward Krehbiel (New York, 1921); rev. and ed. Elliot Forbes, *Thayer's Life of Beethoven* (Princeton, 1964; 2nd edn., 1967).

Berlioz

BARZUN, JACQUES: *Berlioz and the Romantic Century* (London, 1951; rev. 2nd edn., as *Berlioz and his Century*, 1956; rev. 3rd edn., 1969).

BERLIOZ, HECTOR: *Correspondance inédite*, ed. Daniel Bernard (Paris, 1879; 2nd edn., 1879); Eng. trans., H. Mainwaring Dunstan, *Life and Letters of Berlioz* (London, 1882), i.

—— *Grande Traité d'instrumentation et d'orchestration modernes* (Paris, 1843; 2nd edn., 1855); Eng. trans., M. C. Clarke, *A Treatise upon Modern Orchestration and Instrumentation* (London, 1856).

—— *Lettres intimes* (Paris, 1882); Eng. trans., H. Mainwaring Dunstan, *Life and Letters of Berlioz* (London, 1882), ii.

—— *Mémoires de Hector Berlioz* (Paris, 1870; ed. Pierre Citron, 1969); Eng. trans., David Cairns, *The Memoirs of Hector Berlioz* (New York and London, 1969).

BOSCHOT, ADOLPHE: *La Jeunesse d'un romantique* (Paris, 1906).

CONE, EDWARD T.: 'Inside the Saint's Head: The Music of Berlioz', *Musical Newsletter*, 1/3 (1971), 3-12; 1/4 (1971), 16-20; 2/1 (1972), 19-22.

FOSTER, DONALD H.: 'The Oratorio in Paris in the 18th Century', *Acta musicologica*, 47 (1975), 67-133.

HOLOMAN, D. KERN: *Catalogue of the Works of Hector Berlioz* (Kassel, 1987) [part of the New Berlioz Edition].

MACDONALD, HUGH J.: *Berlioz Orchestral Music* (London, 1969).

—— *Berlioz* (London, 1982).

RUSHTON, JULIAN: *The Musical Language of Berlioz* (Cambridge, 1983).

WARRACK, JOHN, MACDONALD, HUGH, and KOHLER, KARL-HEINZ: *The New Grove Early Romantic Masters 2* (London, 1985) [includes Berlioz].

WOTTON, TOM S.: *Hector Berlioz* (London, 1935; repr. 1970).

Berwald

BERWALD, FRANZ: *Franz Berwald: Die Dokumente seines Lebens*, ed. Erling Lomnäs *et al.* (Kassel, 1979).

LAYTON, ROBERT: *Franz Berwald* (Stockholm, 1956); Eng. orig. (London, 1959).

David

BRANCOUR, RENÉ: *Félicien David* (Paris, 1911).

HAGAN, DOROTHY: *Félicien David, 1810–1876: A Composer and a Cause* (Syracuse, NY, 1985).

Glinka

BROWN, DAVID: *Mikhail Glinka: A Biographical and Critical Study* (London, 1974).

GLINKA, MIKHAIL IVANOVICH: *Literaturnoe nasledie Glinki*, ed. Valerian Mikhaylovich Bogdanov-Beryozovsky (Leningrad and Moscow, 1952–3).

—— *Memoirs*, trans. Richard B. Mudge (Norman, Okla., 1963).

Mendelssohn

DAHLHAUS, CARL (ed.): *Das Problem Mendelssohn* (Regensburg, 1974).

ELVERS, RUDOLF: *Felix Mendelssohn Bartholdy Briefe* (Frankfurt, 1984); Eng. trans., Craig Tomlinson, *Felix Mendelssohn: A Life in Letters* (New York, 1986).

GROSSMANN-VENDREY, SUSANNA: *Felix Mendelssohn-Bartholdy und die Musik der Vergangenheit* (Regensburg, 1969).

KLINGEMANN, KARL (ed.): *Felix Mendelssohn Bartholdys Briefwechsel mit Legationsrat Karl Klingemann in London* (Essen, 1909).

KONOLD, WULF: 'Die zwei Fassungen der "Italienischer Symphonie" von Felix Mendelssohn Bartholdy', in Christoph-Hellmut Mahling and Sigrid Wiesmann (eds.), *Kongressbericht Bayreuth 1981: Bericht über den internationalen Kongress der Gesellschaft für Musikforschung* (Kassel, 1984).

MINTZ, DONALD M., '*Melusine*: A Mendelssohn Draft', *Musical Quarterly*, 43 (1957), 480–99.

RADCLIFFE, PHILIP: *Mendelssohn* (London, 1954; rev. 2nd edn., 1967).

THOMAS, MATHIAS; *Das Instrumentalwerk Felix Mendelssohn Bartholdys: Eine systematisch-theoretische Untersuchung unter besonderer Berücksichtigung der zeitgenössischen Musiktheorie* (Kassel, 1972).

TODD, R. LARRY: 'An Unfinished Piano Concerto by Mendelssohn', *Musical Quarterly*, 68 (1982), 80–101.

——'An Unfinished Symphony by Mendelssohn', *Music and Letters*, 61 (1980), 293–309.

—— *Mendelssohn's Musical Education: A Study and Edition of his Exercises in Composition* (Cambridge, 1983).

—— 'Of Sea Gulls and Counterpoint: The Early Versions of Mendelssohn's *Hebrides* Overture', *19th-century Music*, 2 (1979–80), 179–213.

WARRACK, JOHN, MACDONALD, HUGH, and KOHLER, KARL-HEINZ: *The New Grove Early Romantic Masters 2* (London, 1985) [includes Mendelssohn].

WERNER, ERIC: *Mendelssohn: A New Image of the Composer and his Age* (New York, 1963).

Schumann

ABRAHAM, GERALD: 'The Three Scores of Schumann's D Minor Symphony', in *Slavonic and Romantic Music* (London, 1968), 281–7.

BOETTICHER, WOLFGANG: *Robert Schumann: Einführung in Persönlichkeit und Werk* (Berlin, 1941).

ERLER, HERMANN: *Robert Schumanns Leben: Aus seinen Briefen geschildert* (Berlin, 1886–7; 3rd edn., 1927).

FINSON, JON W.: 'The Sketches for the Fourth Movement of Schumann's Second

Symphony, Op. 61', *Journal of the American Musicological Society*, 39 (1986), 143–68.

GEBHARDT, ARMIN: *Robert Schumann als Symphoniker* (Regensburg, 1968).

SCHUMANN, ROBERT: *Jugendbriefe von Robert Schumann*, ed. Clara Schumann (Leipzig, 1885; 4th edn., 1910); Eng. trans., May Herbert, *Early Letters* (London, 1888).

TEMPERLEY, NICHOLAS, ABRAHAM, GERALD and SEARLE, HUMPHREY: *The New Grove Early Romantic Masters 1* (London, 1985) [includes Schumann].

WASIELEWSKI, WILHELM JOSEPH VON: *Robert Schumann: Eine Biographie* (Dresden, 1858; rev. 4th edn., Waldemar von Wasielewski, Leipzig, 1906); Eng. trans., Abby Langdon Alger, *Life of Robert Schumann, with Letters, 1833–1852* (London, 1878; repr. Detroit, 1975).

For further **Schumann** bibliography *see* § II and § IV.

Clara Schumann

LITZMANN, BERTHOLD: *Clara Schumann: Ein Künstlerleben nach Tagebüchern und Briefen*, i (Leipzig, 1902; 8th edn., 1925, repr. 1971); ii (Leipzig, 1905; 7th edn., 1925, repr. 1971); iii (Leipzig, 1908; 6th edn., 1923, repr. 1971); abridged Eng. trans., Grace E. Hadow, *Clara Schumann: An Artist's Life Based on Material Found in Diaries and Letters* (London, 1913; repr. 1979).

Spohr

BROWN, CLIVE: *Louis Spohr: A Critical Biography* (Cambridge, 1984).

SPOHR, LOUIS: *Selbstsbiographie* (Kassel and Göttingen, 1860–1); ed. F. Göthel as *Lebenserinnerungen* (Tutzing, 1968); Eng. trans., *Ludwig Spohr's Autobiography* (London, 1865, repr. 1969; 2nd edn., 1878); part trans., Henry Pleasants, *The Musical Journeys of Louis Spohr* (Norman, Okla., 1961, repr. 1987).

Wagner

ABRAHAM, GERALD: 'Wagner's Second Thoughts', in *Slavonic and Romantic Music* (London, 1968), 294–312.

WAGNER, RICHARD: *Mein Leben* (Munich, 1911; ed. Martin Gregor-Dellin, 1963); Eng. trans., Andrew Gray and Mary Whittall, *My Life* (Cambridge, 1983).

—— 'Über das Dirigieren' (1870), repr. in *Richard Wagner: Gesammelte Schriften und Dichtungen*, viii (Leipzig, 1873), 325–410; Eng. trans., William Ashton Ellis (ed. and trans.), *Richard Wagner's Prose Works*, iv (London, 1895; repr. 1972), 289–364; and Robert L. Jacobs (trans.), *Three Wagner Essays* (London, 1979), 45–93.

For further **Wagner** bibliography *see* § V.

CHAPTER II

CHAMBER MUSIC: 1830–1850

(i) Modern Editions

(a) Anthologies

KRAMARZ, JOACHIM: *Vom Haydn bis Hindemith: Das Streichquartett in Beispielen* (Wolfenbüttel, 1961).

UNVERRICHT, HUBERT: *Die Kammermusik* (Das Musikwerk, 46; Cologne, 1972); Eng. trans., A. Crawford Howie, *Chamber Music* (Anthology of Music, 46; Cologne, 1975).

(b) Works by Individual Composers

BENNETT, W. S.: Piano and Chamber Music, ed. Geoffrey Bush (Musica Britannica, 37; London, 1972).

BERWALD, F.: *Sämtliche Werke*, ed. Berwald Kommittén (Monumenta musicae svecicae, 2nd series; Kassel, 1966-82): *Kammermusikwerke*, 7 vols.

CHOPIN, F. F.: *Fryderyk Chopin: Dzieła wszystkie/Complete Works*, ed. Ignacy Jan Paderewski with Józef Turczyński and Ludwik Bronarski (Warsaw, 1949-61): 16 *Chamber Music* (1961).

—— *Friedrich Chopin's Werke*, ed. Woldemar Bargiel *et al.* (Leipzig, 1878-1902): 11 *Für Pianoforte und Saiteninstrumente*.

GLINKA, M. I.: *Polnoe sobranie sochineniy*, ed. Vissarion Yakovlevich Shebalin *et al.* (Moscow, 1955-69): 3 *Septuor, Kvartet D-dur* (1957).

MENDELSSOHN, F.: *Felix Mendelssohn Bartholdy's Werke: Kritisch durchgesehene Ausgabe*, ed. Julius Rietz (Leipzig, 1874-7; repr. 1967-9): series 5 *Kammermusik für fünf und mehrere Saiteninstrumente*; series 6 *Quartette für 2 Violinen, Bratsche und Violoncell*; series 9 *Für Pianoforte und Saiteninstrumente*.

—— *Leipziger Ausgabe der Werke Felix Mendelssohn Bartholdys*, ed. Internationale Felix-Mendelssohn-Gesellschaft (Leipzig, 1960-): series 3 *Kammermusikwerke*, ed. Gerhard Schuhmacher (1976-7).

—— *Octet*, ed. Jon Newson (Washington, DC, 1973) [facsimile of holograph score].

SCHUMANN, R.: *Robert Schumann's Werke*, ed. Clara Schumann (Leipzig, 1881-93; repr. 1967-8): series 4 *Für Streichinstrumente* (1881); 5 *Für Pianoforte und andere Instrumente* (1880-7).

SMETANA, B.: *Studijní vydání děl Bedřicha Smetany*, ed. František Bartoš, Josef Plavec, and Karel Šolc (Prague, 1977): 15 *Komorní skladby*.

SPOHR, L.: *Ausgewählte Werke*, ed. Friedrich Otto Leinert (Kassel, 1950s): *Klaviertrio Nr. 4* (repr. in *The Nineteenth Century*, no. 19106, Kassel, 1969).

—— *Selected Works of Louis Spohr (1784-1859)*, ed. Clive Brown (New York, 1987-): 9 *Chamber Music for Strings*, 10 *Chamber Music with Piano*.

(ii) Books and Articles

(a) General

ALTMAN, WILHELM: *Kammermusik-Katalog* (6th edn., Leipzig, 1945; repr. 1967).

COBBETT, WALTER WILLSON (ed.): *Cobbett's Cyclopedic Survey of Chamber Music* (2 vols.; London, 1929-30; 2nd rev. edn., with supplement by Colin Mason, 1963).

ELLA, JOHN: *Musical Sketches Abroad and at Home* (London, 1869; 3rd edn., ed. J. Belcher, 1878).

FINSCHER, LUDWIG: *Studien zur Geschichte des Streichquartetts* (Kassel, 1974).

FOSTER, MYLES B.: *History of the Philharmonic Society of London 1813-1912* (London, 1912).

GRIFFITHS, PAUL: *The String Quartet: A History* (London, 1983).

HINSON, MAURICE: *The Piano in Chamber Ensemble: An Annotated Guide* (Bloomington, Ind., 1978).

LÁNG, PAUL HENRY: *Music in Western Civilisation* (New York, 1941; London, 1942; repr. 1963).

MERSMANN, HANS: *Die Kammermusik*, ii. *XIX Jahrhunderts* (Leipzig, 1930-3).

ROBERTSON, ALEC (ed.): *Chamber Music* (Harmondsworth, 1957) [incl. essays on Mendelssohn by Andrew Porter and Schumann by Joan Chissell].

TOVEY, DONALD (FRANCIS): *Essays in Musical Analysis: Chamber Music*, ed. Hubert J. Foss (London, 1944; repr. 1972).

UNVERRICHT, HUBERT: *Geschichte des Streichtrios* (Tutzing, 1969).

(b) *Individual Composers*

Berlioz

BERLIOZ, HECTOR: *Les Soirées de l'orchestre* (Paris, 1852; ed. L. Guichard, Paris, 1968); Eng. trans., Jacques Barzun (trans. and ed.), *Evenings with the Orchestra* (New York, 1956; 2nd edn., 1973).
For further **Berlioz** bibliography *see* § I.

Berwald

NORMAN, LUDWIG: 'Franz Berwalds kammarmusik-verk', *Tidning for teater och musik* (1859), nos. 7, 8, 10; Ger. trans., Erling Lomnäs (ed.), *Franz Berwald: Die Dokumente seines Lebens* (Kassel, 1979), 490-7.

Mendelssohn

GODWIN, JOSCELYN: 'Early Mendelssohn and Late Beethoven', *Music and Letters*, 55 (1974), 272-85.
HORTON, JOHN: *Mendelssohn Chamber Music* (London, 1972).
KRUMMACHER, FRIEDHELM: *Mendelssohn—der Komponist: Studien zur Kammermusik für Streicher* (Munich, 1978).
For further **Mendelssohn** bibliography *see* § I.

Moscheles

MOSCHELES, CHARLOTTE (ed.): *Aus Moscheles' Leben* (Leipzig, 1872); Eng. trans., Arthur D[uke] Coleridge, *The Life of Moscheles* (London, 1873).

Schumann

CHISSELL, JOAN: *Schumann* (London, 1948; rev. edn., 1977).
DICKINSON, A(LAN), E. F.: 'The Chamber Music', in Gerald Abraham (ed.), *Schumann: A Symposium* (London, 1952), 138-75.
FULLER MAITLAND, J(OHN) A.: *Schumann's Concerted Chamber-Music* (London, 1929).
KOHLHASE, HANS: *Die Kammermusik Robert Schumanns: Stilistische Untersuchungen* (Hamburg, 1979).
PLANTINGA, LEON B.: *Schumann as Critic* (New Haven, 1967; repr. 1977).
SCHUMANN, ROBERT: *Gesammelte Schriften über Musik und Musiker*, ed. Martin Kreisig (4 vols., Leipzig, 1854; 4th edn., 2 vols., 1891; repr. 1968; 5th edn. 1914); Eng. trans., Fanny Raymond Ritter, *Music and Musicians: Essays and Criticisms* (London, 1877-80); new selected Eng. trans., Konrad Wolff (ed.) and Paul Rosenfeld (trans.), *On Music and Musicians* (New York, 1947; repr. 1982); selections, Henry Pleasants (ed. and trans.), *The Musical World of Robert Schumann: A Selection from his own Writings* (London, 1965).
WILCKE, G.: *Tonalität und Modulation in Streichquartetten Schumanns und Mendelssohns* (Leipzig, 1933).
For further **Schumann** bibliography *see* § I and § IV.

Spohr

SPOHR, LOUIS: *Selbstsbiographie* (Kassel and Göttingen, 1860-1); ed. F. Göthel as *Lebenserinnerungen* (Tutzing, 1968); Eng. trans., *Ludwig Spohr's Autobiography* (London, 1865, repr. 1969; 2nd edn., 1878); part trans., Henry Pleasants, *The Musical Journeys of Louis Spohr* (Norman, Okla., 1961; repr. 1987).

CHAPTER III
ROMANTIC OPERA: 1830–1850
(a) *GRAND OPÉRA*

(i) Modern Editions

(a) Anthologies

GOSSETT, PHILIP, and ROSEN, CHARLES: *Early Romantic Opera* (New York, 1978–83) [complete operas cited under individual composers].

WOLFF, HELLMUTH CHRISTIAN: *Die Oper III—19. Jahrhundert* (Das Musikwerke, 40; Cologne, 1972); Eng. trans., A. Crawford Howie, *The Opera III—19th Century* (Anthology of Music, 40; Cologne, 1975) [includes extracts from Auber, *La Muette de Portici*, and Meyerbeer, *Les Huguenots*].

(b) Works by Individual Composers

AUBER, D. F.: *La Muette de Portici*, ed. Philip Gossett and Charles Rosen (Early Romantic Opera, 30; New York, 1980).

—— *Gustave ou le Bal Masqué*, ed. Philip Gossett and Charles Rosen (Early Romantic Opera, 31; New York, 1980).

BERLIOZ, H.: *New Berlioz Edition of the Complete Works*, ed. Hugh Macdonald *et al.* (Kassel, 1967–): 1 *Benvenuto Cellini*, ed. Hugh Macdonald (forthcoming).

DONIZETTI, G.: *Collected Works* [Donizetti Society] (London, 1973–): 4 *Les Martyrs* (1975).

—— *Les Martyrs, La Favorite, Dom Sébastien*, ed. Philip Gossett and Charles Rosen (Early Romantic Opera, 27, 28, 29; New York, 1982, 1982, 1980).

HALÉVY, J.-F.: *La Juive*, ed. Philip Gossett and Charles Rosen (Early Romantic Opera, 36; New York, 1980).

—— *La Juive*, ed. Karl Leich-Galland (Saarbrücken).

MEYERBEER, G.: *Robert le Diable, Les Huguenots, Le Prophète*, ed. Philip Gossett and Charles Rosen (Early Romantic Opera, 19, 20, 21; New York, 1980, 1980, 1978).

ROSSINI, G.: *Guillaume Tell*, ed. Philip Gossett and Charles Rosen (Early Romantic Opera, 17; New York, 1980).

(ii) Books and Articles

(a) General

ALLÉVY, MARIE-ANTOINETTE: *La Mise en scène en France dans la première moitié du dix-neuvième siècle* (Paris, 1938).

ARNDT, MICHAEL, and WALTER, MICHAEL (eds.): *Jahrbuch für Opernforschung 1985* (Frankfurt am Main, 1985).

BECKER, HEINZ: 'Die historische Bedeutung der Grand Opéra', in Walter Salmen (ed.), *Beiträge zur Geschichte der Musikanschauung im 19. Jahrhundert* (Regensburg, 1965), 151-9.

BÜCKEN, ERNST: *Der heroische Stil in der Oper* (Leipzig, 1924).

CARLSON, MARVIN: *The French Stage in the Nineteenth Century* (Metuchen, NJ, 1972).

CHARLTON, D. G.: 'The French Romantic Movement', in D. G. Charlton (ed.), *The French Romantics* (Cambridge, 1984), i. 1-32.

—— 'Religious and Political Thought', in D. G. Charlton (ed.), *The French Romantics* (Cambridge, 1984), i. 33-75.

COHEN, H. ROBERT: 'On the Reconstruction of the Visual Elements of French Grand Opera: Unexplored Sources in Parisian Collections', in Daniel Heartz and Bonnie Wade (eds.), *Berkeley 1977: Zwölfter Kongress der Gesellschaft für Musikwissenschaft* (Kassel, 1981), 463–80.

——(ed.): *Les Gravures Musicales dans L'Illustration (1843–1899)* (Quebec, 1983).

——and GIGOU, MARIE-ODILE: 'La Conservation de la tradition scénique sur la scène lyrique en France au XIXe siècle', *Revue de musicologie*, 64 (1978), 253–67.

——and —— *Cent ans de mise en scène lyrique en France (env. 1830–1930): Catalogue descriptif des livrets de mise en scène, des libretti annotés et des partitions annotées dans la Bibliothèque de l'Association de la Régie Théâtrale (Paris)* (New York, 1986).

CROSTEN, WILLIAM L.: *French Grand Opera: An Art and a Business* (New York, 1948; repr. 1972).

FULCHER, JANE: *The Nation's Image: French Grand Opera as Politics and Politicized Art* (Cambridge, 1987).

GAUTIER, THÉOPHILE: *Histoire de l'art dramatique en France depuis vingt-cinq ans* (Paris, 1858–9; repr. 1968).

GERHARD, ANSELM (ed.): 'Victor-Joseph Éteinne de Juoy: *Essay sur l' Opéra français*', *Bollettino del Centro Rossiniano di Studi* (1987), nos. 1–3, pp 63–91.

——'Une véritable révolution opérée à l'Opéra français', *L'Avant-scène opéra*, 81 (Nov. 1985), 19–23.

——'Die französische "Grand Opéra" in der Forschung seit 1945', *Acta musicologica*, 54 (1987), 220–70.

GOSSETT, PHILIP: 'Music at the Théâtre-Italien', in Peter Bloom, *Music in Paris in the Eighteen-Thirties* (New York, 1987), 327–64.

GOURRET, JEAN: *Histoire de l'Opéra de Paris, 1669–1971* (Paris, 1977).

HONOUR HUGH: *Romanticism* (Harmondsworth, 1981).

HOWARTH W. D.: 'Drama', in D. G. Charlton (ed.), *The French Romantics* (Cambridge, 1984), ii. 205–47.

JOIN-DIÉTERLE, CATHERINE: 'La Monarchie, source d'inspiration de l'Opéra à l'époque romantique', *Revue d'histoire du théâtre*, 35 (1983–4), 430–41.

KANTNER, LEOPOLD M.: 'Zur Genese der Marschduette in der Grand Opéra', *Österreichische Akademie der Wissenschaften: Mitteilungen der Kommission für Musikforschung*, 25 (Vienna, 1976), 322–34.

KRAKOVITCH, ODILE: 'Les Romantiques et la censure au théâtre', *Revue d'histoire du théâtre*, 36 (1984), 56–68.

LOCKE, RALPH P.: *Music, Musicians, and the Saint-Simonians* (Chicago, 1986).

'L'Opéra-Comique au XIXe siècle', *La Revue musicale*, 14/4 (1933), no. 140, pp. 243–308 [special issue].

MITCHELL, JEROME: *The Walter Scott Operas* (Alabama, 1977).

MOYNET, J.: *L'Envers du théâtre: Machines et décorations* (Paris, 1873; repr. 1972).

PENDLE, KARIN: *Eugène Scribe and French Opera of the 19th Century* (Ann Arbor, Mich., 1979).

——'The Boulevard Theaters and Continuity in French Opera of the Nineteenth Century', in Peter Bloom (ed.), *Music in Paris in the Eighteen-Thirties* (New York, 1987), 509–36.

PROD'HOMME, JACQUES-GABRIEL: *L'Opéra (1669–1925)* (Paris, 1925; repr. 1972).

SCHMIDGALL, GARY: *Literature as Opera* (Oxford, 1977).

SMITH, PATRICK J.: 'The French Grand Opéra', in *The Tenth Muse: A Historical Study of the Opera Libretto* (London, 1971), 207–32.

SOUBIES, ALBERT: *Soixante-sept ans à l'Opéra en une page* (Paris, 1893).

VÉRON, LOUIS: *Mémoires d'un bourgeois de Paris* (Paris, 1853–5).

Vingt-six livrets de mise en scène datant de créations Parisiennes (Auber, Bellini, Donizetti, Gounod, Halévy, Meyerbeer, Rossini, Thomas, Verdi et Weber), selected and introduced by H. Robert Cohen with a preface by Marie-Odile Gigou (New York, forthcoming).

WALTER, MICHAEL: 'Die Darstellung des Volkes in der französischen Oper von der Revolution bis 1870', *Romanistische Zeitschrift für Literaturgeschichte*, Heft 3/4 (1986), 381–400.

WILD, NICOLE: 'La Recherche de la précision historique chez les décorateurs de l'Opéra de Paris au XIXème siècle', in Daniel Heartz and Bonnie Wade (eds.), *Berkeley 1977: Zwölfter Kongress der Gesellschaft für Musikwissenschaft* (Kassel, 1981), 453–63.

—— *Dictionnaire des théâtres lyriques à Paris au XIXe siècle* (New York, forthcoming).

WOLFF, HELLMUTH CHRISTIAN: *Oper: Szene und Darstellung von 1600 bis 1900* (Musikgeschichte in Bildern, 4; Leipzig, 1968).

WOLFF, STÉPHANE: *L'Opéra au Palais Garnier (1875–1962)* (Paris, 1962; repr. 1983).

For further general bibliography on French opera *see* § VI (b)

(b) *Individual Composers*

Auber

FINSCHER, LUDWIG: 'Aubers *La Muette de Portici* und die Anfänge der Grand-opéra', in Jürgen Schläder and Reinhold Quandt (eds.), *Festschrift Heinz Becker* (n.p., 1982), 87–105.

LONGYEAR, REY: 'La Muette de Portici', *Music Review*, 19 (1958), 37–46.

MALHERBE, CHARLES: *Auber* (Paris, 1911).

MONGRÉDIEN, JEAN: 'Variations sur un thème: Masaniello', in Michael Arndt and Michael Walter (eds.), *Jahrbuch für Opernforschung 1985* (Frankfurt am Main, 1985), 90–121.

WAGNER, RICHARD: 'Erinnerungen an Auber' (1871), repr. in *Richard Wagner: Gesammelte Schriften und Dichtungen*, ix (Leipzig, 1873), 51–73; Eng. trans., William Ashton Ellis (ed. and trans.), *Richard Wagner's Prose Works*, v (London, 1896; repr. 1972), 35–55.

WALTER, MICHAEL, ' "Man überlege sich nur Alles, sehe, wo Alles hinausläuft!" Zu Robert Schumanns "Hugenotten"-Rezension', *Die Musikforschung*, 36 (1983), 127–44.

Berlioz

BERLIOZ, HECTOR: *Correspondance générale*, ed. Pierre Citron, i. *1803–1832* (Paris, 1972); ii. *1832–1842* (Paris, 1975).

DICKINSON, A. E. F.: 'Berlioz's "Bleeding Nun" ', *Musical Times*, 107 (1966), 584–8.

LA MAY, THOMASIN K.: 'A New Look at the Weimar Versions of Berlioz's *Benvenuto Cellini*', *Musical Quarterly*, 65 (1979), 559–72.

MACDONALD, HUGH: 'The Original "Benvenuto Cellini" ', *Musical Times*, 107 (1966), 1042–5.

For further **Berlioz** bibliography *see* § I

David

BRANCOUR, RENÉ: *Félicien David* (Paris, 1911).

Hagan, Dorothy Veinus: *Félicien David, 1810–1876: A Composer and a Cause* (Syracuse NY, 1985).

Donizetti

ASHBROOK, WILLIAM: *Donizetti and his Operas* (Cambridge, 1982).

DEAN, WINTON: 'Donizetti's Serious Operas', *Proceedings of the Royal Musical Association*, 100 (1973–4), 123–41.

MESSENGER, MICHAEL F.: 'Donizetti, 1840: 3 'French' Operas and their Italian

Counterparts', *Journal of the Donizetti Society*, 2 (1975) 99–115.
For further **Donizetti** bibliography *see* § III (c)

Halévy

BERLIOZ, HECTOR: *Les Musiciens et la musique*, ed. A. Hallays (Paris, 1903) [contains several notices of Halévy's operas].

HALÉVY, LEON: *F. Halévy: Sa vie et ses œuvres* (Paris, 1862; 2nd edn., 1863).

'HALÉVY: *La Juive*', *L'Avant-scène opéra*, 100 (July 1987).

WAGNER, RICHARD: '*La Reine de Chypre* d'Halévy' (1842); repr. in Richard Wagner, *Sämtliche Schriften und Dichtungen*, ed. H. von Wolzogen and R. Sternfeld, xii (Leipzig, 1911), 404–11; Eng. trans. William Ashton Ellis (ed. and trans.), *Richard Wagner's Prose Works*, viii (1899), 175–200.

—— 'Bericht über eine neue Pariser Oper: *La Reine de Chypre* von Halévy' (1842); repr. in *Richard Wagner: Gesammelte Schriften und Dichtungen*, i (Leipzig, 1871), 299–319; Eng. trans., Ellis, *Prose Works*, vii (1898), 205–22.

—— 'Halévy und die französiche Oper' (1842); repr. in Richard Wagner, *Sämtliche Schriften und Dichtungen*, xii (Leipzig, 1911), 129–46.

Meyerbeer

BECKER, HEINZ: 'Giacomo Meyerbeers Mitarbeit an den Libretti seiner Opern', in Carl Dahlhaus *et al.* (eds.), *Bericht über den internationalen musik-wissenschaftlichen Kongress Bonn 1970* [Gesellschaft für Musikforschung] (Kassel, 1972). 155–60.

BLOOM, PETER A.: 'Friends and Admirers: Meyerbeer and Fétis', *Revue belge de musicologie*, 32–3 (1978–9), 174–87.

DELACROIX, EUGÈNE: *Journal de Eugène Delacroix: Nouvelle édition publiée d'après le manuscrit original*, ed. André Joubin (Paris, 1932); Eng. trans., Walter Pach, *The Journal of Eugène Delacroix* (New York, 1937).

DIEREN, BERNARD VAN, 'Meyerbeer', in *Down Among the Dead Men* (London, 1935), 142–74.

FRESE, CHRISTHARD.: *Dramaturgie der grossen Opern Giacomo Meyerbeers* (Berlin, 1970).

FULCHER, JANE: 'Meyerbeer and the Music of Society', *Musical Quarterly*, 67 (1981), 213–29.

JOIN-DIÉTERLE, CATHERINE: '*Robert le Diable*: Le Premier Opéra romantique', *Romantisme*, 28/9 (1980), 147–66.

MACDONALD, HUGH: '*Robert le Diable*', in Peter Bloom (ed.), *Music in Paris in the Eighteen-Thirties* (New York, 1987), 457–69.

MEYERBEER, GIACOMO: *Giacomo Meyerbeer: Briefwechsel und Tagebucher*, ed. Heinz Becker (Berlin, 1960–75).

(b) *OPÉRA COMIQUE*

(i) Modern Editions

(*a*) *Anthologies*

WOLFF, HELLMUTH CHRISTIAN: *Die Oper III—19. Jahrhundert* (Das Musikwerke, 40; Cologne, 1972); Eng. trans., A. Crawford Howie, *The Opera III—19th Century* (Anthology of Music, 40; Cologne, 1975) [includes extracts from Meyerbeer's *Fra Diavolo*].

(ii) Books and Articles

(*a*) *General*

BAILBÉ, JOSEPH-MARC: 'Le Bourgeois et la musique au XIX siècle', *Romantisme*, 13 (1977), 123–36.

BOSSUET, PIERRE: *Histoire des théâtres nationaux* (Paris, n.d.).

CHORLEY, HENRY F.: *Thirty Years' Musical Recollections* (London, 1862; rev. and slightly abridged 2nd edn., Ernest Newman, 1926).

CLÉMENT, FÉLIX, and LAROUSSE, PIERRE: *Dictionnaire lyrique, ou Histoire des opéras* (Paris, 1867; enlarged 3rd edn., 1905, repr. 1960; ed. Arthur Pougin as *Dictionnaire des opéras*).

COOPER, MARTIAN: *Opéra comique* (London, 1949).

LEPEINTRE DESROCHES, PIERRE MARIE MICHEL: *Suite du répertoire du théâtre français* (81 vols.; Paris, 1882–3; repr. 1970).

LESURE, FRANÇOIS (ed.): *La Musique à Paris en 1830–1831* (Paris, 1983).

'L'Opéra-Comique au XIXe siècle', *La Revue musicale*, 14/140 (1933), 243–308.

PENDLE, KARIN: *Eugène Scribe and French Opera of the 19th Century* (Ann Arbor, Mich., 1979).

SOUBIES, ALBERT: *Soixante-neuf ans à l'Opéra-Comique en deux pages 1825–94* (Paris, 1893).

WALSH, THOMAS JOSEPH: *Second Empire Opera: The Théâtre Lyrique, Paris, 1851–1870* (London, 1981).

(*b*) *Individual Composers*

Adam

ADAM, ADOLPHE: 'Les Musiciens de Paris' (1834), in *Souvenirs d'un musicien* (Paris, 1857; later edn., 1868).

HALÉVY, FROMENTAL: *Notice sur la vie et les ouvrages de M. Adolphe Adam* (Paris, 1859; repr. as 'Adolphe Adam' in *Souvenirs et portraits*, Paris, 1861).

POUGIN, ARTHUR: *Adolphe Adam: Sa vie, sa carrière, ses mémoires artistiques* (Paris, 1876).

STUDWELL, WILLIAM E.: *Adolphe Adam and Leo Délibes: A Guide to Research* (New York, 1987).

Auber
See § III (a)

Halévy
See § III (a)

Mendelssohn

MENDELSSOHN, FELIX: *Letters*, trans. Gisella Selden-Goth (New York, 1945, London, 1946; repr. 1969).

For further **Mendelssohn** bibliography *see* § I

Thomas

COOPER, MARTIN: 'Charles Louis Ambroise Thomas', in A. L. Bacharach (ed.), *The Music Masters* (London, 1957–8), ii.

DEAN, WINTON: 'Shakespeare and Opera', in Phyllis Hartnoll (ed.), *Shakespeare in Music* (London, 1964), 89–176.

(C) ITALY

(i) Modern Editions

(*a*) *Anthologies*

GOSSETT, PHILIP: *Italian Opera 1810–1840* (New York, 1985) [includes operas and opera excerpts by Raimondi and Vaccai; other operas cited under individual composers].

(b) *Works by Individual Composers*

MERCADANTE, S.: *I Normanni a Parigi, Il guiramento, Le due illustri rivali, Elena da Feltre, Il bravo, La vestale*, ed. Philip Gossett, Italian Opera 1810–1840, 17, 18, (New York, 1986), 19, 20 (1985), 21, 22 (1986).

PACINI, G.: *Saffo*, in Italian Opera 1810–1840, 36, ed. Philip Gossett (New York, 1986).

VERDI, G.: *The Works of Giuseppe Verdi*, ed. Philip Gossett *et al.* (*Chicago and Milan, 1983–*): *series 1*, 5 *Ernani*, ed. Claudio Gallico (1985); 3 *Nabucco*, ed. Roger Parker (1987); 4 *I Lombardi*, 7 *Giovanna d'Arco*, 10 & 25 *Macbeth*, 14 *La battaglia di Legnano* (forthcoming).

—— Full scores of *Ernani, Giovanna d'Arco, I Lombardi, La battaglia, Macbeth*, and *Nabucco* (Milan, *c.* 1882– ; repr. New York, n.d.).

(ii) Books and Articles

(a) *General*

AMBROSE, MARY: 'Walter Scott, Italian Opera and Romantic Stage-setting', *Italian Studies*, 36 (1981) 58–78.

BERLIOZ, HECTOR: *Mémoires de Hector Berlioz* (Paris, 1870; ed. Pierre Citron, 1969); Eng. trans., David Cairns, *The Memoirs of Hector Berlioz* (New York and London, 1969).

BLACK, JOHN N.: *The Italian Romantic Libretto; A Study of Salvadore Cammarano* (Edinburgh, 1984).

D'AZEGLIO, MASSIMO: *I miei ricordi*, with posthumous completion by Giuseppe Torelli (2 vols.; Florence, 1867); Eng. trans., E. R. Vincent, *Things I Remember* (London, 1966).

DEAN, WINTON: 'Shakespeare and Opera', in Phyllis Hartnoll (ed.), *Shakespeare in Music* (London, 1964), 89–175.

DI STEFANO, CARLO: *La censura teatrale in Italia (1600–1962)* (Bologna, 1964).

EINAUDI, GINO (ed.): *Il melodramma italiano dell'Ottocento: Studie e ricerche per Massimo Mila* (Turin., 1977).

FLORIMO, FRANCESCO: *La scuola musicale di Napoli e i suoi conservatorii* (Naples, 1881–3; repr. 1969).

GLINKA, MIKHAIL IVANOVICH: *Memoirs*, trans. Richard B. Mudge (Norman, Okla., 1963).

GOSSETT, PHILIP, *et al.*: *The New Grove Masters of Italian Opera* (London, 1983) [Rossini, Donizetti, Bellini, Verdi, Puccini].

HANSLICK, EDUARD: *Die moderne Oper*, i. *Kritiken und Studien* (Berlin, 1875; repr., 1971).

KIMBELL, DAVID: 'The Setting', in *Verdi in the Age of Italian Romanticism* (Cambridge, 1981), 3–87.

LASTER, ARNAUD: 'Victor Hugo, la musique et les musiciens', *V. Hugo; Œuvres complètes* (Paris, 1967).

LIPPMANN, FRIEDRICH: 'Der italienische Vers und der musikalische Rhythmus: Zum Verhältnis von Vers und Musik in der italienischen Oper des 19. Jahrhunderts, mit einem Rückblick auf die 2. Hälfte des 18. Jahrhunderts', *Analecta musicologica*, 12 (1975), 253–369; 14 (1977), 324–410; 15 (1978), 298–333.

—— 'Zur *italianità* der italienischen Oper im 19. Jahrhundert' *Die 'Couleur locale' in der Oper des 19. Jahrhunderts* (Regensburg, 1976), 229–56.

LONGYEAR, REY M.: *Schiller and Music* (Chapel Hill, NC, 1966).

MAZZINI, GIUSEPPE: 'Della fatalità considerata com'elemento drammatico', *Edizione nazionale degli scritti di Giuseppe Mazzini*, viii (Imola, 1910), 169–200.

—— 'Filosofia di musica', Edizione nazionale degli scritti di Giuseppe Mazzini, viii (Imola, 1910), 119–65.

MENDELSSOHN, FELIX: *Briefe aus den Jahren 1830 bis 1847*, ed. Paul and C. Mendelssohn (Leipzig, 1863-4; 7th edn., 1899); Eng. trans., Lady Wallace, *Letters of Felix Mendelssohn Bartholdy* (London, 1863; 4th edn., 1864, repr. 1970).

RINALDI, MARIO: *Felice Romani: dal melodramma classico al melodramma romantico* (Rome, 1965).

ROSSELLI, JOHN: *The Opera Industry in Italy from Cimarosa to Verdi: The Role of the Impresario* (Cambridge, 1984).

SCHLITZER, FRANCO: *Mondo teatrale dell'Ottocento* (Naples, 1954).

—— *Storia dell'opera*, ed. Alberto Basso, i. *L'opera in Italia* (Turin 1977).

SCHMIDGALL, GARY: *Literature as Opera* (New York, 1977).

ZAMBONI, GIUSEPPE: *Die italienische Romantik: Ihre Auseinandersetzungen mit des Tradition* (Krefeld, 1953).

(*b*) *Individual Composers*

Bellini

ADAMO, MARIA ROSARIA, and LIPPMANN, FRIEDRICH: *Vincenzo Bellini* (Turin, 1981).

BELLINI, VINCENZO: *Vincenzo Bellini: Epistolario*, ed. Luisa Cambi (Verona, 1943).

ORREY, LESLIE: *Bellini* (London, 1969).

WEINSTOCK, HERBERT: *Vincenzo Bellini: his Life and his Operas* (New York, 1971).

Donizetti

ALBORGHETTI, F., and GALLI, M.: *Gaetano Donizetti e G. Simone Mayr: Notizie e documenti* (Bergamo, 1875).

ASHBROOK, WILLIAM: *Donizetti* (London, 1965).

—— *Donizetti and his Operas* (Cambridge, 1982).

Atti del 1° convegno internazionale di studi donizettiani Bergamo 1975.

DENT, EDWARD J.: 'Donizetti: An Italian Romantic', in Herbert Van Thal (ed.), *Fanfare for Ernest Newman* (London, 1955), 86-107.

GOSSETT, PHILIP: '*Anna Bolena*' and the Artistic Maturity of Gaetano Donizetti (Oxford, 1985).

LIPPMANN, FRIEDRICH: 'Die Melodien Donizettis', *Analecta musicologica*, 3 (1966), 80-113.

WEINSTOCK, HERBERT: *Donizetti and the World of Opera in Italy, Paris and Vienna in the First Half of the Nineteenth Century* (London, 1964; repr. 1979).

ZAVADINI, GUIDO: *Donizetti: Vita-musiche-epistolario* (Bergamo, 1948).

Mercadante

CARLI BALLOLA, GIOVANNI: 'Incontro con Mercadante', *Chigiana*, 26-7 (1969-70), 465-500.

FLORIMO, FRANCESCO: *Cenno storico sulla scuola musicale di Napoli* (Naples, 1869-71; rev. enlarged 2nd edn. as *La scuola musicale di Napoli e i suoi conservatorii*, 1880-3, repr. 1969).

NOTARNICOLA, BIAGIO: *Saverio Mercadante, biografico critica* (Rome, 1945, rev. and enlarged as *Saverio Mercadente nella gloria e nella luce*, 1948).

SCHMID, PATRIC: 'Rediscovering Mercandante', *Opera*, 26 (1975), 332-7.

WALKER, FRANK: 'Mercadante and Verdi', *Music and Letters*, 33 (1952), 311-21; 34 (1953), 33-8.

Pacini

LIPPMANN, FRIEDRICH: 'Giovanni Pacini: Bemerkungen zum Stil seiner Opern', *Chigiana*, 24 (1967), 111-24.

PACINI, GIOVANNI: *Le mie memorie artistiche* (Florence, 1865; ed. F. Magnani, Florence 1875).

Rossini

OSBORNE, RICHARD: *Rossini* (London, 1986).

STENDHAL: *Vie de Rossini* (Paris, 1824; rev. 2nd edn. by Henry Prunières, 1922); Eng. trans., Richard N. Coe, *Life of Rossini* (London, 1956; rev. 2nd edn., 1970).

Verdi

ABBATE, CAROLYN, and PARKER, ROGER (eds.): *Analyzing Opera: Verdi and Wagner* (Berkeley and Los Angeles, Calif., 1988).

ABBIATI, FRANCO: *Giuseppe Verdi* (Milan, 1959).

BALDINI, GABRIELE: *Abitare la battaglia: La storia di Giuseppe Verdi* (Milan, 1970); Eng. trans., Roger Parker, *The Story of Giuseppe Verdi* (Cambridge, 1980).

BUDDEN, JULIAN: *The Operas of Verdi*, i. *From Oberto to Rigoletto* (London, 1973).

—— *Verdi* (London, 1985).

CHECCHI, EUGENIO: *Giuseppe Verdi: Le genio e le opere* (Florence, 1887).

CONATI, MARCELLO (ed.): *Interviste e incontri con Verdi* (Milan, 1980); Eng. trans., R. Stokes, *Interviews and Encounters with Verdi* (London, 1984).

—— *La bottega della musica: Verdi e La Fenice* (Milan, 1983).

GARIBALDI, LUIGI AGOSTINO: *Giuseppe Verdi nelle lettere di Emanuele Muzio ad Antonio Barezzi* (Milan, 1931).

GERHARTZ, LEO KARL: *Die Auseinandersetzungen des jungen Giuseppe Verdi mit dem literarischen Drama: Ein Beitrag zur szenischen Strukturbestimmung der Oper* (Berlin, 1968).

GODEFROY, VINCENT: *The Dramatic Genius of Verdi: Studies of Selected Operas*, i. '*Nabucco*' to '*La traviata*' (London, 1975).

HARWOOD, GREGORY W.: 'Verdi's Reform of the Italian Opera Orchestra', *19th-century Music*, 10 (1986–7), 108–34.

KIMBELL, DAVID: 'The Young Verdi and Shakespeare', *Proceedings of the Royal Musical Association*, 101 (1974–5), 59–73.

—— *Verdi in the Age of Italian Romanticism* (Cambridge, 1981).

MEDICI, MARIO (ed.): *Atti del I° congresso internazionale di studi verdiani: Situazione e prospective degli studi verdiani nel mondo* (Parma, 1969).

—— *Atti del III° congresso internazionale di studi verdinai: Il teatro e la musica di Giuseppe Verdi* (Parma, 1974).

MILA, MASSIMO: *Giuseppe Verdi* (Bari, 1958).

—— *La giovinezza di Verdi* (Turin, 1974).

—— *L'arte di Verdi* (Turin, 1980).

MONALDI, GINO: *Verdi* (Stuttgart and Leipzig, 1898; 4th edn., 1951).

POUGIN, ARTHUR: *Giuseppe Verdi: Vita aneddotica con note ed aggiunte di Folchetto* (Milan, 1881).

ROSEN, DAVID, and PORTER, ANDREW (eds.): *Verdi's Macbeth: A Sourcebook* (Cambridge and New York, 1984) [papers given at the 5th international Verdi congress].

VERDI, GIUSEPPE: *Carteggio Verdi–Boito*, ed. Mario Medici and Marcello Conati (Parma, 1978).

—— *I copialettere di Giuseppe Verdi*, ed. Gaetano Cesari and Alessandro Luzio (Milan, 1913; repr. 1973); abridged Eng. trans., Charles Osborne (ed. and trans.), *Letters of Giuseppe Verdi* (London, 1971).

WALKER, FRANK: *The Man Verdi* (London, 1962; repr. 1982).

WEAVER, WILLIAM: *Verdi: A Documentary Study* (London, 1977).

—— and CHUSID, MARTIN (eds.): *The Verdi Companion* (London, 1980).

WERFEL, FRANZ, and STEFAN, PAUL: *Verdi: The Man in his Letters* (New York, 1942; repr., n.d.).

For further **Verdi** bibiography *see* § VI (c)

(d) GERMANY

(i) Modern Editions

(*a*) *Anthologies*

GOSSETT, PHILIP: *Early Romantic Opera* (New York, 1978) [includes operas by Meyerbeer].

WOLFF, HELLMUTH CHRISTIAN: *Die Oper III—19. Jahrhundert* (Das Musikwerke, 40; Cologne, 1972) Eng. trans., A. Crawford Howie, *The Opera III—19th Century* (Anthology of Music, 40; Cologne, 1975) [includes extracts from Lortzing, *Hans Sachs*, and Spohr, *Faust*].

(*b*) *Works by Individual Composers*

SCHUMANN, R.: *Robert Schumann's Werke*, ed. Clara Schumann *et al.* (Leipzig, 1881-93; repr. 1967-8): series 9 *Grössere Gesangwerke*, 1 *Das Paradiso und die Peri* (1883), 3 *Genoveva* (1886).

SPOHR, L.: *Selected Works of Louis Spohr* (*1784-1859*), ed. Clive Brown (New York, 1987-): 1 *Faust*, 2 *Jessonda*, 3 *Pietro von Abano*.

WAGNER, R.: *Richard Wagners Werke: Musikdramen—Jugendopern—musikalische Werke*, ed. Michael Balling (Leipzig, 1912-29; repr. 1971): 3 *Tannhäuser*; 4 *Lohengrin*; 12 *Die Hochzeit*; 3 *Die Geen*; 14 *Das Liebesvot*.

—— *Richard Wagner: Sämtliche Werke*, ed. Carl Dahlhaus, Egon Voss *et al.* (Mainz, 1970-): series A *Musikbände*: 3 *Rienzi*, ed. Reinhard Strohm and Egon Voss (1974-7); 4 *Der fliegende Holländer*, ed. Isolde Vetter (1983); 5-6 *Tannhäuser*, ed. Reinhard Strohm (1980-6); 1 *Die Feen*, 2 *Das Liebesvot*, 7 *Lohengrin*, 15 *Unvollendete Bühnenwerke und Einlage Stucke* (forthcoming).

(ii) Books and Articles

(*a*) *General*

DENT, EDWARD J.: *The Rise of Romantic Opera*, ed. Winton Dean (Cambridge, 1970).

FLAHERTY, MARIA GLORIA: *Opera in the Development of German Cultural Thought* (Princeton, NJ, 1978).

GARLINGTON, AUBREY S.: 'German Romantic Opera and the Problem of Origins', *Musical Quarterly*, 68 (1977), 500-6.

—— 'E. T. A. Hoffmann's "Der Dichter und der Komponist" and the Creation of the German Romantic Opera', *Musical Quarterly*, 65 (1979), 22-47.

GÖPFERT, BERND: *Stimmtypen und Rollencharakten in der deutschen Oper von 1815-1848* (Wiesbaden, 1977).

GOSLICH, SIEGFRIED: *Beiträge zur Geschichte der deutschen romantischen Oper* (Leipzig, 1937; enlarged 2nd edn., as *Die deutsche romantische Oper*, 1975).

HOFFMANN, E. T. A.: 'Der Dichter und der Komponist', *Allgemeine musikalische Zeitung*, 15 (1813), repr. in *E. T. A. Hoffman: Schriften zur Musik: Nachlese*, ed. Friedrich Schnapp (Munich, 1963; 2nd edn., 1978); Eng. trans., Martyn Clarke, *E. T. A. Hoffmann: Writings on Music*, ed. David Charlton (Cambridge, forthcoming).

HORTSCHANSKY, KLAUS: 'Der *Deus ex machina* im Opernlibretto der ersten Hälfte des 19. Jahrhunderts', in Heinz Becker (ed.), *Beiträge zur Geschichte der Oper* (Regensburg, 1965), 45-76.

PALDAMUS, F. G.: *Das deutsche Theater der Gegenwart* (Mainz, 1857).

REICHA, ANTOINE(-JOSEPH): *L'Art du compositeur dramatique, ou cours complet de composition vocale* (Paris, 1883); trans., Carl Czerny (ed. and trans.), *Die Kunst der dramatischen Composition* (Vienna, 1835).

SCHIEDERMAIR, LUDWIG: *Die deutsche Oper: Grundzuge ihres Werdens und Wesens* (Leipzig, 1930; repr. 1971; 3rd edn., 1943), chap. III 'Romantik'.

SCHLETTERER, HANS MICHAEL: *Das deutsche Singspeil* (Augsburg, 1863; repr. 1975).

WAGNER, RICHARD: 'Die deutsche Oper' (1834), repr. in *Richard Wagner: Sämtliche Schriften und Dichtungen*, ed. H. von Wolzogen and R. Sternfeld, xii (Leipzig, 1911), 1–4; Eng. trans., William Ashton Ellis (ed. and trans.), *Richard Wagner's Prose Works*, viii (London, 1899; repr. 1972), 55–8.

—— 'Pasticcio' (1834), Richard Wagner, *Sämtliche Schriften und Dichtungen*, xii (Leipzig, 1911), 5–11; Eng. trans., Ellis, *Prose Works*, viii (London, 1899), 59–67.

—— 'Über die Ouverture' (1840), repr. in *Richard Wagner: Gesammelte Schriften und Dichtungen*, i (Leipzig, 1871), 241–56.; Eng. trans., Ellis, *Prose Works*, vii (London, 1898), 151–65.

—— 'Eine Mitteilung an meine Freunde' (1851), repr. in *Richard Wagner: Gesammelte Schriften und Dichtungen*, iv (Leipzig, 1872), 285–418; Eng. trans., Ellis, *Prose Works*, i (London, 1892), 267–392.

(b) Individual Composers

Beethoven

THAYER, ALEXANDER WHEELOCK: *Ludwig van Beethovens Leben*, ed. and trans. Hermann Dieters, i (Berlin, 1866; rev. 2nd edn., 1901; rev. 3rd edn., Hugo Riemann, 1917); ii–iii (Berlin, 1872–9; rev. 2nd edn., Hugo Riemann, Leipzig, 1910–11); iv–v, ed. Hugo Riemann (Leipzig, 1907–8. Eng. original, ed. Henry Edward Krehbiel (New York, 1921); rev. and ed. Elliot Forbes, *Thayer's Life of Beethoven* (Princeton, NJ, 1964; 2nd edn., 1967).

Flotow

WEISSMAN, JOHN S.: *Flotow* (London, 1950).

Liszt

LISZT, FRANZ: *Franz Liszt: Briefe an die Fürstin Sayn-Wittgenstein* (Leipzig, 1900). For further **Liszt** bibliography *see* § VII

Lortzing

KRUSE, GEORG RICHARD (ed.): *A. Lortzing: Gesammelte Briefe* (Leipzig, 1902; 3rd edn., 1947).

SUBNOTNIK, ROSE ROSENGARD: 'Lortzing and the German Romantics: A Dialectical Assessment', *Musical Quarterly*, 62 (1976), 241–64.

Marschner

PALMER, A. DEAN: *Heinrich August Marschner 1795–1861: His Life and Stage Works* (Ann Arbor, Mich., 1980).

Mendelssohn

MINTZ, DONALD M.: '*Melusine*: A Mendelssohn Draft', *Musical Quarterly*, 43 (1957), 480–99.

WARRACK, JOHN: 'Mendelssohn's Operas', in Nigel Fortune (ed.), *Music and Theatre: Essays in Honour of Winton Dean* (Cambridge, 1987), 263–98.

For further **Mendelssohn** bibliography *see* § I

Meyerbeer

See § III (a)

Nicolai

ALTMANN, WILHELM (ed.): *Otto Nicolais Tagebücher* (Regensburg, 1973).

HANSLICK, EDUARD: *Die Moderne Oper*, viii. *Am Erde des Jahrhunderts* (Berlin, 1899).

KONRAD, ULRICH: *Otto Nicolai, 1810–1849: Studien zu Leben und Werk* (Baden-Baden, 1986).

Schumann

ABRAHAM, GERALD: 'The Dramatic Music', in Gerald Abraham (ed.), *Schumann: A Symposium* (London, 1952), 260–82.

HANSLICK, EDUARD: 'R. Schumann als Opernkomponist', *Die Moderne Oper* (Berlin, 1875; repr. 1971), 256–73.

SIEGEL, LINDA: 'A Second Look at Schumann's *Genoveva*', *Music Review*, 36 (1975), 17–41.

For further **Schumman** bibliography *see* § I, § II, and § IV

Spohr

SPOHR, LOUIS: *Selbstsbiographie* (Kassel and Göttingen, 1860–1); ed. F. Göthel as *Lebenserinnerungen* (Tutzing, 1968); Eng. trans., *Ludwig Spohr's Autobiography* (London 1865, repr. 1969; 2nd edn., 1878); part trans. Henry Pleasants *The Musical Journeys of Louis Spohr* (Norman, Okla., 1961, repr. 1987).

Wagner

BAILEY, ROBERT: 'Wagner's Musical Sketches for *Siegfrieds Tod*', in Harold S. Powers (ed.), *Studies in Music History: Essays for Oliver Strunk* (Princeton, NJ, 1968), 459–95.

DEATHRIDGE, JOHN: *Wagner's Rienzi A Reappraisal Based on a Study of the Sketches and Drafts* (Oxford, 1977).

HOPKINSON, CECIL: *Tannhäuser: An Examination of 36 Editions* (Tutzing, 1973).

KOCH, MAX: 'Die Quellen der "Hochzeit" ', *Richard Wagner-Jahrbuch*, iv (1912), 105–14.

WAGNER, RICHARD: *Richard Wagner: Gesammelte Schriften und Dichtungen*, i–x (Leipzig, 1871–3, 1883; 2nd edn. 1887, repr. 1976; 5th edn., with vols. xi–xii added, *Sämtliche Schriften und Dichtungen*, ed. H. von Wolzogen and R. Sternfeld, 1911; 6th edn., with vols. xiii–xvi added, ed. H. von Wolzogen and R. Sternfeld, 1914).

—— *Richard Wagner's Prose Works*, ed. and trans. William Ashton Ellis (London, 1892–9; repr. 1972).

—— *Richard Wagner: Sämtliche Werke*, ed. Carl Dahlhaus (Mainz, 1970–): series B *Dokumentenbände*: 23 *Rienzi*, ed. Reinhard Strohm (1976); 29 *Der Ring des Nibelungen*, ed. Werner Brieg and Hartmut Fladt (1976); 30 *Parsifal*, ed. Egon Voss and Martin Geck (1972–3); 22 *Die Feen und Das Liebesvot*; 24 *Der fliegender Holländer*; 25 *Tannhäuser*; 26 *Lohengrin*; 27 *Tristan und Isolde*; 28 *Die Meistersinger von Nürnberg* (forthcoming).

—— *Three Wagner Essays*, trans. Robert L. Jacobs (London, 1979).

—— 'Über das Dirigieren' (1870), repr. in *Richard Wagner: Gesammelte Schriften und Dichtungen*, viii (Leipzig, 1873), 325–410; Eng. trans., William Ashton Ellis (ed. and trans.), *Richard Wagner's Prose Works*, iv (London, 1895; repr. 1972), 289–364; and Robert L. Jacobs (trans.), *Three Wagner Essays* (London, 1979), 45–93.

For further **Wagner** bibliography *see* § V

Weber

JÄHNS, FRIEDRICH WILHELM: *Carl Maria von Weber in seinen Werken; Chronologisch-thematisches Verzeichniss seiner sämmtlichen Compositionen* (Berlin, 1871; repr. 1967).

WEBER, CARL MARIA VON: *Sämtliche Schriften von Carl Maria von Weber: Kritische Ausgabe*, ed. Georg Kaiser (Berlin and Leipzig, 1908); Eng. trans. Martin

Cooper, *Carl Maria von Weber: Writings on Music*, ed. John Warrack (Cambridge, 1981).

(e) RUSSIA AND EAST EUROPE

(i) Modern Editions

(a) Anthologies

WOLFF, HELLMUTH CHRISTIAN: *Die Oper III—19. Jahrhundert* (Das Musikwerke, 40; Cologne, 1972); Eng. trans., A. Crawford Howie, *The Opera III—19th Century* (Anthology of Music, 40; Cologne, 1975) [includes extracts from Moniuszko's *Halka*].

(b) Works by Individual Composers

DARGOMÏZHSKY, A. S.: *Esmeralda*, ed. Mikhail Samoylovich Pekelis (Moscow, 1961).
GLINKA, M. I.: *Polnoe sobranie sochineniy*, ed. Vissarion Yakovlevich Shebalin *et al.* (Moscow, 1955–69): 12–13 *Ivan Susanin*, 14–15 *Ruslan i Lyudmila*.
LISINSKI, V.: *Vatroslav Lisinski: Izabrana djela*, ed. Lovro Županović (Zagreb, 1969): 6 *Ljubav i zloba*.
ŠKROUP, F.: *Dráternik* (Prague, 1913; 2nd edn., 1926).

(ii) Books and Articles

(a) General

ABRAHAM, GERALD: 'The Early Development of Opera in Poland', *Essays on Russian and East European Music* (London, 1985), 122–40.
—— et al.: *The New Grove Russian Masters 2* (London, 1986) [Rimsky-Korsakov, Skryabin, Prokofiev, Shostakovich].
BROWN, DAVID et al.: *The New Grove Russian Masters 1* (London, 1986) [Glinka, Borodin, Balakirev, Mussorgsky, Tchaikovsky].
COOPER, MARTIN: *Russian Opera* (London, 1951).
GINZBURG, SEMYON L'VOVICH: *Istoriya russkoy muzïki v notnïkh obraztsakh* (Moscow and Leningrad, 1952; enlarged 2nd edn., 1967–70).
GOSENPUD, ABRAM AKIMOVICH: *Russkiy opernïy teatr XIX veka*, i. *1836–56* (Leningrad, 1969).
MICHAŁOWSKI, KORNEL: *Opery polskie* (Kraków, 1954).
LEVASHOVA, O. E., KELDÏSH, YURY, and KANDINSKY, A. (ed.): *Istoriya russkoy muzïki* (Moscow, 1972).
PEKELIS, MIKHAIL SAMOYLOVICH: *Istoriya russkoy muzïki* (Moscow and Leningrad, 1940; repr. 1963).
SEAMAN, GERALD R.: *History of Russian Music*, i (Oxford, 1967).
SZABOLCSI, BENCE: *A magyar zenetörténet kézikönyve* (Budapest, 1947; 2nd edn., 1955; 3rd edn., 1977); abridged Eng. trans. of 2nd edn., *A Concise History of Hungarian Music* (Budapest, 1964; 2nd edn., 1965).
TYRRELL, JOHN: *Czech Opera* (Cambridge, 1988).

(b) Individual Composers

Dargomïzhsky
PEKELIS, MIKHAIL SAMOYLOVICH: *Aleksandr Sergeevich Dargomïzhskiy i ego okruzhenie* (Moscow, 1966–71).
TARUSKIN, RICHARD: 'Realism as Preached and Practiced: The Russian Opera Dialogue', *Musical Quarterly*, 56 (1970), 431–54.
For further **Dargomïzhsky** bibliography *see* § VI (d)

Glinka
BROWN, DAVID: *Mikhail Glinka: A Biographical and Critical Study* (London, 1974).
GLINKA, MIKHAIL IVANOVICH: *Literaturnoe nasledie Glinki*, ed. Valerian Mikhaylovich Bogdanov-Beryozovsky (Leningrad and Moscow, 1952–3).
—— *Memoirs*, trans. Richard B. Mudge (Norman, Okla., 1963).
TARUSKIN, RICHARD: 'Glinka's Ambiguous Legacy and the Birth Pangs of Russian Opera', *19th-century Music*, 1 (1977–8), 142–62.

Moniuszko
ABRAHAM, GERALD: 'The Operas of Stanisław Moniuszko', *Essays on Russian and East European Music* (Oxford, 1985), 156–71.
MACIEJEWSKI, B. M.: *Moniuszko, Father of Polish Opera* (London, 1979).
RUDZIŃSKI, WITOLD: *'Halka' Stanisława Moniuszko* (Kraków, 1972).
—— *Moniuszko* (Kraków 1971).
—— *Stanisław Moniuszko: Studia i materiały* (Kraków, 1955–61).

Verstovsky
ABRAHAM, GERALD: 'The Operas of Alexei Verstovsky', *19th-century Music*, 7 (1983–4), 326–35.
DOBROKHOTOV, B.: *A. N. Verstovskiy* (Moscow, 1949).
VERSTOVSKY, ALEKSEY NIKOLAEVICH: 'Avtobiografiya kompozitora A. N. Verstovskogo', *Biryuch petrogradskikh gosudarstvennïkh teatrov* (Petrograd, 1921).

(f) BRITAIN AND THE UNITED STATES

(i) Books and Articles

(a) General

BARNETT, JOHN FRANCIS: *Musical Reminiscences and Impressions* (London, 1906).
British Opera in Retrospect (British Music Society, London, 1985).
CHASE, GILBERT: *America's Music: From the Pilgrims to the Present* (New York, 1955; rev. 2nd edn., 1966).
CARR, BRUCE: 'Theatre Music: 1800–1834', in Nicholas Temperley (ed.), *Music in Britain: The Romantic Age 1800–1914* (London, 1981), 288–306.
HAMM, CHARLES: *Music in the New World* (New York, 1983).
HURD, MICHAEL: 'Opera: 1834–1865', in Nicholas Temperley (ed.), *Music in Britain: The Romantic Age 1800–1914* (London, 1981), 307–57.
HOGARTH, GEORGE: *Memoirs of the Musical Drama* (London, 1838; repr. 1972).
MATES, JULIAN: *America's Musical Stage: Two Hundred Years of Musical Theatre* (Westport, Conn., 1985).
REEVES, SIMS (J.): *My Jubilee, or, Fifty Years of Artistic Life* (London, 1889).
SHAW, BERNARD: *London Music in 1888–89 as heard by Corno di Bassetto* (London, 1937).
TEMPERLEY, NICHOLAS: 'Ballroom and Drawing-room Music', in Nicholas Temperley (ed.), *Music in Britain: The Romantic Age 1800–1914* (London, 1981), 109–34.
—— 'The English Romantic Opera', *Victorian Studies*, 9 (1966), 293–301.
WHITE, ERIC WALTER: 'Romantic Operas—XIXth Century', in *A History of English Opera* (London, 1983), 243–59.

(b) Individual Composers

Balfe
BARRETT, WILLIAM ALEXANDER: *Balfe: His Life and Works* (London, 1882).
WHITE, ERIC WALTER: 'Balfe and his Contemporaries', in *A History of English Opera* (London, 1983), 260–94.

Barnett

CARR, BRUCE: 'The First All-sung English 19th-century Opera', *Musical Times*, 115 (1974), 125–6.

Loder

TEMPERLEY, NICHOLAS: 'Raymond and Agnes', *Musical Times*, 107 (1966), 307–10.

Wallace

KLEIN, J. W.: 'Vincent Wallace (1812–65): A Reassessment', *Opera*, 16 (1965), 709–16.

CHAPTER IV

ROMANTIC PIANO MUSIC: 1830–1850

(i) Modern Editions

(a) Anthologies

FARRENC, ARISTIDE and LOUISE: *Le Trésor des pianistes* (Paris, 1861–72; repr. 1977) [23 includes works by Mendelssohn and Chopin].

FERGUSON, HOWARD: *Style and Interpretation: An Anthology of Keyboard Music*, 4 *Romantic Piano Music* (London 1964; 2nd edn., 1972) [includes works by Mendelssohn, Chopin, Schumann, and Liszt].

GEORGII, WALTER: 'Romanticism and the National Efforts in the 19th Century', *400 Jahre europäischer Klaviermusik* (Das Musikwerk, 1; Cologne, 1959); Eng. trans., *400 Years of European Keyboard Music* (Anthology of Music, 1; Cologne, 1959) [includes music by Schumann, Mendelssohn, and Chopin].

GILLESPIE, JOHN: *Nineteenth-century European Piano Music: Unfamiliar Masterworks* (New York, 1977) [includes music by Heller].

KAHL, WILLI: *Lyrische Klavierstücke der Romantik* (Stuttgart, 1926).

—— *Das Charakterstück* (Das Musikwerke, 8; Cologne, 1955); Eng. trans., A. Crawford Howie, *The Character Piece* (Anthology of Music, 8; Cologne, 1961) [includes music by Heller].

NEWMAN, WILLIAM S.: *Thirteen Keyboard Sonatas of the 18th and 19th Centuries* (Chapel Hill, NC, 1947).

POHANKA, JAROSLAV: *Dějiny české hudby v příkladech* (Prague, 1958).

SCHLEUNING, PETER: *Die Fantasie 2* (Das Musikwerk, 43; Cologne, 1971); Eng. trans., A. Crawford Howie, *The Fantasia: 18th to 20th Centuries* (Anthology of Music, 43; Cologne, 1971) [includes music by Czerny].

STEPHENSON, KURT: *Romantik in der Tonkunst* (Das Musikwerk, 21; Cologne, 1961); Eng. trans., Robert Kolben, *Romanticism in Music* (Anthology of Music, 21; Cologne, 1961) [includes music by Heller, Schumann, and Liszt].

TEMPERLEY, NICHOLAS: *The London Pianoforte School 1766–1860* (New York, 1984–7) [includes continental composers in London].

(b) Works by Individual Composers

ALKAN, C. V.: *Œuvres choisies pour piano*, ed. Georges Beck (Le Pupitre, 16; Paris, 1969).

—— *The Piano Music of Alkan*, ed. Raymond Lewenthal (New York, 1964).

BENNETT, W. S.: *Piano and Chamber Music*, ed. Geoffrey Bush (Musica Britannica, 37; London, 1972); selection as *Suite de pieces* (Early Keyboard Music, 32; London, 1972).

—— *Complete Works for Piano Solo* (The London Pianoforte School 1770–1860, ed. Nicholas Temperley, New York, 1985).

CHOPIN, F. F.: *Friedrich Chopin's Werke*, ed. Woldemar Bargiel, Johannes Brahms,

August Franchomme, Franz Liszt, Carl Reinecke, Ernst Rudorff (Leipzig, 1878-1902: vols. 1-10 and 13 [Works for solo piano].

—— *Fryderyk Chopin: Dzieła wszystkie/Complete Works*, ed. Ignacy Jan Paderewski, with Józef Turczyński and Ludwik Bronarski (Warsaw, 1949-61): 1 *Preludes* (1949); 2 *Studies* (1949); 3 *Ballades* (1949); 4 *Impromptus* (1949); 4 *Scherzos* (1950); 6 *Sonatas* (1949); 7 *Nocturnes* (1952); 8 *Polonaises* (1952); 9 *Waltzes* (1950); 10 *Mazurkas* (1953); 11 *Fantasia etc.* (1954); 12 *Rondos* (1954); 13 *Concert Allegro etc.* (1954).

—— *Complete Works for Piano*, ed. Carl Mikuli (New York, 1934).

—— *Sämtliche Werke* (Leipzig, Peters; new edn., ed. Bronislaw von Pozniak).

GLINKA, M. I.: *Polnoe sobranie sochineniy*, ed. Vissarion Yakovlevich Shebalin *et al.* (Moscow, 1955-69): 5 [Piano Duet] (1957); 6 [Piano Solo] (1958).

—— *Complete Works for Piano Solo and Piano 4 Hands* (Moscow and New York, 1952).

LISZT, F.: *Franz Liszts Musikalische Werke*, ed. Franz Liszt-Stiftung (Leipzig, 1907-36; repr. 1966): Part 2 *Pianoforte-Werke*.

—— *Liszt Society Publications* (London, 1950-): 1 *Early and Late Piano Works*.

—— [Works], ed. V. Belov and K. Sorokin (Moscow, 1958-): i/1 [Piano Works].

—— *Franz Liszt: Neue Ausgabe sämtlicher Werke/New Edition of the Complete Works*, 1st series, ed. Zoltán Gárdonyi and István Szelényi, *Works for Piano, Two Hands* (Kassel and Budapest, 1970-85).

—— *Werke für Klavier zu 2 Händern*, ed. Emil von Sauer (Leipzig, 1917).

MENDELSSOHN, F.: *Felix Mendelssohn Bartholdy's Werke: Kritisch durchgesehene Ausgabe*, ed. Julius Rietz (Leipzig, 1874-7; repr. 1967-9): series 10 *Für Pianoforte zu 4 Händen*; series 11 *Für Pianoforte allein* (repr. 1975).

—— *Complete Piano Works* (London, 1909).

—— *Sämtliche Klavierwerke*, ed. Theodor Kullak (Leipzig, Peters).

MONIUSZKO S.: *Stanisław Moniuszko: Dzieła/Werke* (Kraków, 1965-): series E, 34 *Klavierwerke* (1976).

SCHUMANN, R.: *Robert Schumann's Werke*, ed. Clara Schumann (Leipzig, 1881-93; repr. 1967-8: series 7 *Für Pianoforte zu zwei Händen* (1879-87); 6 *Für ein oder zwei pianoforte zu vier Händen* (1887).

—— *Abegg-Variationen*, ed. Robert Münster (Munich, 1976).

—— *Sämtliche Werke für Klavier*, ed. Emil von Sauer (Leipzig, Peters).

—— *Papillons*, ed. Karl Geiringer (Vienna, 1933).

SMETANA, B.: *Studijní vydání děl Bedřicha Smetany*, ed. František Bartoš, Josef Plavec, *et al.* (Prague, 1940-): [Piano Works] 7 vols. (1944-78).

—— *Klavírní dílo Bedřicha Smetany*, ed. Mirko Očadlík *et al.* (Prague 1944-73): 1 *První cykly*; 2 *Polky*; 3 *Skladby studijní*.

WAGNER, R.: *Richard Wagner: Sämtliche Werke*, ed. Carl Dahlhaus (Mainz, 1970-): 19 *Klavierwerke*, ed. Carl Dahlhaus (1970).

(ii) Books and Articles

(a) General

BARENBOYM, L. A., and MUZALEVSKY, V. I.: *Khrestomatiya po istorii fortep'yannoy muziki v Rossii* (Moscow and Leningrad, 1949).

BECKING, GUSTAV: 'Zur musikalischen Romantik', *Deutsche Vierteljahrschrift für Literaturwissenschaft und Geistesgeschichte*, ii (1924), 581-615.

CLOSSON ERNEST: *Histoire du piano* (Brussels, 1944); Eng. trans., Delano Ames, *History of the Piano* (London, 1947; rev. 2nd edn., Robin Golding, London, 1974).

CORTOT, ALFRED: *La Musique française de piano* (Paris, 1930-44).

DALE, KATHLEEN: *Nineteenth-century Piano Music* (London, 1954; repr. 1972).

EGERT, PAUL: *Die Klaviersonate im Zeitalter der Romantik* (Berlin, 1934).

EHRLICH, CYRIL: *The Piano: A History* (London, 1976).

FRIEDLAND, MARTIN: *Zeitstil und Persönlichkeitsstil in den Variationenwerke der musikalischen Romantik* (Leipzig, 1930).

GEORGII, WALTER: *Klaviermusik: Geschichte der Musik für Klavier für zwei und vier Hände* (Berlin and Zurich, 1941; 5th edn., 1976; 6th edn., 1984).

HARDING, ROSAMOND: *The Pianoforte: Its History Traced to the Great Exhibition of 1851* (Cambridge, 1933; rev. 2nd edn., 1978).

KRUEGER, WOLFGANG: *Das Nachtstück: Ein Beitrag zur Entwicklung des einsätzigen Pianofortestückes im 19. Jahrhundert* (Munich, 1971).

LENZ, WILHELM VON: *Die grossen Pianoforte-Virtuosen unserer Zeit aus persönlicher Bekannschaft: Liszt, Chopin, Tausig, Henselt* (Berlin, 1872); Eng. trans., *The Great Piano Virtuosos of our Time* (New York, 1899: rev. Philip Reder, London, 1971).

MERSMANN, HANS: 'Sonaten Form, in der romantischen Kammermusik', in Walter Lott, Helmuth Osthoff, and Werner Wolffheim (eds.), *Musikwissenschaftliche Beiträge: Festschrift für Johannes Wolf zu seinem 60. Geburtstag* (Berlin, 1929; repr. 1973), 112–17.

MÜLLER-BLATAU, JOSEPH M.: *Gestaltung-Umgestaltung: Studien zur Geschichte der musikalischen Variation* (Stuttgart, 1950).

NELSON, ROBERT U.: *The Technique of Variation: A Study of the Instrumental Variation from Cabézon to Reger* (Berkeley and Los Angeles, Calif., 1948; rev. 2nd edn., 1962).

NEWMAN, WILLIAM S.: *A History of the Sonata Idea*, iii. *The Sonata since Beethoven* (Chapel Hill, NC, 1969; rev. 2nd edn., 1972).

PRESSER, DIETHER: 'Die Opernbearbeitung des 19. Jahrhunderts', *Archiv für Musikwissenschaft*, 12 (1955), 228–38.

PUCHELT, GERHARD: *Variationen für Klavier im 19. Jahrhundert* (Hildesheim and New York, 1973).

—— *Verlorene Klänge: Studien zur deutschen Klaviermusik 1830–1880* (Berlin, 1969).

SCHMITZ, ARNOLD: *Das romantische Beethovenbild* (Berlin and Bonn, 1927).

SCHÜNEMANN, GEORG: *Geschichte des Klaviermusik* (Hamburg, 1940; rev. Herbert Gerigk, 1953; 2nd edn., 1956).

SMIRNOV, M.: *Fortep'yannïe proizvedeniya kompozitorov moguchey kuchki* (Moscow, 1971).

(*b*) *Individual Composers*

Alkan

SMITH, RONALD: *Alkan*, i. *The Enigma* (London, 1976), ii. *The Music* (1987).

Burgmüller

ECKERT, HEINRICH: *Norbert Burgmüller: Ein Beitrag zur Stil- und Geistesgeschichte der deutschen Romantik* (Augsburg, 1932).

Chopin

ABRAHAM, GERALD: *Chopin's Musical Style* (London, 1939; rev. 4th edn., 1960).

CHOMIŃSKI, JÓZEF MICHAŁ: *Fryderyk Chopin* (Leipzig, 1980).

CHOPIN, FRYDERYK FRANCISZEK: *Selected Correspondence of Fryderyk Chopin*, ed. and trans. Arthur Hedley (London, 1962).

—— *Korespondencja Fryderyka Chopina z rodziną*, ed. Krystyna Kobylańska (Warsaw, 1972).

—— *Korespondencja Fryderyka Chopina*, ed. Bronisław Edward Sydow (Warsaw, 1955).

EIGELDINGER, JEAN-JACQUES: *Chopin vu par ses élèves* (Neuchâtel, 1970), Eng. trans., Naomi Shohet and Krysia Osostowicz, *Chopin: Pianist and Teacher*, ed. Roy Howat (Cambridge, 1987).

HEDLEY, ARTHUR: *Chopin* (London, 1947; rev. 3rd edn., Maurice J. E. Brown, 1974).

JACHIMECKI, ZDZISŁAW: *Chopin: Rys życia i twórczości* (Warsaw, 1949).

KALLBERG, JEFFREY: 'Chopin's Last Style', *Journal of the American Musicological Society*, 38 (1985), 264–315.

LISSA, ZOFIA (ed.): *The Book of the First International Musicological Congress Devoted to the Works of Frederick Chopin* (Warsaw, 1963).

METHUEN-CAMPBELL, JAMES: *Chopin Playing* (London, 1981).

NIECKS, FRIEDRICH: *Frederick Chopin as a Man and a Musician* (Leipzig, 1888; 3rd edn., 1902, repr. 1973).

OTTICH, MARIA: *Die Bedeutung des Ornaments im Schaffen Friedrich Chopins* (Berlin, 1937).

SAMSON, JIM: *The Music of Chopin* (London, 1985).

—— (ed.): *Chopin Studies* (Cambridge, 1988).

TEMPERLEY, NICHOLAS, ABRAHAM, GERALD, and SEARLE, HUMPHREY: *The New Grove Early Romantic Masters 1* (London, 1985) [includes Chopin].

WALKER, ALAN (ed.): *Frederic Chopin: Profiles of the Man and the Musician* (London, 1966; rev. 2nd edn., as *The Chopin Companion*, 1973).

ŻEBROWSKI, DARIUSZ (ed.): *Studies in Chopin* (Warsaw, 1973) [Proceedings of 1972 Warsaw conference].

Dargomïzhsky

DARGOMÏZHSKY, A. S.: *Sobranie sochineniy dlya fortep'yano*, ed. Mikhail Samoylovich Pekelis (Moscow and Leningrad, 1954).

—— *Sochineniya dlya simfonicheskogo orkestra*, ed. Mikhail Samoylovich Pekelis (Moscow, 1967).

Heller

EIGELDINGER, JEAN-JACQUES: *Stephen Heller: Lettres d'un musicien romantique à Paris* (Paris, 1981).

SCHÜTZ, R.: *Stephen Heller: Ein Künstlerleben* (Leipzig, 1911).

Liszt

BUSONI, FERRUCCIO: 'Die ausgaben der Liszt'schen Klavierwerke', *Allgemeine Musik-Zeitung*, xxvii (1900), repr. in *Gesammelte Aufsatze: Von der Einheit der Musik* (Berlin, 1922).

LONGYEAR, REY M.: 'The Text of Liszt's B Minor Sonata', *Musical Quarterly*, 40 (1974), 435–50.

WINKLHOFER, SHARON: *Liszt's Sonata in B minor: A Study of Autography Sources and Documents* (Ann Arbor, Mich., 1980).

For further **Liszt** bibliography *see* § VII

Mendelssohn

FELLERER, KARL GUSTAV: 'Mendelssohn in der Klaviermusik seiner Zeit', in Carl Dahlhaus (ed.), *Das Problem Mendelssohn* (Regensburg, 1974), 195–200.

KAHL, WILLI: 'Zu Mendelssohn's *Liedern ohne Worte*', *Zeitschrift für Musikwissenschaft*, 3 (1920–1), 459–69.

KLINGEMANN, KARL (ed.): *Felix Mendelssohn-Bartholdys Briefwechsel mit Legationsrat Karl Klingemann in London* (Essen, 1909).

For further **Mendelssohn** bibliography *see* § 1

Schumann

ABERT, HERMANN: *Robert Schumann* (Berlin, 1903; 4th edn., 1920).

BOETTICHER, WOLFGANG: '*Gesänge der Frühe*: Schumanns letztes Klavierwerke', *Neue Zeitschrift für Musik*, 107 (1956), 418–21.

—— *Robert Schumann: Einführung in Persönlichkeit und Werk* (Berlin, 1941).

—— *Robert Schumanns Klavierwerke: Neue biographische und textkritische Untersuchungen*, 1. *Opus 1–6* (Wilhelmshaven, 1976).

CHISSELL, JOAN: *Schumann Piano Music* (London, 1972).

DALE, KATHLEEN: 'The Piano Music', in Gerald Abraham (ed.), *Schumann: A Symposium* (London, 1952), 12–97.

GERTLER, WOLFGANG: *Robert Schumann in seinem frühen Klavierwerken* (Wolfenbüttel and Berlin, 1931).

HOHENEMSER, RICHARD: 'Formale Eigentümlichkeiten in Robert Schumanns Klaviermusik', in *Festschrift zum 50. Geburtstag Adolf Sandberger überreicht von seinem Schülern* (Munich, 1918), 21–50.

KORTE, WERNER: *Robert Schumann* (Potsdam, 1937).

KÖTZ, HANS: *Der Einfluss Jean Pauls auf Robert Schumann* (Munich, 1918).

ROESNER, LINDA CORRELL: 'Schumann's Revisions in the First Movement of the Piano Sonata in G minor, Op. 22', *19th-century Music*, 1 (1977–8), 97–109.

—— 'The Autograph of Schumann's Piano Sonata in F minor, Opus 14', *Musical Quarterly*, 61 (1975), 98–130.

SCHUMANN, ROBERT: *Gesammelte Schriften über Musik und Musiker*, ed. Martin Kreisig (4 vols., Leipzig, 1854; 4th edn., 2 vols., 1891; repr. 1968; 5th edn. 1914); Eng. trans., Fanny Raymond Ritter, *Music and Musicians: Essays and Criticisms* (London, 1877–80); new selected Eng. trans., Konrad Wolff (ed.) and Paul Rosenfeld (trans.), *On Music and Musicians* (New York, 1947; repr. 1982); selections, Henry Pleasants (ed. and trans.), *The Musical World of Robert Schumann: A Selection from his own Writings* (London, 1965).

—— *Robert Schumanns Briefe; Neue Folge*, ed. Friedrich Gustav Jensen (Leipzig, 1886; 2nd edn., 1904); Eng. trans., May Herbert, *The Life of Robert Schumann Told in his Letters* (London, 1890).

SCHWARZ, WERNER: *Robert Schumann und die Variation mit besonderer Berucksichtigung der Klavierwerke* (Kassel, 1932).

WALKER, ALAN (ed.): *Robert Schumann; The Man and his Music* (London, 1972; rev. 2nd edn., 1976) [includes articles on the piano music by Yonty Solomon and Bálint Vázsonyi].

STEGLICH, RUDOLF: *Robert Schumanns Kinderszenen* (Kassel and Basle, 1949).

For further **Schumann** bibliography *see* § I and § II

Wagner
DAUBE, OTTO: '*Ich schreibe keine Symphonien mehr*' (Cologne, 1960).

Weber
GEORGII, WALTER: *Karl Maria von Weber als Klavierkomponist* (Leipzig, 1914).

CHAPTER V
WAGNER'S LATER STAGE WORKS

(i) Modern Editions

WAGNER, R.: *Richard Wagners Werke: Musikdramen—Jugendopern—musikalische Werke*, ed. Michael Balling (Leipzig, 1912–29; repr. 1971): 3 *Tannhäuser*; 5 *Tristan und Isolde*.

—— *Richard Wagner: Sämtliche Werke*, ed. Carl Dahlhaus, Egon Voss, *et al.* (Mainz, 1970–): series A *Musikbände*: 5–6 *Tannhäuser*, ed. Reinhard Strohm (1980–); 9 *Die Meistersinger von Nürnberg*, ed. Egon Voss (1979–8); 13

Götterdämmerung, ed. Hartmut Fladt (1980–2); 14 *Parsifal*, ed. Egon Voss and Martin Geck (1972–3); 8 *Tristan und Isolde*, 10 *Das Rheingold*, 11 *Die Walküre*, 12 *Siegfried*.

(ii) Books and Articles

(a) General

ABRAHAM, GERALD: *A Hundred Years of Music* (London, 1938; rev. 4th edn., 1974).

ADORNO, THEODOR: *Versuch über Wagner* (Berlin, 1952; 2nd edn., 1964); Eng. trans., Rodney Livingstone, *In Search of Wagner* (London, 1981).

BAILEY, ROBERT: 'The Method of Composition', in Peter Burbidge and Richard Sutton (eds.), *The Wagner Companion* (London, 1979), 269–338.

——(ed.): *Prelude and Transfiguration from Tristan and Isolde* (Norton Critical Score; New York, 1985).

BARTH, HERBERT, MACK, DIETRICH, and VOSS, EGON (eds.): *Wagner: Sein Leben und seine Welt in zeitgenössischen Bildern und Texten* (Vienna, 1975); Eng. trans., P. R. J. Ford and Mary Whittall, *Wagner: A Documentary Study* (London, 1975).

BECKETT, LUCY: *Richard Wagner: Parsifal* (Cambridge, 1981).

BERGFELD, JOACHIM (ed.): *Richard Wagner: Tagebuchaufzeichnungen 1865–1882: 'Das braune Buch'* (Zurich, 1975); Eng. trans., George Bird, *The Diary of Richard Wagner 1865–1882: The Brown Book* (London, 1980).

BORETZ, BENJAMIN: 'Meta-Variations, Part IV: Analytic Fallout (I)', *Perspectives of New Music*, 11 (1972), 159–217.

BURBIDGE, PETER, and SUTTON, RICHARD (eds.): *The Wagner Companion* (London, 1979).

DAHLHAUS, CARL: *Die Musikdramen Richard Wagners* (Velber, 1971); Eng. trans., Mary Whittall, *Richard Wagner's Music Dramas* (Cambridge, 1979).

DEATHRIDGE, JOHN: 'The Nomenclature of Wagner's Sketches', *Proceedings of the Royal Musical Association*, 101 (1974–5), 75–83.

——and DAHLHAUS, CARL: *The New Grove Wagner* (London, 1984).

——, GECK, MARTIN, and VOSS, EGON: *Wagner Werk-Verzeichnis* (Mainz, 1986).

FÖRSTER-NIETZSCHE, ELISABETH: *Wagner und Nietzsche zur Zeit ihrer Freundschaft: Erinnerungsgabe zu Friedrich Nietzsches 70. Geburtstag den 15. Oktober 1914* (Munich, 1915; Eng. trans., Caroline V. Kerr (1921, repr. 1970, as *The Nietzsche–Wagner Correspondence*).

HOLLOWAY, ROBIN: *Debussy and Wagner* (London, 1979).

LORENZ, ALFRED: *Das Geheimnis der Form bei Richard Wagner* (Berlin, 1924–33; repr. 1966).

MAGEE, BRYAN: *Aspects of Wagner* (London, 1968; rev. 2nd edn., Oxford, 1988).

MANN, THOMAS: *Wagner und unsere Zeit: Aufsätze, Betrachtungen, Briefe*, ed. E. Mann (Frankfurt am Main, 1963); Eng. trans., (a) Allan Blunden, *Pro and Contra Wagner* (London, 1985) [complete German text]; (b) H. T. Lowe-Porter, 2 essays in *T. Mann: Essays of Three Decades* (London, 1947), and 'The Sufferings and Greatness of Richard Wagner', in *Thomas Mann: Past Masters and other Papers* (London, 1933), 15–96.

MILLINGTON, BARRY: *Wagner* (London, 1984).

MITCHELL, WILLIAM J.: 'The Tristan Prelude: Techniques and Structures', *Music Forum*, 1 (1967), 162–203.

MURRAY, DAVID R.: 'Major Analytical Approaches to Wagner's Musical Style: A Critique', *Music Review*, 39 (1978), 211–22.

NEWCOMB, ANTHONY: 'The Birth of Music out of the Spirt of Drama: An Essay in Wagnerian Formal Analysis', *19th-century Music*, 5 (1980-1), 38–66.

NEWMAN, ERNEST: *The Life of Richard Wagner* (London, 1933–47; repr. 1976).

—— *Wagner Nights* (London, 1949, repr. 1977, as *The Wagner Operas*, New York, 1949, repr. 1963).

—— *Wagner as Man and Artist* (London, 1914; rev. 2nd edn., 1924; repr. 1969).

NIETZSCHE, FRIEDRICH WILHELM: *Die Geburt der Tragödie aus dem Geiste der Musik* (Leipzig, 1872); *Der Fall Wagner* (Leipzig, 1888); Eng. trans., Walter Kaufmann, *The Birth of Tragedy* and *The Case of Wagner* (New York, 1967).

SCHENKER, HEINRICH: *Ein Beitrag zur Ornamentation als Einführung zu Ph. E. Bachs Klavierwerke* (Vienna, 1904; rev. 2nd edn., 1908; repr. 1954); Eng. trans., Hedi Siegel, 'Essay on Ornamentation', *Music Forum*, 4 (1976), 1–140.

SCHOENBERG, ARNOLD: *Structural Functions of Harmony*, ed. Humphrey Searle (London, 1954; rev. 2nd edn., ed. Leonard Stein, 1969).

SKELTON, GEOFFREY: *Wagner at Bayreuth: Experiment and Tradition* (New York, 1965; rev. and enlarged, 1976).

STRAVINSKY, IGOR: *Poétique musicale* (Cambridge, Mass., 1942); Eng. trans., Arthur Knodel and Ingolf Dahl, *Poetics of Music* (Cambridge, Mass., 1947); Eng./Fr. edn., 1970.

WAGNER, COSIMA: *Cosima Wagner: Die Tagebucher 1869-1877*, ed. Martin Gregor-Dellin and Dietrich Mack (Munich and Zurich, 1976-7); Eng. trans., Geoffrey Skelton, *The Diaries of Cosima Wagner* (London, 1978-80).

WAGNER, RICHARD: *Mein Leben* (Munich, 1911; ed. Martin Gregor-Dellin, 1963, repr. 1976): Eng. trans., Andrew Gray, *My Life* (Cambridge, 1983).

—— *Familienbriefe von Richard Wagner 1832-1874*, ed. C. Friedrich Glasenapp (Berlin, 1907); Eng. trans., William Ashton Ellis, *The Family Letters of Richard Wagner* (1911, repr. 1972).

—— *Richard Wagner: Gesammelte Schriften und Dichtungen*, i-x (Leipzig, 1871-3, 1883; 2nd edn., 1887-8, repr. 1976; 5th edn., with vols. xi-xii added, *Sämtliche Schriften und Dichtungen*, ed. H. von Wolzogen and R. Sternfeld, 1911; 6th edn., with vols. xiii-xvi added, ed. H. von Wolzogen and R. Sternfeld, 1914).

—— *Richard Wagner: Sämtliche Briefe*, ed. Gertrud Strobel and Werner Wolf (Leipzig, 1967-).

—— *Richard Wagner: Sämtliche Werke*, ed. Carl Dahlhaus (Mainz, 1970-): series B *Dokumentenbände*: 23 *Rienzi*, ed. Reinhard Strohm (1976); 29 *Der Ring des Nibelungen*, ed. Werner Brieg and Hartmut Fladt (1976); 30 *Parsifal*, ed. Egon Voss and Martin Geck (1972-3); 22 *Die Feen und Das Liebesvot*; 24 *Der fliegender Holländer*; 25 *Tannhäuser*; 26 *Lohengrin*; 27 *Tristan und Isolde*; 28 *Die Meistersinger von Nürnberg*.

—— *Richard Wagner's Prose Works*, ed. and trans. William Ashton Ellis (London, 1892-9; repr. 1972).

—— *Selected Letters of Richard Wagner*, trans. and ed. Stewart Spencer and Barry Millington (London, 1987).

—— *Three Wagner Essays*, trans. Robert L. Jacobs (London, 1979).

—— *Wagner on Music and Drama: A Compendium of Richard Wagner's Prose Works*, ed. Albert Goldman and Evert Sprinchorn (New York, 1964; repr. 1981).

—— 'Das Kunstwerk der Zukunft' (1849); repr. in *Richard Wagner: Gesammelte Schriften und Dichtungen*, iii (Leipzig, 1872), 51–210; Eng. trans., William Ashton Ellis (ed. and trans.), *Richard Wagner's Prose Works*, i (London, 1892; repr. 1972), 69–213.

—— 'Meine Erinnerungen an Ludwig Schnorr von Carolsfeld' (1868); repr. in *Richard Wagner: Gesammelte Schriften und Dichtungen*, iii (Leipzig, 1872), 221–41; Eng. trans., Ellis, *Prose Works*, iv (London, 1895), 225–43.

—— 'Oper und Drama' (1851; rev. 1868); repr. in *Richard Wagner: Gesammelte Schriften und Dichtungen*, iii and iv (Leipzig, 1872), 269–394 and 3–284; Eng. trans., Ellis, *Prose Works*, ii (London, 1893).

—— 'Zukunftsmusik' (1860); repr. in *Richard Wagner: Gesammelte Schriften und Dichtungen*, vii (Leipzig, 1873), 121–80; Eng. trans., Ellis, *Prose Works*, iii (London, 1894), 293–345, and Robert L. Jacobs, *Three Wagner Essays* (London, 1979), 13–44.

WESTERNHAGEN, CURT VON: *Wagner* (Zurich, 1968); Eng. trans., Mary Whittall, *Wagner: A Biography* (Cambridge, 1978).

WOLZOGEN, HANS PAUL VON: *Richard Wagner über den 'Fliegenden Holländer': Die Entstehung, Gestaltung und Darstellung des Werkes aus den Schriften und Briefen des Meisters zusammengestellt* (Leipzig, 1914).

ZUCKERMAN, ELLIOTT: *The First Hundred Years of Wagner's Tristan* (New York, 1964).

(*b*) The 'Ring'

BAILEY, ROBERT: 'The Structure of the *Ring* and its Evolution', *19th-century Music*, 1 (1977–8), 48–61.

COOKE, DERYCK: *I Saw the World End: A Study of Wagner's Ring* (London, 1979).

DEATHRIDGE, JOHN: 'Wagner's Sketches for the *Ring*: Some Recent Studies', *Musical Times*, 118 (1977), 383–9.

—— Review of Recent Wagner Literature, *19th-century Music*, 5 (1981–2), 81–9.

DONINGTON, R.: *Wagner's 'Ring' and its Symbols* (London, 1963; rev. 3rd edn., 1974).

McCRELESS, PATRICK: *Wagner's Siegfried: Its Drama, History, and Music* (Ann Arbor, Mich., 1982).

PORGES, HEINRICH: *Die Bühnenproben zu den Bayreuther Festspielen des Jahres 1876* (Leipzig, 1876); Eng. trans., Robert L. Jacobs, *Wagner Rehearsing the 'Ring': An Eye-Witness Account of the Stage Rehearsals of the First Bayreuth Festival* (Cambridge, 1983).

SHAW, BERNARD: *The Perfect Wagnerite: A Commentary on the Niblung's Ring* (London, 1898; 4th edn., 1923; repr. 1972).

WESTERNHAGEN, CURT VON: *Die Enstehung des 'Ring'* (Zurich, 1973); Eng. trans., Arnold and Mary Whittall, *The Forging of the Ring: Richard Wagner's Composition Sketches for 'Der Ring des Nibelungen'* (Cambridge, 1976).

CHAPTER VI

OPERA: 1850–1890

(a) GERMANY

(i) Modern Editions

(*a*) *Works by Individual Composers*

CORNELIUS, P.: *Peter Cornelius Musikalisches Werke*, ed. Max Hasse (Leipzig, 1905–6; repr. 1971): 3 *Der Barbier von Bagdad*, 4 *Der Cid*, 5 *Gunlöd*.

STRAUSS, J. (ii): *Johann Strauss: Gesamtausgabe*, ed. Fritz Racek (Vienna, 1967–): series 2 *Bühnen- und Vokalwerke*: 3 *Die Fledermaus* (1974).

(ii) Books and Articles

(*a*) *General*

SHAW, BERNARD: *Music in London 1890–94* (London, 1932; repr. 1973).

(b) Individual Composers

Bruch
KÄMPER, DIETRICH: *Max Bruch-Studien: Zum 50. Todestag des Komponisten* (Cologne, 1970).

Cornelius
CORNELIUS, PETER: *Literarische Werke*, ed. C. M. Cornelius, E. Istel, and A. Stern (Leipzig, 1904–5), i. *Ausgewählte Briefe*.
FEDERHOFER, HELLMUT, and OEHL, KURT (eds.): *Peter Cornelius als Komponist, Dichter, Kritiker und Essayist* (Regensburg, 1977).
WAGNER, GÜNTHER: *Peter Cornelius: Verzeichnis seiner musikalischen und literarischen Werken* (Tutzing, 1986).

Goetz
KREUZHAGE, E.: *Hermann Goetz: Seine Leben und seine Werke* (Leipzig, 1916).
KRUSE, G.: *Hermann Goetz* (Leipzig, 1920).

Goldmark
GOLDMARK, KARL: *Erinnerungen aus meinem Leben* (Vienna, 1922; 2nd edn., 1929).
HANSLICK, EDUARD: *Die moderne Oper* (Berlin, 1875–1900; repr. 1971).

Rubinstein
ABRAHAM, GERALD: 'Anton Rubinstein: Russian Composer', *Musical Times*, 86 (1945), 361–5.
BARENBOYM, L.: *Anton Grigor'evich Rubinshteyn* (Leningrad, 1957–62).
—— (ed.): *Izbrannïe pis'ma* (Leningrad, 1954).

Schumann
ABRAHAM, GERALD: 'The Dramatic Music', in Abraham (ed.) *Schumann: A Symposium* (London, 1952), 260–82.
For further **Schumann** bibliography *see* § I, § II, and § IV

(b) FRANCE

(i) Modern Editions

(a) Anthologies

WOLFF, HELLMUTH CHRISTIAN: *Die Oper III–19. Jahrhundert* (Das Musikwerke, 40; Cologne, 1972); Eng. trans., A. Crawford Howie, *The Opera III–19th Century* (Anthology of Music, 40; Cologne, 1975) [includes extracts from Gounod, *Philémon et Baucis*, and Meyerbeer, *Dinorah*].

(b) Works by Individual Composers

BERLIOZ, H.: *Hector Berlioz: Werke*, ed. Charles Malherbe and Felix Weingartner (Leipzig, 1900–10; repr. 1971): series 19 *Opern*: 19–20 *Béatrice et Bénédict*.
—— *New Berlioz Edition of the Complete Works*, ed. Hugh Macdonald *et al.* (Kassel, 1967–): 2 *Les Troyens*, ed. Hugh Macdonald (1969); 3 *Béatrice et Bénédict*, ed. Hugh Macdonald (1980); 4 *Incomplete Operas*, ed. Eric Gräbner and Paul Banks (forthcoming).
DELIBES, L.: *Lakmé* (Biblioteca musica Bononiensis, No. 268; Bologna, 1967–).
MEYERBEER, G.: *L'Étoile du Nord, Le Pardon de Ploërmel, L'Africaine*, ed. Philip Gossett and Charles Rosen (Early Romantic Opera, 22, 23, 24; New York, 1980, 1981, 1980).
VERDI, G.: *The Works of Giuseppe Verdi*, ed. Philip Gossett *et al.* (Chicago and Milan, 1983–): series 1 *Operas*: 10 *Macbeth*, 12 *Jérusalem*, 20 *Les Vêpres Siciliennes*, 26 and 29, *Don Carlos* (forthcoming).

—— Full scores of *Don Carlos*, *Jérusalem*, *Les Vêpres Siciliennes*, and *Macbeth* (Milan, *c*.1882– ; repr. New York, n.d.).

—— *Don Carlos* (Leipzig, 1954).

—— *Don Carlos: Edizione integrate delle varie versioni in cinque e in quattro atti*, ed. Ursula Günther and Luciano Petazzoni (Milan, 1980).

(ii) Books and Articles

(a) General

ABRAHAM, GERALD: *The Concise Oxford History of Music* (London, 1979).

ANSELM, GERHARD: 'Die französische "Grand Opéra" in der Forschung seit 1945', *Acta musicologica*, 59 (1987), 220–70.

BECKER, HEINZ (ed.): *Die Couleur locale in der Oper des 19. Jahrhunderts* (Regensburg, 1976).

CHARLTON, DAVID: 'Revival or Survival?', *19th-century Music*, 2 (1978–9), 159–64.

CLIVE, GEOFFREY (ed.): *The Philosophy of Nietzsche* (New York, 1965).

COOPER, MARTIN: *French Music from the Death of Berlioz to the Death of Fauré* (London, 1951; repr. 1984).

GUICHARD, LÉON: *La Musique et les lettres en France au temps du wagnérisme* (Paris, 1963).

HARDING, JAMES: *Folies de Paris: The Rise and Fall of French Operetta* (London, 1979).

HUGHES, GERVASE: *Composers of Operetta* (London, 1962).

LAVIGNAC, ALBERT: *Le Voyage artistique à Bayreuth* (Paris, 1897; rev. H. Busser, 1951); Eng. trans., Esther Singleton, *The Music Dramas of Richard Wagner and his Festival Theatre in Bayreuth* (London, 1898; 2nd edn., 1904; repr. 1968).

LOCKSPEISER, EDWARD: *The Literary Clef: An Anthology of Letters and Writings by French Composers* (London, 1958).

MACDONALD, HUGH: 'Hoffmann's Melancholy Tale', *Musical Times*, 121 (1980), 662–4.

MITCHELL, JEROME: *The Walter Scott Operas* (University of Alabama, 1977).

NIETZSCHE, FRIEDRICH: Der Fall Wagner (1888), *Friedrich Nietzsche: Der Musikalische Nachlass*, ed. Curt Paul Janz (Basle, 1976).

'Rapport de la Commission chargée d'examiner la situation de l'Opéra', *Le Moniteur universel*, 2 July 1854.

WALSH, THOMAS JOSEPH: *Second Empire Opera: The Théâtre Lyrique, Paris, 1851–1870* (London, 1981).

WILD, NICOLE: *Dictionnaire des théâtres lyriques à Paris au XIXe siècle* (New York, forthcoming).

For further general bibliography on French Opera *see* § III (a) and (b)

(b) Individual Composers

Auber

GIER, ALBERT: ' "Manon Lescaut" als Fabel von der Grille und der Ameise: Eugène Scribes Libretto für Daniel-François-Esprit Auber', in Michael Arndt and Michael Walter (eds.), *Jahrbuch für Opernforschung 1985* (Frankfurt am Main, 1985), 73–89.

For further **Auber** bibliography *see* § III (a)

Berlioz

BERLIOZ, HECTOR: *Mémoires de Hector Berlioz* (Paris, 1870; ed. Pierre Citron, 1969); Eng. trans., David Cairns, *The Memoirs of Hector Berlioz* (New York and London, 1969).

CAIRNS, DAVID: 'Berlioz and Virgil: A Consideration of "Les Troyens" as a Virgilian

Opera', *Proceedings of the Royal Musical Association*, 95 (1968–9), 97–110.

—— 'Les Troyens and the Aeneid', in *Respónses* (London, 1973), 88–110.

FAUQUET, JOËL-MARIE: 'Quatre versions de *Roméo et Juliette*', *L'avant-scène*, 41 (1982), 66–9.

KEMP, IAN: *Hector Berlioz: The Trojans* (Cambridge, 1988).

MACDONALD, HUGH: *Berlioz* (London, 1982).

RUSHTON, JULIAN: 'Berlioz's Swan-Song: Towards a Criticism of *Béatrice et Bénédict*', *Proceedings of the Royal Musical Association*, 109 (1982–3), 105–18.

—— 'The Overture to *Les Troyens*', *Music Analysis*, 4 (1985), 119–44.

For further **Berlioz** Bibliography *see* § I

Bizet

CURTISS, MINA: *Bizet and his World* (London, 1959; repr. 1974).

DEAN, WINTON: 'Bizet's "Ivan IV" ', in Herbert Van Thal (ed.), *Fanfare for Ernest Newman* (London, 1955), 58–85.

—— *Georges Bizet: His Life and Work* (London, 1948; enlarged 3rd edn., 1975).

—— 'The Libretto', in *Carmen: A Romance by Prosper Mérimée: With a Study of the Opera of the Same Name* (London, 1949), 85–108.

—— 'The True "Carmen"?', *Musical Times*, 106 (1965), 846–55.

ISTEL, EDGAR: *Bizet und 'Carmen'* (Stuttgart, 1927).

PARKER, DOUGLAS CHARLES: *Bizet* (London, 1951).

WESTRUP, JACK: 'Bizet's *La Jolie Fille de Perth*', in J. Westrup (ed.), *Essays Presented to Egon Wellesz* (Oxford, 1966), 157–70.

WRIGHT, LESLEY A: 'A New Source for *Carmen*', *19th-century Music*, 2 (1978–9), 61–71.

Chabrier

DELAGE, ROGER: 'Ravel and Chabrier', *Musical Quarterly*, 61 (1975), 546–52.

MOORE, C. H.: 'Verlaine's *Opéra Bouffe*', *Publications of the Modern Language Association of America*, 83 (1968), 305–11.

MYERS, ROLLO: *Emmanual Chabrier and his Circle* (London, 1969).

POULENC, FRANCIS: *Emmanuel Chabrier* (Paris, 1961); Eng. trans., Cynthia Jolly, *Emmanuel Chabrier* (London, 1981).

David

BRANCOUR, RENÉ: *Félicien David* (Paris, 1911).

HAGAN, DOROTHY VEINUS: *Félicien David, 1810–1876: A Composer and a Cause* (Syracuse, NY, 1985).

Delibes

CURZON, HENRI DE: *Léo Delibes, sa vie et ses œuvres* (Paris, 1926).

STUDWELL, WILLIAM E.: *Adolphe Adam and Leo Delibes: A Guide to Research* (New York, 1987).

Gounod

COOPER, MARTIN: 'Charles Gounod and his Influence on French Music', *Music and Letters*, 21 (1940), 50–9.

CURTISS, MINA: 'Gounod before *Faust*', *Musical Quarterly*, 38 (1952), 48–67.

DEAN, WINTON: 'Shakespeare and Opera', in Phyllis Hartnoll (ed.), *Shakespeare in Music* (London, 1964), 89–175.

HARDING, JAMES: *Gounod* (London, 1973).

Lalo

MACDONALD, HUGH: 'A Fiasco Remembered: *Fiesque* Dismembered', in Malcolm H. Brown and Roland J. Wiley (eds.), *Slavonic and Western Music: Essays for Gerald Abraham* (Ann Arbor, Mich., 1985), 163–85.

Massenet

BECKER, HEINZ: 'Zur Frage des Stilverfalls, dargestellt an der französischen Oper', in Carl Dahlhaus (ed.), *Studien zur Trivialmusik des 19. Jahrhunderts* (Regensburg, 1967), 111–20.

Meyerbeer

BECKER, HEINZ: 'Die Couleur locale als Stilkategorie des Oper', in H. Becker (ed.), *Die Couleur locale in der Oper des 19. Jahrhunderts* (Regensburg, 1976), 23–45.

LOPPERT, MAX: 'An Introduction to "L'Étoile du nord" ', *Musical Times*, 116 (1975), 130–3.

For further **Meyerbeer** bibliography, *see* § III (a)

Offenbach

FARIS, ALEXANDER: *Jacques Offenbach* (London, 1980).

HARDING, JAMES: *Jacques Offenbach: A Biography* (London, 1980).

HUFFMAN, RICHARD S.: '*Les Contes d'Hoffmann*: Unity of Dramatic Form in the Libretto', *Studies in Romanticism*, 15 (1976), 97–117.

Reyer

CURZON, HENRI DE: *Ernest Reyer, sa vie et ses œuvres* (Paris, 1924).

—— *La Légende de Sigurd dans l'Edda: L'Opéra d' E. Reyer* (Paris, 1890).

JULLIEN, ADOLPE: *Ernest Reyer: Sa vie et ses œuvres* (Paris, 1909).

Saint-Saëns

HARDING, JAMES: *Saint-Saëns and his Circle* (London, 1965).

LYLE, WATSON: *Camille Saint-Saëns: His Life and Art* (London, 1923; repr. n.d.).

ROLLAND, ROMAIN: *Musiciens d'aujourd'hui* (Paris, 1908, repr. 1946); Eng. trans., Mary Blaiklock, *Musicians of To-day* (London, 1914; repr. 1969).

SAINT-SAËNS, CAMILLE: *Outspoken Essays on Music*, trans. F. Rothwell (New York, 1922; repr. 1970) [collection of Saint-Saëns's writing on music].

WOLFF, STÉPHANE, *Un demi-siècle d'opéra-comique (1900–1950)* (Paris, 1953).

For further **Saint-Saens** bibliography *see* § VII

Thomas

PORTER, ANDREW: 'Travels with Mignon', in *Music of Three Seasons: 1974–1977* (New York, 1978).

Verdi

BUDDEN, JULIAN: *The Operas of Verdi*, ii. *From Il Trovatore to La Forza del destino* (London, 1978); iii. *From Don Carlos to Falstaff* (London, 1981).

DALLAPICCOLA, LUIGI: 'Words and Music in Italian 19th-century Opera', in William Weaver and Martin Chusid (eds.), *The Verdi Companion* (London, 1980), 193–215.

MEDICI, MARIO (ed.): *Atti del II° Congresso internazionale di studi verdiani: Don Carlos/Don Carlo* (Parma, 1971).

NOSKE, FRITS: ' "Don Carlos": The Signifier and the Signified', in *The Signifier and the Signified: Studies in the Operas of Mozart and Verdi* (The Hague, 1977), 294–308.

—— 'The Musical Figure of Death', in *The Signifier and the Signified*, pp. 171–214.

PORTER, ANDREW: '*Les Vêpres siciliennes*: New Letters from Verdi to Scribe', *19th-century Music*, 2 (1978–9), 95–109.

—— 'The Making of *Don Carlos*', *Proceedings of the Royal Musical Association*, 98 (1971–2), 73–88.

WALKER, FRANK: *The Man Verdi* (London, 1962).

For further **Verdi** bibliography *see* § III (c) and § VI (c)

(c) ITALY

(i) Modern Editions

(a) Anthologies

WOLFF, HELLMUTH CHRISTIAN: Die Oper III—19. Jahrhundert (Das Musikwerke, 40; Cologne, 1972); Eng. trans., A. Crawford Howie, The Opera III—19th Century (Anthology of Music, 40; Cologne, 1975) [includes extracts from Verdi, La forza del destino].

(b) Works by Individual Composers

MARCHETTI, F.: Ruy Blas (Biblioteca musica Bononiensis, No. 267; Bologna, 1967-).
MERCADANTE, S.: Virginia (Biblioteca musica Bononiensis, No. 265; Bologna, 1967-).
VERDI, G.: The Works of Giuseppe Verdi, ed. Philip Gossett et al. (Chicago and Milan, 1983-): series 1 Operas: 17 Rigoletto, ed. Martin Chusid (1983); 10 Macbeth, 18 Il trovatore, 19 La traviata, 21 Simon Boccanegra, 23 Un ballo in maschera, 24 La forza del destino, ed. William C. Holmes, 25 Don Carlos, 26 Aida, 27 Otello, 28 Falstaff (forthcoming).
—— Full scores of Aida, Don Carlos, Falstaff, La forza del destino, La traviata, Il trovatore, Macbeth, Otello, Rigoletto, Simon Boccanegra and Un ballo in maschera (Milan, c.1882; repr. New York, n.d.).
—— Study scores of Aida, Falstaff, Il trovatore, La traviata, Otello, Rigoletto, and Un ballo in maschera (Milan, 1913-14; repr. 1950s).
—— L'abbozzo del Rigoletto (Rome, 1941).
—— Falstaff [facsimile of autograph] (Milan, 1951).

(ii) Books and Articles

(a) General

BUDDEN, JULIAN: 'Wagnerian Tendencies in Italian Opera', in Nigel Fortune (ed.), Music and Theatre: Essays in Honour of Winton Dean (Cambridge, 1987), 299-332.
CASELLA, ALFREDO: I segreti della giara (Florence, 1939); Eng. trans., Spencer Norton, Music in my Time: The Memoires of Alfredo Casella (Norman, Okla., 1955).
GOSSETT, PHILIP et al.: The New Grove Masters of Italian Opera (London, 1983) [Rossini, Donizetti, Bellini, Verdi, Puccini].
HADOW, WILLIAM HENRY: Oxford History of Music (London, 1950; 2nd edn., 1932).
LIPPMANN, FRIEDRICH: 'Der italienische Vers und der musikalische Rhythmus: Zum Verhältnis von Vers und Musik in der italienischen Oper des 19. Jahrhunderts, mit einem Rückblick auf die 2. Hälfte des 18. Jahrhunderts', Analecta musicologica, 12 (1975), 253-369; 14 (1977), 324-410; 15 (1978), 298-333.
NICOLAISEN, JAY: Italian Opera in Transition, 1871-1893 (Ann Arbor, Mich., 1980).

(b) Individual Composers

Boito
BOITO, ARRIGO: Tutti gli scritti, ed. Piero Nardi (Verona, 1942).
NARDI, PIERO: Vita di Arrigo Boito (Verona, 1942).

Catalani
CATALANI, ALFREDO: Lettera di Alfredo Catalani a Giuseppe Depanis, ed. Carlo Gatti (Milan, 1946).

GATTI, CARLO: *Alfredo Catalani: La vita e le opere* (Milan, 1953).
ZURLETTI, MICHELANGELO: *Catalani* (Turin, 1982).

Gomes
BRITO, JOLUMA: *Carlos Gomes* (Rio de Janeiro, 1956).

Mercadante
CARLI BALLOLA, GIOVANNI: 'Incontro con Mercadante', *Chigiana*, 26–7 (1969–70), 465–500.
For further **Mercadante** bibliography *see* § III (c)

Pacini
LIPPMANN, FRIEDRICH: 'Giovanni Pacini: Bemerkungen zum Stil seiner Opern', *Chigiana*, 24 (1967), 111–24.
PACINI, GIOVANNI: *Le mie memorie artistiche* (Florence, 1865; ed. F. Magnani, 1875).

Petrella
FLORIMO, FRANCESCO: *Cenno storico sulla scuola musicale di Napoli* (Naples, 1869–71; rev. 2nd edn., 1880–3; repr. 1969, as *La scuola musicale di Napoli e i suoi conservatori*).

Ponchielli
ALBAROSA, NINO (ed.): *Amilcare Ponchielli (1834–1886): Studi e ricerche* (Casalmorano, 1984).
CESARI, GAETANO: *Amilcare Ponchielli nell'arte del suo tempo* (Cremona, 1934).
DE NAPOLI, GIUSEPPE: *Amilcare Ponchielli (1836–1886)* (Cremona, 1936).

Puccini
ADAMI, GUISEPPE: *Giacomo Puccini: Epistolario* (Milan, 1928; Eng. trans., 1931, repr. 1974).
ASHBROOK, WILLIAM: *The Operas of Puccini* (London, 1969; repr., ed. Roger Parker, 1985).
CARNER, MOSCO: *Giacomo Puccini: Tosca* (Cambridge, 1985).
—— *Puccini: A Critical Biography* (London, 1958; rev. 2nd edn., 1974).
GARA, EUGENIO: *Carteggi Pucciniani* (Milan, 1958).
GREENFELD, HOWARD: *Puccini: A Biography* (New York, 1980).
GROOS, ARTHUR, and PARKER, ROGER: *Giacomo Puccini: La Bohème* (Cambridge, 1986).
KAYE, MICHAEL: *The Unknown Puccini* (Oxford, 1987).
MARCHETTI, LEOPOLDO (ed.): *Puccini nelle immagini* (Milan, 1949).
MAREK, GEORGE: *Puccini: a Biography* (New York, 1951).
SARTORI, CLAUDIO (ed.): *Puccini* (Milan, 1959).

Verdi
ABBATE, CAROLYN, and PARKER, ROGER (eds.): *Analyzing Opera: Verdi and Wagner* (Berkeley and Los Angeles, Calif., 1988).
ABBIATI, FRANCO: *Giuseppe Verdi* (Milan, 1959).
Atti dei congressi (Parma, 1969–).
BASEVI, ABRAMO: *Studio sulle opere di Giuseppe Verdi* (Florence, 1859).
BUDDEN, JULIAN: *The Operas of Verdi*, vols. 2 and 3 (London, 1978 and 1981).
—— *Verdi* (London, 1985).
BUSCH, HANS: *Verdi's Aida: The History of an Opera in Letters and Documents* (Minneapolis, 1978).
—— *Verdi's 'Otello' and 'Simon Boccanegra' (Revised Version): A History in Letters and Documents* (Oxford, 1988).
CHUSID, MARTIN: *Giuseppe Verdi: Il trovatore* (Cambridge, 1988).
CONATI, MARCELLO: *La bottega della musica: Verdi e La Fenice* (Milan, 1983).

DE RENSIS, R.: *Franco Faccio e Verdi: Carteggio e documenti inediti* (Milan, 1934).

GATTI, CARLO: *Verdi nelle immagini* (Milan, 1941).

GODEFROY, VINCENT: *The Dramatic Genius of Verdi: Studies of Selected Operas*, ii. '*I vespri siciliani*' *to* '*Falstaff*' (London, 1977).

HEPOKOSKI, JAMES A.: *Giuseppe Verdi: Falstaff* (Cambridge, 1983).

—— *Giuseppe Verdi: Otello* (Cambridge, 1987).

KERMAN, JOSEPH: 'Otello: Traditional Opera and the Image of Shakespeare', in *Opera as Drama* (New York, 1956), 129–67.

LUZIO, ALESSANDRO: *Carteggi Verdiani* (Rome, 1935–47).

MARTIN, GEORGE: *Verdi, his Music Life and Times* (New York, 1964).

—— *Aspects of Verdi* (New York, 1988).

MILA, MASSIMO: *Giuseppe Verdi* (Bari, 1958).

MORELLI, GIOVANNI (ed.): *Tornando a Stiffelio: Atti del convegno internazionale* (Venice, 1985), Quaderni della Rivista Italiana di Musicologia, XIV (1987).

PASCOLATO, ANTONIO: *Re Lear e Ballo in Maschera: Lettere di Giuseppe Verdi* (Città di Castello, 1902).

Quaderni dell'Istituto di studi verdiani (Parma, 1963–).

Studi verdiani, i– (Turin, 1982–).

Verdi: Bollettini dell'Istituto di studi Verdiani (Parma, 1960–).

VERDI, GIUSEPPE: *Carteggio Verdi–Boito*, ed. Mario Medici and Marcello Conati (Parma, 1978).

—— *Carteggio Verdi–Ricordi 1880–1881*, ed. Pierluigi Petrobelli, Marisa Di Gregorio Casati and Carlo Matteo Mossa (Parma, 1988).

—— *I copialettere di Giuseppe Verdi*, ed. Gaetano Cesari and Alessandro Luzio (Milan, 1913; repr. 1973); abridged Eng. trans., Charles Osborne (ed. and trans.), *Letters of Giuseppe Verdi* (London, 1971).

For further **Verdi** bibliography *see* § III (c)

(d) RUSSIA AND EAST EUROPE

(i) Modern Editions

(a) Anthologies

WOLFF, HELLMUTH CHRISTIAN: *Die Oper III—19. Jahrhundert* (Das Musikwerke, 40; Cologne, 1972); Eng. trans., A. Crawford Howie, *The Opera III—19th Century* (Anthology of Music, 40; Cologne, 1975) [includes extracts from Borodin, *Prince Igor*, Moniuszko, *Halka*, and Smetana, *Dalibor*].

(b) Works by Individual Composers

DARGOMÏZHSKY, A. S.: *Rusalka* (Moscow, 1949).

—— *Kamennïy gost'* (Leningrad, 1929).

DVOŘÁK, A.: *Antonín Dvořák: Souborné vydání*, ed. Otakar Šourek *et al.* (Prague, 1955–) [Czech, German, English, French]: series 1 *Theatrical Works*: 1 *Alfred*, 2–3 *Král a uhlíř*, 4 *Tvrdé palice*, 5 *Vanda*, 6 *Šelma sedlák*, 7–8 *Dimitrij*, 10 *Jakobín* (1966).

FIBICH, Z.: *Studijní vydání děl Zdeňka Fibicha*, ed. L. Boháček *et al.* (Prague, 1950–67): libretto of *Nevěsta messinská*.

MUSSORGSKY, M. P.: *Polnoe sobranie sochineniy*, ed. Pavel Aleksandrovich Lamm with Boris Vladimirovich Asaf'ev (Moscow, 1928–34; repr. 1969): 1–3 *Boris Godunov*, 4 *Khovanshchina*, 5–6 *Sorochinskaya yarmarka*.

—— *Boris Godunov*, ed. David Lloyd-Jones (London, 1975).

RIMSKY-KORSAKOV, N.: *Polnoe sobranie sochineniy*, ed. Andrey Nikolaevich Rimsky-Korsakov *et al.* (Moscow, 1946–70): 1 and 29 *Pskovityanka*, ed. A. N. Dmitriev (1966–8 and 1965–7); 2 and 30 *Mayskaya noch'* (1948 and 1951); 3 and 31 *Snegurochka* (1953).

SMETANA, B.: *Souborná díla Bedřicha Smetany*, ed. Otakar Ostrčil (Prague, 1932–6): 2–4 *Prodaná nevěsta*.
—— *Studijní vydáni děl Bedřicha Smetany*, ed. František Bartoš, Josef Plavec, *et al.* (Prague, 1940–): 1 *Prodaná nevěsta* (1940); 3 *Hubička* (1942); 5 *Dalibor* (1945); 6 *Libuše* (1949); 7 *Dvě vdovy* (1950); 9 *Braniboři v Čechách* (1952); 10 *Tajemství* (1953); 12 *Čertova stěna* (1959).
TCHAIKOVSKY, P. I.: *Pyotr Il'ich Chaykovskiy: Polnoe sobranie sochineniy* (Moscow and Leningrad, 1940–71): 1 *Voevoda*, 2 *Undine*, 3 and 34 *Oprichnik*, 4 and 36 *Evgeniy Onegin*, 5 and 37 *Orleanskaya deva*, 6 and 38 *Mazepa*, 8 and 40 *Charodeyka*, 9 and 41 *Pikovaya dama*, 10 and 42 *Iolanta*, 11 and 56 *Lebedinoe ozero*, 12 and 57 *Spyashchaya krasavitsa*, 13 and 54 *Shchelkunchik*.

(ii) Books and Articles

(a) General

ABRAHAM, GERALD: *Essays on Russian and East European Music* (Oxford, 1985).
—— *On Russian Music* (London, 1939; repr. 1982).
—— *The Concise Oxford History of Music* (Oxford, 1979).
—— *et al.*: *The New Grove Russian Masters 2* (London, 1986) [Rimsky-Korsakov, Skryabin, Prokofiev, Shostakovich].
BROWN, DAVID *et al.*: *The New Grove Russian Masters 1* (London, 1986) [Glinka, Borodin, Balakirev, Mussorgsky, Tchaikovsky].
COOPER, MARTIN: *Russian Opera* (London, 1951).
GOZENPUD, ABRAM AKIMOVICH: *Russkiy operniy teatr XIX veka 1857–72* (Leningrad 1971).
LEVASHOVA, OL'GA EVGEN'EVNA, KELDÏSH, YURY VSEVOLODOVICH, and KANDINSKY, A.: *Istoriya russkoy muzïki*, i (Moscow 1972).
MICHAŁOWSKI, KORNEL: *Opery polskie* (Kraków, 1954).
NEWMARCH, ROSA: *The Music of Czechoslovakia* (London, 1942; repr. 1969).
POŹNIAK, WŁODZIMIERZ: 'Główne gatunki i formy muzyki polskiej XIX wieku', in *Z dziejów polskiej kultury muzycznej*, ii (Kraków, 1966), 265–401 and 463–552.
RUBETS, A. I.: *216 narodnïkh ukrainskikh napevov* (Moscow, 1872; 2nd edn., 1882).
SEAMAN, GERALD R.: *History of Russian Music: From its Origins to Dargomyzhsky*, i (Oxford, 1967).
SZABOLCSI, BENCE: *A magyar zenetörténet kézikönyve* (Budapest, 1947; 3rd edn., 1977); abridged Eng. trans. of 2nd edn., 1955, *A Concise History of Hungarian Music* (Budapest, 1964; 2nd edn., 1965).
TARUSKIN, RICHARD: *Opera and Drama in Russia as Preached and Practiced in the 1860s* (Ann Arbor, Mich., 1981).
TYRRELL, JOHN: *Czech Opera* (Cambridge, 1988).

(b) Individual Composers

Borodin
ABRAHAM, GERALD: 'Arab Melodies in Rimsky-Korsakov and Borodin', in *Essays on Russian and East European Music* (Oxford, 1985), 93–8.
—— 'The History of Prince Igor', *On Russian Music* (London, 1939; repr. 1982), 147–68.
BOBETH, MAREK: *Borodin: The Composer and his Music* (London, 1927; repr. n.d.).
—— *Borodin und seine Oper Furst Igor: Geschichte, Analyse, Konsequenzen* (Munich, 1982).
DIANIN, SERGEY A.: *Borodin: Zhizneopisanie, materialï i dokumentï* (Moscow, 1955; rev. 2nd edn., 1960); Eng. trans., Robert Lord, *Borodin* (London, 1963).

SOKHOR, ARNOL'D NAUMOVICH: *Aleksandr Porfir'evich Borodin: Zhizn', deyatel'-nost', muzïkal'noe tvorchestvo* (Moscow, 1965).

Cui

ABRAHAM, GERALD: 'Heine, Cui, and "William Ratcliffe" ', in *Essays on Russian and East European Music* (Oxford, 1985), 56-67.

ANGLÈS, HIGINIO: 'Relations épistolaires entre César Cui et Philippe Pedrell', *Fontes Artis Musicae*, 13 (1966), 15-21.

Dargomïzhsky

ABRAHAM, GERALD: 'Glinka, Dargomïzhsky and *The Rusalka*', *On Russian Music* (London, 1939; repr. 1972), 43-51.

—— 'The Stone Guest', in *Studies in Russian Music* (London, 1936), 68-86.

BAKER, JENNIFER: 'Dargomïzhsky, Realism and *The Stone Guest*', *Music Review*, 37 (1976), 193-208.

DARGOMÏZHSKY, A. S.: *A. S. Dargomïzhskiy: Izbrannïe pis'ma*, ed. Mikhail Samoylovich Pekelis (Moscow, 1952).

TARUSKIN, RICHARD: 'Realism as Preached and Practiced: The Russian Opera Dialogue', *Musical Quarterly*, 56 (1970), 431-54.

Erkel

LEGÁNY, DEZSŐ: *Erkel Ferenc művei* (Budapest, 1974).

VÉBER, GYULA: *Ungarische Elemente in der Opernmusik Ferenc Erkels* (Bilthoven, 1976).

Fibich

HUDEC, VLADIMÍR: *Zdeněk Fibich* (Prague, 1971).

SMACZNY, JAN: 'The Operas and Melodramas of Zdeněk Fibich (1850-1900)', *Proceedings of the Royal Musical Association*, 109 (1982-3), 119-33.

For further **Fibich** bibliography *see* § IX (e)

Kovařovic

NĚMEČEK, J.: *Opera Národního divadla za Karla Kovařovice* (Prague, 1968-9).

Moniuszko

ABRAHAM, GERALD: 'The Operas of Stanisław Moniuszko', in *Essays on Russian and East European Music* (Oxford, 1985), 156-71.

RUDZIŃSKI, WITOLD: *Moniuszko* (Kraków, 1972).

Mussorgsky

ABRAHAM, GERALD: 'Mussorgsky's *Boris* and Pushkin's', in *Slavonic and Romantic Music* (London, 1968), 178-87.

—— 'The Mediterranean Element in *Boris Godunov*', in *Slavonic and Romantic Music* (London, 1968), 188-94.

BROWN, MALCOLM HAMRICK (ed.): *Musorgsky in Memoriam, 1881-1981* (Ann Arbor, Mich., 1982).

CALVOCORESSI, M. D.: *Modest Mussorgsky: His Life and Works* (London, 1956; rev. edn. by Gerald Abraham, 1974).

EMERSON, CARYL: *Boris Godunov: Transpositions of a Russian Theme* (Bloomington, Indiana, 1986).

LEYDA, JAY, and BERTENSSON, SERGEI (eds.): *The Musorgsky Reader: A Life of M. P. Musorgsky in Letters and Documents* (New York, 1947; repr. 1970).

LLOYD-JONES, DAVID: *Boris Godunov: A Critical Commentary* (London, 1975).

Rimsky-Korsakov

ABRAHAM, GERALD: 'Arab Melodies in Rimsky-Korsakov and Borodin', in *Essays on Russian and East European Music* (Oxford, 1985), 93-8.

—— '*Pskovityanka*: The Original Version of Rimsky-Korsakov's First Opera', in

Essays on Russian and East European Music (Oxford, 1985), 68–82.
—— 'Rimsky-Korsakov's *Mlada*', in *On Russian Music* (London, 1939; repr. 1982), 113–21.
—— 'Rimsky-Korsakov's First Opera', in *Studies in Russian Music* (London, 1935; rev. 2nd edn., 1969; repr. 1976), 142–66.
GILSE VAN DER PALS, NIKOLAUS VAN: *N. A. Rimsky-Korssakow: Opernschaffen nebst Skizze über Leben und Werken* (Paris and Leipzig, 1929; repr. 1977).
RIMSKY-KORSAKOV, NIKOLAY ANDREEVICH: *Letopis' moey muzïkal'noy zhizni* (St Petersburg, 1909; enlarged 3rd edn., 1926; ed. Andrey Nikolaevich Rimsky-Korsakov and Aleksandr Vyacheslavovich Ossovsky, *Polnoe sobranie sochineniy*, i (1955); Eng. trans., Judah A. Joffe, *My Musical Life* (New York, 1942; repr. 1974; 5th edn., 1935).
For further **Rimsky-Korsakov** bibliography *see* § VII

Serov
ABRAHAM, GERALD: 'The Operas of Serov', in *Essays on Russian and East European Music* (Oxford, 1985), 40–55.
KHUBOV, GEORGY N.: *Zhizn' A. Serova* (Moscow and Leningrad, 1950).
SEROV, A. N.: *A. N. Serov: Izbrannïe stat'i*, ed. Georgy N. Khubov (Moscow and Leningrad, 1950–7).

Smetana
ABRAHAM, GERALD: 'The Genesis of *The Bartered Bride*', in *Slavonic and Romantic Music* (London, 1968), 28–39.
BARTOŠ, FRANTIŠEK: *Smetana ve vzpomínkách a dopisech* (Prague, 1939; 9th edn., 1953); Eng. trans., Daphne Rusbridge, *Smetana in Letters and Reminiscences* (Prague, 1955).
CLAPHAM, JOHN: *Smetana* (London, 1972).
JARKA, V. H. (ed.): *Kritické dílo Bedřicha Smetany, 1858–65* (Prague, 1948).
LARGE, BRIAN: *Smetana* (London, 1970).
NEJEDLÝ, ZDENĚK: *Zpěvohry Smetanovy* (Prague, 1908; 3rd ed., 1954).
For further **Smetana** bibliography *see* § IX (e)

Tchaikovsky
ABRAHAM, GERALD: 'Tchaikovsky's Operas', in *Slavonic and Romantic Music* (London, 1968), 116–77.
BROWN, DAVID: *Tchaikovsky: A Biographical and Critical Study*, i. *The Early Years (1840–1874)* (London, 1978); ii. *The Crisis Years (1874–1878)* (London, 1982); iii. *The Years of Wandering (1878–1885)* (London, 1986).
DAVÏDOVA, K. YU., PROTOPOPOV, V. V., and TUMANINA, N. V.: *Muzïkal'noe nasledie Chaykovskogo* (Moscow, 1958).
PROTOPOPOV, VLADIMIR VASIL'EVICH, and TUMANINA, NADEZHDA VASIL'EVNA: *Opernoe tvorchestvo Chaykovskogo* (Moscow, 1957).
TCHAIKOVSKY, MODEST: *Zhizn' P. I. Chaykovskogo* (Moscow, 1900–2); abridged Eng. trans., Rosa Newmarch, *The Life and Letters of Peter Ilyich Tchaikovsky* (London, 1906).
TCHAIKOVSKY, PYOTR IL'ICH: *P. I. Chaykovskiy: Perepiska s N. F. fon-Mekk*, ed. Vladimir Aleksandrovich Zhdanov and Nikolay Timofeevich Zhegin (Moscow and Leningrad, 1934–6).
—— *P. I. Chaykovskiy: Perepiska s P. I. Yurgensonom*, ed. Vladimir Aleksandrovich Zhdanov and Nikolay Timofeevich Zhegin (Moscow, 1938–52).
—— *P. I. Chaykovskiy–S. I. Taneev: Pis'ma*, ed. Modest Tchaikovsky (1916); rev. edn. ed. Vladimir Aleksandrovich Zhdanov (Moscow, 1951).
—— *Letters to his Family: An Autobiography*, trans. Galina von Meck (New York, 1981).

WILEY, ROLAND JOHN: *Tchaikovsky's Ballets: Swan Lake, Sleeping Beauty, Nut-cracker* (Oxford, 1985).
For further **Tchaikovsky** bibliography *see* § VIII

(e) BRITAIN AND THE UNITED STATES

(i) Modern Editions

(b) Works by Individual Composers

BRISTOW, G. F.: *Rip Van Winkle*, ed. H. Wiley Hitchcock (Earlier American Music, 25; New York, 1980).
LODER, E. J.: *Raymond and Agnes*, ed. Nicholas Temperley (Cambridge, 1966) [vocal score].
SULLIVAN, A. S.: *The Operas by Arthur Sullivan and W. S. Gilbert: A Critical Edition*, ed. Reginald Allen, Steven Ledbetter, Jane Stedman, and Percy Young (New York, forthcoming).

(ii) Books and Articles

(a) General

British Opera in Retrospect (British Music Society, London, 1985).
BURTON, NIGEL: 'Opera: 1865–1914', in Nicholas Temperley (ed.), *Music in Britain: The Romantic Age 1800–1914* (London, 1981), 330–57.
GÄNZL, KURT: *British Musical Theatre*, i (London, 1986).
HAMM, CHARLES: *Music in the New World* (New York, 1983).
HIPSHER, EDWARD ELLSWORTH: *American Opera and its Composers* (Philadelphia, 1927; repr. 1978).
HURD, MICHAEL: 'Opera: 1834–1865', in Temperley (ed.), *Music in Britain: The Romantic Age 1800–1914* (London, 1981), 307–29.
LAMB, ANDREW: 'Music of the Popular Theatre', in Temperley (ed.) *Music in Britain: The Romantic Age 1800–1914* (London, 1981), 92–108.
MATES, JULIAN: *America's Musical Stage: Two Hundred Years of Musical Theatre* (Westport, Conn., 1985).
MIDGLEY, SAMUEL: *My 70 Years' Musical Memories* (London, 1934).
ROOT, DEANE: *American Popular Stage Music 1860–1880* (Ann Arbor, Mich., 1981).
SONNECK, OSCAR G. T.: 'A Survey from 1781 to 1792', *Early Opera in America*, (New York, 1915; repr. 1963), 57–83.
TEMPERLEY, NICHOLAS: 'The English Romantic Opera', *Victorian Studies*, 9 (1966), 293–301.
WHITE, ERIC WALTER: 'Some National Opera Schemes; and Gilbert and Sullivan', *A History of English Opera* (London, 1983), 295–334.

(b) Individual Composers

Macfarren
BANISTER, HENRY CHARLES: *George Alexander Macfarren: His Life, Works and Influence* (London, 1891).
TEMPERLEY, NICHOLAS: 'George Alexander Macfarren and English Musical Nationalism,' in Temperley (ed.), *The Lost Chord: Studies in Victorian Music* (Bloomington, Ind., 1989).

Sullivan
DUNHILL, THOMAS F.: *Sullivan's Comic Operas: A Critical Appreciation* (Oxford, 1928; repr. 1981).

HAYTER, CHARLES: *Gilbert and Sullivan* (London, 1987).
JACOBS, ARTHUR: *Arthur Sullivan: A Victorian Musician* (Oxford, 1984).

CHAPTER VII

THE SYMPHONIC POEM AND KINDRED FORMS

(i) Modern Editions

(a) Anthologies

STOCKMEIER, WOLFGANG: *Die Programmusik* (Das Musikwerke, 36; Cologne, 1970); Eng. trans., A. Crawford Howie, *The Program Music* (Cologne, 1970) [includes piano score of Liszt's *Manfred*].

(b) Works by Individual Composers

DVOŘÁK, A.: *Antonín Dvořák: Souborné vydání*, ed. Otakar Šourek *et al.* (Prague, 1955) [Czech, German, English, French]: series 3 *Orchestral Works* 24 vols. (1955–63).
FIBICH, Z.: *Studijní vydání děl Zdeňka Fibicha*, ed. L. Boháček *et al.* (Prague, 1950–67): *Orchestrální hudba* (1954–63).
LISZT, F.: *Franz Liszts Musikalische Werke*, ed. Franz Liszt-Stiftung (Leipzig, 1907–36; repr. 1966): Part 1 *Für Orchester* [including Bd 1–6 *Symphonische Dichtungen*].
—— *Neue Ausgabe sämtlicher Werke/New Edition of the Complete Works* (Kassel and Budapest, 1970–): series 6 *Works and Arrangements for Orchestra* (forthcoming).
MUSSORGSKY, M. P.: *Modest Petrovich Musorgskiy: Polnoe sobranie sochineniy*, ed. Pavel Aleksandrovich Lamm, with Boris Vladimirovich Asaf'ev (Moscow, 1928–34): 16 *Six Works for Orchestra*.
RIMSKY-KORSAKOV, N.: *Nikolay Rimskiy-Korsakov: Polnoe sobranie sochineniy*, ed. Andrey Nikolaevich Rimsky-Korsakov *et al.* (Moscow, 1946–70): 19A *Sadko* (1951).
SMETANA, B.: *Studijní vydání děl Bedřicha Smetany*, ed. František Bartoš, Josef Plavec, *et al.* (Prague, 1940–): 14 *Má Vlast* (1966).
TCHAIKOVSKY, P. I.: *Pyotr Il'ich Chaykovskiy: Polnoe sobranie sochineniy* (Moscow and Leningrad, 1940–71; repr. 1974): 18 *Manfred Symphony* (1949); 21–2 *Overtures* [including *Groza* and *Fatum*] (1952); 23 *Romeo and Juliet* (1950); 24 [Including *Tempest* and *Francesca da Rimini*] (1961); 26 *Hamlet*.
—— *Manfred* (London, 1958) [miniature score, with foreword by Gerald Abraham].
WAGNER, R.: *Richard Wagners Werke: Musikdramen—Jugendopern—musikalische Werke*, ed. Michael Balling (Leipzig, 1912–29; repr. 1971): Band 18 & 20 *Orchesterwerke*.
—— *Richard Wagner: Sämtliche Werke*, ed. Carl Dahlhaus (Mainz, 1970–): 18 *Orchesterwerke*, ed. Egon Voss (1973).
WOLF, H.: *Hugo Wolf: Sämtliche Werke*, ed. Internationale Hugo Wolf-Gesellschaft/Hans Jancik (Vienna, 1960–): 16 *Penthesilea* (1971).
—— *Hugo Wolf: Nachgelassene Werke*, ed. Robert Haas and Helmut Schultz (Leipzig and Vienna, 1936): 3 *Instrumentalwerke*; 2 *Penthesilea*.

(ii) Books and Articles

(a) General

COOKE, DERYCK: *The Language of Music* (London, 1959; repr. 1962).
DANCKERT, WERNER: *Das europäische Volkslied* (Berlin, 1939; 2nd edn., 1970).

FINSCHER, LUDWIG: 'Zwischen absoluter und Programmusik: Zur Interpretation der deutschen romantischen Symphone', in Christoph–Hellmut Mahling (ed.), *Über Symphonien: Beiträge zu einer musikalischen Gattung: Festschrift Walter Wiora zum 70. Geburtstag* (Tutzing, 1979), 103–15.

FISKE, ROGER: 'Shakespeare in the Concert Hall', in Phyllis Hartnoll (ed.), *Shakespeare in Music* (London, 1964), 177–241.

KLAUWELL, OTTO: *Geschichte der Programmusk von ihren Anfängen bis zur Gegenwart* (Leipzig, 1910).

KLOIBER, RUDOLF: *Handbuch der symphonischen Dichtung* (Wiesbaden, 1967).

LOCKSPEISER, EDWARD: *Music and Painting* (London, 1973).

MYERS, ROLLO: *Modern French Music* (Oxford, 1971).

ORREY, LESLIE: *Programme Music* (London, 1975).

SCHUBERT, K.: *Die Programmusik* (Wolfenbuttel, 1933; 2nd edn., 1961).

TOVEY, DONALD (FRANCIS): *Essays in Musical Analysis*, iv. *Illustrative Music* (London, 1937; repr. 1972).

YOUNG, PERCY M.: 'Orchestral Music', in Nicholas Temperley (ed.), *Music in Britain: The Romantic Age 1800–1914* (London, 1981), 358–80.

SCRUTON, ROGER: 'Representation in Music', *Philosophy*, 51 (1976), 273–87.

WELLESZ, EGON: *Die neue Instrumentation* (Berlin, 1928).

WIORA, WALTER: 'Zwischen absoluter und Programmusik', in Anna Amalie Abert and Wilhelm Pfannkuch (eds.), *Festschrift Friedrich Blume zum 70. Geburtstag* (Kassel, 1963), 381–8.

(b) *Individual Composers*

Balakirev

GARDEN, EDWARD: *Balakirev: A Critical Study of his Life and Music* (London, 1967).

KARENIN, V. (ed.): *Perepiska M. A. Balakireva s V. V. Stasovïm* (Moscow, 1935).

STASOV, VLADIMIR VASIL'EVICH: 'Nasha muzïka za posledniya 25 let', *Vestnik Evropï* (Oct. 1883), no. 10, pp. 561–623.

TIMOFEEV, GRIGORY: 'M. A. Balakirev: Na osnovanii novïkh materialov', *Russkaya Mïsl'* (1912), no. 6, pp. 38 ff., and no. 7, pp. 55 ff.

D'Indy

VALLAS, LÉON: *Vincent d'Indy* (Paris, 1946–50).

Dvořák

ABRAHAM, GERALD: *The Tradition of Western Music* (London, 1974).

ŠOUREK, OTAKAR: *Dvořákovy skladby orchestrální* (Prague, 1944–6); abridged Eng. trans., Roberta Finlayson Samsour, *The Orchestral works of Antonín Dvořák* (Prague, 1956).

SYCHRA, ANTONÍN: *Estetika Dvořákovy symfonické tvorby* (Prague, 1959).

For further **Dvořák** bibliography see § VIII

Franck

CORTOT, ALFRED: *La Musique française de piano* (Paris, 1930–48); Eng. trans., Hilda Andrews, *French Piano Music* (London, 1932).

DAVIES, LAURENCE: *César Franck and his Circle* (London, 1970).

—— *Franck* (London, 1973).

D'INDY, VINCENT: *César Franck* (Paris, 1906; 8th edn., 1919); Eng. trans., Rosa Newmarch, *César Franck* (London, 1910; repr. 1965).

MOHR, WILHELM: *César Franck* (Stuttgart, 1942; 2nd edn., 1969 incl. thematic catalogue of published works).

SEIPT, ANGELUS: *César Francks Symphonische Dichtungen* (Regensburg, 1981).

TIERSOT, JULIAN: 'Les Œuvres inédites de César Franck', *La Revue musicale*, 4/2 (1922), 97–138.

—— *La Véritable Histoire de César Franck* (Paris, 1950); Eng. trans., Hubert Foss, *César Franck* (London, 1951).

Liszt

BARRY, C. F.: 'Hans von Bülow's *Nirwana*', *Zeitschrift der Internationalen Musik-gesellschaft*, 2/9 (June 1901).

BERGFELD, JOACHIM: *Die formale Struktur der symphonischen Dichtungen Franz Liszts* (Eisenach, 1931).

HEUSS, ALFRED: 'Eine motivisch-thematische Studie über Liszts sinfonische Dichtung *Ce qu'on entend sur le montagne*', *Zeitschrift der Internationalen Musik-Gesellschaft*, 13 (1911–12), 10–21.

LISZT, FRANZ: *Briefwechsel zwischen Franz Liszt und Hans von Bülow*, ed. La Mara (Leipzig, 1898).

—— *Briefe*, ed. La Mara (8 vols.; Leipzig, 1893–1905); Eng. trans., Constance Bache, *Letters* (2 vols.; London, 1894).

—— *Franz Liszt: Correspondence*, ed. Pierre-Antoine Hure and Claude Knepper (Paris, 1987).

—— *Gesammelte Schriften von Franz Liszt*, ed. Lina Ramann (Leipzig, 1880–3).

MERRICK, PAUL: *Revolution and Religion in the Music of Liszt* (Cambridge, 1987).

RAABE, PETER: *Franz Liszt: Leben und Schaffen* (Stuttgart, 1931; rev. 2nd edn., 1968).

RAFF, HELENE: 'Franz Liszt und Joachim Raff im Spiegel ihrer Briefe', *Die Musik*, 1 (1901–2).

SOMFAI, LASZLO: 'Die Gestaltwandlungen der "Faust-Symphone" von Liszt', in Klara Hamburger (ed.), *Franz Liszt: Beiträge von ungarischen Autoren* (Budapest, 1978), 292–324.

TEMPERLEY, NICHOLAS, ABRAHAM, GERALD, and SEARLE, HUMPHREY: *The New Grove Early Romantic Masters 1* (London, 1985) [includes Liszt].

WAGNER, RICHARD: 'Über Franz Liszt's symphonische Dichtungen: Briefe an M. W.' (1857), repr. in *Richard Wagner: Gesammelte Schriften und Dichtungen*, v (Leipzig, 1872), 235–55; Eng. trans., William Ashton Ellis (ed. and trans.), *Richard Wagner's Prose Works*, iii (London, 1894; repr. 1972), 235–54.

WALKER, ALAN: *Franz Liszt: The Man and his Music* (London, 1970; 2nd edn., 1976).

—— *Franz Liszt*, i. *Virtuoso Years, 1811–1847* (London, 1983).

WOOLLETT, H., and PIERNÉ, GABRIEL: 'Histoire de l'orchestration: Franz Liszt (1811–1866)', in Albert Lavignac (ed.), *Encyclopédie de la musique et Dictionnaire du Conservatoire* (Paris, 1920–31), II. iv. 2602–5.

Raff

RAFF, HELENE: *Joachim Raff: Ein Lebensbild* (Regensburg, 1925).

ROMER, MARKUS: *Joseph Joachim Raff (1822–1882)* (Wiesbaden, 1982).

Ritter

HAUSEGGER, SIEGMUND VON: 'Alexander Ritter: Ein Bild seines Charakters und Schaffens', *Die Musik* (Berlin, 1907).

Rimsky-Korsakov

ABRAHAM, GERALD: *Slavonic and Romantic Music* (London, 1968).

JONAS, FLORENCE (trans.): *Reminiscences of Rimsky-Korsakov* (New York, 1985).

OSSOVSKY, ALEKSANDR VYACHESLAVOVICH (ed.): *Rimskiy-Korsakov: Vospominaniya V. V. Yastrebtseva* (Moscow, 1959–60).

RIMSKY-KORSAKOV, NIKOLAY ANDREEVICH: *Letopis' moey muzïkal'noy zhizni*

(St Petersburg, 1909; enlarged 3rd edn., 1928; ed. Andrey Nikolaevich Rimsky-Korsakov and Aleksandr Vyacheslavovich Ossovsky, *Polnoe sobranie sochineniy*, i (1955); Eng. trans., Judah A. Joffe, *My Musical Life* (New York, 1942, repr. 1974; 5th edn., 1935).
For further **Rimsky-Korsakov** bibliography *see* § VI (d)

Saint-Saëns
Catalogue général et thématique des œuvres de Saint-Saëns (Paris, 1897; repr. 1908) [ed. Durand et Cie].
SAINT-SAËNS, CAMILLE: *Portraits et souvenirs* (Paris, 1899; 3rd edn., 1909).
SERVIÈRES, GEORGES: *Saint-Saëns* (Paris, 1923; rev. edn., 1930).
For further **Saint-Saens** bibliography *see* § VI (b)

Smetana
BARTOŠ, FRANTIŠEK: *Smetana ve vzpomínkách a dopisech* (Prague, 1939; 9th edn. 1953); Eng. trans., Daphne Rusbridge, *Letters and Reminiscences* (Prague, 1955).
CLAPHAM, JOHN: *Smetana* (London, 1972).
LARGE, BRIAN: *Smetana* (London, 1970).
SMETANA, BEDŘICH: *Bedřich Smetana a Dr. Ludevít Procházka: Vzájemná korespondence*, ed. Jan Löwenbach (Prague, 1914).
ŠOUREK, OTAKAR: *Smetanova 'Má Vlast': Její vznik a osudy* (Prague, 1939).
ZICH, OTAKAR: *Symfonické Básně Smetanovy: Hudebně estetický rozbor* (Prague, 1924; 2nd edn., 1949).
For further **Smetana** bibliography *see* § IX (e)

Strauss
ARMSTRONG, THOMAS: *Strauss' Tone Poems* (London, 1931).
DEL MAR, NORMAN: *Richard Strauss: A Critical Commentary on his Life and Works* (London, 1962–72; rev. repr. 1978, repr. 1986).
GYSI, FRITZ: *Richard Strauss* (Potsdam, 1934).
KENNEDY, MICHAEL: *Strauss Tone Poems* (London, 1984).
LONGYEAR, REY M.: 'Schiller, Moszkowski and Strauss: Joan of Arc's "Death and Transfiguration" ', *Music Review*, 28 (1967), 209–17.
MAUKE, WILHELM: *Richard Strauss: Symphonien und Tondichtungen* (Berlin, n.d.).
MUELLER VON ASOW, ERICH H.: *Richard Strauss: Thematisches Verzeichnis* (Vienna, 1959–74).
MUSCHLER, REINHOLD KONRAD: *Richard Strauss* (Hildesheim, 1925).
SPECHT, RICHARD: *Richard Strauss und sein Werk* (Vienna and Leipzig, 1921).
STEINITZER, MAX: *Richard Strauss* (Berlin, 1911; 13th edn., 1922; final enlarged edn., 1927).
STRAUSS, RICHARD: *Richard Strauss und Franz Wüllner im Briefwechsel*, ed. Dietrich Kämper (Cologne, 1963).
TRENNER, FRANZ: *Richard Strauss: Werkverzeichnis* (Vienna and Munich, 1985).
WOLLETT, H., and PIERNÉ, GABRIEL: 'Histoire de l'orchestration: Max Reger et Richard Strauss', in Albert Lavignac (ed.), *Encyclopédie de la musique et Dictionnaire du Conservatoire* (Paris, 1920–31), II. iv. 2619–35.

Tchaikovsky
DAVÏDOVA, K. YU. PROTOPOPOV, V. V., and TUMANINA, N. V.: *Muzïkal'noe nasledie Chaykovskogo* (Moscow, 1958).
TCHAIKOVSKY, P.: *P. I. Chaykovskiy o programmnoy muzïke* (Moscow, 1952).
For further **Tchaikovsky** bibliography *see* § VI (d) and § VIII

Wagner
VOSS, EGON: *Richard Wagner und die Instrumentalmusik: Wagners symphonischer*

Ehrgeiz (Wilhelmshaven, 1977).
For further **Wagner** bibliography *see* § V

CHAPTER VIII

MAJOR INSTRUMENTAL FORMS: 1850–1890

(i) Modern Editions

(*a*) *Anthologies*

BEDELL, ROBERT LEECH: *The French Organist* (New York, 1944) [includes music by Widor].

BONNET, JOSEPH: *Historical Organ-Recitals* (New York, 1917–40): 4 *Three Composers of the Romantic Period* [Schumann, Mendelssohn, and Liszt]; 5 *Modern Composers* [includes Franck, Brahms, Saint-Saëns, and Widor].

ENGEL, HANS: *Das Solokonzert* (Das Musikwerk, 25; Cologne, 1964); Eng. trans., Robert Kolben, *The Solo Concerto* (Anthology of Music, 25; Cologne, 1964).

FERGUSON, HOWARD: *Style and Interpretation: An Anthology of Keyboard Music*, 4 *Romantic Piano Music* (London, 1964; 2nd edn., 1972) [includes works by Brahms and Liszt].

GEORGII, WALTER: 'Romanticism and the National Efforts in the 19th Century', *400 Jahre europäischer Klaviermusik* (Das Musikwerk, 1; Cologne, 1959); Eng. trans., *400 Years of European Keyboard Music* (Anthology of Music, 1; Cologne, 1959) [includes works by Brahms, Liszt, Mussorgsky, and Smetana].

GILLESPIE, JOHN: *Nineteenth-century European Piano Music: Unfamiliar Masterworks* (New York, 1977) [includes works by Arensky, Bizet, Chabrier, Dvořák, Gade, Smetana, R. Strauss, and Wagner].

HOFFMANN-ERBRECHT, LOTHAR: 'The Symphony in the 19th Century after Beethoven', *Die Sinfonie* (Das Musikwerk, 29; Cologne, 1967); Eng. trans., Robert Kolben, *The Symphony* (Anthology of Music, 29; Cologne, 1967) [includes extracts from works by Brahms, Bruckner, and Tchaikovsky].

KAHL, WILLI: *Das Charakterstück* (Das Musikwerk, 8; Cologne, 1955); Eng. trans., A. Crawford Howie, *The Character Piece* (Anthology of Music, 8; Cologne, 1961) [includes works by Bizet, Fibich, Jensen, Liszt, and R. Strauss].

—— *Lyrische Klavierstücke der Romantik* (Stuttgart, 1926).

KRAMARZ, JOACHIM: *Vom Haydn bis Hindemith: Das Streichquartett in Beispielen* (Wolfenbüttel, 1961).

LANG, PAUL HENRY: *The Concerto 1800–1900* (New York, 1969).

—— *The Symphony 1800–1900* (New York, 1969) [includes works by Brahms, Bruckner, Dvořák, and Tchaikovsky].

POHANKA, JAROSLAV: *Dějiny české hudby v příkladech* (Prague, 1958).

SCHLEUNING, PETER: *Die Fantasie 2* (Das Musikwerk, 43; Cologne, 1971); Eng. trans., A. Crawford Howie, *The Fantasia 2: 18th to 20th Centuries* (Anthology of Music, 43; Cologne, 1971) [includes music by Liszt].

STEPHENSON, KURT: *Romantik in der Tonkunst* (Das Musikwerk, 21; Cologne, 1961); Eng. trans., Robert Kolben, *Romanticism in Music* (Anthology of Music, 21; Cologne, 1961) [includes piano music by Brahms and Liszt].

TEMPERLEY, NICHOLAS: *The London Pianoforte School 1770–1860* (New York, 1984–7).

UNVERRICHT, HUBERT: *Die Kammermusik* (Das Musikwerk, 46; Cologne, 1972); Eng. trans., A. Crawford Howie, *Chamber Music* (Anthology of Music, 46; Cologne, 1975) [includes music by Herzogenberg and Raff].

(b) *Works by Individual Composers*

ALKAN, C. V.: *Œuvres choisies pour piano*, ed. Georges Beck (Le Pupitre, 16; Paris, 1969).
—— *The Piano Music of Alkan*, ed. Raymond Lewenthal (New York, 1964).
BALAKIREV, M. A.: *Miliy Alekseevich Balakirev: Polnoe sobranie sochineniy dlya fortep'yano*, ed. K. S. Sorokin (Moscow, 1951–4).
BIZET, G.: *Symphony, C Major*, ed. Hans-Hubert Schönzeler (London, 1973).
BORODIN, A.: *First String Quartet* (London, 1976) [Foreword by David Brown].
BRAHMS, J.: *Johannes Brahms: Sämtliche Werke*, 1–10 ed. Hans Gál, 11–26 ed. Eusebius Mandyczewski (Leipzig, 1926–7; repr. 1964–5 and 1971): 1–2 *Symphonien für Orchester* (repr. 1974 with Eng. trans. of text); 3 *Ouvertüren und Variationen für Orchester*; 4 *Serenaden und Tänze für Orchester*; 5 *Konzerte für Streichinstrumente und Orchester*; 6 *Konzerte für Klavier und Orchester*; 7 *Kammermusik für Streichinstrumente*; 8 *Klavier-Quintett und -Quartette*; 9 *Klavier-Trios*; 10 *Klavier-Duos*; 11–15 *Klavierwerke* [including 13 *Sonaten und Variationen für Klavier zu zwei Händen*] (13–15 repr. 1971, 12 repr. 1976, both with Eng. trans. of text); 16 *Orgelwerke* (repr. 1949 with Eng. trans. of text).
—— *Johannes Brahms Autographs: Facsimiles of Eight Manuscripts in the Library of Congress*, with introduction by James Webster and preface by George Bozarth (New York, 1983) [includes chamber and piano works].
—— *Klavierwerke*, ed. Carl Seeman, rev. Kurt Stephenson (Frankfurt, 1974).
—— *Kleine Stücke für Klavier*, ed. Robert Pascall (Diletto musicale No. 819; Vienna and Munich, 1979) [includes Sarabande and Gavottes].
—— *Quintett, H. Moll*, ed. Kurt Herrmann (London, 1938).
—— *Sämtliche Orgelwerke: Neue Ausgabe/Complete Organ Works: New Edition*, ed. Walter E. Buszin and Paul G. Bunjes (New York, 1964).
BRUCKNER, A.: *Anton Bruckner: Sämtliche Werke: Kritische Gesamtausgabe* (Vienna, 1930–50): 1–2, 4–8 *Symphonien*, ed. Robert Haas; 3 *Symphonie*, ed. Fritz Oeser (Wiesbaden, 1950).
—— *Anton Bruckner Sämtliche Werke: Kritische Gesamtausgabe*, ed. Leopold Nowak (Vienna, 1951–): 1–11 *Symphonien* (1951–81); 13/1 *Streichquartett c-Moll* (1955); 13/2 *Streichquintett F-Dur*, *Intermezzo d-Moll für Streichquintett* (1963).
—— *Orgelwerke*, ed. Hans Haselböck (Diletto musicale, No. 364; Vienna and Munich, 1970).
—— *Symphony No. 9*, ed. Hans-Hubert Schönzeler (London, 1963) [Foreword by Hans Ferdinand Redlich].
—— Organ and piano works incl. in Göllerich, August: *Anton Bruckner: Ein Lebens- und Schaffens-Bild*, 1 (Regensburg, 1922), 2–4, ed. Max Auer (Regensburg, 1928–37); all repr. 1974.
DEBUSSY, C.: *Œuvres complètes de Claude Debussy* (Paris, 1985–): series 1: *Piano Works*; series 3 *Chamber Music*; series 5 *Orchestral Works*.
DVOŘÁK, A.: *Antonín Dvořák: Souborné vydání*, ed. Otakar Šourek *et al.* (Prague, 1955–) [Czech, German, English, French]: series 3 *Orchestral Works*: 24 vols. including 1–9 *Symphonies* (1955–63); 4 *Chamber Music:* 11 vols. (1955–79); 5 *Piano Works:* 6 vols. (1955–76).
ELGAR, E.: *Elgar Complete Edition*, ed. Jerrold Northrop Moore and Christopher Kent (London, 1981–): series 1 *Choral Works* (forthcoming); series 4 *Orchestral Works* (1984) [including Symphony No. 1].
FIBICH, Z.: *Studijní vydání děl Zdeňka Fibicha*, ed. L.. Boháček *et al.* (Prague, 1950–67): *Orchestrální hudba* (1954–63); *Klavír na dvě ruce, Klavír na čtyři ruce, Housle a klavír, Klavírní výtahy; Komorní hudba*.
FRANCK, C.: *Œuvres complètes pour orgue*, ed. Marcel Dupré (Paris, 1955–).

—— *Organ Works*, ed. Harvey Grace (London, 1942).

GRIEG, E.: *Edvard Grieg: Gesamtausgabe/Complete Works*, ed. Edvard-Grieg-Komitee (Frankfurt, 1977–): I *Instrumentalmusik*: 1–7 *Klaviermusik*, 8–9 *Kammermusik*, 10–13 *Orchestermusik*.

—— *Sämtliche Klavierwerke* (Leipzig, Peters).

LISZT, F.: *Franz Liszts Musikalische Werke*, ed. Franz Liszt-Stiftung (Leipzig, 1907–36; repr. 1966): Part 1 *Für Orchester*: 1–6 *Symphonische Dichtungen*, 7 *Eine Symphonie zu Dantes Divina commedia*, 8–9 *Eine Faustsymphonie*, 10–12 *Kleinere Orchesterwerke*, 13 *Werke für Pianoforte und Orchester*.

—— *Liszt Society Publications* (London, 1950–): 1 *Late Piano Works*; 2 *Early and Late Piano Works*; 3 *Hungarian and Late Piano Works*; 4 *Dances for Piano*; 5 *Various Piano Pieces* (1968); 7 *Unfamiliar Piano Works*.

—— [Works], ed. V. Belov and K. Sorokin (Moscow, 1958–): i/1 [Piano Works]; iv/3 [Organ Works].

—— *Franz Liszt: Neue Ausgabe sämtlicher Werke/New Edition of the Complete Works*: series 1 *Works for Piano, Two Hands*, ed. Zoltán Gárdonyi and István Szelényi (Kassel and Budapest, 1970–85); *Transcriptions and Arrangements of Original and Other Works*, series 3 *Works including Transcriptions and Arrangements of Original and Other Works for Piano, Four Hands or Two Pianos*; 6 *Works and Arrangements for Orchestra* [20 vols.] (all forthcoming).

—— *Werke für Klavier zu 2 Händen*, ed. Emil von Sauer (Leipzig, 1917).

—— *Complete Organ Works*, ed. Sandor Margittay (Budapest and London, 1970–3).

MAHLER, G.: *Gustav Mahler: Sämtliche Werke: Kritische Gesamtausgabe*, ed. Internationale Gustav-Mahler-Gesellschaft (Vienna, 1960–): 1–8, 10 *Symphonien Nr. 1–9* (1960–9).

MENDELSSOHN, F.: *Felix Mendelssohn Bartholdy's Werke: Kritisch durchgesehene Ausgabe*, ed. Julius Rietz (Leipzig, 1874–7; repr. 1967–9): 12 *Für Orgel*.

MONIUSZKO, S.: *Stanisław Moniuszko: Dzieła/Werke* (Kraków, 1965–): series E *Instrumentalmusik*: 33 *Streichquartett I, II* (1971); 34 *Klavierwerke* (1976).

MUSSORGSKY, M. P.: *Modest Petrovich Musorgskiy: Polnoe sobranie sochineniy*, ed. Pavel Aleksandrovich Lamm, with Boris Vladimirovich Asaf'ev (Moscow, 1928–34; repr. 1969): 16 [Six Works for Orchestra]; 17–18 [Piano Works].

RIMSKY-KORSAKOV, N.: *Nikolay Rimskiy-Korsakov: Polnoe sobranie sochineniy*, ed. Andrey Nikolaevich Rimsky-Korsakov *et al.* (Moscow, 1946–70): 16–18 [Symphonies] (1949–59); 19, 20, 21, 22 [other orchestral works] (1951–8); 27 [Works for Chamber Ensemble] (1955); 28A [Chamber Works] (1951); 49A [Piano Works] (1959).

SCHUMANN, R.: *Robert Schumann's Werke*, ed. Clara Schumann (Leipzig, 1881–93; repr. 1967–8): 8 *Für Orgel* (1881).

—— *Symphony No. 3*, ed. Linda Correll Roesner (London, 1986).

—— *Symphony No. 4*, ed. Linda Correll Roesner (London, 1978).

SMETANA, B.: *Studijní vydání děl Bedřicha Smetany*, ed. František Bartoš, Josef Plavec, *et al.* (Prague, 1940–): 4 *Symf. básně švéds. obdobi* (1942); 8 *Orchestrálni skladby sv. 2* (1952); 11 *Triumfálni symfonie* (1955); [Piano Works] 7 vols. (1944–78).

—— *Studijní vydání děl Bedřicha Smetany*, xv. *Komorni Skladby*, ed. František Bartoš, Josef Plavec, and Karel Šolc (Prague, 1977) [Foreword by František Bartoš].

STRAUSS, JOHANN (ii): *Johann Strauss: Gesamtausgabe*, ed. Fritz Racek (Vienna, 1967–): series 1 *Instrumentalwerke*: 18 Opp. 292–303 (1968); 19 Opp. 304–16 (1967); 20 Opp. 317–29 (1971).

TCHAIKOVSKY, P. I.: *Pyotr Il'ich Chaykovskiy: Polnoe sobranie sochineniy* (Moscow and Leningrad, 1940–71): 14–17 [Symphonies nos. 1–6] (1949–63).

—— *Suite No. 3* (London, 1978) [miniature score].

—— *Ausgewählte Klavierwerke in drei Bänden*, ed. Fritz Weitzmann (Leipzig, n.d.).

WAGNER, R.: *Richard Wagners Werke: Musikdramen—Jugendopern—musikalische Werke*, ed. Michael Balling (Leipzig, 1912–29; repr. 1971): 18 & 20 *Orchesterwerke*.

—— *Richard Wagner: Sämtliche Werke*, ed. Carl Dahlhaus (Mainz, 1970–): 18 *Orchesterwerke*, ed. Egon Voss (1973).

WOLF, H.: *Hugo Wolf: Sämtliche Werke*, ed. Internationale Hugo Wolf-Gesellschaft/Hans Jancik (Vienna, 1960–): 15 [Works for string quartet] (1960–); 17 *Italienische Serenade* (1965); 18 *Klavierkompositionen* (1974).

—— *Hugo Wolf: Nachgelassene Werke*, ed. Robert Haas and Helmut Schultz (Leipzig and Vienna, 1936): 3 *Instrumentalwerke*.

(ii) Books and Articles

(a) General

ABRAHAM, GERALD: *The Concise Oxford History of Music* (Oxford, 1979).

—— *The Tradition of Western Music* (London, 1974).

COBBETT, WALTER WILLSON (ed.): *Cobbett's Cyclopedic Survey of Chamber Music* (2 vols.; London, 1929–30; 2nd rev. edn., with supplement by Colin Mason, 1963).

COOPER, JEFFREY: *The Rise of Insrumental Music and Concert Series in Paris, 1828–1871* (Ann Arbor, Mich., 1983).

DAHLHAUS, CARL: 'Zur Problematik der musikalischen Gattungen im 19. Jahrhundert', in Wulf Arlt, Ernst Lichtenhahn, and Hans Oesch (eds.), *Gattungen der Musik in Einzeldarstellungen: Gedenkschrift Leo Schrade* (Berne and Munich, 1973), 840–95.

GUT, SERGE, and PISTONE, DANIÈLE: *La Musique de chambre en France de 1870 à 1918* (Paris, 1978).

HEIDEGGER, MARTIN: *What is called thinking?*, trans. J. Glenn Gray (New York, 1968).

KOCH, HEINRICH CHRISTOPH: *Musikalisches Lexikon, welches die theoretische und praktische Tonkunst, encyclopädisch bearbeitet, alle alten und neuen Kunstwörter erklärt, und die alten und neuen Instrumente beschrieben, enthält* (Frankfurt am Main, 1802; 2nd edn., 1817, abridged, 1807, as *Kurzgefasstes Handwörterbuch der Musik für praktische Tonkünstler und für Dilettanten*).

—— *Versuch, aus der harten und weichen Tonart jeder Tonstufe der diatonisch-chromatischen Leiter vermittels des enharmonischen Tonwechsels in die Dur- und molltonart der übrigen Stufen auszuweichen* (Rudolstadt, 1812).

—— *Versuch einer Anleitung zur Composition* (Rudolstadt and Leipzig, 1782–93; repr. 1969).

KRETZSCHMAR, HERMANN: *Führer durch den Konzert-Saal* (Leipzig, 1887–90, with later editions).

MÜLLER-REUTER, THEODOR: *Lexikon der deutschen Konzertliteratur* (Leipzig, 1909, supplement, 1921; all repr. 1972).

ROLLAND, ROMAIN: *Musiciens d'aujourd'hui* (Paris, 1908); Eng. trans., Mary Blaiklock, *Musicians of To-day* (London, 1914; repr. 1969).

SALMEN, WALTER: *Zur Orgelmusik im 19. Jahrhundert* (Innsbruck, 1983).

SCRUTON, ROGER: *The Aesthetic Understanding* (London, 1983).

TARUSKIN, RICHARD: 'How the Acorn Took Root: A Tale of Russia', *19th-century Music*, 6 (1982–3), 189–212.

TOVEY, DONALD (F.): *Essays and Lectures on Music*, ed. Hubert J. Foss (London, 1949).

(*b*) *Individual Composers*

Alkan
SMITH, RONALD: *Alkan*, i. *The Enigma* (London, 1976), ii. *The Music* (1987).

Berlioz
BERLIOZ, HECTOR: *À travers chants: Études musicales, adorations, boutades et critiques* (Paris, 1862); Eng. trans. [3 books], Edwin Evans, *A Critical Study of Beethoven's Nine Symphonies* (London, 1913); *Gluck and his Operas* (London, 1913); *Mozart, Weber and Wagner, with Various Essays on Musical Subjects* (London, 1918; repr. 1969).

Borodin
ABRAHAM, GERALD: *Borodin: The Composer and his Music* (London, 1927; 2nd edn., 1935, repr.).
DIANIN, SERGEY A.: *Borodin: Zhizneopisanie, materialï i dokumentï* (Moscow, 1955; rev. 2nd edn., 1960); Eng. trans., Robert Lord, *Borodin* (London, 1963).
For further **Borodin** bibliography *see* § VI (d)

Brahms
BOZARTH, GEORGE (ed.): *Brahms Studies: Proceedings of the Washington Brahms Conference, 1983* (Oxford, 1990).
BRAHMS, JOHANNES: *Johannes Brahms Briefswechsel*, i–xvi (Berlin 1907–22).
COOKE, DERYCK *et al.*: *The New Grove Late Romantic Masters* (London, 1985) [includes Brahms].
DUNSBY, JONATHAN: *Structural Ambiguity in Brahms: Analytic Approaches to Four Works* (Ann Arbor, Mich., 1981).
FRISCH, WALTER: *Brahms and the Principle of Developing Variation* (Berkeley and Los Angeles, Calif., 1984).
GÁL, HANS: *Johannes Brahms* (Frankfurt am Main, 1961); Eng. trans., Joseph Stein, *Johannes Brahms: His Work and Personality* (London, 1963; repr. 1975).
GEIRINGER, KARL: *Brahms: Leben und Schaffen eines deutschen Meisters* (Vienna, 1935; 2nd edn., 1955); Eng. trans., H. B. Weiner and Bernard Miall, *Brahms: His Life and Work* (Boston, Mass.,1936; rev. 2nd edn., 1947).
HERTTRICH, ERNST: 'Johannes Brahms—Klaviertrio H-dur op. 8, Frühfassung und Spätfassung—ein analytischer Vergleich', in Martin Bente (ed.), *Musik, Edition, Interpretation: Gedenkschrift Günter Henle* (Munich, 1980), 218–36.
JENNER, GUSTAV: *Johannes Brahms als Mensch, Lehrer und Künstler: Studien und Erlebnisse* (Marburg, 1905; 2nd edn., 1930).
KAHL, WILLI: 'Viertes rheinisches Kammermusik im Brühler Schloss', *Zeitschriftfür Musikwissenschaft*, 7 (1924–5), 575–80.
KALBECK, MAX: *Johannes Brahms* (4 vols.; Berlin, 1904–14; reprint of latest edition of each vol. (1921, 1921, 1912–13, 1915), Tutzing, 1974).
KROSS, SIEGFRIED: 'Brahms the Symphonist', in Robert Pascall (ed.), *Brahms: Biographical, Documentary and Analytical Studies* (Cambridge, 1983), 125–45.
LITZMANN, BERTHOLD (ed.): *Clara Schumann–Johannes Brahms: Briefe aus den Jahren 1853–1896* (Leipzig, 1927; abridged Eng. trans., *Letters of Clara Schumann and Johannes Brahms, 1853–1896* (New York, 1927; 2nd edn., 1971).
McCORKLE, MARGIT L.: *Johannes Brahms: Thematisch-bibliographisches Werkverzeichnis* (Munich, 1984).
MUSGRAVE, MICHAEL: 'Brahms's First Symphony: Thematic Coherence and its Secret Origin', *Music Analysis*, 2 (1983), 117–33.
—— 'Frei aber Froh: A Reconsideration', *19th-century Music*, 3 (1979–80), 251–8.
—— *The Music of Brahms* (London, 1985).

—— (ed.): *Brahms 2: Biographical, Documentary and Analytical Studies* (Cambridge, 1987).

NIEMANN, WALTER: *Johannes Brahms* (Berlin, 1920); Eng. trans., Catherine Alison Phillips, *Brahms* (New York, 1929; repr. 1969).

PASCALL, ROBERT: 'Brahms's First Symphony Slow Movement: The Initial Performing Version', *Musical Times*, 122 (1981), 664–7.

—— 'Brahms und die Gattung der Symphonie', in Christiane Jacobsen (ed.), *Johannes Brahms: Leben und Werk* (Wiesbaden, 1983), 113–14.

—— 'Unknown Gavottes by Brahms', *Music and Letters*, 57 (1976), 404–11.

—— (ed.): *Brahms: Biographical, Documentary and Analytical Studies* (Cambridge, 1983).

RÉTI, RUDOLPH: *The Thematic Process in Music* (New York, 1951; 2nd edn., 1961).

SCHOENBERG, ARNOLD: 'Brahms the Progressive', in Dika Newlin (ed.), *Style and Idea* (New York, 1950; London, 1951), 52–101.

SPECHT, RICHARD: *Johannes Brahms: Leben und Werk eines deutschen Meisters* (Hellerau, 1928); Eng. trans., Eric Blom, *Johannes Brahms* (London, 1930).

THOMAS-SAN-GALLI, W. A.: *Johannes Brahms* (Munich, 1912; 5th edn., 1922).

WEBSTER, JAMES: 'Schubert's Sonata Form and Brahms's First Maturity', *19th-century Music*, 2 (1977–8), 18–35; 3 (1978–9), 52–71.

Bruckner

AUER, MAX: *Anton Bruckner: Sein Leben und Werk* (Vienna, 1923; 6th edn., 1967).

COOKE, DERYCK: 'The Bruckner Problem Simplified', *Musical Times*, 110 (1969), 20–2, 142–4, 362–5, 479–82, 828.

—— *et al.: The New Grove Late Romantic Masters* (London, 1985) [includes Bruckner].

DECSEY, ERNST: *Bruckner: Versuch eines Lebens* (Berlin, 1921; 3rd edn., 1930).

GÖLLERICH, AUGUST: *Anton Bruckner: Ein Lebens- und Schaffens-Bild*, i (Regensburg, 1922), ii–iv, ed. Max Auer (Regensburg, 1928–37); all repr. 1974.

GRASBERGER, RENATE: *Bruckner-Bibliographie* (Graz, 1988).

KURTH, ERNST: *Bruckner* (Berlin, 1925; repr. 1971).

NEWLIN, DIKA: *Bruckner, Mahler, Schoenberg* (New York, 1947; rev. edn., 1979).

REDLICH, HANS F.: *Bruckner and Mahler* (London, 1955; rev. edn., 1970).

SCHÖNZELER, HANS HUBERT: *Bruckner* (London, 1970).

SIMPSON, ROBERT: *The Essence of Bruckner: An Essay towards the Understanding of his Music* (London, 1967).

WATSON, DEREK: *Bruckner* (London, 1975).

Bülow

BÜLOW, HANS VON: *Hans von Bülow: Briefe und Schriften*, ed. Marie von Bülow (Leipzig, 1896–1908; i–ii, 2nd edn., 1899).

Dargomïzhsky

DARGOMÏZHSKY, A. S.: *Sobranie sochineniy dlya fortep'yano*, ed. Mikhail Samoylovich Pekelis (Moscow and Leningrad, 1954).

—— *Sochineniya dlya simfonicheskogo orkestra*, ed. Mikhail Samoylovich Pekelis (Moscow, 1967).

Dvořák

BURGHAUSER, JARMIL: *Antonín Dvořák: Thematický Katalog, bibliografie, přehled života a díla* (Prague, 1960).

CLAPHAM, JOHN: *Antonín Dvořák: Musician and Craftsman* (London, 1966).

—— *Dvořák* (Newton Abbot, 1979).

COOKE, DERYCK *et al.: The New Grove Late Romantic Masters* (London, 1985) [includes Dvořák].

DVOŘÁK, ANTONÍN, and FINCK, HENRY T.: 'Franz Schubert', *The Century Illustrated Monthly Magazine* (New York, 1894; repr. in Clapham, *Antonín Dvořák*).

FISCHL, VIKTOR (ed.): *Antonín Dvořák: His Achievement* (London, 1942).
HOŘEJŠ, ANTONÍN: *Antonín Dvořák: The Composer's Life and Work in Pictures* (Prague, 1955).
LAYTON, ROBERT: *Dvořák Symphonies and Concertos* (London, 1978).
ŠOUREK, OTAKAR: *Dvořákovy Symfonie* (Prague, 1922; 2nd edn., 1943, 3rd edn., 1948); Eng. trans., Roberta Finlayson Samsour, in *The Orchestral Works of Antonín Dvořák* (Prague, 1956; repr., n.d.).
—— *Dvořák ve vzpomínkách a dopisech* (Prague, 1938; 9th edn., 1951); Eng. trans., Roberta Finlayson Samsour, *Antonín Dvořák: Letters and Reminiscences* (Prague, 1954; repr. 1983).

Franck
DAVIES, LAURENCE: *César Franck and his Circle* (London, 1970).
D'INDY, VINCENT: *César Franck* (Paris, 1906); Eng. trans., Rosa Newmarch, *César Franck* (London, 1910; repr. 1965).

Glinka
BROWN, DAVID: *Mikhail Glinka* (London, 1974).
For further **Glinka** bibliography *see* § III (e)

Goldmark
GOLDMARK, KARL: *Erinnerungen aus meinem Leben* (Vienna and Munich, 1922; 2nd edn., 1929).

Liszt
ALTENBURG, DETLEF: 'Eine Theorie der Musik der Zukunft: Zur Funktion des Programms im symphonischen Werk von Franz Liszt', in Wolfgang Suppan (ed.), *Liszt Studien 1: Kongress-Bericht Eisenstadt 1975* (Graz, 1977), 9–25.
COLLET, ROBERT: 'Works for Piano and Orchestra', in Alan Walker (ed.), *Franz Liszt: The Man and his Music* (London, 1970; 2nd edn., 1976), 248–78.
HARASZTI, EMILE: *Franz Liszt* (Paris, 1967).
LISZT, FRANZ: 'Berlioz und seine Haroldsymphonie', *Neue Zeitschrift für Musik*, 43 (1855), 37–46.
—— *Franz Liszt's Briefe*, ed. La Mara (Leipzig, 1893–1902); Eng. trans., Constance Bache, *Letters of Franz Liszt* (London, 1894).
LONGYEAR, REY M.: 'Liszt's B minor Sonata: Precedents for a Structural Analysis', *Music Review*, 34 (1973), 198–209.
RAABE, PETER: *Franz Liszt: Leben und Schaffen* (Stuttgart, 1931; rev. 2nd edn., 1968).
SEARLE, HUMPHREY: *The Music of Liszt* (London, 1954; rev. 2nd edn., 1966).
WAGNER, RICHARD: 'Über Franz Liszts symphonische Dichtungen: Brief an M. W.' (1857), repr. in *Richard Wagner: Gesammelte Schriften und Dichtungen*, v (Leipzig, 1872), 235–55; Eng. trans., William Ashton Ellis (ed. and trans.), *Richard Wagner's Prose Works*, iii (London, 1894; repr. 1972), 235–54.
WINKLHOFER, SHARON: *Liszt's Sonata in B minor: A Study of Autograph Sources and Documents* (Ann Arbor, Mich., 1980).
For further **Liszt** bibliography *see* § VII

Mahler
BAUER-LECHNER, NATALIE: *Erinnerungen an Gustav Mahler* (Vienna and Zurich, 1923); Eng. trans., Dika Newlin, *Recollections of Gustav Mahler* (London, 1980).
BLAUKOPF, KURT: *Gustav Mahler* (Vienna, 1969); Eng. trans., Inge Goodwin, *Gustav Mahler* (London, 1973; repr. 1985).
—— with ROMAN, ZOLTAN: *Mahler: Sein Leben, sein Werk, und sein Welt in zeitgenössischen Bildern und Texten* (Vienna, 1976); Eng. trans., P. Baker *et al.*, *Mahler: A Documentary Study* (London, 1976).

COOKE, DERYCK: *Gustav Mahler: An Introduction to his Music* (London, 1980).
DE LA GRANGE, HENRI-LOUIS: *Mahler* (London, 1973–); Fr. trans., rev. (1980–).
MAHLER, GUSTAV: *Gustav Mahler: Briefe 1879–1911*, ed. Alma Maria Mahler
    (Berlin, 1924); Eng. trans., Eithne Wilkins, Ernest Kaiser, and Bill Hopkins,
    Selected Letters of Gustav Mahler, ed. Knud Martner (London, 1979).
MITCHELL, DONALD: *Gustav Mahler: The Early Years* (London, 1958; rev. edn.,
    Paul Banks and David Matthews, 1980).
—— *Gustav Mahler: The Wunderhorn Years* (London, 1975).
NEWLIN, DIKA: *Bruckner, Mahler, Schoenberg* (New York, 1947; rev. edn., 1979).
REDLICH, HANS F.: *Bruckner and Mahler* (London, 1955; rev. edn., 1970).
SPONHEUER, BERND: 'Der Durchbruch als primäre Formkategorie Gustav Mahlers:
    Eine Untersuchung zum Finalproblem der Ersten Symphonie', in Klaus
    Hinrich Stahmer (ed.), *Form und Idee in Gustav Mahlers Instrumentalmusik*
    (Wilhelmshaven, 1980), 117–64.

Puccini
CARNER, MOSCO: *Puccini: A Critical Biography* (London, 1958; rev. 2nd edn., 1974).
For further **Puccini** bibliography *see* § VI (c)

Raff
RAFF, HELENE: *Joachim Raff: Ein Lebensbild* (Regensburg, 1925).
RÖMER, MARKUS: *Joseph Joachim Raff (1822–1882)* (Wiesbaden, 1982).
SCHÄFER, A.: *Chronologisch-systematisches Verzeichnis der Werke Joachim Raffs*
    (Wiesbaden, 1888; repr. 1974).

Rimsky-Korsakov
Rimsky-Korsakov, Nikolay Andreevich: *Letopis' moey muzïkal'noy zhizni*
    (St Petersburg, 1909; enlarged 3rd edn., 1926); ed. Andrey Nikolaevich
    Rimsky-Korsakov and Aleksandr Vyacheslavovich Ossovsky, *Polnoe sobranie
    sochineniy*, i (1955); Eng. trans., Judah A. Joffe, *My Musical Life* (New York,
    1942, repr. 1974; 5th edn., 1935).
For further **Rimsky-Korsakov** bibliography *see* § VI (d) and § VII

Saint-Saëns
HERVEY, ARTHUR: *Saint-Saëns* (London and New York, 1921).
For further **Saint-Saëns** bibliography *see* § VI (b) and § VII

Schumann, Robert and Clara
CHISSELL, JOAN: *Clara Schumann: A Dedicated Spirit* (London, 1983).
LITZMANN, BERTHOLD: *Clara Schumann: Ein Künstlerleben nach Tagebüchern und
    Briefen* (Leipzig, 1902–8; all later edns. repr. 1971); abridged Eng. trans., Grace
    E. Hadow, *Clara Schumann: An Artist's Life Based on Material Found in
    Diaries and Letters* (London, 1913; repr. 1979).
REICH, NANCY B.: *Clara Schumann: The Artist and the Woman* (London, 1985).
SAMS, ERIC: 'Did Schumann use Ciphers?, *Musical Times*, 106 (1965), 584–91, 767–
    70, 949.
—— 'The Schumann Ciphers', *Musical Times*, 107 (1966), 392–400, 1050–1.
—— 'The Tonal Analogue in Schumann's Music', *Proceedings of the Royal Musical
    Association*, 96 (1969–70), 103–17.
SCHUMANN, ROBERT: *Gesammelte Schriften über Musik und Musiker*, ed. Martin
    Kreisig (4 vols., Leipzig, 1854; 4th edn., 2 vols., 1892; repr. 1968; 5th edn.
    1914); Eng. trans., Fanny Raymond Ritter, *Music and Musicians: Essays and
    Criticisms* (London, 1877–80); new selected Eng. trans., Konrad Wolff (ed.)
    and Paul Rosenfeld (trans.), *On Music and Musicians* (New York, 1947; repr.
    1982); selections Henry Pleasants (ed. and trans.), *The Musical World of Robert
    Schumann: A Selection from his own Writings* (London, 1965).
For further **Schumann** bibliography *see* § I, § II, and § IV

Smetana

JANEČEK, KAREL: *Smetanova komorni hudba: Kompozični výklad* (Prague, 1978).

LARGE, BRIAN: *Smetana* (London, 1970).

TEIGE, KAREL: *Příspěvky k životopisu a umělecké činnosti mistra Bedřicha Smetany*, i. *Skladby Smetanovy* (Prague, 1893); ii. *Dopisy Smetanovy* (1896).

For further **Smetana** bibliography *see* § VI (d) and § VII

Strauss

DEL MAR, NORMAN: *Richard Strauss: A Critical Commentary on his Life and Works* (London, 1962–72; rev. repr. 1978, repr. 1986).

SCHUH, WILLI: *Richard Strauss: Jugend und frühe Meisterjahre: Lebenschronik 1864–1898* (Zurich, 1976); Eng. trans., Mary Whittall, *Richard Strauss: A Chronicle of the Early Years, 1864–1898* (Cambridge, 1982).

For further **Strauss** bibliography *see* § VIII

Tchaikovsky

ABRAHAM, GERALD: *On Russian Music* (London, 1939; repr. 1982).

—— *Studies in Russian Music* (London, 1935; rev. 2nd edn., 1969, repr., 1976).

—— (ed.): *Tchaikovsky: A Symposium* (London, 1945; repr., 1979).

BROWN, DAVID: *Tchaikovsky: A Biographical and Critical Study*, i. *The Early Years (1840–1874)* (London, 1978); ii. *The Crisis Years (1874–1878)* (London, 1982); iii. *The Years of Wandering (1878–1885)* (London, 1986).

NIKOLAEVA, N. S.: *Simfonii P. I. Chaykovskogo* (Moscow, 1958).

TCHAIKOVSKY, PYOTR IL'ICH: *Letters to his Family: An Autobiography*, trans. Galina von Meck, with additional annotations by Percy M. Young (New York, 1981).

WARRACK, JOHN: *Tchaikovsky* (London, 1973).

—— *Tchaikovsky Symphonies and Concertos* (London, 1969).

WEINSTOCK, HERBERT: *Tchaikovsky* (New York, 1946; repr. 1980).

For further **Tchaikovsky** bibliography *see* § VI (d)

Wagner

WESTERNHAGEN, CURT VON: *Wagner* (Zurich, 1968); Eng. trans., Mary Whittall, *Wagner: A Biography* (Cambridge, 1978).

For further **Wagner** bibliography *see* § V

Wolf

WALKER, FRANK: *Hugo Wolf: A Biography* (London, 1951; enlarged 2nd edn., 1968).

For further **Wolf** bibliography *see* § IX (a)

Widor

THOMPSON, ANDREW: *The Life and Times of Charles-Marie Widor* (Oxford, 1987).

CHAPTER IX

SOLO SONG

(a) GERMANY

(i) Modern Editions

(a) Anthologies

MOSER, HANS-JOACHIM: *Das deutsche Sololied und die Ballade* (Das Musikwerke, 14; Cologne, 1957); Eng. trans., *The German Solo Song and Ballad* (Anthology of Music, 14; Cologne, 1958) [includes works by Brahms, Cornelius, Franz, Mendelssohn, Schumann, and Wolf].

REIMANN, HEINRICH: *Das deutsche Lied: Eine Auswahl aus den Programmen der historischen Lieder-Abends der Frau Amalie Joachim* (Berlin, 1892–3) [includes works by Bernardt Klein, Spohr, and other early 19th-century *Lieder* composers].

STEPHENSON, KURT: *Romantik in der Tonkunst* (Das Musikwerk, 21; Cologne, 1961); Eng. trans., Robert Kolben, *Romanticism in Music* (Anthology of Music, 21; Cologne, 1961) [includes works by Franz, Jensen, Schumann, and Wagner].

THYM, JURGEN: *100 Years of Eichendorf Songs* (Recent Researches in the Music of the Nineteenth and Early Twentieth Centuries, ed. Rufus Hallmark, 5; Madison, Wis., 1983).

(b) Works by Individual Composers

BRAHMS, J.: *Johannes Brahms: Sämtliche Werke* (Leipzig, 1926–7; repr. 1964–5 and 1971): 23–6 *Lieder und Gesänge für eine Singstimme mit Klavierbegleitung*, ed. Eusebius Mandyczewski.

—— *Deutsche Volkslieder*, ed. Franz Kretschmer and Anton Wilhelm von Zuccalmaglio (Berlin, 1840).

—— *Lieder* (Leipzig: Peters).

—— *Neue Volkslieder von Johannes Brames*, ed. Max Friedlaender (Berlin, 1926).

—— *Folk Songs for Women's Voices*, ed. Vernon Gotwals and Philip Keppler (Smith College Music Archives, 15; Northampton, Mass., 1968).

—— *Volksliedbearbeitungen für Frauenchor*, ed. Siegmund Helms (The Nineteenth Century, No. 19302; Kassel, 1970).

CORNELIUS, P.: *Peter Cornelius: Musikalisches Werke*, ed. Max Hasse (Leipzig, 1905–6; repr. 1971): 2 *Merhstimmige Lieder und Gesänge, Duette, Mannerchor, Gemischte Chore*.

—— *Weihnachtslieder und Trauer und Trost*, ed. Gerhard von Westerman (Musikalische Stundenbücher; Munich, 1921).

—— *Weinachtslieder* (The Nineteenth Century, No. 19304; Kassel, 1970).

FRANZ, R.: *Fifty Songs of Robert Franz*, ed. William Apthorp (Boston, Mass., 1900).

LISZT, F.: *Franz Liszts Musikalische Werke*, ed. Franz Liszt Stiftung (Leipzig, 1907–36; repr. 1966): part 7 *Einstimmige Lieder und Gesänge*.

—— *Liszt Society Publications* (London, 1950–): 6 *Selected Songs* (1975).

—— *Neue Ausgabe sämtlicher Werke/New Edition of the Complete Works* (Kassel and Budapest, 1970–): 8 *Lieder, Songs, Choral Works* [with piano, 5 vols.], 9 *Vocal Works with Orchestra* [12 vols.] (forthcoming).

LOEWE, C.: *Carl Loewes Werke: Gesamtausgabe der Balladen, Legenden, Lieder und Gesänge*, ed. Max Runze (Leipzig, 1894–1904; repr. 1970).

MAHLER, G.: *Gustav Mahler: Sämtlicher Werke, Kritische Gesamtausgabe*, ed. Internationale Gustav-Mahler-Gesellschaft (Vienna, 1960–): 9 *Das Lied von der Erde* (1964).

MENDELSSOHN, F.: *Felix Mendelssohn Bartholdy's Werke: Kritisch durchgesehene Ausgabe*, ed. Julius Rietz (Leipzig, 1874–7; repr. 1967–9): 19 *Lieder und Gesänge für eine Singstimme mit Begleitung des Pianoforte*.

SCHUMANN, R.: *Robert Schumann's Werke*, ed. Clara Schumann (Leipzig, 1881–93; repr. 1967–8): series 13 *Für eine Singstimme mit Begleitung des Pianoforte* (1882–95).

—— *Frauen-Liebe und -Leben*, Musikalischer Stundenbücher (Munich, 1921) [with foreword by Walter Courvoisier].

SPOHR, L.: *Selected Works by Louis Spohr (1784–1859)*, ed. Clive Brown (New York, 1987–): 8 *The Complete Lieder Sets*.

—— *Sechs deutsche Lieder für eine Singstimme, Klarinette und Klavier*, ed. Friedrich Leinert (The Nineteenth Century, No. 19306; Kassel, 1971).

STRAUSS, R.: *Richard Strauss: Lieder, Gesamtausgabe/Complete Editions*, ed. Franz

Trenner (London, 1964–5): 1–3 *Lieder für eine Singstimme und Klavier* (1964); 4 *Lieder für eine Singstimme und Orchester* (1965).

WAGNER, R.: *Richard Wagners Werke: Musikdramen—Jugendopern—musikalische Werke*, ed. Michael Balling (Leipzig, 1912–29; repr. 1971): 15 *Lieder und Gesänge*.

—— *Richard Wagner: Sämtliche Werke*, ed. Carl Dahlhaus (Mainz, 1970–): 17 *Klavierlieder*, ed. Egon Voss (1976).

—— *Zehn Lieder aus den Jahren 1838–1858*, ed. Wolfgang Golther (Musikalische Stundenbücher; Munich *c*.1920).

WOLF, H.: *Hugo Wolf: Sämtliche Werke*, ed. Internationale Hugo Wolf-Gesellschaft/Hans Jancik (Vienna, 1960–): 1–9 [*Lieder*] (1963–).

—— *Hugo Wolf: Nachgelassene Werke*, ed. Robert Haas and Helmut Schultz (Leipzig and Vienna, 1936): 1 *Lieder mit Klavierbegleitung*; 2/1 *Zwei Orchesterlieder aus dem Spanischen Liederbuch*.

—— *Hugo Wolf: Lieder aus des Jugendzeit*, ed. F. Foll (Leipzig, 1903).

(ii) Books and Articles

(a) General

BÜCKEN, ERNST: *Das deutsche Lied: Probleme und Gestalten* (Hamburg, 1939).

DALTON, DAVID: 'Goethe and the Composers of his Time', *Music Review*, 34 (1973), 157–74.

GRASBERGER, FRANZ: *Das Lied, Kostbarkeiten der Musik* (Tutzing, 1968).

JOLIZZA, W. K. VON: *Das Lied und seine Geschichte* (Leipzig and Vienna, 1910).

KRAVITT, EDWARDS F.: 'The Lied in 19th-century Concert Life', *Journal of the American Musicological Society*, 17 (1965), 207–18.

KRETZSCHMAR, HERMANN: 'Das deutsche Lied seit dem Tode Richard Wagners', *Jahrbuch der Musikbibliothek Peters*, 4 (Leipzig, 1897), 45–60.

—— *Geschichte des neuen deutschen Liedes* (Leipzig, 1911; repr. 1966).

MOSER, HANS JOACHIM: *Das deutsche Lied seit Mozart* (Berlin and Zurich, 1937; rev. 2nd edn., 1968).

MÜLLER, GÜNTHER: *Geschichte des deutschen Liedes vom Zeitalter des Barocks bis zur Gegenwart* (Munich, 1925; repr. 1959).

PAMER, FRITZ EGON: 'Deutches Lied im 19. Jahrhundert', in Guido Adler (ed.), *Handbuch des Musikgeschichte* (2nd edn., Berlin, 1930; repr. 1961), ii. 939–55.

RADCLIFFE, PHILIP: 'Germany and Austria', in Denis Stevens (ed.), *A History of Song* (London, 1960; repr. 1971), 228–64.

RAUHE, HERMANN: 'Zum volkstümlichen Lied des 19. Jahrhunderts', in Carl Dahlhaus (ed.), *Studien zur Trivialmusik des 19. Jahrhunderts* (Regensburg, 1967), 159–98.

RIEMANN, HUGO: *Musik-Lexikon* (Leipzig, 1882; 8th edn., 1916; 9th–11th edn., ed. Alfred Einstein, 1919–29; 12th edn., ed. Wilibald Gurlitt, Carl Dahlhaus, and Hans Heinrich Eggebrecht, 1959–67; Eng. trans., J. S. Shedlock, *Dictionary of Music* (London, 1897; repr. 1972).

ROSENWALD, HANS HERMANN: *Geschichte des deutschen Liedes zwischen Schubert und Schumann* (Berlin, 1930).

SEATON, DOUGLAS: *The Art Song: A Research and Information Guide* (New York, 1987).

SMEED J. W.: *German Song and its Poetry, 1740–1900* (London 1987).

STEIN, JACK M.: *Poem and Music in the German Lied from Gluck to Hugo Wolf* (Cambridge, Mass., 1971).

WIORA, WALTER: *Das deutsche Lied: Zur Geschichte und Ästhetik einer muikalischen Gattung* (Wolfenbüttel and Zurich, 1971).

(b) Individual Composers

Brahms

FOX STRANGWAYS, A. H.: 'Brahms and Tieck's "Magelone" ', *Music and Letters*, 21 (1940), 211–29.

FRIEDLAENDER, MAX: *Brahms' Lieder: Einführung in seine Gesänge für 1 und 2 Stimmen* (Berlin, 1922); Eng. trans., C. Leonard Leese, *Brahms's Lieder: An Introduction to the Songs for One and Two Voices* (London, 1928).

—— 'Brahms' Volkslieder', *Jahrbuch der Musikbibliothek Peters*, 9 (Leipzig, 1902), 67–88.

JACOBSEN, CHRISTIANE: *Das Verhältnis von Sprache und Musik in ausgewählten Liedern von Johannes Brahms* (Hamburg, 1975).

MAY, FLORENCE: *The Life of Johannes Brahms* (London, 1905; rev. 2nd edn., 1948).

MIES, PAUL: *Stilmomente und Ausdrucksstilformen im Brahmsschen Lied* (Leipzig, 1923).

NIEMANN, WALTER: *Johannes Brahms* (Berlin, 1920); Eng. trans., Catherine Alison Phillips, *Brahms* (New York, 1920; repr. 1969).

OPHÜLS, GUSTAV: *Brahms-Texte: Vollständige Sammlung der von J. Brahms componirten und musikalisch bearbeiteten Dichtungen* (Bonn, 1898; 2nd edn., 1908).

PASCALL, ROBERT (ed.): *Brahms: Biographical, Documentary and Analytical Studies* (Cambridge, 1983).

SAMS, ERIC: *Brahms Songs* (London, 1972).

For further **Brahms** bibliography *see* § VIII

Cornelius

FEDERHOFER, HELLMUT, and OEHL, KURT (eds.): *Peter Cornelius als Komponist, Dichter, Kritiker und Essayist* (Rebensburg, 1977).

WAGNER, GUNTHER: *Peter Cornelius: Verzeichnis musikalischen und literarische Werken* (Tutzing, 1986).

Franz

BOONIN, JOSEPH M.: *An Index to the Solo Songs of Robert Franz* (Hackensack, NJ, 1970).

BRENDEL, FRANZ: *Neue Zeitschrift für Musik*, 47 (1857).

LISZT, FRANZ: *Robert Franz* (Leipzig, 1872).

PORTER, ERNEST G.: 'Robert Franz on Song', *Music Review*, 26 (1965), 15–18.

—— 'The Songs of Robert Franz', *Musical Times*, 104 (1963), 477–9.

WALDMANN, WILHELM (ed.): *Robert Franz: Gespräche aus zehn Jahren* (Leipzig, 1895).

Jensen

BASER, F.: 'Der Nachlass des Liedmeister A. Jensen', *Musica*, 7 (1953), 581–2.

NIGGLI, ARNOLD: *Adolf Jensen* (Zurich, 1895).

Liszt

COOPER, MARTIN: 'Liszt as a Song Writer', *Music and Letters*, 19 (1938), 171–81.

HEADINGTON, CHRISTOPHER: 'The Songs', in Alan Walker (ed.), *Franz Liszt: The Man and his Music* (London, 1970; 2nd edn., 1976), 221–47.

KITTEL, CARL: 'Über das "Gesangliche" in Franz Liszts Vokal-Kompositionen', *Die Musik* (October 1936).

RAABE, PETER: *Franz Liszt: Leben und Schaffen* (Stuttgart, 1931; rev. 2nd edn., 1968).

REUSS, E.: *Liszts Lieder* (Leipzig, 1906; also pub. in *Bayreuther Blätter*, nos. 7–12, 1906).

For further **Liszt** bibliography *see* § VII

Loewe

BROWN, MAURICE J. E.: 'Carl Loewe, 1796–1869', *Musical Times*, 110 (1969), 357–9.

ELSON, JAMES: 'Carl Loewe and the Nineteenth Century German Ballad', *National Association of Teachers of Singing Bulletin*, 28 (1971), 16–19.

ENGEL, HANS: *Karl Loewe: Überblick und Würdigung seines Schaffens* (Greifswald, 1934).

KLEEMAN, HANS: *Beiträge zur Ästhetik und Geschichte der Loeweschen Ballade* (Halle, 1913).

Schumann

COOPER, MARTIN: 'The Songs', in Gerald Abraham (ed.), *Schumann: A Symposium* (London, 1952), pp. 98–137.

DUVAL, RAYMOND: ' "L'Amour du poète" de Schumann-Heine', *Rivista musicale italiana*, 8 (1901), 656–73.

FELBER, RUDOLF: 'Schumann's Place in German Song', *Musical Quarterly*, 26 (1940), 340–54.

FELDMANN, FRITZ: 'Zur Frage des "Liederjahres" bei Robert Schumann', *Archiv für Musikwissenschaft*, 9 (1952), 246–69.

HALLMARK, RUFUS E.: *The Genesis of Schumann's 'Dichterliebe': A Source Study* (Ann Arbor, Mich., 1979).

LITZMANN, BERTHOLD: *Clara Schumann: Ein Künstlerleben*, i (Leipzig, 1902; 8th edn., 1925, repr. 1971); ii (Leipzig, 1905; 7th edn., 1925, repr. 1971); iii (Leipzig, 1908; 6th edn., 1923, repr. 1971); Eng. trans., Grace E. Hadow, *Clara Schumann: An Artist's Life Based on Material Found in Diaries and Letters* (London, 1913; repr. 1979).

SAMS, ERIC: 'Did Schumann use Ciphers?', *Musical Times*, 106 (1965), 584–91, 767–70, 949, and 107 (1966), 392–400, 1050–1.

—— *The Songs of Robert Schumann* (London, 1969; rev. 2nd edn., 1975).

SCHUH, WILLI: *Goethe-Vertonungen: Ein Verzeichnis* (Zurich, 1952; enlarged 2nd edn. in Ernst Beutler (ed.), *Goethe: Gedenkausgabe der Werke, Briefe und Gespräche* (1953), ii. 665–760).

SCHUMANN, ROBERT: *Jugendbriefe von Robert Schumann*, ed. Clara Schumann (Leipzig, 1885; 4th edn., 1910); Eng. trans., May Herbert, *Early Letters* (London, 1888).

—— *Robert Schumanns Briefe: Neue Folge*, ed. F. Gustav Jensen (Leipzig, 1886; 2nd edn., 1904); Eng. trans., May Herbert, *The Life of Robert Schumann Told in his Letters* (London, 1890).

WÖRNER, KARL H.: *Robert Schumann* (Zurich, 1949).

For further **Schumann** bibliography *see* § I, § II, and § IV

Strauss

DEL MAR, NORMAN: *Richard Strauss: A Critical Commentary on his Life and Works* (London, 1962–72; rev. repr. 1978, repr. 1986), iii. 246–404.

JEFFERSON, ALAN: *The Lieder of Richard Strauss* (London, 1971).

PETERSON, BARBARA A.: *Ton und Wort: The Lieder of Richard Strauss* (Ann Arbor, Mich., 1980).

For further **Strauss** bibliography *see* § VII

Wagner

NEWMAN, ERNEST: *Wagner as Man and Artist* (London, 1914; rev. 2nd edn., 1924, repr. 1969).

For further **Wagner** bibliography *see* § V

Wolf

BIERI, GEORG: *Die Lieder von Hugo Wolf* (Berne, 1935).

CARNER, MOSCO: *Hugo Wolf Songs* (London, 1982).

COOKE, DERYCK, *et al.*: *The New Grove Late Romantic Masters* (London, 1985) [includes Wolf].

EGGER, RITA: *Die Deklamationsrhythmik Hugo Wolfs in historischer Sicht* (Vienna, 1963).

LEGGE, WALTER: 'Hugo Wolf's Afterthoughts on his Mörike Lieder', *Music Review*, 2 (1941), 211-14.

MACKWORTH-YOUNG, G.: 'Goethe's "Prometheus" and its Settings by Schubert and Wolf', *Proceedings of the Royal Musical Association*, 78 (1951-2), 53-65.

MARE, MARGARET: *Eduard Mörike: The Man and the Poet* (London, 1957).

NEWMAN, ERNEST: *Hugo Wolf* (London, 1907; repr. 1966).

PLEASANTS, HENRY (ed. and trans.): *The Music Criticism of Hugo Wolf* (New York, 1978) [articles for *Wiener Salonblatt*, 1884-7].

SAMS, ERIC: *The Songs of Hugo Wolf* (London, 1961; 2nd edn., 1983).

STEIN, JACK M.: 'Poem and Music in Hugo Wolf's Mörike Songs', *Musical Quarterly*, 53 (1967), 22-38.

TAUSCHE, ANTON: *Hugo Wolfs Mörike-Lieder in Dichtung, Musik, Vortrag* (Vienna, 1947).

WALKER, FRANK: *Hugo Walker: A Biography* (London, 1951; 2nd edn., 1968).

Gesammelte Aufsatze über Hugo Wolf (Berlin, 1898-1900).

(b) FRANCE

(i) Modern Editions

(a) Anthologies

NOSKE, FRITS: *Das ausserdeutsche Sololied 1500-1900* (Das Musikwerk, 16; Cologne, 1958); Eng. trans., *The Solo Song outside German-speaking Countries* (Anthology of Music, 16; Cologne, 1958) [includes works by David, Debussy, Fauré, Gounod, and Saint-Saëns].

TUNLEY, DAVID: *Le Bel Age: 10 Romantic French Songs* (London, 1985) [includes songs by Berlioz, Reyer, Reber, Massé, Lalo, Saint-Säens, Gounod, Massenet, Bizet, de Castillon].

(b) Works by Individual Composers

BERLIOZ, H.: *New Edition of the Complete Works*, ed. Hugh Macdonald *et al.* (Kassel, 1967-); 13 *Songs for Solo Voice and Orchestra*, ed. Ian Kemp (1975); 15 *Songs for One, Two, or Three Voices and Piano*, ed. Ian Kemp (forthcoming).

—— *Hector Berlioz: Werke*, ed. Charles Malherbe and Felix Malherbe (Leipzig, 1900-10; repr. 1971): series 6 *Gesänge mit Orchesterbegleitung*: 15 *Für eine oder zwei Singstimmen*; series 7 *Gesänge mit Klavier*: 17 *Für eine Singstimme*.

—— *Ausgewählte Lieder*, ed. Karl Blessinger (Musikalische Stundenbücher; Munich, 1920).

DEBUSSY, C.: *Œuvres complètes de Claude Debussy* (Paris, 1985): series 2 *Songs* (forthcoming).

DUPARC, H.: *Cinq mélodies* (Paris, 1869) [Op. 2].

—— *Recueil de mélodies* (Paris, 1894).

—— *Nouvelle édition complète* (Paris, 1911).

(ii) Books and Articles

(*a*) *General*

BERNAC, PIERRE: *The Interpretation of French Song* (London, 1970).

COOPER, MARTIN: *French Music from the Death of Berlioz to the Death of Fauré* (London, 1951; repr. 1984).

COX, DAVID: 'France', in Denis Stevens (ed.), *A History of Song* (London, 1960; repr. 1971), 194–227.

HALL, J.: *The Art Song* (Norman, Okla, 1953).

LOCKSPEISER, EDWARD: 'The French Songs in the 19th Century', *Musical Quarterly*, 26 (1940), 192–9.

MEISTER, BARBARA: *Nineteeth-century French Song: Fauré, Chausson, Duparc and Debussy* (Bloomington, Indiana, 1980).

NOSKE, FRITS: *La Mélodie française de Berlioz à Duparc: Essai de critique historique* (Paris and Amsterdam, 1954); Eng. trans., rev., Rita Benton, *French Song from Berlioz to Duparc: The Origin and Development of the Mélodie* (New York, 1970).

REUTER, EVELYN: *La Mélodie et le Lied* (Paris, 1950).

(*b*) *Individual Composers*

Berlioz

DICKINSON, A. E. F.: 'Berlioz's Songs', *Musical Quarterly*, 55 (1969), 329–43.

WARRACK, JOHN: 'Berlioz's Mélodies', *Musical Times*, 105 (1969), 252–4.

For further **Berlioz** bibliography *see* § I

Bizet

DEAN, WINTON: *Georges Bizet: His Life and Work* (London, 1948; enlarged 3rd edn., 1975).

For further **Bizet** bibliography *see* § VI (*b*)

Debussy

HARDECK, ERWIN: *Untersuchungen zu den Klavierliedern Claude Debussys* (Regensburg, 1967).

Duparc

MORTHCOTE, S.: *The Songs of Henri Duparc* (London, 1949).

Fauré

LOCKSPEISER, EDWARD: 'Fauré and the Song', *Monthly Musical Record*, 75 (1945), 79–84.

ORREY, LESLIE: 'The Songs of Gabriel Fauré', *Music Review*, 6 (1945), 72–84.

Massenet

D'UDINE, J.: *L'Art du Lied et les mélodies de Massenet* (Paris, 1931).

(c) RUSSIA

(i) Modern Editions

(*a*) *Anthologies*

Albums of Russian Songs for Soprano (London, 1917–21) [includes songs by Borodin, Cui, Dargomïzhsky, Glinka, Rimsky-Korsakov, and others].

Albums of Russian Songs for Bass or Baritone (London, 1917–21) [includes songs by Balakirev, Tchaikovsky, and others].

ZHAROV, V. (ed.): *Romansï russkikh kompozitorov* (Moscow, 1979) [includes songs by Borodin, Cui, Dargomïzhsky, Glinka, Gurilyov, Rimsky-Korsakov, Rubinstein, Tchaikovsky, Varlamov, and others].

(b) Works by Individual Composers

BALAKIREV, M.: *Romansï i pesni* ed. R. Rustamov (Moscow, 1968–79).
—— *Russkie narodnïe pesni*, ed. Evgeny Vladimirovich Gippius (Moscow, 1957).
BORODIN, A.: *Romansï i pesni*, ed. Pavel Aleksandrovich Lamm (Moscow, 1967; new edn., ed. M. Gorodetskaya, Moscow, 1985).
DARGOMÏZHSKY, A. S.: *Polnoe sobranie romansov i pesen*, ed. Mikhail Samoylovich Pekelis (Moscow and Leningrad, 1947; rev. edn., ed. E. Stempneveskaya, 1970–1).
GLINKA, M. I.: *Polnoe sobranie sochineniy*, ed. Vissarion Yakovlevich Shebalin and others (Moscow, 1955-69): 10 [songs for voice and piano]; 11 [vocalises].
MUSSORGSKY, M. P.: *Modest Petrovich Musorgskiy: Polnoe sobranie sochineniy*, ed. Pavel Aleksandrovich Lamm and Boris Vladimirovich Asaf'ev (Moscow, 1928–34; repr. 1969); 9–15 [songs]; 20 [folk-songs].
—— *Izbrannïe romansï i pesni*, ed. R. N. Kotlyarevsky and G. V. Krasnov (Leningrad, 1979) [includes most of the songs].
—— song cycles *Nursery, Without Sun, Songs and Dances of Death* (New York, 1951) [Russian/English versions].
RIMSKY-KORSAKOV, N.: *Nikolay Rimskiy-Korsakov: Polnoe sobranie sochineniy*, ed. Andrey Nikolaevich Rimsky-Korsakov *et al.* (Moscow, 1946–70): 45 [complete collection of songs, voice and piano]; 47 [Russian folk-songs, voice and piano].
RUBINSTEIN, A.: *Izbrannïe romansï*, ed. R. Rustamov (Moscow, 1979).
TCHAIKOVSKY, P. I.: *Pyotr Il'ich Chaykovskiy: Polnoe sobranie sochineniy* (Moscow and Leningrad, 1940–71): 44–55 [Songs]; 27 [vocal works with orchestra]; 66 [Russian folk-songs, voice and piano].
VERSTOVSKY, A.: *Izbrannïe romansï i pesni*, ed. M. Gorodetskaya (Moscow, 1980).

(ii) Books and Articles

(a) General

ABRAHAM, GERALD: 'Russia', in Denis Stevens (ed.), *A History of Song* (London, 1960; repr. 1971), 338–75; repr. as 'Russian Song' in *Essays on Russian and East European Music* (Oxford, 1985), 1–39.
SEAMAN, GERALD R.: *History of Russian Music from its Origins to Dargomyzhsky*, i (Oxford, 1967).
TARUSKIN, RICHARD: *Opera and Drama in Russia as Preached and Practiced in the 1860s* (Ann Arbor, Mich., 1981).
VASINA-GROSSMAN, VERA ANDREEVNA: *Russkiy klassicheskiy romans XIX veka* (Moscow, 1956).

(b) Individual Composers

Balakirev
GARDEN, EDWARD: 'Songs', in *Balakirev: A Critical Study of his Life and Music* (London, 1967), 270–90.
VIKHANSKAYA, ANNA: 'Romansï i pesni', in Yuly Anatol'evich Kremlyov and others (ed.), *Miliy Alekseevich Balakirev: Issledovaniya i stat'i* (Leningrad, 1961), 271–340.

Borodin
ABRAHAM, GERALD: 'Borodin's Songs', in *On Russian Music* (London, 1939), 169–78.

DIANIN, SERGEY A.: *Borodin: Zhizneopisanie, materialï i dokumentï* (Moscow, 1955;
    rev. 2nd edn., 1960); Eng. trans., Robert Lord, *Borodin* (London, 1963).
For further **Borodin** bibliography *see* § VI (d)

Dargomïzhsky
DARGOMÏZHSKY, ALEKSANDR: *Aleksandr Sergeevich Dargomïzhskiy (1813–1869):*
    Avtobiografiya, pis'ma, vospominaniya sovremennikov, ed. Nikolay Fyodorovich
    Findeisen (Peterburg, 1921).
PEKELIS, MIKHAIL SAMOYLOVICH: *A. S. Dargomïzhskiy i ego okruzhenie* (Moscow,
    1966–83).
SEROV, ALEKSANDR NIKOLAEVICH: *A. N. Serov: Izbrannïe stat'i*, ed. Georgy N.
    Khubov (Moscow and Leningrad, 1950–7).

Glinka
BROWN, DAVID: *Mikhail Glinka: A Biographical and Critical Study* (London, 1974).
For further **Glinka** bibliography *see* § VI (d)

Mussorgsky
BASMAJIAN, NANCY: 'The Romances', in Malcolm Hamrick Brown (ed.), *Musorgsky
    in Memoriam, 1881–1981* (Ann Arbor, Mich., 1982), 29–56.
CALVOCORESSI, M. D.: *Modest Mussorgsky: His Life and Works* (London, 1956;
    repr. 1967).
—— and ABRAHAM, GERALD: *Mussorgsky* (London, 1946; rev. edn., 1974).
DURANDINA, E. E.: *Vokal'noe tvorchestvo Musorgskogo* (Moscow, 1985).
GORDEEVA, E. (ed.): *M. P. Musorgskiy: Pis'ma* (Moscow, 1981).
HOOPS, RICHARD: 'Musorgsky and the Populist Age', in Malcolm Hamrick Brown
    (ed.), *Musorgsky in Memoriam, 1881–1981* (Ann Arbor, Mich., 1982), 271–306.
TARUSKIN, RICHARD: ' "Little Star": An Etude in the Folk Style', in Malcolm
    Hamrick Brown (ed.), *Musorgsky in Memoriam, 1881–1981* (Ann Arbor, Mich.,
    1982), 57–84.
WALKER, JAMES: 'Musorgsky's "Sunless" Cycle in Russian Criticism: Focus of
    Controversy', *Musical Quarterly*, 67 (1981), 382–91.
For further **Mussorgsky** bibliography *see* § VI (d)

Rimsky-Korsakov
ABRAHAM, GERALD: 'Rimsky-Korsakov's Songs', in *Slavonic and Romantic Music*
    (London, 1968), 202–11.
RIMSKY-KORSAKOV, NIKOLAY ANDREEVICH: *Letopis' moey muzïkal'noy zhizni*
    (St Petersburg, 1909; enlarged 3rd edn., 1926); ed. Andrey Nikolaevich
    Rimsky-Korsakov and Aleksandr Vyacheslavovich Ossovsky, in *Polnoe sobranie
    sochineniy*, i (1955); Eng. trans., Judah A. Joffe, *My Musical Life* (New York,
    1942, repr. 1974).
For further **Rimsky-Korsakov** bibliography *see* § VI (d) and § VII

Rubinstein
BARENBOYM, LEV ARONOVICH: *Anton Grigor'evich Rubinshteyn* (Leningrad, 1957–
    62).

Tchaikovsky
ALSHVANG, A.: 'The Songs', in Gerald Abraham (ed.), *Tchaikovsky: A Symposium*
    (London, 1945; repr. 1979), 197–229.
ORLOVA E.: *Romansï Chaykovskogo* (Moscow and Leningrad, 1948).
For further **Tchaikovsky** bibliography *see* § VI (d) and § VIII

(d) POLAND

(i) Modern Editions

Works by Individual Composers

CHOPIN, F. F.: *Friedrich Chopin's Werke*, ed. Woldemar Bargiel, Johannes Brahms, August Franchomme, Franz Liszt, Carl Reinecke, and Ernst Rudorff (Leipzig, 1878–1902): 14 *Lieder für eine Singstimme*.
—— *Fryderyk Chopin: Dzieła wszystkie/Complete Works*, ed. Ignacy Jan Paderewski, with Józef Turczyński and Ludwik Bronarski (Warsaw and Kraków, 1949–61): 17 *Songs for Solo Voice with Piano Accompaniment* (1959).
GALL, J.: *Pieśni wybrane* (Kraków, 1957): *Zeszyt* 1, ed. Stanisław Lachowicz (Kraków, 1957).
KARŁOWICZ, M.: *Pieśni zebrane*, ed. Jerzy Młodziejowski (Kraków, 1953).
MONIUSZKO, S.: *Stanisław Moniuszko: Dzieła/Werke*, ed. Witold Rudziński (Kraków, 1965): series A *Lieder* (1965–70).
PADEREWSKI, I. J.: *Sześć pieśni do słów Adama Mickiewicza*, op. 18 (Kraków).
—— *Vier Lieder*, Op. 7, No. 1 (Berlin, 1888).
PANKIEWICZ, E.: *Pieśni wybrane*, ed. Włodzimierz Poźniak (Kraków, 1957).
ŻELEŃSKI, W.: *Pieśni wybrane* (Kraków, 1958): *Zeszyt* 1 (1958).

(ii) Books and Articles

(a) General

ABRAHAM, GERALD: 'Poland', in Denis Stevens (ed.), *A History of Song* (London, 1960; repr. 1971), 323–37.
BARBAG, SEWERYN: 'Polska pieśń artystyczna', in Mateusz Gliński (ed.), *Muzyka polska* (Warsaw, 1927), 91–107.
DZIĘBOWSKA, ELŻBIETA: 'O polskiej szkole narodowej', *Szkice o kulturze muzycznej XIX wieku*, ed. Zofia Chechlińska (Warsaw, 1971), 20–6.
GABRYŚ, JERZY, and CYBULSKA, JANINA: *Z dziejów polskiej pieśni solowej* (Kraków, 1960).
JACHIMECKI, ZDZISŁAW: 'Muzyka polska od roku 1796 do roku 1930', *Polska, Jej dzieje i kultura od czasów najdawniejszych do chwili obecnej*, ed. Stanisław Lam, 3 (Warsaw, 1937).
MATRACKA-KOŚCIELNA, ALICJA: 'Twórzcość pieśniarska warszawskiego środowiska kompozytorskiego w drugiej połowie XIX wieku', *Kultura muzyczna Warszawy drugiej połowy XIX wieku*, ed. Andrzej Spóz (Warsaw, 1980), 202–16.
SIMON, ALICJA: *The Polish Songwriters* (Warsaw, 1936).

(b) Individial Composers

Chopin
BARBAG, SEWERYN: *Studium o pieśniach Chopina* (Lwów, 1927).
JACOBSON, BERNARD: 'The Songs', in Alan Walker (ed.), *Frederic Chopin: Profiles of the Man and the Musician* (London, 1966), 187–211.
PRISILAUER, RICHARD: 'Frédéric Chopins "Polnische Lieder" ', *Chopin-Jahrbuch*, ii (1963), 117–32.
STOOKES, SACHA: 'Chopin, the Song-writer', *Monthly Musical Record*, 53 (1950), 96–9.
For further **Chopin** bibliography *see* § IV

Karłowicz
ANDERS, HENRYK (ed.): *Karłowicz w listach i wspomnieniach* (Kraków, 1960).

—— 'Pieśni solowe Mieczysława Karłowicza', *Studia muzykologiczne*, 4 (1955), 292–415.

CHMARA-ŻACZKIEWICZ, BARBARA, SPÓZ, ANDRZEJ, and MICHAŁOWSKI, KORNEL: *Mieczysław Karłowicz: katalog tematyczny dzieł i bibliografia* (Kraków, 1986).

CHYBIŃSKI, ADOLF: *Mieczysław Karłowicz: Kronika życia artysty i taternika* (Kraków, 1949).

DZIĘBOWSKA, ELŻBIETA (ed.): *Z życia i twórczości Mieczysława Karłowicza* (Kraków, 1970).

KĘCKI, FELIKS: *Mieczysław Karłowicz: Szkic monograficzny* (Warsaw, 1934).

POLONY, LESZEK: *Poetyka muzyczna Mieczysława Karłowicza: program literacki, ekspresja i symbol w poemacie symfonicznym* (Kraków, 1986).

Moniuszko

JACHIMECKI, ZDZISŁAW: *Moniuszko* (Kraków, 1921; 2nd edn., 1983).

MAZUR, KRZYSZTOF: *Pierwodruki Stanisława Moniuszki* (Warsaw, 1970).

NOWACZYK, ERWIN: *Pieśni solowe S. Moniuszki* (Kraków, 1954).

RUDZIŃSKI, WITOLD: *Moniuszko* (Kraków, 1971).

—— *Stanisław Moniuszko: studia i materiały* (Kraków, 1955-61).

—— and PROSNAK, JAN: *Almanach moniuszkowski* (Kraków, 1952).

—— and STOKOWSKA, MAGDALENA: *Stanisław Moniuszko: listy zebrane* (Kraków, 1969).

Noskowski

SUTKOWSKI, ADAM: *Zygmunt Noskowski* (Kraków, 1957).

Pankiewicz

POŹNIAK, WŁODIMIERZ: *Eugeniusz Pankiewicz* (Kraków, 1958).

Szymanowska

IWANEJKO, MARIA: *Maria Szymanowska* (Kraków, 1959).

MIRSKI, JÓZEF: 'Zapomniana artystka polska: W setną rocznicę śmierci Marji Szymanowskiej', *Muzyka*, 11-12 (1931), pp.

SYGA, TEOFIL, and SZENIC, STANISŁAW: *Maria Szymanowska i jej czasy* (Warsaw, 1960).

Żeleński

JACHIMECKI, ZDZISŁAW: *Władysław Żleleński: Życie i twórczość* (Kraków, 1952).

(e) CZECHOSLOVAKIA

(i) Modern Editions

(a) Anthologies

POHANKA, JAROSLAV: *Dějiny české hudby v příkladech* (Prague, 1958).

(b) Works by Individual Composers

DVOŘÁK, A.: *Antonín Dvořák: Souborné vydání*, ed. Otakar Šourek *et al.* (Prague, 1955-) [Czech, German, English, French]: 6 *Vocal Music*.

FIBICH, Z.: *Studijní vydání děl Zdeňka Fibicha*, ed. L. Boháček *et al.* (Prague, 1950-67): *Zpěv a klavír*.

ŠKROUP, F: *Věnec*, ed. Josef Plavec (Prague, 1960).

SMETANA, B.: *Studijní vydání děl Bedřicha Smetany*, ed. František Bartoš, Josef Plavec, *et al.* (Prague, 1940-):

—— *Písně*, ed. Josef Plavec (Prague, 1962).

(ii) Books and Articles

(a) General

ABRAHAM, GERALD: 'Czechoslovakia' in Denis Stevens (ed.), *A History of Song* (London, 1960; repr. 1971), 181–93.

(b) Individual Composers

Bendl

POLAK, JOSEF: *Karel Bendl* (Prague, 1938).

Dvořák

CLAPHAM, JOHN: *Antonín Dvořák: Musician and Craftsman* (London, 1966).
—— *Dvořák* (Newton Abbot, 1979).
ROBERTSON, ALEC: 'Dvořák's Songs', *Music and Letters*, 24 (1943); repr. in Robertson, *Dvořák* (London, 1945; 2nd edn., 1964).
ŠOUREK, OTAKAR: *Dvořákova čítanka: články a skladby* (Prague, 1929) [includes 10th *Cypresses* song].
—— *Život a dílo Antonína Dvořáka* (Prague, 1916–33; 2nd edn., 1955–8).
For further **Dvořák** bibliography *see* § VIII

Fibich

DOLEŽIL, HUBERT (ed.): *Fibichova čítanka: články a skladby* (Prague, 1930) [includes 3 songs from 1871–2].
HUDEC, VLADIMÍR: *Zdeněk Fibich* (Prague, 1971).
JIRÁNEK, JAROSLAV: 'Die Beziehung von Musik und Wort im Schaffen Zdeněk Fibichs', *Music and Word IV, 1969*, ed. Rudolf Pečman (Brno, 1973), 159–70.
—— *Zdeněk Fibich* (Prague, 1971).
PLAVEC, JOSEF: *Zdeněk Fibich: Mistr české balady* (Prague, 1940).
REKTORYS, ARTUŠ (ed.): *Zdeněk Fibich: Sborník dokumentů a studií o jeho životě a díle* (Prague, 1951–2).
TOMÁŠEK, J.: 'Písňová tvorba Zd. Fibicha', *Hudební rozhledy*, 2/3–4 (1925–6).

Škroup

PLAVEC, JOSEF: *František Škroup* (Prague, 1941).
NEJEDLÝ, ZDENĚK: *Bedřich Smetana* (Prague, 1924–33; 2nd edn., 1950–4) [includes list of contents of *Věnec*].

Smetana

BALTHASAR, VLADIMÍR: *Bedřich Smetana* (Prague, 1924).
BARTOŠ, FRANTIŠEK: *Smetana ve vzpomínkách a dopisech* (Prague, 1954).
CLAPHAM, JOHN: *Smetana* (London, 1972).
HOLZKNECHT, VÁCLAV: *Bedřich Smetana: Život a dílo* (Prague, 1979).
JIRÁNEK, JOSEF: *Vzpomínky a korespondence s Bedřichem Smetanou* (Prague, 1957).
LARGE, BRIAN: *Smetana* (London, 1970).
MALÝ, MIROSLAV: *Jabkenická léta Bedřicha Smetany* (Prague, 1968).
NEJEDLÝ, ZDENĚK: *Smetanova čítanka: články a skladby* (Prague, 1924) [Includes *Evening Songs* nos. 1 and 2].
RYCHNOVSKY, ERNST: *Smetana* (Stuttgart, 1924).
SMOLKA, JAROSLAV: *Smetanova vokální tvorba: Písně, sbory, Kantáta* (Prague, 1980).

(i) Modern Editions

(a) Works by Individual Composers

BERWALD, F.: *Sämtliche Werke*, ed. Berwald Kommittén (Monumenta musicae svecicae, 2nd series; Kassel, 1966-82): 17-24 *Vokalwerke*.

GRIEG, E. *Edvard Grieg: Gesamtausgabe/Complete Works*, ed. Edvard-Grieg-Komitee (Frankfurt, 1977-): II *Vokalmusik*: 14-15 *Lieder mit Klavierbegleitung*, 16 *Vokalwerke mit Orchesterbegleitung*.

LANGE-MÜLLER, P. E.: *Sange* (Copenhagen, 1911-12).

NORDRAAK, R.: *Samlede verker* (Oslo, n.d.).

SINDING, C.: *50 sanger*, ed. Øystein Gaukstad and David Monrad Johansen (Oslo, 1978).

SÖDERMAN, J. A.: *Songs*, ed. Axel Helmer (Monumenta musica svecicae; forthcoming).

WEYSE, C. E. F.: *Romancer og Sange* (Copenhagen, 1852 and 1860).

(ii) Books and Articles

(a) General

BRUUN, K. A.: *Dansk musiks historie* (Copenhagen, 1969).

GRINDE, NILS: *Norsk musikkhistorie* (Oslo, 1971; 3rd edn., 1981).

HELMER, AXEL: *Svensk solosång 1850-1890* (Stockholm, 1972).

HORTON, JOHN: *Scandinavian Music: A Short History* (London, 1963; repr. 1975).

JENSEN, NIELS MARTIN: *Den danske romance 1800-1850 og dens musikalske forudsætninger* (Copenhagen, 1964).

LANGE, KRISTIAN, and Østvedt, Arne: *Norwegian Music* (London, 1958).

MAASOLA, K.: *Suomalaisia sävellyksia* (Porvoo, 1964-9).

MAKINEN, TIMO, and NUMMI, SEPPO: *Musica fennica* (Helsinki, 1965) [in English].

MOBERG, CARL-ALLAN: 'Från kämpevisa till locklåt', *Svensk tidskrift för musikforskning*, 33 (1951), 5-52.

RADCLIFFE, PHILIP: 'Scandinavia and Finland', in Denis Stevens (ed.) *A History of Song* (London, 1960; repr. 1971), 376-81.

SCHIØRRING, NILS: *Musikkens Historie i Danmark* (Copenhagen, 1977-8).

(b) Individual Composers

Berwald

LOMNÄS, ERLING (ed.): *Franz Berwald: Die Dokumente seines Lebens* (Kassel, 1979).

Grieg

DESMOND, ASTRA: 'The Songs', in Gerald Abraham (ed.), *Grieg: A Symposium* (London, 1948), 17-92.

HORTON, JOHN: *Grieg* (London, 1974).

MURADOVA, E.: *Romansï i pesni Edvarda Griga* (Baku, 1962).

SCHJELDERUP-EBBE, DAG: *Edvard Grieg 1858-1867, with Special Reference to the Evolution of his Harmonic Style* (Oslo and London, 1964).

Heise

BEHREND, WILLIAM: 'Peter Heise; ein dänischer Liederkomponist', in *Riemann-Festschrift* (Leipzig, 1909), 496-503.

Lindblad

NYBLOM, CARL RUPERT: *Adolf Fredrik Lindblad* (Stockholm, 1881).

Weyse

Fog, Dan: *Kompositionen von C. E. F. Weyse* (Copenhagen, 1979).

Larsen, Jens Peter: *Weyses sang: deres betydning for sangen i hjem, skole og kirke* (Copenhagen, 1942).

(g) BRITAIN AND THE UNITED STATES

(i) Modern Editions

(a) Anthologies

Bouchelle, Joan Hoiness: *With Tennyson at the Keyboard: A Victorian Songbook* (New York, 1985) [includes songs by Parry, Pease, Somervell, Stanford, and Sullivan].

Bush, Geoffrey, and Temperley, Nicholas: *English Songs 1800–1860* (Musica Britannica, 43; London, 1979) [includes works by Balfe, Barnett, Sterndale Bennett, Hatton, Loder, Macfarren, Pierson, and S. S. Wesley].

Marrocco, William Thomas: *Music in America: An Anthology from the Landing of the Pilgrims to the Close of the Civil War* (New York, 1964): chap. 10 'Romantic Ballads and Nationalist Composers' [includes music by Bristow].

(b) Works by Individual Composers

Bennett, W. S.: *Twelve Songs with English and German Words Op. 23 and Op. 35*, ed. Arthur O'Leary (London [1877].).

Chadwick, G. W.: *Songs to Poems by Arlo Bates* [with introduction by Steven Ledbetter] (Earlier American Music, ed. H. Wiley Hitchcock, 16; New York, 1980).

Foster, S. C.: *Stephen Foster Song Book: Original Sheet Music of 40 Songs*, compiled by Richard Jackson (New York, 1974).

Macdowell, E.: *Songs* (Earlier American Music, ed. H. Wiley Hitchcock, 7; New York, 1972).

Parry, H.: *Hubert Parry: Songs*, ed. Geoffrey Bush (Musica Britannica, 49; London, 1982).

Pierson, H. H.: *H. Hugo Pierson Album* (Leipzig, *c.*1875).

Stanford, C. V.: *C. V. Stanford: Songs* (Musica Britannica, in preparation).

(ii) Books and Articles

(a) General

Banfield, Stephen: *Sensibility and English Song* (Cambridge, 1985).

Bush, Geoffrey: 'Songs', in Nicholas Temperley (ed.), *Music in Britain: The Romantic Age 1800–1914* (London, 1981), 266–87.

Carman, J. E., Gaeddert, W. K., and Resch, R. M.: *Art Song in the United States 1801–1976: An Annotated Bibliography* (New York, 1976; supplement, 1978).

Chase, Gilbert: *America's Music from the Pilgrims to the Present* (New York, 1955; rev. 2nd edn., 1966).

Hitchcock, H. Wiley: *Music in the United States: A Historical Introduction* (Englewood Cliffs, NJ, 1969; rev. 2nd edn., 1974).

Howard, John Tasker: *Our American Music: Three Hundred Years of It* (New York, 1931; 3rd edn., 1946, repr. 1954 with supplement by J. Lyons).

Nathan, Hans: 'United States of America', in Denis Stevens (ed.) *A History of Song* (London, 1960; repr. 1971), 408–60.

Simpson, Harold: *A Century of Ballads 1810–1910: Their Composers and Singers* (London, 1910).

'Sketch of Music in London', *Quarterly Musical Magazine and Review*, 5 (1823), 241-75.

UPTON, WILLIAM T.: *Art-song in America: A Study in the Development of American Music* (Boston, Mass., and New York, 1930; supplement 1938; all repr. 1969).

WALKER, ERNEST: *A History of Music in England* (4th edn.), rev. J. A. Westrup (Oxford, 1952).

(*b*) *Individual Composers*

Balfe
BARRETT, WILLIAM ALEXANDER: *Balfe: His Life and Works* (London, 1882).

Barnett
CHORLEY, HENRY F.: Review of John Barnett, *Lyric Illustrations of the Modern Poets*, *Athenaeum* (1834), 753 ff

Bennett
STERNDALE BENNETT, JAMES ROBERT: *The Life of William Sterndale Bennett* (*Cambridge, 1907*).

TEMPERLEY, NICHOLAS: 'Sterndale Bennett and the Lied', *Musical Times*, 106 (1975), 958-61, 1060-3.

Chadwick
ENGEL, CARL: 'George W. Chadwick', *Musical Quarterly*, 10 (1924), 438-57.

Macdowell
SUMMERVILLE, SUZANNE: 'The Songs of Edward Macdowell', *NAB Bulletin*, 35/4 (March/April 1979), 36-40.

Macfarren
BANISTER, HENRY CHARLES: *George Alexander Macfarren: His Life, Works and Influence* (London, 1891).

Parry
COLLES, H. C.: 'Parry, as Song-writer', *Musical Times*, 62 (1921), 82-7, 155-8, 235-8; repr. in *Essays and Lectures* (London, 1945), 55-75.

FULLER MAITLAND, J. A.: *The Music of Parry and Stanford* (Cambridge, 1934).

HOWELLS, HERBERT: 'Hubert Parry', *Music and Letters*, 50 (1969), 223-9.

Pierson
POLLIN, ALICE and BURTON: 'In Pursuit of Pearson's Shelley Songs', *Music and Letters*, 46 (1965), 322-31.

SCHUMANN, ROBERT: *Gesammelte Schriften über Musik und Musiker*, ed. Martin Kreisig (Leipzig, 1854; 4th edn. 1891; repr. 1968; 5th edn. 1914); Eng. trans., Fanny Raymond Ritter, *Music and Musicians: Essays and Criticisms* (London, 1877-80); new selected Eng. trans., ed. Konrad Wolff, trans. Paul Rosenfeld, *On Music and Musicians* (New York, 1947; repr. 1982).

TEMPERLEY, NICHOLAS: 'Henry Hugo Pierson, 1815-73', *Musical Times*, 104 (1973), 1217-20 and 105 (1974), 31-4.

Somervell
BANFIELD, STEPHEN: 'The Immortality Odes of Finzi and Somervell', *Musical Times*, 116 (1975), 527-31.

HUGHES, LINDA: 'From Parlor to Concert Hall: Arthur Somervell's Song-cycle on Tennyson's *Maud*', *Victorian Studies*, 30 (1986-7), 113-29; repr. in Nicholas Temperley (ed.), *The Lost Chord: Studies in Victorian Music* (Bloomington, Ind., 1989).

Stanford
FULLER MAITLAND, J. A.: *The Music of Parry and Stanford* (Cambridge, 1934).
GREENE, HARRY PLUNKET: 'Stanford's Songs', *Music and Letters*, 2 (1921), 94–106.

Sullivan
JACOBS, ARTHUR: *Arthur Sullivan: A Victorian Musician* (Oxford, 1984).

CHAPTER X

CHORAL MUSIC

(i) Modern Editions

(*a*) *Anthologies*

KNIGHT, GERALD H., and REED, WILLIAM LEONARD: *The Treasury of English Church Music 1760–1900*, iv (London, 1965) [includes anthems by Bennett, Stanford, Sullivan, and Wesley].

(*b*) *Works by Individual Composers*

BENNETT, W. S.: *Anthems* (London, *c*.1885).
BERLIOZ, H.: *New Berlioz Edition of the Complete Works*, ed. Hugh Macdonald *et al.* (Kassel, 1967–): 8 *La Damnation de Faust*, ed. Julian Rushton (1979); 9 *Grande Messe des Morts*, ed. Jürgen Kindermann (1978); 10 *Te Deum*, ed. Denis McCaldin (1973); 19 *Grande Symphonie funèbre et triomphale*, ed. Hugh Macdonald (1967); 7 *Lélio*, ed. David Cairns; 11 *L'Enfance du Christ*; 12 *Works for Chorus and Orchestra*, A. ed. Julian Rushton, B. ed. David Charlton; 14 *Choruses Unaccompanied or with Piano*, 18 *Roméo et Juliette*, ed. D. Kern Holoman (1988).
—— *Hector Berlioz: Werke*, ed. Charles Malherbe and Felix Weingartner (Leipzig, 1900–10; repr. 1971): series 4 *Geistliche Werke*: 3 *Grande Messe des Morts*, 6 *Te deum*, 7 *L'Enfance du Christ*; series 5 *Weltliche Kantaten*: 3 *La Damnation de Faust*, 4 *Lélio*, 6 *L'Impériale*; series 6: *Gesänge mit Orchesterbegleitung*: 14 *Für Chor*; series 7 *Gesänge mit Klavier*; 16A *Für Chor*.
BRAHMS, J.: *Johannes Brahms: Sämtliche Werke*, ed. Eusebius Mandyczewski (Leipzig, 1926–7; repr. 1964–5 and 1971): 17 *Ein deutsches Requiem*; 18 *Rinaldo*; 19 *Ave Maria, Rhapsodie, Schicksalslied, Nänie, Gesang der Parzen*; 20 *Mehrstimmige Gesänge mit Klavier oder Orgel*; 21 *Mehrstimmige Gesänge ohne Begleitung*; 22 *Duette mit Klavierbegleitung*.
BRUCKNER, A.: *Anton Bruckner: Sämtliche Werke: Kritische Gesamtausgabe*: 13 *Messe e-Moll, Grosse Messe f-Moll*, ed. Robert Haas and Leopold Nowak (Leipzig, 1940); 14 *Messe d-Moll*, 15 *Requiem d-Moll, Missa solemnis b-Moll*, ed. Robert Haas (Vienna, 1930–49).
—— *Anton Bruckner: Sämtliche Werke: Kritische Werke*, ed. Leopold Nowak (Vienna, 1951–): 14 *Requiem d-Moll* (1966); 15 *Missa solemnis b-Moll* (1975); 16 *Messe d-Moll* (1957); 17 *Messe e-Moll*; 18 *Grosse Messe f-Moll*; 19 *Te deum*; 21 *Kleine Kirchenmusik 1835–1892* (1984); 22 incl. *Psalm 150*, ed. Franz Grasberger (1964).
—— *Chorwerke aus dem Nachlasse Anton Bruckners*, ed. Viktor Keldorfer (Vienna, 1911).
—— Choral music incl. in Göllerich, August: *Anton Bruckner: Ein lebens- und Schaffens-Bild*, 1 (Regensburg, 1922), 2–4, ed. Max Auer (Regensburg, 1928–37); all repr. 1974.
DEBUSSY, C.: *Œuvres complètes de Claude Debussy* (Paris, 1985–): series 4 [Choral Works].

DVOŘÁK, A.: *Antonín Dvořák: Souborné vydání*, ed. Otakar Šourek *et al.* (Prague, 1955–) [Czech, German, English, French]: series 2 *Oratorios, Cantatas, Mass*: 1 *Stabat mater* (1958), 2 *Svatební košile* (1967), 3 *Svatá Ludmila* (1964), *Requiem* (1961), 5 incl. *The American Flag*, 6 *Te deum*; series 6 *Vocal Music*: 4 *Male, Female, and Mixed Choruses.*

ELGAR, E.: *Elgar Complete Edition*, ed. Jerrold Northrop Moore and Christopher Kent (London, 1981–): series 1 *Choral Works* [including *The Dream of Gerontius* (1982)].

ESLAVA, H.: *Oficio de difuntos, Te deum* in *Lira sacro-hispana*, ed. Hilarión Eslava, Siglo, 2nd series, 1 (Madrid, 1869)..

GLINKA, M. I.: *Polnoe sobranie sochineniy*, ed. Vissarion Yakovlevich Shebalin *et al.* (Moscow, 1955–69): 8 [Vocal Works with Orchestra] (1960); 9 [Vocal Works with Piano and *a capella*] (1960); 17 [Unfinished Works] (1968).

LISZT, F.: *Franz Liszts Musikalische Werke*, ed. Franz Liszt-Stiftung (Leipzig, 1907– 36; repr. 1966): Part 5 *Kirchliche und geistliche Gesangwerke* incl.: 1 *Missa solemnis*, 3 *Messen und Requiem mit Orgel*; Part 6 *Weltliche mehrstimmige Gesangwerke.*

—— *Franz Liszt: Neue Ausgabe sämtlicher Werke/New Edition of the Complete Works*, ed. Zoltán Gárdonyi (Kassel and Budapest, 1970–): series 8 *Lieder, Songs, Choral Works with piano*; series 10 *A capella Choral Works*; series 16 *Die Legende von der heiligen Elisabeth, Christus* (all forthcoming).

—— *Die Legende von der heiligen Elisabeth*, ed. Olivér Nagy (Budapest, 1975) [vocal score].

MENDELSSOHN, F.: *Felix Mendelssohn Bartholdy's Werke: Kritisch durchgesehene Ausgabe*, ed. Julius Rietz (Leipzig, 1874–7; repr. 1967–9): series 13 *Oratorien*: 85 *Paulus*, 86 *Elias*; series 14 *Geistliche Gesangwerke*: 93 *Lobgesang*, 94 *Lauda Sion*; series 17 *Lieder und Gesänge für vier Männerstimmen*; series 18 *Lieder und Gesänge für zwei Singstimmen mit Begleitung des Pianoforte*; series 16 *Lieder, für Sopran, Alt, Tenor und Bass.*

—— *Leipziger Ausgabe der Werke Felix Mendelssohn Bartholdys*, ed. Internationale Felix-Mendelssohn-Gesellschaft (Leipzig, 1960–): series 6 *Geistliche Vokalmusik* (1977–).

—— anthems, ed. Brian W. Pritchard (Hilversum, 1972).

MONIUSZKO, S.: *Stanisław Moniuszko: Dzieła/Werke*, ed. Witold Rudziński (Kraków, 1965–): series D. *Chormusik.*

MUSSORGSKY, M. P.: *Polnoe sobranie sochineniy*, ed. Pavel Aleksandrovich Lamm with Boris Vladimirovich Asaf'ev (Moscow, 1928–34; repr. 1969): 19 *Salammbô*;. 21 [Choral Works, with piano].

PARKER, H. W.: *Hora novissima* (Early American Music, ed. H. Wiley Hitchcock, 2; New York, 1972).

RIMSKY-KORSAKOV, N.: *Polnoe sobranie sochineniy*, ed. Andrey Nikolaevich Rimsky-Korsakov *et al.* (Moscow, 1946–70): 24 and 44 [Cantatas] (1952 and 1953); 46A [Duets and Trios] (1949); 46B [Choruses, *a capella*] (1954); 47 [Russian Folk-songs] (1952).

SCHUMANN, R.: *Robert Schumann's Werke*, ed. Clara Schumann *et al.* (Leipzig, 1881–93; repr. 1967–8): series 9 *Grössere Gesangwerke* (1882–7); series 10 *Mehrstimmige Gesangwerke mit Pianoforte* (1883–4); 11 *Für Männerchor* (1887); 12 *Für Sopran, Alt, Tenor und Bass* (1886).

SMETANA, B.: *Studijní vydání děl Bedřicha Smetany*, ed. František Bartoš, Josef Plavec *et al.* (Prague, 1940–): 2 *Česká píseň* (1941).

SPOHR, L.: *Selected Works of Louis Spohr (1784–1859)*, ed. Clive Brown (New York, 1987–): 4 *Die Letzten Dinge*; 5 *Des Heilands Letzte Stunden.*

TCHAIKOVSKY, P. I.: *Pyotr Il'ich Chaykovskiy: Polnoe sobranie sochineniy* (Moscow and Leningrad, 1940–71): 27 [Vocal Works with Orchestra].

VERDI, G.: *The Works of Giuseppe Verdi*, ed. Philip Gossett *et al.* (Chicago and Milan, 1983–): series 3 *Sacred Music* [includes *Messa de Requiem*, ed. David Rosen (1966)]; series 4 *Cantatas and Hymns*.
WESLEY, S. S.: *Anthems* (London, 1853).
—— *The European Psalmist* (London, 1872) [includes service music by Wesley].

(ii) Books and Articles

(a) General

BLUME, FRIEDRICH (ed.): *Die evangelische Kirchenmusik* (Potsdam, 1931; 2nd edn., 1965, as *Geschichte der evanglischen Kirchenmusik*); Eng. trans. enlarged as *Protestant Church Music: A History* (New York, 1974).
BURBACH, HERMANN-JOSEPH: 'Das "triviale" in der katholischen Kirchenmusik des 19. Jahrhunderts', in Carl Dahlhaus (ed.), *Studien zur Trivialmusik des 19. Jahrhunderts* (Regensburg, 1967), 71–82.
FELLERER, KARL: *Geschichte der katholischen Kirchenmusik* (Düsseldorf, 1939; 2nd edn., 1949); Eng. trans., Francis A. Brunner, *The History of Catholic Church Music* (Baltimore, Md., 1961).
—— 'Das deutsche Chorlied im 19. Jahrhundert', in Wulf Arlt *et al.* (eds.), *Gattungen der Musick in Einzeldarstellungen: Gedenkschrift für Leo Schrade* (Berne and Munich, 1973), 785–812.
GATENS, WILLIAM J.: *Victorian Cathedral Music in Theory and Practice* (Cambridge, 1986).
HUTCHINGS, ARTHUR: *Church Music in the Nineteenth Century* (London, 1967).
JACOBS, ARTHUR (ed.): *Choral Music: A Symposium* (Harmondsworth, 1963).
KRABBE, WILHELM: 'Chormusik (Lied und kleinere Chorwerke)', in Guido Adler (ed.), *Handbuch der Musikgeschichte*, ii (Frankfurt, 1924; 2nd edn., 1930, repr. 1961), 955–63.
KRUMMACHER, FRIEDHELM: 'Kunstreligion und religiöse Musik: Zur ästhetischen Problematick geistlicher Musik im 19. Jahrhundert', *Die Musikforschung*, 32 (1979), 365–93.
MOSER, HANS-JOACHIM: *Die evangelische Kirchenmusik in Deutschland* (Berlin, 1954).
TEMPERLEY, NICHOLAS: *The Music of the English Parish Church* (Cambridge, 1979) i; chap. 8 'The Rediscovery of Tradition (1800–50)', pp. 244–67; chap. 9 'The Victorian Settlement (1850–1900)', pp. 268–314.
URSPRUNG, OTTO: *Die katholische Kirchenmusik* (Potsdam, 1931, repr. 1949).
VALENTIN, ERICH (ed.): *Handbuch der Chormusik* (Regensburg, 1953–8).
WIORA, WALTER (ed.): *Religiöse Musik in nichtliturgischen Werken von Beethoven bis Reger* (Regensburg, 1978).

(b) Individual Composers

Berlioz
PROD'HOMME, J.-G.: *Le Cycle Berlioz*, i. *La Damnaton de Faust*, ii. *L'Enfance du Christ* (Paris, 1898–9).
RUSHTON, JULIAN: 'The Genesis of Berlioz's "La Damnation de Faust" ', *Music and Letters*, 56 (1975), 129–46.
For further **Berlioz** bibliography *see* § I

Brahms
BLUM, KLAUS: *Hundert Jahre Ein deutsches Requiem von Johannes Brahms: Entstehung, Uraufführung, Interpretation, Würdidung* (Tutzing, 1971).
HANCOCK, VIRGINIA: *Brahms's Choral Compositions and his Library of Early Music* (Ann Arbor, Mich., 1983).

KALBECK, MAX: *Johannes Brahms* (4 vols; Berlin, 1904–14; reprint of latest edition of each vol. (1921, 1921, 1912–13, 1915), Tutzing, 1974).

KROSS, SIEGFRIED: *Die Chorwerke von Johannes Brahms* (Berlin, 1958; 2nd edn., 1963).

For further **Brahms** bibliography *see* § VIII

Bruckner

AUER, MAX: *Anton Bruckner als Kirchenmusiker* (Regensburg, 1927).

HOWIE, A. CRAWFORD: 'Traditional and Novel Elements in Bruckner's Sacred Music', *Musical Quarterly*, 66 (1981), 544–67.

SINGER, KURT: *Bruckners Chormusik* (Stuttgart, 1924).

For further **Bruckner** bibliography *see* § VIII

Cherubini

ALBERTI, LUCIANO: 'I tempi e i modi della produzione sacra di Luigi Cherubini', in Adelmo Damerini (ed.), *Luigi Cherubini nel II centenario della nascita* (Florence, 1962), 70–92.

DEANE, BASIL: *Cherubini* (Oxford, 1965).

Dvořák

CLAPHAM, JOHN: *Antonín Dvořák: Musician and Craftsman* (London, 1966).

KOUBA, JAN: 'Nejstarší český tištěný kancionál z roku 1501 jako hudební pramen', in *Studie a materiály k dějinám starší české hudby* (Prague, 1965).

ROBERTSON, ALEC: *Dvořák* (London, 1945; 2nd edn., 1964).

For further **Dvořák** bibliography *see* § VIII

Elsner

NOWAK-ROMANOWICZ, ALINA: *Józef Elsner* (Kraków, 1957).

Franck

D'INDY, VINCENT: *César Franck* (Paris, 1906; 8th edn. 1919); Eng. trans., Rosa Newmarch, *César Franck* (London, 1910; repr. 1965).

LANDGRAF, ARMIN: *Musica sacra zwischen Symphonie und Improvisation: César Franck und seine Musik für den Gottesdienst* (Tutzing, 1975).

Gounod

PROD'HOMME, J.-G., and DANDELOT, ARTHUR: *Gounod (1818–1893): Sa vie et ses œuvres* (Paris, 1911; repr. 1973).

WAGENER, HEINZ: 'Die Messen Charles Gounods', *Kirchenmusikalisches Jahrbuch*, 51 (1967), 145–53.

Liszt

LISZT, FRANZ: *Gesammelte Schriften von Franz Liszt*, ed. Lina Ramann (Leipzig, 1880–3).

MERRICK, PAUL: *Revolution and Religion in the Music of Liszt* (Cambridge, 1987).

SEGNITZ, E.: *Franz Liszts Kirchenmusik* (Langensalza, 1911).

SZABOLCSI, BENCE: *A magyar zenetörténet kézikönyve* (Budapest, 1947; 3rd edn., 1977); Eng. trans. of 2nd edn., 1955, abridged as *A Concise History of Hungarian Music* (Budapest, 1964; 2nd edn., 1.965).

For further **Liszt** bibliography *see* § VII

Loewe

BITTER, CARL HERMANN (ed.): *Dr. Carl Loewe's Selbstbiographie* (Berlin, 1870; repr. 1976).

Mendelssohn

Über Felix Mendelssohn Bartholdys Oratorium Paulus (Kiel, 1842).

PRITCHARD, BRIAN W.: 'Mendelssohn's Chorale Cantatas: An Appraisal', *Musical Quarterly*, 62 (1976), 1–24.

RADCLIFFE, PHILIP: *Mendelssohn* (London, 1954; rev. 2nd edn., 1967).

WERNER, JACK: *Mendelssohn's 'Elijah': A Historical and Analytical Guide to the Oratorio* (London, 1965).

WERNER, RUDOLF: *Felix Mendelssohn-Bartholdy als Kirchenmusiker* (Frankfurt, 1930).

For further **Mendelssohn** bibliography *see* § I

Moniuszko

JACHIMECKI, ZDZISŁAW: *Muzyka kościelna Moniuszki* (Warsaw, 1947).

Rossini

AMBROS, AUGUST WILHELM: 'Die "Messe solennelle" von Rossini', *Bunte Blätter* (Leipzig, 1872; 2nd edn., 1896), i. 81–92.

D'ORTIGUE, JOSEPH L.: *Le 'Stabat' de Rossini* (Paris, 1841).

Saint-Saëns

SAINT-SAËNS, CAMILLE: *École buissonnière: notes et souvenirs* (Paris, 1913); abridged Eng. trans., Edwin Giles Rich, *Musical Memories* (London, 1919, repr. 1969).

For further **Saint-Saens** bibliography *see* § VI (b)

Schumann

HALSEY, LOUIS: 'The Choral Music', in Alan Walker (ed.), *Robert Schumann: The Man and his Music* (London, 1972; rev. 2nd edn., 1976), 350–89.

HORTON, JOHN: 'The Choral Works', in Gerald Abraham (ed.), *Schumann: A Symposium* (London, 1952), 283–99.

For further **Schumann** bibliography *see* § I, § II, and § IV

Verdi

CONATI, MARCELLO: 'Le *Ave Maria* su scala enigmatica di Verdi dalla prima alla seconda stesura (1889–1897)', *Rivista italiana di musicologia*, 13 (1978), 280–311.

GIRARDI, MICHELE and PETROBELLI, PIERLUIGI (ed.): *Messa per Rossini: La storia, il testo, la musica*, Quaderni dell'Istituto di Studi Verdiani, 5 (Parma and Milan, 1988).

PIZZETTI, ILDEBRANDO: 'La religiosita di Verdi: Introduzione alla Messa da Requiem', *Nuova antologia* (Jan.–Feb. 1941), 209–13.

ROSEN, DAVID: 'Verdis "Liber scriptus" Re-written', *Musical Quarterly*, 55 (1969), 151–59.

—— 'La *Messa* a Rossini e il *Requiem* per Manzoni', *Rivista Italiana di Musicologia*, 4 (1969), 127–37; 5 (1970), 216–33.

WALKER, FRANK: 'Verdi's *Four Sacred Pieces*', *Ricordiana*, vi/2 (1961), 1–3.

For further **Verdi** bibliography *see* § III (c) and § VI (c)

INDEX

Compiled by FREDERICK SMYTH

Page numbers in bold type indicate the more important references.
Operas and oratorios are indexed under composers and librettists, the latter
being identified as such.